AUSTRALIAN SCHOOLMATE

THE FUTURE OF AUSTRALIAN ENGLISH

OXFORD THESAURUS

THIRD EDITION

Compiled by Anne Knight

OXFORD
UNIVERSITY PRESS
AUSTRALIA & NEW ZEALAND

OXFORD
UNIVERSITY PRESS

Oxford University Press is a department of the University of Oxford.
It furthers the University's objective of excellence in research,
scholarship, and education by publishing worldwide. Oxford is a registered
trademark of Oxford University Press in the UK and in certain other
countries.

Published in Australia by
Oxford University Press
253 Normanby Road, South Melbourne, Victoria 3205, Australia

First published 1992
Second edition published 2001
Third edition published 2006
Reprinted 2007, 2008, 2009, 2010, 2011, 2012 (twice)

National Library of Australia Cataloguing-in-Publication data

The Australian schoolmate Oxford thesaurus

3rd ed.
For secondary students.
ISBN 978 0 19 555023 8

1. English Language—Australia—Synonyms and antonyms.
2. English language—Synonyms and antonyms. I. Knight, Anne.

423.12

Reproduction and communication for educational purposes

Compiled by Anne Knight
Typeset by Promptset Pty Ltd
Printed in Hong Kong by Sheck Wah Tong Printing Press Ltd

OWLS
OXFORD
DICTIONARY
WORD AND
LANGUAGE
SERVICE

Do you have a query about words,
their origin, meaning, use, spelling,
pronunciation, or any other aspect
of international English? Then write
to OWLS at the Australian National
Dictionary Centre, Australian
National University, Canberra ACT
0200 (email ANDC@anu.edu.au).
All queries will be answered using
the full resources of *The Australian
National Dictionary* and *The Oxford
English Dictionary.*
The Australian National Dictionary
Centre and Oxford University Press
also produce *Ozwords*, a
biannual newsletter which contains
interesting items about Australian
words and language. Subscription is
free – please contact the *Ozwords*
subscription manager at Oxford
University Press, GPO Box 2784,
Melbourne, VIC 3001, or
ozwords.au@oup.com

Preface

The *Australian Schoolmate Oxford Thesaurus* is an alphabetical collection of words with their synonyms (words of the same or nearly the same meaning) and antonyms (words of opposite meaning). Each entry provides a set of words of similar or related meaning to the word you look up, so that you can choose the word which best expresses what you want to say. You may want to find an alternative word for an overused one, a more formal word for an everyday word, a slang alternative to a standard word, or a more specific word for a general one.

In using the thesaurus it is important to recognise that perfect synonyms—words that have exactly the same meaning and are substitutable in any context—are in fact rare. Care must be taken in order to select the most appropriate word for the particular context, and it is wise to check the meaning and usage of any unfamiliar word in a dictionary. The *Australian Schoolmate Oxford Thesaurus* draws its vocabulary largely from the *Australian Schoolmate Oxford Dictionary*, and the two books should serve as useful companions.

AK

Guide to the thesaurus

Headword —

wilt *verb* **1** *The flowers wilted in the heat.* become limp, deteriorate, droop, shrivel, wither. OPPOSITE thrive. **2** *The runners wilted after ten kilometres.* droop, flag, languish, tire.

— **Example**

wily *adjective* *He was as wily as a fox.* artful, astute, clever, crafty, cunning, devious, foxy, knowing, scheming, shrewd, sly, tricky, underhand. OPPOSITE straightforward.

— **Synonyms**

Part of speech —

wimp *noun* (*informal*) *He's such a wimp when it comes to injections.* baby, coward, milksop, sissy, sook (*Australian informal*), wuss (*slang*).

win *verb* **1** *May the best team win.* be victorious, come first, come top, prevail, succeed, triumph. **2** *He won first prize.* attain, earn, gain, get, land, obtain, pick up, receive, secure, walk away with (*informal*). OPPOSITE lose. — *noun They scored another win.* conquest, success, triumph, victory. OPPOSITE loss. □ **win over** *He won his audience over.* convert, convince, persuade, sway, talk round.

Sense number —

— **Opposite**

wince *verb* *She winced as the splinter was removed.* blench, cringe, flinch, grimace, recoil, start.

winch *verb* *The tow-truck winched the car from the gully.* hoist, lift, pull.

wind¹ *noun* **1** *The wind blew.* air current, blast, breeze, draught, gale, gust, squall, zephyr; [*various winds*] cyclone, doctor (*Australian*), hurricane, mistral, monsoon, sirocco, southerly buster (*Australian*), tornado, typhoon, whirlwind, willy willy (*Australian*). **2** *After eating cabbage he has a lot of wind.* flatulence, gas. **3** *The piper has run out of wind to keep playing.* air, breath, puff.

— **Related words**

Homograph number —

wind² *verb* **1** *The river winds through pretty country.* bend, curve, meander, snake, twist, wander, zigzag. **2** *She wound the wool over her hand.* coil, curl, loop, roll, turn, twine, twirl, twist, wrap. OPPOSITE unwind. □ **wind up 1** *He wound up the business.* close down, dissolve, liquidate. **2** (*informal*) *He wound up in jail.* end up, finish up, land.

Phrase —

— **Usage label**

windbreak *noun* *The trees act as a windbreak.* barrier, breakwind, screen.

windcheater *noun* *Their windcheaters keep out wind and spray.* anorak, cagoule, jacket, parka; see also SWEATER.

— **Cross-reference**

windfall *noun* *He has spent his little windfall.* bonanza, godsend.

winding *adjective* *a winding road.* corkscrew, crooked, serpentine, sinuous, tortuous, twisting, zigzag. OPPOSITE straight.

Headwords

The headword is the first word of each entry and is printed in bold type. Entries are arranged in alphabetical order of headwords.

Homograph numbers

Words that have the same spelling but different meaning or origin are called homographs. They have separate entries in the thesaurus and their headwords are distinguished by raised numbers.

Parts of speech

The headword is followed by a part-of-speech label indicating how the word is used in a sentence, for example as a *noun, verb, adverb, adjective, preposition, pronoun, interjection,* or *conjunction.* Within an entry a dash introduces a new part of speech.

Sense numbers

Different senses of the headword are numbered, and a new numbering sequence is used for each part of speech within an entry.

Examples

Example phrases or sentences printed in italics help to identify the different senses of the headword or show how the word is used in context.

Synonyms

Synonyms are words that have the same or nearly the same meaning. They are arranged in alphabetical order for each sense of the headword or phrase. Sometimes one or more synonyms are also offered for the plural form of the headword indicated in square brackets. In choosing a synonym remember that no two words have exactly the same meaning or tone, so take care that the word you select is the most appropriate one for the particular context.

Opposites

Opposites and contrasting words are given for many headwords and are introduced by the labels OPPOSITE or CONTRASTS WITH.

Phrases

Where a word is often used as part of a phrase, the phrase is printed in bold type and found at the entry for the main word in the phrase. Synonyms and opposites are given for the phrase.

Usage labels

If a synonym is restricted in use, it is followed by a label printed in italics in brackets. A label following either the part of speech or a sense number applies to the headword or phrase printed in bold type. Words may be restricted to a particular region or subject area, or may be classed as *formal, informal, slang, old use,* or *derogatory. Informal* indicates that the word is normally used in informal or spoken English rather than formal writing, while *slang* warns that it is used very informally, or restricted to a particular group. A *derogatory* use is one that is intentionally insulting.

Cross-references

Cross-references printed in small capitals and introduced by 'see' or 'see also' are provided at some entries instead of, or to supplement, a list of synonyms.

Related words

As well as synonyms and opposites, some entries offer lists of words related to the headword in other ways, e.g. different kinds or varieties of a thing, words for the male and female of an animal, etc. These lists are preceded by an explanatory note in italics in square brackets.

Proprietary terms

This book includes some words which are, or are asserted to be, proprietary names or trade marks. Their inclusion does not imply that they have acquired for legal purposes a non-proprietary or general significance, nor is any other judgement implied concerning their legal status. In cases where the editor has some evidence that a word is used as a proprietary name or trade mark this is indicated by the label *trade mark*, but no judgement concerning the legal status of such words is made or implied thereby.

Aa

abandon *verb* **1** *He would never abandon his family.* desert, ditch (*informal*), forsake, jilt, leave, leave in the lurch, run out on (*informal*), walk out on (*informal*). **2** *We were told to abandon ship.* desert, evacuate, leave, quit, vacate. **3** *The search was abandoned because of the storm.* cancel, discontinue, drop, give up, scrap. OPPOSITE continue.

abate *verb* *The wind abated.* decrease, die down, ease, moderate, subside, weaken. OPPOSITE intensify.

abbey *noun* convent, friary, monastery, nunnery, priory, religious house.

abbreviate *verb* *Elizabeth is abbreviated to 'Liz'.* abridge, contract, cut, reduce, shorten, truncate. OPPOSITE lengthen.

abbreviation *noun* *Use the full name rather than the abbreviation.* acronym, contraction, shortening.

abdicate *verb* **1** *The king abdicated the throne.* give up, relinquish, renounce. **2** *The king abdicated.* quit, resign, stand down, step down.

abdomen *noun* belly, gut (*informal*), insides (*informal*), intestines, paunch, stomach, tummy (*informal*).

abduct *verb* *The man abducted the girl.* carry off, kidnap, seize, snatch (*informal*).

abet *verb* *He was charged with abetting the murderer.* aid, assist, encourage, help, incite, support. OPPOSITE hinder.

abhor *verb* *He abhors wastefulness.* abominate, detest, hate, loathe, recoil from, shrink from. OPPOSITE love.

abhorrent *adjective* *Cannibalism is an abhorrent practice.* abominable, detestable, disgusting, hateful, horrid, loathsome, odious, repugnant, repulsive, revolting.

abide *verb* **1** (*old use*) *They had to abide in the same house.* dwell, live, remain, reside, stay. **2** *She can't abide the smell of garlic.* bear, endure, put up with, stand, stomach, suffer, take, tolerate. ☐ **abide by** *We must abide by the rules.* accept, adhere to, agree to, comply with, conform to, follow, keep to, obey, observe, stick to. OPPOSITE disobey.

abiding *adjective* *an abiding love.* endless, enduring, eternal, everlasting, lasting, permanent, steadfast, unending. OPPOSITE ephemeral.

ability *noun* *mathematical ability.* aptitude, capability, capacity, cleverness, competence, expertise, facility, flair, genius, gift, knack, know-how, potential, proficiency, prowess, skill, talent. OPPOSITE inability, incompetence.

able *adjective* **1** *He is able to attend the class.* allowed, authorised, available, eligible, fit, free, permitted. OPPOSITE unable. **2** *an able student.* accomplished, adept, adroit, capable, clever, competent, gifted, intelligent, proficient, qualified, skilful, talented. OPPOSITE incompetent.

abnormal *adjective* *an abnormal reaction.* anomalous, atypical, bizarre, curious, deviant, eccentric, exceptional, extraordinary, freakish, irregular, odd, peculiar, queer, rare, singular, strange, uncommon, unconventional, unnatural, unusual, weird. OPPOSITE normal.

abnormality *noun* *a physical abnormality.* anomaly, deformity, irregularity, malformation, peculiarity.

abolish *verb* *The group's aim is to abolish duck shooting.* cancel, do away with, eliminate, end, eradicate, extinguish, get rid of, put an end to, remove, stamp out, wipe out. OPPOSITE retain.

abolition *noun* *the abolition of capital punishment.* cancellation, elimination, ending, eradication, removal. OPPOSITE retention.

abominable *adjective* **1** *an abominable crime.* abhorrent, appalling, atrocious, base, contemptible, despicable, detestable, disgusting, execrable, foul, hateful, heinous, horrible, loathsome, obnoxious, odious, repugnant, repulsive, vile. **2** (*informal*) *abominable weather.* atrocious (*informal*), awful (*informal*), bad, crook (*Australian informal*), dreadful (*informal*), foul, frightful (*informal*), lousy (*informal*), shocking (*informal*), terrible (*informal*), unpleasant.

abominate *verb* *We abominate mediocrity.* abhor, detest, hate, loathe. OPPOSITE approve of, love.

aboriginal *adjective* *the aboriginal inhabitants.* earliest, first, indigenous, native, original. OPPOSITE immigrant.

abortion *noun* *The woman decided not to have an abortion.* termination.

abortive *adjective* *an abortive attempt.* failed, fruitless, futile, ineffective, unsuccessful, vain. OPPOSITE successful.

abound *verb* **1** *Weeds abound in the backyard.* be abundant, be plentiful, flourish, proliferate, thrive. **2** *The river abounds with fish.* be full, overflow, swarm, teem.

about *preposition* **1** *Look about you.* around, close to, near. **2** *an article about obesity.* concerning, connected with, dealing with, involving, on, regarding, relating to. — *adverb* **1** *She is about 150 centimetres tall.* almost, approximately, around, more or less, nearly, roughly. **2** *They're somewhere about.* around, hereabouts, near, nearby. ☐ **be about to** *He was about to leave.* be going to, be on the brink of, be on the point of, be on the verge of, be ready to.

about-face *noun* *The government did an about-face on its election promise.* about-turn, backflip, U-turn.

above *adverb* **1** *noises from above.* overhead, upstairs. **2** *discussed above.* before, earlier, previously. OPPOSITE below. — *preposition* **1** *above the clouds.* above the bridge. higher than, on top of, over, upstream from. **2** *above 50,000.* beyond, exceeding, greater than, higher than, more than, over. OPPOSITE below. **3** *the officer above corporal.* higher than, superior to. ☐ **above board** *All his business dealings were above board.* clean, fair, honest, honourable, legal, legitimate, open, straight. OPPOSITE underhand.

abrasion *noun* *The victim suffered slight abrasions.* graze, lesion, scrape, scratch.

abridge *verb* *The novel was abridged for the magazine.* abbreviate, condense, cut, edit, reduce, shorten, trim. OPPOSITE expand.

abroad *adverb* *He travelled abroad.* overseas.

abrupt *adjective* **1** *an abrupt halt.* hasty, precipitate, quick, rapid, sharp, sudden, swift, unexpected. OPPOSITE gradual. **2** *an abrupt manner.* blunt, brisk, brusque, curt, gruff, impolite, rude, short. OPPOSITE polite.

abscond *verb* *The accountant absconded with the money.* bolt, disappear, do a bunk (*slang*), escape,

flee, make off, nick off (*Australian slang*), run off, shoot through (*Australian informal*).

absence *noun* **1** *an absence of three weeks.* absenteeism, non-attendance, truancy. OPPOSITE attendance, presence. **2** *an absence of evidence.* dearth, deficiency, lack, want. OPPOSITE existence.

absent *adjective* *Five children were absent.* away, elsewhere, missing, off. OPPOSITE present. — *verb* **absent yourself from** *Peter absented himself from school.* bludge (*Australian informal*), play hookey from (*informal*), play truant from, skive off (*informal*), stay away from, wag (*informal*). OPPOSITE attend.

absent-minded *adjective* *The old lady is becoming absent-minded.* abstracted, daydreaming, distracted, dreamy, far-away, forgetful, inattentive, oblivious, preoccupied, scatterbrained, scatty (*informal*). OPPOSITE alert.

absolute *adjective* **1** *an absolute delight. an absolute disaster.* complete, downright, out-and-out, outright, perfect, positive, pure, sheer, thorough, total, unmitigated, unqualified, utter. OPPOSITE qualified. **2** *They needed absolute proof.* categorical, certain, conclusive, definite, firm, positive, reliable, sure, unequivocal, unquestionable. OPPOSITE dubious. **3** *The monarch has absolute power.* autocratic, complete, omnipotent, sovereign, supreme, total, unconditional, unlimited, unqualified, unrestricted. OPPOSITE limited.

absolution *noun* *The priest pronounced the absolution of their sins.* forgiveness, pardon, remission.

absolve *verb* **1** *He was absolved of the crime.* acquit, clear, exonerate, vindicate. OPPOSITE blame. **2** *The priest has authority to absolve sins.* forgive, pardon, remit. **3** *She was absolved from all responsibility.* discharge, excuse, exempt, free, release, set free.

absorb *verb* **1** *The sponge absorbs water.* draw up, mop up, soak up, suck up, take up. **2** *The student absorbed the information.* assimilate, digest, take in. **3** *The TV show absorbed his attention.* captivate, capture, engross, monopolise, occupy, preoccupy. ☐ **absorbed in** *absorbed in thought.* engrossed in, immersed in, interested in, lost in, preoccupied with.

absorbing *adjective* *an absorbing book.* captivating, engrossing, fascinating, gripping, interesting, riveting. OPPOSITE boring.

abstain *verb* **abstain from** *She abstained from drink.* avoid, decline, desist from, do without, forgo, go without, refrain from. OPPOSITE indulge in.

abstinence *noun* *As a reformed alcoholic he preaches total abstinence.* non-indulgence, self-denial, sobriety, teetotalism, temperance.

abstract *adjective* *abstract ideas.* academic, conceptual, intangible, intellectual, theoretical. OPPOSITE concrete, practical. — *noun* *an abstract of the book.* outline, précis, résumé, summary, synopsis.

absurd *adjective* *We laughed at his absurd suggestion.* comic, crazy, farcical, foolish, funny, illogical, inane, laughable, ludicrous, mad, nonsensical, outrageous, preposterous, ridiculous, senseless, silly, strange, stupid, unreasonable, zany. OPPOSITE reasonable.

abundance *noun* *an abundance of food.* heaps (*informal*), lashings (*informal*), loads (*informal*), lots (*informal*), oodles (*informal*), plenty, stacks (*informal*), tons

(*informal*), wealth. OPPOSITE lack, shortage.

abundant *adjective* *an abundant supply of fruit.* ample, bountiful, copious, generous, large, lavish, liberal, plentiful, profuse. OPPOSITE inadequate, insufficient. ☐ **abundant in** *The river is abundant in fish.* abounding in, full of, overflowing with, teeming with. OPPOSITE deficient in, lacking in.

abuse *noun* **1** *physical abuse. child abuse.* assault, exploitation, ill-treatment, maltreatment, mistreatment. **2** *verbal abuse.* calumny, curses, denigration, insults, invective, obscenities, revilement, slander, swearing, vilification, vituperation. OPPOSITE compliments. — *verb* **1** *She abused her position.* exploit, misuse. **2** *The man had abused the child physically.* assault, damage, harm, hurt, ill-treat, maltreat, mistreat, molest. **3** *She abused the person on the telephone.* attack, be rude to, curse, denigrate, disparage, insult, revile, slander, swear at. OPPOSITE compliment.

abusive *adjective* *abusive language.* derogatory, disparaging, foul-mouthed, impolite, insulting, obscene, offensive, pejorative, rude, scornful, scurrilous, slanderous. OPPOSITE complimentary, polite.

abysmal *adjective* (*informal*) *The food was abysmal.* abominable (*informal*), appalling (*informal*), atrocious (*informal*), dreadful (*informal*), shocking (*informal*), terrible (*informal*); see also BAD.

abyss *noun* *It sank into the abyss.* bottomless pit, chasm, hole, void.

academic *adjective* **1** *academic books.* educational, pedagogic, scholastic. **2** *an academic person.* bookish, erudite, highbrow, intellectual, learned, scholarly, studious. OPPOSITE practical. **3** *The question is purely academic.* abstract, hypothetical, speculative, theoretical. OPPOSITE practical. — *noun* *a university academic.* don, lecturer, professor, reader.

accelerate *verb* **1** *The driver accelerated to overtake.* go faster, quicken, speed up, step on it (*informal*). OPPOSITE decelerate, slow down. **2** *Work on the project was accelerated.* expedite, hasten, intensify, speed up, step up. OPPOSITE slow down.

accent *noun* **1** *The accent is on the first syllable in the word 'tangent'.* emphasis, prominence, stress. **2** *She speaks with an Irish accent.* brogue, inflection, intonation, pronunciation. — *verb* *Accent the first syllable.* accentuate, emphasise, stress.

accentuate *verb* *The report accentuates the problems in the company.* accent, draw attention to, emphasise, highlight, stress, underline.

accept *verb* **1** *She accepted the prize.* get, receive, take. OPPOSITE refuse, reject. **2** *He accepted responsibility.* admit, assume, bear, shoulder, take, undertake. OPPOSITE evade. **3** *She finds it hard to accept change.* agree to, consent to, go along with, put up with, reconcile yourself to, resign yourself to, take, tolerate, welcome. OPPOSITE reject. **4** *Do you accept that I am right?* acknowledge, admit, agree, believe, think. OPPOSITE dispute.

acceptable *adjective* *acceptable behaviour.* adequate, admissible, appropriate, passable, pleasing, proper, satisfactory, seemly, suitable, tolerable. OPPOSITE unacceptable, unsatisfactory.

access *noun* *Access to the house was restricted.* admission, admittance, approach, entrance, entry, way in.

— verb *She was unable to access the information.* retrieve.

accessible *adjective The computer is down and the information is not accessible.* attainable, available, handy, obtainable, retrievable. OPPOSITE inaccessible, irretrievable.

accessory *noun* **1** *accessories for the vacuum cleaner.* attachment, extension, extra, fitting. **2** *an accessory to murder.* abetter, accomplice, assistant, associate, confederate, partner.

accident *noun* **1** *a tragic accident.* calamity, catastrophe, disaster, misadventure, misfortune, mishap. **2** *a car accident.* collision, crash, pile-up (*informal*), prang (*slang*), smash. **3** *It happened by accident.* chance, coincidence, fluke, fortune, luck.

accidental *adjective an accidental discovery.* chance, coincidental, fluky, fortuitous, inadvertent, serendipitous, unexpected, unforeseen, unintentional, unplanned. OPPOSITE deliberate, planned.

accident-prone *adjective* disaster-prone, hapless, jinxed (*informal*), unlucky.

acclaim *verb The spectators acclaimed the winning team.* applaud, cheer, clap, hail, praise, salute, welcome. **— noun** *The book met with universal acclaim.* acclamation, applause, approval, commendation, ovation, praise, welcome.

acclimatise *verb He has acclimatised to the cold.* adapt, adjust, become accustomed, become inured, get used.

accolade *noun The pianist received high accolades.* acclaim, compliment, honour, praise, tribute. OPPOSITE censure.

accommodate *verb* **1** *The family can accommodate two visitors.* billet, board, house, put up, take in. **2** *The cottage accommodates eight.* fit, house, sleep. **3** *We will accommodate your request.* furnish, grant, provide, supply.

accommodation *noun rented accommodation.* billet, digs (*informal*), home, house, housing, lodgings, premises, quarters, residence.

accompaniment *noun a musical accompaniment.* background, backing, support.

accompany *verb* **1** *A bodyguard accompanies the singer everywhere.* attend, be with, chaperone, escort, go with, partner, tag along with, travel with. **2** *The teacher accompanied the cellist on the piano.* back up, play with, support.

accomplice *noun an accomplice in crime.* abetter, accessory, assistant, collaborator, helper, partner, sidekick (*informal*).

accomplish *verb She accomplished what was required.* achieve, attain, bring off, carry out, complete, do, effect, execute, finish, fulfil, perform, succeed in. OPPOSITE fail.

accomplished *adjective an accomplished writer.* able, adept, brilliant, consummate, experienced, expert, gifted, proficient, skilful, skilled, talented. OPPOSITE amateurish, inexpert.

accomplishment *noun* **1** *social accomplishments.* ability, attainment, gift, skill, talent. **2** *Climbing Mount Everest was her latest accomplishment.* achievement, attainment, deed, exploit, feat.

accord *noun All parties signed the accord.* agreement, compact, pact, treaty. **— verb** *His views accorded with mine.* agree, be consistent, coincide, concur, correspond, harmonise, tally. □ **of your own accord** *She wrote the letter of her own accord.* off your own bat, of your own free will, of your own volition,

spontaneously, unasked, voluntarily, willingly.

accordingly *adverb She stopped at the shops and accordingly was late.* consequently, hence, so, therefore, thus.

accost *verb A stranger accosted him outside the meeting.* bail up (*Australian*), buttonhole, confront, hail, stop, waylay.

account *noun* **1** *He paid the account.* bill, invoice, receipt, statement. **2** *We read an account of these events.* chronicle, description, explanation, history, log, narrative, record, report, story, tale. **— verb** **account for** *Not even a headache could account for his rudeness.* excuse, explain, give grounds for, justify. □ **take into account** *His age will be taken into account.* allow for, consider, take into consideration. OPPOSITE disregard.

accountable *adjective You will be held accountable for your actions.* answerable, liable, responsible.

accumulate *verb* **1** *They accumulated books over the years.* acquire, amass, collect, gather, hoard, stockpile, store up. **2** *The miser's funds accumulated.* accrue, build up, grow, increase, multiply, pile up. OPPOSITE diminish.

accumulation *noun an accumulation of dirty dishes.* build-up, collection, heap, hoard, mass, pile, stack, stockpile, store.

accuracy *noun I can't vouch for the accuracy of the figures.* correctness, exactitude, exactness, faithfulness, fidelity, meticulousness, precision, truth. OPPOSITE inaccuracy.

accurate *adjective an accurate representation of events.* careful, correct, exact, factual, faithful, meticulous, perfect, precise, right, spot on (*informal*), true. OPPOSITE inaccurate.

accusation *noun a false accusation.* allegation, charge, imputation, indictment.

accuse *verb He was accused of spying.* blame, charge, denounce, impeach, incriminate, indict, point the finger at (*informal*). OPPOSITE acquit, exonerate.

accustomed *adjective* **1** *Andrew arrived at the accustomed time.* customary, established, expected, familiar, fixed, habitual, normal, regular, set, usual. **2** *The family were soon accustomed to the conditions.* acclimatised, adjusted, habituated, inured, used. OPPOSITE unused.

ace *noun He's an ace at golf.* champion, expert, master, star, winner.

ache *verb Her head ached.* be painful, be sore, hurt, pound, throb. **— noun** **1** *Rest relieved the ache in her body.* discomfort, hurt, pain, pang, soreness. **2** *the ache of a broken heart.* agony, anguish, distress, grief, misery, pain, sorrow, suffering.

achieve *verb* **1** *She achieved her goal.* accomplish, attain, carry out, fulfil, reach, realise, succeed in. **2** *He achieved fame.* acquire, attain, earn, gain, get, obtain, win.

achievement *noun proud of his achievements.* accomplishment, attainment, deed, feat; see also SUCCESS. OPPOSITE failure.

acid *adjective* **1** *an acid taste.* acidic, sharp, sour, tangy, tart, vinegary. OPPOSITE sweet. **2** *acid remarks.* acerbic, bitter, caustic, cutting, sarcastic, sharp, stinging.

acknowledge *verb* **1** *He acknowledged that they were right.* accept, admit, agree, allow, concede, confess, grant, recognise. OPPOSITE deny. **2** *She acknowledged all her sympathy cards.* answer, reply to, respond to, show appreciation of.

acknowledgement *noun* **1** *an acknowledgement of guilt.* acceptance, admission, confession. OPPOSITE denial. **2** *All applications received a written acknowledgement.* answer, reply, response. **3** *an acknowledgement for bravery.* notice, recognition, reward, thanks.

acme *noun the acme of her career.* apex, climax, culmination, height, peak, pinnacle, summit, top, zenith. OPPOSITE nadir.

acne *noun* see PIMPLE.

acquaint *verb* **acquaint with** *He acquainted him with the facts.* advise of, enlighten about, familiarise with, fill in on (*informal*), inform of, make aware of, tell. **be acquainted with** *He was not acquainted with the rules.* be aware of, be familiar with, be versed in, know.

acquaintance *noun I wouldn't call her a friend, simply an acquaintance.* associate, colleague, contact.

acquiesce *verb* see AGREE.

acquire *verb He acquired many possessions.* buy, collect, come by, gain, get, obtain, pick up, procure, purchase, secure. OPPOSITE dispose of.

acquisition *noun the library's acquisitions.* accession, possession, purchase.

acquit *verb The judge acquitted him after new evidence.* absolve, clear, exonerate, let off, release, vindicate. OPPOSITE convict.

acrimonious *adjective an acrimonious dispute.* bitter, cutting, embittered, hostile, nasty, spiteful, tart, virulent. OPPOSITE genial.

acrobat *noun a circus acrobat.* gymnast, tightrope walker, trapeze artist.

across *preposition He travelled across Europe.* over, through, throughout.

act *noun* **1** *his brave acts.* accomplishment, achievement, action, deed, exploit, feat, undertaking. **2** *an act of parliament.* decree, edict, law, statute. **3** *the comedian's act.* performance, routine, show, sketch, skit. **4** (*informal*) *Her tears were just an act.* deception, front, hoax, pretence, sham, show. **— verb** **1** *Act sensibly!* behave, conduct yourself. **2** *The brakes did not act.* function, have an effect, operate, work. **3** *The children acted as fairies in the play.* appear, impersonate, perform, play, portray. **4** *She's not really upset: she's just acting.* fake, feign, make believe, pretend, sham.

acting *adjective the acting principal.* deputy, interim, provisional, substitute, temporary. OPPOSITE permanent.

action *noun* **1** *They put the plan into action.* activity, motion, operation, performance, practice, work. **2** *brave actions.* act, deed, effort, endeavour, exploit, feat, move, step, undertaking. **3** *a holiday packed with action.* activity, adventure, drama, events, excitement, happenings, incidents. **4** *legal action.* lawsuit, litigation, proceedings, prosecution. **5** *He was killed in action.* battle, combat, conflict, fighting, warfare.

activate *verb Pressing the button activates the brakes.* actuate, set off, start, switch on, trigger, turn on.

active *adjective* **1** *an active toddler. an active eighty-year-old.* dynamic, energetic, full of beans (*informal*), hyperactive, lively, sprightly, spry, vivacious. OPPOSITE inactive. **2** *active games such as tennis.* energetic, lively, physical, strenuous, vigorous. OPPOSITE passive. **3** *an active member.* busy, diligent, hardworking, industrious, involved, occupied, participating. OPPOSITE inactive, nominal. **4** *an active vol-*

cano. functioning, operative, working. OPPOSITE dormant, extinct.

activist *noun a political activist.* agitator, campaigner, crusader, firebrand, lobbyist, militant, protester, stirrer.

activity *noun* **1** *The hall was a hive of activity.* action, bustle, excitement, hurly-burly, hustle, industry, liveliness, movement. OPPOSITE inactivity. **2** *physical activity.* exercise, exertion. OPPOSITE inactivity. **3** *leisure activities.* enterprise, hobby, occupation, pastime, project, pursuit, undertaking, venture.

actor *noun* actress, performer, player, star, trouper; [*group of actors*] cast, company, troupe.

actual *adjective an actual incident.* authentic, confirmed, factual, genuine, real, true, verified. OPPOSITE fictitious.

actually *adverb He was actually surprised.* genuinely, indeed, in fact, really, truly.

acute *adjective* **1** *acute pain.* excruciating, extreme, intense, keen, piercing, severe, sharp, shooting, stabbing. OPPOSITE mild. **2** *an acute mind.* astute, canny, clever, discerning, discriminating, incisive, keen, penetrating, perceptive, sharp, shrewd, subtle. OPPOSITE dull.

adamant *adjective He was adamant that they would not have a dog.* determined, firm, immovable, inflexible, intransigent, resolute, resolved, stubborn, unyielding. OPPOSITE flexible.

adapt *verb* **1** *The play was adapted for television.* adjust, alter, change, convert, edit, modify, remake, rewrite, transform. **2** *The koalas adapted to their new habitat.* acclimatise, adjust, become accustomed to, become used to.

adaptable *adjective an adaptable person.* accommodating, amenable, easygoing, flexible, malleable, versatile. OPPOSITE inflexible.

add *verb* **1** *He added the figures.* add up, combine, sum, total, tot up (*informal*). OPPOSITE subtract. **2** *He added his name to the list.* affix, append, attach, join, tack on. OPPOSITE remove. □ **add to** *This added to the weight of the parcel.* augment, enlarge, increase, swell. OPPOSITE reduce. **add up** *She added up the bill.* calculate, compute, count, reckon, total, tot up (*informal*), work out. **add up to** *It added up to $5.* amount to, come to, make, total.

addendum *noun The reprint of the book has an addendum at the back.* appendix, postscript, supplement.

addict *noun* **1** *a drug addict.* druggie (*informal*), junkie (*slang*), user (*informal*). **2** *a television addict.* devotee, enthusiast, fan, fanatic, freak (*informal*), lover, nut (*informal*).

addicted *adjective She is addicted to heroin.* dependent on, hooked on (*slang*).

addiction *noun drug addiction.* dependence, habit, obsession.

addition *noun* **1** *He did the addition in his head.* calculation, computation, totalling, totting up (*informal*). OPPOSITE subtraction. **2** *an addition to a building.* annexe, extension, wing. **3** *an addition to a document.* appendix, attachment, codicil, postscript, rider, supplement.

additional *adjective additional help.* added, backup, extra, further, more, new, other, supplementary.

address *noun* **1** *He lives at a new address.* abode (*old use*), domicile, location, residence. **2** *The minister's address was brief.* discourse, lecture, oration, sermon, speech, talk. **— verb** **1** *She addressed her students.* lecture, speak to, talk to. **2** *He eventually addressed the problem.*

apply yourself to, attend to, devote yourself to, focus on, tackle, turn to.

adept *adjective Jane is adept at handling complaints.* accomplished, capable, competent, expert, masterful, masterly, proficient, skilful, skilled, talented. OPPOSITE inept.

adequate *adjective* **1** *They have adequate supplies for a month.* ample, enough, sufficient. OPPOSITE insufficient. **2** *an adequate standard.* acceptable, all right, fair, OK (*informal*), passable, satisfactory, tolerable. OPPOSITE inadequate, unsatisfactory.

adhere *verb The chewing gum adhered to the shoe.* attach, cling, hold fast, stick. □ **adhere to** *We must adhere to the rules.* abide by, comply with, follow, keep to, stick to.

adhesive *adjective adhesive tape.* gummed, sticky. — *noun The tiles were fixed to the wall with adhesive.* cement, fixative, glue, gum, paste.

adjacent *adjective adjacent blocks of land.* adjoining, bordering, contiguous, neighbouring, next-door.

adjoin *verb Our land adjoins theirs.* abut on, be adjacent to, be next to, border on.

adjourn *verb They adjourned the meeting until next week.* break off, defer, discontinue, interrupt, postpone, put off, suspend.

adjudicate *verb The teacher adjudicated the debate.* arbitrate, judge, referee, umpire.

adjudicator *noun* arbitrator, judge, referee, umpire.

adjust *verb* **1** *She adjusted the volume.* alter, regulate, set. **2** *The dress needed adjusting.* adapt, alter, change, fit, modify, reshape, tailor. **3** *She had to adjust to being at home again.* acclimatise, adapt, become accustomed, get used, reconcile yourself.

ad lib *adverb She spoke ad lib.* extempore, impromptu, off the cuff, off the top of your head (*informal*). — *adjective ad lib remarks.* extempore, impromptu, improvised, off the cuff, unrehearsed. OPPOSITE prepared. — *verb* (*informal*) *She had not learned the music, but she ad libbed very well.* extemporise, improvise, play it by ear (*informal*).

administer *verb* **1** *He administers a trust fund.* conduct, control, direct, govern, look after, manage, operate, oversee, run, supervise. **2** *The teacher administered the punishment.* carry out, deal out, dispense, give, hand out, mete out, provide.

administration *noun* **1** *the administration of the company.* control, direction, management, running, supervision. **2** *the Bush administration in the United States.* government, ministry, regime.

administrator *noun the territory's administrator.* chief, controller, director, executive, governor, head, manager, superintendent.

admirable *adjective admirable conduct.* commendable, excellent, exemplary, honourable, laudable, praiseworthy, worthy. OPPOSITE deplorable.

admiration *noun He was full of admiration for their achievements.* approval, commendation, praise, respect, veneration.

admire *verb The people admire their leader.* appreciate, approve of, esteem, idolise, look up to, praise, regard highly, respect, revere, think highly of, venerate. OPPOSITE despise.

admirer *noun* **1** *a woman's admirers.* beau, boyfriend, lover, suitor, sweetheart. **2** *The actor has many admirers.* devotee, fan, follower, supporter.

admission *noun* **1** *free admission.* access, admittance, entrance, entry. **2** *an admission of guilt.* acceptance, acknowledgement, confession, declaration, disclosure, statement. OPPOSITE denial.

admit *verb* **1** *Only people over eighteen are admitted.* allow in, let in, permit entry, take in. OPPOSITE exclude. **2** *I admit that I don't know the answer.* accept, acknowledge, concede, confess, grant, own up. OPPOSITE deny.

admittance *noun Strictly no admittance!* access, admission, entrance, entry.

admonish *verb She admonished the child for touching the switches.* chide (*old use*), rebuke, reprimand, reproach, reprove, scold, tell off (*informal*), tick off (*informal*). OPPOSITE commend.

ado *noun without further ado.* bother, commotion, fuss, kerfuffle (*informal*), to-do, trouble.

adolescence *noun* puberty, teens, youth.

adolescent *adjective* teenage, youthful. — *noun* minor, teenager, youngster, youth.

adopt *verb* **1** *He adopted a false name.* assume, choose, take up, use. **2** *The committee adopted the report's recommendations.* accept, approve, embrace, endorse, espouse, ratify.

adorable *adjective an adorable baby.* appealing, cute (*informal*), darling, dear, delightful, irresistible, likeable, lovable, lovely, sweet (*informal*).

adore *verb* **1** *The man adored his wife.* cherish, dote on, idolise, love. OPPOSITE hate. **2** *They adore God.* exalt, extol, glorify, hallow, honour, laud (*formal*), magnify (*old use*), praise, revere, venerate, worship. **3** (*informal*) *She adores jazz.* be fond of, enjoy, like, love. OPPOSITE hate.

adorn *verb They adorned the hall with flowers.* array, deck out, decorate, festoon, ornament.

adult *adjective an adult penguin.* developed, full-sized, fully grown, grown-up, mature. OPPOSITE immature. — *noun* grown-up. OPPOSITE child, minor.

adulterated *adjective adulterated juice.* contaminated, diluted, impure, watered down, weakened. OPPOSITE pure, unadulterated.

adultery *noun He divorced his wife on the grounds of adultery.* infidelity, unfaithfulness. OPPOSITE fidelity.

advance *verb* **1** *They advanced towards the city.* approach, go ahead, go forward, go on, make headway, move forward, proceed, progress. OPPOSITE retreat. **2** *They advanced the date of the wedding.* bring forward, hasten. OPPOSITE defer, postpone. **3** *She advanced a month's pocket money.* lend, prepay. — *noun* **1** *a scientific advance.* breakthrough, development, headway, improvement, progress. **2** *an advance on next week's pocket money.* loan, prepayment. □ **in advance** *She paid her fees in advance.* ahead, beforehand, up front. OPPOSITE later.

advanced *adjective* **1** *an advanced age.* elderly, mature, old, ripe. OPPOSITE tender, young. **2** *advanced studies.* complicated, difficult, hard, higher. OPPOSITE elementary. **3** *advanced technology.* avant-garde, innovative, modern, new, progressive, revolutionary, sophisticated, up-to-date. OPPOSITE obsolete.

advantage *noun* **1** *Language skills are an advantage.* asset, benefit, blessing, bonus, boon, help, plus. OPPOSITE disadvantage, handicap. **2** *It will be to your advantage.* benefit, gain, profit. □ **take advantage of** *She took advantage of the fine day and went parasailing.* capitalise on, cash in on, exploit, make the most of, make use of, use.

advantageous *adjective an advantageous position.* beneficial, favourable, good, helpful, profitable, useful, valuable. OPPOSITE unhelpful.

advent *noun Their grandparents were born before the advent of television.* appearance, arrival, coming, dawn. OPPOSITE departure.

adventure *noun* **1** *an unforgettable adventure.* escapade, experience, exploit, incident. **2** *a life filled with adventure.* danger, excitement, risk, uncertainty.

adventurous *adjective an adventurous explorer.* bold, brave, daring, enterprising, intrepid, venturesome.

adversary *noun She defeated her adversary.* enemy, foe, opponent, rival.

adverse *adjective She suffered no adverse effects.* bad, detrimental, harmful, ill, injurious, unfavourable, untoward. OPPOSITE favourable, good.

adversity *noun in sickness and adversity.* affliction, calamity, catastrophe, disaster, distress, hardship, misfortune, trouble. OPPOSITE prosperity.

advertise *verb The company advertises their products on TV.* make known, plug (*informal*), promote, publicise, push (*informal*), tout.

advertisement *noun a newspaper advertisement. an advertisement at the cinema.* ad (*informal*), advert (*informal*), announcement, blurb, commercial, notice, plug (*informal*), promotion, publicity, trailer.

advice *noun* **1** *She asked for my advice as to what to do.* counsel, guidance, opinion, recommendation, suggestion, tip. **2** *We received advice that the goods had been sent.* information, news, notification, word.

advisable *adjective It is advisable to remain silent.* expedient, judicious, politic, prudent, recommended, sensible, wise. OPPOSITE foolish, inadvisable.

advise *verb* **1** *He advised them to sell the house.* counsel, recommend, suggest, urge, warn. **2** *She advised them of their rights.* acquaint (with), inform, notify, tell.

adviser *noun a financial adviser.* consultant, counsellor, guide, mentor.

advocate *verb She advocates free education.* be in favour of, champion, endorse, favour, recommend, support. OPPOSITE oppose. — *noun* **1** *an advocate of reform.* backer, champion, promoter, proponent, supporter. OPPOSITE opponent. **2** *an advocate in a court of law.* attorney (*American*), barrister, counsel, lawyer.

aegis *noun under the aegis of the United Nations.* auspices, patronage, protection, sponsorship.

aerial *adjective an aerial view.* bird's-eye, overhead. — *noun a TV aerial.* antenna.

aeroplane *noun* plane; see also AIRCRAFT.

affable *adjective an affable person.* amiable, amicable, congenial, cordial, courteous, easygoing, friendly, genial, good-tempered, kindly, pleasant. OPPOSITE disagreeable, unfriendly.

affair *noun* **1** *That's not your affair.* business, concern, responsibility, thing. **2** *business affairs.* activity, business, concern, dealing, interest, matter, operation, undertaking. **3** *a* sad and sorry affair. business, case, episode, event, happening, incident, occurrence. **4** *an affair with a married woman.* fling, liaison, love affair, relationship, romance.

affect *verb* **1** *The changes did not affect them.* concern, have an effect on, have an impact on, impinge on, touch. **2** *Tuberculosis affected his lungs.* attack, damage, infect, strike. **3** *His death affected them deeply.* disturb, move, stir, touch, upset.

affected *adjective an affected laugh.* artificial, fake, feigned, insincere, phoney (*informal*), pretended, sham, studied, unnatural. OPPOSITE genuine.

affection *noun They show great affection for one another.* caring, devotion, fondness, liking, love, tenderness, warmth.

affectionate *adjective an affectionate husband.* caring, devoted, doting, fond, kind, loving, tender-hearted, warm-hearted. OPPOSITE cold-hearted, indifferent.

affiliate *verb The club affiliated with the larger one.* ally, associate, combine, connect, join, unite.

affinity *noun* **1** *an affinity between the two languages.* closeness, connection, correspondence, likeness, relationship, resemblance, similarity. **2** *They felt an affinity for one another.* attraction, fondness, liking, rapport, sympathy.

affirm *verb He affirmed that he had written the letter.* assert, confirm, declare, state, swear.

affirmative *adjective an affirmative reply.* agreeing, assenting, favourable, positive. OPPOSITE negative.

affix *verb* **1** *Affix a stamp to the envelope.* attach, fasten, join, stick, tack. **2** *Affix your signature to the agreement.* add, append.

afflict *verb The disease afflicted her in childhood.* affect, distress, oppress, plague, strike, torment, trouble.

affliction *noun* **1** *She bore affliction bravely.* adversity, distress, hardship, misery, misfortune, pain, suffering, trouble. **2** *Doctors tried to treat her affliction.* ailment, condition, disease, disorder, illness, malady, sickness, trouble.

affluent *adjective the affluent society.* moneyed, opulent, prosperous, rich, wealthy, well-heeled (*informal*), well off, well-to-do. OPPOSITE poor.

afford *verb They can't afford the money for the tickets.* bear the expense of, manage, pay for, spare.

affront *verb He was affronted by the suggestion.* insult, offend, outrage, scandalise. — *noun an affront to her pride.* insult, offence, slap in the face (*informal*), slight, snub.

afraid *adjective* **1** *She is afraid of the dark.* alarmed, anxious, apprehensive, fearful, frightened, nervous, panic-stricken, scared, terrified, timid, worried. OPPOSITE brave, unafraid. **2** *I'm afraid there isn't any more.* apologetic, regretful, sorry.

after *preposition* **1** *Close the door after you.* behind. **2** *He rang after my bedtime.* following, later than, past. OPPOSITE before. **3** *He asked after you.* about, concerning, regarding.

aftermath *noun the aftermath of the cyclone.* after-effects, consequences, follow-up, outcome, sequel, upshot, wake.

afterwards *adverb What happened afterwards?* after, later, next, subsequently.

again *adverb* **1** *Try again.* afresh, anew, another time, once more. **2** *Then again, there is another reason.* also, besides, furthermore, in addition, moreover.

against *preposition* **1** *We're against capital punishment.* anti, averse to, opposed to. OPPOSITE for, in favour of. **2** *the A team against the B team.* in opposition to, opposing, versus.

age *noun* **1** *the age in which we live.* days, epoch, era, period, time. **2** (*informal*) *I haven't seen him for ages.* donkey's years (*informal*), eternity (*informal*), years, yonks (*slang*). — *verb The wine has aged well.* develop, grow older, mature, mellow, ripen.

aged *adjective* **1** *aged people.* elderly, old, retired. OPPOSITE young. **2** *an aged cheddar.* mature, ripe, vintage.

agency *noun a travel agency.* bureau, business, company, firm, office, organisation.

agenda *noun the agenda for the meeting.* list, plan, programme, schedule.

agent *noun* **1** *an agent for a company. an actor's agent.* broker, delegate, envoy, go-between, intermediary, middleman, negotiator, proxy, representative, spokesperson. **2** *a secret agent.* intelligence officer, mole (*informal*), spy.

aggravate *verb* **1** *Washing with soap aggravated the rash.* compound, exacerbate, inflame, intensify, worsen. OPPOSITE improve. **2** (*informal*) *Rock music aggravates some people.* annoy, bother, exasperate, get on someone's nerves, irritate, provoke, rile (*informal*), vex. OPPOSITE please.

aggregate *adjective the aggregate score.* combined, cumulative, total, whole.

aggressive *adjective* **1** *aggressive behaviour.* attacking, bellicose, belligerent, combative, hostile, militant, pugnacious, warlike. OPPOSITE friendly. **2** *an aggressive salesperson.* assertive, forceful, insistent, persistent, pushy, self-assertive, zealous. OPPOSITE retiring.

aghast *adjective Aghast at the terrible news.* appalled, dismayed, horrified, shocked, stunned.

agile *adjective an agile dancer.* flexible, limber, lissom, lithe, nimble, quick-moving, sprightly, spry, supple. OPPOSITE clumsy, stiff.

agitate *verb* **1** *Agitate the mixture.* beat, churn, shake, stir, toss, whisk. **2** *The patient became agitated.* disturb, excite, fluster, perturb, ruffle, stir up, trouble, unsettle, upset, work up, worry. OPPOSITE pacify. **3** *The students were agitating against logging.* campaign, lobby, protest, stir.

agitator *noun political agitators.* activist, campaigner, demagogue, firebrand, lobbyist, protester, rabble-rouser, stirrer.

agonising *adjective agonising pain.* acute, excruciating, harrowing, intolerable, painful, severe, unbearable. OPPOSITE mild.

agony *noun The injured boy was in agony.* anguish, distress, pain, suffering, torment, torture.

agree *verb* **1** *Father and son never agree.* be of the same mind, be unanimous, concur, see eye to eye. OPPOSITE differ. **2** *They agreed that we had grounds for complaint.* accept, admit, allow, concede, grant. **3** *He agreed to speak at the ceremony.* consent, undertake. **4** *Their answers agree.* accord, be consistent, be in harmony, coincide, conform, correspond, fit, harmonise, match, tally. OPPOSITE disagree. □ **agree to** *She agreed to our plan.* accede to, accept, acquiesce in, approve, assent to, back, consent to, endorse, OK (*informal*), support. OPPOSITE reject. **agree with** *Curry does not agree with me.* be good for, suit.

agreeable *adjective* **1** *an agreeable person.* amiable, congenial, friendly, likeable, nice, pleasant; see also PLEASANT. **2** *We'll go ahead*

if you're agreeable. amenable, in accord, in agreement, in favour, willing. OPPOSITE against, unwilling.

agreement *noun* **1** *No agreement could be reached on what to do.* accord, concord, consensus, harmony, unanimity. OPPOSITE disagreement. **2** *An agreement was signed by both parties.* accord, arrangement, bargain, compact, contract, covenant, deal, pact, settlement, treaty.

aground *adverb The ship had run aground on the island.* beached, grounded, marooned, shipwrecked, stranded.

ahead *adverb* **1** *moving ahead.* forwards, on, onwards. OPPOSITE backwards. **2** *Their team is ahead.* in advance, in front, in the lead. OPPOSITE behind.

aid *verb* **1** *He aided the robber.* abet, assist, collaborate with, cooperate with, help. OPPOSITE hinder. **2** *The computer aids their essay writing.* advance, facilitate, further, promote. **3** *The government aids their organisation.* back, contribute to, give to, subscribe to, subsidise. **4** *He aided the injured man.* assist, help, lend a hand to, minister to, relieve, succour. — *noun* **1** *She could not have managed without their aid.* assistance, backing, collaboration, cooperation, encouragement, help, succour, support. OPPOSITE hindrance, opposition. **2** *financial aid.* charity, contribution, donation, funding, grant, relief, sponsorship, subsidy, support.

aide *noun a nurse's aide.* assistant, helper.

ailing *adjective He looked after his ailing parents.* crook (*Australian informal*), ill, indisposed, infirm, poorly, sick, unwell. OPPOSITE healthy.

ailment *noun The doctor treated his ailment.* affliction, complaint, condition, disease, disorder, illness, indisposition, infection, infirmity, malady, sickness, trouble.

aim *verb* **1** *He aimed the gun at the bird.* direct, focus, level, point, train. **2** *She aims to be famous.* aspire, endeavour, intend, plan, purpose, seek, strive, try. — *noun What is his aim?* ambition, design, end, goal, intention, object, objective, plan, point, purpose, target.

aimless *adjective an aimless existence.* drifting, goalless, pointless, purposeless. OPPOSITE purposeful.

air *noun* **1** *flying through the air.* aerospace, atmosphere, sky. **2** *Open the window and let in some air.* breeze, draught, wind. **3** *an air of mystery.* ambience, appearance, atmosphere, aura, feeling, impression, look, mood. **4** *He whistled a happy air.* melody, strain, tune. — *verb* **1** *She aired the room.* freshen, open up, ventilate. **2** *You can air your grievances.* express, get off your chest, make known, reveal, say, tell, vent, voice. □ **air hostess** flight attendant, hostess, hostie (*Australian informal*), steward, stewardess. **in the air 1** *Rumours are in the air.* abroad, around, circulating, current. **2** *Plans are still in the air.* uncertain, undecided, unresolved.

aircraft *noun* [*kinds of aircraft*] aeroplane, airliner, airship, biplane, bomber, fighter, glider, helicopter, jet, jumbo jet, jump jet, microlight, monoplane, plane, seaplane, turbojet.

airport *noun The plane landed at Sydney Airport.* aerodrome, airfield, airstrip, landing strip.

airtight *adjective an airtight container.* hermetically sealed, impermeable.

airy *adjective an airy room.* breezy, draughty, fresh, ventilated, well-ventilated. OPPOSITE stuffy.

aisle *noun The theatre has two aisles for ease of access.* corridor, gangway, gap, passage, passageway, path.

alarm *noun* **1** *The fire alarm sounded.* alert, bell, signal, siren, tocsin, warning. **2** *He jumped up in alarm.* anxiety, apprehension, consternation, dismay, dread, fear, fright, panic, terror, trepidation, worry. — *verb The loud knock alarmed them.* agitate, dismay, disturb, frighten, panic, perturb, petrify, put the wind up (*informal*), scare, startle, terrify, unnerve. OPPOSITE reassure.

album *noun* **1** *a photo album.* book, display book. **2** *the group's latest album.* collection, compilation, disc, record, recording.

alcohol *noun He prefers soft drinks to alcohol.* booze (*informal*), drink, grog (*Australian informal*), liquor, spirits, wine.

alcoholic *adjective alcoholic drinks.* intoxicating, spirituous. — *noun a reformed alcoholic.* boozer (*informal*), dipsomaniac, drunk, drunkard, soak (*informal*), sot, wino (*informal*). OPPOSITE teetotaller.

alcove *noun an alcove in a room.* bay, niche, nook, recess.

alert *adjective A nurse must be alert.* attentive, awake, aware, careful, observant, on the ball (*informal*), on the lookout, on your guard, on your toes, ready, vigilant, wary, watchful. OPPOSITE careless, inattentive. — *noun They sounded the alert.* alarm, signal, siren, warning. — *verb He alerted them to the dangers.* caution, forewarn, prepare, warn.

alias *noun Her real name was Beatrice Brown but she went by various aliases.* assumed name, false name, nickname, nom de plume, pen-name, pseudonym, stage name.

alien *noun* **1** *enemy aliens.* foreigner, outsider, stranger. OPPOSITE native. **2** *an alien from another planet.* extraterrestrial. — *adjective* **1** *an alien practice.* exotic, foreign, outlandish, strange, unfamiliar. OPPOSITE familiar. **2** *Cruelty is alien to her character.* contrary, foreign, inconsistent, uncharacteristic. OPPOSITE consistent.

alienate *verb She alienated people with her rudeness.* antagonise, estrange, turn away, turn off.

alight[1] *adjective The house was alight.* ablaze, blazing, burning, on fire.

alight[2] *verb* **1** *The passengers alighted from the bus.* descend, disembark, get down, get off. OPPOSITE board. **2** *The bird alighted on a branch.* land, perch, settle.

align *verb* **1** *They aligned the cars for a photo.* line up, straighten up. **2** *They aligned themselves with the Liberals.* affiliate, ally, associate, join, side.

alike *adjective The girls are alike in many ways.* comparable, equivalent, identical, indistinguishable, similar. OPPOSITE different, unlike.

alive *adjective The animal was still alive.* animate, breathing, existing, live, living, quick (*old use*), surviving. OPPOSITE dead. □ **alive to** *He is alive to the possible dangers.* alert to, aware of, conscious of, mindful of, sensitive to. OPPOSITE unaware of. **alive with** *The river was alive with boats.* crawling with (*informal*), full of, packed with, swarming with, teeming with.

allay *verb He allayed their fears.* alleviate, calm, diminish, ease, lessen, quell, reduce, subdue. OPPOSITE heighten.

allegation *noun There was no substance to his allegations.* accusation, assertion, charge, claim, statement.

allege *verb He alleged that he was innocent.* affirm, assert, avow, claim, declare, profess, state.

allegiance *noun They swore allegiance to the king.* devotion, duty, faithfulness, fidelity, loyalty. OPPOSITE disloyalty, treason.

allegory *noun The story is an allegory.* fable, parable.

allergy *noun an allergy to dust.* reaction, sensitivity.

alleviate *verb The treatment alleviated the pain.* assuage, diminish, ease, lessen, mitigate, moderate, reduce, relieve, soften. OPPOSITE aggravate.

alley *noun An alley runs behind the houses.* back street, lane, passage, passageway, path.

alliance *noun The two parties formed an alliance.* affiliation, association, coalition, confederation, league, partnership, union.

allocate *verb see* ALLOT.

allocation *noun an allocation of funds.* allotment, allowance, cut (*informal*), lot, portion, quota, ration, share, slice (*informal*).

allot *verb A committee allots the money to the various charities.* allocate, apportion, assign, dispense, distribute, dole out, give out, mete out, ration, share out.

allotment *noun* **1** *an annual allotment of $10,000.* allocation, allowance, quota, ration, share. **2** *a building allotment.* block, lot, plot, section (*Australian historical*).

allow *verb* **1** *They allowed her to come.* approve, authorise, enable, let, permit. OPPOSITE forbid. **2** *He was allowed $200 a year for expenses.* allocate, allot, assign, give, grant, permit, provide.

allowance *noun* **1** *They used up their water allowance.* allocation, allotment, portion, quota, ration. **2** *He was paid an allowance.* annuity, benefit, dole, endowment, grant, payment, pension, pocket money, stipend, subsidy. □ **make allowances for** *You must make allowances for her failing eyesight.* allow for, bear in mind, make concessions for, take into account, take into consideration; see also EXCUSE.

all right *adjective* **1** *The car was badly damaged but the driver was all right.* fine, OK (*informal*), safe, safe and sound, unharmed, uninjured, unscathed. **2** *The food at camp was all right.* acceptable, fine, OK (*informal*), passable, satisfactory.

allude *verb* **allude to** *He alluded to his problem.* hint at, mention, refer to, touch on.

alluring *adjective an alluring smile.* attractive, beguiling, captivating, charming, enchanting, fascinating.

allusion *noun an allusion to past problems.* hint, intimation, mention, reference.

ally *noun They are friends and allies.* associate, colleague, confederate, friend, partner. OPPOSITE enemy. — *verb They allied themselves against the common enemy.* affiliate, band together, combine, join forces, side, team up, unite.

almighty *adjective Almighty God.* all-powerful, omnipotent, sovereign, supreme.

almost *adverb They ate almost half of the cake.* all but, approximately, close to, nearly, not quite, practically, virtually, wellnigh.

alone *adjective She likes to be alone.* apart, by yourself, isolated, on your own, separate, single, solitary, solo, unaccompanied, unaided, unassisted; see also LONELY. — *adverb You alone can help.* exclusively, just, only, solely.

alongside *preposition His car was parked alongside ours.* adjacent to, beside, close to, next to.

aloof *adjective an aloof manner.* cool, distant, remote, reserved, standoffish, unapproachable, unfriendly, unsociable, unsympathetic.

aloud *adverb The children read aloud.* audibly, out loud. OPPOSITE silently.

also *adverb* additionally, as well, besides, furthermore, in addition, moreover, too.

alter *verb She had her dress altered to fit better. He altered his story for the police.* adapt, adjust, amend, change, convert, modify, remodel, reshape, revise, transform, vary.

altercation *noun The children had an altercation over toys.* argument, barney (*informal*), clash, disagreement, dispute, fight, quarrel, row, scrap (*informal*), set-to, squabble.

alternate *adjective The cleaner comes on alternate Tuesdays.* every other, every second. — *verb Her mood alternates between happiness and despair.* change, interchange, oscillate, rotate, swing, switch, take turns, vary.

alternative *noun The two alternatives are Sydney or Melbourne.* choice, option, possibility. — *adjective* **1** *an alternative proposal.* different, other, second. **2** *alternative sources of energy.* non-conventional, unconventional.

altitude *noun an altitude of 2000 metres.* elevation, height.

altogether *adverb* **1** *He was not altogether satisfied.* absolutely, completely, entirely, on the whole, perfectly, quite, thoroughly, totally, utterly, wholly. OPPOSITE partially. **2** *There were ten altogether.* all told, in all, in total, in toto.

always *adverb* **1** *He always arrives late.* consistently, every time, invariably, regularly. **2** *They are always arguing.* constantly, continually, continuously, eternally, forever, perpetually, repeatedly. **3** *You can always cancel your appointment.* in any case, in any event, whatever happens.

amalgamate *verb Their club amalgamated with ours.* blend, combine, incorporate, integrate, join, merge, mix, unite. OPPOSITE separate.

amass *verb He amassed great wealth.* accumulate, collect, gather, heap up, hoard, pile up, stock up, store up.

amateur *noun This is a job for professionals, not amateurs.* dabbler, dilettante, layman, layperson, non-professional. OPPOSITE professional.

amateurish *adjective an amateurish performance.* clumsy, incompetent, inexpert, unprofessional, unskilful. OPPOSITE professional.

amaze *verb She was amazed by the amount of support she received.* astonish, astound, bewilder, confound, dumbfound, flabbergast, nonplus, overwhelm, shock, stagger, startle, stun, stupefy, surprise, take aback.

amazement *noun To our amazement no one was hurt.* astonishment, bewilderment, shock, stupefaction, surprise, wonder.

ambassador *noun* attaché, consul, diplomat, envoy, legate, plenipotentiary, representative.

ambiguous *adjective an ambiguous answer.* equivocal, imprecise, indefinite, uncertain, unclear, vague. OPPOSITE clear, unambiguous.

ambition *noun* **1** *His ambition is to be a doctor.* aim, aspiration, desire, dream, goal, intention, object, objective, purpose. **2** *He lacks ambition.* drive, enterprise, enthusi-

asm, get-up-and-go (*informal*), motivation, push, zeal.

ambitious *adjective* **1** *an ambitious person.* aspiring, eager, enterprising, go-ahead, high-flying, keen, pushy, zealous. OPPOSITE apathetic. **2** *an ambitious project.* bold, challenging, daring, difficult, formidable, grandiose. OPPOSITE modest.

amble *verb She has the time to amble to the shops.* dawdle, ramble, saunter, stroll, walk, wander.

ambush *noun set up an ambush.* snare, trap. — *verb The bushrangers ambushed the gold escort.* attack, ensnare, lie in wait for, pounce on, swoop on, trap, waylay.

ameliorate *verb These changes ameliorated his situation.* enhance, improve, make better, upgrade. OPPOSITE worsen.

amend *verb He amended the text where necessary.* adapt, adjust, alter, change, correct, edit, improve, modify, rectify, revise.

amends *plural noun* **make amends for** *He said he was sorry and wanted to make amends for his crime.* atone for, compensate for, expiate, make reparation for, make restitution for, recompense for.

amenity *noun a resort with many amenities.* convenience, facility, feature.

amiable *adjective an amiable person.* affable, agreeable, amicable, friendly, genial, good-natured, kind, kindly, pleasant. OPPOSITE unfriendly.

amicable *adjective They parted on amicable terms.* cordial, friendly, harmonious, peaceful. OPPOSITE hostile.

amiss *adjective There was something amiss with the TV.* awry, defective, faulty, incorrect, out of order, wrong.

ammunition *noun The soldiers were running out of ammunition.* bullets, cartridges, grenades, missiles, projectiles, rounds, shells, shot, shrapnel.

amnesty *noun an amnesty for all political prisoners.* pardon, reprieve.

among *preposition a rose among thorns.* amid, amidst, amongst, in the middle of, in the midst of, surrounded by.

amorous *adjective an amorous glances.* affectionate, loving, passionate, tender. OPPOSITE cold.

amount *noun a large amount.* extent, lot (*informal*), mass, measure, quantity, sum, total, volume. — *verb* **amount to** *It amounted to $99.20.* add up to, come to, equal, make, total.

ample *adjective* **1** *They have ample supplies of food.* abundant, bountiful, copious, enough, generous, lavish, liberal, plentiful, profuse, sufficient. OPPOSITE insufficient. **2** *a person of ample build.* big, large, stout. OPPOSITE slight.

amplify *verb* **1** *We need to amplify the sound in the hall.* boost, enhance, increase, intensify, magnify, strengthen. OPPOSITE reduce. **2** *Please amplify your story.* add to, develop, elaborate on, enlarge upon, expand, fill out, supplement. OPPOSITE condense.

amputate *verb The surgeon had to amputate the man's leg.* chop off, cut off, remove.

amuse *verb A clown came to amuse the patients.* cheer up, delight, divert, entertain.

amusement *noun* **1** *a source of amusement.* delight, enjoyment, entertainment, fun, hilarity, merriment, mirth, pleasure. **2** *They each found different amusements.* distraction, diversion, entertainment,

game, hobby, interest, pastime, recreation, sport.

amusing *adjective see* FUNNY.

anaemic *adjective The child looked rather anaemic.* colourless, pale, pallid, pasty, sickly, wan, white. OPPOSITE ruddy.

analogous *adjective Her situation is analogous to mine.* akin, comparable, corresponding, like, parallel, similar. OPPOSITE dissimilar.

analogy *noun the analogy between the human heart and a pump.* comparison, likeness, metaphor, parallel, resemblance, similarity.

analyse *verb* **1** *The specimen was analysed in the laboratory.* break down, dissect, divide, separate, take apart. **2** *He analysed the data.* examine, interpret, investigate, study.

analysis *noun an analysis of the causes.* breakdown, examination, interpretation, investigation, study.

anarchy *noun The country fell into a state of anarchy.* chaos, confusion, disorder, lawlessness. OPPOSITE law, order.

ancestor *noun She discovered her ancestors were Scottish.* forebear, forefather, predecessor, progenitor. OPPOSITE descendant.

ancestry *noun He was proud of his French ancestry.* ancestors, blood, descent, extraction, forebears, genealogy, lineage, origin, pedigree, roots, stock. OPPOSITE progeny.

anchor *verb The fisherman anchored the boat.* berth, moor, secure, tie up.

ancient *adjective* **1** *in ancient times.* bygone, early, former, old, olden, prehistoric, primeval, primitive, primordial. OPPOSITE modern. **2** *an ancient encyclopedia.* antiquated, antique, archaic, obsolete, old, old-fashioned, out-of-date. OPPOSITE modern, new.

ancillary *adjective ancillary services.* auxiliary, subordinate, subsidiary, support, supporting.

anecdote *noun He told an amusing anecdote.* narrative, story, tale, yarn (*informal*).

angel *noun a host of angels.* archangel, cherub, messenger of God, seraph.

angelic *adjective* **1** *the angelic choir.* celestial, cherubic, heavenly, seraphic. **2** *an angelic child.* good, innocent, kind, pure. OPPOSITE devilish.

anger *noun He could not hide his anger.* annoyance, displeasure, exasperation, fury, indignation, ire, irritation, outrage, pique, rage, temper, vexation, wrath. — *verb His arrogance angered them.* annoy, bug (*informal*), displease, enrage, exasperate, gall, incense, infuriate, irritate, madden, outrage, pique, provoke, rile (*informal*), vex. OPPOSITE pacify, please.

angle *noun* **1** *an angle of 45 degrees.* bend, corner. **2** *written from a woman's angle.* approach, outlook, perspective, point of view, position, slant, standpoint, viewpoint. — *verb He angled the screen towards them.* slant, slope, tilt, turn, twist.

angry *adjective He was angry when he found out what they'd done.* annoyed, bad-tempered, cross, displeased, enraged, exasperated, furious, hot under the collar (*informal*), incensed, indignant, infuriated, irascible, irate, irritated, livid (*informal*), mad (*informal*), outraged, resentful, riled (*informal*), ropeable (*Australian informal*), shirty (*informal*), snaky (*Australian informal*), up in arms, wild, wrathful. OPPOSITE calm, pleased. □ **be or become angry** blow your stack (*informal*), blow your top (*informal*), do your block (*Australian*

informal), do your lolly (*informal*), explode, flare up, flip your lid (*informal*), fly off the handle (*informal*), freak (out) (*informal*), fume, get steamed up (*informal*), go ballistic (*slang*), go crook (*Australian informal*), go off the deep end (*informal*), hit the roof (*informal*), lose your temper, rage, rave, seethe.

anguish *noun She suffered severe mental anguish.* agony, distress, grief, misery, pain, sorrow, suffering, torment, torture, woe.

animal *noun The wild animals are protected.* beast, brute, creature; [*animals*] fauna, livestock, wildlife.

animate *adjective an animate being.* alive, breathing, live, living, sentient. OPPOSITE inanimate. — *verb A new leader was needed to animate the group.* buck up (*informal*), energise, enliven, excite, fire up, galvanise, inspire, liven up, motivate, perk up (*informal*), rouse, stimulate.

animated *adjective an animated conversation.* active, bright, energetic, enthusiastic, excited, exuberant, lively, passionate, spirited, vigorous, vivacious. OPPOSITE lifeless.

animation *noun She spoke with great animation.* dynamism, energy, enthusiasm, excitement, liveliness, spirit, verve, vigour, vitality, vivacity, zest. OPPOSITE apathy.

animosity *noun He showed no animosity towards his replacement.* acrimony, antagonism, antipathy, bitterness, enmity, hatred, hostility, ill will, malevolence, malice, rancour, resentment. OPPOSITE friendliness.

annex *verb The country was annexed by its neighbour.* conquer, occupy, seize, take over, take possession of.

annexe *noun the hotel annexe.* addition, extension, wing.

annihilate *verb The bomb annihilated the entire population.* destroy, eliminate, eradicate, exterminate, extinguish, get rid of, kill, liquidate, murder, obliterate, slaughter, wipe out.

anniversary *noun* birthday, jubilee.

annotation *noun He filled the margins of the essay with annotations.* comment, explanation, footnote, note.

announce *verb* **1** *The couple announced their engagement.* advertise, broadcast, declare, disclose, divulge, make known, proclaim, promulgate, publicise, publish, report, reveal, tell. **2** *The MC announced the next item.* introduce, present.

announcement *noun an official announcement.* advertisement, bulletin, communiqué, declaration, disclosure, notice, notification, proclamation, pronouncement, publication, report, statement.

announcer *noun a radio announcer.* broadcaster, compère, disc jockey, DJ, herald, master of ceremonies, MC, newsreader, presenter.

annoy *verb Her housemate's untidiness annoyed her greatly.* aggravate (*informal*), anger, badger, bother, bug (*informal*), distress, drive someone mad (*informal*), drive someone up the wall (*informal*), exasperate, gall, get on someone's nerves, get under someone's skin (*informal*), get up someone's nose (*informal*), harass, hassle, infuriate, irk, irritate, madden, nark (*informal*), needle (*informal*), pester, pique, plague, provoke, rankle, rile (*informal*), rub someone up the wrong way (*informal*), trouble, try, upset, vex, worry. OPPOSITE please.

annoyed *adjective He was annoyed with the shop for losing his order.* angry, cheesed off (*slang*), cranky, crook (*Australian informal*), cross, displeased, exasperated, fed up (*informal*), irritated, mad, miffed (*informal*), narked (*informal*), needled (*informal*), peeved (*informal*), put out, riled (*informal*), shirty (*informal*), upset, vexed. OPPOSITE pleased.

annual *adjective an annual holiday.* yearly.

annul *verb The contract was annulled.* abolish, cancel, invalidate, nullify, rescind, revoke, void. OPPOSITE validate.

anoint *verb She anointed his head with oils.* grease, oil, rub, smear.

anomaly *noun They have removed some of the anomalies in the tax system.* abnormality, deviation, inconsistency, irregularity, oddity, peculiarity.

anonymous *adjective an anonymous caller.* incognito, nameless, unidentified, unknown, unnamed. OPPOSITE familiar.

another *adjective* 1 *They each had another helping.* additional, extra, further, second. 2 *There is another kind you can buy.* alternative, different. OPPOSITE same.

answer *noun* 1 *the answer to my letter. the answer to my question.* acknowledgement, rejoinder, reply, response, retort, riposte. 2 *the answer to all her problems.* explanation, solution. — *verb* 1 *He answered the letter. He answered aggressively.* acknowledge, rejoin, reply, respond, retort. 2 *She answered the problem.* resolve, solve, work out. □ **answer back** *It's rude to answer back.* argue, be cheeky, contradict, disagree, talk back. **answer to** *This bag answers to the description of the stolen one.* conform to, correspond to, fit, match.

answerable *adjective We are answerable for our actions.* accountable, liable, responsible.

antagonism *noun There was antagonism between the two families.* animosity, antipathy, conflict, discord, friction, hatred, hostility, opposition, rivalry. OPPOSITE harmony.

antenna *noun* 1 *an insect's antenna.* feeler. 2 *a TV antenna.* aerial.

anthem *noun The choir sang the anthem.* canticle, chorale, hymn, psalm.

anthology *noun an anthology of poetry.* collection, compendium, compilation, miscellany, selection, treasury.

anticipate *verb* 1 *The man anticipated the journalist's question.* forestall, pre-empt. 2 *The authorities anticipated trouble.* expect, forecast, foresee, predict.

anticlimax *noun The party was an anticlimax.* comedown, disappointment, flop (*informal*), let-down.

antics *plural noun She was not amused by their silly antics.* capers, fooling around, mischief, pranks, shenanigans (*informal*), tomfoolery, tricks.

antidote *noun* 1 *an antidote to a poison.* antitoxin, antivenene. 2 *an antidote to depression.* corrective, countermeasure, cure, remedy.

antipathy *noun an antipathy towards furry creatures.* abhorrence, aversion, detestation, dislike, hatred, hostility, loathing, revulsion. OPPOSITE love.

antiquated *adjective His ideas are antiquated.* ancient, antediluvian (*informal*), antique, archaic, behind the times, obsolete, old, old-fashioned, outdated, outmoded, out of date, prehistoric, primitive, quaint, unfashionable. OPPOSITE modern.

antique *adjective an antique bicycle. antique furniture.* ancient, antiquated, archaic, old, old-fashioned, veteran, vintage. — *noun The shop*

sells antiques. collectable, collector's item, heirloom, relic.

antiseptic *noun The surfaces were wiped with antiseptic.* bactericide, disinfectant, germicide.

antisocial *adjective Spitting is antisocial behaviour.* inconsiderate, objectionable, offensive, unacceptable, unfriendly.

anxiety *noun The thought of the interview filled him with anxiety.* apprehension, concern, dismay, disquiet, dread, foreboding, fear, misgiving, nervousness, stress, tension, trepidation, uneasiness, worry. OPPOSITE calmness.

anxious *adjective* 1 *anxious about the outcome.* afraid, apprehensive, concerned, fearful, nervous, tense, troubled, uneasy, uptight (*informal*), worried. OPPOSITE carefree. 2 *anxious to please.* desirous, desperate, eager, keen, longing, wanting. OPPOSITE loath.

apart *adverb* 1 *Husband and wife live apart now.* independently, separately. OPPOSITE together. 2 *The bomb tore the hotel apart.* asunder, to bits, to pieces. □ **apart from** *They all attended apart from Maria.* aside from, except, excluding, not counting, not including, other than, save. OPPOSITE including.

apartment *noun* bedsit (*British*), condominium (*American*), flat, home unit (*Australian*), penthouse, rooms, unit (*Australian*).

apathetic *adjective The audience was bored and apathetic.* impassive, indifferent, listless, passive, unconcerned, unemotional, uninterested, unmoved, unresponsive. OPPOSITE enthusiastic.

apathy *noun voter apathy.* coolness, impassivity, indifference, listlessness, passivity, unconcern. OPPOSITE enthusiasm.

ape *verb The child aped the teacher.* copy, imitate, mimic.

aperture *noun Mia peeped through the aperture.* crack, gap, hole, opening, slit.

apex *noun the apex of the roof.* crest, peak, pinnacle, summit, tip, top, vertex, zenith.

apologetic *adjective She was apologetic for being late.* contrite, penitent, regretful, remorseful, repentant, sorry. OPPOSITE unrepentant.

apologise *verb He apologised for the trouble he had caused.* beg pardon, express regret, repent, say sorry.

apology *noun He offered an apology for his behaviour.* defence, excuse, explanation, justification, plea.

apostle *noun Paul was an apostle of Christ.* evangelist, messenger, missionary, preacher.

appal *verb They were appalled by the destruction.* disgust, dismay, horrify, outrage, shock, sicken, terrify.

appalling *adjective an appalling crime.* abominable, atrocious, awful, dire, dreadful, frightful, ghastly, hideous, horrendous, horrible, horrifying, outrageous, repulsive, shocking, sickening, terrible.

apparatus *noun He set up the apparatus for the job.* appliance, contraption, device, equipment, gear, instrument, machine, machinery, tool.

apparel *noun see* ATTIRE.

apparent *adjective* 1 *His unhappiness is apparent.* clear, conspicuous, discernible, evident, manifest, obvious, patent, plain, unmistakable, visible. 2 *Do not be deceived by her apparent reluctance.* ostensible, outward, seeming, superficial.

apparition *noun At night he was haunted by apparitions.* ghost, hallucination, phantom, spectre, spirit, spook (*informal*), vision.

appeal *verb* 1 *After the earthquake Pakistan appealed for international*

help. apply, ask, beg, entreat, implore, petition, plead, request, solicit. 2 *Cruises do not appeal to me.* attract, entice, fascinate, interest, lure, tempt. — *noun* 1 *an appeal for help.* call, entreaty, petition, plea, request. 2 *Swimming does not hold much appeal for Sharon.* attraction, charm, fascination, interest, temptation.

appear *verb* 1 *The cat always appears at mealtimes.* arrive, attend, be present, come, emerge, front up (*informal*), materialise, show up, surface, turn up. 2 *Janet appears as Eliza in the school play.* act, perform, play, star, take the part of. 3 *His story appeared in the newspapers.* be published, be reported, come out. 4 *My aunt appeared unwell.* give an impression of being, look, seem.

appearance *noun* 1 *Music heralded the appearance of the official party.* advent, arrival, coming. OPPOSITE disappearance. 2 *Jake always has a sad appearance.* air, aspect, demeanour, expression, look, manner, mien. 3 *an appearance of normality.* front, guise, illusion, impression, pretence, semblance, show.

appease *verb The manager appeased the angry customer.* calm, mollify, pacify, placate, quiet, quieten, soothe, tranquillise.

appendix *noun an appendix to a report.* addendum, addition, attachment, supplement.

appetiser *noun* 1 *eat an appetiser.* hors d'oeuvre, starter. 2 *drink an appetiser.* aperitif, pre-dinner drink.

appetising *adjective appetising food.* appealing, delicious, mouth-watering, palatable, tasty, tempting.

appetite *noun an appetite for spicy food. an appetite for power.* craving, desire, fondness, hunger, inclination, keenness, liking, longing, passion, relish, stomach, taste, thirst.

applaud *verb* 1 *The audience applauded enthusiastically.* clap, give an ovation, give someone a big hand (*informal*), put your hands together. 2 *We applaud your action.* acclaim, approve, commend, compliment, congratulate, praise. OPPOSITE condemn.

applause *noun The pianist received thunderous applause.* clapping, hand (*informal*), ovation, plaudits; see also APPROVAL.

appliance *noun kitchen appliances.* apparatus, contraption, device, equipment, gadget, implement, instrument, machine, utensil.

applicable *adjective The rules were not applicable to his case.* apposite, appropriate, fitting, germane, pertinent, relevant, suitable. OPPOSITE inapplicable.

applicant *noun an applicant for a job. an applicant for a scholarship.* candidate, competitor, entrant, interviewee.

application *noun* 1 *His application for assistance was refused.* appeal, claim, petition, request, submission. 2 *The student shows great application.* assiduity, commitment, dedication, diligence, effort, industry, perseverance, persistence.

applied *adjective applied mathematics.* practical. OPPOSITE pure, theoretical.

apply *verb* 1 *Apply the ointment twice daily.* put on, smear, spread. 2 *They had to apply force to open the door.* employ, exercise, use, utilise. 3 *You must apply the rules fairly.* administer, enforce, put into effect. 4 *It does not apply to me.* be relevant, concern, pertain, refer, relate. □ **apply for** *Twenty people applied for the job.* ask for, audition for, put

in for, register for, request, seek, solicit.

appoint *verb* 1 *They appointed him secretary.* choose, designate, elect, name, nominate, select. 2 *They appointed a time for the next meeting.* arrange, assign, decide on, determine, establish, fix, organise, settle on.

appointment *noun* 1 *an appointment to see someone.* arrangement, assignation, date, engagement, interview, meeting, rendezvous. 2 *The appointment of Mary Jones as new state secretary was welcomed.* choice, election, selection. 3 *Phil took up his new appointment.* job, office, position, post, situation.

appraise *verb see* ASSESS.

appreciable *adjective an appreciable difference.* considerable, noticeable, perceptible, significant, substantial. OPPOSITE imperceptible.

appreciate *verb* 1 *She knows she's appreciated.* be grateful for, be thankful for, cherish, prize, think highly of, treasure, value. 2 *I appreciate your desire for privacy.* acknowledge, realise, recognise, understand. 3 *House values are appreciating all the time.* escalate, gain, go up, improve, increase, inflate, mount, rise. OPPOSITE depreciate.

appreciative *adjective an appreciative customer.* grateful, obliged, thankful.

apprehend *verb* 1 *The police apprehended the culprit.* arrest, capture, catch, detain, nab (*informal*), nail, nick (*slang*), seize, take into custody. 2 *I could see she had apprehended my meaning.* comprehend, grasp, perceive, realise, understand.

apprehension *noun* 1 *She faced the exam with apprehension.* anxiety, concern, dread, fear, foreboding, nervousness, trepidation, uneasiness, worry. 2 *an apprehension of the facts.* appreciation, comprehension, realisation, recognition, understanding. 3 *the apprehension of the culprits.* arrest, capture, seizure.

apprehensive *adjective Ellie is apprehensive about flying.* afraid, anxious, edgy (*informal*), fearful, frightened, nervous, troubled, uneasy, worried.

apprentice *noun The electrician has taken on an apprentice.* beginner, cadet, learner, novice, probationer, pupil, tiro, trainee.

approach *verb* 1 *The holidays are approaching.* advance, come near, draw near, loom, near. 2 *They approached the problem from a different angle.* go about, handle, set about, tackle. 3 *They approached the bank for a loan.* appeal to, apply to, ask. — *noun* 1 *The dog barked at the approach of strangers.* advance, advent, arrival, coming, nearing. 2 *The northern approach to the city is congested.* access, entry, way, way in. OPPOSITE exit. 3 *a different approach to the problem.* attitude, manner, method, procedure, style, technique, way.

approachable *adjective an approachable boss.* accessible, affable, easygoing, friendly. OPPOSITE aloof.

appropriate *adjective an appropriate comment. an appropriate time.* applicable, apposite, apropos, apt, befitting, fitting, pertinent, proper, relevant, right, seemly, suitable, timely. OPPOSITE inappropriate, unsuitable. — *verb They appropriated my car.* commandeer, confiscate, requisition, seize, take; see also STEAL.

approval *noun* 1 *Their performance won the audience's approval.* acclaim, acclamation, admiration, applause, appreciation, approbation, commendation, favour, praise. OPPOSITE condemnation. **2** *The plans received council approval.* acceptance, agreement, assent, authorisation, blessing, consent, endorsement, go-ahead, OK (*informal*), permission, ratification, sanction, support, validation.

approve *verb The committee approved the expenditure.* agree to, allow, assent to, authorise, back, consent to, endorse, pass, permit, ratify, sanction, support, validate. OPPOSITE reject. □ **approve of** *He approves of what they are doing.* acclaim, admire, applaud, be pleased with, commend, favour, like, praise. OPPOSITE disapprove.

approximate *adjective an approximate figure.* ballpark (*informal*), close, estimated, inexact, rough.

approximately *adverb The tree is approximately 200 years old.* about, almost, approaching, around, circa, close to, nearly, roughly.

apt *adjective* **1** *an apt remark.* applicable, apposite, appropriate, apropos, felicitous, fitting, relevant, suitable. OPPOSITE inappropriate. **2** *He is apt to be careless.* inclined, liable, likely, tending. OPPOSITE unlikely. **3** *an apt student.* bright, clever, intelligent, quick, sharp, smart. OPPOSITE slow.

aptitude *noun an aptitude for mathematics.* ability, capability, capacity, facility, flair, gift, knack, skill, talent.

arbitrary *adjective an arbitrary choice.* capricious, chance, indiscriminate, random, subjective, unreasoned, whimsical. OPPOSITE reasoned.

arbitrator *noun The dispute was settled by an arbitrator.* adjudicator, arbiter, judge, referee, umpire.

arc *noun the arc of a rainbow.* arch, bend, bow, crescent, curve.

arcade *noun* cloister, colonnade, gallery, mall, passage, portico, walk.

arcane *adjective an arcane subject.* abstruse, esoteric, inscrutable, mysterious, obscure, secret.

arch[1] *noun* **1** *a single-arch bridge.* archway, span, vault. **2** *He bent over to form an arch.* arc, bow, curve, semicircle. — *verb The cat arched her back.* bend, bow, curve, hump.

arch[2] *adjective an arch smile.* mischievous, playful, roguish, saucy, teasing.

archaic *adjective archaic words. an archaic lawnmower.* ancient, antiquated, antique, obsolete, old, olden, old-fashioned, outmoded, out of date. OPPOSITE modern.

archetype *noun the archetype of dictionaries.* model, original, pattern, prototype, standard.

archives *plural noun the state's archives.* annals, chronicles, documents, papers, records, registers.

ardent *adjective an ardent football fan.* avid, eager, earnest, enthusiastic, fervent, impassioned, keen, passionate, vehement, zealous.

ardour *noun She spoke of her experiences with great ardour.* eagerness, earnestness, enthusiasm, fervour, keenness, passion, warmth, zeal.

arduous *adjective an arduous task.* difficult, exacting, exhausting, formidable, gruelling, hard, herculean, laborious, onerous, strenuous, taxing, tough. OPPOSITE easy, effortless.

area *noun* **1** *the area of a playing field.* extent, measurement, size. **2** *They live in the same area.* district, locality, neighbourhood, precinct, quarter, region, territory, vicinity, zone. **3** *a picnic area.* place, space, spot. **4** *His expertise is in the area of information technology.* domain, field, realm, sphere.

arena *noun The athletes entered the arena.* amphitheatre, field, ground, pitch, ring, stadium.

arguable *adjective Whether sanctions will work is an arguable point.* contentious, controversial, debatable, disputable, doubtful, moot, uncertain. OPPOSITE incontrovertible.

argue *verb* **1** *They argued over everything.* barney (*informal*), bicker, debate, differ, disagree, dispute, feud, fight, haggle, have words, quarrel, quibble, row (*informal*), spar, squabble, wrangle. **2** *He argued that all people are born equal.* assert, claim, contend, declare, maintain, reason, show.

argument *noun* **1** *two people having an argument over trivia.* altercation, barney (*informal*), blue (*Australian informal*), clash, controversy, debate, disagreement, dispute, feud, fight, quarrel, row (*informal*), spat (*informal*), squabble, tiff, wrangle. **2** *There's a strong argument for free education.* case, defence, grounds, justification, reason, reasoning.

argumentative *adjective He became unpleasant and argumentative.* belligerent, contentious, contrary, disputatious, pugnacious, quarrelsome.

arid *adjective the world's arid regions.* desert, dry, parched, waterless; see also BARREN. OPPOSITE well-watered.

arise *verb* **1** *A problem has arisen.* appear, come up, crop up, emerge, occur, originate, present itself. **2** (*old use*) *He arose and walked away.* get up, rise, stand up.

aristocracy *noun* elite, gentry, nobility, peerage, upper class.

aristocrat *noun* grandee, lady, lord, noble, nobleman, noblewoman, peer, peeress.

aristocratic *adjective an aristocratic gentleman.* blue-blooded, courtly, high-born, noble, titled, upperclass. OPPOSITE plebeian.

arm[1] *noun* **1** *an animal's arms.* appendage, forelimb, limb, tentacle (*of an octopus*). **2** *an arm of a tree.* bough, branch, limb. **3** *a different arm of the organisation.* branch, department, division, offshoot, section, wing.

arm[2] *verb The men armed themselves with batons.* equip, furnish, provide, supply. □ **armed services** air force, armed forces, army, defence forces, forces, marines, military, navy, services, troops.

armada *noun an armada of ships.* convoy, fleet, flotilla, navy, squadron.

armaments *plural noun* see WEAPONS.

armistice *noun The countries signed an armistice.* ceasefire, peace, peace treaty, truce.

armour *noun a knight in armour.* chain mail, mail, protective covering.

arms *plural noun* **1** *the arms race.* armaments, firearms, weapons. **2** *The flag features the family's arms.* coat of arms, crest, emblem, insignia, shield.

army *noun* **1** *The army kept the peace in the town.* armed forces, armed services, military, soldiers, troops. **2** *an army of helpers.* crowd, horde, host, mob, multitude, throng.

aroma *noun The food has a delicious aroma.* bouquet, fragrance, odour, perfume, savour, scent, smell.

aromatic *adjective an aromatic curry.* fragrant, pungent, spicy, strong-smelling.

around *adverb* **1** *He's never around when you want him.* about, at hand, close by, in the vicinity, near, nearby. **2** *He travels around.* about,

here and there, hither and thither. **3** *an audience of around 500 people.* about, approximately, circa, close to, nearly, roughly. — *preposition The nurse drew the curtains around the bed.* encircling, on all sides of, round, surrounding.

arouse *verb* **1** *The noise aroused the neighbours.* awake, awaken, rouse, stir, waken, wake up. **2** *Try not to arouse suspicion.* cause, excite, inspire, provoke, rouse, stimulate, stir up.

arrange *verb* **1** *The books are arranged according to subject.* array, categorise, classify, display, dispose, group, lay out, line up, order, organise, position, put in order, rank, set out, sort. **2** *He arranged a meeting.* contrive, fix, organise, plan, prepare, schedule, settle, set up, wangle (*slang*). **3** *The music has been arranged for two recorders.* adapt, orchestrate, score, set.

arrangement *noun* **1** *the arrangement of books on the shelves.* array, categorisation, classification, display, grouping, layout, line-up, order, organisation, set-up, system. **2** *a financial arrangement.* agreement, bargain, contract, deal, plan, provision, settlement, understanding. **3** *a musical arrangement.* adaptation, orchestration, setting, version.

array *verb She was arrayed in all her finery.* adorn, attire, clothe, deck, dress, garb, robe. — *noun an array of ornaments.* arrangement, collection, display, exhibit, line-up, series, show.

arrears *plural noun* **1** *The company paid the man's arrears.* back pay, debt, outstanding amount. **2** *They caught up on the arrears of work.* accumulation, backlog, build-up, pile-up. □ **in arrears** *in arrears with the rent.* behind, late, overdue. OPPOSITE in advance, up to date.

arrest *verb* **1** *The progress of the cancer was arrested.* block, check, curb, halt, inhibit, prevent, retard, stem, stop. **2** *The police arrested the thief.* apprehend, capture, catch, collar (*informal*), detain, nab (*informal*), nail, nick (*slang*), seize, take into custody.

arrival *noun the arrival of the official party.* advent, appearance, approach, coming, entrance, entry. OPPOSITE departure.

arrive *verb They finally arrived in Sydney at eight o'clock.* appear, come, disembark, enter, get in, land, roll up (*informal*), show up, touch down, turn up; see also REACH. OPPOSITE depart.

arrogant *adjective* cocky, conceited, condescending, contemptuous, disdainful, egotistic, haughty, high and mighty, lofty, overbearing, presumptuous, proud, scornful, self-important, snobbish, snooty (*informal*), stuck-up (*informal*), supercilious, vain. OPPOSITE modest.

arsenal *noun an arsenal of weapons.* ammunition dump, armoury, arms depot, magazine, ordnance depot, store.

arsonist *noun* firebug (*informal*), pyromaniac.

art *noun the art of saying a lot in a few words.* craft, flair, gift, knack, skill, talent, technique, trick.

artful *adjective as artful as a fox.* astute, clever, crafty, cunning, deceitful, ingenious, scheming, shifty, shrewd, sly, tricky, wily. OPPOSITE artless.

article *noun* **1** *an article of jewellery.* item, object, piece, thing. **2** *a newspaper article.* essay, feature, item, piece, report, story, write-up.

articulate *adjective an articulate speaker.* clear, coherent, compre-

hensible, eloquent, fluent, intelligible, lucid, understandable. OPPOSITE inarticulate. — *verb She articulated each word with care.* enunciate, pronounce, say, speak, utter.

artifice *noun a clever artifice.* dodge (*informal*), ruse, stratagem, subterfuge, trick, wile.

artificial *adjective* **1** *artificial grass.* bogus, counterfeit, fake, false, imitation, man-made, manufactured, mock, phoney (*informal*), pseudo, sham, synthetic. OPPOSITE natural, real. **2** *His sympathy is artificial.* affected, false, feigned, forced, hollow, insincere, phoney (*informal*), pretended, simulated, skin-deep, superficial. OPPOSITE genuine, sincere.

artisan *noun* craftsman, craftswoman, technician, tradesman, tradeswoman.

artist *noun* **1** *an exhibition of the artist's work.* cartoonist, engraver, graphic designer, illustrator, painter, photographer, sculptor. **2** *The concert artists appeared on stage.* artiste, entertainer, musician, performer.

artistic *adjective an artistic design.* aesthetic, attractive, beautiful, creative, decorative, imaginative, tasteful.

artless *adjective an artless child.* genuine, guileless, honest, ingenuous, innocent, natural, open, simple, sincere, straightforward, unaffected, unsophisticated. OPPOSITE artful, artificial.

ascend *verb They ascended the mountain. The plane ascended.* climb, go up, mount, rise, scale, soar. OPPOSITE descend.

ascent *noun a steep ascent.* climb, gradient, hill, incline, rise, slope. OPPOSITE descent.

ascertain *verb Try to ascertain what is wrong.* confirm, determine, discover, establish, find out, identify, learn, uncover, verify, work out.

ascetic *adjective The monks lead an ascetic life.* abstemious, austere, frugal, harsh, puritanical, self-disciplined, spartan, strict, temperate. OPPOSITE self-indulgent.

ascribe *verb The failure was ascribed to carelessness.* attribute, impute, put down.

ashamed *adjective He was ashamed about what happened.* abashed, embarrassed, humiliated, mortified, red-faced, shamefaced, sheepish.

ashes *plural noun* cinders, embers, remains.

aside *adverb Step aside.* away, out of the way, to one side, to the side. □ **aside from** *Aside from milk, what do you drink?* apart from, besides, in addition to, other than.

ask *verb* **1** *Ask the teacher.* enquire of, inquire of, interrogate, query, question, quiz. OPPOSITE answer. **2** *He asked for help.* appeal, apply, beg, beseech, demand, entreat, implore, petition, plead, pray, request, seek, solicit, supplicate. **3** *She asked me to dinner.* invite, summon.

askew *adjective The painting is askew.* awry, cock-eyed (*informal*), crooked, lopsided, on an angle, out of line, slanting. OPPOSITE level, straight.

asleep *adverb & adjective* **1** *Dad was asleep in the hammock.* dormant, dozing, hibernating, napping, resting, sleeping, slumbering, snoozing. OPPOSITE awake. **2** *My foot is asleep.* deadened, numb. □ **fall asleep** doze off, drop off, flake out (*informal*), go to sleep, nod off.

aspect *noun* **1** *All aspects of the problem had been considered.* angle, detail, facet, feature, side. **2** *The*

room has a northerly aspect. orientation, outlook, prospect, view.

aspiration noun He has aspirations to be a politician. aim, ambition, desire, dream, goal, hope, longing, objective, wish, yearning.

aspire verb **aspire to** He aspired to the top job. aim for, desire, hanker after, hope for, long for, set your sights on, wish for, yearn for.

ass noun **1** He rode an ass. donkey, jackass (male), jenny (female). **2** (informal) Don't be an ass. see FOOL.

assail verb The rioters assailed the police with stones. assault, attack, bombard, lay into, set upon.

assailant noun assaulter, attacker, mugger.

assassin noun executioner, hit man (slang), killer, murderer.

assassinate verb The President was assassinated. execute, kill, murder, slay.

assault noun They launched an assault on the enemy's military buildings. attack, blitz, charge, incursion, offensive, onslaught, raid, strike. — verb **1** He assaulted the police officer. assail, attack, beat up, hit, mug, set upon, strike. **2** The woman had been sexually assaulted. molest, rape.

assemble verb **1** A crowd assembled to welcome Princess Mary. accumulate, collect, come together, congregate, flock, gather, group, meet, muster, rally, swarm, throng. OPPOSITE scatter. **2** They assembled the students in the school hall. bring together, collect, gather, marshal, mobilise, muster, rally, round up. **3** The machines are assembled in Adelaide. build, construct, erect, fabricate, fit together, make up, manufacture, put together. OPPOSITE dismantle.

assembly noun The mayor spoke to the assembly. conference, congregation, congress, convention, council, crowd, gathering, group, meeting, mob, multitude, rally, synod, throng.

assent verb She assented to the changes. accede, accept, acquiesce, agree, approve, consent, permit, sanction. OPPOSITE dissent. — noun The act was given royal assent. acceptance, accord, acquiescence, agreement, approval, consent, permission, sanction. OPPOSITE refusal.

assert verb He asserted that he was innocent. allege, argue, attest, claim, contend, declare, insist, maintain, proclaim, state, swear.

assertive adjective She became more confident and assertive. aggressive, authoritative, bold, dogmatic, forceful, insistent, pushy, self-assertive, strong-willed. OPPOSITE submissive.

assess verb **1** The teacher assessed the student's work. appraise, evaluate, grade, judge, mark, rate. **2** The damage was assessed at $10,000. appraise, calculate, compute, estimate, gauge, reckon, value, work out.

asset noun Brains are definitely an asset. advantage, benefit, blessing, boon, help, strength. OPPOSITE disadvantage, liability. □ **assets** plural noun The company was forced to sell some of its assets. capital, holdings, means, possessions, property, resources, securities, wealth. OPPOSITE liabilities.

assiduous adjective an assiduous employee. diligent, hard-working, indefatigable, industrious, persevering. OPPOSITE slack.

assign verb **1** Books were assigned to each pupil. allocate, allot, deal out, dispense, distribute, give out. **2** Andrew was assigned the job of

library monitor. appoint, delegate, designate, nominate, select.

assignment noun He completed his assignment just before the deadline. homework, job, project, task, work.

assimilate verb **1** The students assimilated the information. absorb, digest, take in; see also LEARN. **2** The immigrants assimilated quickly. become absorbed, blend in, integrate.

assist verb He likes to assist people. abet, advance, aid, back, collaborate with, cooperate with, help, lend a hand, relieve, serve, succour, support. OPPOSITE hinder.

assistance noun I couldn't have done it without your assistance. aid, backing, backup, collaboration, cooperation, help, reinforcement, relief, service, succour, support. OPPOSITE hindrance.

assistant noun The boss has two assistants. abetter, accessory, accomplice, aide, auxiliary, deputy, helper, offsider (Australian), sidekick (informal), subordinate, underling.

associate verb **1** She associates with many different people. consort, fraternise, hang around (informal), hang out (informal), hobnob, keep company, mix, socialise. **2** They associated summer with swimming. connect, identify, link, relate. — noun a business associate. colleague, co-worker, fellow-worker, partner, workmate; see also COMPANION.

association noun **1** an association between the two ideas. connection, link, relation, relationship, tie-up. **2** She belongs to a sporting association. alliance, body, club, federation, group, league, organisation, society, union.

assorted adjective a box of assorted chocolates. different, diverse, miscellaneous, mixed, sundry, varied.

assortment noun an assortment of graphic novels. array, collection, hotchpotch, medley, miscellany, mixture, pot-pourri, range, selection, variety.

assuage verb **1** The pills assuaged the pain. alleviate, calm, ease, lessen, mitigate, relieve, soothe. OPPOSITE intensify. **2** Water will assuage your thirst. appease, quench, relieve, satisfy, slake.

assume verb **1** We assumed that you knew the way. believe, expect, guess, imagine, presume, presuppose, suppose, surmise, think. **2** He has assumed that responsibility. accept, adopt, take on, undertake. **3** He assumed a grave expression. acquire, adopt, affect, put on.

assumed adjective an assumed name. false, fictitious, made-up, phoney (informal).

assumption noun His assumption proved to be wrong. guess, hypothesis, presumption, presupposition, supposition, surmise, theory.

assurance noun **1** They gave an assurance that the parcel would be delivered. commitment, guarantee, oath, pledge, promise, undertaking. **2** life assurance. see INSURANCE. **3** She conducts herself with assurance. aplomb, confidence, poise, self-assurance, self-confidence.

assure verb **1** He assured her that he would come. declare, give your word, guarantee, pledge, promise, swear, vow. **2** He tried the door to assure himself that it was locked. convince, persuade, prove to, reassure. **3** Preparation assures success. ensure, guarantee, make sure of, secure.

assured adjective an assured manner. bold, cocksure, confident, cool, self-assured, self-confident, unafraid. OPPOSITE timorous.

astonish verb The news astonished her. amaze, astound, confound, dumbfound, flabbergast, nonplus, shock, stagger, startle, stun, stupefy, surprise, take aback.

astonishment noun They gazed in astonishment. amazement, surprise, wonder.

astound verb see ASTONISH.

astray adverb **go astray** Her purse has gone astray. be lost, be mislaid, be misplaced, go missing, go walkabout (informal).

astronaut noun cosmonaut, spaceman, spacewoman.

astronomical adjective an astronomical amount of money. colossal, enormous, exorbitant, huge, incredible (informal), massive, unbelievable, vast. OPPOSITE tiny.

astute adjective an astute journalist. canny, clever, discerning, intelligent, knowing, observant, perceptive, quick, sharp, shrewd, sly. OPPOSITE obtuse.

asylum noun **1** The refugees sought political asylum. protection, refuge, safety, sanctuary, shelter. **2** (old use) an asylum for the criminally insane. lunatic asylum (old use), mental home, mental hospital, mental institution, psychiatric hospital.

asymmetrical adjective an asymmetrical design. irregular, lopsided, unbalanced, uneven. OPPOSITE symmetrical.

atheist noun see NON-BELIEVER.

athletic adjective an athletic person. active, brawny, husky, muscular, robust, sporty (informal), strapping, strong.

athletics plural noun school athletics. games, races, sport, sports, track and field events.

atmosphere noun **1** the earth's atmosphere. aerospace, air, heavens, sky. **2** Their home has a happy atmosphere. air, ambience, aura, climate, environment, feeling, mood, tone, vibes (informal).

atom noun He does not have an atom of common sense. bit, iota, jot, molecule, ounce, particle, scrap, skerrick (Australian informal), speck, trace, whit.

atone verb **atone for** He has atoned for his sins. compensate for, expiate, make amends for, make up for, pay for, pay the penalty for.

atrocious adjective **1** an atrocious crime. abominable, appalling, barbaric, brutal, cruel, despicable, evil, heinous, horrific, monstrous, savage, vicious, wicked. **2** (informal) atrocious weather. abominable (informal), bad, dreadful (informal), foul, shocking (informal), terrible (informal), unpleasant.

atrocity noun wartime atrocities. crime, cruelty, evil, horror, offence, outrage.

attach verb She attached the documents to the letter. affix, append, bind, connect, couple, fasten, fix, glue, join, link, pin, secure, staple, stick, tack, tie. OPPOSITE detach.

attached adjective They are very attached to one another. close, devoted, fond (of).

attachment noun The vacuum cleaner came with various attachments. accessory, appendage, extra, fitting.

attack verb **1** The thieves attacked the travellers. ambush, assail, assault, beat up, fall upon, molest, mug, pounce on, set upon. OPPOSITE defend. **2** The city was attacked at night. besiege, bombard, invade, raid, storm, strike. **3** The critics attacked the artist and his work. condemn, criticise, denounce, knock (informal), malign, pan (informal), revile, slam (informal), slate (informal), vilify. OPPOSITE praise. **4** The

disease attacked his liver. affect, afflict, damage, harm, infect, injure. **5** Let's attack the washing-up. begin, embark on, get stuck into (informal), make inroads on, set about, start, tackle. — noun **1** an attack on the city. ambush, assault, blitz, bombardment, charge, foray, incursion, invasion, offensive, onslaught, raid, rush, sortie, strike. OPPOSITE defence. **2** an attack of sneezing. bout, fit, outbreak, seizure, spell.

attacker noun aggressor, assailant, assaulter, mugger.

attain verb He attained the required standard. accomplish, achieve, arrive at, gain, obtain, reach.

attainment noun Robert's sporting attainments. accomplishment, achievement, deed, exploit, success.

attempt verb He attempted to climb the mountain. endeavour, strive, try, venture. — noun Their first attempt met with failure. bid, effort, endeavour, go, try.

attend verb **1** She attends their meetings. appear at, be present at, go to, show up at (informal), turn up at, visit. **2** The doctor is attending the patient. care for, look after, take care of, tend. **3** She is always attended by one of her staff. accompany, chaperone, escort, guard, wait on. □ **attend to** He is attending to the problem. deal with, handle, see to, take care of.

attendance noun Her attendance at the function was requested. appearance, presence. OPPOSITE absence.

attendant noun aide, assistant, chaperone, companion, escort, helper, servant, steward, usher.

attention noun **1** attention to detail. care, concentration, concern, heed, notice, regard, thought. **2** We don't want to attract attention. notice, publicity, recognition. □ **pay attention** attend, concentrate, listen, pay heed, watch.

attentive adjective **1** an attentive pupil. alert, careful, diligent, observant, vigilant, watchful. OPPOSITE inattentive. **2** Sue is attentive to the guests' needs. aware, considerate, mindful, thoughtful.

attest verb The witness attested its authenticity. affirm, assert, certify, confirm, swear to, testify to, verify, vouch for. OPPOSITE deny.

attic noun garret, loft.

attire noun (formal) Jeans are not suitable attire for a formal dinner. apparel (formal), clothes, clothing, costume, dress, garb, garments, gear (informal), outfit, raiment (old use), wear. — verb see CLOTHE.

attitude noun **1** Her attitude is always cheerful. demeanour, disposition, frame of mind, manner, mien, mood, outlook. **2** the government's attitude towards climate change. feeling, opinion, position, stance, stand, standpoint, thoughts, view, viewpoint.

attorney noun see LAWYER.

attract verb **1** A magnet attracts iron. draw, pull. OPPOSITE repel. **2** The bright lights of the big city attracted him. allure, appeal to, draw, entice, fascinate, interest, lure.

attraction noun **1** the attraction of visiting new places. allure, appeal, attractiveness, charm, enticement, fascination, lure, pull. **2** tourist attractions. crowd-pleaser, drawcard, feature, interest.

attractive adjective **1** an attractive offer. appealing, enticing, interesting, inviting, pleasing, tempting. OPPOSITE unattractive. **2** an attractive woman. alluring, appealing, beautiful, bonny (Scottish), captivating, charming, comely, enchanting, fascinating, fetching, good-looking, handsome, irresistible, lovely, nice, pleasant, pretty, striking, stunning, sweet (*informal*), winsome. OPPOSITE plain, ugly. **3** *an attractive outfit.* becoming, flattering.

attribute *verb He attributed his success to his upbringing.* ascribe, credit, impute, put down to. — *noun Kindness is one of his attributes.* characteristic, feature, property, quality, trait, virtue.

audacious *adjective an audacious stuntman.* adventurous, bold, brave, confident, courageous, daredevil, daring, fearless, game, heroic, intrepid, plucky, reckless, venturesome. OPPOSITE cowardly, fainthearted.

audacity *noun He had the audacity to suggest she had cheated.* boldness, cheek, effrontery, gall (*slang*), hide (*informal*), impertinence, impudence, insolence, nerve, temerity.

audible *adjective audible sounds.* clear, discernible, distinct, perceptible. OPPOSITE inaudible.

audience *noun The singer spoke to the audience between items.* congregation, crowd, listeners, spectators, viewers.

audit *noun an audit of the accounts.* check, examination, inspection, review, scrutiny. — *verb The books are audited annually.* check, examine, go over, inspect, review, scrutinise.

audition *noun an audition for a film.* screen test, test, trial, try-out.

auditorium *noun* hall, theatre.

augment *verb You can augment your earnings by working overtime.* add to, boost, eke out, increase, supplement, swell. OPPOSITE decrease.

augur *verb That does not augur well for the future.* be a sign of, bode, foreshadow, portend, presage, promise.

august *adjective an august establishment.* dignified, grand, imposing, impressive, majestic, noble, venerable.

aura *noun The place has an aura of tranquillity.* air, ambience, atmosphere, feeling, mood, spirit, vibes (*informal*).

auspices *plural noun under the auspices of the Red Cross.* aegis, authority, control, patronage, protection, sponsorship.

auspicious *adjective an auspicious beginning.* favourable, promising, propitious. OPPOSITE inauspicious.

austere *adjective an austere way of life.* abstemious, ascetic, frugal, hard, harsh, plain, puritanical, restrained, rigorous, self-denying, self-disciplined, severe, simple, spartan, strict. OPPOSITE indulgent.

authentic *adjective an authentic passport.* actual, dinkum (*Australian informal*), genuine, real, true, trustworthy. OPPOSITE fake.

authenticate *verb He authenticated their story.* certify, confirm, endorse, prove, substantiate, validate, verify, vouch for. OPPOSITE invalidate.

author *noun the author of a literary work.* biographer, composer, creator, dramatist, essayist, novelist, playwright, poet, writer.

authorise *verb* **1** *He authorised the sale.* agree to, allow, approve, give permission for, OK (*informal*), permit, sanction. OPPOSITE forbid. **2** *She is authorised to collect the rent.* commission, empower, entitle, license, permit.

authoritarian *adjective She was frightened of her authoritarian father.* autocratic, bossy, dictatorial, dogmatic, domineering, severe, strict. OPPOSITE permissive.

authority *noun* **1** *Wendy is in a position of authority.* command, control, dominion, influence, jurisdiction, power, right, sovereignty, suprem-

acy. **2** *The detective had authority to search the house.* approval, authorisation, consent, licence, permission, sanction, warrant. **3** *Verity is an authority on wines.* arbiter, connoisseur, expert, judge, pundit, scholar, specialist.

autocratic *adjective an autocratic leader.* absolute, despotic, dictatorial, domineering, high-handed, imperious, tyrannical.

autograph *noun* signature.

automatic *adjective* **1** *an automatic device.* automated, computerised, electronic, mechanised, programmed, pushbutton, self-operating, self-regulating. OPPOSITE manual. **2** *an automatic reaction.* instinctive, involuntary, mechanical, reflex, spontaneous, unconscious, unthinking. OPPOSITE conscious. **3** *an automatic penalty.* compulsory, inevitable, mandatory, necessary, obligatory.

autonomous *adjective an autonomous state.* free, independent, self-governing.

autopsy *noun An autopsy was conducted to discover the cause of death.* necropsy, post-mortem.

autumn *noun Autumn follows summer.* fall (*American*).

auxiliary *adjective auxiliary services.* ancillary, assisting, backup, helping, reserve, supplementary, support, supporting. — *noun She works as a medical auxiliary.* aide, assistant, helper.

available *adjective Is the car available?* accessible, at hand, at your disposal, free, handy, obtainable, ready, usable.

avalanche *noun an avalanche of letters.* deluge, flood, inundation, torrent.

avaricious *adjective* see GREEDY.

avenge *verb He wanted to avenge the crime.* get even for, get your own back for (*informal*), repay, take revenge for; see also RETALIATE. OPPOSITE forgive.

avenue *noun* see ROAD.

average *adjective* **1** *The average mark for the class was 65.* mean. **2** *a man of average intelligence.* intermediate, mediocre, medium, middling, normal, ordinary, regular, standard, usual. OPPOSITE exceptional.

averse *adjective He is not averse to hard work.* disinclined, loath, opposed, reluctant, unwilling.

aversion *noun* **1** *She has an aversion to snakes.* antipathy, dislike, hatred, hostility, loathing, revulsion. OPPOSITE liking. **2** *Strong perfume is her pet aversion.* bugbear, dislike, hate (*informal*). OPPOSITE like (*informal*).

avert *verb* **1** *People averted their eyes.* turn away. **2** *They managed to avert disaster.* fend off, prevent, stave off, ward off.

aviator *noun* airman, airwoman, aviatrix (*female, old use*), flyer, pilot.

avid *adjective an avid reader.* eager, enthusiastic, fervent, keen, passionate, zealous. OPPOSITE reluctant.

avoid *verb* **1** *He avoided the tidying.* bypass, circumvent, dodge, escape, evade, get out of, shirk, sidestep, skirt. OPPOSITE face. **2** *You must avoid alcohol.* abstain from, eschew, keep off, refrain from. **3** *He avoided the new boy.* cold-shoulder, elude, give a wide berth to, ignore, keep away from, leave alone, shun, steer clear of. OPPOSITE confront.

awake *verb* **1** *I awoke to the sound of thunder.* awaken, stir, wake, wake up. **2** *The noise awoke us.* arouse, awaken, rouse, wake, wake up. — *adjective He lay awake for hours.* conscious, open-eyed, sleepless, wakeful, wide awake. OPPOSITE asleep.

awaken *verb* **1** see AWAKE. **2** *The music awakened strong feelings.* arouse, call forth, excite, kindle, revive, rouse, stimulate, stir up.

award *verb The prize is awarded to the top student.* accord, allot, assign, bestow, confer, give, grant, present. — *noun the presentation of awards.* badge, colours, cup, decoration, honour, medal, prize, scholarship, trophy.

aware *adjective* **aware of** *I am aware of the risks.* acquainted with, alert to, alive to, conscious of, familiar with, informed about, mindful of, sensible of. OPPOSITE ignorant.

awe *noun They were filled with awe.* admiration, amazement, fear, respect, reverence, veneration, wonder. OPPOSITE contempt.

awe-inspiring *adjective an awe-inspiring sight.* amazing, astonishing, awesome, breathtaking, impressive, magnificent, marvellous, stupendous, wonderful, wondrous (*poetical*).

awesome *adjective an awesome responsibility.* daunting, fearsome, formidable, intimidating, overwhelming, terrible.

awful *adjective* **1** *an awful accident. awful weather.* abominable, appalling, atrocious, bad, disgusting, dreadful, foul, frightful, ghastly, horrible, lousy (*informal*), nasty, rotten (*informal*), shocking, terrible, unpleasant. **2** (*informal*) *an awful lot of money.* big, excessive, huge, impressive, inordinate, large, tremendous.

awfully *adverb* **1** *He behaved awfully.* abominably, appallingly, atrociously, badly, deplorably, dreadfully, frightfully, horribly, lousily (*informal*), nastily, poorly, reprehensibly, shockingly, terribly, unpleasantly. **2** (*informal*) *She's awfully pretty.* exceedingly, extremely, really, terribly (*informal*), very.

awkward *adjective* **1** *an awkward tool.* cumbersome, inconvenient, unmanageable, unwieldy. OPPOSITE user-friendly. **2** *an awkward spot to get to.* difficult, hard, inconvenient, ticklish, tricky, troublesome. OPPOSITE convenient. **3** *an awkward person, always having accidents.* bumbling, bungling, clumsy, gauche, gawky, ham-fisted (*informal*), maladroit, uncoordinated, ungainly. OPPOSITE coordinated. **4** *He felt awkward about it.* embarrassed, ill at ease, self-conscious, uncomfortable, uneasy. OPPOSITE comfortable.

awry *adverb* **1** *The paintings hung awry.* askew, crookedly, on an angle, out of line, unevenly. OPPOSITE straight. **2** *Plans had gone awry.* amiss, wrong. OPPOSITE right.

axe *noun Bob chopped the tree with an axe.* adze, battleaxe, chopper, cleaver, hatchet, mogo, tomahawk. — *verb The programme was axed.* abolish, cancel, discontinue, do away with, eliminate, get rid of, give the chop (*informal*), remove, scrap, terminate, wind up.

axiom *noun The statement was accepted as an axiom.* fundamental, principle, truth; see also PROVERB.

axle *noun The wheel turned on the axle.* arbor, rod, shaft, spindle.

Bb

babble *verb* **1** *I can't understand what she's babbling about.* chatter, gabble, gibber, jabber, mumble, yabber (*Australian informal*). **2** *the sooth-*

ing sound of a creek babbling along. burble, gurgle, murmur.

baby *noun* **1** *The mother fed her baby.* babe, bairn (*Scottish*), child, infant, toddler, tot. OPPOSITE adult. **2** *an animal's baby.* offspring, young. — *verb They baby the child too much.* coddle, cosset, indulge, mollycoddle, pamper, spoil.

babyish *adjective babyish behaviour.* childish, immature, infantile, juvenile, sooky (*Australian informal*). OPPOSITE mature.

babysit *verb* see MIND.

babysitter *noun* carer, childminder, minder, nanny, sitter.

back *noun* **1** *His back was injured.* backbone, spinal column, spine, vertebral column. **2** *They stood at the back of the line.* end, rear, tail. OPPOSITE front. **3** *the back of a ship.* poop, stern. OPPOSITE bow. **4** *the back of the painting.* reverse, underside. OPPOSITE front. — *adjective* **1** *back legs.* hind, rear. OPPOSITE front. **2** *a back issue.* earlier, former, past, previous. OPPOSITE current, future. — *verb* **1** *She backed the car into the space.* move backwards, reverse. **2** *The government is backing their new venture.* aid, assist, encourage, endorse, help, promote, sponsor, subsidise, support, underwrite. OPPOSITE oppose. **3** *Which horse did he back in the race?* bet on, gamble on. □ **back away** *He backed away from the others.* move backwards, pull back, recede, recoil, retire, retreat, withdraw. **back down** *It was an unpopular decision, but he refused to back down.* back-pedal, backtrack, concede, give in, retreat, submit, surrender, yield. **back out of** *He found a way to back out of the agreement.* escape from, get out of, go back on, renege on, withdraw from, wriggle out of. **back up** *She backed up everything he said.* affirm, confirm, corroborate, document, reinforce, second, substantiate, support, verify. OPPOSITE contradict.

backblocks *plural noun* (*Australian*) *The family moved from the city to the backblocks.* back of beyond, backwoods, bush (*Australian*), interior, never-never (*Australian*), outback (*Australian*), the sticks (*Australian informal*), up country, Woop Woop (*Australian informal*).

backbone *noun* **1** *an animal's backbone.* back, spinal column, spine, vertebral column. **2** *The country needs a leader with backbone.* courage, determination, fortitude, grit, guts (*informal*), pluck, resolve.

backer *noun The scheme has several backers.* benefactor, patron, promoter, sponsor, supporter, underwriter. OPPOSITE opponent.

backfire *verb Their plan backfired.* boomerang, fail, rebound, recoil.

background *noun* **1** *The painting has a pale blue background.* backcloth, backdrop, setting. OPPOSITE foreground. **2** *the historical background of the play.* circumstances, context, environment, setting. **3** *The applicant's background suited him to the job.* education, experience, history, training, upbringing.

backing *noun* **1** *The club receives the school's backing.* aid, approval, assistance, endorsement, funding, help, patronage, sponsorship, subsidy, support. OPPOSITE opposition. **2** *musical backing.* accompaniment.

backlash *noun The proposed legislation provoked a strong backlash.* counteraction, reaction, response.

backlog *noun a backlog of letters to answer.* accumulation, arrears, build-up, stockpile.

backpack *noun* haversack, knapsack, pack, rucksack.

backpacker noun see HIKER, TRAVELLER.

back-pedal verb The premier back-pedalled on his proposal when he met resistance. back down, backtrack, do a backflip (informal), do an about-face, retreat.

backside noun see BOTTOM.

backup noun The team provides the driver with backup. aid, assistance, help, support. — adjective backup supplies. emergency, reserve, spare, stand-by.

backward adjective 1 a backward glance. rearward. OPPOSITE forward. 2 a backward place. primitive, underdeveloped, undeveloped. OPPOSITE advanced. 3 a backward child. handicapped, retarded, slow. OPPOSITE precocious.

backwards adverb in reverse, rearwards. OPPOSITE forwards. □ **backwards and forwards** back and forth, hither and thither, to and fro. **go backwards** see DETERIORATE, REVERSE.

bad adjective 1 a bad person. a bad deed. abhorrent, abominable, atrocious, awful, base, beastly, corrupt, criminal, cruel, deplorable, depraved, despicable, detestable, disgraceful, dishonest, dishonourable, evil, hateful, immoral, infamous, loathsome, malevolent, malicious, mean, nasty, naughty, notorious, reprehensible, sinful, ungodly, unrighteous, unworthy, vile, villainous, wicked. OPPOSITE good, virtuous. 2 bad weather. appalling (informal), atrocious (informal), dreadful (informal), foul, grim, inclement, lousy (informal), rotten (informal), shocking (informal), terrible (informal), unpleasant. OPPOSITE fair, fine. 3 a bad accident. appalling, awful, dire, disastrous, dreadful, frightful, ghastly, grave, hideous, horrendous, horrible, horrific, nasty, serious, severe, shocking, terrible. 4 The food had gone bad. decayed, foul, mildewed, mouldy, off, putrid, rancid, rotten, spoiled, tainted. OPPOSITE fresh. 5 a bad smell. foul, nauseating, noxious, obnoxious, offensive, on the nose (Australian informal), repulsive, revolting, stinking, vile. OPPOSITE fragrant. 6 The workman did a bad job. defective, deficient, faulty, inadequate, incompetent, inferior, poor, shoddy, substandard, unacceptable, unsatisfactory, unsound. OPPOSITE good. 7 She went to the doctor because she felt bad. crook (Australian informal), ill, off colour, poorly, sick, unhealthy, unwell. OPPOSITE well. 8 He felt bad about what happened. ashamed, conscience-stricken, contrite, guilty, regretful, remorseful, rueful, sad, sorry, unhappy, upset. 9 Lollies are bad for your teeth. damaging, dangerous, deleterious, destructive, detrimental, harmful, hurtful, injurious, ruinous, unhealthy. OPPOSITE beneficial. □ **bad language** The player was penalised for using bad language. abuse, curses, expletives, invective, obscenities, profanities, swear words, vituperation.

baddy noun (informal) the goodies and the baddies. criminal, crook (informal), miscreant, rogue, villain.

badge noun a school badge. crest, emblem, insignia, logo, medal, shield, sign, symbol.

badger verb He badgered them into going. bully, harass, hassle (informal), hound, nag, pester.

bad-tempered adjective angry, cantankerous, crabby, cranky, cross, crotchety, grouchy, gruff, grumpy, hot-tempered, ill-tempered, irascible, irritable, moody, peevish, pet-

ulant, quarrelsome, shirty (informal), short-tempered, snaky (Australian informal), snappy (informal), stroppy (informal), sullen, surly, testy. OPPOSITE easygoing, good-humoured.

baffle verb The problem had me baffled. bamboozle (informal), bewilder, confound, confuse, flummox (informal), mystify, perplex, puzzle, stump.

bag noun receptacle; [kinds of bag] attaché case, backpack, briefcase, carpet bag, carry bag, case, dilly bag (Australian), duffel bag, grip, handbag, haversack, holdall, kitbag, knapsack, pack, port (Australian), pouch, purse (American), rucksack, sack, satchel, schoolbag, shopping bag, shoulder bag, suitcase, swag (Australian), travelling bag, tucker bag (Australian informal).

baggage noun They checked in their baggage at the airport. bags, cases, luggage, suitcases, trunks.

baggy adjective baggy trousers. floppy, loose, roomy, shapeless. OPPOSITE tight.

bail¹ noun He was released on bail. bond, guarantee, security, surety. — verb **bail out** They wanted us to bail the firm out. assist, help, relieve, rescue.

bail² verb **bail up** (Australian) 1 She gets bailed up by her friends at the shops. buttonhole, corner, detain, waylay. 2 The bushrangers bailed them up on a lonely track. hold up, rob, stick up (informal).

bait noun Cheese was used as a bait to catch the mouse. attraction, decoy, enticement, lure, temptation. — verb Baiting bears is a cruel sport. badger, goad, provoke, tantalise, tease, torment.

bake verb 1 The chicken was baked in the oven. cook, roast. 2 The bricks were baked in the sun. dry, fire, harden.

balance noun 1 She weighed the ingredients on the balance. scales, weighing machine. 2 The skater lost her balance and fell. equilibrium, poise, stability, steadiness. 3 We took what we needed and gave away the balance. difference, excess, leftovers, remainder, residue, rest, surplus. — verb The two sides balanced each other. cancel out, counteract, counterbalance, equalise, even out, level, neutralise, offset.

balanced adjective The journalist was commended for his balanced reporting. even-handed, fair, impartial, unbiased.

balcony noun 1 The house has a balcony outside the bedroom. deck, terrace, veranda. 2 a balcony in the theatre. gallery, the gods (informal), upper dress circle.

bald adjective 1 a bald head. hairless, shaved. OPPOSITE hairy, hirsute. 2 a bald tyre. smooth, worn.

bale¹ noun a bale of wool. bundle, pack, package, parcel, truss.

bale² verb **bale out** The airman baled out before the plane crashed. eject, jump out, parachute.

ball¹ noun a ball of wool. a ball of spit. bead, drop, globe, globule, orb, pellet, sphere.

ball² noun Cinderella wasn't invited to the ball. dance, formal, social.

balloon verb Her skirt ballooned in the wind. billow, bulge, puff out, swell.

ballot noun They held a secret ballot. election, plebiscite, poll, referendum, vote.

balm noun He rubbed balm on the man's wounds. balsam, embrocation, liniment, ointment, salve.

balmy adjective a balmy spring day. gentle, mild, pleasant, warm.

bamboozle verb (informal) 1 The problem had them bamboozled.

baffle, bewilder, confound, mystify, perplex, puzzle. 2 Don't be bamboozled by the advertiser's claims. cheat, con (informal), deceive, dupe, fool, hoax, hoodwink, mislead, take in, trick.

ban verb The government banned smoking in restaurants. forbid, outlaw, prohibit, proscribe. OPPOSITE permit. — noun a ban on the sale of fireworks. embargo, moratorium, prohibition, proscription, veto.

banal adjective The reviewer made some banal comments. clichéd, commonplace, hackneyed, humdrum, trite, unimaginative, uninteresting, unoriginal. OPPOSITE interesting.

band noun 1 a band of red on each sleeve. annulus, circle, hoop, line, loop, ring, strip, stripe. 2 The books were tied together with a band. belt, brace, cord, elastic, ligature, loop, ribbon, strap, string, tie. 3 a band of gangsters. body, bunch, clique, company, gang, group, mob, pack, party, push (Australian old use). 4 She plays flute in the band. ensemble, group, orchestra. — verb The newcomers banded together for moral support. affiliate, ally, associate, gather, group, join, team up, unite.

bandage noun dressing, gauze, plaster, tourniquet.

bandit noun We were attacked by bandits. brigand, buccaneer, bushranger, criminal, crook (informal), desperado, gangster, highwayman, outlaw, pirate, robber, thief.

bandstand noun platform, rotunda, stage.

bandy verb **bandy about** The story was bandied about. circulate, pass about, put about, spread.

bandy-legged adjective bow-legged. OPPOSITE knock-kneed.

bane noun Tax returns are the bane of his life. curse, plague, scourge, trial, woe.

bang verb 1 Some fireworks bang; others fizz. blast, boom, crash, detonate, explode, pop. 2 Don't bang the door down. bash, hammer, hit, knock, pound, punch, slam, strike, thump. — noun 1 We were startled by a loud bang. blast, boom, clap, clatter, crash, detonation, explosion, pop, report, shot, thud. 2 The bang on the head gave him a nasty lump. blow, bump, hit, knock, punch, whack.

banish verb He was banished from the country. cast out, deport, dismiss, drive out, excommunicate (from a church), exile, expatriate, expel, oust, remove, send away, transport. OPPOSITE admit.

banisters plural noun It's fun to slide down the banisters. handrail, railing, stair-rail.

bank¹ noun 1 a river bank. brink, edge, embankment, shore, side, slope, verge. 2 a sand bank. mass, mound, pile. 3 a bank of switches. group, row, series, set. — verb 1 The leaves banked up in the gutters. accumulate, amass, collect, heap, pile, stack. 2 The plane banked as it prepared to land. incline, lean, list, pitch, tilt.

bank² noun money in the bank. kitty, pool, reserve, store. — verb He banks $100 each week. deposit, invest, put aside, save. □ **bank on** We are banking on your success. bargain on, count on, depend on, pin your hopes on, rely on.

bankrupt adjective The company is bankrupt. broke (informal), bust (informal), failed, in liquidation, insolvent, ruined. OPPOSITE solvent.

banner noun 1 Supporters waved the team's banner. flag, pennant, standard. 2 The protesters carried banners. placard, sign.

banquet noun The conference ended with a banquet. dinner, feast, meal, repast (formal).

banter noun friendly classroom banter. badinage, chiacking (Australian informal), jesting, joking, kidding (informal), raillery, repartee, ribbing (informal), teasing.

baptise verb He was baptised John. christen, name.

bar noun 1 a wooden bar. bail, batten, beam, block, girder, pole, rail, rod, stake, stick. 2 The chart shows bars of different colours. band, column, oblong, rectangle, strip, stripe. 3 a bar of soap. block, cake, hunk, lump, piece, slab. 4 a bar to progress. barrier, block, hindrance, impediment, obstacle, obstruction, restriction. 5 They drank at the bar. counter, saloon. 6 a snack bar. kiosk, shop, stall. — verb 1 He was barred from entering the meeting. ban, exclude, forbid, keep out, outlaw, prevent, prohibit. 2 The policeman barred our way. block, impede, obstruct. □ **behind bars** imprisoned, incarcerated, in jail, in prison. OPPOSITE free.

barbarian adjective a barbarian tribe. barbarous, primitive, savage, uncivilised, uncultivated, uncultured. OPPOSITE civilised.

barbaric adjective barbaric customs. barbarous, brutal, cruel, inhuman, rough, savage, vicious, wild. OPPOSITE civilised.

barbarity noun atrocity, brutality, cruelty, inhumanity, savagery, viciousness.

barber noun haircutter, hairdresser.

bare adjective 1 bare bodies. exposed, naked, nude, unclothed, uncovered, undressed. OPPOSITE clad, dressed. 2 bare trees. defoliated, denuded, leafless, stripped. 3 the bare facts. bald, plain, unadorned, unembellished, unvarnished. OPPOSITE embellished. 4 The house was bare. empty, unfurnished, uninhabited, unoccupied, vacant. 5 the bare necessities of life. basic, meagre, mere, scant. — verb The dog bared its teeth. expose, reveal, show.

barefaced adjective a barefaced lie. blatant, brazen, downright, flagrant, shameless, unconcealed, undisguised.

barely adverb He barely had time to eat. hardly, only just, scarcely.

bargain noun 1 The two sides struck a bargain. accord, agreement, compact, contract, covenant, deal, pact. 2 There were some bargains at the sales. give-away (informal), good buy, snip (informal), special, steal (informal). — verb The customer bargained with the salesman. barter, discuss terms, haggle, negotiate. □ **bargain for** She got more than she bargained for. anticipate, be prepared for, envisage, expect, foresee. **bargain on** He can't bargain on their support. bank on, count on, depend on, expect, reckon on, rely on.

barge verb They barged into another boat. bump, collide, crash, knock, lurch, slam. □ **barge in** He barged in on our conversation. burst in, butt in, interrupt, intrude.

bark noun a dog's bark. bay, bow-wow, growl, woof, yap, yelp. — verb The dog barked. bay, growl, woof, yap, yelp.

barmy adjective see CRAZY.

barn noun outbuilding, outhouse, shed.

barney noun (informal) They had a barney over money. altercation, argument, fight, quarrel, row, squabble.

baron noun see NOBLEMAN.

barrack verb **barrack for** (Australian) They barracked for the local team.

cheer on, egg on, encourage, support.

barracks noun *army barracks.* billet, camp, garrison, quarters.

barrage noun **1** *a barrage across a river.* barrier, dam, wall. **2** *a barrage of bullets.* battery, bombardment, fusillade, gunfire, hail, salvo, volley. **3** *a barrage of questions.* flood, onslaught, stream, torrent, volley.

barrel noun *a wine barrel.* butt, cask, drum, hogshead, keg, tun; see also CONTAINER.

barren adjective **1** *barren land.* arid, bare, desert, infertile, lifeless, unproductive, waste. OPPOSITE fertile. **2** *a barren couple.* childless, infertile, sterile. OPPOSITE fertile.

barricade noun *The road was blocked off with barricades.* barrier, blockade, fence, obstacle. — verb *The police barricaded the building.* block off, fence off, obstruct, shut off.

barrier noun **1** *We were not allowed past the barrier.* bar, barricade, boom, fence, gate, obstruction, partition, rail, screen, wall. **2** *a barrier to communication.* bar, block, hindrance, impediment, obstacle, restriction, stumbling block.

barrister noun advocate, attorney (*American*), counsel; see also LAWYER.

barrow noun *He filled his barrow with soil.* cart, handcart, wheelbarrow.

barter verb *They bartered cigarettes for food.* exchange, swap, trade.

base noun **1** *The ornament has a flat base.* bottom, foot, foundation, pedestal, plinth, stand, support. OPPOSITE apex. **2** *The soldiers returned to their base.* camp, depot, headquarters, installation, post, station. — verb **1** *The story was based on fact.* build, establish, found, ground, root. **2** *The manager is based in Canberra.* locate, post, station. — adjective *base motives.* bad, contemptible, cowardly, despicable, dishonourable, evil, ignoble, immoral, low, mean, selfish, shabby, sordid, underhand, wicked. OPPOSITE honourable.

basement noun *Wine is stored in the basement.* cellar, crypt, vault.

bash verb *The intruder bashed the householder.* assault, attack, batter, beat, clout, hit, mug, punch, strike, thump. — noun **1** *a bash on the head.* blow, hit, knock, punch, thump. **2** (*informal*) *Have a bash at it.* see TRY.

bashful adjective *He was young and bashful, lacking in confidence.* coy, demure, diffident, reserved, reticent, self-conscious, sheepish, shy. OPPOSITE bold.

basic adjective **1** *the basic problem.* fundamental, primary, root, underlying; see also CENTRAL. OPPOSITE secondary. **2** *basic mathematics.* elementary, fundamental, rudimentary, simple. OPPOSITE advanced. **3** *The house is very basic.* no-frills (*informal*), plain, primitive, simple, spartan. **4** *a basic income for survival.* essential, minimum, necessary.

basically adverb *Basically he's a nice man.* at bottom, at heart, essentially, for the most part, fundamentally.

basics plural noun *the basics of trigonometry.* ABC, elements, essentials, fundamentals, nitty-gritty (*informal*), nuts and bolts (*informal*), rudiments.

basin noun *a basin of water.* bowl, container, dish, font, sink, washbasin, washbowl.

basis noun **1** *The proposal lacked a solid basis.* base, footing, foundation, grounds, premise, principle,

support. **2** *the basis of a good story.* base, beginning, starting point.

bask verb **1** *The dog basked in the sun.* sunbake, sunbathe, sun yourself, warm yourself. **2** *The writer basked in popularity.* delight, glory, luxuriate, revel, wallow.

basket noun carrier, hamper, pannier, punnet.

bass adjective *a bass sound.* deep, low, sonorous.

bastion noun see STRONGHOLD.

bat noun *a bat used in games.* club, racquet, stick.

batch noun *a batch of scones.* bunch, collection, group, lot, number, set.

bathe verb **1** *The nurse bathed the wound.* clean, cleanse, rinse, wash. **2** *They bathed in the river.* bogey (*Australian*), paddle, swim, take a dip.

bathers plural noun (*informal*) *They can't go swimming without their bathers.* bathing costume, bathing suit, bikini, cossie (*Australian informal*), one-piece, swimmers (*Australian informal*), swimming costume, swimsuit, togs (*Australian informal*), trunks, two-piece.

baton noun *a conductor's baton. a policeman's baton.* cane, rod, staff, stick, truncheon, wand.

batter verb *He battered his wife when he was drunk.* abuse, assault, bash, beat, belt (*slang*), clobber (*slang*), hit, pound, pummel, strike, thump, wallop (*informal*), whack.

battery noun **1** *a battery of tests.* sequence, series, set. **2** *assault and battery.* assault, attack, bashing, beating, violence.

battle noun *He died in the battle.* action, affray, campaign, clash, combat, conflict, confrontation, crusade, encounter, engagement, fighting, fray, hostilities, offensive, skirmish, strife, war, warfare; see also FIGHT. — verb see FIGHT.

battler noun (*Australian*) *the little Aussie battler.* fighter, struggler, toiler, worker.

battleship noun see WARSHIP.

bauble noun *We hung baubles on the Christmas tree.* decoration, ornament, trinket.

baulk verb *The horse baulked at the fence.* hesitate, jib, prop, pull up, shy, stop.

bawl verb **1** *The sergeant bawled his orders.* bellow, cry out, roar, shout, yell. **2** *The child bawled her eyes out.* cry, howl, sob, wail, weep.

bay[1] noun *ships in the bay.* bight, cove, estuary, gulf, inlet.

bay[2] noun **1** *a parking bay.* compartment, division, space. **2** *The piano sits in a bay of the lounge room.* alcove, niche, nook, recess.

bay[3] verb *The dogs bayed.* bark, cry, howl, yelp. □ **keep at bay** see WARD OFF (at WARD).

bazaar noun *The school bazaar raised $3000.* charity sale, fair, fête, flea market (*informal*), garage sale, jumble sale, trash and treasure market.

be verb **1** *He is still in Sydney.* be alive, dwell, exist, live, remain, reside. **2** *The box is on the shelf.* be found, be located, be situated, sit. **3** *Easter will be in March this year.* fall, happen, occur, take place. **4** *She won't be at school today.* attend, be present. **5** *He wants to be a doctor.* become.

beach noun coast, sands, seashore, seaside, shore, strand.

beacon noun *The beacon alerted us to the danger.* flare, lighthouse, signal fire, signal light, signal station.

bead noun *beads of perspiration.* bubble, drop, droplet. □ **beads** plural noun necklace, necklet, rosary.

beady adjective *beady eyes.* bright, shiny, small.

beaker noun *a beaker of water.* cup, glass, tumbler.

beam noun **1** *roof beams.* board, girder, joist, plank, rafter, support, timber. **2** *a beam of light.* gleam, ray, shaft, streak, stream. — verb **1** *The programme is beamed across the world.* broadcast, send out, transmit. **2** *Light beamed from the lighthouse.* emit, radiate, shine. **3** *She beamed with pleasure.* grin, smile.

bear verb **1** *The tree-house cannot bear a heavy weight.* carry, hold up, support, sustain, take. **2** *They came bearing gifts.* bring, carry, convey, deliver, transport. **3** *He bore the scars.* have, possess, show, wear. **4** *He can't bear the pain.* abide, cope with, endure, put up with, stand, stomach, suffer, tolerate. **5** *She bore a set of twins.* bring forth, give birth to, have, produce. □ **bear out** *Their story bears out what he said.* confirm, prove, substantiate, uphold, verify.

bearable adjective *The pain is bearable.* acceptable, endurable, sustainable, tolerable. OPPOSITE intolerable.

beard noun facial hair, goatee, whiskers, ziff (*Australian slang*).

bearing noun **1** *soldierly bearing.* air, behaviour, carriage, demeanour, deportment, manner, mien, posture, stance. **2** *What you say has no bearing on the matter.* connection, relation, relationship, relevance.

bearings plural noun *You need to find your bearings.* location, orientation, position, whereabouts.

beast noun **1** *A country vet looks after big beasts.* animal, brute, creature, quadruped. **2** *The person who did this was a beast.* brute, fiend, monster, savage.

beastly adjective **1** *the man's beastly instinct.* animal, bestial. **2** (*informal*) *That was a beastly thing to do.* abominable, awful, disgusting, hateful, horrible, mean, nasty, rotten, unpleasant.

beat verb **1** *He beat the boy until he cried.* bash, batter, belt (*slang*), cane, clobber (*slang*), clout (*informal*), club, cudgel, drub, flog, hit, knock, lash, lay into (*informal*), pound, quilt (*Australian slang*), slap, smack, smite, spank, stoush (*Australian slang*), strike, thrash, thump, thwack, trounce, wallop (*informal*), whack, whip. **2** *The sun beat down.* burn, shine. **3** *Beat the eggs.* agitate, mix, stir, whip, whisk. **4** *Her heart beat unevenly.* flutter, palpitate, pound, pulsate, throb, thump. **5** *He beat all his opponents.* clobber (*slang*), conquer, crush, defeat, euchre, get the better of, lick (*informal*), outdo, outstrip, outwit, overcome, overwhelm, prevail over, pulverise, rout, slaughter, stonker (*Australian slang*), surpass, thrash, triumph over, trounce, vanquish; see also WIN. **6** *It beats me.* baffle, bamboozle (*informal*), bewilder, perplex, puzzle, stump. — noun **1** *the beat in music.* accent, pulse, rhythm, stress. **2** *a police officer's beat.* circuit, course, path, round, route. □ **beat up** *He beat up the driver and robbed him.* assault, attack, bash up, batter, mug.

beautiful adjective **1** *She was beautiful to look at.* appealing, attractive, bonny (*Scottish*), captivating, charming, comely, delightful, exquisite, fair (*old use*), fetching, glorious, good-looking, gorgeous, handsome, irresistible, lovely, pleasing, pretty, radiant, stunning. OPPOSITE ugly. **2** *The student does beautiful work.* brilliant, excellent, fine, good; see also EXCELLENT. **3** *beautiful landscapes.* picturesque, pretty, scenic.

beautify verb *They beautified the house before selling it.* adorn, decorate, embellish, enhance, improve, prettify, smarten up, titivate (*informal*), tizzy up (*Australian*).

beauty noun **1** *a thing of beauty. a woman's beauty.* attractiveness, elegance, glamour, glory, good looks, handsomeness, loveliness, magnificence, prettiness, radiance, splendour. OPPOSITE ugliness. **2** *The beauty of this method is that it is simple.* advantage, attraction, benefit, blessing, good point. OPPOSITE disadvantage.

because conjunction *He was sad because his cat had died.* as, for, since. □ **because of** *She was absent because of illness.* as a result of, by reason of, on account of, owing to, thanks to.

beckon verb *He beckoned to the child to come to him.* gesture, motion, signal.

become verb **1** *The tadpole became a frog.* change into, develop into, grow into, turn into. **2** *Yellow becomes her.* befit, be right for, flatter, look good on, suit. □ **become of** *What became of Henry?* befall (*formal*), happen to.

bed noun **1** *a bed to sleep in.* berth, bunk, camp bed, cot, cradle, crib, divan, folding bed, four-poster, futon, hammock, sofa bed, stretcher, trundle bed, waterbed. **2** *The curry was served on a bed of rice.* base, bottom, foundation. **3** *a dry river bed.* bottom, channel, course. **4** *a garden bed.* border, patch, plot, strip.

bedclothes plural noun bedding, bed linen, bedspread, blankets, covers, linen, pillows, quilt, sheets.

bedlam noun *With so many performers it was bedlam backstage.* chaos, confusion, madhouse (*informal*), mayhem, pandemonium, rumpus, uproar.

bedraggled adjective *He came in bedraggled after his walk in the rain.* dishevelled, messy, ruffled, scruffy, unkempt, untidy, wet. OPPOSITE well-groomed.

bedroom noun chamber (*old use*), dormitory.

bee noun *a hive of bees.* bumble-bee, drone, honey bee, queen, worker.

beefy adjective *a beefy footballer.* brawny, burly, hefty, muscular, nuggety (*Australian*), solid, stocky, strapping, strong, sturdy, thickset. OPPOSITE skinny, weak.

bee-keeper noun apiarist.

beer noun ale, bitter, lager, stout.

befall verb (*formal*) *He will be with you whatever befalls.* come about, come to pass, crop up, eventuate, happen, occur, take place.

befitting adjective *She spoke in a befitting manner.* appropriate, becoming, fitting, proper, right, seemly, suitable.

before adverb *They had been there before.* beforehand, earlier, formerly, hitherto, in the past, previously. — preposition *Thunder comes before lightning.* ahead of, earlier than, in front of, prior to. OPPOSITE after.

beforehand adverb *The meal was prepared beforehand.* ahead, earlier, in advance, in anticipation, in readiness.

befriend verb *She is good at befriending newcomers.* look after, make a friend of, take care of, welcome.

beg verb **1** *He's always begging for money.* cadge, scrounge, sponge. **2** *She begged them to stay.* ask, beseech, entreat, implore, plead, pray, request.

beget verb (*literary*) **1** *Abraham begat Isaac.* father, procreate, sire. **2** *War begets misery.* breed, bring about, cause, create, engender, generate, give rise to, produce, result in.

beggar *noun* **1** *She gave money to the beggar in the street.* cadger, down-and-out, mendicant, scrounger, sponger, tramp. **2** (*informal*) *You cheeky beggar!* fellow, person, rascal, wretch (*informal*).

begin *verb* **1** *The game begins at twelve o'clock.* commence, get going, get under way, kick off (*informal*), open, start. OPPOSITE end, finish. **2** *He began a pizza delivery service.* commence, create, embark on, establish, found, inaugurate, initiate, introduce, launch, open, originate, set up, start. **3** *The problems begin when people cannot agree.* appear, arise, commence, crop up, emerge, originate, spring up, start.

beginner *noun* *Tony teaches beginners.* apprentice, learner, new chum (*Australian informal*), novice, recruit, starter, tiro, trainee. OPPOSITE old hand.

beginning *noun* **1** *the beginning of the race.* commencement, opening, outset, start. **2** *the beginning of a new movement.* birth, creation, dawn, founding, genesis, inception, introduction, onset, origin, rise, root, source, starting point. **3** *the beginning of a novel.* introduction, opening, preamble, preface, prelude, prologue. OPPOSITE end.

begrudge *verb* *She begrudges him his promotion.* envy, grudge, mind, object to, resent.

beguiling *adjective a beguiling smile.* bewitching, captivating, charming, enthralling, seductive.

behalf *noun* **on behalf of** *Henry spoke on behalf of his class.* as a representative of, for, representing.

behave *verb* **1** *She can predict how you will behave.* act, conduct yourself, react. **2** *The car behaved well in the snow.* function, operate, perform, run, work. **3** *We hope you all can behave yourselves.* be polite, be well-mannered, mind your manners. OPPOSITE misbehave.

behaviour *noun* *They were on their best behaviour.* actions, conduct, demeanour, deportment, manners.

behead *verb* decapitate, guillotine; see also EXECUTE.

behind *adverb* *He is behind with his payment.* behindhand, in arrears, late, overdue. — *preposition* **1** *He ran behind the main group.* after, at the back of, at the rear of, following. **2** *Our car is parked behind the red one.* beyond, on the far side of, on the other side of. **3** *What is behind his comment?* at the bottom of, underlying. **4** *Some countries are behind others in development.* less advanced than, trailing. — *noun He fell on his behind.* see BOTTOM. □ **behind someone's back** *They did a deal behind his back.* covertly, deceitfully, in secret, secretly, slyly, sneakily, surreptitiously. **behind the times** antediluvian, antiquated, obsolete, old-fashioned, outdated, outmoded, out of date.

behold *verb* (*old use*) *They beheld an amazing sight.* observe, see, survey, view, witness.

beige *adjective a beige colour.* biscuit, buff, coffee, fawn, neutral.

being *noun* **1** *The recorder group came into being two years ago.* existence, life. **2** *living beings.* animal, creature, entity, individual, living thing, mortal, person.

belch *verb* **1** *He belched after drinking the lemonade.* bring up wind, burp (*informal*). **2** *The funnel belched black smoke.* discharge, emit, give off, send out, spew.

belief *noun* **1** *Her belief in God will always remain firm.* confidence, credence, faith, reliance, trust.

OPPOSITE disbelief. **2** *It was her belief that the man was innocent.* conviction, impression, judgement, opinion, thought, view. **3** *people of many different beliefs.* conviction, credo, creed, doctrine, dogma, faith, ideology, persuasion, philosophy, religion.

believable *adjective Lee's excuse was believable.* acceptable, convincing, credible, plausible. OPPOSITE incredible, unlikely.

believe *verb* **1** *I would not believe all that he says.* accept, credit, rely on, trust. OPPOSITE disbelieve, mistrust. **2** *I believe that you can do it.* be certain, be convinced, be sure, have faith. OPPOSITE doubt. **3** *I believe it's going to rain.* guess (*informal*), reckon, suppose, think.

believer *noun* *religious believers.* adherent, convert, disciple, follower, supporter, zealot. OPPOSITE unbeliever.

belittle *verb* *He was always belittling her friends.* denigrate, depreciate, disparage, knock (*informal*), put down, run down, sling off at (*Australian informal*). OPPOSITE praise.

bell *noun an alarm bell. the church bells.* alarm, carillon, chime, knell, peal, ring, signal, tocsin.

belligerent *adjective* **1** *The belligerent countries agreed to a ceasefire.* fighting, militant, warmongering, warring. **2** *a belligerent reply.* aggressive, argumentative, bellicose, hostile, provocative, pugnacious, quarrelsome, truculent. OPPOSITE peaceable.

bellow *verb* *The leader bellowed his instructions.* bawl, roar, scream, shout, yell.

belly *noun a pain in the belly.* abdomen, guts (*informal*), paunch, stomach, tummy (*informal*).

belong *verb* *The clothes belong in the wardrobe.* go, have a place. □ **belong to 1** *The house belongs to me.* be owned by, be the property of. **2** *We belong to the club.* be a member of, be a part of, be associated with.

belongings *plural noun You must take care of your belongings.* chattels, effects, gear (*informal*), goods, possessions, property, stuff (*informal*), things (*informal*).

beloved *adjective a beloved child.* adored, cherished, darling, dear, loved, precious, treasured.

below *adverb* **1** *go below.* beneath, downstairs, downstream, underneath. **2** *see chapter 2 below.* further on. OPPOSITE above. — *preposition* **1** *The landing stage is located below the bridge.* beneath, downstream from, under, underneath. **2** *temperatures below zero.* less than, lower than. OPPOSITE above.

belt *noun* **1** *a leather belt.* band, cummerbund, girdle, sash, strap. **2** *They live in the wheat belt.* area, district, region, strip, zone. — *verb He belted the child.* beat, flog, hit, lash, strap, thrash, whip; see also HIT.

bemused *adjective His note left her somewhat bemused.* bewildered, confused, perplexed, puzzled.

bench *noun* **1** *The children sat on a bench.* form, pew, seat, settle. **2** *She chopped the meat on the kitchen bench.* counter, table, work surface, worktop.

bend *verb* **1** *The force bent the metal.* angle, arch, bow, buckle, contort, curl, curve, distort, flex, kink, loop, twist, warp. OPPOSITE straighten. **2** *The plant bent towards the light.* incline, lean. **3** *The road bends sharply.* curve, turn, twist, veer, wind. **4** *She bent down to tie her laces.* bow, crouch, duck, hunch, kneel, lean, stoop. — *noun a bend in the road.* angle, arc, corner, crook, curve, kink, loop, turn, twist.

beneath *preposition* **1** *beneath the surface.* below, under, underneath. OPPOSITE above. **2** *He considered the work beneath him.* unbefitting, unfit for, unworthy of.

benefactor *noun The costs were paid by an anonymous benefactor.* backer, donor, patron, philanthropist, sponsor, supporter.

beneficial *adjective the beneficial effects of walking.* advantageous, constructive, favourable, good, helpful, positive, profitable, rewarding, useful, valuable. OPPOSITE harmful.

beneficiary *noun a beneficiary under a will.* heir, heiress, inheritor, legatee, recipient.

benefit *noun* **1** *It was a benefit to know some French.* advantage, asset, blessing, boon, help, profit, use. OPPOSITE handicap. **2** *He was paid a government benefit.* allowance, assistance, dole (*informal*), handout (*informal*), income support, payment. — *verb* **1** *The discovery will benefit mankind.* advance, aid, assist, further, help, serve. **2** *Who benefited from the sale?* gain, profit.

benevolent *adjective They were lucky to find a benevolent sponsor.* benign, caring, charitable, compassionate, friendly, generous, good, gracious, helpful, humane, humanitarian, kind, kindly, liberal, magnanimous, merciful, philanthropic, warm-hearted. OPPOSITE malevolent.

benign *adjective* **1** *a benign smile.* benevolent, caring, kind, sympathetic. **2** *a benign tumour.* harmless, non-malignant. OPPOSITE malignant.

bent *noun She has a mathematical bent.* ability, aptitude, flair, gift, inclination, leaning, liking, skill, talent. — *adjective a bent back. a bent knitting needle.* arched, bowed, contorted, crooked, curved, distorted, hunched, twisted, warped. □ **bent on** *He was bent on winning.* determined on, intent on, set on.

bequeath *verb* *She bequeathed her jewellery to her daughter.* hand down, leave, make over, pass on, will.

bequest *noun He made several bequests in his will.* endowment, gift, inheritance, legacy, settlement.

bereaved *adjective* orphaned, widowed.

bereft *adjective* **bereft of** *bereft of hope.* deprived of, devoid of, lacking, robbed of, without.

berserk *adjective The man went berserk with a machete.* beside yourself, crazy, demented, deranged, frantic, frenzied, insane, mad, maniacal, manic, wild. OPPOSITE calm.

berth *noun* **1** *a six-berth cabin.* bed, bunk. **2** *a berth for a ship.* anchorage, dock, landing stage, moorings, pier, quay, wharf. — *verb The ship berthed in Sydney.* anchor, dock, land, moor, tie up.

beseech *verb They beseeched God to save them.* appeal to, ask, beg, entreat, implore, plead with, pray, supplicate.

beside *preposition The car drew up beside ours.* alongside, close to, near to, next to. □ **beside the point** immaterial, irrelevant, unconnected. OPPOSITE to the point.

besides *preposition There were five applicants besides her.* apart from, aside from, as well as, excluding, in addition to, not counting. — *adverb We don't want to go; and besides, we weren't invited.* also, anyway, furthermore, in addition, in any case, moreover, too.

besiege *verb* **1** *The enemy besieged the town.* blockade, encircle, encompass, lay siege to, surround.

2 *He was besieged with requests for autographs.* assail, badger, beleaguer, beset, harass, hound, pester.

besotted *adjective He was besotted with the new girl.* enamoured, infatuated, smitten (*informal*).

best *adjective best practice. the best doctor in the field.* finest, first-rate, foremost, greatest, leading, optimal, optimum, pre-eminent, superlative, supreme, top, top-notch (*informal*), unequalled, unrivalled, unsurpassed. OPPOSITE worst.

bestial *adjective bestial instincts.* animal, beastly, brutish, depraved, inhuman, savage, wild. OPPOSITE human.

bestow *verb The Governor bestowed the honour on him.* award, confer, give, grant, present.

bet *noun He had a bet on a horse.* flutter (*informal*), gamble, punt, risk, stake, wager. — *verb* **1** *She bet $2 on the winning horse.* gamble, punt, risk, stake, venture, wager. **2** (*informal*) *I bet he'll be late.* be certain, be convinced, be sure, predict.

betray *verb* **1** *She could never betray a friend.* be disloyal to, denounce, dob in (*Australian informal*), double-cross, grass (on) (*slang*), inform on, rat on (*informal*), shop (*informal*), tell on (*informal*). **2** *You must not betray our secret.* blab, disclose, divulge, expose, give away, let slip, reveal, tell. OPPOSITE keep.

betrayal *noun* denunciation, disloyalty, perfidy, treachery, treason, unfaithfulness.

better *adjective* **1** *better quality.* finer, greater, superior. OPPOSITE worse. **2** *She feels better now.* cured, fitter, healed, healthier, improved, on the mend (*informal*), recovered, stronger, well. — *verb He bettered the world record by two seconds.* beat, do better than, exceed, improve on, surpass, top. □ **get better** *The patient is getting better.* convalesce, improve, rally, recover, recuperate. OPPOSITE deteriorate. **get the better of** *I won't let her get the better of me.* beat, conquer, defeat, outdo, outwit, overcome.

beverage *noun non-alcoholic beverages.* drink, liquid, refreshment.

bevy *noun a bevy of beauties.* collection, company, gathering, group, mob (*Australian*).

beware *verb Buyer beware! Beware of the dog!* be careful, be cautious, be on your guard, be wary, look out, mind, take heed, watch out.

bewilder *verb We were bewildered by his behaviour.* baffle, bamboozle (*informal*), bemuse, confound, confuse, nonplus, perplex, puzzle, stump.

bewitch *verb* **1** *The sorcerer bewitched the cat.* cast a spell on, jinx (*informal*), point the bone at (*Australian*). **2** *He was bewitched by Jane's beauty.* beguile, captivate, charm, delight, enchant, enthral, entrance, fascinate, spellbind.

beyond *preposition* **1** *They walked beyond the town.* farther than, further than, past. **2** *They won't insure beyond the age of 75.* after, later than, over, past.

bias *noun* **1** *The newspaper shows a bias towards the Coalition.* favouritism, inclination, leaning, partiality, prejudice, slant. OPPOSITE impartiality. **2** *The skirt is cut on the bias.* angle, cross, diagonal, slant.

biased *adjective biased reporting.* distorted, one-sided, partial, prejudiced, slanted, unbalanced, unfair. OPPOSITE impartial.

Bible *noun a verse from the Bible.* Holy Writ, Scripture, the Scriptures, the Word of God.

bicker *verb* see QUARREL.

bicycle *noun* bike (*informal*), cycle, push-bike (*informal*), two-wheeler (*informal*); [*kinds of bicycle*] BMX, moped, mountain bike, penny farthing, racing bike, tandem.

bid[1] *noun* **1** *She put in a bid of $10 for the vase.* offer, proposal, submission, tender. **2** *He made a bid for the presidency.* attempt, effort, try. — *verb He bid $200 for the stamp collection.* offer, proffer, propose, tender.

bid[2] *verb* **1** *Bid them come in.* ask, command, instruct, invite, order, tell. **2** *We bade them farewell.* say, tell, wish.

big *adjective* **1** *a big building. a big man.* ample, broad, bulky, colossal, enormous, fat, gargantuan, giant, gigantic, ginormous (*slang*), great, hefty, huge, hulking, humungous (*slang*), immense, jumbo (*informal*), king-sized, large, lofty, mammoth, massive, mighty, monstrous, monumental, outsize, spacious, stupendous, tall, tremendous, vast. OPPOSITE little, small. **2** *a big amount.* astronomical, colossal, considerable, enormous, excessive, exorbitant, extravagant, handsome, hefty, immeasurable, incalculable, large, prodigious, sizeable, staggering, substantial, tidy (*informal*). OPPOSITE small. **3** *my big brother.* elder, grown-up, older. OPPOSITE little. **4** *It was the big match.* critical, grand, great, important, major, momentous, significant, vital. OPPOSITE minor. **5** (*informal*) *That's big of you.* altruistic, big-hearted, generous, kind, magnanimous, unselfish. OPPOSITE mean.

bigoted *adjective A conversation was impossible with this bigoted man.* biased, dogmatic, intolerant, narrow-minded, opinionated, prejudiced. OPPOSITE open-minded.

bilious *adjective He felt bilious.* ill, nauseous, queasy, sick.

bill[1] *noun* **1** *She can't pay the bill.* account, invoice, statement, tab (*informal*). **2** *The billposters had stuck new bills over old ones.* advertisement, flyer, notice, placard, poster. **3** *a parliamentary bill.* draft legislation, proposed legislation. **4** *a $20 bill.* banknote, note. — *verb You will be billed for your purchases.* charge, debit, invoice.

bill[2] *noun a bird's bill.* beak.

billet *verb The students were billeted with families.* accommodate, house, lodge, put up.

billow *noun* see WAVE. — *verb* **1** *Smoke billowed forth.* rise, roll, surge, swell. **2** *The wind caused skirts to billow.* balloon, puff out, swell.

billycart *noun* (*Australian*) go-cart, hill trolley.

bin *noun* **1** *a storage bin.* can, container, crate, drum, receptacle, skip, tin. **2** *a household bin for rubbish.* dustbin, garbage bin, garbage can, garbage tin, rubbish bin, Sulo (*trade mark*), trash can, wheelie bin.

bind *verb* **1** *He bound the parcel with string.* attach, fasten, hold together, secure, strap, tie, truss. **2** *They were bound by ties of friendship.* connect, join, link, unite. **3** *Bind his wounds.* bandage, cover, dress, swathe, wrap. **4** *The blanket was bound with satin.* edge, finish, hem, trim. **5** *The contract bound him to stay in the job for three years.* compel, constrain, force, oblige, require. — *noun* (*informal*) *I'm in a bit of a bind.* difficulty, dilemma, fix, jam (*informal*), predicament, quandary, spot (*informal*).

binder *noun He put all his papers into a binder.* cover, file, folder.

binge *noun* see SPREE.

biography *noun* life story, memoirs, profile, reminiscences.

bird *noun a feathered bird.* birdie (*informal*), chick, cock, fledgeling, fowl, hen, nestling.

birth *noun* **1** *The hospital has a special birth unit.* childbirth, confinement, delivery, labour, nativity. **2** *the birth of a new industry.* beginning, creation, founding, genesis, origin, start. **3** *He is of noble birth.* ancestry, blood, descent, extraction, lineage, origin, parentage, pedigree, stock. □ **give birth to** *Mary gave birth to a son and they named him Jesus.* bear, bring forth, deliver, produce, reproduce.

birthday *noun* anniversary.

biscuit *noun* bickie (*informal*), cookie, cracker, wafer.

bistro *noun They ate a meal at the bistro.* bar, brasserie, café, restaurant.

bit *noun* **1** *It doesn't make a bit of difference.* iota, jot, ounce, scrap, skerrick (*Australian informal*), speck. **2** *a bit of cheese.* chip, chunk, crumb, fragment, hunk, lump, morsel, particle, piece, portion, segment, slice. **3** *Wait a bit.* jiffy (*informal*), minute, moment, second, tick (*informal*). □ **bit by bit** *Debbie's health improved bit by bit.* by degrees, gradually, little by little, progressively.

bitchy *adjective a bitchy comment.* catty (*informal*), malicious, mean, nasty, spiteful, vindictive.

bite *verb* **1** *He bit into his apple.* champ, crunch, gnaw, munch, nibble; see also EAT. **2** *The insect bit him.* nip, sting, wound. — *noun* **1** *an insect bite.* nip, sting, wound. **2** *a bite of apple.* morsel, mouthful, piece.

biting *adjective* **1** *a biting wind.* bitter, cold, harsh, penetrating, piercing, sharp. OPPOSITE mild. **2** *He made some biting remarks.* caustic, critical, cutting, incisive, sarcastic, sharp, stinging, trenchant.

bitter *adjective* **1** *a bitter taste.* acrid, harsh, sharp. OPPOSITE sweet. **2** *bitter memories.* distressing, galling, heartbreaking, painful, poignant, sad, sorrowful, unpleasant. OPPOSITE happy. **3** *bitter comments.* acrimonious, embittered, hostile, rancorous, resentful, spiteful, vicious, virulent. **4** *a bitter wind.* biting, cold, freezing, harsh, piercing, sharp.

bizarre *adjective People stared at her bizarre costume.* curious, eccentric, fantastic, grotesque, odd, outlandish, peculiar, strange, unusual, weird. OPPOSITE ordinary.

blab *verb* **1** *She blabbed the whole story.* blurt out, disclose, divulge, let out, reveal. **2** *He promised not to blab.* blow the gaff (*slang*), let the cat out of the bag (*informal*), spill the beans (*slang*), squeal (*slang*), tattle, tell, tittle-tattle.

black *adjective* **1** *a black colour.* dusky, ebony, inky, jet-black, pitch-black, raven, sable, sooty, swarthy. OPPOSITE white. **2** *The sky was black.* dark, moonless, overcast, starless. **3** *The chimney sweep's hands were black.* blackened, dirty, filthy, grimy, grubby, sooty. OPPOSITE clean. **4** *She gave me a black look.* angry, furious, glowering, hostile, menacing, sullen, threatening. **5** *He was in a black mood.* depressed, dismal, gloomy, glum, lugubrious, melancholy, sad, sombre. OPPOSITE bright. **6** *He committed a black deed.* deadly, evil, hateful, malicious, nefarious, sinister, wicked. □ **black out** see FAINT.

blacken *verb* **1** *The wall was blackened by the fire.* darken, dirty, soil, stain. **2** *The newspapers blackened his character.* besmirch, defame, denigrate, discredit, libel, malign, slander, smear, speak ill of, sully, tarnish.

blackguard *noun* knave (*old use*), miscreant, rascal, rogue, scoundrel, villain.

blacklist *verb The company was blacklisted because they use whale products.* ban, bar, blackball, boycott, debar, exclude, ostracise.

blackmail *verb* hold to ransom, threaten. — *noun He won't give in to blackmail.* extortion, intimidation.

blackout *noun* **1** *When there is a blackout we use candles.* power cut, power failure. **2** *He suffers occasional blackouts.* faint, loss of consciousness, swoon.

blade *noun* **1** *The knife has a sharp blade.* cutting edge, edge. **2** *a blade of grass.* frond, leaf, shoot.

blame *verb They blamed him for the accident.* accuse, charge, condemn, criticise, find guilty, hold responsible, make accountable, reproach, reprove. — *noun She took the blame for what happened.* censure, criticism, culpability, fault, guilt, liability, rap (*informal*), reprimand, reproach, reproof, responsibility.

blameless *adjective blameless conduct.* guiltless, innocent, irreproachable, unimpeachable.

bland *adjective The food tastes bland.* flavourless, insipid, mild, plain, tasteless, uninteresting, wishy-washy. OPPOSITE tasty.

blank *adjective* **1** *a blank sheet of paper.* clean, empty, plain, unfilled, unmarked, unused. **2** *a blank face.* deadpan, emotionless, expressionless, impassive, poker-faced, vacant, vacuous. — *noun fill the blanks.* gap, space, void.

blanket *noun* **1** *We need extra blankets on the bed.* cover, covering, rug. **2** *a thick blanket of fog.* cloak, covering, layer, mantle, sheet. — *adjective a blanket agreement.* comprehensive, general, inclusive, overall.

blare *verb The trumpets blared.* blast, boom, resound, roar, sound, trumpet.

blasé *adjective The spoilt child was blasé about treats.* bored, indifferent, nonchalant, unexcited, unimpressed, uninterested. OPPOSITE excited.

blasphemous *adjective His remarks were considered blasphemous.* disrespectful, impious, irreligious, irreverent, profane, sacrilegious, ungodly. OPPOSITE reverent.

blasphemy *noun* disrespect, impiety, irreverence, profanity, sacrilege. OPPOSITE reverence.

blast *noun* **1** *a blast of wind.* draught, gust, rush. **2** *a blast from the horns.* blare, boom, honk, toot. **3** *a bomb blast.* detonation, discharge, explosion. — *verb The miners blasted the rock.* blow up, break up, detonate, explode, shatter.

blast-off *noun the blast-off of the spacecraft.* launch, lift-off, take-off.

blatant *adjective blatant dishonesty.* barefaced, flagrant, obvious, open, overt, unashamed, unconcealed. OPPOSITE concealed.

blaze *noun* **1** *The firemen extinguished the blaze.* conflagration, fire, flames, inferno. **2** *a blaze of anger.* burst, fit, outburst, rage. — *verb Lights were blazing.* burn, flame, flare, glow, shine.

blazer *noun* coat, jacket.

bleach *verb The clothes were bleached by the sun. Her hair is bleached.* blanch, fade, lighten, peroxide, whiten.

bleak *adjective* **1** *bleak weather.* bitter, chilly, cold, dreary, wintry. OPPOSITE sunny. **2** *a bleak setting.* bare, barren, desolate, dismal, windswept. **3** *The future looks bleak.* black, depressing, dismal, gloomy, grim, hopeless, unpromising. OPPOSITE bright.

bleary *adjective bleary eyes.* blurred, cloudy, filmy, fuzzy, misty, watery. OPPOSITE clear.

bleed *verb The patient bled.* haemorrhage, lose blood.

bleep *noun She woke up when she heard the bleep.* beep, signal.

blemish *noun skin without blemishes.* blotch, defect, discoloration, disfigurement, fault, flaw, imperfection, mark, scar, spot, stain.

blend *verb* **1** *The ingredients are blended in the machine.* combine, fuse, incorporate, intermingle, mingle, mix, synthesise. OPPOSITE separate. **2** *The colours blend well.* fit, go together, harmonise. OPPOSITE clash. — *noun a blend of flavours.* amalgam, combination, composite, compound, fusion, mix, mixture, synthesis.

bless *verb The priest blessed the house.* consecrate, dedicate, hallow, sanctify. OPPOSITE curse.

blessed *adjective* **1** *the Blessed Virgin Mary.* beatified, consecrated, hallowed, holy, revered, sacred, sanctified. **2** (*old use*) *Blessed are the pure in heart.* fortunate, happy.

blessing *noun* **1** *The project had his blessing.* approval, consent, favour, OK (*informal*), sanction, support. OPPOSITE disapproval. **2** *The minister pronounced the blessing.* benediction, grace, prayer, thanksgiving. **3** *The rain was a blessing to farmers.* asset, boon, gift, godsend, help. OPPOSITE misfortune.

blight *noun* **1** *Blight had affected the plants.* disease, fungus, mildew, pestilence, rust. **2** *a blight on society.* affliction, bane, curse, plague, scourge. — *verb His plans were blighted by a family tragedy.* damage, dash, frustrate, mar, ruin, spoil, wreck. OPPOSITE enhance.

blind *adjective* **1** *a blind person.* sightless, unsighted, visually impaired. OPPOSITE sighted. **2** *blind obedience.* mindless, uncritical, unreasoning, unthinking. — *verb He tried to blind them with science.* bamboozle (*informal*), confuse, dazzle, overawe, overwhelm; see also DECEIVE. — *noun The blinds are sold with the house.* holland blind, screen, shade, shutter, venetian blind, vertical blind. □ **blind alley** *He drove the car into a blind alley.* cul-de-sac, dead end, no through road.

blink *verb The lights blinked.* flash, flicker, glimmer, shimmer, sparkle, twinkle, wink.

bliss *noun Six weeks of holidays will be bliss.* delight, ecstasy, euphoria, happiness, heaven, joy, paradise, pleasure, rapture. OPPOSITE hell, misery.

blissful *adjective The honeymoon was blissful.* delightful, happy, heavenly, joyous, rapturous, wonderful.

blithe *adjective* **1** *With the exams over they were in a blithe mood.* carefree, cheerful, gay, happy, joyous, light-hearted, merry. OPPOSITE gloomy. **2** *blithe ignorance.* careless, casual, heedless, indifferent, nonchalant.

blitz *noun The police had a blitz on speeding drivers.* attack, campaign, crackdown (*informal*), offensive, onslaught.

bloated *adjective a bloated stomach.* distended, enlarged, inflated, puffed up, swollen.

blob *noun a blob of mayonnaise.* bead, dollop, drop, globule, splash, splotch, spot.

block *noun* **1** *a block of wood. a block of soap. a block of gold.* bar, brick, cake, chunk, cube, hunk, ingot, slab, wedge. **2** (*Australian*)

Their house is on a large suburban block. acreage, allotment, plot, section (*Australian historical*). **3** *Their house is built on blocks.* pile, stilt, support. **4** *The police set up a road block.* barrier, blockade, obstacle, obstruction. — *verb* **1** *Parked trucks blocked the traffic.* bar, blockade, halt, hamper, hinder, hold back, impede, obstruct, stop. **2** *The leaves blocked the drain.* bung up, choke, clog, fill up, jam, obstruct, stop up. OPPOSITE clear.

blockade *noun The soldiers set up a blockade.* barricade, barrier, block, siege.

blockage *noun* barrier, block, blockade, bottleneck, impediment, jam, obstacle, obstruction, stoppage.

bloke *noun* (*informal*) *He's a nice bloke.* boy, chap (*informal*), character, fellow (*informal*), guy (*informal*), man.

blond, blonde *adjective blond hair.* fair, flaxen, golden, light, tow-coloured. OPPOSITE dark.

blood *noun* **1** *blood at the crime scene.* gore. **2** *of royal blood.* ancestry, birth, descent, family, line, lineage, parentage, race, stock. **3** *my own flesh and blood.* family, kinsfolk, kith and kin, relations, relatives.

bloodbath *noun* see MASSACRE.

blood-curdling *adjective a blood-curdling scream.* chilling, frightening, hair-raising, horrific, horrifying, spine-chilling, terrifying.

bloodshed *noun* carnage, killing, massacre, murder, slaughter, slaying, wounding.

bloodthirsty *adjective bloodthirsty soldiers.* brutal, ferocious, fierce, homicidal, murderous, sanguinary, savage, vicious.

bloody *adjective* **1** *bloody hands.* bleeding, bloodstained. **2** *a bloody battle.* cruel, gory, sanguinary, violent; see also BLOODTHIRSTY. OPPOSITE bloodless.

bloom *noun a bouquet of red blooms.* blossom, bud, flower. — *verb Her plants are blooming.* blossom, burgeon, flower.

blossom *noun* peach blossom. bloom, flower. — *verb* **1** *The tree blossomed.* bloom, burgeon, flower. **2** *Her talent has blossomed.* bloom, develop, flourish, grow, thrive.

blot *noun* **1** *blots of ink.* blotch, mark, smudge, splotch, spot, stain. **2** *a blot on the landscape.* blight, eyesore. **3** *a blot on his character.* blemish, defect, fault, stain. — *verb* **1** *The page was blotted with ink.* smudge, spot, stain. **2** *Blot the spill with paper towel.* absorb, dry, soak up. □ **blot out** *He tried to blot out the bad memories.* cover, efface, mask, obliterate, obscure, wipe out.

blotch *noun blotches of ink.* skin blotches. blemish, blot, mark, patch, spot.

blow[1] *verb* **1** *The wind blew very fiercely.* blast, bluster, gust, roar, whistle. **2** *The breeze blew the fumes our way.* carry, convey, drive, move, send, sweep, waft. **3** *He blew his trumpet.* blare, blast, play, sound, toot. **4** *She stopped her hiccups by blowing into a paper bag.* breathe out, exhale, puff. **5** (*slang*) *I blew it.* botch, bungle, muff, ruin, spoil, wreck. □ **blow out** *He blew out the candle.* extinguish, put out, snuff. **blow up** **1** *He blew up the tyres.* fill, inflate, pump up. OPPOSITE deflate. **2** *They blew up the photograph.* enlarge. OPPOSITE reduce. **3** *The story was blown up by the newspapers.* exaggerate, magnify, overstate. OPPOSITE play down. **4** *The bomb blew up.* detonate, explode, go off. **5** *The building was blown up.* blast, bomb, burst apart, destroy, shatter.

blow[2] *noun* **1** *He was knocked out by a heavy blow.* bang, bash, belt (*slang*), box, buffet, clout (*informal*), hit, king-hit (*Australian informal*), knock, punch, rap, slap, smack, stroke, thump, thwack, wallop (*informal*), whack. **2** *Losing his house was a terrible blow.* body blow, bombshell, calamity, disappointment, disaster, misfortune, setback, shock, upset.

blubber *noun The diet got rid of his blubber.* fat, flab (*informal*). — *verb* cry, snivel, sob, weep.

bludge *verb* (*Australian informal*) **1** *Some work hard while others bludge.* idle, loaf, skive (*informal*), slack, take it easy. **2** *He hasn't any money and is forced to bludge off others.* borrow, cadge, scab (*Australian slang*), scrounge, sponge. — *noun* (*Australian informal*) *The job was a bludge.* breeze (*informal*), child's play, cinch (*informal*), doddle (*informal*), piece of cake (*informal*), pushover (*informal*), snack (*Australian informal*), snap (*informal*).

bludgeon *noun* see CLUB.

bludger *noun* (*Australian informal*) *He was generally seen as a lazy bludger.* freeloader (*informal*), hanger-on, idler, layabout, loafer, parasite, shirker, slacker, sponger.

blue *adjective* **1** *a blue colour.* aqua, aquamarine, azure, cobalt (blue), indigo, navy (blue), powder blue, Prussian blue, royal blue, sapphire, sky blue, turquoise, ultramarine. **2** *blue skies.* clear, cloudless. **3** *feeling blue.* depressed, despondent, downcast, down in the dumps (*informal*), gloomy, low, melancholy, sad, unhappy. **4** *blue jokes.* bawdy, coarse, dirty, indecent, lewd, obscene, risqué, rude. OPPOSITE clean. — *noun* **1** *They had a blue over the handling of the money.* see ARGUMENT. **2** *He made a terrible blue.* see MISTAKE. □ **blues** *plural noun* see DEPRESSION.

blueprint *noun a blueprint for change.* design, outline, pattern, plan, scheme.

bluey *noun* (*Australian*) *The swagman's bluey contains all his possessions.* drum (*Australian*), matilda (*Australian*), shiralee (*Australian*), swag (*Australian*).

bluff[1] *verb* **1** *The card player bluffed his opponent.* deceive, dupe, fool, hoodwink, mislead, take in, trick. **2** *I knew he was only bluffing.* fake, feign, pretend, sham. — *noun We weren't sure whether what he said was just a bluff.* deception, pretence, sham, trick.

bluff[2] *noun We climbed the bluff to admire the view.* cliff, escarpment, headland, precipice, scarp.

blunder *verb She blundered about in the dark.* lumber, lurch, stagger, stumble. — *noun He committed a blunder.* blue (*Australian informal*), booboo (*slang*), bungle, error, clanger (*informal*), gaffe, howler (*informal*), mistake, slip-up (*informal*).

blunt *adjective* **1** *a blunt knife.* dull, unsharpened. OPPOSITE sharp. **2** *a blunt refusal.* abrupt, candid, curt, direct, frank, open, outspoken, upfront (*informal*). OPPOSITE subtle. — *verb She blunted the knife.* dull. OPPOSITE sharpen, whet.

blurred *adjective The picture is blurred.* blurry, confused, dim, distorted, foggy, fuzzy, hazy, indistinct, misty, out of focus, unclear. OPPOSITE clear.

blurt *verb blurt out He blurted out the answer.* blab, burst out with, call out, utter; see also SAY.

blush *verb She blushed when he looked at her.* colour, flush, glow, go red, redden. OPPOSITE pale.

blustery *adjective blustery conditions.* blowy, gusty, rough, squally, stormy, wild, windy.

board *noun* **1** *wooden boards.* beam, plank, sheet, slat, timber. **2** *on the company's board.* committee, council, panel. — *verb* **1** *They boarded the ferry.* catch, embark, get on, go on board. OPPOSITE alight, disembark. **2** *Some country students board with city families.* live, lodge, reside.

boarding house *noun* guest house, hostel, lodging house.

boast *verb He boasted about his successes.* be conceited, blow your own trumpet, brag, congratulate yourself, crow, have tickets on yourself (*Australian informal*), show off, skite (*Australian informal*), swagger, swank (*informal*), talk big (*informal*). OPPOSITE hide your light under a bushel.

boastful *adjective* big-headed, bragging, cocky (*informal*), conceited, egotistical, proud, swaggering, swanky (*informal*), vain. OPPOSITE modest.

boat *noun* craft, vessel; [*various boats*] barge, canoe, catamaran, cutter, dinghy, ferry, gondola, houseboat, hydrofoil, junk, kayak, ketch, launch, lifeboat, motor boat, pontoon, punt, raft, rowing boat, sailing boat, sampan, skiff, sloop, speedboat, trawler, tug, yacht, yawl; see also SHIP.

bob *verb* **1** *bob up and down.* bounce, curtsy, jerk, jig, jump, leap. **2** *bob your head.* duck, nod. □ **bob up** *Look who bobbed up?* appear, come up, show up, turn up.

bobbin *noun* reel, spool.

bode *verb It bodes well for their future.* augur, indicate, portend, presage, promise.

bodily *adjective having a bodily form.* corporal, physical.

body *noun* **1** *The artist studied the human body.* anatomy, figure, form, frame, physique, shape. **2** *The body was taken to the morgue.* cadaver, carcass, corpse, remains. **3** *The spots are on his body and not on his limbs or face.* torso, trunk. **4** *an aeroplane body.* fuselage, hull, shell. **5** *He belongs to a student body.* see GROUP. **6** *a foreign body in your eye.* object, thing. **7** *This fabric lacks body.* density, solidity, strength, substance.

bodyguard *noun The Governor's bodyguard was injured.* escort, guard, minder, protector.

bog *noun* fen, marsh, mire, morass, mudflat, quagmire, quicksand, slough, swamp, wetlands. — *verb The car was bogged in the mud.* immobilise, stick, trap.

boggy *adjective boggy ground.* marshy, miry, muddy, spongy, swampy, wet.

bogus *adjective a bogus diamond.* counterfeit, fake, false, forged, imitation, phoney (*informal*), sham. OPPOSITE genuine.

bogyman *noun She is frightened of the bogyman.* bogy, devil, evil spirit, goblin.

boil[1] *verb The casserole is boiling.* bubble, cook, heat, seethe, simmer, stew.

boil[2] *noun Her skin was covered in painful boils.* abscess, carbuncle, gumboil, inflammation, pustule.

boiling *adjective* see HOT.

boisterous *adjective boisterous children.* active, energetic, exuberant, high-spirited, lively, noisy, rough, rowdy, unruly, vivacious, wild. OPPOSITE quiet.

bold *adjective* **1** *a bold leader.* brave, confident, courageous, daring, fearless, game, heroic, intrepid, unafraid, undaunted. OPPOSITE timid. **2** *bold behaviour.* assertive, auda-

cious, brazen, cheeky, forward, immodest, impudent, presumptuous, shameless. OPPOSITE coy, shy. **3** *bold colours.* bright, conspicuous, showy, striking, strong, vibrant, vivid. OPPOSITE pale.

bolster *noun The child sat on a bolster.* cushion, pillow, support. — *verb The government's new measures should bolster the economy.* boost, encourage, prop up, reinforce, shore up, strengthen, support.

bolt *noun* **1** *the bolt on a door.* bar, catch, latch, lock, snib. **2** *a bolt of lightning.* flash, shaft. — *verb* **1** *Have you bolted the door?* fasten, latch, lock, secure, snib. **2** *The animal bolted.* dart off, dash off, escape, run away, run off, scarper, take off, tear off. **3** *She bolts her food.* gobble, gulp, guzzle, shovel in, wolf. □ **a bolt from the blue** bombshell, shock, surprise, thunderbolt.

bomb *noun* **1** *The building was destroyed by a bomb.* device (*euphemism*), explosive, grenade, incendiary, missile. **2** (*Australian informal*) *They drive an old bomb.* heap (*informal*), jalopy (*informal*), rattletrap (*informal*), rust bucket (*informal*), wreck. — *verb The city was bombed at night.* attack, blitz, blow up, bombard, shell.

bombard *verb* **1** *The soldiers bombarded the building.* attack, besiege, blitz, bomb, fire at, pelt, shell. **2** *They bombarded her with questions.* assail, attack, besiege, hound.

bombastic *adjective bombastic language.* extravagant, grandiloquent, grandiose, high-flown, inflated, ostentatious, pompous.

bombshell *noun The news of his death came as a bombshell.* bolt from the blue, jolt, shock, surprise.

bonanza *noun* bonus, godsend, windfall.

bond *noun* **1** *a bond of friendship.* attachment, connection, link, relationship, tie. **2** *The trainee enters into a bond with the employer.* agreement, bargain, contract, deal. **3** *a bond on a flat.* bond money, deposit, guarantee, security. — *verb The glue bonds the two surfaces together.* adhere, bind, cement, connect, fasten, fuse, join, link, stick, tie. □ **bonds** *plural noun The prisoner burst his bonds.* chains, fetters, handcuffs, manacles, ropes, shackles.

bondage *noun freed from bondage.* captivity, enslavement, serfdom, servitude, slavery. OPPOSITE freedom.

bonnet *noun* **1** *She knitted the baby a bonnet.* cap, hat. **2** *the car bonnet.* hood (*American*).

bonus *noun* **1** *The boss gave everyone a bonus.* bounty, gratuity, perk (*informal*), premium, reward, supplement, tip. OPPOSITE penalty. **2** *The fine weather was a bonus.* addition, advantage, benefit, extra, plus.

bony *adjective After dieting she had a bony look.* angular, emaciated, gaunt, lean, raw-boned, scrawny, skinny, thin. OPPOSITE plump.

boo *verb The audience booed.* heckle, hoot, jeer, scoff. OPPOSITE cheer.

book *noun* **1** *We read his latest book.* publication, tome, volume, work; [*kinds of book*] almanac, annual, anthology, atlas, concordance, dictionary, digest, directory, encyclopedia, guidebook, handbook, hymnal, manual, missal, novel, omnibus, primer, textbook, thesaurus, yearbook. **2** *She records everything in her book.* account book, album, daybook, diary, exercise book, journal, ledger, logbook, memo book, notebook, passbook, pocketbook, scrapbook, sketchbook. **3** *The Old Testament is made up of thirty-nine books.* division, part, section. — *verb* **1** *The police booked him for speeding.* charge, fine. **2** *We booked seats for the concert.* order, reserve.

booklet *noun a booklet explaining immunisation.* brochure, handbook, handout, leaflet, pamphlet.

boom *verb* **1** *Her voice boomed in the empty cave.* echo, resonate, resound, reverberate. **2** *Business is booming.* expand, flourish, grow, prosper, thrive. OPPOSITE slacken. — *noun* **1** *the boom of the drums.* bang, blast, reverberation, roar, rumble, thunder. **2** *a boom in the film industry.* expansion, growth, improvement, upturn. OPPOSITE decline.

boomerang *verb The plan boomeranged on the instigators.* backfire, rebound, recoil.

boon *noun What a boon the telephone can be!* advantage, asset, benefit, blessing, help. OPPOSITE nuisance.

boost *verb* **1** *He boosted the boy up to see over the wall.* hoist, lift, push, raise. **2** *The visit boosted morale.* assist, bolster, encourage, heighten, improve, increase, lift, raise, strengthen. OPPOSITE lower. — *noun a financial boost from the government.* assistance, encouragement, help, impetus, shot in the arm, stimulus.

booster *noun You need a tetanus booster.* immunisation, injection, inoculation, jab (*informal*), shot, vaccination.

boot *noun* **1** *He wore boots in the rain.* gumboot, wellington; see also SHOE. **2** *the boot of the car.* trunk (*American*). — *verb He booted the ball.* kick, punt. □ **boot out** (*slang*) *He was booted out of his job.* chuck out (*informal*), dismiss, eject, expel, kick out (*informal*), remove, sack (*informal*), throw out.

booth *noun* **1** *a booth selling magazines.* kiosk, stall, stand. **2** *a telephone booth.* box, compartment, cubicle, enclosure.

booty *noun The thieves shared the booty.* gains, haul, loot, pickings, plunder, spoils, swag (*informal*), takings.

booze *noun* (*informal*) *There was no booze at the party.* alcohol, drink, grog (*Australian*), liquor.

border *noun* **1** *They crossed the border of the country.* boundary, frontier, limit. **2** *the border of a lake.* brink, circumference, edge, margin, perimeter, periphery, rim, verge. **3** *a decorative border.* binding, edge, edging, frame, frieze, fringe, hem, margin, mount, strip, surround. — *verb Their land borders ours.* abut on, adjoin, be next to, flank.

borderline *noun the borderline between good and bad taste.* boundary, dividing line, limit, threshold. — *adjective a borderline case.* doubtful, line-ball (*Australian*), marginal, touch-and-go, uncertain.

bore[1] *verb He bored through the surface.* drill, gouge, penetrate, perforate, pierce. — *noun* **1** *the bore of a gun.* calibre, diameter, gauge. **2** (*Australian*) *Their water comes from a bore.* artesian bore, artesian well.

bore[2] *verb He bores me stiff.* send to sleep, tire, weary. OPPOSITE interest.

bored *adjective She was bored with everything.* blasé, fed up, jaded, tired.

boredom *noun Books relieved his boredom.* apathy, dreariness, dullness, monotony, tedium.

boring *adjective a boring job.* dreary, dull, monotonous, repetitious, rou-

tine, soul-destroying, tedious, tiresome, unexciting, uninteresting. OPPOSITE exciting.

borrow *verb* **1** *He had to borrow the tools.* be lent, have the loan of; see also CADGE. OPPOSITE lend. **2** *He borrowed their methods.* adopt, appropriate, copy, plagiarise, take over, use.

bosom *noun a woman's bosom.* breasts, bust, chest.

boss *noun* (*informal*) *The boss gave him the time off.* administrator, chief, director, employer, foreman, governor (*slang*), head, leader, manager, master, overseer, proprietor, superintendent, supervisor. — *verb* (*informal*) *She bosses her friends around.* control, give orders to, order about, push around, tell what to do.

bossy *adjective She leads without being bossy.* autocratic, despotic, dictatorial, domineering, imperious, masterful, officious, overbearing, tyrannical.

botch *verb She botched the job.* bungle, make a hash of (*informal*), make a mess of, mess up, muck up (*informal*), muff (*informal*), ruin, spoil, wreck.

bother *verb* **1** *Everyone must stop bothering her.* annoy, disturb, harass, hassle (*informal*), hound, irritate, nag, pester, plague, trouble, upset, worry. **2** *She didn't even bother to phone.* care, concern yourself, take the time, take the trouble, trouble yourself. **3** *He didn't seem bothered that they hadn't arrived.* concern, disconcert, distress, disturb, perturb, put out (*informal*), trouble, upset, worry. — *noun* **1** *The bus strike was a bit of a bother.* inconvenience, irritation, nuisance, pest, problem. **2** *He found the house without any bother.* difficulty, fuss, hassle (*informal*), to-do, trouble, worry.

bottle *noun* **1** *a bottle of wine.* carafe, container, cruet, decanter, flagon, flask, magnum. **2** *a bottle of perfume.* phial, vial. □ **bottle up** *She bottled up her grief.* conceal, hide, keep back, suppress. OPPOSITE give vent to.

bottleneck *noun traffic bottlenecks.* blockage, hold-up, jam, obstruction.

bottom *noun* **1** *the bottom of a statue.* base, foot, foundation, pedestal, support. OPPOSITE top. **2** *the bottom of the ocean.* bed, depths, floor. **3** *the bottom of a vase.* underneath, underside. **4** *He fell and bruised his bottom.* backside (*informal*), behind (*informal*), bum (*slang*), butt (*slang*), buttocks, posterior, rear (*informal*), rump, seat. — *adjective the bottom level.* base, ground, lowest. OPPOSITE top.

bottomless *adjective a bottomless purse.* deep, inexhaustible, infinite.

bough *noun the tree's boughs.* branch, limb.

boulder *noun The ground was strewn with boulders.* gibber (*Australian*), rock, stone.

boulevard *noun a tree-lined boulevard.* avenue, parade, road, street.

bounce *verb* **1** *The ball bounced quite unexpectedly.* rebound, recoil, ricochet. **2** *She bounced out of bed.* bob, bound, hop, jump, leap, spring.

bouncing *adjective a bouncing baby.* bonny, healthy, thriving.

bouncy *adjective a bouncy surface.* elastic, resilient, springy.

bound[1] *verb The dog bounded over the gate.* bob, bounce, gallop, hurdle, jump, leap, lope, spring, vault. — *noun He cleared the fence in a single bound.* bob, bounce, gallop, hurdle, jump, leap, lope, spring, vault.

bound[2] *adjective house-bound.* confined, restricted, tied. □ **bound to** *He is bound to win.* certain to, destined to, sure to.

bound[3] *adjective* **bound for** *bound for Australia.* destined for, en route for, heading for, off to, travelling to.

bound[4] *verb The school is bounded by four streets.* border, circumscribe, enclose, limit, surround. □ **bounds** *plural noun His generosity knew no bounds.* boundaries, limitations, limits.

boundary *noun The boundary of the property is fenced.* border, borderline, bounds, circumference, confines, demarcation, edge, fringes, frontier, limit, margin, perimeter, threshold.

boundless *adjective boundless energy.* endless, infinite, limitless, unbounded, unlimited, vast. OPPOSITE finite, limited.

bountiful *adjective a bountiful supply of fresh vegetables.* abundant, ample, copious, generous, lavish, liberal, plentiful, prolific. OPPOSITE meagre.

bounty *noun* **1** *The poor depend on the bounty of the rich.* benevolence, charity, generosity, goodness, kindness, largesse, liberality, philanthropy. OPPOSITE stinginess. **2** *A bounty was offered for his capture.* gift, gratuity, premium, reward.

bouquet *noun The bride carried a bouquet of flowers.* bunch, corsage, posy, spray.

bout *noun* **1** *bouts of work.* period, session, spell, stint, stretch, turn. **2** *a bout of hayfever.* attack, fit, outbreak. **3** *a boxing bout.* competition, contest, fight, match, round.

boutique *noun see* SHOP.

bow[1] *verb He bowed as a sign of respect.* bend, bob, curtsy, genuflect, kneel, nod, salaam, stoop.

bow[2] *noun a ship's bow.* fore, front, prow. OPPOSITE stern.

bowels *plural noun an animal's bowels.* entrails, guts, innards (*informal*), insides (*informal*), intestines, viscera.

bower *noun a garden bower.* arbour, gazebo, pavilion, pergola, shelter, summer house.

bowl[1] *noun a bowl of soup.* basin, dish, tureen.

bowl[2] *verb He bowled a bouncer.* deliver, fling, hurl, lob, pitch, roll, throw, toss. □ **bowl over** *I was bowled over by the news.* flabbergast, floor, overwhelm, stun, surprise.

box[1] *noun* **1** *She put her papers in a box.* carton, case, chest, coffer, container, crate, pack, package, receptacle, trunk. **2** *a witness box.* compartment, stall, stand. **3** *a sentry-box.* *a telephone box.* booth, cabin, cubicle, hut, shelter. □ **box in** *She feels boxed in living in a flat.* box up, confine, coop up, enclose, hem in, shut in, surround.

box[2] *verb* **1** *He boxes as a sport.* fight, spar. **2** *He threatened to box the boy's ears.* clout (*informal*), cuff, punch, slap, thump; see also HIT.

boxer *noun* fighter, prizefighter, pugilist, sparring partner.

boxing *noun* fighting, fisticuffs, pugilism.

boy *noun* child, fellow, guy (*informal*), kid (*informal*), lad, male, schoolboy, youngster, youth.

boycott *verb People boycotted the company in protest.* avoid, ban, blacklist, ostracise, shun, stay away from. — *noun a boycott on the company's products.* ban, blacklist, embargo, prohibition.

boyfriend *noun Kate brought her boyfriend home.* admirer, beau, date (*informal*), escort, fellow, male companion, suitor, swain (*poetical*).

boyish *adjective* **1** *a man with a boyish face.* childish, childlike, immature, juvenile, young, youthful. OPPOSITE mature. **2** *a girl with a boyish appearance.* masculine. OPPOSITE feminine, girlish.

brace *noun* **1** *The shelf was supported by a brace.* bracket, buttress, calliper, prop, splint, stay, strut, support. **2** *a brace of partridge.* couple, pair. — *verb The wobbly chair needs to be braced.* reinforce, shore up, strengthen, support, tighten. □ **braces** *plural noun trousers kept up with braces.* straps, suspenders (*American*). **brace yourself** *He braced himself for the bad news.* prepare yourself, steady yourself, steel yourself.

bracing *adjective bracing sea air.* invigorating, refreshing, stimulating.

bracket *noun* **1** *a bracket on the wall.* shelf, support. **2** *He read the words in the brackets.* brace, parenthesis. **3** *an income bracket.* category, class, division, group, range, set.

brackish *adjective brackish water.* briny, slightly saline, slightly salty.

brag *verb He likes to brag about his successes.* blow your own trumpet (*informal*), boast, crow, show off, skite (*Australian informal*), swagger, swank (*informal*).

braid *noun* **1** *The dress is trimmed with braid.* ribbon, trimming. **2** *hair in braids.* plait.

brain *noun* **1** *He wanted a job which used his brain.* intellect, intelligence, mind, reason, sense, wit. **2** *He was labelled a brain.* egghead (*informal*), genius, intellectual, mastermind, whiz-kid (*informal*).

brainwash *verb The cult members had been brainwashed.* condition, indoctrinate.

brainwave *noun* brainstorm, idea, inspiration, thought; see also IDEA.

brainy *adjective a brainy kid.* bright, brilliant, clever, gifted, intellectual, intelligent, smart, studious. OPPOSITE stupid.

brake *verb You must brake at a stop sign.* halt, pull up, slow down, stop.

branch *noun* **1** *a tree branch.* bough, limb, offshoot. **2** *a branch of a river.* anabranch, arm, billabong, distributary. **3** *a branch of an organisation.* arm, department, division, office, part, section, subdivision. — *verb The river branches here.* divide, fork, split, subdivide. □ **branch out** *The business branched out into new areas.* diversify, expand, extend, open out, spread.

brand *noun a brand of car.* make, marque, sort, trade mark, type. — *verb He brands his cattle.* identify, label, mark, stamp.

brandish *verb The robber was brandishing a knife.* flourish, swing, wave.

brash *adjective His brash manner put us off.* arrogant, audacious, bold, brazen, bumptious, cocky (*informal*), impertinent, impudent, self-assertive. OPPOSITE unassuming.

bravado *noun acts of bravado.* boldness, daring, front, show, showing off.

brave *adjective a brave soldier.* bold, courageous, daring, dauntless, fearless, gallant, game, heroic, intrepid, lion-hearted, plucky, undaunted, valiant. OPPOSITE cowardly. — *noun an Indian brave.* fighter, warrior. — *verb He braved the cold.* defy, endure, face, weather, withstand.

bravery *noun an award for bravery.* boldness, courage, daring, fearlessness, fortitude, gallantry, grit (*informal*), guts (*informal*), heroism, intrepidity, mettle, nerve, pluck, prowess, valour. OPPOSITE cowardice.

brawl *noun The argument turned into a brawl.* clash, confrontation, fight, fisticuffs, free-for-all, mêlée, punch-up (*informal*), quarrel, row, scrap (*informal*), scuffle, set-to (*informal*), skirmish, stoush (*Australian slang*), struggle, tussle.

brawny *adjective a brawny rower.* beefy, burly, hefty, muscular, nuggety (*Australian*), sinewy, stocky, strong, sturdy, thickset. OPPOSITE scrawny.

bray *noun a donkey's bray.* hee-haw, neigh, whinny.

brazen *adjective a brazen hussy.* audacious, bold, cheeky, forward, impertinent, impudent, insolent, saucy, shameless, unashamed. OPPOSITE modest.

breach *noun* **1** *a breach of the rules.* breaking, contravention, infringement, transgression, violation. **2** *a breach in the fence.* aperture, break, crack, fissure, gap, hole, opening, space, split. — *verb He breached the agreement.* break, contravene, infringe, transgress, violate.

breadth *noun* broadness, extent, magnitude, range, scope, span, spread, thickness, width. CONTRASTS WITH depth, length.

break *verb* **1** *The vase fell and broke into pieces.* burst, bust (*informal*), collapse, come apart, crack, crash, crumble, demolish, disintegrate, fall apart, fracture, fragment, shatter, smash, snap, splinter, split; see also DIVIDE. OPPOSITE join. **2** *They broke the remote control.* bust (*informal*), damage, destroy, ruin, wreck. OPPOSITE mend. **3** *She wouldn't break a promise.* dishonour, go back on, renege on. OPPOSITE honour, keep. **4** *If you break the law you will be punished.* breach, contravene, disobey, flout, infringe, transgress, violate. OPPOSITE abide by, obey. **5** *Let's break for coffee.* adjourn, discontinue, interrupt, pause, stop. **6** *He has broken the record.* beat, exceed, outdo, outstrip, surpass. — *noun* **1** *a break in a hose. a break in the rock.* breach, breakage, burst, chink, cleft, crack, fissure, fracture, gash, leak, rent, rift, rupture, slit, smash, split, tear. **2** *They made a break for it.* bolt, dash, run; see also ESCAPE. **3** *a break in the line of cars.* gap, hole, interruption, opening, space. **4** *a break from work.* breather, interlude, intermission, interruption, interval, let-up (*informal*), lull, pause, playtime, recess, respite, rest, smoko (*Australian informal*), spell (*Australian*); see also HOLIDAY. **5** *a break in transmission.* discontinuity, disruption, hiatus, interruption, lapse, suspension. **6** *Give him a break.* chance, opening, opportunity. □ **break down** **1** *Break down the barriers of prejudice.* destroy, do away with, eliminate, get rid of. OPPOSITE build up. **2** *The engine broke down.* conk out (*informal*), fail, go bung (*Australian informal*), go on the blink (*informal*), malfunction, pack up (*informal*), seize up, stop working. **3** *When he heard the news he broke down.* burst into tears, collapse, crack up (*informal*), cry, go to pieces (*informal*), weep. **4** *Vegetable matter breaks down.* decay, decompose, rot. **break in** **1** *She broke in on a private discussion.* barge in, burst in, butt in, interrupt, intrude. **2** *The horse needs breaking in.* discipline, tame, train. **break off** **1** *He broke off a piece.* detach, pull off, sever, snap off. **2** *She broke off the engagement.* cease, discontinue, end, finish, stop, terminate. **break out** **1** *Fighting broke out.* begin, commence, erupt, start. **2** *They broke out of jail.* see ESCAPE. **break up** **1** *The couple broke up.* divorce, part, separate, split up. OPPOSITE reunite. **2** *School breaks up in December.* adjourn, discontinue, end, finish, stop. OPPOSITE resume.

breakable *adjective breakable plastic.* brittle, delicate, flimsy, fragile, weak. OPPOSITE indestructible, unbreakable.

breakdown *noun* **1** *mechanical breakdown.* collapse, crash (*Computing*), failure, hitch, malfunction, stoppage. **2** *a breakdown of the figures.* analysis, dissection, itemisation, run-down.

break-in *noun The police investigated the break-in.* burglary, forced entry, robbery.

breakneck *adjective breakneck speed.* dangerous, fast, headlong, reckless.

breakthrough *noun a breakthrough in the treatment of cancer.* advance, development, discovery, progress.

break-up *noun* **1** *a marriage break-up.* breakdown, collapse, dissolution, failure, separation, split-up. **2** *school break-up.* end of term.

breakwater *noun The beach is protected by a breakwater.* jetty, mole, pier.

breast *noun a woman's breast.* bosom, bust, chest.

breath *noun a deep breath.* exhalation, gasp, inhalation, pant, puff, respiration.

breathe *verb* **1** *The walkers breathed deeply.* exhale, inhale, pant, puff, respire. **2** *You mustn't breathe a word of it.* let out, utter, whisper.

breather *noun The workers have a short breather once an hour.* break, interval, pause, recess, rest, spell (*Australian*).

breathless *adjective Walking uphill makes her breathless.* gasping, out of breath, panting, puffed, short of breath, winded.

breathtaking *adjective a breathtaking performance.* amazing, astounding, awe-inspiring, exciting, overwhelming, spectacular, stupendous.

breed *verb* **1** *These animals breed well.* bear young, multiply, procreate, produce young, reproduce. **2** *They breed roses.* cultivate, propagate. **3** *He breeds dogs.* raise, rear. **4** *Lies only breed more lies.* create, engender, generate, give rise to, lead to, result in, yield. — *noun a rare breed of dog.* kind, sort, strain, type, variety.

breeze *noun* **1** *a cool breeze.* draught, wind, zephyr. **2** (*informal*) *She found the task a breeze.* bludge (*Australian informal*), child's play, cinch (*informal*), doddle (*informal*), piece of cake (*informal*), pushover (*informal*), snack (*Australian informal*), snap (*informal*), walkover. — *verb* (*informal*) *They breezed in late again.* drift, flit, float, sail, saunter, waltz (*informal*), wander.

breezy *adjective* **1** *a breezy place.* airy, draughty, exposed, windswept. OPPOSITE sheltered. **2** *a breezy day.* blowy, fresh, windy.

brevity *noun the brevity of a speech.* briefness, conciseness, curtness, shortness, succinctness, terseness. OPPOSITE long-windedness.

brew *verb* **1** *I'll brew the tea.* infuse, make, prepare. **2** *He brews his own beer.* ferment, make. **3** *Trouble is brewing.* develop, fester, gather force, hatch.

bribe *noun The official had accepted a bribe.* backhander (*informal*), carrot, enticement, graft (*informal*), hush money, incentive, inducement, kickback (*informal*), pay-off (*informal*), sling (*Australian informal*), sweetener (*informal*). — *verb He tried to bribe the policeman.* buy, buy off, corrupt, grease someone's palm (*slang*), influence, pervert, sling (*Australian informal*), tempt.

bridal *adjective the bridal party.* marriage, matrimonial, nuptial, wedding.

bridge *noun* **1** *a bridge over the river.* crossing, span; [*kinds of bridge*] aqueduct, drawbridge, flyover, footbridge, overpass, pontoon bridge, suspension bridge, swing bridge, viaduct. **2** *She is building bridges between cultures.* bond, connection, link, tie. — *verb The road bridges the chasm.* cross, extend across, span, straddle, traverse.

brief[1] *adjective* **1** *brief happiness.* ephemeral, fleeting, momentary, passing, short-lived, temporary, transient, transitory. OPPOSITE lasting. **2** *a brief report.* abridged, concise, short, succinct, terse. OPPOSITE long, wordy. □ **in brief** briefly, concisely, in a nutshell, in short, in summary, succinctly.

brief[2] *noun* **1** *a barrister's brief.* case. **2** *an architect's brief to design a fireproof house.* directions, guidelines, instructions. — *verb They briefed the premier before he addressed the meeting.* advise, fill in (*informal*), inform, instruct, prepare, put in the picture (*informal*).

briefs *plural noun a clean pair of briefs.* drawers (*old use*), jocks (*informal*), knickers, panties, pants, trunks, underpants.

brigade *noun the fire brigade.* band, corps, crew, force, group, squad, team.

brigand *noun The brigands attacked and robbed the travellers.* bandit, buccaneer, bushranger, desperado, gangster, highwayman, outlaw, pirate, robber, thief.

bright *adjective* **1** *Summer is full of bright days.* clear, cloudless, fair, fine, sunny. OPPOSITE dull, overcast. **2** *a bright colour.* bold, brilliant, flashy, gaudy, intense, showy, strong, vivid. OPPOSITE dull. **3** *bright lights.* beaming, blazing, dazzling, glaring, gleaming, glistening, glittering, glowing, incandescent, luminous, lustrous, radiant, resplendent, shining, sparkling. OPPOSITE dull. **4** *a bright personality.* animated, cheerful, gay, happy, jolly, light-hearted, lively, merry, sparkling, vivacious. OPPOSITE dreary, dull. **5** *a bright student.* able, astute, brainy, brilliant, clever, gifted, ingenious, intelligent, quick-witted, sharp, smart, talented. OPPOSITE dull, slow.

brighten *verb* **1** *The room needs brightening.* illuminate, lighten, light up. **2** *Visitors brighten the patients.* animate, buck up (*informal*), buoy up, cheer up, enliven, liven up, perk up.

brilliant *adjective* **1** *brilliant lights.* blazing, bright, dazzling, glaring, gleaming, radiant, resplendent, scintillating, shining, sparkling. **2** *a brilliant scholar.* brainy, bright, clever, exceptional, gifted, ingenious, intelligent, outstanding, smart, talented. OPPOSITE dim-witted. **3** (*informal*) *a brilliant party.* see EXCELLENT.

brim *noun The jar was full to the brim.* brink, edge, lip, rim, top.

bring *verb* **1** *The postman brings the mail.* bear, carry, convey, deliver. **2** *She brought her friend home.* accompany, conduct, escort, fetch, lead, take, transport, usher. **3** *War brings sadness and loss.* beget, cause, create, generate, give rise to, lead to, produce, result in, yield. □ **bring about** *The new government brought about many changes.* accomplish, achieve, cause, effect, produce. **bring forward** *They brought forward their wedding date.* advance. OPPOSITE defer, postpone. **bring in** **1** *They brought in a new rule.* initiate, institute, introduce, start. **2** *The scheme brought in a lot of money.* earn, net, produce, realise, yield. **bring off** *Can he bring off his plan?* accomplish, achieve, carry off, pull off, succeed in. **bring out** **1** *The article brought out the consequences of passive smoking.* draw attention to, emphasise, highlight, point out, point up, reveal, show. **2** *The students bring out a weekly newsletter.* issue, produce, publish, release. **bring up** **1** *Harry was brought up by his aunt and uncle.* care for, look after, nurture, raise, rear, train. **2** *He brought up the subject.* broach, introduce, mention, raise. OPPOSITE drop. **3** *She brought up her dinner.* see VOMIT.

brink *noun the brink of a lake.* bank, border, brim, edge, margin, perimeter, threshold, verge.

brisk *adjective They worked at a brisk pace.* bustling, energetic, fast, keen, lively, quick, rapid, snappy, spanking (*informal*), vigorous. OPPOSITE slow.

bristle *noun His face was covered with bristles.* hair, stubble, whisker.

brittle *adjective The plastic had become brittle in the sun.* breakable, crisp, fragile, hard.

broach *verb He broached the subject.* bring up, introduce, mention, raise.

broad *adjective* **1** *a broad area.* big, expansive, extensive, great, large, sweeping, vast, wide. OPPOSITE narrow. **2** *a broad Australian accent.* clear, explicit, marked, obvious, strong, unmistakable. **3** *the broad outline.* basic, general, overall, vague. OPPOSITE detailed.

broadcast *verb The programme is broadcast on Tuesdays.* air, relay, screen, send out, telecast, televise, transmit. — *noun radio and television broadcasts.* programme, show, telecast, transmission.

broaden *verb The river broadened out.* enlarge, expand, extend, open out, spread out, widen. OPPOSITE narrow.

broad-minded *adjective* flexible, liberal, open-minded, permissive, tolerant, understanding, unprejudiced. OPPOSITE narrow-minded.

brochure *noun travel brochures.* booklet, catalogue, flyer, handout, leaflet, pamphlet, prospectus.

brogue *noun She spoke with an Irish brogue.* accent, dialect.

broke *adjective* (*informal*) *She is broke until next pay day.* bankrupt, destitute, penniless, skint (*informal*), stony-broke (*slang*), strapped for cash (*informal*); see also POOR.

broken-hearted *adjective* desolate, devastated, disconsolate, forlorn, grief-stricken, heartbroken, woebegone, wretched.

broker *noun They bought the shares through a broker.* agent, dealer, intermediary, middleman, negotiator.

brooch *noun She wore a brooch on her lapel.* badge, clasp, pin.

brood *noun The mother bird looks after her brood.* clutch, family, litter, offspring, young. — *verb He's brooding over his loss.* dwell (on), fret, meditate, mull, ponder, reflect, stew (*informal*), sulk, think, worry.

broody *adjective He's been broody lately.* depressed, gloomy, pensive, thoughtful.

brook[1] *noun a fast-flowing brook.* creek (*Australian*), rill, rivulet, stream, watercourse.

brook[2] *verb She won't brook any interruptions.* allow, endure, permit, put up with, stand, tolerate. OPPOSITE prohibit.

broth *noun chicken broth.* bouillon, consommé, potage, soup, stock.

brother *noun* **1** *He has a brother and a sister.* male sibling. **2** see MONK.

brotherhood *noun a religious brotherhood.* association, community, fraternity, order, society.
brotherly *adjective* fraternal; see also FRIENDLY.
brow *noun* **1** *She plucks her brows.* eyebrow. **2** *He wrinkled his brow.* forehead.
brown *adjective* **1** *a brown colour.* auburn, bay, beige, biscuit, bronze, buff, camel, chestnut, chocolate, coffee, copper, fawn, hazel, khaki, mocha, ochre, rust, sepia, tan, tawny, umber, walnut. **2** *brown bodies on the beach.* bronzed, dark-skinned, suntanned, tanned. — *verb* **1** *His skin browns in summer.* bronze, suntan, tan. **2** *Brown the cheese.* cook, grill, toast.
brown-haired *adjective* brunette, dark-haired.
browse *verb* **1** *The cattle are browsing.* feed, graze. **2** *He browsed through his notes.* flick through, flip through, glance through, leaf through, look through, scan, skim (through), thumb through.
bruise *noun a bruise on her cheek.* contusion, discoloration, shiner (*informal*). — *verb He bruised his leg.* blacken, damage, discolour, injure, mark.
brumby *noun* (*Australian*) bronco, mustang, warrigal (*Australian*), wild horse.
brunt *noun They bore the brunt of the attack.* force, impact, strain, stress.
brush *noun a brush with the law.* clash, confrontation, dealings, encounter, skirmish. — *verb* **1** *She brushed the table.* clean, dust, polish, scrub, smooth, sweep, tidy. **2** *The bullet brushed her arm.* graze, touch. □ **brush aside** *He brushed the problem aside.* dismiss, disregard, ignore, reject, sweep aside. **brush up on** *She's brushing up on her French before going overseas.* bone up on (*informal*), go over, revise, study.
brusque *adjective a brusque manner.* abrupt, blunt, curt, offhand, short, terse.
brutal *adjective a brutal attack.* atrocious, barbarous, beastly, bloodthirsty, callous, cruel, ferocious, inhuman, inhumane, merciless, ruthless, sadistic, savage, vicious. OPPOSITE humane.
brute *noun The man was an absolute brute.* animal, beast, bully, monster, ogre, sadist.
bubble *verb The liquid bubbled.* boil, effervesce, fizz, foam, froth, seethe, simmer.
bubbly *adjective* **1** *Lemonade is bubbly.* aerated, carbonated, effervescent, fizzy, foamy, frothy, sparkling. OPPOSITE flat, still. **2** *a bubbly personality.* animated, buoyant, exuberant, sparkling, vivacious.
buccaneer *noun* adventurer, brigand, corsair (*old use*), marauder, pirate, privateer.
buck *verb* **1** *The horse bucked.* jump, leap, start. **2** (*informal*) *Don't buck the system.* fight, oppose, resist. □ **buck up** (*informal*) **1** *You'd better buck up, or we'll be late.* get a move on (*informal*), hasten, hurry up, make haste, rush. **2** *Rosemary bucked up when her visitors arrived.* brighten, cheer up, liven up, perk up.
bucket *noun* pail, scuttle.
buckle *noun a shoe buckle.* catch, clasp, clip, fastening. — *verb* **1** *She buckled her shoes.* do up, fasten. OPPOSITE unbuckle. **2** *The car's bonnet had buckled in the smash.* bend, cave in, collapse, contort, crumple, distort, give way, twist, warp.
bud *noun The plant has lots of buds.* shoot, sprout. — *verb The tree is starting to bud.* burgeon, develop, grow, sprout.
budding *adjective a budding poet.* developing, promising, up-and-coming. OPPOSITE established.
buddy *noun* (*informal*) *The boys have been buddies since kindergarten.* chum (*informal*), cobber (*Australian informal*), companion, comrade, confidant, confidante, crony, friend, mate, pal (*informal*).
budge *verb* **1** *He refused to budge from his spot.* move, shift, stir. **2** *Once she had made up her mind she would not budge.* back down, change your mind, yield.
budget *noun* **1** *The Treasurer prepared the Budget.* estimate, plan. **2** *She has a budget of $100 for stationery.* allocation, allowance. — *verb The committee budgeted $5000 for painting.* allocate, allow, estimate, plan, set aside.
buffer *noun The bumper bar is fitted with rubber buffers.* cushion, damper, guard, pad, shield.
buffet[1] *noun* **1** *We ate in the buffet.* café, cafeteria, snack bar; see also RESTAURANT. **2** *The glasses are in the buffet.* china cupboard, sideboard.
buffet[2] *verb The boat was buffeted by the waves.* batter, hit, knock, pound, strike.
buffoon *noun Martin played the buffoon.* clown, comic, fool, jester, wag.
bug *noun* (*informal*) **1** *bed bugs.* insect, mite. **2** *She was sick with a tummy bug.* bacterium, germ, infection, microbe, micro-organism, virus, wog (*Australian informal*). **3** *a bug in the software.* defect, error, fault, flaw, problem. — *verb* (*informal*) **1** *Our phone calls were bugged.* eavesdrop on, listen in on, tap. **2** *What's bugging you?* annoy, bother, exasperate, irritate, trouble.
bugbear *noun The interview was his biggest bugbear.* bane, bogy, dread, nightmare, pet hate.
buggy *noun* (*old use*) *a horse and buggy.* carriage, gig, trap.
build *verb* **1** *They built their own house.* assemble, construct, erect, fabricate, form, make, put together, put up, raise. OPPOSITE destroy, dismantle. **2** *a relationship built on trust.* base, establish, found, ground. — *noun a person of slender build.* figure, frame, physique, shape. □ **build up** **1** *Their funds are building up.* accrue, accumulate, amass, grow. OPPOSITE dwindle. **2** *The pressure built up.* escalate, grow, increase, intensify, rise, strengthen. **3** *They have steadily built up their business.* develop, enlarge, establish, expand, increase. OPPOSITE wind down.
building *noun new buildings in the city.* construction, edifice, premises, structure.
bulge *noun The black top covers up the bulges.* bump, curve, hump, lump, protrusion, protuberance, swelling. — *verb His stomach bulged.* bloat, distend, enlarge, expand, protrude, stick out, swell.
bulk *noun* **1** *The pizza dough was left to double in bulk.* magnitude, mass, size, volume, weight. **2** *He had finished the bulk of the work.* best part, greater part, lion's share, majority, most. □ **in bulk** *He buys dog food in bulk.* in quantity, in volume, wholesale.
bulky *adjective a bulky parcel.* big, cumbersome, heavy, huge, large, massive, unwieldy, voluminous. OPPOSITE small.
bulldoze *verb They bulldozed the burnt-out building.* clear, demolish, flatten, level, raze.
bulletin *noun* **1** *a news bulletin.* announcement, broadcast, communiqué, dispatch, message, notice, report, statement. **2** *He edits the school bulletin.* magazine, newsletter.
bullfighter *noun* matador, picador, toreador.
bull's-eye *noun Her dart hit the bull's-eye.* bull, centre, middle.
bully *noun Stay away from that bully.* intimidator, persecutor, ruffian, tormentor, tough, tyrant. — *verb He bullies the other boys.* cow, frighten, harass, hector, intimidate, oppress, persecute, pick on, push around (*informal*), stand over, terrorise, threaten, torment, tyrannise.
bulwark *noun* **1** *a bulwark surrounding a fortress.* barrier, earthwork, fortification, rampart, wall. **2** *a bulwark against inflation.* barrier, buffer, defence, guard, protection, safeguard, security.
bum *noun* see BOTTOM.
bumble *verb* **1** *He bumbled up the hallway in the dark.* blunder, flounder, lumber, lurch, stumble. **2** *She kept bumbling on about something.* babble, mumble, mutter, ramble.
bump *verb* **1** *She's always bumping herself on things.* hit, hurt, injure, knock. **2** *We bumped along on the gravel road.* bounce, bucket, jerk, jolt, shake. — *noun* **1** *I heard a bump.* bang, collision, crash, knock, thud, thump. **2** *bumps and bruises.* bulge, hump, lump, protrusion, protuberance, swelling. □ **bump into** (*informal*) *I bumped into an old friend today.* come across, meet, run into, see. **bump off** see KILL.
bumpkin *noun a country bumpkin.* hick (*informal*), hill-billy (*American informal*), peasant, rustic, yokel.
bumptious *adjective a bumptious young man.* arrogant, brash, cocky (*informal*), conceited, overbearing, self-assertive, self-important. OPPOSITE humble.
bumpy *adjective* **1** *a bumpy road.* corrugated, potholed, rough, uneven. OPPOSITE smooth. **2** *a bumpy trip.* bouncy, jarring, jolting, rough. OPPOSITE smooth.
bunch *noun* **1** *a bunch of flowers.* bouquet, corsage, nosegay, posy, spray. **2** *a bunch of bananas.* cluster, hand. **3** *a bunch of papers.* batch, bundle, collection, lot, pack, quantity, set, sheaf, wad. **4** *hair tied in bunches.* pigtail. **5** (*informal*) *a noisy bunch of people.* band, crowd, gang, group, lot, mob, team. — *verb The people bunched together to keep warm.* cluster, congregate, crowd, gather, herd, huddle, squash up.
bundle *noun a bundle of papers.* bale, bunch, collection, package, parcel, set, sheaf, swag (*Australian*). — *verb* **1** *They bundled the books together.* pack, package, tie, wrap. **2** *They bundled him into a taxi.* pack off, push, shove, thrust.
bung[1] *noun a bung for a cask.* cork, plug, stopper. — *verb* (*informal*) *Bung it in the bin.* put, shove, stick (*informal*), throw, toss. □ **bunged up** *My nose is bunged up.* blocked (up), clogged up, congested, stuffed up.
bung[2] *adjective* **go bung** (*Australian informal*) *The fridge has gone bung.* be on the blink (*informal*), be out of order, break down, conk out (*informal*), fail, go kaput (*informal*), pack up (*informal*), seize up.
bungle *verb The robbers bungled the job.* botch, fluff (*slang*), foul up (*informal*), goof (*slang*), make a mess of, mess up, mismanage, muff (*informal*), ruin, spoil, wreck. — *noun an administrative bungle.* blunder, botch, mess, mistake, mix-up.
bunk[1] *noun* bed, berth.
bunk[2] *noun* **do a bunk** (*slang*) *The employee did a bunk with the day's takings.* abscond, bolt, escape, flee, make off, nick off (*Australian slang*), run off, scarper (*informal*), shoot through (*Australian informal*), vanish.
buoy *noun The ship's course was marked out with buoys.* float, marker. — *verb* **buoy up** *They were buoyed up with new hope.* boost, cheer, encourage, hearten, sustain, uplift. OPPOSITE weigh down.
buoyant *adjective* **1** *a buoyant object.* floating, light. **2** *a buoyant mood.* bouncy, carefree, cheerful, light-hearted, lively, resilient. OPPOSITE depressed.
burden *noun* **1** *The horse carried a heavy burden.* load, weight. **2** *They share each other's burdens.* care, concern, problem, strain, trial, trouble, worry. — *verb He was burdened with problems.* encumber, load, lumber, oppress, saddle, weigh down, worry.
bureau *noun a travel bureau.* agency, branch, department, division, office.
bureaucracy *noun* **1** *a member of the bureaucracy.* administration, officialdom, public service. **2** *Her pension claim was complicated by unnecessary bureaucracy.* formalities, paperwork, red tape, regulations.
bureaucrat *noun* administrator, functionary, official, public servant.
burglar *noun The owner disturbed the burglar.* housebreaker, intruder, robber, thief.
burglary *noun* break-in, breaking and entering, larceny, robbery, stealing, theft.
burial *noun* entombment, interment; see also FUNERAL. □ **burial ground** see CEMETERY.
burlesque *noun* caricature, imitation, mockery, parody, send-up (*informal*), spoof (*informal*), take-off (*informal*).
burly *adjective a burly footballer.* beefy, brawny, hefty, husky, muscular, nuggety (*Australian*), stocky, stout, strapping, strong, sturdy, thickset, tough. OPPOSITE skinny, weak.
burn *verb* **1** *She burnt the toast. She burnt herself.* blacken, brown, char, scald, scorch, sear, set alight, set fire to, set on fire, singe, toast. **2** *They burnt the corpse.* cremate. **3** *Their house was burnt in the bushfire.* consume, destroy, gut, incinerate. **4** *The bush was burning.* be ablaze, be alight, be on fire, blaze, catch fire, flame, flare, ignite, kindle, smoulder. **5** *This fabric burns.* be flammable, be inflammable. **6** *Her cheeks were burning.* feel hot, flush, redden.
burning *adjective* **1** *a burning ambition.* ardent, deep, fervent, intense, passionate, strong. **2** *a burning question.* crucial, important, pressing, urgent, vital.
burnish *verb He burnished the silver.* buff, polish, rub, shine.
burp *verb* (*informal*) *He burped loudly.* belch, bring up wind.
burrow *noun an animal's burrow.* den, hole, lair, tunnel, warren. — *verb* **1** *The wombat burrowed under the fence.* dig, excavate, tunnel. **2** *He burrowed into the box to find the letter.* delve, fossick (*Australian informal*), rummage, search.
bursar *noun the school bursar.* accountant, financial controller, treasurer.
bursary *noun The college awarded her a bursary.* allowance, endowment, grant, scholarship.
burst *verb* **1** *The tyre burst.* blow out, break, bust (*informal*), disintegrate,

explode, puncture, rip, rupture, split, tear. **2** *He burst the bag.* break open, bust (*informal*), force open, pop open. **3** *He burst into the room.* barge, fly, run, rush. **4** *She burst into tears.* break, collapse, dissolve, erupt. — *noun* **1** *a burst of gunfire.* blaze, explosion, fusillade, outbreak, outburst, round, volley. **2** *a burst of activity.* effort, rush, spurt.

bursting *adjective* see FULL.

bury *verb* **1** *She was buried in the town cemetery.* entomb, inter, lay to rest. OPPOSITE exhume. **2** *He tried to bury the evidence.* conceal, cover up, hide, submerge. OPPOSITE unearth.

bus *noun* coach, minibus, omnibus.

bush *noun* **1** *She has several small bushes in her garden.* plant, shrub. **2** *Large areas of the country are bush.* brush, forest, scrub, woodland, woods. **3** (*Australian*) *They sold their house in the city to live in the bush.* backblocks (*Australian*), country, donga (*Australian*), inland, interior, mallee (*Australian*), mulga (*Australian*), outback (*Australian*), sticks (*Australian informal*).

bushed *adjective* **1** (*Australian*) *The walkers were bushed.* lost. **2** (*informal*) *It's been a long day, and I'm bushed.* dog-tired, done in (*informal*), exhausted, tired out, whacked (*informal*), worn out.

bushfire *noun* *Fifty houses were destroyed in the bushfire.* blaze, conflagration, fire; see also FIRE.

bushie *noun* (*Australian informal*) *Bushies came to the city for the show.* bush-dweller, bushwhacker, countryman, countrywoman, farmer. OPPOSITE city-dweller.

bushranger *noun* *The carriage was held up by bushrangers.* bandit, brigand, escapee, highwayman, outlaw, robber.

bushwalker *noun* *an injured bushwalker.* hiker, rambler, trekker, walker.

bushy *adjective* **1** *bushy land.* scrubby, shrubby. **2** *a bushy tail.* bristly, fluffy, fuzzy, hairy, shaggy, thick, woolly.

business *noun* **1** *It's not his business to mend fuses.* concern, duty, function, job, province, responsibility, task, work. **2** *He's in the plumbing business.* calling, career, employment, field, industry, job, line, occupation, profession, trade, vocation, work. **3** *Business was brisk before Christmas.* buying and selling, commerce, trade, trading. **4** *They run their own printing business.* company, concern, corporation, enterprise, establishment, firm, outfit (*informal*), practice, undertaking, venture. **5** *This business has nothing to do with you.* affair, concern, issue, matter, situation, subject, topic.

businesslike *adjective* *a businesslike approach.* efficient, methodical, organised, practical, professional, systematic. OPPOSITE unprofessional.

businessman, businesswoman *noun* entrepreneur, executive, industrialist, magnate, merchant, trader, tycoon.

busker *noun* *She threw a dollar into the busker's hat.* street entertainer, street performer.

bust[1] *noun* **1** *a marble bust of the King.* sculpture. **2** *a woman's bust.* bosom, breast, chest.

bust[2] *verb* (*informal*) **1** *With his weight he'll bust the chair.* break, burst, collapse, crack. **2** *The police busted the dealer.* arrest, capture, catch, nab (*informal*), nick (*slang*), raid. □ **go bust** *The business went bust.* fail, go bankrupt, go broke (*informal*).

bustle *verb* *She bustled round the house tidying up.* dash, hasten, hurry, hustle, rush, tear. — *noun* *He likes the bustle of the big city.* activity, busyness, commotion, excitement, hurly-burly, hurry, hustle.

busy *adjective* **1** *He is kept busy.* active, employed, engaged, industrious, involved, occupied, on the go (*informal*), snowed under (*informal*), working. OPPOSITE idle. **2** *a busy life.* active, bustling, frenetic, frenzied, full, hectic, lively. OPPOSITE quiet.

busybody *noun* interferer, meddler, mischief-maker, Nosy Parker (*informal*), snooper (*informal*), stickybeak (*Australian informal*).

but *adverb* *We can but try.* only. — *conjunction* *He studied hard but he failed the test.* however, nevertheless, still, yet. — *preposition* *There is no one here but me.* apart from, aside from, except, other than, save. — *noun* *ifs and buts.* objection.

butch *adjective* (*informal*) *The woman is rather butch.* mannish, masculine, tough-looking. OPPOSITE feminine.

butcher *verb* *The soldiers butchered the enemy.* kill, massacre, murder, slaughter, slay.

butt[1] *noun* **1** *a rifle butt.* handle, shaft, stock. **2** *cigarette butts.* end, remnant, stub. OPPOSITE tip. **3** *cheque butts.* counterfoil, stub.

butt[2] *noun* *a wine butt.* barrel, cask, hogshead, tun.

butt[3] *noun* *He is often the butt of their jokes.* object, subject, target, victim. — *verb* *The goat is butting her.* bump, knock, poke, prod, push, ram. □ **butt in** *Stop butting in!* chip in (*informal*), interfere, interrupt, intervene, meddle, poke your nose in (*informal*).

buttocks *plural noun* backside (*informal*), behind (*informal*), bottom, bum (*slang*), butt (*slang*), haunches, posterior, rear (*informal*), rump, seat.

button *noun* *All at the press of a button.* control, knob, switch. — *verb* *Button your cardigan!* do up, fasten.

buttonhole *verb* *The teacher buttonholed the boy in the corridor.* accost, bail up (*Australian*), corner, detain, waylay.

buttress *noun* *a church wall with flying buttresses.* prop, reinforcement, stay, support. — *verb* *The walls of the church were buttressed.* brace, prop up, reinforce, shore up, support.

buxom *adjective* *a buxom woman.* bosomy, busty, plump, shapely, voluptuous.

buy *verb* **1** *She is buying a car.* acquire, come by, gain, get, obtain, pay for, procure, purchase. OPPOSITE sell. **2** (*slang*) *No one would buy that excuse.* accept, believe, swallow. OPPOSITE reject. — *noun* *The car was a good buy.* acquisition, deal, purchase; see also BARGAIN.

buyer *noun* client, consumer, customer, patron, purchaser, shopper. OPPOSITE seller, vendor.

buzz *noun* **1** *the buzz of traffic.* burr, drone, hum, vibration, whirr. **2** (*informal*) *Give me a buzz.* bell (*informal*), call, ring (*informal*), telephone call. — *verb* *Bees buzz.* burr, drone, hum, throb, whirr. □ **buzz off** see LEAVE.

by *preposition* **1** *They live by the river.* alongside, beside, near, next to. **2** *They drove to Melbourne by the coast road.* along, via. **3** *They came by night.* at, during. **4** *by artificial means.* through, using. **5** *Cinderella had to be home by midnight.* before, no later than. **6** *They do things by the book.* according to, following. — *adverb* **1** *Put a little by for the future.* aside, away, in reserve. **2** *They walk by every day.* past. □ **by and by** before long, presently, soon. **by and large** all things considered, generally speaking, on the whole. **by yourself** alone, single-handed, unaccompanied, unaided, unassisted.

bye-bye *interjection* see GOODBYE.

bygone *adjective* *in bygone days.* ancient, former, olden, past. OPPOSITE future.

bypass *noun* *The bypass avoids the city traffic.* detour, deviation, diversion, ring road, ring route. — *verb* **1** *They chose to bypass the major cities.* avoid, miss. **2** *He cleverly bypassed the problem.* avoid, circumvent, dodge, evade, ignore, sidestep, skirt.

by-product *noun* *Her increased fitness was a by-product of losing her driver's licence.* consequence, offshoot, repercussion, side benefit, side effect, spin-off.

bystander *noun* *an innocent bystander.* eyewitness, observer, onlooker, passer-by, spectator, witness. OPPOSITE participant.

byword *noun* **1** *The firm became a byword for mismanagement.* example, model, symbol. **2** *Their byword is 'Natural is good'.* adage, catchphrase, maxim, motto, proverb, saying, slogan.

Cc

cabin *noun* **1** *a log cabin.* chalet, hut, lodge, shack, shanty, shelter. **2** *a cabin on a ship.* berth, compartment, room.

cabinet *noun* *a china cabinet.* buffet, case, chest, closet, console, cupboard, locker, sideboard, wall unit.

cable *noun* **1** *electrical cables.* cord, flex, lead, wire. **2** *a mooring cable.* chain, cord, guy, hawser, line, rope.

cache *noun* **1** *The shed was used as a cache for the stolen goods.* depot, hiding place, repository. **2** *They found their cache of ammunition.* hoard, reserve, stash (*informal*), stockpile, store, supply.

cackle *verb* **1** *The hen cackled.* cluck, squawk. **2** *The woman cackled.* see LAUGH.

cadet *noun* *a police cadet.* learner, novice, recruit, trainee.

cadge *verb* *He has no money of his own, so he's always cadging off his friends.* beg, bludge (*Australian informal*), bot (*Australian slang*), hum (*Australian slang*), put the bite on (*Australian informal*), scab (*Australian slang*), scrounge, sponge.

café *noun* bistro, brasserie, buffet, cafeteria, coffee shop, eatery (*informal*), milk bar, restaurant, snack bar, tea room.

cage *noun* *The animals are in cages.* aviary, coop, enclosure, hutch, pen. — *verb* *He caged the animals.* confine, coop up, lock up, pen, shut in.

cajole *verb* *He cajoled them into coming along.* beguile, coax, entice, persuade, seduce, sweet-talk (*informal*), wheedle.

cake *noun* **1** *a cake to eat with coffee.* baba, bun, cheesecake, cupcake, doughnut, éclair, flan, gateau, lamington, muffin, pastry, scone, sponge, tart, torte. **2** *fish cakes.* croquette, patty. **3** *a cake of soap.* bar, block, hunk, lump, piece, slab. — *verb* *The car was caked with mud.* coat, cover, encrust.

calamity *noun* *The town has not recovered from the calamity.* accident, catastrophe, disaster, misadventure, misfortune, mishap, tragedy.

calculate *verb* **1** *He calculated the cost.* add up, assess, compute, count, determine, estimate, figure out, reckon, total, tot up (*informal*), work out. **2** *The statement was calculated to annoy people.* aim, design, intend, mean, plan.

calculating *adjective* *a calculating person.* crafty, cunning, designing, devious, plotting, scheming, shrewd, sly, wily. OPPOSITE guileless.

calculation *noun* *His calculation was out by 10%.* answer, computation, estimate, forecast, result, sum.

calendar *noun* *a pocket calendar.* daybook, diary, programme, schedule, timetable.

calf *noun* heifer, mickey (*Australian*), poddy (*Australian*).

call *noun* **1** *He heard a call for help.* bellow, cooee (*informal*), cry, exclamation, roar, scream, shout, shriek, signal, yell. **2** *They paid a call on her.* visit. **3** *He responded to the call for volunteers.* appeal, invitation, plea, request, summons. **4** *There's no call for concern.* cause, grounds, justification, need, occasion, reason. **5** *He gave me a call.* bell (*informal*), buzz (*informal*), phone call, ring, telephone call. — *verb* **1** *He called to the people below.* bellow, cooee (*informal*), cry, cry out, exclaim, roar, scream, shout, shriek, yell. **2** *They called their cat 'Puss'.* address as, baptise, christen, dub, label, name, nickname. **3** *What is that thing called?* describe as, designate, name, term. **4** *She slept until she was called for breakfast.* arouse, awaken, rouse, waken. **5** *Call the doctor.* contact, fetch, page, phone, ring, send for, summon, telephone. **6** *We were called to board the aircraft.* ask, bid, command, invite, order, summon. □ **call for** **1** *Such behaviour calls for strong discipline.* demand, deserve, justify, necessitate, occasion, require, warrant. **2** *Her friend called for her at 8.* collect, fetch, get, pick up. **call off** *The police called off the search.* abandon, cancel, discontinue, drop, stop. **call on** **1** *The nurse will call on you tomorrow.* drop in on, look in on, pay a visit to, see, visit. **2** *They called on people to give generously.* appeal to, ask, entreat, implore, invite, request. **call up** *He was called up to serve in the war.* conscript, draft (*American*), recruit, summon.

calling *noun* *He had found his calling in life.* career, employment, job, mission, niche, occupation, profession, trade, vocation.

callous *adjective* *a callous person.* cold-hearted, cruel, hard-hearted, harsh, heartless, insensitive, merciless, pitiless, ruthless, thick-skinned, uncaring, unfeeling, unsympathetic. OPPOSITE sensitive.

calm *adjective* **1** *a calm day.* balmy, halcyon, mild, quiet, still. OPPOSITE windy. **2** *calm seas.* even, flat, motionless, quiet, smooth, steady, still. OPPOSITE choppy, wild. **3** *He stays calm in a crisis.* collected, composed, cool, imperturbable, level-headed, nonchalant, peaceful, phlegmatic, placid, relaxed, sedate, self-possessed, serene, stoical, tranquil, unexcited, unfazed (*informal*), unflappable (*informal*), unruffled. OPPOSITE agitated, excited. — *noun* *the calm before the storm.* calmness, lull, peace, quietness, repose, serenity, stillness, tranquillity; see also CALMNESS. — *verb* *He tried to calm their fears.* allay, alleviate, appease, lull, mollify, pacify, quell, quieten, relieve, soothe, still, subdue. OPPOSITE arouse. □ **calm down** *She needed to calm down before responding.* collect yourself, compose yourself, cool off, relax, settle, simmer down.

calmness *noun His calmness in a crisis is appreciated.* calm, composure, coolness, equanimity, imperturbability, nonchalance, poise, presence of mind, serenity. OPPOSITE panic.

camouflage *verb His green clothes camouflaged him in the bush.* conceal, cover up, disguise, hide, mask, screen.

camp *noun They set up camp by the creek.* base, bivouac, encampment, tent. — *verb They camped by the river.* encamp, pitch your tent.

campaign *noun a military campaign. an advertising campaign.* action, battle, blitz, crusade, drive, fight, manoeuvre, offensive, operation, strategy, war. — *verb They campaigned for the release of political prisoners.* agitate, battle, canvass, crusade, fight, lobby, press, push, strive, work.

campus *noun The school has two campuses.* grounds, property, site.

can *noun a sugar can.* caddy, canister, tin; see also CONTAINER. — *verb She cans the fruit.* preserve, tin.

canal *noun* **1** *boating on a canal.* channel, watercourse, waterway. **2** *the alimentary canal.* duct, passage, tube.

cancel *verb* **1** *The game was cancelled.* abandon, call off, scrap, scrub (*informal*), stop, wash out (*informal*); see also DISCONTINUE. **2** *He cancelled the order.* abolish, annul, countermand, quash, repeal, rescind, retract, revoke. **3** *She cancelled her subscription.* discontinue, give up, stop, withdraw. OPPOSITE continue, renew. **4** *He cancelled the amount on the docket.* cross out, delete, erase, obliterate, scratch out, wipe out. □ **cancel out** *The two actions cancel out one another.* balance out, counteract, counterbalance, negate, neutralise, nullify, offset, undo.

cancer *noun diagnosed with cancer.* carcinoma, growth, malignancy, melanoma, tumour.

candid *adjective a candid reply.* blunt, direct, forthright, frank, honest, open, outspoken, plain, sincere, straight, straightforward, upfront (*informal*). OPPOSITE evasive.

candidate *noun They interviewed all the candidates.* applicant, competitor, contender, contestant, entrant, examinee, interviewee, nominee, runner.

candy *noun* see LOLLY.

cane *noun He walked with a cane.* rod, staff, stick, walking stick. — *verb The teacher caned the boy.* beat, hit, flog, lash, strike, thrash, whack.

canister *noun a tea canister.* caddy, can, tin.

canopy *noun a bed with a canopy.* awning, cover, covering, tester.

canteen *noun* **1** *the office canteen.* cafeteria, dining room, refectory, restaurant, snack bar. **2** *the school canteen.* tuckshop.

canvass *verb Politicians canvassed up to the eve of the election.* campaign, electioneer, solicit votes.

canyon *noun They hiked through a deep canyon.* chasm, defile, gorge, gully, pass, ravine, valley.

cap *noun* **1** *He wears a cap.* hat, headcovering, headgear; [*kinds of cap*] beanie, beret, bonnet, busby, deerstalker, fez, mob cap, mortarboard, nightcap, skullcap, yarmulke. **2** *a cap for a bottle.* cover, lid, top.

capability *noun a student of great capability.* ability, aptitude, calibre, capacity, competence, potential, proficiency, prowess, skill, talent.

capable *adjective a capable secretary.* able, accomplished, adept, clever, competent, effective, efficient, expert, gifted, proficient, skilful, skilled, smart, talented. OPPOSITE inept.

capacity *noun* **1** *the capacity of the trunk.* dimensions, magnitude, size, volume. **2** *the capacity to think critically.* ability, aptitude, capability, competence, gift, potential, power, skill, talent. **3** *in his capacity as chairman.* duty, function, office, position, post, role.

cape[1] *noun She wore a cape.* cloak, cope, mantle, poncho, shawl, stole, wrap.

cape[2] *noun They sailed round the cape.* head, headland, point, promontory.

caper *verb The baby animals capered about in the paddock.* bound, cavort, dance, frisk, frolic, gambol, hop, jump, leap, play, prance, romp, scamper, skip.

capital *adjective* **1** *the capital city.* chief, foremost, important, leading, main, major, principal. **2** *capital letters.* big, block, upper case. — *noun The business needs more capital.* assets, cash, finance, funds, means, money, principal, resources, stock, wealth.

capitalise *verb* **capitalise on** *They capitalised on the situation.* cash in on, exploit, make the most of, profit from, take advantage of.

capitulate *verb The enemy capitulated.* cave in, give in, give up, submit, succumb, surrender, throw in the towel, yield. OPPOSITE persevere.

capricious *adjective It was hard to live with such a capricious woman.* changeable, erratic, fickle, flighty, impulsive, inconstant, mercurial, temperamental, unpredictable, unreliable, variable, volatile, whimsical. OPPOSITE constant, predictable.

capsize *verb The boat capsized.* flip over, invert, keel over, overturn, tip over, turn over, turn turtle.

capsule *noun The doctor prescribed capsules.* pill, tablet; see also MEDICINE.

captain *noun the ship's captain.* commander, master, skipper; see also CHIEF.

caption *noun She read the caption accompanying the picture.* heading, headline, subtitle, surtitle, title.

captivate *verb She captivated him with her smile.* attract, capture, charm, delight, enchant, enthral, entrance, fascinate, mesmerise, seduce. OPPOSITE repel.

captive *noun The chief released the captives after ten days.* convict, detainee, hostage, prisoner.

captivity *noun held in captivity.* bondage, confinement, custody, detention, imprisonment, incarceration, internment, servitude, slavery. OPPOSITE freedom.

captor *noun He escaped from his captors.* abductor, kidnapper.

capture *verb* **1** *The police captured the burglar.* apprehend, arrest, catch, collar (*informal*), nab (*informal*), nail, nick (*slang*), seize. **2** *The film captured their interest.* catch, hold, take, win. — *noun the capture of the criminal.* apprehension, arrest, seizure.

car *noun He drives a car.* auto (*informal*), automobile (*American*), motor, motor car, motor vehicle, vehicle, wheels (*slang*); [*an old or dilapidated car*] banger, bomb (*Australian*), heap, jalopy, rattletrap, rust bucket, wreck; [*kinds of car*] convertible, coupé, fastback, four-wheel drive, hatchback, hearse, hot rod, limousine, panel van (*Australian*), saloon, sedan, soft-top, sports car, station wagon (*Australian*), ute (*Australian informal*), utility (*Australian*), van, wagon (*informal*).

caravan *noun* **1** *a holiday caravan.* camper, campervan, mobile home, trailer (*American*). **2** *a gypsy caravan.* carriage, cart, van, wagon.

carcass *noun a sheep's carcass.* body, cadaver, corpse, remains.

care *noun* **1** *She always works with care.* attention, carefulness, caution, circumspection, concentration, diligence, meticulousness, precision, thoroughness, thought. OPPOSITE carelessness. **2** *She left the children in her sister's care.* charge, control, custody, guardianship, hands, keeping, protection, responsibility, supervision. **3** *not a care in the world.* anxiety, bother, burden, concern, problem, trouble, woe, worry. OPPOSITE delight. — *verb She cares about what happens.* be concerned, be interested, bother, concern yourself, mind, worry. □ **care for** **1** *She cares for sick children.* attend to, look after, mind, mother, nurse, take care of, tend, watch over. **2** *He cares for her.* be fond of, be keen on, cherish, like, love. **take care** *Take care not to be deceived.* be careful, be cautious, beware, be wary, look out, take heed, take pains, watch out. **take care of** **1** *He took good care of the children.* keep an eye on, look after, mind, supervise, take charge of, watch over. OPPOSITE neglect. **2** *He took care of the banking.* attend to, deal with, take charge of.

career *noun a career in engineering.* calling, employment, job, occupation, profession, trade, vocation, work. — *verb The car careered into the wall.* hurtle, run, rush, shoot, speed.

carefree *adjective a carefree youth.* blithe, breezy, casual, cheerful, contented, easygoing, footloose, happy-go-lucky, laid-back (*informal*), light-hearted, nonchalant, relaxed, untroubled. OPPOSITE troubled.

careful *adjective* **1** *a careful worker.* accurate, conscientious, diligent, fastidious, methodical, meticulous, neat, organised, painstaking, pernickety (*informal*), precise, punctilious, rigorous, scrupulous, systematic, thorough. OPPOSITE slapdash. **2** *a careful driver. Be careful not to say too much.* alert, attentive, cautious, chary, circumspect, guarded, mindful, on guard, prudent, vigilant, wary, watchful. OPPOSITE negligent, reckless.

careless *adjective* **1** *careless work.* cursory, disorganised, hasty, hit-or-miss, imprecise, inaccurate, inexact, lax, messy, perfunctory, shoddy, slapdash, slipshod, sloppy, slovenly, untidy. OPPOSITE meticulous. **2** *a careless driver.* absent-minded, inattentive, incautious, irresponsible, lax, negligent, rash, reckless, slack. OPPOSITE cautious. **3** *a careless comment.* imprudent, inconsiderate, indiscreet, insensitive, tactless, thoughtless, uncaring, unguarded, unthinking.

caress *verb He caressed her tenderly.* cuddle, embrace, fondle, hug, kiss, pat, pet, stroke, touch.

caretaker *noun a caretaker of the church buildings.* curator, custodian, janitor, keeper, sexton, steward, verger, warden.

cargo *noun a ship carrying a cargo of cars.* consignment, freight, goods, load, shipment.

caricature *noun a clever caricature of a famous person.* burlesque, cartoon, parody, satire, send-up (*informal*), spoof (*informal*), take-off (*informal*).

carnage *noun The fighting ended in carnage.* bloodbath, bloodshed, butchery, holocaust, killing, massacre, murder, slaughter.

carnival *noun There is a lively atmosphere during the carnival.* celebration, fair, festival, fête, fiesta, gala, jamboree, Mardi Gras, pageant, show.

carol *noun Christmas carols.* canticle, hymn, song.

carpentry *noun* cabinetmaking, joinery, woodwork.

carpet *noun* **1** *the hall carpet.* floor covering, mat, rug, runner. **2** *a carpet of leaves.* blanket, covering, layer.

carriage *noun* **1** *a horse-drawn carriage.* brougham, buggy, chaise, chariot, coach, curricle, gig, hansom, landau, phaeton, post-chaise, stagecoach, sulky, trap, wagon. **2** *a railway carriage.* car, coach. **3** *The entrants were marked on beauty and carriage.* bearing, deportment, posture, stance.

carrier *noun* **1** *She sent the package with the carrier.* carter, courier, dispatch rider, haulier, messenger. **2** *a parcel carrier on a bicycle.* basket, container, holder, pannier, receptacle.

carry *verb* **1** *She carried the TV from the sitting room.* bring, cart (*informal*), fetch, lift, lug, move, remove, take, transfer. **2** *Ships and trucks carry live sheep.* bear, cart, convey, ferry, freight, haul, ship, transport. **3** *She always carries a bag.* bring, have, take. **4** *The floor could not carry the weight of the piano.* bear, hold up, support, sustain, take. □ **carry on** **1** *He carried on working till he was eighty.* continue, go on, keep on, persevere, persist, remain. **2** *They are carrying on a business.* conduct, manage, operate, run. **3** (*informal*) *What's he carrying on about now?* bang on (*informal*), complain, go on, rant, rave, spout. **carry out** *He carried out his duties.* accomplish, complete, conduct, discharge, do, execute, finish, fulfil, perform, undertake.

cart *noun The produce is loaded into a cart.* barrow, billycart, dray, float, go-cart, handcart, trolley, tumbrel, wagon, wheelbarrow. — *verb* see CARRY.

carton *noun The tins are packed in a carton.* box, case, container, pack, package, packet.

cartoon *noun* **1** *a political cartoon.* caricature, comic, comic strip, drawing. **2** *TV cartoons.* animated film, animation.

carve *verb* **1** *He carved the ornament out of wood.* chip, chisel, fashion, hew, sculpt, sculpture, shape, whittle. **2** *She carved her name on the base.* engrave, etch, inscribe. **3** *He carved the roast.* cut, slice.

cascade *noun* cataract, falls, rapids, waterfall.

case[1] *noun* **1** *The case protects its contents.* box, cabinet, canteen (*of cutlery*), capsule, carton, cartridge, casing, casket, chest, coffer, container, covering, crate, envelope, holder, holster, housing, jacket, pack, packaging, receptacle, sheath, shell, skin, sleeve, wrapper. **2** *The travellers were laden with cases.* attaché case, bag, briefcase, holdall, port (*Australian*), portmanteau, suitcase, trunk; [*cases*] baggage, luggage.

case[2] *noun* **1** *He cited many cases of injustice.* example, illustration, instance, occasion, occurrence, situation. **2** *a court case.* action, dispute, hearing, lawsuit, proceedings, suit, trial. **3** *the case against smoking.* arguments, facts.

cash *noun* **1** *He does not carry any cash.* banknotes, change, coins, currency, money, notes, paper money, ready money. **2** (*informal*) *They are short of cash.* capital, dosh (*slang*), dough (*slang*), finance, funds, lucre (*derogatory*), means, money, resources, riches, wealth, wherewithal (*informal*). — *verb They cashed their investment.* redeem, turn into cash. □ **cash in on** *He cashed in on the situation.* capitalise on, exploit, make the most of, profit from, take advantage of.

cask *noun a cask of wine.* barrel, butt, hogshead, keg, tub, tun, vat.

casket *noun a jewellery casket.* box, case, chest, coffer, container.

casserole *noun Dinner was a hearty casserole.* cassoulet, fricassee, goulash, hotpot, ragout, stew.

cast *verb* **1** *He cast the box into the sea.* chuck (*informal*), drop, eject, fling, heave, hurl, launch, pitch, shy, sling, throw, toss. **2** *The snake cast its skin.* discard, shed, slough, throw off. **3** *He was able to cast light on the situation.* shed, throw. **4** *He cast his eyes on the box.* direct, turn. **5** *She cast a statue in bronze.* fashion, form, model, mould, sculpt, shape. — *noun* **1** *a bronze cast of the animal's foot.* form, mould, shape. **2** *The play has a famous cast.* actors, company, performers, players, troupe. □ **cast off** *She cast off her old clothes.* discard, get rid of, give away, pass on, reject, throw away.

caste *noun* see CLASS.

castigate *verb He castigated the boy for his mistake.* admonish, censure, chastise, chide (*old use*), criticise, haul over the coals, punish, rebuke, reprimand, reproach, reprove, scold, tear strips off (*informal*), tell off (*informal*), tick off (*informal*). OPPOSITE praise.

castle *noun* château, citadel, fort, fortress, mansion, palace, stronghold.

casual *adjective* **1** *a casual encounter.* accidental, chance, fortuitous, serendipitous, unexpected, unforeseen, unintentional, unplanned. OPPOSITE arranged. **2** *a casual comment.* offhand, passing, random, spontaneous, unthinking. **3** *a casual manner.* apathetic, blasé, carefree, careless, easygoing, happy-go-lucky, lackadaisical, laid-back (*informal*), lax, light-hearted, nonchalant, offhand, relaxed, slap-happy (*informal*), unconcerned. OPPOSITE serious. **4** *casual clothes.* informal, leisure, sports. OPPOSITE dressy, formal. **5** *casual work.* erratic, irregular, occasional, temporary. OPPOSITE permanent.

casualty *noun the casualties of war.* fatality, victim.

cat *noun a pet cat.* feline, kitten, moggie (*informal*), puss, pussy (*informal*), tom, tomcat.

catalogue *noun The books are listed in the catalogue.* directory, file, index, inventory, list, register. — *verb He catalogued all their compact discs.* index, list, record, register.

catapult *noun He killed a bird with his catapult.* ging (*Australian informal*), shanghai (*Australian*), sling, slingshot. — *verb The impact catapulted the passenger through the window.* fling, hurl, propel, throw.

cataract *noun* cascade, falls, waterfall.

catastrophe *noun flood, fire, and other catastrophes.* accident, blow, calamity, disaster, misadventure, misfortune, mishap, tragedy.

catastrophic *adjective a catastrophic nuclear accident.* calamitous, devastating, dire, disastrous.

catch *verb* **1** *He caught a big fish.* bag, capture, ensnare, gaff, hook, land, net, snare, trap. OPPOSITE release. **2** *They caught the thief.* apprehend, arrest, capture, collar (*informal*), cop (*informal*), corner, grab, intercept, nab (*informal*), nail, nick (*slang*), pick up, seize. **3** *She caught him as he fell.* clutch, grab, grasp, grip, hang on to, hold on to, seize, snatch. OPPOSITE drop. **4** *She could not catch the person in front.* catch up with, draw level with, overtake, reach. **5** *They caught him raiding the fridge.* detect, discover, find, spot, surprise. **6** *Her jumper caught on a wire.* entangle, jam, snag, stick. **7** *He caught hepatitis.* become infected with, come down with, contract, get. — *noun* **1** *The fisherman had a good catch.* bag, booty, haul, prize, take. **2** *The proposal looks good, but there must be a catch.* difficulty, disadvantage, drawback, hitch, problem, snag, trap. **3** *He fastened the catch.* bolt, clasp, clip, fastener, hasp, hook, latch, lock. □ **catch on** (*informal*) **1** *Short skirts have caught on.* become fashionable, become popular, take off. **2** *The pupil caught on quickly.* comprehend, cotton on (*informal*), get it (*informal*), latch on (*informal*), learn, understand.

catching *adjective a disease that is catching.* communicable, contagious, infectious, transmissible.

catchword *noun the politician's catchword.* byword, catchphrase, motto, proverb, slogan, watchword.

catchy *adjective a catchy tune.* attractive, haunting, memorable, popular, tuneful.

categorical *adjective a categorical refusal.* absolute, definite, emphatic, explicit, express, unambiguous, unequivocal, unqualified, unreserved. OPPOSITE equivocal.

category *noun The questions fell into different categories.* class, classification, division, group, grouping, kind, rank, set, sort, type.

cater *verb They cater for weddings.* cook, provide food, supply food. □ **cater to** *The staff cater to their every whim.* indulge, pander to, satisfy.

catholic *adjective His tastes are catholic.* all-embracing, broad, comprehensive, eclectic, liberal, universal, varied, wide. OPPOSITE narrow.

cattle *plural noun The farmer lost a lot of cattle in the flood.* bullocks, bulls, calves, cows, heifers, livestock, oxen, steers, stock.

catty *adjective a catty person.* bitchy (*informal*), malicious, mean, nasty, sly, spiteful, vicious.

cause *noun* **1** *the cause of the problem.* basis, bottom, genesis, origin, root, source. OPPOSITE effect. **2** *no cause for concern.* basis, call, grounds, justification, need, occasion, reason. **3** *a worthy cause.* aim, end, goal, object, principle, purpose. — *verb Her attitude causes problems.* bring about, create, effect, generate, give rise to, induce, lead to, occasion, precipitate, produce, provoke, result in, spark off.

caustic *adjective* **1** *a caustic substance.* burning, corrosive. **2** *caustic criticism.* acrimonious, biting, bitter, cutting, sarcastic, scathing, sharp, stinging, virulent.

caution *noun* **1** *Caution is needed when handling guns.* alertness, attention, attentiveness, care, carefulness, circumspection, discretion, heed, prudence, vigilance, wariness. OPPOSITE carelessness. **2** *The policeman gave him a caution.* admonition, reprimand, warning. — *verb* **1** *She cautioned him about the dangers.* advise, alert, counsel, forewarn, warn. **2** *The policeman cautioned the driver.* admonish, reprimand, warn.

cautious *adjective a cautious driver. He was cautious when questioned.* alert, attentive, careful, chary, circumspect, discreet, guarded, heedful, mindful, prudent, vigilant, wary, watchful. OPPOSITE heedless, rash.

cave *noun Hugh explores caves on weekends.* cavern, cavity, den, dugout, grotto, hole, hollow, pothole. — *verb* **cave in 1** *The roof caved in.* collapse, fall in, subside. **2** *They pestered him until he caved in.* capitulate, give in, submit, surrender, yield.

cavity *noun* **1** *a cavity in the rock.* cave, crater, gap, hole, hollow, pit, pocket. **2** *The dentist found no cavities.* caries, decay, hole.

cease *verb* **1** *The noise ceased.* cut out, die away, peter out, stop. **2** *He ceased work.* break off, conclude, desist, discontinue, end, finish, halt, knock off (*informal*), leave off, quit, refrain from, stop, suspend, terminate. OPPOSITE begin, continue.

ceasefire *noun The warring parties declared a ceasefire.* armistice, peace, truce.

ceaseless *adjective her ceaseless complaining.* constant, continual, continuous, endless, eternal, everlasting, incessant, interminable, non-stop, permanent, perpetual, persistent, relentless.

cede *verb He ceded his rights to his brother.* give up, grant, hand over, relinquish, surrender, yield. OPPOSITE keep.

ceiling *noun a wage ceiling.* cap, limit, upper limit.

celebrate *verb* **1** *She celebrated her birthday with a party.* commemorate, keep, mark, observe, remember. **2** *It's your birthday, so let's celebrate.* make merry, party, rejoice, revel. **3** *The priest celebrated the wedding.* officiate at, perform, solemnise.

celebrated *adjective a celebrated musician.* acclaimed, distinguished, eminent, famous, illustrious, notable, noted, popular, prominent, renowned, respected, well-known. OPPOSITE unknown.

celebration *noun* **1** *They attended an anniversary celebration.* carnival, festival, gala, jamboree, jubilee, observance, party. **2** *a night of celebration.* festivity, jollification, merrymaking, partying, revelry.

celebrity *noun* **1** *a television celebrity.* big name, identity (*Australian informal*), luminary, notable, personage, personality, star. OPPOSITE nonentity. **2** *The show brought him celebrity.* eminence, fame, popularity, prestige, prominence, renown, stardom. OPPOSITE obscurity.

celestial *adjective* **1** *celestial bodies.* astral, heavenly, stellar. OPPOSITE earthly. **2** *celestial music.* angelic, beatific, divine, heavenly, spiritual, sublime. OPPOSITE mundane.

celibate *adjective The priest vowed to remain celibate.* chaste, single, unmarried, unwed, virginal. OPPOSITE married.

cell *noun* **1** *The prisoners are confined in cells.* compartment, cubicle, den, dungeon, room. **2** *cells in honeycomb.* cavity, compartment, hole.

cellar *noun The cellar is cool and dry.* basement, crypt, dugout, vault.

cement *verb He cemented the pieces together.* bond, braze, fuse, glue, join, paste, solder, stick, unite, weld.

cemetery *noun Many famous people are buried in this cemetery.* burial ground, churchyard, graveyard, necropolis.

censor *verb Some parts of the book have been censored.* ban, bowdlerise, cut out, delete, expurgate, remove.

censure *noun Such behaviour warrants her parents' censure.* condemnation, criticism, disapproval, rebuke, reprimand, reproach, reproof. OPPOSITE approval. — *verb He was censured for his disobedience.* castigate, chide (*old use*), condemn, criticise, rap over the knuckles, rebuke, reprimand, reproach, reprove, scold, upbraid. OPPOSITE commend.

central *adjective* **1** *a central position.* innermost, medial, median, mid, middle. OPPOSITE outer. **2** *the central issue.* cardinal, chief, core, essential, foremost, fundamental, key, main, major, paramount, primary, principal. OPPOSITE marginal, minor.

centre *noun the centre of a target. the centre of the city.* bull's-eye, core, focus, headquarters, heart, hub, middle, midpoint, nucleus. OPPOSITE edge, perimeter. — *verb Attention was centred on the main arena.* concentrate, focus, home in.

ceremonial *adjective a ceremonial occasion.* formal, ritual, ritualistic, solemn, stately.

ceremonious *adjective The butler's ceremonious manner irritated people.* dignified, formal, over-polite, pompous, prim, proper, punctilious, solemn, starchy, stiff. OPPOSITE casual, informal.

ceremony *noun* **1** *They attended the wedding ceremony.* celebration, event, function, observance, occasion, rite, ritual, sacrament, service. **2** *He served us without ceremony.* decorum, formality, pageantry, pomp, protocol, ritual. OPPOSITE informality.

certain *adjective* **1** *He is certain that he is right.* assured, confident, convinced, definite, positive, sure. OPPOSITE uncertain, unsure. **2** *Victory was certain.* assured, destined, fated, guaranteed, inescapable, inevitable, sure, unavoidable. **3** *It is certain that he is lying.* definite, indisputable, indubitable, irrefutable, plain, undeniable, undoubted, unquestionable. OPPOSITE doubtful. **4** *a certain cure.* dependable, fail-safe, guaranteed, infallible, reliable, sure, sure-fire (*informal*), trustworthy, unfailing. OPPOSITE doubtful. **5** *a certain person who will remain nameless.* particular, specific.

certainly *adverb* **1** *There is certainly some truth in that.* assuredly, clearly, definitely, indubitably, surely, undoubtedly, without doubt. **2** *'Will you come to his concert?' 'Certainly.'* absolutely, by all means, of course, yes.

certainty *noun* **1** *He couldn't say with certainty.* assurance, certitude, confidence, conviction. OPPOSITE doubt. **2** *He's a certainty to win.* cert (*slang*), cinch (*informal*), foregone conclusion, moral certainty, sure thing (*informal*).

certificate *noun Successful candidates receive a certificate.* award, credentials, degree, diploma, document, licence, paper, qualification.

certified *adjective a certified practitioner.* accredited, authorised, chartered, licensed, official, qualified.

certify *verb He certified that this was a true copy.* affirm, attest, bear witness, confirm, declare, endorse, guarantee, testify, verify, vouch, warrant.

chafe *verb The straps chafed his shoulders.* abrade, fret, gall, rub.

chain *noun* **1** *The rescuers formed a human chain.* column, cordon, line, row. **2** *a chain of mountains.* line, range, row, series, tier. **3** *a chain of events.* combination, progression, sequence, series, set, string, succession, train. — *verb The prisoners were chained together.* bind, fasten, fetter, handcuff, join, link, secure, tie. □ **chains** *plural noun The pris-*

oner was in chains. bonds, fetters, handcuffs, irons, manacles, shackles.

chair *noun He sat in his chair.* place, seat; [*kinds of chair*] armchair, banana chair, chaise longue, deckchair, dining chair, easy chair, high chair, recliner chair, rocking chair, throne, wheelchair. — *verb The principal chaired the meeting.* conduct, direct, lead, preside over, run.

chairperson *noun the chairperson of a meeting.* chair, chairman, chairwoman, moderator, president, speaker (*in a legislative assembly*).

challenge *noun He issued a challenge.* dare, invitation, provocation, summons, trial. — *verb* **1** *He challenged the man to a fight.* dare, defy, invite, provoke, summon. **2** *The problem challenged the students.* stimulate, stretch, tax, test, try. **3** *He challenged the judge's decision.* contest, dispute, object to, protest against, query, question. OPPOSITE accept.

challenging *adjective challenging work.* demanding, exacting, inspiring, stimulating, testing, thought-provoking. OPPOSITE easy.

chamber *noun* **1** *a council chamber.* hall, meeting room. **2** *The parliament has two chambers.* assembly, council, house, legislative body. **3** *a lawyer's chambers.* office, room. **4** (*old use*) *a lady's chamber.* bedchamber, bedroom, boudoir, room.

champion *noun* **1** *a racing champion.* ace, conqueror, hero, titleholder, victor, winner. **2** *a champion of citizens' rights.* advocate, backer, defender, guardian, patron, protector, supporter, upholder.

championship *noun* see COMPETITION.

chance *noun* **1** *They met by chance.* accident, coincidence, destiny, fate, fluke, fortune, luck. OPPOSITE design. **2** *There is a chance that he could lose.* danger, likelihood, possibility, probability, prospect, risk. OPPOSITE certainty. **3** *She wasn't given a chance to speak.* break (*informal*), look-in (*informal*), occasion, opening, opportunity, turn. — *adjective a chance meeting.* accidental, casual, coincidental, fortuitous, lucky, unexpected, unintentional, unplanned. OPPOSITE planned.

chancy *adjective a chancy operation.* dangerous, dicey (*slang*), hazardous, perilous, precarious, risky, uncertain. OPPOSITE safe.

change *verb* **1** *They changed their plans.* adapt, adjust, alter, amend, chop and change, modify, rearrange, reform, reorganise, revise, transform, vary. OPPOSITE keep, maintain. **2** *These events changed her attitude to life.* affect, alter, have an effect on, have an impact on, influence, revolutionise. **3** *Their relationship changed.* alter, develop, evolve; see also DETERIORATE, IMPROVE. **4** *His mood changes.* fluctuate, shift, swing. **5** *The frog changed into a handsome prince.* become, be transformed, convert, metamorphose, mutate, transform, turn. **6** *They changed places.* exchange, interchange, replace, substitute, swap, switch, trade. — *noun* **1** *a change of policy. a noticeable change.* about-turn, adjustment, alteration, amendment, conversion, deviation, difference, fluctuation, innovation, metamorphosis, modification, mutation, rearrangement, reform, reorganisation, reversal, revision, revolution, shift, swing, transfiguration, transformation, transition, transmutation, U-turn, variation, variety. **2** *a change of clothes.* exchange, interchange, replacement, substitution, swap, switch. **3** *He pocketed the change.* coins, coppers, silver.

changeable *adjective a changeable person.* capricious, erratic, fickle, fitful, flighty, inconsistent, inconstant, mercurial, moody, temperamental, unpredictable, unreliable, unsteady, variable, volatile. OPPOSITE constant, steady.

channel *noun* **1** *He sailed the boat through the channel.* narrows, passage, strait, watercourse, waterway. **2** *The water runs away in a channel.* aqueduct, canal, conduit, culvert, ditch, drain, duct, dyke, furrow, groove, gully, gutter, outlet, sluice, trench, trough. **3** *a television channel.* band, frequency, station, wavelength. — *verb Their energies were channelled into fundraising.* direct, guide, lead, steer.

chant *noun religious chants.* canticle, psalm, song. — *verb The crowd chanted their slogan.* intone, recite, sing.

chaos *noun The hurricane left New Orleans in chaos.* anarchy, bedlam, confusion, disarray, disorder, havoc, mayhem, mess, muddle, pandemonium, tumult, turmoil, upheaval. OPPOSITE order.

chaotic *adjective Life was chaotic after the earthquake hit.* confused, disorderly, disorganised, haphazard, haywire (*informal*), jumbled, messy, muddled, out of control, topsy-turvy, uncontrolled, unruly. OPPOSITE orderly.

chap *noun* (*informal*) *Sally is going out with a nice chap.* bloke (*informal*), boy, fellow, guy (*informal*), lad (*informal*), man, person.

chapel *noun* see CHURCH.

chaperone *noun & verb* see ESCORT.

chaplain *noun a prison chaplain.* clergyman, clergywoman, minister, padre, pastor, priest.

chapter *noun a chapter of a book.* division, part, section, subdivision.

char *verb The meat was charred.* blacken, brown, scorch, sear, singe, toast.

character *noun* **1** *Adelaide has a distinctive character.* attributes, characteristics, features, feel, flavour, individuality, make-up, nature, peculiarities, qualities, traits. **2** *She has a cheerful character.* attitude, disposition, manner, nature, personality, spirit, temperament. **3** *He was an unpleasant character.* chap (*informal*), fellow, human being, individual, person, specimen, type (*informal*). **4** *The old man was a real character.* card (*informal*), eccentric, individual, oddball (*informal*), oddity, weirdo (*informal*). **5** *She played several characters in the show.* part, persona, role. **6** *printed characters.* figure, letter, sign, symbol.

characteristic *adjective her characteristic walk.* distinctive, idiosyncratic, individual, particular, peculiar, recognisable, singular, special, typical, unique. — *noun He described the butterfly's characteristics.* aspect, attribute, feature, hallmark, mark, peculiarity, property, quality, trait.

charade *noun The negotiations were a complete charade.* farce, mockery, pretence, sham.

charge *noun* **1** *high charges for services.* cost, expense, fare, fee, levy, payment, price, rate, tariff, terms, toll. **2** *The children were left in her charge.* care, command, control, custody, keeping, protection, responsibility, supervision. **3** *The charge was assault.* accusation, allegation, complaint, imputation, indictment. — *verb* **1** *They charged $100 as a deposit.* ask, debit, demand, levy, require. **2** *She was charged with the responsibility.* burden, encumber, entrust, give, saddle. **3** *The police charged her with the crime.* accuse, blame, book, impeach, indict. OPPOSITE absolve, acquit. **4** *The troops charged the building.* assault, attack, rush, storm.

charitable *adjective* see GENEROUS.

charity *noun* **1** *She refused to accept charity.* alms (*old use*), assistance, contributions, donations, financial assistance, handouts. **2** *He does not give to any charity.* fund, good cause, institution. **3** *She shows charity to all people.* altruism, benevolence, compassion, generosity, goodwill, humanity, kindness, love, philanthropy, sympathy. OPPOSITE ill will.

charlatan *noun The so-called doctor turned out to be a charlatan.* cheat, con man (*informal*), fake, fraud, humbug, impostor, phoney (*informal*), quack, swindler, trickster.

charm *noun* **1** *a person with great charm.* allure, appeal, attractiveness, charisma, magnetism. **2** *The fairy's charm had worn off.* incantation, magic, sorcery, spell, witchcraft, witchery, wizardry. **3** *She carried a lucky charm.* amulet, mascot, talisman, trinket. — *verb She charmed them with her dance.* allure, attract, beguile, bewitch, captivate, delight, enchant, enthral, entrance, fascinate, hold spellbound, hypnotise, mesmerise, seduce.

charming *adjective a charming young lady.* appealing, attractive, beguiling, captivating, delightful, enchanting, enthralling, fascinating, likeable, pleasant, pleasing, sweet (*informal*). OPPOSITE repulsive.

chart *noun* **1** *a chart of the seas.* map, plan. **2** *The figures are set out in the chart.* diagram, graph, histogram, table, tabulation. — *verb They charted their progress.* graph, map, plot, record, register.

charter *verb They chartered a bus.* hire, lease, rent.

chase *verb They chased the thief.* follow, hound, hunt, pursue, run after, track, trail.

chasm *noun a chasm in the rock.* abyss, breach, canyon, cavity, cleft, crack, crevasse, fissure, gap, gorge, hole, opening, ravine, rift.

chassis *noun a car chassis.* frame, framework, skeleton, substructure.

chaste *adjective a chaste woman.* celibate, pure, virginal, virtuous. OPPOSITE promiscuous.

chastise *verb He chastised them for their rudeness.* beat, castigate, censure, chasten, chide (*old use*), discipline, flog, lash, punish, rebuke, reprimand, reproach, reprove, scold, tell off (*informal*), thrash, upbraid. OPPOSITE praise.

chastity *noun a nun's vow of chastity.* celibacy, purity, sexual abstinence, virginity, virtue. OPPOSITE promiscuity.

chat *noun Her friend popped in for a chat.* chinwag (*informal*), conversation, gossip, natter (*informal*), talk, yabber (*Australian informal*), yak (*informal*). — *verb They chatted for hours.* chatter, converse, gossip, have a word, mag (*Australian informal*), natter (*informal*), prattle, talk, yabber (*Australian informal*), yak (*informal*).

chatter *verb The audience chattered until the lights went out.* babble, chat, gabble, gossip, jabber, natter (*informal*), prattle, talk, yak (*informal*). — *noun idle chatter.* chit-chat, gossip, talk, tattle, tittle-tattle.

chatterbox *noun* chatterer, gasbag (*informal*), magpie, windbag (*informal*).

chatty *adjective She can be very chatty at awkward times.* communicative, garrulous, loquacious, talkative, voluble.

cheap *adjective* **1** *cheap prices.* bargain, budget, competitive, cut-price, discount, economical, inexpensive, keen, low, reasonable, reduced, sale. OPPOSITE dear. **2** *He bought a cheap and nasty camera which did not work well.* gimcrack, inferior, poor, rubbishy, second-rate, shoddy, tacky (*informal*), tinny, tinpot, trashy, worthless. OPPOSITE first-rate. **3** *a cheap joke.* contemptible, crude, despicable, low, tasteless, vulgar.

cheat *verb* **1** *He cheated in the test.* break the rules, copy, crib (*informal*). **2** *The salesman cheated his customers.* bamboozle (*informal*), bilk, bluff, con (*informal*), deceive, defraud, diddle (*informal*), double-cross, dupe, fleece, have on (*informal*), hoax, hoodwink, outwit, rip off (*informal*), rob, rook, rort (*Australian slang*), short-change, swindle, take for a ride (*informal*), trick, welsh on. — *noun They caught the cheats.* charlatan, con man (*informal*), crook (*informal*), embezzler, extortioner, fraud, racketeer, rogue, shark, sharp (*informal*), sharper, shicer (*Australian slang*), shyster (*informal*), swindler, trickster, welsher.

check *verb* **1** *The supervisor checks their work.* audit, correct, double-check, examine, inspect, look over, mark, monitor, screen, scrutinise, test, verify, vet. **2** *She checked how he was going.* ascertain, check on, check out, check up, find out, inquire, investigate, suss out (*informal*). **3** *His progress was checked by his health problems.* curb, frustrate, hamper, hinder, hold back, impede, inhibit, limit, restrict, retard, slow down, stop, stunt, thwart. OPPOSITE accelerate. — *noun* **1** *He gave the car a thorough check.* check-up, examination, going-over (*informal*), inspection, investigation, once-over (*informal*), probe, scrutiny, search, test. **2** *They imposed checks on their spending.* brake, constraint, control, curb, limitation, restraint, restriction. □ **check in** *They checked in at reception.* arrive, book in, register. **check out** *Next morning they checked out of the hotel.* depart, go, leave.

checked *adjective* see CHEQUERED.

cheek *noun* **1** *He had food on his cheek.* chap, jowl. **2** *She had the cheek to say that!* audacity, boldness, effrontery, front, gall (*slang*), hide (*informal*), impertinence, impudence, insolence, nerve, presumption, temerity.

cheeky *adjective cheeky behaviour. a cheeky person.* arrogant, audacious, bold, brazen, discourteous, disrespectful, forward, fresh (*informal*), impertinent, impolite, impudent, insolent, pert, presumptuous, rude, saucy, shameless. OPPOSITE polite.

cheer *noun happy and full of good cheer.* cheerfulness, gaiety, gladness, glee, good spirits, happiness, jollity, joy, merriment, mirth, pleasure. OPPOSITE gloom. — *verb* **1** *They cheered their team.* applaud, barrack for (*Australian*), clap, encourage, shout for, support. OPPOSITE hiss at, jeer. **2** *The cards cheered the sick man.* brighten, buck up (*informal*), buoy up, comfort, console, divert, encourage, gladden, hearten, perk up, uplift. OPPOSITE sadden.

cheerful *adjective a cheerful person. a cheerful manner.* blithe, bright, buoyant, carefree, cheery, chirpy, contented, elated, exhilarated, exuberant, gay, glad, gleeful, good-humoured, happy, happy-go-lucky, jaunty, jolly, jovial, joyful, joyous, jubilant, light-hearted, lively, merry, optimistic, perky, positive, radiant, upbeat (*informal*). OPPOSITE dismal, sad.

chemist noun **1** *The chemist dispenses the medicine.* apothecary (*old use*), dispenser, druggist, pharmacist. **2** *She picked up her medicine at the chemist.* dispensary, drugstore (*American*), pharmacy.

chequered adjective **1** *a chequered pattern.* check, checked, chequerboard, criss-cross, plaid, tartan. **2** *a chequered career.* fitful, fluctuating, uneven, up-and-down, varied.

cherish verb **1** *He cherished his wife and children.* adore, be fond of, care for, dote on, hold dear, love, nurture, prize, protect, treasure, value. OPPOSITE despise. **2** *He cherished the hope that they would return.* cling to, foster, harbour, nourish, nurse, nurture, sustain. OPPOSITE abandon.

chest noun **1** *a toy chest. a treasure chest.* ark, box, case, casket, coffer, crate, ottoman, strongbox, trunk. **2** *The jumper fits over her chest.* bosom, breast, bust, ribcage, thorax. □ **chest of drawers** bureau, chest, dresser, lowboy, tallboy.

chew verb *The dog chewed the slipper.* champ, chomp, crunch, gnaw, grind, masticate, munch, nibble; see also EAT.

chic adjective *chic clothes.* classy (*informal*), elegant, fashionable, smart, sophisticated, stylish. OPPOSITE dowdy.

chick noun *The birds look after their chicks.* fledgeling, nestling.

chicken noun **1** *Chickens are kept for their flesh.* chook (*Australian informal*), fowl, hen, rooster. **2** *Don't be a chicken.* see COWARD. — verb **chicken out** *He chickened out of entering the competition.* back out, opt out, pike out (*Australian informal*), pull out, withdraw.

chief noun *The people respect their chief.* boss, captain, chieftain, commander, director, employer, governor, head, leader, manager, master, overseer, president, principal, ruler, superintendent, supervisor. — adjective **1** *the chief engineer.* head, leading, senior. **2** *of chief importance.* basic, cardinal, central, dominant, essential, first, foremost, fundamental, greatest, highest, key, leading, main, major, overriding, paramount, predominant, primary, prime, principal, supreme. OPPOSITE least, secondary.

chiefly adverb *She was chiefly responsible for the mix-up.* especially, for the most part, generally, in the main, mainly, mostly, particularly, primarily, principally.

child noun **1** *A child must be accompanied by an adult.* babe, baby, bairn (*Scottish*), boy, girl, infant, juvenile, kid (*informal*), lad, lass, minor, piccaninny, toddler, tot, youngster, youth. OPPOSITE adult. **2** *The estate passed to his children.* daughter, offspring, son; see also DESCENDANTS.

childhood noun *a friend since childhood.* boyhood, girlhood, infancy, youth. OPPOSITE adulthood.

childish adjective *Her behaviour was childish.* babyish, immature, infantile, juvenile, naive, puerile, silly. OPPOSITE mature.

childlike adjective *childlike pleasure. childlike innocence.* artless, guileless, ingenuous, innocent, naive, simple, trusting, youthful.

chill noun *a chill in the air.* chilliness, coldness, crispness, iciness, nip. — verb *They chilled the drinks.* cool, refrigerate. OPPOSITE warm.

chilling adjective *a chilling experience.* frightening, harrowing, horrifying, nightmarish, spine-chilling, terrifying.

chilly adjective **1** *chilly weather.* cold, crisp, freezing, frosty, icy, nippy (*informal*), raw, wintry. OPPOSITE warm. **2** *a chilly reception.* aloof, cold, cool, frosty, hostile, icy, stony, unfriendly, unwelcoming. OPPOSITE friendly.

chime verb *The clock chimed midnight.* ding, dong, peal, ring, sound, strike, toll.

china noun *They ate off her best china.* crockery, dinner service, porcelain, pottery, tableware.

chink noun *a chink in the wall.* aperture, breach, cleft, crack, cranny, fissure, gap, hole, opening, rift, slit, split.

chip noun **1** *chips of wood. chips of glass.* bit, flake, fragment, piece, shard, shaving, sliver, splinter. **2** *a potato chip.* crisp, French fry. — verb *She chipped the plate.* break, damage, nick, splinter.

chirp verb *The sparrows chirped.* cheep, chirrup, peep, tweet, twitter.

chirpy adjective *He was feeling quite chirpy.* bright, cheerful, happy, light-hearted, lively, perky, vivacious. OPPOSITE depressed.

chivalrous adjective *chivalrous behaviour.* considerate, courteous, courtly, gallant, gentlemanly, heroic, honourable, noble, polite. OPPOSITE boorish.

chock noun *Put a chock under the wheel.* block, wedge.

chock-a-block adjective *The room was chock-a-block with reporters.* chockers (*informal*), chock-full, crammed, crowded, full, jam-packed (*informal*), packed.

choice noun **1** *I have no choice.* alternative, option. **2** *a wide choice of holidays.* array, assortment, collection, range, selection, variety. **3** *He found it hard to make a choice.* decision, election, pick, preference, selection. — adjective *a choice steak.* excellent, fine, first-class, first-rate, prime, prize, select, superior.

choir noun *Anne sings in a choir.* choral group, choristers, chorus, ensemble, singers.

choke verb **1** *He choked the man.* asphyxiate, smother, stifle, strangle, suffocate, throttle. **2** *She choked in the thick smoke.* gag, gasp. **3** *The roads were choked with cars.* block, clog, congest, crowd, jam, obstruct, pack.

chook noun (*Australian informal*) *Alex keeps chooks for the eggs.* chicken, fowl, poultry.

choose verb *They chose him as their spokesperson.* adopt, appoint, decide on, draw lots for, elect, name, nominate, opt for, pick, plump for, prefer, select, settle on, single out, vote for.

choosy adjective (*informal*) *a choosy customer.* fastidious, finicky, fussy, particular, pernickety (*informal*), picky (*informal*), selective. OPPOSITE indifferent.

chop verb **1** *He chopped the wood.* cleave, cut, fell, hack, hew, split. **2** *He chopped the vegetables.* chip, cube, cut, dice, mince.

chopper noun **1** *He cut the bone with a chopper.* axe, cleaver, hatchet, tomahawk. **2** (*informal*) *They flew in a chopper.* helicopter.

choppy adjective *choppy seas.* rough, stormy, turbulent. OPPOSITE smooth.

chore noun *a domestic chore.* duty, errand, job, task, work.

chorus noun **1** *They all joined in the chorus.* jingle, refrain. **2** *a member of the chorus.* see CHOIR.

christen verb *He was christened 'Peter'.* baptise, name; see also CALL.

christening noun *a baby's christening.* baptism.

Christmas noun Noel, Xmas, yule (*old use*), yuletide (*old use*).

chronic adjective *a chronic problem.* ceaseless, constant, continuing, continuous, lifelong, lingering, long-standing, perennial, permanent, persistent, unending. OPPOSITE intermittent, temporary.

chubby adjective *a chubby child.* dumpy, fat, obese, overweight, plump, podgy, rotund, round, stout, tubby. OPPOSITE skinny.

chuck verb (*informal*) **1** *She chucked the rubbish in the bin.* cast, fling, heave, hurl, pitch, sling, throw, toss. **2** *He chucked his job.* chuck in (*informal*), give up, jack in (*slang*), leave, pack in (*informal*), quit, resign, throw in, toss in (*informal*). □ **chuck out** (*informal*) **1** *She chucked out her old clothes.* discard, ditch (*informal*), get rid of, throw away, throw out. **2** *He was chucked out of school.* boot out (*slang*), cast out, expel, kick out (*informal*), throw out (*informal*).

chuckle verb *The cartoon made her chuckle.* chortle, giggle, laugh, snigger, titter.

chum noun (*informal*) *They were old school chums.* buddy (*informal*), cobber (*Australian informal*), companion, comrade, confidant(e), crony, friend, mate, pal (*informal*).

chunk noun *a chunk of cheese.* hunk, lump, mass, piece, slab, wedge, wodge.

church noun **1** *They visited several churches.* abbey, basilica, cathedral, chapel, minster, sanctuary, shrine, tabernacle, temple. **2** *Church is at 11 o'clock.* devotions, divine service, service, worship. **3** *leaders of all the Christian churches.* denomination. — adjective *church music.* ecclesiastical, religious, sacred. OPPOSITE secular.

churlish adjective *a churlish person.* bad-tempered, boorish, ill-bred, ill-mannered, impolite, mean, rude, surly, uncivil, unfriendly, unsociable. OPPOSITE agreeable.

churn verb **1** *He churned the cream.* beat, stir, whip, whisk. **2** *The waters churned.* foam, heave, seethe, swirl, toss. **3** *The waiting had churned her up inside.* agitate, disturb, stir up, upset.

cigarette noun ciggy (*informal*), fag (*slang*), smoke (*informal*).

cinch noun (*informal*) *Getting into the finals will be a cinch.* breeze (*informal*), certainty, child's play, doddle (*informal*), piece of cake (*informal*), pushover (*informal*), snack (*Australian informal*), snap (*informal*), walkover.

cinders plural noun *The cinders were still hot.* ashes, clinker, embers.

cinema noun *She works in cinema.* films, flicks (*informal*), motion pictures, movies (*informal*), pictures (*informal*), the screen.

circle noun **1** *A circle was painted above the saint's head.* band, disc, halo, hoop, loop, ring, round. **2** *The craft completed its circle of the earth.* circuit, circumnavigation, lap, loop, orbit, revolution. **3** *a circle of friends.* clique, company, group, set, sphere, world. — verb **1** *The explorer circled the globe.* circumnavigate, go round, orbit, tour. **2** *She circled the mistakes.* circumscribe, encircle, ring.

circuit noun **1** *a racing circuit.* course, ring, track. **2** *The car broke down on the fiftieth circuit.* circle, lap, loop, orbit, revolution.

circular adjective *a circular shape.* discoid, round. — noun *Office circulars consume a lot of paper.* bulletin, flyer, leaflet, memorandum, newsletter, notice.

circulate verb **1** *Blood circulates through the body.* flow, go round, move round. **2** *They circulated the letter.* distribute, issue, pass round, release, send round.

circumference noun *the circumference of a circle.* boundary, edge, limit, margin, perimeter.

circumstance noun *the circumstances of the case.* background, condition, context, detail, event, fact, particular, position, situation.

citadel noun *The people took refuge in the citadel.* acropolis, bastion, castle, fort, fortress, garrison, stronghold.

cite verb *He cited several examples to support his argument.* adduce, mention, name, put forward, quote, refer to, specify.

citizen noun **1** *She became an Australian citizen.* national. **2** *the citizens of Sydney.* denizen, dweller, inhabitant, native, resident.

city noun *He grew up in the country but now lives in the city.* big smoke (*slang*), metropolis, town. OPPOSITE country.

civic adjective *a civic centre.* civic pride. citizen's, communal, community, local, municipal, public.

civil adjective **1** *civil rights.* citizen's, civic. **2** *civil aviation.* civilian, non-military. **3** *civil marriage ceremony.* lay, secular. OPPOSITE religious. **4** *civil war.* domestic, home, internal. **5** *They are always civil to visitors.* cordial, courteous, obliging, polite, respectful, well-mannered. OPPOSITE rude.

civilised adjective *a civilised society.* cultivated, cultured, developed, educated, enlightened, refined, sophisticated. OPPOSITE barbaric.

clad adjective *The people are warmly clad.* attired, clothed, dressed. OPPOSITE naked.

claim verb **1** *She claimed her share.* ask for, bags (*informal*), demand, lay claim to, request, require. OPPOSITE renounce. **2** *He claimed that he was innocent.* allege, assert, contend, declare, insist, maintain, make out, pretend, profess, state. OPPOSITE deny. — noun **1** *They pursued a claim for higher wages.* application, call, demand, request. **2** *He has no claim on the land.* entitlement, right, title.

clairvoyance noun *The woman claimed to have the gift of clairvoyance.* ESP, extrasensory perception, second sight, sixth sense.

clamber verb *They clambered over the fence.* climb, crawl, scramble, shin.

clammy adjective *His body felt clammy.* damp, dank, humid, moist, sticky, sweaty, wet.

clamour noun *The clamour in the streets woke the neighbourhood.* commotion, din, hubbub, hullabaloo, noise, outcry, racket, row, rumpus, shouting, uproar. — verb *They were clamouring for justice.* call, cry out, demand, protest, shout.

clamp noun *The pieces were held together with a clamp.* brace, clasp, clip, fastener, grip, support, vice. — verb *The pieces were clamped together in a vice.* clasp, clip, fasten, grip, secure.

clan noun *a Scottish clan.* family, group, line, tribe.

clang noun *the clang of bells.* chime, clangour, clank, clash, clink, jangle, peal, ringing.

clank noun *the clank of metal chains.* clang, clash, clatter, clunk, jangle, rattle.

clap noun **1** *a thunder clap.* bang, burst, crack, crash, explosion, peal. **2** *Give them a big clap.* applause, hand (*informal*). — *verb The audience clapped the performers.* applaud, cheer. OPPOSITE boo.

clarify *verb* **1** *She clarified what she meant.* clear up, elucidate, explain, make clear, shed light on, spell out. OPPOSITE confuse, obscure. **2** *He clarified the butter.* clear, filter, purify, refine. OPPOSITE cloud.

clarity *noun the clarity of the water.* clearness, limpidity, purity, transparency. OPPOSITE murkiness.

clash *verb* **1** *The cymbals clashed.* bang, clang, clank, clatter, crash, jangle, rattle. **2** *The two parties clashed over use of the reserve.* argue, battle, contend, disagree, dispute, feud, fight, quarrel, squabble, wrangle. **3** *Their views clashed.* be opposed, conflict, differ, diverge. OPPOSITE harmonise. — *noun* **1** *a clash between rivals.* altercation, battle, combat, conflict, confrontation, contest, disagreement, fight, skirmish. **2** *a clash of colours. a personality clash.* conflict, discord, disharmony, incompatibility, mismatch. OPPOSITE harmony, match.

clasp *noun The clasp on the necklace is broken.* brooch, buckle, catch, clip, fastener, hook, lock. — *verb* **1** *She clasped the two edges together with a pin.* catch, clip, fasten, join, secure. **2** *They clasped one another tightly.* clutch, embrace, enfold, grasp, grip, hold, hug, squeeze.

class *noun* **1** *The objects were sorted into classes.* category, classification, division, family, genre, genus, group, kind, league, order, set, sort, species, subset, type, variety. **2** *a social class.* caste, level, order, rank, station, stratum. **3** *The girls are in the same class at school.* form, grade, group, set, year. **4** *He missed the class and had to catch up.* lecture, lesson, seminar, session, tutorial. — *verb She classed the specimens according to colour.* arrange, categorise, classify, grade, group, label, rank, sort.

classic *adjective* **1** *a classic performance.* excellent, exemplary, firstclass, first-rate, model, outstanding. **2** *a classic case of malnutrition.* archetypal, characteristic, model, standard, typical. **3** *a classic recipe.* abiding, enduring, established, immortal, lasting, time-honoured, traditional. — *noun Some books are considered classics.* masterpiece, masterwork.

classical *adjective* **1** *classical studies.* Greek, Latin, Roman. **2** *classical works.* ageless, enduring, standard, traditional. OPPOSITE modern.

classification *noun the classification of birds.* arrangement, categorisation, grouping; see also CLASS.

classify *verb He classified the books according to subject.* arrange, categorise, class, grade, group, label, order, organise, pigeon-hole, rank, sort.

clatter *noun the clatter of plates in the sink.* banging, clack, clang, clangour, clank, jangle, rattle.

clause *noun a clause of a contract.* article, condition, paragraph, provision, proviso, section, stipulation.

claw *noun a crab's claws. a bird's claws.* nail, nipper, pincer, talon. — *verb The lion clawed its victim.* lacerate, maul, scratch, slash, tear.

clean *adjective* **1** *a clean bathroom.* disinfected, fresh, hygienic, immaculate, sanitary, sanitised, scoured, scrubbed, spick and span, spotless, sterilised. OPPOSITE dirty. **2** *clean clothes.* fresh, laundered, unsoiled, washed. OPPOSITE dirty. **3** *a clean sheet of paper.* blank, fresh, new, unmarked, unused. OPPOSITE used. **4** *clean air.* clear, fresh, pure, purified, uncontaminated, unpolluted. OPPOSITE polluted. **5** *a clean fighter.*

above board, fair, honest, honourable, sporting, sportsmanlike. **6** *a clean joke.* decent, innocent, inoffensive, respectable. OPPOSITE dirty, rude. — *verb* **1** *They cleaned the kitchen.* brush, disinfect, dust, mop, sanitise, scour, scrub, sponge, sweep, tidy (up), vacuum, wash, wipe. OPPOSITE dirty. **2** *He had his clothes cleaned.* dry-clean, launder. OPPOSITE soil. **3** *They cleaned the car.* shampoo, sponge, vacuum, wash. **4** *She cleaned the wound.* bathe, cleanse, decontaminate, disinfect, purify, rinse, sanitise, sterilise, swab, wash.

cleanser *noun bathroom cleanser.* antiseptic, bactericide, detergent, disinfectant, germicide, sanitiser, soap, steriliser.

clear *adjective* **1** *a clear liquid.* clean, crystal-clear, crystalline, limpid, pure, see-through, transparent. OPPOSITE opaque. **2** *clear skies.* blue, bright, cloudless, fair, starry, sunny, unclouded. OPPOSITE cloudy, overcast. **3** *clear skin.* immaculate, perfect, spotless, unblemished. OPPOSITE spotty. **4** *a clear conscience.* blameless, easy, guilt-free, guiltless, untroubled. OPPOSITE guilty. **5** *a clear call.* audible, clarion, discernible, distinct. OPPOSITE indistinct. **6** *clear handwriting.* bold, legible, neat, plain, precise, readable. OPPOSITE illegible. **7** *a clear picture.* focused, precise, sharp, well-defined. OPPOSITE blurred. **8** *a clear contrast.* definite, distinct, marked, noticeable, obvious, pronounced, sharp, stark, strong, visible, vivid. OPPOSITE fuzzy. **9** *a clear case of cheating.* apparent, blatant, clear-cut, definite, evident, glaring, manifest, obvious, palpable, patent, plain, straightforward, unmistakable. OPPOSITE doubtful. **10** *The message was clear.* coherent, comprehensible, crystal-clear, intelligible, lucid, perspicuous, plain, unambiguous, unconcealed, understandable, unequivocal, unmistakable. OPPOSITE vague. **11** *a clear path.* empty, free, open, passable, unimpeded, unobstructed. OPPOSITE blocked. **12** *His clear pay is $300.* net. OPPOSITE gross. — *verb* **1** *The fog cleared.* disappear, dissipate, evaporate, fade, lift, melt, vanish. **2** *He cleared the pipe.* clean, free, unblock, unclog. **3** *The building must be cleared.* empty, evacuate, vacate. **4** *The athletes cleared the hurdles.* bound over, jump over, leap over, spring over, vault. **5** *The plans were cleared by the council.* approve, authorise, OK (*informal*), pass, sanction. OPPOSITE reject. **6** *He was cleared of any wrongdoing.* absolve, acquit, exonerate, vindicate. OPPOSITE accuse. **7** *They cleared $100.* make, make a profit of, net, realise. □ **clear off** see LEAVE. **clear up** **1** *She cleared up her desk.* clean up, sort out, straighten up, tidy up. **2** *They cleared up the matter.* clarify, explain, resolve, settle, sort out.

clearing *noun a clearing in the forest.* gap, glade, opening, space.

cleaver *noun a butcher's cleaver.* chopper, hatchet, meat-axe; see also KNIFE.

clench *verb He clenched his teeth.* clamp together, close, grit, set.

clergy *noun a member of the clergy.* ministry, priesthood; [*various members of the clergy*] archbishop, archdeacon, bishop, canon, cardinal, chaplain, churchman, churchwoman, clergyman, clergywoman, cleric, curate, deacon, deaconess, dean, minister, padre, parson, pastor, preacher, prelate, priest, primate, rector, vicar. OPPOSITE laity.

clerical *adjective* **1** *clerical work.* administrative, bookkeeping, office, paper, secretarial, stenographic, white-collar. **2** *The minister does not wear clerical clothes.* ecclesiastical, ministerial, priestly, sacerdotal.

clever *adjective* **1** *a clever person.* able, accomplished, adept, adroit, artful, astute, brainy, bright, brilliant, canny, crafty, cunning, deft, dexterous, expert, gifted, intelligent, perceptive, quick-witted, resourceful, sharp-witted, shrewd, skilful, slick, sly, smart, talented, wily, wise, witty. OPPOSITE slow, stupid. **2** *a clever plan.* ingenious, inventive, neat, nifty (*informal*), smart, strategic, subtle. OPPOSITE stupid.

cleverness *noun* ability, adroitness, astuteness, brains, brilliance, cunning, dexterity, expertise, ingenuity, intelligence, mastery, quickness, resourcefulness, shrewdness, skill, wit, wizardry.

cliché *noun His speech was full of clichés.* banality, commonplace, hackneyed phrase, platitude.

click *verb The two parts click together.* catch, fasten, snap.

client *noun The company looks after its clients.* consumer, customer, patron, shopper, user; [*clients*] clientele.

cliff *noun a house perched on the cliffs.* bluff, crag, escarpment, precipice, rock face, scarp.

climate *noun The place has a mild climate.* clime (*literary*), weather.

climax *noun The film reached its climax.* apex, crisis, culmination, highlight, peak, pinnacle, summit, zenith.

climb *verb* **1** *He climbed the fence.* clamber over, go over, mount, scale, shin. **2** *The plane was climbing steadily.* ascend, go up, rise, soar. OPPOSITE descend.

clinch *verb He clinched the deal.* close, conclude, finalise, secure, settle, sew up (*informal*).

cling *verb The plastic clings to the bowl.* adhere, attach, stick. □ **cling to** *The child clung to her mother.* clasp, cleave to (*old use*), clutch, embrace, grasp, grip, hang on to, hold on to, hug. OPPOSITE let go of.

clinic *noun He saw a doctor at the clinic.* health centre, hospital, infirmary, medical centre, surgery.

clink *verb The coins clinked in the bowl.* jangle, jingle, ring, tinkle.

clip[1] *noun The bag does up with a clip.* clasp, fastener, grip, hook. — *verb He clipped the papers together.* attach, fasten, fix, join, pin, secure, staple.

clip[2] *verb* **1** *She clipped her hair. Clip the hedge.* bob, crop, cut, prune, shear, shorten, snip, trim. **2** (*informal*) *He threatened to clip his ears.* see HIT. — *noun a film clip.* excerpt, extract, segment, snippet, trailer.

clippers *plural noun hair clippers. hedge clippers.* cutters, scissors, secateurs, shears, snips.

clique *noun He did not belong to their clique.* circle, crowd, faction, group, mob, set.

cloak *noun* **1** *She wore a cloak.* burnous, cape, coat, cope, mantle, poncho, shroud, wrap. **2** *a cloak of secrecy.* cloud, cover, mantle, pall, screen, shroud, veil.

clock *noun The clocks show different times.* chronometer, timepiece.

clog *verb Leaves clogged the gutters.* block, bung up, choke, jam, obstruct, stop up.

close[1] *adjective* **1** *Christmas is close.* at hand, imminent, impending, near, nigh. **2** *The shops are close.* accessible, adjacent, near, neighbouring. OPPOSITE distant. **3** *The* man was shot at close range. point-blank, short. OPPOSITE long. **4** *close friends.* affectionate, attached, dear, devoted, familiar, fond, inseparable, intimate. **5** *a close contest.* even, level-pegging, narrow, neck and neck, tight. **6** *a close fit.* cramped, narrow, tight. OPPOSITE loose. **7** *a close inspection.* careful, concentrated, detailed, minute, searching, thorough. OPPOSITE cursory, superficial. **8** *Keep a close eye on the bags.* alert, attentive, careful, keen, sharp, vigilant, watchful. **9** *a close atmosphere.* airless, humid, muggy, oppressive, stale, stifling, stuffy, sultry. OPPOSITE airy. — *adverb Don't come too close.* alongside, close by, near, within cooee (*Australian informal*). □ **close to** *There were close to fifty people present.* almost, approaching, approximately, nearly.

close[2] *verb* **1** *She closed the door.* bar, bolt, fasten, latch, lock, seal, secure, shut, slam. OPPOSITE open. **2** *He closed up all the holes.* block, bung, clog, cork, fill, plug, seal, stop. **3** *The police closed off the area.* barricade, cordon off, rope off, seal off. **4** *The speaker closed the meeting.* conclude, end, finish, stop, terminate, wind up. OPPOSITE open. — *noun The concert came to a close.* completion, conclusion, culmination, end, finale, finish, halt, stop, termination. OPPOSITE beginning, opening.

closeness *noun* **1** *the closeness of the copy to the original.* likeness, resemblance, similarity. **2** *closeness to the shops.* nearness, proximity.

closet *noun* cupboard, wardrobe.

clot *verb The cream clotted.* coagulate, solidify, thicken.

cloth *noun She bought cloth to make a dress.* fabric, material, stuff, textile.

clothe *verb They were clothed in their Sunday best.* array, attire, deck, dress, garb, robe.

clothes *plural noun She enjoys wearing new clothes.* apparel (*formal*), attire (*formal*), clobber (*slang*), clothing, costume, dress, finery, garb, garments, gear (*informal*), get-up (*informal*), kit, outfit, raiment (*old use*), rig (*informal*), togs (*informal*), uniform, vestments, wardrobe, wear.

cloud *noun* **1** *flying through the clouds.* fog, haze, mist, vapour. **2** *a cloud of secrecy.* cloak, mantle, pall, shroud, veil. — *verb* **1** *The sky clouded over.* darken, dim, grow overcast. OPPOSITE clear. **2** *Tears clouded his vision.* blur, distort, fog, impair, muddy, obscure.

cloudless *adjective a cloudless sky.* blue, bright, clear, fair, starlit, starry, sunny, unclouded. OPPOSITE cloudy.

cloudy *adjective* **1** *a cloudy sky.* dull, gloomy, grey, heavy, leaden, louring, overcast. OPPOSITE cloudless. **2** *a cloudy liquid.* hazy, milky, muddy, murky, opaque. OPPOSITE clear, transparent.

clout *noun* (*informal*) **1** *a clout on the head.* bash, box, hit, slap, smack, thump, whack. **2** *an organisation with political clout.* influence, muscle, power, strength, sway, weight. — *verb He was clouted on the head.* see HIT.

clown *noun We were amused by the clown.* buffoon, comedian, comic, fool, jester, joker, wag, zany.

club *noun* **1** *He hit the snake with his club.* bat, baton, bludgeon, cudgel, nulla-nulla, stick, truncheon, waddy. **2** *a student club.* alliance, association, fellowship, group, guild, league, organisation, society, union. — *verb He clubbed the animal to death.* batter, beat, bludgeon, clobber (*informal*), cudgel, hit, strike, wallop (*informal*).

clue *noun no clues to the mystery.* cue, guide, hint, idea, indication, inkling, key, lead, pointer, sign, suggestion, tip.

clump *noun a clump of hair. a clump of weeds.* bunch, cluster, group, mass, tuft.

clumsy *adjective a clumsy worker.* awkward, blundering, bungling, fumbling, gawky, ham-fisted (*informal*), heavy-handed, inept, maladroit, uncoordinated, ungainly, unskilful. OPPOSITE deft.

cluster *noun a cluster of people.* assembly, batch, bunch, collection, congregation, crowd, gathering, group, herd, huddle, swarm, throng. — *verb They clustered together to keep warm.* assemble, bunch, collect, congregate, crowd, flock, gather, group, herd, huddle, throng. OPPOSITE scatter.

clutch *verb He clutched his case.* clasp, cling to, grasp, grip, hang on to, hold, hug. OPPOSITE let go.

clutter *noun They tidied up the clutter.* jumble, litter, mess, muddle. — *verb His desk is cluttered with papers.* crowd, litter, mess up, scatter, strew. OPPOSITE tidy up.

coach *noun* **1** *a horse-drawn coach.* carriage, stagecoach. **2** *She saw Europe by coach.* bus. **3** *a maths coach.* instructor, teacher, trainer, tutor. — *verb He coached the chess team.* drill, instruct, teach, train, tutor.

coagulate *verb The mixture has coagulated.* clot, congeal, curdle, solidify, stiffen, thicken.

coalition *noun a coalition of two political parties.* alliance, amalgamation, association, bloc, partnership, union.

coarse *adjective* **1** *a coarse material.* harsh, loose-weave, prickly, rough, scratchy. OPPOSITE fine, smooth. **2** *coarse manners. coarse language.* boorish, common, crude, foul, impolite, improper, indecent, low, offensive, rough, rude, uncouth, unrefined, vulgar. OPPOSITE polite, refined.

coast *noun The road follows the coast.* beach, coastline, foreshore, seaboard, seashore, seaside, shore. — *verb He turned off the engine and coasted down the hill.* cruise, drift, freewheel, glide.

coat *noun* **1** *You will need to wear a coat.* [*kinds of coat*] anorak, blazer, cagoule, dinner-jacket, doublet, duffel coat, greatcoat, jacket, mackintosh, overcoat, parka, raincoat, tailcoat, topcoat, trench coat, tuxedo, waistcoat, windcheater, wrap; see also CLOAK. **2** *an animal's coat.* fleece, fur, hair, hide, pelt, skin. **3** *a coat of paint.* coating, cover, film, layer, overlay. — *verb He coated the chair with the paint. The car was coated with mud.* cover, daub, encase, encrust, laminate, paint, plaster, protect, seal, smear, spread, veneer. □ **coat of arms** blazon, crest, emblem, heraldic device, shield.

coating *noun a protective coating.* coat, cover, covering, film, glaze, layer, outside, overlay, sealant, skin, surface, veneer.

coax *verb They coaxed her into giving a speech.* beguile, cajole, charm, entice, induce, inveigle, persuade, sweet-talk (*informal*), talk into, tempt.

cobber *noun see* FRIEND.

cock *noun the cock and the hens.* cockerel, rooster. — *verb The dog cocked his ears.* prick up, raise, tilt, tip.

cock-eyed *adjective* (*informal*) **1** *a cock-eyed painting.* askew, awry, crooked, lopsided. OPPOSITE straight. **2** *a cock-eyed scheme.* absurd, crazy, foolish, hare-brained, ludicrous, mad, stupid, wild. OPPOSITE sensible.

cocky *adjective The new fellow is too cocky.* arrogant, brash, bumptious, cocksure, conceited, impudent, opinionated, overconfident, self-assured, self-confident, vain. OPPOSITE modest.

code *noun* **1** *a code of ethics.* laws, principles, regulations, rules, system. **2** *a message in code.* cipher, signs. — *verb He coded the message.* encode, encrypt. OPPOSITE decipher.

codicil *noun a codicil to a will.* addendum, appendix, postscript, rider, supplement.

coerce *verb They coerced her into signing the form.* bludgeon, browbeat, bulldoze (*informal*), bully, compel, constrain, dragoon, force, intimidate, lean on (*informal*), press, pressure, railroad.

coffin *noun The body was placed in a coffin for burial.* box, casket, sarcophagus.

cogent *adjective see* CONVINCING.

coherent *adjective a coherent speech.* articulate, clear, connected, consistent, intelligible, logical, lucid, rational, structured, systematic, understandable. OPPOSITE incoherent, rambling.

coil *verb He coiled the wire round the spool.* bend, curl, entwine, kink, loop, roll, turn, twine, twirl, twist, wind, wrap. — *noun a coil of wire.* circle, convolution, curl, helix, kink, loop, ring, spiral, twist, whorl.

coin *noun* **1** *a 20-cent coin.* bit, piece. **2** *a purse bursting with coins.* cash, change, copper, money, silver. — *verb* **1** *A special $5 piece has been coined.* mint, strike. **2** *She coined the word.* create, devise, invent, make up, originate.

coincide *verb* **1** *The two events coincided.* be concurrent, clash, happen simultaneously, happen together, synchronise. **2** *Their accounts coincide.* accord, agree, be the same, concur, correspond, match, square, tally. OPPOSITE disagree.

coincidence *noun They were on the same bus by coincidence.* accident, chance, fluke, luck.

coincidental *adjective Any resemblance to real people is purely coincidental.* accidental, chance, fortuitous, unintentional, unplanned. OPPOSITE deliberate.

cold *adjective* **1** *cold weather.* arctic, biting, bitter, bleak, chill, chilly, cool, crisp, freezing, frigid, frosty, glacial, icy, nippy (*informal*), perishing (*informal*), raw, subzero, wintry. OPPOSITE hot. **2** *She feels cold.* chilly, cool, freezing, frozen, numb, shivery. OPPOSITE hot. **3** (*informal*) *knocked out cold.* insensible, unconscious. **4** *a cold person.* aloof, callous, clinical, cold-hearted, cool, distant, frigid, frosty, hard-hearted, heartless, hostile, indifferent, inhuman, insensitive, severe, standoffish, stony, uncaring, undemonstrative, unemotional, unenthusiastic, unfeeling, unfriendly, unkind, unsympathetic. OPPOSITE ardent, warm.

cold-blooded *adjective a cold-blooded killer.* brutal, callous, cruel, heartless, inhuman, inhumane, merciless, pitiless, ruthless, sadistic, savage. OPPOSITE humane.

cold-shoulder *verb He cold-shouldered his replacement.* freeze out (*informal*), ostracise, rebuff, send to Coventry, snub.

collaborate *verb The two teams collaborated on the work.* cooperate, join forces, team up, work together.

collaborator *noun* **1** *collaborators on the project.* ally, assistant, associate, colleague, co-worker, fellow worker, helper, partner. **2** *a wartime collaborator.* fraterniser, quisling, traitor.

collapse *verb* **1** *The runner collapsed after the race.* faint, fall down, flake out (*informal*), keel over, pass out, swoon. **2** *She collapsed into the chair.* crumple, drop, fall, flop, sink, slump. **3** *The building collapsed with an explosion.* buckle, cave in, crumble, crumple, disintegrate, fall down, give way, subside, tumble down. **4** *The financial system has collapsed.* break down, crash, fail, fold, founder, go bung (*Australian informal*), go bust (*informal*). — *noun* **1** *the collapse of the building.* cave-in, destruction, fall, ruin, subsidence. **2** *the collapse of a political system.* breakdown, disintegration, downfall, failure.

collate *verb She collated the survey findings.* arrange, collect, sort, systematise.

colleague *noun a business colleague.* associate, co-worker, fellow worker, partner, workmate; see also COLLABORATOR.

collect *verb* **1** *He collected antiques.* accumulate, acquire, amass, garner, heap up, hoard, pile up, save, stockpile, store. **2** *A crowd of shoppers collected at the door.* assemble, cluster, come together, congregate, convene, flock, gather, group, herd, rally, swarm, throng. OPPOSITE disperse. **3** *She collected the dry-cleaning.* bring, fetch, get, obtain, pick up. **4** *She collects money for charities.* ask for, obtain, raise, receive, solicit. OPPOSITE distribute.

collection *noun* **1** *the rubbish collection.* pick-up. **2** *the church collection.* alms (*old use*), contributions, donations, gifts, offering, offertory. **3** *a collection of things.* accumulation, anthology, arrangement, array, assortment, batch, bundle, compendium, compilation, conglomeration, corpus, group, heap, hoard, jumble, library, mass, medley, miscellany, mixture, pile, selection, series, set, stack, stockpile, store, storehouse, swag (*Australian*), treasury, variety. **4** *a collection of people.* assembly, band, bevy, body, bunch, cluster, company, congregation, crowd, flock, gathering, group, herd, horde, host, mass, mob, multitude, pack, swarm, throng.

college *noun* academy, conservatorium, institute, school, seminary, university.

collide *verb* **collide with** *The car collided with a bus.* bump into, cannon into, crash into, hit, knock into, ram into, run into, slam into, smash into, strike.

collision *noun People were hurt in the collision.* accident, bingle (*Australian informal*), crash, impact, pile-up (*informal*), prang (*informal*), smash.

colloquial *adjective a colloquial expression.* casual, chatty, conversational, everyday, familiar, informal, vernacular. OPPOSITE formal.

colonist *noun British colonists in Australia.* immigrant, pioneer, settler.

colony *noun* **1** *the colony of South Australia.* dependency, dominion, possession, province, settlement, territory. **2** *a colony of bees.* community, group, hive.

colossal *adjective a colossal amount. a colossal building.* big, enormous, extensive, gargantuan, giant, gigantic, ginormous (*slang*), great, huge, humungous (*slang*), immense, large, mammoth, massive, mighty, monstrous, monumental, prodigious, stupendous, towering, tremendous, vast, whopping (*slang*). OPPOSITE small.

colour *noun* **1** *bright colours.* dye, hue, paint, pigment, shade, tinge, tint, tone. **2** *The colour has come back to her cheeks.* bloom, blush, flush, glow, redness, ruddiness. OPPOSITE pallor. — *verb* **1** *They coloured the eggs for Easter.* dye, paint, stain, tinge, tint. **2** *Her cheeks coloured with embarrassment.* blush, flush, glow, redden. **3** *The information coloured his judgement.* affect, bias, distort, influence, prejudice, taint.

colourful *adjective* **1** *a colourful drawing.* bright, brilliant, flashy, gaudy, gay, loud, multicoloured, showy, vibrant, vivid. OPPOSITE colourless. **2** *a colourful story.* descriptive, graphic, interesting, lively, picturesque, vivid. OPPOSITE dull.

colourless *adjective* **1** *a colourless liquid.* clear, transparent. **2** *The invalid was colourless.* anaemic, ashen, pale, pallid, pasty, sickly, wan, washed out, waxen, white. OPPOSITE ruddy. **3** *a colourless performance.* boring, drab, dreary, dull, insipid, lacklustre, lifeless, monotonous, nondescript, ordinary, tame, unexciting, unimaginative, wishy-washy. OPPOSITE colourful.

column *noun* **1** *Columns support the roof.* pile, pillar, pole, post, shaft, support, upright. **2** *He writes a newspaper column.* article, feature, leader, piece. **3** *a column of armoured vehicles.* file, line, motorcade, parade, procession, queue, row, string, train.

comb *verb* **1** *She combed her hair.* groom, tidy. **2** *He combed the ruins for evidence.* fossick through (*Australian informal*), ransack, rummage through, scour, search.

combat *noun Their son was killed in combat.* action, battle, clash, conflict, confrontation, contest, duel, engagement, fight, hostility, skirmish, struggle, war. — *verb Doctors are trying to combat the disease.* battle, counter, fight, oppose, resist, tackle.

combination *noun a combination of colours.* alliance, amalgam, amalgamation, association, blend, coalition, composite, conjunction, fusion, marriage, merger, mix, mixture, partnership, synthesis, union.

combine *verb* **1** *She combined the ingredients.* bind, blend, incorporate, lump together, mix, put together, synthesise. **2** *The two schools combined to form a new one.* amalgamate, band together, consolidate, federate, integrate, join forces, merge, team up, unite. OPPOSITE separate.

combined *adjective* **1** *a combined score.* aggregate, composite, total. OPPOSITE individual. **2** *their combined efforts.* collective, concerted, corporate, group, joint, united. OPPOSITE individual.

come *verb* **1** *Come here.* advance, approach, draw near. **2** *The guests came on time.* appear, arrive, blow in (*informal*), drop in, lob in (*Australian slang*), materialise, roll up (*informal*), show up, turn up. **3** *The bus eventually came to my stop.* arrive at, get to, reach. **4** *What came next?* happen, occur, take place. □ **come about** *He told us how the meeting came about.* arise, come to pass, happen, occur, take place. **come across** (*informal*) *He came across the evidence by accident.* chance upon, come upon, discover, find, happen on, stumble on. **come back** *The rash came back.* reappear, recur, resurface, return. **come down** **1** *The plane came down quickly.* descend, land. **2** *Prices* *came down.* drop, fall, nosedive, plunge. **come out 1** *The sun came out.* appear, become visible, emerge. **2** *The truth eventually came out.* become known, be published, be revealed, emerge, leak out. **3** *The stain came out.* be removed, disappear, wash out. **come round** *The patient is coming round.* come to, rally, recover, regain consciousness, revive. **come to 1** *The bill came to $50.* add up to, amount to, equal, tot up to. **2** *The boxer came to.* see COME ROUND. **come up 1** *The diver came up for air.* ascend, pop up, rise, surface. **2** *A problem has come up.* arise, crop up, occur. **come up with** *She came up with a new idea.* contribute, produce, propose, put forward, submit, suggest.

comedian, comedienne *noun The comedian entertained us with his jokes.* comic, humorist, jester, joker, wag, wit.

comedy *noun Dan appreciated the comedy of the situation.* farce, fun, hilarity, humour, joking, satire, slapstick. OPPOSITE tragedy.

comfort *noun* **1** *They live in comfort.* contentment, ease, luxury, opulence, well-being. OPPOSITE discomfort, hardship. **2** *He provided comfort to the grieving family.* commiseration, condolence, consolation, reassurance, relief, solace, support, sympathy. OPPOSITE aggravation. *— verb She comforted them with kind words.* cheer, console, encourage, gladden, reassure, relieve, solace, soothe, sympathise with. OPPOSITE distress.

comfortable *adjective* **1** *a comfortable bed.* comfy (*informal*), cosy, luxurious, relaxing, restful, snug, soft. OPPOSITE uncomfortable. **2** *a comfortable job.* cushy (*informal*), easy, pleasant, soft (*informal*). OPPOSITE demanding, hard. **3** *He makes his guests feel comfortable.* at ease, at home, contented, relaxed. OPPOSITE uneasy.

comic *noun* see COMEDIAN.

comical *adjective a comical situation.* absurd, amusing, comic, droll, farcical, funny, hilarious, humorous, laughable, ludicrous, nonsensical, ridiculous, silly, zany. OPPOSITE serious, tragic.

coming *noun the coming of the king.* advent, approach, arrival.

command *noun* **1** *They follow his commands.* bidding, commandment, decree, dictate, direction, directive, edict, injunction, instruction, order, precept, summons. **2** *Who is in command?* authority, charge, control, leadership, power, rule. **3** *She has a good command of English.* control, grasp, mastery, understanding. *— verb* **1** *She commanded them to be silent.* bid, call upon, charge, decree, direct, instruct, order, prescribe, require, summon, tell. **2** *Stephens was the officer commanding the expedition.* be in charge of, control, direct, govern, head, lead, manage, rule, supervise. **3** *He commands their respect.* compel, deserve, earn, get.

commandment *noun the Ten Commandments.* command, law, order, precept, principle, rule.

commemorate *verb They like to commemorate Anzac Day.* celebrate, mark, observe, remember. OPPOSITE forget, ignore.

commence *verb* **1** *The show commenced at 8 o'clock.* begin, get going, get under way, kick off (*informal*), open, start. OPPOSITE finish. **2** *He commenced the negotiations.* begin, embark on, enter upon, inaugurate, initiate, launch, open, start. OPPOSITE conclude.

commencement *noun the commencement of proceedings.* begin-

ning, birth, dawn, founding, genesis, inauguration, inception, onset, opening, origin, outset, start. OPPOSITE end.

commend *verb The judges commended the book.* acclaim, applaud, approve, extol, laud (*formal*), praise, recommend. OPPOSITE condemn.

commendable *adjective commendable behaviour.* admirable, laudable, meritorious, praiseworthy, worthy.

comment *noun He wrote his comments in the margin.* annotation, note, observation, opinion, reference, reflection, remark, statement. *— verb He merely commented that they were late.* mention, observe, remark, say.

commentary *noun The broadcaster provided a commentary on the game.* account, description, narration, report, voice-over.

commentator *noun a sports commentator.* broadcaster, commenter, journalist, narrator, presenter, reporter.

commerce *noun* business, trade.

commercial *adjective a commercial venture.* business, economic, money-making, profitable, profit-making. *— noun a show without commercials.* ad (*informal*), advert (*informal*), advertisement, plug (*informal*).

commission *noun* **1** *a commission to paint a portrait.* assignment, authority, duty, job, mission, order, task, warrant. **2** *The government has set up a commission of inquiry.* board, committee, council, panel. **3** *An insurance salesman earns a commission.* brokerage, cut (*informal*), fee, percentage, share.

commit *verb* **1** *He committed the crime.* carry out, do, perform, perpetrate. **2** *She committed the children to her sister's care.* commend, consign, entrust, hand over. **3** *He committed himself to big repayments.* bind, pledge, promise.

commitment *noun* **1** *He is trying to reduce his commitments.* duty, engagement, obligation, responsibility, task, tie. **2** *She honoured her commitment to make a donation.* pledge, promise, undertaking, vow, word. **3** *The party expects members' total commitment.* allegiance, dedication, devotion, loyalty.

committee *noun The club appointed a committee.* board, cabinet, council, panel, working party.

commodity *noun They have no commodities to sell.* article, item, product; [*commodities*] goods, merchandise, produce, wares.

common *adjective* **1** *It was common knowledge.* general, open, popular, public, universal, well-known. OPPOSITE private. **2** *a common interest.* communal, joint, mutual (*informal*), shared. **3** *a common problem. a common occurrence.* commonplace, customary, everyday, familiar, frequent, general, habitual, prevalent, regular, routine, standard, universal, usual, widespread. OPPOSITE rare, unusual. **4** *the common house spider.* common or garden (*informal*), conventional, normal, ordinary, plain, simple, standard, typical. OPPOSITE special. **5** (*derogatory*) *common behaviour.* boorish, coarse, crude, ill-bred, low, plebeian, rude, uncouth, unrefined, vulgar. OPPOSITE refined. □ **common sense** gumption (*informal*), intelligence, judgement, nous (*informal*), sense.

commonplace *adjective a commonplace event.* common, customary, everyday, familiar, mundane, normal, ordinary, regular, routine, usual. OPPOSITE rare.

commotion *noun She was woken by the commotion outside.* ado, ballyhoo, clamour, din, disturbance, fracas, furore, fuss, hubbub, hullabaloo, kerfuffle (*informal*), noise, pandemonium, racket, riot, rumpus, shindy (*informal*), stir, to-do, tumult, turmoil, unrest, uproar.

communal *adjective a communal kitchen.* common, joint, public, shared. OPPOSITE private.

communicate *verb* **1** *She communicated her views.* announce, broadcast, convey, declare, disclose, disseminate, divulge, express, impart, indicate, make known, pass on, promulgate, relate, relay, report, reveal, say, show, signal, speak, state, voice. OPPOSITE withhold. **2** *He does not communicate with people.* commune, confer, converse, correspond, get in touch, make contact, speak, talk, write.

communication *noun* **1** *a lack of communication.* contact, conversation, correspondence, dialogue, speaking, writing. **2** *a handwritten communication from the Premier.* advice, announcement, bulletin, communiqué, dispatch, information, letter, memorandum, message, news, note, notice, notification, report, statement.

communicative *adjective He was not very communicative.* chatty, forthcoming, garrulous, informative, loquacious, open, talkative. OPPOSITE reserved.

Communion *noun* Eucharist, Holy Communion, Lord's Supper, Mass.

communiqué *noun The leaders issued a communiqué after the meeting.* announcement, bulletin, communication, dispatch, message, report, statement.

community *noun* **1** *The police appealed to the community for information.* citizens, nation, people, populace, public, residents, society. **2** *They live in a quiet community.* area, district, environment, locality, municipality, neighbourhood, suburb. **3** *the business community.* group, people, sector, set. *— adjective* **1** *widespread community support.* popular, public. **2** *a community centre.* civic, local, municipal, neighbourhood.

compact *adjective* **1** *The house is compact.* poky, small, tiny. OPPOSITE spacious. **2** *a compact calculator.* little, neat, portable, small. OPPOSITE bulky. **3** *a compact style.* brief, concise, condensed, laconic, pithy, succinct, terse. OPPOSITE long-winded.

companion *noun He has been a faithful lifelong companion.* assistant, associate, attendant, buddy (*informal*), chaperone, chum (*informal*), cobber (*Australian informal*), comrade, consort, crony, escort, friend, mate, pal (*informal*), partner, playmate, sidekick (*informal*).

company *noun* **1** *They enjoy his company.* companionship, fellowship, friendship, society. **2** *They're expecting company.* callers, guests, visitors. **3** *a theatrical company.* crew, ensemble, group, society, troupe. **4** *He spoke to the assembled company.* assembly, audience, congregation, crowd, gathering, group, mob, party, throng, troop. **5** *an insurance company.* business, concern, corporation, establishment, firm, institution, organisation.

comparable *adjective a comparable situation.* analogous, corresponding, equivalent, like, parallel, similar. OPPOSITE different.

compare *verb* **1** *He compared the two plans.* contrast, juxtapose, weigh up. **2** *He compared the human body to a machine.* liken.

□ **compare with** *His latest book does not compare with his earlier ones.* approach, be on a par with, compete with, match, rival.

comparison *noun* **1** *He made a comparison of the two schemes.* contrast, juxtaposition. **2** *There is no comparison between the two things.* analogy, likeness, parallel, resemblance, similarity.

compartment *noun The room is divided into compartments.* area, bay, booth, box, carrel, cell, chamber, cubby hole, cubicle, division, niche, part, pigeon-hole, pocket, recess, section, slot, space, stall.

compassion *noun He had compassion for the injured man.* concern, feeling, humanity, mercy, pity, sympathy, tenderness. OPPOSITE indifference.

compassionate *adjective a compassionate judge.* humane, kind-hearted, lenient, merciful, soft-hearted, sympathetic, tender-hearted, warm-hearted. OPPOSITE hard-hearted, pitiless.

compatible *adjective* **1** *a compatible couple.* harmonious, like-minded, well-matched, well-suited. OPPOSITE incompatible. **2** *Their explanations are not compatible.* consistent, in accord, in agreement, reconcilable. OPPOSITE contradictory, inconsistent.

compel *verb They compelled him to leave.* coerce, constrain, drive, force, impel, make, oblige, press, pressure, push, require.

compelling *adjective* **1** *a compelling argument.* cogent, convincing, forceful, persuasive, powerful, strong. OPPOSITE weak. **2** *The book makes compelling reading.* gripping, irresistible, riveting.

compensate *verb* **1** *The company compensated her for the loss.* indemnify, make amends, make up, recompense, reimburse, repay. **2** *This success compensates for previous failures.* cancel out, counterbalance, make up for, neutralise, offset.

compensation *noun She received $10,000 in compensation for the injury.* compo (*Australian slang*), damages, indemnity, recompense, redress, reparation, restitution.

compère *noun the compère of a programme.* anchorperson, announcer, host, master of ceremonies, MC, presenter.

compete *verb* **1** *Four teams are competing.* enter, participate, take part. **2** *The cars competed for pole position.* battle, contend, contest, fight, rival, strive, struggle, vie.

competent *adjective a competent worker.* able, adept, capable, effective, efficient, handy, practical, proficient, qualified, skilful, skilled, trained. OPPOSITE inept.

competition *noun* **1** *a spelling competition. a tennis competition.* challenge, championship, contest, game, match, meet, quiz, rally, tournament. **2** *competition for export markets.* opposition, rivalry.

competitor *noun Matt has an advantage over the other competitors.* adversary, candidate, challenger, contender, contestant, entrant, opponent, participant, player, rival.

compile *verb He is compiling the material for the book.* accumulate, assemble, collate, collect, gather, organise, put together.

complacent *adjective You must keep striving and not allow yourself to be complacent.* content, pleased with yourself, self-satisfied, smug.

complain *verb He complained that it was unfair.* beef (*slang*), bitch (*informal*), carp, gripe (*informal*), grizzle (*informal*), groan, grumble, moan, object, protest, rail, wail, whine, whinge (*informal*).

complaint *noun* **1** *no complaints about the food.* beef (*slang*), criticism, grievance, gripe (*informal*), grizzle (*informal*), grumble, objection, protest. **2** *He suffers from a chest complaint.* affliction, ailment, disease, disorder, illness, malady, sickness.

complement *verb The necklace complemented the outfit.* complete, round off, set off.

complete *adjective* **1** *a complete jigsaw set.* entire, full, intact, total, unbroken, whole. OPPOSITE incomplete. **2** *the complete story.* comprehensive, full, unabridged, uncut, whole. OPPOSITE incomplete, partial. **3** *The work is now complete.* accomplished, concluded, done, ended, finished. OPPOSITE unfinished. **4** *complete stupidity.* absolute, downright, out-and-out, outright, perfect, positive, proper, pure, sheer, thorough, total, utter. — *verb* **1** *He completed the work in time.* accomplish, achieve, carry out, conclude, end, finalise, finish, fulfil, round off, wind up, wrap up (*informal*). OPPOSITE begin. **2** *Complete the form in black ink.* fill in, fill out.

completely *adverb completely satisfied.* absolutely, altogether, entirely, fully, perfectly, quite, thoroughly, totally, utterly, wholly.

complex *adjective a complex structure.* complicated, composite, compound, elaborate, intricate, involved, multiple, sophisticated. OPPOSITE simple. — *noun She has a complex about her ears.* fixation, hang-up (*informal*), obsession, preoccupation, thing (*informal*).

complexion *noun a healthy complexion.* colour, skin, tone.

compliant *adjective She was trained to be compliant.* biddable, deferential, docile, obedient, submissive, tractable, yielding. OPPOSITE disobedient.

complicated *adjective* **1** *a complicated machine.* complex, elaborate, intricate, sophisticated. OPPOSITE simple. **2** *a complicated issue.* complex, difficult, intricate, involved, knotty, messy, problematical, tricky. OPPOSITE straightforward.

complication *noun Things proceeded without any complications.* difficulty, hitch, obstacle, problem, setback, snag, stumbling block.

compliment *noun Lois received many compliments for her work.* acclamation, accolade, bouquet, commendation, congratulations, flattery, honour, plaudits, praise, tribute. OPPOSITE insult. — *verb He complimented the students on their fine results.* applaud, commend, congratulate, flatter, pay tribute to, praise. OPPOSITE criticise, reproach.

complimentary *adjective* **1** *a complimentary review.* admiring, approving, commendatory, congratulatory, favourable, flattering, positive. OPPOSITE critical. **2** *a complimentary drink.* free, free of charge, gratis, on the house (*informal*).

comply *verb* **comply with** *The car complies with safety standards.* accord with, conform to, follow, fulfil, meet, obey, satisfy. OPPOSITE infringe.

component *noun Spare components are expensive.* bit, constituent, element, ingredient, module, part, piece, unit.

compose *verb* **1** *A jury is composed of twelve ordinary people.* constitute, form, make up. **2** *She composed a story.* compile, concoct, construct, create, devise, fashion,

formulate, invent, make up, produce, put together, write.

composed *adjective He remained composed while they told him the news.* calm, collected, controlled, cool, nonchalant, placid, sedate, self-controlled, serene, stoical, tranquil, unruffled. OPPOSITE agitated.

composition *noun* **1** *The children wrote a composition.* article, essay, paper, story. **2** *a musical composition.* creation, opus, piece, work. **3** *the composition of the group.* constitution, make-up, structure.

composure *noun He regained his composure.* calmness, control, cool (*informal*), coolness, equanimity, poise, self-control, serenity.

compound¹ *adjective a compound substance.* complex, composite, multiple. OPPOSITE simple. — *noun a chemical compound. a compound of two words.* alloy, amalgam, blend, combination, composite, mixture, synthesis. — *verb Worry compounded her problems.* add to, aggravate, complicate, exacerbate, increase, worsen.

compound² *noun The animals are kept in the compound.* enclosure, pen, pound, yard.

comprehend *verb She did not comprehend the seriousness of the situation.* appreciate, conceive, fathom, follow, grasp, perceive, realise, see, take in, understand.

comprehension *noun He has some comprehension of the problem.* awareness, conception, grasp, insight, perception, realisation, understanding.

comprehensive *adjective a comprehensive account.* all-inclusive, broad, complete, detailed, exhaustive, extensive, full, inclusive, sweeping, thorough. OPPOSITE incomplete.

compress *verb She compressed the foam to fill the cushion.* compact, condense, cram, crush, pack down, press, squash, squeeze.

comprise *verb The house comprises eight rooms.* be composed of, be made up of, consist of, contain, include.

compromise *noun The negotiator helped them to reach a compromise.* bargain, deal, happy medium, middle course, trade-off. — *verb They agreed to compromise.* come to terms, give and take, make a deal, make concessions, meet halfway, strike a bargain.

compulsive *adjective* **1** *a compulsive desire to eat.* compelling, driving, irresistible, overpowering, uncontrollable. **2** *a compulsive gambler.* addicted, habitual, incorrigible, obsessive.

compulsory *adjective a compulsory suspension.* mandatory, necessary, obligatory, prescribed, required, unavoidable. OPPOSITE optional.

compute *verb He computed the petrol consumption for the trip.* add up, calculate, reckon, total, tot up, work out.

comrade *noun They remained comrades throughout their lives.* ally, associate, buddy (*informal*), chum (*informal*), cobber (*Australian informal*), colleague, companion, crony, fellow, friend, mate, pal (*informal*), partner.

con *verb* (*informal*) *She felt she'd been conned.* cheat, deceive, have (*slang*), hoax, hoodwink, mislead, rip off (*informal*), swindle, trick. — *noun* (*informal*) *The deal turned out to be a con.* confidence trick, deception, hoax, swindle, swizz (*informal*), trick. □ **con man** (*informal*) *Don't be deceived by that con man.* charlatan, cheat, confidence man, fraud, humbug, illywhacker (*Australian informal*), impostor,

phoney (*informal*), quack, swindler, trickster.

conceal *verb* **1** *He concealed the microphone.* bury, camouflage, cover up, hide, obscure, plant, screen, secrete. OPPOSITE expose. **2** *She concealed her feelings.* bottle up, cover up, disguise, hide, keep secret, mask, repress, suppress, withhold. OPPOSITE reveal.

concede *verb* **1** *They conceded that he was right.* accept, acknowledge, admit, confess. OPPOSITE deny. **2** *They conceded us the right to cross their land.* allow, give, grant, yield. OPPOSITE deny. **3** *Their team was forced to concede.* admit defeat, give in, give up, resign, surrender.

conceit *noun He was clever but full of conceit.* arrogance, boastfulness, egotism, pride, vanity. OPPOSITE modesty.

conceited *adjective a conceited champion.* arrogant, boastful, bumptious, cocky, egotistical, haughty, immodest, proud, self-important, self-satisfied, smug, stuck-up (*informal*), swollen-headed (*informal*), vain. OPPOSITE humble, modest.

conceive *verb* **1** *The woman conceived.* become pregnant. **2** *He conceived a way to save the building.* contrive, create, devise, dream up, envisage, formulate, hatch, imagine, plan, think up.

concentrate *verb* **concentrate on** *They all concentrated on the lesson.* apply yourself to, attend to, be absorbed in, focus on, pay attention to, put your mind to.

concentrated *adjective concentrated chicken stock.* condensed, intense, reduced, strong. OPPOSITE dilute.

concept *noun She grasped the concept.* belief, idea, notion, principle, thought.

conception *noun* **1** *She was involved in the scheme from its conception.* beginning, birth, creation, formulation, genesis, inception, origin, outset, start. OPPOSITE termination. **2** *His conception of the future was different from theirs.* concept, idea, image, impression, notion, picture, understanding, vision.

concern *verb* **1** *The story concerns the plight of children suffering with AIDS.* be about, deal with, have to do with, involve, refer to, surround. **2** *The news concerns everybody.* affect, apply to, be important to, interest, matter to, relate to, touch. **3** *His disappearance concerned them.* bother, disturb, perturb, trouble, worry. — *noun* **1** *Their safety is his concern.* affair, business, responsibility. **2** *She showed no concern for their feelings.* attention, care, consideration, heed, interest, regard, solicitude. OPPOSITE indifference. **3** *He hasn't a concern in the world.* anxiety, burden, care, problem, trouble, worry. **4** *a going concern.* business, company, corporation, enterprise, establishment, firm, organisation.

concerned *adjective concerned parents.* anxious, caring, distressed, interested, involved, solicitous, troubled, uneasy, worried. OPPOSITE unconcerned.

concerning *preposition a discussion concerning capital punishment.* about, re, regarding, relating to, with reference to, with regard to.

concert *noun The group gave a free concert.* gig (*informal*), performance, recital, show.

concerted *adjective a concerted effort.* collaborative, combined, cooperative, coordinated, joint, united.

concession *noun travel concessions.* discount, privilege, reduction, right.

concise *adjective a concise description.* abridged, brief, compact, condensed, pithy, short, succinct, summary, terse. OPPOSITE wordy.

conclude *verb* **1** *The service concluded with the blessing.* cease, close, come to an end, end, finish, stop, terminate. OPPOSITE begin, start. **2** *He concluded the interview.* bring to an end, close, complete, end, finish, round off, stop, terminate, wind up. OPPOSITE begin, start. **3** *She concluded that something had gone wrong.* decide, deduce, gather, infer, judge, reason.

conclusion *noun* **1** *the conclusion of the show.* close, completion, end, ending, finish, termination. OPPOSITE start. **2** *The researcher announced his conclusions.* decision, deduction, finding, inference, judgement, verdict.

conclusive *adjective conclusive evidence.* absolute, convincing, decisive, definitive, incontrovertible, indisputable, unequivocal. OPPOSITE inconclusive.

concoct *verb He concocted a good story.* cook up, create, devise, fabricate, invent, make up, put together, think up.

concoction *noun The dessert was a delicious concoction of fruit and cream.* blend, confection, creation, mixture, preparation.

concord *noun living in concord.* accord, agreement, harmony, peace, unity. OPPOSITE discord, strife.

concrete *adjective concrete evidence.* actual, definite, factual, material, objective, palpable, physical, real, solid, specific, substantial, tangible. OPPOSITE abstract.

concur *verb* see AGREE.

concurrent *adjective concurrent events.* coexistent, coincident, parallel, simultaneous.

condemn *verb* **1** *She condemned them for their destructive behaviour.* blame, censure, criticise, denounce, disapprove of, rebuke. OPPOSITE praise. **2** *The judge condemned him.* convict, declare guilty, sentence. OPPOSITE acquit.

condense *verb* **1** *He condensed the pan juices to make a sauce.* boil down, concentrate, reduce, thicken. **2** *He condensed his speech.* abbreviate, abridge, compress, cut, précis, reduce, shorten, summarise. OPPOSITE lengthen.

condescending *adjective a condescending person.* disdainful, haughty, high and mighty, hoity-toity, patronising, snobbish, snooty (*informal*), supercilious, superior. OPPOSITE humble.

condition *noun* **1** *He sold the car in good condition.* nick (*informal*), order, repair, shape, state. **2** *The runner was in fine condition.* fettle, fitness, form, health, shape, trim. **3** *She has a heart condition.* affliction, ailment, complaint, disease, disorder, illness, malady, problem. **4** *The contract specified certain conditions.* prerequisite, provision, proviso, qualification, requirement, stipulation, term. — *verb He was conditioned to respond to the bell.* accustom, teach, train. □ **conditions** *plural noun Working conditions are good.* circumstances, environment, situation, surroundings.

condolence *noun He offered his condolences to the widow.* commiseration, pity, sympathy.

condone *verb They cannot condone stealing.* connive at, disregard, forgive, ignore, overlook, tolerate, turn a blind eye to.

conduct *verb* **1** *She conducted them to their seats.* direct, escort, guide, lead, pilot, show, steer, take, usher. **2** *She conducted the meeting.* be in charge of, chair, direct, lead, preside over. **3** *He conducts the business from home.* administer, carry on, control, direct, manage, operate, organise, run. — *noun an award for good conduct.* actions, behaviour, deportment, manners. □ **conduct yourself** *He knew how to conduct himself in public.* acquit yourself, act, behave.

conductor *noun an orchestral conductor.* director, maestro.

confer *verb* **1** *The degree was conferred the following year.* award, bestow, give, grant, present. **2** *She conferred with the others.* consult, converse, discuss, speak, talk.

conference *noun the annual dental conference.* assembly, congress, convention, forum, gathering, meeting, symposium.

confess *verb He confessed that he had smashed the window.* acknowledge, admit, declare, disclose, own up. OPPOSITE conceal, deny.

confide *verb She confided her secret to her friend.* confess, disclose, divulge, impart, tell, trust.

confidence *noun* **1** *He has confidence in his staff.* belief, faith, reliance, trust. OPPOSITE mistrust. **2** *She went into the exam with confidence.* aplomb, boldness, coolness, courage, self-assurance, self-confidence, self-reliance. OPPOSITE diffidence. **3** *She said it with such confidence.* assurance, authority, certainty, certitude, conviction. OPPOSITE uncertainty. □ **confidence trick** see CON.

confident *adjective* **1** *They were confident about the outcome.* certain, positive, sure. OPPOSITE unsure. **2** *a confident player.* bold, cocksure, daring, fearless, self-assured, self-confident. OPPOSITE diffident.

confidential *adjective The information is confidential.* classified, hush-hush (*informal*), intimate, off the record, personal, private, secret. OPPOSITE public.

confine *verb* **1** *The problem was confined to a small area.* contain, keep, limit, localise, restrict. **2** *The animals are confined in cages.* box in, coop up, enclose, hold captive, imprison, intern, jail, keep, lock up, pen, shut in, shut up. OPPOSITE let loose.

confirm *verb Others confirmed what the boy said.* attest to, authenticate, back up, bear out, corroborate, establish, prove, reinforce, substantiate, support, validate, verify, witness to. OPPOSITE contradict, disprove.

confirmed *adjective a confirmed vegetarian.* dyed-in-the-wool, established, habitual, inveterate, seasoned.

confiscate *verb She confiscated the comics.* appropriate, commandeer, impound, seize, take away.

conflict *noun* **1** *Lives were lost in the conflict.* action, battle, clash, combat, encounter, engagement, fight, fray, strife, struggle, war. **2** *a conflict of interests.* clash, difference, divergence. OPPOSITE harmony. **3** *Their different beliefs caused conflict.* antagonism, confrontation, contention, disagreement, discord, dispute, dissension, friction, hostility, opposition, strife. — *verb His story conflicts with theirs.* be at odds, be at variance, be incompatible, clash, contradict, differ, disagree, diverge. OPPOSITE agree.

conform *verb She refuses to conform.* comply, fit in, toe the line (*informal*). OPPOSITE rebel. □ **conform to** **1** *He won't conform to the rules.* abide by, comply with, follow, keep to, obey, submit to. OPPOSITE disobey. **2** *The box does not conform to the standard measurements.* accord with, coincide with, comply with, correspond to, fit, match. OPPOSITE differ from.

conformity *noun Their procedures are in conformity with the standards.* accord, accordance, agreement, compliance, harmony, keeping.

confound *verb She was confounded by the strange events.* astonish, astound, baffle, bewilder, confuse, disconcert, flummox (*informal*), mystify, nonplus, perplex, puzzle, surprise.

confront *verb* **1** *They confronted many problems.* encounter, face, meet. **2** *He confronted his rival.* accost, brave, challenge, defy, face up to, oppose, stand up to, take on. OPPOSITE avoid.

confuse *verb* **1** *He confused the socks in the drawer.* jumble, mix up, muddle, scramble. OPPOSITE sort out. **2** *The changes confused her.* baffle, bewilder, confound, disconcert, disorientate, flummox (*informal*), fluster, mislead, mix up, mystify, nonplus, perplex, puzzle, rattle (*informal*). **3** *She confused her with someone else.* mistake, mix up, muddle. OPPOSITE distinguish.

confused *adjective* **1** *The man was confused.* baffled, bemused, bewildered, bushed (*Australian informal*), disoriented, flummoxed (*informal*), flustered, hazy, mixed-up, muddled, perplexed. OPPOSITE lucid. **2** *a confused account of what happened.* chaotic, disorganised, garbled, higgledy-piggledy, incoherent, jumbled, messy, muddled, topsy-turvy, unclear, vague. OPPOSITE clear.

confusion *noun* **1** *a scene of confusion.* anarchy, bedlam, chaos, commotion, disorder, disorganisation, havoc, jumble, mayhem, mess, muddle, pandemonium, riot, shambles, tumult, turmoil, upheaval, uproar. OPPOSITE order. **2** *Labels will eliminate confusion.* misunderstanding, mix-up, muddle.

congeal *adjective The sauce congealed on the plate.* coagulate, set, solidify, thicken.

congenial *adjective a congenial travelling companion.* agreeable, amiable, compatible, friendly, genial, nice, pleasant, sympathetic.

congenital *adjective a congenital defect.* inborn, innate.

congested *adjective* **1** *The roads were congested.* blocked, chock-a-block, choked, crowded, jammed, overcrowded, packed. OPPOSITE empty. **2** *Her nose was congested.* blocked, clogged up, stuffed up. OPPOSITE clear.

congratulate *verb He congratulated the winner.* applaud, commend, compliment, praise.

congratulations *plural noun Congratulations on your birthday.* compliments, felicitations, good wishes, greetings.

congregate *verb The people congregated at the entrance.* assemble, cluster, collect, converge, crowd, flock, gather, group, herd, huddle, mass, meet, muster, rally, swarm, throng. OPPOSITE disperse.

congregation *noun The minister spoke to his congregation.* flock, parishioners.

congress *noun He attended the annual congress of church leaders.* assembly, conference, convention, council, gathering, meeting, symposium, synod.

congruence *noun an amazing congruence of opinions.* accord, agreement, coincidence, conformity, consistency, correspondence. OPPOSITE divergence.

conjecture *verb He conjectured that she would be late.* guess, hypothesise, speculate, suppose, surmise, suspect, theorise. — *noun His conjecture proved to be correct.* assumption, guess, hunch, hypothesis, speculation, supposition, surmise, suspicion, theory.

conjure *verb* **conjure up** *Hearing his story conjured up happy holiday memories.* bring to mind, call up, evoke, produce.

conjuring *noun a performer skilled at conjuring.* legerdemain, magic, sleight of hand, tricks.

conjuror *noun The conjuror performed many tricks.* illusionist, magician.

connect *verb* **1** *She connected the ends.* attach, couple, fasten, hitch, interlock, join, link, secure, tie, unite. OPPOSITE disconnect. **2** *He connected the two ideas.* associate, bracket together, correlate, link, relate. OPPOSITE separate.

connection *noun* **1** *a faulty connection.* bond, hook-up, join, joint, junction, link. **2** *a connection between the two events.* association, correlation, correspondence, interconnection, link, relation, relationship, tie-up.

connive *verb* **connive at** *He connived at their eating in the library.* condone, ignore, overlook, turn a blind eye to, wink at.

connoisseur *noun a wine connoisseur.* authority, buff (*informal*), expert, specialist.

conquer *verb* **1** *They conquered the enemy.* beat, crush, defeat, get the better of, lick (*informal*), master, overcome, overpower, overthrow, prevail over, rout, stonker (*Australian slang*), subdue, subjugate, thrash, triumph over, trounce, vanquish. OPPOSITE surrender to. **2** *She conquered her disability.* overcome, rise above, surmount. OPPOSITE give in to.

conqueror *noun William the Conqueror.* champion, vanquisher, victor, winner. OPPOSITE loser.

conquest *noun the conquest of a country.* annexation, capture, defeat, invasion, occupation, subjugation, takeover. OPPOSITE surrender.

conscience *noun You must vote according to your conscience.* ethics, morals, principles, scruples.

conscientious *adjective a conscientious worker.* careful, dedicated, diligent, dutiful, hard-working, honest, meticulous, painstaking, particular, punctilious, responsible, rigorous, scrupulous, thorough. OPPOSITE careless.

conscious *adjective* **1** *The patient was conscious.* alert, awake, aware. OPPOSITE unconscious. **2** *a conscious insult.* calculated, deliberate, intended, intentional, premeditated, studied, wilful. OPPOSITE unintentional.

conscript *verb Her father had been conscripted to serve in Vietnam.* call up, draft (*American*). OPPOSITE volunteer.

consecrate *verb The building was consecrated to God.* bless, dedicate, hallow, sanctify.

consecutive *adjective five consecutive wins.* in a row, straight, successive, uninterrupted.

consensus *noun a consensus of opinion.* agreement, harmony, unanimity. OPPOSITE divergence.

consent *verb* **consent to** *They consented to his marrying their daughter.* accede to, acquiesce in, agree to, allow, approve, authorise, concur with, permit. OPPOSITE refuse. — *noun He signed the form to give his consent.* acceptance, acquiescence, agreement, approval, assent, authorisation, concurrence, endorsement, go-ahead, leave, OK (*informal*), permission, sanction. OPPOSITE refusal.

consequence *noun* **1** *The consequences of his mistake were felt for a long time.* aftermath, effect, outcome, ramification, repercussion, result, sequel, upshot. OPPOSITE cause. **2** *The matter is of no consequence.* account, gravity, import, importance, moment, seriousness, significance. OPPOSITE unimportance.

consequent *adjective the consequent damage.* consequential, ensuing, following, resultant, resulting.

consequently *adverb The car broke down. Consequently he arrived late.* accordingly, as a result, hence, so, therefore, thus.

conservation *noun conservation of the environment.* maintenance, preservation, protection, safe keeping, saving. OPPOSITE destruction.

conservationist *noun* environmentalist, green (*informal*), greenie (*Australian informal*), preservationist.

conservative *adjective* **1** *a conservative attitude.* conventional, hidebound, middle-of-the-road, old-fashioned, orthodox, reactionary, traditional. OPPOSITE progressive. **2** *a conservative estimate.* cautious, low, moderate, understated. OPPOSITE excessive.

conservatory *noun a tropical conservatory.* glasshouse, greenhouse, hothouse.

conserve *verb They tried to conserve their supplies.* hold on to, husband, keep, maintain, preserve, save. OPPOSITE waste. — *noun apricot conserve.* jam, jelly, preserve.

consider *verb* **1** *They considered the merits of the case.* contemplate, deliberate over, examine, look at, meditate on, mull over, ponder, reflect on, ruminate over, study, think about, weigh. **2** *You must consider people's feelings.* allow for, bear in mind, pay heed to, respect, take into account. OPPOSITE disregard. **3** *She considered herself lucky.* believe, deem, judge, rate, reckon, regard, think.

considerable *adjective a considerable amount.* appreciable, big, decent, extensive, fair, goodly, large, noticeable, respectable, significant, sizeable, substantial, tidy (*informal*). OPPOSITE slight.

considerate *adjective A considerate guest helps the host.* attentive, helpful, kind, neighbourly, obliging, polite, sensitive, solicitous, thoughtful, unselfish. OPPOSITE inconsiderate, thoughtless.

consignment *noun a consignment of books.* batch, cargo, delivery, load, shipment.

consist *verb* **consist of** *The flat consists of three rooms.* be composed of, comprise, contain, include.

consistency *noun the consistency of whipped cream.* density, firmness, solidity, stiffness, texture, thickness, viscosity.

consistent *adjective* **1** *The quality is consistent.* constant, dependable, invariable, predictable, reliable, stable, steady, unchanging, uniform. OPPOSITE variable. **2** *Her version was consistent with his.* compatible, corresponding, in accordance, in agreement, in keeping. OPPOSITE inconsistent.

console *verb He consoled the losers with a small gift.* cheer, comfort, encourage, relieve, solace, soothe. OPPOSITE upset.

consolidate *verb* **1** *He consolidated his position as leader.* fortify, reinforce, strengthen. OPPOSITE weaken. **2** *The two schools were consolidated to form one for the area.* amalgamate, combine, incorporate, join, merge, unite. OPPOSITE separate.

conspicuous *adjective* **1** *a conspicuous building.* impressive, noticeable, obtrusive, ostentatious, prominent, showy, striking, visible. OPPOSITE inconspicuous. **2** *a conspicuous mistake.* apparent, blatant, clear, evident, flagrant, glaring, manifest, obvious, patent, pronounced, unconcealed. OPPOSITE hidden. **3** *conspicuous bravery.* distinguished, notable, outstanding, remarkable.

conspiracy *noun a conspiracy to blow up the building.* collusion, intrigue, plot, scheme.

conspire *verb They conspired to overthrow the government.* collaborate, collude, connive, intrigue, plot, scheme.

constant *adjective* **1** *constant problems.* ceaseless, chronic, continual, continuous, endless, everlasting, incessant, never-ending, non-stop, perennial, permanent, perpetual, persistent, regular, repeated, unending. OPPOSITE occasional. **2** *a constant friend.* dependable, devoted, faithful, firm, loyal, reliable, steadfast, true, trustworthy. OPPOSITE fickle. **3** *a constant speed.* even, fixed, invariable, level, stable, steady, unchanging, uniform, unvarying. OPPOSITE variable.

consternation *noun To his consternation he found himself stranded on a rock.* alarm, anxiety, dismay, fear, panic, shock, terror.

constituent *noun He analysed the substance into its constituents.* component, element, ingredient, material, part, unit.

constitute *verb Twelve months constitute a year.* compose, form, make up.

constitution *noun* **1** *a society's constitution.* charter, laws, principles, rules. **2** *She has a strong constitution.* health, physique. **3** *The constitution of the burgers is a secret.* composition, make-up, structure.

constrain *verb* **1** *He was constrained to remain silent.* bind, compel, force, make, oblige, press, pressure, urge. **2** *The research was constrained by a lack of funds.* curb, hamper, hamstring, hinder, impede, limit, restrict.

constraint *noun* **1** *He acted under constraint rather than from choice.* compulsion, force, obligation, pressure. **2** *financial constraints.* check, curb, limitation, restriction.

constrict *verb Her shoes constrict her feet painfully.* compress, cramp, pinch, squeeze.

construct *verb The builders constructed the house in a month.* assemble, build, create, erect, fabricate, fashion, form, make, manufacture, produce, put up. OPPOSITE demolish, destroy.

construction *noun a concrete construction.* building, edifice, structure.

constructive *adjective constructive criticism.* beneficial, helpful, positive, practical, productive, useful, valuable. OPPOSITE destructive.

consult *verb He consulted his lawyer.* confer with, discuss with, refer to, seek advice from, speak to, talk with.

consultant *noun a financial consultant.* adviser, expert, specialist.

consultation *noun The members held a consultation over the matter.* conference, discussion, hearing, interview, meeting, talk.

consume *verb* **1** *He consumed all their supper.* devour, eat up, gobble up, guzzle, knock back, swallow. **2** *Writing letters consumed her time.* eat into, take up, use up. **3** *Their supplies were consumed in no time.* deplete, drain, exhaust, expend, use up, utilise. **4** *Fire consumed the building.* burn, demolish, destroy, devastate, gut, ravage, raze.

consumer *noun Manufacturers need feedback from consumers.* buyer, client, customer, end-user, patron, purchaser, user.

consumption *noun petrol consumption.* use, utilisation.

contact *noun* **1** *The two surfaces must be in contact.* connection, touch. **2** *There is no contact between the two groups.* communication, liaison. — *verb He tried to contact his friend.* communicate with, correspond with, get hold of, get in touch with, reach, speak to, talk to, write to.

contagious *adjective a contagious disease.* catching, communicable, infectious, transmittable.

contain *verb* **1** *The box contains jewels.* enclose, hold, house. **2** *The cake contains butter and eggs.* be composed of, consist of, include, incorporate. **3** *Try to contain your laughter.* control, curb, hold back, keep in, repress, restrain, stifle, suppress. OPPOSITE vent.

container *noun It all fitted in the container.* holder, receptacle, repository, vessel; [*various containers*] bag, barrel, basket, bin, bottle, box, bucket, caddy, can, canister, carton, cartridge, case, cask, casket, chest, coffer, crate, cup, dish, drum, jar, keg, packet, pot, pouch, punnet, sachet, sack, skip, tank, tin, trunk, tub, vat.

contaminate *verb The water was contaminated by the chemicals.* adulterate, defile, foul, infect, poison, pollute, spoil, taint. OPPOSITE purify.

contemplate *verb* **1** *He contemplated the scene.* eye, gaze at, look at, observe, regard, stare at, study, survey, view, watch. **2** *She contemplated her next step.* cogitate on, consider, deliberate over, meditate on, mull over, ponder, reflect on, ruminate on, think over. **3** *He did not contemplate marriage.* envisage, have in mind, intend, plan.

contemporary *adjective contemporary designs.* current, latest, modern, new, present-day, recent, trendy (*informal*), up-to-date, up-to-the-minute. OPPOSITE old-fashioned.

contempt *noun He treated the visitor with contempt.* disdain, disgust, dislike, disrespect, hatred, loathing, scorn. OPPOSITE respect.

contemptible *adjective a contemptible scoundrel.* abominable, base, dastardly, despicable, detestable, hateful, loathsome, low, mean, miserable, odious, pitiful, shabby, shameful, vile, worthless. OPPOSITE honourable.

contemptuous *adjective She gave the others a contemptuous look.* derisive, disdainful, haughty, insolent, scornful, sneering, snooty (*informal*), supercilious. OPPOSITE respectful.

contend *verb* **1** *Two teams contended for the trophy.* battle, clash, compete, contest, fight, strive, struggle, vie. **2** *He contends that he is innocent.* allege, argue, assert, claim, declare, insist, maintain. □ **contend with** *He has to contend with many problems.* cope with, deal with, face, grapple with, tackle.

content[1] *adjective She is content with what she has.* contented, fulfilled, gratified, happy, pleased, satisfied. OPPOSITE discontented. — *verb Nothing seems to content him.* gratify, please, satisfy.

content[2] *noun The essay is marked on form and content.* gist, material, matter, substance. □ **contents** *plural noun The contents are listed on the back of the packet.* components, constituents, content, elements, ingredients, parts.

contest *noun a close contest.* battle, bout, challenge, championship, combat, competition, conflict, duel, fight, game, match, race, rally, struggle, tournament. — *verb* **1** *Five people contested the seat.* battle for, compete for, contend for, fight for, struggle for, vie for. **2** *He will contest the point.* argue, challenge, debate, dispute, question. OPPOSITE accept.

contestant *noun There were ten contestants in the competition.* candidate, challenger, competitor, contender, entrant, opponent, participant, player, rival.

context *noun This event must be seen in its social context.* background, circumstances, environment, setting, situation, surroundings.

continual *adjective their continual arguments.* constant, endless, everlasting, frequent, habitual, incessant, perpetual, persistent, recurrent, regular, repeated. OPPOSITE occasional.

continuation *noun the continuation of the story.* extension, postscript, resumption, sequel, supplement.

continue *verb* **1** *They continued with the treatment.* carry on, keep going, keep on, persevere, persist, proceed. OPPOSITE discontinue, stop. **2** *He continued as captain.* keep on, remain, stay, survive. **3** *The dry weather continued.* endure, go on, hold, last, persist. OPPOSITE cease. **4** *They continued the story after the break.* pick up, recommence, resume, take up. OPPOSITE break off. **5** *They continued the contract.* extend, maintain, prolong, protract, renew. OPPOSITE terminate.

continuous *adjective* **1** *a continuous line.* connected, unbroken. OPPOSITE broken. **2** *continuous rain.* ceaseless, constant, endless, everlasting, incessant, interminable, never-ending, non-stop, permanent, perpetual, persistent, relentless, solid, steady, unceasing, uninterrupted, unrelieved. OPPOSITE intermittent.

contorted *adjective a contorted body.* bent, deformed, misshapen, twisted, wry.

contour *noun the contours of her body.* form, lines, outline, profile, shape.

contract *noun They signed the contract.* agreement, bargain, bond, charter, compact, covenant, deal, deed, pact, policy, treaty, understanding, undertaking. — *verb* **1** *The metal contracted as it cooled.* become smaller, shrink. OPPOSITE expand. **2** *The muscle contracted.* tense, tighten. OPPOSITE relax. **3** *She contracted to do the work at home.* agree, arrange, negotiate, undertake. **4** *He contracted bronchitis.* acquire, catch, come down with, develop, get, pick up.

contradict *verb She contradicted what he said.* counter, deny, gainsay (*formal*), oppose. OPPOSITE agree with, back up.

contradictory *adjective contradictory explanations.* conflicting, incompatible, inconsistent, irreconcilable, opposing. OPPOSITE consistent.

contraption *noun* (*informal*) *He invented a new kitchen contraption.* apparatus, appliance, device, gadget, gizmo (*informal*), implement, machine, tool.

contrary *adjective* **1** *the contrary view.* conflicting, contradictory, converse, opposing, opposite. OPPOSITE same. **2** *a contrary child.* cantankerous, defiant, disobedient, headstrong, intractable, obstinate, perverse, pigheaded, rebellious, recalcitrant, refractory, stroppy (*informal*), stubborn, unreasonable, wayward, wilful. OPPOSITE biddable. — *noun The contrary is true.* antithesis, converse, opposite, reverse.

contrast *noun* **1** *a contrast of the two poems.* comparison. **2** *a marked contrast in their attitudes.* difference, disparity, dissimilarity, distinction. OPPOSITE similarity. — *verb* **1** *He contrasted their styles.* compare, differentiate, distinguish, set against each other. **2** *Her ideas contrasted with theirs.* differ (from), disagree. OPPOSITE resemble.

contribute *verb Everyone contributed money for the present.* chip in (*informal*), donate, fork out (*slang*), give, pitch in (*informal*), provide, put in, subscribe, supply. □ **contribute to** *Good teaching contributed to his success.* advance, have a hand in, lead to, play a part in, promote.

contribution *noun a financial contribution.* donation, gift, grant, handout, help, input, offering, offertory, subscription.

contrite *adjective a contrite sinner.* penitent, regretful, remorseful, repentant, sorry. OPPOSITE unrepentant.

contrive *verb He contrived a meeting between them.* arrange, engineer, manage, plan, plot, scheme, wangle (*slang*).

control *noun* **1** *He has control of his class. The company is under overseas control.* authority, charge, command, direction, domination, influence, jurisdiction, leadership, management, mastery, power, rule, supervision, sway. **2** *the machine's controls.* button, dial, instrument, joystick, knob, lever, switch. — *verb* **1** *She controls the organisation.* administer, command, direct, dominate, govern, head, lead, manage, oversee, preside over, rule, supervise. **2** *He controls the machine.* handle, manage, manipulate, operate, regulate. **3** *He could not control his temper.* bridle, check, contain, curb, hold back, master, repress, restrain, subdue. OPPOSITE unleash.

controversial *adjective Climate change is a controversial subject.* contentious, debatable, disputable, moot.

controversy *noun His actions sparked off a controversy.* argument, debate, disagreement, dispute, quarrel, row (*informal*), wrangle.

convalesce *verb She convalesced in a nursing home.* get better, improve, mend, recover, recuperate.

convenient *adjective* **1** *a convenient arrangement.* handy, helpful, practical, suitable, timely, useful, well-timed. OPPOSITE inconvenient. **2** *a convenient set of shops.* accessible, handy, nearby. OPPOSITE inaccessible.

convent *noun The nuns live in a convent.* abbey, cloister, nunnery, priory, religious community.

convention *noun* **1** *She attended the annual convention.* assembly, conference, congress, council, gathering, jamboree, meeting, rally, synod. **2** *He did not follow social conventions.* custom, etiquette, formality, practice, protocol, rule, tradition.

conventional *adjective conventional methods.* accepted, accustomed, customary, established, mainstream, normal, ordinary, orthodox, regular, standard, traditional, usual. OPPOSITE unconventional.

converge *verb Five roads converge at the roundabout.* come together, intersect, join, meet, merge. OPPOSITE diverge, radiate.

conversation noun *They had a long conversation on the phone.* chat, chatter, chinwag (*informal*), confabulation, dialogue, discourse, discussion, gossip, natter (*informal*), talk, tête-à-tête, yabber (*Australian informal*), yak (*informal*).

converse verb *They conversed for hours.* chat, chatter, gossip, natter (*informal*), prattle, speak, talk, yabber (*Australian informal*), yak (*informal*). — noun *The converse of her statement is true.* antithesis, contrary, opposite, reverse.

convert verb *He converted the sofa into a bed.* adapt, change, modify, switch, transform, turn.

convey verb **1** *The truck conveys army supplies.* bear, bring, carry, deliver, fetch, haul, shift, take, transfer, transport. **2** *The wires convey electricity.* carry, conduct, transmit. **3** *The writer conveyed his message clearly.* communicate, impart, make known, put across, tell.

convict verb *She was convicted of the crime.* condemn, declare guilty. OPPOSITE acquit. — noun *The convicts were transported to Australia.* criminal, felon, lag (*slang*), prisoner.

conviction noun **1** *She spoke with conviction.* assurance, certainty, confidence, earnestness, fervour. OPPOSITE doubt. **2** *They do not share the same convictions.* belief, creed, faith, opinion, persuasion, tenet, view.

convince verb *She convinced the others that she was right.* assure, persuade, prove to, satisfy, sway, win over.

convinced adjective *I am not convinced that we should do this.* certain, confident, definite, positive, sure.

convincing adjective *a convincing argument.* cogent, compelling, forceful, irresistible, persuasive, powerful, sound, strong, telling.

convoy noun *a convoy of ships.* armada, company, fleet, flotilla, group.

convulsion noun *The child had a fever with convulsions.* fit, paroxysm, seizure, spasm.

cook verb *He decided to cook the dinner.* make, prepare, put together; [*various ways to cook*] bake, barbecue, boil, braise, broil, casserole, flambé, fry, grill, parboil, poach, roast, sauté, simmer, steam, stew, toast. — noun *He works as a cook.* chef. □ **cook up** *She cooked up an excuse.* concoct, devise, fabricate, invent, make up, plan, plot.

cookery noun *French cookery.* cooking, cuisine.

cool adjective **1** *cool weather.* chilly, cold, nippy (*informal*). OPPOSITE warm. **2** *She remains cool in a crisis.* calm, collected, composed, laidback (*informal*), level-headed, nonchalant, relaxed, sedate, self-possessed, serene, unemotional, unexcited, unflappable (*informal*), unflustered, unruffled. OPPOSITE excited. **3** *She received a cool reception.* cold, frosty, half-hearted, hostile, icy, indifferent, lukewarm, offhand, unenthusiastic, unfriendly, unwelcoming. OPPOSITE friendly, warm. **4** (*informal*) *The party was cool.* see EXCELLENT. **5** (*informal*) *She tries to look cool.* see TRENDY. — noun (*informal*) *He lost his cool.* calmness, composure, poise, self-control. — verb *He cooled the drinks.* chill, freeze, refrigerate. OPPOSITE heat, warm.

coop noun *a chicken coop.* cage, enclosure, pen. — verb □ **coop up** *He was cooped up in his room.* box in, cage in, confine, imprison, keep, lock up, pen in, shut up.

cooperate verb *The people cooperated with the police.* collaborate, join forces, pull together, unite, work together; see also HELP.

cooperation noun *The biography was written with the subject's cooperation.* assistance, collaboration, contribution, help, involvement, participation, support, teamwork.

cooperative adjective **1** *a cooperative person.* accommodating, helpful, obliging, willing. OPPOSITE uncooperative. **2** *a cooperative venture.* collaborative, combined, joint. OPPOSITE individual.

coordinate verb *The leader coordinates the work of the various groups.* integrate, orchestrate, organise, synchronise.

coordinator noun *a project coordinator.* controller, director, manager, organiser.

cope verb **cope with** *He copes with all sorts of problems.* contend with, deal with, endure, face, handle, manage, withstand.

copious adjective *copious supplies.* abundant, ample, bountiful, generous, lavish, liberal, plentiful, profuse. OPPOSITE sparse.

copy noun *He could not distinguish the copy from the original.* carbon copy, counterfeit, double, duplicate, facsimile, fake, forgery, imitation, likeness, photocopy, print, replica, reproduction, twin. OPPOSITE original. — verb **1** *He copied the document.* duplicate, forge, photocopy, print, reproduce. **2** *The student copied his friend's essay.* crib, plagiarise. **3** *The actor copies people's mannerisms.* ape, imitate, mimic, parody, take off (*informal*).

cord noun *The parcel was tied with cord.* cable, lace, line, rope, string, twine.

cordial adjective *a cordial welcome.* affable, amiable, amicable, friendly, genial, heartfelt, kind, sincere, warm. OPPOSITE unfriendly.

cordon noun *a police cordon around the house.* chain, circle, line, ring. — verb **cordon off** *The police cordoned off the area.* close off, enclose, seal off, shut off, surround.

core noun **1** *the core of an object.* centre, heart, inside, middle. **2** *the core of the problem.* centre, crux, essence, gist, heart, kernel, nitty-gritty (*informal*), nub, nucleus.

cork noun *He closed the cask with a cork.* bung, plug, stopper.

corkscrew noun *The road into the valley was a corkscrew.* helix, spiral.

corner noun **1** *the corners of a room.* angle. **2** *The car approached the corner.* bend, crossroads, curve, intersection, junction, turn. — verb **1** *They cornered him in the shop.* bail up (*Australian*), buttonhole, capture, catch, trap. **2** *He has cornered the market.* control, dominate, monopolise.

corny adjective **1** *a corny joke.* banal, feeble, hackneyed, outworn, trite, weak. **2** *a corny film.* mawkish, old-fashioned, over-sentimental, schmaltzy, soppy (*informal*).

corollary noun *Job losses were the corollary of expenditure cuts.* consequence, effect, result, upshot.

coronation noun crowning, enthronement.

corporal adjective *corporal punishment.* bodily, physical.

corporation noun **1** *a business corporation.* company, firm, organisation. **2** *a municipal corporation.* council.

corpse noun *The corpse was buried.* body, cadaver, carcass, remains.

correct adjective **1** *His answer was correct.* accurate, exact, faultless, flawless, perfect, precise, proper, right, spot on (*informal*), true. OPPOSITE incorrect, wrong. **2** *correct behaviour.* acceptable, appropriate, conventional, decent, decorous, fitting, impeccable, proper, right, seemly, suitable. OPPOSITE improper. — verb **1** *The fault can be corrected.* cure, fix, mend, put right, rectify, remedy, repair. **2** *He corrected the draft.* adjust, alter, amend, improve, revise. **3** *The teacher corrected their work.* assess, check, mark. **4** *She was always correcting her child.* admonish, censure, chasten, chastise, discipline, rebuke, reprimand, reprove, scold.

correlation noun *a correlation between the crime and unemployment figures.* connection, correspondence, interdependence, link, relationship, tie-up.

correspond verb **1** *This information corresponds with what I'd previously heard.* accord, agree, be consistent, coincide, concur, conform, fit, match, square, tally. OPPOSITE disagree. **2** *They corresponded regularly.* communicate, exchange letters, keep in touch, send letters, write.

correspondence noun *She answers her correspondence promptly.* communications, letters, mail, messages.

correspondent noun *the newspaper's European correspondent.* journalist, reporter, writer.

corresponding adjective *corresponding positions.* analogous, equivalent, homologous, like, matching, parallel, similar.

corridor noun *We met in the corridor.* hall, hallway, lobby, passage, passageway.

corroborate verb *He corroborated the other man's account.* back up, bear out, confirm, substantiate, support, validate, verify. OPPOSITE disprove.

corrode verb *The car was corroded by rust.* consume, destroy, eat away, erode, oxidise, rot, rust, wear away.

corrugated adjective *corrugated cardboard.* fluted, furrowed, grooved, ribbed, ridged, wrinkled. OPPOSITE flat.

corrupt adjective **1** *a corrupt official.* bent (*slang*), crooked, dishonest, fraudulent, shady, shonky (*Australian informal*), unscrupulous, venal. OPPOSITE honest. **2** *He was leading a corrupt life.* decadent, degenerate, depraved, dissolute, evil, immoral, iniquitous, perverted, sinful, wicked. OPPOSITE moral. — verb **1** *He tried to corrupt the official.* bribe, buy off, influence, lead astray, pervert, tempt. **2** *The text was corrupted by a careless scribe.* alter, spoil, tamper with, vitiate.

corruption noun *police corruption, moral corruption.* bribery, decadence, degeneracy, depravity, dishonesty, fraud, graft, immorality, perversion, sinfulness, unscrupulousness, venality, vice, wickedness. OPPOSITE honesty, morality.

cortège noun *a funeral cortège.* procession, train.

cosmetics plural noun beauty products, make-up.

cosmonaut noun *a Russian cosmonaut.* astronaut, space traveller.

cosmopolitan adjective **1** *a cosmopolitan city.* international, multicultural, multiracial. **2** *a cosmopolitan outlook.* broad-minded, liberal, sophisticated, urbane, worldly. OPPOSITE parochial.

cosmos noun universe, world.

cost noun *He cannot meet the cost.* charge, expenditure, expense, fare, fee, outlay, overheads, payment, price, rate, tariff, toll. — verb **1** *The book costs $30.* be priced at, be worth, fetch, sell for. **2** *She costed the holiday at $1000.* estimate, price, value.

costly adjective *costly presents.* dear, exorbitant, expensive, extravagant, precious, pricey (*informal*), valuable. OPPOSITE cheap.

costume noun **1** *ceremonial costume.* apparel (*formal*), attire (*formal*), clothes, clothing, dress, garb, garments, gear (*informal*), livery, outfit, raiment, regalia, uniform, vestments. **2** *a swimming costume.* suit.

cosy adjective *a cosy house.* comfortable, comfy (*informal*), friendly, homely, relaxing, secure, snug, warm. OPPOSITE uncomfortable.

cot noun *a baby's cot.* cradle, crib.

cottage noun *a holiday cottage.* cabin, chalet, hut, lodge, shack, weekender (*Australian*); see also HOUSE.

couch noun *He reclined on the couch.* chaise longue, chesterfield, divan, ottoman, settee, sofa.

council noun **1** *the school council, the council of elders.* assembly, board, committee, conference, congress, synod. **2** *a municipal council.* corporation.

counsel noun *He was given wise counsel.* advice, direction, guidance. — verb *His job is to counsel students on careers.* advise, direct, guide.

counsellor noun *a careers counsellor.* adviser, guide, mentor.

count¹ verb **1** *She counted the items.* add up, calculate, compute, enumerate, number, sum up, tally, total, tot up (*informal*). **2** *He did not count the visitors in his calculations.* consider, include, reckon with, take into account. OPPOSITE exclude. **3** *Looks don't count.* be important, carry weight, matter, rate highly, signify. **4** *He counted it an honour.* consider, deem, judge, look upon, rate, reckon, regard, think. — noun **1** *an official count.* census, poll, stocktaking. **2** *The final count was 500.* aggregate, amount, figure, number, reckoning, tally, total. **3** *He was found guilty on four counts.* charge, point. □ **count on** *She counted on their support.* assume, bank on, depend on, expect, reckon on, rely on.

count² noun see NOBLEMAN.

counter¹ noun **1** *a shop counter.* bar, checkout, stand. **2** *The game uses counters.* chip, disc, piece, token.

counter² verb **1** *She countered his statement with the facts.* contradict, negate, oppose, rebut. **2** *He learned to counter in boxing.* counter-attack, fight back, hit back, parry, retaliate.

counteract verb *The drug will counteract the effect of the poison.* cancel out, counter, counterbalance, negate, neutralise, offset, oppose, undo. OPPOSITE reinforce.

counterfeit adjective *a counterfeit note.* bogus, dud (*informal*), fake, forged, imitation, phoney (*informal*), sham, spurious. OPPOSITE genuine. — verb *They counterfeited $50 notes.* copy, fake, forge, imitate, reproduce.

counterpart noun *She spoke to her counterpart in the other office.* equivalent, opposite number.

countess noun see NOBLEWOMAN.

countless adjective *They met on countless occasions.* endless, frequent, incalculable, innumerable, many, myriad, numerous. OPPOSITE few.

country noun **1** *He rules the country.* commonwealth, democracy, duchy, emirate, kingdom, land, monarchy, nation, principality, realm, republic, state, territory. **2** *Forty per cent of the country voted for him.* citizens, community, inhabitants, nation, people, populace, population, public. **3** *They left the city to live in the country.* backblocks (*Australian*), backwoods, bush (*Australian*), inland, interior, outback (*Australian*), rural district, sticks (*informal*). OPPOSITE city, town. **4** *rugged country.* countryside, land, landscape, region, scenery, terrain, territory. — *adjective country life.* agricultural, bucolic, farming, pastoral, provincial, rural, rustic. OPPOSITE urban.

countryman, countrywoman *noun* **1** *The countryman rarely visits the city.* bushie (*Australian informal*), farmer, rustic. OPPOSITE city-dweller. **2** *a fellow countryman.* compatriot.

couple *noun* **1** *a couple of birds.* brace, pair. **2** *They toasted the happy couple.* duo, pair, twosome. — *verb He coupled the cars together.* connect, fasten, hitch, join, link, tie, yoke.

coupon *noun She sent in the coupons to collect the refund.* entry form, form, ticket, token, voucher.

courage *noun The policeman showed great courage.* boldness, bottle (*slang*), bravery, daring, determination, fearlessness, fortitude, gallantry, grit, guts (*informal*), heroism, mettle, nerve, pluck, prowess, spirit, spunk (*informal*), valour. OPPOSITE cowardice.

courageous *adjective a courageous rescue worker.* bold, brave, daring, dauntless, determined, fearless, gallant, game, heroic, intrepid, lion-hearted, mettlesome, plucky, resolute, spirited, stoical, stout-hearted, unafraid, undaunted, valiant. OPPOSITE cowardly.

courier *noun The documents were brought by the courier.* carrier, dispatch rider, messenger, runner.

course *noun* **1** *in the ordinary course of events.* development, flow, march, passage, progression, succession, unfolding. **2** *The spacecraft was on course.* direction, line, orbit, path, route, track. **3** *a language course.* classes, curriculum, lessons, programme. **4** *a course of blood transfusions.* sequence, series. **5** *The cars tested out the course.* circuit, racecourse, track. □ **of course** *Of course you can.* by all means, certainly, naturally, obviously, without a doubt.

court *noun* **1** *the royal court.* attendants, courtiers (*old use*), entourage, household, retinue, train. **2** *He was summoned to appear before the court.* bar, bench, lawcourt, tribunal. — *verb He courted the lady for two years before proposing.* date (*informal*), go out with, woo (*old use*).

courteous *adjective He was brought up to be courteous.* chivalrous, civil, considerate, diplomatic, gallant, gracious, polite, proper, respectful, tactful, thoughtful, well-behaved, well-bred, well-mannered. OPPOSITE discourteous, rude.

courtesy *noun He treats everyone with courtesy.* chivalry, civility, consideration, deference, diplomacy, gallantry, good manners, politeness, respect, tact, thoughtfulness. OPPOSITE discourtesy, rudeness.

courtyard *noun The party was held in the courtyard.* court, forecourt, patio, quad (*informal*), quadrangle, yard.

cove *noun The ship sheltered in the cove.* bay, inlet.

covenant *noun He made a covenant with God.* agreement, bargain, compact, contract, deal, pact, pledge, promise, undertaking.

cover *verb* **1** *He covered the books in plastic.* encase, enclose, overlay, protect, shield, wrap. **2** *The body was covered with clothes.* attire, clothe, drape, dress, garb, swaddle, swathe, wrap. **3** *She covered the wound with gauze.* bandage, bind, dress. OPPOSITE expose. **4** *The hills are covered in mist.* blanket, blot out, bury, camouflage, cloak, cloud, conceal, envelop, hide, mask, obscure, screen, shroud, surround, veil. **5** *His shoes are covered with mud.* cake, coat, encrust, plaster, smear, spread. **6** *The forest covers a large area.* extend over, occupy, span, stretch over, take up. **7** *They covered five kilometres in an hour.* travel, traverse. **8** *This policy covers you against fire.* indemnify, insure, protect. **9** *The report covers the main issues.* deal with, encompass, include, survey, take in. OPPOSITE exclude. — *noun* **1** *a protective cover.* armour, canopy, cap, case, casing, cladding, coating, cocoon, covering, cowl, hood, housing, lid, mantle, mask, outside, overlay, pall, roof, screen, sheath, shell, shield, shroud, skin, sleeve, slip, surface, top, veneer, wrapping. **2** *a cover for a book.* binding, jacket, wrapper. **3** *a cover for papers.* binder, envelope, file, folder, portfolio. **4** *He ran for cover.* hiding place, protection, refuge, sanctuary, shelter. **5** *His business was a cover for his Resistance activities.* camouflage, disguise, façade, front, pretence, screen, smokescreen. □ **cover up** *He tried to cover up the truth.* bury, conceal, hide, hush up, suppress, whitewash. OPPOSITE expose.

covert *adjective a covert signal.* clandestine, concealed, disguised, furtive, hidden, secret, secretive, surreptitious. OPPOSITE open, overt.

covet *verb She coveted his car.* crave, desire, fancy, hanker after, long for, want, yearn for.

covetous *adjective covetous of his neighbour's car.* avaricious, desirous, envious, grasping, greedy. OPPOSITE content.

coward *noun He was a coward in the face of danger.* baby, chicken (*informal*), cry-baby, scaredy-cat (*informal*), sissy, sook (*Australian informal*), wimp (*informal*), wuss (*slang*). OPPOSITE hero.

cowardly *adjective It was cowardly to run away.* chicken-hearted, craven, dastardly, faint-hearted, fearful, gutless (*informal*), lily-livered, pusillanimous, spineless, timid, timorous, yellow (*informal*). OPPOSITE brave, heroic.

cower *verb He cowered when he saw the cane.* cringe, crouch, draw back, flinch, quail, recoil, shrink.

coy *adjective She was coy with strangers.* bashful, demure, diffident, modest, self-conscious, sheepish, shy, timid, underconfident. OPPOSITE forward.

crabby *adjective a crabby person.* bad-tempered, cantankerous, cross, crotchety, grouchy (*informal*), grumpy, irritable, maggoty (*Australian informal*), peevish, snaky (*Australian informal*), sour, sullen, surly. OPPOSITE cheerful.

crack *noun* **1** *a crack of a whip.* crackle, pop, snap. **2** *cracks in the walls. a crack in the rock.* breach, break, chink, cleft, cranny, crevasse, crevice, fissure, fracture, gap, hole, hollow, opening, rift, rupture, slit, split. **3** (*informal*) *She had a crack at it.* attempt, bash (*informal*), go, shot, stab (*informal*), try, whack (*informal*). — *verb* **1** *The thunder cracked.* clap, crackle, strike. **2** *The glass cracked.* break, chip, cleave, fracture, shatter, splinter, split. **3** *She cracked the code.* break, decipher, solve, work out. **4** *He finally cracked under the strain.* break down, collapse, crack up, fall apart, give way, go to pieces.

cracked *adjective cracked skin.* broken, chapped, rough. OPPOSITE smooth.

crackle *noun The radio show was marred by crackle.* atmospherics, interference, static.

cradle *noun a baby's cradle.* basket, bassinet, cot, crib.

craft *noun* **1** *the craft of lacemaking.* art, handicraft, skill, technique, trade. **2** *travel in a craft.* aircraft, boat, raft, ship, spacecraft, vessel.

craftsman, craftswoman *noun* artisan, artist, maker, smith, technician.

craftsmanship *noun She admired the craftsmanship.* artistry, expertise, handiwork, skill, workmanship.

crafty *adjective as crafty as a fox.* artful, astute, calculating, canny, clever, cunning, deceitful, devious, foxy, guileful, knowing, machiavellian, shifty (*informal*), shrewd, sly, sneaky, subtle, tricky, underhand, wily. OPPOSITE guileless.

crag *noun The goat was perched on a crag.* bluff, cliff, precipice, rock, scarp.

cram *verb* **1** *He crammed his clothes in the case.* force, jam, pack, push, ram, squash, squeeze, stuff. **2** *The lift was crammed with people.* crowd, fill, overfill, pack. **3** *She crammed for two weeks before the exams.* revise, study, swot (*informal*).

cramp *verb Lack of money cramped his style.* hamper, hinder, impede, inhibit, limit, restrict, stunt, thwart.

cramped *adjective* **1** *cramped living conditions.* confined, crowded, narrow, poky, tight. OPPOSITE spacious. **2** *cramped writing.* crabbed, illegible, small.

crane *noun A crane is used for moving heavy objects.* cherry picker, davit, derrick, hoist. — *verb She craned her neck to see.* stretch.

crank *noun a health-food crank.* eccentric, fanatic, freak (*informal*), maniac, nut (*informal*), weirdo (*informal*).

cranky *adjective* **1** *She became cranky and impatient.* bad-tempered, cantankerous, crabby, cross, crotchety, grouchy (*informal*), ill-tempered, irritable, peevish, snaky (*Australian informal*), surly. OPPOSITE agreeable. **2** *He has cranky ideas.* bizarre, eccentric, odd, peculiar, quirky, strange, weird. OPPOSITE conventional.

crash *noun* **1** *They heard a loud crash.* bang, boom, clang, clangour, clank, clatter, smash, wham. **2** *a car crash.* accident, bingle (*Australian informal*), collision, pile-up (*informal*), prang (*slang*), smash. **3** *a financial crash.* collapse, failure. — *verb* **1** *The plates crashed to the floor during the earthquake.* clatter, fall, shatter, smash, topple, tumble. **2** *The thunder crashed.* bang, boom, clap, clatter, crack, peal. **3** *The car crashed into a bus.* bang, bump, knock, plough, ram, run, slam, smash; see also COLLIDE. **4** *The plane crashed into a field.* crash-land, nosedive, plummet, plunge.

crate *noun a crate of bottles.* box, carton, case, packing case, tea chest.

crater *noun moon craters. the crater of a volcano.* cavity, hole, hollow, pit.

crave *verb He craved love.* desire, hanker after, hunger for, long for, pine for, thirst for, want, wish for, yearn for. OPPOSITE spurn.

craving *noun a craving for chocolates.* desire, fancy, hankering, hunger, longing, thirst, wish, yearning, yen.

crawl *verb* **1** *She crawled under the bed.* creep, move on all fours, slither, squirm, worm your way, wriggle, writhe. **2** *The cars crawled along.* edge forward, go at a snail's pace, inch forward, move slowly. **3** (*informal*) *He was unpopular because he crawled to the teacher.* grovel, kowtow, lick someone's boots, suck up (*informal*), toady.

crawler *noun* (*informal*) *The other students despised crawlers.* flatterer, groveller, lackey, sycophant, toady, truckler, yes-man.

craze *noun iPods were the latest craze.* enthusiasm, fad, fashion, mania, obsession, passion, rage, thing (*informal*), vogue.

crazy *adjective* **1** *crazy people.* barmy (*slang*), batty (*slang*), berserk, bonkers (*slang*), crackers (*slang*), crazed, cuckoo (*informal*), daft (*informal*), demented, deranged, dotty (*informal*), flaky (*slang*), insane, loony (*informal*), loopy (*informal*), mad, mental (*informal*), nuts (*informal*), nutty (*informal*), off your head, out of your mind, potty (*informal*), round the bend (*informal*), screwy (*informal*), troppo (*Australian slang*), unbalanced, unhinged, wacky (*slang*). OPPOSITE sane. **2** *a crazy plan.* absurd, cock-eyed (*informal*), crackpot (*informal*), daft (*informal*), foolish, half-baked (*informal*), hare-brained, idiotic, impractical, imprudent, inane, lunatic, mad, outrageous, preposterous, ridiculous, senseless, silly, stupid, unwise, unworkable, zany. OPPOSITE sensible. **3** *She is crazy about tennis.* enthusiastic, fanatical, infatuated, keen, mad, nuts (*informal*), obsessed, passionate, wild.

creak *verb The door creaked.* screech, squeak.

cream *noun She applied sunburn cream.* emollient, lotion, ointment, salve.

crease *noun He smoothed out the creases.* corrugation, crinkle, crumple, fold, furrow, groove, line, pucker, ridge, ruck, wrinkle. — *verb He creased the paper.* crimp, crinkle, crumple, fold, furrow, pleat, pucker, ruck, rumple, wrinkle. OPPOSITE smooth.

create *verb* **1** *He created a masterpiece.* bring into being, compose, conceive, construct, design, devise, fashion, form, invent, make, originate, produce, think up. **2** *She created a fund to help the bushfire victims.* establish, found, initiate, institute, pioneer, set up. **3** *The solution created more problems.* beget, engender, generate, give rise to, lead to, make, produce.

creation *noun The creation of the world is described in Genesis.* beginning, birth, formation, foundation, genesis, invention, making, origin.

creative *adjective a creative mind.* fertile, imaginative, ingenious, inventive, original, productive, resourceful. OPPOSITE unimaginative.

creator *noun the creator of the universe.* architect, author, designer, inventor, maker, originator, producer.

creature *noun They care for all creatures.* animal, beast, being, living thing, organism.

crèche *noun Her children go to a crèche while she works.* child care centre, nursery, preschool.

credible *adjective Her story was credible.* believable, conceivable, plausible, reasonable. OPPOSITE incredible.

credit *noun She brought credit to her family.* acclaim, distinction, esteem, glory, honour, merit, praise, recognition, reputation. OPPOSITE disgrace, reproach. □ **on credit** *He bought the TV on credit.* by instalments, on hire purchase, on the never-never (*informal*), on the slate (*informal*), on tick (*informal*).

creditable *adjective a creditable performance.* admirable, commendable, honourable, laudable, meritorious, praiseworthy, respectable, worthy. OPPOSITE discreditable, shameful.

creed *noun regardless of colour or creed.* belief(s), conviction(s), doctrine, dogma, faith, principles, religion, tenets.

creek *noun* (*Australian*) *The creek dries up in summer.* brook, rill, river, rivulet, stream, tributary, watercourse.

creep *verb* **1** *She crept under the sofa.* crawl, move on all fours, slither, squirm, worm your way, wriggle, writhe. **2** *He crept quietly out of the room.* edge, inch, slink, slip, sneak, steal, tiptoe.

creepy *adjective a creepy film.* disturbing, eerie, frightening, hair-raising, scary, sinister, spooky (*informal*), terrifying, uncanny, weird.

crest *noun* **1** *The cockatoo has a yellow crest.* comb, topknot, tuft. **2** *The walkers reached the crest of the hill.* apex, brow, crown, peak, pinnacle, summit, top. OPPOSITE base. **3** *He designed the school crest.* badge, emblem, insignia, symbol.

crevice *noun a rock crevice.* chink, cleft, crack, cranny, fissure, gap, opening, rift, split.

crew *noun* **1** *the ship's crew. the camera crew.* company, corps, party, personnel, squad, staff, team, workforce. **2** *Come and join our happy crew.* band, bunch, crowd, gang, group, mob, troop.

crib *noun a baby's crib.* cot, cradle. — *verb She cribbed off the top student.* cheat, copy, lift (*informal*), plagiarise.

crime *noun He was guilty of the crime.* felony (*old use*), misdeed, misdemeanour, offence, wrong, wrongdoing; see also SIN.

criminal *noun The police caught the criminal.* baddy (*informal*), convict, crim (*Australian informal*), crook (*informal*), culprit, delinquent, desperado, felon, jailbird, lawbreaker, malefactor, miscreant, offender, outlaw, transgressor, villain, wrongdoer. — *adjective criminal behaviour.* corrupt, crooked, dishonest, illegal, illicit, shady, unlawful, wrong. OPPOSITE legal.

cringe *verb The sight of the cane made him cringe.* cower, crouch, draw back, flinch, quail, recoil, shrink back, wince.

crinkle *verb & noun* see CREASE.

cripple *verb* **1** *The disease is gradually crippling him.* debilitate, disable, incapacitate, lame, maim, paralyse, weaken. **2** *The strike crippled industry.* bring to a standstill, damage, hamstring, hurt, immobilise, paralyse.

crippled *adjective a crippled person.* disabled, handicapped, incapacitated, invalid, lame, maimed, paralysed.

crisis *noun* **1** *the crisis in an illness.* climax, crunch (*informal*), crux, danger period, height, turning point. **2** *He can handle any crisis.* calamity, catastrophe, difficulty, disaster, emergency, predicament.

crisp *adjective* **1** *crisp pastry.* brittle, crispy, crunchy, crusty. OPPOSITE soft, soggy. **2** *a crisp winter morning.* bracing, chilly, cold, cool, fresh, nippy (*informal*). OPPOSITE balmy, warm. **3** *a crisp manner.* abrupt, brisk, brusque, curt, sharp, snappy (*informal*), terse.

criterion *noun judged according to several criteria.* benchmark, measure, principle, rule, standard, touchstone, yardstick.

critic *noun* **1** *The scheme has its critics.* attacker, detractor, fault-finder, knocker (*informal*), objector, opponent. OPPOSITE supporter. **2** *a film critic.* evaluator, judge, reviewer.

critical *adjective* **1** *critical comments.* captious, censorious, disapproving, disparaging, judgemental, nit-picking (*informal*), uncomplimentary. OPPOSITE complimentary. **2** *an event of critical importance.* acute, crucial, decisive, key, main, major, momentous, pivotal, serious, vital. **3** *The patient is in a critical condition.* dangerous, grave, perilous, precarious, risky, serious.

criticise *verb He criticised their work. She's always criticising people.* bag (*Australian informal*), belittle, censure, condemn, decry, denounce, disparage, find fault with, knock (*informal*), object to, pan (*informal*), pick holes in, rebuke, reprimand, rubbish, slam (*informal*), slate (*informal*), tell off (*informal*), tick off (*informal*). OPPOSITE praise.

criticism *noun* **1** *He faced hostile criticism over his decision.* censure, condemnation, disapproval, disparagement, fault-finding, flak (*informal*), nit-picking (*informal*), reproach. OPPOSITE approval, praise. **2** *literary criticism.* analysis, appraisal, commentary, critique, evaluation, review.

croaky *adjective a croaky voice.* hoarse, husky, rasping, rough, throaty. OPPOSITE mellow.

crockery *noun They washed the crockery.* china, dishes, earthenware, plates, pottery, tableware.

crook *noun* **1** *a shepherd's crook.* crosier, staff, stick. **2** (*informal*) *Don't trust him. He's a crook.* baddy (*informal*), cheat, criminal, knave (*old use*), lawbreaker, malefactor, rogue, scoundrel, swindler, thief, villain, wrongdoer. — *adjective* (*Australian informal*) **1** *She did a crook job.* bad, inferior, poor, shoddy, slipshod, unsatisfactory. OPPOSITE good. **2** *He feels crook.* ailing, ill, indisposed, lousy (*informal*), poorly, rotten (*informal*), sick, unwell. OPPOSITE well. □ **go crook at** or **on** (*Australian informal*) *His parents went crook on him for smashing the window.* castigate, chastise, get mad with, rebuke, reprimand, reproach, rouse on (*Australian informal*), scold, tick off (*informal*), upbraid. OPPOSITE praise.

crooked *adjective* **1** *a crooked path.* bent, curved, serpentine, sinuous, tortuous, twisted, winding, zigzag. OPPOSITE straight. **2** *The painting is crooked.* askew, awry, cock-eyed (*informal*), lopsided, off-centre, slanting, uneven. OPPOSITE level, straight. **3** *a man with a crooked back.* bent, bowed, contorted, crippled, deformed, lopsided. OPPOSITE straight. **4** *a crooked accountant.* bent (*slang*), corrupt, criminal, dishonest, fraudulent, shady, shifty, shonky (*Australian informal*), underhand, unscrupulous, untrustworthy. OPPOSITE honest, straight.

crop *noun* **1** *The farmer's crop was affected by the hail.* harvest, produce, vintage, yield. **2** *a new crop of weeds.* batch, outcrop. — *verb* **1** *The sheep crop the grass closely.* browse, eat, graze, nibble. **2** *She had her hair cropped.* bob, clip, cut, shear, snip, trim. □ **crop up** *A problem has cropped up.* appear, arise, come up, emerge, happen, occur, turn up.

cross *noun* **1** *In the church there is a wooden cross.* crucifix, rood. **2** *The dog is a cross between a German shepherd and a Great Dane.* bitser (*Australian informal*), blend, combination, cross-breed, hybrid, mixture, mongrel. — *verb* **1** *The lines cross.* criss-cross, intersect. **2** *He crossed the road.* cut across, go across, traverse. **3** *The bridge crosses the river.* extend across, pass over, span, straddle. **4** *He crossed a Great Dane with a German shepherd.* cross-breed, interbreed, mate. — *adjective a cross old lady.* angry, annoyed, bad-tempered, cantankerous, crabby, cranky, crotchety, disagreeable, fractious, grouchy (*informal*), grumpy, ill-tempered, impatient, irascible, irate, irritable, maggoty (*Australian informal*), peevish, petulant, shirty (*informal*), snaky (*Australian informal*), surly, testy, tetchy. OPPOSITE agreeable. □ **cross out** *They crossed out her name.* cancel, delete, obliterate, scratch out, strike out.

crossing *noun* **1** *The travellers had a rough crossing.* journey, passage, voyage. **2** *the crossing of two paths.* crossroads, intersection, junction. **3** *a shallow river crossing.* causeway, ford.

crosspatch *noun The crosspatch was all alone again.* curmudgeon, grouch (*informal*), grump, malcontent, sourpuss (*informal*).

crossroads *noun There are traffic lights at the crossroads.* crossing, interchange, intersection, junction.

cross-section *noun a cross-section of the community.* sample, section.

crouch *verb She crouched under the bed.* bend, cower, duck, huddle, hunch, squat, stoop. OPPOSITE stand up.

crow *verb nothing to crow about.* blow your own trumpet, boast, brag, gloat, show off, skite (*Australian informal*), swagger, swank (*informal*).

crowd *noun* **1** *He spoke to the crowd.* assembly, company, congregation, crush, flock, gathering, herd, horde, host, mass, mob, multitude, pack, rabble, swarm, throng. **2** *The game drew a big crowd.* attendance, audience, onlookers, spectators, turnout. **3** *He's not one of their crowd.* bunch (*informal*), circle, crew, gang, group, lot, mob, set, troop. — *verb* **1** *The people crowded along the streets to watch the parade.* assemble, cluster, collect, congregate, flock, gather, herd, mill, swarm, throng. OPPOSITE disperse. **2** *We were crowded onto a ferry.* cram, huddle, jam, pack, pile, press, shove, squash, squeeze, stuff.

crowded *adjective* **1** *a crowded train.* congested, full, jam-packed, overflowing, packed. OPPOSITE empty. **2** *a crowded city.* over-populated, populous. OPPOSITE uninhabited.

crown *noun* **1** *the Queen's crown.* coronet, diadem, tiara. **2** *the crown of the hill.* apex, brow, crest, peak, pinnacle, summit, top. — *verb* **1** *He was crowned the new king.* enthrone, install, invest. **2** *The publication of the book crowned an illustrious career.* cap, complete, consummate, top off.

crowning *noun* coronation, enthronement.

crucial *adjective a crucial matter.* critical, decisive, important, key, momentous, pivotal, serious, significant, vital. OPPOSITE unimportant.

crude *adjective* **1** *crude oil.* natural, raw, unprocessed, unrefined. OPPOSITE refined. **2** *crude tools.* improvised, makeshift, primitive, rough, rudimentary, simple, unsophisticated. OPPOSITE sophisticated. **3** *a crude joke.* blue, coarse, improper, indecent, lewd, obscene, ribald, rude, vulgar. OPPOSITE polite.

cruel *adjective a cruel person. a cruel act.* atrocious, barbaric, beastly, bloodthirsty, brutal, callous, cold-blooded, ferocious, fiendish, hard-hearted, harsh, heartless, inhuman, inhumane, mean, merciless, monstrous, pitiless, ruthless, sadistic, savage, severe, tyrannical, unkind, vicious, violent. OPPOSITE humane, kind.

cruelty *noun The refugees recounted instances of great cruelty they had suffered.* atrocity, barbarity, bestiality, brutality, callousness, ferocity, fiendishness, hard-heartedness, harshness, heartlessness, inhumanity, meanness, mercilessness, monstrousness, pitilessness, ruthlessness, sadism, savagery, severity, tyranny, unkindness, viciousness, violence. OPPOSITE humanity, kindness.

cruise *verb They cruised the Pacific.* sail, travel, voyage. — *noun a harbour cruise.* journey, sail, trip, voyage.

crumb *noun bread crumbs.* bit, fragment, morsel, particle, piece, scrap, speck.

crumble *verb* **1** *She crumbled the stock cube.* crush, grind, pulverise. **2** *The rock crumbled.* break up, decompose, disintegrate, fall apart, go to pieces.

crumbly *adjective crumbly soil.* friable.

crumple *verb* **1** *He crumpled his shirt.* crease, crinkle, crush, rumple, screw up, wrinkle. OPPOSITE smooth. **2** *She crumpled into a heap.* collapse, fall down, flop.

crunch *verb* **1** *She crunched an apple.* chew, chomp, gnaw, masticate, munch. **2** *He crunched the leaves as he walked.* crush, scrunch, squash. — *noun When it comes to the crunch what will you do?* acid test, moment of truth, showdown, test.

crusade *noun She led the crusade against tobacco advertising.* campaign, drive, movement, push, struggle, war.

crush *verb* **1** *The machine crushed the metal.* buckle, compress, mangle, press, smash, squash, squeeze. **2** *She crushed the clothes in packing them.* crease, crinkle, crumple, rumple, wrinkle. **3** *He crushed the fruit.* liquidise, mash, pound, pulp, squash. **4** *She crushed the biscuits.* crumble, crunch, grind, pound, pulverise, shatter. **5** *They crushed the enemy.* conquer, defeat, overcome, overpower, overthrow, overwhelm, rout, subdue, suppress, thrash, trounce, vanquish.

crust *noun a crust on a kettle. a crust on a wound.* coating, incrustation, outside, scab, skin.

crutch *noun He used crutches when he walked.* prop, support.

cry *noun* **1** *She let out a cry.* bellow, call, exclamation, howl, scream, screech, shout, shriek, squawk, squeak, squeal, wail, whimper, whine, whoop, yell, yelp, yowl. **2** *a cry for help.* appeal, call, demand, entreaty, plea, request. — *verb* **1** *He cries over little things.* bawl, blubber, break down, grizzle, howl, shed tears, snivel, sob, wail, weep, whimper. **2** *She cried out from across the road.* bellow, call out, exclaim, roar, scream, shout, yell.

cry-baby *noun* sissy, sook (*Australian informal*), wimp (*informal*), wuss (*slang*).

crypt *noun He was buried in the church crypt.* undercroft, vault.

cryptic *adjective a cryptic comment.* baffling, coded, enigmatic, hidden, inscrutable, mysterious, obscure, perplexing, puzzling. OPPOSITE straightforward.

crystallise *verb His ideas are beginning to crystallise.* take form, take shape.

cubby hole *noun He put the file in Simon's cubby hole.* carrel, compartment, cubicle, niche, nook, pigeon-hole.

cube *noun a baby's building cubes.* block, brick. — *verb She cubed the carrots.* chop, cut, dice.

cubicle *noun Each cubicle is fitted with a tape recorder.* booth, carrel, compartment, cubby hole, stall.

cuddle *verb* **1** *The mother cuddled her child.* caress, clasp, embrace, fondle, hug, nurse, squeeze. **2** *She cuddled up to him in bed.* huddle, nestle, snuggle.

cue *noun She missed her cue to speak.* hint, prompt, reminder, sign, signal.

cuff *noun* **off the cuff** *He spoke off the cuff.* ad lib, extempore, impromptu, off the top of your head, spontaneously, unprepared, unrehearsed.

cul-de-sac *noun They live in a quiet cul-de-sac.* blind alley, close, dead end.

culminate *verb The argument culminated in a fight.* climax, close, conclude, end up, finish, terminate, wind up.

culprit *noun They caught the culprit.* lawbreaker, malefactor, miscreant, offender, troublemaker, wrongdoer.

cult *noun members of a new cult.* religion, sect.

cultivate *verb* **1** *He cultivated the land.* farm, till, work. **2** *They cultivated wheat.* grow, produce, raise, tend. **3** *She cultivated the skill.* develop, foster, nurture, refine, work on.

culture *noun* **1** *They studied French language and culture.* art, arts, civilisation, customs, literature, music, society, traditions. **2** *classes in physical culture.* development, education, training.

cultured *adjective a cultured person.* civilised, cultivated, educated, enlightened, highbrow, intellectual, refined, sophisticated, well-bred. OPPOSITE uncouth.

cumbersome *adjective a cumbersome package.* awkward, bulky, clumsy, heavy, inconvenient, ponderous, unwieldy, weighty. OPPOSITE manageable.

cumulative *adjective the cumulative effect.* accumulated, aggregate, combined.

cunning *adjective a cunning ploy. a cunning person.* artful, astute, calculating, clever, crafty, deceitful, devious, dodgy (*informal*), foxy, guileful, ingenious, knowing, machiavellian, scheming, sharp, shifty, shrewd, sly, sneaky, subtle, tricky, underhand, wily. OPPOSITE guileless. — *noun The fox is noted for his cunning.* cleverness, craftiness, deceitfulness, deviousness, guile, ingenuity, shrewdness, slyness, subtlety, trickery, wiliness.

cup *noun* **1** *He drank from the cup.* beaker, chalice, goblet, mug, tankard, teacup. **2** *Their team won the cup.* award, prize, trophy.

cupboard *noun [kinds of cupboard]* buffet, built-in, cabinet, chest, chiffonier, closet, dresser, larder, linen press, locker, pantry, safe, sideboard, wardrobe.

curator *noun the museum curator.* conservator, custodian, keeper, manager.

curb *verb They tried to curb their spending.* check, contain, control, curtail, hold back, limit, moderate, rein in, restrain, restrict, slow down.

cure *verb* **1** *She could not cure the patient's problem.* heal, make better, remedy. **2** *The technician cured the fault.* correct, fix, mend, put right, rectify, remedy, repair. — *noun a cure for the disease.* anti-

dote, corrective, medicine, remedy, restorative, therapy, treatment.

curiosity *noun* **1** *Curiosity killed the cat.* inquisitiveness, interest, nosiness (*informal*), prying, snooping (*informal*). OPPOSITE indifference. **2** *The shop sells curiosities.* curio, novelty, oddity, rarity.

curious *adjective* **1** *a curious neighbour.* inquiring, inquisitive, interested, nosy (*informal*), prying, snoopy (*informal*). OPPOSITE uninterested. **2** *frightened by curious noises.* abnormal, bizarre, extraordinary, funny, mysterious, odd, peculiar, queer, strange, unusual, weird. OPPOSITE normal.

curl *verb* **1** *The snake curled round the branch.* bend, coil, curve, loop, spiral, turn, twist, wind. **2** *She curled her hair.* crimp, frizz, perm, wave. OPPOSITE straighten. — *noun She has curls in her hair.* dreadlock, kink, ringlet, wave.

curly *adjective curly hair.* crimped, frizzed, frizzy, permed, wavy.

currency *noun She exchanged a traveller's cheque for the local currency.* cash, coinage, legal tender, money.

current *adjective current practices.* actual, contemporary, existing, latest, modern, present, present-day, prevailing, prevalent, up-to-date. OPPOSITE past. — *noun The river has a strong current.* flow, stream, tide.

curse *noun* **1** *The bad fairy's curse came to pass.* evil spell, hex, jinx (*informal*), malediction. OPPOSITE blessing. **2** *The injured man uttered a curse.* blasphemy, expletive, oath, obscenity, profanity, swear word. — *verb He cursed the other driver.* damn, revile, swear at. OPPOSITE bless. □ **be cursed with** *He was cursed with poor eyesight.* be afflicted with, be blighted with, be plagued with, be troubled with, suffer from.

cursory *adjective a cursory examination.* brief, hasty, hurried, perfunctory, quick, slapdash, superficial. OPPOSITE thorough.

curt *adjective He gave a curt answer.* abrupt, blunt, brief, brusque, gruff, offhand, short, snappy (*informal*), terse.

curtail *verb* **1** *She curtailed her speech.* abbreviate, abridge, cut short, shorten, truncate. OPPOSITE extend. **2** *He curtailed their spending.* check, curb, cut back, decrease, reduce, restrain, restrict, trim. OPPOSITE increase.

curtain *noun He drew the curtains.* drape, hanging, screen.

curtsy *noun She made a curtsy to the Queen.* bob, bow, obeisance. — *verb Emma curtsied before the altar.* bob, bow, genuflect.

curve *noun The wire was bent in the form of a curve.* arc, arch, bend, bow, crescent, crook, curl, curvature, kink, loop, spiral, turn, twist. — *verb* arc, arch, bend, bow, circle, coil, kink, loop, spiral, turn, twist, wind.

curved *adjective* **1** *a curved path.* crescent-shaped, crooked, looped, serpentine, sinuous, spiral, tortuous, twisting, winding. OPPOSITE straight. **2** *a curved surface.* arched, bent, bowed, concave, convex, humped, rounded. OPPOSITE flat.

cushion *noun He knelt on a cushion.* bolster, hassock, kneeler, pad, pillow. — *verb A rubber pad cushioned the impact.* absorb, buffer, damp, dampen, deaden, lessen, reduce, soften.

cushy *adjective (informal) a cushy job.* easy, pleasant, soft (*informal*), undemanding.

custodian *noun the gallery's custodian.* caretaker, curator, guardian, keeper, steward, warden.

custody *noun* **1** *She has custody of the children.* care, charge, guardianship. **2** *The papers are in safe custody.* care, hands, keeping. **3** *He was being held in custody.* detention, imprisonment, jail, prison.

custom *noun* **1** *It is their custom to shake hands.* convention, habit, practice, routine, tradition, way, wont. **2** *The owner appreciated their custom.* business, patronage, support, trade.

customary *adjective She answered with her customary politeness.* accustomed, habitual, normal, ordinary, regular, routine, standard, traditional, typical, usual, wonted. OPPOSITE unusual.

customer *noun The shop attracts male customers.* buyer, client, consumer, patron, purchaser, shopper. OPPOSITE vendor.

customs *noun The government collects customs on imports.* duty, import tax, levy, tariff.

cut *verb* **1** amputate, bisect, carve, chip, chisel, chop, cleave, clip, crop, cube, detach, dice, dissect, divide, dock, engrave, fell, gash, gouge, guillotine, hack, hew, incise, knife, lacerate, lance, lop, mangle, mince, mow, mutilate, nick, notch, pare, pierce, pink, prune, reap, remove, saw, score, scythe, sever, shave, shear, shred, slash, slice, slit, snick, snip, split, stab, trim, truncate, whittle, wound. **2** *The lines cut at right angles.* cross, go across, intersect. **3** *He cut his paper by 1000 words.* abbreviate, abridge, condense, curtail, reduce, shorten. OPPOSITE lengthen. — *noun* **1** *She had a cut on her leg.* gash, incision, laceration, nick, slash, snick, wound. **2** *He made a cut in the timber.* channel, furrow, groove, indentation, nick, notch, slit. **3** *a cut in interest rates.* decline, decrease, fall, lowering, reduction. OPPOSITE increase. **4** *a power cut.* disruption, failure, stoppage. **5** *(informal) a cut of the profits.* commission, percentage, portion, rake-off (*informal*), share, slice. □ **cut back** *The company was forced to cut back staff.* downsize (*informal*), rationalise, reduce, retrench; see also ECONOMISE. **cut down on** *He has to cut down on fat intake.* decrease, lessen, lower, reduce. OPPOSITE increase. **cut in** *He cut in on our conversation.* break in, butt in, interrupt, intervene. **cut off** **1** *The gas supply has been cut off.* disconnect, discontinue, halt, stop, suspend. **2** *The farm was cut off from the town by the floods.* isolate, maroon, separate. **cut out** *She cut out the offending part.* censor, delete, eliminate, excise, exclude, leave out, omit, remove. OPPOSITE include.

cutback *noun government cutbacks.* cut, economy, rationalisation, reduction, retrenchment.

cute *adjective (informal) a cute baby.* adorable, attractive, pretty, sweet (*informal*).

cutthroat *adjective a cutthroat competition.* competitive, dog-eat-dog (*informal*), fierce, merciless, ruthless.

cutting *adjective cutting remarks.* acrimonious, caustic, harsh, hurtful, sarcastic, scathing, sharp, stinging, wounding. — *noun* **1** *a newspaper cutting.* clipping, extract, piece, section. **2** *a plant cutting.* slip.

cycle *noun* **1** *the cycle of the seasons.* repetition, revolution, rotation, round, sequence, series. **2** *He rides a cycle.* bicycle, moped, motorcycle, motor scooter, penny farthing, scooter, tandem, tricycle. — *verb He cycles to work.* bicycle, bike (*informal*), pedal, ride.

cyclone *noun The cyclone destroyed hundreds of homes.* hurricane, tropical cyclone, typhoon.

cynical *adjective a cynical view of politicians.* jaundiced, sardonic, sceptical, scoffing, sneering, suspicious. OPPOSITE optimistic.

Dd

dab *noun a dab of polish.* bit, pat, touch. — *verb She dabbed paint on the wall.* apply, daub, pat.

dabble *verb* **1** *They dabbled at the water's edge.* dip, paddle, splash. **2** *She dabbles in photography.* play, potter, tinker.

dagger *noun He was killed with a dagger.* dirk, knife, kris, stiletto.

daily *adjective a daily occurrence.* day-to-day, diurnal, everyday.

dainty *adjective dainty coffee cups.* delicate, dinky (*informal*), exquisite, fine, pretty, small.

dais *noun He spoke to the audience from the dais.* platform, podium, rostrum, stage.

dally *verb They dallied on the way home.* dawdle, delay, dilly-dally (*informal*), hang about, linger, loiter, take your time, tarry. OPPOSITE hurry.

dam *noun* **1** *A dam was built across the river.* bank, barrage, barrier, embankment, wall, weir. **2** *(Australian) The farmer's dam is full after rain.* pond, reservoir, tank (*Australian*).

damage *noun The accident caused a lot of damage.* destruction, devastation, harm, havoc, hurt, injury, loss, mutilation, ruin. — *verb* **1** *Public property has been damaged.* blemish, blight, break, bruise, bust (*informal*), chip, cripple, deface, dent, destroy, devastate, flaw, harm, hurt, impair, injure, mangle, mar, mutilate, ravage, ruin, sabotage, scar, scratch, spoil, vandalise, wound, wreck. OPPOSITE mend. **2** *The incident has damaged his reputation.* blemish, smirch, stain, sully, tarnish. OPPOSITE enhance. □ **damages** *plural noun The court ordered the guilty party to pay damages.* compensation, costs, indemnity, reparation, restitution.

damnation *noun condemned to suffer damnation.* eternal punishment, hell, perdition.

damp *adjective damp weather. damp clothes.* clammy, dank, humid, moist, muggy, sodden, soggy, steamy, sticky, wet. OPPOSITE dry. — *verb* **1** *He damped the clothes before ironing them.* dampen, moisten, sprinkle, wet. **2** *She damped their enthusiasm.* cool, dampen, dash, discourage, dull, restrain. OPPOSITE kindle.

dance *verb The children danced around.* bob, caper, cavort, frolic, gambol, jig, jump, leap, pirouette, prance, romp, skip, trip, twirl. — *noun They went to a dance.* ball, disco (*informal*), formal, prom (*American*), social.

danger *noun* **1** *There is no danger of losing.* chance, possibility, risk, threat. **2** *the dangers of diving in shallow water.* hazard, jeopardy, peril, pitfall, risk, snare, trouble. OPPOSITE safety.

dangerous *adjective* **1** *a dangerous undertaking.* chancy, dicey (*slang*), dodgy (*informal*), hairy (*slang*), hazardous, perilous, precarious, risky, tricky, uncertain, unsafe. OPPOSITE safe. **2** *a dangerous animal.* destructive, ferocious, savage, treacherous, vicious, wild. OPPOSITE harmless. **3** *a dangerous criminal.* desperate, menacing, threatening, violent.

dangle *verb The apples dangled from strings.* hang, sway, swing.

dapper *adjective a dapper little man.* chic, natty (*informal*), neat, smart, snazzy (*informal*), spruce, trim, well-dressed.

dappled *adjective a dappled horse.* mottled, piebald, pied, skewbald, spotted.

dare *verb* **1** *She wouldn't dare to interrupt.* be bold enough, be game, have the nerve, presume, venture. **2** *They dared him to jump.* challenge, defy, taunt.

daring *noun He was rewarded for his daring.* audacity, boldness, bravery, courage, intrepidity, nerve, pluck, prowess, valour. OPPOSITE cowardice. — *adjective a daring rescuer.* adventurous, audacious, bold, brave, courageous, fearless, game, heroic, intrepid, plucky, reckless, valiant, venturesome. OPPOSITE cowardly.

dark *adjective* **1** *a dark night.* black, dim, dingy, dull, dusky, gloomy, moonless, murky, overcast, pitch-dark, shadowy, shady, starless, unlit. OPPOSITE bright. **2** *dark skin.* black, brown, dusky, olive, swarthy, tanned. OPPOSITE fair. **3** *dark hair.* black, brown, brunette. OPPOSITE blond. **4** *Keep it dark.* confidential, hidden, hush-hush (*informal*), secret. — *noun She was out after dark.* darkness, dusk, evening, gloaming, night, nightfall, night-time, sunset, twilight.

darken *verb The sky darkened.* become overcast, blacken, cloud over. OPPOSITE brighten.

darling *noun Good night, darling.* beloved, dear, love, pet, sweet, sweetheart. — *adjective her darling husband.* beloved, dear, lovable, loved, precious.

darn *verb He darned his socks.* mend, repair, sew.

dart *noun a poisoned dart.* arrow, missile, projectile, shaft. — *verb She darted out in front of a car.* bolt, dash, jump, leap, race, run, scoot, shoot, spring, streak, tear, zip.

dash *verb* **1** *The runners dashed past him.* bolt, dart, fly, gallop, hasten, hurry, hurtle, hustle, race, run, rush, scoot, shoot, speed, sprint, stampede, streak, sweep, tear, whiz, zip, zoom. **2** *She dashed the glass against the wall.* fling, hurl, knock, shatter, smash, strike, throw. **3** *Their hopes were dashed.* blight, destroy, disappoint, frustrate, put paid to, ruin, shatter, spoil. OPPOSITE fulfil, raise. — *noun* **1** *a last-minute dash.* bolt, run, rush, sprint, spurt. **2** *a dash of vanilla.* drop, hint, splash, sprinkling, suggestion, touch.

dashing *adjective a dashing young man.* bold, debonair, gallant, plucky, smart, spirited, stylish.

data *plural noun He analysed the data.* evidence, facts, figures, information, material.

date *noun* **1** *objects of prehistoric date.* age, epoch, era, period, time, vintage. **2** (*informal*) *They had a date for lunch together.* appointment, arrangement, assignation, booking, commitment, engagement, meeting, rendezvous. **3** (*informal*) *Lots of people go to the formal without a date.* boyfriend, companion, escort, girlfriend, partner. — *verb* **date from** *The custom dates from ancient times.* come from, exist from, originate in.

daub *verb She daubed sunscreen on her face.* paint, plaster, slap, slop, smear.

daunt *verb The darkness daunted the children.* alarm, discourage, dis-

hearten, dismay, frighten, intimidate, perturb, put off, scare, unnerve.

daunting *adjective a daunting task.* awesome, fearsome, forbidding, formidable, frightening, overwhelming.

dauntless *adjective a dauntless warrior.* bold, brave, courageous, fearless, gallant, game, heroic, intrepid, plucky, unafraid, undaunted, valiant. OPPOSITE timid.

dawdle *verb They were late home because they dawdled.* dally, delay, dilly-dally (*informal*), hang about, lag behind, linger, loiter, straggle, take your time. OPPOSITE hurry.

dawdler *noun We can't wait for dawdlers.* laggard, slowcoach, sluggard, straggler.

dawn *noun* **1** *He woke up at dawn.* break of day, cock-crow, crack of dawn, daybreak, first light, sunrise, sun-up. OPPOSITE dusk. **2** *the dawn of an era.* beginning, birth, inception, onset, origin, start, threshold. OPPOSITE end. — *verb* **dawn on** *The truth dawned on him.* occur to, strike.

day *noun* **1** *She works during the day.* daylight, daytime. OPPOSITE night. **2** *He died on this day last year.* date. **3** *the olden days.* the present day. age, epoch, era, period, time.

daybreak *noun* SEE DAWN.

daydream *noun The whole idea was only a daydream.* castle in the air, dream, fantasy, illusion, pipe dream, reverie. — *verb She was daydreaming instead of concentrating.* dream, fantasise, muse.

daylight *noun* **1** *eight hours of daylight.* daytime, light, sunlight, sunshine. **2** *He was up before daylight.* break of day, dawn, morning, sunrise.

daze *verb The knock on the head dazed him.* bewilder, confuse, stun, stupefy. — *noun She walked around in a daze.* bewilderment, confusion, muddle, shock, stupor, trance.

dazzle *verb* **1** *The headlights dazzled the pedestrian.* blind, daze. **2** *He dazzled them with his knowledge.* amaze, awe, blind, confuse, impress, overawe, stun.

dazzling *adjective a dazzling light.* blinding, brilliant, radiant, resplendent, sparkling.

dead *adjective* **1** *a dead person.* deceased, departed, late, lifeless. OPPOSITE alive, living. **2** *Her foot felt dead.* numb, paralysed. **3** *a dead language.* defunct, disused, extinct, obsolete. OPPOSITE living. **4** *Business is dead.* dormant, inactive, inert, quiet, slow, sluggish, stagnant, static. OPPOSITE active, booming. **5** *dead silence.* absolute, complete, thorough, total, utter. □ **dead end** *Their street is a dead end.* blind alley, close, cul-de-sac.

deaden *verb* **1** *The medicine deadened the pain.* anaesthetise, dull, kill, numb, subdue. OPPOSITE intensify. **2** *The muffler deadens the noise.* damp, muffle, mute, quieten, soften, stifle, suppress. OPPOSITE amplify.

deadline *noun a deadline for the work.* time limit.

deadlock *noun The talks reached a deadlock.* halt, impasse, stalemate, stand-off, standstill.

deadly *adjective a deadly disease.* fatal, lethal, mortal, terminal.

deaf *adjective* hard of hearing, hearing-impaired, stone-deaf.

deafening *adjective a deafening sound.* booming, ear-piercing, loud, noisy, thunderous.

deal *verb* **1** *She dealt the cards.* allocate, allot, apportion, distribute, divide, dole out, give out, hand out, share out. **2** *They deal in antiques.*

do business, handle, market, sell, trade, traffic. — *noun* **1** *a deal of cards.* distribution, hand, round. **2** *The two parties made a deal.* agreement, arrangement, bargain, contract, pact, settlement, transaction. **3** (*informal*) *a great deal of money.* amount, lot, quantity, volume. □ **deal with 1** *He dealt with the problem.* attend to, cope with, grapple with, handle, look after, manage, see to, sort out, tackle, take care of, treat. OPPOSITE ignore. **2** *The book deals with various subjects.* be about, be concerned with, consider, cover, touch on, treat.

dealer *noun* **1** *a car dealer.* distributor, merchant, retailer, salesperson, seller, shopkeeper, stockist, supplier, trader, vendor, wholesaler. **2** *a drug dealer.* peddler, seller, supplier, trafficker.

dear *adjective* **1** *a dear friend.* beloved, cherished, close, darling, loved, precious, treasured, valued. **2** *Everything they sell is dear.* costly, exorbitant, expensive, extortionate, pricey (*informal*). OPPOSITE cheap.

dearth *noun a dearth of good books.* absence, deficiency, lack, paucity, scarcity, shortage, want. OPPOSITE surfeit.

death *noun She became Queen after the death of her father.* decease (*formal*), demise (*formal*), dying, end, passing. OPPOSITE birth, life. □ **put to death** execute, kill, slay.

deathly *adjective He looked deathly.* ashen, cadaverous, deathlike, ghostly, pale.

debatable *adjective a debatable point.* arguable, contentious, controversial, disputable, dubious, moot, questionable. OPPOSITE incontrovertible.

debate *noun a political debate.* argument, conference, controversy, discussion, dispute, wrangle. — *verb They debated the issue.* argue, contest, discuss, dispute, wrangle over.

debilitate *verb She was debilitated by the illness.* cripple, disable, enervate, enfeeble, incapacitate, pull down, weaken. OPPOSITE strengthen.

debris *noun They cleaned up the debris.* detritus, flotsam, fragments, litter, remains, rubbish, rubble, wreckage.

debt *noun He paid off his debts.* due, liability, obligation.

decadent *adjective an increasingly decadent society.* corrupt, debased, degenerate, depraved, immoral. OPPOSITE moral.

decapitate *verb* behead, guillotine.

decay *verb The food decayed in the heat.* break down, decompose, deteriorate, disintegrate, go bad, go off, go rotten, moulder, perish, putrefy, rot, spoil. — *noun tooth decay.* caries, cavity, rot.

deceased *adjective the deceased man.* dead, departed, late. OPPOSITE alive, living.

deceit *noun full of lies and deceit.* artifice, cheating, chicanery, cunning, deceitfulness, deception, dishonesty, double-dealing, duplicity, fraud, guile, humbug, hypocrisy, lies, misrepresentation, pretence, skulduggery (*informal*), treachery, trickery, untruthfulness, wiliness. OPPOSITE honesty, openness.

deceitful *adjective a deceitful person.* crafty, crooked, cunning, devious, dishonest, false, hypocritical, lying, machiavellian, phoney (*informal*), shifty, sneaky, treacherous, tricky, two-faced, underhand, unfaithful, untrustworthy. OPPOSITE honest

deceive *verb He cannot easily be deceived.* bamboozle (*informal*), beguile, bluff, cheat, con (*informal*), defraud, delude, diddle (*informal*), double-cross, dupe,

fool, have (*slang*), have on (*informal*), hoax, hoodwink, kid (*informal*), mislead, rip off (*informal*), string along (*informal*), suck in (*informal*), swindle, take for a ride (*informal*), take in, trick.

decent *adjective* **1** *decent behaviour.* acceptable, appropriate, becoming, correct, decorous, honourable, law-abiding, proper, respectable, seemly, upright. OPPOSITE immodest. **2** *a decent joke.* clean, inoffensive, polite. OPPOSITE indecent, obscene. **3** (*informal*) *That's very decent of you.* civil, considerate, fair, generous, good, kind, obliging, sporting. **4** *a decent meal.* adequate, satisfactory, square. OPPOSITE unsatisfactory.

deception *noun We could see through this little deception.* bluff, con (*informal*), fraud, hoax, lie, pretence, ruse, sham, subterfuge, swindle, swizz (*informal*), trick; see also DECEIT.

deceptive *adjective Appearances can be deceptive.* deceiving, false, illusory, misleading, specious, unreliable. OPPOSITE trustworthy.

decide *verb* **1** *She decided on the red dress.* choose, elect, opt for, pick, plump for, select. **2** *The jury decided that he was guilty.* adjudicate, conclude, determine, judge, resolve, rule, settle. **3** *The goal decided the match.* clinch, determine, seal, settle.

decided *adjective* **1** *He has decided ideas about things.* adamant, determined, firm, fixed, resolute. OPPOSITE indecisive. **2** *There was a decided difference between the two contestants.* clear, clear-cut, definite, distinct, marked, noticeable, obvious, pronounced, unmistakable.

decipher *verb She deciphered the message.* crack, decode, figure out, interpret, make out, read, translate. OPPOSITE code, encode.

decision *noun The judge's decision is final.* adjudication, conclusion, determination, finding, judgement, resolution, ruling, sentence, verdict; see also CHOICE.

decisive *adjective* **1** *a decisive battle.* conclusive, critical, crucial, deciding, significant. **2** *a decisive person.* decided, determined, firm, resolute, unhesitating. OPPOSITE indecisive, non-committal.

deck[1] *noun the top deck.* floor, level, platform, storey.

deck[2] *verb The hall was decked with streamers.* adorn, decorate, festoon, trim.

declaration *noun a declaration of innocence.* affirmation, announcement, assertion, attestation, avowal, confession, proclamation, profession, pronouncement, protestation, statement, testimony.

declare *verb She declared her intentions. He declared that he was leaving.* affirm, announce, assert, avow, confess, contend, disclose, make known, proclaim, profess, pronounce, reveal, state, testify, voice. OPPOSITE hide.

decline *verb* **1** *He declined the invitation.* pass up, refuse, reject, turn down. OPPOSITE accept. **2** *Business declined. His health declined.* decrease, deteriorate, diminish, dwindle, ebb, fall off, flag, go downhill, go to the pack (*Australian informal*), sink, slip, slump, wane, weaken, worsen. OPPOSITE improve, increase. — *noun a decline in interest. a decline in business.* decrease, deterioration, downturn, drop, falling off, recession, slump, wane. OPPOSITE improvement.

decode *verb* SEE DECIPHER.

decompose *verb The food decomposed in the heat.* decay, disintegrate, go bad, go off, go rotten, moulder, perish, putrefy, rot, spoil.

decorate verb **1** *They decorated the Christmas tree.* adorn, deck, dress, embellish, festoon, ornament, tizzy (*Australian informal*), trim. **2** *The house has been newly decorated.* do up (*informal*), paint, paper, redecorate, refurbish, renovate.

decoration noun **1** *Christmas decorations.* adornment, ornament, trimming. **2** *a decoration for bravery.* award, badge, medal, medallion.

decorative adjective *The roof was both decorative and functional.* fancy, ornamental, ornate, pretty.

decorous adjective *decorous behaviour.* becoming, correct, decent, honourable, polite, proper, refined, respectable, seemly. OPPOSITE indecorous.

decorum noun *He behaved with decorum.* correctness, decency, dignity, politeness, propriety, respectability, seemliness.

decoy noun *The police used a decoy to catch the criminal.* bait, enticement, lure, stool-pigeon, trap. — verb *He was decoyed into enemy territory and arrested.* allure, bait, entice, lure, trap.

decrease verb **1** *They decreased the number of holidays.* cut, cut back, lower, reduce, shorten. OPPOSITE increase. **2** *Interest has decreased.* abate, drop off, ease off, ebb, lessen, slacken, subside, wane. OPPOSITE intensify. **3** *The numbers have decreased.* contract, decline, diminish, drop, dwindle, fall, reduce, shrink, taper off. OPPOSITE increase. — noun *a decrease in numbers attending.* contraction, cut, cutback, decline, drop, ebb, fall, reduction. OPPOSITE increase.

decree noun **1** *They obeyed the royal decree.* command, commandment, dictate, direction, directive, edict, instruction, law, order, ordinance, proclamation, statute. **2** *the judge's decree.* decision, judgement, ruling, verdict. — verb *The government decreed that the day would be a holiday.* command, declare, dictate, direct, enact, ordain, order, prescribe, proclaim, rule.

decrepit adjective *a decrepit old house.* battered, derelict, dilapidated, ramshackle, rickety, rundown, tumbledown.

dedicate verb **1** *She dedicated her life to God's service.* commit, consecrate, devote, give, pledge. **2** *The book is dedicated to her father.* address, inscribe.

dedicated adjective *a dedicated tennis player.* committed, devoted, enthusiastic, single-minded, wholehearted, zealous.

deduce verb *He deduced that the plane had been delayed.* conclude, gather, infer, reason, suss out (*informal*), work out.

deduct verb *She deducted $5 from the total.* knock off (*informal*), remove, subtract, take away, take off. OPPOSITE add.

deduction noun **1** *a deduction of $5 from the bill.* discount, rebate, removal, subtraction. **2** *a logical deduction.* conclusion, inference, reasoning.

deed noun **1** *praised for his good deeds.* accomplishment, achievement, act, action, exploit, feat, work. **2** *the deeds to the house.* contract, document, paper.

deem verb (*formal*) *She deemed it an honour.* consider, count, judge, rate, reckon, regard, think.

deep adjective **1** *a deep crater.* bottomless, cavernous, profound, unfathomed. OPPOSITE shallow. **2** *a deep sleep.* heavy, profound, sound. OPPOSITE light. **3** *a deep colour.*

dark, intense, rich, strong, vivid. OPPOSITE pale. **4** *a deep voice.* bass, booming, low, resonant, sonorous. OPPOSITE high-pitched. **5** *deep in thought.* absorbed, engrossed, immersed, lost, occupied, preoccupied, rapt. **6** *a deep interest.* burning, earnest, extreme, fervent, heartfelt, intense, keen, profound, serious. OPPOSITE superficial. **7** *a deep discussion.* erudite, intellectual, learned, penetrating, profound, thoughtful. OPPOSITE superficial.

deer noun [*male deer*] buck, hart, stag; [*female deer*] doe, hind; [*young deer*] fawn.

deface verb *Vandals defaced the front of the building.* damage, disfigure, mar, spoil.

defame verb *His opponents tried to defame him.* blacken, denigrate, discredit, disparage, libel, malign, slander, smear, vilify.

defeat verb **1** *Their team defeated the others.* beat, clobber (*slang*), conquer, crush, euchre, get the better of, lick (*informal*), outclass, outdo, outwit, overcome, overpower, overthrow, overwhelm, paste (*slang*), prevail over, pulverise (*informal*), rout, slaughter (*informal*), stonker (*Australian slang*), surpass, thrash, triumph over, trounce, vanquish. OPPOSITE lose to. **2** *The problem defeats me.* baffle, beat, confound, frustrate, perplex, puzzle. — noun *Our team suffered defeat.* beating, conquest, downfall, drubbing, failure, licking (*informal*), loss, overthrow, pasting (*informal*), reverse, thrashing. OPPOSITE victory.

defect noun **1** *a defect in the paintwork.* a mechanical defect. blemish, bug (*informal*), fault, flaw, imperfection, mark, spot, stain. **2** *a personality defect.* deficiency, failing, fault, flaw, shortcoming, weakness. — verb *The traitor defected to the other country.* change sides, desert, go over.

defective adjective *a defective machine.* crook (*Australian informal*), deficient, dud (*informal*), faulty, imperfect, malfunctioning, on the blink (*informal*), out of order. OPPOSITE perfect.

defector noun *a defector from the Democrats.* apostate, deserter, renegade, traitor, turncoat.

defence noun **1** *The soldiers ensured the country's defence.* preservation, protection, security. **2** *The wall acts as a defence against attack.* buffer, bulwark, cover, fortification, guard, protection, safeguard, shield. **3** *What was his defence when you challenged him?* excuse, explanation, justification, plea.

defenceless adjective *defenceless children.* helpless, powerless, vulnerable, weak.

defend verb **1** *They defended the city against attack.* fortify, guard, preserve, protect, safeguard, secure, shelter, shield. OPPOSITE attack. **2** *He defended their right to speak.* champion, justify, stand up for, support, uphold, vindicate.

defer verb *The programme was deferred to next month.* adjourn, delay, hold over, postpone, put off, shelve.

deferential adjective *deferential behaviour.* courteous, dutiful, meek, obsequious, polite, respectful, submissive. OPPOSITE disrespectful.

defiant adjective *The child was strong-willed and defiant.* contrary, disobedient, insubordinate, mutinous, obstinate, rebellious, recalcitrant, refractory, truculent. OPPOSITE compliant, obedient.

deficiency noun **1** *a calcium deficiency.* absence, dearth, deficit, insufficiency, lack, shortage, want.

OPPOSITE abundance. **2** *aware of his own deficiencies.* failing, fault, flaw, imperfection, shortcoming, weakness. OPPOSITE strength.

deficient adjective **1** *deficient in vitamins.* insufficient, lacking, light on (*Australian informal*), short, wanting. OPPOSITE abundant, rich. **2** *a deficient memory.* defective, faulty, imperfect, inadequate, unsatisfactory.

deficit noun *a budget deficit.* deficiency, shortfall. OPPOSITE surplus.

defile verb **1** *The river has been defiled with chemicals.* contaminate, dirty, poison, pollute, soil, taint. **2** *He has misused and defiled the high altar.* corrupt, desecrate, dishonour, profane, violate.

define verb **1** *The dictionary defines words.* clarify, explain. **2** *The document defines the conditions.* delineate, describe, detail, set out, specify, spell out, state.

definite adjective **1** *Fix a definite time.* defined, exact, explicit, fixed, particular, precise, specific. OPPOSITE indefinite. **2** *He has a definite accent.* clear, discernible, distinct, marked, noticeable, obvious, plain, pronounced, unmistakable. OPPOSITE vague. **3** *Is it definite that we are to move?* assured, certain, decided, fixed, positive, settled, sure. OPPOSITE uncertain.

definition noun *a dictionary definition.* description, elucidation, explanation, interpretation.

deflect verb *He deflected the blow.* avert, divert, parry, turn aside.

deformed adjective *a deformed body.* contorted, crooked, disfigured, distorted, grotesque, lopsided, malformed, misshapen, twisted, warped.

deformity noun *She was born with a spinal deformity.* abnormality, contortion, defect, disfigurement, distortion, malformation.

defraud verb *They were defrauded by a con man.* bilk, cheat, con (*informal*), deceive, diddle (*informal*), dupe, fleece, have (*slang*), hoodwink, rip off (*informal*), rook, swindle, take for a ride (*informal*), trick.

deft adjective *deft movements.* adept, adroit, agile, dexterous, expert, neat, nimble, proficient, skilful. OPPOSITE clumsy.

defunct adjective *a defunct organisation.* dead, extinct, obsolete. OPPOSITE alive.

defy verb **1** *He defied his teachers.* confront, disobey, flout, oppose, resist, stand up to. OPPOSITE obey. **2** *He defied them to try it.* challenge, dare.

degenerate verb *The debate degenerated into a brawl.* decline, deteriorate, regress, retrogress, sink, worsen. OPPOSITE improve.

degrade verb *She degrades herself by the way she speaks.* abase, cheapen, debase, demean, disgrace, humiliate, lower. OPPOSITE dignify, upgrade.

degrading adjective *degrading work.* demeaning, humiliating, menial, undignified.

degree noun **1** *the degree of difficulty.* grade, level, order, rank. **2** *They moved up by degrees.* stage, step.

dehydrated adjective *dehydrated food.* desiccated, dried.

deify verb *They deified their heroes.* enshrine, exalt, glorify, idolise, revere, venerate, worship.

deign verb *She did not deign to reply.* condescend, lower yourself, stoop, vouchsafe.

deity noun *They worshipped several deities.* divinity, god, goddess.

dejected adjective *She felt alone and dejected.* crestfallen, depressed, despondent, disconsolate, discour-

aged, disheartened, dispirited, doleful, downcast, down-hearted, forlorn, gloomy, glum, heavyhearted, melancholy, miserable, morose, sad, sorrowful. OPPOSITE happy.

delay verb **1** *We were delayed by an accident.* detain, hamper, hinder, hold up, impede, inhibit, obstruct, retard, slow. OPPOSITE advance. **2** *He delayed leaving until the weather became cooler.* defer, postpone, put off, shelve. OPPOSITE hasten. **3** *Act now. Do not delay.* dillydally (*informal*), hang back, hesitate, pause, procrastinate, stall, temporise, wait. OPPOSITE hurry. — noun *Bad weather caused delays.* hold-up, interruption, lull, pause, postponement, setback, wait.

delegate noun *We dealt with the union delegate.* agent, ambassador, deputy, emissary, envoy, proxy, representative, spokesperson. — verb *He delegated responsibility to his staff.* assign, depute, entrust, hand over, transfer.

delete verb *She deleted the offending words.* cancel, cross out, cut out, edit out, efface, erase, expunge, obliterate, remove, rub out, strike out, take out, wipe out. OPPOSITE insert.

deliberate adjective **1** *a deliberate insult.* calculated, conscious, intended, intentional, planned, premeditated, studied, wilful. OPPOSITE accidental. **2** *Her footsteps were deliberate.* careful, cautious, measured, painstaking, slow, unhurried. OPPOSITE hasty. — verb *They are still deliberating about what to do.* cogitate, confer about, consider, debate, discuss, meditate, mull over, muse, ponder, reflect, ruminate, think.

delicate adjective **1** *a delicate fabric.* filmy, fine, flimsy, lacy, light, sheer, thin. OPPOSITE coarse. **2** *a delicate ornament.* breakable, dainty, flimsy, fragile, frail. OPPOSITE sturdy. **3** *delicate workmanship.* exquisite, fine, intricate, precise. OPPOSITE rough. **4** *a delicate flavour.* faint, gentle, mild, subtle. OPPOSITE intense, strong. **5** *delicate colours.* faint, muted, pale, pastel, soft, subdued. OPPOSITE strong, vivid. **6** *a delicate child.* feeble, frail, infirm, sickly, unhealthy, weak. OPPOSITE healthy, strong. **7** *delicate plants.* frail, tender. OPPOSITE hardy. **8** *a delicate situation.* awkward, hazardous, precarious, sensitive, ticklish, touchy, tricky. **9** *The situation requires delicate handling.* careful, diplomatic, discreet, sensitive, skilful, tactful. OPPOSITE insensitive.

delicious adjective *a delicious meal.* appetising, delectable, luscious, mouth-watering, palatable, scrumptious (*informal*), tasty, yummy (*informal*). OPPOSITE revolting.

delight verb **1** *The performers delighted the audience.* amuse, captivate, charm, divert, enchant, enrapture, entertain, entrance, fascinate, please, thrill. OPPOSITE disappoint. **2** *She delights in teasing people.* revel, take pleasure; see also ENJOY. — noun *a source of great delight.* bliss, ecstasy, enjoyment, gratification, happiness, joy, pleasure, satisfaction. OPPOSITE displeasure.

delightful adjective **1** *Gina is a delightful girl.* adorable, agreeable, attractive, beautiful, captivating, charming, enchanting, lovable, lovely. **2** *We had a delightful time.* delectable, enjoyable, heavenly, lovely, marvellous, nice, pleasant, pleasurable, wonderful.

delinquent noun *a home for delinquents.* criminal, hooligan, lawbreaker, miscreant, offender, troublemaker, wrongdoer.

delirious *adjective* **1** *The fever made him delirious.* demented, deranged, frantic, frenzied, hysterical, incoherent, light-headed, mad, raving. **2** *She was delirious with joy.* ecstatic, euphoric, excited, wild.

deliver *verb* **1** *He delivered the letters.* bear, bring, carry, convey, distribute, give out, hand over, take, transport. OPPOSITE receive. **2** *The head girl delivered the speech.* give, make, present, utter. **3** *The attacker delivered a nasty blow.* aim, deal, inflict, strike. **4** *The bowler delivered a fast ball.* bowl, throw, toss. **5** *Deliver us from evil.* emancipate, free, liberate, release, rescue, save, set free.

delivery *noun* **1** *The price includes free delivery.* conveyance, dispatch, distribution, transport. **2** *He received a new delivery of goods.* batch, consignment, load, shipment. **3** *the delivery of a baby.* birth, childbirth.

delude *verb* *He was deluded into thinking he needed a new car.* beguile, bluff, con (*informal*), deceive, dupe, fool, have on (*informal*), hoax, hoodwink, kid (*informal*), mislead, trick.

deluge *noun* **1** *The shed was washed away in the deluge.* flood, inundation, spate. **2** *Sunshine followed the deluge.* cloudburst, downpour, rain, torrent. **3** *a deluge of fan mail.* flood, rush, shower, spate, stream, torrent. — *verb* *She was deluged with letters.* flood, inundate, overrun, overwhelm, swamp.

delusion *noun* *delusions of grandeur.* fantasy, illusion, misbelief, misconception.

de luxe *adjective* *a de luxe hotel.* elegant, first-class, grand, luxurious, posh (*informal*), superior, upmarket. OPPOSITE basic, ordinary.

delve *verb* *They delved into his past.* dig, examine, investigate, probe, research, search.

demand *noun* **1** *They complied with his demands.* command, order, request, summons. **2** *a demand for their goods.* call, need, requirement, want. — *verb* **1** *He demanded his money.* ask for, claim, clamour for, insist on, order, press for, request, require. **2** *This work demands great skill.* call for, need, require.

demanding *adjective* *a demanding job.* arduous, challenging, difficult, exacting, hard, onerous, strenuous, taxing, tough. OPPOSITE easy.

demean *verb* *She won't demean herself to ask for help.* debase, degrade, humble, humiliate, lower.

demeanour *noun* *pleasant demeanour.* bearing, behaviour, conduct, deportment, manner, mien.

demented *adjective* *He was behaving as if he were demented.* berserk, bonkers (*slang*), crazy, deranged, insane, lunatic, mad, nutty (*informal*), out of your mind, potty (*informal*), screwy (*informal*), unbalanced, unhinged. OPPOSITE sane.

democratic *adjective* *democratic government.* elected, popular, representative.

demolish *verb* *The workmen demolished the old house.* destroy, dismantle, knock down, level, pull down, raze, tear down; see also WRECK. OPPOSITE construct, erect.

demon *noun* *The demons were imaginary.* bogy, devil, evil spirit, fiend, goblin, hobgoblin, imp.

demonic *adjective* *a demonic laugh.* devilish, diabolical, evil, fiendish, satanic, wicked.

demonstrate *verb* **1** *He demonstrated that sugar dissolves in water.* confirm, establish, prove, show. **2** *He demonstrated his invention.* display, exhibit, present, show.

3 *She demonstrated how it worked.* describe, explain, illustrate, show, teach. **4** *The students demonstrated against increased fees.* march, parade, protest, rally.

demonstration *noun* **1** *a ballet demonstration.* display, exhibition, presentation, show. **2** *an anti-war demonstration.* demo (*informal*), march, parade, protest, rally, sit-in.

demoralise *verb* *She was demoralised by her poor results.* crush, depress, discourage, dishearten. OPPOSITE encourage.

demure *adjective* *a demure person.* bashful, coy, diffident, modest, prim, quiet, reserved, shy, unassuming. OPPOSITE brash.

den *noun* **1** *an animal's den.* burrow, hole, lair, nest. **2** *He sought the privacy of his den.* hideaway, hide-out (*informal*), retreat, sanctum, study.

denial *noun* **1** *a denial of the statement.* contradiction, disclaimer, negation, rejection, repudiation. OPPOSITE affirmation. **2** *a denial of rights.* deprivation, refusal, withholding.

denigrate *verb* *He denigrates people whom he dislikes.* belittle, defame, discredit, disparage, knock (*informal*), malign, run down, smear, smirch, vilify. OPPOSITE praise.

denomination *noun* *various Christian denominations.* church, persuasion, sect.

denote *verb* *A red symbol denotes danger.* express, indicate, mean, represent, signal, signify, stand for, symbolise.

denounce *verb* **1** *He denounced their harsh policies.* attack, censure, condemn, criticise, decry, object to. OPPOSITE praise. **2** *She denounced him as a spy.* accuse, betray, dob in (*Australian informal*), incriminate, inform against, report.

dense *adjective* **1** *dense fog.* heavy, impenetrable, thick. OPPOSITE light. **2** *a dense weave.* close, compact, heavy. OPPOSITE loose, open. **3** *a dense crowd.* packed, solid, thick. OPPOSITE sparse. **4** *She was too dense to understand.* bovine, dim (*informal*), dull, dumb (*informal*), feeble-minded, foolish, obtuse, slow, stupid, thick, unintelligent. OPPOSITE bright.

dent *noun* *a dent in the bodywork.* depression, dimple, dint, hollow, indentation.

deny *verb* **1** *She denied the statement.* contradict, disclaim, gainsay (*formal*), negate, reject, repudiate. OPPOSITE affirm. **2** *He was denied his rights.* deprive of, disallow, refuse, withhold. OPPOSITE grant.

depart *verb* **1** *They packed their bags and departed.* clear off (*informal*), decamp, embark, emigrate, escape, exit, go away, leave, make off, make tracks (*informal*), nick off (*Australian slang*), push off (*informal*), quit, retire, run away, run off, scarper (*informal*), scram (*informal*), set off, set out, shoot through (*Australian informal*), skedaddle (*informal*), take your leave, withdraw. OPPOSITE arrive, stay. **2** *They departed from normal procedure.* break, deviate, diverge. OPPOSITE stick (to).

department *noun* *the departments of a hospital. a government department.* branch, bureau, division, office, part, section, unit.

departure *noun* *They were packed and ready for departure.* exit, exodus, going away, leaving, retreat, withdrawal. OPPOSITE arrival, return.

depend *verb* **depend on 1** *Whether we can swim depends on the weather.* hang on, hinge on, rest on, turn on. **2** *She depends on my help.*

bank on, count on, need, reckon on, rely on.

dependable *adjective* *a dependable person.* consistent, constant, faithful, loyal, reliable, stalwart, steadfast, steady, true, trustworthy. OPPOSITE unreliable.

dependent *adjective* **dependent on 1** *Promotion is dependent on ability.* conditional on, contingent on, determined by, subject to. OPPOSITE independent of. **2** *He is dependent on drugs.* addicted to, hooked on (*slang*), reliant on.

depict *verb* **1** *The artist depicted the scene in bright colours.* draw, illustrate, paint, picture, portray, represent, show, sketch. **2** *The writer depicted life in Victorian times.* describe, narrate, outline, record, relate.

deplorable *adjective* **1** *deplorable behaviour.* abominable, disgraceful, lamentable, regrettable, reprehensible, shameful. OPPOSITE praiseworthy. **2** *deplorable conditions.* appalling, awful, dire, dreadful, pathetic, shocking, wretched; see also BAD. OPPOSITE good.

deplore *verb* **1** *We deplore his death.* bewail, grieve over, lament, mourn, regret. **2** *She deplores waste.* condemn, deprecate, disapprove of, regret.

deploy *verb* *Troops were deployed along the border.* arrange, dispose, organise, position, spread out.

deport *verb* *The illegal immigrants were deported.* banish, exile, expatriate, expel, send away, transport.

deportment *noun* *The girls were assessed on dress and deportment.* bearing, behaviour, carriage, conduct, demeanour, manner, mien.

depose *verb* *The leader was deposed by his deputy.* dethrone, get rid of, oust, remove. OPPOSITE enthrone.

deposit *noun* **1** *He paid a deposit on the car.* down payment, first instalment. **2** *a deposit of mud.* alluvium, crust, dregs, lees, precipitate, sediment, silt. — *verb* **1** *They deposited their bags inside the door.* drop, dump, lay, leave, park (*informal*), place, put down, set down. **2** *She deposits her wages in the account.* bank, pay in, save. OPPOSITE withdraw.

depot *noun* **1** *Extra supplies are kept at the depot.* base, cache, headquarters, repository, store, storehouse, warehouse. **2** *a bus depot.* garage, station, terminal, terminus.

depraved *adjective* *a depraved murderer.* base, corrupt, degenerate, dissolute, evil, immoral, perverted, vile, wicked. OPPOSITE virtuous.

depreciate *verb* *The computer has depreciated in value.* decrease, devalue, drop, go down, lower, reduce. OPPOSITE appreciate.

depress *verb* **1** *His circumstances depressed him.* discourage, dishearten, oppress, sadden, weigh down. OPPOSITE cheer. **2** *depress the lever.* lower, press down, push down. OPPOSITE raise.

depressed *adjective* *feeling depressed.* blue, dejected, desolate, despondent, disconsolate, disheartened, dismal, dispirited, down, downcast, down-hearted, down in the dumps, gloomy, glum, heavy-hearted, hopeless, in the doldrums, low, melancholy, miserable, morose, out of sorts, pessimistic, sad, unhappy, woebegone, wretched. OPPOSITE elated, exhilarated.

depression *noun* **1** *He was overcome by depression.* the blues, dejection, despair, despondency, gloom, hopelessness, low spirits, melancholy, pessimism, sadness, unhappiness, wretchedness. OPPOSITE light-heartedness. **2** *Economists forecast*

a depression. decline, downturn, recession, slump. OPPOSITE boom. **3** *The weather map shows a depression.* cyclone, low, trough. OPPOSITE anticyclone, high. **4** *a depression in the ground.* basin, cavity, crabhole (*Australian*), crater, dent, dip, gilgai (*Australian*), hole, hollow, indentation, pit, trough. OPPOSITE elevation.

deprive *verb* **deprive of** *The war had deprived them of their childhood.* deny, dispossess of, refuse, rob of, take away.

depth *noun* **depth of feeling.* deepness, intensity, profundity, strength. ☐ **in depth** *study a subject in depth.* comprehensively, extensively, in detail, intensively, thoroughly.

deputise *verb* **deputise for** *He deputises for the boss.* fill in for, hold the fort for, stand in for, substitute for, take the place of.

deputy *noun* *Her deputy has to stand in for her quite often.* assistant, delegate, lieutenant, locum, offsider (*Australian*), proxy, relief, replacement, representative, reserve, stand-in, substitute, surrogate, understudy.

deranged *adjective* *The crime was committed by a deranged person.* berserk, crazy, demented, insane, irrational, lunatic, mad, unbalanced, unhinged. OPPOSITE sane.

derelict *adjective* *a derelict building.* abandoned, decrepit, deserted, dilapidated, forsaken, neglected, run-down, tumbledown. — *noun* *The derelict slept on a park bench.* down-and-out, outcast, tramp, vagrant.

deride *verb* see RIDICULE.

derision *noun* *They treated his idea with derision.* contempt, disdain, mockery, ridicule, sarcasm, scorn.

derivation *noun* *the derivation of a word.* etymology, origin, root, source.

derive *verb* **1** *She derives pleasure from cooking.* draw, gain, get, glean, obtain, receive. **2** *The word derives from Latin.* come, originate, stem.

derogatory *adjective* *a derogatory comment.* belittling, contemptuous, disparaging, insulting, pejorative, uncomplimentary. OPPOSITE complimentary.

descend *verb* **1** *We descended the mountain.* climb down, come down, go down. OPPOSITE climb. **2** *The plane suddenly descended.* come down, drop, fall, nosedive, plummet, plunge, sink, swoop down. OPPOSITE ascend.

descendants *plural noun* *Abraham was promised many descendants.* children, heirs, issue, offspring, progeny, scions, seed (*old use*). OPPOSITE ancestors.

descent *noun* **1** *the parachuter's descent.* coming down, dive, drop, fall, plunge. **2** *a steep descent in the road.* decline, downward slope. OPPOSITE ascent, rise. **3** *a person of noble descent.* ancestry, birth, blood, extraction, genealogy, lineage, origin, parentage, stock, strain.

describe *verb* *He described the events and the people.* characterise, depict, detail, elaborate, explain, express, narrate, outline, portray, recount, relate, represent, tell (about).

description *noun* *a description of a person. a description of an event.* account, characterisation, commentary, depiction, explanation, outline, picture, portrait, portrayal, profile, record, report, representation, sketch, story.

desecrate *verb* *Someone broke in and desecrated the church.* debase, defile, degrade, profane, violate. OPPOSITE honour.

desert[1] *noun an oasis in the desert.* wasteland, wilderness. — *adjective* **1** *The interior is desert country.* arid, barren, dry, infertile, uncultivated, waste, wild. **2** *a desert island.* desolate, uninhabited. OPPOSITE inhabited.

desert[2] *verb* **1** *He deserted his wife.* abandon, ditch (*informal*), dump (*informal*), forsake, jilt, leave, leave in the lurch, walk out on. OPPOSITE stand by. **2** *He was disillusioned with the party and deserted.* abscond, defect, run away. OPPOSITE stay.

deserter *noun an army deserter.* absconder, defector, escapee, fugitive, runaway.

deserts *plural noun He received his just deserts.* come-uppance (*informal*), due, nemesis, punishment, retribution, reward.

deserve *verb The CFS deserves our thanks and praise.* be entitled to, be worthy of, command, earn, justify, merit, warrant.

design *noun* **1** *She drew a design of the finished structure.* blueprint, diagram, draft, drawing, outline, pattern, plan, sketch. **2** *fashion design.* couture. **3** *an efficient kitchen design.* arrangement, configuration, form, layout. **4** *the newest design of blender.* model, style, type, version. **5** *fabric with a floral design.* composition, motif, pattern. — *verb* **1** *He designed the building.* conceive, draft, draw, lay out, plan, sketch, visualise. **2** *The speech was designed to make an impact.* aim, calculate, intend, mean, plan, tailor.

designate *verb He designated his son as his successor.* appoint, choose, name, nominate, select, specify, stipulate.

designation *noun Anthony's designation is Systems Administrator.* epithet, name, title.

designer *noun* **1** *an interior designer.* architect, inventor, originator, planner. **2** *a dress designer.* couturier, creator.

desirable *adjective* **1** *a desirable person. a desirable quality.* alluring, appealing, attractive, popular, sought-after, worthwhile. **2** *It is desirable that you wear a tie.* advisable, preferable, recommended.

desire *noun satisfy a desire for adventure.* ambition, appetite, aspiration, craving, fancy, hunger, itch, longing, lust, passion, thirst, urge, wish, yen. — *verb She desires fame.* covet, crave, fancy, hanker after, hope for, hunger for, long for, lust after, set your heart on, thirst for, want, wish for, yearn for.

desist *verb He asked the interjectors to desist.* cease, discontinue, leave off, refrain, stop. OPPOSITE persist.

desolate *adjective* **1** *a desolate landscape.* barren, bleak, deserted, dismal, dreary, empty, inhospitable, isolated, lonely, remote, stark, uninhabited, wild, windswept. **2** *Her father's death left her feeling desolate.* dejected, depressed, despondent, disconsolate, forlorn, forsaken, glum, heavy-hearted, lonely, melancholy, miserable, unhappy, wretched. OPPOSITE cheerful.

despair *noun She wrung her hands in despair.* depression, desperation, despondency, hopelessness. — *verb Do not despair. It will all work out.* give up, lose heart, lose hope.

desperate *adjective* **1** *The situation is desperate.* acute, bad, critical, dire, grave, hopeless, serious, urgent. **2** *a desperate criminal.* dangerous, daring, foolhardy, impetuous, rash, reckless, violent, wild.

despicable *adjective a despicable crime.* abominable, bad, base, contemptible, detestable, evil, hateful,

loathsome, low, mean, odious, outrageous, reprehensible, rotten, shameful, vile, wicked. OPPOSITE admirable.

despise *verb She despised them because they dobbed her in.* detest, disdain, dislike, feel contempt for, hate, loathe, look down on, scorn, spurn. OPPOSITE revere.

despondent *adjective She's been despondent since she lost her job.* dejected, depressed, discouraged, disheartened, dispirited, doleful, down, downcast, down-hearted, forlorn, gloomy, glum, heavy-hearted, melancholy, miserable, morose, sad, sorrowful, unhappy, wretched. OPPOSITE happy.

despot *noun They were ruled by a cruel despot.* autocrat, dictator, tyrant.

despotic *adjective a despotic ruler.* absolute, authoritarian, autocratic, dictatorial, domineering, imperious, oppressive, tyrannical.

dessert *noun afters* (*informal*), pudding, sweet.

destination *noun They reached their destination.* end, goal, objective, target.

destined *adjective destined to happen.* doomed, fated, intended, meant, ordained, predestined, preordained.

destiny *noun* **1** *She left it to destiny.* chance, fate, fortune, luck, providence. **2** *Her destiny was to be a martyr.* doom, fate, fortune, karma, kismet, lot, portion.

destitute *adjective Unemployment has left him destitute.* bankrupt, broke (*informal*), down and out, hard up (*informal*), impecunious, impoverished, insolvent, needy, penniless, penurious, poor, poverty-stricken. OPPOSITE rich.

destroy *verb* **1** *They destroyed the city's oldest buildings.* annihilate, blow up, demolish, devastate, dismantle, eliminate, exterminate, knock down, lay waste, level, obliterate, pull down, pull to pieces, ravage, raze, ruin, sabotage, smash, tear down, vandalise, wipe out, wreck, zap (*slang*). OPPOSITE construct. **2** *The vet destroyed the sick cow.* finish off, kill, put down, put to sleep, slaughter, slay. OPPOSITE save. **3** *The sharp criticism destroyed her confidence.* crush, dash, erode, extinguish, put an end to, shatter, undermine. OPPOSITE build.

destruction *noun weapons of mass destruction.* annihilation, damage, demolition, devastation, elimination, extermination, extinction, havoc, holocaust, killing, massacre, obliteration, ruin, sabotage, slaughter, vandalism, wreckage.

destructive *adjective a destructive influence.* adverse, baleful, damaging, dangerous, deleterious, detrimental, devastating, disastrous, harmful, injurious, malign, malignant, negative, pernicious, ruinous. OPPOSITE constructive.

detach *verb He detached the wheels from the suitcase.* disconnect, disengage, part, pull off, release, remove, separate, slip off, take off, undo, unfasten. OPPOSITE attach.

detached *adjective* **1** *a detached house.* free-standing, separate. OPPOSITE attached. **2** *a detached view of the matter.* aloof, disinterested, impartial, neutral, objective, unbiased, uninvolved, unprejudiced. OPPOSITE involved.

detail *noun a minor detail.* aspect, circumstance, element, fact, factor, feature, item, particular, point, respect.

detailed *adjective a detailed account.* blow-by-blow, comprehensive, elaborate, exact, exhaustive, full,

graphic, in-depth, itemised, minute, rigorous, thorough. OPPOSITE sketchy.

detain *verb* **1** *The police detained the suspect.* arrest, capture, confine, hold in custody, imprison, jail. OPPOSITE release. **2** *Her friend detained her at the shops.* bail up (*Australian*), buttonhole, delay, hold up, keep, waylay.

detect *verb She detected the leak. He detected that something was wrong.* discern, discover, find, identify, locate, note, notice, observe, perceive, see, sense, spot, track down, uncover. OPPOSITE overlook.

detective *noun* cop (*slang*), investigator, policeman, police officer, policewoman, private eye (*informal*), sleuth.

detention *noun kept in police detention.* captivity, confinement, custody, imprisonment.

deter *verb The fear of punishment deterred them.* daunt, discourage, dissuade, hinder, impede, obstruct, prevent, put off, scare off. OPPOSITE encourage.

deteriorate *verb Her health has deteriorated.* decline, degenerate, diminish, go backwards, go downhill, go to the dogs (*informal*), go to the pack (*Australian informal*), retrogress, sink, slip, wane, weaken, worsen. OPPOSITE improve.

determination *noun He will succeed because he has determination.* backbone, courage, doggedness, fortitude, grit, guts (*informal*), perseverance, persistence, pertinacity, resolve, spirit, tenacity, willpower.

determine *verb* **1** *He determined how much he would get.* ascertain, calculate, discover, establish, find out, work out. **2** *The committee determined what had to be done.* agree on, decide, fix on, resolve, settle. **3** *Many factors determine the result.* affect, control, decide, dictate, influence, regulate, shape.

determined *adjective a determined person.* adamant, dogged, firm, headstrong, intransigent, persistent, pertinacious, purposeful, resolute, single-minded, steadfast, strong-willed, stubborn, tenacious. OPPOSITE irresolute.

detest *verb He detests work.* abhor, abominate, despise, dislike, hate, loathe. OPPOSITE love.

detestable *adjective a detestable man.* abhorrent, abominable, atrocious, contemptible, deplorable, despicable, disgusting, hateful, horrid, intolerable, loathsome, objectionable, obnoxious, odious, repugnant, repulsive, revolting, vile. OPPOSITE lovable.

detonate *verb They detonated a bomb.* discharge, explode, let off, set off.

detour *noun a detour to avoid the roadworks.* bypass, deviation, diversion.

detract *verb* **detract from** *The weather did not detract from their enjoyment of the day.* diminish, lessen, reduce, take away from. OPPOSITE enhance.

detrimental *adjective The work had a detrimental effect on his health.* adverse, damaging, deleterious, destructive, harmful, injurious, pernicious, prejudicial. OPPOSITE beneficial.

devastate *verb The city was devastated by war.* damage, demolish, destroy, lay waste, level, ravage, raze, ruin, wreck.

devastated *adjective devastated by the news.* appalled, dismayed, overcome, overwhelmed, shattered, shocked, traumatised.

devastating *adjective a devastating earthquake.* catastrophic, destructive, disastrous.

develop *verb* **1** *The child developed.* advance, blossom, grow, mature. **2** *He developed the business.* build up, cultivate, diversify, enlarge, expand, improve, increase. **3** *The company developed rapidly.* advance, evolve, expand, flourish, grow, mushroom, progress. OPPOSITE stagnate. **4** *She developed a sore throat.* acquire, contract, get, pick up.

development *noun* **1** *the development of the business.* building, evolution, expansion, growth, progress, spread. **2** *the latest developments.* circumstance, event, happening, incident, occurrence.

deviant *adjective deviant behaviour.* aberrant, abnormal, freakish, kinky (*informal*), odd, peculiar, perverted, unusual. OPPOSITE normal.

deviate *verb She deviated from the rules.* depart, digress, diverge, stray, turn aside. OPPOSITE adhere to.

device *noun a kitchen full of modern devices.* apparatus, appliance, contraption (*informal*), gadget, implement, instrument, invention, machine, tool, utensil.

devil *noun* **1** *He was plagued by devils.* bogy, demon, evil spirit, fiend. **2** *He was a little devil.* imp, monster, rascal, rogue, scamp, scoundrel. □ **the Devil** Lucifer, Old Nick, Satan.

devilish *adjective devilish practices.* demonic, diabolical, evil, fiendish, hellish, infernal, satanic, ungodly, villainous, wicked. OPPOSITE angelic.

devious *adjective* **1** *a devious route.* circuitous, indirect, roundabout, tortuous, winding. OPPOSITE direct. **2** *a devious person.* calculating, crafty, cunning, deceitful, dishonest, sly, sneaky, underhand, wily. OPPOSITE straightforward.

devise *verb He devised a scheme.* conceive, concoct, contrive, cook up (*informal*), create, design, dream up, formulate, hatch, invent, make up, plan, plot, produce, think up, work out.

devoid *adjective* **devoid of** *The plan was devoid of merit.* bereft of, free from, lacking, without. OPPOSITE full of.

devote *verb She devotes her time to helping others.* commit, consecrate, dedicate, give, set aside.

devoted *adjective a devoted friend.* close, committed, constant, dedicated, enthusiastic, faithful, loving, loyal, reliable, staunch, true. OPPOSITE disloyal.

devotee *noun a devotee of tennis.* aficionado, buff (*informal*), enthusiast, fan, fanatic, follower, lover, supporter.

devotion *noun devotion to the party.* affection, allegiance, attachment, commitment, dedication, fervour, fondness, love, loyalty, zeal. □ **devotions** *plural noun He joined in morning devotions.* prayers, worship.

devour *verb They devoured the food in five minutes.* bolt, consume, demolish (*informal*), eat, gobble, gorge, gulp down, guzzle, knock back, scoff (*informal*), swallow, wolf.

devout *adjective a devout Jew.* ardent, committed, dedicated, devoted, earnest, fervent, genuine, godly, holy, pious, religious, sincere, staunch. OPPOSITE impious.

dexterous *adjective a dexterous cabinetmaker.* adept, adroit, agile, deft, nimble, skilful. OPPOSITE clumsy.

diabolical *adjective a diabolical deed.* devilish, evil, fiendish, hellish, infernal, inhuman, satanic, ungodly, villainous, wicked.

diagnose *verb The technician was able to diagnose the problem.* detect, determine, identify, name, recognise.

diagonal *adjective a diagonal line.* oblique, slanting, sloping.

diagram *noun* chart, drawing, figure, graph, illustration, outline, picture, plan, representation, sketch.

dial *verb She dialled her friend's house.* call, phone, ring, telephone.

dialect *noun They speak the local dialect.* accent, brogue, idiom, lingo (*informal*), patois, variety, vernacular; see also LANGUAGE.

dialogue *noun A dialogue between the parties resolved the matter.* communication, conference, conversation, discourse, discussion, talk.

diameter *noun the diameter of a gun.* bore, calibre, thickness, width.

diary *noun He kept a diary of daily happenings.* chronicle, journal, log, record.

dice *verb Dice the vegetables.* chop, cube.

dictate *verb He tried to dictate what she should wear.* command, decree, lay down the law on, ordain, order, prescribe.

dictator *noun The country is ruled by a dictator.* autocrat, despot, tyrant.

dictatorial *adjective His dictatorial approach made people resentful.* authoritarian, autocratic, bossy, despotic, domineering, imperious, overbearing, peremptory, totalitarian, tyrannical. OPPOSITE democratic.

dictatorship *noun a military dictatorship.* autocracy, despotism, tyranny.

dictionary *noun He could not find the word in his dictionary.* glossary, lexicon, phrase book, thesaurus, vocabulary.

die *verb* 1 *He died at eighty.* bite the dust (*slang*), breathe one's last, croak (*slang*), depart this world, expire, fall (*in war*), go to glory (*slang*), kick the bucket (*slang*), lose one's life, pass away, pass on, perish, snuff it (*slang*). OPPOSITE live, survive. 2 *The engine died.* break down, conk out (*informal*), fail. 3 *She is dying for an ice cream.* hanker, hunger, long, thirst, yearn. □ **die down** *Interest died down.* decline, decrease, diminish, ebb, fade, fizzle out, lessen, peter out, subside, taper off, wane. OPPOSITE grow. **die out** *The custom has died out.* cease, disappear, end, pass, vanish. OPPOSITE endure, survive.

diet *noun She eats a healthy diet.* fare, food intake, nourishment, nutrition.

differ *verb* 1 *The twins differ in temperament.* be different, be dissimilar, be distinguishable, be poles apart, be unlike, contrast. OPPOSITE be alike. 2 *They differed on the matter.* be at odds, clash, conflict, disagree, quarrel. OPPOSITE agree.

difference *noun* 1 *a difference in meaning.* contrast, deviation, disparity, dissimilarity, distinction, divergence, nuance. OPPOSITE likeness, similarity. 2 *They agreed to make up the difference.* balance, deficit, gap. 3 *a difference in her mood.* alteration, change, modification, transformation, variation. 4 *They settled their differences.* argument, conflict, disagreement, dispute, quarrel, strife, tiff. OPPOSITE agreement.

different *adjective* 1 *They have completely different ideas.* conflicting, contradictory, contrary, contrasting, disparate, dissimilar, distinct, divergent, unlike. OPPOSITE identical. 2 *a collection of different stamps.* assorted, diverse, heteroge-

neous, miscellaneous, mixed, sundry, various. OPPOSITE identical. 3 *a different way of looking at things.* alternative, new, novel, other. OPPOSITE same. 4 *He's different now.* altered, changed, modified, transformed. 5 *There is a different peg for each person's coat.* discrete, distinct, individual, particular, separate, special, unique.

differentiate *verb* 1 *the features that differentiate the two models.* contrast, distinguish, separate, set apart. 2 *He cannot differentiate between blue and green.* contrast, discriminate, distinguish, tell apart. OPPOSITE confuse.

difficult *adjective* 1 *a difficult maths problem.* abstruse, baffling, challenging, complex, complicated, confusing, hard, knotty, perplexing, problematical, puzzling, thorny, ticklish, tough, tricky. OPPOSITE easy. 2 *Moving the piano is a difficult task.* arduous, demanding, exacting, exhausting, formidable, gruelling, hard, herculean, laborious, onerous, strenuous, taxing, tiring, tough, uphill. OPPOSITE easy. 3 *difficult times.* bad, hard, harsh, oppressive, rough, severe, tough, troubled. 4 *a difficult person to deal with.* awkward, demanding, fussy, intractable, obstreperous, recalcitrant, refractory, stroppy (*informal*), stubborn, troublesome, trying, uncooperative.

difficulty *noun He overcame many difficulties.* adversity, complication, hang-up (*informal*), hardship, hassle (*informal*), hindrance, hitch, hurdle, impediment, obstacle, ordeal, pitfall, pressure, problem, snag, stumbling block, trouble. □ **in difficulties** *If you are in difficulties ask for help.* in a bind (*informal*), in a fix, in a jam (*informal*), in a mess, in a pickle (*informal*), in a plight, in a predicament, in a quandary, in a spot (*informal*), in dire straits, in hot water (*informal*), in strife (*Australian informal*), in the soup (*informal*), in trouble, up the creek (*informal*).

diffident *adjective a diffident applicant.* bashful, coy, hesitant, meek, modest, reserved, reticent, shy, tentative, timid, timorous, unassertive. OPPOSITE confident.

diffuse *adjective* 1 *diffuse light.* dispersed, scattered, spread out. OPPOSITE concentrated. 2 *a diffuse style.* long-winded, rambling, verbose, wordy. OPPOSITE concise. — *verb The ink diffused through the water.* circulate, disperse, spread.

dig *verb* 1 *The wombat dug under the fence.* burrow, delve (*old use*), excavate, tunnel. 2 *He dug a hole.* gouge out, hollow out, scoop out. 3 *He dug his fork into the meat.* jab, plunge, poke, prod, stab, thrust. — *noun* 1 *an archaeological dig.* excavation. 2 *a dig in the ribs.* nudge, poke, prod, thrust. □ **dig up** 1 *They dug up the body.* disinter, exhume, unearth. OPPOSITE bury. 2 *She dug up some useful facts.* discover, dredge up, ferret out, find, fossick out (*Australian informal*), root out, seek, uncover, unearth.

digest *verb* 1 *He has trouble digesting certain foods.* absorb, assimilate, break down. 2 *It took time to digest the information.* absorb, assimilate, comprehend, grasp, take in, understand.

digit *noun* 1 *a number with four digits.* figure, integer, number, numeral. 2 *an animal's digits.* finger, toe.

dignified *adjective a dignified air. a dignified person.* calm, decorous, elegant, formal, grand, honourable, imposing, majestic, noble, proper,

sedate, serious, sober, solemn, staid, stately. OPPOSITE undignified.

dignitary *noun The wedding was attended by many foreign dignitaries.* bigwig (*informal*), celebrity, luminary, personage, VIP, worthy.

dignity *noun* 1 *He behaved with dignity.* decorum, formality, gravity, majesty, nobility, poise, propriety, self-respect, solemnity, stateliness. 2 *a job beneath his dignity.* position, rank, standing, station, status.

digress *verb The speaker digressed several times.* deviate, diverge, drift, ramble, stray, wander.

dike *noun* see DYKE.

dilapidated *adjective a dilapidated old house. a dilapidated car.* battered, broken down, decrepit, derelict, ramshackle, rickety, ruined, run-down, tumbledown.

dilate *verb The blood vessels dilated.* broaden, distend, enlarge, expand, swell, widen. OPPOSITE constrict.

dilemma *noun* (*informal*) *in a dilemma.* bind (*informal*), catch-22 (*informal*), difficulty, fix, hole (*informal*), jam (*informal*), mess, plight, predicament, problem, quandary, spot (*informal*).

diligent *adjective a diligent student.* assiduous, attentive, careful, conscientious, earnest, hard-working, indefatigable, industrious, meticulous, painstaking, persevering, scrupulous, sedulous, steady, studious, thorough. OPPOSITE slack.

dilute *verb She diluted the soup.* adulterate, thin, water down, weaken. OPPOSITE concentrate.

dim *adjective* 1 *dim light.* cloudy, dark, dingy, dull, dusky, faint, gloomy, low, murky, pale, shadowy, weak. OPPOSITE bright. 2 *a dim memory.* blurred, faint, fuzzy, hazy, indistinct, obscure, vague. OPPOSITE clear. 3 *He's too dim to understand that.* see STUPID.

dimension *noun A solid has three dimensions.* breadth, depth, height, length, measurement, thickness, width. □ **dimensions** *plural noun* 1 *the room's dimensions.* area, capacity, measurements, proportions, size, volume. 2 *the dimensions of a problem.* extent, magnitude, scale, scope, size.

diminish *verb Interest has diminished.* abate, contract, decline, decrease, dwindle, fade, lessen, reduce, shrink, subside, wane. OPPOSITE increase.

din *noun She could not hear her friend above the din.* bedlam, clamour, clatter, commotion, hubbub, hullabaloo, noise, pandemonium, racket, row (*informal*), rumpus, shindy (*informal*), tumult, uproar. OPPOSITE silence.

dine *verb They dine at 7.30 p.m.* eat, feast, have dinner, sup.

dingy *adjective He felt depressed in his dingy office.* dark, dirty, dismal, drab, dreary, dull, gloomy, shabby. OPPOSITE bright.

dinkum *adjective* (*Australian informal*) *a dinkum Aussie.* authentic, bona fide, dinky-di (*Australian informal*), genuine, honest-to-goodness (*informal*), real, true, veritable. OPPOSITE fake.

dinner *noun a farewell dinner.* banquet, feast, meal, repast (*formal*), supper, tea.

dip *verb* 1 *She dips her biscuit in her tea.* dunk, immerse, plunge, sink, steep, submerge, wet. 2 *The road dips.* decline, descend, drop, go down, slope downwards. OPPOSITE rise. — *noun* 1 *a dip in the pool.* bathe, bogey (*Australian*), plunge, swim. 2 *a dip in the road.* depression, hollow. OPPOSITE hump. □ **dip into** *He dipped into the book.* browse, glance at, sample, skim.

diploma *noun* award, certificate, qualification.

diplomacy *noun She handled a tricky situation with diplomacy.* courtesy, delicacy, discretion, tact, tactfulness. OPPOSITE tactlessness.

diplomat *noun an Australian diplomat in Iraq.* ambassador, attaché, consul, envoy, representative.

diplomatic *adjective He was diplomatic in his reply.* courteous, delicate, discreet, judicious, polite, politic, sensitive, tactful. OPPOSITE tactless.

dire *adjective* 1 *dire consequences.* appalling, calamitous, catastrophic, disastrous, dreadful, horrible, serious, terrible. 2 *dire warnings.* gloomy, grave, grim, ominous. 3 *in dire need.* critical, desperate, drastic, extreme, pressing, urgent.

direct *adjective* 1 *a direct route.* straight, unswerving. OPPOSITE indirect, roundabout. 2 *a direct way of speaking.* blunt, candid, explicit, forthright, frank, honest, open, outspoken, plain, straight, straightforward, to the point. OPPOSITE evasive. 3 *direct opposites.* absolute, complete, diametrical, exact, polar. — *verb* 1 *She directed me to the office.* conduct, guide, lead, navigate, point, show, steer, usher. 2 *They directed their guns at the crowd.* aim, level, point, target, train, turn. 3 *She directed the proceedings.* administer, command, control, govern, head, lead, manage, mastermind, oversee, preside over, regulate, run, superintend, supervise. 4 *He directed them to leave.* bid, command, instruct, order, tell.

direction *noun* 1 *Things improved under her direction.* administration, charge, command, control, guidance, leadership, management, supervision. 2 *travelling in a northerly direction.* course, line, route, tack, way. □ **directions** *plural noun He followed the directions.* guidelines, instructions, orders, recipe, rules.

director *noun the director of a company.* administrator, boss, captain, chairperson, chief, commander, coordinator, executive, governor, head, leader, manager, superintendent, supervisor.

directory *noun Her name is in the directory.* index, list, register.

dirge *noun They sang a dirge at the funeral.* elegy, keen, lament.

dirt *noun* 1 *Clean the dirt off your shoes.* dust, filth, grime, mire, muck, mud, soot. 2 *a heap of dirt.* clay, earth, loam, soil.

dirty *adjective* 1 *dirty clothes. a dirty place.* blackened, dingy, dusty, filthy, foul, grimy, grotty (*slang*), grubby, insanitary, messy, muddy, soiled, sooty, sordid, squalid, stained, unclean, unwashed. OPPOSITE clean. 2 *a dirty trick.* base, contemptible, despicable, dishonest, dishonourable, low, low-down, mean, nasty, shabby, underhand, unfair, unsporting. OPPOSITE above board. 3 *a dirty joke.* bawdy, blue, coarse, crude, filthy, improper, indecent, lewd, obscene, offensive, pornographic, rude, smutty, tasteless, vulgar. OPPOSITE clean. — *verb Mud dirtied the water.* blacken, foul, muddy, pollute, soil, stain, sully, tarnish. OPPOSITE clean.

disability *noun mental or physical disability.* handicap, impairment, incapacity.

disabled *adjective a disabled person.* crippled, handicapped, incapacitated, lame, maimed. OPPOSITE able-bodied.

disadvantage *noun Her shortness was a disadvantage in netball.* drawback, handicap, hindrance, impediment, inconvenience, liability, minus. OPPOSITE advantage, benefit.

disadvantaged *adjective a disadvantaged group in society.* deprived, underprivileged. OPPOSITE favoured.

disagree *verb* **1** *the right to disagree.* differ, dissent, diverge. OPPOSITE agree. **2** *His statement disagrees with theirs.* be at odds, be at variance, be incompatible, clash, conflict, contrast, differ (from). OPPOSITE coincide. **3** *The sisters disagree over everything.* argue, be at loggerheads, differ, quarrel, squabble, wrangle. OPPOSITE agree.

disagreeable *adjective* **1** *a disagreeable smell.* disgusting, distasteful, nasty, objectionable, obnoxious, offensive, repugnant, repulsive, revolting, unpleasant. OPPOSITE pleasant. **2** *He is disagreeable when he first gets up.* bad-tempered, crabby, cross, crotchety, fractious, grouchy (*informal*), grumpy, irritable, shirty (*informal*), snaky (*Australian informal*), stroppy (*informal*), surly, unfriendly. OPPOSITE affable.

disagreement *noun* There was a disagreement over boundaries. altercation, argument, clash, conflict, controversy, dispute, quarrel, row, squabble, tiff, wrangle. OPPOSITE consensus.

disappear *verb* **1** *The man disappeared before we could find out his name.* clear off (*informal*), flee, go away, nick off (*Australian slang*), retire, retreat, run away, run off, scarper (*informal*), scram (*informal*), shoot through (*Australian informal*), vanish, withdraw. OPPOSITE appear, arrive. **2** *The fog disappeared.* clear, dissipate, evaporate, fade, melt away, pass, vanish.

disappoint *verb* **1** *The attendance disappointed the organisers.* discourage, dishearten, disillusion, let down, sadden. OPPOSITE gratify. **2** *He disappointed their hopes.* dash, destroy, frustrate, shatter, thwart. OPPOSITE satisfy.

disappointed *adjective* With such high expectations Eve was bound to be disappointed. discontented, disenchanted, disheartened, disillusioned, dissatisfied, frustrated, let down, saddened, unhappy. OPPOSITE satisfied.

disappointment *noun* **1** *He did not hide his disappointment.* chagrin, discontent, disenchantment, disillusionment, dissatisfaction, frustration, regret, sadness, unhappiness. OPPOSITE fulfilment. **2** *The actual event was a bit of a disappointment.* anticlimax, comedown, damp squib, failure, fiasco, fizzer (*Australian informal*), flop (*informal*), letdown, non-event, swizz (*informal*), washout (*informal*). OPPOSITE success.

disapproval *noun* She viewed the deal with disapproval. censure, condemnation, criticism, disapprobation, disfavour, dissatisfaction; see also OPPOSITION.

disapprove *verb* **disapprove of** *He disapproved of what they did.* censure, condemn, criticise, denounce, deplore, deprecate, frown on, object to, take a dim view of (*informal*). OPPOSITE approve.

disarming *adjective* a disarming smile. charming, enchanting, engaging, winning.

disarray *noun* Her house was in disarray. chaos, confusion, disorder, havoc, mess, muddle, shambles. OPPOSITE order.

disaster *noun* **1** *natural disasters.* accident, adversity, calamity, cataclysm, catastrophe, misfortune, mishap, reverse, tragedy. **2** *The din-*

ner was a disaster. failure, fiasco, fizzer (*Australian informal*), flop (*informal*), washout (*informal*). OPPOSITE success.

disastrous *adjective* disastrous consequences. appalling, calamitous, cataclysmic, catastrophic, devastating, dire, dreadful, ruinous, terrible, tragic.

disband *verb* The group disbanded. break up, disperse, dissolve, separate, split up.

disbelieve *verb* She disbelieved their explanation. distrust, doubt, mistrust, question. OPPOSITE believe.

disc *noun* **1** *The game is played with coloured discs.* circle, counter, token. **2** *music discs.* album, compact disc, record, recording, single.

discard *verb* They discarded their old clothes. cast off, chuck out (*informal*), dice (*Australian informal*), dispose of, ditch (*informal*), dump, get rid of, jettison, reject, scrap, shed, throw away. OPPOSITE keep.

discern *verb* It was easy to discern his displeasure. detect, make out, notice, observe, perceive, recognise, see, sense.

discerning *adjective* the discerning viewer. critical, discriminating, intelligent, judicious, perceptive, sharp, shrewd, wise. OPPOSITE undiscerning.

discharge *verb* **1** *The factory discharged its waste into the river.* belch, eject, emit, empty out, expel, exude, give out, leak, ooze, pour out, release, secrete, send out, spurt. **2** *He accidentally discharged the missile.* detonate, explode, fire, let off, set off, shoot, trigger. **3** *He was discharged from his job.* dismiss, fire, kick out (*informal*), sack (*informal*). OPPOSITE hire. **4** *The patient was discharged from hospital.* free, liberate, release. OPPOSITE admit. **5** *With the payout she was able to discharge her debts.* clear, meet, pay, settle, square.

disciple *noun* a disciple of Rousseau. adherent, apprentice, devotee, follower, pupil, supporter.

disciplinarian *noun* The teacher was a disciplinarian. authoritarian, hard-liner, martinet, stickler, taskmaster.

discipline *noun* The teacher maintains good discipline. control, order, routine, system. — *verb* **1** *She disciplined them to say 'Please'.* coach, drill, educate, indoctrinate, instruct, train. **2** *He disciplined them harshly.* chastise, correct, penalise, punish, rebuke, reprimand.

disclaim *verb* The company disclaimed all responsibility. deny, disown, refuse, reject, repudiate. OPPOSITE acknowledge.

disclose *verb* You must not disclose this information to anyone. air, betray, blab, blow (*slang*), bring to light, divulge, expose, give away, impart, leak, let out, let slip, make known, make public, publish, reveal, tell, uncover. OPPOSITE cover up.

disco *noun* (*informal*) club, discothèque, nightclub; see also DANCE.

discolour *verb* The material has discoloured. bleach, fade, scorch, stain, tarnish, tinge.

discomfort *noun* physical or mental discomfort. ache, affliction, distress, hardship, irritation, misery, pain, soreness, suffering, uneasiness. OPPOSITE comfort.

disconcert *verb* The noises did not seem to disconcert him. agitate, confuse, discomfit, disturb, faze (*informal*), fluster, perturb, put off, rattle (*informal*), ruffle, throw (*informal*), trouble, unnerve, upset, worry.

disconnect *verb* They need to disconnect the power supply. cut off, detach, disengage, switch off, turn

off, uncouple, undo, unplug. OPPOSITE connect.

disconnected *adjective* disconnected thoughts. disjointed, disorganised, garbled, haphazard, incoherent, jumbled, rambling, random, unsystematic. OPPOSITE connected.

discontent *noun* The workers voiced their discontent. disenchantment, displeasure, disquiet, dissatisfaction, misery, regret, resentment, restlessness, unhappiness. OPPOSITE contentment.

discontented *adjective* He was discontented with his job. browned off (*slang*), cheesed off (*slang*), disenchanted, disgruntled, displeased, dissatisfied, fed up (*informal*), miserable, unhappy. OPPOSITE contented.

discontinue *verb* They discontinued the ballet class. abandon, break off, cancel, cease, cut, end, finish, interrupt, stop, suspend, terminate. OPPOSITE continue.

discord *noun* There was discord over the new toy. argument, conflict, disagreement, disharmony, dissension, disunity, friction, quarrelling, strife. OPPOSITE accord, concord.

discordant *adjective* discordant sounds. cacophonous, dissonant, grating, harsh, jarring, strident. OPPOSITE harmonious.

discount *noun* a 5% discount on the full price. concession, cut, deduction, rebate, reduction.

discourage *verb* **1** *She was discouraged by her failure.* daunt, demoralise, depress, dishearten, dismay, intimidate. OPPOSITE encourage. **2** *They discouraged him from applying.* deter, dissuade, put off, talk out of. OPPOSITE persuade.

discourse *noun* **1** *a scholarly discourse on plant classification.* address, dissertation, essay, lecture, monograph, oration, paper, sermon, speech, talk, thesis, treatise. **2** *polite discourse.* see CONVERSATION.

discourteous *adjective* It would be discourteous to refuse her aunt's invitation. bad-mannered, boorish, cheeky, disrespectful, ill-mannered, impertinent, impolite, impudent, insolent, insulting, rude, uncivil, uncouth. OPPOSITE polite.

discover *verb* She discovered the solution by accident. come across, come upon, detect, dig up, ferret out, find, find out, hear of, hit on, identify, learn, light on, locate, perceive, read of, realise, spot, stumble on, suss out (*informal*), track down, uncover, unearth, work out.

discredit *verb* **1** *They tried to discredit the Opposition.* blacken, defame, denigrate, disgrace, disparage, malign, slander, smear, sully, vilify. **2** *The theory has been discredited.* challenge, debunk (*informal*), disprove, explode, invalidate, question.

discreet *adjective* She was discreet in her comments. careful, cautious, chary, circumspect, diplomatic, guarded, judicious, prudent, tactful, wary. OPPOSITE indiscreet.

discrepancy *noun* a discrepancy in the figures. difference, disagreement, disparity, inconsistency.

discrete *adjective* discrete entities. disconnected, distinct, separate.

discretion *noun* He acted with discretion. care, discernment, judgement, prudence, sense, sensitivity, tact, wisdom. OPPOSITE indiscretion.

discriminate *verb* He can't discriminate between the two brands. differentiate, distinguish, tell apart.

discrimination *noun* sexual discrimination. bias, favouritism, inequity, intolerance, prejudice, unfairness. OPPOSITE impartiality.

discuss *verb* They discussed the matter. argue, confer on, consider, converse about, debate, deliberate, examine, have out, speak about, talk about, thrash out.

discussion *noun* **1** *a discussion between management and the union.* argument, conference, consultation, conversation, debate, dialogue, exchange, talk. **2** *The author presents a detailed discussion of the issues.* analysis, examination, scrutiny, study.

disdain *noun* They treated his idea with disdain. contempt, derision, scorn. OPPOSITE respect. — *verb* He disdained their attempts at reconciliation. despise, look down on, rebuff, reject, scorn, sneer at, spurn.

disdainful *adjective* a disdainful look. arrogant, contemptuous, derisive, haughty, hoity-toity, proud, scornful, sneering, snobbish, snooty (*informal*), supercilious, superior.

disease *noun* suffering from a rare disease. affliction, ailment, bug (*informal*), complaint, condition, disorder, illness, infection, malady, plague, sickness.

disembark *verb* The passengers disembarked at Fremantle. alight, get off, get out, go ashore, land. OPPOSITE board.

disentangle *verb* **1** *She disentangled the rope.* sort out, straighten out, unravel, untangle, untie, untwist. OPPOSITE entangle. **2** *He disentangled the animal from the net.* detach, extricate, free, liberate.

disfigured *adjective* The accident left him disfigured. defaced, deformed, mutilated, scarred.

disgrace *noun* He brought disgrace upon himself. discredit, dishonour, disrepute, humiliation, ignominy, reproach, scandal, shame, stigma. OPPOSITE honour. — *verb* He disgraced his family. bring dishonour to, bring shame on, degrade, embarrass, humiliate, let down.

disgraceful *adjective* disgraceful conduct. contemptible, degrading, discreditable, dishonourable, ignominious, outrageous, scandalous, shameful, unbecoming, unseemly. OPPOSITE creditable.

disgruntled *adjective* a disgruntled customer. browned off (*slang*), cheesed off (*slang*), cross, discontented, displeased, dissatisfied, fed up (*informal*), unhappy. OPPOSITE satisfied.

disguise *verb* **1** *He disguised himself as a priest.* dress up, masquerade; see also IMPERSONATE. **2** *He could not disguise his true feelings.* camouflage, conceal, cover up, hide, mask, veil. — *noun* We were taken in by the disguise. camouflage, costume, cover, mask, masquerade.

disgust *noun* They had to overcome feelings of disgust. abhorrence, antipathy, aversion, contempt, dislike, distaste, hatred, loathing, nausea, repugnance, repulsion, revulsion. — *verb* The battle scene disgusted them. appal, horrify, nauseate, offend, repel, revolt, shock, sicken, turn someone's stomach.

disgusting *adjective* a disgusting habit. appalling, detestable, distasteful, dreadful, filthy, foul, gross (*informal*), loathsome, nauseating, objectionable, obnoxious, offensive, off-putting, repellent, repugnant, repulsive, revolting, shocking, sickening, unpleasant, vile, yucky (*informal*). OPPOSITE delightful.

dish *noun* basin, bowl, casserole, container, coolamon (*Australian*), plate, platter, ramekin, receptacle, tureen; [*dishes*] crockery. ☐ **dish out** see DISTRIBUTE.

dishearten *verb* The failure disheartened him. demoralise, depress, discourage, dismay, sadden. OPPOSITE encourage.

dishevelled *adjective The runners were dishevelled after the race.* bedraggled, messy, ruffled, scruffy, tangled, tousled, unkempt, untidy. OPPOSITE neat.

dishonest *adjective a dishonest person. a dishonest act.* bent (*slang*), corrupt, criminal, crooked, deceitful, deceptive, dodgy (*informal*), false, fraudulent, hypocritical, insincere, lying, mendacious, misleading, shady, shonky (*Australian informal*), two-faced, underhand, unscrupulous, untrustworthy, untruthful. OPPOSITE honest.

dishonour *noun* see DISGRACE.

dishonourable *adjective dishonourable behaviour.* base, despicable, discreditable, disgraceful, disreputable, ignominious, improper, low, opprobrious, reprehensible, shabby, shameful, unprincipled. OPPOSITE honourable.

disillusion *verb They were full of hope and he did not want to disillusion them.* disabuse, disappoint, disenchant, enlighten, undeceive.

disincentive *noun Losing your licence is a disincentive to drink-drive.* deterrent, discouragement. OPPOSITE incentive.

disinfect *verb The bathroom has been disinfected.* clean, cleanse, fumigate, purify, sanitise, sterilise.

disinfectant *noun* antiseptic, bactericide, germicide, sanitiser, steriliser.

disintegrate *verb The structure disintegrated after many years.* break up, collapse, crumble, decay, decompose, deteriorate, fall apart, perish, rot, shatter.

disinterested *adjective The adjudicator must be a disinterested party.* detached, dispassionate, impartial, neutral, objective, unbiased, uninvolved, unprejudiced. OPPOSITE biased, interested.

disjointed *adjective a disjointed speech.* desultory, disconnected, disorganised, fragmented, incoherent, jumbled, mixed up, rambling. OPPOSITE coherent.

dislike *noun He took a strong dislike to me.* abhorrence, animosity, antipathy, aversion, contempt, detestation, disgust, distaste, hatred, horror, hostility, loathing, repugnance, resentment, revulsion. OPPOSITE liking. — *verb She dislikes liars.* abominate, despise, detest, hate, have an aversion to, loathe, object to, resent, take exception to. OPPOSITE like.

disloyal *adjective He was disloyal to his friends.* faithless, false, perfidious, treacherous, two-faced, unfaithful, untrue. OPPOSITE loyal.

disloyalty *noun She was dismissed for disloyalty.* betrayal, infidelity, perfidy, treachery, treason, unfaithfulness. OPPOSITE loyalty.

dismal *adjective dismal songs.* black, bleak, cheerless, depressing, dreary, funereal, gloomy, grim, lugubrious, melancholy, miserable, mournful, sad, sombre. OPPOSITE cheerful.

dismantle *verb They dismantled the trampoline for storage.* demolish, knock down, pull to pieces, take apart, take down, undo. OPPOSITE assemble, erect.

dismay *noun The thought of war filled them with dismay.* agitation, alarm, anxiety, apprehension, consternation, discouragement, dread, fear, horror, shock, terror, trepidation. OPPOSITE delight. — *verb The amount of work dismayed her.* alarm, appal, daunt, depress, disconcert, discourage, dishearten, distress, frighten, horrify, scare, shock, terrify, unnerve. OPPOSITE cheer.

dismiss *verb* **1** *The teacher dismissed the class.* disband, let go, release, send away. **2** *The boss dismissed him.* discharge, fire, get rid of, give notice to, give the boot to (*slang*), give the sack to (*informal*), kick out (*informal*), lay off, make redundant, pension off, remove, sack (*informal*). OPPOSITE hire, reinstate. **3** *He was quick to dismiss the idea.* discard, give up, pooh-pooh, reject, set aside. OPPOSITE accept.

dismount *verb The rider dismounted.* alight, descend, get down, get off. OPPOSITE mount.

disobedient *adjective a disobedient person.* contrary, defiant, insubordinate, intractable, mutinous, naughty, obstreperous, perverse, rebellious, recalcitrant, refractory, unmanageable, unruly, wayward. OPPOSITE compliant, obedient.

disobey *verb She disobeyed the rules.* break, contravene, defy, disregard, flout, ignore, infringe, transgress, violate. OPPOSITE obey, observe.

disorder *noun* **1** *The room was in disorder.* chaos, confusion, disarray, mess, muddle, shambles, untidiness. OPPOSITE order. **2** *public disorder.* anarchy, bedlam, chaos, commotion, confusion, disturbance, havoc, lawlessness, mayhem, pandemonium, rioting, trouble, turmoil, unrest, uproar. OPPOSITE order, peace. **3** *a nervous disorder.* ailment, complaint, condition, disease, illness, malady, sickness.

disorderly *adjective* **1** *a disorderly crowd.* badly-behaved, boisterous, lawless, obstreperous, riotous, rowdy, turbulent, undisciplined, unruly, wild. OPPOSITE well-behaved. **2** *a disorderly office.* chaotic, confused, disorganised, higgledy-piggledy, jumbled, messy, muddled, topsy-turvy, unsystematic, untidy. OPPOSITE tidy.

disorganised *adjective disorganised work.* careless, confused, disorderly, haphazard, messy, slipshod, sloppy, unmethodical, unsystematic. OPPOSITE methodical.

disown *verb He disowned his former friend.* cast off, deny, disclaim, ostracise, reject, renounce, repudiate. OPPOSITE acknowledge.

disparaging *adjective disparaging comments.* critical, derogatory, insulting, pejorative, uncomplimentary. OPPOSITE complimentary.

disparity *noun a disparity in their ages.* contrast, difference, discrepancy, gap, inequality. OPPOSITE equality, similarity.

dispassionate *adjective He took a dispassionate view of events.* calm, clinical, composed, detached, disinterested, impartial, neutral, objective, unbiased, unemotional, uninvolved, unprejudiced.

dispatch *verb* **1** *They dispatched the parcel.* consign, convey, deliver, forward, mail, post, send, transmit. OPPOSITE receive. **2** *The farmer dispatched the sick cow.* see KILL. — *noun a government dispatch.* bulletin, communication, communiqué, letter, message, report.

dispel *verb The phone call dispelled her fears.* allay, banish, drive away, remove, scatter.

dispense *verb* **1** *She dispensed their pocket money.* allocate, allot, apportion, deal out, dish out (*informal*), distribute, dole out, give out, hand out, issue, mete out. **2** *The chemist dispenses medicines.* give out, make up, prepare, provide, supply. □ **dispense with** *We can dispense with the car.* dispose of, do without, forgo, get rid of, relinquish. OPPOSITE retain.

disperse *verb The crowd dispersed.* break up, disband, scatter, spread out. OPPOSITE congregate, gather.

displace *verb She was displaced in his affections.* oust, replace, supersede, supplant.

display *verb He displayed his knowledge to the examiners.* demonstrate, exhibit, flaunt, manifest, parade, present, reveal, show. OPPOSITE conceal. — *noun a doll display. a ballet display.* array, demonstration, exhibition, exposition, pageant, presentation, show, spectacle.

displease *verb His behaviour displeased them.* anger, annoy, exasperate, irk, irritate, offend, trouble, upset, vex, worry. OPPOSITE please.

displeasure *noun He could not hide his displeasure.* anger, annoyance, chagrin, disapproval, disfavour, exasperation, indignation, irritation, wrath. OPPOSITE pleasure.

disposable *adjective* **1** *disposable income.* available, net, usable. **2** *disposable cups.* discardable, throw-away. OPPOSITE reusable.

dispose *verb The singers were disposed in three rows according to height.* arrange, array, group, marshal, order, organise, place, set out. □ **dispose of** *She disposed of her old car.* discard, dispatch, ditch (*informal*), dump, get rid of, give away, scrap, sell, throw away, throw out. OPPOSITE keep.

disposition *noun a kindly disposition.* attitude, character, make-up, nature, personality, spirit, temperament.

disprove *verb He disproved the theory.* confute, debunk (*informal*), discredit, explode, negate, rebut, refute. OPPOSITE confirm, prove.

dispute *verb* **1** *Emily disputed with her sister about who owned the ring.* argue, bicker, clash, debate, disagree, haggle, quarrel, squabble, wrangle. **2** *He disputed their right to be there.* challenge, contest, doubt, query, question. OPPOSITE accept. — *noun a dispute about ownership.* altercation, argument, battle, conflict, controversy, debate, disagreement, feud, quarrel, row, squabble, wrangle.

disqualify *verb Tina was disqualified from driving for six months.* ban, bar, debar, outlaw, preclude, prohibit.

disregard *verb He disregarded my wishes.* brush aside, forget, ignore, neglect, overlook, pay no attention to; see also DISOBEY. OPPOSITE heed.

disrepair *noun The house was in a state of disrepair.* decay, dilapidation, neglect, ruin.

disreputable *adjective* **1** *a disreputable firm.* discreditable, dishonourable, dodgy (*informal*), dubious, notorious, shady, shonky (*Australian informal*), suspect, untrustworthy. OPPOSITE reputable. **2** *He looked disreputable.* dirty, scruffy, seedy, shabby, sleazy, slovenly, unkempt, untidy. OPPOSITE respectable.

disrespect *noun He meant no disrespect.* contempt, impiety, impoliteness, insolence, irreverence, rudeness. OPPOSITE respect.

disrespectful *adjective She was disrespectful to her mother.* cheeky, contemptuous, discourteous, impertinent, impolite, impudent, insolent, irreverent, offensive, rude, uncivil. OPPOSITE respectful.

disrupt *verb The strike disrupted progress on the site.* break up, cut into, disturb, interfere with, interrupt, obstruct, upset.

dissatisfied *adjective dissatisfied patrons.* browned off (*slang*), cheesed off (*slang*), disappointed, discontented, disenchanted, disgruntled, displeased, fed up (*informal*), frustrated, unhappy. OPPOSITE contented, satisfied.

dissect *verb The students dissected a rat.* cut up, dismember.

disseminate *verb The council uses leaflets and their website to disseminate information.* broadcast, circulate, distribute, promulgate, publicise, publish, spread.

dissent *verb Only one member dissented.* differ, disagree, object, protest. OPPOSITE assent.

disservice *noun He has done a disservice to his neighbour.* bad turn, injury, injustice, unkindness, wrong. OPPOSITE favour.

dissident *noun a political dissident.* apostate, dissenter, nonconformist, objector, protester, rebel.

dissipate *verb* **1** *The smoke dissipated.* clear, disappear, disperse, evaporate, scatter. **2** *He dissipated his fortune.* blow (*slang*), fritter away, squander, waste.

dissociate *verb She dissociated herself from them.* cut off, detach, distance, divorce, isolate, separate. OPPOSITE associate.

dissolve *verb* **1** *The crystals dissolve in hot water.* liquefy, melt. **2** *He dissolved into thin air.* disappear, fade, melt, vanish. **3** *She dissolved into tears.* break, collapse, melt. **4** *The partnership was dissolved.* annul, break up, cancel, end, sever, terminate, wind up.

dissuade *verb* **dissuade from** *He dissuaded them from running.* advise against, deter from, discourage from, put off. OPPOSITE persuade to.

distance *noun the distance between Adelaide and Perth.* gap, haul, interval, length, range, space, span, stretch.

distant *adjective* **1** *a distant place.* far, far-away, far-flung, far-off, outlying, remote. OPPOSITE close. **2** *The friends had become distant with one another.* aloof, cold, cool, detached, estranged, formal, offhand, remote, reserved, standoffish, unfriendly, withdrawn. OPPOSITE close.

distaste *noun* see DISLIKE.

distasteful *adjective He found cleaning toilets distasteful.* detestable, disagreeable, disgusting, loathsome, nauseating, objectionable, offensive, off-putting, repugnant, repulsive, revolting, sickening, unpalatable, unpleasant, vile. OPPOSITE pleasant.

distended *adjective a distended stomach.* bloated, bulging, enlarged, expanded, puffed up, swollen.

distinct *adjective* **1** *a distinct improvement.* clear, clear-cut, definite, marked, noticeable, obvious, plain, pronounced, sharp, strong, unmistakable. OPPOSITE vague. **2** *two distinct problems.* different, discrete, individual, separate, unconnected.

distinction *noun* **1** *a distinction between the two groups.* contrast, difference. OPPOSITE similarity. **2** *an author of distinction.* class, eminence, excellence, fame, importance, merit, note, prestige, prominence, quality, renown, superiority, worth. OPPOSITE mediocrity.

distinctive *adjective She recognised the distinctive footsteps.* characteristic, different, distinguishing, idiosyncratic, individual, peculiar, personal, singular, special, specific, unique. OPPOSITE nondescript.

distinguish *verb* **1** *He cannot distinguish between blue and black.* differentiate, discriminate, separate, tell apart. **2** *His voice distinguished him from the others.* characterise, differentiate, identify, mark, set apart. **3** *She distinguished his foot-*

steps. discern, identify, make out, perceive, pick out, recognise, single out.

distinguished *adjective* **1** *a distinguished pianist.* celebrated, eminent, famed, famous, great, illustrious, important, legendary, notable, noted, outstanding, preeminent, prominent, renowned, respected, well-known. OPPOSITE unknown. **2** *He had a distinguished air.* aristocratic, dignified, grand, noble, refined, regal, stately.

distort *verb* **1** *The heat distorted the metal.* bend, buckle, contort, deform, skew, twist, warp. **2** *He distorted the facts for the sake of a good story.* colour, falsify, garble, misrepresent, pervert, slant, twist.

distract *verb* *She was distracted by another customer.* divert, draw away, sidetrack.

distraction *noun* *Television can be a useful distraction.* amusement, diversion, entertainment, escape, pastime, recreation.

distraught *adjective* *The police spoke to the distraught parents.* agitated, distressed, frantic, hysterical, overwrought, upset.

distress *noun* **1** *The man was in distress.* affliction, agony, anguish, discomfort, misery, pain, sorrow, suffering, torment, torture, woe. OPPOSITE comfort. **2** *a ship in distress.* adversity, danger, difficulty, trouble. OPPOSITE safety. — *verb The news distressed them.* afflict, bother, dismay, disturb, grieve, hurt, pain, perturb, sadden, shake, shock, torment, torture, trouble, upset, worry. OPPOSITE cheer.

distressing *adjective* *a distressing sight of starving children.* appalling, disturbing, grievous, harrowing, heartbreaking, heart-rending, horrific, painful, pathetic, poignant, sad, terrible, tragic, traumatic, upsetting. OPPOSITE heartening.

distribute *verb* *He distributed the food.* allocate, allot, apportion, assign, circulate, deal out, deliver, dish out (*informal*), dispense, divide up, dole out, give out, hand out, issue, mete out, pass round, serve, share out.

district *noun* *They live in the same district.* area, community, electorate (*Australian*), locality, municipality, neighbourhood, place, precinct, province, quarter, region, sector, shire, suburb, territory, vicinity, ward, zone.

distrust *noun* *a general distrust of politicians.* doubt, mistrust, scepticism, suspicion. OPPOSITE trust. — *verb He distrusted their motives.* be wary of, doubt, have misgivings about, mistrust, question, suspect. OPPOSITE trust.

distrustful *adjective* *She was distrustful of strangers.* chary, mistrustful, paranoid, sceptical, suspicious, wary. OPPOSITE trusting.

disturb *verb* **1** *The news disturbed him.* alarm, discomfit, disconcert, distress, fluster, perturb, rattle (*informal*), ruffle, startle, trouble, unsettle, upset, worry. **2** *Don't disturb her while she's studying.* annoy, bother, disrupt, hassle (*informal*), interrupt, pester. **3** *The surface of the water was disturbed by a boat.* agitate, churn up, ripple, rock, ruffle, shake.

disturbance *noun* *The youths created a disturbance at the shops.* commotion, fracas, hullabaloo, kerfuffle (*informal*), racket, riot, row, rumpus, stir, to-do, trouble, tumult, turmoil, unrest, uproar.

disturbed *adjective* *mentally disturbed.* deranged, neurotic, unbalanced, unstable.

disunity *noun* *party disunity.* conflict, disagreement, discord, dishar-mony, dissension, division, strife. OPPOSITE solidarity.

disused *adjective* *a disused building.* abandoned, idle, neglected, obsolete.

ditch *noun* *He dug a ditch.* channel, drain, dyke, gutter, moat, trench. — *verb* (*informal*) *She ditched her boyfriend.* abandon, dice (*Australian informal*), discard, drop, dump (*informal*), get rid of, reject. OPPOSITE keep.

dither *verb* *He dithered about signing the contract.* hesitate, hum and haw, shilly-shally, vacillate, waver.

dive *verb* **1** *She dived under water.* dip, plunge, submerge. **2** *The aircraft suddenly dived.* descend, drop, nosedive, pitch, plummet, plunge, swoop. OPPOSITE rise.

diverge *verb* **1** *The paths diverged.* branch, divide, fork, separate, split. OPPOSITE converge. **2** *His story diverged from the truth.* depart, deviate, digress, stray, turn aside.

diverse *adjective* **1** *a diverse group.* heterogeneous, miscellaneous, mixed, motley, varied. OPPOSITE uniform. **2** *people of diverse backgrounds.* assorted, different, various. OPPOSITE similar.

diversion *noun* **1** *Reading is her favourite diversion.* amusement, distraction, entertainment, escape, game, hobby, pastime, recreation, sport. **2** *a traffic diversion.* bypass, detour, deviation.

divert *verb* **1** *The police diverted traffic.* deflect, redirect, shunt, sidetrack, switch, turn aside. **2** *The clown diverted the audience.* amuse, cheer up, distract, entertain, interest, occupy.

divide *verb* **1** *She divided the chicken into even portions.* break up, carve up, cut up, joint, part, partition, separate, split, subdivide. **2** *The road divides here.* bifurcate, branch, diverge, fork, split. **3** *He divided the food amongst them.* allot, apportion, deal out, dish out (*informal*), distribute, divvy (*informal*), dole out, parcel out, share. **4** *He divided his books according to subject.* arrange, categorise, class, classify, group, sort.

divine *adjective* *a divine being. divine intervention.* celestial, godlike, heavenly, holy, sacred, spiritual, superhuman, supernatural. OPPOSITE human.

division *noun* **1** *the division of the profits.* allocation, apportionment, distribution, sharing, splitting. **2** *arranged in separate divisions.* compartment, part, partition, section, segment. **3** *the divisions of an organisation.* branch, department, section, sector, subdivision. **4** *The issue caused division in the party.* disagreement, discord, dissension, disunity, schism, split. OPPOSITE unity.

divorce *verb* *The couple divorced.* break up, part, separate, split up. OPPOSITE marry.

divulge *verb* *Do not divulge the secret.* betray, blab, blow (*slang*), disclose, expose, give away, impart, leak, let out, let slip, make known, publish, reveal, tell.

dizziness *noun* *The dizziness passed after she lay down.* faintness, giddiness, light-headedness, vertigo.

dizzy *adjective* *He felt dizzy on the roof.* faint, giddy, light-headed, reeling, unsteady, woozy (*informal*). OPPOSITE steady.

do *verb* **1** *She did her duty reluctantly.* accomplish, carry out, complete, discharge, execute, fulfil, perform, undertake. **2** *What wrong has he done?* commit, perpetrate. **3** *He did five copies.* make, prepare, produce, turn out. **4** *He does the cleaning.* attend to, deal with, handle, look after, manage. **5** *She couldn't do this problem.* answer, solve, work out. **6** *Do as I say.* act, behave, conduct yourself, practise. **7** *How is the patient doing?* fare, get on, make out. **8** *That will never do.* be acceptable, be adequate, be enough, be satisfactory, be sufficient, be suitable, suffice. — *noun* (*informal*) *a farewell do.* event, function, occasion, party, reception. □ **do away with** *They did away with that law.* abolish, axe, discard, discontinue, get rid of, scrap, stop. OPPOSITE retain. **do up 1** *He did up his boots.* buckle, fasten, lace up, zip. **2** *They did up the house.* redecorate, refurbish, renovate, repair, restore. **do without** *They did without sugar.* abstain from, dispense with, forgo, go without.

dob *verb* (*Australian informal*) **dob in 1** *He dobs in cheats.* blow the whistle on, denounce, grass (on) (*slang*), inform on, report, shelf (*Australian slang*), shop (*slang*), split on (*slang*), tell on. **2** *We all dobbed in $5 for his present.* chip in (*informal*), contribute, donate, give, pitch in (*informal*), put in.

docile *adjective* *a docile creature.* biddable, compliant, gentle, manageable, meek, mild, obedient, passive, submissive, tame, tractable. OPPOSITE intractable.

dock *noun* *The ship is in the dock.* berth, jetty, landing stage, pier, quay, slipway, wharf. — *verb The ship docked at Sydney.* berth, moor, put in. □ **docks** *plural noun* dockyard, harbour, marina, port, shipyard.

docker *noun* longshoreman, stevedore, watersider (*Australian*), waterside worker, wharfie (*Australian informal*), wharf labourer.

docket *noun* *Keep the docket with your purchase.* invoice, receipt.

doctor *noun* consultant, general practitioner, GP, intern, locum, medic (*informal*), medical practitioner, medico (*informal*), physician, quack (*slang*), registrar, specialist, surgeon.

doctrine *noun* *a religious doctrine.* belief, conviction, credo, creed, dogma, philosophy, precept, principle, teaching, tenet.

document *noun* *official documents.* certificate, charter, contract, deed, form, instrument, licence, paper, policy, record, report. — *verb* **1** *They documented their claims with receipts.* back up, corroborate, prove, substantiate, support. **2** *He documented the interview.* chronicle, record, report, write up.

doddery *adjective* *a doddery old man.* decrepit, frail, infirm, shaky, tottering, trembling, unsteady.

dodge *verb* **1** *She dodged out of the way of the ball.* bob, duck, escape, sidestep, swerve, veer. **2** *He dodged their questions.* avoid, evade, fend off, parry, sidestep, skirt round. **3** *She dodged work.* avoid, evade, get out of, shirk, shun, shy away from. — *noun* (*informal*) *a tax dodge.* lurk (*Australian informal*), racket, rort (*Australian slang*), ruse, scam (*slang*), scheme, trick.

dog *noun* *Brian loved his dog.* bitch (*female*), cur, hound, mongrel, mutt (*informal*), pooch (*slang*), pup, puppy, whelp.

dogged *adjective* *She finished by dogged determination.* determined, firm, obstinate, patient, persistent, pertinacious, resolute, single-minded, stubborn, tenacious, unwavering.

dogma *noun* *He could not accept this dogma.* belief, credo, creed, doctrine, principle, teaching, tenet.

dogmatic *adjective* *She was very dogmatic and not interested in my opinion.* assertive, authoritarian, authoritative, categorical, cocksure, dictatorial, doctrinaire, opinionated, peremptory.

dogsbody *noun* (*informal*) *He was treated as the office dogsbody.* drudge, gofer (*slang*), menial, slave.

dole *verb* **dole out** *He doles out the money.* allocate, allot, apportion, deal out, deliver, dish out (*informal*), dispense, distribute, give out, hand out, issue, mete out, share out. — *noun* (*informal*) *She finds it hard to live on the dole.* benefit, social security, unemployment benefit.

doleful *adjective* *She looked doleful.* dismal, down in the dumps (*informal*), gloomy, glum, lugubrious, melancholy, mournful, rueful, sad, sorrowful, unhappy, woebegone. OPPOSITE happy.

dollop *noun* *a dollop of cream.* blob, lump.

domain *noun* **1** *the king's domain.* dominion, empire, kingdom, land, province, realm, territory. **2** *the domain of science.* area, field, province, sphere.

dome *noun* *a church with a dome.* cupola.

domestic *adjective* **1** *domestic duties.* family, home, household. **2** *a domestic flight.* internal, national. OPPOSITE international. **3** *domestic animals.* domesticated, house-trained, pet, tame. OPPOSITE wild.

domicile *noun* abode (*old use*), accommodation, address, dwelling, habitation, home, house, residence.

dominant *adjective* *the dominant person in a group. the dominant features.* chief, commanding, controlling, influential, leading, main, outstanding, paramount, predominant, prevailing, principal, ruling.

dominate *verb* *The television dominates their lives.* control, govern, monopolise, rule.

domineering *adjective* *a domineering woman.* authoritarian, bossy, dictatorial, imperious, masterful, overbearing, peremptory, tyrannical. OPPOSITE meek.

dominion *noun* **1** *He has dominion over the country.* ascendancy, authority, control, jurisdiction, power, rule, sovereignty, supremacy, sway. **2** *the King's dominions.* domain, empire, kingdom, realm, state, territory.

donate *verb* *She donated $2000 to their cause.* bequeath, bestow, chip in (*informal*), contribute, fork out (*slang*), give, grant, present, provide, subscribe. OPPOSITE receive.

donation *noun* *All donations will be gratefully received.* alms (*old use*), bequest, contribution, gift, handout, offering, present, subscription.

donkey *noun* ass, jackass (*male*), jenny (*female*).

donor *noun* *The money came from an anonymous donor.* benefactor, contributor, giver, provider, sponsor. OPPOSITE recipient.

doom *noun* *He faced his doom with stoicism.* death, destiny, destruction, end, fate, fortune, lot, ruin. — *verb The project was doomed to failure.* condemn, destine, fate, ordain, predestine.

door *noun* doorway, entrance, entry, exit, gate, hatch, portal, trapdoor.

doorstep *noun* step, threshold.

dope *noun* **1** (*informal*) *They found dope in his possession.* drug, narcotic, opiate. **2** (*informal*) *She knew she'd been a dope.* ass (*informal*), clot (*informal*), fool, idiot (*informal*), imbecile, mug (*informal*), nincompoop, twit (*slang*). — *verb The man was heavily doped.* anaesthetise, drug, sedate.

dopey *adjective* (*informal*) **1** *He is dopey when he first gets up.* groggy, half asleep, sleepy, somnolent. **2** *a dopey thing to do.* dumb (*informal*), foolish, idiotic, imprudent, reckless, senseless, silly, stupid, unwise. OPPOSITE sensible.

dormant *adjective a dormant animal.* asleep, hibernating, inactive, inert, quiescent, resting, sleeping. OPPOSITE active, awake.

dose *noun a dose of medicine.* amount, dosage, measure, portion, quantity.

dossier *noun They keep a dossier on their clients.* file, records.

dot *noun painted dots.* fleck, mark, point, speck, speckle, spot.

dote *verb* **dote on** *She dotes on her children.* adore, cherish, idolise, love, treasure, worship.

dotted *adjective dotted material.* flecked, freckled, speckled, spotted, stippled.

double *adjective* **1** *double lines.* duplicate, paired, twin. OPPOSITE single. **2** *a double purpose.* dual, twin, twofold. OPPOSITE single. — *noun She was shocked to see her double.* clone, copy, dead spit, duplicate, lookalike, ringer (*informal*), spitting image, twin. — *verb* (*Australian*) *He doubled his friend on his bike.* dink (*Australian*), dinky (*Australian*), donkey (*Australian*), double-bank (*Australian*), double-dink (*Australian*).

double-cross *verb The scoundrel double-crossed him.* betray, cheat, deceive, trick.

doubt *noun* **1** *They have some doubts about the situation.* anxiety, concern, hesitation, misgiving, qualm, reservation, uncertainty, worry. OPPOSITE certainty. **2** *Her faith was strengthened by working through her doubt.* disbelief, distrust, incredulity, mistrust, scepticism, suspicion. OPPOSITE conviction. **3** *There is no doubt about what he meant.* ambiguity, confusion, question, uncertainty. OPPOSITE certainty. — *verb He doubted their honesty.* distrust, mistrust, question, suspect.

doubtful *adjective He felt doubtful about the job.* distrustful, dubious, hesitant, mistrustful, sceptical, suspicious, uncertain, undecided, unsure. OPPOSITE certain.

dour *adjective a dour person.* forbidding, gloomy, grim, harsh, morose, severe, stern, sullen, unfriendly. OPPOSITE cheerful.

douse *verb She doused the shirt with soapy water.* drench, immerse, saturate, soak, submerge, wet.

dowdy *adjective dowdy clothes.* daggy (*Australian informal*), drab, dull, frumpish, old-fashioned, shabby, sloppy, unattractive, unfashionable. OPPOSITE smart.

down¹ *verb* (*informal*) *He downed a glass of beer.* drain, drink, gulp down, swallow. □ **down and out** *The rich man helps those who are down and out.* broke (*informal*), destitute, hard up (*informal*), impoverished, needy, penniless, poor, poverty-stricken. OPPOSITE rich.

down² *noun a quilt made of goose down.* feathers, fluff, plumage.

downcast *adjective He was downcast and needed cheering up.* blue, crestfallen, dejected, depressed, despondent, disconsolate, discouraged, disheartened, dispirited, down, down-hearted, down in the dumps, gloomy, heavy-hearted, low, melancholy, miserable, sad, unhappy, wretched. OPPOSITE elated, happy.

downfall *noun Greed caused his downfall.* collapse, destruction, fall, ruin, undoing.

downpour *noun caught in a downpour.* cloudburst, deluge, rainstorm, shower, storm.

downright *adjective downright nonsense.* absolute, arrant, complete, out-and-out, outright, pure, sheer, thorough, utter.

down-to-earth *adjective matter-of-fact, no-nonsense, practical, realistic, sensible.* OPPOSITE airy-fairy.

doze *verb She dozed in a chair.* drop off, kip (*slang*), nap, nod off, sleep, slumber, snooze.

drab *adjective The place looks drab.* cheerless, colourless, dingy, dismal, dreary, dull, sombre, unattractive. OPPOSITE bright.

draft *noun a draft of the thesis.* outline, plan, sketch. — *verb* **1** *She drafted a proposal.* draw up, frame, outline, plan. **2** (*American*) *He was drafted into the army.* call up, conscript.

drag *verb He dragged a heavy bag.* draw, haul, lug, pull, tow, tug. — *noun He found the work a drag.* bind (*informal*), bore, nuisance, pain in the neck (*informal*), strain. □ **drag out** *They dragged out the discussions.* draw out, extend, prolong, protract, spin out. OPPOSITE shorten.

drain *verb* **1** *He drained the water from the can.* draw off, empty, pour off, remove, siphon off. **2** *The bath water drained out.* discharge, empty, flow out, seep out, trickle away. **3** *The mowing drained his energy.* consume, deplete, exhaust, sap, spend, use up. — *noun The drain is blocked.* channel, conduit, culvert, ditch, gutter, outlet, pipe, sewer, trench.

drama *noun* **1** *a three-act drama.* play. **2** *They study drama at school.* acting, dramatics, stagecraft, theatre. **3** *Her life is full of drama.* action, excitement, suspense.

dramatic *adjective* **1** *dramatic works.* stage, theatrical. **2** *a dramatic change.* impressive, marked, noticeable, radical, spectacular, startling, striking.

dramatist *noun playwright, screenwriter, scriptwriter.*

drastic *adjective drastic measures.* desperate, dire, extreme, radical, severe, strong.

draught *noun He felt a cold draught.* breeze, wind.

draw *verb* **1** *He drew the scene. She likes to draw.* delineate, depict, doodle, illustrate, outline, picture, portray, represent, scribble, sketch, trace. **2** *The car drew a heavy load.* drag, haul, lug, pull, tow, tug. **3** *The show drew a large crowd.* attract, bring in, entice, lure, pull. **4** *The waiter drew the cork.* extract, remove, pull out, take out. **5** *Our team drew with theirs.* be equal, tie. **6** *They drew their own conclusions.* come to, formulate, reach; see also DEDUCE. — *noun* **1** *The band proved quite a draw.* attraction, drawcard, enticement, lure. **2** *The contest ended in a draw.* dead heat, deadlock, stalemate, tie. □ **draw back** *He drew back in fear.* cringe, recoil, retreat, shrink back, withdraw. **draw out** *He drew out the meeting with unnecessary questions.* drag out, extend, lengthen, prolong, protract, spin out. OPPOSITE shorten. **draw up** **1** *The taxi drew up.* come to a stop, halt, pull up, stop. **2** *He drew up a contract.* compose, draft, formulate, prepare, write out.

drawback *noun The plan has no drawbacks.* catch, disadvantage, handicap, hindrance, inconvenience, liability, minus, shortcoming. OPPOSITE advantage.

drawing *noun cartoon, design, diagram, illustration, pattern, picture, plan, portrait, sketch.*

drawing room *noun The house had a drawing room for entertaining*

guests. parlour (*old use*), reception room, salon, sitting room.

dread *noun He faced the exams with dread.* alarm, anxiety, apprehension, consternation, dismay, fear, foreboding, horror, panic, terror, trepidation. OPPOSITE confidence. — *verb She dreaded the punishment.* be afraid of, be scared of, fear.

dreadful *adjective* **1** *a dreadful accident.* appalling, awful, bad, calamitous, catastrophic, dire, disastrous, fearful, frightful, ghastly, grisly, hideous, horrendous, horrible, horrific, terrible, tragic. **2** (*informal*) *dreadful weather.* abominable (*informal*), abysmal (*informal*), appalling (*informal*), atrocious (*informal*), bad, foul, lousy (*informal*), miserable, nasty, rotten (*informal*), shocking (*informal*), terrible (*informal*). OPPOSITE good, pleasant.

dream *noun* **1** *lost in a dream.* daydream, fantasy, hallucination, illusion, nightmare, reverie, trance, vision. **2** *His dream is to own a sports car.* ambition, aspiration, desire, goal, hope, wish. — *verb He dreamt he was flying.* daydream, fancy, fantasise, hallucinate, imagine. □ **dream up** *He dreamt up a silly scheme.* conceive, concoct, create, devise, hatch, imagine, invent, think up.

dreary *adjective* **1** *a dreary performance.* boring, deadly (*informal*), dull, humdrum, lacklustre, lifeless, monotonous, mundane, stodgy, tedious, tiresome, uninteresting. **2** *a dreary place.* bleak, cheerless, colourless, depressing, dingy, dismal, drab, dull, gloomy, miserable, sombre. OPPOSITE bright.

dregs *plural noun The dregs were left in the glasses.* deposit, grounds, lees, remains, residue, sediment.

drench *verb The sprinkler drenched them.* douse, saturate, soak, souse, wet.

dress *noun* **1** *appropriate dress for the occasion.* apparel (*formal*), attire (*formal*), clobber (*slang*), clothes, clothing, costume, garb, garments, gear (*informal*), get-up (*informal*), outfit, raiment, rig (*informal*), togs (*informal*), vestments, wear. **2** *a woman's dress.* frock, gown, kimono, robe, sari. — *verb* **1** *They were dressed in their best clothes.* array, attire, clothe, deck out, doll up (*informal*), robe. **2** *The nurse dressed his wounds.* bandage, bind.

dresser *noun We put the dishes in the dresser.* buffet, cupboard, sideboard.

dressing *noun* **1** *salad dressing.* mayonnaise, sauce, vinaigrette. **2** *the dressing on a wound.* bandage, plaster, poultice.

dressing gown *noun bath robe, brunch coat, housecoat, negligée, robe, wrapper.*

dressmaker *noun couturier, couturière, seamstress, tailor.*

dressy *adjective dressy clothes.* chic, classy (*informal*), elegant, formal, smart, snazzy (*informal*), stylish. OPPOSITE casual.

dribble *verb* **1** *He dribbled as he looked at the food.* drool, salivate, slaver, slobber. **2** *The juice dribbled down his chin.* drip, flow, ooze, run, trickle.

dried *adjective dried coconut.* dehydrated, desiccated.

drift *verb* **1** *The raft drifted downstream.* coast, float, waft. **2** *He drifted idly through the streets.* meander, mosey (*slang*), ramble, roam, rove, saunter, stray, wander. — *noun* **1** *They tried to stop the drift of people away from the town.* movement, shift, tide. **2** *Did you catch the drift of his speech?* gist, meaning, point, tenor, trend.

drill *noun army drill.* exercises, practice, training. — *verb* **1** *He drilled through the timber.* bore, penetrate, pierce. **2** *The students were drilled in vocabulary.* coach, instruct, teach, train.

drink *verb He drank his juice.* down, drain, gulp, guzzle, lap, quaff, sip, swallow, swig (*informal*), swill. — *noun* **1** *hot or cold drinks.* beverage, liquid, refreshment. **2** *His work was affected by drink.* alcohol, booze (*informal*), grog (*Australian*), liquor. **3** *She took a drink from her glass.* gulp, mouthful, sip, swallow, swig (*informal*).

drip *verb Water dripped through the ceiling.* dribble, drizzle, filter, leak, sprinkle, trickle. — *noun* **1** *She cleaned up the drips.* drop, droplet, splash. **2** (*informal*) *She thinks he's a drip.* dope (*informal*), dork (*slang*), geek (*slang*), jerk (*slang*), nerd (*slang*), twit (*slang*), wally (*slang*), weed, wimp (*informal*), wuss (*slang*).

drive *verb* **1** *He drove the animals into the yard.* herd, push, send, urge. **2** *He drove the ball a great distance.* hit, propel, push, strike. **3** *He drove the stake into the ground.* hammer, push, ram, send, sink, thrust. **4** *He can't drive the vehicle.* control, guide, handle, operate, pilot, steer. **5** *She drives to work.* motor, travel by car. **6** *He drives the boss to the office.* chauffeur, convey, run. **7** *What drove him to steal?* compel, constrain, force, impel, motivate, oblige, pressure, push, spur. — *noun* **1** *Let's go for a drive.* excursion, jaunt, journey, outing, run, spin, trip. **2** *We need a leader with drive.* ambition, determination, energy, enterprise, enthusiasm, go, initiative, motivation, push, vigour, zeal. **3** *a sales drive.* campaign, crusade, push. □ **drive out** *He was driven out of his own home.* banish, evict, expel, kick out (*informal*), remove, turn out.

driver *noun chauffeur, motorist.*

drizzly *adjective drizzly weather.* damp, misty, rainy, showery, wet.

droll *adjective see* FUNNY.

drone *verb The machines droned continuously.* buzz, hum, purr, whirr.

drool *verb The smell of fish makes the cat drool.* dribble, salivate, slaver, slobber.

droop *verb The plant drooped in the heat.* dangle, flop, hang down, sag, wilt, wither.

drop *noun* **1** *a drop of water.* bead, drip, droplet, globule, spot. **2** *a drop of chilli sauce.* dash, hint, splash, sprinkling, touch, trace. **3** *a drop in prices.* cut, decline, decrease, fall, reduction, slump. OPPOSITE rise. **4** *a steep drop to the sea.* descent. OPPOSITE climb. — *verb* **1** *He dropped the parcel on the floor.* let fall, let go of, plonk. **2** *The engines failed and the plane dropped to the ground.* collapse, crash, descend, dive, fall, plummet, plunge, sink, tumble. OPPOSITE soar. **3** *Prices dropped.* crash, decline, decrease, diminish, fall, nosedive, plummet, plunge, slump. OPPOSITE rise. **4** *The salesman dropped the price.* lower, reduce. OPPOSITE increase. **5** *She dropped behind the others.* fall, lag, straggle, trail. **6** *He dropped his middle name.* eliminate, exclude, leave out, omit. OPPOSITE include. **7** *He dropped his girlfriend.* abandon, desert, ditch (*informal*), dump, forsake, jilt, leave, reject. **8** *They dropped the idea.* abandon, discard, give up, scrap. □ **drop in on** *They dropped in on grandmother.* call in on, look in on, pop in on, visit. **drop off** *She dropped off in front of the*

TV. doze, drowse, fall asleep, kip (*slang*), nap, nod off, sleep, snooze.

drove *noun The visitors came in droves.* crowd, flock, herd, horde, mob, swarm.

drown *verb* **1** *The fields were drowned by the floodwaters.* drench, engulf, flood, inundate, submerge, swamp. **2** *Their noise drowned ours.* overpower, overwhelm.

drowsy *adjective She stopped work when she felt drowsy.* dopey (*informal*), dozy, lethargic, sleepy, somnolent, tired, weary. OPPOSITE wide awake.

drudge *noun a harmless drudge.* dogsbody (*informal*), hack, labourer, menial, servant, worker.

drug *noun The doctor prescribed the drugs.* medicament, medication, medicine, pill. — *verb The patient was drugged.* anaesthetise, dope, knock out (*informal*), sedate, stupefy. □ **drug user** addict, druggie (*informal*), junkie (*slang*).

drum *noun* **1** *He plays the drums.* bongo, kettledrum, side drum, snare drum, tabor, tambour, timpano, tom-tom. **2** *He used the drum for storage.* barrel, cask, container, cylinder, keg, tub. — *verb* **1** *She drummed on the table.* beat, pound, rap, tap, thump. **2** *The teacher drummed the rules into them.* din, drive, hammer, instil. □ **drum up** *They tried to drum up support for the candidate.* canvass, gather, obtain, round up, solicit, summon, whip up.

drummer *noun* timpanist.

drunk *adjective* drunken, full (*slang*), full as a goog (*Australian slang*), happy (*informal*), inebriated, intoxicated, jolly (*informal*), legless (*slang*), merry (*informal*), paralytic (*informal*), pickled (*slang*), plastered (*slang*), shickered (*Australian slang*), sloshed (*slang*), smashed (*slang*), sozzled (*slang*), tanked (*slang*), tiddly (*informal*), tipsy, under the influence (*informal*), under the weather. OPPOSITE sober.

drunkard *noun* alcoholic, boozer (*informal*), dipsomaniac, drunk, inebriate, soak (*informal*), sot, tippler, wino (*informal*). OPPOSITE teetotaller.

dry *adjective* **1** *dry land.* arid, bonedry, dehydrated, parched, scorched, thirsty, waterless. OPPOSITE wet. **2** *a dry book.* boring, dull, prosaic, tedious, uninteresting. OPPOSITE interesting. **3** *a dry sense of humour.* ironic, laconic, subtle, wry. — *verb* **1** *The swimmer dried himself.* towel, wipe. **2** *She dried the food to preserve it.* cure, dehydrate, desiccate. **3** *The plant dried.* shrivel, wilt, wither.

dual *adjective a dual purpose.* binary, double, twin, twofold. OPPOSITE single.

dub *verb Robert was dubbed 'Professor'.* christen, name, nickname, rename.

dubious *adjective* **1** *She was dubious about his motives.* disbelieving, distrustful, doubtful, mistrustful, sceptical, suspicious, uncertain, unsure. OPPOSITE certain. **2** *a dubious character.* dodgy (*informal*), fishy (*informal*), questionable, shady, shifty (*informal*), suspect, suspicious, unreliable, untrustworthy. OPPOSITE reliable.

duchess *noun* see NOBLEWOMAN.

duck *noun* drake (*male*), duckling (*young*). — *verb* **1** *She ducked under water.* bob, dip, dive, plunge, submerge. **2** *He ducked to avoid hitting his head.* bend down, bob down, crouch, stoop. **3** *He ducked his responsibility.* avoid, dodge, evade, get out of, shirk, sidestep.

duct *noun The liquid flows through ducts.* canal, channel, conduit, pipe, tube.

dud *adjective* (*informal*) **1** *a dud $10 note.* counterfeit, fake, forged, phoney (*informal*). OPPOSITE genuine. **2** *a dud machine.* bung (*Australian informal*), defective, inoperative, unusable, useless, worthless. OPPOSITE working.

due *adjective* **1** *Pay the amount due.* outstanding, owed, owing, payable, unpaid. **2** *with due respect.* adequate, appropriate, deserved, fitting, merited, proper, rightful, suitable. **3** *When is the bus due?* expected, scheduled. □ **dues** *plural noun Pay your membership dues.* fee, levy, sub (*informal*), subscription.

duel *noun He challenged his rival to a duel.* combat, contest, fight.

duffer *noun What a duffer she's been!* clot (*informal*), fool, goose (*informal*), idiot, mug (*informal*), muggins (*informal*), nincompoop, nitwit (*informal*), silly, twit (*slang*).

duke *noun* see NOBLEMAN.

dull *adjective* **1** *a dull day.* bleak, cloudy, dismal, grey, overcast, sunless. OPPOSITE sunny. **2** *a dull student.* bovine, dense, dim, dumb (*informal*), obtuse, slow, stupid, thick. OPPOSITE bright, intelligent. **3** *a dull edge.* blunt, blunted. OPPOSITE keen, sharp. **4** *a dull colour.* dark, dingy, drab, dreary, faded, gloomy, sombre, subdued. OPPOSITE bright. **5** *a dull sound.* deadened, indistinct, muffled, muted. OPPOSITE sharp. **6** *a dull finish.* flat, matt, tarnished. OPPOSITE glossy. **7** *a dull book.* bland, boring, dreary, dry, humdrum, lacklustre, lifeless, monotonous, mundane, ordinary, prosaic, routine, stodgy, tedious, tiresome, unimaginative, uninteresting, vapid. OPPOSITE exciting. — *verb The drugs dulled the pain.* deaden, numb, relieve, soothe, subdue. OPPOSITE accentuate.

dumb *adjective* **1** *The child is deaf and dumb.* mute, silent, speechless, tongue-tied. **2** (*informal*) *Don't be so dumb.* dense, dim (*informal*), foolish, obtuse, slow, stupid, thick, unintelligent. OPPOSITE clever.

dumbfounded *adjective They were dumbfounded by the news.* amazed, astonished, astounded, confounded, flabbergasted, nonplussed, speechless, staggered, stunned, surprised, thunderstruck.

dummy *noun* **1** *The clothes were put on the dummy.* lay figure, mannequin, model. **2** *a baby's dummy.* pacifier.

dump *verb* **1** *He dumped the old car.* chuck out (*informal*), discard, dispose of, ditch (*informal*), get rid of, offload, scrap, throw out. OPPOSITE keep. **2** *She dumped the things on the counter.* deposit, drop, place, plonk, put down, set down, throw down, unload. **3** *She dumped her boyfriend.* abandon, desert, ditch (*informal*), jilt, leave. — *noun She took the rubbish to the dump.* garbage dump, garbage tip, rubbish tip, scrap heap, tip.

dumpy *adjective a dumpy person.* chubby, fat, plump, podgy, pudgy, rotund, squat, stout, tubby. OPPOSITE slim, thin.

dunce *noun He thought he was a dunce at maths.* blockhead, bonehead, clot (*informal*), dill (*Australian informal*), dimwit (*informal*), dolt, dope (*informal*), dullard, dummy (*informal*), dunderhead, fool, half-wit, idiot, ignoramus, imbecile, moron (*informal*), nincompoop, nitwit (*informal*), nong (*Australian informal*), simpleton, twit (*slang*).

dung *noun fresh cattle dung.* droppings, excrement, faeces, manure, muck.

dungeon *noun The prisoner is in the dungeon.* cell, lock-up, prison.

dunk *verb He dunked the bread in the sauce.* dip, immerse, sop.

duo *noun a comedy duo.* couple, pair.

dupe *verb The quack duped him into believing he was sick.* bluff, cheat, con (*informal*), deceive, delude, fool, hoax, hoodwink, kid (*informal*), mislead, string along (*informal*), suck in (*informal*), swindle, take in, trick.

duplicate *noun a duplicate of the original.* copy, facsimile, photocopy, replica, reproduction. — *verb* **1** *He duplicated the letter.* copy, photocopy, reproduce. **2** *They duplicated our work.* redo, repeat, replicate.

durable *adjective durable work shoes.* hard-wearing, indestructible, long-lasting, serviceable, solid, stout, strong, sturdy, tough. OPPOSITE fragile.

duration *noun She slept for the duration of the concert.* length, period, span, term, time.

duress *noun She made the commitment under duress.* coercion, compulsion, force, pressure, threat.

dusk *noun They worked from dawn to dusk.* evening, gloaming, nightfall, sundown, sunset, twilight. OPPOSITE dawn.

dust *noun The car was covered in dust.* bulldust (*Australian*), dirt, grime, grit, powder, sawdust, soot. — *verb* **1** *Dust the cake with icing sugar.* dredge, sprinkle. **2** *Dust the table.* brush, clean, wipe. □ **dust storm** Darling shower (*Australian*), dust devil, sandstorm, willy willy (*Australian*).

dutiful *adjective a dutiful daughter.* compliant, conscientious, devoted, diligent, faithful, loyal, obedient, reliable, responsible. OPPOSITE remiss.

duty *noun* **1** *He acted out of a sense of duty.* allegiance, loyalty, obligation, responsibility. **2** *We each have a list of duties to perform.* assignment, charge, chore, function, job, office, role, task. **3** *You must pay a duty on these goods.* customs, excise, levy, tariff, tax, toll.

duvet *noun a duvet for the bed.* continental quilt, Doona (*trade mark*), eiderdown, quilt.

dwarf *noun a fairy tale about a dwarf.* elf, gnome, leprechaun, midget, pygmy, troll. OPPOSITE giant. — *adjective a dwarf tree.* bonsai, little, miniature, small, stunted. OPPOSITE giant. — *verb The new tower dwarfs the older buildings.* dominate, overshadow, tower over.

dwell *verb She dwells in an old house.* abide (*old use*), live, reside; see also INHABIT. □ **dwell on** *She dwelt on their faults.* concentrate on, focus on, harp on, linger over. OPPOSITE pass over.

dwelling *noun a comfortable dwelling.* abode (*old use*), domicile, habitation, home, house, lodging, residence; see also FLAT, HOUSE.

dwindle *verb The number of members has dwindled.* contract, decline, decrease, diminish, lessen, reduce, shrink, wane. OPPOSITE increase.

dye *verb He dyed his shoes black.* colour, paint, stain, tint. — *noun fabric dye.* colour, colouring, pigment, stain, tint.

dying *adjective Letter writing is a dying art.* moribund, obsolescent, passing, vanishing, waning. OPPOSITE thriving.

dyke *noun* **1** *They built a dyke to hold back the flood waters.* embankment, levee, stopbank, wall. **2** *The water*

runs away in a dyke. canal, channel, ditch, furrow, gutter, watercourse.

dynamic *adjective a dynamic person.* active, energetic, forceful, go-ahead, high-powered, lively, powerful, progressive, vigorous.

dynasty *noun a royal dynasty.* family, house, line, lineage.

Ee

eager *adjective* **1** *The teacher was pleased to have such eager students.* ardent, avid, earnest, enthusiastic, fervent, interested, keen, motivated, passionate, willing, zealous. OPPOSITE apathetic. **2** *He was eager to find out more.* anxious, bursting, desirous, dying (*informal*), impatient, itching, keen, longing, raring (*informal*), yearning. OPPOSITE reluctant.

eagerness *noun Paul showed an eagerness to learn.* alacrity, ardour, desire, earnestness, enthusiasm, fervour, hunger, impatience, keenness, longing, readiness, yearning, zeal. OPPOSITE reluctance.

earl *noun* see NOBLEMAN.

earlier *adverb He left earlier.* before, beforehand, previously. OPPOSITE later. — *adjective an earlier conversation.* previous, prior. OPPOSITE later.

earliest *adjective the earliest inhabitants.* aboriginal, first, initial, original. OPPOSITE latest.

early *adverb The baby arrived early.* ahead of time, prematurely, too soon. OPPOSITE late, punctually. — *adjective* **1** *an early arrival.* premature. OPPOSITE late, punctual. **2** *in the early days.* ancient, old, olden, prehistoric, primeval, primitive, primordial. OPPOSITE modern. **3** *We received an early warning.* advance, first, initial, preliminary. OPPOSITE later.

earmark *verb The money has been earmarked for a holiday.* assign, designate, reserve, set aside, specify, tag.

earn *verb* **1** *She earned their respect.* be entitled to, be worthy of, deserve, gain, merit, win. **2** *He earns $400 a week.* bring in, clear, collect, draw, get, gross, make, net, obtain, rake in (*informal*), receive, take home, work for.

earnest *adjective* **1** *an earnest desire.* ardent, fervent, heartfelt, impassioned, intense, passionate, serious, sincere, strong, wholehearted. OPPOSITE half-hearted. **2** *an earnest person.* conscientious, determined, diligent, grave, serious, sober, solemn, staid, thoughtful, zealous. OPPOSITE frivolous.

earnings *plural noun* income, pay, remuneration, salary, wages.

earth *noun* **1** *life on earth.* globe, planet, world. **2** *The earth is hard to dig.* clay, dirt, ground, land, loam, soil.

earthenware *noun* ceramics, crockery, pottery, terracotta.

earthly *adjective our earthly existence.* mortal, mundane, physical, secular, terrestrial, worldly. OPPOSITE heavenly, spiritual.

earthquake *noun Buildings collapsed during the earthquake.* quake (*informal*), shock, tremor.

ease *noun* **1** *He did it with ease.* deftness, dexterity, effortlessness, facility. OPPOSITE difficulty. **2** *a life of ease.* comfort, contentment, leisure, luxury, prosperity, relaxation, repose, rest. OPPOSITE hardship. — *verb* **1** *The medicine eased the* *pain.* allay, alleviate, assuage, calm, lessen, lighten, mitigate, palliate, quell, reduce, relieve, soothe, subdue. OPPOSITE aggravate, exacerbate. **2** *They eased the pressure.* decrease, reduce, relax, slacken. OPPOSITE tighten. **3** *The pain eased.* abate, diminish, let up, moderate, slacken. OPPOSITE intensify.

easy *adjective* **1** *an easy job.* cushy (*informal*), effortless, elementary, light, painless, soft (*informal*), undemanding. OPPOSITE hard. **2** *The gadget is easy to use.* foolproof, simple, straightforward, uncomplicated, user-friendly. OPPOSITE difficult. **3** *an easy conscience.* carefree, clear, trouble-free, untroubled, unworried. OPPOSITE troubled. **4** *She has an easy existence.* carefree, comfortable, cosy, leisurely, peaceful, relaxed, restful, soft (*informal*), tranquil, untroubled. OPPOSITE hard.

easygoing *adjective* *Her flatmate is a pleasant easygoing person.* calm, carefree, casual, even-tempered, happy-go-lucky, indulgent, laid-back (*informal*), lenient, liberal, nonchalant, open-minded, permissive, placid, relaxed, soft, tolerant, unflappable (*informal*). OPPOSITE strict, tense.

eat *verb* **1** *He ate his food.* bite, bolt, chew, chomp, consume, devour, feast on, feed on, gnaw, gobble, gorge, gulp, guzzle, ingest, knock back (*informal*), masticate, munch, nibble, partake of, peck, pick at, polish off, scoff, stuff, swallow, tuck into (*informal*), wolf. **2** *She eats at a set time.* breakfast, dine, lunch, snack, sup. □ **eat into** *1* *Acids eat into metals.* attack, corrode, destroy, erode, rot, wear away. **2** *The expenses gradually ate into their savings.* consume, erode, make a hole in, use up.

eatable *adjective* *The dinner had dried out and was no longer eatable.* digestible, edible.

eavesdrop *verb* **eavesdrop on** *He eavesdropped on their conversation.* bug (*informal*), listen in on, monitor, overhear, tap.

ebb *verb* **1** *The tide ebbed.* flow back, go out, recede, retreat, subside. OPPOSITE flow, rise. **2** *His strength was ebbing as he became more ill.* decline, decrease, diminish, dwindle, fade, wane, weaken. OPPOSITE grow.

eccentric *adjective* *an eccentric person. eccentric habits.* abnormal, bizarre, cranky, dotty (*informal*), freakish, idiosyncratic, irregular, nutty (*informal*), odd, offbeat, outlandish, peculiar, queer, singular, strange, unconventional, unusual, way-out, weird, zany. OPPOSITE normal, ordinary. — *noun* *He was regarded as an eccentric.* character, crackpot (*informal*), crank, dag (*Australian informal*), dingbat (*informal*), freak, hard case (*Australian informal*), nonconformist, nut (*informal*), oddball (*informal*), oddity, screwball (*informal*), weirdo (*informal*).

echo *noun* *The circular wall created an echo.* resonance, reverberation. — *verb* **1** *The music echoed in the valley.* reflect, resound, reverberate. **2** *The clown echoed everything she said.* ape, copy, imitate, mimic, parrot, repeat, reproduce.

eclipse *noun* *an eclipse of the sun.* blocking out, covering, darkening, obscuring, shadowing. — *verb* *Her beauty was eclipsed by Snow White's.* exceed, outshine, overshadow, surpass.

economic *adjective* **1** *economic policy.* budgetary, financial, fiscal, monetary, trade. **2** *It is not economic to stay open late.* cost-

effective, profitable. OPPOSITE uneconomic.

economical *adjective* **1** *She is very economical with her pocket money.* careful, frugal, provident, sparing, thrifty. OPPOSITE extravagant, wasteful. **2** *The larger pack is more economical than the small one.* cost-efficient, inexpensive, reasonable. OPPOSITE expensive.

economise *verb* *They had to economise on heating.* be economical, conserve, cut back, cut costs, retrench, save, scrimp, skimp, stint, tighten your belt. OPPOSITE splash out.

ecstasy *noun* *She was in ecstasy at the news.* bliss, delight, elation, euphoria, happiness, joy, rapture. OPPOSITE misery.

ecstatic *adjective* *He was ecstatic at the results.* blissful, delighted, elated, euphoric, exultant, happy, joyful, overjoyed, over the moon, rapt, rapturous. OPPOSITE miserable.

eddy *noun* *The leaf was caught in an eddy.* swirl, vortex, whirl, whirlpool.

edge *noun* **1** *the edge of the cup.* brim, brink, lip, rim. **2** *the edge of the town.* border, boundary, circumference, end, extremity, fringe, limit, margin, outskirts, perimeter, periphery. OPPOSITE centre, interior. **3** *the edge of the road.* kerb, roadside, shoulder, side, verge. **4** *a fabric edge.* selvedge. — *verb* **1** *The blanket is edged with satin.* bind, border, fringe, hem, trim. **2** *She edged her way out of the room.* crawl, creep, inch, sidle, slink, steal, worm.

edgy *adjective* *The long wait for any news made her edgy.* anxious, irritable, jittery (*informal*), jumpy, nervous, nervy, on edge, on tenterhooks, tense, uptight (*informal*). OPPOSITE calm.

edible *adjective* *Witchetty grubs are edible.* digestible, eatable. OPPOSITE inedible.

edifice *noun* *The new parliament house is an imposing edifice.* building, construction, structure.

edify *verb* SEE EDUCATE.

edit *verb* **1** *The text was edited before publication.* adapt, adjust, alter, check, correct, modify, polish, revise, rewrite. **2** *He edited a set of essays on language.* assemble, collate, compile, put together.

edition *noun* **1** *the paperback edition of the book.* copy, form, version. **2** *this month's edition of the magazine.* issue, number, publication.

educate *verb* *The child was educated by both parents and school.* bring up, coach, edify, enlighten, indoctrinate, inform, instruct, nurture, rear, school, teach, train, tutor.

educated *adjective* *He was addressing an educated audience.* cultivated, cultured, enlightened, erudite, informed, knowledgeable, learned, literate, scholarly. OPPOSITE ignorant, uneducated.

education *noun* *He received a well-rounded education.* cultivation, development, edification, enlightenment, instruction, schooling, teaching, training, tuition, upbringing.

educational *adjective* **1** *an educational institution.* academic, pedagogical, scholastic. **2** *The programme was both educational and entertaining.* edifying, educative, enlightening, informative, instructive.

eerie *adjective* *an eerie atmosphere.* creepy, frightening, ghostly, mysterious, scary, spooky (*informal*), uncanny, weird.

efface *verb* *The writing had been effaced.* delete, erase, expunge, obliterate, rub out, wipe out.

effect *noun* **1** *the effect of his decision.* consequence, impact, outcome, repercussion, result, upshot. OPPOSITE cause. **2** *Special lighting gave the effect of moonlight.* illusion, impression, sensation. **3** *The law came into effect last week.* force, operation, play. — *verb* *The doctor effected a cure.* accomplish, achieve, bring about, cause, perform, produce.

effective *adjective* **1** *an effective manager.* capable, competent, effectual, efficient, productive, strong, successful. **2** *an effective advertisement.* compelling, convincing, forceful, impressive, persuasive, potent, powerful, striking, successful. OPPOSITE ineffective.

effeminate *adjective* *The man has an effeminate manner.* camp, unmanly, womanish. OPPOSITE macho, manly.

effervescent *adjective* *an effervescent drink.* aerated, bubbly, carbonated, fizzy, foaming, gassy, sparkling. OPPOSITE still.

efficient *adjective* *an efficient worker.* businesslike, capable, competent, effective, effectual, organised, productive, proficient, skilful. OPPOSITE inefficient.

effigy *noun* *They burned an effigy of Guy Fawkes.* dummy, figure, guy, image, likeness, model, puppet, statue.

effort *noun* **1** *The job required a lot of effort.* elbow grease, energy, exertion, labour, pains, strain, struggle, toil, trouble, work. **2** *He made no effort to help us.* attempt, endeavour, try.

effortless *adjective* *an effortless achievement.* easy, painless, simple, undemanding. OPPOSITE difficult.

egg *verb* **egg on** *They egged him on to do it.* encourage, goad, incite, prompt, push, sool on (*Australian informal*), spur on, urge. OPPOSITE discourage.

egotism *noun* conceit, narcissism, pride, self-admiration, self-centredness, self-importance, self-love, vanity.

egotistic *adjective* conceited, egocentric, egotistical, narcissistic, proud, self-centred, self-important, vain.

eiderdown *noun* continental quilt, Doona (*trade mark*), duvet, quilt.

eject *verb* **1** *The guns eject spent cartridges.* discharge, emit, expel, send out, spew, spit out (*informal*). **2** *The police ejected them from the disco.* banish, chuck out (*informal*), evict, expel, get rid of, kick out (*informal*), oust, remove, throw out, turf out (*informal*), turn out.

elaborate *adjective* **1** *The wallpaper had an elaborate design.* busy, detailed, fancy, fussy, intricate, ornate, showy. OPPOSITE plain, simple. **2** *an elaborate technique for solving these puzzles.* complex, complicated, intricate, involved, sophisticated. OPPOSITE simple. — *verb* **elaborate on** *He elaborated on his idea.* enlarge on, expand on, flesh out, work out.

elapse *verb* *Years elapsed before they saw each other again.* go by, pass, roll by, slip by.

elastic *adjective* *an elastic material.* expandable, resilient, rubbery, springy, stretchy. OPPOSITE rigid.

elated *adjective* *She was elated at the news.* chuffed (*slang*), delighted, ecstatic, enraptured, euphoric, exhilarated, exultant, happy, joyful, jubilant, overjoyed, over the moon, rapt, rapturous, thrilled. OPPOSITE depressed.

elbow *verb* *He elbowed his way past the others.* jostle, nudge, push, shove, thrust.

elder *adjective* *an elder brother.* big, older. OPPOSITE younger. — *noun*

He is my elder by one year. senior. OPPOSITE junior.

elderly *adjective* *elderly people.* aged, ageing, old, oldish, retired, senior. OPPOSITE young.

eldest *adjective* *the eldest child.* first-born, oldest. OPPOSITE youngest.

elect *verb* *They elected a new Prime Minister.* appoint, choose, opt for, pick, select, vote for.

election *noun* *a federal election.* ballot, poll, vote.

elective *adjective* *elective surgery.* chosen, non-essential, optional. OPPOSITE essential.

electorate *noun* **1** *The electorate decides who the government will be.* constituents, electors, people, voters. **2** (*Australian*) *The MP has a city electorate.* constituency, seat.

elegant *adjective* **1** *an elegant person.* chic, dignified, fashionable, graceful, gracious, handsome, refined, smart, stylish. OPPOSITE unrefined. **2** *elegant surroundings.* grand, luxurious, opulent, plush, posh (*informal*), stately, stylish, sumptuous, tasteful.

elegy *noun* *The poet wrote an elegy for the dead statesman.* dirge, lament, requiem.

element *noun* *the different elements of her job.* component, constituent, factor, ingredient, part, unit. □ **elements** *plural noun* **1** *Man against the elements.* weather. **2** *He has mastered the elements of the subject.* basics, essentials, fundamentals, principles, rudiments.

elementary *adjective* *elementary mathematics.* basic, fundamental, introductory, primary, rudimentary, simple. OPPOSITE advanced.

elevate *verb* **1** *The foot needs to be elevated.* lift, raise. OPPOSITE lower. **2** *He was elevated to the position of supervisor.* exalt, move up, promote, raise, upgrade. OPPOSITE demote.

elevation *noun* *a mountain's elevation.* altitude, height.

elevator *noun* *The elevator holds twelve people.* lift.

elf *noun* *The elf played a trick on the man.* fairy, gnome, goblin, gremlin (*informal*), hobgoblin, imp, leprechaun, pixie, spirit, sprite.

elicit *verb* *His question did not elicit the desired response.* call forth, draw out, evoke, extract, get, obtain.

eligible *adjective* *Anna is eligible to compete in the tournament.* acceptable, allowed, authorised, entitled, qualified, suitable. OPPOSITE ineligible.

eliminate *verb* **1** *We cannot eliminate all errors.* abolish, cut out, delete, do away with, eradicate, get rid of, omit, remove, root out, stamp out, weed out. OPPOSITE include, retain. **2** *He was eliminated in the second round.* defeat, exclude, knock out.

elite *noun* *the elite of society.* best, choice, chosen, cream, pick.

ellipse *noun* oval.

elocution *noun* *His elocution was improved by participating in debates.* articulation, delivery, diction, enunciation, oratory, public speaking, speech.

elongate *verb* *She elongated the shape.* draw out, extend, lengthen, protract, stretch out. OPPOSITE shorten.

eloquent *adjective* *an eloquent speech. an eloquent speaker.* articulate, expressive, fluent, forceful, persuasive, powerful. OPPOSITE inarticulate.

elude *verb* *He eluded his pursuers.* avoid, dodge, escape from, evade, give the slip to, shake off.

elusive *adjective* *an elusive quality.* fugitive, indefinable, intangible, subtle, transient.

emaciated *adjective emaciated prisoners-of-war.* cadaverous, gaunt, scrawny, skinny, thin.

emanate *verb The order emanated from this office.* come, flow, issue, originate, proceed, spring, stem.

emancipate *verb They emancipated the slave.* deliver, free, liberate, release, set free. OPPOSITE enslave.

embankment *noun The flood waters rushed over the embankment.* bank, levee, stopbank.

embargo *noun An embargo was imposed on live animal exports.* ban, moratorium, prohibition, proscription.

embark *verb The travellers embarked in Sydney.* board ship, get on, go aboard. OPPOSITE disembark. □ **embark on** *He embarked on further study.* begin, commence, enter on, start, undertake.

embarrass *verb She embarrassed them by mentioning the matter.* abash, chagrin, discomfit, disconcert, distress, humiliate, mortify, shame.

embarrassed *adjective He felt embarrassed about what he had done.* abashed, ashamed, awkward, chagrined, discomfited, disconcerted, distressed, flustered, humiliated, mortified, self-conscious, shamefaced, sheepish, uncomfortable, upset.

embed *verb The post was embedded in concrete.* fix, implant, insert, lodge, set, stick.

embellish *verb* **1** *She embellished the dress with lace.* adorn, beautify, decorate, dress up, enhance, ornament, prettify, tizzy (*Australian*). **2** *There is no need to embellish the facts.* embroider, enhance, exaggerate, improve upon.

embezzle *verb He was jailed for embezzling the company's money.* misappropriate, steal.

embittered *adjective The man felt embittered by the experience.* bitter, disillusioned, rancorous, resentful, sour.

emblem *noun a school emblem.* badge, coat of arms, crest, device, hallmark, insignia, logo, seal, sign, symbol.

embodiment *noun He was the embodiment of unselfishness.* epitome, model, personification, quintessence, soul.

embody *verb* **1** *The house embodied her idea of a home.* exemplify, express, represent. **2** *Parts of the old treaty are embodied in the new one.* contain, include, incorporate, integrate.

embossed *adjective an embossed ceiling.* chased, fretted, moulded.

embrace *verb He embraced his wife affectionately.* clasp, cuddle, enfold, hold, hug.

embroider *verb* **1** *She embroidered the cloth.* sew, stitch, work. **2** *He embroidered the truth.* embellish, enhance, improve upon.

embroidery *noun* needlework, sewing.

embroil *verb He got embroiled in their argument.* catch up, drag in, draw in, entangle, involve, mix up.

embryonic *adjective The town is still at an embryonic stage.* early, immature, incipient, rudimentary, undeveloped. OPPOSITE advanced.

emerge *verb* **1** *The child emerged from behind the curtain.* appear, come out, materialise, peep out, show up, surface. OPPOSITE disappear. **2** *It emerged that several people were involved in the crime.* become apparent, become known, be revealed, come out, come to light, transpire, turn out.

emergency *noun She stays calm in an emergency.* crisis, danger, difficulty, predicament. — *adjective an*

emergency supply of food. backup, reserve, spare.

emigrant *noun an emigrant from Germany.* émigré, expatriate, refugee, settler. OPPOSITE immigrant.

emigrate *verb He emigrated from England.* depart, leave, migrate, move, quit, relocate. OPPOSITE immigrate.

eminence *noun The conference attracted a professor of some eminence.* celebrity, distinction, fame, importance, note, pre-eminence, prominence, renown, repute, standing, stature. OPPOSITE unimportance.

eminent *adjective an eminent scholar.* celebrated, distinguished, famous, great, illustrious, important, notable, noted, outstanding, pre-eminent, prominent, renowned, respected, well-known. OPPOSITE undistinguished.

emit *verb Light is emitted from the tube. The chimney emits noxious fumes.* discharge, expel, exude, give off, give out, issue, leak, ooze, pour forth, radiate, send out, shed, transmit.

emotion *noun He showed no emotion when the cat died.* feeling, passion, sentiment.

emotional *adjective* **1** *an emotional speech.* emotive, impassioned, moving, passionate, poignant, sentimental, stirring, touching. **2** *an emotional person.* ardent, demonstrative, excitable, fervent, passionate, sensitive, sentimental, temperamental. OPPOSITE unemotional.

emotive *adjective The reporter used highly emotive language.* emotional, moving, stirring. OPPOSITE matter-of-fact.

emperor *noun* Caesar, czar, head of state, kaiser, mikado, monarch, ruler, sovereign, tsar.

emphasis *noun The emphasis is on quality.* accent, attention, importance, priority, prominence, stress, weight.

emphasise *verb The doctor emphasised the importance of exercise.* accent, accentuate, draw attention to, highlight, impress, insist on, point up, stress, underline. OPPOSITE play down.

emphatic *adjective His answer was an emphatic 'No'.* categorical, decisive, definite, forceful, strong, unequivocal, vigorous. OPPOSITE tentative.

empire *noun These countries were once part of the Austro-Hungarian empire.* domain, dominion, kingdom, realm, territory.

employ *verb* **1** *The company employed extra workers.* appoint, contract, engage, give work to, hire, sign up, take on. **2** *He employed a new technique for treating burns.* apply, make use of, use, utilise.

employee *noun The firm has 100 employees.* hand, wage-earner, worker; [*employees*] human resources, labour, personnel, staff, workforce. OPPOSITE employer.

employer *noun* **1** *He was a kind employer.* boss, chief, manager, master, proprietor. OPPOSITE employee. **2** *Her new employer was one of the big banks.* business, company, corporation, establishment, firm, organisation.

employment *noun She was looking for new employment.* business, calling, career, job, occupation, profession, pursuit, trade, vocation, work; see also POSITION. OPPOSITE leisure, unemployment.

empower *verb* **1** *Police are empowered to arrest people.* authorise, commission, license. **2** *Knowledge empowers people to act.* enable, equip, give power to.

empty *adjective* **1** *an empty box.* hollow, unfilled, void. OPPOSITE full. **2** *an empty house.* bare, deserted, unfurnished, uninhabited, unoccupied, vacant. OPPOSITE occupied. **3** *an empty page.* blank, clean, clear, unused. OPPOSITE used. **4** *empty promises.* hollow, idle, insincere, insubstantial, meaningless, vain. OPPOSITE meaningful. — *verb* **1** *She emptied the contents of her purse.* pour out, remove, tip out. **2** *She emptied the bath water.* drain, let out, pour out. **3** *The police emptied the building.* clear, evacuate.

enable *verb* **1** *The gift enabled her to visit Italy.* allow, assist, facilitate, let, permit. **2** *The visa enables him to work in Australia.* allow, authorise, entitle, license, permit, qualify. OPPOSITE prevent (from).

enact *verb* **1** *Parliament enacted the bill.* decree, legislate, ordain, pass. OPPOSITE repeal. **2** *They enacted the balcony scene from Romeo and Juliet.* act out, perform, play.

enchant *verb She enchanted the audience with her singing.* bewitch, captivate, charm, delight, enrapture, enthral, entrance, fascinate, hold spellbound, hypnotise, mesmerise, thrill.

enchanter *noun* magician, sorcerer, warlock, wizard.

enchantress *noun* magician, siren, sorceress, witch.

encircle *verb Troops encircled the city.* besiege, circle, enclose, encompass, hem in, ring, surround.

enclose *verb* **1** *He enclosed the area with a fence.* circle, encircle, encompass, ring, surround, wall in. **2** *The animals are enclosed in cages.* box in, close in, confine, fence in, pen, restrict, shut in. **3** *She enclosed a card with the parcel.* include, insert, send with.

enclosure *noun The animals are kept in enclosures.* cage, compound, coop, corral, fold, hutch, paddock, pen, pound, run, stall, sty, yard.

encompass *verb The book encompasses many subjects.* contain, cover, embrace, include, incorporate. OPPOSITE exclude.

encounter *verb* **1** *They encountered a stranger on the path.* bump into (*informal*), chance upon, meet, run into. **2** *He encountered many problems.* be faced with, come up against, confront, contend with, experience, face, grapple with, meet with, run into. — *noun* **1** *a brief encounter.* meeting. **2** *an encounter with the authorities.* battle, brush, clash, conflict, confrontation, fight, run-in.

encourage *verb* **1** *She encourages her students.* buck up (*informal*), build up, buoy up, cheer up, comfort, hearten, inspire, reassure. OPPOSITE discourage. **2** *They encouraged him to keep trying.* egg on, exhort, persuade, spur, urge. OPPOSITE deter, dissuade. **3** *Cutting back encourages new growth.* aid, assist, boost, foster, further, help, promote, stimulate. OPPOSITE hinder.

encouragement *noun His praise was all the encouragement she needed.* boost, incentive, inspiration, reassurance, shot in the arm, stimulus, support.

encroach *verb We mustn't encroach on his territory.* impinge, infringe, intrude, invade, make inroads, poach, trespass.

encumber *verb The family was encumbered with a large mortgage.* burden, hamper, load down, lumber, saddle, weigh down.

encyclopedic *adjective encyclopedic knowledge.* comprehensive, extensive, vast, wide-ranging.

end *noun* **1** *the end of the bus route.* boundary, limit, terminus. OPPOSITE start. **2** *the end of the queue.* back, rear, tail. OPPOSITE beginning, head. **3** *The pencil has a sharp end.* extremity, point, tip. **4** *cigarette ends.* butt, remains, remnant, stub. **5** *the end of the session.* breakup, cessation, close, completion, conclusion, culmination, ending, finale, finish, termination. OPPOSITE beginning, opening. **6** *the end of the lending period.* expiration, expiry, termination. **7** *He came to an unfortunate end.* death, demise (*formal*), destruction, downfall, extinction, fall, passing, ruin. **8** *The end does not justify the means.* aim, design, goal, intention, object, objective, purpose. — *verb* **1** *He ended the concert with an old favourite.* bring to an end, close, complete, conclude, finish, round off, terminate, wind up. OPPOSITE begin. **2** *They campaigned to end the cruel practice.* abolish, eliminate, eradicate, get rid of, put an end to, put a stop to, stamp out, stop, wipe out. **3** *They ended their relationship.* break off, cut, discontinue, dissolve, sever, terminate. OPPOSITE commence. **4** *Work has ended for the day.* cease, come to an end, finish, halt, peter out, run out, stop. OPPOSITE start. **5** *The contract ended.* cease, expire, run out. □ **end up** *He ended up in jail.* finish up, land, wind up. **in the end** *You will succeed in the end.* eventually, finally, in the long run, ultimately.

endanger *verb Their lives were endangered by his driving.* imperil, jeopardise, put at risk, threaten. OPPOSITE safeguard.

endearing *adjective an endearing smile.* appealing, attractive, charming, disarming, engaging, likeable, lovable, winsome.

endeavour *verb We endeavour to please our customers.* aim, attempt, make an effort, strive, try. — *noun Her endeavour to please them succeeded.* attempt, effort, try.

ending *noun* **1** *The book has a surprise ending.* conclusion, denouement, end, finale, finish, resolution. OPPOSITE beginning. **2** *The -ed ending on verbs shows past tense.* suffix, termination.

endless *adjective* **1** *endless love.* abiding, boundless, ceaseless, constant, eternal, everlasting, immeasurable, inexhaustible, infinite, limitless, never-ending, permanent, perpetual, unending. OPPOSITE finite. **2** *an endless din.* constant, continual, continuous, incessant, interminable, non-stop, ongoing, perpetual, persistent. OPPOSITE passing.

endorse *verb* **1** *He endorsed the cheque.* countersign, sign. **2** *The councillors have endorsed the plan.* agree with, approve, assent to, back, confirm, OK (*informal*), ratify, sanction, second, subscribe to, support, uphold.

endow *verb She is endowed with intelligence.* bestow, bless, provide, supply.

endurance *noun The race was a test of endurance.* fortitude, hardiness, patience, perseverance, persistence, stamina, staying power, strength, tenacity.

endure *verb* **1** *He endured great hardship.* bear, brave, cope with, experience, suffer, undergo, weather, withstand. OPPOSITE escape. **2** *She cannot endure their insolence.* abide, bear, brook, put up with, stand, stomach, tolerate. **3** *The tradition has endured.* carry on, continue, last, live on, persist, prevail, remain, stay, survive. OPPOSITE die.

enemy *noun These former enemies have now overcome their differences.* adversary, antagonist, foe, opponent, opposition, rival. OPPOSITE ally, friend.

energetic *adjective* **1** *an energetic person.* active, animated, dynamic, forceful, full of beans (*informal*), go-ahead, hard-working, high-powered, indefatigable, industrious, lively, perky, spirited, sprightly, spry, tireless, vibrant, vigorous, zippy. OPPOSITE listless. **2** *an energetic game of tennis.* brisk, strenuous, vigorous.

energy *noun He never runs out of energy.* drive, enthusiasm, force, go, gusto, liveliness, oomph (*informal*), pep, power, stamina, steam, verve, vigour, vim (*informal*), vitality, vivacity, zeal, zest, zing (*informal*), zip. OPPOSITE lethargy.

enforce *verb He enforces the rules.* administer, apply, carry out, implement, impose, insist on. OPPOSITE waive.

engage *verb* **1** *He engaged a personal assistant.* appoint, employ, hire, recruit, take on. OPPOSITE dismiss. **2** *They engaged her in conversation.* absorb, engross, involve, occupy.

engaged *adjective* **1** *an engaged couple.* affianced (*formal*), betrothed (*formal*). **2** *The line is engaged.* busy, in use, occupied. OPPOSITE free.

engagement *noun* **1** *the couple's engagement.* betrothal. **2** *He could not attend because of a previous engagement.* appointment, arrangement, assignation, booking, commitment, date (*informal*), meeting, rendezvous.

engaging *adjective an engaging manner.* appealing, attractive, charming, delightful, disarming, enchanting, endearing, likeable, lovable, winning, winsome.

engender *verb Injustice engenders resentment.* beget, breed, bring about, cause, create, generate, give rise to, lead to, produce.

engine *noun* **1** *a car engine.* motor. **2** *a railway engine.* locomotive.

engineer *verb He engineered a meeting.* arrange, bring about, contrive, fix, mastermind, orchestrate, organise, plan, rig, wangle (*slang*).

engrave *verb Her name was engraved on the medal.* carve, chisel, cut, etch, incise, inscribe.

engrossed *adjective Brian was engrossed in his book.* absorbed, immersed, involved, lost, occupied, preoccupied.

engulf *verb The waters engulfed the town.* cover, flood, inundate, overrun, overwhelm, submerge, swallow up, swamp.

enhance *verb Salt enhances the flavour.* boost, enrich, heighten, improve, increase, intensify, reinforce, strengthen. OPPOSITE detract from, diminish.

enigma *noun Nobody could solve the enigma.* conundrum, mystery, problem, puzzle, riddle, secret.

enigmatic *adjective an enigmatic comment.* arcane, baffling, cryptic, inscrutable, mysterious, obscure, perplexing, puzzling, unfathomable. OPPOSITE straightforward.

enjoy *verb She enjoys the attention.* appreciate, bask in, be fond of, be keen on, delight in, fancy, lap up, like, love, luxuriate in, relish, revel in, savour, wallow in. OPPOSITE dislike. □ **enjoy yourself** be happy, have a ball (*informal*), have a good time, have fun.

enjoyable *adjective an enjoyable evening.* agreeable, cool (*informal*), delightful, good, lovely (*informal*), nice, pleasant, pleasurable, satisfying. OPPOSITE unpleasant.

enjoyment *noun She gets enjoyment out of life.* amusement, delectation, delight, entertainment, fun, happiness, joy, kick (*informal*), pleasure, recreation, satisfaction, thrill, zest.

enlarge *verb* **1** *The new owners enlarged the shop.* add to, broaden, expand, extend, lengthen, widen. **2** *Her stomach has enlarged over the years.* bulge, distend, expand, fill out, grow, stretch, swell. OPPOSITE diminish. **3** *She enlarged the photo.* blow up (*informal*), magnify. OPPOSITE reduce. □ **enlarge upon** *He will enlarge upon this subject in his address.* amplify, elaborate on, expand on, expatiate on.

enlighten *verb He enlightened his readers on prison life.* edify, educate, inform, instruct, teach.

enlist *verb* **1** *He enlisted as a soldier.* enrol, join up, register, sign on, volunteer. **2** *The government enlisted troops.* call up, conscript, draft (*American*), enrol, recruit. **3** *Try to enlist their support.* drum up, gather, get, mobilise, muster, obtain, secure.

enmity *noun centuries of enmity between the nations.* acrimony, animosity, antagonism, antipathy, bitterness, hatred, hostility, ill will, malevolence, opposition, rancour. OPPOSITE friendship.

enormous *adjective an enormous house. an enormous amount.* astronomical, big, colossal, gargantuan, giant, gigantic, ginormous (*slang*), great, huge, humungous (*slang*), immeasurable, immense, incalculable, jumbo, king-sized, large, mammoth, massive, mighty, monstrous, monumental, outsize, prodigious, spacious, staggering, stupendous, sweeping, tremendous, vast. OPPOSITE tiny.

enough *adjective They have enough money to live on.* adequate, ample, sufficient. OPPOSITE insufficient.

enquire *verb He enquired about the patient's condition.* ask, inquire, query, question.

enquiry *noun The counter officer handles enquiries.* inquiry, query, question.

enrage *verb His lateness enraged his team mates.* anger, annoy, exasperate, incense, infuriate, irritate, madden, outrage, provoke, rile (*informal*). OPPOSITE mollify.

enrol *verb* **1** *He enrolled in the swimming club.* enlist, join up, register, sign on. OPPOSITE withdraw (from). **2** *The college enrolled her as a student.* accept, admit, enlist, recruit, take on. OPPOSITE expel.

ensemble *noun a string ensemble.* band, group, orchestra.

ensign *noun the Australian Navy's ensign.* banner, flag, jack, standard.

ensue *verb A quarrel ensued.* follow, result.

ensuing *adjective the ensuing weeks.* following, next, subsequent, succeeding. OPPOSITE previous.

ensure *verb Good food will ensure good health.* guarantee, make certain, make sure, secure.

entail *verb These plans entail great expense.* call for, involve, mean, necessitate, require.

entangle *verb* **1** *The strands of cotton became entangled.* entwine, interlace, intertwine, ravel, snarl, tangle, twist. OPPOSITE unravel. **2** *The animal was entangled in the net.* catch, ensnare, snare, trap. **3** *He became entangled in a dangerous situation.* catch up, embroil, involve, mix up.

enter *verb* **1** *Enemy forces entered the country.* come in, go in, infiltrate, intrude in, invade, penetrate. OPPOSITE leave. **2** *He entered the army.* enlist in, enrol in, join, register for, sign up for. OPPOSITE leave. **3** *She entered his name in her book.*

inscribe, jot, list, note, record, register, write. **4** *They will enter the race.* compete in, go in, participate in, register for, take part in. OPPOSITE withdraw (from).

enterprise *noun* **1** *a difficult enterprise.* endeavour, mission, operation, project, undertaking, venture. **2** *The new person shows enterprise.* drive, get-up-and-go, initiative, push, resourcefulness. **3** *He works for a large enterprise.* business, company, concern, corporation, establishment, firm, operation, organisation.

enterprising *adjective There's an opportunity here for an enterprising person.* adventurous, bold, daring, energetic, go-ahead, imaginative, industrious, intrepid, resourceful, venturesome.

entertain *verb* **1** *She entertained her audience.* amuse, delight, divert, please. **2** *They enjoy entertaining visitors.* play host to, receive, regale, welcome, wine and dine. **3** *He refused to entertain the idea.* consider, contemplate, harbour, think about. OPPOSITE reject.

entertainer *noun a career as an entertainer.* artist, artiste, performer, player; [*various entertainers*] actor, actress, busker, clown, comedian, comic, conjuror, dancer, instrumentalist, jester, juggler, magician, minstrel, musician, singer, vocalist.

entertainment *noun The hotel organises entertainment for guests.* amusement, distraction, diversion, enjoyment, fun, pastime, pleasure, recreation, sport.

enthral *verb The lady enthralled him with her beauty.* beguile, bewitch, captivate, charm, enchant, enrapture, entrance, fascinate, hold spellbound, hypnotise, mesmerise.

enthrone *verb The Queen was enthroned with all pomp and ceremony.* crown, install. OPPOSITE depose.

enthusiasm *noun She does everything with enthusiasm.* ardour, eagerness, excitement, exuberance, fervour, gusto, keenness, passion, relish, verve, zeal, zest.

enthusiast *noun a tennis enthusiast.* addict, aficionado, buff (*informal*), devotee, fan, fanatic, follower, freak (*informal*), lover, nut (*informal*), supporter, zealot.

enthusiastic *adjective* **1** *an enthusiastic supporter.* ardent, avid, committed, eager, excited, exuberant, fervent, keen, passionate, zealous. OPPOSITE apathetic. **2** *The party guests received an enthusiastic welcome.* hearty, warm, wholehearted. OPPOSITE half-hearted.

entice *verb He enticed the cat inside with a fish.* allure, attract, bribe, cajole, coax, decoy, inveigle, lure, persuade, seduce, tempt.

entire *adjective an entire tea set.* complete, full, intact, total, unbroken, whole. OPPOSITE incomplete, partial.

entirely *adverb You are entirely correct.* absolutely, altogether, completely, fully, one hundred per cent, perfectly, quite, totally, utterly, wholly. OPPOSITE partially.

entitle *verb* **1** *The book is entitled 'Cats'.* call, name, title. **2** *The ticket entitles you to a seat.* allow, authorise, permit, qualify.

entitlement *noun an entitlement to a pension.* claim, eligibility, prerogative, right.

entity *noun separate entities.* being, body, object, thing.

entourage *noun the Queen's entourage.* attendants, court, escort, followers, retinue, train.

entrance[1] *noun* **1** *the entrance to a house.* access, door, doorway, entry, foyer, gate, gateway, opening, pas-

sage, porch, portal, postern, threshold, way in. OPPOSITE exit. **2** *She made a grand entrance.* appearance, arrival, entry. OPPOSITE departure, exit. **3** *Entrance is refused to people in thongs.* access, admission, admittance, entry.

entrance[2] *verb She entranced them with her song.* beguile, bewitch, captivate, charm, delight, enchant, enrapture, enthral, fascinate, hold spellbound, hypnotise, mesmerise, transport.

entrant *noun ten entrants in the competition.* applicant, candidate, competitor, contestant, participant.

entreat *verb He entreated the giant to have mercy on him.* appeal to, beg, beseech, implore, plead with, pray, request, supplicate.

entrench *verb The idea became entrenched in his mind.* establish, fix, root, settle.

entrust *verb* **1** *He entrusted them with the job.* assign, charge, delegate, trust. **2** *She entrusted the children to the nanny's care.* commend, commit, consign, hand over.

entry *noun* **1** *She was refused entry.* admission, admittance, entrance. **2** *The actor made his entry.* appearance, arrival, entrance. **3** *Keep the entry clear.* access, approach, door, doorway, entrance, gate, gateway, opening, way in. **4** *an entry in a diary.* item, jotting, note, record.

entwine *verb The ivy was entwined in the trellis.* entangle, intertwine, interweave, snarl, tangle, twine, twist, weave.

envelop *verb Mist enveloped the hills.* blanket, cloak, cocoon, conceal, cover, obscure, shroud, surround, veil.

envelope *noun He put the letter in an envelope.* case, cover, covering, holder, jacket, pocket, sheath, wrapper.

envious *adjective She was envious of their good fortune.* covetous, green, grudging, jealous, resentful.

environment *noun a change of environment.* ambience, atmosphere, circumstances, conditions, context, ecosystem, element, environs, habitat, medium, milieu, setting, situation, surroundings.

environmentalist *noun* conservationist, ecologist, green, greenie (*Australian informal*).

environs *noun a map of Brisbane and environs.* district, neighbourhood, outskirts, surroundings, vicinity.

envisage *verb They did not envisage any problems.* conceive of, contemplate, foresee, imagine, picture, predict, visualise.

envoy *noun The minister sent an envoy.* agent, ambassador, delegate, diplomat, emissary, messenger, representative.

envy *noun She was green with envy.* covetousness, jealousy, resentment. — *verb She envies them their independence.* begrudge, be jealous of, covet, grudge, resent.

ephemeral *adjective A good dinner is an ephemeral pleasure.* brief, fleeting, impermanent, momentary, passing, short-lived, temporary, transient, transitory. OPPOSITE lasting.

epidemic *noun a flu epidemic.* outbreak, pestilence, plague.

epigram *noun He invented some clever epigrams.* aphorism, pun, quip, saying, witticism.

epilogue *noun The play has an epilogue.* conclusion, postscript. OPPOSITE prologue.

episode *noun* **1** *a memorable episode in history.* affair (*informal*), event, happening, incident, occasion, occurrence. **2** *the second episode in* *the series.* chapter, instalment, part, scene, section.

epistle *noun He wrote them a long epistle.* communication, letter, note.

epoch *noun the dawn of a new epoch.* age, era, period, time.

equal *adjective equal amounts.* equivalent, even, identical, level, like, matching, parallel, same, uniform. OPPOSITE unequal. — *noun At chess he has no equal.* match, parallel, peer, rival. — *verb* **1** *Two plus two equals four.* add up to, be equivalent to, come to, make, total. **2** *He equalled his opponent's score.* draw with, match, reach, tie with.

equality *noun equality in pay and conditions.* egalitarianism, equivalence, evenness, parity, sameness, uniformity. OPPOSITE inequality.

equilibrium *noun The see-saw is in a state of equilibrium.* balance, poise, stability, steadiness.

equip *verb We were equipped for our journey.* arm, fit out, furnish, kit out, prepare, provide, rig out, stock, supply.

equipment *noun the equipment for a job.* apparatus, appliances, gear, hardware, implements, instruments, kit, machinery, materials, outfit, paraphernalia, plant, rig, supplies, tackle, tools.

equitable *adjective an equitable distribution of the proceeds.* even-handed, fair, impartial, just, proper, reasonable, right, unbiased.

equity *noun They treated all their children with equity.* even-handedness, fairness, impartiality, justice. OPPOSITE inequity.

equivalent *adjective* **1** *two items of equivalent value.* commensurate, comparable, corresponding, equal, identical, interchangeable, matching, same. OPPOSITE different. **2** *His request was equivalent to an order.* tantamount.

equivocal *adjective David's answer was deliberately equivocal.* ambiguous, imprecise, indefinite, uncertain, unclear, vague.

era *noun They belonged to a different era.* age, day, epoch, period, time.

eradicate *verb He cannot eradicate the weeds.* annihilate, destroy, eliminate, exterminate, get rid of, obliterate, remove, root out, uproot, weed out, wipe out.

erase *verb She erased her mistake.* blot out, cancel, delete, efface, expunge, obliterate, remove, rub out, wipe out.

erect *adjective an erect stance.* bolt upright, perpendicular, standing, upright, vertical. — *verb* **1** *It doesn't take long to erect a tent.* pitch, put up, set up. OPPOSITE dismantle. **2** *The house was erected in two months.* build, construct, raise. OPPOSITE demolish.

erode *verb The surface is being eroded by rain and wind.* abrade, corrode, destroy, eat away, grind down, rub away, wear away, weather.

erosion *noun soil erosion.* abrasion, corrosion, wearing away, weathering.

erotic *adjective an erotic painting.* seductive, sensual, sexy, suggestive, titillating.

err *verb* **1** *He erred in his calculations.* be incorrect, go wrong, make a mistake, miscalculate, slip up. **2** *He confessed that he had erred.* do wrong, go astray, sin, transgress, trespass (*old use*).

errand *noun She sent the child on an errand.* chore, job, mission, task.

erratic *adjective erratic behaviour.* capricious, changeable, fickle, inconsistent, irregular, spasmodic, uneven, unpredictable, variable. OPPOSITE consistent.

error *noun He corrected the errors.* bloomer (*slang*), blue (*Australian informal*), blunder, booboo (*slang*), clanger (*informal*), fault, flaw, gaffe, howler (*informal*), inaccuracy, lapse, miscalculation, misprint, mistake, oversight, slip, slip-up (*informal*), typo (*informal*).

erupt *verb Lava erupted from the volcano.* be discharged, belch, burst out, gush out, issue, pour out, shoot forth, spew, spurt out.

escalate *verb* **1** *Prices have escalated.* increase, jump, multiply, rise, skyrocket, soar. OPPOSITE drop. **2** *The tension escalated.* blow up, heighten, intensify, mount, rise, step up, worsen. OPPOSITE lessen.

escapade *noun The friends had some exciting escapades.* adventure, caper, exploit, lark, prank, scrape.

escape *verb* **1** *The prisoner escaped.* abscond, bolt, break free, break out, flee, get away, run away, scarper, slip away, take flight. **2** *The air escaped from the tyre.* discharge, drain, get out, leak, seep. **3** *He escaped punishment.* avoid, dodge, elude, evade, get out of, wriggle out of. — *noun* **1** *They planned their escape from prison.* breakout, flight, getaway. OPPOSITE capture. **2** *a fire escape.* exit, way out. **3** *Reading is a pleasant escape from the chores.* distraction, diversion, outlet, relief.

escapee *noun a prison escapee.* absconder, bolter, escaper, fugitive, runaway.

escort *noun* **1** *The President was given a police escort.* bodyguard, chaperone, convoy, guard, minder, protector. **2** *The girl has a charming escort.* companion, date (*informal*), partner. — *verb He escorted them to the police station.* accompany, chaperone, conduct, guide, lead, take, usher.

especially *adverb* **1** *He made it especially for them.* chiefly, expressly, particularly, primarily, specially, specifically. **2** *It was not especially good.* exceptionally, extraordinarily, outstandingly, particularly.

essay *noun She wrote an essay.* article, composition, critique, dissertation, paper, thesis.

essence *noun* **1** *the essence of her argument.* core, crux, gist, heart, kernel, nub, pith, quintessence, substance. **2** *vanilla essence.* concentrate, extract.

essential *adjective* **1** *A toothbrush is essential.* imperative, indispensable, necessary, requisite, vital. OPPOSITE dispensable. **2** *He outlined the essential features of the system.* basic, central, chief, fundamental, inherent, intrinsic, key, main, primary, principal. OPPOSITE incidental. — *noun Tact is an essential for this job.* must, necessity, prerequisite, requirement, requisite.

establish *verb* **1** *She established a new company.* begin, build, construct, create, found, inaugurate, initiate, institute, introduce, originate, pioneer, set up, start. **2** *You must establish your innocence.* confirm, demonstrate, prove, show, substantiate, verify. OPPOSITE disprove.

establishment *noun They run a large establishment.* business, company, concern, corporation, enterprise, firm, institution, organisation, plant.

estate *noun* **1** *a housing estate.* area, development. **2** *His estate was left to the children.* assets, fortune, money, property, wealth.

esteem *noun His father was held in high esteem.* admiration, appreciation, approval, estimation, regard, respect, reverence, veneration. OPPOSITE disdain.

estimate *noun* **1** *an estimate of a thing's worth.* appraisal, approximation, assessment, calculation, evaluation, guesstimate (*informal*), judgement, opinion, valuation. **2** *a builder's estimate.* quotation, quote (*informal*), tender. — *verb She estimated the watch's value at $500.* appraise, assess, calculate, evaluate, guess, judge, put, rate, reckon, size up, value.

estrange *verb Bitterness estranged him from his friend.* alienate, drive apart. OPPOSITE unite.

estuary *noun the river estuary.* firth, inlet, mouth.

etch *verb The scene is etched on my mind.* carve, engrave, impress, imprint, inscribe, stamp.

eternal *adjective see* EVERLASTING.

ethical *adjective His behaviour was not ethical.* above board, correct, honourable, moral, principled, proper, right, righteous, upright, virtuous. OPPOSITE unethical.

ethics *plural noun medical ethics.* moral code, morality, morals, principles, scruples.

ethnic *adjective ethnic differences.* cultural, national, racial.

etiquette *noun wedding etiquette.* code of behaviour, conventions, decorum, form, manners, proprieties, protocol, rules.

Eucharist *noun* Holy Communion, Lord's Supper, Mass.

evacuate *verb* **1** *The townspeople were evacuated.* move out, relocate, remove, send away. **2** *The police evacuated the nursing home.* clear, empty. **3** *The residents evacuated the building.* abandon, desert, flee, leave, quit, vacate.

evade *verb Steve could no longer evade his responsibilities.* avoid, dodge, duck, elude, escape from, shirk, shun, sidestep. OPPOSITE face.

evaluate *verb* **1** *Evaluate 'x' in these equations.* calculate, compute. **2** *She evaluated the scheme.* appraise, assess, judge, rate, review, size up, value, weigh up.

evangelist *noun* missionary, preacher.

evaporate *verb* **1** *The water evaporated in the sun.* dry up, vaporise. OPPOSITE condense. **2** *Their hopes evaporated.* disappear, fade away, melt away, vanish. OPPOSITE increase.

evasive *adjective Her answers were evasive.* ambiguous, cagey (*informal*), devious, equivocal, non-committal, oblique, prevaricating, roundabout. OPPOSITE frank, straight.

even *adjective* **1** *an even surface.* flat, flush, level, plane, smooth. OPPOSITE rough, uneven. **2** *an even temperature.* consistent, constant, regular, steady, unchanging, uniform, unvarying. OPPOSITE variable. **3** *The scores were even.* balanced, drawn, equal, identical, level, neck and neck, square, the same, tied. OPPOSITE different. — *verb* **1** *The hairdresser evened the ends.* level, straighten. **2** *The last point evened the scores.* balance, equalise, level, tie.

evening *noun They went for a walk in the evening after dinner.* dusk, eventide (*old use*), gloaming, night, nightfall, sundown, sunset, twilight. OPPOSITE dawn, morning.

event *noun* **1** *an unlikely event.* affair, circumstance, episode, eventuality, experience, happening, incident, occasion, occurrence. **2** *a sporting event.* championship, competition, contest, fixture, meet, meeting, tournament. **3** *The next event in the carnival is the relay.* competition, contest, item, race.

even-tempered *adjective Janet is an even-tempered girl and easy to live*

with. calm, easygoing, equable, imperturbable, placid, serene, steady, tranquil, unfazed (*informal*), unflappable (*informal*). OPPOSITE volatile.

eventful *adjective an eventful holiday.* action-packed, busy, exciting, full, memorable, momentous, unforgettable. OPPOSITE uneventful.

eventuality *noun He was prepared for any eventuality.* contingency, possibility; see also EVENT.

eventually *adverb She arrived at the party eventually.* at last, finally, in the end, ultimately.

everlasting *adjective* **1** *everlasting life.* endless, eternal, immortal, infinite, limitless, never-ending, timeless, unending, unlimited. OPPOSITE finite, transitory. **2** *an everlasting problem.* abiding, ceaseless, chronic, constant, continual, continuous, endless, eternal, incessant, interminable, non-stop, perennial, permanent, perpetual, persistent, recurrent, repeated. OPPOSITE occasional, temporary.

everybody *pronoun You can tell everybody.* all, all and sundry, everyone, one and all, the world. OPPOSITE nobody.

everyday *adjective A visit from royalty was not an everyday occurrence.* common, commonplace, customary, daily, day-to-day, familiar, mundane, normal, ordinary, regular, routine, usual. OPPOSITE unusual.

everywhere *adverb* extensively, far and wide, globally, high and low, near and far, ubiquitously, universally.

evict *verb The landlord evicted his tenant.* chuck out (*informal*), drive out, eject, expel, get rid of, kick out (*informal*), remove, throw out, turf out (*informal*), turn out.

evidence *noun* **1** *They had enough evidence to support their claim.* data, documentation, facts, grounds, information. **2** *Her tears were evidence of her true feelings.* indication, manifestation, proof, sign, symptom, testimony, token.

evident *adjective It was evident that she enjoyed reading.* apparent, clear, manifest, noticeable, obvious, patent, plain, undeniable, unmistakable. OPPOSITE dubious.

evil *adjective an evil person. an evil act.* abominable, atrocious, bad, base, beastly, corrupt, demonic, depraved, despicable, detestable, diabolical, foul, hateful, heinous, immoral, infamous, iniquitous, loathsome, malevolent, malicious, nefarious, satanic, sinful, sinister, ungodly, unrighteous, vicious, vile, villainous, wicked. OPPOSITE good. — *noun He wanted to root out evil.* corruption, depravity, immorality, iniquity, sin, turpitude, ungodliness, vice, wickedness, wrong, wrongdoing. OPPOSITE goodness.

evoke *verb The smell evoked pleasant memories.* arouse, awaken, call up, conjure up, elicit, inspire, rouse, stimulate, stir up, suggest.

evolve *verb The scheme evolved gradually.* develop, grow, unfold.

exact *adjective* **1** *an exact answer.* accurate, correct, literal, perfect, precise, right, spot-on (*informal*), true. OPPOSITE approximate. **2** *exact instructions.* detailed, explicit, minute, particular, precise, rigorous, specific, strict. **3** *an exact worker.* careful, fastidious, meticulous, painstaking, punctilious, scrupulous. OPPOSITE careless. — *verb They exacted their payment.* claim, demand, extort, extract, insist on.

exacting *adjective an exacting task.* arduous, demanding, difficult, hard, onerous, stiff, taxing, tough.

exaggerate *verb* **1** *He exaggerated the size of the problem.* blow up, inflate, magnify, overdo, overestimate, overstate. OPPOSITE understate. **2** *She likes to exaggerate.* ham it up (*informal*), lay it on thick (*informal*), make a mountain out of a molehill, pile it on (*informal*).

exaggeration *noun His description was full of exaggeration.* hyperbole, magnification, overstatement. OPPOSITE understatement.

exalt *verb* **1** *He was quickly exalted to a senior position.* advance, elevate, promote, raise, upgrade. OPPOSITE demote. **2** *Christians exalt Jesus.* adore, extol, glorify, hallow, honour, laud (*formal*), magnify (*old use*), praise, revere, venerate, worship.

examination *noun* **1** *an examination of the college records.* analysis, audit, check, inspection, investigation, observation, perusal, probe, review, scrutiny, study, survey. **2** *school examinations.* exam (*informal*), oral (*informal*), quiz, test. **3** *examination of the witness.* cross-examination, interrogation, questioning.

examine *verb* **1** *He examined the accounts, evidence, etc.* analyse, audit, check, consider, go over, inquire into, inspect, investigate, look at, look over, peruse, pore over, probe, research, review, scan, scrutinise, sift, study, survey, vet. **2** *The students are examined on their knowledge.* question, quiz, sound out, test. **3** *He examined the witness.* cross-examine, cross-question, grill, interrogate, question.

example *noun* **1** *The lawyer cited several examples of the same situation.* case, illustration, instance, model, precedent. **2** *She sent in an example of her work.* prototype, sample, specimen. **3** *He is not a good example of right behaviour.* model, paragon, pattern, standard.

exasperate *verb He was exasperated by their slowness.* anger, annoy, bug (*informal*), enrage, get on someone's nerves, infuriate, irk, irritate, madden, needle (*informal*), peeve (*informal*), provoke, rile (*informal*), vex. OPPOSITE appease, please.

excavate *verb* **1** *He excavated a cellar under the kitchen.* burrow, dig, hollow out, scoop out, shovel out, tunnel. OPPOSITE fill in. **2** *He excavated some old bones.* dig up, exhume, uncover, unearth. OPPOSITE bury.

exceed *verb The attendance exceeded last year's record.* beat, better, excel, go beyond, go over, outdo, outnumber, overtake, pass, surpass, top, transcend.

excel *verb Clare excels at music.* be outstanding, shine, stand out.

excellence *noun They strive for excellence.* greatness, merit, perfection, pre-eminence, quality, superiority.

excellent *adjective an excellent performance. an excellent idea.* ace (*informal*), admirable, awesome (*informal*), beaut (*Australian informal*), brilliant (*informal*), capital, choice, classic, cool (*informal*), exceptional, fabulous, fantastic, far-out (*informal*), fine, first-class, first-rate, great, groovy (*slang*), impressive, magnificent, marvellous, masterly, matchless, meritorious, model, out of the box (*Australian informal*), outstanding, peerless, perfect, prize, remarkable, select, sensational, splendid, sterling, super (*informal*), superb, superior, superlative, supreme, swell (*informal*), terrific (*informal*), top-notch (*informal*), tremendous, wicked (*slang*), wizard (*informal*), wonderful. OPPOSITE bad, inferior.

except *preposition No one was left except me.* apart from, bar, besides, but, excluding, other than, save. OPPOSITE including.

exception *noun a rule without exceptions.* anomaly, departure, deviation, exclusion, inconsistency, irregularity.

exceptional *adjective* **1** *an exceptional case.* abnormal, anomalous, atypical, extraordinary, odd, phenomenal, rare, remarkable, singular, special, uncommon, unusual. OPPOSITE normal, typical. **2** *an exceptional pianist.* see EXCELLENT.

excerpt *noun* **1** *excerpts from a book.* citation, extract, passage, quotation, selection. **2** *an excerpt from the film.* clip, trailer.

excess *noun* **1** *an excess of grapes.* glut, over-abundance, overflow, oversupply, superfluity, surfeit, surplus. OPPOSITE shortage. **2** *Take what you need and dispose of the excess.* balance, leftovers, remainder, residue, surplus. OPPOSITE deficit.

excessive *adjective* **1** *excessive prices.* exorbitant, extortionate, extreme, inordinate, outrageous, steep, unreasonable. OPPOSITE reasonable. **2** *excessive drinking.* heavy, immoderate, intemperate. OPPOSITE moderate. **3** *excessive flattery.* exaggerated, extravagant, fulsome, overdone, profuse, superfluous.

exchange *verb The children exchanged stamps.* barter, change, interchange, substitute, swap, trade.

excitable *adjective an excitable person.* emotional, highly-strung, hot-headed, mercurial, nervous, temperamental, volatile. OPPOSITE placid.

excite *verb* **1** *Do not excite the patient.* agitate, animate, arouse, disturb, fluster, rouse, stir up, thrill, upset, wind up (*informal*), work up. OPPOSITE lull. **2** *The snippet of news excited curiosity.* arouse, awaken, generate, incite, inspire, kindle, provoke, stimulate, whet. OPPOSITE dampen.

excitement *noun There was great excitement on the streets.* action, activity, ado, adventure, agitation, ferment, flurry, frenzy, furore, fuss, kerfuffle, sensation, stir, to-do, unrest.

exciting *adjective an exciting story.* breathtaking, electrifying, exhilarating, gripping, heady, moving, riveting, rousing, sensational, spectacular, stimulating, stirring, suspenseful, thrilling. OPPOSITE boring.

exclaim *verb "Look out!" he exclaimed.* bawl, bellow, call out, cry out, shout, yell.

exclude *verb* **1** *He was excluded from the group.* ban, bar, debar, expel, forbid, keep out, leave out, ostracise, oust, prohibit, shut out. OPPOSITE admit, include. **2** *She excluded that possibility.* eliminate, omit, preclude, reject, rule out. OPPOSITE admit.

exclusive *adjective* **1** *He belongs to an exclusive club.* closed, private, restricted, select. OPPOSITE open. **2** *an exclusive boutique.* expensive, high-class, upmarket. **3** *They have the exclusive rights.* complete, full, sole, undivided, unique. OPPOSITE shared.

excrete *verb* defecate, urinate, void.

excruciating *adjective an excruciating headache.* acute, agonising, insufferable, intolerable, painful, severe, unbearable.

excursion *noun an excursion into the hills.* drive, expedition, hike, holiday, jaunt, journey, outing, pleasure-trip, ramble, ride, run, tour, trek, trip, walk.

excusable *adjective an excusable mistake.* forgivable, pardonable, venial. OPPOSITE inexcusable.

excuse *verb* **1** *The teacher excused her for being late.* exonerate, forgive, let off, make allowances for, pardon. OPPOSITE punish. **2** *Nothing can excuse such rudeness.* condone, explain, justify, mitigate, vindicate, warrant. **3** *He was excused from attending the lesson.* exempt, free, let off, release. OPPOSITE compel. — *noun an excuse for her absence.* defence, explanation, justification, pretext, reason.

execute *verb* **1** *He executes the boss's orders.* accomplish, carry out, complete, do, effect, fulfil, implement, perform. **2** *The murderer was executed.* kill, put to death, slay; [*various ways to execute*] behead, crucify, electrocute, garrotte, gas, guillotine, hang, lynch, shoot, stone.

executive *noun a business executive.* administrator, chief, director, manager.

exemplify *verb She exemplifies the perfect secretary.* embody, epitomise, illustrate, personify, represent, typify.

exempt *adjective He is exempt from paying tax.* excused, freed, immune, released, relieved, spared. OPPOSITE liable. — *verb They exempted him from playing football.* excuse, free, let off, release, relieve, spare.

exemption *noun You can claim a tax exemption.* dispensation, immunity, privilege. OPPOSITE obligation.

exercise *noun* **1** *She keeps fit through exercise.* activity, aerobics, callisthenics, exertion, games, gymnastics, physical education, physical training, sport. **2** *military exercises.* drill, manoeuvres, movements, practice, training. — *verb* **1** *He exercised his power of veto.* apply, employ, exert, use, utilise, wield. **2** *She exercises daily at the gym.* limber up, loosen up, practise, train, work out.

exert *verb He exerted all his strength.* apply, employ, exercise, use, utilise, wield.

exertion *noun physical and mental exertion.* effort, exercise, labour, strain, toil, work. OPPOSITE inertia.

exhale *verb Take a deep breath, hold it, and exhale slowly.* blow, breathe out, expire, pant, puff. OPPOSITE inhale.

exhaust *verb* **1** *Playing in the heat exhausted them.* drain, fatigue, tire out, weaken, wear out, weary. OPPOSITE refresh. **2** *He exhausted their funds.* blow (*slang*), consume, deplete, dissipate, expend, spend, use up. OPPOSITE replenish. — *noun car exhaust.* emissions, fumes, gases, smoke.

exhausted *adjective The players were exhausted.* all in (*informal*), burnt out, bushed (*informal*), dog-tired, done in (*informal*), drained, fagged out (*informal*), fatigued, knackered (*slang*), played out, pooped (*informal*), run down, sapped, spent, tired out, washed out, weak, weary, whacked (*informal*), worn out, zapped (*slang*), zonked (*slang*). OPPOSITE invigorated.

exhausting *adjective an exhausting job.* arduous, difficult, gruelling, hard, heavy, laborious, strenuous, tiring. OPPOSITE easy.

exhaustive *adjective an exhaustive study.* complete, comprehensive, detailed, full, in-depth, intensive, minute, thorough. OPPOSITE cursory.

exhibit *verb They exhibited their paintings.* display, present, show.

exhibition *noun an art exhibition.* demonstration, display, expo, exposition, fair, presentation, show.

exhilarated *adjective The winner was exhilarated.* cheerful, delighted, ecstatic, elated, euphoric, excited, happy, joyful, overjoyed, thrilled. OPPOSITE depressed.

exhort *verb He exhorted them to attend.* advise, appeal to, beseech, encourage, entreat, implore, plead with, urge.

exile *noun* **1** *She lived in exile.* banishment, deportation, expatriation, expulsion. **2** *a political exile.* deportee, expatriate, outcast, refugee. — *verb He was exiled for political reasons.* banish, deport, expatriate, expel, send away.

exist *verb* **1** *Do fairies exist?* be, be real, live, occur. **2** *They cannot exist on that income.* keep going, live, subsist, survive. OPPOSITE die.

existence *noun* **1** *He does not believe in the existence of fairies.* actuality, presence, reality. OPPOSITE non-existence. **2** *the struggle for existence.* being, life, subsistence, survival. OPPOSITE death.

exit *noun* **1** *She made her exit.* departure, escape, retreat. OPPOSITE entrance. **2** *The room has an emergency exit.* door, outlet, way out. OPPOSITE entrance. — *verb We exited by the rear door.* depart, go out, leave.

exonerate *verb She was exonerated from all blame.* absolve, acquit, clear, free, pardon, vindicate. OPPOSITE convict.

exorbitant *adjective exorbitant prices.* excessive, expensive, extortionate, high, inordinate, outrageous, preposterous, steep, unreasonable. OPPOSITE cheap.

exotic *adjective exotic plants.* alien, foreign, imported; see also UNUSUAL. OPPOSITE native.

expand *verb* **1** *The business expanded.* build up, develop, enlarge, grow, increase. OPPOSITE contract. **2** *His stomach expanded.* bloat, broaden, distend, fatten, grow, stretch, swell, widen. OPPOSITE shrink. **3** *The pelican expanded its wings.* extend, open out, spread out, stretch out, unfurl. OPPOSITE close up. **4** *He expanded his story.* amplify, elaborate upon, enlarge upon, expatiate on, flesh out, pad out. OPPOSITE abridge.

expanse *noun She painted an expanse of blue.* area, extent, sea, stretch, sweep, tract.

expect *verb* **1** *She didn't expect these problems.* anticipate, bargain for, contemplate, envisage, forecast, foresee, predict. **2** *He expects obedience.* count on, demand, insist on, rely on, require. **3** *He expected that she would ring up.* assume, believe, guess, imagine, presume, suppose, think.

expectant *adjective* **1** *an expectant mother.* expecting, pregnant. **2** *expectant fans.* eager, hopeful, ready, waiting, watchful.

expectation *noun little expectation of success.* anticipation, hope, likelihood, outlook, probability, prospect.

expedition *noun a polar expedition.* excursion, exploration, journey, mission, outing, safari, tour, trek, trip, voyage.

expel *verb He was expelled from school. Foreign journalists were expelled from the country.* banish, chuck out (*informal*), deport, discharge, dismiss, drive out, eject, evict, exile, get rid of, kick out (*informal*), remove, send away, throw out, turf out (*informal*). OPPOSITE admit.

expenditure *noun They cut their expenditure.* expenses, outgoings, outlay, overheads, spending. OPPOSITE income.

expense noun Expenses were high and income was low. charge, cost, fee, payment, price; see also EXPENDITURE.

expensive adjective an expensive watch. costly, dear, exorbitant, extravagant, luxurious, precious, priceless, pricey (informal), valuable. OPPOSITE cheap.

experience noun 1 Has he any experience in caring for old people? background, familiarity, involvement, practice. 2 a frightening experience. adventure, episode, event, happening, incident, occurrence, ordeal. — verb She experienced severe pain. bear, encounter, endure, face, feel, go through, know, meet with, suffer, sustain, undergo.

experienced adjective an experienced teacher. accomplished, competent, expert, fully-fledged, practised, proficient, seasoned, skilled, veteran, well-versed. OPPOSITE inexperienced, raw.

experiment noun a scientific experiment. investigation, test, trial. — verb They experimented on rats. investigate, research, test, try.

experimental adjective an experimental programme. pilot, test, trial.

expert noun an expert in economics. a wine expert. ace, adept, authority, buff (informal), connoisseur, consultant, dab hand (informal), genius, know-all (informal), maestro, master, old hand, past master, pro (informal), professional, pundit, scholar, specialist, virtuoso, whiz (informal). OPPOSITE novice. — adjective an expert jeweller. accomplished, capable, competent, experienced, knowledgeable, practised, professional, proficient, qualified, skilful, skilled, talented. OPPOSITE incompetent.

expertise noun She has the expertise for the job. know-how, knowledge, mastery, proficiency, skill.

expire verb 1 The sick man finally expired. breathe your last, die, pass away, perish. 2 His permit has expired. cease, end, finish, lapse, run out, stop, terminate. OPPOSITE continue, start. 3 expire air. breathe out, exhale. OPPOSITE inhale.

explain verb 1 He explained what the writer meant. clarify, clear up, decipher, define, demonstrate, describe, detail, elaborate, elucidate, expound, illustrate, interpret, show, spell out, teach. 2 That explains his strange behaviour. account for, excuse, justify.

explanation noun 1 an explanation of a word, theory, etc. account, clarification, commentary, definition, description, elucidation, interpretation, key. 2 She gave no explanation for her behaviour. account, excuse, justification, reason.

explicit adjective explicit instructions. categorical, clear, definite, exact, express, particular, plain, positive, precise, specific, unambiguous, unequivocal. OPPOSITE implicit, vague.

explode verb 1 The army bomb squad exploded the bomb. detonate, discharge, let off, set off. 2 The bomb exploded. blast, blow up, burst, detonate, erupt, go off. 3 Her father exploded with anger. see BECOME ANGRY (at ANGRY).

exploit noun his noble exploits. achievement, act, adventure, deed, escapade, feat. — verb 1 He exploited the opportunity. capitalise on, cash in on, make the most of, profit from, take advantage of, use, utilise. 2 The company exploits their

workers. abuse, misuse, take advantage of, use.

explore verb 1 Sturt explored the Murray River. check out, inspect, look around, prospect, reconnoitre, scout, survey, tour, travel about. 2 She explored the problem. analyse, examine, inquire into, investigate, look into, probe, research, study, survey.

explorer noun discoverer, pioneer, prospector, surveyor, trailblazer, traveller.

explosion noun 1 We heard an explosion. bang, blast, boom, detonation, discharge, eruption, outburst, pop, report, shot. 2 an explosion of laughter. burst, eruption, fit, outburst.

explosive adjective an explosive situation. charged, dangerous, dicey (slang), precarious, tense, unstable, volatile. — noun He used explosives to open the safe. dynamite, gelignite, gunpowder, jelly (slang), nitroglycerine, TNT.

expose verb 1 He exposed himself to danger. lay open, put at risk, subject. 2 She did not expose her legs. bare, display, reveal, show, uncover. OPPOSITE cover. 3 He exposed the plot. betray, disclose, divulge, leak, let out, make known, reveal, uncover. OPPOSITE conceal.

express[1] adjective 1 an express train. direct, fast, high-speed, non-stop, rapid-transit, through. OPPOSITE slow. 2 an express postal service. expeditious, fast, hasty, prompt, quick, rapid, speedy, swift. 3 He left express instructions. clear, definite, exact, explicit, particular, plain, precise, specific, unequivocal. OPPOSITE implicit.

express[2] verb They expressed their feelings honestly. air, articulate, communicate, convey, disclose, indicate, put into words, reveal, speak, state, utter, vent, verbalise, voice.

expression noun 1 a slang expression. idiom, phrase, saying, term, word. 2 a sad expression on her face. air, appearance, aspect, countenance, face, look, mien. 3 He read it with expression. eloquence, emotion, feeling, intonation, meaning, sensitivity.

expressionless adjective an expressionless stare. blank, deadpan, empty, poker-faced, vacant, vacuous, wooden. OPPOSITE expressive.

expressive adjective an expressive look. eloquent, meaningful, revealing, significant, telling. OPPOSITE vacant.

expulsion noun expulsion from school. banishment, eviction, exclusion, removal.

exquisite adjective an exquisite ring. beautiful, dainty, delicate, elegant, fine, lovely, perfect. OPPOSITE ugly.

extend verb 1 He extended the line. continue, elongate, enlarge, lengthen, stretch. OPPOSITE shorten. 2 They extended their stay. drag out, lengthen, prolong, protract, spin out. OPPOSITE curtail. 3 He extended his arm. hold out, reach out, straighten out, stretch out. 4 Their land extends to the river. carry on, continue, reach, stretch. 5 The load extended beyond the end of the truck. jut out, project, protrude, stick out. 6 He extended a warm welcome. accord, bestow, confer, give, grant, impart, offer, proffer.

extension noun They built an extension to their house. addition, annexe, wing.

extensive adjective 1 extensive gardens. ample, big, huge, immense, large, spacious, vast. OPPOSITE small. 2 extensive knowledge. broad, comprehensive, encyclope-

dic, thorough, vast, wide, wide-ranging. OPPOSITE restricted. 3 extensive damage. sweeping, vast, wholesale, widespread. OPPOSITE slight.

extent noun 1 the extent of the property. area, breadth, expanse, length, size, spread, stretch, width. 2 the extent of the problem. amount, degree, limit, range, scale, scope.

extenuating adjective extenuating circumstances. mitigating.

exterior adjective the exterior wall. external, outer, outside, outward, superficial. OPPOSITE interior. — noun the house exterior. façade, face, outside, shell, surface. OPPOSITE interior.

exterminate verb He exterminated the blowflies. annihilate, destroy, eliminate, eradicate, get rid of, kill, liquidate, murder, root out, slaughter, wipe out.

external adjective an external appearance. exterior, outer, outside, outward, superficial. OPPOSITE internal.

extinct adjective 1 an extinct volcano. extinguished, inactive. OPPOSITE active. 2 extinct animals. dead, died out. OPPOSITE extant.

extinguish verb Please extinguish your fire before leaving. douse, put out, quench, smother, snuff out. OPPOSITE kindle, light.

extort verb He extorted the money from them. exact, extract, squeeze, wring.

extortionate adjective House prices are extortionate. excessive, exorbitant, immoderate, inordinate, outrageous, steep, unreasonable.

extra adjective extra supplies. additional, auxiliary, excess, further, more, other, reserve, spare, superfluous, supplementary, surplus. — adverb It is extra cold today. especially, exceptionally, extremely, particularly, unusually. — noun 1 You have to pay for the extras. accessory, addition, add-on, attachment, bonus, luxury, supplement. 2 He kept what he needed and gave away the extra. excess, remainder, rest, surplus.

extract verb The dentist extracted the tooth. draw out, pull out, remove, take out. OPPOSITE insert. — noun 1 a vegetable extract. concentrate, distillate, essence. 2 an extract from the article. citation, clip, clipping, cutting, excerpt, passage, quotation, snippet.

extraordinary adjective an extraordinary person. extraordinary events. abnormal, amazing, astonishing, astounding, bizarre, curious, exceptional, incredible, miraculous, odd, outstanding, peculiar, phenomenal, rare, remarkable, singular, special, strange, striking, uncommon, unusual, weird. OPPOSITE everyday, ordinary.

extravagant adjective 1 He is extravagant when buying presents. improvident, lavish, munificent, over-generous, prodigal, profligate, spendthrift, wasteful. OPPOSITE economical, mean. 2 an extravagant present. costly, expensive, sumptuous. OPPOSITE cheap.

extreme adjective 1 extreme pain. acute, excessive, great, intense, severe. OPPOSITE mild. 2 the extreme end of the hall. farthest, furthermost, furthest, utmost, uttermost. OPPOSITE closest. 3 extreme measures. desperate, dire, Draconian, drastic, harsh, radical, severe, stiff, stringent. OPPOSITE moderate. 4 an extreme view. extremist, fanatical, hard-line, immoderate, intemperate, radical, uncompromising, unreasonable, way-out (informal). OPPOSITE moderate. — noun mid-

way between the two extremes. boundary, end, extremity, limit, maximum, minimum, pole.

extremely adverb extremely lucky. awfully (informal), especially, exceedingly, exceptionally, extraordinarily, remarkably, terribly (informal), very.

extroverted adjective An extroverted person usually enjoys parties. gregarious, outgoing, sociable. OPPOSITE introverted.

exuberant adjective exuberant children. animated, boisterous, energetic, excited, exhilarated, full of beans (informal), high-spirited, irrepressible, lively, spirited, vivacious. OPPOSITE listless, subdued.

exude verb 1 The tree exuded a resin. drip, ooze, secrete, seep. 2 She exudes confidence. display, emanate, ooze, radiate.

exult verb They exulted in their success. crow, gloat, glory, rejoice, revel.

exultant adjective an exultant winner. delighted, ecstatic, elated, gleeful, jubilant, overjoyed, triumphant.

eye verb The boy eyed the girl curiously. behold (old use), contemplate, gaze at, look at, observe, ogle, peer at, stare at, study, view, watch.

eyesight noun good eyesight. sight, vision.

eyesore noun The building is an eyesore. blight, blot, monstrosity.

eyewitness noun an eyewitness to the crash. bystander, looker-on, observer, onlooker, spectator, witness.

Ff

fable noun Aesop's fables. allegory, legend, myth, parable, story, tale.

fabric noun The fabric was draped over the dummy. cloth, material, stuff, textile.

fabricate verb 1 The company fabricates refrigerators. assemble, build, construct, make, manufacture, produce. 2 He fabricated a story. concoct, devise, hatch, invent, make up, manufacture.

fabulous adjective 1 stories of fabulous creatures. fabled, fanciful, fictional, fictitious, imaginary, legendary, mythical. OPPOSITE real. 2 a fabulous sum of money. extraordinary, great, inconceivable, incredible, mind-boggling (informal), phenomenal, prodigious, stupendous, tremendous, unbelievable. 3 (informal) We had a fabulous time. see EXCELLENT.

façade noun 1 the building façade. exterior, face, front, frontage, outside. 2 the patient's brave façade. appearance, exterior, front, mask, pretence, show, veneer.

face noun 1 a pretty face. a cheerful face. air, countenance, expression, look, physiognomy, visage. 2 the northern face of the building. façade, front, side, surface. — verb 1 The house faces a park. front on, lie opposite, look out on, overlook. 2 She faced many trials. brave, confront, encounter, experience, meet, weather, withstand. □ **face up to** He couldn't face up to his problems. accept, come to terms with, cope with, deal with. OPPOSITE evade.

facet noun The problem has many facets. aspect, face, feature, side.

facetious adjective a facetious comment. amusing, comical, flippant, funny, humorous, jocular, joking, witty. OPPOSITE serious.

facilitate *verb A food processor facilitates making mayonnaise.* aid, assist, ease, expedite, help, simplify. OPPOSITE complicate, hamper.

facility *noun* **1** *laundry facilities.* amenity, convenience, resource. **2** *She reads music with great facility.* competence, ease, effortlessness, fluency, proficiency, skill. OPPOSITE difficulty.

facsimile *noun a facsimile of the original book.* copy, duplicate, photocopy, replica, reproduction.

fact *noun* **1** *Sort out fact from fiction.* actuality, certainty, reality, truth. OPPOSITE fiction. **2** *He gave me the facts.* circumstance, detail, particular; [*facts*] data, evidence, information, low-down (*slang*).

faction *noun opposing factions in the party.* camp, clique, division, group, lobby, set, wing.

factor *noun The human factor must be taken into account.* aspect, circumstance, component, element, influence, ingredient, part.

factory *noun* forge, foundry, mill, plant, refinery, works, workshop.

factual *adjective a factual account.* accurate, faithful, objective, strict, true, truthful. OPPOSITE false, fanciful.

faculty *noun* **1** *the faculty of sight.* capacity, power, sense. **2** *a faculty for learning languages.* ability, aptitude, bent, capability, capacity, facility, flair, gift, knack, skill, talent.

fad *noun Skateboarding was not just a fad.* craze, cult, fashion, mania, passion, rage, trend, vogue.

fade *verb* **1** *Her jeans have faded.* bleach, dull, lighten, pale, wash out, whiten. OPPOSITE brighten. **2** *The image faded.* dim, disappear, grow faint, vanish, weaken. **3** *Interest faded. The sound faded.* decline, decrease, die away, diminish, dwindle, ebb, peter out, trail away, wane. OPPOSITE increase. □ **fade away** *You'll fade away if you don't eat.* die, shrivel, waste away, wither.

fail *verb* **1** *She failed her exam.* be unsuccessful in, bomb out in (*informal*), flunk (*informal*). OPPOSITE pass. **2** *Their plan failed.* abort, backfire, be unsuccessful, come unstuck (*informal*), fall through, flop (*informal*), founder, miscarry, misfire. OPPOSITE succeed, work. **3** *The supply failed.* be exhausted, be insufficient, be used up, run out. OPPOSITE hold out. **4** *Her eyesight is failing.* decline, deteriorate, dim, diminish, dwindle, ebb, fade, wane, weaken. OPPOSITE improve. **5** *The engine failed.* break down, conk out (*informal*), malfunction, pack up (*informal*). OPPOSITE work. **6** *Ali was worried when he failed to write.* forget, neglect, omit.

failing *noun Pride was one of his failings.* fault, flaw, foible, imperfection, shortcoming, vice, weakness. OPPOSITE strength.

failure *noun The programme was a failure.* damp squib, disaster, fiasco, fizzer (*Australian informal*), flop (*informal*), non-event, washout (*informal*). OPPOSITE success.

faint *adjective* **1** *a faint picture.* blurred, dim, hazy, indistinct, misty, unclear. OPPOSITE clear, distinct. **2** *a faint colour.* delicate, faded, light, pale, pastel, soft, subdued, subtle. OPPOSITE intense. **3** *a faint sound.* indistinct, low, muffled, muted, soft, subdued. OPPOSITE loud. **4** *a faint hope.* feeble, remote, slender, slight, slim, small, vague, weak. OPPOSITE strong. **5** *He felt faint.* dizzy, giddy, light-headed, unsteady, weak, woozy (*informal*). — *verb He fainted at the sight of blood.* black out, collapse, flake out (*informal*), keel over, lose consciousness, pass out (*informal*), swoon. OPPOSITE come round.

faint-hearted *adjective A war zone is not for the faint-hearted.* chicken-hearted, cowardly, diffident, fearful, lily-livered, pusillanimous, timid, timorous. OPPOSITE bold.

fair[1] *adjective* **1** *fair hair.* blond, flaxen, golden, light, tow-coloured. OPPOSITE dark. **2** *fair weather.* bright, clear, cloudless, fine, sunny, unclouded. OPPOSITE cloudy. **3** *a fair decision. a fair judge.* above board, disinterested, equitable, even-handed, honest, impartial, just, legitimate, objective, open-minded, proper, reasonable, right, sporting, sportsmanlike, unbiased, unprejudiced. OPPOSITE unfair. **4** *The meal was fair.* all right, average, indifferent, mediocre, middling, OK (*informal*), passable, reasonable, satisfactory, so-so (*informal*), tolerable.

fair[2] *noun* **1** *a craft stall at the school fair.* bazaar, fête, gala, market. **2** *a book fair.* exhibition, expo, exposition, sale, show. **3** *a merry-go-round at the fair.* carnival, funfair, show.

fairly *adverb* **1** *They acted fairly.* equitably, honestly, impartially, justly, objectively, properly, reasonably. **2** *Rowan drives fairly fast.* moderately, pretty, quite, rather, reasonably, somewhat.

fairness *noun* disinterest, equity, even-handedness, impartiality, justice, neutrality, objectivity.

fairy *noun The fairies in the story help the shoemaker.* elf, imp, pixie, sprite.

faith *noun* **1** *He has faith in you.* belief, confidence, reliance, trust. **2** *people of many faiths.* belief, church, conviction, creed, doctrine, persuasion, religion.

faithful *adjective* **1** *a faithful supporter.* committed, constant, dedicated, dependable, devoted, dutiful, loyal, reliable, stalwart, staunch, steadfast, true, trustworthy, trusty. OPPOSITE disloyal, unfaithful. **2** *a faithful account.* accurate, correct, factual, honest, strict, true, truthful. OPPOSITE inaccurate.

faithfulness *noun* see FIDELITY.

fake *noun* **1** *The note was a fake.* copy, counterfeit, duplicate, forgery, fraud, hoax, imitation, phoney (*informal*), replica, reproduction, sham. **2** *The doctor was a fake.* charlatan, cheat, con man (*informal*), fraud, humbug, impostor, phoney (*informal*), quack. — *adjective fake diamonds.* artificial, bogus, counterfeit, false, forged, imitation, phoney (*informal*), pretend (*informal*), pseudo, sham, synthetic. OPPOSITE authentic, genuine. — *verb* **1** *They faked the document.* copy, counterfeit, fabricate, forge, reproduce. **2** *He faked a cold to get out of sport.* affect, feign, pretend, simulate.

fall *verb* **1** *He fell down the hill.* collapse, come a buster (*Australian informal*), come a cropper (*informal*), come a gutser (*Australian slang*), crash, founder, overbalance, plummet, plunge, slide, slip, spill, stumble, topple, trip, tumble. **2** *Night fell.* descend. **3** *The material falls gracefully.* cascade, dangle, hang. **4** *Prices fell. The numbers fell.* crash, decline, decrease, diminish, drop, dwindle, nosedive, plummet, plunge, reduce, slump. OPPOSITE rise. **5** *Many men fell in the battle.* be killed, die, perish. **6** *Easter fell early.* happen, occur, take place. — *noun* **1** *the fall of the government.* collapse, defeat, downfall, overthrow. **2** *a fall in interest rates.* decline, decrease, dip, dive, downturn, drop, nosedive, plunge, reduction, slump. □ **fall out** *The couple fell out over the incident.* argue, disagree, fight, quarrel, squabble. **fall through** *Their plan fell through at the last minute.* be unsuccessful, collapse, fail, founder. OPPOSITE succeed.

fallacy *noun* **1** *That people can't change their nature is a fallacy.* delusion, misconception, mistake, myth. **2** *a fallacy in the reasoning.* error, flaw, inaccuracy, inconsistency, mistake.

falls *plural noun* cascade, cataract, waterfall.

false *adjective* **1** *a false argument.* erroneous, fallacious, faulty, inaccurate, incorrect, invalid, misleading, spurious, unsound, untrue, wrong. OPPOSITE correct, true. **2** *a false friend.* deceitful, dishonest, disloyal, duplicitous, faithless, hypocritical, insincere, lying, perfidious, treacherous, two-faced, unfaithful, untruthful. OPPOSITE faithful, true. **3** *false pearls.* artificial, bogus, counterfeit, fake, imitation, phoney (*informal*), pretend (*informal*), pseudo, sham, synthetic. OPPOSITE genuine. **4** *a false name.* assumed, fictitious, made-up; see also PSEUDONYM. OPPOSITE real.

falsehood *noun She has been telling falsehoods.* fabrication, fairy story, fairy tale, fib, fiction, lie, myth, porky (*slang*), story, untruth. OPPOSITE truth.

falsify *verb The accountant falsified the books.* alter, cook (*informal*), doctor, fiddle (*slang*), tamper with.

falter *verb* **1** *The old man faltered and fell.* stagger, stumble, totter. **2** *She faltered in front of the microphone.* hesitate, pause, stammer, stutter.

fame *noun The actor rose rapidly to fame.* celebrity, distinction, eminence, glory, honour, kudos (*informal*), prestige, prominence, recognition, renown, reputation, repute. OPPOSITE obscurity.

familiar *adjective* **1** *a familiar experience.* common, commonplace, customary, everyday, habitual, normal, regular, routine, usual, well-known. OPPOSITE strange, unfamiliar. **2** *They are on familiar terms.* chummy (*informal*), close, friendly, informal, intimate, matey, pally (*informal*). OPPOSITE distant, formal. **3** *He is too familiar with his elders.* disrespectful, forward, free and easy, impertinent, impudent, informal, presumptuous. □ **be familiar with** *He is familiar with computers.* be acquainted with, be at home with, be conversant with, be used to, be versed in, know about.

familiarise *verb* **familiarise with** *She familiarised herself with the road rules.* accustom to, acquaint with, instruct in, teach.

family *noun* **1** *a single-income family.* household. **2** *The couple want to raise a family.* brood, children, kids (*informal*), offspring, progeny. **3** *a reunion of the whole family.* clan, flesh and blood, folk, kin, kindred, kinsmen, kinswomen, kith and kin, people, relations, relatives, tribe. **4** *He comes from a noble family.* ancestry, dynasty, forebears, genealogy, house, line, lineage, parentage, pedigree, roots, stock.

famished *adjective The children were famished after school.* hungry, peckish (*informal*), ravenous, starving.

famous *adjective a famous person.* acclaimed, celebrated, distinguished, eminent, famed, great, illustrious, important, legendary, notable, noted, outstanding, preeminent, prominent, renowned, well-known. OPPOSITE unknown.

fan *noun jazz fans. tennis fans.* addict, admirer, aficionado, buff (*informal*), devotee, enthusiast, fanatic, follower, lover, nut (*informal*), supporter.

fanatic *noun a religious fanatic.* enthusiast, extremist, maniac, zealot.

fanciful *adjective fanciful ideas.* curious, fabulous, fantastic, imaginative, romantic, unrealistic, visionary, whimsical, wild. OPPOSITE realistic.

fancy *noun* **1** *flights of fancy.* delusion, fantasy, illusion, imagination, make-believe, unreality. OPPOSITE reality. **2** *He had a fancy for a hamburger.* craving, desire, hunger, liking, longing. OPPOSITE dislike. — *adjective a fancy design.* complicated, decorative, detailed, elaborate, intricate, ornamental, ornate, showy. OPPOSITE plain, simple. — *verb* **1** *He fancied that he was in another place.* dream, fantasise, imagine, picture. **2** *I fancy you're right.* believe, guess, reckon, suppose, suspect, think. **3** *She fancies the red dress.* desire, hanker after, like, long for, prefer, want, wish for, yearn for. **4** (*informal*) *He fancies her.* be attracted to, like, take a fancy to, take a liking to, take a shine to (*informal*). OPPOSITE dislike.

fantasise *verb He fantasised about being rich.* daydream, dream, imagine.

fantastic *adjective* **1** *a fantastic story involving wizards and dragons.* absurd, amazing, bizarre, extraordinary, fanciful, far-fetched, implausible, incredible, outlandish, preposterous, strange, unbelievable, unreal, unrealistic, weird, whimsical, wild. OPPOSITE credible. **2** *a fantastic sum of money.* enormous, extravagant, great, huge, immense, terrific (*informal*), tremendous, vast. **3** (*informal*) *a fantastic show.* exceptional, fabulous (*informal*), first-rate, great, magnificent, marvellous, remarkable, sensational, splendid, wonderful; see also EXCELLENT.

fantasy *noun in the realms of fantasy.* daydream, delusion, dream, fancy, hallucination, illusion, imagination, invention, make-believe, reverie. OPPOSITE reality.

far *adjective in a far country.* distant, far-away, far-off, remote. OPPOSITE near.

farce *noun He described the proceedings as a farce.* charade, joke, mockery, sham.

farcical *adjective a farcical situation.* absurd, comical, laughable, ludicrous, nonsensical, preposterous, ridiculous.

fare *noun* **1** *bus fares.* charge, cost, fee, payment, price, rate. **2** *The café provides stodgy fare.* food, meals, tucker (*Australian informal*). — *verb How did he fare?* do, get on, make out, manage.

farewell *interjection* adieu, au revoir, bye (*informal*), bye-bye (*informal*), cheerio (*informal*), cheers (*informal*), ciao (*informal*), goodbye, hooray (*Australian informal*), see you (*informal*), see you later (*informal*), so long (*informal*). — *noun They all went to Tim's farewell.* departure, goodbye, send-off. — *adjective a farewell speech.* leave-taking, parting, valedictory.

far-fetched *adjective a far-fetched explanation.* dubious, fanciful, implausible, improbable, incredible, strained, unconvincing, unlikely, unrealistic. OPPOSITE plausible.

farm *noun* plantation, property, ranch, run (*Australian*), smallholding, station (*Australian*). — *verb They farm the land.* cultivate, till, work.

farmer *noun* agriculturalist, cocky (*Australian informal*), grazier (*Australian*), pastoralist (*Australian*), peasant, sharefarmer (*Australian*), smallholder.

farming *noun* agribusiness, agriculture, agronomy, cultivation, husbandry.

far-reaching *adjective far-reaching policy changes.* broad, extensive, sweeping, wide-ranging.

far-sighted *adjective* **1** *A far-sighted person wears glasses for close work.* hypermetropic, hyperopic, longsighted, presbyopic. OPPOSITE myopic, short-sighted. **2** *a far-sighted politician.* far-seeing, prescient, provident, prudent, shrewd. OPPOSITE short-sighted.

fascinate *verb The dancer fascinated the audience.* attract, beguile, bewitch, captivate, charm, enchant, enthral, entrance, hold spellbound, hypnotise, mesmerise, rivet.

fashion *noun* **1** *Continue in this fashion.* manner, method, mode, way. **2** *the fashion of short skirts.* craze, fad, mode, rage, style, trend, vogue. — *verb She fashions new things out of scrap.* carve, construct, create, devise, form, make, manufacture, model, mould, produce, shape, work.

fashionable *adjective fashionable clothes.* chic, classy (*informal*), contemporary, elegant, in, in fashion, latest, modern, smart, stylish, swish (*informal*), trendy (*informal*), up-to-date, with it (*informal*). OPPOSITE old-fashioned.

fast[1] *adjective* **1** *a fast pace.* breakneck, brisk, express, fleet, hasty, high-speed, nippy (*informal*), quick, rapid, rattling, speedy, swift, zippy. OPPOSITE slow. **2** *fast colours.* fixed, indelible, permanent. — *adverb* **1** *Run as fast as you can.* at full pelt, at full speed, at the double, briskly, hastily, hell for leather (*informal*), hurriedly, like lightning (*informal*), like mad (*informal*), like the clappers (*informal*), posthaste, quickly, rapidly, speedily, swiftly. OPPOSITE slowly. **2** *The car was stuck fast.* firmly, securely, solidly, tightly.

fast[2] *verb They binged after fasting.* go without food, starve. OPPOSITE eat.

fasten *verb* **1** *Fasten the door.* bolt, chain, close, latch, lock, seal, secure, shut. OPPOSITE open. **2** *The dress fastens at the back.* button, do up, zip up. **3** *Fasten your shoes.* buckle, do up, lace, tie. **4** *He fastened the sign on the gate.* affix, attach, fix, nail, pin, screw, secure, staple, stick, tack, tape, tie. **5** *We fastened the boxes on the roof rack.* attach, bind, hitch, lash, secure, strap, tether, tie, truss. OPPOSITE unfasten.

fastidious *adjective He is fastidious about his food.* choosy (*informal*), finicky, fussy, particular, pernickety (*informal*), picky (*informal*), selective.

fat *noun* **1** *excess body fat.* blubber, corpulence, flab (*informal*). **2** *He cooks with fat.* butter, dripping, grease, lard, margarine, suet. — *adjective* **1** *a fat person.* chubby, corpulent, dumpy, flabby, gross, heavy, large, obese, overweight, plump, podgy, portly, roly-poly, rotund, squat, stout, tubby. OPPOSITE slim, thin. **2** *a fat book.* bulky, thick, weighty. OPPOSITE thin.

fatal *adjective a fatal disease.* deadly, lethal, mortal, terminal.

fatality *noun road fatalities.* casualty, death.

fate *noun* **1** *Fate had brought them together.* chance, destiny, fortune, luck, predestination, providence. **2** *a person's fate.* destiny, doom, fortune, karma, kismet, lot, portion.

fated *adjective He was fated to lose.* destined, doomed, predestined, preordained.

fateful *adjective that fateful day.* decisive, important, momentous, significant; see also DISASTROUS.

father *noun* **1** patriarch; [*informal terms of address*] dad, daddy, pa, papa, pater, pop. **2** *land of our fathers.* ancestor, forebear, forefather, patriarch, progenitor. **3** *the father of modern medicine.* creator, founder, inventor, originator. — *verb He fathered fourteen children.* beget, procreate, sire.

fatherhood *noun* paternity.

fatherly *adjective He showed fatherly concern.* fatherlike, kindly, paternal, protective, tender.

fathom *verb* **1** *They fathomed the harbour depths.* measure, plumb, sound. **2** *She could not fathom what he meant.* comprehend, get to the bottom of, penetrate, understand, work out.

fatigue *noun After working for twenty hours he was overcome with fatigue.* exhaustion, lassitude, lethargy, tiredness, weariness. OPPOSITE energy.

fatty *adjective fatty food.* greasy, oily.

fault *noun* **1** *faults in the paintwork.* blemish, defect, flaw, imperfection. OPPOSITE perfection. **2** *a mechanical fault.* bug (*informal*), defect, glitch (*informal*), malfunction, trouble. **3** *He forgave their faults.* error, failing, foible, imperfection, lapse, misdeed, misdemeanour, mistake, offence, shortcoming, sin, slip-up (*informal*), transgression, trespass (*old use*), vice, weakness, wrongdoing. OPPOSITE strength. **4** *The other driver admitted fault.* blame, responsibility. — *verb You can't fault his work.* censure, criticise, find fault with, knock (*informal*), pick holes in. OPPOSITE commend. □ **at fault** *Both drivers were at fault.* culpable, guilty, in the wrong, liable, responsible, to blame.

faultless *adjective a faultless performance.* consummate, correct, exemplary, flawless, ideal, immaculate, perfect, unblemished. OPPOSITE imperfect.

faulty *adjective The toaster is faulty.* defective, imperfect, kaput (*informal*), malfunctioning, on the blink (*informal*), out of order. OPPOSITE sound, working.

fauna *noun native fauna.* animals, wildlife.

favour *noun* **1** *He was looked upon with favour.* approval, goodwill, support, sympathy. OPPOSITE disfavour. **2** *Can you do me a favour?* courtesy, good deed, good turn, kindness, service. OPPOSITE disservice. **3** *The umpire showed favour to one team.* bias, favouritism, partiality, preference. OPPOSITE evenhandedness. — *verb* **1** *Which method do you favour?* advocate, approve, back, choose, endorse, espouse, opt for, prefer, recommend, select, support. OPPOSITE oppose. **2** *The wet track favoured our horse.* assist, benefit, give an advantage to, help. OPPOSITE hinder.

favourable *adjective* **1** *a favourable response.* approving, encouraging, good, pleasing, positive, reassuring, supportive, sympathetic. OPPOSITE hostile, unfavourable. **2** *favourable conditions for starting a business.* advantageous, auspicious, beneficial, conducive, helpful, promising, propitious. OPPOSITE adverse.

favourite *adjective her favourite doll.* chosen, pet, preferred. — *noun* **1** *the teacher's favourite.* darling, pet. **2** *the favourite in the race.* front runner. OPPOSITE outsider.

favouritism *noun The teacher was accused of favouritism.* bias, nepotism (*towards relatives*), partiality, positive discrimination, preference, prejudice. OPPOSITE even-handedness.

fawn *adjective a fawn colour.* beige, buff, camel, khaki, light brown, neutral.

faze *verb Nothing seems to faze Jamie.* daunt, discomfit, disconcert, fluster, perturb, rattle (*informal*), throw (*informal*), trouble, unnerve, upset, worry.

fear *noun* **1** *trembling with fear.* alarm, anxiety, apprehension, awe, consternation, dismay, dread, foreboding, fright, horror, panic, terror, trepidation, worry. OPPOSITE courage. **2** *a fear of flying.* aversion, dread, phobia. — *verb He feared the punishment.* be afraid of, be frightened of, be scared of, dread, worry about.

fearful *adjective* **1** *Tina is fearful in new situations.* afraid, alarmed, anxious, apprehensive, cowardly, fainthearted, frightened, nervous, panicky, pusillanimous, scared, terrified, timid, timorous, worried. OPPOSITE fearless. **2** *The town was rocked by a fearful explosion.* alarming, appalling, awful, dreadful, fearsome, frightening, frightful, ghastly, horrendous, horrific, scary, shocking, terrible, terrific, terrifying.

fearless *adjective a fearless policeman.* bold, brave, courageous, daring, dauntless, gallant, game, heroic, intrepid, lion-hearted, plucky, unafraid, undaunted, valiant, valorous. OPPOSITE cowardly.

fearlessness *noun* boldness, bravery, courage, daring, grit, guts (*informal*), intrepidity, nerve, pluck, valour. OPPOSITE cowardice.

feasible *adjective I don't think the idea is feasible.* achievable, possible, practicable, viable, workable. OPPOSITE impossible.

feast *noun* **1** *a ten-course feast.* banquet, dinner, meal, repast (*formal*), spread. **2** *a religious feast.* celebration, festival, fête, holiday. — *verb They feasted on smoked salmon.* dine, eat, gorge, tuck in (*informal*).

feat *noun the amazing feats of the riders.* achievement, act, action, deed, exploit, performance, stunt.

feather *noun a bird's feather.* hackle, plume, quill; [*feathers*] down, plumage.

feature *noun The plan has good and bad features.* aspect, attribute, characteristic, detail, facet, point, property, quality, respect, trait. □ *features plural noun The girl has fine features.* countenance, face, lineaments, physiognomy, visage.

federation *noun He belongs to a federation of driving instructors.* alliance, association, confederation, league, syndicate, union.

fee *noun He paid his membership fees. The bill includes a fee for the service.* brokerage, charge, commission, cost, dues, levy, payment, price, rate, remuneration, subscription, sum, tariff, toll.

feeble *adjective* **1** *He was too feeble to carry the suitcase.* debilitated, decrepit, delicate, frail, helpless, infirm, listless, poorly, puny, sickly, weak, weedy. OPPOSITE strong. **2** *She gave a feeble excuse.* flimsy, lame, paltry, poor, tame, unconvincing, weak. OPPOSITE convincing. **3** *He's too feeble to stand up to them.* feckless, impotent, ineffective, ineffectual, powerless, soft, spineless, weak, wimpish (*informal*). OPPOSITE powerful, strong.

feed *verb* **1** *She fed the baby.* nourish, nurse, suckle. OPPOSITE starve. **2** *The animals are feeding.* browse, eat, graze. **3** *They feed on insects.* dine, live, prey, subsist; see also EAT.

feedback *noun The business welcomes customer feedback.* reaction, response.

feel *verb* **1** *She felt the parcel and guessed its contents.* finger, handle, manipulate, maul, paw, stroke, touch. **2** *He felt his way.* fumble, grope. **3** *He felt a severe pain.* be aware of, be conscious of, experience, notice, perceive, sense, suffer, undergo. **4** *I feel that you're right.* believe, consider, reckon, think.

feeler *noun the insect's feelers.* antenna, tentacle.

feeling *noun* **1** *a tingling feeling in his fingers.* awareness, sensation. **2** *a feeling of calm about the place.* air, ambience, atmosphere, aura, climate, feel, mood, spirit, tone, vibes (*informal*). **3** *He showed no feeling for those who were suffering.* compassion, concern, emotion, empathy, passion, sensitivity, sympathy, tenderness, understanding. OPPOSITE apathy. **4** *He had a feeling that they would not turn up.* hunch, idea, impression, inkling, instinct, intuition, notion, premonition, sense, suspicion, thought. **5** *The feeling of the meeting was against it.* attitude, opinion, sentiment, view.

feign *verb He feigned remorse.* affect, fake, pretend, sham, simulate.

fell *verb He felled the tree.* chop down, cut down, knock down.

fellow *noun* **1** *She gets on well with her fellows.* associate, colleague, companion, comrade, mate, peer. **2** (*informal*) *He was a strange fellow.* bloke (*informal*), boy, chap (*informal*), character, gentleman, guy (*informal*), individual, lad, man, person.

fellowship *noun* **1** *She enjoys the fellowship of others.* camaraderie, companionship, company, friendship, society. **2** *He belongs to a student fellowship.* association, brotherhood, club, fraternity, league, sisterhood, society, sorority.

felon *noun The felon is serving his sentence.* criminal, culprit, lawbreaker, miscreant, offender, outlaw.

female *adjective* feminine, womanly. OPPOSITE male. — *noun* see GIRL, WOMAN.

feminine *adjective a girl who likes being feminine.* female, girlish, ladylike, womanly; see also EFFEMINATE. OPPOSITE masculine.

fence *noun The garden is enclosed by a fence.* barricade, barrier, hoarding, palings, palisade, railing, stockade, wall. — *verb* **fence in** *They fenced in the rabbits.* box in, close in, confine, coop up, enclose, hedge in, hem in.

fend *verb* **fend for** *They were left to fend for themselves.* look after, shift for, support, take care of. **fend off** *They fended off their attackers.* fight off, hold at bay, keep off, parry, repel, repulse, ward off.

ferocious *adjective* **1** *Lions are ferocious.* fierce, savage, vicious, wild. OPPOSITE gentle, tame. **2** *a ferocious assault.* barbarous, bestial, bloodthirsty, brutal, cruel, fierce, ruthless, sadistic, savage, vicious, violent.

ferret *verb* **1** *She ferreted about in the drawer.* forage, fossick (*Australian informal*), hunt, rummage, search. **2** *He managed to ferret out the information.* dig out, discover, root out, unearth.

ferry *verb They ferried the cars across the river.* carry, convey, ship, shuttle, take, transfer, transport.

fertile *adjective* **1** *fertile soil.* fruitful, productive, rich. OPPOSITE barren. **2** *a fertile animal.* fruitful, productive. OPPOSITE infertile, sterile. **3** *a fertile imagination.* creative, imaginative, inventive, productive, prolific, rich. OPPOSITE unimaginative.

fertilise *verb* **1** *We need to fertilise the garden.* compost, dress, feed, manure, top-dress. **2** *The cow has been fertilised.* impregnate, inseminate. **3** *Bees fertilise the plant.* pollinate.

fervent *adjective a fervent supporter.* ardent, devout, eager, earnest, emotional, enthusiastic, fanatical, fervid, impassioned, keen, passionate, vehement, warm, zealous. OPPOSITE apathetic.

fester *verb* **1** *The cut festered.* become infected, discharge, gather, putrefy, suppurate. **2** *Resentment festered inside her.* grow, intensify, rankle, smoulder.

festival *noun An arts festival takes place annually.* anniversary, carnival, celebration, eisteddfod, fair, fête, fiesta, gala, holiday, jamboree, jubilee, pageant, party, show.

festive *adjective a festive spirit.* cheerful, gay, happy, jolly, jovial, joyous, light-hearted, merry. OPPOSITE gloomy.

festivity *noun They joined in the festivities.* celebration, gaiety, jollification, merrymaking, mirth, party, rejoicing, revelry, revels, roistering, wassailing (*old use*).

festoon *noun The bridge was decorated with festoons of roses.* garland, wreath.

fetch *verb* **1** *He fetched the luggage.* bring, call for, carry, collect, get, pick up, retrieve. **2** *The car won't fetch much.* bring in, go for, raise, sell for, yield.

fête *noun the school fête.* bazaar, fair, gala, jumble sale; see also FESTIVAL.

fetters *plural noun The prisoners are in fetters.* bonds, chains, irons, manacles, shackles.

feud *noun a feud between the two families.* conflict, dispute, quarrel, row, vendetta.

feverish *adjective* **1** *The patient was feverish.* burning, febrile, hot. **2** *feverish preparations for Grandma's visit.* agitated, excited, frantic, frenetic, frenzied, hectic, restless. OPPOSITE calm.

few *adjective The old lady has few visitors.* infrequent, rare, scarce, sparse, sporadic. OPPOSITE many. — *noun We have only a few left.* handful, remnant, sprinkling. OPPOSITE lot.

fiancé, fiancée *noun* betrothed, husband-to-be, intended, wife-to-be.

fiasco *noun The party was a fiasco.* catastrophe, disaster, failure, fizzer (*Australian informal*), flop (*informal*), non-event, washout (*informal*). OPPOSITE success.

fib *noun They knew she was telling fibs.* fabrication, fairy story, falsehood, fiction, lie, porky (*slang*), story, untruth, white lie (*informal*). OPPOSITE truth.

fibre *noun The fibre is spun.* filament, strand, thread.

fickle *adjective a fickle person. fickle weather.* capricious, changeable, erratic, inconsistent, inconstant, mercurial, mutable, temperamental, unfaithful, unpredictable, unreliable, vacillating, variable. OPPOSITE constant.

fiction *noun* **1** *His explanation was pure fiction.* fabrication, fib, invention, lie, make-believe. OPPOSITE fact. **2** *She prefers to read fiction.* fable, fairy story, fantasy, legend, myth, novel, romance, story, tale. OPPOSITE non-fiction.

fictitious *adjective a fictitious character. a fictitious account.* apocryphal, bogus, fabled, false, fanciful, fictional, imaginary, invented, legendary, made-up, mythical, phoney (*informal*), spurious, untrue. OPPOSITE factual, true.

fiddle *noun* **1** (*informal*) *He plays the fiddle.* violin. **2** (*slang*) *The accountant was involved in a big fiddle.* fraud, racket, rort (*Australian slang*), scam (*slang*), swindle, swizz (*informal*). — *verb* **1** *She fiddled with the beads.* fidget, finger, jiggle, juggle, play, toy, twiddle. **2** *He fiddled with the radio to make it work.* mess about, muck around, tamper, tinker, twiddle. **3** (*slang*) *He fiddled the books.* alter, cook (*informal*), doctor, falsify, fix.

fiddly *adjective* (*informal*) *Threading beads is a fiddly job.* awkward, intricate, messy, ticklish, tricky.

fidelity *noun* **1** *marital fidelity. fidelity to the king.* allegiance, devotion, faithfulness, loyalty. OPPOSITE disloyalty, infidelity. **2** *fidelity in newspaper reporting.* accuracy, faithfulness, honesty, integrity, truthfulness. OPPOSITE inaccuracy.

fidget *verb They fidgeted nervously.* fiddle, jiggle around, shuffle, squirm, twitch, wriggle.

fidgety *adjective a fidgety audience.* jittery (*informal*), nervous, restive, restless, twitchy.

field *noun* **1** *sheep in the field.* lea (*poetical*), meadow, paddock, paddy (*for rice*), pasture. **2** *a sports field.* arena, ground, oval, pitch, stadium. **3** *her field of vision.* range, scope. **4** *an expert in his field.* area, domain, province, sphere, subject.

fiend *noun* **1** *The hero saved them from the fiend.* brute, demon, devil, monster, ogre. **2** *a fitness fiend.* addict, crank, devotee, enthusiast, fanatic, freak (*informal*), maniac, nut (*informal*).

fierce *adjective* **1** *a fierce battle.* bloodthirsty, bloody, brutal, cutthroat, ferocious, merciless, relentless, savage, vicious, violent, wild. OPPOSITE gentle. **2** *the fierce heat.* extreme, great, intense, severe, strong. OPPOSITE mild.

fiery *adjective* **1** *a fiery incinerator.* blazing, burning, flaming, hot, red-hot. **2** *a fiery speech.* ardent, emotional, fervent, impassioned, intense, passionate, spirited, tempestuous, vehement. **3** *a fiery temper.* hot, impetuous, irascible, passionate, pugnacious, violent. OPPOSITE calm.

fight *verb* **1** *The enemies fought. The boys were always fighting.* argue, battle, be at loggerheads, bicker, box, brawl, clash, combat, contend, duel, feud, grapple, joust, quarrel, scrap (*informal*), scuffle, skirmish, spar, squabble, stoush (*Australian slang*), strive, struggle, tussle, war, wrestle. **2** *The two countries were fighting a war.* carry on, conduct, engage in, prosecute, wage. **3** *He is fighting for justice.* campaign, crusade, strive, struggle, take a stand. **4** *You can't fight progress.* defy, oppose, resist. — *noun* **1** *He was injured in a fight.* action, affray, aggression, altercation, argument, barney (*informal*), battle, blue (*Australian informal*), brawl, brush, campaign, clash, combat, conflict, confrontation, contest, dispute, duel, dust-up (*informal*), encounter, engagement, feud, fisticuffs, fracas, fray, free-for-all, hostilities, joust, mêlée, punch-up (*informal*), quarrel, row, scrap (*informal*), scrimmage, scuffle, set-to, skirmish, squabble, stoush (*Australian slang*), strife, struggle, tussle, war, wrestle. **2** *The boxers began their fight.* bout, boxing match, contest. □ **fight back** *Having been punched he was set to fight back.* counter, counter-attack, hit back, retaliate.

fighter *noun* aggressor, battler, boxer, campaigner, combatant, duellist, gladiator, guerrilla, marine, mercenary, partisan, pugilist, soldier, warrior, wrestler.

figurative *adjective a figurative sense of a word.* metaphorical. OPPOSITE literal.

figure *noun* **1** *She wrote down the figures.* digit, integer, number, numeral. **2** *The figure was carved out of wood.* effigy, figurine, image, sculpture, statue. **3** *He was an important figure in politics.* character, identity (*Australian*), person, personage, personality. **4** *She has a good figure.* body, build, form, outline, physique, shape. — *verb Where does he figure in the story?* appear, feature, play a part. □ **figure out** **1** *She figured out what was owing.* add up, calculate, compute, total, work out. **2** *He can't figure out what's going on.* comprehend, fathom, grasp, interpret, suss out (*informal*), understand, work out.

filament *noun* fibre, strand, thread, wire.

file[1] *verb He filed the metal.* rub, shape, smooth.

file[2] *noun* **1** *She keeps her papers in a file.* binder, folder, holder, portfolio. **2** *They keep a file on each person.* dossier, papers, records. **3** *a long file of cars.* column, line, queue, rank, row, string, train. — *verb* **1** *The clerk filed the papers.* arrange, catalogue, organise, pigeon-hole, put away, store. **2** *The competitors filed past the flag.* march, parade, troop.

fill *verb* **1** *He filled his case with clothes.* cram, jam, load up, pack, stuff. OPPOSITE empty. **2** *The builders filled the hole.* block up, bung up, close, plug, seal, stop up. OPPOSITE excavate, hollow out. **3** *He was appointed to fill the position.* hold, occupy, take up. OPPOSITE vacate. **4** *The new bus service fills a need.* answer, fulfil, meet, satisfy. **5** *He filled the time wisely.* pass, spend, use. □ **fill in** **1** *She filled in the form.* answer, complete, fill out. **2** (*informal*) *He filled me in on what had happened.* acquaint, advise, brief, inform, tell. **3** *Another player filled in for her.* cover, deputise, relieve, stand in, substitute, take the place of.

filling *noun cushion filling.* contents, padding, stuffing, wadding.

film *noun* **1** *plastic film.* coating, covering, layer, sheet, skin. **2** *They watched a film about the war.* feature, flick (*informal*), motion picture, movie, picture, video. — *verb They filmed the scene four times.* photograph, record, shoot, video.

filter *noun Pass the liquid through a filter.* colander, screen, sieve, strainer. — *verb* **1** *They filter the water.* clarify, purify, refine, sieve, strain. **2** *The water filters through the soil.* leach, ooze, percolate, seep, trickle.

filth *noun The gardener wiped the filth off his boots.* dirt, grime, gunge, gunk (*informal*), muck (*informal*), mud, slime, sludge.

filthy *adjective* **1** *filthy buildings.* blackened, dirty, dusty, grimy, grubby, muddy, soiled, squalid. OPPOSITE clean. **2** *filthy language.* blue, coarse, crude, dirty, foul, improper, indecent, obscene, offensive, rude, smutty, vile, vulgar.

final *adjective* **1** *the final chapter.* closing, concluding, end, finishing, last, ultimate. OPPOSITE opening. **2** *The judge's decision is final.* conclusive, decisive, definitive, indisputable, irrevocable, unalterable.

finale *noun* see ENDING.

finalise *verb He finalised the deal.* clinch, complete, conclude, finish, settle, sew up (*informal*), wrap up (*informal*).

finally *adverb Finally they decided to leave.* at last, eventually, in the end, once and for all, ultimately.

finance *verb The bank financed the scheme.* back, fund, pay for, sponsor, subsidise, underwrite. □ **finances** *plural noun His finances are limited.* assets, capital, cash, funds, means, money, resources.

financial *adjective* **1** *financial planning.* budgetary, economic, fiscal, monetary, pecuniary. **2** *He can pay, but the others are not financial.* in funds, solvent. OPPOSITE broke.

find *verb* **1** *He found his missing keys.* chance upon, come across, come upon, dig up, discover, light on, locate, recover, regain, retrieve, spot, stumble on, uncover, unearth. OPPOSITE lose. **2** *The technician found the cause of the problem.* detect, determine, diagnose, discover, identify, trace, track down, work out. **3** *They can't find work.* acquire, gain, get, obtain, procure. **4** *The court found her innocent.* declare, judge, pronounce, rule. □ **find out** **1** *She found out the results.* ascertain, discover, hear, learn. **2** *He found out their secret.* bring to light, detect, discover, expose, reveal.

findings *plural noun the findings of a court.* conclusion, decision, judgement, verdict.

fine[1] *adjective* **1** *a fine performance.* accomplished, brilliant, consummate, excellent, exceptional, fantastic, first-class, first-rate, great, high-quality, impressive, magnificent, marvellous, masterly, meritorious, meticulous, outstanding, peerless, praiseworthy, prize, sensational, skilful, splendid, sterling, super (*informal*), superb, superior, superlative, top-notch (*informal*), wonderful. OPPOSITE inferior, poor. **2** *fine weather.* balmy, bright, clear, fair, sunny. OPPOSITE overcast, wet. **3** *fine material.* delicate, diaphanous, filmy, flimsy, gauzy, gossamer, lacy, light, sheer, thin, transparent. OPPOSITE coarse, heavy. **4** *a fine line.* narrow, slender, slim, thin. OPPOSITE thick. **5** *fine workmanship.* beautiful, dainty, delicate, exquisite, flawless. **6** *I'm fine, thank you.* all right, comfortable, OK (*informal*), well.

fine[2] *noun I have to pay a parking fine.* charge, penalty, ticket. — *verb He was fined for speeding.* book, charge, penalise.

finicky *adjective a finicky eater.* choosy (*informal*), fastidious, fussy, particular, pernickety (*informal*), picky (*informal*).

finish *verb* **1** *He finished the lecture with a question.* close, complete, conclude, discontinue, end, halt, round off, terminate, wind up, wrap up (*informal*). OPPOSITE begin. **2** *The lesson finished early.* cease, close, come to an end, conclude, end, stop, terminate. OPPOSITE start. **3** *The work was finished on time.* accomplish, achieve, carry out, complete, finalise, get through. OPPOSITE start. **4** *Who finished the biscuits?* consume, eat up, get through, knock off (*informal*), polish off. — *noun* **1** *the finish of a race. the finish of a job.* cessation, close, completion, conclusion, culmination, end, ending, finale, termination. OPPOSITE beginning. **2** *The shelves have a glossy finish.* coating, exterior, surface, veneer.

finite *adjective They have a finite number of seats available.* bounded, limited, measurable, restricted. OPPOSITE infinite.

fire *noun* **1** *Where there's smoke there's fire.* burning, combustion, flames. **2** *The firemen fought the fire.* blaze, bonfire, bushfire (*Aus-*

tralian), conflagration, holocaust, inferno. **3** *The leader was full of fire.* ardour, energy, enthusiasm, fervour, inspiration, passion, spirit, vigour. **4** *The soldier was wounded by enemy fire.* flak, fusillade, gunfire, salvo, shelling, shooting, volley. — *verb* **1** *The soldier fired at the crowd.* open fire, shoot, snipe. **2** *They fired their missiles.* detonate, discharge, explode, launch, let off, set off. **3** *The boss fired her.* discharge, dismiss, give someone notice, give someone the boot (*informal*), remove, sack (*informal*). OPPOSITE hire. **4** *He fired the pile of sticks.* ignite, kindle, light, set ablaze, set fire to, set on fire. **5** *He fired the students with enthusiasm.* animate, excite, inspire, motivate, stimulate. □ **on fire** *The house is on fire.* ablaze, aflame, alight, blazing, burning, in flames.

firebug *noun The fire was the work of firebugs.* arsonist, fire-raiser, pyromaniac.

fireplace *noun* fire, grate, hearth.

fireproof *adjective a fireproof container.* flameproof, incombustible, non-flammable, non-inflammable. OPPOSITE flammable, inflammable.

fireworks *plural noun* crackers, pyrotechnics.

firm[1] *noun They are partners in a firm.* business, company, concern, corporation, enterprise, establishment, organisation, partnership.

firm[2] *adjective* **1** *a firm mixture.* compact, dense, hard, rigid, set, solid, stable, stiff, unyielding. OPPOSITE soft. **2** *a firm grip.* secure, steady, strong, sure, tenacious, tight. OPPOSITE loose. **3** *He remained firm in his opinion.* adamant, definite, dogged, inflexible, obstinate, persistent, resolute, rigid, steadfast, stubborn, unshakeable, unwavering, unyielding. OPPOSITE irresolute. **4** *a firm arrangement.* agreed, definite, established, fixed, settled, unalterable, unchangeable. OPPOSITE tentative. **5** *firm friends.* constant, dependable, faithful, loyal, reliable, solid, staunch, steadfast. — *verb The mixture firmed up.* compact, harden, jell, set, solidify, stiffen.

first *adjective* **1** *the first child in the family.* eldest, first-born, oldest. OPPOSITE last, youngest. **2** *a ship's first voyage.* initial, maiden, original. OPPOSITE last. **3** *the first stage.* earliest, initial, introductory, opening, preliminary. OPPOSITE final. **4** *of first importance.* basic, cardinal, chief, foremost, fundamental, greatest, highest, leading, main, major, premier, primary, prime, principal, supreme. OPPOSITE least.

first-class *adjective* see EXCELLENT.

fish *verb* **1** *He fished from the side of the boat.* angle, go fishing, trawl. **2** *He's fishing for clues.* fossick (*Australian informal*), hunt, look, probe, search, seek.

fishy *adjective* (*informal*) *There's something fishy about him.* doubtful, dubious, questionable, shady, strange, suspect, suspicious, suss (*informal*).

fissure *noun a fissure in the rock.* cleft, crack, cranny, crevasse, crevice, opening, rift, slit, split.

fit[1] *adjective* **1** *a dinner fit for a king.* appropriate, fitting, proper, right, suitable, worthy. OPPOSITE unfit, unsuitable. **2** *She does not feel fit to take on the job.* able, capable, competent, prepared, qualified, ready. **3** *He keeps fit by running daily.* hardy, healthy, in condition, in fine fettle, in training, robust, well. OPPOSITE unfit, unhealthy. — *verb* **1** *The tailor fitted the jacket on him.* adapt, adjust, alter, modify, shape. **2** *He fitted a lock on the door.* install. **3** *They fitted the pieces together.* assemble, connect, join, put together. **4** *The pieces fitted together.* connect, dovetail, go, interlock, join. **5** *This fits our requirements.* conform to, correspond to, match, meet, satisfy, suit. □ **fit in 1** *The doctor fitted us in.* accommodate, make room for, make time for, slot in, squeeze in. **2** *He feels he doesn't fit in.* belong, conform, feel at home. **fit out** *They fitted out the team.* equip, kit out, rig out, supply.

fit[2] *noun a fit of sneezing.* attack, bout, burst, convulsion, outbreak, outburst, seizure, spasm, spell.

fitful *adjective He showed fitful interest.* erratic, haphazard, intermittent, irregular, occasional, spasmodic, sporadic, variable. OPPOSITE constant.

fitting *adjective a fitting comment.* apposite, appropriate, apt, fit, proper, right, suitable, timely. OPPOSITE unsuitable.

fix *verb* **1** *He fixed the mirror to the wall.* anchor, attach, cement, fasten, fit, glue, install, mount, nail, peg, pin, rivet, screw, secure, stick, tape. **2** *The number is fixed in her mind.* implant, plant, root. **3** *They fixed a time for their next meeting.* agree on, appoint, arrange, decide on, establish, organise, set, settle on, specify. **4** *He fixed the car's problem.* correct, cure, mend, put right, rectify, remedy, repair, sort out. — *noun* (*informal*) *He was in a real fix.* bind (*informal*), catch-22 (*informal*), difficulty, dilemma, hole (*informal*), jam (*informal*), mess, pickle (*informal*), plight, predicament, quandary, spot (*informal*).

fixation *noun a fixation about fast cars.* infatuation, mania, obsession, preoccupation, thing (*informal*).

fixed *adjective* **1** *fixed cupboards.* built-in, permanent. OPPOSITE movable. **2** *fixed prices.* constant, firm, invariable, level, pegged, set, stable, static. OPPOSITE fluctuating. **3** *a fixed look.* intent, steady, stony, unblinking.

fixture *noun* **1** *The insurance covers fixtures.* fitment, fitting. OPPOSITE movable. **2** *a sporting fixture.* engagement, event, match, meet, meeting.

fizz *verb The lemonade fizzed when he opened the bottle.* bubble, effervesce, fizzle, froth, hiss, sparkle, sputter.

fizzer *noun* (*Australian informal*) *The party was a fizzer because of poor publicity.* damp squib, disappointment, failure, fiasco, flop (*informal*), non-event.

fizzy *adjective a fizzy drink.* aerated, bubbly, carbonated, effervescent, sparkling. OPPOSITE still.

flabbergasted *adjective We were flabbergasted at the results.* astonished, astounded, confounded, dumbfounded, nonplussed, overwhelmed, speechless, staggered, stunned, surprised, thunderstruck.

flabby *adjective a flabby stomach.* flaccid, limp, soft, weak. OPPOSITE firm, taut.

flag[1] *noun a team's flag.* banner, colours, ensign, jack, pennant, standard, streamer. — *verb We flagged down their car.* hail, signal, wave.

flag[2] *verb* **1** *He started to flag after the third lap.* droop, languish, tire, weary, wilt. **2** *Their interest never flagged.* decline, fail, wane, weaken.

flagrant *adjective a flagrant misdemeanour.* barefaced, blatant, brazen, conspicuous, glaring, gross, obvious, open, patent, scandalous, shameless, undisguised.

flair *noun He has a flair for arranging flowers.* ability, aptitude, faculty, gift, knack, talent.

flake *noun soap flakes.* bit, leaf, piece, scale, shaving, sliver.

flamboyant *adjective* **1** *flamboyant clothes.* bright, colourful, flashy, gaudy, lairy (*Australian informal*), ostentatious, showy. OPPOSITE dull. **2** *flamboyant gestures.* bold, exaggerated, extravagant, showy, theatrical.

flame *verb The fire began to flame more brightly.* blaze, burn, flare. □ **in flames** *Their house was in flames.* ablaze, aflame, alight, blazing, burning, on fire.

flammable *adjective flammable material.* combustible, inflammable. OPPOSITE non-flammable, non-inflammable.

flan *noun a savoury flan.* pie, quiche, tart.

flank *noun The eastern flank of the mountain.* face, side. — *verb Rose bushes flanked the path.* border, edge, line.

flap *verb The clothes flapped on the line.* flutter, swing, wave. — *noun* (*informal*) *She got herself in a flap about the arrangements.* bother, flat spin (*informal*), fluster, panic, state, stew (*informal*), tizzy (*informal*).

flare *verb* **1** *The bushfire flared.* blaze, burn, flame. **2** *Tempers flared.* blow up, erupt, rage; see also BECOME ANGRY (at ANGRY). **3** *Her jeans flared.* broaden, widen. OPPOSITE taper.

flash *verb The lights flashed.* blink, flicker, gleam, glimmer, glint, sparkle, twinkle, wink. — *noun* **1** *a flash of light.* blaze, flare, gleam, ray, shaft. **2** *a flash of inspiration.* burst, display, spark. **3** *He was back in a flash.* instant, jiffy (*informal*), moment, second, split second, tick (*informal*), trice.

flashy *adjective The singer wore a flashy outfit.* flamboyant, flash (*informal*), garish, gaudy, jazzy, lairy (*Australian informal*), loud, ostentatious, pretentious, showy, snazzy (*informal*), tacky (*informal*), tasteless, tawdry.

flask *noun* see BOTTLE.

flat *adjective* **1** *a flat surface.* even, horizontal, level, plane, smooth. OPPOSITE uneven. **2** *a flat dish.* low-sided, shallow. OPPOSITE deep. **3** *a flat refusal.* absolute, categorical, definite, firm, unqualified. **4** *flat seas.* calm, smooth, unruffled. OPPOSITE choppy. **5** *She answered in a flat voice.* boring, dull, lacklustre, lifeless, monotonous, unemotional, uninteresting. OPPOSITE excited. **6** *The drink has gone flat.* stale, still. OPPOSITE fizzy. — *noun She lives in a flat.* apartment, bedsit (*British*), condominium (*American*), home unit (*Australian*), penthouse, tenement, unit (*Australian*).

flatten *verb* **1** *The machine flattens the ground.* compress, iron out, level, pat down, press, roll, smooth. **2** *He accidentally stepped in the flower bed and flattened her flowers.* crush, run over, squash, trample. **3** *The storm flattened the building.* demolish, destroy, knock down, level, raze.

flatter *verb* **1** *She flattered him to get his help.* butter up (*informal*), compliment, crawl to, fawn on, humour, play up to, praise, suck up to (*informal*), sweet-talk (*informal*). **2** *The dress flatters her.* become, do something for, suit.

flattery *noun Flattery does not always get you what you want.* adulation, blandishments, cajolery, compliments, obsequiousness, praise, smooth talk, soft soap (*informal*), sweet talk (*informal*), sycophancy.

flaunt *verb She flaunted her jewellery.* display, exhibit, parade, show off, sport. OPPOSITE hide.

flavour *noun* **1** *Salt brings out the flavour of the food.* piquancy, relish, savour, tang, taste. **2** *The author has captured the flavour of Singapore.* aspect, atmosphere, character, essence, feel, quality, spirit, tone. — *verb The cook flavoured the food.* season, spice.

flaw *noun* **1** *a flaw in the work.* blemish, bug, defect, error, fault, imperfection, mistake. **2** *a flaw in his character.* failing, fault, foible, shortcoming, weakness.

flawless *adjective a flawless presentation.* faultless, immaculate, impeccable, perfect, spotless, unblemished. OPPOSITE flawed, imperfect.

fleck *noun flecks of a different colour.* dot, freckle, patch, speck, speckle, spot.

flee *verb He took his bags and fled.* abscond, beat it (*slang*), bolt, decamp, disappear, do a bunk (*slang*), escape, leave, make tracks (*slang*), retreat, run away, scarper (*slang*), scram (*slang*), shoot through (*Australian informal*), skedaddle (*informal*), take flight, vanish.

fleece *noun a sheep's fleece.* coat, wool. — *verb The con man fleeced them.* cheat, con (*informal*), defraud, diddle (*informal*), rip off (*informal*), rob, swindle.

fleet[1] *noun a fleet of ships.* argosy (*poetical*), armada, convoy, flotilla, line, navy, squadron.

fleet[2] *adjective* fast, nimble, quick, rapid, speedy, swift. OPPOSITE slow.

fleeting *adjective fleeting sadness.* brief, ephemeral, momentary, passing, short-lived, temporary, transient, transitory. OPPOSITE lasting.

flesh *noun* **1** *the flesh of animals.* meat. **2** *the flesh of the apricot.* pulp, substance.

flex *noun electrical flex.* cable, cord, lead, wire.

flexible *adjective* **1** *a flexible wire.* bendable, elastic, pliable, resilient, springy. OPPOSITE rigid, stiff. **2** *a flexible body.* limber, lithe, supple. OPPOSITE stiff. **3** *a flexible arrangement.* adaptable, adjustable, changeable, open, versatile. OPPOSITE inflexible.

flick *verb* **1** *He flicked the dust off the table.* brush, flip, sweep, whisk. **2** *She flicked through the cards.* flip, leaf, skim, thumb.

flicker *verb The candle flickered.* blink, glimmer, quiver, shimmer, tremble, twinkle, waver, wink.

flight[1] *noun* **1** *the science of flight.* aeronautics, aviation, flying. **2** *a one-hour flight between cities.* hop, journey, trip. □ **flight attendant** air hostess, hostess, hostie (*Australian informal*), steward, stewardess.

flight[2] *noun a hasty flight from danger.* departure, escape, exit, exodus, fleeing, getaway, retreat.

flighty *adjective a flighty woman.* capricious, changeable, erratic, fickle, frivolous, scatterbrained, scatty (*informal*), temperamental, unpredictable. OPPOSITE staid.

flimsy *adjective* **1** *a flimsy structure.* breakable, fragile, frail, gimcrack, jerry-built, ramshackle, rickety, shaky, weak. OPPOSITE solid, strong. **2** *flimsy curtains.* delicate, diaphanous, filmy, fine, gossamer, lacy, see-through, sheer, thin. OPPOSITE thick. **3** *a flimsy excuse.* feeble, implausible, inadequate, lame, paltry, poor, unconvincing, weak. OPPOSITE sound.

flinch *verb He flinched when he saw the whip.* cower, cringe, draw back, duck, quail, recoil, shrink, wince.

fling *verb* **1** *Don't fling stones.* cast, catapult, chuck (*informal*), heave, hurl, launch, pitch, shy, sling, throw, toss. OPPOSITE catch. **2** *She flung her bags down.* bung (*informal*), chuck (*informal*), plonk, shove, throw, toss (*informal*).

flip *verb* **1** *Let's flip a coin.* flick, spin, throw, toss. **2** *He flipped through the pages of his magazine.* flick, leaf, skim, thumb. □ **flip over** *The boat flipped over.* capsize, overturn, roll over, topple over, turn over, turn turtle.

flippant *adjective flippant comments.* cheeky, disrespectful, frivolous, glib, impertinent, jocular, light-hearted, offhand, pert. OPPOSITE serious.

flirt *verb* **flirt with** *He flirted with the woman.* chat up, dally with, lead on, philander with, trifle with. — *noun an incorrigible flirt.* coquette (*female*), philanderer (*male*), tease.

flit *verb Moths flitted round the light.* dart, flitter, flutter, fly.

float *verb* **1** *The dinghies floated on the water.* bob, drift, sail. OPPOSITE sink. **2** *The balloon floated out the window.* drift, glide, hover, waft.

flock *noun* **1** *a flock of sheep.* drove, herd, mob. **2** *a flock of birds.* flight, gaggle (*of geese*). **3** *a flock of tourists.* assembly, band, bevy, bunch, cluster, collection, community, company, congregation, contingent, crowd, gathering, herd, horde, mob, multitude, pack, swarm, throng, troop. — *verb People flocked to see the fireworks.* assemble, cluster, collect, congregate, converge, crowd, gather, herd, huddle, mass, mob, swarm, throng.

flog *verb The prisoner was flogged.* beat, belt (*slang*), birch, cane, chastise, lash, scourge, thrash, whip.

flood *noun* **1** *Houses were washed away in the flood.* deluge, inundation, spate, torrent. **2** *a flood of questions.* deluge, outpouring, rush, shower, spate, stream, torrent, wave. — *verb* **1** *The town was flooded when the river burst its banks.* cover, deluge, drown, engulf, inundate, submerge, swamp. **2** *The river flooded.* overflow, run a banker (*Australian*). **3** *Letters flooded in.* flow, pour.

floor *noun a building with five floors.* deck, level, storey. — *verb* **1** *The boxer floored his opponent.* bowl over, fell, knock down. **2** *The problem completely floored him.* baffle, bamboozle (*informal*), confound, confuse, dumbfound, flummox (*informal*), nonplus, perplex, stump (*informal*), throw.

flop *verb* **1** *The doll's arms flop.* dangle, droop, hang down, sag. **2** *She flopped into a chair.* collapse, drop, fall, loll, slump, tumble. — *noun* (*informal*) *The show was a flop.* disaster, failure, fiasco, fizzer (*Australian informal*), non-event, washout (*informal*). OPPOSITE hit, success.

floppy *adjective* baggy, drooping, flaccid, limp, loose, wilting. OPPOSITE firm, rigid.

flora *noun* botany, plants, vegetation.

flounce[1] *verb Evelyn flounced out of the room.* march, stamp, stomp, storm, strut.

flounce[2] *noun The skirt has a flounce.* frill, furbelow, ruffle.

flounder *verb The walkers floundered in the mud.* bumble, fumble, stagger, struggle, stumble, wallow.

flourish *verb* **1** *The plants flourished.* bloom, blossom, burgeon, flower, grow, thrive. **2** *Business flourished.* be successful, boom, grow, prosper, succeed, thrive. OPPOSITE decline. **3** *He flourished the trophy.* brandish, display, flaunt, wave.

flout *verb He flouts the rules.* see DISOBEY.

flow *verb* **1** *Water flows through the pipes.* circulate, course, move, proceed, run. **2** *The water flowed from the hose.* dribble, drip, gush, leak, ooze, pour, run, rush, seep, spill, spout, spurt, squirt, stream, trickle. — *noun* **1** *carried by the river's flow.* course, current, drift, stream. **2** *a flow of tears. a flow of words.* flood, gush, outflow, outpouring, stream, torrent. **3** *a steady flow of visitors.* influx, spate, stream, succession, tide, train.

flower *noun* **1** *The plant is covered in flowers.* bloom, blossom, bud. **2** *She was presented with flowers.* bouquet, corsage, garland, nosegay, posy, spray, wreath. — *verb The plant flowers in spring.* bloom, blossom.

flowery *adjective flowery language.* elaborate, embellished, florid, grandiloquent, high-flown, ornate.

fluctuate *verb His mood fluctuates.* alternate, change, oscillate, see-saw, shift, swing, vacillate, vary, waver.

fluent *adjective a fluent speaker.* articulate, eloquent, smooth-spoken, voluble. OPPOSITE hesitant.

fluff *noun The clothes had fluff on them.* down, fuzz, lint.

fluffy *adjective a fluffy dressing gown.* downy, fleecy, furry, fuzzy, woolly.

fluid *noun* gas, liquid, solution. OPPOSITE solid. — *adjective a fluid substance.* flowing, gaseous, liquid, molten, runny, sloppy, watery. OPPOSITE solid, stiff.

fluke *noun It was a fluke that he passed his exam.* accident, chance, stroke of luck.

flush *verb* **1** *Her cheeks flushed with embarrassment.* blush, colour, glow, redden. OPPOSITE pale. **2** *The plumber flushed the drains.* clean out, rinse out, wash out. — *adjective* **1** *The mirror needs to be flush with the wall.* flat, level. **2** (*informal*) *He has just been paid and is feeling flush.* rich, wealthy, well in (*Australian informal*), well off. OPPOSITE hard up (*informal*).

flushed *adjective He was flushed after his run.* florid, red, rosy, ruddy. OPPOSITE pale.

flustered *adjective He gets flustered easily.* agitated, bothered, confused, disconcerted, fazed (*informal*), in a dither, in a flap (*informal*), in a state, in a tizzy (*informal*), nervous, panicky, rattled (*informal*), ruffled, thrown (*informal*), upset.

flutter *verb* **1** *The butterfly fluttered away.* flit, flitter, fly. **2** *The insect fluttered its wings.* bat, beat, flap, vibrate, wave. **3** *Her heart fluttered.* palpitate, quiver, shake, tremble. — *noun* **1** *The cast were all in a flutter before the show started.* dither, flap (*informal*), fluster, tizzy (*informal*). **2** *The news caused a flutter in the classroom.* commotion, ripple, sensation, stir. **3** (*informal*) *We had a flutter at the races.* bet, gamble, punt, wager.

fly *verb* **1** *The bird flew from tree to tree.* flit, flitter, flutter, glide, hover, soar, swoop, wing. **2** *She flew to London.* go by plane, jet. **3** *The flag is flying at half-mast.* flap, flutter, wave. **4** *She flew out of the room.* burst, dart, dash, hurry, hurtle, race, run, rush, scoot, shoot, speed, sweep, tear, whiz, zoom.

flyer *noun They sent out flyers about their next play.* bulletin, handout, leaflet, pamphlet.

flying *noun* aeronautics, aviation, flight.

foal *noun a horse and foal.* colt (*male*), filly (*female*).

foam *noun* **1** *The water was covered in foam.* bubbles, froth, lather, suds. **2** *a cushion made of foam.* rubber, sponge. — *verb The drink foamed.* bubble, effervesce, fizz, froth.

fob *verb* **fob off** *He tried to fob off the superseded model on an unsuspecting customer.* get rid of, offload, palm off (*informal*), pass off, unload.

focus *noun the focus of their attention.* centre, core, hub. — *verb He focused his attention on this issue.* centre, concentrate, fix, home in, zero in.

fodder *noun animal fodder.* feed, food, forage, provender, silage.

foe *noun They have more friends than foes.* adversary, antagonist, enemy, opponent, rival. OPPOSITE ally, friend.

fog *noun We couldn't see through the fog.* cloud, haze, mist, murkiness, smog. — *verb Her glasses fogged up when she entered the greenhouse.* cloud, mist, steam.

foggy *adjective* **1** *foggy weather.* hazy, misty, murky. OPPOSITE clear. **2** *only a foggy idea.* fuzzy, hazy, imprecise, inexact, obscure, vague. OPPOSITE clear.

foible *noun They put up with each other's foibles.* failing, flaw, idiosyncrasy, peculiarity, quirk, shortcoming, weakness.

foil *verb He foiled their plans.* baffle, baulk, frustrate, hamper, hinder, obstruct, stonker (*Australian slang*), thwart.

fold[1] *verb* **1** *Origami involves folding paper to make things.* bend, crease, crimp, double over, pleat, wrinkle. OPPOSITE unfold. **2** *The bed folds for storage.* collapse. — *noun folds in the material.* crease, crinkle, gather, pleat, pucker, tuck, wrinkle.

fold[2] *noun the sheep fold.* compound, enclosure, pen, yard.

folder *noun The papers are in a folder.* binder, cover, file, portfolio, ringbinder.

folk *noun* **1** *ordinary folk.* human beings, people. **2** *Her folk are in England.* family, kin, kinsfolk, parents, people, relations, relatives.

folklore *noun* beliefs, legends, lore, myths, traditions.

follow *verb* **1** *The police followed the suspect.* chase, go after, hound, hunt, pursue, run after, shadow, stalk, tail (*informal*), track, trail. OPPOSITE lead. **2** *She followed the path.* go along, keep to, proceed along, take. OPPOSITE stray from. **3** *Which king followed Henry VII?* come after, replace, succeed, supersede, supplant. OPPOSITE precede. **4** *Follow her example.* copy, emulate, imitate. **5** *Follow the rules.* abide by, comply with, conform to, heed, keep, obey, observe. OPPOSITE disobey. **6** *She didn't follow what you said.* comprehend, cotton on to (*informal*), get (*informal*), grasp, latch on to (*informal*), take in, understand. OPPOSITE misunderstand. **7** *He follows cricket.* be interested in, support. **8** *What followed is history.* come next, ensue, result.

follower *noun The great man had many followers.* adherent, admirer, devotee, disciple, fan, hanger-on, supporter. OPPOSITE leader.

following *adjective in the following days.* ensuing, next, subsequent, succeeding, successive. OPPOSITE preceding, previous.

folly *noun To attempt such a dangerous act would be folly.* foolishness, idiocy, imprudence, insanity, lunacy, madness, recklessness, silliness, stupidity. OPPOSITE wisdom.

fond *adjective* **1** *fond parents.* adoring, affectionate, caring, devoted, doting, indulgent, loving, tender, warm. OPPOSITE unloving. **2** *fond hopes.* absurd, foolish, naive, silly, vain. □ **fond of** *fond of jazz.* crazy about, enamoured of, keen on, nuts about (*informal*), partial to.

fondle *verb The cat likes to be fondled.* caress, cuddle, pat, pet, stroke, touch.

fondness *noun* **1** *a fondness for chocolates.* liking, partiality, taste, weakness. OPPOSITE dislike. **2** *fondness for a person.* affection, attachment, devotion, love, tenderness, warmth. OPPOSITE hostility.

food *noun* chow (*slang*), delicacies, diet, eats (*informal*), fare, feed, fodder, foodstuff, forage, grub (*slang*), nosh (*slang*), nourishment, nutriment, produce, provender, provisions, rations, refreshments, sustenance, tucker (*Australian informal*), victuals.

fool *noun* **1** *He realised what a fool he'd been.* ass (*informal*), blockhead, bonehead, boofhead (*Australian informal*), chump (*informal*), clot (*informal*), cretin, dill (*Australian informal*), dimwit (*informal*), dingbat (*informal*), dodo (*informal*), dolt, dope (*informal*), drongo (*Australian informal*), duffer, dummy (*informal*), dunce, fat-head (*informal*), galah (*Australian slang*), gig (*Australian informal*), git (*informal*), goof (*slang*), goon (*slang*), goose (*informal*), half-wit, idiot (*informal*), ignoramus, imbecile, jerk (*slang*), lunatic, moron (*informal*), mug (*informal*), muggins (*informal*), nincompoop, ninny, nitwit (*informal*), nong (*Australian informal*), numskull, nut (*informal*), sap (*informal*), silly (*informal*), silly billy (*informal*), simpleton, sucker (*informal*), thickhead (*informal*), tomfool, twerp (*slang*), twit (*slang*), wally (*slang*). **2** *the court fool.* buffoon, clown, comic, entertainer, jester, zany. — *verb* **1** *They didn't mean it seriously: they were just fooling.* jest, joke, kid (*informal*), make believe, pretend, tease. **2** *You can't fool her.* bluff, con (*informal*), deceive, delude, dupe, hoax, hoodwink, mislead, take in, trick. □ **fool around** *They had nothing to do and were just fooling around.* clown around, mess around, monkey about, play around, play the fool.

foolhardy *adjective a foolhardy action.* bold, daredevil, daring, impetuous, imprudent, irresponsible, madcap, precipitate, rash, reckless, unwise. OPPOSITE cautious.

foolish *adjective a foolish person. a foolish scheme.* absurd, barmy (*slang*), crazy, daft (*informal*), dopey (*informal*), fatuous, goofy (*slang*), half-witted, hare-brained, idiotic, illogical, imprudent, inane, insane, irrational, ludicrous, lunatic, mad, madcap, misguided, nonsensical, nutty (*informal*), potty (*informal*), ridiculous, senseless, short-sighted, silly, stupid, unintelligent, unwise, witless. OPPOSITE wise.

foolishness *noun* see FOLLY.

foot *noun* **1** *an animal's foot.* hoof, pad, paw, trotter. **2** *the foot of the hill.* base, bottom. OPPOSITE top.

foothold *noun She got a foothold and clambered up.* footing, purchase, toehold.

footing *noun The two groups are now on an equal footing.* basis, standing, status, terms.

footloose *adjective She was footloose and fancy-free.* carefree, independent, unencumbered, without ties. OPPOSITE tied-down.

footpath *noun* footway, path, pavement, sidewalk (*American*).

footprint *noun* footmark, footstep, track.

footwear *noun* see SHOE.

forage *noun forage for the beasts.* feed, fodder, food, provender. — *verb She foraged in the cupboard and eventually found some chocolate.* fossick (*Australian informal*), hunt, poke around, ransack, rummage, scrounge, search.

foray noun The soldiers made a foray on the town. assault, attack, incursion, invasion, offensive, raid.

forbearance noun The teacher looked on their mistakes with forbearance. indulgence, lenience, mercy, patience, tolerance. OPPOSITE intolerance.

forbearing adjective a forbearing parent. forgiving, lenient, long-suffering, merciful, patient, tolerant. OPPOSITE intolerant.

forbid verb She forbids talking in class. ban, bar, outlaw, prohibit, proscribe, veto. OPPOSITE allow.

forbidding adjective a forbidding appearance. a forbidding manner. grim, harsh, hostile, inhospitable, menacing, off-putting, ominous, severe, stern, threatening, unfriendly, uninviting.

force noun 1 Force was needed to shift it. effort, energy, exertion, might, power, pressure, strength, vigour. 2 a police force. a force of workers. body, corps, posse, squad, team, unit. 3 The new rules come into force next week. effect, operation, play, use. — verb 1 They forced him to sign the paper. bully, coerce, compel, constrain, dragoon, drive, make, oblige, order, pressure. 2 He forced a confession from her. drag, extort, extract, wrest, wring. 3 He forced the lock. break open, burst open, prise open, push open, wrench open.

forced adjective The conversation was forced. artificial, contrived, laboured, stilted, strained, unnatural. OPPOSITE spontaneous.

forceful adjective 1 a forceful personality. aggressive, assertive, dynamic, energetic, masterful, powerful, pushy, strong, vigorous. OPPOSITE weak. 2 a forceful argument. cogent, compelling, convincing, effective, persuasive, potent, powerful, strong, telling, weighty. OPPOSITE feeble.

forebear noun ancestor, forefather, predecessor, progenitor.

foreboding noun an uncomfortable foreboding about the exam. apprehension, forewarning, intuition, misgiving, omen, portent, premonition, presentiment.

forecast verb They forecast that it would rain. foretell, forewarn, predict, prophesy. — noun a gloomy economic forecast. outlook, prediction, prognosis, projection, prophecy.

forefather noun ancestor, forebear, predecessor, progenitor.

forefront noun in the forefront of genetic research. cutting edge, fore, lead, van, vanguard.

forehead noun brow.

foreign adjective 1 foreign goods. alien, exotic, imported, overseas, strange, unfamiliar. OPPOSITE native. 2 foreign affairs. external, international, overseas. OPPOSITE domestic. 3 Jealousy is foreign to her nature. alien, outside, uncharacteristic, unnatural. OPPOSITE intrinsic.

foreigner noun Rose meets many foreigners in her job as a tour guide. alien, immigrant, new chum (Australian informal), newcomer, outsider, stranger, visitor. OPPOSITE native.

foreman noun 1 a factory foreman. boss, overseer, superintendent, supervisor. 2 a jury foreman. leader, spokesman, spokesperson, spokeswoman.

foremost adjective the country's foremost scientists. best, chief, greatest, leading, main, major, pre-eminent, premier, principal, supreme, top.

forerunner noun 1 the forerunner of the modern aeroplane. ancestor, antecedent, precursor, predecessor, prototype. 2 The darkness was a forerunner to the storm. harbinger, herald, precursor.

foresee verb She foresaw the dangers. anticipate, envisage, expect, forecast, foretell, predict, prophesy.

foresight noun They showed foresight in their town planning. farsightedness, forethought, prescience, providence, vision. OPPOSITE hindsight, short-sightedness.

forest noun diminishing areas of forest. brush, jungle, plantation, thicket, wood, woodland, woods.

forestall verb The boss forestalled their plan to strike. anticipate, foil, pre-empt, prevent, thwart.

foretaste noun a foretaste of future joy. preview, sample, token.

foretell verb The prophets foretold future events. forecast, foresee, predict, prophesy.

forethought noun He showed forethought in bringing a drink for the walk. foresight, planning, preparation.

forever adverb They are forever arguing. always, constantly, continually, eternally, everlastingly, incessantly, permanently, perpetually.

foreword noun the foreword to a book. introduction, preamble, preface, prologue.

forfeit noun If you cancel you have to pay a forfeit. fine, penalty. — verb She forfeited her rights. cede, forgo, give up, relinquish, renounce, sacrifice, surrender, waive.

forge noun a blacksmith's forge. furnace, smithy, workshop. — verb 1 The blacksmith forged the horse's shoes. fashion, form, hammer out, mould, shape. 2 The crooks forged $20 notes. copy, counterfeit, fake.

forged adjective a forged $20 bill. bogus, counterfeit, dud (informal), fake, false, imitation, phoney (informal), sham. OPPOSITE genuine.

forgery noun The passport was a forgery. copy, counterfeit, fake, fraud, imitation, phoney (informal), replica, reproduction, sham.

forget verb 1 He forgot a few people. leave out, miss, neglect, omit, overlook, pass over, skip. OPPOSITE remember. 2 He forgot his umbrella. leave behind. OPPOSITE remember, take.

forgetful adjective absent-minded, careless, inattentive, neglectful, negligent, oblivious, remiss, scatterbrained, vague.

forgivable adjective a forgivable sin. excusable, pardonable, venial. OPPOSITE unforgivable.

forgive verb Forgive us our sins as we forgive those who sin against us. absolve, excuse, exonerate, let off, overlook, pardon, remit. OPPOSITE condemn.

forgiveness noun forgiveness for past wrongs. absolution, amnesty, exoneration, pardon, remission.

forgo verb You will have to forgo rich food. abandon, abstain from, give up, go without, renounce.

fork noun We came to a fork in the road. bifurcation, Y-junction. — verb The road forks. bifurcate, branch, divide, separate, split.

forlorn adjective She was forlorn after he left. dejected, depressed, desolate, disconsolate, forsaken, heavy-hearted, lonely, melancholy, miserable, sad, unhappy, woebegone, wretched. OPPOSITE happy.

form noun 1 He is more interested in the form of things than their substance. appearance, arrangement, composition, configuration, construction, contour, design, figure, format, formation, layout, mould, organisation, outline, pattern, profile, shape, silhouette, structure. 2 different forms of the same thing. brand, breed, class, edition, genre, genus, kind, model, sort, species, style, type, variety, version. 3 Sixth form at school. class, grade, year. 4 We were asked to fill in a form. application, document, paper, questionnaire, sheet. 5 The runners were in fine form. condition, fettle, fitness, health, shape, trim. 6 We sat on wooden forms. bench, seat. — verb 1 The sculptor formed a horse out of clay, stone, etc. build, carve, cast, construct, create, fabricate, fashion, forge, make, model, mould, produce, sculpt, shape, work. 2 We formed a fundraising committee. establish, found, set up. 3 Twelve members form a team. compose, constitute, make up. 4 He is forming bad habits. acquire, develop, pick up.

formal adjective 1 She wears a hat on formal occasions. ceremonial, official, solemn, stately. OPPOSITE informal. 2 a formal manner. ceremonious, conventional, dignified, pompous, prim, proper, punctilious, reserved, starchy, stiff, stilted, strait-laced. OPPOSITE casual.

formality noun 1 She behaved with formality. ceremoniousness, ceremony, conventionality, decorum, punctiliousness, stiffness. OPPOSITE informality. 2 They had to go through the formalities. convention, custom, form, procedure, regulation, rite, ritual, rule.

format noun the format of a book. arrangement, design, form, layout, organisation, shape, size, structure.

former adjective in former times. ancient, bygone, earlier, old, olden, past, previous.

formerly adverb Their house was formerly a nursing home. in the past, once, previously.

formidable adjective a formidable task. arduous, challenging, daunting, difficult, herculean, mammoth, onerous, overwhelming, tough. OPPOSITE easy.

formula noun 1 a formula for success. blueprint, method, prescription, recipe. 2 a mathematical formula. algorithm, rule, statement, theorem.

formulate verb She formulated her response carefully. articulate, compose, express, form, frame, phrase, work out.

forsake verb He promised never to forsake her. abandon, desert, leave, reject.

fort noun see FORTRESS.

forte noun Debating is her forte. speciality, specialty, strength, strong point.

forthcoming adjective 1 The flyer publicised forthcoming attractions. coming, future, imminent, impending, prospective, upcoming. OPPOSITE past. 2 (informal) The interviewee was not very forthcoming. communicative, expansive, responsive, talkative. OPPOSITE reticent.

forthright adjective He has a reputation for being forthright. blunt, candid, direct, frank, open, outspoken, plain-spoken, straightforward, truthful, upfront (informal). OPPOSITE evasive, reticent.

forthwith adverb see IMMEDIATELY.

fortification noun bastion, battlement, bulwark, parapet, rampart, stronghold.

fortify verb 1 They fortified the town against the invaders. defend, garrison, protect, reinforce, secure, strengthen. 2 The hot food fortified the walkers. boost, invigorate, strengthen, sustain.

fortitude noun He bore his troubles with fortitude. boldness, bravery, courage, determination, endurance, grit, guts (informal), pluck, resoluteness, stoicism. OPPOSITE weakness.

fortress noun acropolis, castle, citadel, fort, fortification, garrison, stronghold.

fortuitous adjective a fortuitous meeting. accidental, casual, chance, coincidental, random, serendipitous, unexpected, unintentional, unplanned. OPPOSITE planned.

fortunate adjective 1 a fortunate person. blessed, favoured, happy, lucky, prosperous. 2 a fortunate choice. auspicious, favourable, lucky, opportune, propitious, providential, timely. OPPOSITE disastrous.

fortune noun 1 Fortune smiled on their venture. chance, destiny, fate, luck, providence. 2 He inherited the family fortune. assets, estate, inheritance, property, riches, wealth. 3 It cost a fortune. He made a fortune. big bickies (Australian informal), bundle (informal), heaps (informal), megabucks (informal), mint, packet (informal), pile (informal), pots (informal).

fortune-teller noun astrologer, clairvoyant, crystal-gazer, diviner, palmist, prophet, seer, sibyl (female), soothsayer.

forum noun see MEETING.

forward adjective She was too forward for her own good. assertive, audacious, bold, brazen, cheeky, fresh (informal), impertinent, impudent, pert, presumptuous, pushy, saucy; see also PRECOCIOUS. OPPOSITE retiring. — verb 1 The neighbours forwarded the mail. readdress, redirect, send on. 2 The company forwards parcels to Europe. deliver, dispatch, freight, send, ship, transport. 3 She did all that she could to forward their cause. advance, assist, foster, further, help, promote, support. OPPOSITE hinder.

forwards adverb Go forwards. ahead, forth, forward, frontwards, onwards. OPPOSITE backwards.

fossick verb (Australian informal) He was fossicking in the pile for anything useful. ferret, fish, forage, hunt, poke around, rake through, rummage, scavenge, scrounge, search.

fossil noun plant and animal fossils. relic, remains.

foster verb The school tries to foster students' creativity. advance, cultivate, encourage, further, nurture, promote.

foul adjective 1 a foul smell. bad, disgusting, horrible, nauseating, noisome (literary), objectionable, obnoxious, off (informal), offensive, on the nose (Australian informal), putrid, rank, revolting, rotten, smelly, stinking, vile. OPPOSITE fragrant, sweet. 2 a foul crime. abhorrent, abominable, appalling, atrocious, beastly, contemptible, despicable, detestable, evil, loathsome, monstrous, shocking, terrible, vicious, vile, villainous, violent, wicked. 3 foul language. abusive, bad, blasphemous, coarse, crude, dirty, disgusting, filthy, impolite, indecent, obscene, offensive, rude, smutty, vulgar. OPPOSITE polite. 4 foul weather. atrocious (informal), crook (Australian informal), dreadful (informal), lousy (informal), rough, shocking (informal), stormy, terrible (informal), wild. OPPOSITE fair, fine. — verb 1 The sewage fouled the water. contaminate, pollute, taint. OPPOSITE cleanse. 2 His fishing line fouled theirs. entangle, snarl, tangle.

found verb 1 The hospital was founded in 1946. begin, create, establish, inaugurate, initiate, institute, originate, set up, start. 2 The *story is founded on fact.* base, build, ground, root.

foundation *noun* **1** *a foundation for medical research.* establishment, institution, organisation. **2** *The building has a strong foundation.* base, footing, substructure. **3** *Her claims are without foundation.* base, basis, grounds, justification, support.

fountain *noun* **1** *a fountain of water.* jet, shower, spout, spray, spring. **2** *the fountain of wisdom.* beginning, fount, origin, source.

fowl *noun* bird, chook (*Australian informal*); [*fowls*] poultry.

fox *noun* cub (*young*), kit (*young*), vixen (*female*). — *verb The riddle had them foxed.* baffle, bamboozle (*informal*), confound, flummox (*informal*), perplex, puzzle, stump, trick.

foxy *adjective* see CUNNING.

foyer *noun the hotel foyer.* entrance hall, lobby, vestibule.

fracas *noun There was a fracas over the money.* altercation, brawl, commotion, disturbance, fight, hullabaloo, quarrel, row, skirmish, squabble, storm, uproar.

fraction *noun Only a fraction was left.* bit, fragment, part, piece, portion, section.

fracture *noun a fracture in the rock.* break, cleft, crack, fissure, rift, rupture, split. — *verb She fell and fractured her arm.* break, crack.

fragile *noun a fragile vase.* breakable, brittle, delicate, flimsy, frail, weak. OPPOSITE strong.

fragment *noun* **1** *fragments of glass.* bit, chip, part, particle, piece, remnant, scrap, shred, sliver, speck, splinter; [*fragments*] smithereens. **2** *a fragment of the conversation.* bit, snatch, snippet.

fragrance *noun the fragrance of roses.* aroma, balm, bouquet, odour, perfume, redolence, scent, smell. OPPOSITE stink.

frail *adjective* **1** *a frail structure.* delicate, flimsy, fragile, rickety, unsound, weak. OPPOSITE strong. **2** *a frail old lady.* ailing, decrepit, feeble, infirm, sickly, weak. OPPOSITE robust.

frame *noun* **1** *a house with a timber frame. a car frame.* chassis, framework, shell, skeleton, structure, substructure. **2** *a picture frame. a window frame.* border, case, edge, margin, mount, mounting, surround. **3** *a woman with a large frame.* body, build, figure, physique, skeleton. — *verb* **1** *She framed the photo.* enclose, mount, surround. **2** *He framed the questions carefully.* compose, construct, devise, draft, formulate. □ **frame of mind** *He was not in the right frame of mind for dealing with these problems.* attitude, disposition, humour, mood, outlook, state, temper.

framework *noun* **1** *the timber framework of a house.* chassis, frame, shell, skeleton, structure, substructure. **2** *the framework of a book.* outline, plan, skeleton, structure.

franchise *noun When were women given the franchise?* suffrage, right to vote, vote.

frank *adjective He was frank in his criticism.* blunt, candid, direct, forthright, honest, open, outspoken, plain-spoken, straightforward, truthful, upfront (*informal*). OPPOSITE evasive.

frantic *adjective Their mother was frantic when they didn't arrive.* agitated, anxious, berserk, beside yourself, crazy, desperate, distraught, frenzied, hysterical, overwrought, panic-stricken, worried. OPPOSITE calm.

fraternise *verb He fraternises with all sorts of people.* associate, consort, hobnob, mingle, mix, socialise.

fraud *noun* **1** *She was found guilty of fraud.* cheating, deceit, deception, dishonesty, duplicity, fraudulence, rorting (*Australian slang*), swindling, trickery. **2** *The doctor was found to be a fraud.* charlatan, cheat, con man (*informal*), fake, humbug, impostor, phoney (*informal*), quack, sham, swindler, trickster.

fraudulent *adjective a fraudulent insurance claim.* crooked, deceitful, dishonest, false, phoney (*informal*), shady, shonky (*Australian informal*), unscrupulous. OPPOSITE honest.

frayed *adjective The towel is old and frayed.* ragged, shabby, tattered, tatty (*informal*), threadbare, unravelled, worn.

freak *noun* **1** *He was considered a freak because he had an extra toe.* monster, monstrosity, mutant, oddity, weirdo (*informal*). **2** (*informal*) *a fitness freak.* crank, eccentric, fanatic, fiend, maniac, nut (*informal*). — *verb* (*informal*) **1** *He freaked when he saw the damage to his car.* see BECOME ANGRY (at ANGRY). **2** *Exams freak me out.* see FRIGHTEN.

freakish *adjective freakish behaviour.* abnormal, atypical, bizarre, eccentric, exceptional, extraordinary, freak, odd, outlandish, peculiar, queer, strange, unusual, weird. OPPOSITE normal.

free *adjective* **1** *a free person.* emancipated, liberated, released. OPPOSITE enslaved. **2** *a free country.* autonomous, democratic, independent, self-governing, sovereign. **3** *the free end of the rope.* loose, unattached, untied. **4** *free of responsibility.* absolved, exempt (from), immune (from), rid, without. **5** *a free sample.* complimentary, gratis, on the house (*informal*), unpaid. **6** *free time.* leisure, spare, uncommitted. **7** *The toilet is free.* available, unoccupied, vacant. OPPOSITE engaged. **8** *He was free to leave.* able, allowed, at liberty, permitted. OPPOSITE forbidden. **9** *She is very free with her money.* bountiful, generous, lavish, liberal, open-handed, unstinting. OPPOSITE stingy. — *verb* **1** *He freed the slaves.* deliver, emancipate, liberate, release, rescue, save, set free. OPPOSITE capture. **2** *He freed the animals.* let loose, let out, uncage, unchain, unleash. OPPOSITE confine. **3** *He was freed from his obligations.* excuse, exempt, let off, release, relieve, save, spare. **4** *He freed his line from the tangled mess.* clear, detach, disengage, disentangle, extricate, loosen, remove, untangle.

freebie *noun* see GIFT.

freedom *noun* **1** *political freedom.* autonomy, independence, liberty, self-determination, self-government. OPPOSITE dependence. **2** *freedom of speech.* candour, directness, frankness, openness, outspokenness. OPPOSITE censorship. **3** *freedom after captivity.* deliverance, emancipation, liberation, liberty, release. OPPOSITE captivity. **4** *freedom to do as you wish.* discretion, free hand, free rein, latitude, licence, scope.

freeway *noun driving on the freeway.* expressway, highway, motorway.

freewheel *verb The cyclist freewheeled down the hill.* coast, drift, glide.

freeze *verb* **1** *The lake froze.* ice over, turn to ice. OPPOSITE thaw. **2** *She froze the drinks.* chill, cool, refrigerate. OPPOSITE thaw. **3** *He froze on the spot.* halt, petrify, stop. **4** *Prices have been frozen.* fix, hold, peg.

freezing *adjective freezing weather.* arctic, bitter, chilly, cold, frigid, frosty, ice-cold, icy, nippy (*informal*), perishing (*informal*), subzero. OPPOSITE sweltering.

freight *noun* **1** *The price includes freight.* carriage, cartage, conveyance, haulage, shipment, shipping, transport. **2** *The train carries freight and passengers.* cargo, consignment, goods, lading, load. — *verb The company freights goods overseas.* carry, cart, dispatch, forward, move, send, ship, transport.

frenzied *adjective frenzied activity. a frenzied crowd.* agitated, berserk, crazy, demented, distraught, excited, feverish, frantic, frenetic, hectic, hysterical, mad, wild. OPPOSITE calm.

frenzy *noun He worked himself into a frenzy.* agitation, excitement, fever, hysteria, insanity, madness, mania.

frequent *adjective* **1** *a frequent problem.* common, continual, eternal, perpetual, persistent, recurrent, repeated. OPPOSITE rare. **2** *They had frequent phone calls.* constant, continual, countless, incessant, many, numerous. OPPOSITE few. **3** *a frequent visitor.* familiar, habitual, regular. OPPOSITE infrequent, occasional. — *verb He frequents the local pizzeria.* haunt, patronise, visit.

frequently *adverb They go out to dinner frquently.* again and again, commonly, constantly, continually, habitually, often, regularly, repeatedly.

fresh *adjective* **1** *fresh news.* hot, latest, new, recent, up-to-date, up-to-the-minute. OPPOSITE old, stale. **2** *a fresh approach.* alternative, different, innovative, new, newfangled (*derogatory*), novel, original, untried. OPPOSITE old. **3** *a fresh sheet of paper.* clean, pristine, untouched, unused. OPPOSITE used. **4** *fresh air.* clean, cool, crisp, pure, refreshing, unpolluted. OPPOSITE stale. **5** *He was fresh after his rest.* alert, energetic, invigorated, lively, perky, refreshed, revived. OPPOSITE weary.

freshen *verb She freshened the room.* air, clean, deodorise, ventilate.

fret *verb She fretted when her friend went away.* brood, distress yourself, grieve, mope, pine, worry.

fretful *adjective The patient was fretful.* anxious, distressed, miserable, peevish, restless, troubled, upset.

friar *noun* brother, monk, religious.

friction *noun* **1** *The sore was caused by friction.* abrasion, chafing, fretting, rubbing. **2** *There was friction between the sisters.* antagonism, conflict, contention, disagreement, discord, dissension, quarrelling, strife.

friend *noun* **1** *Liz confided in her friend.* acquaintance, ally, boyfriend, buddy (*informal*), chum (*informal*), cobber (*Australian informal*), companion, comrade, confidant, confidante, crony, girlfriend, mate, pal (*informal*), partner, penfriend, playmate, steady. OPPOSITE enemy. **2** *He belongs to the friends of the library.* backer, benefactor, helper, patron, supporter, sympathiser.

friendliness *noun The group members are known for their friendliness.* affability, affection, amiability, amicability, brotherliness, camaraderie, conviviality, cordiality, geniality, goodwill, hospitality, kindness, neighbourliness, sociability, warmth. OPPOSITE hostility.

friendly *adjective* **1** *a friendly person.* affable, affectionate, amiable, amicable, approachable, brotherly, chummy (*informal*), companionable, convivial, genial, good-natured, gracious, hospitable, kind, kind-hearted, kindly, loving, matey, neighbourly, outgoing, pally (*informal*), sisterly, sociable, sympathetic, tender, warm-hearted, welcoming. OPPOSITE hostile. **2** *We are on friendly terms.* amicable, close, cordial, familiar, good, harmonious, intimate. OPPOSITE unfriendly.

friendship *noun* **1** *The club aims to promote friendship.* amity, camaraderie, companionship, comradeship, cordiality, friendliness, harmony, mateship. OPPOSITE hostility. **2** *a long-standing friendship.* alliance, association, partnership, relationship.

fright *noun* **1** *The noise made her jump in fright.* alarm, anxiety, apprehension, consternation, dismay, dread, fear, horror, panic, terror, trepidation. **2** *He gave me a fright.* scare, shock, start, turn.

frighten *verb Dogs frighten him.* alarm, cow, daunt, dismay, freak out (*informal*), horrify, intimidate, menace, perturb, petrify, put the wind up (*informal*), rattle (*informal*), scare, shock, startle, terrify, terrorise, unnerve. OPPOSITE reassure.

frightened *adjective Patrick was all alone and frightened.* afraid, alarmed, anxious, apprehensive, chicken (*informal*), faint-hearted, fearful, nervous, panic-stricken, petrified, scared, terrified, terror-stricken. OPPOSITE unafraid.

frightening *adjective a frightening experience.* alarming, chilling, creepy, daunting, dreadful, eerie, fearful, fearsome, frightful, hair-raising, horrifying, nightmarish, scary, sinister, spine-chilling, spooky, terrifying. OPPOSITE reassuring.

frightful *adjective Something frightful has happened.* appalling, awful, bad, dreadful, fearful, fearsome, ghastly, grisly, gruesome, hideous, horrendous, horrible, horrid, horrific, shocking, terrible.

frigid *adjective* see COLD.

frill *noun* **1** *a frill on a dress.* flounce, ruff, ruffle. **2** *simple accommodation with no frills.* addition, extra, supplement, trimming.

fringe *noun* **1** *the fringe of a scarf.* border, edge, edging, tassels. **2** *the fringe of a town.* borders, edge, limits, margin, outskirts, perimeter, periphery. □ **fringe benefit** *A company car is one of his fringe benefits.* bonus, extra, perk (*informal*), perquisite, side benefit.

frisk *verb* **1** *The lambs frisked about in the field.* caper, cavort, dance, frolic, gambol, jump, leap, play, prance, romp, skip. **2** *The police frisked everyone.* check, inspect, search.

frisky *adjective a frisky kitten.* active, frolicsome, lively, perky, playful, skittish, spirited.

fritter *verb* **fritter away** *She frittered away all her money.* dissipate, misspend, squander, waste.

frivolous *adjective* **1** *frivolous conversation.* facetious, flippant, inane, petty, ridiculous, silly, superficial, trivial, unimportant. OPPOSITE serious. **2** *a frivolous person.* flighty, giddy, irresponsible, light-hearted, shallow, silly, superficial. OPPOSITE earnest.

frizzy *adjective frizzy hair.* Afro, bushy, curly, fuzzy.

frock *noun Julie wore a green frock.* dress, gown, robe.

frolic *verb The children frolicked in the yard.* caper, cavort, frisk, gambol, let off steam, play, romp, skip.

front *noun* **1** *the front of an object.* face, head, nose. OPPOSITE back. **2** *a ship's front.* bow, fore, prow. OPPO-

SITE stern. **3** *a house front.* façade, face, frontage. **4** *the front of the line.* beginning, head, start, top. OPPOSITE back. **5** *The young soldier was sent to the front.* front line, van, vanguard. OPPOSITE rearguard. **6** *She put on a brave front.* air, appearance, exterior, façade, face, look, show. — *adjective* **1** *front legs.* fore. OPPOSITE hind, rear. **2** *the front page.* first, initial, leading. OPPOSITE back.

frontier *noun a country's frontier.* border, boundary, limits.

frost *noun The ground was covered in frost.* hoar-frost, rime.

frosty *adjective* see COLD.

froth *noun The detergent created a thick layer of froth.* bubbles, foam, lather, scum, suds.

frown *verb He looked ugly when he frowned.* glare, glower, grimace, knit your brow, lour, scowl. OPPOSITE smile. □ **frown on** *They frown on gambling.* disapprove of, look askance at, take a dim view of. OPPOSITE approve of.

frozen *adjective* see COLD.

frugal *adjective* **1** *She is a frugal housekeeper.* economical, parsimonious, penny-pinching, provident, sparing, thrifty. OPPOSITE wasteful. **2** *a frugal meal.* meagre, paltry, scanty, skimpy. OPPOSITE lavish.

fruit *noun the fruit of his hard work.* consequence, harvest, outcome, product, result, reward, upshot.

fruitful *adjective* **1** *fruitful soil.* fertile, productive, rich. OPPOSITE barren. **2** *The two parties had a fruitful discussion.* productive, profitable, rewarding, successful, useful, valuable, worthwhile. OPPOSITE fruitless.

fruitless *adjective a fruitless attempt.* abortive, barren, futile, ineffective, pointless, unproductive, unsuccessful, useless, vain. OPPOSITE fruitful.

frustrate *verb The weather frustrated their efforts.* baffle, baulk, block, check, foil, hamper, hamstring, hinder, impede, prevent, stonker (*Australian slang*), stop, stymie, thwart. OPPOSITE facilitate.

fry *verb She fried the meat.* brown, sauté.

fuddy-duddy *noun* (*informal*) *In spite of being old he's not a fuddy-duddy.* conservative, old fogy, square (*informal*), stick-in-the-mud.

fugitive *noun The police finally caught the fugitive.* deserter, escapee, renegade, runaway.

fulfil *verb* **1** *She fulfilled her task.* accomplish, achieve, carry out, complete, discharge, execute, perform. **2** *He fulfilled all the requirements.* answer, comply with, conform to, fill, meet, satisfy. **3** *She fulfilled her promise.* abide by, keep, live up to. OPPOSITE break.

full *adjective* **1** *a full glass of water.* brimming, filled, overflowing. OPPOSITE empty. **2** *The place was full.* bursting, chock-a-block, chockers (*Australian informal*), chock-full, congested, crammed, crowded, filled, jam-packed, overcrowded, packed, stuffed. OPPOSITE empty. **3** *full of ideas.* abounding (in), rich (in), teeming (with). OPPOSITE devoid (of). **4** *He felt full after his meal.* gorged, replete, sated, satiated, stuffed. OPPOSITE hungry. **5** *She wrote a full account of the day's proceedings.* complete, comprehensive, detailed, entire, exhaustive, thorough, total, unabridged, whole. OPPOSITE partial.

fumbling *adjective a fumbling attempt at fielding.* awkward, bumbling, bungling, clumsy, inept.

fume *verb He fumed when they were late again.* blow up (*informal*), blow your stack (*informal*), blow your

top (*informal*), explode, flare up, lose your temper, rage, seethe, smoulder. □ **fumes** *plural noun She choked on the fumes of the car in front.* exhaust, gas, smoke, vapour.

fun *noun They just wanted to relax and have fun.* amusement, diversion, enjoyment, entertainment, frivolity, frolic, gaiety, hilarity, joking, jollity, kicks (*informal*), laughter, merriment, merrymaking, mirth, play, pleasure, recreation, relaxation, sport. OPPOSITE misery. □ **make fun of** *It was mean to make fun of his sister.* chiack (*Australian informal*), deride, jeer at, joke about, laugh at, mock, parody, poke borak at (*Australian informal*), poke fun at, rib (*informal*), ridicule, satirise, send up (*informal*), sling off at (*Australian informal*), take the mickey out of (*informal*), taunt, tease.

function *noun* **1** *a person's function. a thing's function.* activity, duty, job, purpose, role, task, use. **2** *Most people attended the Christmas function.* affair (*informal*), ceremony, do (*informal*), event, gathering, occasion, party, reception. — *verb* **1** *The machine is not functioning correctly.* behave, go, operate, perform, run, work. **2** *It functions as an office and play room.* act, serve.

functional *adjective functional furniture.* practical, serviceable, useful, utilitarian. OPPOSITE decorative.

fund *noun* **1** *his retirement fund.* kitty, nest egg, pool, reserve. **2** *a fund of jokes.* hoard, mine, reserve, reservoir, stock, store, supply. — *verb The company funded the project.* back, finance, pay for, sponsor, subsidise. □ **funds** *plural noun He manages the company's funds.* capital, cash, finances, means, money, resources, savings, wealth.

fundamental *adjective a fundamental rule.* basic, cardinal, central, crucial, elementary, essential, important, key, primary, principal, underlying, vital. OPPOSITE secondary. □ **fundamentals** *plural noun The course deals with the fundamentals of programming.* basics, elements, essentials, principles, rudiments.

funeral *noun The funeral was held a week after he died.* burial, cremation, interment.

funnel *noun a ship's funnel.* chimney, smokestack.

funny *adjective* **1** *She told a funny joke.* absurd, amusing, comical, crazy, droll, entertaining, facetious, hilarious, humorous, laughable, ludicrous, priceless (*informal*), ridiculous, witty, zany. OPPOSITE sad. **2** *A funny thing happened.* abnormal, bizarre, curious, extraordinary, odd, peculiar, queer, strange, unusual, weird.

fur *noun an animal's fur.* coat, down, fleece, hair, hide, pelt, skin.

furious *adjective* **1** *Dad was furious when he found out.* angry, cross, enraged, hopping mad (*informal*), incensed, indignant, infuriated, irate, livid, mad, rabid, ropeable (*Australian informal*), wrathful. OPPOSITE calm. **2** *a furious storm.* fierce, intense, raging, savage, tempestuous, violent, wild.

furnace *noun The rubbish is burnt in the furnace.* boiler, forge, incinerator, kiln, oven.

furnish *verb* **1** *She furnished the house luxuriously.* equip, fit out. **2** *Each person was furnished with stationery.* arm, equip, provide, supply.

furniture *noun The removalists shifted the furniture.* effects, furnishings, movables.

furore *noun The incident caused a furore.* commotion, hullabaloo, rumpus, stir, storm, to-do, uproar.

furphy *noun* see RUMOUR.

furrow *noun* **1** *Plant in the furrows.* channel, corrugation, ditch, drill, groove, rut, trench. **2** *skin furrows.* crease, line, wrinkle.

furry *adjective furry skin.* downy, fleecy, fluffy, fuzzy, hairy, woolly.

further *adjective further details.* additional, extra, fresh, more, new, other, supplementary. — *verb They furthered the cause.* advance, aid, assist, boost, champion, forward, foster, help, promote. OPPOSITE hinder.

furthermore *adverb* also, besides, in addition, moreover, too.

furthest *adjective the furthest point.* extreme, farthest, furthermost, outermost, ultimate, uttermost. OPPOSITE closest.

furtive *adjective a furtive glance.* clandestine, covert, secretive, shifty, sly, sneaky, stealthy, surreptitious, wily. OPPOSITE open.

fury *noun* **1** *Her eyes were wild with fury.* anger, exasperation, frenzy, ire, rage, temper, wrath. **2** *the fury of the storm.* ferocity, intensity, might, violence.

fuse *verb The parts fused together.* amalgamate, blend, bond, coalesce, combine, consolidate, incorporate, merge, stick, synthesise, unite, weld. OPPOSITE separate.

fuss *noun a lot of fuss over nothing.* ado, bother, bustle, commotion, excitement, flurry, fluster, furore, hue and cry, hullabaloo, kerfuffle (*informal*), palaver (*informal*), rumpus, stir, to-do, uproar. — *verb She fussed over every little thing.* carry on, complain, create (*slang*), flap (*informal*), fret, niggle, quibble, worry.

fussy *adjective* **1** *a fussy person.* choosy (*informal*), faddy, fastidious, finicky, hard to please, particular, pernickety (*informal*), picky (*informal*), selective. OPPOSITE easygoing. **2** *a fussy design.* busy, cluttered, detailed, elaborate, fancy, intricate, ornate. OPPOSITE simple.

futile *adjective a futile attempt.* fruitless, ineffective, ineffectual, pointless, senseless, unproductive, unsuccessful, useless, vain, worthless. OPPOSITE effective.

future *adjective future programmes.* approaching, coming, forthcoming, prospective, subsequent. CONTRASTS WITH past, present. — *noun* **1** *no worries about the future.* hereafter, tomorrow. **2** *The future is promising.* outlook, prospect.

fuzzy *adjective* **1** *fuzzy material.* downy, fleecy, fluffy, frizzy, furry, woolly. **2** *fuzzy images.* blurred, dim, hazy, imprecise, indistinct, unclear, vague, woolly. OPPOSITE clear.

Gg

gabble *verb She gabbled unintelligibly.* babble, chatter, jabber, prattle, yabber (*Australian informal*).

gadget *noun a useful kitchen gadget.* apparatus, appliance, contraption (*informal*), device, gizmo (*informal*), implement, instrument, machine, tool, utensil.

gag *noun They laughed at his gags.* jest, joke, quip, wisecrack, witticism. — *verb* **1** *We cannot gag the press.* keep quiet, muzzle, silence, stifle. **2** *He gagged at the stench.* choke, gasp, retch.

gaiety *noun Christmas is a time of gaiety.* celebration, cheer, cheerfulness, festivity, fun, glee, happiness, hilarity, jollity, joy, merriment, merrymaking, mirth, revelry. OPPOSITE melancholy.

gain *verb* **1** *He gained the prize. She gained recognition.* achieve, acquire, attain, earn, get, obtain, procure, receive, score, secure, win. OPPOSITE forfeit, lose. **2** *They gained out of the sale.* make a profit, profit. OPPOSITE lose. **3** *He gained two kilos.* add on, increase, put on. OPPOSITE lose. **4** *The swimmer finally gained the shore.* arrive at, get to, reach. — *noun* **1** *a financial gain.* advantage, benefit, dividend, income, profit, return, reward, yield. OPPOSITE loss. **2** *a gain in weight.* increase, jump, rise. OPPOSITE loss. □ **gains** *plural noun illgotten gains.* booty, earnings, income, loot, proceeds, profits, takings, winnings.

gait *noun a distinctive gait.* carriage, pace, step, stride, tread, walk.

gala *noun The annual gala attracts a large crowd.* carnival, fair, festival, fête, pageant.

gale *noun The tree was blown over in the gale.* blast, cyclone, gust, hurricane, storm, tempest, tornado, typhoon, wind.

gall[1] *noun* (*slang*) *She had the gall to tell him he was wrong.* audacity, boldness, cheek, effrontery, hide, impertinence, impudence, nerve, temerity.

gall[2] *verb The strap galled the horse.* abrade, chafe, fret, rub.

gallant *adjective* **1** *a gallant officer.* brave, courageous, daring, dauntless, fearless, heroic, intrepid, lionhearted, manly, noble, valiant. OPPOSITE cowardly. **2** *a gallant man.* attentive, chivalrous, considerate, courteous, gentlemanly, gracious, kind, polite, suave. OPPOSITE discourteous.

gallery *noun* **1** *a gallery in a theatre.* balcony, circle, gods (*informal*). **2** *A gallery was attached to the building.* arcade, cloister, colonnade, loggia, portico, veranda. **3** *an art gallery.* hall, museum.

gallop *verb The horse galloped home.* bolt, bound, dash, fly, hurry, hurtle, race, run, rush, shoot, speed, sprint, tear, whiz.

gallows *noun He was hanged on the gallows.* gibbet, scaffold.

gamble *verb* **1** *She gambles on the horses.* bet, have a flutter (*informal*), punt. **2** *He gambled his week's wages.* bet, chance, risk, stake, venture, wager. — *noun The enterprise is a bit of a gamble.* chance, lottery, punt, risk, speculation, uncertainty.

gambler *noun Problem gamblers can be helped.* better, punter, speculator.

game *noun* **1** *They enjoy games.* amusement, diversion, entertainment, pastime, playing, recreation, sport. **2** *They won all their games in the tournament.* bout, competition, contest, event, match, round. — *adjective He wasn't game to tell them.* bold, brave, courageous, daring, fearless, intrepid, plucky; see also WILLING. OPPOSITE afraid.

gang *noun* **1** *a gang of road workers.* crew, relay, squad, team, troop. **2** *a gang of ruffians.* band, bunch, group, mob (*informal*), pack, push (*Australian old use*), set.

gangling *adjective a gangling youth.* gawky, lanky, lean, skinny, tall, thin, ungainly.

gangster *noun He got mixed up with a group of gangsters.* bandit, brigand, criminal, crook (*informal*), desperado, robber, ruffian, thug, tough.

gangway noun *A gangway was left between the seats.* aisle, gap, passage.

gaol noun & verb see JAIL.

gaoler noun see JAILER.

gap noun **1** *a narrow gap.* aisle, aperture, breach, break, chasm, crack, cranny, crevice, discontinuity, fissure, gangway, hole, opening, space. **2** *a gap between items in the concert.* break, hiatus, interlude, intermission, interval, lull, pause, recess. **3** *the gap between their views on religion.* chasm, difference, disparity, divergence, gulf.

gape verb **1** *He gaped at the magician.* gawp (*informal*), gaze, goggle, stare. **2** *The seam gaped.* come apart, open up, part, split open.

garage noun **1** *He parked the car in the garage.* shed. **2** *The garage serves petrol.* filling station, petrol station, service station, servo (*Australian informal*).

garbage noun *The garbage is collected once a week.* debris, junk, litter, refuse, rubbish, scraps, trash, waste.

garbled adjective *a garbled account.* confused, incoherent, jumbled, mixed-up, muddled, unclear.

garden noun *Each house has a garden.* allotment, grounds, lawn, patch, plot, yard.

garish adjective *a garish green car.* bright, flashy, gaudy, lairy (*Australian informal*), loud, showy, vivid. OPPOSITE unobtrusive.

garland noun *a garland of flowers.* festoon, lei, wreath.

garments plural noun *The shop sells ladies' garments.* apparel (*formal*), attire (*formal*), clothes, clothing, costume, dress, garb, gear (*informal*), outfit, raiment (*old use*), vestments, wear.

garnish verb *The soup was garnished with coriander.* decorate, embellish.

garrison noun *an army garrison.* citadel, fort, fortress, stronghold. — verb *Troops garrisoned the town.* defend, guard, occupy, protect.

garrulous adjective *a garrulous companion.* chatty, long-winded, loquacious, talkative, verbose, voluble, wordy. OPPOSITE taciturn.

gas noun *He breathed in the gas.* exhaust, fumes, vapour.

gash noun *a deep gash in the leg.* cut, laceration, slash, slit, tear, wound. — verb *She gashed her arm on the spikes.* cut, lacerate, slash, slit, tear, wound.

gasp verb *He gasped for air.* choke, pant, puff, wheeze.

gate noun *Enter via gate 2.* barrier, door, entrance, entry, exit, gateway, portal, portcullis, postern, turnstile.

gather verb **1** *The people gathered outside the church.* assemble, cluster, concentrate, congregate, convene, crowd, flock, herd, mass, meet, rally, rendezvous, swarm, throng. OPPOSITE disperse. **2** *He gathered his forces.* marshal, mobilise, muster, rally, round up, summon. **3** *He gathered supplies for the winter.* accumulate, amass, collect, hoard, pile up, stack up, stockpile, store. **4** *They gathered mushrooms.* collect, garner, glean, harvest, pick, pluck, reap. **5** *The car gathered speed.* gain, increase, pick up. **6** *I gather your proposal was accepted.* conclude, infer, learn, surmise, take it, understand. **7** *She gathered the fabric.* ruffle, shirr.

gathering noun *a gathering of all her relatives.* assembly, collection, congregation, congress, convention, crowd, flock, get-together (*informal*), group, meeting, mob, muster, party, rally, reunion, social, swarm, throng.

gaudy adjective *He wore a gaudy orange shirt.* bright, colourful, flamboyant, flashy, garish, jazzy, lairy (*Australian informal*), loud, lurid, showy, tawdry, vivid. OPPOSITE drab.

gauge noun **1** *heavy-gauge wire.* diameter, thickness. **2** *a gauge of their support.* guide, indicator, measure, yardstick. **3** *The amount registered on the gauge.* meter, scale. — verb *It is easy to gauge their interest.* assess, determine, estimate, judge, measure.

gaunt adjective *He lost too much weight and looked gaunt.* bony, cadaverous, emaciated, haggard, lanky, lean, scraggy, scrawny, skeletal, skinny, thin. OPPOSITE fat.

gauzy adjective *gauzy fabric.* diaphanous, fine, flimsy, light, see-through, sheer, thin, transparent. OPPOSITE coarse, thick.

gay adjective **1** *The mood was gay.* blithe, bright, carefree, cheerful, happy, jolly, jovial, light-hearted, lively, merry. OPPOSITE glum, unhappy. **2** *gay colours.* bright, colourful, gaudy, showy, vivid. OPPOSITE dull. **3** *gay rights.* homosexual, lesbian (*female*). OPPOSITE heterosexual.

gaze verb *gaze at* *They gazed at the scene.* behold (*old use*), contemplate, eye, gape at, gawp at (*informal*), look at, observe, peer at, stare at, study, survey, view, watch. — noun *She shifted her gaze.* look, stare.

gear noun **1** *fishing gear.* apparatus, appliances, equipment, implements, instruments, kit, materials, outfit, paraphernalia, rig, stuff, tackle, things, tools. **2** (*informal*) *Dress in casual gear.* apparel (*formal*), attire (*formal*), clothes, clothing, dress, garments, get-up (*informal*), outfit, rig (*informal*), wear.

geld verb *The vet gelded the animal.* castrate, desex, doctor, neuter, spay, sterilise.

gem noun *a bangle studded with gems.* gemstone, jewel, precious stone.

genealogy noun *She traced her genealogy back 200 years.* ancestry, family history, lineage, pedigree.

general adjective **1** *His idea received general support.* broad, common, extensive, global, overall, popular, public, sweeping, universal, wholesale, widespread, worldwide. OPPOSITE local. **2** *good general knowledge.* all-round, broad, comprehensive, encyclopedic. OPPOSITE specialised. **3** *She drives them to school as a general rule.* customary, everyday, familiar, habitual, normal, ordinary, regular, standard, typical, usual. OPPOSITE exceptional. **4** *She spoke only in general terms.* broad, imprecise, indefinite, vague. OPPOSITE specific. **5** *the general secretary.* chief, head, principal.

generally adverb **1** *He is generally happy.* by and large, for the most part, in general, largely, mainly, mostly, normally, on the whole, usually. OPPOSITE rarely. **2** *The rules apply generally.* across the board, always, everywhere, globally, universally. OPPOSITE locally.

generate verb *She could not generate any enthusiasm.* bring about, create, drum up, give rise to, inspire, produce, whip up.

generosity noun *The institution relies on your generosity.* benevolence, bounty, charity, largesse, liberality, magnanimity, munificence, philanthropy.

generous adjective **1** *a generous giver.* benevolent, big-hearted, bountiful, charitable, kind-hearted, lavish, magnanimous, munificent, open-handed, philanthropic, selfless, unselfish, unstinting. OPPOSITE

mean. 2 *a generous amount.* abundant, ample, copious, lavish, liberal, plentiful, sizeable. OPPOSITE meagre.

genesis noun *the genesis of an idea.* beginning, birth, commencement, creation, inception, origin, start. OPPOSITE end.

genial adjective *genial people.* affable, amiable, congenial, convivial, cordial, easygoing, friendly, hospitable, kind, outgoing, pleasant, sociable, warm-hearted. OPPOSITE unfriendly.

genius noun **1** *She was a true genius.* brain (*informal*), expert, know-all, mastermind, prodigy, virtuoso, whiz-kid (*informal*). OPPOSITE moron. **2** *a man of genius.* ability, aptitude, brains, brilliance, intellect, intelligence, talent. OPPOSITE stupidity.

genteel adjective *They were taught to be genteel.* civil, courteous, courtly, gentlemanly, ladylike, mannerly, polite, posh (*informal*), refined, well-bred, well-mannered. OPPOSITE boorish.

gentle adjective **1** *a gentle breeze.* balmy, faint, light, mild, moderate, soft. OPPOSITE strong. **2** *a gentle voice.* calm, mild, pleasant, quiet, soft, soothing, sweet, tender. OPPOSITE raucous. **3** *a gentle person.* benign, compassionate, humane, kind, kind-hearted, kindly, lenient, meek, merciful, mild, peaceful, placid, serene, soft-hearted, sympathetic, tender-hearted. OPPOSITE harsh, rough. **4** *a gentle animal.* docile, harmless, manageable, meek, placid, tame. OPPOSITE wild. **5** *a gentle slope.* easy, gradual, moderate, slight. OPPOSITE steep. **6** *a gentle hint.* faint, indirect, mild, slight, subtle. OPPOSITE strong.

genuine adjective **1** *the genuine article.* actual, authentic, bona fide, dinkum (*Australian informal*), dinky-di (*Australian informal*), honest-to-goodness (*informal*), kosher (*informal*), real, ridgy-didge (*Australian informal*), true. OPPOSITE fake. **2** *He showed genuine concern.* heartfelt, honest, real, sincere, true. OPPOSITE insincere.

germ noun *Cleanliness prevents the spread of these germs.* bacterium, bug (*informal*), microbe, micro-organism, virus.

germinate verb *The seeds germinated after a week.* come up, grow, shoot, spring up, sprout.

gesture noun *Her gestures indicated her true feelings.* action, gesticulation, motion, movement, sign, signal. — verb *He gestured to them to approach.* beckon, gesticulate, motion, nod, point, signal, wave.

get verb **1** *She got a new book.* acquire, be given, buy, come by, get hold of, obtain, procure, purchase, receive. **2** *He got all the prizes.* earn, gain, land, receive, scoop, score, take, win. OPPOSITE lose. **3** *Go and get your umbrella.* bring, collect, fetch, pick up, retrieve. **4** *She has got a cold.* be afflicted with, catch, come down with, contract, develop, pick up, suffer from. **5** *The police will get the culprit.* arrest, capture, catch, grab, nab (*informal*), seize. **6** *Try to get his attention.* attract, capture, catch, draw. **7** (*informal*) *He didn't get what I meant.* comprehend, cotton on to (*informal*), fathom, follow, grasp, realise, understand. OPPOSITE misunderstand. **8** *I'll get lunch now.* fix, make ready, prepare. **9** *Try to get him to eat.* cause, convince, induce, influence, make, persuade. OPPOSITE dissuade. **10** *The days are getting longer.* become, grow. **11** *How do you get to work?* go, journey, travel. **12** *He got home late.* arrive at,

reach. □ **get at** (*informal*) *What are you getting at?* drive at, hint at, imply, insinuate, mean, suggest. **get away** *The thieves got away in a stolen car.* abscond, bolt, break free, decamp, depart, do a bunk (*slang*), escape, flee, leave, nick off (*Australian slang*), push off (*informal*), scarper, shoot through (*Australian informal*), slip away. OPPOSITE stay. **get back 1** *She got her money back.* recoup, recover, regain, retrieve. **2** *Things got back to normal.* go back, return. **get down** *The rider got down.* dismount, get off. **get off** *The passengers all got off.* alight, descend, disembark, get out. **get on 1** *The man got on the bus.* board, climb on. **2** *He got on his horse.* mount. **3** *How's she getting on?* cope, fare, get along, make out (*informal*), manage. **get out of** *She got out of doing the cleaning again.* avoid, dodge, escape, evade, shirk, wriggle out of. **get over 1** *He got over the problem.* master, overcome, surmount. **2** *He has got over his illness.* pull through, recover from, survive. **get through** *He got through his exam.* pass, succeed in. OPPOSITE fail. **get up** *She gets up at 7 o'clock.* arise (*old use*), rise, surface. OPPOSITE retire. **get your own back** (*informal*) *He was determined to get his own back.* get even, have your revenge, pay back, retaliate.

getaway noun *He made a quick getaway.* escape, flight, retreat.

get-together noun (*informal*) *The friends arranged a get-together.* function, gathering, meeting, party, rendezvous, reunion, social.

ghastly adjective **1** *a ghastly accident.* appalling, awful, dreadful, frightful, gruesome, hideous, horrendous, horrible, repulsive, shocking, terrible. **2** *He looked ghastly.* ashen, deathly, ghostly, pale, pallid, pasty, sickly, wan, washed out. OPPOSITE blooming, healthy.

ghost noun *He doesn't believe in ghosts.* apparition, phantom, poltergeist, shade, spectre, spirit, spook (*informal*), vision, wraith.

ghostly adjective *ghostly noises.* creepy, eerie, sinister, spooky (*informal*), uncanny, unearthly, weird.

ghoulish adjective *a ghoulish interest in accidents.* gruesome, macabre, morbid.

giant noun *a fairy-tale giant.* monster, ogre, Titan. OPPOSITE dwarf. — adjective see GIGANTIC.

gibberish noun *He was talking gibberish.* babble, double Dutch, drivel, gobbledegook (*informal*), jabber, mumbo-jumbo, nonsense, poppycock (*slang*), rubbish, twaddle.

gibe verb *gibe at* *They gibed at the boy's mispronunciations.* chiack (*Australian informal*), jeer at, make fun of, mock, poke borak at (*Australian informal*), ridicule, scoff at, sling off at (*Australian informal*), sneer at, taunt, tease.

giddiness noun dizziness, light-headedness, unsteadiness, vertigo.

giddy adjective *He felt giddy standing on the roof.* dizzy, faint, light-headed, unsteady. OPPOSITE steady.

gift noun **1** *a generous gift.* alms, bequest, bonus, contribution, donation, endowment, freebie (*informal*), give-away (*informal*), gratuity, handout, legacy, offering, offertory, present, tip. **2** *He has a gift for mathematics.* ability, aptitude, facility, flair, genius, head, knack, talent.

gifted adjective *a gifted pupil.* able, accomplished, bright, brilliant, capable, clever, intelligent, skilful, skilled, talented. OPPOSITE inept.

gig *noun* (*informal*) *The band has a gig at our local pub.* performance, show.

gigantic *adjective a gigantic building.* big, boomer (*Australian informal*), colossal, enormous, extensive, gargantuan, giant, ginormous (*slang*), huge, humungous (*slang*), immeasurable, immense, jumbo-sized, king-sized, large, mammoth, massive, mighty, monstrous, monumental, prodigious, stupendous, tremendous, vast, whopping (*slang*). OPPOSITE small, tiny.

giggle *verb She giggled nervously.* chuckle, laugh, snicker, snigger, titter. — *noun He let out a giggle.* chuckle, laugh, snicker, snigger, titter.

gimmick *noun an advertising gimmick.* device, ploy, stratagem, trick.

gingerly *adverb She touched the controls gingerly.* carefully, cautiously, charily, timidly, warily. OPPOSITE confidently.

gird *verb The city is girded by a wall.* encircle, enclose, encompass, ring, surround. □ **gird yourself** *The soldiers girded themselves for battle.* brace yourself, gird up your loins, prepare yourself, steel yourself.

girdle *noun* **1** *He tied the robe with a girdle.* belt, cord. **2** *She wears a girdle to pull her stomach in.* corset, stays (*old use*), truss.

girl *noun* babe (*informal*), bird (*informal*), chick (*slang*), damsel (*old use*), female, gal (*informal*), lass, lassie (*informal*), maid (*old use*), maiden (*old use*), miss, schoolgirl, sheila (*Australian slang*); see also CHILD, WOMAN.

girlfriend *noun Sam took his girl friend to dinner.* date (*informal*), female friend, fiancée, steady, sweetheart.

girth *noun He measured his girth.* circumference, perimeter.

gist *noun the gist of a speech.* content, core, drift, essence, meaning, pith, point, substance.

give *verb* **1** *He gave them money.* allot, allow, award, bestow, deal out, dish out (*informal*), distribute, dole out, endow with, entrust with, equip with, furnish with, grant, hand out, hand over, offer, pay, present, proffer, provide with, ration out, supply with. OPPOSITE receive, take. **2** *They give to various charities.* contribute, donate, subscribe. **3** *He gave me the message.* communicate, convey, deliver, impart, pass on, report, tell, transmit. **4** *She gave a scream.* emit, let out, utter. **5** *The children give an annual show.* perform, play, present, put on, stage. **6** *They gave a party.* hold, host, organise, provide, put on, throw (*informal*). **7** *The chair will give under her weight.* break, buckle, collapse, crack, fold up, give way, yield. □ **give away 1** *She gave away the old clothes.* cast off, discard, part with, throw out, toss out. **2** *She gave away their secret.* betray, blab, divulge, leak, let out, make known, reveal. **give back** *They gave back the deposit.* pay back, refund, reimburse, repay, return. OPPOSITE retain. **give in** *He will fight and not give in.* capitulate, cave in, concede, give up, submit, succumb, surrender, yield. **give off** *It gave off a strong smell.* discharge, emit, exude, give out, release. **give out 1** *The candle gives out light.* emit, produce, put out, radiate, shed. **2** *The supply gave out.* dry up (*informal*), fail, peter out, run out, stop. **give up 1** *He gave up smoking.* cease, discontinue, give away (*Australian*), quit, stop. OPPOSITE continue. **2** *She gave up her job.* abandon, chuck in (*informal*), leave, quit, resign, retire from. OPPOSITE keep. **3** *He gave up his rights.* cede, forfeit, forgo, relinquish, renounce, sacrifice, surrender, waive. OPPOSITE retain. **4** *Her opponent gave up.* capitulate, concede, give in, retire, surrender, throw in the towel, throw up the sponge, yield. OPPOSITE persevere. **give way** *The bridge gave way under the car's weight.* break, buckle, cave in, collapse, crumble, give, snap.

giver *noun a generous giver.* benefactor, contributor, donor, sponsor.

glad *adjective* **1** *They were glad to hear he was well.* delighted, gratified, happy, joyful, pleased, thrilled. OPPOSITE sorry. **2** *the glad tidings.* cheerful, good, happy, joyful, pleasing, welcome. OPPOSITE sad.

gladden *verb The news gladdened their hearts.* brighten, cheer, delight, please. OPPOSITE sadden.

glamorous *adjective a glamorous woman.* attractive, beautiful, bewitching, charming, elegant, exciting, fascinating. OPPOSITE unattractive.

glance *verb He glanced through the advertisements.* look, peek, peep, scan, skim. — *noun He took a glance at the paper.* glimpse, look, peek, peep, squiz (*Australian slang*).

glare *verb She glared at them.* frown, glower, lour, scowl, stare. — *noun* **1** *sun glare.* brightness, dazzle, radiance. **2** *He gave them a hard glare.* black look, frown, glower, lour, scowl, stare.

glaring *adjective* **1** *glaring headlights.* blinding, bright, dazzling, harsh, strong. OPPOSITE dim. **2** *glaring inconsistencies.* blatant, conspicuous, flagrant, obvious, patent, plain, unmistakable. OPPOSITE subtle.

glass *noun* **1** *She polished the glass.* crystal, pane, plate glass. **2** *She admired herself in the glass.* looking-glass, mirror. **3** *She drinks from a glass.* beaker, goblet, tumbler, wineglass. □ **glasses** *plural noun optical glasses.* binoculars, field glasses, goggles, opera glasses, pince-nez, specs (*informal*), spectacles, sunglasses.

glasshouse *noun These plants grow best in a glasshouse.* conservatory, greenhouse, hothouse.

glassy *adjective* **1** *a glassy surface.* reflective, shiny, smooth, vitreous. **2** *a glassy look.* blank, deadpan, expressionless, fixed, glazed, vacant.

glaze *noun the glaze on the pots.* enamel, finish, lustre.

gleam *noun a gleam of light.* beam, flash, glimmer, glint, ray, shaft, shimmer, spark. — *verb The sink gleamed.* flash, glimmer, glisten, shimmer, shine, sparkle.

glean *verb They were in the fields gleaning grain. He did not glean any information.* collect, garner, gather, harvest, obtain, pick up.

glee *noun She jumped with glee.* cheerfulness, delight, ecstasy, elation, excitement, exhilaration, happiness, joy, jubilation, mirth. OPPOSITE misery.

gleeful *adjective the gleeful birthday girl.* cheerful, chuffed (*slang*), delighted, ecstatic, elated, excited, exhilarated, exuberant, exultant, glad, happy, joyful, jubilant, merry, pleased. OPPOSITE miserable.

glib *adjective a glib answer.* facile, offhand, pat, ready, slick, smooth. OPPOSITE considered, sincere.

glide *verb* **1** *The skaters glided on the ice.* aquaplane, coast, glissade, skate, skid, skim, slide, slip. **2** *The trapeze artists glide through the air.* drift, float, fly, sail, soar.

glimmer *noun* **1** *a glimmer of light.* flash, flicker, gleam, glint, glow, ray, shimmer, sparkle. **2** *a glimmer of hope.* flicker, gleam, ray, spark, speck. — *verb The city lights glimmered.* flicker, gleam, glint, glow, shimmer, shine, twinkle.

glimpse *noun He caught a brief glimpse.* glance, look, peek, peep, squiz (*Australian slang*), view. — *verb She glimpsed a bird in the tree.* catch sight of, discern, espy, notice, peep at, see, sight, spot.

glint *noun the glint in his eye.* flash, gleam, sparkle. — *verb The metal glinted in the sun.* flash, gleam, glimmer, glisten, glitter, shine, sparkle, twinkle.

glisten *verb The bath glistened after being cleaned.* gleam, shimmer, shine, sparkle.

glitch *noun* (*informal*) *a computer glitch.* bug (*informal*), fault, hitch, irregularity, malfunction, problem.

glitter *verb All that glitters is not gold.* glimmer, scintillate, shimmer, shine, sparkle, twinkle. — *noun the glitter of crystal.* gleam, sparkle, twinkle. OPPOSITE dullness.

glittering *adjective a glittering display.* brilliant, dazzling, glitzy (*slang*), resplendent, splendid.

gloat *verb She gloated over her success.* crow, delight, exult, glory, rejoice, revel; see also BOAST.

global *adjective a global problem.* general, international, universal, widespread, worldwide. OPPOSITE local.

globe *noun* **1** *a light globe.* ball, bulb, sphere. **2** *He has travelled the globe.* earth, world.

gloom *noun* **1** *He could not see much in the gloom.* darkness, dimness, dusk, gloaming, semi-darkness, shadows, twilight. OPPOSITE brightness. **2** *a feeling of gloom.* dejection, depression, despair, glumness, melancholy, misery, pessimism, sadness, unhappiness, woe. OPPOSITE cheerfulness.

gloomy *adjective* **1** *a gloomy day.* black, bleak, cheerless, cloudy, dark, depressing, dismal, dreary, dull, murky, overcast. OPPOSITE sunny. **2** *a gloomy man. a gloomy expression.* depressed, desolate, dismal, doleful, down-hearted, funereal, glum, heavy-hearted, lugubrious, melancholy, moody, morbid, morose, mournful, pessimistic, sad, saturnine, sombre, sullen, unhappy. OPPOSITE cheerful.

glorify *verb The people glorified God.* adore, exalt, extol, hallow, honour, laud (*formal*), magnify (*old use*), praise, revere, venerate, worship. OPPOSITE denigrate.

glorious *adjective* **1** *a glorious achievement.* famous, grand, heroic, illustrious, impressive, noble. OPPOSITE inglorious. **2** *a glorious day.* beautiful, brilliant, excellent, fine, gorgeous, grand, magnificent, majestic, marvellous, spectacular, splendid, stunning, sublime, superb, terrific (*informal*), wonderful. OPPOSITE dull.

glory *noun* **1** *Her success brought glory to her school.* credit, distinction, esteem, fame, honour, kudos (*informal*), prestige, renown. OPPOSITE shame. **2** *glory to God.* adoration, exaltation, honour, praise, reverence, veneration, worship. OPPOSITE blasphemy. **3** *the glory of a sunset.* beauty, grandeur, greatness, magnificence, majesty, splendour. — *verb They gloried in their success.* delight, exult, pride yourself, rejoice, revel, take pride.

gloss *noun The woodwork has a high gloss.* brightness, gleam, lustre, polish, sheen, shine, sparkle. □ **gloss over** *He glossed over their faults.* conceal, cover up, hide, make light of, whitewash. OPPOSITE emphasise, highlight.

glossy *adjective glossy paint.* gleaming, glistening, lustrous, shining, shiny, sleek. OPPOSITE matt.

glove *noun* gauntlet, mitt, mitten.

glow *verb* **1** *The fire glowed.* gleam, radiate, shine, smoulder. **2** *Her cheeks glowed.* blush, colour, flush, redden, shine. OPPOSITE pale. — *noun* **1** *the glow from the fire.* brightness, gleam, heat, incandescence, light, luminosity, radiance, warmth. **2** *a healthy glow.* blush, colour, flush, radiance, redness, rosiness, ruddiness. OPPOSITE pallor.

glower *verb She stopped speaking when he glowered at her.* frown, glare, lour, scowl, stare. OPPOSITE smile.

glue *noun stuck with glue.* adhesive, cement, gum, paste. — *verb She glued the parts together.* affix, attach, cement, fasten, gum, paste, stick.

gluey *adjective a gluey mixture.* adhesive, gluggy (*informal*), glutinous, sticky, tacky, viscous.

glum *adjective He was all alone, feeling glum.* cheerless, crestfallen, depressed, despondent, doleful, down-hearted, down in the mouth, forlorn, gloomy, melancholy, miserable, moody, morose, mournful, sad, unhappy, woebegone. OPPOSITE cheerful.

glut *verb* **1** *The suppliers glutted the market.* flood, inundate, oversupply, saturate, swamp. **2** *They glutted themselves with cake.* cram, gorge, overfill, satiate, stuff. — *noun a glut of potatoes.* excess, overabundance, oversupply, superfluity, surfeit, surplus. OPPOSITE shortage.

glutton *noun* gormandiser, gourmand, greedy-guts (*informal*), guts (*informal*), guzzler, hog (*informal*), pig (*informal*).

gluttonous *adjective* greedy, gutsy (*slang*), insatiable, voracious.

gnarled *adjective a gnarled tree trunk.* distorted, knobbly, knotty, lumpy, misshapen, rough, twisted. OPPOSITE smooth.

gnash *verb He gnashed his teeth in fury.* grate, grind.

gnaw *verb She gnawed a carrot.* bite, chew, chomp, crunch, eat, munch, nibble.

gnome *noun* dwarf, elf, goblin, troll.

go *verb* **1** *He is going home.* head for, journey, make for, nip (*informal*), pop, proceed, set out for, start for, take yourself off, travel, visit, wend your way, zip off; see also ADVANCE. **2** *It's time to go.* beat it (*slang*), be off, buzz off (*slang*), clear off (*informal*), decamp, depart, disappear, exit, get away, go away, hop it (*slang*), leave, make tracks (*informal*), make yourself scarce, nick off (*Australian slang*), push off (*informal*), retire, retreat, run off, scarper (*informal*), scoot, scram (*informal*), set off, shoot through (*Australian informal*), shove off (*informal*), skedaddle (*informal*), take your leave, take yourself off, vanish, withdraw. OPPOSITE arrive. **3** *The road goes to Mannum.* extend, lead, reach, run, stretch. **4** *The car won't go.* function, move, operate, perform, run, work. **5** *The time went quickly.* elapse, pass, slip by. **6** *The glasses go in this case.* belong, fit. **7** *The milk went sour.* become, turn. **8** *Things went well.* fare, proceed, progress, turn out, work out. **9** *The money has all gone.* be spent, be used, dry up, run out. **10** *The elastic has gone.* disintegrate, fail, give way, perish. — *noun* **1** *a man with plenty of go.* dash, drive, dynamism, energy, get-up-and-go (*informal*), oomph (*informal*), pep, vigour, vim (*informal*), vivacity, zip.

2 (*informal*) *Have a go at it.* attempt, bash (*informal*), crack (*informal*), shot, stab (*informal*), try, turn. □ **go about** *He went about the task the wrong way.* approach, attack, deal with, handle, set about, tackle, undertake. **go across** *He went across their land.* cross, cut across, traverse. **go after** *The police went after the speeding motorist.* chase, follow, pursue, tail (*informal*), track, trail. OPPOSITE precede. **go along with** *We don't go along with their ideas.* agree with, be in sympathy with, concur with, subscribe to. **go back on** *She went back on her word.* break, recant, renege on, repudiate. OPPOSITE keep. **go back to** *He went back to his former habits.* resume, return to, revert to. **go before** *I allowed her to go before me on the path.* lead, precede. OPPOSITE follow. **go beyond** *The amount we raised went beyond our expctations.* exceed, pass, surpass, transcend. **go for** *She always goes for the dearest item.* choose, opt for, plump for, prefer. **go off** **1** *The bomb went off.* blow up, detonate, explode. **2** *The meat went off.* decay, deteriorate, go bad, go rotten, perish, rot, spoil. OPPOSITE keep. **go on** **1** *They went on with their work.* carry on, continue, keep on, persevere, persist, proceed. **2** (*informal*) *He kept going on about the olden days.* bang on (*informal*), carry on (*informal*), drone on, harp on, rabbit on (*informal*), ramble on, waffle (*informal*), witter on (*informal*). **go over 1** *Let's go over the evidence.* examine, recap (*informal*), recapitulate, review. **2** *The actor goes over his lines.* practise, rehearse, run through. **go round** *The wheel goes round.* circle, gyrate, orbit, revolve, rotate, spin, swirl, swivel, turn, twirl, whirl. **go through 1** *The arrow went through his heart.* enter, penetrate, pierce, puncture. **2** *He has gone through an ordeal.* bear, endure, experience, suffer, undergo. **3** *They went through his papers.* check, inspect, look through, search, sift through. **go up 1** *We'll go up the stairs.* ascend, climb, mount. OPPOSITE descend. **2** *Prices are going up.* escalate, increase, rise, rocket, soar. OPPOSITE fall. **go with 1** *She went with them.* accompany, escort. **2** *The shoes go with the dress.* match, suit. OPPOSITE clash with. **go without** *She went without meat during Lent.* be deprived of, deny yourself, do without, forgo, give up, sacrifice.

goad *verb His friends goaded him into retaliating.* drive, egg on, incite, prod, prompt, provoke, sool (*Australian informal*), spur, stimulate, urge.

go-ahead *adjective a go-ahead employee.* ambitious, dynamic, energetic, enterprising, forward-looking, progressive.

goal *noun They worked towards a common goal.* aim, ambition, end, object, objective, purpose, target.

goat *noun* billy goat, he-goat, kid, nanny goat.

gobble *verb He gobbled his food and left.* bolt, devour, gulp, guzzle, scoff (*informal*), wolf.

gobbledegook *noun* (*informal*) *He didn't understand any of their gobbledegook.* double Dutch, gibberish, humbug, jargon, mumbo-jumbo, nonsense.

go-between *noun The two sides appointed Darren to act as a go-between.* agent, broker, intermediary, liaison, mediator, messenger, middleman, negotiator.

goblin *noun Goblins only exist in fairy tales.* bogy, elf, gnome, hobgoblin, imp, leprechaun, sprite.

go-cart *noun* billycart, hill trolley.

god *noun The Greeks worshipped many gods.* deity, divinity. □ **God** *They worship God as creator and ruler of the universe.* Allah, the Almighty, the Creator, the Father, Jehovah, the Lord, our Maker, Yahweh.

goddess *noun a Roman goddess.* deity, divinity.

godless *adjective a godless society.* atheistic, evil, heathen, impious, irreligious, pagan, sacrilegious, ungodly, wicked. OPPOSITE God-fearing.

godly *adjective a godly man.* devout, God-fearing, holy, pious, religious, saintly. OPPOSITE ungodly.

godsend *noun The lottery prize was a godsend.* blessing, bonanza, boon, windfall.

gold *adjective a gold frame.* gilded, gilt, golden, gold-plated.

golden *adjective* **1** *golden curls.* blond, flaxen, gold, yellow. **2** *a golden opportunity.* excellent, favourable, precious, priceless, valuable, wonderful.

good *adjective* **1** *good food.* beneficial, delicious, healthy, nutritious, scrumptious (*informal*), tasty, wholesome. OPPOSITE harmful. **2** *a good reason for not attending.* cogent, genuine, legitimate, powerful, satisfactory, solid, sound, strong, valid. OPPOSITE weak. **3** *He made a good decision.* appropriate, fitting, judicious, proper, prudent, right, sensible, wise. OPPOSITE bad. **4** *You have called at a good time.* advantageous, auspicious, beneficial, convenient, desirable, favourable, fortunate, lucky, opportune, propitious, suitable. OPPOSITE adverse, bad. **5** *a good person.* benevolent, benign, blameless, considerate, decent, ethical, godly, holy, honest, honourable, innocent, just, kind, law-abiding, moral, noble, righteous, upright, virtuous, well-intentioned, well-meaning, worthy. OPPOSITE wicked. **6** *good conduct.* admirable, commendable, correct, exemplary, honourable, meritorious, praiseworthy, worthy. OPPOSITE unseemly. **7** *a good child.* biddable, courteous, dutiful, helpful, obedient, polite, well-behaved, well-mannered. OPPOSITE ill-mannered, naughty. **8** *We had a good time.* agreeable, cool (*informal*), delightful, enjoyable, excellent, fabulous (*informal*), fantastic (*informal*), fine, great (*informal*), happy, lovely, marvellous, nice, outstanding, pleasant, satisfying, superb, swell (*informal*), terrific (*informal*), tremendous (*informal*), wonderful. OPPOSITE rotten. **9** *a good player. a good worker.* able, accomplished, adept, capable, competent, conscientious, dependable, diligent, effective, efficient, expert, first-rate, professional, proficient, reliable, skilful, skilled, sound, thorough. OPPOSITE poor. — *noun* **1** *Look for the good in people.* goodness, merit, virtue. OPPOSITE bad, evil. **2** *The exercise is for his own good.* advantage, benefit, interest, profit, welfare, well-being. OPPOSITE harm. □ **good point** *The plan has its good points.* advantage, merit, strength, strong point, virtue. OPPOSITE drawback, weakness.

goodbye *interjection & noun* adieu, au revoir, bon voyage, bye-bye (*informal*), cheerio (*informal*), cheers (*informal*), ciao (*informal*), farewell, hooray (*Australian informal*), see you (*informal*), see you later (*informal*), so long (*informal*), ta-ta (*informal*).

good-looking *adjective* attractive, beautiful, bonny (*Scottish*), comely, fair (*old use*), fetching, handsome, lovely, personable, pretty. OPPOSITE plain.

good-natured *adjective* benevolent, big-hearted, compassionate, easy-going, forgiving, friendly, generous, genial, gracious, helpful, kind, kind-hearted, kindly, obliging, sympathetic, tender-hearted, thoughtful, tolerant, unselfish. OPPOSITE unkind.

goodness *noun She trusted in the goodness of strangers.* benevolence, generosity, honour, integrity, kindness, merit, morality, probity, rectitude, righteousness, virtue. OPPOSITE evil.

goods *plural noun* **1** *one's worldly goods.* belongings, chattels, effects, possessions, property, things. **2** *a tax on goods and services.* articles, commodities, merchandise, products, wares. **3** *a goods train.* cargo, freight.

good-tempered *adjective* affable, amiable, amicable, cheerful, easy-going, even-tempered, gentle, good-humoured, happy, happy-go-lucky, jovial, mild, pleasant. OPPOSITE peevish, testy.

goodwill *noun an act of goodwill towards a stranger.* benevolence, charity, friendliness, grace, kindness. OPPOSITE hostility.

gooey *adjective* (*informal*) *a gooey mixture.* gluey, mushy, slimy, sloppy, sludgy, slushy, squidgy, sticky, tacky, viscous.

goose *noun* gander (*male*), gosling (*young*).

gore *verb The bull gored the man.* pierce, poke, puncture, wound.

gorge *noun They drove through the gorge.* canyon, chasm, gully, pass, ravine, valley. — *verb She gorged herself on cakes.* feast, fill, glut, overeat, satiate, stuff. OPPOSITE starve.

gorgeous *adjective* **1** *a gorgeous tapestry.* colourful, exquisite, magnificent, rich, splendid, sumptuous. OPPOSITE drab. **2** *a gorgeous woman.* attractive, beautiful, good-looking, smashing (*informal*), stunning (*informal*). OPPOSITE ugly.

gory *adjective a gory film.* bloody, grisly, gruesome, macabre, sanguinary, violent.

gossamer *adjective gossamer wings.* delicate, diaphanous, fine, flimsy, gauzy, light, sheer, transparent.

gossip *noun* **1** *a piece of idle gossip.* backbiting, chit-chat, hearsay, rumour, scandal, talk, tittle-tattle. **2** *Don't tell her your secrets. She's a gossip.* busybody, gossip-monger, rumour-monger, scandalmonger, tattler. — *verb They gossiped for hours.* blab, chat, natter (*informal*), prattle, tattle, tell tales, tittle-tattle.

got see GET.

gouge *verb She gouged out a hole in the log.* bore, chisel, cut, dig, groove, hollow, incise, scoop.

gourmet *noun The restaurant tries to please gourmets.* connoisseur, epicure, foodie (*informal*), gastronome.

govern *verb Who governs the country?* administer, be in charge of, command, control, direct, guide, head, lead, manage, reign over, rule, run, superintend, supervise.

government *noun the government of the country.* administration, command, control, leadership, management, regime, rule.

governor *noun the governor of a province, state, etc.* administrator, chief, head, ruler, viceroy.

gown *noun The woman was wearing a long gown.* dress, frock, habit, kimono, robe, vestment.

grab *verb He grabbed her handbag.* clasp, clutch, grasp, hold, nab (*informal*), pluck, seize, snatch, swipe (*informal*). OPPOSITE release.

grace *noun* **1** *She dances with grace.* elegance, gracefulness, poise, smoothness. OPPOSITE clumsiness. **2** *The teacher gave him a week's grace.* extension, postponement, reprieve. **3** *the grace of God.* favour, forbearance, forgiveness, goodness, goodwill, lenience, mercy. **4** *They said grace before eating.* benediction, blessing, prayer, thanksgiving.

graceful *adjective a graceful dancer.* agile, elegant, limber, lissom, lithe, nimble, supple. OPPOSITE clumsy, ungainly.

gracious *adjective* **1** *a gracious person.* amiable, benevolent, benign, courteous, friendly, good-natured, hospitable, kind, kindly, merciful, polite, tactful. **2** *gracious living.* elegant, luxurious, refined.

grade *noun* **1** *several grades of potatoes.* category, class, level, quality, standard. **2** *a student's grade for an essay.* assessment, mark, rank, rating, result, score. **3** *What grade are you in at school?* class, form, year. — *verb* **1** *The wool has been graded.* class, classify, rank, sort. **2** *The teacher graded the assignments.* assess, mark, rate, score.

• **gradient** *noun The road has a steep gradient.* grade, hill, incline, slope.

gradual *adjective a gradual increase.* gentle, piecemeal, progressive, slow, steady. OPPOSITE sharp, sudden.

gradually *adverb The patient gradually improved.* bit by bit, by degrees, little by little, progressively, slowly, steadily, step by step.

grain *noun* **1** *Birds eat grain.* cereal, corn, granule, grist, kernel, seed. **2** *a grain of sand.* bit, particle, speck. **3** *a grain of truth.* bit, hint, jot, ounce, shred, skerrick (*Australian informal*), trace.

grand *adjective* **1** *a grand house.* elegant, glorious, imposing, impressive, large, luxurious, magnificent, majestic, opulent, palatial, posh (*informal*), splendid, stately, sumptuous, superb. OPPOSITE humble. **2** (*informal*) *We had a grand time.* brilliant (*informal*), excellent, fine, first-rate, great (*informal*), marvellous, splendid, superb. OPPOSITE bad. **3** *the grand total.* all-inclusive, complete, comprehensive, full.

grandeur *noun the grandeur of the occasion.* dignity, magnificence, majesty, pomp, splendour.

grandiose *adjective grandiose schemes.* ambitious, grand, impressive, ostentatious, pretentious. OPPOSITE modest.

grant *verb* **1** *She granted them permission to leave.* accord, allow, give. OPPOSITE refuse. **2** *The government granted subsidies.* allocate, award, bestow, donate, give, pay, provide. **3** *The bank granted that they had made a mistake.* acknowledge, admit, agree, concede. OPPOSITE deny. — *noun She receives a study grant.* allowance, award, bursary, endowment, scholarship, subsidy.

grapevine *noun I heard it on the grapevine.* bush telegraph, mulga wire, network.

graphic *adjective* **1** *a graphic presentation.* diagrammatic, drawn, illustrated, pictorial, visual. **2** *The witness gave a graphic account of the accident.* colourful, descriptive, detailed, explicit, vivid.

grapple *verb* **grapple with 1** *He grappled with the man.* fight, struggle with, tackle, wrestle with. **2** *She grappled with the problem.* address, come to grips with, contend with, deal with, struggle with, tackle, wrestle with.

grasp verb **1** *She grasped his hand.* clasp, clench, cling to, clutch, grab, grip, hang on to, hold, seize, snatch, take, take hold of. OPPOSITE release. **2** *He couldn't grasp the point.* apprehend, comprehend, cotton on to (*informal*), fathom, follow, get (*informal*), latch on to (*informal*), see, understand. — noun **1** *a powerful grasp.* clasp, clutch, grip, hold. **2** *a good grasp of the subject.* command, comprehension, mastery, understanding.

grasping adjective *He's mean and grasping.* acquisitive, avaricious, covetous, greedy, mercenary. OPPOSITE generous.

grass noun *a picnic on the grass.* green, lawn, pasture, sward, turf. — verb **grass on** (*slang*) *He grassed on his mates.* betray, blow the whistle on (*informal*), dob in (*Australian informal*), inform on, rat on (*informal*), shelf (*Australian slang*), shop (*slang*), sneak on (*informal*), split on (*slang*).

grassland noun field, meadow, pampas, pasture, plain, prairie, range, savannah, steppe.

grate verb **1** *She grated the ginger.* grind, mince, shred. **2** *His finger grated on the blackboard.* grind, rasp, rub, scrape, scratch. □ **grate on** *Her laugh grates on people.* annoy, get on someone's nerves, irritate, jar on, rub someone up the wrong way.

grateful adjective *She was grateful for their concern.* appreciative, thankful. OPPOSITE resentful.

gratify verb **1** *The results gratified her.* content, delight, gladden, please, satisfy. **2** *He gratified his desire for chocolates.* fulfil, give in to, indulge, pander to, satisfy.

grating[1] noun *A grating covers the hole.* grate, grid, grille.

grating[2] adjective *a grating voice.* discordant, harsh, jarring, rasping, raucous, shrill, strident.

gratitude noun *He showed his gratitude by sending flowers.* appreciation, thankfulness, thanks. OPPOSITE ingratitude.

gratuity noun *extra income from gratuities.* bonus, gift, present, tip.

grave[1] noun *buried in a grave.* burial place, crypt, mausoleum, sepulchre, tomb, vault.

grave[2] adjective **1** *a grave matter.* critical, crucial, important, momentous, serious, weighty. OPPOSITE petty. **2** *grave faces.* earnest, funereal, gloomy, grim, pensive, serious, sober, solemn, sombre, staid, thoughtful. OPPOSITE merry.

gravel noun *a path of gravel.* pebbles, road metal, shingle, stones.

gravestone noun headstone, monument, tombstone.

graveyard noun burial ground, cemetery, churchyard, necropolis.

graze[1] verb *The sheep are grazing in the paddock.* browse, feed.

graze[2] verb *He fell and grazed his knee.* bark, scrape, scratch, skin. — noun *a graze on the knee.* abrasion, scrape, scratch.

grazier noun (*Australian*) cattle farmer, pastoralist (*Australian*), sheep farmer.

grease verb *He greased the engine.* lubricate, oil.

greasy adjective *greasy food.* fatty, oily.

great adjective **1** *a great amount.* big, colossal, enormous, gigantic, huge, humungous (*slang*), immense, large, massive, monumental, phenomenal, prodigious, stupendous, vast. OPPOSITE slight. **2** *The storm caused great damage.* considerable, extensive, immeasurable, sweeping, vast, widespread. OPPOSITE minor. **3** *a great success.* notable, outstanding, profound, remarkable, re-

sounding, splendid, stupendous, tremendous. **4** *great joy.* deep, indescribable, ineffable, intense, profound, unspeakable. **5** *great pain.* acute, extreme, intense, severe, strong. OPPOSITE mild. **6** *a great mathematician.* brilliant, celebrated, distinguished, eminent, firstclass, gifted, illustrious, important, leading, noted, outstanding, pre-eminent, prominent, renowned, superior, talented, well-known. **7** *one of the great events of history.* grand, historic, important, momentous, significant. OPPOSITE unimportant. **8** *Vicki's a great reader.* avid, eager, keen, passionate. **9** (*informal*) *It was a great party.* brilliant (*informal*), cool (*informal*), delightful, enjoyable, excellent, fabulous (*informal*), fantastic (*informal*), fine, first-rate, good, grand (*informal*), lovely, magnificent, marvellous, outstanding, pleasant, splendid, super (*informal*), superb, swell (*informal*), terrific (*informal*), tremendous (*informal*), wonderful. OPPOSITE bad, lousy (*informal*).

greatest adjective best, chief, highest, main, maximum, paramount, supreme, top, utmost. OPPOSITE least.

greatness noun *Some people achieve greatness.* distinction, eminence, grandeur, importance, pre-eminence, stature.

greed noun *greed for food. greed for money.* avarice, covetousness, cupidity, gluttony, rapacity, voraciousness. OPPOSITE unselfishness.

greedy adjective **1** *The greedy child ate all the biscuits.* gluttonous, ravenous, voracious. **2** *greedy moneylenders.* avaricious, covetous, grasping, miserly, money-hungry, on the make (*informal*), rapacious. OPPOSITE generous.

greedy-guts noun see GLUTTON.

green adjective **1** *a green colour.* apple green, aquamarine, beryl, bottle green, chartreuse, emerald, jade, lime, olive, pea green, sea green. **2** *green pastures. green trees.* leafy, lush, verdant. **3** *The new recruits are a bit green.* callow, immature, inexperienced, naive, raw. OPPOSITE experienced. — noun *a political green.* conservationist, environmentalist, greenie (*Australian informal*).

greenhouse noun *He grows tomatoes in the greenhouse.* conservatory, glasshouse, hothouse.

greet verb **1** *She greeted her friend.* address, receive, welcome. **2** *the sight that greeted their eyes.* appear to, meet, present itself to.

greeting noun *They were given a warm greeting.* reception, salutation, welcome. □ **greetings** plural noun *birthday greetings.* compliments, congratulations, regards, wishes.

gregarious adjective *The receptionist was gregarious.* extroverted, friendly, outgoing, sociable, social. OPPOSITE unsociable.

grey adjective **1** *a grey colour. grey hair.* charcoal grey, dun, grizzled, grizzly, gunmetal, hoary, mousy, silver, slate, smoky, steely. **2** *grey skies.* cloudy, dark, dull, gloomy, heavy, leaden, louring, overcast. OPPOSITE sunny. **3** *a grey area.* doubtful, hazy, intermediate, uncertain, unclear.

grid noun **1** *The drain was covered with a grid.* grating, grille. **2** *The cables are laid in a grid.* lattice, network.

grief noun *overcome with grief.* anguish, desolation, distress, heartache, heartbreak, misery, regret, remorse, sadness, sorrow, suffering, unhappiness, woe. OPPOSITE joy.

grievance noun *He aired his grievances.* beef (*slang*), complaint, gripe (*informal*), objection.

grieve verb **1** *She grieved them with her thoughtlessness.* distress, hurt, pain, sadden, upset. OPPOSITE hearten. **2** *He grieved for his dead friend.* fret, lament, mope, mourn, pine, weep. OPPOSITE rejoice.

grill verb **1** *He grilled the meat.* barbecue, broil, brown, toast. **2** *The police grilled them over the incident.* cross-examine, interrogate, question.

grim adjective **1** *grim faces.* dour, forbidding, gloomy, glum, harsh, severe, stern. OPPOSITE smiling. **2** *The future looks grim.* bleak, desolate, dire, dismal, dreadful, forbidding, frightful, ghastly, gloomy, horrible, unpleasant.

grimace verb *She grimaced with pain.* frown, pull a face, scowl, wince.

grimy adjective *grimy hands.* blackened, dirty, filthy, grubby, soiled, sooty. OPPOSITE clean.

grin verb *She grinned with pleasure.* beam, smile, smirk.

grind verb **1** *She ground the pepper.* crush, granulate, mill, pound, pulverise. **2** *a tool for grinding metal.* file, polish, rub, sharpen, smooth, whet. **3** *He grinds his teeth.* gnash, grate.

grip verb **1** *She gripped his arm.* clasp, clutch, grab, grasp, hang on to, hold, seize, snatch, take hold of. OPPOSITE let go. **2** *The story gripped him.* absorb, captivate, engross, enthral, hold spellbound, rivet. — noun **1** *He had a powerful grip.* clasp, clutch, grasp, hold. **2** *She has a good grip of her subject.* command, comprehension, grasp, hold, mastery, understanding.

gripe verb see GRUMBLE.

grisly adjective *a grisly murder.* appalling, dreadful, frightful, ghastly, gory, grim, gruesome, hideous, horrendous, horrible, horrid, macabre, repugnant, repulsive, shocking, vile. OPPOSITE pleasant.

gristly adjective *gristly meat.* leathery, tough.

grit noun **1** *She had grit in her eyes.* dirt, dust, sand. **2** *a man of true grit.* backbone, courage, determination, endurance, fortitude, guts (*informal*), mettle, pluck, spirit, spunk (*informal*). OPPOSITE cowardice. — verb *He gritted his teeth.* clench, set.

grizzle verb (*informal*) *The child grizzled continuously.* cry, fret, moan, whimper, whine, whinge (*informal*); see also COMPLAIN.

groan verb *He groaned in pain.* bellow, cry, howl, moan, wail.

grog noun (*Australian informal*) *bring your own grog.* alcohol, liquor.

groggy adjective *The patient was groggy from the anaesthetic.* dazed, dopey (*informal*), shaky, unsteady, wonky (*informal*), woozy (*informal*).

groom noun *the bride and groom.* bridegroom, husband. — verb **1** *He groomed the horse.* brush, comb, curry. **2** *The cat groomed herself.* clean up, preen, spruce up, tidy, wash. **3** *He was being groomed for the job.* prepare, prime, train.

groove noun *a groove in the wood.* channel, cut, furrow, rut, score, slot. OPPOSITE ridge.

grope verb *He groped for a match in the dark.* feel about, fish, fossick (*Australian informal*), fumble, rummage, scrabble, search.

gross adjective **1** *He became gross through overeating.* corpulent, enormous, fat, flabby, huge, obese, overweight, rotund. OPPOSITE emaciated. **2** *gross manners.* boorish,

coarse, crass, crude, rude, unrefined, vulgar. OPPOSITE refined. **3** *gross negligence.* blatant, clear, flagrant, glaring, manifest, obvious, outrageous. **4** *gross income.* entire, pre-tax, total, whole. OPPOSITE net. **5** (*informal*) *The food was gross.* see DISGUSTING.

grotesque adjective *a grotesque face.* absurd, bizarre, deformed, distorted, fantastic, freakish, hideous, misshapen, monstrous, odd, ugly, weird.

grouch noun (*informal*) *Who invited that old grouch?* crosspatch, grumbler, grump (*informal*), killjoy, malcontent, misery (*informal*), sourpuss (*informal*), spoilsport, wet blanket, whinger (*informal*).

grouchy adjective *a grouchy person.* badtempered, cantankerous, churlish, crabby, cranky, cross, crotchety, crusty, discontented, disgruntled, fractious, grumpy, irritable, peevish, shirty (*informal*), snaky (*Australian informal*), stroppy (*informal*), sullen, surly, testy, tetchy.

ground noun **1** *She kept her feet on the ground.* earth, land. **2** *Plant the rose in the ground.* dirt, earth, loam, soil. **3** *a sports ground.* arena, field, oval, pitch, stadium. — verb **1** *The ship was grounded in the storm.* beach, run aground, shipwreck, strand. OPPOSITE launch. **2** *The children were grounded in grammar.* drill, educate, instruct, teach, train. **3** *The story is grounded on fact.* base, establish, found, root. □ **grounds** plural noun **1** *the house and grounds.* campus, estate, garden(s), lawn(s), surroundings. **2** *coffee grounds.* deposit, dregs, lees, sediment. **3** *He has no grounds for complaint.* basis, cause, evidence, justification, reason.

groundless adjective *Your fears are groundless.* baseless, irrational, unfounded, unjustified, unwarranted. OPPOSITE justified.

groundwork noun *Others had done the groundwork.* preparation, spadework.

group noun **1** *The specimens were classified into four groups.* category, class, classification, division, family, genus, kind, order, sort, species, type, variety. **2** *a group of people, animals, things, etc.* alliance, assembly, association, assortment, band, batch, battery, bevy, body, bracket, brigade, brood, bunch, circle, clan, clique, club, cluster, cohort, collection, colony, combination, community, company, congregation, consortium, constellation (*of stars*), contingent, convoy, corps, crew, crop, crowd, drove, ensemble, faction, federation, fleet, flock, flotilla, force, gaggle (*of geese*), galaxy (*of stars*), gang, gathering, herd, horde, host, league, legion, litter, lot, mass, mob, movement, multitude, organisation, pack, panel, party, phalanx, platoon, pod (*of seals, dolphins, or whales*), posse, pride (*of lions*), rabble, ring, school (*of fish, dolphins, or whales*), series, set, shoal (*of fish*), society, squad, subset, swarm (*of bees*), syndicate, team, throng, tribe, troop, troupe (*of actors*), union. — verb **1** *They were grouped by age.* arrange, class, classify, organise, sort. **2** *The new children grouped together.* associate, band, cluster, collect, congregate, gather. OPPOSITE disperse.

grove noun *an olive grove.* orchard, plantation.

grovel verb *He was not prepared to grovel to the boss.* crawl (*informal*), fawn (on), ingratiate yourself (with), kowtow, suck up (*informal*), toady.

grow *verb* **1** *The child grew quickly.* become bigger, become taller, develop, fill out, grow up, mature, shoot up. OPPOSITE shrink. **2** *The line of people grew.* become longer, extend, lengthen. OPPOSITE shorten. **3** *The business has grown.* boom, build up, develop, enlarge, evolve, expand, flourish, increase, mushroom, progress, prosper, snowball, spread, thrive. OPPOSITE decline. **4** *The plants won't grow without water.* burgeon, flourish, germinate, live, shoot, spring up, sprout, survive, thrive. OPPOSITE die. **5** *He grew resentful.* become, get, turn. **6** *She grows vegetables.* cultivate, produce, propagate, raise.

growl *verb The dog growled.* snarl.

grown-up *adjective* grown-up *behaviour.* adult, mature. OPPOSITE immature. — *noun* adult, oldie (*informal*). OPPOSITE child.

growth *noun* **1** *growth in numbers.* enlargement, expansion, increase, proliferation. OPPOSITE decrease. **2** *strong economic growth.* advancement, development, improvement, progress. OPPOSITE decline. **3** *The doctor removed the growth.* cancer, cyst, lump, polyp, tumour.

grub *noun* caterpillar, larva, maggot.

grubby *adjective grubby feet.* blackened, dirty, dusty, filthy, grimy, soiled. OPPOSITE clean.

grudge *noun She bore no grudges.* animosity, bitterness, grievance, hard feelings, ill will, rancour, resentment. □ **hold a grudge against** *He continues to hold a grudge against his successor.* have a derry on (*Australian informal*), have a down on (*informal*), have a set on (*Australian informal*).

grudging *adjective grudging in his praise.* envious, jealous, reluctant, resentful, sparing, unwilling. OPPOSITE generous.

gruelling *adjective a gruelling task.* arduous, demanding, exhausting, hard, laborious, strenuous, tiring, tough. OPPOSITE easy.

gruesome *adjective the gruesome details of the murder.* ghastly, ghoulish, gory, grisly, hideous, horrible, macabre, repulsive, revolting, shocking, sickening. OPPOSITE pleasant.

gruff *adjective* **1** *a gruff voice.* gravelly, guttural, harsh, hoarse, husky, rough, throaty. **2** *a gruff reply. a gruff manner.* abrupt, bad-tempered, blunt, brusque, crabby, crusty, curt, grouchy (*informal*), grumpy, sullen, surly, unfriendly. OPPOSITE friendly.

grumble *verb She grumbled about everything.* beef (*slang*), bitch (*informal*), carp, cavil, complain, find fault with, gripe (*informal*), grizzle (*informal*), groan, moan, object, protest, whine, whinge (*informal*).

grumpy *adjective He was feeling tired and grumpy.* bad-tempered, cantankerous, churlish, crabby, cranky, cross, crotchety, grouchy, irritable, peevish, petulant, shirty (*informal*), snaky (*Australian informal*), sullen, surly, testy, tetchy.

grunt *verb The pig grunted.* snort.

guarantee *noun* **1** *She gave her guarantee that it would be finished.* assurance, pledge, promise, undertaking, word. **2** *a 12-month guarantee on all parts.* warranty. — *verb* **1** *Your privacy is guaranteed.* ensure, protect, secure. **2** *He guaranteed that they were genuine.* certify, pledge, promise, swear, vouch, vow.

guard *verb* **1** *The cat guarded her kittens.* defend, look after, mind, preserve, protect, safeguard, shelter, shield, watch over. **2** *He guarded the prisoner.* keep an eye on, supervise, watch over. — *noun* **1** *an armed guard.* bodyguard, chaperone, escort, garrison, guardian, guardsman, lookout, minder, patrol, picket, security officer, sentinel, sentry, warder, watchman. **2** *a mouth guard.* protector, screen, shield. □ **off (your) guard** *Don't be caught off guard.* napping, unprepared, unready. **on (your) guard** *Be on your guard for pickpockets.* alert, careful, on the watch, ready, vigilant, wary, watchful. **stand guard** *She stood guard while the others went in.* guard, keep a lookout, keep nit (*slang*), keep watch, patrol.

guardian *noun the guardian of their faith.* custodian, defender, keeper, preserver, protector, trustee, warden, watchdog.

guess *verb* **1** *She guessed the answer.* estimate, have a stab at (*informal*). OPPOSITE know. **2** *I guess he'll be back.* assume, conjecture, expect, imagine, predict, reckon, speculate, suppose, surmise, suspect, think. — *noun Her guess turned out to be correct.* assumption, conjecture, estimate, guesstimate (*informal*), hunch, hypothesis, prediction, shot in the dark, supposition, surmise, suspicion, theory.

guest *noun* **1** *a house guest.* billet, caller, company, visitor. OPPOSITE host, hostess. **2** *a hotel guest.* patron, resident, visitor. □ **guest house** *They stayed in a guest house.* hostel, hotel, pension.

guidance *noun guidance on careers.* advice, counselling, direction, help, information, instruction.

guide *noun* **1** *a tour guide.* conductor, courier, director, escort, leader, pilot, usher. **2** *a friend and guide.* adviser, counsellor, guru, mentor, teacher. — *verb She guided them through the town.* conduct, direct, escort, lead, manoeuvre, navigate, pilot, show the way, steer, usher.

guidebook *noun a restaurant guidebook.* directory, guide, handbook, manual.

guidelines *plural noun They followed the guidelines.* instructions, principles, regulations, requirements, rules, standards.

guild *noun the pharmacists' guild.* association, federation, league, organisation, society, union.

guile *noun He acted without guile.* artifice, craftiness, cunning, deceit, duplicity, slyness, trickery. OPPOSITE honesty.

guilt *noun* **1** *They could not establish his guilt.* blame, fault, responsibility. OPPOSITE innocence. **2** *She was overcome by feelings of guilt.* compunction, contrition, disgrace, remorse, self-reproach, shame.

guilty *adjective* **1** *He was proven guilty.* blameworthy, culpable, responsible. OPPOSITE innocent. **2** *a guilty look.* ashamed, contrite, hangdog, remorseful, shamefaced, sheepish. OPPOSITE innocent.

guise *noun under the guise of friendship.* cover, disguise, masquerade, pretence, show.

gulf *noun* **1** *ships in the gulf.* bay, cove, inlet. **2** *a gulf between people.* chasm, gap, rift.

gullet *noun The food was stuck in his gullet.* craw, oesophagus, throat.

gullible *adjective With experience she became less gullible.* believing, credulous, green, naive, trusting, unsuspecting. OPPOSITE suspicious.

gully *noun* **1** *a stormwater gully.* channel, ditch, drain, gutter. **2** (*Australian*) *The car rolled down the gully.* gorge, ravine, valley.

gulp *verb He gulped his food greedily.* bolt, devour, gobble, guzzle, wolf. — *noun She took a big gulp.* draught, mouthful, swallow, swig (*informal*).

gum *noun The pictures are stuck with gum.* adhesive, glue, paste. — *verb He gummed the pieces together.* glue, paste, stick.

gumption *noun He didn't have the gumption to do it.* common sense, enterprise, initiative, nous (*informal*), sense, wit.

gun *noun* arm, firearm; [*various guns*] airgun, automatic, blunderbuss, cannon, carbine, flintlock, handgun, howitzer, machine-gun, mortar, musket, pistol, revolver, rifle, semi-automatic, shotgun, submachine-gun, tommy-gun.

gunfire *noun caught in the gunfire.* broadside, cannonade, fire, flak, fusillade, salvo, shooting.

gunman *noun The gunman threatened the police.* assassin, gunslinger, marksman, sniper.

gurgle *noun a gurgle of water in the pipe.* babble, burble.

guru *noun They respected him as their guru.* leader, master, mentor, sage, teacher.

gush *verb* **1** *Water gushed from the hose.* flow, pour, run, rush, spout, spurt, stream, surge. OPPOSITE trickle. **2** *She gushed about her new friend.* babble on, get carried away (*informal*), go overboard (*informal*), rave (*informal*). — *noun a gush of water.* cascade, flood, jet, outflow, outpouring, rush, spurt, stream, torrent.

gust *noun a gust of wind.* blast, puff, rush, squall.

gusto *noun He does everything with gusto.* enjoyment, enthusiasm, relish, spirit, verve, vigour, zeal, zest. OPPOSITE apathy.

gusty *adjective a gusty day.* blowy, blustery, squally, stormy, windy. OPPOSITE calm.

gut *noun a pain in the gut.* abdomen, bowel, insides (*informal*), intestine, stomach. — *adjective a gut reaction.* instinctive, intuitive, spontaneous, subconscious. — *verb The building was gutted by fire.* destroy, devastate, ravage. □ **guts** *plural noun* (*informal*) *It took guts to say that.* audacity, boldness, bravery, courage, daring, determination, grit (*informal*), nerve, pluck, spunk (*informal*).

gutter *noun Water runs off in the gutters.* channel, culvert, ditch, drain, gully, sewer, trench, trough.

guy *noun* (*informal*) *The party was only for guys.* bloke (*informal*), boy, chap (*informal*), fellow (*informal*), gentleman, lad, male, man.

guzzle *verb They guzzled their dinner.* bolt, devour, gobble, gulp, scoff (*informal*), wolf.

gymnastics *plural noun* acrobatics, callisthenics.

gypsy *noun He sold all his possessions and joined the gypsies.* nomad, Romany, traveller, vagabond, wanderer.

gyrate *verb She gyrated until she was dizzy.* circle, pirouette, revolve, rotate, spin, spiral, turn, twirl, wheel, whirl.

Hh

habit *noun* **1** *He had a habit of putting his foot in it.* custom, inclination, practice, predisposition, propensity, routine, tendency, way, wont. **2** *Jane has kicked her drug habit.* addiction, dependence. **3** *a nun's habit.* costume, dress, garb, robe.

habitat *noun the koala's native habitat.* domain, environment, habitation, home, setting, surroundings, territory.

habitual *adjective* **1** *habitual lying.* constant, continual, frequent, persistent, regular, repeated, routine, standard, usual. OPPOSITE occasional. **2** *He was waiting in his habitual place.* accustomed, customary, established, familiar, fixed, normal, regular, set, traditional, usual. **3** *a habitual smoker.* addicted, chronic, confirmed, hardened, inveterate. OPPOSITE occasional.

hack *verb He hacked the shrub to pieces.* chop, cut, hew, mutilate, slash.

hackneyed *adjective a hackneyed phrase.* banal, clichéd, common, commonplace, conventional, overused, pedestrian, stale, stereotyped, stock, trite. OPPOSITE original.

hag *noun She was an old hag.* bag (*slang*), battleaxe (*informal*), crone, witch.

haggard *adjective She looked haggard after her illness.* careworn, drawn, emaciated, exhausted, gaunt, thin, worn. OPPOSITE radiant.

haggle *verb They haggled over the price.* argue, bargain, dispute, negotiate, quarrel, quibble, wrangle.

hail[1] *noun a hail of bullets.* barrage, shower, storm, torrent, volley.

hail[2] *verb She hailed a taxi.* call to, flag down, signal to, wave to. □ **hail from** *He hails from South Africa.* be born in, come from, originate from.

hair *noun* **1** *Each hair is extremely fine.* bristle, filament, strand. **2** *He admired her hair.* curls, locks, ringlets, tresses. **3** *facial hair.* beard, bristles, fuzz, moustache, sideburns, whiskers. **4** *an animal's hair.* coat, down, fleece, fur, mane, pelt, wool.

hairdresser *noun* barber, haircutter, hair stylist.

hair-raising *adjective a hair-raising experience.* frightening, hairy (*slang*), nerve-racking, scary, spine-chilling, terrifying.

hairy *adjective* **1** *hairy skin.* bristly, bushy, downy, fleecy, furry, fuzzy, hirsute, shaggy, stubbly, unshaven, whiskery, woolly. OPPOSITE bald, hairless. **2** (*slang*) *The drive through the hills was rather hairy.* dangerous, dicey (*slang*), difficult, frightening, hair-raising, nerve-racking, scary, terrifying.

hale *adjective hale and hearty.* fit, healthy, lively, robust, sprightly, spry, strong, vigorous, well. OPPOSITE frail.

half *adverb His story was only half true.* partially, partly, slightly. OPPOSITE completely.

half-hearted *adjective a half-hearted attempt. half-hearted support.* apathetic, feeble, indifferent, lackadaisical, lukewarm, unenthusiastic. OPPOSITE hearty, wholehearted.

halfway *adjective They have reached the halfway point.* intermediate, median, mid, middle, midway.

hall *noun* **1** *They left their coats in the hall.* corridor, entrance hall, foyer, lobby, passage, vestibule. **2** *The hall was packed for the concert.* assembly hall, auditorium, chamber, concert hall, room, theatre.

hallmark *noun This attack bears all his hallmarks.* badge, brand, characteristic, mark, stamp, trade mark.

hallow *verb* **1** *The ground has been hallowed.* bless, consecrate, make holy, make sacred, sanctify. OPPOSITE desecrate. **2** *God's name is hallowed.* honour, respect, revere, venerate.

hallucination *noun This drug produces hallucinations.* apparition, dream, fantasy, illusion, mirage, nightmare, phantasm, vision.

halo *noun He painted a halo over the saint's head.* aureole, nimbus.

halt *noun a halt in proceedings.* break, close, delay, hiatus, intermission, interruption, pause, recess, shutdown, standstill, stop, stoppage, suspension, termination. — *verb* **1** *The cars must halt at a red light.* come to a stop, pull up, stop, wait. OPPOSITE proceed, start. **2** *They have halted the spread of the disease.* arrest, block, check, stem, stop.

halve *verb* **1** *Draw a line which halves the square.* bisect, divide in two. **2** *The price was halved.* cut by half, reduce to half. OPPOSITE double.

hammer *noun Hit the nail with a hammer.* claw hammer, gavel, mallet, sledgehammer. — *verb* **1** *He hammered the nails back in.* bang, drive, hit, knock, nail, tack. **2** *She hammered the table.* bash, batter, beat, hit, knock, pound, strike, thump. □ **hammer out** *They hammered out a plan.* devise, thrash out, work out.

hamper[1] *noun a picnic hamper.* basket, pannier.

hamper[2] *verb The splint hampered his movements.* check, curb, hinder, impede, inhibit, interfere with, limit, obstruct, restrict. OPPOSITE assist.

hand *noun* **1** *a clean pair of hands.* fist, mitt (*slang*), palm, paw (*informal*). **2** *The jewels are in safe hands.* care, charge, control, custody, keeping, possession. **3** *The matter is out of my hands.* authority, control, jurisdiction, power, responsibility. **4** *Please give me a hand.* aid, assistance, help, support. **5** *He was employed as a factory hand.* assistant, employee, labourer, worker. **6** (*informal*) *They gave her a big hand.* applause, clap, ovation. — *verb She handed him his hat.* give, pass. □ **at hand 1** *There is a deli at hand.* accessible, close, handy, near, nearby. **2** *The exams are at hand.* approaching, close, coming, imminent, near, soon. **by hand** *She whipped the cream by hand.* manually. **hand in** *She handed in her essay.* deliver, give, present, submit. **hand out** *He handed out the lollies.* deal out, dish out (*informal*), dispense, distribute, dole out, give out, share out. **hand over 1** *He handed over the money.* donate, give, pass, pay, surrender. **2** *He was handed over to the authorities.* deliver, present, turn over. **hands down** *They won hands down.* easily, effortlessly. **on hand** *We have a helper on hand.* accessible, available, handy, present. **out of hand** *Things have got out of hand.* chaotic, out of control, out of order.

handbag *noun ladies' handbags.* bag, purse (*American*).

handbook *noun a motorist's handbook.* guidebook, manual.

handcuffs *plural noun* manacles, shackles.

handful *noun A handful of students remained.* few, remnant, sprinkling. OPPOSITE crowd.

handicap *noun* **1** *a physical handicap.* disability, disadvantage, impairment. **2** *Lack of experience was a handicap.* barrier, disadvantage, drawback, hindrance, impediment, limitation, obstacle, stumbling block. OPPOSITE advantage. — *verb Lack of light handicapped the search party.* disadvantage, hamper, hinder, impede, limit, restrict. OPPOSITE help.

handle *noun The knife is held by the handle.* grip, haft, helve, hilt, knob, shaft, stock. — *verb* **1** *Please do not handle the fruit.* feel, finger, pick up, poke, touch. **2** *He can handle the car well.* control, drive, manage, manoeuvre, operate, steer. **3** *She can handle any problem.* cope with,

deal with, look after, manage, tackle, take care of.

handout *noun* **1** *He survives on handouts.* alms, donation, freebie (*informal*), gift. **2** *She never reads the handouts.* brochure, bulletin, circular, leaflet, pamphlet.

handsome *adjective* **1** *a handsome man.* attractive, fine-looking, good-looking. OPPOSITE ugly. **2** *a handsome woman.* attractive, beautiful, comely, elegant, good-looking, smart. **3** *a handsome amount of money.* ample, considerable, generous, large, lavish, liberal, sizeable. OPPOSITE stingy.

handwriting *noun* calligraphy, copperplate, hand, longhand, scrawl, scribble, script, writing.

handy *adjective* **1** *a handy gadget.* convenient, helpful, practical, useful. OPPOSITE useless. **2** *The pens are handy by the telephone.* accessible, at hand, available, convenient, near, on hand, to hand. OPPOSITE inaccessible. **3** *He is handy with cars.* adept, adroit, capable, competent, deft, dexterous, expert, good, proficient, skilful. OPPOSITE inept.

hang *verb* **1** *She hung the lights on the tree.* dangle, drape, string, suspend. **2** *The material hangs well.* drape, fall. **3** *She hung her head in shame.* bend, bow, droop, drop, incline, lower. **4** *The smoke is hanging over the city.* hover, linger, remain, rest, stay. OPPOSITE disperse. □ **get the hang of** (*informal*) *He has finally got the hang of it.* come to grips with, comprehend, figure out, get the knack of, grasp, master, understand. **hang around** *They were still hanging around when we left.* hang about, linger, loiter, lurk, remain, stay, wait. OPPOSITE leave. **hang back** *If you hang back you might miss out.* hesitate, hold back, wait. **hang on** (*informal*) *He asked me to hang on.* hold on, hold the line, wait. **hang on to 1** *The child hung on to my hand.* cling to, clutch, grip, hold on to. **2** *He hung on to his job.* hold on to, keep, remain in, retain. OPPOSITE lose. **hang out** (*informal*) *He found somewhere else to hang out.* dwell, live, reside.

hang-up *noun* (*informal*) *He has a hang-up about eating in public.* difficulty, inhibition, mental block, phobia, problem, thing (*informal*).

hanker *verb* **hanker after** *She hankers after fame and riches.* covet, crave, desire, have a yen for, hunger for, long for, thirst for, want, yearn for.

haphazard *adjective She works in a haphazard fashion.* arbitrary, careless, casual, chaotic, disorganised, hit-or-miss, indiscriminate, random, slapdash, unorganised, unplanned, unsystematic. OPPOSITE methodical, systematic.

happen *verb An accident is bound to happen.* arise, come about, come to pass, crop up, ensue, eventuate, occur, result, take place. □ **happen to** *Whatever will happen to her?* become of, befall (*formal*).

happening *noun strange happenings.* episode, event, incident, occasion, occurrence, proceeding.

happiness *noun* bliss, cheerfulness, contentment, delight, ecstasy, elation, enjoyment, euphoria, exhilaration, exuberance, felicity, gladness, glee, joy, jubilation, light-heartedness, merriment, mirth, pleasure, rapture, satisfaction. OPPOSITE sadness.

happy *adjective* **1** *She was happy when the exams were over.* blissful, blithe, cheerful, contented, delighted, ecstatic, elated, enraptured, euphoric, exhilarated, glad, gleeful, gratified, joyful, joyous, jubilant, light-hearted, merry, over-

joyed, pleased, rapturous, satisfied, thrilled. OPPOSITE sad. **2** *a happy coincidence.* auspicious, convenient, favourable, fortunate, lucky, opportune, propitious, timely. OPPOSITE unfortunate. **3** *I am happy to help.* delighted, eager, glad, keen, pleased, willing. OPPOSITE reluctant.

happy-go-lucky *adjective* see CAREFREE.

harangue *noun He was subjected to constant harangues.* diatribe, ear-bashing (*Australian informal*), lecture, sermon, speech, tirade. — *verb He couldn't stand being harangued any more.* berate, ear-bash (*Australian informal*), lecture, nag, scold.

harass *verb He'll work better if you stop harassing him.* annoy, badger, bother, bug (*informal*), disturb, harry, hassle (*informal*), hound, importune, pester, plague, stand over (*Australian*), trouble, worry.

harbour *noun The harbour was filled with ships.* anchorage, dock, haven, marina, port, shelter. — *verb* **1** *He harboured the escapee.* conceal, hide, house, protect, shelter, shield. **2** *He harboured a grudge.* cling to, foster, hold, maintain, nurse, nurture, retain.

hard *adjective* **1** *hard cardboard.* dense, firm, inflexible, rigid, solid, stiff, tough. OPPOSITE soft. **2** *hard facts.* definite, indisputable, irrefutable, solid, true. OPPOSITE disputable. **3** *a hard job.* arduous, back-breaking, demanding, difficult, exacting, gruelling, heavy, herculean, laborious, onerous, rigorous, strenuous, taxing, tiring, tough. OPPOSITE easy. **4** *a hard question.* awkward, baffling, complex, complicated, confusing, cryptic, difficult, knotty, puzzling, thorny, ticklish, tricky. OPPOSITE easy, simple. **5** *She has gone through hard times.* bad, difficult, grim, harsh, oppressive, painful, rough, severe, tough, unbearable, unpleasant. OPPOSITE pleasant. **6** *The Tax Office takes a hard line on tax evasion.* severe, stern, strict, unbending, uncompromising. OPPOSITE lenient. **7** *a hard worker.* assiduous, conscientious, diligent, earnest, energetic, indefatigable, industrious, painstaking, sedulous, unflagging, untiring. OPPOSITE lazy. **8** *a hard voice.* grating, harsh, sharp, shrill, unpleasant. OPPOSITE gentle, pleasant. — *adverb* **1** *He worked hard.* assiduously, conscientiously, diligently, doggedly, energetically, indefatigably, industriously, sedulously, strenuously, untiringly, vigorously. OPPOSITE lazily. **2** *She pressed the lid down hard.* firmly, forcefully, forcibly, powerfully, strongly, violently. OPPOSITE gently, lightly. **3** *It's raining hard.* heavily, intensely. OPPOSITE lightly. □ **hard up** (*informal*) *too hard up to be able to give a donation.* broke (*informal*), impecunious, impoverished, penniless, poor, poverty-stricken, skint (*informal*). OPPOSITE well off.

harden *verb The mixture hardened in the sun.* firm, set, solidify, stiffen, strengthen, toughen. OPPOSITE soften.

hard-hearted *adjective How can you be so hard-hearted?* callous, cold, cruel, hard, harsh, heartless, indifferent, inhuman, insensitive, mean, merciless, pitiless, remorseless, ruthless, stony-hearted, uncaring, unfeeling, unforgiving, unkind, unrepentant, unsympathetic. OPPOSITE compassionate.

hardly *adverb There is hardly any petrol left.* barely, scarcely.

hardship *noun The family suffered severe financial hardship.* adversity, affliction, deprivation, difficulty,

distress, misery, misfortune, need, poverty, privation, strain, suffering, trials, tribulation, woe. OPPOSITE ease.

hardware *noun The shop sells hardware.* equipment, implements, instruments, ironmongery, machinery, tools.

hard-wearing *adjective hard-wearing shoes.* durable, heavy-duty, long-lasting, stout, strong, tough. OPPOSITE flimsy.

hardy *adjective a hardy plant.* drought-resistant, frost-resistant, resilient, robust, strong, sturdy, tough, vigorous. OPPOSITE tender.

hare *noun* buck (*male*), doe (*female*), leveret (*young*).

hark *verb Hark! the dogs are barking.* listen. □ **hark back** *He keeps harking back to his favourite subject.* go back, return, revert.

harlequin *adjective a harlequin design.* motley, multicoloured, variegated.

harm *noun* **1** *grievous bodily harm.* hurt, injury, pain, suffering. **2** *Clearing the land has caused a great deal of harm.* damage, destruction, detriment, havoc. OPPOSITE benefit, good. — *verb* **1** *Do not harm the cat.* abuse, hurt, ill-treat, injure, maltreat, mistreat, molest, wound. **2** *Smoking can harm your health.* damage, destroy, impair, injure, ruin, spoil, undermine. OPPOSITE benefit, improve.

harmful *adjective harmful practices. harmful chemicals.* adverse, bad, damaging, dangerous, deleterious, destructive, detrimental, hurtful, injurious, noxious, pernicious, ruinous, unhealthy. OPPOSITE beneficial, harmless.

harmless *adjective* **1** *a harmless drug.* non-toxic, safe. OPPOSITE dangerous, harmful. **2** *a bit of harmless fun.* gentle, innocent, innocuous, inoffensive, mild.

harmonious *adjective* **1** *harmonious sounds.* dulcet, euphonious, melodious, musical, sweet, tuneful. OPPOSITE cacophonous, discordant. **2** *a harmonious relationship.* amicable, compatible, congenial, friendly, pleasant. OPPOSITE incompatible.

harmony *noun a state of harmony among the people.* accord, agreement, compatibility, concord, friendliness, peace, sympathy, unanimity, unity. OPPOSITE conflict.

harness *verb* **1** *He harnessed the horse.* bridle, hitch up, yoke. **2** *They are able to harness the energy of the waterfall.* capture, control, exploit, use.

harp *verb* **harp on** *He's always harping on about manners.* bang on (*informal*), dwell on, get on your hobby horse, go on (*informal*), keep on, nag.

harrowing *adjective a harrowing film.* alarming, chilling, distressing, disturbing, horrifying, spine-chilling, terrifying.

harry *verb* see HARASS.

harsh *adjective* **1** *a harsh voice.* cacophonous, discordant, grating, gravelly, gruff, guttural, jarring, rasping, raucous, rough, shrill, stern, strident. OPPOSITE gentle. **2** *a harsh light.* bright, brilliant, dazzling, glaring. OPPOSITE soft. **3** *a harsh environment.* austere, hard, inhospitable, rough, severe, stark, tough, unpleasant. OPPOSITE mild, pleasant. **4** *harsh words. harsh treatment.* acrimonious, aggressive, bitter, brutal, cruel, cutting, hard, hostile, hurtful, malicious, mean, merciless, nasty, severe, spiteful, stern, unfeeling, unfriendly, unkind, unsympathetic, vicious, vindictive. OPPOSITE gentle, lenient.

harvest *noun We expect a good tomato harvest this year.* crop, produce, vintage, yield. — *verb The crops have all been harvested.* collect, garner, gather, glean, pick, reap. OPPOSITE plant, sow.

hash *noun* **make a hash of** (*informal*) botch, bungle, make a mess of, mess up, muff (*informal*), ruin, spoil.

hassle *noun* (*informal*) **1** *She had no hassles exchanging the present.* bother, difficulty, problem, trouble, worry. **2** *They're always having hassles about the rent money.* argument, disagreement, fight, quarrel, squabble, wrangle. — *verb* (*informal*) *He keeps on hassling her when she is trying to work.* annoy, badger, bother, bug (*informal*), harass, hound, nag, pester, worry.

haste *noun He came with haste.* alacrity, dispatch, promptness, rapidity, speed, swiftness, urgency. OPPOSITE delay.

hasten *verb* **1** *He hastened back home.* dash, fly, hurry, make haste, race, rush, scurry, scuttle, speed. OPPOSITE dawdle. **2** *Bad management hastened the shop's demise.* accelerate, bring forward, expedite, precipitate, quicken, speed up. OPPOSITE delay.

hasty *adjective* **1** *a hasty retreat.* fast, hurried, prompt, quick, rapid, speedy, sudden, swift. OPPOSITE slow. **2** *a hasty decision.* careless, headlong, hurried, impetuous, impulsive, precipitate, quick, rash, rushed, snap. OPPOSITE considered.

hat *noun* [kinds of hat] Akubra (*trade mark*), beanie, bearskin, beret, boater, bonnet, bowler hat, busby, cabbage-tree hat (*Australian*), cap, deerstalker, fez, mortarboard, panama, slouch hat, sombrero, sou'wester, stetson, sunhat, tam o'shanter, top hat, trilby; see also HEADGEAR.

hatch[1] *noun He passed the boxes through the hatch.* aperture, manhole, opening.

hatch[2] *verb* **1** *hatch eggs.* brood, incubate, sit on. **2** *They have hatched a money-making scheme.* conceive, concoct, cook up (*informal*), design, devise, dream up, invent, plan, think up.

hatchet *noun* axe, chopper, mogo (*Australian*), tomahawk.

hate *noun* **1** *He was filled with hate.* see HATRED. **2** (*informal*) *a pet hate.* abomination, aversion, dislike. OPPOSITE love. — *verb* **1** *They hate one another.* abhor, abominate, despise, detest, dislike, loathe. OPPOSITE love. **2** (*informal*) *She hated to wake the baby.* be averse, be loath, be reluctant, be unwilling, dislike. OPPOSITE like.

hateful *adjective a hateful person. a hateful job.* abhorrent, abominable, atrocious, contemptible, despicable, detestable, disgusting, execrable, horrid, loathsome, nasty, objectionable, obnoxious, odious, offensive, repugnant, repulsive, revolting, vile. OPPOSITE lovable, pleasant.

hatred *noun filled with hatred.* abhorrence, abomination, animosity, antagonism, antipathy, aversion, bitterness, contempt, detestation, disgust, dislike, enmity, hate, hostility, loathing, malevolence, odium, repugnance, resentment, revulsion. OPPOSITE affection, love.

haughty *adjective He has a haughty manner.* arrogant, conceited, condescending, contemptuous, disdainful, high and mighty, hoity-toity, lofty, lordly, patronising, proud, scornful, self-important, snobbish, snooty (*informal*), stuck-up (*informal*), supercilious, superior. OPPOSITE humble.

haul *verb* **1** *He was hauled out of the wreckage.* drag, draw, heave, hoick (*slang*), pull, tug, wrench, yank (*informal*). **2** *The truck was hauling a heavy load.* carry, cart, convey, lug, tow, transport. — *noun* **1** *The robbers made a good haul.* booty, profit, swag (*informal*), takings. **2** *a long haul to the next town.* distance, stretch.

haunt *verb* **1** *She haunts the gift shop.* frequent, hang around, loiter around, patronise. **2** *The memory haunts me.* linger with, obsess, plague, prey on, stay with. — *noun one of their favourite haunts.* hangout (*informal*), meeting-place, resort, retreat, stamping ground (*informal*).

have *verb* **1** *They have two cars.* keep, own, possess. **2** *The library has many rare books.* contain, hold, include. **3** *She's had a nasty shock.* endure, experience, go through, suffer, undergo. **4** (*slang*) *You've been had.* cheat, con (*informal*), deceive, swindle, take for a ride (*informal*), trick. **5** *They had a conversation.* carry on, conduct, engage in. **6** *I won't have any more nonsense.* accept, allow, permit, put up with, stand for (*informal*), take, tolerate. **7** *She asked me to have a biscuit.* eat, take. □ **have on** (*informal*) *You're having me on!* fool, hoax, kid (*informal*), pull someone's leg, tease. **have to** *We have to go.* be forced to, be obliged to, must, need to.

haven *noun His home was a haven from his fans.* asylum, hide-out, refuge, retreat, sanctuary, shelter; see also HARBOUR.

haversack *noun Chris carried her lunch in her haversack.* backpack, knapsack, pack, rucksack, satchel.

havoc *noun The floods caused widespread havoc.* chaos, confusion, destruction, devastation, disorder, mayhem, ruin, upheaval.

hawker *noun He doesn't buy anything from hawkers.* huckster, pedlar, travelling salesman.

haywire *adjective* (*informal*) *The system's gone haywire.* awry, chaotic, confused, disorganised, out of control, wrong.

hazard *noun Beware of unseen hazards.* danger, peril, pitfall, risk, threat.

hazardous *adjective a hazardous undertaking.* chancy, dangerous, dicey (*slang*), hairy (*slang*), perilous, precarious, risky, tricky, uncertain. OPPOSITE safe.

haze *noun We couldn't see the view through the haze.* cloud, fog, mist, smog.

hazy *adjective* **1** *a hazy day.* foggy, misty, smoggy. OPPOSITE clear. **2** *a hazy idea.* blurred, confused, faint, fuzzy, imprecise, indefinite, indistinct, nebulous, sketchy, unclear, vague. OPPOSITE precise.

head *noun* **1** *He fell and hit his head.* cranium, pate (*old use*), scone (*Australian informal*), skull. **2** *Use your head!* brain, intellect, intelligence, loaf (*slang*), mind, nut (*informal*). **3** *He has a good head for figures.* ability, aptitude, capacity, faculty, gift, intellect, mind, talent. **4** *It costs $50 per head.* capita, person. **5** *the head of the line.* front, top. OPPOSITE end. **6** *the head of the river.* beginning, headwater(s), origin, source. OPPOSITE mouth. **7** *the head of the organisation.* boss, captain, CEO, chairman, chief, commander, director, leader, manager, superintendent, supervisor. OPPOSITE subordinate. **8** *The school has a new head.* headmaster, headmistress, head teacher, principal. **9** *heads of countries. heads of governments.* emperor, governor, king, leader,

monarch, premier, president, prime minister, queen, ruler, sovereign. **10** *Matters have come to a head.* climax, crisis. — *verb* **1** *He heads the organisation.* be in charge of, command, control, direct, govern, lead, manage, rule, superintend, supervise. **2** *She headed the procession.* be at the front of, begin, lead, start. **3** *They headed home.* aim for, go, make for, make tracks for (*informal*), proceed, set off for, start for, steer for, turn for. □ **head off 1** *Let's head them off.* block, cut off, divert, intercept, turn aside. **2** *They headed off a disaster.* avert, fend off, forestall, prevent, ward off.

headache *noun* (*informal*) *a major headache for the government.* bugbear, difficulty, nightmare (*informal*), nuisance, pain (*informal*), problem, worry.

headgear *noun* [kinds of headgear] balaclava, cap, crown, hat, headdress, headscarf, helmet, hood, keffiyeh, kerchief, mantilla, scarf, skullcap, snood, tiara, turban, veil, wimple, yarmulke, yashmak; see also HAT.

heading *noun Each chapter has a heading.* caption, headline, title.

headland *noun* cape, head, point, promontory.

headline *noun a newspaper headline.* caption, heading, title.

headlong *adverb* **1** *They ran headlong into one another.* head first, head-on. **2** *He rushed headlong into the decision.* hastily, impetuously, impulsively, precipitately, rashly, recklessly.

headmaster, headmistress *noun* head, head teacher, principal.

headquarters *plural noun* base, central office, depot, head office.

headstrong *adjective a headstrong child.* determined, intractable, obstinate, pigheaded, recalcitrant, refractory, self-willed, strong-willed, stubborn, uncontrollable, wilful. OPPOSITE docile, tractable.

headway *noun* **make headway** *They're making headway with the investigation.* advance, get ahead, get on, have a breakthrough, make inroads, progress.

heal *verb* **1** *The wound has healed.* knit, mend. **2** *The doctor healed the sick people.* cure, restore, treat.

health *noun* **1** *They promised to love each other in sickness and in health.* fitness, healthiness, robustness, vitality, well-being. OPPOSITE sickness. **2** *After a long illness he is now in good health again.* condition, constitution, fettle, form, shape, state.

healthy *adjective* **1** *a healthy person.* fit, hale, hearty, robust, strapping, well. OPPOSITE sick, sickly. **2** *a healthy climate.* beneficial, bracing, health-giving, invigorating, salubrious, wholesome. OPPOSITE unhealthy. **3** *a healthy economy.* flourishing, sound, strong, thriving. OPPOSITE unsound.

heap *noun A heap of rubbish lay on the ground.* accumulation, bundle, mass, mound, mountain, pile, stack, stockpile. — *verb* **1** *We heaped the leaves under the trees.* accumulate, bank, collect, gather, pile, stack. OPPOSITE scatter. **2** *She heaped his plate with food.* fill, load, pile. **3** *They heaped praise upon him.* bestow, lavish, pour, shower. □ **heaps** *plural noun* (*informal*) *There's heaps of food.* loads (*informal*), lots (*informal*), masses, mountains, oodles (*informal*), piles (*informal*), plenty, stacks (*informal*), tons (*informal*), whips (*Australian informal*). OPPOSITE little.

hear *verb* **1** *We heard their conversation.* catch, listen to, overhear, pick up. **2** *I heard about it in the paper.*

discover, find out, gather, learn, read.

hearing *noun* **1** *in her hearing.* earshot, presence. **2** *an official hearing in the court.* inquiry, investigation, trial.

hearsay *noun The evidence is based on hearsay.* gossip, rumour, tittle-tattle. OPPOSITE fact.

heart *noun* **1** *a healthy heart.* ticker (*informal*). **2** *That was cruel: have you no heart?* compassion, consideration, emotions, feelings, humanity, love, pity, sympathy, tenderness. **3** *He was losing heart.* courage, determination, enthusiasm, guts (*informal*), nerve, pluck, spirit, spunk (*informal*). **4** *the heart of the problem.* core, crux, essence, nitty-gritty (*informal*), nub. **5** *the heart of the city.* centre, hub, middle, nucleus. OPPOSITE outskirts. □ **by heart** *learn by heart.* by memory, by rote, parrot-fashion.

heartbreak *noun* anguish, distress, grief, heartache, misery, pain, sadness, sorrow, suffering. OPPOSITE joy.

heartbroken *adjective* see BROKEN-HEARTED.

hearten *verb She was heartened by the news.* buck up (*informal*), buoy up, cheer, comfort, encourage, please. OPPOSITE dishearten.

heartfelt *adjective heartfelt thanks.* deep, earnest, fervent, genuine, profound, sincere, warm. OPPOSITE superficial.

hearth *noun They warmed themselves by the hearth.* fireplace, fireside.

heartily *adverb He was heartily sick of it.* absolutely, completely, thoroughly, utterly, very.

heartless *adjective a heartless person.* callous, cold, cruel, hardhearted, harsh, merciless, pitiless, ruthless, unfeeling, unkind, unsympathetic. OPPOSITE kind.

heart-warming *adjective a heart-warming story.* cheering, encouraging, heartening, inspiring, pleasing, touching. OPPOSITE disheartening.

hearty *adjective* **1** *hearty applause. a hearty welcome.* effusive, enthusiastic, exuberant, heartfelt, lively, sincere, vigorous, warm, whole-hearted. OPPOSITE half-hearted. **2** *a hale and hearty eighty-year-old.* energetic, hardy, healthy, robust, sprightly, spry, strong, vigorous. OPPOSITE frail. **3** *a hearty meal.* big, large, solid, substantial. OPPOSITE skimpy.

heat *noun* **1** *A thermometer measures heat.* hotness, temperature, warmth. **2** *He won his heat.* preliminary, round. — *verb She heated the pie.* reheat, warm up. OPPOSITE cool down.

heated *adjective a heated argument.* angry, ardent, emotional, excited, fervent, fierce, passionate, stormy, tense, vehement, violent. OPPOSITE calm.

heathen *noun He preached to the heathens.* infidel, non-believer, pagan, unbeliever.

heave *verb* **1** *He heaved the case on to the platform.* drag, draw, haul, hoick (*slang*), hoist, lift, pull, raise, yank (*informal*). **2** *She heaved a sigh.* emit, let out, utter. **3** *He heaved a rock at it.* cast, chuck (*informal*), fling, hurl, pitch, sling, throw, toss.

heaven *noun* **1** *Heaven is the abode of God.* Elysium, hereafter, next world, paradise. OPPOSITE hell. **2** *A dip in the pool is heaven on a hot day.* bliss, delight, ecstasy, happiness, joy, paradise. OPPOSITE hell. □ **the heavens** the firmament, the sky.

heavenly *adjective* **1** *heavenly creatures.* angelic, celestial, divine. OPPOSITE earthly. **2** (*informal*) *The* *music was heavenly.* beautiful, blissful, delightful, divine (*informal*), exquisite, glorious, sublime, wonderful.

heavy *adjective* **1** *a heavy parcel.* bulky, cumbersome, hefty, massive, ponderous, unwieldy, weighty. OPPOSITE light. **2** *a heavy man.* big, burly, fat, hefty, hulking, large, overweight, solid, stocky, stout, sturdy, thickset. OPPOSITE lean. **3** *heavy rain.* copious, hard, pouring, profuse, torrential. OPPOSITE light. **4** *a heavy drinker.* excessive, immoderate, intemperate, unrestrained. OPPOSITE moderate. **5** *heavy work.* arduous, exhausting, hard, laborious, onerous, strenuous, tiring. OPPOSITE light. **6** *Their army suffered heavy losses.* considerable, extensive, severe, substantial. OPPOSITE small. **7** *heavy fighting.* concentrated, intense, relentless, severe, unrelenting. OPPOSITE sporadic. **8** *heavy mist.* dense, thick. OPPOSITE fine. **9** *a heavy heart.* depressed, downcast, forlorn, gloomy, melancholy, miserable, sad, sorrowful, unhappy. OPPOSITE happy, light.

heckle *verb The demonstrators heckled the speaker.* harass, harry, interrupt, jeer at, shout down, taunt.

hectic *adjective a hectic holiday.* active, busy, exciting, frantic, frenzied, lively, wild. OPPOSITE leisurely.

hedge *noun They planted a hedge.* hedgerow, screen, windbreak. — *verb He keeps hedging on the issue.* beat about the bush, dodge, equivocate, play for time, prevaricate, stall, temporise. OPPOSITE commit yourself.

heed *verb Heed his advice.* bear in mind, listen to, mark, mind, pay attention to, take notice of. OPPOSITE disregard, ignore. — *noun He paid no heed to their advice.* attention, notice, regard, thought.

heedless *adjective heedless of the dangers.* careless, inattentive, negligent, oblivious, rash, reckless, unthinking, unwary. OPPOSITE mindful, wary.

hefty *adjective* **1** *a hefty footballer.* beefy, big, brawny, burly, heavy, husky, muscular, solid, strong, sturdy, tough. OPPOSITE weedy. **2** *a hefty blow.* forceful, heavy, mighty, powerful, strong, vigorous. OPPOSITE light. **3** *a hefty amount.* big, huge, large, massive, sizeable, substantial. OPPOSITE little.

height *noun* **1** *a person's height.* stature, tallness. **2** *The mountain's height is 1500 metres.* altitude, elevation. **3** *the view from the heights.* cliff, highland, hill, hilltop, peak, pinnacle, rise, summit, top. **4** *at the height of her career.* acme, apex, climax, heyday, peak, pinnacle, zenith. OPPOSITE nadir.

heighten *verb Her fears heightened.* grow, increase, intensify. OPPOSITE diminish.

heir, heiress *noun heir to a large fortune.* beneficiary, inheritor, legatee, successor.

hell *noun* **1** *They believe in heaven and hell.* Hades, inferno, underworld. OPPOSITE heaven. **2** *He made their life hell.* agony, misery, torment, torture. OPPOSITE bliss.

hellish *adjective a hellish job.* awful (*informal*), devilish, diabolical, dreadful (*informal*), frightful (*informal*), ghastly (*informal*), horrible (*informal*), infernal, unpleasant. OPPOSITE heavenly (*informal*), pleasant.

help *verb* **1** *He helped the criminal to escape. He helped to write the book.* abet, aid, assist, collaborate, cooperate, lend a hand. **2** *They helped the cause.* advance, back, boost, champion, further, promote, serve, stand up for, support. OPPOSITE hinder. **3** *These pills should help the headache.* alleviate, cure, ease, improve, relieve, remedy, soothe. OPPOSITE aggravate. **4** *He couldn't help laughing.* avoid, keep from, prevent, refrain from, resist. — *noun* **1** *She could not have managed without their help.* advice, aid, assistance, backing, backup, collaboration, contribution, cooperation, encouragement, succour, support. OPPOSITE opposition. **2** *Knowledge of another language is a help.* advantage, asset, benefit, boon. OPPOSITE handicap.

helper *noun She couldn't manage without her helper.* abetter, accessory, accomplice, aid, aide, assistant, auxiliary, collaborator, helpmate, offsider (*Australian*), partner, sidekick (*informal*), supporter.

helpful *adjective* **1** *He was only trying to be helpful.* accommodating, considerate, cooperative, kind, neighbourly, obliging, supportive, willing. OPPOSITE unhelpful. **2** *a helpful gadget.* convenient, handy, practical, useful. OPPOSITE useless. **3** *helpful criticism.* constructive, instructive, useful, valuable, worthwhile. OPPOSITE useless.

helping *noun a second helping of dessert.* portion, ration, serving.

helpless *adjective helpless as a baby.* defenceless, dependent, feeble, impotent, incapable, powerless, vulnerable. OPPOSITE capable.

hem *verb* **hem in** *He was hemmed in by reporters.* beset, besiege, box in, encircle, enclose, fence in, hedge in, restrict, surround.

hence *adverb Emily has a broken leg and hence cannot drive.* accordingly, consequently, so, therefore, thus.

henchman *noun The gangster leaves all his dirty work to his henchmen.* attendant, follower, hanger-on, lackey, retainer (*old use*), stooge (*informal*), supporter, yes-man.

herald *noun* **1** *The herald proclaimed the king's message.* announcer, messenger, town crier. **2** *heralds of spring.* forerunner, harbinger, portent, precursor, sign. — *verb John the Baptist heralded the coming of Jesus.* announce, foretell, proclaim, signal, usher in.

herb *noun She uses herbs in cooking.* flavouring, seasoning, spice.

herd *noun* **1** *a herd of animals.* drove, flock, mob (*Australian*), pack. **2** *a herd of shoppers.* army, company, crowd, drove, flock, group, horde, host, mass, mob, multitude, swarm, throng. — *verb* **1** *The people herded together under the shelter.* assemble, congregate, crowd, flock, gather, group, huddle, mob, muster, throng. **2** *He herded the sheep into the yard.* drive, guide, lead, round up, shepherd.

hereditary *adjective a hereditary disease.* genetic, inbred, inherited. OPPOSITE acquired.

heretic *noun Religious heretics were burnt at the stake.* apostate, dissenter, iconoclast, nonconformist, rebel, renegade. OPPOSITE conformist.

heritage *noun proud of his country's heritage.* background, history, inheritance, legacy, past, tradition.

hermit *noun a religious hermit.* loner, recluse, solitary.

hero, heroine *noun* **1** *The firefighters were honoured as heroes.* celebrity, champion, idol, legend (*informal*), star, superstar. OPPOSITE coward. **2** *the hero in the film.* goody (*informal*), protagonist. OPPOSITE villain.

heroic *adjective a heroic act. a heroic person.* bold, brave, chivalrous, courageous, daring, dauntless, doughty, fearless, gallant, intrepid, lion-hearted, plucky, valiant. OPPOSITE cowardly.

hero-worship *noun the object of hero-worship.* adulation, idolatry, idolisation, lionisation.

hesitant *adjective* **1** *Her speech was hesitant.* faltering, halting, slow, stammering, stuttering. OPPOSITE fluent. **2** *He was hesitant about interfering.* diffident, dubious, indecisive, in two minds, irresolute, reluctant, uncertain, unsure. OPPOSITE confident.

hesitate *verb He who hesitates is lost.* delay, dilly-dally (*informal*), dither, falter, hang back, hum and haw, pause, shilly-shally, vacillate, waver.

hew *verb She hewed a statue from the lump of wood.* carve, chisel, sculpt, sculpture, shape.

heyday *noun in its heyday.* height, peak, pinnacle, prime, zenith. OPPOSITE eclipse.

hiatus *noun* see GAP.

hibernate *verb The animal hibernates for six months.* be dormant, be inactive, sleep.

hidden *adjective a hidden meaning.* arcane, concealed, cryptic, dark, disguised, obscure, secret, veiled. OPPOSITE obvious.

hide[1] *verb* **1** *She hid her money.* bury, conceal, put away, secrete, stash (*informal*). OPPOSITE display. **2** *He hid his true feelings.* bottle up, conceal, cover up, disguise, mask, repress, suppress. OPPOSITE reveal. **3** *She hid until they'd gone.* conceal yourself, go into hiding, go underground, hole up (*informal*), lie low, take cover.

hide[2] *noun* **1** *a cow's hide.* fell, pelt, skin. **2** (*informal*) *Fancy having the hide to do that.* audacity, boldness, cheek, effrontery, gall (*slang*), impertinence, nerve, temerity.

hideous *adjective a hideous crime. a hideous picture.* abominable, appalling, atrocious, dreadful, frightful, ghastly, grim, grisly, grotesque, gruesome, horrendous, horrible, horrid, monstrous, objectionable, odious, repulsive, revolting, shocking, sickening, ugly, unsightly, vile. OPPOSITE beautiful, pleasant.

hideout *noun* (*informal*) *He thought they would never discover his hideout.* den, hidey-hole (*informal*), hiding place, lair, refuge, sanctuary.

hiding *noun* (*informal*) *He was going to get a hiding.* beating, caning, flogging, spanking, thrashing, whipping.

higgledy-piggledy *adjective* chaotic, confused, disorderly, jumbled, mixed-up, muddled, topsy-turvy. OPPOSITE orderly.

high *adjective* **1** *a high building.* high-rise, lofty, soaring, tall, towering. OPPOSITE low. **2** *a high platform.* elevated, raised. OPPOSITE low. **3** *She has a high position in the company.* exalted, important, powerful, prominent, senior, top. OPPOSITE lowly. **4** *high quality.* best, first, superior, supreme, top. OPPOSITE inferior, low. **5** *high temperatures.* above average, extreme, great, intense. OPPOSITE low. **6** *high prices.* dear, excessive, exorbitant, expensive, steep (*informal*), stiff (*informal*). OPPOSITE cheap. **7** *a high voice.* high-pitched, piercing, sharp, shrill, soprano, treble. OPPOSITE deep, low. **8** (*slang*) *high on drugs.* delirious, euphoric, high as a kite (*slang*), spaced out (*slang*); see also INTOXICATED.

highbrow *adjective a highbrow publication.* cultured, erudite, intellectual, learned, scholarly, sophisticated. OPPOSITE lowbrow.

highlands *plural noun* heights, hills, mountains, plateau, ranges, tableland, uplands. OPPOSITE lowlands.

highlight *noun It was the highlight of the trip.* climax, feature, high point, high spot. — *verb This case highlighted the problem.* accent, accentuate, emphasise, point up, spotlight, stress, underline. OPPOSITE play down.

highly-strung *adjective* edgy, excitable, jumpy, nervous, nervy, stressed, tense, touchy, uneasy, uptight (*informal*), volatile. OPPOSITE calm, placid.

high-spirited *adjective* boisterous, elated, excited, exhilarated, exuberant, full of beans (*informal*), jolly, lively, merry, vivacious. OPPOSITE depressed.

highway *noun a national highway.* expressway, freeway, main road, motorway, tollway.

highwayman *noun Travellers feared being held up by a highwayman.* bandit, brigand, bushranger, robber, thief.

hike *noun an afternoon hike through the bush.* bushwalk, ramble, tramp, trek, walk. — *verb They hiked for seven hours through the scrub.* backpack, ramble, roam, rove, tramp, trek, walk.

hiker *noun* backpacker, bushwalker, rambler, trekker, walker.

hilarious *adjective* **1** *We had a hilarious time.* boisterous, exuberant, jolly, lively, merry, noisy, riotous, rollicking. OPPOSITE dull. **2** *a hilarious story.* amusing, comical, funny, humorous, witty. OPPOSITE sad, serious.

hill *noun* **1** *They climbed the hill to admire the view.* bluff, dune, elevation, fell, foothill, headland, hillock, mesa, mountain, peak, promontory, rise, summit, tor; [*hills*] downs, heights, highlands, ranges, tiers (*Tasmania & early South Australia*). OPPOSITE valley. **2** *The cyclist struggled to get up the hill.* gradient, incline, rise, slope.

hillock *noun The land was basically flat with a few hillocks.* hummock, knoll, mound, rise.

hind *adjective hind legs.* back, hinder, posterior, rear. OPPOSITE fore, front.

hinder *verb The accident hindered progress.* block, curb, delay, frustrate, hamper, handicap, hold back, hold up, impede, inhibit, obstruct, prevent, restrict, slow, stonker (*Australian slang*), stop, thwart. OPPOSITE advance, help.

hindrance *noun The roadworks were a hindrance to traffic.* barrier, handicap, impediment, obstacle, obstruction, restriction, snag, stumbling block. OPPOSITE help.

hinge *verb It all hinges on the examination.* depend, hang, pivot, rest, revolve (around), turn.

hint *noun* **1** *He gave no hint of his plans.* allusion, clue, implication, indication, inkling, innuendo, insinuation, intimation, lead, suggestion. **2** *cleaning hints.* pointer, suggestion, tip, wrinkle (*informal*). — *verb She hinted that he was unwelcome.* imply, indicate, insinuate, intimate, suggest.

hire *verb* **1** *She hires the workers.* appoint, employ, engage, take on. OPPOSITE dismiss. **2** *They hired a car for their holiday.* charter, lease, rent.

hiss *verb The audience hissed.* boo, deride, heckle, hoot, jeer. OPPOSITE applaud.

historic *adjective a historic event.* celebrated, famous, important, memorable, momentous, significant. OPPOSITE unimportant.

historical *adjective a study based on historical evidence.* actual, authentic, documented, factual, real, recorded, true. OPPOSITE fictional, fictitious.

history noun **1** *He has written a history of Australia.* account, annals, chronicle, record, saga, study. **2** *She told them a little of her history.* background, biography, life story, memoirs, past, story.

hit verb **1** *He hit his opponent.* bash, batter, beat, belt (*slang*), box, buffet, butt, clip (*informal*), clobber (*informal*), clout (*informal*), club, cuff, dong (*Australian informal*), flog, hammer, job (*informal*), knock, lash, lay into (*informal*), pound, pummel, punch, quilt (*Australian slang*), rap, slap, slog, slug, smack, smite, sock (*slang*), spank, stoush (*Australian slang*), strike, swat, swipe (*informal*), tap, thrash, thump, thwack, trounce, wallop (*informal*), whack, whip. **2** *The truck hit the car.* bang into, bump into, collide with, crash into, ram into, run into, slam into, smash into. OPPOSITE miss. **3** *The loss hit her deeply.* affect, move, touch, upset, wound. — noun **1** *He received such a hit that he couldn't get up.* bash, blow, buffet, bump, clip (*informal*), clout (*informal*), dong (*Australian informal*), king-hit (*Australian informal*), knock, knockout, punch, slap, slog, slug, smack, stroke, swipe (*informal*), thump, thwack, wallop (*informal*), whack. **2** *The play was a big hit.* sell-out, sensation, smash hit (*informal*), success, triumph, winner. OPPOSITE failure. □ **hit back** see RETALIATE. **hit on** *He hit on a method which worked.* chance on, come up with, discover, stumble on. **hit out at** *He hit out at the authorities.* attack, condemn, criticise, denounce, lash out at.

hitch verb **1** *He hitched the animal to the cart.* attach, connect, couple, fasten, harness, join, tie, yoke. OPPOSITE unfasten. **2** see HITCHHIKE. **3** *He hitched up his trousers.* jerk, pull, tug, yank (*informal*). — noun *a slight hitch in the proceedings.* catch, complication, difficulty, hiccup, hold-up, interruption, obstacle, problem, snag, stumbling block.

hitchhike verb *He hitchhiked from Adelaide to Darwin.* hitch, thumb a lift.

hit-or-miss adjective *His methods were rather hit-or-miss.* careless, casual, haphazard, indiscriminate, random. OPPOSITE precise.

hive noun *a hive of bees.* apiary, beehive.

hoard noun *He kept a hoard of chocolate in the cupboard.* cache, fund, reserve, stash (*informal*), stock, stockpile, store, supply, treasure trove. — verb *He hoards tiny jars.* accumulate, amass, collect, gather, hang on to, hold on to, keep, lay up, save, stash away (*informal*), stockpile, store.

hoarding noun *They attached an advertisement to the hoarding.* billboard, fence.

hoarse adjective *a hoarse voice.* croaky, gravelly, gruff, harsh, husky, rasping, rough, scratchy. OPPOSITE smooth.

hoax verb *Don't let him hoax you.* bluff, con (*informal*), deceive, delude, dupe, fool, have on (*informal*), hoodwink, pull someone's leg, swindle, take in (*informal*), trick. — noun *We soon realised that it was a hoax.* con (*informal*), confidence trick, deception, fraud, prank, scam (*slang*), spoof (*informal*), swindle, trick.

hobble verb *He hobbled about in plaster for six weeks.* limp, shamble, shuffle, stumble.

hobby noun *Building boats is his hobby, not his job.* diversion, inter-

est, leisure activity, pastime, recreation, relaxation, sideline. OPPOSITE job.

hobby horse noun *He's on his hobby horse again.* fixation, obsession, pet subject, preoccupation.

hog noun (*informal*) *Don't be such a hog.* glutton, greedy-guts (*slang*), pig (*informal*).

hoist verb *He hoisted the box on to his shoulder.* haul, heave, hoick (*slang*), lift, pull up, raise, winch. OPPOSITE lower.

hold verb **1** *He held the bag.* bring, carry, clasp, clutch, grasp, grip, hang on to, keep, retain, seize, take. OPPOSITE let go. **2** *The police held the suspect for questioning.* arrest, confine, detain, keep, lock up. OPPOSITE release. **3** *The hall holds 1000 people.* accommodate, have a capacity of, house, seat, take. **4** *This beam won't hold the roof.* bear, carry, support, take. **5** *The fine weather is expected to hold until the weekend.* carry on, continue, endure, last, persist, stay. **6** *The play held their interest.* captivate, capture, keep, maintain, sustain. OPPOSITE lose. **7** *He held an important job.* have, hold down, occupy, possess. **8** *They held a meeting about local heritage issues.* call, conduct, convene, run. **9** *Hold your tongue.* check, control, curb, restrain. **10** *She holds me responsible.* believe, consider, deem, judge, regard, think. — noun **1** *He kept a firm hold on the railing.* clasp, clutch, grasp, grip. **2** *The blackmailer has a hold over them.* control, dominance, influence, power, sway. □ **hold back** *She held back her tears. They held back information.* block, check, control, curb, halt, keep back, repress, restrain, stop, suppress, withhold. **hold forth** *He held forth on his pet subject.* declaim, harangue, lecture, preach, sermonise, sound off (*informal*), speak, spout. **hold off** *They held off making a decision.* defer, delay, postpone, put off, stall. **hold out** **1** *She held out her hand.* extend, put out, reach out, stretch out. **2** *He can hold out indefinitely.* continue, hang on (*informal*), last, persevere, persist, stick it out (*informal*). **hold up** **1** *The work was held up by the wet weather.* delay, hinder, obstruct, slow down. **2** *The bushrangers held them up.* bail up (*Australian*), mug, rob, stick up (*informal*), waylay.

holder noun see CONTAINER.

hold-up noun **1** *a traffic hold-up.* delay, jam, snarl, stoppage. **2** *an armed hold-up.* burglary, robbery, stick-up (*informal*).

hole noun **1** *a hole in the wall.* aperture, breach, break, cavity, chink, crack, fissure, gap, opening, orifice, slit, slot, space. **2** *The ground was uneven with holes.* cavity, crabhole (*Australian*), depression, gilgai (*Australian*), gnamma hole (*Australian*), hollow, melon hole (*Australian*), pit, pocket, pothole, tunnel. OPPOSITE mound. **3** *a hole in the tyre.* gash, leak, perforation, puncture, split, tear. **4** *The animals returned to their holes.* burrow, den, hideout (*informal*), lair, warren.

holiday noun **1** *Christmas and Easter are holidays.* feast day, festival. **2** *a holiday from school and work.* break, furlough, leave, rest, time off, vacation. **3** *an overseas holiday.* cruise, excursion, honeymoon, safari, tour, trip.

hollow adjective **1** *a hollow Easter egg.* empty, unfilled, void. OPPOSITE solid. **2** *hollow cheeks.* concave, sunken. OPPOSITE rounded. **3** *hollow promises.* empty, false, hypocritical, insincere. OPPOSITE genuine. — noun **1** *a hollow in the*

ground. basin, bunker (*Golf*), cave, cavern, cavity, crabhole (*Australian*), crater, depression, ditch, gilgai (*Australian*), gnamma (*Australian*), hole, pit, pothole, trough. OPPOSITE mound. **2** *It is cool in the hollows.* dell, glen, gully (*Australian*), valley. OPPOSITE hill. — verb *He hollowed out a spot for the plant.* dig, excavate, gouge, scoop. OPPOSITE fill.

holocaust noun *the nuclear holocaust. millions of Holocaust victims.* annihilation, carnage, conflagration, destruction, devastation, genocide, massacre, mass murder.

holy adjective **1** *holy ground.* blessed, consecrated, divine, hallowed, sacred, sacrosanct. **2** *He led a holy life.* blameless, devout, godly, pious, religious, righteous, saintly, virtuous. OPPOSITE sinful.

homage noun *The people paid homage to the king.* honour, obeisance, respect, tribute. OPPOSITE disrespect.

home noun **1** *The family moved into a new home.* abode (*old use*), domicile, dwelling, habitation, house, place, residence; see also FLAT, HOUSE. **2** *He left his home to come to Australia.* see HOMELAND. **3** *a home for sick or elderly people.* hospice, hostel, institution, nursing home, rest home, retirement home. **4** *the home of the quokka.* domain, habitat, habitation, haunt, territory. — verb **home in on** *He homed in on the target.* aim at, concentrate on, focus on, zero in on, zoom in on. □ **at home** *He made his guests feel at home.* at ease, comfortable, relaxed. **home unit** apartment, condominium (*American*), flat, unit.

homeland noun *She longed to return to her homeland.* birthplace, fatherland, home, mother country, native land.

homeless adjective **1** *a homeless kitten.* abandoned, lost, stray. **2** *a homeless person.* displaced, evicted, exiled, itinerant, nomadic, outcast, vagabond, vagrant, wandering.

homely adjective **1** *a homely guest house.* comfortable, cosy, friendly, informal, liveable, simple, unpretentious, welcoming. OPPOSITE formal. **2** (*American*) *a homely girl.* ordinary, plain, unattractive. OPPOSITE attractive.

homestead noun *the homestead on a sheep station.* farmhouse, home, house, residence.

homework noun *two hours' homework per night.* assignment, prep, preparation, study, work.

homicide noun *The man was found guilty of homicide.* assassination, killing, manslaughter, murder, slaying.

homily noun *The chapel service includes a homily.* address, lecture, sermon, speech.

homogeneous adjective *They form a homogeneous group.* consistent, uniform, unvarying. OPPOSITE heterogeneous.

homosexual adjective gay, lesbian (*female*). CONTRASTS WITH bisexual, heterosexual.

honest adjective **1** *an honest businessman.* honourable, law-abiding, principled, scrupulous, straight, trustworthy, truthful, upright, upstanding, veracious. OPPOSITE corrupt, dishonest. **2** *an honest opinion.* blunt, candid, direct, forthright, frank, genuine, open, sincere, straightforward, truthful. OPPOSITE dishonest, insincere. **3** *honest dealings.* above board, ethical, fair, honourable, lawful, legal, legitimate, proper. OPPOSITE fraudulent, unethical.

honesty noun *She was admired for her complete honesty.* frankness, genuineness, integrity, openness, probity, rectitude, sincerity, trustworthiness, truthfulness, uprightness, veracity. OPPOSITE dishonesty.

honour noun **1** *She treated him with great honour.* admiration, esteem, homage, respect, reverence, veneration, worship. OPPOSITE contempt. **2** *He brought great honour to his school.* acclaim, credit, distinction, fame, glory, prestige, recognition, renown, repute. OPPOSITE discredit, dishonour. **3** *He deemed it an honour to have been chosen.* compliment, privilege. OPPOSITE insult. **4** *a man of honour.* decency, fairness, honesty, integrity, morality, principle, probity, rectitude, scruples, virtue. OPPOSITE dishonour. — verb **1** *They honoured the dead with two minutes' silence.* pay homage to, pay tribute to, pay your respects to, praise, salute. OPPOSITE insult. **2** *She honours God before people.* admire, esteem, glorify, hallow, praise, respect, revere, value, venerate, worship. OPPOSITE disrespect. **3** *She would always honour a promise.* abide by, fulfil, keep, stand by, stick to. OPPOSITE break.

honourable adjective *an honourable businessman.* above board, decent, ethical, high-minded, honest, principled, reputable, respectable, scrupulous, upright. OPPOSITE dishonourable.

hoodwink verb *Be careful not to be hoodwinked.* bamboozle (*informal*), bluff, cheat, con (*informal*), deceive, defraud, dupe, fool, hoax, swindle, trick.

hook noun *Hang your hat on the hook.* nail, peg. — verb **1** *He hooked a large fish.* capture, catch, take. **2** *He hooked the gate behind him.* fasten, hitch, latch, secure. OPPOSITE unhook. □ **be hooked on** (*slang*) *He is hooked on dope.* be addicted to, be dependent on.

hooked adjective *a hooked nose.* aquiline.

hooligan noun *The police arrested the young hooligans.* delinquent, hoodlum, hoon (*Australian informal*), larrikin (*Australian*), lout, ruffian, tearaway, thug, tough, troublemaker, vandal, yob (*informal*).

hoon noun *She was upset by the hoon's reckless driving.* delinquent, hooligan, yob (*informal*).

hoop noun *He jumped through a series of hoops.* band, circle, ring.

hoot noun **1** *The owl's hoots woke the other animals.* cry, scream, screech, shriek, whoop. **2** *The audience sent him off the stage with hoots.* boo, catcall, hiss, jeer. OPPOSITE cheer. — verb **1** *The train hooted as it neared the station.* screech, whistle. **2** *The audience hooted the speaker off the stage.* boo, deride, heckle, hiss, jeer, mock. OPPOSITE cheer. **3** *The driver hooted his horn.* blast, blow, honk, sound, toot.

hooter noun *The hooter sounded.* horn, siren, whistle.

hop verb *The rabbit hopped out of the way.* bob, bound, jump, leap, skip, spring. — noun **1** *With one hop he reached the chair.* bob, bounce, bound, jump, leap, spring. **2** *a short hop between towns.* distance, flight, journey, stage, trip.

hope noun **1** *They live in hope that one day he'll return.* confidence, expectation, faith, optimism, trust. OPPOSITE despair. **2** *no hope of winning.* chance, likelihood, probability, prospect. **3** *filled with hopes of happiness.* ambition, aspiration, desire, dream, longing, wish. — verb *He is hoping for a promotion.* aspire, desire, dream, expect, hanker, long, trust, want, wish. OPPOSITE despair of.

hopeful *adjective* **1** *They were hopeful of a cure.* confident, expectant, optimistic, sanguine, trusting. OPPOSITE pessimistic. **2** *a hopeful sign.* auspicious, encouraging, favourable, heartening, positive, promising, propitious, reassuring. OPPOSITE discouraging.

hopeless *adjective* **1** *He felt hopeless in the face of all these problems.* dejected, demoralised, depressed, despairing, despondent, downcast, forlorn, pessimistic, wretched. OPPOSITE hopeful, optimistic. **2** *The situation is hopeless.* bad, desperate, incurable, irredeemable, irreparable, irretrievable, irrevocable. **3** *a hopeless cook.* feeble, inadequate, incompetent, poor, useless. OPPOSITE competent, good.

horde *noun She avoided the hordes of shoppers.* crowd, drove, mass, mob, multitude, swarm, throng.

horizon *noun a ship on the horizon.* skyline.

horizontal *adjective a horizontal surface.* flat, level. OPPOSITE vertical.

horrible *adjective* **1** *a horrible crime.* abhorrent, abominable, appalling, atrocious, awful, despicable, detestable, dreadful, foul, frightful, ghastly, grisly, gruesome, hideous, horrendous, horrid, horrific, loathsome, monstrous, odious, repugnant, repulsive, revolting, shocking, sickening, terrible, vile. OPPOSITE pleasant. **2** (*informal*) *a horrible person.* awful, disagreeable, horrid, mean, nasty, objectionable, obnoxious, offensive, unbearable, unkind, unpleasant. OPPOSITE charming, kind.

horrify *verb The news horrified her.* alarm, appal, disgust, frighten, revolt, scare, shock, terrify. OPPOSITE delight, please.

horror *noun* **1** *He felt horror at the sight of the bushfire.* alarm, consternation, dismay, dread, fear, panic, terror, trepidation. **2** *He has a horror of spiders.* abhorrence, antipathy, aversion, dislike, dread, fear, hatred, loathing, revulsion. OPPOSITE liking. **3** *The little horror had locked them out.* devil, rascal, scallywag, scamp, scoundrel, terror (*informal*), wretch. OPPOSITE angel.

horse *noun* bronco, brumby (*Australian*), carthorse, charger, draughthorse, gee-gee (*informal*), hack, moke (*Australian*), mount, mustang, nag (*informal*), nanto (*Australian old use*), neddy (*informal*), pacer, palfrey (*old use*), pony, racehorse, steed (*poetical*), trotter, yarraman (*Australian*); [*male horses*] colt, gelding, sire, stallion; [*female horses*] filly, mare; [*young horses*] colt, filly, foal.

horse-rider *noun* equestrian, hoop (*Australian informal*), horseman, horsewoman, jockey, rider.

hospice *noun She spent her last months in a hospice.* home, hospital, institution, nursing home.

hospitable *adjective hospitable hosts.* amiable, cordial, friendly, generous, genial, gracious, kind, sociable, warm, welcoming. OPPOSITE inhospitable.

hospital *noun The city is served by several hospitals.* clinic, hospice, infirmary, medical centre, nursing home, sanatorium.

host[1] *noun the host of the show.* anchorperson, announcer, compère, disc jockey, DJ, Master of Ceremonies, MC, presenter.

host[2] *noun A host of people attended.* army, crowd, horde, lot, mass, mob, multitude, myriad, swarm, throng; see also GROUP. OPPOSITE handful.

hostage *noun The aid worker was taken as a hostage.* captive, prisoner.

hostel *noun They stayed at a students' hostel.* boarding house, guest house, home.

hostess *noun She works as a hostess with the airline.* air hostess, flight attendant, hostie (*Australian informal*), steward, stewardess.

hostile *adjective* **1** *hostile aircraft.* attacking, enemy, opposing, warring. OPPOSITE friendly. **2** *We were given a hostile reception.* chilly, cold, cool, frosty, icy, unfriendly. OPPOSITE friendly, warm. **3** *They exchanged hostile words.* aggressive, angry, belligerent, spiteful, unfriendly, unkind, vicious. OPPOSITE kind.

hostility *noun There was open hostility between the former friends.* aggression, animosity, antagonism, antipathy, belligerence, enmity, friction, opposition, rancour, resentment, unfriendliness. OPPOSITE friendship. □ **hostilities** *plural noun* see WAR.

hot *adjective* **1** *hot weather.* boiling, scorching, sultry, summery, sweltering, torrid, warm. OPPOSITE cold. **2** *a hot fire. a hot pan.* baking, blazing, boiling, burning, fiery, flaming, glowing, piping hot, red-hot, roasting, scalding, scorching, searing, sizzling, steaming. OPPOSITE cold. **3** *a hot curry.* burning, peppery, piquant, pungent, sharp, spicy. OPPOSITE mild. **4** *a hot debate.* angry, animated, ardent, emotional, excited, fervent, fiery, heated, intense, lively, passionate, stormy. OPPOSITE calm. **5** *The news is hot off the press.* fresh, latest, new, recent. OPPOSITE stale. **6** *He's not too hot at chess any more.* capable, competent, good, skilful. — *verb* (*informal*) *She hotted up the bath.* heat up, reheat, warm up. OPPOSITE cool.

hotel *noun They stayed the night at the hotel in the town centre.* guest house, inn, local (*informal*), motel, pub (*informal*), public house, tavern.

hotheaded *adjective* excitable, fiery, impetuous, impulsive, rash, reckless, wild.

hothouse *noun Tomatoes may be cultivated in a hothouse.* conservatory, glasshouse, greenhouse.

hotpot *noun She cooked a beef hotpot.* casserole, goulash, ragout, stew.

hot-tempered *adjective* angry, bad-tempered, fiery, irritable, quick-tempered, short-tempered, tempestuous. OPPOSITE placid.

hound *noun a pack of hounds.* beagle, bloodhound, dog, foxhound, greyhound, hunting dog, wolfhound. — *verb He hounded them for the money.* badger, chase, dog, harass, hunt, keep at, nag, pester, pursue.

house *noun* **1** *They have moved into a new house.* abode (*old use*), accommodation, domicile, dwelling, habitation, home, place, residence; [*kinds of house*] bungalow, chalet, cottage, farmhouse, homestead, hut, igloo, maisonette, manor, manse, mansion, presbytery, rectory, shack, shanty, terrace house, town house, vicarage, villa. **2** *two houses of parliament.* assembly, chamber, council, legislative body. **3** *They played to a packed house.* auditorium, hall, theatre. **4** *the House of Windsor.* dynasty, family, line, lineage. — *verb Several families housed the students.* accommodate, billet, put up, shelter.

housebreaker *noun* burglar, intruder, robber, thief.

household *noun The work is shared in their household.* family, home, house. — *adjective a household name.* familiar, well-known.

householder *noun a letter addressed to the householder.* occupant, owner, resident, tenant.

housework *noun* cleaning, cooking, home duties, housekeeping.

housing *noun* **1** *The government provides housing.* accommodation, dwellings, homes, houses, lodging(s), quarters, residences, shelter. **2** *The machine's housing is cracked.* case, casing, container, cover.

hovel *noun The poor man lived in a dreadful hovel.* dump (*informal*), hole (*informal*), hut, shack, shanty, shed. OPPOSITE palace.

hover *verb* **1** *The butterfly hovered over the flower.* float, flutter. **2** *The sales assistant hovered over the customer.* hang about, linger, wait near.

however *adverb Later, however, she changed her mind.* nevertheless, none the less, though.

howl *noun* **1** *the howl of a dog.* bay, cry, wail, whine, yelp, yowl. **2** *a howl of pain.* bellow, cry, groan, scream, shout, shriek, wail, yell, yowl. — *verb* **1** *He howled in pain.* bawl, bellow, cry, roar, scream, shout, shriek, wail, whine, yell, yelp, yowl; see also WEEP. **2** *They howled with laughter.* cry, hoot, roar, scream, shriek. □ **howl down** *The speaker was howled down.* boo, heckle, hiss, hoot, jeer, shout down.

hub *noun a transport hub.* centre, core, focus, heart, pivot.

hubbub *noun The hubbub in the hall ceased as the speaker stood up.* babble, clamour, din, hullabaloo, noise, racket. OPPOSITE silence.

huddle *verb* **1** *Fifteen people huddled into a lift.* cluster, cram, crowd, flock, herd, jam, pile, press, squash, squeeze, throng. **2** *He huddled up in a chair by the fire.* curl up, nestle, snuggle.

hue[1] *noun The paper comes in various hues.* colour, shade, tinge, tint, tone.

hue[2] *noun* **hue and cry** *There was a great hue and cry over the incident.* clamour, commotion, furore, fuss, hullabaloo, outcry, protest, to-do, uproar.

huffy *adjective He gets huffy when criticised.* annoyed, grumpy, in a huff, miffed (*informal*), offended, peevish, petulant, piqued, resentful, shirty (*informal*), sulky, testy, touchy. OPPOSITE good-humoured.

hug *verb He hugged her and kissed her.* clasp, cuddle, embrace, hold, squeeze.

huge *adjective a huge amount. a huge object.* astronomical, big, colossal, enormous, exorbitant, gargantuan, giant, gigantic, great, humungous (*slang*), immense, jumbo, large, mammoth, massive, mighty, monstrous, staggering, stupendous, sweeping, vast, whopping (*slang*). OPPOSITE tiny.

hulking *adjective* (*informal*) *a hulking weightlifter.* bulky, burly, heavy, hefty, husky, large, massive.

hull *noun a ship's hull.* body, frame, framework, skeleton.

hullabaloo *noun They made such a hullabaloo when she left.* clamour, commotion, din, fracas, fuss, hubbub, racket, rumpus, uproar.

hum *verb The motor hummed.* buzz, drone, purr, vibrate, whirr. — *noun There was an unpleasant hum in the amplifier.* buzz, drone, purr, vibration, whirr.

human *adjective* **human being** child, human, individual, man, mortal, person, woman.

humane *adjective a humane judge.* benevolent, compassionate, humanitarian, kind, kind-hearted, merciful, sympathetic, understanding. OPPOSITE cruel, inhumane.

humanitarian *adjective motivated by humanitarian ideals.* benevolent, humane, philanthropic.

humanity *noun* **1** *crimes against humanity.* humankind, human race, man, mankind, people, society. **2** *The politician was admired for his humanity.* benevolence, compassion, goodness, humaneness, kindness, mercy, sympathy, understanding. OPPOSITE cruelty, inhumanity.

humble *adjective* **1** *He is humble about his talents.* meek, modest, self-effacing, unassertive, unassuming. OPPOSITE proud. **2** *a humble house.* modest, ordinary, plain, simple, unpretentious. OPPOSITE grand. **3** *a man of humble rank.* insignificant, low, lowly, unimportant. OPPOSITE high. — *verb The experience humbled him.* abase, chasten, disgrace, humiliate, mortify, shame, subdue, take down a peg (*informal*). OPPOSITE exalt.

humbug *noun* **1** *Don't believe all that humbug.* blarney, boloney (*informal*), bull (*slang*), bunkum, claptrap, deceit, deception, fraud, hocus-pocus, lies, mumbo-jumbo, nonsense, pretence, rubbish, rot (*slang*), sham, trickery. OPPOSITE truth. **2** *He was exposed as a humbug.* charlatan, cheat, con man (*informal*), fake, fraud, phoney (*informal*), quack, sham, swindler, trickster.

humdrum *adjective a humdrum packing job.* boring, commonplace, dreary, dull, monotonous, mundane, ordinary, repetitive, routine, tedious, unexciting, uninteresting, wearisome. OPPOSITE interesting.

humid *adjective The humid atmosphere was oppressive.* clammy, close, damp, dank, moist, muggy, steamy, sticky, sultry. OPPOSITE dry.

humiliate *verb He humiliated his son by correcting him in public.* abase, chasten, demean, disgrace, embarrass, humble, mortify, put down, shame, take down a peg (*informal*). OPPOSITE exalt.

humiliation *noun He suffered humiliation at the announcement.* abasement, disgrace, embarrassment, indignity, mortification, shame. OPPOSITE pride.

humility *noun a great man with true humility.* deference, humbleness, lowliness, meekness, modesty, unpretentiousness. OPPOSITE pride.

humorous *adjective a humorous story.* amusing, comic, comical, droll, facetious, farcical, funny, hilarious, laughable, ridiculous, witty. OPPOSITE serious.

humour *noun* **1** *She appreciated the humour of the situation.* absurdity, comedy, farcicalness, funniness, ludicrousness, ridiculousness. OPPOSITE gravity. **2** *His stories are full of humour.* comedy, jokes, wit, wittiness. OPPOSITE seriousness. **3** *Is he in a good humour?* disposition, mood, spirits, temper. — *verb They only agreed to attend in order to humour him.* go along with, indulge, pamper, pander to, play up to.

hump *noun a camel's hump.* bulge, bump, hunch, lump, swelling. — *verb He humped his back.* arch, curve, hunch.

hunch *verb She was hunched over her work.* arch, bend, crouch, hump. — *noun I have a hunch about that.* feeling, idea, inkling, intuition, premonition, suspicion.

hunger *noun* **1** *He nearly died of hunger.* malnutrition, starvation. OPPOSITE overeating. **2** *a hunger for knowledge.* appetite, craving, desire, longing, thirst.

hungry *adjective After their long walk they were hungry.* famished, peckish (*informal*), ravenous, starved, starving. OPPOSITE full.

hunk *noun a big hunk of cake.* block, chunk, lump, piece, slab, wedge.

hunt *verb* **1** *He is hunting wild pigs.* chase, pursue, stalk, track, trail. **2** *She was hunting for her stapler.* ferret out, forage for, fossick for (*Australian informal*), look for, rummage for, search for, seek. — *noun the hunt for clues.* chase, pursuit, quest, search.

hunter *noun* huntsman, predator, tracker.

hurdle *noun* **1** *He jumped all the hurdles.* barricade, barrier, fence. **2** *The language was another hurdle to overcome.* barrier, difficulty, impediment, obstacle, problem, snag, stumbling block.

hurl *verb He hurled a ball through the window.* cast, chuck (*informal*), fling, heave, pitch, propel, sling (*informal*), throw, toss.

hurly-burly *noun the hurly-burly of the playground.* activity, bustle, commotion, hubbub, hustle and bustle, tumult.

hurricane *noun The hurricane caused extensive damage.* cyclone, tropical cyclone, typhoon; see also STORM, WIND[1].

hurry *noun No need for all the hurry.* bustle, haste, hurry-scurry, hustle, rush, scurry, urgency. OPPOSITE delay. — *verb* **1** *He hurried home.* bolt, dash, fly, hasten, hurtle, hustle, race, run, rush, scoot, scurry, scuttle, speed, whiz, zip, zoom. OPPOSITE dawdle. **2** *He told me to hurry.* be quick, get a move on (*informal*), get cracking (*informal*), get your skates on (*informal*), make haste, make it snappy (*informal*), step on it (*informal*). OPPOSITE slow down. **3** *They hurried the work along.* accelerate, expedite, fast-track (*informal*), hasten, push, quicken, speed up. OPPOSITE delay.

hurt *verb* **1** *He hurt his leg. He was severely hurt.* bruise, cripple, cut, damage, disable, injure, maim, mutilate, scratch, sprain, wound. **2** *Oil won't hurt the machine.* damage, harm, impair, spoil. OPPOSITE improve. **3** *She was hurt by his tactless remark.* distress, grieve, offend, pain, trouble, upset, wound. OPPOSITE cheer. **4** *My head hurts.* ache, be painful, be sore, smart, sting, throb. — *noun mental hurt. physical hurt.* ache, affliction, agony, anguish, damage, discomfort, distress, grief, harm, injury, misery, pain, sadness, soreness, sorrow, suffering, torment, torture.

hurtful *adjective a hurtful comment.* brutal, cruel, cutting, distressing, malicious, mean, nasty, unkind, upsetting. OPPOSITE helpful, kind.

hurtle *verb The car hurtled along.* fly, race, shoot, speed, tear, whiz, zip, zoom. OPPOSITE crawl.

husband *noun The woman does not have a husband.* bridegroom, consort, groom, mate, partner, spouse. — *verb They husbanded their resources.* conserve, hoard, preserve, save. OPPOSITE waste.

hush *verb She hushed the baby.* calm, lull, quieten, shush (*informal*), silence, soothe. — *noun There was a hush in the room.* quietness, silence, stillness. OPPOSITE noise. □ **hush up** *He was paid to hush things up.* conceal, cover up, keep secret, suppress.

hushed *adjective They spoke in hushed voices.* low, quiet, soft, subdued. OPPOSITE loud.

husk *noun He removed the seeds from the husks.* case, hull, pod, shell.

husky *adjective* **1** *a husky voice.* croaking, dry, gravelly, gruff, guttural, harsh, hoarse, rasping, rough, throaty. **2** *a husky young man.* beefy, brawny, burly, hefty, hulking, muscular, nuggety (*Australian*), solid, stocky, strapping, strong, sturdy, thickset, tough. OPPOSITE puny.

hustle *verb* **1** *They hustled the man out of the building.* bundle, bustle, jostle, push, shove, thrust. **2** *He hustled her into buying the computer.* force, pressure, push, rush. — *noun the hustle of the big city.* activity, bustle, haste, hurly-burly, hurry, hurry-scurry, rush, tumult.

hut *noun a bush hut.* cabin, chalet, gunyah (*Australian*), house, hovel, humpy (*Australian*), lean-to, mia mia (*Australian*), shack, shanty, shed, shelter, skillion (*Australian*), wurley (*Australian*).

hutch *noun a rabbit hutch.* box, cage, coop, enclosure, pen.

hybrid *noun The gardener has produced a hybrid.* blend, cross, crossbreed, half-breed, mixture. OPPOSITE thoroughbred.

hygienic *adjective a hygienic hospital ward.* aseptic, clean, disinfected, germ-free, healthy, sanitary, sterile, sterilised. OPPOSITE dirty.

hymn *noun Hymns are sung in church.* anthem, canticle, carol, chorus, introit, psalm, song.

hype *noun* (*slang*) *There was a lot of hype about the new book.* advertising, plug (*informal*), promotion, publicity.

hyperbole *noun The novelist uses hyperbole to good effect.* exaggeration, overstatement. OPPOSITE understatement.

hypnotic *adjective hypnotic music.* mesmerising, soporific, spellbinding.

hypnotise *verb He was hypnotised by her looks.* bewitch, enthral, entrance, fascinate, mesmerise.

hypocrisy *noun His speech was full of hypocrisy.* deceit, dishonesty, dissembling, falseness, insincerity. OPPOSITE sincerity.

hypocritical *adjective It is hypocritical not to practise what you preach.* false, inconsistent, insincere, pharisaical, two-faced. OPPOSITE sincere.

hypothesis *noun He is investigating a new hypothesis.* assumption, conjecture, idea, proposition, speculation, supposition, theory, thesis. OPPOSITE fact.

hypothetical *adjective a hypothetical example.* academic, theoretical. OPPOSITE real.

hysterical *adjective The woman was hysterical after the accident.* berserk, crazed, distraught, frantic, frenzied, overwrought, raving, uncontrollable. OPPOSITE composed.

Ii

ice *noun Ice is frozen water.* black ice, floe, frost, glacier, iceberg, icicle, pack ice, rime.

icing *noun lemon icing on the cake.* frosting, glaze.

icon *noun a religious icon.* idol, image, statue.

icy *adjective* **1** *icy winds. icy temperatures.* biting, bitter, chilly, cold, freezing, frigid, frosty, glacial, nippy (*informal*), subzero. OPPOSITE blazing, hot. **2** *icy roads.* frosty, frozen, slippery.

idea *noun* **1** *Cathy has lots of good ideas.* brainwave (*informal*), concept, notion, plan, proposal, scheme, suggestion, thought. **2** *Can you give him some idea of what is needed?* clue, hint, impression, indication, inkling, intimation. **3** *He tested his idea.* hunch, hypothesis, suspicion, theory. **4** *They have different ideas about discipline.* attitude, belief, conviction, notion, opinion, thought, view.

ideal *adjective ideal conditions.* excellent, exemplary, faultless, model, optimal, optimum, perfect.

idealistic *adjective an idealistic view of how things could be.* impractical, optimistic, romantic, unrealistic, Utopian, visionary. OPPOSITE realistic.

identical *adjective The two suitcases look identical.* alike, indistinguishable, matching, the same. OPPOSITE different.

identify *verb* **1** *The victim was able to identify her attacker in the line-up.* distinguish, name, pick out, recognise, single out, spot. **2** *The mechanic identified the problem.* detect, diagnose, discover, pinpoint, work out. □ **identify with** *She could not identify with the characters.* empathise with, relate to, respond to, sympathise with.

identity *noun* **1** *proof of identity.* ID, name. **2** *She worried about losing her identity.* individuality, personality, uniqueness. **3** (*Australian informal*) *a television identity.* celebrity, personage, personality, star. OPPOSITE nonentity.

ideology *noun Marxist ideology.* beliefs, creed, doctrine, ideas, philosophy, principles, tenets.

idiom *noun Some idioms are hard to translate.* expression, phrase.

idiosyncrasy *noun He got to know her idiosyncrasies.* characteristic, eccentricity, foible, habit, mannerism, peculiarity, quirk, trait.

idiot *noun* (*informal*) *Don't be such an idiot!* ass (*informal*), blockhead, bonehead, chump (*informal*), clot (*informal*), cretin, dill (*Australian informal*), dimwit (*informal*), dodo (*informal*), dolt, dope (*informal*), drongo (*Australian informal*), dummy (*informal*), dunce, fat-head (*informal*), fool, galah (*Australian slang*), half-wit, ignoramus, imbecile, jerk (*slang*), lunatic, moron (*informal*), nincompoop, ninny, nitwit (*informal*), nong (*Australian informal*), numskull, nut (*informal*), simpleton, thickhead (*informal*), twerp (*slang*), twit (*slang*). OPPOSITE genius.

idiotic *adjective Driving across the broken bridge was an idiotic thing to do.* absurd, crazy, dumb (*informal*), foolhardy, foolish, inane, irrational, lunatic, mad, nutty (*informal*), reckless, ridiculous, senseless, silly, stupid, unintelligent, unwise. OPPOSITE sensible.

idle *adjective* **1** *The tractor lay idle.* inactive, out of action, unused. **2** *an idle fellow.* indolent, lazy, shiftless, slothful, sluggish. OPPOSITE busy. **3** *idle time.* free, unfilled, unoccupied, unproductive. **4** *idle chatter.* empty, frivolous, pointless, superficial, trivial, useless, worthless. — *verb* **1** *He spends a lot of time just idling.* laze, loaf, potter, slack, take it easy, vegetate. OPPOSITE work. **2** *He idled away the time.* fritter away, waste, while away.

idler *noun The boss doesn't want any idlers.* bludger (*Australian informal*), good-for-nothing, layabout, lazybones (*informal*), loafer, malingerer, shirker, skiver (*informal*), slacker, slouch (*informal*).

idol *noun* **1** *The people worshipped idols.* effigy, graven image, icon, image, statue. **2** *a sporting idol.* celebrity, heart-throb (*slang*), hero, heroine, star, superstar.

idolise *verb She idolised her brother.* adore, deify, dote on, glorify, lionise, look up to, love, revere, venerate, worship. OPPOSITE despise.

ignite *verb The wood was slow to ignite.* burn, catch fire, kindle.

ignominious *adjective Their army suffered an ignominious defeat.* degrading, disgraceful, dishonourable, humiliating, infamous, inglorious, shameful. OPPOSITE honourable.

ignorant *adjective* **1** *ignorant of the road rules.* oblivious, unaware, unfamiliar (with), uninformed (about). OPPOSITE aware. **2** *She felt ignorant through lack of schooling.* illiterate, uneducated, uninformed, unschooled, untaught. OPPOSITE educated.

ignore *verb* **1** *She ignored his rudeness.* close your eyes to, disregard, neglect, overlook, pass over, shrug off, take no notice of. **2** *He ignored the new boy.* cold-shoulder, send to Coventry, slight, snub, spurn.

ill *adjective* **1** *She felt ill.* ailing, crook (*Australian informal*), diseased, indisposed, infirm, nauseous, off colour, out of sorts, poorly, queasy, rotten, seedy (*informal*), sick, sickly, under the weather, unhealthy, unwell. OPPOSITE well. **2** *no ill effects.* adverse, bad, damaging, destructive, detrimental, evil, harmful, unfavourable. OPPOSITE good. □ **ill will** *The freed hostage showed no ill will towards her captors.* animosity, antipathy, hostility, malevolence, malice, rancour, resentment, spite.

illegal *adjective an illegal activity. an illegal drug.* banned, criminal, forbidden, illegitimate, illicit, outlawed, prohibited, proscribed, unauthorised, unlawful. OPPOSITE legal.

illegible *adjective Her writing is illegible.* indecipherable, unreadable. OPPOSITE clear, legible.

illegitimate *adjective* **1** *an illegitimate child.* bastard (*old use*), love. **2** *an illegitimate move in chess.* illegal, improper, inadmissible, wrong. OPPOSITE legal, legitimate.

illicit *adjective* see ILLEGAL.

illiterate *adjective computer illiterate.* ignorant, uneducated, uninformed, unknowledgeable, untrained. OPPOSITE literate.

illness *noun Pedro was suffering from a rare illness.* affliction, ailment, bug (*informal*), complaint, condition, disease, disorder, indisposition, infection, infirmity, malady, sickness, trouble, wog (*Australian informal*). OPPOSITE health.

illogical *adjective Their findings were illogical.* absurd, irrational, unreasonable, unsound. OPPOSITE logical.

ill-treat *verb The child was ill-treated.* abuse, harm, injure, maltreat, mistreat, molest, persecute, wrong.

illuminate *verb* **1** *The castle was illuminated at night.* brighten up, floodlight, light up. OPPOSITE darken. **2** *He illuminated the subject.* clarify, elucidate, explain, shed light on, throw light on.

illusion *noun an optical illusion.* deception, hallucination, mirage, trick.

illusory *adjective Any success is illusory.* deceptive, fancied, illusive, imaginary, imagined, unreal. OPPOSITE real.

illustrate *verb* **1** *The artist illustrated the courtroom scene.* depict, draw, picture, portray, represent. **2** *The sentence illustrates the word's usage.* clarify, demonstrate, elucidate, exemplify, explain, show.

illustration *noun* **1** *The book has coloured illustrations.* diagram, drawing, figure, picture, plate. **2** *The dictionary includes illustrations of usage.* example, instance, sample, specimen.

illustrious *adjective our illustrious president.* celebrated, distinguished, eminent, famous, notable, prominent, renowned, well-known. OPPOSITE unknown.

image noun **1** *a graven image of a god.* carving, effigy, figure, icon, idol, representation, statue. **2** *She studied her image in the mirror.* appearance, likeness, reflection. **3** *She is the image of her mother.* copy, dead ringer (*informal*), duplicate, replica, spit, spitting image. **4** *a mental image.* concept, conception, idea, impression, perception, picture, vision.

imaginary *adjective My sister talked to her imaginary friend.* fancied, fanciful, fictitious, hypothetical, illusory, invented, legendary, made-up, mythical, mythological, non-existent, pretend (*informal*), unreal. OPPOSITE real.

imagination noun **1** *The story shows imagination.* creativity, ingenuity, innovation, inspiration, inventiveness, vision. **2** *in your imagination.* fancy, fantasy, mind's eye.

imaginative *adjective an imaginative architect.* creative, ingenious, innovative, inspired, inventive, original, visionary. OPPOSITE unimaginative.

imagine verb **1** *He imagined what his life would be like.* conceive, dream up, envisage, fantasise, picture, speculate, think up, visualise. **2** *What do you imagine has happened?* assume, believe, expect, fancy, guess, presume, suppose, think.

imbalance *noun an imbalance of girls and boys in the class.* disproportion, inequality, unevenness. OPPOSITE balance.

imbecile *noun see* IDIOT.

imitate verb **1** *He imitated the professor.* ape, copy, echo, emulate, impersonate, mimic, parody, send up (*informal*), take off. **2** *They imitated the sound of the sea.* copy, counterfeit, duplicate, replicate, reproduce, simulate.

imitation noun **1** *She could not distinguish the imitation from the real article.* copy, counterfeit, duplicate, fake, forgery, replica, reproduction. **2** *He does imitations of celebrities.* burlesque, impersonation, impression, mimicry, parody, send-up (*informal*), spoof (*informal*), take-off. — *adjective imitation cream.* artificial, fake, mock, phoney (*informal*), sham, synthetic. OPPOSITE real.

immaculate *adjective* **1** *an immaculate room.* clean, neat, spick and span, spotless, tidy. OPPOSITE dirty. **2** *an immaculate record.* faultless, flawless, impeccable, perfect, unblemished. OPPOSITE flawed.

immature *adjective an immature attitude.* babyish, callow, childish, green, inexperienced, infantile, juvenile, naive, puerile, youthful. OPPOSITE mature.

immediate *adjective* **1** *an immediate reply.* direct, instant, instantaneous, prompt, speedy, swift, unhesitating. OPPOSITE delayed. **2** *in the immediate neighbourhood.* adjacent, closest, nearest, next.

immediately *adverb She paid up immediately.* at once, directly, forthwith, instantly, on the knocker (*Australian informal*), on the spot, promptly, right away, straight away, then and there.

immense *adjective an immense amount of money.* astronomical, big, colossal, considerable, enormous, excessive, exorbitant, extensive, gigantic, great, hefty, huge, immeasurable, large, mammoth, massive, monstrous, prodigious, staggering, stupendous, terrific, tremendous, vast. OPPOSITE small.

immerse verb **1** *She immersed the clothes in soapy water.* dip, drench,

---

dunk, plunge, soak, steep, submerge, wet. **2** *He immersed himself in history.* absorb, bury, engross, occupy, preoccupy.

immigrant *noun Ingrid teaches English to immigrants.* migrant, newcomer, settler. CONTRASTS WITH emigrant.

imminent *adjective War was imminent.* approaching, close, impending, looming, near, nigh, threatening. OPPOSITE distant.

immobile *adjective* **1** *With its wheels clamped, the car was immobile.* fast, fixed, immobilised, immovable, stationary, stuck. **2** *The patient was immobile.* motionless, paralysed, still. OPPOSITE mobile.

immoderate *adjective immoderate drinking.* excessive, heavy, inordinate, intemperate, unrestrained. OPPOSITE moderate.

immodest *adjective* **1** *People were shocked by her immodest behaviour.* brazen, forward, improper, indecent, shameless, wanton. OPPOSITE modest. **2** *She is immodest about her achievements.* see CONCEITED.

immoral *adjective immoral behaviour.* bad, base, corrupt, degenerate, depraved, evil, iniquitous, shameless, sinful, unethical, unprincipled, unscrupulous, wicked. OPPOSITE moral, virtuous.

immortal *adjective God is immortal.* abiding, enduring, eternal, everlasting, undying. OPPOSITE mortal.

immovable *adjective an immovable rock.* fixed, immobile, stationary.

immune *adjective immune to criticism. immune to mumps.* exempt (from), free (from), impervious (to), invulnerable (to), protected (from), resistant (to), safe (from). OPPOSITE liable, susceptible.

immunisation *noun rubella immunisation.* inoculation, vaccination; see also INJECTION.

immunity *noun an immunity to mumps.* protection, resistance. OPPOSITE susceptibility.

imp noun **1** *fairy-tale imps.* demon, devil, elf, fairy, goblin, hobgoblin, pixie, spirit, sprite. **2** *The little imp had tied his shoelaces together.* devil, monkey, rascal, scallywag, scamp.

impact noun **1** *The impact caused severe injuries.* bump, collision, crash, knock, smash. **2** *The war had a big impact on their lives.* consequence, effect, impression, influence, repercussions.

impair *verb Smoking impairs your health.* damage, harm, hurt, injure, ruin, spoil, undermine, weaken. OPPOSITE improve.

impart verb **1** *The spices impart a delicious flavour to the dish.* contribute, give. **2** *He was eager to impart the information.* communicate, convey, disclose, divulge, make known, pass on, report, reveal, tell, transmit. OPPOSITE withhold.

impartial *adjective an impartial observer.* disinterested, even-handed, fair, just, neutral, non-aligned, non-partisan, objective, unbiased. OPPOSITE biased.

impasse *noun The talks have reached an impasse.* deadlock, stalemate, standstill.

impassioned *adjective The mother made an impassioned plea for her son's release.* ardent, earnest, emotional, emotive, fervent, heartfelt, passionate, stirring, zealous. OPPOSITE apathetic.

impassive *adjective The accused man remained impassive during the trial.* apathetic, cool, dispassionate, indifferent, phlegmatic, stolid, stony, unemotional, unmoved,

---

unresponsive, wooden. OPPOSITE emotional.

impatient *adjective* **1** *They were impatient to leave.* anxious, eager, itching, keen, raring. **2** *The audience was getting impatient.* edgy, fidgety, nervous, nervy, restive, restless, toey (*Australian informal*). OPPOSITE patient.

impeccable *adjective impeccable behaviour.* blameless, exemplary, faultless, flawless, irreproachable, perfect, unimpeachable. OPPOSITE blameworthy.

impede *verb The weather has impeded progress on the building.* block, check, curb, delay, hamper, handicap, hinder, hold up, inhibit, obstruct, prevent, restrict, retard, slow, stonker (*Australian slang*), thwart. OPPOSITE assist.

impediment noun **1** *Racist attitudes are an impediment to progress.* bar, barrier, hindrance, hitch, hurdle, obstacle, obstruction, snag, stumbling block. **2** *a speech impediment.* defect, handicap, lisp, stammer, stutter.

impel *verb Curiosity impelled her to investigate.* compel, drive, force, make, prompt, urge.

impending *adjective They ignored the warnings of the impending disaster.* approaching, coming, forthcoming, imminent, looming, threatening.

impenetrable *adjective an impenetrable jungle.* dense, impassable, impervious, inaccessible, thick. OPPOSITE penetrable.

impenitent *adjective an impenitent sinner.* hardened, remorseless, unrepentant. OPPOSITE contrite.

imperative *adjective It is imperative that you attend.* compulsory, essential, mandatory, necessary, obligatory. OPPOSITE optional.

imperceptible *adjective She grew by an imperceptible amount.* indiscernible, minuscule, minute, negligible, slight, subtle, tiny, unnoticeable. OPPOSITE noticeable.

imperfect *adjective imperfect work.* defective, deficient, faulty, flawed, incomplete, shoddy, substandard, unfinished. OPPOSITE perfect.

imperfection noun *The polish showed up the imperfections.* blemish, defect, deficiency, fault, flaw, shortcoming, weakness.

imperious *verb an imperious manner.* bossy, commanding, dictatorial, domineering, lordly, magisterial, masterful, overbearing, peremptory. OPPOSITE meek.

impersonate *verb He can impersonate anyone once he's seen them.* ape, imitate, masquerade as, mimic, portray, pose as, pretend to be, take off.

impertinence *noun He was offended by her impertinence.* cheek, effrontery, gall, hide, impudence, insolence, nerve, presumptuousness, rudeness.

impertinent *adjective an impertinent person. an impertinent question.* cheeky, disrespectful, forward, impolite, impudent, insolent, presumptuous, rude. OPPOSITE polite.

impervious *adjective* **1** *impervious to water.* impenetrable, impermeable, resistant, waterproof. OPPOSITE pervious. **2** *impervious to criticism.* immune, invulnerable, unaffected (by), unresponsive. OPPOSITE susceptible.

impetuous *adjective* **1** *an impetuous decision.* hasty, headlong, impulsive, precipitate, quick, reckless, spontaneous, spur-of-the-moment, sudden, wild. **2** *an impetuous person.* foolhardy, headstrong, hot-headed, impulsive, rash, reckless, spontaneous. OPPOSITE cautious.

impetus *noun He needs a fresh impetus to complete the work.* boost,

---

drive, impulse, incentive, momentum, motivation, push, spur, stimulus.

impinge verb **impinge on 1** *How will the government's policy impinge on families?* affect, have an effect on, have an impact on, impact on, touch. **2** *The new law impinges on people's privacy.* encroach on, infringe on, intrude on, trespass on.

impious *adjective He was offended by their impious talk.* blasphemous, disrespectful, irreligious, irreverent, profane, sacrilegious. OPPOSITE godly, pious.

implant *verb She implanted the idea in his head.* inculcate, insert, insinuate, instil, introduce, plant, put, sow.

implausible *adjective an implausible explanation.* far-fetched, improbable, incredible, unconvincing, unlikely. OPPOSITE plausible.

implement *noun cooking implements.* appliance, device, gadget, instrument, tool, utensil. — *verb They implemented the proposed changes.* accomplish, carry out, effect, enforce, execute, put into effect.

implicate *verb The offender implicated others.* dob in (*Australian informal*), embroil, grass on (*slang*), incriminate, inform on, involve.

implication *noun I resent the implication that I did not pay.* innuendo, insinuation, intimation, overtone, suggestion.

implicit *adjective implicit agreement.* implied, tacit, understood, unsaid, unspoken. OPPOSITE explicit.

implore *verb She implored them to stay.* appeal to, ask, beg, beseech, entreat, plead with, request.

imply *verb He implied that he thought they were wrong.* hint, indicate, insinuate, intimate, suggest.

impolite *adjective It was impolite not to express his thanks.* bad-mannered, boorish, cheeky, churlish, coarse, discourteous, disrespectful, impudent, insolent, insulting, loutish, rude, tactless, uncivil, vulgar. OPPOSITE polite.

importance noun **1** *a person of importance.* distinction, eminence, influence, note, prominence, renown, standing, stature, status. **2** *Her parents place importance on manners.* emphasis, priority, stress, value, weight. **3** *matters of little importance.* account, consequence, import, moment, significance.

important *adjective* **1** *an important decision.* big, consequential, critical, crucial, fateful, grave, historic, key, life and death, major, momentous, newsworthy, noteworthy, pivotal, pressing, primary, serious, significant, urgent, vital, weighty. OPPOSITE trivial. **2** *an important person.* celebrated, distinguished, eminent, famed, famous, great, high-ranking, influential, leading, notable, outstanding, powerful, pre-eminent, prominent, renowned, well-known. OPPOSITE unimportant.

impose verb **1** *They imposed a tax on clothing.* enforce, exact, inflict, lay, levy, prescribe, put. **2** *He imposed his ideas on the class.* foist, force, inflict. □ **impose on** *We don't want to impose on your hospitality.* abuse, exploit, presume on, take advantage of.

imposing *adjective The town hall is an imposing building.* big, grand, impressive, magnificent, majestic, ostentatious, splendid, stately, striking. OPPOSITE unimposing.

impossible *adjective an impossible task.* hopeless, impracticable, inconceivable, insoluble, out of the question, unachievable, unattainable, unthinkable. OPPOSITE feasible, possible.

impostor *noun They got rid of the impostor.* charlatan, con man (*informal*), fraud, impersonator, phoney (*informal*), pretender.

impotent *adjective She was impotent to help.* helpless, powerless, unable; see also WEAK.

impound *verb The police impounded their car.* confiscate, seize, take, take possession of.

impoverished *adjective He was out of work and impoverished.* destitute, down and out, hard up (*informal*), impecunious, needy, penniless, penurious, poor, poverty-stricken. OPPOSITE affluent.

impractical *adjective* **1** *an impractical person.* airy-fairy, idealistic, starry-eyed, unrealistic, visionary. OPPOSITE practical, realistic. **2** *an impractical scheme.* half-baked, hare-brained, impossible, impracticable, unviable, unworkable. OPPOSITE feasible, workable.

imprecise *adjective an imprecise idea.* approximate, fuzzy, general, hazy, indefinite, inexact, nebulous, rough, sketchy, vague. OPPOSITE precise.

impregnable *adjective an impregnable fortress.* invincible, invulnerable, safe, secure, unassailable, unconquerable. OPPOSITE vulnerable.

impregnate *verb* **1** *impregnate a cow.* fertilise, inseminate. **2** *The rag was impregnated with teak oil.* fill, imbue, permeate, saturate, soak, steep.

impress *verb* **1** *They were impressed by her singing.* affect, move, stir, strike, touch. **2** *He impressed on them the need for haste.* bring home to, emphasise to, instil in, stress to.

impression *noun* **1** *He wanted to make a good impression.* effect, impact, mark. **2** *He had an impression that they knew the way.* belief, feeling, hunch, idea, notion, opinion, sense, suspicion. **3** *She does impressions of famous people.* imitation, impersonation, parody, send-up (*informal*), take-off.

impressionable *adjective an impressionable person.* gullible, receptive, suggestible, susceptible.

impressive *adjective an impressive display. an impressive occasion.* august, awe-inspiring, grand, great, imposing, magnificent, majestic, memorable, moving, outstanding, remarkable, sensational, spectacular, splendid, stately, striking, superb. OPPOSITE ordinary.

imprint *noun the imprint of a paw.* impression, indentation, mark, print, seal, stamp. — *verb The scene is imprinted on his mind.* engrave, etch, implant, impress, stamp.

imprison *verb The murderer was imprisoned for life.* confine, detain, incarcerate, intern, jail, lock up, place in custody, shut up. OPPOSITE free.

imprisonment *noun The murderer was sentenced to life imprisonment.* confinement, custody, detention, incarceration, internment, jail.

improbable *adjective an improbable explanation.* far-fetched, implausible, incredible, unbelievable, unlikely. OPPOSITE likely.

impromptu *adjective an impromptu speech.* ad lib, extempore, off the cuff, spontaneous, unprepared, unrehearsed, unscripted. OPPOSITE prepared.

improper *adjective improper conduct. improper language.* coarse, crude, inappropriate, indecent, irreverent, obscene, offensive, rude, unbecoming, unseemly, unsuitable, vulgar. OPPOSITE decent, proper.

improve *verb* **1** *Business is improving.* advance, develop, look up, pick

up, progress. OPPOSITE decline. **2** *The patient is improving.* be on the mend, get better, perk up, rally, recover, recuperate, take a turn for the better. OPPOSITE deteriorate. **3** *He improved his work.* ameliorate, amend, enhance, fix up, polish, refine, revise, touch up, upgrade. OPPOSITE spoil, worsen. **4** *They promised to improve standards.* boost, lift, raise. OPPOSITE lower.

improvement *noun a noticeable improvement.* advance, amelioration, amendment, development, enhancement, progress, rally, recovery, refinement, reform, revamp, revision, touch-up, upgrade, upturn.

improvise *verb They had no music, but they improvised an accompaniment.* ad lib (*informal*), extemporise, invent, make up, play by ear.

imprudent *adjective His action was imprudent.* foolhardy, foolish, ill-advised, impolitic, inadvisable, indiscreet, reckless, short-sighted, unintelligent, unwise. OPPOSITE prudent, wise.

impudent *adjective Don't be impudent!* brazen, cheeky, discourteous, disrespectful, fresh (*informal*), impertinent, impolite, insolent, pert, presumptuous, rude, saucy. OPPOSITE polite.

impulsive *adjective* **1** *an impulsive person.* capricious, hotheaded, impetuous, rash, reckless. OPPOSITE cautious. **2** *an impulsive action.* automatic, hasty, headlong, impetuous, instinctive, precipitate, rash, reckless, spontaneous, spur-of-the-moment, unplanned. OPPOSITE premeditated.

impure *adjective The water was impure.* adulterated, contaminated, dirty, filthy, foul, polluted, tainted, unclean. OPPOSITE clean, pure.

in *adjective Hats are in again.* fashionable, in fashion, in vogue, trendy (*informal*). OPPOSITE out of fashion.

inability *noun an inability to speak.* helplessness, impotence, incapacity, powerlessness. OPPOSITE ability.

inaccessible *adjective The area was inaccessible even by boat.* cut off, isolated, out of reach, remote, unreachable. OPPOSITE accessible.

inaccuracy *noun inaccuracies in the text.* error, fault, misprint, mistake, slip-up (*informal*), typo (*informal*).

inaccurate *adjective inaccurate reporting.* careless, false, imprecise, incorrect, inexact, sloppy, untruthful, wrong. OPPOSITE accurate.

inactive *adjective The animals are inactive in the daytime.* asleep, dormant, hibernating, idle, indolent, inert, lazy, lethargic, listless, passive, resting, sedentary, sleepy, slothful, sluggish, torpid. OPPOSITE active.

inadequate *adjective inadequate information.* deficient, insufficient, scanty, sketchy, skimpy, sparse, wanting. OPPOSITE adequate.

inadvertent *adjective an inadvertent slip.* accidental, involuntary, unconscious, unintentional, unwitting. OPPOSITE deliberate.

inadvisable *adjective It is inadvisable to walk alone here.* foolish, ill-advised, imprudent, unwise.

inane *adjective see SILLY.*

inanimate *adjective an inanimate object.* lifeless. OPPOSITE animate.

inappropriate *adjective an inappropriate remark.* improper, incongruous, irrelevant, unbecoming, unsuitable, wrong. OPPOSITE appropriate.

inattentive *adjective Inattentive driving causes accidents.* absent-minded, careless, distracted, heedless, incautious, negligent. OPPOSITE attentive, cautious.

inborn *adjective an inborn ability.* congenital, hereditary, inbred, inherent, innate, native, natural. OPPOSITE acquired.

incalculable *adjective The problems are incalculable.* countless, enormous, immeasurable, inestimable, infinite, innumerable.

incapable *adjective an incapable worker.* incompetent, ineffective, ineffectual, inept, useless. OPPOSITE capable, competent.

incapacitate *verb The accident incapacitated him for a year.* cripple, disable, immobilise, lay up, maim.

incense *verb He was incensed by their selfish attitude.* anger, enrage, exasperate, infuriate, madden, outrage, provoke, rile (*informal*), vex.

incentive *noun The workers are offered incentives to work harder.* carrot, encouragement, goad, inducement, lure, reward, spur, stimulus. OPPOSITE deterrent.

incessant *adjective Dad was exhausted by their incessant chatter.* ceaseless, chronic, constant, continual, continuous, endless, eternal, everlasting, interminable, non-stop, permanent, perpetual, persistent, relentless. OPPOSITE occasional.

incidence *noun an increased incidence of TB.* frequency, occurrence, prevalence, rate.

incident *noun an amusing incident.* affair, episode, event, experience, happening, occasion, occurrence.

incidental *adjective incidental costs.* ancillary, minor, secondary, subsidiary. OPPOSITE major.

incision *noun The doctor stitched up the incision.* cut, slit.

incite *verb He incited the crowd to revolt.* arouse, egg on, encourage, excite, goad, provoke, rouse, spur, stimulate, stir up, urge.

inclement *adjective inclement weather.* bad, foul, rough, stormy, wet. OPPOSITE fine.

inclination *noun* **1** *He has an inclination to overeat.* habit, predisposition, propensity, tendency. **2** *She has an inclination for the sciences.* fondness, liking, partiality, penchant, predilection, preference. OPPOSITE aversion. **3** *the inclination of the land.* angle, gradient, incline, slant, slope.

incline *verb* **1** *The roof inclines steeply.* cant, pitch, slant, slope. **2** *He inclined his head to see.* bend, bow, lean, tilt, tip. — *noun a steep incline.* grade, gradient, hill, inclination, pinch (*Australian*), pitch, rise, slant, slope. □ **be inclined** *She was inclined to give up easily.* be apt, be liable, be prone, be wont (*old use*), tend.

include *verb* **1** *The course includes practical and theoretical subjects.* comprise, consist of, contain, cover, embrace, encompass, incorporate, take in. OPPOSITE exclude. **2** *He included her on his birthday list.* add, count, list, number. OPPOSITE omit.

incoherent *adjective When he was tired his speech became incoherent.* confused, garbled, illogical, inarticulate, incomprehensible, jumbled, muddled, rambling, unclear, unintelligible. OPPOSITE coherent.

income *noun Income exceeds expenditure.* earnings, livelihood, pay, receipts, revenue, salary, stipend, takings, wages. OPPOSITE expenditure.

incomparable *adjective the lady's incomparable beauty.* inimitable, matchless, peerless, superlative, supreme, unequalled, unparalleled, unrivalled, unsurpassed.

incompatible *adjective* **1** *The two people are incompatible.* inharmonious, mismatched, unsuited. OPPOSITE compatible. **2** *incompatible*

statements. conflicting, contradictory, incongruous, inconsistent, irreconcilable. OPPOSITE consistent.

incompetent *adjective an incompetent cook.* clueless (*informal*), hopeless, inadequate, incapable, ineffectual, inefficient, inept, inexpert, unskilful, useless. OPPOSITE competent, skilful.

incomplete *adjective an incomplete manuscript.* abridged, fragmentary, imperfect, partial, sketchy, unfinished. OPPOSITE complete.

incomprehensible *adjective an incomprehensible theory.* abstruse, bewildering, complicated, inexplicable, inscrutable, unfathomable, unintelligible. OPPOSITE comprehensible.

inconceivable *adjective It was inconceivable that he would miss the match.* impossible, improbable, incredible, unbelievable, unimaginable, unthinkable. OPPOSITE conceivable.

incongruous *adjective The log cabin looked incongruous in suburbia.* absurd, inappropriate, odd, out of keeping, out of place. OPPOSITE congruous.

inconsiderate *adjective an inconsiderate person. an inconsiderate action.* careless, insensitive, rude, selfish, tactless, thoughtless, uncaring, unthinking. OPPOSITE considerate.

inconsistent *adjective* **1** *inconsistent behaviour.* capricious, changeable, erratic, fickle, patchy, temperamental, unpredictable, unreliable, variable. **2** *These actions are inconsistent with his philosophy.* at odds, conflicting, contradictory, incompatible, irreconcilable. OPPOSITE consistent.

inconspicuous *adjective The shy man tried to be inconspicuous.* unnoticeable, unobtrusive, unostentatious. OPPOSITE prominent.

inconvenience *noun They put up with many inconveniences.* bother, disruption, disturbance, hassle (*informal*), irritation, nuisance, trouble. — *verb He didn't mean to inconvenience us.* bother, disrupt, disturb, hassle (*informal*), impose on, put out (*informal*), trouble.

inconvenient *adjective an inconvenient time.* awkward, bothersome, ill-timed, inopportune, troublesome, unsuitable, untimely. OPPOSITE convenient.

incorporate *verb The three councils were incorporated into one.* amalgamate, blend, combine, consolidate, integrate, merge, mix, subsume, unite; see also INCLUDE.

incorrect *adjective an incorrect answer.* erroneous, false, inaccurate, mistaken, untrue, wrong. OPPOSITE correct.

incorrigible *adjective an incorrigible liar.* hardened, hopeless, incurable, inveterate, unreformable.

increase *verb* **1** *They increased the size of the club.* add to, augment, boost, build up, enlarge, expand, lift, raise, supplement, swell. OPPOSITE decrease, reduce. **2** *The shares increased in value.* appreciate, escalate, gain, go up, grow, improve, jump, multiply, rise, skyrocket, soar. OPPOSITE decrease, drop. **3** *The treatment increased the pain.* aggravate, compound, exacerbate, heighten, intensify, step up, strengthen. OPPOSITE ease. **4** *He increased the time allowed for the project.* extend, lengthen, prolong, protract. OPPOSITE decrease, shorten. — *noun* **1** *an increase in size. an increase in demand.* boost, build-up, enlargement, escalation, expansion, explosion, extension, growth, inflation, rise, upsurge. **2** *an increase of $20.* addition, gain, increment, jump, rise. OPPOSITE decrease.

incredible *adjective an incredible story.* amazing, extraordinary, far-fetched, implausible, improbable, inconceivable, miraculous, unbelievable, unlikely. OPPOSITE credible.

incredulous *adjective He was incredulous when they told him.* disbelieving, distrustful, doubtful, dubious, sceptical, unbelieving. OPPOSITE credulous.

incriminate *verb He said nothing which might incriminate his friends.* accuse, blame, implicate, inculpate.

incurable *adjective* **1** *an incurable squint.* inoperable, uncorrectable, untreatable. OPPOSITE curable. **2** *an incurable flirt.* hopeless, incorrigible, inveterate.

indebted *adjective She was indebted to her friend for her help.* beholden, grateful, obliged, thankful.

indecent *adjective an indecent joke. indecent language.* blue, coarse, crude, dirty, filthy, foul, improper, indelicate, lewd, obscene, offensive, pornographic, risqué, rude, suggestive, tasteless, unprintable, unseemly, vulgar. OPPOSITE decent.

indecisive *adjective It was hard to work with such an indecisive person.* hesitant, in two minds, irresolute, tentative, uncertain, undecided, unsure. OPPOSITE decisive.

indefinable *adjective an indefinable quality.* elusive, indescribable, obscure, vague. OPPOSITE definable.

indefinite *adjective* **1** *The exhibition will continue for an indefinite period.* indeterminate, open-ended, unlimited, unspecified. OPPOSITE fixed. **2** *He was indefinite about his return date.* non-committal, tentative, uncertain, undecided, unsure, vague. OPPOSITE specific. **3** *an indefinite idea.* confused, fuzzy, general, hazy, imprecise, inexact, obscure, vague. OPPOSITE precise.

indelible *adjective indelible ink.* fast, fixed, lasting, permanent.

indentation *noun indentations in the timber.* cut, groove, nick, notch, recess, score.

independent *adjective* **1** *She had the money to be independent.* self-reliant, self-sufficient, self-supporting. **2** *an independent state.* autonomous, free, self-determining, self-governing, self-ruling, sovereign. OPPOSITE dependent. **3** *an independent school.* non-government, private. OPPOSITE public. **4** *an independent commentator.* impartial, neutral, non-aligned, non-partisan.

indescribable *adjective indescribable joy.* ineffable, inexpressible, unspeakable, unutterable.

indestructible *adjective* **1** *indestructible plastic.* durable, strong, sturdy, tough, unbreakable. OPPOSITE breakable, fragile. **2** *an indestructible friendship.* enduring, eternal, everlasting, lasting, permanent, undying.

index *noun an index of names.* catalogue, concordance, directory, gazetteer, inventory, list, register.

indicate *verb* **1** *The signs indicate the way.* make known, point out, reveal, show, signal, specify, tell. **2** *A nod indicates agreement.* be a sign of, denote, imply, mean, show, signify, spell, suggest.

indication *noun The tears were an indication of tiredness.* clue, evidence, hint, mark, sign, signal, symptom, token, warning.

indicator *noun* **1** *an indicator of public feeling.* barometer, gauge, guide, index. **2** *a water-level indicator.* dial, display, gauge, meter.

indifferent *adjective* **1** *The official was indifferent to their suffering.* apathetic, blasé, cold, cool, dispassionate, half-hearted, lukewarm, neutral, nonchalant, uncaring, unconcerned, uninterested. OPPOSITE interested. **2** *indifferent playing.* fair, mediocre, middling, ordinary, passable, so-so, unexceptional, uninspired. OPPOSITE exceptional.

indigenous *adjective indigenous plants. indigenous people.* aboriginal, native, original. OPPOSITE foreign, imported.

indignant *adjective an indignant customer.* angry, cross, disgruntled, infuriated, irate, irritated, livid (*informal*), riled (*informal*), ropeable (*Australian informal*), up in arms (*informal*), vexed. OPPOSITE delighted.

indignation *noun righteous indignation.* anger, dudgeon, fury, ire, irritation, outrage, rage, umbrage, wrath.

indirect *adjective an indirect route.* circuitous, devious, meandering, rambling, roundabout, tortuous. OPPOSITE straight.

indiscreet *adjective It was indiscreet to speak about the matter.* impolitic, imprudent, injudicious, tactless, thoughtless, untactful, unwise. OPPOSITE discreet.

indispensable *adjective an indispensable gadget.* essential, key, necessary, required, requisite, vital. OPPOSITE redundant.

indisposed *adjective A relief teacher replaced our teacher who was indisposed.* ailing, crook (*Australian informal*), ill, off colour, poorly, sick, unwell. OPPOSITE well.

indisputable *adjective indisputable evidence.* certain, conclusive, incontestable, incontrovertible, indubitable, irrefutable, undeniable, unquestionable. OPPOSITE questionable.

indistinct *adjective indistinct shapes.* blurred, confused, dim, faint, fuzzy, hazy, indefinite, nebulous, obscure, unclear, vague. OPPOSITE clear, distinct.

individual *adjective* **1** *individual serves.* separate, single. OPPOSITE shared. **2** *The artist has his individual style.* characteristic, distinct, distinctive, exclusive, idiosyncratic, own, particular, peculiar, personal, special, specific, unique. OPPOSITE universal. — *noun* (*informal*) *an unpleasant individual.* character, fellow, human being, man, person, woman.

indoctrinate *verb The sect indoctrinates its members.* brainwash; see also TEACH.

indolent *adjective He was indolent throughout the summer.* idle, inactive, inert, lazy, lethargic, slothful, sluggish. OPPOSITE active.

indubitable *adjective The evidence was indubitable.* certain, definite, indisputable, undeniable, undoubted, unquestionable. OPPOSITE doubtful.

induce *verb I don't know what induced him to buy a car.* cause, coax, influence, inspire, lead, motivate, move, persuade, prompt, provoke, sway, tempt. OPPOSITE deter.

inducement *noun The company offered him inducements to stay.* attraction, carrot, enticement, goad, incentive, spur, stimulus. OPPOSITE deterrent.

indulge *verb* **1** *He indulges his children.* cosset, mollycoddle, pamper, pander to, spoil. **2** *She indulged her craving for chocolate.* cater to, give in to, gratify, satisfy.

indulgent *adjective an indulgent father.* easygoing, forbearing, forgiving, kind, lenient, liberal, merciful, permissive, soft, tolerant. OPPOSITE strict.

industrious *adjective an industrious worker.* assiduous, conscientious, diligent, energetic, hard-working, indefatigable, tireless, unflagging, zealous. OPPOSITE lazy.

industry *noun the car industry.* business, commerce, manufacturing, trade.

inebriated *adjective* see DRUNK.

inedible *adjective The food was inedible.* uneatable, unpalatable. OPPOSITE edible.

ineffective *adjective* **1** *The treatment was ineffective.* futile, unavailing, unsuccessful, useless. **2** *an ineffective employee.* feckless, incapable, incompetent, ineffectual, inefficient, unproductive, useless. OPPOSITE effective.

ineffectual *adjective an ineffectual leader.* feckless, feeble, hopeless, impotent, incapable, incompetent, ineffective, weak. OPPOSITE effectual.

inefficient *adjective* **1** *an inefficient system.* ineffective, uneconomic, unproductive, wasteful. **2** *an inefficient worker.* disorganised, incapable, incompetent, ineffective, ineffectual. OPPOSITE efficient.

inept *adjective* **1** *an inept workman.* bungling, clumsy, incompetent, inefficient, inexpert, unskilful. OPPOSITE competent. **2** *an inept remark.* absurd, inappropriate, unsuitable. OPPOSITE apt.

inequality *noun Poverty and inequality were the causes of this unrest.* bias, difference, discrimination, disparity, imbalance, prejudice. OPPOSITE equality.

inertia *noun a feeling of inertia.* inactivity, indolence, languor, laziness, lethargy, listlessness, passivity, sluggishness, torpor. OPPOSITE action, vitality.

inevitable *adjective an inevitable accident.* certain, fated, inescapable, sure, unavoidable. OPPOSITE avoidable.

inexact *adjective an inexact translation of the poem.* approximate, imprecise, inaccurate, loose, rough. OPPOSITE exact.

inexcusable *adjective Her bad behaviour was inexcusable.* indefensible, unforgivable, unjustifiable, unpardonable. OPPOSITE excusable.

inexhaustible *adjective an inexhaustible supply.* boundless, endless, everlasting, infinite, never-ending, unending, unlimited. OPPOSITE finite.

inexpensive *adjective an inexpensive hotel.* budget-priced, cheap, economical, low-priced, reasonable. OPPOSITE expensive.

inexperienced *adjective an inexperienced youth.* callow, green, immature, naive, raw, unsophisticated, unworldly. OPPOSITE experienced.

inexplicable *adjective The disappearance was inexplicable.* baffling, enigmatic, incomprehensible, insoluble, mysterious, puzzling, unaccountable, unexplainable, unfathomable.

infallible *adjective an infallible cure.* certain, dependable, foolproof, guaranteed, perfect, reliable, sure, unfailing. OPPOSITE fallible, uncertain.

infamous *adjective an infamous villain. his infamous deeds.* disgraceful, dishonourable, disreputable, evil, nefarious, notorious, outrageous, scandalous, wicked. OPPOSITE honourable.

infancy *noun His son died in infancy.* babyhood, childhood.

infant *noun The infant was seated on his mother's lap.* babe, baby, bairn (*Scottish*), child, piccaninny, toddler, tot.

infantile *adjective His behaviour is infantile.* babyish, childish, immature, juvenile, puerile. OPPOSITE mature.

infatuated *adjective* **infatuated with** *Lisa was infatuated with him.* besotted with, crazy about, enamoured of, in love with, keen on, mad about, rapt in, smitten with.

infatuation *noun* crush (*informal*), obsession, passion.

infect *verb The water was infected by the chemicals.* contaminate, poison, pollute, taint.

infection *noun She caught a respiratory infection.* ailment, bug (*informal*), disease, illness, virus, wog (*Australian informal*).

infectious *adjective infectious diseases.* catching, communicable, contagious, transmittable.

infer *verb From the state of his clothes we inferred that it was raining.* conclude, deduce, gather, reason, surmise, work out.

inferior *adjective* **1** *inferior rank.* junior, lower, subordinate. OPPOSITE superior. **2** *inferior work. inferior quality.* cheap, crook (*Australian informal*), faulty, imperfect, inadequate, indifferent, mediocre, poor, second-rate, shoddy, substandard, third-rate. OPPOSITE superior.

infertile *adjective infertile soil.* barren, poor, sterile, unproductive. OPPOSITE fertile.

infest *verb Rats infested the shed.* invade, overrun, swarm, take over.

infidelity *noun his wife's infidelity.* adultery, disloyalty, unfaithfulness. OPPOSITE faithfulness, fidelity.

infinite *adjective* **1** *an infinite number of possibilities.* countless, endless, immeasurable, immense, incalculable, inexhaustible, innumerable, limitless, myriad, unlimited. **2** *He believes that space is infinite.* boundless, endless, interminable, never-ending, unbounded, unending. OPPOSITE finite.

infinitesimal *adjective an infinitesimal difference.* little, microscopic, miniature, minuscule, minute, small, teeny, tiny. OPPOSITE large.

infirm *adjective A nurse looks after the infirm people.* ailing, decrepit, feeble, frail, ill, poorly, senile, unwell, weak. OPPOSITE healthy.

inflame *verb His speech inflamed the crowd.* anger, arouse, enrage, fire up, incense, incite, infuriate, provoke, rouse, stir up. OPPOSITE calm.

inflamed *adjective an inflamed tonsil.* festering, infected, red, sore, swollen.

inflammable *adjective Petrol is highly inflammable.* combustible, flammable. OPPOSITE non-flammable, non-inflammable.

inflate *verb* **1** *The tyres are fully inflated.* blow up, fill, pump up. OPPOSITE deflate. **2** *Rumours of shortages have inflated the price of fuel.* boost, increase, raise.

inflexible *adjective* **1** *The ruler is made of inflexible plastic.* firm, hard, rigid, solid, stiff. **2** *an inflexible person. an inflexible attitude.* adamant, firm, immutable, intractable, intransigent, obstinate, pig-headed, rigid, stubborn, unbending, uncompromising, unyielding. OPPOSITE flexible.

inflict *verb The judge inflictd a severe penalty.* administer, deal out, impose, mete out, wreak.

influence *noun* **1** *Television had an influence on her.* effect, hold, impact. **2** *political influence.* authority, clout (*informal*), control, leverage, muscle, power, pressure, sway, weight. — *verb Don't try to influence her.* affect, bias, change, control, lead, manipulate, motivate, move, persuade, predispose, prejudice, sway.

influential *adjective an influential person.* authoritative, important, persuasive, powerful, strong. OPPO-SITE weak.

influx *noun an influx of tourists.* flood, inflow, inrush, rush, stream.

inform *verb The lawyer informed them of their rights.* acquaint, advise, apprise (*formal*), brief, enlighten, fill in (*informal*), instruct, keep posted, notify, tell, warn. □ **inform on** *He informed on his colleague.* betray, blow the whistle on (*informal*), denounce, dob in (*Australian informal*), grass (on) (*slang*), rat on (*informal*), report, shelf (*Australian slang*), shop (*slang*), sneak on (*informal*), split on (*slang*), tell on.

informal *adjective* **1** *an informal atmosphere.* casual, easygoing, free and easy, homely, natural, relaxed, unofficial. **2** *informal language.* colloquial, everyday, slangy, vernacular. OPPOSITE formal.

information *noun The police received new information. She read the information she was given.* advice, communication, data, evidence, facts, info (*informal*), intelligence, knowledge, low-down (*informal*), material, message, news, notice, notification, particulars, report, tidings.

informer *noun a police informer.* dobber (*Australian informal*), dog (*slang*), grass (*slang*), informant, source, stool-pigeon, tell-tale, whistle-blower (*informal*).

infrequent *adjective infrequent visits.* irregular, occasional, rare, sporadic, uncommon. OPPOSITE frequent.

infringe *verb She infringed the parking laws.* breach, break, contravene, disobey, transgress, violate. OPPOSITE obey.

infringement *noun a parking infringement.* breach, contravention, transgression, violation.

infuriate *verb Her selfishness infuriated the others.* anger, enrage, exasperate, gall, incense, irritate, madden, needle (*informal*), outrage, rile (*informal*), vex.

ingenious *adjective an ingenious idea.* artful, brilliant, clever, crafty, cunning, imaginative, inventive, neat, nifty (*informal*), resourceful, shrewd, skilful, smart. OPPOSITE unimaginative.

ingenuous *adjective an ingenuous manner.* artless, guileless, innocent, naive, simple, unaffected, unsophisticated. OPPOSITE artful.

ingrained *adjective an ingrained scepticism.* confirmed, deep-rooted, deep-seated.

ingratiate *verb* **ingratiate yourself with** *He ingratiated himself with the boss.* crawl to, curry favour with, fawn on, grovel to, kowtow to, play up to, suck up to (*informal*), toady to.

ingratitude *noun* thanklessness, unappreciativeness, ungratefulness. OPPOSITE gratitude.

ingredient *noun Mix all the ingredients.* component, constituent, element, part.

inhabit *verb The island was inhabited by fishermen.* dwell in, live in, occupy, people, populate, reside in, settle in.

inhabitant *noun the city's inhabitants.* citizen, denizen, dweller, native, occupant, resident; see also POPULATION.

inhale *verb She inhaled the fumes.* breathe in, draw in, suck in. OPPOSITE exhale.

inherent *adjective inherent goodness.* essential, inborn, inbred, innate, intrinsic, native, natural.

inheritance *noun He received an inheritance.* bequest, birthright, estate, heritage, legacy.

inheritor *noun* beneficiary, heir, heiress.

inhibit *verb Poor teaching inhibited the child's progress.* block, check, curb, hamper, hinder, hold back, impede, limit, obstruct, prevent, restrain, restrict, retard, stunt. OPPOSITE promote.

inhibition *noun They overcame their inhibitions.* hang-up (*informal*), mental block, reserve, self-consciousness, shyness.

inhospitable *adjective* **1** *inhospitable people.* cool, unfriendly, unsociable, unwelcoming. OPPOSITE hospitable. **2** *an inhospitable place.* bleak, desolate, forbidding, uninviting.

inhuman *adjective inhuman treatment of prisoners.* barbarous, brutal, cold-hearted, cruel, heartless, inhumane, merciless, ruthless, savage, unfeeling, vicious. OPPOSITE human, humane.

inimitable *adjective her inimitable style.* incomparable, matchless, singular, unique.

iniquity *noun forgiven for his iniquities.* crime, evil, injustice, offence, sin, transgression, trespass, wickedness, wrong, wrongdoing.

initial *adjective the initial stage.* beginning, early, first, introductory, opening, original, preliminary, starting. OPPOSITE final.

initiate *verb He initiated the discussions.* begin, commence, embark on, inaugurate, instigate, institute, kick off (*informal*), launch, open, originate, set in motion, start. OPPOSITE conclude.

initiative *noun The employer encourages initiative.* drive, dynamism, enterprise, resourcefulness. □ **take the initiative** begin, commence, make the first move, start, take the lead.

inject *verb The leader tried to inject enthusiasm into the group.* bring in, infuse, instil, introduce.

injection *noun a tetanus injection.* booster, immunisation, inoculation, jab (*informal*), shot, vaccination.

injure *verb He injured his leg.* bruise, cripple, cut, damage, disable, fracture, harm, hurt, impair, lacerate, maim, mangle, mutilate, scar, sprain, strain, wound.

injurious *adjective an injurious effect.* adverse, damaging, deleterious, destructive, detrimental, harmful, hurtful. OPPOSITE beneficial.

injury *noun minor injuries.* abrasion, bruise, contusion, cut, damage, fracture, harm, hurt, laceration, lesion, scrape, scratch, wound.

injustice *noun* **1** *the injustice of the system.* bias, discrimination, inequity, prejudice, unfairness, unjustness. OPPOSITE justice. **2** *They committed many injustices.* abuse, injury, offence, wrong.

inkling *noun She had no inkling of what was happening.* clue, hint, idea, knowledge, notion, suspicion.

inland *noun He lives in the inland.* backblocks (*Australian*), back of beyond, bush, interior, never-never (*Australian*), outback (*Australian*), sticks (*informal*).

inlet *noun They rowed up the inlet.* bay, cove, creek (*British*), estuary, fiord, firth, harbour, sound.

inn *noun We had a meal at the inn.* hotel, pub (*informal*), public house, tavern.

innate *adjective innate ability.* congenital, hereditary, inborn, inbred, inherent, inherited, intrinsic, native, natural. OPPOSITE acquired.

inner *adjective an inner wall.* central, inside, interior, internal. OPPOSITE outer.

innkeeper *noun* hotelier, hotel-keeper, landlady, landlord, proprietor, publican.

innocent *adjective* **1** *innocent until proven guilty.* blameless, guiltless. OPPOSITE guilty. **2** *as innocent as a baby.* angelic, moral, pure, righteous, sinless, virtuous. OPPOSITE sinful. **3** *an innocent remark.* harmless, innocuous, inoffensive. OPPOSITE harmful. **4** *young and innocent.* green, gullible, inexperienced, ingenuous, naive, trusting, unworldly. OPPOSITE experienced.

innocuous *adjective an innocuous remark.* harmless, inoffensive, safe, unobjectionable.

innovative *adjective an innovative design.* creative, imaginative, new, novel, original. OPPOSITE unoriginal.

innuendo *noun a destructive campaign of lies and innuendoes.* hint, insinuation, intimation, overtone, suggestion.

innumerable *adjective innumerable grains of sand.* countless, infinite, myriad, numberless, numerous.

inoculate *verb inoculate against disease.* immunise, vaccinate.

inoffensive *adjective an inoffensive remark.* bland, harmless, innocuous, safe, unobjectionable, unoffending. OPPOSITE objectionable.

inordinate *adjective an inordinate amount of money.* disproportionate, excessive, exorbitant, undue, unreasonable. OPPOSITE moderate.

inquest *noun* see INQUIRY.

inquire *verb The man inquired about her health.* ask, check, enquire, query, question, quiz. □ **inquire into** *He inquired into their financial dealings.* examine, explore, inspect, investigate, look into, probe, research, study.

inquiry *noun* **1** *an official inquiry.* enquiry, hearing, inquest, inquisition, investigation, post-mortem, probe, review, study. **2** *a telephone number for inquiries.* enquiry, query, question.

inquisitive *adjective The stranger was too inquisitive.* curious, nosy (*informal*), prying, snoopy (*informal*). OPPOSITE uninterested.

insane *adjective The murderer was insane.* berserk, crazy, demented, deranged, irrational, lunatic, mad, mental (*informal*), nutty (*informal*), unbalanced, unhinged. OPPOSITE sane.

insatiable *adjective an insatiable appetite.* greedy, ravenous, unquenchable, voracious.

inscribe *verb He inscribed his name in the wood.* carve, engrave, etch, write.

inscription *noun an inscription on a tombstone.* engraving, epitaph, words, writing.

inscrutable *adjective an inscrutable expression.* arcane, baffling, cryptic, enigmatic, impenetrable, incomprehensible, mysterious, puzzling, unfathomable. OPPOSITE transparent.

insect *noun* bug (*informal*), creepy-crawly (*informal*).

insecure *adjective* **1** *The ladder is insecure.* dangerous, precarious, rickety, rocky, shaky, unsafe, unsteady, wobbly. OPPOSITE secure. **2** *She feels insecure.* anxious, diffident, fearful, timid, vulnerable. OPPOSITE confident.

insensible *adjective* **1** *The man was insensible after the blow to his head.* comatose, knocked out, senseless, unconscious. OPPOSITE conscious. **2** *He seemed insensible of the danger.* ignorant, oblivious, unaware, unconscious. OPPOSITE aware.

insensitive *adjective an insensitive person.* callous, cold-hearted, hard-hearted, heartless, indifferent, tactless, thick-skinned, thoughtless, uncaring, unfeeling, unsympathetic. OPPOSITE sensitive.

inseparable *adjective The friends were inseparable.* attached, close, thick as thieves (*informal*).

insert *verb* **1** *They inserted an extra phrase.* add, interject, interpolate, interpose, introduce, put in. OPPOSITE remove. **2** *She inserted old coins in the pudding.* implant, put in, slip in, stick in, tuck in. OPPOSITE remove.

inside *noun the inside of an object.* centre, core, heart, interior, middle. OPPOSITE outside. — *adjective the inside surface.* inmost, inner, innermost, interior, internal. OPPOSITE outside. □ **insides** *plural noun* (*informal*) *the animal's insides.* bowels, entrails, guts, innards (*informal*), intestines, stomach, tummy (*informal*), viscera.

insight *noun He showed great insight into human behaviour.* acumen, discernment, intuition, judgement, perception, perspicacity, understanding.

insignificant *adjective* **1** *an insignificant increase.* inconsequential, little, minor, minute, negligible, paltry, petty, slight, tiny, trifling, trivial. OPPOSITE substantial. **2** *an insignificant person.* unimportant, useless, worthless. OPPOSITE important.

insincere *adjective insincere words. an insincere person.* deceitful, dishonest, false, hypocritical, phoney (*informal*), two-faced. OPPOSITE sincere.

insinuation *noun an insinuation that she was lying.* hint, implication, innuendo, intimation, suggestion.

insipid *adjective* **1** *insipid tea.* bland, tasteless, watery, weak, wishy-washy. OPPOSITE strong, tasty. **2** *an insipid person.* characterless, colourless, dull, uninteresting, vapid, wishy-washy. OPPOSITE interesting.

insist *verb* **1** *She insisted that she was right.* assert, claim, contend, declare, emphasise, maintain, stress. **2** *He insisted that we attend the ceremony.* command, demand, put your foot down, require, stipulate.

insolence *noun She won't put up with his insolence.* arrogance, audacity, backchat (*informal*), cheek, effrontery, impertinence, impudence, insubordination, lip (*slang*), rudeness.

insolent *adjective The insolent boy had to apologise.* arrogant, brazen, cheeky, contemptuous, disrespectful, impertinent, impolite, impudent, insubordinate, presumptuous, rude. OPPOSITE polite.

insoluble *adjective an insoluble problem.* baffling, inexplicable, mysterious, perplexing, puzzling, unanswerable, unfathomable, unsolvable. OPPOSITE soluble.

inspect *verb They inspected the site.* check, examine, investigate, look over, scrutinise, survey, suss out (*informal*), view.

inspection *noun The car passed the inspection.* check, check-up, examination, going-over (*informal*), investigation, once-over (*informal*), review, scrutiny.

inspire *verb His action was inspired by jealousy.* animate, drive, encourage, influence, motivate, move, prompt, provoke, spur, stimulate, stir.

install *verb* **1** *The machine was installed in its correct position.* establish, fit, fix, mount, place, put, set up. OPPOSITE remove. **2** *Eric was installed as chairman.* inaugurate, induct, invest, ordain.

instalment *noun We read the first instalment of the novel.* chapter, episode, part, section.

instance *noun She gave an instance of their carelessness.* case, example, illustration, sample.

instant *adjective instant answers.* immediate, instantaneous, prompt, quick, ready, speedy, unhesitating. OPPOSITE slow. — *noun It happened in an instant.* flash, jiffy (*informal*), moment, split second, trice, twinkling of an eye. OPPOSITE age.

instantaneous *adjective Death was instantaneous.* immediate, instant, quick, swift. OPPOSITE gradual, slow.

instead *adverb* **instead of** in place of, in lieu of.

instigate *verb The minister instigated a public inquiry.* bring about, initiate, institute, set up, start.

instil *verb She instilled kindness in her children.* implant, inculcate, infuse.

instinct *noun* **1** *She knows what to do by instinct.* intuition, nature, sixth sense. **2** *He has an instinct for finding a good place.* aptitude, gift, knack, skill, talent.

instinctive *adjective an instinctive reaction.* automatic, inborn, innate, intuitive, natural, reflex, spontaneous, subconscious, unlearned. OPPOSITE learned.

institute *noun an institute for learning.* academy, college, establishment, institution, organisation, school, society. — *verb They instituted a new practice.* begin, create, establish, found, inaugurate, initiate, originate, start. OPPOSITE abolish.

institution *noun* **1** *a charitable institution.* establishment, foundation, organisation, society. **2** *Bedtime stories were a family institution.* convention, custom, habit, practice, ritual, routine, tradition.

instruct *verb* **1** *He instructed the class in life-saving.* coach, drill, educate, ground, lecture, school, teach, train, tutor. **2** *He instructed them to start.* bid, charge, command, direct, enjoin, order, tell.

instruction *noun* **1** *religious instruction.* education, guidance, lessons, schooling, teaching, training, tuition. **2** *He followed the instructions.* command, direction, guideline, order, prescription, recipe, rule.

instructive *adjective an instructive film.* edifying, educational, enlightening, helpful, illuminating, informative.

instructor *noun* coach, educator, lecturer, mentor, teacher, trainer, tutor.

instrument *noun The technician uses many instruments.* apparatus, appliance, device, gadget, implement, machine, tool, utensil; see also EQUIPMENT.

instrumentalist *noun* musician, performer, player.

insubordinate *adjective an insubordinate worker.* contrary, defiant, disobedient, insurgent, mutinous, rebellious, recalcitrant. OPPOSITE obedient.

insufferable *adjective The man beside her was an insufferable bore.* intolerable, obnoxious, unbearable, unendurable.

insufficient *adjective insufficient money.* deficient, inadequate, meagre, scant, scanty, scarce, wanting. OPPOSITE enough.

insular *adjective insular people.* cutoff, isolated, narrow-minded, parochial, provincial. OPPOSITE cosmopolitan.

insulate *verb* **1** *The pipes are insulated for energy efficiency.* clad, cover, encase, lag, protect, wrap. **2** *The inmates are insulated from the outside world.* cut off, isolate, protect, segregate, separate, shelter, shield.

insult *verb He was reprimanded for insulting his sister.* abuse, affront, be rude to, disparage, malign, offend, put down, slight, snub. OPPOSITE compliment. — *noun She tried to ignore his insults.* abuse, affront, insolence, put-down (*informal*), rudeness, slight, snub.

insulting *adjective an insulting remark.* abusive, derogatory, disparaging, offensive, rude, uncomplimentary. OPPOSITE complimentary.

insuperable *adjective insuperable problems.* insurmountable, overwhelming, unconquerable.

insurance *noun life insurance. car insurance.* assurance, cover, indemnity, protection.

insurgent *adjective insurgent forces.* dissident, insubordinate, mutinous, rebellious, revolutionary, seditious. — *noun The military dealt harshly with the insurgents.* dissident, insurrectionist, mutineer, rebel, revolutionary.

insurmountable *adjective insurmountable difficulties.* insuperable, overwhelming, unconquerable.

insurrection *noun an armed insurrection.* mutiny, rebellion, revolt, revolution, riot, rising, uprising.

intact *adjective The ornament was no longer intact after being dropped.* complete, entire, perfect, sound, unbroken, undamaged, whole. OPPOSITE broken, damaged.

intangible *adjective intangible qualities.* abstract, elusive, impalpable, indefinable, subtle. OPPOSITE tangible.

integral *adjective an integral part of the organisation.* basic, constituent, essential, indispensable, necessary, vital. OPPOSITE dispensable.

integrate *verb The two plans were integrated into one.* amalgamate, blend, combine, consolidate, incorporate, join, merge, mix, unite. OPPOSITE separate.

integrity *noun Friends vouched for his integrity.* honesty, honour, morality, probity, rectitude, scrupulousness, trustworthiness, truthfulness, uprightness, veracity, virtue. OPPOSITE dishonesty.

intellect *noun Use your intellect.* brains, intelligence, mental ability, mind, nous (*informal*), reason, sense, understanding, wits.

intellectual *adjective* **1** *an intellectual challenge.* academic, mental. **2** *an intellectual person.* academic, bookish, brainy, erudite, highbrow, intelligent, learned, scholarly, studious, thinking. — *noun a discussion among intellectuals.* academic, brain (*informal*), highbrow, scholar, thinker.

intelligence *noun* **1** *The test measures intelligence.* acumen, brains, cleverness, intellect, mental ability, nous (*informal*), reason, sense, understanding, wisdom, wits. **2** *The government acted on secret intelligence.* advice, information, knowledge, low-down (*informal*), news, notification, report, tidings, word. **3** *He works in intelligence.* espionage, spying.

intelligent *adjective an intelligent person.* astute, brainy, bright, clever, discerning, intellectual, perceptive, perspicacious, quick, reasoning, sagacious, sensible, sharp, shrewd, smart, thinking, wise. OPPOSITE stupid.

intelligible *adjective Her speech was not intelligible.* clear, coherent, comprehensible, lucid, plain, understandable. OPPOSITE incoherent, unintelligible.

intend *verb* **1** *She intends to become a dentist.* aim, mean, plan, propose. **2** *The comment was intended to shock.* calculate, design, mean.

intense *adjective* **1** *intense pain.* acute, concentrated, excruciating, extreme, great, piercing, raging, severe, sharp, strong, violent. OPPOSITE mild. **2** *an intense love.* ardent, burning, deep, earnest, fervent, keen, passionate, powerful, profound, strong, vehement. OPPOSITE cool, indifferent.

intensify *verb* **1** *The troubles intensified.* escalate, mount, multiply, worsen. OPPOSITE ease. **2** *The humidity intensified her breathing problem.* aggravate, boost, compound, exacerbate, heighten, increase, magnify, reinforce, strengthen. OPPOSITE reduce.

intensive *adjective intensive care.* comprehensive, concentrated, in-depth, thorough.

intent *noun with intent to kill.* intention, object, objective, plan, purpose. — *adjective* **1** *The man was intent on destruction.* bent, determined, hell-bent, resolved, set. **2** *an intent gaze.* absorbed, concentrated, engrossed, fixed, intense, keen, steadfast, steady, watchful.

intention *noun The intention was to please.* aim, ambition, design, end, goal, intent, object, objective, plan, purpose.

intentional *adjective an intentional insult.* conscious, deliberate, intended, planned, premeditated, purposeful, wilful. OPPOSITE accidental.

intentionally *adverb The damage was done intentionally.* consciously, deliberately, on purpose, wilfully, wittingly. OPPOSITE accidentally.

inter *verb inter a body.* bury, entomb, lay to rest. OPPOSITE exhume.

intercept *verb The bus was intercepted before it reached its destination.* ambush, block, cut off, head off, obstruct, stop, waylay.

interchange *verb She interchanged the items on the two shelves.* exchange, substitute, swap, transpose. — *noun a traffic interchange.* crossroads, intersection, junction.

interest *noun* **1** *He has no interest in the subject.* concern, curiosity, enthusiasm, fascination. OPPOSITE indifference. **2** *His interests are philately and reading.* activity, diversion, hobby, pastime, preoccupation, pursuit. **3** *She looks after her own interests.* advantage, benefit, gain, good. — *verb The subject interests him.* absorb, appeal to, attract, concern, engage, engross, excite, fascinate, intrigue, preoccupy. OPPOSITE bore.

interested *adjective* **1** *an interested student.* absorbed, attentive, concerned, curious, engrossed, enthusiastic, inquisitive, keen. OPPOSITE uninterested. **2** *an interested party.* concerned, involved, partial, partisan. OPPOSITE disinterested, neutral.

interesting *adjective an interesting book.* absorbing, engrossing, exciting, fascinating, gripping, intriguing, readable, riveting, stimulating. OPPOSITE uninteresting.

interfere *verb* **1** *Do not interfere in their business.* butt in, intervene, intrude, meddle, poke your nose in, pry. **2** *Someone has interfered with the radio.* fiddle, tamper, tinker. **3** *He doesn't let his problems interfere with his work.* get in the way of, hamper, hinder, impede, inhibit.

interim *noun in the interim.* interval, meantime, meanwhile. — *adjective an interim measure.* provisional, stopgap, temporary. OPPOSITE permanent.

interior *adjective the interior surface.* inner, inside, internal. OPPOSITE exterior. — *noun They explored the country's interior.* backblocks (*Australian*), centre, inland, outback (*Australian*). OPPOSITE coast.

interlude *noun a refreshing interlude.* break, gap, intermission, interval, pause, recess, rest.

intermediary *noun They settled the dispute through an intermediary.* agent, go-between, intercessor, mediator, middleman.

intermediate *adjective an intermediate position.* halfway, medial, middle, midway, neutral.

interminable *adjective an interminable conversation.* ceaseless, endless, everlasting, lengthy, long, never-ending, unending. OPPOSITE brief.

intermission *noun* see INTERVAL.

intermittent *adjective intermittent rain.* fitful, occasional, on and off, periodic, spasmodic, sporadic. OPPOSITE continuous.

intern *verb They interned aliens.* confine, detain, imprison, jail, lock up. OPPOSITE free.

internal *adjective an internal wall.* inner, inside, interior. OPPOSITE external.

international *adjective* **1** *an international phone call.* long-distance, overseas. OPPOSITE domestic. **2** *an international problem.* global, universal, worldwide. OPPOSITE local, national.

interpret *verb He interpreted the words incorrectly.* construe, decipher, decode, explain, read, take, translate, understand.

interrogate *verb The police interrogated the suspect.* cross-examine, examine, grill, question, quiz.

interrogation *noun a lengthy interrogation at the police station.* cross-examination, examination, inquisition, questioning, third degree.

interrupt *verb* **1** *A phone call interrupted the game.* break up, disrupt, disturb, halt, hold up, interfere with, stop. **2** *The speaker asked her to stop interrupting.* barge in, break in, butt in, chip in, cut in, interject.

interruption *noun a short interruption to her work.* break, disruption, gap, halt, hiatus, pause, stop, stoppage, suspension.

intersect *verb The two roads intersect.* converge, cross, cut.

intersection *noun an intersection without traffic lights.* corner, crossing, crossroads, interchange, junction.

intertwine *verb The three threads were intertwined.* braid, entwine, interweave, plait, twine, twist.

interval *noun* **1** *an interval of half an hour.* break, gap, hiatus, interlude, intermission, interruption, lapse, lull, pause, recess, respite, rest, space, spell. **2** *the interval measured two centimetres.* gap, opening, space.

intervene *verb She does not intervene in their disputes.* butt in, intercede, interfere, intrude, meddle, mediate, step in.

interview *noun a job interview.* conversation, dialogue, discussion, meeting.

intestines *plural noun* bowels, colon, entrails, gut, guts, innards (*informal*), insides (*informal*), viscera.

intimate[1] *adjective* **1** *intimate friends.* affectionate, bosom, close, familiar. OPPOSITE distant. **2** *an intimate conversation.* confidential, heart-to-heart, personal, private. OPPOSITE public. **3** *an intimate knowledge of computers.* deep, detailed, firsthand, in-depth, thorough. OPPOSITE superficial.

intimate[2] *verb She intimated that she was going to resign.* hint, imply, indicate, insinuate, make known, suggest.

intimidate *verb They were intimidated into signing the consent form.*

browbeat, bully, coerce, cow, frighten, hector, menace, scare, stand over (*Australian*), terrorise, threaten.

intolerable *adjective intolerable pain.* agonising, excruciating, insufferable, insupportable, unbearable. OPPOSITE tolerable.

intolerant *adjective He was intolerant of people with different views.* bigoted, illiberal, narrow-minded, prejudiced. OPPOSITE tolerant.

intoxicated *adjective* drunk, drunken, fuddled, full (*slang*), happy (*informal*), high (*informal*), high as a kite (*informal*), inebriated, merry (*informal*), off one's face (*Australian slang*), plastered (*slang*), shickered (*Australian slang*), smashed (*slang*), sozzled (*slang*), stoned (*slang*), tiddly (*informal*), tipsy, under the influence, under the weather. OPPOSITE sober.

intoxicating *adjective intoxicating drinks.* alcoholic, heady, spirituous, strong. OPPOSITE soft.

intractable *adjective an intractable person.* headstrong, mulish, obstinate, perverse, rebellious, recalcitrant, refractory, stubborn, uncontrollable, unmanageable, unruly, wayward, wild, wilful. OPPOSITE submissive.

intrepid *adjective an intrepid knight.* bold, brave, courageous, daring, fearless, gallant, game, heroic, plucky, valiant. OPPOSITE cowardly.

intricate *adjective an intricate design.* complex, complicated, detailed, elaborate, fancy, involved, ornate. OPPOSITE simple.

intrigue *verb The story intrigued her.* appeal to, fascinate, interest. — *noun a political intrigue.* conspiracy, machination, plot, scheme.

intrinsic *adjective The ring has little intrinsic value.* basic, essential, inherent, natural. OPPOSITE extrinsic.

introduce *verb 1 She introduced her boyfriend to her mother.* acquaint (with), make known, present. **2** *The MC introduced the next item.* announce, present. **3** *The council introduced a new recycling service.* begin, bring in, establish, inaugurate, initiate, institute, launch, phase in, pioneer, set up, start.

introduction *noun the introduction of a book.* beginning, foreword, opening, preamble, preface, prelude, prologue. OPPOSITE epilogue.

introductory *adjective introductory remarks.* opening, prefatory, preliminary, preparatory. OPPOSITE concluding.

introverted *adjective He was introverted and did not enjoy parties.* introspective, inward-looking, reserved, shy, unsociable, withdrawn. OPPOSITE extroverted.

intrude *verb They intruded on a private meeting.* barge in, break in, butt in, encroach, gatecrash, interfere, intervene, muscle in (*slang*), trespass.

intruder *noun The owner came home and surprised the intruder.* burglar, gatecrasher, housebreaker, interloper, invader, robber, thief, trespasser.

intuition *noun He acted on his intuition.* feeling, hunch, instinct, sixth sense.

intuitive *adjective* see INSTINCTIVE.

inundate *verb 1 The river inundated the town.* drown, engulf, flood, overflow, submerge, swamp. **2** *She was inundated with letters of condolence.* deluge, overwhelm, swamp.

invade *verb 1 Enemy forces invaded the country.* attack, enter, infiltrate, occupy, overrun, penetrate, raid. **2** *Do not invade their privacy.* encroach on, impinge on, infringe

upon, intrude on, trespass on, violate.

invalid¹ *noun The invalid is bedridden.* patient, sufferer.

invalid² *adjective His licence is invalid.* expired, illegal, out of date, unusable, useless, void, worthless. OPPOSITE valid.

invalidate *verb 1 The new evidence invalidated his theory.* disprove, negate, rebut, refute, undermine. **2** *The contract has been invalidated.* annul, cancel, nullify, rescind, revoke, void. OPPOSITE validate.

invaluable *adjective His support was invaluable.* inestimable, precious, useful, valuable. OPPOSITE useless, worthless.

invariable *adjective her invariable response.* consistent, constant, immutable, predictable, regular, set, unchangeable, unchanging, unfailing, uniform.

invasion *noun 1 an invasion into a neighbouring country.* attack, foray, incursion, infiltration, inroad, onslaught, raid. **2** *an invasion of privacy.* encroachment, infringement, intrusion, violation.

invent *verb 1 He invented a new gadget. She invented a useful word.* coin, conceive, contrive, create, design, devise, make, manufacture, mint, originate. **2** *He had to invent an excuse.* concoct, cook up (*informal*), dream up, fabricate, make up, think up.

invention *noun a useful invention.* coinage, contraption, contrivance, creation, device, innovation.

inventive *adjective an inventive person.* clever, creative, enterprising, imaginative, ingenious, innovative, resourceful. OPPOSITE unimaginative.

inventor *noun* architect, creator, designer, discoverer, innovator, maker, originator.

invest *verb 1 He invested his money in the business.* place, put. **2** *He invested much time in study.* devote, expend, give, put in, spend.

investigate *verb They investigated his disappearance.* check on, examine, explore, go into, inquire into, look into, probe, research, study, suss out (*informal*).

investigation *noun a police investigation. a scientific investigation.* examination, exploration, inquest, inquiry, inspection, research, review, scrutiny, study, survey.

investment *noun a good return on an investment.* capital, outlay, principal, stake.

inveterate *adjective an inveterate liar.* chronic, confirmed, established, habitual, incorrigible.

invigorate *verb The walk invigorated her.* enliven, pep up (*informal*), perk up, refresh, rejuvenate, strengthen. OPPOSITE tire.

invigorating *adjective an invigorating walk.* bracing, healthy, refreshing, stimulating. OPPOSITE exhausting.

invincible *adjective an invincible team.* strong, unbeatable, unconquerable, undefeatable, unstoppable. OPPOSITE conquerable.

invisible *adjective invisible stitching.* concealed, hidden, imperceptible, inconspicuous, undetectable, unnoticeable, unseen. OPPOSITE visible.

invite *verb 1 They invited him to speak.* ask, bid, call on, request, summon, urge. **2** *He's inviting trouble.* ask for, attract, court, provoke, tempt.

inviting *adjective an inviting place.* appealing, attractive, enticing, tempting. OPPOSITE uninviting.

invoice *noun The goods came with an invoice.* account, bill, statement.

involuntary *adjective an involuntary movement.* automatic, impulsive,

instinctive, mechanical, reflex, spontaneous, unconscious, unintentional. OPPOSITE deliberate, voluntary.

involve *verb 1 The plan involves much expense.* entail, mean, necessitate, require. **2** *The scheme involves ordinary people.* affect, concern, include, touch. **3** *He was not involved in the robbery.* embroil, entangle, implicate, incriminate, mix up.

involved *adjective 1 a long and involved story.* complex, complicated, convoluted, elaborate, intricate. OPPOSITE straightforward. **2** *Pam was deeply involved in her work.* absorbed, busy, caught up, engaged, engrossed, occupied, preoccupied, wrapped up.

inward *adjective a feeling of inward happiness.* inner, mental, personal, spiritual. OPPOSITE outward, superficial.

irascible *adjective* see IRRITABLE.

irate *adjective an irate customer.* angry, annoyed, cross, enraged, furious, indignant, infuriated, livid (*informal*), mad, ropeable (*Australian informal*).

irk *verb It irked them to have to postpone their holiday.* annoy, exasperate, gall, irritate, pique, rile (*informal*), vex. OPPOSITE please.

iron *verb He ironed the clothes.* press, smooth. □ **irons** *plural noun The prisoner was in irons.* bonds, chains, fetters, manacles, shackles.

ironic *adjective 'You're a fine one to talk,' he said in an ironic tone.* derisory, mocking, sarcastic, satirical, wry.

irrational *adjective irrational behaviour.* crazy, illogical, insane, mad, nonsensical, senseless, unreasonable. OPPOSITE rational.

irreconcilable *adjective irreconcilable opinions.* conflicting, contradictory, incompatible, opposing. OPPOSITE reconcilable.

irrefutable *adjective an irrefutable argument.* incontrovertible, indisputable, undeniable, watertight. OPPOSITE refutable.

irregular *adjective 1 an irregular surface.* bumpy, lumpy, pitted, rough, rugged, uneven. OPPOSITE even, level. **2** *an irregular shape.* asymmetric, lopsided. OPPOSITE regular. **3** *Jan made irregular visits.* erratic, haphazard, infrequent, intermittent, occasional, random, spasmodic, sporadic. OPPOSITE regular. **4** *They were concerned about their aunt's irregular behaviour.* aberrant, abnormal, anomalous, deviant, eccentric, extraordinary, odd, peculiar, strange, unconventional, unorthodox, unusual. OPPOSITE normal.

irrelevant *adjective This information is irrelevant.* beside the point, extraneous, immaterial, inapplicable, neither here nor there, unconnected. OPPOSITE pertinent.

irreligious *adjective an irreligious person.* agnostic, atheistic, godless, heathen, impious, irreverent, pagan, unbelieving, ungodly. OPPOSITE religious.

irrepressible *adjective an irrepressible person.* boisterous, buoyant, ebullient, exuberant, lively, spirited, unrestrained. OPPOSITE restrained.

irreproachable *adjective His conduct was irreproachable.* beyond reproach, blameless, faultless, impeccable, unimpeachable. OPPOSITE blameworthy.

irresistible *adjective an irresistible desire.* compelling, overpowering, overwhelming, powerful; see also TEMPTING.

irresolute *adjective A leader should not be irresolute.* hesitant, indeci-

sive, spineless, tentative, uncertain, undecided, unsure, vacillating, wavering. OPPOSITE resolute.

irrespective *adjective* **irrespective of** disregarding, ignoring, regardless of.

irresponsible *adjective an irresponsible babysitter.* careless, negligent, reckless, thoughtless, unthinking, untrustworthy. OPPOSITE responsible.

irreverent *adjective an irreverent joke.* blasphemous, disrespectful, impious, irreligious, profane, sacrilegious, ungodly. OPPOSITE reverent.

irrevocable *adjective an irrevocable decision.* binding, final, immutable, irreversible, settled, unalterable. OPPOSITE alterable.

irritable *adjective He is irritable when tired.* bad-tempered, cantankerous, crabby, cranky, cross, crotchety, fractious, grouchy (*informal*), grumpy, irascible, peevish, petulant, prickly, ratty (*informal*), shirty (*informal*), short-tempered, snaky (*Australian informal*), snappy, stroppy (*informal*), surly, testy, tetchy. OPPOSITE cheerful.

irritate *verb She finds that lots of little things irritate her.* anger, annoy, bother, bug (*informal*), drive someone mad (*informal*), drive someone up the wall (*informal*), exasperate, get on someone's nerves, give someone the pip (*informal*), harass, infuriate, irk, nark (*informal*), needle (*informal*), pester, plague, provoke, rankle, rile (*informal*), rub someone up the wrong way (*informal*), trouble, upset, vex.

irritating *adjective an irritating habit.* annoying, bothersome, exasperating, irksome, tiresome, trying, upsetting.

irritation *noun He could not hide his irritation.* anger, annoyance, chagrin, displeasure, exasperation, impatience, vexation.

island *noun* isle, islet; [*group of islands*] archipelago.

isolate *verb He isolated himself from the community.* cut off, detach, insulate, quarantine, segregate, separate, set apart, shut off.

isolated *adjective an isolated homestead.* cut-off, desolate, lone, lonely, outlying, remote, secluded, solitary.

issue *noun 1 the latest issue of the magazine.* edition, number, publication. **2** *The talks had a satisfactory issue.* conclusion, consequence, outcome, result. **3** *They discussed serious issues.* affair, matter, point, question, subject, topic. — *verb* **1** *Muddy water issued from the tap.* come out, discharge, emanate, emerge, erupt, escape, flow out, gush, pour, stream. **2** *They issued safety helmets to visitors.* distribute, give out, provide, supply. **3** *The principal issues a weekly bulletin.* circulate, distribute, publish, put out, release, send out.

itch *noun 1 The bite left an itch.* irritation, prickling, tickle, tingling. **2** *She has an itch to fly.* desire, longing, urge, yearning, yen. — *verb* **1** *Scratch where it itches.* prickle, tickle, tingle. **2** *He is itching to find out.* be desperate, be eager, hanker, long, thirst, yearn.

item *noun 1 The sale items were listed individually.* article, object, piece, product, thing. **2** *a news item.* article, feature, piece, report, story. **3** *items for discussion.* aspect, detail, matter, point, subject, topic.

itemise *verb Phone calls are itemised on the bill.* detail, enumerate, list, specify, spell out.

itinerant *adjective an itinerant fruit picker.* nomadic, peripatetic, roving, travelling, wandering. OPPOSITE resident.

Jj

jab *verb He jabbed the needle into her arm.* poke, prod, stab, thrust. — *noun* **1** *He received a jab in his side.* dig, nudge, poke, prod, stab, thrust. **2** (*informal*) *a tetanus jab.* immunisation, injection, shot, vaccination.

jabber *verb I couldn't understand what she was jabbering about.* babble, blather, chatter, gabble, gibber, prattle, yabber (*Australian informal*); see also TALK.

jack *verb* **jack up** *You need to jack up the car to change the tyre.* hoist, lift, raise.

jacket *noun* **1** *They wore jackets.* anorak, blazer, bolero, cagoule, coat, parka, tuxedo, windcheater. **2** *a book jacket.* cover, dust cover, dust jacket, wrapper.

jaded *adjective He was feeling jaded.* done in (*informal*), fatigued, spent, tired, weary, worn out. OPPOSITE energetic, fresh.

jagged *adjective a jagged edge.* broken, chipped, indented, notched, ragged, rough, serrated, uneven. OPPOSITE smooth.

jail gaol *noun* **1** *The jail was built by convicts.* detention centre, lock-up, nick (*slang*), penitentiary (*American*), prison, remand centre, watchhouse. **2** *He was sentenced to two years' jail.* confinement, custody, imprisonment, incarceration, internment, porridge (*slang*), prison. — *verb He was jailed for ten years.* imprison, incarcerate, intern, lock up, put away, put behind bars, send down. OPPOSITE release.

jailer gaoler *noun* guard, keeper, prison officer, warder.

jam[1] *noun toast and jam.* conserve, jelly, marmalade, preserve.

jam[2] *verb* **1** *She jammed the books in tightly.* pack, push, ram, squash, squeeze, stuff, wedge. **2** *The tape has jammed.* catch, snarl, stick. **3** *The shoppers jammed the entrance to the store.* block, choke, clog, cram, crowd, fill, jam-pack, obstruct, pack. — *noun* **1** *a traffic jam.* bottleneck, build-up, congestion, gridlock, hold-up, snarl. **2** (*informal*) *I'm in a jam.* bind (*informal*), difficulty, fix (*informal*), hole (*informal*), mess, pickle (*informal*), plight, predicament, quandary, spot (*informal*).

jamboree *noun They attended the Scout jamboree.* carnival, celebration, convention, gathering, rally.

jam-packed *adjective* (*informal*) *The hall was jam-packed.* chock-a-block, chockers (*informal*), crammed, crowded, filled, full, packed. OPPOSITE empty, half-empty.

jangle *noun We heard the jangle of keys.* clang, clangour, clank, clink, jingle, rattle. — *verb The keys jangled in her pocket.* clang, clank, clink, jingle, rattle.

janitor *noun The building has a janitor.* caretaker, concierge, doorkeeper, doorman.

jar[1] *noun a glass jar.* bottle, container, crock, jug, pot, receptacle, vase, vessel.

jar[2] *verb* **1** *The music jarred on her nerves.* grate, irritate, jangle. **2** *She jarred her neck in the accident.* jerk, jolt, shake.

jargon *noun He didn't understand the scientist's jargon.* cant, gobbledegook (*informal*), idiom, lingo (*informal*), slang.

jarring *adjective a jarring noise.* discordant, grating, harsh, irritating, raucous.

jaunt *noun a Sunday afternoon jaunt in the car.* drive, excursion, expedition, outing, trip.

jaunty *adjective a jaunty manner.* breezy, bright, cheerful, energetic, lively, perky, sprightly.

jaw *noun* jawbone, mandible, maxilla.

jazz *verb* **jazz up** *She jazzes up her clothes with ribbons.* adorn, brighten up, liven up.

jazzy *adjective a jazzy sports car.* flash (*informal*), flashy, gaudy, showy, smart, snazzy (*informal*).

jealous *adjective* **1** *He was jealous of his brother's popularity.* covetous, envious, grudging, resentful. **2** *He was jealous of his rights.* protective, vigilant, watchful.

jeer *verb The crowd jeered the Prime Minister.* boo, chiack (*Australian informal*), deride, gibe, heckle, hiss, laugh at, make fun of, mock, poke borak at (*Australian informal*), ridicule, scoff at, sneer at, taunt. OPPOSITE cheer. — *noun He was driven off the stage with jeers.* boo, catcall, gibe, hiss, scoff, sneer, taunt. OPPOSITE cheer.

jelly *noun quince jelly.* conserve, jam, preserve.

jeopardise *verb His reckless driving jeopardised their lives.* endanger, imperil, put on the line, risk, threaten.

jeopardy *noun Their lives were in jeopardy.* danger, peril, risk, threat. OPPOSITE safety.

jerk *noun* **1** *The jar opened with a jerk.* jig, jiggle, jog, jolt, pull, rock, shake, thrust, tug, twist, twitch. **2** (*slang*) *He's such a jerk.* see FOOL. — *verb* **1** *She jerked the handle and the door opened.* jiggle, move, pull, shake, tug, tweak, twist, wrench, yank. **2** *The car jerked down the road.* bounce, bump, jolt, kangaroo, kangaroo-hop, lurch.

jerky *adjective jerky movements.* disconnected, rough, spasmodic, uncoordinated, uneven. OPPOSITE smooth.

jersey *noun He wore a jersey over his singlet.* jumper, pullover, sweater, top.

jest *noun He told a jest.* gag, joke, quip, wisecrack (*informal*), witticism. — *verb He didn't mean it: he was only jesting.* joke, kid (*informal*), pull someone's leg (*informal*), tease.

jester *noun the court jester.* buffoon, clown, comedian, comic, entertainer, fool, joker, wag, zany.

jet *noun* **1** *a jet of water.* fountain, gush, spray, spurt, stream. **2** *a blocked jet.* nozzle, spout, sprinkler. **3** *They travelled on a jet.* jumbo, jumbo jet, plane; see also AIRCRAFT.

jettison *verb The cargo had to be jettisoned.* discard, dump, eject, get rid of, throw away, throw overboard, toss out. OPPOSITE keep.

jetty *noun They boarded the ferry at the jetty.* landing stage, pier, quay, wharf.

jewel *noun a gold ring set with jewels.* gem, gemstone, precious stone.

jewellery *noun Michelle likes to wear jewellery.* adornments, jewels, ornaments, trinkets; [*kinds of jewellery*] anklet, bangle, beads, bracelet, brooch, chain, charm, cuff link, earring, locket, necklace, pendant, ring, stud, tiepin.

jib *verb The horse jibbed at the fence.* baulk, prop (*Australian*), pull up, stop.

jiffy *noun* (*informal*) *I'll be there in a jiffy.* flash, instant, minute, moment, second (*informal*), tick (*informal*), trice.

jig *verb The toddler jigged up and down.* bob, bounce, dance, hop, jump.

jiggle *verb He jiggled the key in the lock.* jerk, shake, wiggle.

jilt *verb After a long courtship he jilted her.* abandon, drop (*informal*), dump (*informal*), forsake, reject.

jingle *verb The coins jingled in his pocket.* clink, jangle, rattle, ring, tinkle. — *noun* **1** *the jingle of coins.* the jingle of sleigh bells. clink, jangle, rattle, ring, tinkle. **2** *a catchy advertising jingle.* chorus, poem, rhyme, song, tune, verse.

jinx *noun There seems to be a jinx on them.* curse, hex, spell.

jinxed *adjective He felt that he was jinxed.* bewitched, cursed, ill-fated, unlucky.

jitters *plural noun* (*informal*) *He had the jitters before his driving test.* butterflies (*informal*), collywobbles (*informal*), heebie-jeebies (*informal*), jim-jams (*informal*), nerves, shakes, willies (*informal*).

jittery *adjective* (*informal*) *The dentist calmed the jittery patient.* anxious, apprehensive, frightened, jumpy, nervous, nervy, quaking, quivering, shaky, uneasy. OPPOSITE calm.

job *noun* **1** *He is paid at the end of each job.* activity, assignment, chore, errand, piece of work, project, task. **2** *He changed his job.* appointment, career, employment, occupation, position, post, profession, situation, trade, vocation, work. **3** *It's his job to lock up.* duty, function, responsibility, role.

jobless *adjective* out of work, unemployed. OPPOSITE employed.

jockey *noun a horse and jockey.* hoop (*Australian informal*), horseman, horse-rider, horsewoman, rider.

jocular *adjective a jocular remark. a jocular person.* amusing, funny, humorous, jesting, joking, playful, witty. OPPOSITE serious.

jog *verb* **1** *She needed to jog him a little to wake him up.* jerk, jolt, knock, nudge, prod, push, shake. **2** *Let me jog your memory.* prompt, refresh, stimulate, stir. **3** *He jogs for exercise.* run, trot.

join *verb* **1** *He joined the two bits together.* add, attach, bind, bracket, cement, combine, connect, couple, dovetail, fasten, fit, fuse, glue, knit, link, put together, solder, splice, stick, tack, tie, unite, weld, yoke. OPPOSITE separate. **2** *The two roads join at Hay.* come together, converge, meet, merge. **3** *She joined in the fun.* partake, participate, share, take part. **4** *She joined the army.* enlist in, enrol in, enter, register for, sign up for, volunteer for. OPPOSITE leave. — *noun You can't see the join.* connection, joint, knot, link, seam.

joint *adjective a joint decision. a joint effort.* collective, combined, common, concerted, cooperative, shared, united. OPPOSITE individual.

jointly *adverb They do everything jointly.* as a team, cooperatively, in partnership, together. OPPOSITE individually.

joke *noun* **1** *He peppered his talk with jokes.* gag, jest, pun, quip, wisecrack (*informal*), witticism. **2** *She played a joke on them.* hoax, practical joke, prank, trick. — *verb Don't joke: this is serious.* crack jokes, jest, kid (*informal*), pun, quip, tease.

joker *noun The joker cheered them up.* buffoon, clown, comedian, comic, jester, prankster, wag, wit, zany.

jolly *adjective a jolly person.* bright, cheerful, cheery, exuberant, good-humoured, happy, high-spirited, jocular, jovial, joyful, merry. OPPOSITE miserable.

jolt *verb* **1** *They were jolted out of their seats by the impact.* bump, dislodge, jerk, shake. **2** *The car jolted along the road.* bounce, bump, jerk, judder, kangaroo, kangaroo-hop, lurch. — *noun* **1** *The jolts of the train kept the passengers awake.* bounce, bump, jerk, lurch. **2** *The news of the accident gave her a jolt.* shock, start, surprise.

jostle *verb They jostled their way through the crowd.* bump, elbow, knock, push, shove.

jot *verb* **jot down** *He jotted down the address.* note, record, scribble, take down, write down.

jotter *noun She wrote the name on the jotter.* notebook, notepad, pad, writing pad.

journal *noun* **1** *The explorer kept a journal of his expedition.* chronicle, diary, logbook, record. **2** *an article in a scientific journal.* gazette, magazine, newspaper, paper, periodical.

journalist *noun* columnist, commentator, correspondent, editor, journo (*Australian informal*), reporter, roundsman (*Australian*), writer.

journey *noun They went on a long journey.* cruise, drive, excursion, expedition, flight, jaunt, mission, outing, pilgrimage, ride, safari, tour, trek, trip, voyage, walk. — *verb* see TRAVEL.

jovial *adjective a jovial person.* breezy, bright, cheerful, convivial, good-humoured, happy, jolly, joyful, lively, merry. OPPOSITE melancholy.

joy *noun The news of the birth filled them with joy.* bliss, contentment, delight, ecstasy, elation, euphoria, exultation, gladness, happiness, jubilation, pleasure, rapture.

joyful *adjective She was joyful at the news.* blithe, cheerful, content, delighted, ecstatic, elated, euphoric, exultant, glad, happy, jolly, jovial, joyous, jubilant, merry, overjoyed. OPPOSITE miserable.

jubilant *adjective the jubilant prize-winner.* delighted, elated, exultant, gleeful, happy, joyful, overjoyed, rejoicing, triumphant.

jubilation *noun We shared in the team's jubilation after they won the match.* delight, elation, exultation, glee, happiness, joy, rejoicing, triumph.

jubilee *noun the State's jubilee.* anniversary, celebration, commemoration, festival.

judge *noun* **1** *a judge of a court.* justice, magistrate. **2** *a judge of a competition.* adjudicator, arbiter, arbitrator, referee, umpire. **3** *He cannot claim to be a judge of wine.* authority, connoisseur, expert. — *verb* **1** *Who is judging the case?* decide, hear, try. **2** *The local vet was asked to judge the pet show.* adjudicate, arbitrate, referee, umpire. **3** *You can't judge a book by its cover.* appraise, assess, evaluate, rate, size up (*informal*). **4** *He judged the distance accurately.* assess, estimate, gauge, guess.

judgement *noun* **1** *The judgement was in his favour.* adjudication, decision, decree, finding, ruling, sentence, verdict. **2** *He lacks judgement.* acumen, discernment, discretion, discrimination, good sense, insight, sagacity, shrewdness, wisdom. **3** *He was guilty in the judgement of most people.* assessment, belief, mind, opinion, view.

judgemental *adjective* see CRITICAL.

judicial *adjective the judicial system.* legal.

judicious *adjective a judicious decision.* discerning, politic, prudent, sensible, shrewd, sound, wise. OPPOSITE unwise.

jug *noun a jug of water.* carafe, decanter, ewer, pitcher, vessel.

juggle *verb He juggled the figures to suit his purposes.* alter, cook (*infor-

mal), doctor, falsify, fiddle (*slang*), fix, manipulate, rearrange, rig, tamper with.

juice noun **1** *fruit or vegetable juice.* drink, extract, liquid, nectar, sap. **2** *digestive juices.* fluid, secretion.

juicy adjective *a juicy pear.* moist, ripe, succulent. OPPOSITE dry.

jumble verb *All their clothes were jumbled up.* confuse, disorganise, mix, mix up, muddle. — noun *a jumble of papers.* confusion, hotch-potch, mess, mixture, muddle. □ **jumble sale** bazaar, boot sale, bring-and-buy-sale, garage sale, rummage sale.

jump verb **1** *The cat jumped on to the bed.* bounce, bound, hop, leap, pounce, spring. **2** *She can jump the fence.* clear, go over, hurdle, pass over, vault. **3** *The reader jumped a line.* leave out, miss, omit, overlook, pass over, skip. **4** *The horse jumped when he heard the shot.* buck, flinch, rear, recoil, shy, start. **5** *Prices have jumped recently.* escalate, increase, rise, shoot up. — noun **1** *a running jump.* bounce, bound, hop, leap, pounce, spring, vault. **2** *a jump in house prices.* boost, escalation, increase, rise, upturn. **3** *The horse baulked at the last jump.* fence, gate, hurdle, obstacle. □ **jump at** *She jumped at the opportunity.* grab, leap at, seize, snatch.

jumper noun *Ben wore a jumper and jeans.* guernsey, jersey, pullover, skivvy, sweater, top.

jumpy adjective *She sat by the phone feeling jumpy.* anxious, edgy, jittery (*informal*), nervous, nervy, tense, twitchy (*informal*), uneasy, uptight (*informal*). OPPOSITE calm.

junction noun *a road junction.* corner, crossroads, interchange, intersection, meeting point, T-junction, Y-junction.

juncture noun *at this juncture.* point, point in time, stage, time; see also NOW.

jungle noun *a tropical jungle.* forest, rainforest.

junior adjective **1** *John Smith junior.* younger. OPPOSITE older, senior. **2** *a junior officer.* inferior, lower-ranking, subordinate. OPPOSITE senior, superior. **3** *junior primary school.* lower.

junk noun *They threw out their junk.* cast-offs, clutter, garbage, odds and ends, rubbish, scrap, trash.

jurisdiction noun *The matter comes within the other state's jurisdiction.* authority, control, dominion, power, rule.

just adjective **1** *a just decision.* equitable, even-handed, fair, impartial, neutral, reasonable, unbiased, unprejudiced. OPPOSITE unjust. **2** *a just reward.* appropriate, deserved, due, fair, fitting, merited, right, rightful. — adverb **1** *It happened just at that spot.* exactly, precisely, right. **2** (*informal*) *We are just good friends.* merely, no more than, only, simply. □ **just about** (*informal*) *just about ready.* almost, close to, more or less, nearly, practically.

justice noun **1** *She appealed to his sense of justice.* equity, even-handedness, fairness, fair play, impartiality, right. OPPOSITE injustice. **2** *the Chief Justice.* judge, magistrate.

justifiable adjective *He has a justifiable complaint.* fair, legitimate, reasonable, valid. OPPOSITE unjustifiable.

justification noun *There was no justification for his actions* defence, excuse, explanation, grounds, reason.

justify verb *His actions could not be justified.* defend, excuse, explain, rationalise, vindicate, warrant.

jut verb *The bags jutted into the aisle.* poke out, project, protrude, stick out.

juvenile adjective **1** *juvenile behaviour.* childish, immature, infantile, puerile, youthful. OPPOSITE mature. **2** *juvenile offenders.* adolescent, junior, teenage, young. OPPOSITE adult. — noun *The crime was committed by juveniles.* adolescent, child, kid (*informal*), minor, teenager, youngster, youth. OPPOSITE adult.

Kk

kangaroo noun *a mob of kangaroos.* boomer (*male*), doe (*female*), joey (*young*), old man (*male*), roo (*informal*).

keel noun *the ship's keel.* base, bottom, underside. — verb **keel over** *The ship keeled over.* capsize, collapse, fall over, heel over, overturn, tilt, turn over, upset. □ **on an even keel** *A month after the crisis and things were on an even keel once again.* balanced, calm, level, stable, steady.

keen adjective **1** *The knife had a keen edge.* sharp. OPPOSITE blunt. **2** *A keen wind was blowing.* biting, bitter, cold, piercing, severe. OPPOSITE gentle. **3** *He showed a keen interest in their work.* ardent, avid, deep, eager, enthusiastic, fervent, intense, lively, strong, zealous. OPPOSITE apathetic. **4** *She is keen to start work.* anxious, eager, impatient, itching, raring. **5** *The blind man has a keen sense of smell.* acute, penetrating, sensitive, sharp. OPPOSITE poor. □ **keen on** (*informal*) *He is keen on her.* attracted to, fond of, infatuated by, interested in, mad about, nuts about (*informal*), rapt in, taken with. OPPOSITE uninterested in.

keep verb **1** *You must keep some for later.* conserve, hang on to, hold on to, preserve, put aside, put away, reserve, retain, save, store, withhold. OPPOSITE get rid of. **2** *The patient must keep still.* hold, remain, stay. **3** *What kept you?* delay, detain, hinder, hold up, impede, obstruct, prevent. **4** *He keeps his promises. Keep to the rules.* abide by, comply with, conform to, fulfil, honour, obey, respect, stick to. OPPOSITE break. **5** *They keep the Passover.* celebrate, commemorate, honour, observe. OPPOSITE ignore. **6** *She keeps goal for the team.* defend, guard, protect. **7** *He can't keep a family on his income.* feed, maintain, provide for, support. **8** *He keeps bees.* care for, look after, own, tend. **9** *They keep trying.* carry on, continue, go on, persevere in, persist in. OPPOSITE give up. **10** *Margarine will keep for a long time.* be usable, last, stay fresh. OPPOSITE deteriorate, go off. — noun **1** *She earns her keep.* board, food, maintenance, subsistence. **2** *the castle's keep.* donjon, stronghold, tower. □ **for keeps** (*informal*) *The trophy was hers for keeps.* forever, for good, permanently. OPPOSITE temporarily. **keep away from** *He tried to keep away from her.* avoid, dodge, evade, shun, stay away from, steer clear of. **keep down** *We have to keep the numbers down.* control, curb, limit, restrict. OPPOSITE increase. **keep on** *He just keeps on doing it.* carry on, continue, go on, keep, persist in. OPPOSITE stop. **keep on at** *He keeps*

on at me. badger, harass, hassle (*informal*), nag, pester. **keep up** *Keep up the good work.* carry on with, continue, maintain.

keeper noun **1** *a zoo keeper. a museum keeper.* caretaker, curator, custodian, guardian, ranger. **2** *a jail keeper.* guard, jailer, warder, watchman.

keeping noun *The painting is in safe keeping.* care, charge, custody, guardianship, hands. □ **in keeping with** *a house in keeping with its surroundings.* conforming with, fitting, in harmony with, in line with, in step with, in tune with, suiting.

keepsake noun *a keepsake from her grandmother.* memento, reminder, souvenir.

keg noun *a keg of beer.* barrel, cask, hogshead.

kerb noun *She parked close to the kerb.* edge, roadside, verge.

kernel noun *almond kernels.* nut, seed.

key noun **1** *the key to the door.* latch-key, master key, passkey, skeleton key. **2** *the key to the mystery.* answer, clue, secret, solution. **3** *a key to the symbols used in the book.* code, explanation, guide, interpretation, legend. **4** *Press the keys on the pad.* button. — verb **key in** *She keyed in the data.* enter, input, type. — adjective *a key industry.* critical, crucial, essential, important, major, vital.

keystone noun *Deregulation is the keystone of their policy.* basis, cornerstone, foundation, linchpin.

kick verb **1** *Greg kicked the ball.* boot, punt. **2** *The gun kicked.* recoil, spring back. **3** (*informal*) *He has kicked the habit.* abandon, cease, give up, quit, stop. — noun **1** *She gave the ball a hard kick.* boot, punt. **2** (*informal*) *She gets a kick out of giving presents.* buzz (*informal*), enjoyment, excitement, fun, pleasure, satisfaction, thrill. □ **kick out** (*informal*) *She broke the rules and was kicked out.* dismiss, drive out, evict, expel, fire, oust, sack, throw out.

kid noun (*informal*) *a film for kids.* child, youngster. OPPOSITE adult. — verb (*informal*) **1** *He tried to kid them that he was really sick.* bluff, deceive, fool, have on (*informal*), hoax, hoodwink, lie to, trick. **2** *He was just kidding.* jest, joke, pull someone's leg (*informal*), tease.

kidnap verb *They kidnapped his child.* abduct, carry off, seize, snatch.

kill verb **1** *He had killed someone.* annihilate, assassinate, bump off (*slang*), butcher, destroy, dispatch, do away with, do in (*slang*), eliminate, execute, exterminate, finish off, knock off (*informal*), liquidate, martyr, massacre, mow down, murder, put to death, slaughter, slay, take someone's life, wipe out, zap (*slang*); [*various ways to kill*] asphyxiate, behead, choke, crucify, decapitate, drown, electrocute, gas, guillotine, gun down, hang, knife, poison, shoot, stab, starve, stifle, stone, strangle, suffocate, throttle. **2** *The farmer had to kill some of the animals.* cull, put down, put to sleep. **3** *The medicine killed the pain.* deaden, dull, numb, put an end to, stop.

killer noun *The police hunted for the killer.* assassin, executioner, hit man (*slang*), murderer, slayer.

killing noun *annihilation, assassination, bloodshed, butchery, carnage, destruction, euthanasia, execution, extermination, genocide, homicide, manslaughter, massacre, murder, pogrom, slaughter, slaying, suicide.*

killjoy noun *Who invited that killjoy to the party?* party-pooper (*infor-*

mal), spoilsport, wet blanket, wowser (*Australian*).

kin noun *They notified his next of kin.* family, kindred, kinsfolk, kith and kin, relations, relatives.

kind[1] noun *of the same kind.* brand, breed, category, class, classification, form, genre, genus, ilk (*informal*), make, nature, order, set, sort, species, strain, style, type, variety.

kind[2] adjective *a kind person. a kind deed.* affectionate, altruistic, amiable, avuncular, benevolent, benign, big-hearted, caring, charitable, compassionate, considerate, father-ly, friendly, generous, genial, gentle, good, good-natured, gracious, helpful, hospitable, humane, kind-hearted, kindly, lenient, loving, merciful, motherly, neighbourly, nice, obliging, philanthropic, soft-hearted, sympathetic, tender-hearted, thoughtful, understanding, unselfish, warm-hearted. OPPOSITE unkind.

kindergarten noun nursery school, preschool.

kindle verb **1** *He kindled the fire.* fire, ignite, light, set alight, set fire to. OPPOSITE extinguish. **2** *The teacher kindled his interest in history.* arouse, awaken, excite, inspire, spark off, stimulate, stir. OPPOSITE extinguish.

king noun monarch, ruler, sovereign; see also RULER.

kingdom noun **1** *The King was respected throughout his kingdom.* country, domain, dominion, empire, land, monarchy, nation, realm, state, territory. **2** *a member of the animal kingdom.* classification, division, world.

kingly adjective regal, royal.

kink noun **1** *a kink in a piece of wire.* bend, coil, crinkle, curve, loop, tangle, twist. **2** *a kink in his personality.* eccentricity, foible, idiosyncrasy, peculiarity, quirk.

kinky adjective **1** *kinky hair.* crimped, curly, frizzy, permed, wavy. OPPOSITE straight. **2** (*informal*) *kinky behaviour.* abnormal, depraved, deviant, perverted, unnatural, warped.

kiosk noun **1** *a newspaper kiosk.* booth, stall, stand. **2** (*Australian*) *They had Devonshire tea at the kiosk.* café, snack bar, tea room.

kiss noun *a kiss on the cheek.* caress, peck, smack, smooch (*informal*).

kit noun *Each recruit is supplied with his kit.* clothing, equipment, gear, outfit, paraphernalia, rig, tackle, things.

kitchen noun galley, kitchenette, scullery.

kitty noun *Each person contributes $5 to the kitty.* fund, pool, reserve.

knack noun *She has a knack for making people laugh.* ability, aptitude, art, expertise, flair, gift, skill, talent, trick.

knapsack noun *She travels with a knapsack on her back.* backpack, haversack, pack, rucksack; see also BAG.

knave noun *The knave in the story got his just deserts.* baddy (*informal*), blackguard, miscreant, rascal, rogue, scoundrel, villain.

kneel verb *She knelt to say her prayers.* bend, bow, crouch, genuflect, stoop.

knickers plural noun *ladies' knickers.* briefs, drawers, panties, pants, underpants, underwear, undies (*informal*).

knick-knack noun *She bought some knick-knacks as souvenirs.* bagatelle, curio, ornament, trifle, trinket.

knife noun *cut with a sharp knife.* blade, cutter; [*kinds of knife*] bowie knife, carving knife, chopper, clasp-knife, cleaver, flick knife, jackknife, lancet, machete, paperknife, penknife, pocket knife, scalpel, sheath knife, switchblade. — *verb The victim was knifed.* cut, gash, slash, slit, stab.

knit *verb The broken bones will knit in six weeks.* grow together, heal, join, mend.

knob *noun* **1** *the door knob.* handle. **2** *He turned the knobs on the radio.* button, control, switch. **3** *a smooth surface without any knobs.* bulge, bump, knot, lump, node, nodule, projection, protuberance, swelling. **4** *a knob of butter.* lump, nub, pat.

knobbly *adjective The tree has a knobbly trunk.* gnarled, knotty, lumpy, rough, uneven. OPPOSITE smooth.

knock *verb* **1** *He knocked the man unconscious.* bash, batter, beat, belt, clip (*informal*), clout (*informal*), dong (*Australian informal*), hit, kick, pummel, punch, smite, sock (*slang*), strike, thrash, wallop (*informal*), whack. **2** *She knocked at the door.* bang, hammer, hit, pound, rap, strike, tap, thud, thump. **3** *He knocked a nail in the wall.* drive, hammer, hit. **4** (*informal*) *He knocks everything they do.* bag (*Australian informal*), belittle, bucket (*Australian informal*), criticise, disparage, find fault with, insult, pan (*informal*), pick holes in, rubbish (*Australian informal*), run down, slam (*informal*), tear to pieces. — *noun He received a knock on the head. He heard a loud knock.* bang, blow, bump, clip (*informal*), clout (*informal*), dong (*Australian informal*), hit, kick, punch, rap, slap, smack, tap, thud, thump, thwack, wallop (*informal*), whack, wham (*informal*). □ **knock back** (*informal*) *She knocked back his offer.* decline, rebuff, refuse, reject, scorn, spurn, turn down. **knock down 1** *They knocked down the old building.* demolish, destroy, pull down, raze. OPPOSITE erect. **2** *He knocked down the price to $20.* bring down, decrease, lower, reduce. OPPOSITE raise. **knock into** *He knocked into another car.* bang into, bump into, collide with, crash into, run into, slam into, smash into. **knock off 1** (*informal*) *He has knocked off work for today.* cease, finish, stop. OPPOSITE start. **2** (*informal*) *She knocked $10 off the bill.* deduct, subtract, take off. OPPOSITE add on. **3** (*slang*) *He knocked off the jewels.* nick (*slang*), pinch (*informal*), steal, thieve. **knock out 1** *The top player was knocked out in the second round.* beat, defeat, eliminate. **2** *He knocked himself out running the marathon.* exhaust, tire out, wear out.

knockabout *noun* (*Australian*) *He works as a knockabout on a sheep station.* blue tongue (*Australian slang*), handyman, loppy (*Australian*), odd-job man, rouseabout (*Australian*).

knockback *noun* (*informal*) *He was depressed by the knockbacks he received.* rebuff, refusal, rejection, turndown.

knot *noun* **1** *She tied a knot in the rope.* bow, hitch, loop, twist. **2** *She has knots in her hair.* snarl, tangle. **3** *knots on a tree trunk.* knob, lump, node, nodule. — *verb* **1** *He knotted one string to the other.* bind, fasten, hitch, join, lash, loop, tie. **2** *Her hair has knotted.* entangle, snarl up, tangle.

knotty *adjective* **1** *knotty timber.* gnarled, knobbly, uneven. OPPOSITE smooth. **2** *a knotty problem.* baffling, complex, complicated, difficult, intricate, perplexing, puzzling, thorny, tricky. OPPOSITE straightforward.

know *verb* **1** *They know their tables.* have learnt, have memorised, remember. **2** *He knew what was going on.* be aware of, be in on (*informal*), comprehend, perceive, realise, understand. OPPOSITE be ignorant of. **3** *He knows which twin is which.* discern, discriminate, distinguish, identify, recognise, remember. **4** *I know I left it here.* be certain, be confident, be positive, be sure. OPPOSITE be unsure. **5** *She did not know any of the other people.* be acquainted with, be a friend of, be familiar with. **6** *Does he know French?* comprehend, have a grasp of, speak, understand.

know-all *noun* expert, genius, smart alec (*informal*), wise guy (*informal*).

know-how *noun They need someone with the technical know-how.* ability, competence, expertise, knack, knowledge, skill.

knowing *adjective She gave her a knowing look.* artful, astute, aware, crafty, cunning, eloquent, expressive, meaningful, perceptive, shrewd, significant, sly, wily. OPPOSITE innocent.

knowledge *noun* **1** *She has the knowledge but lacks experience.* education, erudition, learning, scholarship, science; see also INFORMATION. OPPOSITE ignorance. **2** *He had a working knowledge of computers.* comprehension, experience, expertise, familiarity, grasp, know-how, understanding. **3** *He had no knowledge of what had happened.* awareness, consciousness, inkling, memory, perception, realisation.

knowledgeable *adjective a knowledgeable speaker.* educated, enlightened, erudite, intelligent, learned, well-informed. OPPOSITE ignorant.

kowtow *verb He refused to kowtow to the boss.* bow and scrape, crawl (*informal*), grovel, lick someone's boots, suck up (*informal*), toady.

kudos *noun* (*informal*) *She liked the kudos that went with the job.* acclaim, fame, glory, honour, prestige, renown, respect.

Ll

label *noun* **1** *The clothes have labels on them.* sticker, tag, ticket. **2** *She recognised the company's label.* brand, logo, trade mark. — *verb* **1** *All the goods are clearly labelled.* identify, mark, name, stamp, tag. **2** *He was labelled a bully.* brand, call, categorise, describe, identify.

laborious *adjective* **1** *Writing up his research was extremely laborious.* arduous, difficult, exhausting, hard, onerous, strenuous, taxing, tiring. OPPOSITE easy. **2** *The writer has a laborious style.* forced, laboured, ponderous, strained, studied. OPPOSITE spontaneous.

labour *noun* **1** *One cannot put a price on his labour.* effort, exertion, industry, slog, toil, work, yakka (*Australian informal*). **2** *She went to hospital when labour started.* childbirth, contractions, travail (*old use*). **3** *Relations between labour and management are good.* employees, workers, workforce. — *verb* **1** *She laboured over the hot stove.* exert oneself, grind away, slave, sweat, toil, work. **2** *I do not need to labour the point.* dwell on, elaborate, emphasise, harp on, impress, stress.

labourer *noun He prefers to work as a labourer.* blue-collar worker, hand, manual worker, navvy, unskilled worker, worker, workman.

labyrinth *noun They were lost in the labyrinth.* maze, network, warren.

lace *verb* **1** *She can now lace her own shoes.* do up, fasten, tie. **2** *The plant's shoots are laced through the wire.* entwine, intertwine, weave. **3** *Her drink was laced with vodka.* fortify, spike (*informal*).

lacerate *verb Her leg was badly lacerated by the broken glass.* cut, gash, injure, mangle, rip, slash, tear, wound.

lack *noun a lack of knowledge on the subject.* absence, dearth, deficiency, insufficiency, need, paucity, scarcity, shortage, want. OPPOSITE abundance. — *verb She lacks some of the ingredients.* be short of, be without, miss, need. OPPOSITE have.

lackadaisical *adjective She has a lackadaisical approach to her studies.* apathetic, blasé, careless, casual, half-hearted, indifferent, listless, lukewarm, unconcerned, unenthusiastic. OPPOSITE enthusiastic.

lacking *adjective lacking in intelligence.* deficient, inadequate, short, wanting.

laconic *adjective The writer has a laconic style.* brief, concise, economical, succinct, terse. OPPOSITE verbose.

lacquer *noun* gloss, varnish.

lacy *adjective lacy curtains.* delicate, fine, flimsy, net.

lad *noun* **1** *a lad of school age.* boy, child, kid (*informal*), youngster, youth. **2** (*informal*) *They like the lad she's marrying.* bloke (*informal*), boy, chap (*informal*), fellow (*informal*), guy (*informal*), young man.

ladder *noun* stepladder, steps.

laden *adjective We were laden with parcels.* burdened, encumbered, loaded, weighed down.

lady *noun* see WOMAN.

ladylike *adjective Eating in the street is not very ladylike.* dignified, genteel, polite, posh (*informal*), proper, refined, respectable.

lag[1] *verb Some of the younger children lagged behind.* dawdle, drag the chain (*Australian*), drop back, drop behind, fall behind, go slow, straggle, trail. OPPOSITE keep up.

lag[2] *verb They lag the pipes to prevent heat loss.* encase, insulate, wrap.

lagoon *noun They swam in the lagoon.* billabong, lake, pond, pool.

laid-back *adjective* (*informal*) *He is very laid-back about his studies.* calm, casual, easygoing, nonchalant, relaxed, unfazed (*informal*). OPPOSITE uptight (*informal*).

lair[1] *noun an animal's lair.* burrow, den, hideout (*informal*), hidey-hole (*informal*), hiding place, hole, home, shelter.

lair[2] *noun* see LARRIKIN, SHOW-OFF.

lairy *adjective* (*Australian informal*) *a lairy shirt.* bright, flash (*informal*), flashy, garish, gaudy, loud, showy. OPPOSITE subdued.

lake *noun* lagoon, loch (*Scottish*), mere (*poetical*), pond, reservoir, sea, tarn.

lame *adjective* **1** *He has been lame since the accident.* crippled, disabled, maimed, paralysed, paraplegic. OPPOSITE able-bodied. **2** *Don't give me that lame excuse.* feeble, flimsy, unconvincing, unsatisfactory, weak. OPPOSITE persuasive.

lament *noun The choir sang a lament at the funeral.* dirge, elegy, keen, lamentation, requiem. — *verb We lament the death of our friend.* bewail, grieve over, mourn, regret, wail over, weep over.

lamentable *adjective a lamentable state of affairs.* deplorable, regrettable, sad, sorry, terrible, unfortunate.

lamp *noun* see LIGHT[1].

lampoon *verb The councillor was lampooned by the local newspaper.* caricature, make fun of, ridicule, satirise, send up (*informal*), take off.

lance *noun They spear fish with lances.* harpoon, javelin, pike, shaft, spear. — *verb The doctor will have to lance that boil.* cut open, incise, jab, pierce, prick.

land *noun* **1** *good farming land.* earth, ground, soil. **2** *forest land.* area, country, region, terrain, tract. **3** *people from different lands.* country, empire, nation, state, territory. **4** *They own land in the south-east.* property, real estate. — *verb* **1** *The ship landed at Perth.* arrive, berth, dock, moor, put into port. **2** *The aircraft landed on time.* arrive, touch down. **3** *We landed in Hobart.* alight, arrive, disembark, go ashore. **4** *He was lucky to land the job.* clinch, get, obtain, secure, win. **5** *He landed in jail.* end up, fetch up (*informal*), find yourself, finish up, wind up. **6** *He got landed with the job of sorting out the mess.* give, present.

landlady, landlord *noun The tenant paid his rent to his landlady.* owner, proprietor.

landmark *noun* **1** *From the lookout we could see all the important landmarks.* feature. **2** *a landmark in world history.* milestone, turning point, watershed.

landowner *noun* grazier (*Australian*), laird (*Scottish*), landholder, pastoralist (*Australian*), squire.

landscape *noun The artist painted landscapes.* panorama, scene, scenery, view, vista. — *verb The garden has been landscaped professionally.* design, lay out, plan.

landslide *noun The hillside has been eroded by landslides.* avalanche, landslip.

lane *noun Their house is on a quiet lane.* alley, path, road, track.

language *noun* **1** *The people spoke an unfamiliar language.* dialect, speech, tongue. **2** *scientific language.* idiom, jargon, lingo (*informal*), slang, terminology, vocabulary, words.

languid *adjective He feels languid in the hot weather.* apathetic, drained, inert, lazy, lethargic, listless, sluggish, torpid, weak, weary. OPPOSITE energetic.

languish *verb* **1** *The plants languished without water.* droop, wilt, wither. **2** *The business languished.* decline, deteriorate, fail, go downhill, stagnate. OPPOSITE thrive.

lank *adjective lank hair.* lifeless, limp, long, straight, thin.

lanky *adjective a lanky young man.* gangling, gawky, lank, lean, skinny, thin.

lantern *noun a gas lantern.* lamp, light.

lap[1] *noun* **1** *They ran a lap of the oval.* circuit, orbit, tour. **2** *This is the last lap of our journey.* part, section, stage.

lap[2] *verb* **1** *The cat lapped up all the milk.* drink, lick, sip. **2** *The waves lapped against the shore.* splash, wash.

lapse *noun* **1** *He can be forgiven for this lapse.* error, fault, mistake, omission, oversight, slip, slip-up. **2** *a lapse in moral standards.* backsliding, decline, deterioration, drop, regression, slip. **3** *Anna returned to her studies after a lapse of five years.* break, gap, hiatus, interlude, interruption, interval, passage. — *verb* **1** *He lapsed into baby talk.* degenerate, fall, regress, relapse, slip. **2** *She let her membership lapse.* expire, run out, stop, terminate. OPPOSITE continue.

larceny *noun* *His crime was larceny.* robbery, stealing, theft.

larder *noun* *Food is kept in the larder.* food cupboard, pantry.

large *adjective* **1** *a large meal. a large amount.* ample, big, colossal, considerable, copious, enormous, extensive, gargantuan, generous, giant, gigantic, ginormous (*slang*), great, handsome, huge, humungous (*slang*), immeasurable, immense, infinite, jumbo-sized, king-sized, mammoth, massive, monstrous, outsize, oversized, prodigious, stupendous, substantial, tremendous, unlimited, vast, whopping (*slang*). OPPOSITE small. **2** *a large person.* big, broad, bulky, fat, hefty, huge, hulking (*informal*), obese, overweight, portly, stout. OPPOSITE small. **3** *a large house.* big, capacious, commodious, grand, imposing, roomy, sizeable, spacious. OPPOSITE compact, small. □ **at large 1** *At night the dogs are at large.* free, loose, unconfined, unrestrained. **2** *the population at large.* as a whole, in general.

largely *adverb* *He did it largely for his own family.* chiefly, in the main, mainly, mostly, primarily, principally.

large-scale *adjective* *a large-scale review.* big, comprehensive, extensive, major, wholesale, wide-ranging. OPPOSITE small-scale.

largesse *noun* *The millionaire was known for his largesse.* benevolence, bounty, generosity, liberality, munificence, philanthropy.

lark *noun* *They only did it for a bit of a lark.* game, joke, prank, tease, trick.

larrikin *noun* (*Australian*) *The damage was done by a bunch of larrikins.* hooligan, hoon (*Australian informal*), lair (*Australian informal*), rowdy, ruffian, tearaway.

larva *noun* caterpillar, grub, maggot.

lash *verb* **1** *He lashed the boy for his rudeness.* beat, belt, cane, flog, hit, lay into (*informal*), strike, thrash, whip. **2** *The blind was lashed down.* fasten, secure, tie. — *noun* *He received forty lashes as punishment.* blow, cut, stroke.

lass *noun* *a lover and his lass.* damsel (*old use*), girl, lassie (*informal*), maid (*old use*), maiden (*old use*), young woman.

lassitude *noun* *He was overcome with lasssitude.* languor, lethargy, listlessness, tiredness, weariness. OPPOSITE vitality.

lasso *noun* lariat, rope.

last¹ *adjective* **1** *the last item on the programme.* closing, concluding, final, ultimate. OPPOSITE first. **2** *replying to your last letter.* latest, most recent. **3** *our last hope.* only remaining. □ **at last** eventually, finally, in the end, ultimately.

last² *verb* **1** *How long can this pain last?* carry on, continue, endure, go on, keep on, persist. **2** *There is enough water to last us for up to a week.* do, suffice.

lasting *adjective* *a lasting relationship.* abiding, enduring, everlasting, long-lasting, long-lived, long-term, permanent. OPPOSITE short-lived, temporary.

lastly *adverb* finally, in conclusion.

latch *noun* *a latch on a gate.* bar, bolt, catch, lock, snib. — *verb* *Each night he latches the doors.* bar, bolt, fasten, lock, secure, snib. □ **latch on to** (*informal*) *Has he latched on to the idea yet?* catch on to, come to grips with, cotton on to (*informal*), get (*informal*), grasp, understand.

late *adjective* **1** *late birthday wishes.* belated, delayed, held up, overdue, tardy. OPPOSITE early. **2** *her late husband.* dead, deceased, departed. OPPOSITE living.

lately *adverb* *Michael has lost weight lately.* latterly, of late, recently.

latent *adjective* *latent talent.* concealed, dormant, hidden, invisible, potential, undeveloped. OPPOSITE manifest.

later *adverb* *Their friends arrived later.* after, afterwards, presently, subsequently. OPPOSITE earlier.

latest *adjective* *Have you heard the latest news?* current, freshest, most recent, newest, up-to-date, up-to-the-minute.

lather *noun* *shampoo lather.* bubbles, foam, froth, suds.

latitude *noun* *The children are given latitude in the use of their pocket money.* freedom, independence, leeway, liberty, scope.

lattice *noun* *The plant grows on a lattice.* framework, trellis.

laudable *adjective* *a very laudable action.* admirable, commendable, creditable, meritorious, praiseworthy. OPPOSITE despicable.

laugh *verb* *The clown made them laugh.* be in stitches (*informal*), cackle, chortle, chuckle, crack up (*informal*), giggle, guffaw, snicker, snigger, split your sides, titter. — *noun* **1** *The joke raised a few laughs.* cackle, chortle, chuckle, giggle, guffaw, snicker, snigger, titter. **2** (*informal*) *What a laugh that was!* hoot (*informal*), joke, scream (*informal*). □ **laugh at** *They were laughing at him.* deride, jeer at, joke about, make fun of, mock, poke borak at (*Australian informal*), poke fun at, ridicule, satirise, sling off at (*Australian informal*), take the mickey out of (*informal*), taunt, tease. **laugh off** *He laughed off the criticism.* dismiss, disregard, ignore, make light of, shrug off.

laughable *adjective* *The amount being offered is laughable.* absurd, derisory, farcical, ludicrous, nonsensical, outrageous, preposterous, ridiculous.

laughter *noun* *We were cheered by the sound of laughter.* cackling, chuckling, giggling, glee, hilarity, hysterics, laughing, merriment, mirth, sniggering.

launch¹ *verb* **1** *They've launched the spacecraft.* blast off, fire, project, propel, send forth, send off. **2** *The ship was launched.* float, set afloat. OPPOSITE ground. **3** *They launched their campaign.* begin, embark upon, initiate, introduce, open, set going, start. OPPOSITE stop. — *noun* *The launch of the spacecraft was set for noon.* blast-off, lift-off, take-off.

launch² *noun* motor boat; see also BOAT.

launder *verb* *He pays to have his clothes laundered.* clean, wash.

lavatory *noun* see TOILET.

lavish *adjective* **1** *He was always lavish with his money.* extravagant, generous, liberal, unstinting. OPPOSITE stingy. **2** *There were lavish supplies of food in the cupboards.* abundant, bountiful, copious, plentiful, profuse. — *verb* *He lavished affection on his family.* bestow, heap, pour, shower.

law *noun* **1** *the laws of a country.* act, by-law, commandment, decree, edict, regulation, rule, statute. **2** *the laws of physics.* axiom, formula, principle, rule, theorem.

law-abiding *adjective* *a decent law-abiding citizen.* honest, obedient, orderly, upstanding. OPPOSITE lawless.

lawbreaker *noun* criminal, delinquent, felon, miscreant, offender, transgressor, wrongdoer.

lawful *adjective* *It is not lawful to smoke in the airport.* allowable, authorised, constitutional, legal, legitimate, permissible, permitted, sanctioned, valid. OPPOSITE illegal, unlawful.

lawless *adjective* **1** *a lawless country.* anarchic, chaotic, ungoverned. **2** *lawless brigands.* disorderly, insubordinate, rebellious, riotous, rowdy, uncontrolled, unruly, wild. OPPOSITE law-abiding.

lawn *noun* grass, sward, turf.

lawsuit *noun* action, case, legal proceedings, litigation, suit, trial.

lawyer *noun* *You will need to consult a lawyer.* advocate, attorney, barrister, counsel, legal adviser, Queen's Counsel (QC), solicitor.

lax *adjective* *They had been far too lax about discipline.* careless, casual, easygoing, indulgent, lenient, permissive, relaxed, remiss, slack. OPPOSITE strict.

lay¹ *verb* **1** *Lay your bags on the bed.* deposit, leave, place, put, rest, set down. **2** *Lay the table.* arrange, set, spread. **3** *He laid the blame on the new person.* ascribe, assign, attribute, impute, place. **4** *We laid plans for our next fundraiser.* concoct, design, devise, formulate, hatch, make. □ **lay down 1** *He laid down his life for his country.* give up, relinquish, sacrifice, surrender, yield. **2** *She laid down the rules.* dictate, establish, prescribe, set, stipulate. **lay off** *Workers were laid off when business went quiet.* stand down, suspend; see also DISMISS. **lay on** *Meals were laid on.* provide, supply. **lay out** *The editor laid out the page.* arrange, design, plan, set out.

lay² *adjective* **1** *a lay preacher.* non-clerical, non-ordained. OPPOSITE ordained. **2** *Some doctors use different language when talking to lay people.* non-professional, non-specialist. OPPOSITE professional.

layabout *noun* *He was not a layabout. He was just resting between jobs.* bludger (*Australian informal*), bum (*slang*), good-for-nothing, idler, lazybones (*informal*), loafer, malingerer, shirker, skiver (*informal*), slacker.

layer *noun* *Peel off the top layer.* coating, film, level, ply, sheet, stratum, thickness, tier.

layout *noun* *The office has an efficient layout.* arrangement, composition, design, organisation, plan, structure.

layperson *noun* *a layperson's guide to astronomy.* amateur, layman, non-professional, non-specialist.

laze *verb* *They lazed in the sun for the afternoon.* loaf, lounge, put your feet up, relax, rest, take it easy.

lazy *adjective* *The less he has to do, the more lazy he becomes.* idle, inactive, indolent, inert, languid, lethargic, listless, shiftless, slack, slothful, sluggish, torpid. OPPOSITE energetic, industrious.

lazybones *noun* couch potato (*informal*), good-for-nothing, idler, layabout, loafer, slacker, sluggard.

lead *verb* **1** *The usher leads people to their seats.* conduct, escort, guide, pilot, steer, usher. **2** *What led you to take this on?* cause, induce, influence, persuade, prompt. **3** *He led the attack.* be in charge of, command, control, direct, head, spearhead, supervise. — *noun* **1** *Follow his lead.* direction, example, guidance, leadership. **2** *He gave us a lead.* clue, hint, indication, tip-off. **3** *a dog's lead.* leash.

leader *noun* *They look up to their leader.* boss, captain, chief, chieftain, commander, conductor, director, governor, head, manager, overseer, premier, president, prime minister, principal, ringleader, ruler, supervisor. OPPOSITE follower.

leaf *noun* **1** *a leaf of a plant.* blade, frond, needle; [*leaves*] foliage, greenery. **2** *a leaf of a book.* folio, page, sheet.

leaflet *noun* *an information leaflet.* booklet, brochure, flyer, handout, pamphlet.

league *noun* *the league of old scholars.* alliance, association, group, organisation, society, union.

leak *noun* **1** *a leak in a tyre.* crack, fissure, gash, hole, puncture, split. **2** *Towels were used to mop up the leak.* discharge, leakage, seepage. **3** *a government leak.* disclosure, revelation. — *verb* **1** *Water leaked from the tap.* discharge, drip, escape, ooze, seep, trickle. **2** *The employee leaked the news to a journalist.* disclose, divulge, let out, reveal.

lean¹ *adjective* *a lean animal or person.* angular, bony, emaciated, gaunt, lanky, scraggy, scrawny, skinny, slender, slim, thin, weedy, wiry. OPPOSITE fat, hefty.

lean² *verb* **1** *The ship leaned to one side.* incline, list, slant, slope, tilt, tip. **2** *He leans on his stick.* prop yourself, rest, support yourself. **3** *He leans heavily on his wife for her support.* depend, rely.

leaning *noun* *She had a leaning towards the arts.* bent, inclination, partiality, penchant, predilection, preference, proclivity, tendency.

leap *verb* *He leapt into the air.* bounce, bound, jump, pounce, spring, vault. — *noun* *The cat took a huge leap.* bounce, bound, jump, pounce, spring, vault.

learn *verb* **1** *She learned the road rules.* assimilate, grasp, master, memorise, pick up, study. **2** *He learned that his friend had died.* ascertain, become aware, discover, find out, gather, hear.

learned *adjective* *learned people.* clever, educated, erudite, informed, intellectual, knowledgeable, scholarly, well-informed, well-read. OPPOSITE uneducated.

learner *noun* apprentice, beginner, cadet, novice, pupil, rookie (*informal*), student, trainee.

learning *noun* *a man of great learning.* education, erudition, knowledge, scholarship.

lease *verb* *lease a property. lease a car.* hire, let, rent.

leash *noun* *a dog's leash.* lead.

least *adjective* *the least amount.* barest, faintest, littlest, lowest, minimum, scantiest, slightest, smallest, tiniest. OPPOSITE greatest.

leather *noun* *shoes made of leather.* hide, skin, suede.

leave *verb* **1** *He left without saying goodbye.* abscond, beat it (*slang*), buzz off (*slang*), clear off (*informal*), decamp, depart, disappear, do a bunk (*slang*), escape, exit, flee, get away, go away, head off, make off, make yourself scarce, nick off (*Australian slang*), push off (*informal*), quit, rack off (*Australian slang*), retire, retreat, run away, run off, scarper (*informal*), set off, shoot through (*Australian informal*), shove off (*informal*), skedaddle (*informal*), slope off (*informal*), take off, take your leave, vanish, withdraw. OPPOSITE arrive, enter. **2** *He left his job.* chuck in (*informal*), give up, quit, resign, retire from, walk out of. OPPOSITE retain. **3** *She left the house to a nephew.* bequeath, give, hand down, will. **4** *He left his wife and children.* abandon, desert, forsake, leave in the lurch, part from, separate from. — *noun* **1** *He begged leave to speak.* consent, permission.

2 *He has not returned from his leave.* break, exeat, furlough, holiday, sabbatical, vacation. □ **leave off** *Leave off nagging.* cease, desist, lay off (*informal*), quit, refrain from, stop. OPPOSITE continue. **leave out** *If you leave out a word it doesn't make sense.* drop, exclude, miss out, omit, skip. OPPOSITE include.

lecherous *adjective a lecherous man.* lascivious, lewd, lustful, randy, salacious.

lecture *noun* **1** *a physics lecture.* address, discourse, lesson, speech, talk. **2** *He knew he was in for a lecture over the incident.* dressing down (*informal*), earbashing (*Australian informal*), reprimand, reproof, scolding, sermon, serve (*Australian informal*), talking-to (*informal*), telling-off (*informal*).

ledge *noun Heidi placed the vase on the ledge.* mantelpiece, projection, shelf, sill.

leer *verb She felt uncomfortable when he leered at her.* goggle, ogle, smirk, stare.

lees *plural noun wine lees.* deposit, dregs, precipitate, residue, sediment.

leeway *noun These instructions give us plenty of leeway.* freedom, latitude, margin, play, room, scope.

left *adjective the ship's left side.* larboard (*old use*), port. OPPOSITE right, starboard.

leftovers *plural noun* dregs, excess, remainder(s), residue, scraps, surplus.

leg *noun* **1** *quick on his legs.* limb, pin (*informal*), shank. **2** *The first leg of the trip was the most strenuous.* lap, part, section, stage.

legacy *noun Her aunt left her a legacy of $5000 in her will.* bequest, inheritance.

legal *adjective* **1** *Is it legal to drive without wearing a seat belt?* allowed, authorised, lawful, permissible, permitted. OPPOSITE illegal. **2** *the legal heir.* legitimate, proper, rightful.

legalise *verb The use of the drug has not been legalised.* allow, authorise, decriminalise, permit. OPPOSITE prohibit.

legend *noun* **1** *an old Russian legend.* folk tale, myth, saga, story, tale. **2** *the legend on a map.* code, key.

legendary *adjective* **1** *a legendary figure.* fabled, fictional, fictitious, mythical, traditional. OPPOSITE historical. **2** (*informal*) *His soufflés were legendary.* famous, renowned, well-known.

legible *adjective His writing is legible.* clear, neat, plain, readable, tidy. OPPOSITE illegible.

legislation *noun the Native Title legislation.* act, bill, law, statute.

legislative *adjective a legislative assembly.* law-making, parliamentary.

legitimate *adjective* **1** *legitimate business activities.* lawful, legal, permissible. OPPOSITE illegal. **2** *a legitimate excuse.* acceptable, fair, reasonable, valid. OPPOSITE unacceptable.

leisure *noun She has achieved a good balance between work and leisure.* free time, recreation, relaxation, spare time, time off. OPPOSITE work.

leisurely *adjective He walked at a leisurely pace.* calm, easy, gentle, relaxed, restful, slow, unhurried. OPPOSITE brisk.

lend *verb The bank will lend you the money.* advance, loan. OPPOSITE borrow.

length *noun* **1** *The bridge is a kilometre in length.* distance, extent, measurement, size, span. CONTRASTS WITH breadth, depth. **2** *the length of his life.* duration, period, span, term, time. □ **at length 1** *At length the jury came to a decision.* at last, eventually, finally, in the end. **2** *He spoke at length about his problems.* fully, in depth, in detail.

lengthen *verb* **1** *The teacher lengthened the music lesson.* draw out, prolong, protract, spin out, stretch out. **2** *Lengthen the sides.* elongate, extend, increase. OPPOSITE shorten.

lengthways *adverb* lengthwise, longitudinally, longways, longwise. OPPOSITE widthways.

lengthy *adjective a lengthy explanation.* drawn-out, extended, interminable, long, long-winded, prolonged, protracted, verbose, wordy. OPPOSITE brief.

lenient *adjective The judge was lenient.* compassionate, easygoing, forbearing, indulgent, merciful, mild, soft, sparing. OPPOSITE harsh, severe.

leprechaun *noun* elf, fairy, sprite.

lesbian *adjective* gay, homosexual.

less *adjective of less importance.* slighter, smaller. OPPOSITE more. — *preposition She is paid $500, less tax.* deducting, minus, subtracting, taking away.

lessen *verb* **1** *The cushions lessen the impact.* cut down, deaden, decrease, diminish, minimise, reduce. OPPOSITE intensify. **2** *The wind has lessened.* abate, die down, ease, let up, moderate, subside, weaken. OPPOSITE strengthen.

lesser *adjective a lesser problem.* minor, secondary, slighter, smaller, subsidiary. OPPOSITE greater.

lesson *noun* **1** *The school day is divided into eight lessons.* class, period, session. **2** *There was a lesson to be learnt from the accident.* message, moral, principle, rule, warning. **3** *the New Testament lesson.* passage, reading.

let *verb* **1** *They let her see the baby.* agree to, allow, consent to, enable, permit. OPPOSITE forbid. **2** *a house to let.* lease, rent. □ **let down 1** *He let down the tyres.* deflate. OPPOSITE inflate, pump up. **2** *I don't want to let him down.* disappoint, fail, leave high and dry, leave in the lurch. **3** *She let down her dress.* lengthen. OPPOSITE shorten, take up. **let go** *She let all the animals go.* free, let loose, liberate, release, set free. **let off 1** *They let off a bomb.* detonate, discharge, explode, set off. **2** *They knew he was guilty, but they let him off.* excuse, exempt, pardon, release, reprieve, spare. **let on** (*informal*) *She never let on what had happened.* admit, confess, disclose, divulge, give away, let slip, reveal. **let out 1** *She opened the cage and let the bird out.* free, let go, liberate, release, set free. **2** *The dress needs letting out.* enlarge, loosen. **let up** (*informal*) *The rain let up after lunch.* abate, ease, lessen, subside.

let-down *noun* see DISAPPOINTMENT.

lethal *adjective a lethal injection.* deadly, fatal, mortal, poisonous, toxic. OPPOSITE harmless.

lethargy *noun The heat can cause lethargy.* indolence, inertia, languor, lassitude, listlessness, sluggishness, torpor, weariness. OPPOSITE vitality.

letter *noun* **1** *How many letters fit on one line?* character, symbol. **2** *What did the letter say?* communication, dispatch, epistle, message, missive, note; [*letters*] correspondence, mail, post.

letterbox *noun* mailbox, pillar box (*old use*), postbox.

levee *noun The levees saved the town from being flooded.* dyke, embankment, stopbank (*Australian*).

level *noun* **1** *We climbed to a higher level.* altitude, elevation, height. **2** *the level of alcohol in the blood.* amount, degree, measure, value. **3** *He reached a high level in his job.* degree, grade, position, rank, rung, stage, standard. **4** *He works on the third level of the building.* floor, storey, tier. — *adjective* **1** *a level surface.* even, flat, horizontal, plane, smooth. OPPOSITE bumpy, undulating. **2** *They are level in first place.* equal, even, neck and neck, tied. **3** *The volume remained level.* constant, steady, unchanging, uniform. OPPOSITE variable. — *verb* **1** *The last shot levelled the scores.* even out, tie. **2** *The workers levelled the building.* demolish, flatten, knock down, raze, tear down, topple. **3** *He levelled the gun at him.* aim, direct, point, train.

lever *noun It opens with a lever.* control, handle. — *verb He levered the lid off the tea chest.* prise, wrench.

levy *verb The library levied a small fine.* charge, collect, exact, impose. — *noun The government funded the scheme by imposing a levy.* charge, duty, excise, impost, tariff, tax, toll.

lewd *adjective His lewd jokes were inappropriate at dinner.* bawdy, blue, crude, dirty, indecent, obscene, ribald, salacious, vulgar. OPPOSITE decent.

liability *noun* **1** *He must accept liability for their mistakes.* accountability, answerability, responsibility. **2** *the company's liabilities.* debt, obligation, responsibility. OPPOSITE asset. **3** (*informal*) *He's a liability to the team.* burden, disadvantage, drawback, encumbrance, handicap, millstone. OPPOSITE asset.

liable *adjective* **1** *She was liable for the debts.* accountable, answerable, responsible. **2** *He is liable to migraines.* prone, subject, susceptible. **3** *She is liable to cry.* apt, inclined, likely, prone.

liaison *noun* **1** *There is close liaison between the two departments.* communication, contact, cooperation. **2** *She acts as a liaison between the two groups.* contact, coordinator, go-between, link, mediator.

liar *noun You can't trust him: he's a liar.* fibber, storyteller (*informal*).

libel *noun He sued the newspaper for libel.* calumny, defamation, denigration, false statement, slander, slur, smear, vilification. — *verb* defame, denigrate, discredit, malign, slander, smear, vilify.

liberal *adjective* **1** *liberal quantities of food.* abundant, ample, copious, extravagant, generous, lavish, plentiful. OPPOSITE skimpy. **2** *a liberal interpretation of the rules.* broad, flexible, lax, loose. OPPOSITE strict. **3** *liberal in his attitude.* broad-minded, enlightened, open-minded, permissive, tolerant, unbiased, unprejudiced. OPPOSITE narrow-minded.

liberate *verb The prisoners were liberated by the new president.* deliver, emancipate, free, let go, release, set free. OPPOSITE enslave, imprison.

liberation *noun liberation from slavery.* deliverance, emancipation, freedom, liberty, release. OPPOSITE imprisonment.

liberty *noun They fought to preserve their country's liberty.* autonomy, freedom, independence, self-determination, self-rule.

licence *noun You need a licence to sell those goods.* authorisation, franchise, permit, warrant.

license *verb The shop is licensed to sell liquor.* allow, authorise, permit. OPPOSITE forbid.

lick *verb The cat licked up her milk.* lap, tongue.

licking *noun* (*informal*) **1** *Their team came in for a licking.* beating, clobbering (*slang*), defeat, thrashing, trouncing. **2** *He got a licking for being cheeky.* beating, belting, flogging, hiding (*informal*), spanking, thrashing.

lid *noun All the jars had lids.* cap, cover, top.

lie[1] *noun She was punished for telling lies.* falsehood, fib, porky (*slang*), story (*informal*), untruth, whopper (*slang*). OPPOSITE fact, truth. — *verb You never know when she's lying.* bluff, deceive, dissemble, fib, perjure yourself, prevaricate.

lie[2] *verb* **1** *She is lying on the bed.* recline, rest, sprawl. **2** *The machinery lay idle.* be, remain, stay. **3** *The land lies to the east.* be, be found, be located, be situated. □ **lie low** *The thieves lay low till the police had left the scene.* go into hiding, go to ground, hide, keep a low profile (*informal*), take cover.

lieu *noun* **in lieu of** *He received gifts in lieu of money.* instead of, in the place of.

lieutenant *noun* assistant, deputy.

life *noun* **1** *the right to life.* being, existence, survival. OPPOSITE death. **2** *Is there life on Mars?* flora and fauna, living things. **3** *The child is full of life.* animation, energy, exuberance, go, liveliness, vigour, vitality, vivacity. **4** *The life of Luther makes interesting reading.* autobiography, biography.

lifeless *adjective* **1** *a lifeless body.* dead, deceased, inanimate, inert, non-living; see also UNCONSCIOUS. OPPOSITE living. **2** *a lifeless performance.* boring, dull, lacklustre, soulless, unexciting. OPPOSITE lively.

lifelike *adjective The wax models are lifelike.* accurate, authentic, realistic, true to life.

lifelong *adjective a lifelong friendship.* abiding, enduring, lasting, permanent. OPPOSITE short-lived.

lifetime *noun* existence, life, life span.

lift *verb* **1** *He can lift heavy objects.* elevate, hoist, jack up, pick up, raise. OPPOSITE lower. **2** *The music lifted her spirits.* boost, buoy up, cheer up, improve, raise. OPPOSITE depress. **3** (*informal*) *He was caught lifting jewellery.* see STEAL. **4** *The fog lifted.* disperse, dissipate, rise. OPPOSITE descend. **5** *The ban has been lifted.* cancel, remove, revoke, withdraw. OPPOSITE enforce. — *noun* **1** *He gave her a lift to the station.* ride. **2** *Tall buildings need lifts.* elevator. **3** *The compliment gave her a lift.* boost, encouragement, reassurance, shot in the arm.

lift-off *noun* blast-off, launch, take-off.

light[1] *noun* **1** *the light from the fire. the light of the sun.* blaze, brightness, brilliance, flash, glare, glow, illumination, incandescence, radiance, reflection. OPPOSITE darkness. **2** *a light to read by.* beacon, candle, floodlight, headlight, lamp, lantern, spotlight, torch. — *adjective* **1** *The room was very light.* bright, illuminated, well-lit. OPPOSITE dark. **2** *light blue.* delicate, pale, pastel, soft. OPPOSITE dark. — *verb Light the fire.* ignite, kindle, set alight, start. OPPOSITE extinguish. □ **bring to light** *New evidence was brought to light.* disclose, expose, reveal, uncover. **come to light** *It came to light that he had been at the scene of the crime.* appear, become apparent, come out, emerge, transpire. **light up** *Fireworks lit up the sky.* brighten, illuminate, lighten. OPPOSITE darken.

light[2] *adjective* **1** *a light parcel.* lightweight, portable. OPPOSITE heavy. **2** *a light blanket.* flimsy, lightweight, thin. OPPOSITE heavy. **3** *light rainfall.* low, moderate, slight. OPPOSITE heavy. **4** *light duties.* easy, effortless, simple, undemanding. OPPO-

SITE arduous. **5** *light mist.* faint, fine, thin. OPPOSITE dense. **6** *She is light on her feet.* agile, graceful, lithe, nimble, supple. OPPOSITE clumsy. **7** *light music.* entertaining, frivolous, superficial. OPPOSITE serious. □ **light on 1** *We're light on bread.* low on, short on. **2** (*Australian informal*) *The drinks were a bit light on.* in short supply, scarce. OPPOSITE plentiful.

lighten[1] *verb The new paint lightened the room.* brighten, illuminate, light up. OPPOSITE darken.

lighten[2] *verb* **1** *They tossed the cargo overboard to lighten the load.* cut down, diminish, ease, reduce. OPPOSITE increase. **2** *The tablets lightened the pain.* alleviate, ease, lessen, mitigate, reduce, relieve. OPPOSITE increase. **3** *Her spirits were lightened by the news.* lift, raise, uplift. OPPOSITE depress.

light-headed *adjective The medication made him feel light-headed.* dizzy, faint, giddy, woozy (*informal*).

light-hearted *adjective* blithe, bright, carefree, cheerful, gay, happy, jolly, merry. OPPOSITE gloomy, heavy-hearted.

like[1] *verb* **1** *He likes her.* admire, appreciate, approve of, be fond of, be keen on, fancy; see also LOVE. **2** *She doesn't like housework.* be keen on, enjoy, fancy, relish. OPPOSITE dislike, hate. **3** *Would you like to try abseiling?* care, desire, have a mind, want, wish.

like[2] *adjective The twins are of like temperament.* corresponding, identical, matching, similar, the same. OPPOSITE unlike.

likeable *adjective a likeable person.* agreeable, amiable, attractive, charming, congenial, friendly, genial, pleasant, pleasing, winsome. OPPOSITE disagreeable.

likelihood *noun There is a strong likelihood of his winning.* chance, possibility, probability, prospect.

likely *adjective* **1** *I knew that was likely to happen.* bound, destined, expected, liable. **2** *That doesn't sound very likely.* believable, credible, plausible, probable. OPPOSITE dubious. **3** *She was the most likely person for the job.* appropriate, fitting, promising, qualified, suitable.

liken *verb He likened eating to fuelling a car.* compare, draw an analogy between, equate.

likeness *noun* **1** *There is a strong family likeness.* resemblance, sameness, similarity. OPPOSITE difference. **2** *She drew a good likeness of him.* copy, picture, portrait, replica, representation.

liking *noun She has developed a liking for poetry.* affinity, appetite, appreciation, fondness, partiality, penchant, preference, taste. OPPOSITE aversion, dislike.

limb *noun* **1** *an animal with long limbs.* appendage, arm, leg, wing. **2** *the limb of a tree.* bough, branch. □ **out on a limb** alone, isolated, stranded.

limber *verb* **limber up** *You need to limber up before the big race.* exercise, loosen up, prepare, warm up.

limbo *noun* in limbo *The project has been left in limbo.* half-finished, in abeyance, suspended, unfinished, up in the air.

limelight *noun George does not like being in the limelight.* prominence, public eye, publicity, spotlight. OPPOSITE background.

limit *noun* **1** *the city limits.* border, boundary, bounds, confines, edge, frontier, perimeter. **2** *Mum had reached the limit of her patience.* breaking-point, end, extent. **3** *a limit on the number of books you can borrow.* ceiling, cut-off, limita-

tion, maximum, quota, restriction. — *verb We need to limit our spending.* check, confine, contain, control, curb, restrain, restrict.

limitation *noun He is aware of his own limitations.* deficiency, shortcoming, weakness.

limited *adjective limited resources.* minimal, restricted, scanty, small. OPPOSITE unlimited.

limp[1] *verb He limped after injuring his knee.* falter, hobble, shuffle.

limp[2] *adjective The flowers are looking limp.* droopy, flaccid, floppy, lifeless, wilted.

line *noun* **1** *Draw a line through the word.* dash, mark, score, slash, stroke. **2** *Paint a line of red.* band, streak, strip, stripe. **3** *lines on his face.* crease, crow's-foot, furrow, wrinkle. **4** *a dividing line.* border, borderline, boundary, limit. **5** *a line of people.* chain, column, cordon, crocodile, file, procession, queue, row, series. **6** *She dropped me a line at Christmas.* card, letter, note, postcard. **7** *a railway line.* branch, route, track. **8** *a shipping line.* company, fleet. **9** *a line of kings.* dynasty, family, lineage. **10** *a line of inquiry.* course, direction, path, tack, tendency, track, trend, way. **11** *The goat was tied to the end of a line.* cable, cord, hawser, lead, rope, string, wire. — *verb The street is lined with trees.* border, edge, fringe. □ **in line with** *They refunded the money in line with company policy.* conforming with, in accordance with, in agreement with, in keeping with, in step with. **line up 1** *The passengers lined up.* form a line, queue up. **2** *She lined the chairs up.* align, straighten. **3** *He lined up a surprise for her birthday.* arrange, organise, prepare, set up.

lineage *noun He has traced his lineage.* ancestry, descent, extraction, family, genealogy, line, origins, pedigree.

linen *noun table linen.* manchester, napery.

linger *verb* **1** *She knew she must not linger as she was due home shortly.* dally, dawdle, delay, dilly-dally, hang about, loiter, remain, stay, take your time, tarry. **2** *He lingered on until he was 99.* hang on, last, survive. **3** *The smell lingered for days.* continue, hang around, persist, remain, stay.

lingerie *noun* corsetry, underclothes, undergarments, underwear, undies (*informal*).

linguist *noun* **1** *a gifted linguist, speaking several languages.* polyglot. **2** *a research linguist, studying language and its structure.* etymologist, grammarian, lexicographer, philologist, phonetician, semanticist.

liniment *noun The liniment soothed his aching joints.* balm, embrocation, ointment, salve.

lining *noun coat lining.* backing, facing, interfacing.

link *noun* **1** *a link in a chain.* loop, ring. **2** *She was his only link with the outside world.* bond, connection, tie. **3** *a link between diet and the disease.* association, connection, relationship, tie-up. — *verb* **1** *The two rooms are linked by telephone.* connect, join, unite. OPPOSITE separate. **2** *The disease is linked with poor diet.* associate, connect, identify, relate, tie up.

lion *noun* cub (*young*), king of beasts, lioness (*female*).

lip *noun the lip of a jug.* brim, edge, rim.

liquid *noun Pour off the liquid.* fluid, juice, liquor, solution. OPPOSITE solid. — *adjective a liquid substance.* flowing, fluid, molten, runny, watery. OPPOSITE solid.

liquidate *verb* **1** *I can now liquidate my debts.* clear, discharge, pay, settle. **2** *The business has been liquidated.* close down, dissolve, wind up. **3** *They liquidate those who don't toe the line.* do away with, eliminate, exterminate, get rid of, remove; see also KILL.

liquidise *verb The food was liquidised for the invalid.* crush, liquefy, pulp, purée.

liquor *noun under the influence of liquor.* alcohol, drink, grog (*Australian*), spirits.

list[1] *noun a list of names.* catalogue, directory, index, inventory, register, roll, schedule, series, table. — *verb He listed the students' names in his book.* catalogue, enter, enumerate, index, itemise, note, record, register, write down.

list[2] *verb The ship was listing in the storm.* heel, lean, tilt, tip over.

listen *verb If you listen you'll find out.* lend an ear, pay attention, pay heed, take notice, tune in. □ **listen in** *She listened in on their conversation.* bug (*informal*), eavesdrop, overhear, tap.

listener *noun* auditor, hearer; [*listeners*] audience. OPPOSITE speaker, talker.

listless *adjective He was listless following his illness.* apathetic, languid, lethargic, lifeless, sluggish, tired, torpid, unenthusiastic. OPPOSITE energetic, lively.

literal *adjective* **1** *the literal meaning.* basic, main, original, primary. OPPOSITE figurative, metaphorical. **2** *a literal translation.* exact, precise, strict, true, verbatim, word for word. OPPOSITE free.

literate *adjective highly literate people.* educated, well-read. OPPOSITE illiterate.

literature *noun* **1** *He studies literature as well as language.* letters, writings, written works. **2** (*informal*) *The tourist office provides literature on the city's attractions.* booklets, brochures, handouts, information, leaflets, material, pamphlets.

lithe *adjective a lithe ballet dancer.* agile, flexible, limber, lissom, nimble, pliant, supple. OPPOSITE stiff.

litter *noun* **1** *The streets were strewn with litter.* debris, garbage, mess, refuse, rubbish, trash, waste. **2** *the prettiest kitten in the litter.* brood, family, group. — *verb The room was littered with toys.* clutter, mess up, scatter, strew.

little *adjective* **1** *a little object.* compact, concise, diminutive, dwarf, microscopic, midget, mini, miniature, minuscule, minute, petite, pocket-sized, puny, short, slight, small, stunted, tiny, undersized, wee. OPPOSITE big. **2** *It only took a little time.* brief, short. OPPOSITE long. **3** *It made only a little difference.* insignificant, marginal, minimal, negligible, slight. OPPOSITE considerable. **4** *It was only a little point.* minor, petty, trivial, unimportant. OPPOSITE major. **5** *The restaurant gives little portions.* inadequate, meagre, measly (*informal*), scanty, small, stingy. OPPOSITE ample. **6** *She loves her little brother.* baby, young, younger. OPPOSITE big, older. □ **little by little** bit by bit, by degrees, gradually, progressively, slowly.

live[1] *verb* **1** *Do you eat to live or live to eat?* be, be alive, breathe, exist, survive. OPPOSITE die. **2** *The memory will live with me.* continue, endure, last, persist, remain, stay. **3** *She lives on fruit.* feed, keep going, subsist, survive. **4** *Where does he live?* abide (*old use*), dwell, reside; see also INHABIT.

live[2] *adjective* **1** *live specimens.* alive, animate, breathing, living, surviving. OPPOSITE dead. **2** *live embers.* burning, glowing, hot. **3** *very much a live issue.* active, burning, current, topical. **4** *a live broadcast.* direct. OPPOSITE pre-recorded.

livelihood *noun You need to earn a livelihood.* crust (*Australian informal*), income, living, means of support.

lively *adjective a lively person.* active, animated, boisterous, cheerful, chirpy, energetic, enthusiastic, full of beans (*informal*), irrepressible, perky, spirited, sprightly, spry, vigorous, vivacious. OPPOSITE listless.

liven *verb She livened up when her visitors came.* brighten up, buck up (*informal*), cheer up, perk up.

livestock *noun* animals, stock.

livid *adjective* see ANGRY.

living *adjective living creatures.* alive, animate, breathing, live, quick (*old use*). OPPOSITE dead. — *noun* **1** *the joy of living.* being alive, existence, life. OPPOSITE dying. **2** *What do you do for a living?* crust (*Australian informal*), income, livelihood, means of support; see also JOB. □ **living room** drawing room, family room, lounge, lounge room, parlour (*old use*), sitting room.

load *noun* **1** *a load of timber.* cargo, consignment, freight, shipment. **2** *You have taken a load off her mind.* burden, care, weight. — *verb They loaded the car with the luggage.* fill, pack, pile up. □ **loads** *plural noun* (*informal*) *loads of room.* heaps (*informal*), lots (*informal*), masses, oodles (*informal*), piles (*informal*), plenty.

loading *noun* (*Australian*) *He is paid a holiday loading.* allowance, margin.

loaf *verb He spends the weekend loafing around.* idle, laze, lounge, take it easy, veg out (*slang*).

loafer *noun He was nothing but an idle loafer.* bludger (*Australian informal*), bum (*slang*), couch potato (*informal*), good-for-nothing, idler, layabout, lazybones (*informal*), shirker, skiver (*informal*), slacker.

loan *noun They took out a loan with the bank.* advance, mortgage. — *verb* see LEND.

loath *adjective He was loath to pay up.* disinclined, reluctant, unwilling. OPPOSITE keen.

loathe *verb She loathes cigarette smoke.* abhor, abominate, despise, detest, dislike, hate. OPPOSITE love.

loathsome *adjective The man had a loathsome habit of spitting.* abhorrent, abominable, despicable, detestable, disgusting, hateful, odious, offensive, repugnant, repulsive. OPPOSITE delightful, lovable.

lob *verb He lobbed the ball.* see THROW. □ **lob in** (*Australian slang*) *Alex lobbed in an hour late.* appear, arrive, rock up (*slang*), show up (*informal*), turn up.

lobby *noun* **1** *We waited in the lobby.* corridor, entrance hall, foyer, hall, porch, vestibule. **2** *He is the spokesperson for the euthanasia lobby.* force, pressure group. — *verb They lobbied for free bus travel.* campaign, petition, push.

local *adjective* **1** *the local newspaper.* area, community, district, neighbourhood, provincial, regional. OPPOSITE national. **2** *local pain. a local anaesthetic.* confined, localised, restricted. OPPOSITE general. — *noun If you need directions ask one of the locals.* inhabitant, native, resident.

localise *verb He managed to localise the bleeding.* confine, contain, limit, restrict. OPPOSITE spread.

locality noun They live in the same locality. area, community, district, neighbourhood, region, suburb, vicinity.

locate verb The mechanic located the problem. detect, discover, find, identify, pinpoint. □ **be located** The church is located on a hill. be, be found, be situated.

location noun 1 The house is in a beautiful location. area, locality, place, position, setting, site, spot. 2 Can you give your location to help us find you? bearings, position, whereabouts.

lock¹ noun The locks were broken. bar, bolt, catch, latch, padlock, snib. — verb He locked the door. bar, bolt, fasten, secure, snib. OPPOSITE unlock. □ **lock up** He will be locked up for life. imprison, incarcerate, intern, jail, put away.

lock² noun a lock of hair. tress, tuft.

locker noun cabinet, compartment, cupboard.

locomotion noun mobility, motion, movement, moving, transport, travel.

locomotive noun a diesel locomotive. engine.

locum noun Our own doctor was away, so we had to see his locum. deputy, replacement, stand-in, substitute.

lodge noun 1 the gatekeeper's lodge. cottage, gatehouse, home, house, residence. 2 a new lodge for skiers. cabin, chalet, hostel, hotel, motel, resort. — verb 1 He lodges with a family. board, live, reside, stay. 2 The bone has lodged in her throat. become embedded, get stuck, stick. 3 You must lodge a complaint. file, lay, make, register, submit.

lodger noun She takes in lodgers to supplement her income. boarder, guest, tenant.

lodging noun His allowance covers board and lodging. accommodation, housing, shelter. □ **lodgings** plural noun He returned to his lodgings for the night. accommodation, billet, digs (informal), quarters, residence, room(s).

loft noun The house has a loft. attic, garret.

lofty adjective 1 a lofty building. high, soaring, tall, towering. 2 lofty sentiments. exalted, high-minded, noble, sublime. OPPOSITE base. 3 a lofty manner. arrogant, disdainful, haughty, high and mighty, hoity-toity, proud, scornful, snooty (informal), supercilious. OPPOSITE humble, lowly.

log noun 1 He cut the branch into logs. block, piece, stump. 2 They kept a log of their trip. diary, journal, logbook, record.

logger noun The loggers were at work in the forest. lumberjack (American), timber-getter, tree-feller.

logical adjective 1 a logical argument. coherent, rational, reasoned, sound, valid. OPPOSITE illogical. 2 a logical person. intelligent, rational, reasonable, sensible, thinking.

logo noun They designed a new logo for their company. emblem, symbol, trade mark.

loiter verb The people were asked not to loiter, but to return home quickly. dally, dawdle, hang around, linger, lurk, skulk.

loll verb She lolled on the sofa. lie, lounge, recline, relax, slump, sprawl.

lolly noun Most lollies contain a lot of sugar. candy (American), confection, sweet, toffee.

lone adjective a lone passenger on the bus. alone, lonely, single, sole, solitary, unaccompanied.

lonely adjective 1 She often felt lonely after her husband died. forlorn, forsaken, friendless, lone-some. OPPOSITE befriended. 2 a hermit's lonely life. companionless, isolated, solitary. 3 a lonely place. deserted, isolated, remote, secluded, unfrequented, uninhabited. OPPOSITE busy, crowded.

long¹ adjective 1 There was a long silence before she spoke. big, drawn-out, endless, interminable, lengthy, prolonged, protracted, sustained, unending. OPPOSITE short. 2 a long table. elongated, extended. OPPOSITE short. 3 a long friendship. abiding, enduring, lasting, long-lasting, long-lived, long-standing, long-term. OPPOSITE brief.

long² verb **long for** I long for the sunshine. crave, desire, hanker after, hunger for, pine for, thirst for, want, wish for, yearn for.

longing noun The trip satisfied a deep longing. appetite, craving, desire, hunger, thirst, urge, wish, yearning, yen.

long-sighted adjective far-sighted, hypermetropic. OPPOSITE myopic, short-sighted.

long-suffering adjective a long-suffering partner. forbearing, patient, tolerant. OPPOSITE impatient.

long-term adjective a long-term illness. chronic, long, long-lasting, persistent. OPPOSITE short-term, temporary.

long-winded adjective a long-winded speaker. garrulous, loquacious, rambling, tedious, verbose, wordy. OPPOSITE succinct.

look verb 1 He couldn't help looking. gape, gawp (informal), gaze, glance, glare, goggle, leer, ogle, peek, peep, peer, see, squint, stare; see also LOOK AT. 2 Look to the front. face. 3 The work looked easy. appear, seem. — noun 1 Take a look at this. gaze, glance, glare, glimpse, peek, peep, squint (informal), squiz (Australian slang), stare, stickybeak (Australian informal). 2 Have a look for it. check, rummage, search. 3 She had a strange look. appearance, countenance, expression, face. □ **look after** She looks after her elderly parents. attend to, care for, guard, mind, protect, take care of. OPPOSITE neglect. **look at** 1 They looked at the painting. behold (old use), contemplate, examine, eye, inspect, observe, scrutinise, see, study, survey, view, watch. 2 The department will look at your case. see CONSIDER. **look down on** He looks down on other people. despise, disdain, look down your nose at, patronise, scorn. OPPOSITE look up to. **look for** She looked for her purse. check for, fossick for (Australian informal), hunt for, rummage for, search for, seek. **look forward to** I look forward to your letter. anticipate, await, long for. **look in** The doctor looked in every day. call in, drop in, visit. **look into** The police are looking into the matter. check on, examine, explore, go into, inquire into, investigate, probe, research. **look on** The crowd looked on helplessly. observe, stand by, view, watch, witness. OPPOSITE participate. **look out** Look out when you cross the road. beware, keep your eyes open, pay attention, take care, watch out. **look up** 1 You'll need to look up the address in my book. check, find, search for. 2 Look up the book. check, consult, refer to. 3 Things are looking up. get better, improve, pick up. 4 When he was in town he looked us up. call on, drop in on, look in on, visit. **look up to** He looks up to his brother. admire, esteem, idolise, respect, revere, worship. OPPOSITE look down on.

lookalike noun dead spit, double, ringer (informal), spitting image, twin.

looker-on noun an innocent looker-on. bystander, observer, onlooker, spectator, viewer, witness. OPPOSITE participant.

look-in noun He didn't give anyone else a look-in. chance, go (informal), show (informal).

lookout noun 1 He was appointed lookout. guard, picket, sentinel, sentry, watchman. 2 It's a poor lookout for us. future, outlook, prospect.

loom verb 1 Giant trees loomed before him. appear, rise, soar, stand out, tower. 2 The trial was looming. be imminent, be impending, menace, threaten.

loop noun She tied a loop in the cord. circle, circuit, coil, curl, knot, noose, ring, twirl, twist. — verb The wire had looped around the chair. coil, curl, entwine, kink, twist, wind.

loophole noun He looked for loopholes in the contract. escape, get-out, let-out, way out.

loose adjective 1 The animals were loose. at large, free, uncaged, unconfined, unleashed, unrestrained, untethered, untied. OPPOSITE enclosed, tethered. 2 His shirt has a loose button. detached, unattached, unfastened, unstuck. OPPOSITE fixed. 3 a loose floor board. rickety, shaky, unsteady, wobbly. OPPOSITE secure. 4 loose clothes. baggy, floppy, roomy. OPPOSITE tight. 5 The shop sells loose biscuits. bulk, unpackaged. OPPOSITE packaged. 6 The rope is too loose. slack. OPPOSITE taut, tight. 7 a loose definition. broad, imprecise, inexact, rough, sloppy, vague. OPPOSITE precise. — verb 1 They loosed the dogs. free, let go, let loose, liberate, release, set free. OPPOSITE shut in, tie up. 2 The ropes were loosed. loosen, undo, unfasten, untie. OPPOSITE tie, tighten.

loosen verb 1 He loosened his grip. ease, relax, slacken. OPPOSITE tighten. 2 He managed to loosen the screw. free, loose, release, undo, unfasten. OPPOSITE tighten.

loot noun The thief ran off with the loot. booty, goods, pillage, plunder, spoils, swag (informal), takings. — verb After the earthquake many people looted the damaged buildings. pillage, plunder, raid, ransack, rob, sack.

lop verb The trees were lopped to clear the power lines. chop, cut, prune.

lopsided adjective The painting is lopsided. askew, asymmetrical, awry, crooked, unbalanced, uneven. OPPOSITE even, symmetrical.

lord noun 1 The lion is considered lord of the jungle. king, master, monarch, ruler, sovereign. 2 He was made a lord. aristocrat, noble, nobleman, peer. □ **the Lord** God, Jehovah, Jesus Christ, Yahweh.

lordly adjective We've all had enough of his lordly ways. arrogant, bossy, disdainful, haughty, high and mighty, imperious, lofty, overbearing, snobbish, stuck-up (informal). OPPOSITE humble.

lore noun He had studied the lore of these people. folklore, legends, myths, traditions.

lorry noun He drives a lorry. pick-up, road train (Australian), semi (Australian informal), semitrailer, transport, truck, van.

lose verb 1 He has lost his pen. mislay, misplace. OPPOSITE find. 2 So much was lost in the accident. destroy, obliterate, wipe out. OPPOSITE save. 3 They lost their way. miss, stray from, wander from. 4 He lost his opportunity. forfeit, let slip,

miss, pass up (informal), waste. 5 She has lost weight. get rid of, shed. OPPOSITE gain. 6 It doesn't matter whether you win or lose. be defeated, get beaten. OPPOSITE win.

loss noun 1 loss of sight. deprivation, disappearance, forfeiture, impairment, reduction. OPPOSITE gain. 2 a widow's loss. bereavement. 3 Both armies suffered heavy losses. casualty, death, fatality. 4 The pancake stall made a loss. debit, debt, deficit, shortfall. OPPOSITE profit. □ **at a loss** I am at a loss as to how it could have happened. baffled, mystified, nonplussed, perplexed, puzzled.

lost adjective 1 a lost child. a lost purse. mislaid, misplaced, missing, strayed, vanished. OPPOSITE found. 2 lost in wonder. absorbed, engrossed, preoccupied, rapt.

lot¹ noun 1 We were each given our lot. allocation, allotment, part, portion, quota, ration, share. 2 Sarah was happy with her lot in life. destiny, fate, fortune, portion. 3 a building lot. allotment, block, plot. 4 We took delivery of a new lot of chairs. batch, collection, group, set.

lot² noun (informal) 1 a lot of letters. lots of lollies. dozens (informal), heaps (informal), loads (informal), many, masses, oodles (informal), piles (informal), plenty, scores, stacks (informal), swag (Australian informal), tons (informal). 2 Brian's a lot happier now. a good deal, a great deal, much.

lotion noun hand lotion. balm, cream, liniment, moisturiser, ointment, salve.

loud adjective 1 loud music. loud voices. amplified, blaring, booming, deafening, noisy, penetrating, piercing, raucous, resounding, rowdy, sonorous, stentorian, strident, thundering. OPPOSITE soft. 2 loud colours. bold, bright, flashy, garish, gaudy, lurid, obtrusive, showy. OPPOSITE pastel, subdued.

loudness noun volume.

lounge verb On the weekend she just lounges around. laze, lie, loaf, loll, recline, relax, sprawl, veg out (slang). — noun 1 They waited in the airport lounge. waiting room. 2 The lounge is a room for all the family. drawing room, living room, lounge room, parlour (old use), sitting room.

louring adjective louring skies. black, cloudy, dark, gloomy, grey, heavy, leaden, overcast.

lousy adjective (informal) He had a lousy time. awful (informal), bad, dreadful (informal), miserable, nasty, rotten (informal), terrible (informal); see also BAD. OPPOSITE wonderful.

loutish adjective loutish behaviour. boorish, churlish, discourteous, ill-mannered, impolite, rough, rude, uncouth. OPPOSITE polite.

lovable adjective a lovable child. adorable, appealing, charming, darling, dear, delightful, endearing, likeable, lovely, sweet. OPPOSITE detestable.

love noun 1 His love for her is strong. adoration, affection, devotion, fondness, tenderness, warmth; see also PASSION. OPPOSITE hate, hatred. 2 He developed a love of reading. delight, enjoyment, fondness, liking, pleasure, taste. 3 She is his one true love. beloved, darling, lover, sweetheart. — verb 1 She loves him. adore, be devoted to, be fond of, care for, cherish, dote on, hold dear, idolise, revere, treasure. OPPOSITE hate. 2 He loves good books. appreciate, be fond of, delight in, enjoy, like, relish, treasure. OPPOSITE hate. □ **in love** It's easy to tell they're in love. besotted, devoted, enamoured, infatuated, smitten.

lovely adjective **1** *The bride looked lovely.* adorable, attractive, beautiful, charming, good-looking, gorgeous, pretty, winsome. OPPOSITE unattractive. **2** (*informal*) *I had a lovely time.* cool (*informal*), delightful, enjoyable, excellent, fantastic (*informal*), good, great (*informal*), nice, pleasant, terrific (*informal*), wonderful. OPPOSITE terrible.

lover noun **1** *Send a valentine to your lover.* admirer, beloved, boyfriend, girlfriend, suitor, sweetheart. **2** *art lovers.* admirer, buff (*informal*), devotee, enthusiast, fan.

loving adjective *a loving friend. a loving embrace.* adoring, affectionate, amorous, ardent, caring, close, devoted, doting, fond, friendly, kind, kind-hearted, passionate, sympathetic, tender, warm, warm-hearted. OPPOSITE indifferent, unloving.

low[1] adjective **1** *low trees.* dwarf, little, miniature, short, small, squat, stunted. OPPOSITE high, tall. **2** *His position in the firm is quite low.* humble, inferior, junior, lowly, unimportant. OPPOSITE high, superior. **3** *low prices.* budget, cheap, cut-price, inexpensive, modest, reduced. OPPOSITE high. **4** *a low opinion of somebody.* adverse, bad, negative, poor, unfavourable. OPPOSITE high. **5** *The singer has a low voice.* bass, deep. OPPOSITE high-pitched. **6** *He spoke in a low voice so as not to be overheard.* faint, hushed, muffled, quiet, soft, subdued. OPPOSITE loud. **7** *She's feeling rather low.* blue, dejected, depressed, despondent, down, downcast, forlorn, gloomy, glum, listless, melancholy, miserable, sad. OPPOSITE happy.

low[2] verb *The cattle are lowing.* moo.

lower verb **1** *He lowered the flag.* bring down, drop, let down, pull down, take down. OPPOSITE hoist, raise. **2** *She lowered her voice.* quieten, soften, subdue, tone down. OPPOSITE raise. **3** *The lights may be lowered.* dim, dip, fade, subdue, turn down. OPPOSITE turn up. **4** *The company lowered their prices.* cut, decrease, discount, drop, mark down, reduce. OPPOSITE increase.

lowly adjective *She came from a lowly background.* humble, modest, unassuming, unpretentious.

loyal adjective *He remained a loyal friend.* constant, dedicated, dependable, devoted, faithful, patriotic, staunch, steadfast, true, true-blue, trustworthy. OPPOSITE disloyal.

loyalty noun *the man's loyalty to his wife.* allegiance, constancy, devotion, faithfulness, fidelity, steadfastness, trustworthiness. OPPOSITE disloyalty.

lozenge noun *a cough lozenge.* drop, lolly, pastille, sweet, tablet.

lubricate verb *All the moving parts need to be lubricated.* grease, oil.

lucid adjective **1** *a lucid speech.* clear, comprehensible, intelligible, straightforward, understandable. OPPOSITE unintelligible. **2** *Sadly, the old man is no longer lucid.* all there, rational, sane, sensible. OPPOSITE confused.

luck noun **1** *We found it by sheer luck.* accident, chance, coincidence, destiny, fate, fluke, good fortune, serendipity. **2** *We wish you luck.* good fortune, prosperity, success.

luckless adjective *a luckless adventurer.* doomed, fated, hapless, ill-fated, jinxed, unfortunate, unlucky. OPPOSITE lucky.

lucky adjective **1** *a lucky person.* blessed, charmed, favoured, fortunate. OPPOSITE unfortunate. **2** *a*

lucky find. accidental, chance, fluky, fortuitous, serendipitous.

lucrative adjective *a lucrative job.* profitable, remunerative, well-paid. OPPOSITE unprofitable.

ludicrous adjective *a ludicrous proposal.* absurd, crazy, derisory, farcical, laughable, nonsensical, preposterous, ridiculous. OPPOSITE sensible, serious.

lug verb *She lugged the parcel up the stairs.* carry, drag, haul, heave, pull.

luggage noun *They search through all your luggage.* baggage, bags, cases, gear, ports (*Australian*), suitcases, trunks; see also BELONGINGS.

lukewarm adjective **1** *She likes her tea lukewarm.* tepid, warm. **2** *He got a lukewarm reception.* apathetic, cool, half-hearted, indifferent, unenthusiastic. OPPOSITE enthusiastic.

lull verb *The music lulled her to sleep.* calm, hush, pacify, quieten, relax, soothe. OPPOSITE excite. — noun *a lull in the conversation.* break, gap, hiatus, interval, let-up (*informal*), pause, silence.

lumber verb **1** *They lumbered him with the job.* burden, encumber, land, load, saddle. **2** *The man lumbered up the stairs.* clump, plod, shuffle, trudge, waddle.

luminous adjective *The hands of the clock are luminous.* bright, glowing, luminescent, phosphorescent, radiant, shining.

lump[1] noun **1** *a lump of cheese.* ball, bit, chunk, cube, hunk, piece, wedge. **2** *The doctor examined the lump on her arm.* bulge, bump, growth, protrusion, swelling, tumour. — verb *They lumped them together.* combine, group, mix.

lump[2] verb (*informal*) *Like it or lump it!* accept, endure, put up with, suffer, tolerate, wear (*informal*).

lumpy adjective *a lumpy mixture.* bumpy, chunky, uneven. OPPOSITE smooth.

lunacy noun **1** *The murderer suffered from lunacy.* insanity, madness, mania, mental illness. OPPOSITE sanity. **2** *It is sheer lunacy to ride at night without lights.* folly, foolhardiness, foolishness, idiocy, imprudence, madness, recklessness, stupidity. OPPOSITE prudence.

lunatic noun crackpot (*informal*), loony (*informal*), madman, madwoman, maniac, nut (*informal*), nutter (*informal*), psychopath.

lunch noun *He likes a hot lunch at about one o'clock.* dinner, luncheon (*formal*), midday meal.

lunge noun **1** *He made a lunge to catch the ball.* dive, plunge, stretch. **2** *a lunge with the sword.* charge, jab, stab, thrust. — verb *He lunged towards the man with his knife.* charge, dive, plunge, pounce, rush.

lurch[1] verb *The drunken man lurched and fell.* flounder, reel, stagger, stumble, sway, totter.

lurch[2] noun **leave in the lurch** *He moved away, leaving his family in the lurch.* abandon, desert, forsake, leave high and dry, leave stranded.

lure noun *the lure of a big salary.* attraction, bait, decoy, draw, drawcard, enticement. — verb *People are often lured by money.* attract, draw, entice, seduce, tempt.

lurid adjective **1** *a lurid pink.* bright, flashy, garish, gaudy, loud, showy. **2** *the lurid details.* explicit, gory, graphic, horrifying, sensational, shocking, vivid.

lurk verb *There was someone lurking in the bushes.* hide, lie in wait, linger, skulk. — noun (*Australian informal*) *The officer knew all the lurks and perks.* dodge (*informal*), racket, rort (*Australian slang*), scam (*slang*), scheme, stratagem.

luscious adjective *luscious grapes.* delectable, delicious, juicy, rich, succulent, sweet.

lush adjective *The grass is lush after the winter rains.* green, luxuriant, profuse, prolific, strong, thick.

lust noun *a lust for money.* appetite, craving, desire, greed, hunger, longing, passion.

lustre noun *The table had a lustre after polishing.* brightness, brilliance, gleam, gloss, sheen, shine, sparkle.

luxuriant adjective *a luxuriant growth.* abundant, dense, lush, profuse, strong, thick. OPPOSITE sparse.

luxuriate verb *She spent the holidays luxuriating in the sunshine.* bask, delight, enjoy yourself, indulge yourself, relax, wallow.

luxurious adjective *luxurious hotels.* de luxe, elegant, expensive, first-class, grand, opulent, plush, posh (*informal*), sumptuous, swish (*informal*), upmarket. OPPOSITE cheap.

luxury noun **1** *They live a life of luxury.* affluence, comfort, ease, opulence, self-indulgence. **2** *An overseas holiday is a luxury.* extra, extravagance, indulgence, treat. OPPOSITE necessity.

lying noun *Matilda was punished for lying.* deception, dishonesty, fibbing, mendacity, perjury, prevarication. — adjective *the lying scoundrel.* deceitful, dishonest, mendacious, untruthful. OPPOSITE truthful.

lynch verb *He was lynched by the angry mob.* execute, put to death.

lyrical adjective *a lyrical description.* melodic, melodious, musical, poetic, songlike.

lyrics plural noun *the lyrics of a song.* libretto, text, words.

Mm

macabre adjective *a macabre tale of witchcraft and murder.* eerie, frightening, ghastly, ghoulish, gory, grim, grisly, gruesome, hideous, horrific, morbid, spooky (*informal*), weird.

machine noun *The tedious work is now done by a machine.* apparatus, appliance, computer, contraption, device, engine, gadget, instrument, mechanism, robot, tool.

machinery noun *farm machinery.* equipment, gear, machines, plant.

macho adjective *Macho men don't cry.* manly, masculine, tough, virile. OPPOSITE effeminate.

mad adjective **1** *She has gone mad.* bananas (*slang*), barmy (*slang*), batty (*slang*), berserk, bonkers (*slang*), crackers (*slang*), crazy, demented, deranged, dotty (*informal*), flaky (*slang*), frenzied, insane, irrational, loony (*informal*), lunatic, manic, mental (*informal*), nuts (*informal*), nutty (*informal*), off your head, out of your mind, potty (*informal*), psychotic, round the bend (*informal*), screwy (*informal*), troppo (*Australian slang*), unbalanced, unhinged. OPPOSITE sane. **2** *a mad plan.* absurd, crazy, daft (*informal*), foolhardy, foolish, harebrained, idiotic, illogical, insane, lunatic, nonsensical, preposterous, rash, reckless, silly, stupid, unwise, wild. OPPOSITE sensible. **3** *She is mad about horses and riding.* crazy, enthusiastic, fanatical, infatuated, keen, nuts (*informal*), obsessed, passionate, wild. OPPOSITE indifferent. **4** (*informal*) *He'll be really mad when he finds out.* angry, annoyed,

cross, enraged, furious, incensed, infuriated, irate, livid, riled (*informal*), ropeable (*Australian informal*), wild. OPPOSITE calm.

madden verb *His hesitation maddens me.* anger, annoy, bug (*informal*), drive someone mad, enrage, exasperate, incense, infuriate, irritate, needle (*informal*), rile (*informal*), vex, wind up (*informal*). OPPOSITE soothe.

madman, madwoman noun crackpot (*informal*), loony (*slang*), lunatic, maniac, nut (*informal*), nutcase (*informal*), nutter (*informal*), psychopath.

madness noun **1** *The hospital cured his madness.* dementia, derangement, insanity, lunacy, mania, mental illness, psychosis. OPPOSITE sanity. **2** (*informal*) *It was sheer madness to buy it.* folly, foolishness, idiocy, lunacy, stupidity.

maelstrom noun *The boat was caught in a maelstrom.* eddy, swirl, vortex, whirlpool.

maestro noun *a maestro in the kitchen.* ace (*informal*), adept, expert, genius, master, virtuoso, whiz (*informal*), wizard.

magazine noun *She likes to read magazines.* bulletin, journal, newsletter, pamphlet, periodical.

maggot noun grub, larva.

magic noun *She doesn't believe in magic.* black magic, conjuring, divination, illusion, sleight of hand, sorcery, spells, trickery, voodoo, witchcraft, wizardry.

magician noun *We were captivated by the magician's tricks.* conjuror, enchanter, enchantress, illusionist, medicine man, sorcerer, sorceress, warlock (*old use*), witch, witchdoctor, wizard.

magisterial adjective *He speaks with a magisterial air.* assertive, authoritative, bossy (*informal*), domineering, high-handed, imperious, lordly, masterful, overbearing, peremptory. OPPOSITE deferential.

magnanimous adjective *Paying her friend's debts was a magnanimous gesture.* benevolent, big-hearted, bountiful, charitable, generous, kind, noble. OPPOSITE mean, petty.

magnate noun *a newspaper magnate.* baron, big shot (*informal*), bigwig (*informal*), leader, mogul (*informal*), tycoon; see also BUSINESSMAN.

magnetic adjective *a magnetic personality.* alluring, attractive, captivating, charismatic, charming, enchanting, enthralling, fascinating, irresistible, seductive. OPPOSITE repulsive.

magnetism noun *personal magnetism.* allure, appeal, attraction, charisma, charm, fascination, seductiveness.

magnificent adjective *a magnificent house. a magnificent performance.* beautiful, brilliant, excellent, exquisite, extraordinary, fine, glorious, gorgeous, grand, great, imposing, impressive, majestic, marvellous, opulent, spectacular, splendid, stately, striking, stunning, sumptuous, superb, terrific (*informal*), wonderful. OPPOSITE ordinary.

magnify verb **1** *The lens magnifies objects.* blow up (*informal*), enlarge. OPPOSITE reduce. **2** *The newspaper magnified the seriousness of the incident.* amplify, blow up (*informal*), exaggerate, overstate. OPPOSITE understate.

magnitude noun *the magnitude of the problem.* extent, importance, scale, significance, size.

maid noun *The lady employs a maid.* chambermaid, domestic, help, housemaid, lady's maid, maidservant, parlourmaid, servant.

maiden noun (*old use*) *young maidens and lads.* damsel (*old use*), girl, lass, lassie (*informal*), maid (*old use*). — *adjective* **1** *a maiden aunt.* spinster, unmarried, unwed. **2** *a maiden voyage.* first, inaugural, initial.

mail[1] *noun The mail is delivered daily.* correspondence, letters, packages, parcels, post. — *verb She mailed the letter immediately.* dispatch, post, send.

mail[2] *noun a knight's coat of mail.* armour, chain mail.

maim *verb The accident maimed him for life.* cripple, disable, incapacitate, injure, lame, mutilate, wound.

main *adjective the main problem. the main office.* biggest, central, chief, critical, crucial, essential, first, foremost, greatest, head, largest, leading, major, most important, outstanding, paramount, predominant, primary, prime, principal, vital. OPPOSITE minor, secondary.

mainly *adverb The concert was attended mainly by teenagers.* chiefly, especially, generally, in the main, largely, mostly, predominantly, primarily, principally.

mainstay *noun She is the mainstay of the club.* anchor, backbone, foundation, linchpin, pillar, support.

mainstream *noun the mainstream of political opinion.* current, direction, tide, trend.

maintain *verb* **1** *They maintained the custom.* carry on, continue, keep, keep up, perpetuate, preserve, prolong, uphold. OPPOSITE break. **2** *He maintains his car.* care for, keep in good repair, look after, preserve, service, take care of. OPPOSITE neglect. **3** *They maintain three children at university.* finance, keep, provide for, support. **4** *He still maintains that he is right.* assert, claim, contend, declare, hold, insist. OPPOSITE deny.

maintenance *noun* **1** *He looks after the maintenance of the car.* care, preservation, repairs, running, servicing, upkeep. **2** *She is paid maintenance for the children.* alimony, allowance.

majestic *adjective a majestic house. a majestic air.* august, dignified, glorious, grand, imperial, imposing, impressive, kingly, lordly, magnificent, noble, regal, royal, splendid, stately. OPPOSITE humble.

majesty *noun the majesty of the occasion.* dignity, glory, grandeur, magnificence, nobility, pomp, royalty, splendour, stateliness.

major *adjective* **1** *The major part of the work is finished.* bigger, greater, larger, main. **2** *the major consideration.* central, chief, crucial, important, key, main, paramount, primary, prime, principal, significant. OPPOSITE minor.

majority *noun* **1** *He ate the majority of the chocolates.* bulk, greater part, lion's share, most. OPPOSITE minority. **2** *They won by a handsome majority.* margin.

make *verb* **1** *She makes dresses. He makes toys.* assemble, build, carve, construct, create, erect, fabricate, fashion, forge, form, invent, manufacture, model, mould, produce, put together, sculpture, sew, shape. **2** *She made the dessert.* bake, concoct, cook, prepare, produce. **3** *Who made the rules? Make a list.* compile, compose, devise, draw up, establish, formulate, frame, invent, think up, write. **4** *They made a time for their next meeting.* agree on, arrange, decide on, fix, organise, settle on. **5** *They made him their leader.* appoint, elect, nominate, ordain. **6** *Please make your bed.* arrange, prepare, straighten, tidy. **7** *He likes to make difficulties.* bring about, cause, create, provoke. **8** *Five and five make ten.* add up to, amount to, come to, equal, total. **9** *Can she make her goal?* accomplish, achieve, arrive at, attain, reach. **10** *He made a good teacher.* become, end up, turn into, turn out. **11** *He made a lot of money.* acquire, earn, gain, get, obtain, realise, win. **12** *She made him sign it.* cause, coerce, compel, force, oblige, order, pressure. **13** *She made a curtsy.* do, execute, perform. **14** *He made a speech.* deliver, give, present, utter. — *noun The car is a French make.* brand, kind, sort, type. □ **make do** *They had to make do with what they had.* get by, improvise, manage. **make for** *They made for home.* aim for, go towards, head for, proceed towards. **make out** **1** *I can't make out his writing.* decipher, figure out, read, understand, work out. **2** *She made out a shadowy figure.* discern, distinguish, espy, perceive, see. **3** *They made out that the vase was an antique.* allege, assert, claim, imply, pretend. **make over** *He made the car over to his daughter.* sign over, transfer. **make up** **1** *The seven of us made up a team.* compose, constitute, form. **2** *He made up the whole story.* concoct, cook up (*informal*), dream up, fabricate, invent, manufacture, think up. **make up for** *Nothing will make up for the loss.* atone for, compensate for, offset, recompense, redeem. **make up your mind** choose, come to a decision, decide, resolve, settle. OPPOSITE vacillate.

make-believe *noun He lives in a world of make-believe.* daydreaming, dreaming, fantasy, imagination, play-acting, pretence.

make-over *noun a bathroom make-over.* redecoration, remodelling, renovation, transformation, upgrade.

maker *noun a kite maker.* builder, constructor, creator, inventor, manufacturer, producer.

makeshift *adjective a makeshift shelter.* improvised, provisional, stopgap, temporary. OPPOSITE permanent.

make-up *noun* **1** *Actors wear make-up.* cosmetics, face paint, greasepaint. **2** *Depression is in his make-up.* character, nature, personality, temperament.

maladjusted *adjective maladjusted children.* disturbed, mixed-up (*informal*), neurotic, screwed-up (*informal*).

malady *noun He is suffering from a terrible malady.* affliction, ailment, complaint, condition, disease, disorder, illness, infirmity, sickness.

malcontent *noun The riot was started by a group of malcontents.* agitator, complainer, dissenter, grouch (*informal*), grumbler, moaner, rebel, stirrer (*Australian informal*), troublemaker, whinger (*informal*).

male *adjective* manly, masculine. OPPOSITE female. — *noun* see BOY, MAN.

malefactor *noun Malefactors will be punished.* baddy (*informal*), criminal, crook (*informal*), delinquent, evildoer, felon, lawbreaker, miscreant, offender, outlaw, sinner, villain, wrongdoer.

malevolent *adjective a malevolent character. a malevolent look.* hostile, malicious, malignant, nasty, sinister, spiteful, vicious, vindictive. OPPOSITE benevolent, kind.

malformed *adjective a malformed foot.* crooked, deformed, distorted, misshapen, twisted.

malfunction *noun A computer malfunction delayed the project.* breakdown, failure, fault, glitch (*informal*), hiccup, hitch. — *verb The traffic lights malfunctioned.* break down, conk out (*informal*), fail, go bung (*Australian slang*), stop working.

malice *noun done with malice aforethought.* animosity, bitterness, enmity, hostility, ill will, malevolence, maliciousness, spite, spitefulness, vindictiveness. OPPOSITE benevolence, kindness.

malicious *adjective malicious gossip.* bitchy (*informal*), hostile, malevolent, malignant, mean, mischievous, nasty, spiteful, unkind, vicious, vindictive. OPPOSITE benevolent, friendly.

malign *adjective a malign influence.* bad, baleful, damaging, deleterious, destructive, evil, harmful, injurious, noxious, pernicious, sinister. OPPOSITE benign, good. — *verb The report maligned him.* defame, denigrate, disparage, knock (*informal*), libel, revile, run down, slander, smear, vilify. OPPOSITE praise.

malignant *adjective* **1** *a malignant tumour.* cancerous, deadly, fatal. OPPOSITE benign, non-malignant. **2** *a malignant look.* destructive, evil, harmful, hostile, malevolent, malicious, pernicious, spiteful, venomous, vicious, vindictive. OPPOSITE benign, kindly.

malingerer *noun* see SHIRKER.

mall *noun a shopping mall.* arcade, centre, complex, plaza, precinct.

malleable *adjective* **1** *a malleable metal.* plastic, soft, workable. OPPOSITE brittle. **2** *He has a malleable character.* adaptable, biddable, docile, impressionable, manageable, pliable, suggestible, tractable. OPPOSITE intractable.

malnutrition *noun She was suffering from malnutrition.* emaciation, hunger, starvation, undernourishment.

malpractice *noun The doctor was sued for malpractice.* dereliction, misconduct, negligence, wrongdoing.

maltreat *verb The child was not maltreated.* abuse, bully, harm, ill-treat, ill-use, mistreat, oppress.

mammoth *adjective Cleaning the garage was a mammoth task.* colossal, enormous, gargantuan, giant, gigantic, herculean, huge, immense, large, massive, mighty, stupendous, tremendous. OPPOSITE tiny.

man *noun* **1** *All men are equal. Every man for himself.* human, human being, individual, mortal, person. **2** *Man is responsible for the welfare of animals.* human beings, humanity, humankind, human race, humans, mankind, people. **3** *The club is for men only: women are not allowed.* bloke (*informal*), chap (*informal*), fellow (*informal*), gentleman, guy (*informal*), lad (*informal*), male. — *verb The students manned the counter.* attend, operate, staff.

manage *verb* **1** *He manages the business.* administer, be in charge of, command, conduct, control, direct, govern, head, oversee, run, superintend, supervise. **2** *Can she manage scissors yet?* control, handle, manipulate, operate, use, wield. **3** *She manages on a very small wage.* cope, get along, get by, make do, make ends meet, survive. **4** *He is good at managing people.* cope with, deal with, handle. **5** *She managed the task.* accomplish, carry out, do, perform, succeed in, undertake. OPPOSITE fail.

manageable *adjective* **1** *a manageable size.* convenient, handy. OPPOSITE unwieldy. **2** *a manageable task.* feasible, possible, practicable. OPPOSITE impossible. **3** *a manageable child.* biddable, compliant, controllable, docile, governable, pliable, tractable. OPPOSITE rebellious.

management *noun* **1** *experts in project management.* administration, control, direction, handling, organisation, running, supervision. **2** *a disagreement between management and the workers.* administrators, bosses, directors, employers, executives, managers.

manager *noun* **1** *the manager of the repair division.* administrator, boss, chief, director, foreman, head, overseer, proprietor, superintendent, supervisor. **2** *A singer needs a manager.* agent, organiser.

manchester *noun* bedlinen, linen, napery, table linen.

mandate *noun The Government was given a mandate to reform the tax system.* approval, authorisation, authority, direction, permission.

manger *noun The horse's hay was in the manger.* feeding trough.

mangle *verb His body was mangled in the accident.* crush, cut, damage, disfigure, injure, lacerate, maim, mutilate.

manhole *noun Access to the pipe is through a manhole.* hatch, opening, trapdoor.

manhood *noun* **1** *He has reached manhood.* adulthood, majority, maturity. OPPOSITE childhood. **2** *a test of manhood.* bravery, courage, machismo, manliness, masculinity, strength, valour, virility.

mania *noun tennis mania.* craze, enthusiasm, fad, obsession, passion; see also MADNESS.

maniac *noun The fire was started by a maniac.* crackpot (*informal*), loony (*slang*), lunatic, madman, madwoman, nut (*informal*), nutcase (*informal*), nutter (*informal*), psychopath.

manifest *adjective Her disapproval was manifest.* apparent, blatant, clear, conspicuous, evident, obvious, patent, plain, transparent, undisguised, unmistakable, visible. OPPOSITE hidden. — *verb The crowd manifested its support by cheering.* declare, demonstrate, display, exhibit, express, indicate, make known, reveal, show. OPPOSITE hide.

manifesto *noun the party's manifesto.* declaration, platform, policy statement, programme.

manipulate *verb* **1** *She is good at manipulating the gadget.* control, handle, manage, operate, use, wield, work. **2** *He manipulated the figures.* adjust, cook (*informal*), falsify, fiddle (*slang*), juggle, massage, rig.

mankind *noun the history of mankind.* human beings, humanity, humankind, human race, man, people, society.

manly *adjective* **1** *a manly appearance.* male, mannish, masculine. OPPOSITE effeminate, feminine. **2** *He was expected to behave in a manly fashion.* brave, chivalrous, courageous, fearless, gallant, heroic, macho, manful, valiant. OPPOSITE cowardly.

man-made *adjective a man-made product.* artificial, made, manufactured, synthetic. OPPOSITE natural.

manner *noun* **1** *He described the manner in which he makes the dough.* fashion, method, procedure, style, technique, way. **2** *She has a friendly manner.* air, attitude, bearing, demeanour, disposition, mien. **3** *We deal with all manner of things.* category, class, kind, sort, type, variety. □ **manners** *plural noun* **1** *bad manners. good manners.* behaviour, conduct, form. **2** *He hasn't learned any manners.* courtesy, decorum, etiquette, politeness, social graces, tact.

mannerism *noun He had a mannerism of twirling his moustache as he*

spoke. habit, idiosyncrasy, peculiarity, quirk, trait.
mannish *adjective She had a mannish appearance.* butch (*informal*), masculine. OPPOSITE feminine.
manoeuvre *noun* **1** *army manoeuvres.* exercise, movement, operation. **2** *He used a clever manoeuvre to achieve his ends.* device, dodge (*informal*), move, ploy, ruse, scheme, stratagem, tactic, trick. — *verb* **1** *He manoeuvred the car into the front position.* guide, jockey, move, negotiate, position, steer. **2** *She manoeuvred the conversation towards money.* direct, guide, manipulate, steer.
manpower *noun a shortage of manpower.* employees, hands, human resources, labour, personnel, staff, workers, workforce.
manse *noun The minister is provided with a manse.* house, rectory, residence.
mansion *noun The original homestead was a grand two-storeyed mansion.* castle, château, manor, manor house, palace. OPPOSITE hovel.
manslaughter *noun He was tried for manslaughter.* homicide, killing. CONTRASTS WITH murder.
mantle *noun* **1** *He wore a mantle.* cape, cloak, shawl. **2** *a mantle of secrecy.* cloak, cloud, mask, screen, shroud, veil.
manual *adjective* **1** *The car has a manual gear-change.* hand-operated. OPPOSITE automatic. **2** *manual labour.* blue-collar, physical. OPPOSITE mental. — *noun a manual for the car.* handbook, primer, reference book, textbook.
manufacture *verb* **1** *They manufacture cars.* assemble, build, construct, fabricate, make, process, produce. **2** *He manufactured an excuse.* concoct, cook up (*informal*), dream up, fabricate, invent, make up, think up. — *noun the manufacture of cars.* assembly, building, construction, fabrication, making, production.
manure *noun He spread the manure over the garden.* compost, dung, fertiliser, muck.
manuscript *noun He studies ancient manuscripts.* document, script.
many *adjective He received many letters.* a lot of (*informal*), copious, countless, dozens of (*informal*), heaps of (*informal*), innumerable, lots of (*informal*), myriad, numbers of, numerous, oodles of (*informal*), piles of (*informal*), plenty of, scores of, umpteen (*informal*). OPPOSITE few.
map *noun a map of the world.* chart, diagram, plan, projection. — *verb Cook mapped the east coast of Australia.* chart, survey. □ **map out** *He had to map out a programme.* arrange, devise, organise, plan, plot, prepare.
mar *verb* **1** *A scratch marred the surface.* blemish, damage, deface, disfigure, flaw, scar, spoil, stain. **2** *A poor accompaniment marred the performance.* detract from, ruin, spoil, tarnish. OPPOSITE enhance.
marauder *noun The town was raided by marauders.* bandit, buccaneer, looter, pillager, pirate, plunderer, robber.
marbled *adjective a marbled pattern.* mottled, variegated, veined.
march *verb The soldiers marched past.* file, parade, stride, tramp, troop, walk. — *noun a protest march.* demo (*informal*), demonstration, parade, procession.
margin *noun* **1** *The writing filled the page leaving a narrow margin.* border, boundary, edge, frame, fringe. **2** *She won by a narrow margin.* difference, gap.
marginal *adjective This finding is of marginal importance.* little, minimal, minor, negligible, slight. OPPOSITE central, major.
marine *adjective* **1** *marine creatures.* oceanic, salt-water, sea. CONTRASTS WITH freshwater, terrestrial. **2** *marine vessels.* maritime, nautical, naval, ocean-going, seafaring, seagoing.
mariner *noun* sailor, seafarer, seaman.
marital *adjective a happy marital relationship.* conjugal, married, matrimonial, nuptial, wedded.
maritime *adjective a maritime nation. a maritime museum.* marine, nautical, naval, seafaring, seagoing, shipping.
mark *noun* **1** *The vase left a mark on the table. There were paint marks on his clothes.* blemish, blotch, dot, impression, line, patch, scar, scratch, smear, smudge, spatter, speck, speckle, splash, splotch, spot, stain, streak, trace. **2** *a mark of respect.* indication, proof, sign, signal, token. **3** *The clock bears the mark of the maker.* badge, brand, emblem, hallmark, imprint, label, logo, seal, stamp, symbol, trade mark. **4** *The student was pleased with his mark for English.* assessment, grade, rating, result, score. **5** *His dart hit the mark.* bull's-eye, goal, objective, target. — *verb* **1** *Something has marked the surface.* blemish, deface, disfigure, mar, scar, score, scratch, scuff, smudge, spot, stain. **2** *A tree marks the spot.* designate, identify, indicate, show, signify. **3** *She marked all her belongings.* brand, identify, label, name. **4** *The teacher marked the students' work.* assess, correct, evaluate, grade, judge, rate, score. **5** *Mark my words!* heed, mind, note, pay attention to, take notice of. OPPOSITE ignore.
marked *adjective a marked accent.* clear, definite, distinct, noticeable, obvious, pronounced, strong, unmistakable. OPPOSITE imperceptible.
market *noun a craft market.* bazaar, fair, mart, sale. — *verb* see SELL.
marksman, markswoman *noun He was shot by a skilled marksman.* gunman, sharpshooter, shooter, shot, sniper.
maroon *verb He was marooned on an island.* abandon, desert, forsake, isolate, leave, strand.
marriage *noun* **1** *the state of marriage.* matrimony, wedlock. **2** *a long and happy marriage.* match, partnership, union. **3** *We attended their marriage.* marriage ceremony, wedding.
married *adjective* see MARITAL.
marry *verb Let's get married.* become husband and wife, become man and wife, get hitched (*informal*), tie the knot (*informal*), wed.
marsh *noun The marsh was full of bird life.* bog, fen, mire, morass, quagmire, slough, swamp.
marshal *noun The starters reported to the marshal for the event.* controller, officer, official, organiser. — *verb* **1** *The speaker marshalled his thoughts.* arrange, assemble, collect, gather, muster, organise. **2** *He marshalled his troops.* align, array, assemble, deploy, dispose, gather, mobilise, muster, organise. **3** *The host marshalled the guests into the room.* conduct, escort, lead, usher.
marshy *adjective The land was marshy.* boggy, spongy, swampy, waterlogged.
martial *adjective* **1** *martial law.* military. **2** *martial behaviour.* belligerent, combative, fighting, militant, pugnacious, warlike.
martyr *verb Stephen was martyred for his faith.* kill, put to death, torment, torture.
marvel *noun the marvels of modern medicine.* miracle, wonder. — *verb* **marvel at** *They marvelled at his achievements.* admire, be amazed by, be astonished by, be staggered by, be surprised by, wonder at.
marvellous *adjective a marvellous view. a marvellous achievement.* amazing, astonishing, astounding, breathtaking, brilliant (*informal*), cool (*informal*), excellent, extraordinary, fabulous (*informal*), fantastic (*informal*), fine, first-rate, glorious, grand, great, magnificent, miraculous, outstanding, phenomenal, prodigious, remarkable, sensational, spectacular, splendid, staggering, stunning (*informal*), stupendous, superb, terrific (*informal*), tremendous (*informal*), wonderful. OPPOSITE ordinary, terrible.
mascot *noun The team's mascot was a teddy bear.* charm, emblem, symbol, talisman.
masculine *adjective* **1** *a masculine hero.* macho, male, manly, virile; see also MANLY. OPPOSITE effeminate, feminine. **2** *She is masculine-looking.* butch (*informal*), mannish. OPPOSITE feminine.
mash *verb He mashed the pumpkin.* crush, pound, pulp, purée, squash.
mask *noun* **1** *a dentist's protective mask.* covering, goggles, shield, visor. **2** *I could not tell who was behind the mask.* cover-up, disguise. — *verb The robber's face was masked.* camouflage, conceal, cover up, disguise, hide, obscure, screen. OPPOSITE reveal.
mass[1] *noun* **1** *a mass of soap.* blob, block, cake, chunk, hunk, lump. OPPOSITE fragments. **2** *a mass of papers.* bundle, collection, heap, mound, mountain, pile, quantity, stack. **3** *a mass of people.* body, congregation, crowd, flock, gathering, herd, horde, host, mob, multitude, sea, swarm, throng. — *verb People massed outside Parliament House.* assemble, collect, congregate, flock, gather, herd, muster, rally. OPPOSITE disperse. — *adjective weapons of mass destruction.* extensive, general, large-scale, universal, wholesale, widespread.
Mass[2] *noun They go to Mass every Sunday.* Communion, Eucharist, Holy Communion, Lord's Supper.
massacre *noun the senseless massacre of thousands of people.* bloodbath, carnage, extermination, killing, murder, pogrom, slaughter, slaying. — *verb Thousands were massacred.* butcher, execute, exterminate, kill, murder, slaughter, slay.
massage *noun The massage relieved his aching back.* kneading, manipulation, rubbing.
massive *adjective* **1** *a massive statue.* colossal, enormous, giant, gigantic, heavy, hefty, hulking, immense, large, mammoth, monumental, solid. OPPOSITE tiny. **2** *a massive telephone bill.* astronomical, enormous, exorbitant, hefty, high, huge, large. OPPOSITE tiny. **3** *massive changes.* considerable, extensive, far-reaching, substantial, sweeping, vast, wide-ranging. OPPOSITE slight.
mast *noun a ship's mast.* pole, post, spar.
master *noun* **1** *He is the master of the house.* head, leader, lord, owner, ruler. **2** *masters and servants.* boss (*informal*), chief, employer, governor (*slang*), overseer. **3** *a ship's master* captain, skipper. **4** *the senior science master.* schoolmaster, teacher. **5** *a master at the piano.* ace, expert, genius, maestro, past master, professional, virtuoso, wizard. **6** *Many copies may be made from the master.* original. — *verb* **1** *She has mastered her fear of the dark.* conquer, control, overcome, subdue, tame, vanquish. OPPOSITE surrender to. **2** *He has mastered the secrets of Asian cookery.* get the hang of (*informal*), get the knack of, grasp, learn, understand.
masterful *adjective a masterful personality.* authoritative, bossy, commanding, controlling, dictatorial, domineering, forceful, imperious, magisterial, overbearing, powerful. OPPOSITE submissive.
masterly *adjective a masterly performance.* accomplished, adept, brilliant, consummate, deft, excellent, expert, skilful, virtuoso. OPPOSITE inept.
mastermind *noun* **1** *a mastermind at bridge.* ace, brain (*informal*), expert, genius, master, wizard. **2** *the scheme's mastermind.* architect, creator, designer, engineer, originator, planner. — *verb He masterminded the attack.* conceive, devise, direct, engineer, lead, orchestrate, organise, plan.
masterpiece *noun He studied the masterpieces of literature.* *chef-d'œuvre*, classic, masterwork, treasure.
mastery *noun* **1** *He had mastery over the people.* authority, control, domination, dominion, power, rule, supremacy, sway, the upper hand. OPPOSITE subservience. **2** *She had acquired a mastery of the language.* ability, command, competence, expertise, grasp, proficiency, skill, understanding. OPPOSITE incompetence.
mat *noun* carpet, doormat, matting, rug.
match *noun* **1** *His team won the match.* bout, competition, contest, game, rubber, tournament. **2** *He met his match.* equal, equivalent, peer, rival. CONTRASTS WITH inferior, superior. — *verb* **1** *Her qualifications matched the requirements of the job.* agree with, coincide with, correspond with, equal, fit, meet, suit. OPPOSITE differ from. **2** *The jacket matches the dress.* coordinate with, go with, harmonise with, team with, tone with. OPPOSITE clash with. **3** *He matched the names with the faces.* connect, couple, fit, join, link, pair, put together, unite. OPPOSITE mismatch.
mate *noun* **1** *A man always looks after his mates.* buddy (*informal*), chum (*informal*), cobber (*Australian informal*), companion, comrade, crony, friend, pal (*informal*). **2** (*informal*) *a single person in search of a mate.* husband, partner, spouse, wife. — *verb The animals mate once a year.* breed, copulate, couple, pair up.
material *noun* **1** *one of the raw materials.* constituent, element, ingredient, matter, stuff, substance. **2** *The dress is made from a fine material.* cloth, fabric, textile. **3** *She is gathering material for her project.* data, facts, ideas, information, observations.
materialise *verb* **1** *The ghost did not materialise.* appear, emerge, show up (*informal*), turn up. OPPOSITE vanish. **2** *The promised holiday did not materialise.* come to pass, eventuate, happen, occur, take place.
materialistic *adjective a materialistic person.* acquisitive, greedy, mercenary, worldly. OPPOSITE spiritual.
maternal *adjective* see MOTHERLY.
maternity *noun* **1** motherhood, motherliness. **2** *a maternity hospital.* see BIRTH.
mateship *noun* (*Australian*) *A spirit of mateship existed between the workers.* camaraderie, comradeship, friendship.

matey *adjective He found the new neighbour very matey.* chummy (*informal*), familiar, friendly, pally (*informal*), sociable. OPPOSITE unsociable.

matilda *noun* see SWAG.

matrimony *noun united in holy matrimony.* marriage, wedlock.

matt *adjective The walls are covered with a matt paint.* dull, flat. OPPOSITE gloss, glossy.

matted *adjective matted hair.* knotted, knotty, tangled, unkempt.

matter *noun* **1** *foreign matter.* vegetable matter. material, stuff, substance, thing. **2** *It's a serious matter.* affair, business, concern, issue, question, situation, subject, topic. **3** *What is the matter?* difficulty, problem, trouble, worry. — *verb It doesn't matter.* be important, count, signify.

matter-of-fact *adjective He was matter-of-fact about the accident.* down-to-earth, factual, unemotional. OPPOSITE emotional.

mature *adjective* **1** *a mature animal.* adult, developed, fully-fledged, grown, grown-up. OPPOSITE immature. **2** *a mature cheddar.* ripe, ripened. OPPOSITE unripe. — *verb* **1** *The child matured.* develop, grow up. **2** *The cheese matured.* age, mellow, ripen.

maturity *noun The child has reached maturity.* adulthood, coming of age, majority, manhood, womanhood.

maudlin *adjective After a drink he becomes maudlin.* mawkish, sentimental, soppy (*informal*), tearful, weepy (*informal*).

maul *verb The lion mauled the boy.* claw, lacerate, mutilate, savage, tear to pieces.

maverick *noun* dissenter, dissident, eccentric, individualist, law unto yourself, nonconformist, rebel. OPPOSITE conformist.

maxim *noun 'Many hands make light work' is his maxim.* adage, aphorism, axiom, motto, principle, proverb, rule, saying, slogan.

maximise *verb They want to maximise their profits.* boost, build up, enhance, improve, increase. OPPOSITE minimise.

maximum *noun* **1** *The temperature reached a maximum of 35°.* peak, top. OPPOSITE minimum. **2** *They allow a maximum of three visitors at a time.* ceiling, upper limit. — *adjective maximum speed. maximum security.* extreme, full, greatest, highest, most, top, utmost. OPPOSITE least, minimal.

maybe *adverb Maybe it will rain.* perchance (*old use*), perhaps, possibly. OPPOSITE definitely.

mayhem *noun There was mayhem in the streets after the rally.* bedlam, chaos, commotion, confusion, disorder, havoc, pandemonium, tumult, uproar, violence.

maze *noun The children were lost in the maze.* labyrinth, network, warren.

meadow *noun* field, grassland, lea (*poetical*), paddock, pasture.

meagre *adjective a meagre serving of peas.* mean, measly (*informal*), mingy (*informal*), paltry, scanty, skimpy, small, stingy. OPPOSITE ample, generous.

meal *noun The meal was served in the dining room.* banquet, breakfast, brunch, dinner, feast, lunch, luncheon, repast (*formal*), spread, supper, tea.

mean¹ *verb* **1** *I didn't mean to hurt you.* aim, intend, plan. **2** *Helmets are meant to protect cyclists.* design, intend. **3** *What does that word mean to you?* communicate, connote, convey, denote, express, imply, indicate, say, signify, stand for, symbolise.

mean² *adjective* **1** *She's too mean to make a donation.* miserly, niggardly, parsimonious, penny-pinching, stingy, tight-fisted. OPPOSITE generous. **2** *a mean trick. a mean person.* base, beastly (*informal*), contemptible, cruel, despicable, hard-hearted, lousy (*informal*), low-down, malicious, nasty, spiteful, unkind. OPPOSITE kind. **3** *a mean cottage.* humble, inferior, lowly, miserable, poor, shabby, sordid, squalid. OPPOSITE luxurious.

mean³ *adjective The mean mark was 65%.* average.

meander *verb* **1** *The stream meanders.* loop, snake, twist, wind, zigzag. **2** *They meandered through the bush.* ramble, roam, rove, wander.

meaning *noun* **1** *the meaning of what he said.* drift, gist, implication, import, purport, sense, significance. **2** *a life full of meaning.* importance, point, purpose, significance, value. OPPOSITE absurdity.

meaningful *adjective* **1** *a meaningful look.* deep, eloquent, expressive, pointed, significant, telling. OPPOSITE meaningless. **2** *He was seeking more meaningful work.* rewarding, satisfying, useful, worthwhile.

meaningless *adjective* **1** *meaningless words.* empty, hackneyed, hollow, superficial, trite. OPPOSITE meaningful. **2** *The abbreviations were meaningless to outsiders.* baffling, incomprehensible, inexplicable, nonsensical, puzzling, unintelligible. OPPOSITE comprehensible. **3** *His existence was no longer meaningless.* absurd, aimless, pointless, senseless, useless, worthless. OPPOSITE meaningful.

means *noun a means of achieving change.* agency, manner, medium, method, mode, process, way. — *plural noun a man of some means.* assets, funds, income, money, property, resources, riches, wealth.

meanwhile *adverb* **1** *Dinner won't be ready until 7 o'clock. We could play canasta meanwhile.* for now, in the interim, in the interval, in the meantime, in the meanwhile, meantime. **2** *She was reading a book. Her sister, meanwhile, was watching TV.* at the same time, concurrently, simultaneously.

measly *adjective* (*informal*) *a measly amount.* meagre, mean, mingy (*informal*), miserable, paltry, stingy. OPPOSITE generous, lavish.

measurable *adjective* **1** *a measurable improvement.* appreciable, considerable, discernible, noticeable, perceptible, significant. OPPOSITE imperceptible. **2** *The distance is measurable.* calculable, determinable, mensurable, quantifiable.

measure *noun* **1** *the measure of an object.* amount, capacity, dimensions, extent, magnitude, mass, measurement, proportions, quantity, size. **2** *The metre is a measure of length.* standard, unit. **3** *We used the measure to find out the object's size.* callipers, gauge, rule, ruler, scale, tape-measure, yardstick. **4** *measures to prevent accidents.* action, course, law, means, method, procedure, process, step, way. — *verb* **1** *He measured the rock's size.* assess, calculate, compute, determine, estimate, gauge, quantify, weigh. **2** *He measured the depth.* fathom, plumb, sound. □ **measure out** *She measured out their drinks.* apportion, deal out, dispense, distribute, dole out, mete out, ration out. **measure up to** *He doesn't measure up to their standards.* come up to, fulfil, meet, pass, reach, satisfy.

measurement *noun* **1** *the measurement of performance.* assessment, evaluation. **2** *He recorded the measurements of each of the items.* area, breadth, capacity, depth, dimension, extent, height, length, magnitude, mass, size, volume, weight, width.

meat-eating *adjective* carnivorous, flesh-eating. CONTRASTS WITH herbivorous, vegetarian.

mechanic *noun The mechanic fixed the washing machine.* repairman, technician, workman.

mechanical *adjective* **1** *a mechanical device.* automated, automatic, mechanised. OPPOSITE manual. **2** *a mechanical response.* automatic, instinctive, involuntary, reflex, unconscious, unthinking. OPPOSITE conscious.

mechanism *noun the clock mechanism.* action, machinery, movement, workings, works.

medal *noun a medal for bravery.* award, decoration, gong (*slang*), medallion, prize.

medallist *noun* champion, prizewinner, winner.

meddle *verb She likes to meddle in people's affairs.* butt in, interfere, intervene, intrude, poke your nose in, pry.

meddler *noun* busybody, interloper, intruder, Nosy Parker, stickybeak (*Australian informal*).

median *adjective the median score.* mid, middle.

mediate *verb The counsellor mediated between the two parties.* arbitrate, conciliate, intercede, intervene, liaise, negotiate.

mediator *noun He acted as mediator between the two sides.* arbitrator, broker, conciliator, go-between, intercessor, intermediary, middleman, negotiator, referee, umpire.

medical *adjective medical insurance.* health. — *noun* (*informal*) *The applicants had to undergo a medical.* check-up, health check, medical examination, physical (*informal*).

medication *noun The pharmacist dispensed the medication.* drug, medicament, medicine.

medicinal *adjective The herb has medicinal properties.* curative, healing, restorative, therapeutic.

medicine *noun The doctor prescribed a new medicine.* capsule, cure, drug, elixir, linctus, medicament, medication, pill, remedy, tablet, treatment.

mediocre *adjective The entries were of mediocre quality.* average, fair, indifferent, middling, ordinary, passable, run-of-the-mill, second-rate, so-so (*informal*). OPPOSITE outstanding.

meditate *verb* **1** *She meditated on his words.* cogitate, deliberate, muse, ponder, reflect, ruminate, think. **2** *He was meditating what action he would take.* consider, contemplate, plan, think over.

medium *noun* **1** *the happy medium.* average, compromise, mean, middle ground. OPPOSITE extreme. **2** *the use of television as a medium for advertising.* agency, channel, instrument, means, vehicle. — *adjective of medium size.* average, intermediate, middle, middling, moderate.

medley *noun a musical medley.* anthology, assortment, collection, miscellany, mixture, pot-pourri.

meek *adjective a meek and mild person.* compliant, deferential, docile, gentle, humble, mild, obedient, submissive, tame, unassuming. OPPOSITE assertive.

meet *verb* **1** *The friends meet every Friday in the mall.* assemble, come together, congregate, convene, gather, get together, join up, muster, rally, rendezvous. **2** *She met an old acquaintance today.* bump into (*informal*), come across, encounter, run into, see. **3** *There is a line where the two pieces meet.* abut, butt, connect, converge, intersect, join, touch. **4** *Have you met the new teacher?* be introduced to, make the acquaintance of. **5** *Australia meets England at the MCG.* compete against, oppose, play, take on. **6** *He did not know what dangers he would meet.* come up against, confront, encounter, experience, face, run into. **7** *This does not meet our standards.* come up to, comply with, measure up to, reach, satisfy. OPPOSITE fall short of. **8** *She agreed to meet the costs.* cover, deal with, pay, take care of.

meeting *noun* **1** *It was our first meeting.* appointment, date (*informal*), encounter, engagement, get-together (*informal*), rendezvous. **2** *a meeting of heads of churches.* assembly, conference, congregation, congress, convention, council, forum, gathering, rally, summit, synod. **3** *an athletics meeting.* competition, contest, event, fixture, meet.

melancholy *noun His melancholy gradually lifted.* blues, dejection, depression, despondency, gloom, misery, sadness, woe. OPPOSITE happiness. — *adjective She remained melancholy for years after her husband's death.* dejected, depressed, despondent, dismal, doleful, down, down in the dumps (*informal*), forlorn, gloomy, glum, heavy-hearted, in the doldrums, in low spirits, miserable, sad. OPPOSITE happy.

mellow *adjective* **1** *mellow fruit.* juicy, luscious, mature, ripe, sweet. OPPOSITE unripe. **2** *mellow sounds.* dulcet, rich, smooth, velvety. OPPOSITE harsh. **3** *He has become more mellow with age.* affable, amiable, easygoing, genial, gentle, kindly, pleasant, sympathetic. — *verb The wine has mellowed.* develop, mature, soften.

melodious *adjective melodious music.* dulcet, euphonious, harmonious, lyrical, musical, sweet, tuneful. OPPOSITE cacophonous.

melodramatic *adjective a melodramatic account of a minor incident.* exaggerated, histrionic, overdone, sensational, theatrical. OPPOSITE matter-of-fact.

melody *noun We sang familiar melodies.* air, strain, theme, tune.

melt *verb* **1** *The ice melted.* liquefy, thaw. OPPOSITE freeze, solidify. **2** *The lolly melts in the mouth.* dissolve, soften. OPPOSITE harden. **3** *Her compassion melted his hard heart.* disarm, mollify, soften, touch. OPPOSITE harden. □ **melt away** *Gradually the crowd melted away.* disappear, disperse, evaporate, fade away, vanish. OPPOSITE gather.

member *noun* **1** *a member of an association.* associate, fellow, subscriber. **2** *members of the same subset.* component, constituent, element.

membrane *noun The membrane is ruptured.* film, integument, lining, sheet, skin, tissue.

memento *noun mementoes of a holiday.* keepsake, remembrance, reminder, souvenir.

memoirs *plural noun You don't have to be famous to write your memoirs.* autobiography, diary, life story, memories, recollections, reminiscences.

memorable *adjective a memorable speech. a memorable holiday.* historic, impressive, momentous, noteworthy, outstanding, remarkable, significant, striking, unforgettable. OPPOSITE unimpressive.

memorial *noun* see MONUMENT.

memorise *verb She memorised the address.* commit to memory, learn by heart, learn by rote, remember.

memory *noun* **1** *He is losing his memory.* recall, retention. **2** *memories of childhood.* recollection, remembrance, reminder, reminiscence, souvenir.

menace *noun* **1** *a menace to civilisation.* danger, hazard, risk, threat. **2** *She finds the cat a menace.* nuisance, pest. — *verb The dog menaced the visitor.* bully, frighten, intimidate, terrify, terrorise, threaten.

menacing *adjective a menacing look.* baleful, black, forbidding, hostile, intimidating, malignant, ominous, sinister, threatening. OPPOSITE friendly.

mend *verb* **1** *He mends cars.* fix, patch up, put right, repair, restore. OPPOSITE break, damage. **2** *You must mend your manners.* ameliorate, correct, improve, rectify, reform. □ **on the mend** *The patient is on the mend.* convalescing, getting better, improving, recovering, recuperating.

menial *adjective menial tasks.* degrading, demeaning, humble, lowly, servile, unskilled. OPPOSITE dignified. — *noun He was treated as a menial.* dogsbody (*informal*), domestic, drudge, lackey, minion, servant, underling.

mental *adjective* **1** *a mental challenge.* intellectual. **2** *mental illness.* psychiatric. OPPOSITE physical. **3** (*informal*) *The work is driving him mental.* see MAD.

mentality *noun* **1** *a child of above-average mentality.* ability, brains, intellect, intelligence, IQ. **2** *He has a strange mentality.* attitude, disposition, mindset, outlook.

mention *verb He didn't mention the incident.* allude to, bring up, comment on, hint at, refer to, speak of, touch on. — *noun She made no mention of her discovery.* allusion, hint, indication, reference, remark.

mentor *noun He looked up to the professor as his mentor.* adviser, counsellor, guide, guru, instructor, supervisor, teacher, tutor.

mercenary *adjective a mercenary person.* avaricious, grasping, greedy, money-grubbing.

merchandise *noun Don't handle the merchandise.* commodities, goods, produce, stock, wares.

merchant *noun a wine merchant.* dealer, distributor, exporter, importer, salesman, supplier, trader, wholesaler.

merciful *adjective a merciful judge.* compassionate, forbearing, forgiving, gentle, humane, kind, lenient, mild, sympathetic, tender-hearted, tolerant. OPPOSITE merciless.

merciless *adjective a merciless judge.* callous, cruel, hard-hearted, harsh, heartless, implacable, inhuman, inhumane, pitiless, relentless, remorseless, ruthless, severe, strict, unforgiving, unsympathetic. OPPOSITE merciful.

mercy *noun He showed great mercy towards the offender.* clemency, compassion, forbearance, forgiveness, grace, kindness, lenience, pity, sympathy, tolerance. OPPOSITE harshness.

merge *verb* **1** *The two companies merged.* amalgamate, combine, consolidate, join forces, unite. OPPOSITE separate. **2** *The two lanes merge.* converge, join, meet.

merit *noun* **1** *This book shows merit.* excellence, goodness, quality, value, worth. **2** *Each of the proposals had its merits.* advantage, good point, strength, virtue. OPPOSITE fault. — *verb This article merits your attention.* be entitled to, be worthy of, deserve, justify, warrant.

meritorious *adjective a prize for meritorious achievement.* commendable, creditable, excellent, good, honourable, laudable, praiseworthy. OPPOSITE reprehensible.

merriment *noun* see MIRTH.

merry *adjective a merry group of people.* cheerful, convivial, gleeful, happy, high-spirited, jolly, jovial, joyous, light-hearted, lively. OPPOSITE sad.

merry-go-round *noun* carousel, roundabout, whirligig.

merrymaking *noun The merrymaking went on until two in the morning.* celebrations, festivities, fun, partying, revelry, roistering, wassailing (*old use*).

mesh *noun The bag was made of mesh.* lacework, net, netting, network.

mesmerise *verb He was mesmerised by her smile.* bewitch, captivate, enthral, fascinate, hypnotise, magnetise.

mess *noun* **1** *The bedroom was in a mess.* chaos, confusion, disarray, muddle, shambles, shemozzle (*informal*), untidiness. **2** *Mess lay everywhere.* clutter, jumble, litter. **3** *He was in a mess.* difficulty, fix (*informal*), hot water (*informal*), pickle (*informal*), plight, predicament, spot (*informal*), trouble. **4** *They ate in the officers' mess.* canteen, dining room, refectory. — *verb* **1** *They messed up their desks.* clutter up, jumble, litter, muck up, untidy. OPPOSITE tidy. **2** *He messed up our plans.* botch, bungle, muck up (*informal*), ruin, spoil. **3** *The clock doesn't work since he messed around with it.* fiddle, interfere, meddle, play, tamper, tinker. □ **make a mess of** botch, bungle, make a hash of (*informal*), mess up, muddle, muff (*informal*), ruin, spoil.

message *noun* **1** *He sent a message to the minister.* announcement, bulletin, communication, communiqué, dispatch, letter, memo (*informal*), missive, news, note, notice, report, statement, tidings, word. **2** *She missed the book's message.* meaning, moral, point, teaching, theme. □ **get the message** (*informal*) *I had to tell him many times before he got the message.* catch on, comprehend, cotton on (*informal*), get it (*informal*), grasp it, latch on (*informal*), twig (*informal*), understand.

messenger *noun He acted as a messenger between the two parties.* ambassador, courier, envoy, go-between, herald.

messy *adjective* **1** *a messy room.* chaotic, cluttered, dirty, disorderly, jumbled, littered, mucked-up, muddled, topsy-turvy, untidy. OPPOSITE clean, neat, tidy. **2** *The customer had a messy appearance.* bedraggled, dirty, dishevelled, sloppy, slovenly, unkempt. OPPOSITE neat. **3** *a messy situation.* awkward, complicated, difficult, embarrassing, problematical, sticky (*informal*), ticklish, tricky.

metallic *adjective* **1** *metallic paint.* gleaming, glistening, lustrous, shiny. **2** *a metallic sound.* brassy, clanging, clanking, clinking, jangling, ringing, tinny.

metamorphosis *noun the metamorphosis of a grub into a butterfly.* change, conversion, mutation, transfiguration, transformation, transmutation.

metaphorical *adjective a metaphorical use of a word.* figurative. OPPOSITE literal.

mete *verb* **mete out** *He metes out their rewards.* allocate, allot, apportion, deal out, dispense, distribute, dole out, measure out.

meteoric *adjective a meteoric rise to fame.* brilliant, fast, overnight, quick, rapid, speedy, sudden, swift. OPPOSITE gradual, slow.

meter *noun The man read the electricity meter.* clock, dial, gauge, indicator.

method *noun* **1** *a research method.* approach, knack, manner, means, procedure, process, routine, system, technique, way. **2** *There's method in her madness.* design, order, orderliness, pattern, plan, structure, system.

methodical *adjective a methodical approach to his work.* careful, disciplined, logical, meticulous, orderly, organised, precise, structured, systematic, tidy. OPPOSITE careless, haphazard.

meticulous *adjective a meticulous worker.* accurate, careful, exact, fastidious, fussy, methodical, orderly, painstaking, precise, punctilious, scrupulous, thorough. OPPOSITE careless, slipshod.

mettle *noun He showed his mettle in the time of crisis.* boldness, bravery, courage, gameness, grit, guts (*informal*), intrepidity, nerve, pluck, spirit.

microbe *noun The microbe was examined under a microscope.* bacterium, bug (*informal*), germ, micro-organism, virus.

microphone *noun He installed a hidden microphone.* bug (*informal*), mike (*informal*).

microscopic *adjective microscopic writing.* little, minuscule, minute, small, tiny. OPPOSITE large.

middle *adjective in middle position.* central, halfway, intermediate, medial, median, mid, midway. — *noun* **1** *in the middle of Melbourne.* centre, core, heart, hub, nucleus. OPPOSITE outskirts. **2** *The belt goes round your middle.* midriff, stomach, waist.

middleman *noun They dealt directly with the supplier, avoiding the middleman.* agent, broker, distributor, go-between, intermediary.

middling *adjective The book is in middling condition.* average, fair, indifferent, mediocre, medium, ordinary, so-so (*informal*), unremarkable. OPPOSITE outstanding.

midget *noun The film starred a midget.* dwarf, lilliputian, pygmy. OPPOSITE giant. — *adjective a midget television set.* diminutive, little, miniature, minuscule, minute, small, tiny. OPPOSITE gigantic.

midst *noun* **in the midst of** **1** *in the midst of her friends.* amid, amidst, among, amongst, surrounded by. **2** *In the midst of their discussion the telephone rang.* during, halfway through, in the middle of.

mien *noun He has a distinguished mien.* air, appearance, bearing, demeanour, expression, look, manner.

might *noun He tugged with all his might.* energy, force, power, strength.

mighty *adjective* **1** *a mighty army.* indomitable, invincible, powerful, robust, strong, sturdy. OPPOSITE feeble. **2** *a mighty aircraft.* big, bulky, colossal, enormous, huge, immense, large, mammoth, massive, monstrous. OPPOSITE small.

migrant *noun* emigrant, immigrant, newcomer.

migrate *verb The birds migrate each winter.* emigrate, go overseas, immigrate, move, relocate, travel.

mild *adjective* **1** *In spring the weather is mild.* balmy, moderate, temperate, warm. OPPOSITE severe. **2** *She has a mild nature.* calm, docile, easygoing, gentle, kind, placid, serene, unassuming. OPPOSITE harsh. **3** *mild flavours.* bland, delicate, faint, subtle. OPPOSITE sharp, strong.

milestone *noun* **1** *The distance is engraved on the milestone.* distance marker, milepost. **2** *a milestone in her career.* landmark, red-letter day, turning point, watershed.

militant *adjective militant unionists.* aggressive, assertive, belligerent, defiant, pugnacious, pushy (*informal*), uncompromising. OPPOSITE passive.

military *adjective military personnel.* armed, army, defence, service. — *noun The country is being ruled by the military.* armed forces, army, defence forces, soldiers.

milky *adjective a milky liquid.* cloudy, opaque, white, whitish. OPPOSITE clear.

mill *noun a pepper mill.* grinder. — *verb* **1** *They are milling the corn.* crush, granulate, grind, pulverise. **2** *People milled around the entrance.* congregate, crowd, hover, mass, swarm, throng.

millstone *noun* **millstone round your neck** burden, load, responsibility, trouble, worry.

mimic *verb He mimics the politicians brilliantly.* ape, caricature, copy, imitate, impersonate, parody, send up (*informal*), take off.

mimicry *noun The comedian specialises in mimicry.* burlesque, caricature, imitation, impersonation, parody, send-up (*informal*), spoof (*informal*), take-off.

mince *verb The butcher minced the beef finely.* chop, cut, grind, hash.

mind *noun* **1** *He doesn't use his mind sometimes.* brain, common sense, head, imagination, intellect, intelligence, reasoning, sense, understanding, wits. **2** *He changed his mind.* attitude, intention, judgement, opinion, outlook, point of view, position, thoughts, view. **3** *She has a suspicious mind.* attitude, mentality, mindset. — *verb* **1** *He is minding the baby.* babysit, keep an eye on, look after, take care of, tend. OPPOSITE neglect. **2** *He doesn't mind the music.* be bothered by, dislike, object to, resent, take exception to. OPPOSITE like. **3** *Mind the low ceilings.* be careful of, beware of, look out for, take care with, watch out for. **4** *Mind what she says.* heed, listen to, mark, note, pay attention to, remember, take notice of. OPPOSITE ignore. □ **bring to mind** *He can't bring the name to mind.* recall, recollect, remember.

mind-boggling *adjective* amazing, astonishing, astounding, incredible, staggering, startling, unbelievable.

minder *noun* babysitter, bodyguard, carer, child-minder.

mindful *adjective She is mindful of the feelings of others.* alert (to), attentive (to), aware, careful, conscious, considerate, heedful, thoughtful, wary, watchful. OPPOSITE heedless.

mindless *adjective* **1** *the mindless dumping of waste into rivers.* careless, heedless, senseless, thoughtless, unintelligent, unthinking. **2** *Packing bags is a mindless job.* boring, mechanical, routine, tedious. OPPOSITE stimulating.

mine *noun* **1** *a coal mine.* colliery, excavation, pit, quarry, workings. **2** *a mine of information.* fund, source, storehouse, supply, treasury. — *verb He made his fortune mining gold.* dig for, excavate, extract.

mingle *verb* **1** *The flavours mingled in the cooking.* blend, combine, intermingle, merge, mix. OPPOSITE separate. **2** *The host got his guests to mingle.* circulate, mix, socialise.

mingy adjective (informal) a mingy increase of $2. meagre, mean, measly (informal), niggardly, paltry, stingy.

miniature adjective a doll's house with miniature furniture. diminutive, dwarf, little, microscopic, minuscule, minute, pocket-size, small, small-scale, tiny. OPPOSITE full-scale, large.

minimal adjective minimal change. imperceptible, marginal, minuscule, minute, negligible, slight, small, subtle, token. OPPOSITE maximum.

minimise verb The firm tried to minimise costs. cut, decrease, diminish, keep down, lessen, reduce. OPPOSITE maximise.

minimum noun 1 The minimum required to be present is fifteen. least, lowest. 2 an overnight minimum of 5°. low. OPPOSITE maximum. — adjective a minimum wage. basic, least, lowest, smallest. OPPOSITE maximum.

minister noun a church minister. archbishop, archdeacon, bishop, chaplain, clergyman, clergywoman, cleric, curate, deacon, dean, evangelist, father, padre, parson, pastor, preacher, priest, rector, vicar. OPPOSITE layperson. — verb minister to She ministers to the needy. attend to, care for, cater to, help, tend.

minor adjective a minor issue. inconsequential, insignificant, lesser, petty, slight, small, subordinate, trivial, unimportant. OPPOSITE major. — noun Minors are not allowed in the club. adolescent, child, juvenile, teenager, youngster, youth. OPPOSITE adult.

minstrel noun a medieval minstrel. bard, entertainer, musician, performer, singer, troubadour.

mint verb 1 They minted a new dollar coin. cast, coin, make, produce, strike. 2 The word has been recently minted. coin, invent, make up.

minute¹ noun It was all over in a minute. flash, instant, jiffy (informal), moment, tick (informal), trice. ☐ minutes plural noun We read the minutes of the last meeting. account, notes, proceedings, record, summary.

minute² adjective 1 She took minute sips. little, microscopic, minuscule, small, tiny. OPPOSITE huge. 2 a minute examination of the specimen. close, detailed, exhaustive, meticulous, thorough. OPPOSITE superficial.

miracle noun Jesus performed many miracles. marvel, wonder.

miraculous adjective a miraculous recovery. amazing, astonishing, astounding, extraordinary, incredible, marvellous, mysterious, phenomenal, remarkable, supernatural, unbelievable, wonderful.

mirage noun a mirage in the desert. hallucination, illusion, phantasm, vision.

mirror noun He admired himself in the mirror. glass, looking-glass. — verb The trees were mirrored in the lake. reflect.

mirth noun The mood at the party was one of mirth. amusement, cheerfulness, festivity, fun, gaiety, glee, happiness, hilarity, jollity, joviality, laughter, merriment, merrymaking, rejoicing, revelry. OPPOSITE sadness.

misappropriate verb The clerk was accused of misappropriating funds. embezzle, misuse, steal, take.

misbehaviour noun Unhappiness was the cause of her misbehaviour. bad manners, delinquency, disobedience, misconduct, naughtiness, playing up (informal), rebelliousness, unruliness.

miscalculate verb He miscalculated the quantities. misjudge, overestimate, overvalue, underestimate, undervalue.

miscarriage noun 1 The pregnancy ended in a miscarriage. spontaneous abortion. 2 a miscarriage of justice. breakdown, collapse, error, failure.

miscellaneous adjective a miscellaneous collection of games. assorted, different, diverse, mixed, motley, varied, various.

mischief noun 1 Left alone, they got up to mischief. high jinks, misbehaviour, misconduct, naughtiness, playfulness, playing up (informal), pranks, shenanigans (informal). 2 He caused a lot of mischief with this rumour. damage, harm, hurt, injury, trouble.

mischievous adjective 1 a mischievous child. devilish, impish, naughty, playful, roguish. OPPOSITE goody-goody. 2 mischievous gossip. destructive, harmful, hurtful, injurious, malicious, malignant, spiteful. OPPOSITE harmless.

misconduct noun 1 The child's misconduct disrupted his schooling. misbehaviour, naughtiness, playing up (informal), unruliness. 2 The doctor was guilty of professional misconduct. impropriety, malpractice, mishandling, mismanagement.

misconstrue verb He misconstrued all that was said. misapprehend, misinterpret, misread, misunderstand.

miscreant noun They caught the miscreant. baddy (informal), criminal, evildoer, rascal, scoundrel, villain, wretch, wrongdoer.

misdemeanour noun punished for her misdemeanours. crime, misdeed, offence, sin, transgression, wrongdoing.

miser noun That miser won't give you anything. cheapskate (informal), hoarder, scrooge, skinflint, tightwad (informal). OPPOSITE spendthrift.

miserable adjective 1 He was miserable while his friend was away. crestfallen, dejected, depressed, desolate, despondent, disconsolate, doleful, downcast, down-hearted, forlorn, gloomy, glum, heavy-hearted, melancholy, sad, sorrowful, unhappy, woebegone, wretched. OPPOSITE happy. 2 miserable weather. abysmal (informal), appalling (informal), atrocious (informal), depressing, dismal, dreadful (informal), dreary, inclement, lousy (informal), terrible (informal), unpleasant. OPPOSITE fine.

miserly adjective a miserly person. close-fisted, mean, mingy (informal), niggardly, parsimonious, penny-pinching, stingy, tight-fisted. OPPOSITE generous.

misery noun 1 Nothing will lift her out of her misery. blues, depression, despair, distress, gloom, grief, melancholy, sadness, sorrow, torment, unhappiness, woe, wretchedness. OPPOSITE happiness. 2 the misery associated with poverty. adversity, affliction, deprivation, discomfort, hardship, misfortune, suffering, trouble. OPPOSITE comfort. 3 (informal) She's such a misery! complainer, grouch (informal), grumbler, malcontent, moaner, wet blanket, whinger (informal).

misfit noun The new boy was a complete misfit. fish out of water, maverick, nonconformist, square peg in a round hole.

misfortune noun 1 a series of misfortunes. accident, affliction, blow, calamity, catastrophe, disaster, misadventure, mishap, reverse, setback, trial, tribulation, trouble. 2 Amy saw herself as a victim of mis-

fortune. adversity, bad luck, mischance. OPPOSITE good luck.

misgiving noun We have serious misgivings about the project. anxiety, apprehension, doubt, fear, hesitation, qualm, question, reservation, second thoughts, uncertainty, worry.

misguided adjective The officer was well-intentioned but misguided. foolish, misdirected, misinformed, misled, mistaken, unwise.

mishap noun see MISFORTUNE.

misinterpret verb He deliberately misinterpreted the rules. misapprehend, misconstrue, misread, misunderstand.

misjudge verb She misjudged the distance and crashed into the wall. exaggerate, get wrong, miscalculate, overestimate, underestimate.

mislay verb Joe has mislaid his keys. lose, misplace.

mislead verb The advertiser misled people about the product's usefulness. bluff, con (informal), deceive, delude, dupe, fool, hoax, hoodwink, kid (informal), lead astray, lie, misguide, misinform, take for a ride (informal), take in, trick.

misleading adjective a misleading comment. ambiguous, confusing, deceptive, equivocal.

mismanagement noun He was blamed for the mismanagement of the project. bungling, maladministration, mishandling.

misplace verb Simon has misplaced his keys. lose, mislay.

misprint noun see MISTAKE.

misrepresent verb The papers misrepresented the committee's findings. distort, falsify, misquote, misreport, twist.

miss verb 1 He missed football to play chess. absent yourself from, forgo, give up, skip. OPPOSITE attend. 2 She missed her opportunity. let go, let pass, let slip, lose, pass up. OPPOSITE seize. 3 Miss a line. leave, omit, skip. 4 He never misses a mistake. disregard, gloss over, ignore, overlook, pass over. 5 Would you miss television if you didn't have a set? crave for, long for, pine for, want, yearn for. 6 If we go this way we can miss the centre of the city. avoid, bypass, dodge, steer clear of. OPPOSITE hit, reach. ☐ miss out He missed out a word. forget, leave out, omit, overlook, pass over, skip. OPPOSITE include.

misshapen adjective a misshapen foot. contorted, crooked, deformed, distorted, malformed, twisted, warped.

missile noun They attacked the target with missiles. projectile; [kinds of missile] arrow, ballistic missile, bomb, boomerang, bullet, dart, grenade, guided missile, harpoon, javelin, rocket, shell, spear, torpedo.

missing adjective 1 One volume was missing. gone, lost, mislaid, misplaced, removed. 2 The cat is missing. absent, disappeared, gone, gone astray, lost. OPPOSITE present.

mission noun 1 The group was sent on a fact-finding mission. assignment, campaign, exercise, expedition, operation, quest, undertaking. 2 Cathie knows her mission in life. calling, purpose, vocation.

missionary noun apostle, evangelist, preacher.

mist noun It was hard to see through the mist. cloud, fog, haze, smog, steam, vapour.

mistake noun He made a mistake. blooper (informal), blue (Australian informal), blunder, booboo (slang), clanger (informal), error, faux pas, gaffe, howler (informal), miscalculation, misjudgement, misprint, mix-up, oversight, slip, slip-up (informal), typo (informal).

— verb 1 He mistook my meaning. confuse, get wrong, misapprehend, misconstrue, misinterpret, misunderstand. 2 I mistook her for her sister. confuse with, mix up with, take for.

mistreat verb He was fined for mistreating the dog. abuse, harm, hurt, ill-treat, maltreat, manhandle, molest, torment.

mistress noun 1 the cat's mistress. keeper, owner. 2 the senior science mistress. schoolmistress, teacher. 3 His wife discovered he had a mistress. girlfriend, lover.

mistrust verb She mistrusted their methods. distrust, doubt, have misgivings about, question, suspect. OPPOSITE trust. — noun a mistrust of science. distrust, scepticism, suspicion, wariness. OPPOSITE trust.

misty adjective a misty day. foggy, hazy. OPPOSITE clear.

misunderstand verb The student misunderstood the teacher's comments. get wrong, misapprehend, misconstrue, misinterpret, misjudge, misread, mistake. OPPOSITE understand.

misunderstanding noun a misunderstanding of the rules. confusion, misapprehension, misconception, misinterpretation, misjudgement, misreading, mistake, mix-up.

misuse noun a misuse of funds. a misuse of power. abuse, misappropriation, squandering, waste.

mitigate verb 1 The drug mitigated the pain. alleviate, appease, assuage, diminish, ease, lessen, lighten, moderate, mollify, palliate, reduce, relieve, soften, soothe, subdue, weaken. OPPOSITE increase, intensify. 2 The circumstances mitigated the crime. excuse, extenuate.

mix verb 1 Mix the eggs into the butter and sugar mixture. add, beat, blend, combine, fold, incorporate, integrate, stir, whip, whisk. 2 She mixes business with pleasure. combine, join, merge, mingle, unite. OPPOSITE separate. 3 He mixes well at parties. be sociable, fraternise, mingle, socialise. — noun The correct mix of oil and vinegar. proportions, ratio; see also MIXTURE. ☐ mix up 1 They mixed up the cards. jumble up, muddle up, rearrange, shuffle. 2 He mixed up their names. confuse, muddle. 3 She was mixed up in the robbery. embroil, implicate, involve, tie up.

mixed adjective 1 a mixed group of people. assorted, diverse, miscellaneous, motley, varied. OPPOSITE uniform. 2 a mixed breed. crossbred, hybrid, mongrel.

mixed-up adjective (informal) He's not crazy: just a bit mixed-up. confused, maladjusted, muddled, screwed-up (informal).

mixture noun a mixture of things. alloy, amalgam, assortment, blend, collection, combination, compound, concoction, cross, hash, hotchpotch, hybrid, jumble, medley, mix, patchwork, pot-pourri, rag-bag, variety.

moan noun 1 The patient's moans were pitiful. groan, wail, whimper. 2 She had a moan about the amount of homework. beef (slang), complaint, grievance, gripe (informal), grizzle (informal), grumble, whine, whinge (informal). — verb 1 The dog moaned with pain. groan, howl, wail, whimper, whine. 2 He's always moaning about something. beef (slang), complain, gripe (informal), grizzle (informal), grumble, whine, whinge (informal).

mob noun 1 an angry mob of protesters. bunch, crowd, crush, gathering, herd, horde, lot, mass, multitude, pack, rabble, throng. 2 (Australian) a mob of animals. flock, group, herd. — *verb The princess's admirers mobbed her.* besiege, crowd round, gather round, surround, swarm round.

mobile *adjective a mobile toy library.* movable, portable, transportable, travelling. OPPOSITE stationary.

mobilise *verb They mobilised their troops.* assemble, gather, marshal, muster, organise, rally. OPPOSITE demobilise.

mock *verb The spectators mocked the player when he dropped the ball.* chiack (*Australian informal*), deride, imitate, jeer at, make fun of, mimic, pay out (*informal*), poke fun at, ridicule, scoff at, scorn, sling off at (*Australian informal*), sneer at, take the mickey out of (*informal*), taunt. OPPOSITE praise. — *adjective a mock battle.* fake, imitation, pretend (*informal*), pretended, sham, simulated. OPPOSITE real.

mockery *noun* **1** *He was subjected to public mockery.* derision, disdain, jeering, ridicule, scorn. **2** *They made a mockery of justice.* farce, joke, pretence, travesty.

mode *noun* **1** *a mode of instruction.* approach, form, manner, means, method, practice, procedure, system, technique, way. **2** *the latest mode.* custom, fashion, style, trend, vogue.

model *noun* **1** *an architect's model of the finished house.* archetype, copy, dummy, miniature, mock-up, prototype, replica, representation. **2** *the latest model of car.* design, style, type, version. **3** *The clothes are displayed by the models.* mannequin. **4** *a model of a student.* archetype, epitome, exemplar, ideal, paragon. — *adjective a model pupil.* excellent, exemplary, ideal, perfect. — *verb* **1** *He modelled a pig out of clay.* cast, form, make, mould, sculpt, shape. **2** *The Australian show is modelled on a British one.* base, copy.

moderate *adjective* **1** *moderate prices.* average, fair, intermediate, medium, middling, modest, reasonable. OPPOSITE excessive. **2** *a moderate climate.* mild, temperate. OPPOSITE extreme. — *verb* **1** *He moderated his behaviour. She moderated her voice.* check, curb, quieten down, restrain, soften, subdue, tame, temper, tone down. **2** *The wind moderated.* abate, calm down, die down, ease, subside.

moderately *adverb moderately fast.* fairly, pretty, quite, rather, reasonably, slightly, somewhat.

modern *adjective modern ideas.* contemporary, current, fashionable, innovative, new, newfangled (*derogatory*), present, progressive, recent, trendy (*informal*), up-to-date, with it (*informal*). OPPOSITE old, old-fashioned.

modernise *verb The new owners modernised the bathroom.* rejuvenate, renovate, update.

modest *adjective* **1** *Neil was modest about his achievements.* humble, quiet, unassertive, unassuming. OPPOSITE conceited. **2** *a modest increase.* moderate, slight, small. OPPOSITE substantial. **3** *a modest house.* humble, lowly, ordinary, simple, unpretentious. OPPOSITE ostentatious. **4** *The modest ones undressed in the cubicles.* bashful, coy, self-conscious, shy. OPPOSITE brazen, immodest.

modify *verb* **1** *They modified their original design.* adapt, adjust, alter, change, refine, revise, transform, vary. **2** *The adjective modifies the noun.* limit, qualify, restrict.

modulate *verb She modulated her voice.* adjust, alter, change, moderate, regulate, temper, tone down, vary.

module *noun The furniture comes in modules.* component, part, piece, unit.

moist *adjective a moist atmosphere.* clammy, damp, dank, dewy, humid, muggy, steamy, wet. OPPOSITE dry.

moisten *verb Moisten the soil before planting.* damp, dampen, irrigate, soak, spray, water, wet. OPPOSITE dry.

moisture *noun The timber was damaged by moisture.* condensation, damp, dampness, dew, humidity, liquid, steam, vapour, water, wetness. OPPOSITE dryness.

molest *verb The child molested the cat.* abuse, annoy, bother, harass, ill-treat, maltreat, mistreat, persecute, pester, tease, torment.

mollify *verb He knows how to mollify angry customers.* appease, calm, pacify, placate, quiet, soothe, subdue. OPPOSITE incense.

molten *adjective molten gold.* liquefied, liquid, melted. OPPOSITE solidified.

moment *noun* **1** *I'll be with you in a moment.* flash, instant, jiffy (*informal*), minute, second, tick (*informal*), trice, two shakes (*informal*). OPPOSITE eternity (*informal*). **2** *At this moment he walked in.* instant, juncture, point, stage. **3** *a matter of great moment.* consequence, gravity, import, importance, significance.

momentary *adjective a momentary feeling of happiness.* brief, ephemeral, fleeting, passing, short, short-lived, temporary, transient. OPPOSITE lasting.

momentous *adjective a momentous decision.* crucial, fateful, grave, historic, important, significant, weighty. OPPOSITE unimportant.

momentum *noun The campaign is gathering momentum.* force, impetus, strength.

monarch *noun the reigning monarch.* emperor, empress, head, king, queen, ruler, sovereign.

monarchist *noun* royalist.

monarchy *noun* empire, kingdom, realm.

monastery *noun Monks live in a monastery.* abbey, cloister, friary, lamasery (*Buddhism*), priory, religious house.

monastic *adjective He enjoys the monastic life.* ascetic, austere, cloistered, reclusive, secluded, solitary, spartan.

money *noun* **1** *He never carries any money.* banknotes, cash, coins, currency, dosh (*slang*), dough (*slang*), lucre (*derogatory*), notes, paper money, ready money. **2** *You need money to start a business.* assets, capital, finance, funds, means, resources, riches, wealth.

mongrel *noun Our dog is a mongrel.* bitser (*Australian informal*), crossbreed, hybrid. OPPOSITE pedigree dog.

monitor *noun* **1** *a school monitor.* prefect. **2** *a computer monitor.* display terminal, screen, VDU, visual display unit. — *verb The doctor monitored the baby's progress.* check, keep an eye on, keep track of, observe, record, watch.

monk *noun* abbot, brother, friar, lama (*Buddhism*), prior, religious.

monkey *noun* **1** *We saw the monkeys at the zoo.* simian. **2** *The child's a little monkey.* devil, imp, rascal, rogue, scallywag, scamp.

monolithic *adjective a monolithic statue.* colossal, enormous, gigantic, huge, large, massive, monumental.

monologue *noun They listened patiently to his monologue.* address, lecture, oration, sermon, soliloquy, speech.

monopolise *verb The project monopolised his time.* dominate,

preoccupy, take over. OPPOSITE share.

monotonous *adjective* **1** *a monotonous voice.* boring, droning, dull, expressionless, flat, singsong, soporific, unexpressive. OPPOSITE expressive. **2** *monotonous work.* boring, dreary, dull, humdrum, mechanical, repetitive, routine, tedious, unvarying. OPPOSITE interesting, varied.

monster *noun He was frightened by the monster in the story.* beast, bogyman, brute, bunyip (*Australian*), demon, devil, dragon, fiend, giant, ogre.

monstrosity *noun The new skyscraper is a monstrosity.* eyesore, horror, monster.

monstrous *adjective* **1** *a monstrous plant.* abnormal, freakish, grotesque, misshapen, odd, ugly, unnatural, weird. **2** *a monstrous building.* colossal, enormous, gigantic, huge, immense, massive. **3** *a monstrous crime.* abhorrent, appalling, atrocious, brutal, cruel, despicable, detestable, fiendish, ghastly, heinous, hideous, horrible, horrid, outrageous, repulsive, savage, shocking, vile, wicked.

monument *noun a monument to our forefathers.* cairn, cenotaph, gravestone, headstone, mausoleum, memorial, obelisk, plaque, shrine, statue, tombstone.

monumental *adjective* **1** *a monumental novel.* classic, enduring, great, impressive, lasting, major. **2** *a monumental waste of money.* colossal, enormous, great, huge, immense, large, massive, monstrous, stupendous, terrific (*informal*), tremendous.

mood *noun* **1** *Her mood changed.* disposition, frame of mind, humour, spirits, state of mind, temper. **2** *the mood of the meeting.* atmosphere, attitude, feeling.

moody *adjective* **1** *His financial problems made him moody.* blue, depressed, dismal, gloomy, glum, irritable, melancholy, morose, peevish, sulky, sullen, testy, tetchy, unhappy. OPPOSITE cheerful. **2** *You don't know what to expect with such a moody person.* changeable, erratic, inconsistent, mercurial, temperamental, unpredictable, volatile. OPPOSITE stable.

moon *noun Triton is a moon of Neptune.* satellite.

moor[1] *noun* (*British*) *They walked on the moor.* fell, heath.

moor[2] *verb He moored the boat.* anchor, berth, dock, secure, tie up.

moorings *plural noun a boat's moorings.* anchorage, berth.

moot *adjective a moot point.* arguable, controversial, debatable, disputable, undecided, unresolved. OPPOSITE indisputable.

mop *verb She mopped the floor.* clean, sponge, wash, wipe.

mope *verb She spent days moping after her friend left.* brood, fret, languish, mooch (*informal*), moon, pine.

moral *adjective* **1** *a moral code.* ethical. **2** *His behaviour was entirely moral.* above board, blameless, decent, ethical, good, honourable, principled, proper, right, righteous, upright, virtuous. OPPOSITE immoral, unethical. — *noun The story has a moral.* lesson, message, principle, teaching.

morale *noun The team's morale is high.* confidence, self-confidence, spirit.

morality *noun a person of the highest morality.* decency, ethics, fairness, goodness, honour, integrity, morals, principles, rectitude, scruples, standards, virtue.

morbid *adjective* **1** *morbid thoughts.* ghoulish, grim, gruesome, macabre, sick, unwholesome. **2** *She was feeling morbid.* depressed, gloomy, glum, melancholy, morose, pessimistic. OPPOSITE cheerful. **3** *a morbid growth.* diseased, pathological, unhealthy. OPPOSITE healthy.

more *adjective more lollies. more income.* additional, extra, further, other, reserve, spare, supplementary. OPPOSITE fewer, less.

moreover *adverb It was an unkind remark; moreover, it was untrue.* also, besides, further, furthermore, in addition.

morgue *noun* mortuary.

moron *noun* see IDIOT.

morose *adjective He is always sourfaced and morose.* bad-tempered, churlish, depressed, dismal, dour, gloomy, glum, lugubrious, moody, sour, sulky, sullen, surly, taciturn, unsociable. OPPOSITE happy.

morsel *noun a morsel of cheese.* bit, bite, fragment, mouthful, nibble, piece, scrap, sliver, taste, titbit.

mortal *adjective* **1** *our mortal existence.* earthly, ephemeral, human, transient, worldly. OPPOSITE immortal. **2** *a mortal wound.* deadly, fatal, lethal. **3** *He lived in mortal fear.* deep, extreme, grave, intense, severe. — *noun I am only a mere mortal.* human being, man, person, woman.

mortify *verb She was mortified when they found out.* abase, abash, chagrin, discomfit, embarrass, humble, humiliate, shame.

mortuary *noun* morgue.

most *noun He received the most.* bulk, lion's share, majority. OPPOSITE least. — *adverb Her story was most amusing.* exceedingly, extremely, highly, very. □ **make the most of** *He makes the most of every opportunity.* capitalise on, exploit, profit by, take advantage of.

mostly *adverb She works mostly at home.* chiefly, for the most part, generally, in general, largely, mainly, on the whole, predominantly, primarily, principally, usually.

motel *noun They spent the night at a motel.* hotel, inn, motor inn.

mother *noun* matriarch; [*informal terms of address*] ma, mama, mamma, mammy, mom (*American*), mum, mummy. — *verb She was good at mothering her children.* care for, fuss over, look after, nurse, nurture, protect, raise, rear, tend.

motherly *adjective The child had a motherly way with the kittens.* caring, gentle, kind, loving, maternal, protective, tender.

motif *noun* **1** *The fabric has a paisley motif.* decoration, design, feature, pattern. **2** *The motif recurs throughout the work.* idea, leitmotif, subject, theme.

motion *noun* **1** *All motion is restricted.* locomotion, mobility, movement. **2** *The motion was put to the meeting.* proposal, recommendation, suggestion. — *verb He motioned to her to come forward.* beckon, gesticulate, gesture, indicate, nod, signal, wave.

motionless *adjective He remained motionless.* at rest, immobile, inert, paralysed, static, stationary, still, stock-still, transfixed. OPPOSITE moving.

motivate *verb* **1** *His action was motivated by self-interest.* actuate, drive, influence, inspire, prompt, provoke. **2** *The teacher wasn't able to motivate her pupils.* galvanise, inspire, stimulate.

motivation *noun She was lacking in motivation.* ambition, drive, impetus, inspiration, stimulus.

motive *noun* *a motive for the crime.* grounds, motivation, purpose, reason.
motley *adjective* **1** *The clown was dressed in motley material.* harlequin, mottled, multicoloured, variegated. OPPOSITE plain. **2** *a motley collection.* assorted, disparate, diverse, heterogeneous, miscellaneous, mixed, varied. OPPOSITE homogeneous.
motor *noun* engine.
motorcycle *noun* bike (*informal*), motor bike (*informal*).
motorcyclist *noun* biker, bikie (*Australian informal*).
mottled *adjective* *mottled eggs.* blotchy, dappled, flecked, marbled, motley, speckled, spotty, variegated. OPPOSITE plain.
motto *noun* *The school motto is 'Semper fidelis'.* adage, maxim, proverb, saying, slogan, watchword.
mould[1] *verb* **1** *She moulded a cup out of clay.* cast, fashion, forge, form, model, sculpt, shape. **2** *The school helped to mould his character.* develop, form, influence, make, shape.
mould[2] *noun* *The bread was stale and had mould on it.* fungus, mildew.
mouldy *adjective* **1** *The food went mouldy.* bad, mildewed, off, rotten, stale. **2** *The cupboard smelt mouldy.* damp, musty, stale.
mound *noun* **1** *a mound of stones.* cairn, heap, pile, pyramid, stack. **2** *We climbed the mound.* hill, hillock, hummock, knoll.
mount *verb* **1** *She mounted the stairs.* ascend, clamber up, climb, go up. OPPOSITE descend. **2** *He mounted the horse.* climb on, get astride, get on, straddle. OPPOSITE dismount. **3** *Fears mounted for their safety.* escalate, grow, heighten, increase, rise. OPPOSITE diminish. **4** *They mounted the photographs in the album.* fix, install, place, position, put. **5** *They mounted an attack.* arrange, carry out, launch, organise, set up, stage.
mountain *noun* **1** *He climbed the mountain.* alp, ben (*Scottish*), bluff, elevation, hill, mount, peak, pinnacle, range, tier (*Tasmania & early South Australia*). **2** *a mountain of letters. mountains of work.* heap (*informal*), load (*informal*), lot (*informal*), pile (*informal*), stack (*informal*), swag (*Australian informal*), ton (*informal*).
mourn *verb* *He mourned for his dead wife.* grieve, lament, sorrow, weep. OPPOSITE rejoice.
mournful *adjective* *She had a mournful expression.* dismal, doleful, funereal, gloomy, lugubrious, melancholy, sad, sombre, sorrowful. OPPOSITE joyful.
mouth *noun* **1** *She closed her mouth.* gob (*slang*), jaws, lips, trap (*slang*). **2** *the mouth of a cave.* entrance, opening, outlet, portal. **3** *the mouth of the river.* estuary. OPPOSITE head, source.
mouthful *noun* **1** *only one mouthful of pie left.* bit, bite, morsel, nibble, spoonful. **2** *He took a mouthful of tea.* gulp, sip, sup, swallow, swig (*informal*).
movable *adjective* *movable furniture.* mobile, portable, transportable. OPPOSITE built-in, fixed.
move *verb* **1** *They've moved things around.* change, remove, shift, swap, switch, transfer, transport, transpose. **2** *I moved out of the way of the ball.* bolt, dart, jump, leap, shift, step; see also RUN. **3** *Don't move!* budge, fidget, flinch, jerk, quiver, shift, stir, sway, tremble, turn, twitch, wince, wriggle. **4** *The snake moved through the grass.* slink, slip, slither, wiggle, wriggle, writhe. **5** *The skater moves gracefully on the ice.* dance, flow, glide, skate, slide. **6** *They sold their house and moved to a new suburb.* relocate, shift, transfer, transplant; see also MIGRATE. **7** *The work moves slowly.* advance, develop, go on, proceed, progress. OPPOSITE stagnate. **8** *I was moved to say something.* drive, impel, induce, influence, motivate, persuade, prompt, provoke, stimulate, stir. OPPOSITE deter. **9** *He moved that the report be accepted.* propose, put forward, recommend, suggest. — *noun* **1** *You mustn't make a move.* gesture, motion, movement. **2** *Each player has had his move.* chance, go, opportunity, shot (*informal*), turn. **3** *a wise move.* act, action, initiative, measure, step, tactic.
movement *noun* **1** *Every movement is painful to him.* action, activity, gesture, motion, move, step, stroke. **2** *army movements.* exercise, manoeuvre, operation. **3** *the anti-war movement.* faction, group, lobby, organisation, party; see also CAMPAIGN. **4** *a movement towards shorter working hours.* evolution, progress, shift, swing, tendency, trend. **5** *the movements of a symphony.* division, part, section.
movie *noun* (*informal*) *They watched a movie.* film, flick (*informal*), motion picture, moving picture, picture, video.
moving *adjective* *a very moving performance.* emotional, inspiring, poignant, rousing, stirring, touching. OPPOSITE unemotional.
mow *verb* *He mowed the grass.* clip, cut, trim.
much *adjective* *They don't have much money.* abundant, a lot of (*informal*), ample, copious, plentiful. OPPOSITE little. — *noun* *He has much to say.* a great deal, heaps (*informal*), loads (*informal*), lots (*informal*), plenty, stacks (*informal*), volumes. OPPOSITE little. — *adverb* **1** *He feels much better.* a great deal, a lot, considerably, decidedly, far, greatly. OPPOSITE slightly. **2** *Their answers were much the same.* about, almost, approximately, nearly, virtually.
muck *noun* **1** *The farmer's boots were covered in muck.* droppings, dung, manure. **2** (*informal*) *The children traipsed muck into the house.* dirt, filth, mud. — *verb* **muck up 1** *The children mucked up the room in five minutes.* disorganise, jumble, mess up, muddle, turn upside down. OPPOSITE tidy up. **2** *We mucked up the dinner.* botch, bungle, mess up, ruin, spoil.
mud *noun* *Her boots were covered in mud from the garden.* dirt, filth, mire, muck (*informal*), silt, slime, sludge.
muddle *verb* **1** *Her papers were muddled.* disorganise, jumble, mess up, mix up, muck up. **2** *He gets muddled when you interrupt him.* bewilder, confuse, disorient, fluster, mix up. — *noun* *The place is in a muddle.* chaos, clutter, confusion, disarray, jumble, mess, shambles.
muddy *adjective* **1** *muddy ground.* boggy, slimy, waterlogged, wet. OPPOSITE dry. **2** *muddy shoes.* dirty, filthy, mucky (*informal*). **3** *muddy liquid.* cloudy, impure, murky, turbid. OPPOSITE clear.
muff *verb* (*informal*) *He had his opportunity but he muffed it.* blow (*slang*), botch, bungle, fluff (*slang*), mess up, spoil.
muffle *verb* **1** *He muffled himself up before going out in the cold.* cover, wrap. **2** *The blanket muffled the sounds.* dampen, deaden, dull, mute, quieten, soften, stifle, suppress. OPPOSITE amplify.
muffler *noun* **1** *She wore a muffler.* scarf, wrap. **2** *a sound muffler.* deadener, silencer.
mug *noun* **1** *She drank from a mug.* beaker, cup, tankard. **2** (*informal*) *There's always some mug who'll buy it.* bunny (*Australian informal*), duffer, dupe, fool, muggins (*informal*), simpleton, soft touch, sucker (*informal*). — *verb* *The lady was mugged outside the bank.* assault, attack, rob.
muggy *adjective* *The muggy weather made people irritable.* close, humid, oppressive, steamy, sticky, stuffy, sultry.
mulga *noun* (*Australian*) *They live out in the mulga.* backblocks (*Australian*), bush, country, donga (*Australian*), mallee (*Australian*), nevernever (*Australian*), outback (*Australian*), scrub, sticks (*informal*).
mull *verb* **mull over** *He kept mulling it over.* consider, contemplate, deliberate on, dwell on, meditate on, ponder, reflect on, review, think over.
multicoloured *adjective* *a multicoloured shirt.* harlequin, motley, particoloured, pied, variegated. OPPOSITE plain.
multicultural *adjective* *a multicultural society.* cosmopolitan, multiracial, pluralist.
multinational *adjective* *a multinational company.* international, worldwide.
multiple *adjective* *This gadget has multiple uses.* manifold, many, numerous, several, sundry, various.
multiply *verb* *Rabbits multiply rapidly.* breed, increase, proliferate, propagate, reproduce.
multitude *noun* **1** *He was greeted by an angry multitude.* crowd, horde, mob, rabble, swarm, throng. **2** *a multitude of problems.* host, mass, myriad, swag (*Australian informal*).
mumble *verb* *He mumbled something unintelligible.* babble, murmur, mutter. — *noun* *All he heard was a mumble.* babble, murmur, mutter.
mumbo-jumbo *noun* *His lecture was all mumbo-jumbo to me.* bunkum, double Dutch, gibberish, gobbledegook (*informal*), hocus-pocus, humbug, nonsense, poppycock (*informal*).
munch *verb* *He munched a carrot.* bite, chew, chomp, crunch, eat, gnaw.
mundane *adjective* *mundane tasks such as cleaning and shopping.* commonplace, dreary, dull, everyday, ordinary, prosaic, routine, unexciting, uninspiring, uninteresting.
municipal *adjective* *a municipal library.* civic, community, council, district, local.
munificent *adjective* *a munificent gift.* bountiful, generous, lavish, liberal, philanthropic. OPPOSITE stingy.
munitions *plural noun* *The factory supplies munitions to the army.* ammunition, arms, ordnance, weapons.
mural *noun* *They painted a mural on the old building.* fresco, wall-painting.
murder *noun* *He was found guilty of murder.* assassination, extermination, genocide, homicide, killing, massacre, slaughter, slaying. CONTRASTS WITH manslaughter. — *verb* *He murdered many people.* assassinate, bump off (*slang*), do in (*slang*), exterminate, kill, massacre, slaughter, slay.
murderer *noun* *The police caught the murderer.* assassin, cutthroat, hit man (*slang*), killer, murderess.
murderous *adjective* *murderous tendencies.* bloodthirsty, brutal, deadly, homicidal, savage, vicious.
murky *adjective* **1** *It was too murky to see clearly.* dark, dim, dull, dusky, foggy, gloomy, shadowy. OPPOSITE bright. **2** *murky waters.* cloudy, dirty, impure, muddy, turbid. OPPOSITE clear.
murmur *noun* **1** *the murmur of the stream.* babble, burble, drone, hum. **2** *There wasn't a murmur from them.* peep, sigh, sound. **3** *murmurs of discontent.* complaint, grumble, muttering, rumbling, undercurrent, whisper. — *verb* *He murmured something to the person next to him.* mumble, mutter, whisper.
muscle *noun* **1** *It takes a bit of muscle to lift an engine.* brawn, might, muscularity, strength. **2** *Trade unions with plenty of muscle.* clout (*informal*), influence, might, power, strength. — *verb* **muscle in on** (*informal*) *He muscled in on our game.* butt in on, force your way into, intrude on, push your way into.
muscular *adjective* *He became more muscular through rowing.* athletic, beefy, brawny, burly, hefty, nuggety (*Australian*), robust, sinewy, strapping, strong, sturdy, thickset. OPPOSITE weedy.
muse *verb* *He mused upon the meaning of life.* contemplate, meditate, ponder, reflect, ruminate, speculate, think.
mush *noun* *The vegetables were a mush through overcooking.* mash, pap, pulp, purée.
mushroom *verb* *Cinema complexes mushroomed in the suburbs.* burgeon, develop, expand, grow, pop up, proliferate, shoot up, spring up, sprout.
mushy *adjective* **1** *mushy vegetables.* mashed, puréed, sloppy, soft, squidgy (*informal*), squishy (*informal*). **2** *a mushy film.* corny (*informal*), maudlin, mawkish, romantic, schmaltzy, sentimental, soppy (*informal*).
music *noun* **1** *music-making.* harmony, melody. **2** *the music for the film.* score, soundtrack.
musical *adjective* *musical sounds.* dulcet, euphonious, harmonious, lyrical, melodic, melodious, sweet, tuneful. OPPOSITE cacophonous.
musician *noun* artist, busker, composer, entertainer, instrumentalist, maestro, muso (*slang*), performer, player, soloist, virtuoso, vocalist.
must *noun* (*informal*) *An umbrella is a must.* essential, necessity, requirement.
muster *verb* **1** *He mustered his troops.* assemble, collect, gather, marshal, mobilise, rally. **2** *She finally mustered the courage to tell him.* find, gather, screw up, summon. **3** (*Australian*) *The stockman mustered the cattle.* herd, round up.
musty *adjective* *The house had a musty smell.* damp, fusty, mildewed, mouldy, stale, stuffy. OPPOSITE fresh.
mutation *noun* *a gene mutation.* alteration, change, metamorphosis, transformation, variation.
mute *adjective* **1** *He has been mute from birth.* dumb, speechless. **2** *She remained mute during the discussion.* mum (*informal*), quiet, silent, tight-lipped, tongue-tied, uncommunicative. OPPOSITE vocal.
muted *adjective* *muted colours.* pale, pastel, soft, subdued, toned down. OPPOSITE intense.
mutilate *verb* *The body was badly mutilated.* damage, destroy, disfigure, dismember, injure, maim, mangle.
mutinous *adjective* *The crew became mutinous.* defiant, disobedient, insubordinate, rebellious. OPPOSITE compliant.

mutiny *noun The sailors planned a mutiny.* insurrection, rebellion, revolt, riot, rising, uprising. — *verb They mutinied soon after leaving port.* rebel, revolt, riot, rise up.

mutter *verb He muttered his disapproval.* grumble, mumble, murmur. — *noun We heard a mutter from behind us.* complaint, grumble, mumble, murmur.

mutual *adjective* **1** *The feeling is mutual.* reciprocal, reciprocated, requited. **2** *(informal) our mutual friend.* common, joint, shared.

muzzle *noun an animal's muzzle.* jaws, mouth, nose, snout. — *verb He has to muzzle his greyhound.* bridle, control, gag, restrain.

myriad *adjective myriad consequences.* countless, incalculable, infinite, innumerable, manifold, numerous, untold. OPPOSITE few.

myriads *plural noun myriads of insects.* army, horde, host, millions, multitude, scores, swarm, thousands, throng.

mysterious *adjective* **1** *mysterious events.* arcane, baffling, bizarre, curious, incomprehensible, inexplicable, mystical, mystifying, puzzling, strange, supernatural, uncanny, weird. OPPOSITE straightforward. **2** *He was mysterious about his past.* cagey (*informal*), cryptic, enigmatic, evasive, inscrutable, secretive. OPPOSITE open.

mystery *noun* **1** *the mystery of their disappearance.* conundrum, enigma, problem, puzzle, riddle, secret. **2** *divine mysteries.* miracle, wonder.

mystical *adjective These rites have a mystical significance.* allegorical, arcane, cryptic, esoteric, hidden, mysterious, mystic, occult, spiritual, supernatural, symbolic, transcendental.

mystify *verb The police were mystified by the disappearance.* baffle, bamboozle (*informal*), bewilder, confound, confuse, perplex, puzzle.

myth *noun* **1** *He is reading the Greek myths.* fable, legend, narrative, story, tale. **2** *It is a myth that all natural foods are good for you.* delusion, fallacy, falsehood, fantasy, fiction, lie, untruth.

mythical *adjective* **1** *Theseus was a mythical hero.* fabled, legendary, mythological. **2** *a mythical friend.* fictitious, imaginary, invented, made-up, non-existent. OPPOSITE real.

Nn

nab *verb* (*informal*) *The police nabbed the culprit.* apprehend, arrest, capture, catch, collar (*informal*), nail, nick (*slang*), seize.

nag *verb He nagged them to clean their rooms.* badger, harass, harp on at, hassle (*informal*), henpeck, hound, keep on at, pester, scold.

nagging *adjective a nagging suspicion. a nagging toothache.* continuous, niggling, persistent.

nail *verb She nailed the top to the uprights.* attach, fasten, fix, hammer, join, pin, tack. □ **nail down** *It was hard to nail him down to a time.* bind, commit, pin down.

naive *adjective* **1** *naive children.* artless, ingenuous, innocent, simple, unaffected, unsophisticated. OPPOSITE sophisticated. **2** *He must be naive to believe that.* credulous, green, gullible, inexperienced, unsuspecting, unworldly. OPPOSITE wary.

naked *adjective The swimmers were naked.* bare, in the altogether (*informal*), in your birthday suit

(*informal*), nude, starkers (*slang*), unclothed, uncovered, undressed. OPPOSITE clothed.

name *noun* **1** *What name does she go by?* alias, appellation, assumed name, Christian name, false name, family name, first name, given name, last name, maiden name, nickname, nom de plume, penname, pet name, pseudonym, surname, title. **2** *Another name for a 'Nosy Parker' is a 'stickybeak'.* label, term, word. **3** *He made a name for himself.* see REPUTATION. — *verb* **1** *They named her Bronwyn.* baptise, call, christen, dub, nickname. **2** *He was named as the next leader.* appoint, choose, designate, nominate, pick, select. **3** *The report named the culprits.* identify, mention, specify.

nameless *adjective The donor wished to remain nameless.* anonymous, unidentified, unnamed.

nanny *noun A nanny looks after their children.* nurse, nursemaid.

nap *noun He has a nap after lunch.* catnap, doze, forty winks, kip (*slang*), lie-down, rest, shut-eye (*informal*), siesta, sleep, slumber, snooze.

napkin *noun table napkins.* serviette.

nappy *noun a baby's nappy.* diaper (*American*), napkin.

narcotic *adjective The drug has a narcotic effect.* anaesthetic, dulling, hypnotic, numbing, sedative, soporific.

narrate *verb She narrated the episode to me.* describe, recount, relate, tell.

narrative *noun a narrative of her misfortunes.* account, chronicle, report, saga, story, tale, yarn.

narrow *adjective* **1** *a narrow passage.* confined, constricted, cramped, strait (*old use*), tight. OPPOSITE broad, wide. **2** *a narrow tube.* fine, slender, slim, thin. OPPOSITE thick. **3** *a narrow circle of friends.* exclusive, limited, restricted, small. OPPOSITE wide. **4** *a narrow escape.* close, near. — *verb They have narrowed the gap.* close up, diminish, lessen, reduce. OPPOSITE widen.

narrow-minded *adjective* biased, bigoted, blinkered, hidebound, illiberal, inflexible, intolerant, parochial, petty, prejudiced, rigid, small-minded. OPPOSITE broad-minded.

nasty *adjective* **1** *a nasty taste.* awful, disagreeable, disgusting, foul, nauseating, objectionable, offensive, repulsive, revolting, sickening, unpalatable, unpleasant, vile, yucky (*informal*). OPPOSITE pleasant. **2** *nasty weather.* appalling (*informal*), atrocious (*informal*), bad, dreadful (*informal*), foul, lousy (*informal*), rotten (*informal*), shocking (*informal*), stormy, terrible (*informal*). OPPOSITE fair, fine. **3** *a nasty person.* beastly, contemptible, dastardly, ill-tempered, malevolent, malicious, malignant, mean, obnoxious, sinister, spiteful, unkind, vicious, vindictive. OPPOSITE kind.

nation *noun people of all nations.* community, country, land, people, race, society, state.

national *adjective* **1** *national costume.* ethnic. **2** *a national strike.* countrywide, general, nationwide. — *noun Australian nationals.* citizen, native, resident, subject.

nationalism *noun* chauvinism, jingoism, patriotism.

native *adjective* **1** *She developed her native talent.* inborn, inherent, innate, natural. OPPOSITE acquired. **2** *a native inhabitant.* aboriginal, indigenous, original. — *noun If you want to know the way, ask a native.* inhabitant, local, resident.

natural *adjective* **1** *natural resources.* crude, raw, unprocessed, unrefined.

OPPOSITE man-made, refined. **2** *Her reaction was quite natural.* normal, ordinary, reasonable, understandable. OPPOSITE surprising, unnatural. **3** *natural leadership skills.* inborn, inherent, innate, instinctive, intuitive, native. OPPOSITE acquired. **4** *He's a very natural person.* artless, authentic, down-to-earth, genuine, spontaneous, unaffected, unpretentious, unsophisticated. OPPOSITE artificial.

nature *noun* **1** *She has a kind nature.* character, disposition, make-up, personality, spirit, temperament. **2** *the nature of the disease.* character, characteristics, features, peculiarities, properties, qualities. **3** *things of this nature.* kind, sort, type, variety.

naughty *adjective a naughty child.* bad, contrary, disobedient, impish, incorrigible, mischievous, perverse, undisciplined, unruly, wayward, wilful. OPPOSITE well-behaved.

nausea *noun Her nausea was caused by the rocking of the ship.* biliousness, motion-sickness, queasiness, seasickness, sickness, travel-sickness.

nauseating *adjective a nauseating smell.* disgusting, foul, objectionable, offensive, repulsive, revolting, sickening.

nauseous *adjective feeling nauseous.* bilious, carsick, queasy, seasick, sick.

nautical *adjective* marine, maritime, naval, seafaring, seagoing.

navel *noun* belly button (*informal*), umbilicus.

navigate *verb* **1** *The boat navigated the river.* cross, sail, traverse. **2** *He navigated the boat through the channel.* direct, guide, manoeuvre, pilot, sail, steer.

navy *noun* armada, fleet, flotilla.

near *adverb She came near.* alongside, at close quarters, close, nigh, within close range, within cooee (*Australian informal*). — *preposition They live near the school.* adjacent to, around, close to, in the vicinity of. — *adjective* **1** *The end is near.* approaching, at hand, close, imminent, impending, in sight, looming. **2** *a near escape.* close, narrow. — *verb We neared the shore.* approach, draw near to.

nearby *adjective a nearby field.* adjacent, adjoining, close, neighbouring.

nearly *adverb* **1** *nearly a thousand people.* about, almost, approximately, around, close to, in the region of, in the vicinity of, roughly. **2** *He is nearly forty.* almost, approaching, nigh on, pushing (*informal*). **3** *He is nearly ready.* almost, practically, virtually.

near-sighted *adjective* myopic, short-sighted. OPPOSITE hypermetropic, long-sighted.

neat *adjective* **1** *a neat appearance.* clean, dapper, natty (*informal*), smart, spruce, tidy, trim. OPPOSITE scruffy, untidy. **2** *a neat office.* orderly, organised, shipshape, straight, tidy. OPPOSITE disorderly. **3** *neat writing.* careful, legible, readable. OPPOSITE messy. **4** *a neat solution.* clever, deft, dexterous, elegant, nifty (*informal*), simple, skilful. OPPOSITE clumsy. **5** *neat brandy.* pure, straight, unadulterated, undiluted. OPPOSITE diluted.

nebulous *adjective nebulous ideas.* fuzzy, hazy, imprecise, indefinite, obscure, uncertain, unclear, vague, woolly. OPPOSITE precise.

necessarily *adverb It does not necessarily follow.* automatically, inevitably, naturally, of necessity, perforce.

necessary *adjective* **1** *the necessary items for a trip.* compulsory, essen-

tial, indispensable, needed, obligatory, required, requisite, vital. OPPOSITE non-essential, unnecessary. **2** *the necessary consequence.* inevitable, inexorable, unavoidable.

necessitate *verb The new job will necessitate moving house.* call for, entail, involve, mean, require.

necessity *noun* **1** *A degree in computing is not a necessity.* essential, must (*informal*), need, prerequisite, requirement, requisite. **2** *She stole food out of dire necessity.* destitution, hardship, need, poverty, straits, want.

necklace *noun* beads, chain, choker, necklet.

need *noun* **1** *Her needs are few.* demand, desire, necessity, requirement, want. **2** *There is no need to worry.* call, cause, necessity, reason. **3** *The charity helps people in need.* crisis, destitution, hardship, poverty, want. — *verb* **1** *He needs a torch.* be short of, lack, require, want. **2** *They need your help.* depend on, rely on. **3** *Do you need to ask permission?* be compelled to, be obliged to, be required to, have to, must.

needle *noun a sewing needle.* bodkin, crewel, sharp.

needless *adjective needless worry.* inessential, pointless, uncalled-for, unjustifiable, unnecessary, useless. OPPOSITE necessary.

needlework *noun* embroidery, sewing.

needy *adjective The family is very needy.* deprived, destitute, disadvantaged, down and out, hard up (*informal*), impecunious, impoverished, indigent, penniless, poor, poverty-stricken, skint (*informal*). OPPOSITE affluent.

nefarious *adjective nefarious deeds.* abominable, atrocious, base, criminal, despicable, diabolical, evil, heinous, immoral, infamous, iniquitous, odious, vile, villainous, wicked. OPPOSITE good.

negate *verb The theory was negated by new evidence.* annul, cancel, contradict, disprove, invalidate, nullify, refute, void. OPPOSITE confirm.

negative *adjective* **1** *a negative reply.* contradictory, dissenting, objecting, opposing, refusing, rejecting. OPPOSITE affirmative, positive. **2** *a negative attitude.* antagonistic, defeatist, gloomy, pessimistic, reluctant, uncooperative, unenthusiastic, unwilling. OPPOSITE optimistic, positive.

neglect *verb* **1** *Don't neglect your duty.* disregard, forget, ignore, let go, let slide, let slip, overlook, shirk. OPPOSITE attend to. **2** *I neglected to tell you.* fail, forget, omit.

negligence *noun The accident was caused by negligence.* carelessness, forgetfulness, inattention, laxity, slackness, thoughtlessness. OPPOSITE attention, care.

negligent *adjective negligent in his duty.* careless, heedless, inattentive, neglectful, remiss, slack, thoughtless, unthinking. OPPOSITE careful.

negligible *adjective He drank a negligible amount.* imperceptible, insignificant, minuscule, minute, small, tiny, trifling, unimportant. OPPOSITE substantial.

negotiate *verb* **1** *The two sides are negotiating.* bargain, discuss, haggle, talk. **2** *They negotiated a contract.* agree on, arrange, settle, transact, work out. **3** *She easily negotiated the fence.* clear, cross, get over.

negotiator *noun* broker, facilitator, go-between, intermediary, mediator, peacemaker.

neighbourhood *noun The house is in a quiet neighbourhood.* area, community, district, locality, quarter, spot, suburb.

neighbouring *adjective a neighbouring block.* adjacent, adjoining, close, contiguous, nearby.

neighbourly *adjective a neighbourly person.* affable, considerate, friendly, helpful, hospitable, kind, kindly, obliging, sociable, thoughtful. OPPOSITE unfriendly.

nerve *noun* **1** *You need nerve to be a stuntman.* bravery, coolness, courage, daring, fearlessness, grit, guts (*informal*), intrepidity, mettle, pluck, spunk (*informal*). **2** (*informal*) *She had the nerve to ask for more.* audacity, boldness, cheek, effrontery, gall (*slang*), hide (*informal*), impertinence, impudence, insolence, presumption, temerity. □ **get on someone's nerves** annoy, drive someone up the wall (*informal*), exasperate, irritate, worry.

nerve-racking *adjective a nerve-racking experience.* stressful, tense, testing, trying, unnerving, worrying.

nervous *adjective Sam has always been a nervous type. The strange noises made him feel nervous.* afraid, agitated, alarmed, anxious, apprehensive, edgy, fidgety, flustered, frightened, highly-strung, jittery (*informal*), jumpy, nervy, neurotic, restive, shaky, tense, timid, timorous, twitchy, uneasy, uptight (*informal*), worried. OPPOSITE calm.

nervousness *noun Clare's nervousness disappeared after a minute on stage.* agitation, anxiety, apprehension, butterflies (*informal*), heebie-jeebies (*informal*), jitters (*informal*), nerves, stage fright, tension, trembling, uneasiness. OPPOSITE composure.

nest *noun a bird's nest.* eyrie, perch, roost.

nestle *verb She nestled in my arms.* cuddle, curl up, huddle, snuggle.

net[1] *noun Little creatures were caught in the net.* dragnet, drift-net, mesh, netting, network, trawl, web. — *verb He netted a big fish.* capture, catch, ensnare, snare, trap.

net[2] *adjective net income.* clear, disposable, take-home. OPPOSITE gross. — *verb We netted $50 from the sale.* clear, earn, gain, make, realise.

network *noun a network of highways.* complex, grid, system.

neurotic *adjective He has become neurotic.* anxious, irrational, obsessive, unbalanced, unstable.

neuter *verb The animals have been neutered.* castrate, desex, doctor, geld, spay, sterilise.

neutral *adjective* **1** *a neutral umpire.* detached, disinterested, impartial, independent, non-aligned, non-partisan, unbiased, uninvolved. OPPOSITE interested. **2** *Beige and grey are neutral colours.* colourless, dull, indefinite, intermediate, wishy-washy. OPPOSITE strong.

neutralise *verb The acid neutralises the alkali.* cancel (out), counteract, counterbalance, offset.

never-ending *adjective a never-ending supply of jokes.* constant, continuous, endless, everlasting, inexhaustible, infinite, limitless, unlimited. OPPOSITE limited.

never-never *noun* (*Australian informal*) *They live in the never-never.* backblocks, back of beyond, outback, the sticks (*informal*).

nevertheless *adverb It was strange, nevertheless true.* but, however, none the less, still, yet.

new *adjective* **1** *He bought a new car.* brand-new, unused. OPPOSITE second-hand, used. **2** *new ideas.* fresh, hot, innovative, latest, modern, newfangled (*derogatory*), novel, original, recent, red-hot, trendy (*informal*), up-to-date. OPPOSITE old. **3** *Everything was new to me.* strange, unfamiliar, unheard-of. OPPOSITE familiar. **4** *The club has a new member.* additional, another, extra. OPPOSITE long-standing. **5** *the new president.* incoming, succeeding. OPPOSITE past, retiring. **6** *The house was given a new appearance.* altered, changed, different, rejuvenated, renewed, renovated, restored, transformed. OPPOSITE same.

newcomer *noun* **1** *The town welcomes newcomers.* immigrant, migrant, new chum (*Australian informal*), stranger. **2** *a newcomer to the job.* beginner, novice, probationer, tiro, trainee. OPPOSITE old hand.

newly *adverb The house was newly painted.* freshly, just, lately, recently.

news *noun* **1** *She was anxious for news from home.* information, intelligence, tidings, word. **2** *He read the news.* announcement, bulletin, communication, communiqué, dispatch, message, press release, report, statement, story.

newsletter *noun Members are sent a monthly newsletter.* bulletin, magazine, report.

newspaper *noun Suzy writes for a newspaper.* broadsheet, daily, gazette, journal, paper, rag (*derogatory*), tabloid, weekly.

newsworthy *adjective a newsworthy story.* important, interesting, noteworthy, significant.

newsy *adjective* (*informal*) *a newsy letter.* gossipy, informative, interesting.

next *adjective* **1** *She was in the next room.* adjacent, adjoining, closest, nearest, neighbouring, next-door. **2** *the next day.* following, subsequent, succeeding. OPPOSITE preceding. — *adverb What happened next?* afterwards, subsequently, then. □ **next to 1** *He placed his chair next to mine.* alongside, beside, by, closest to, nearest to. **2** *next to impossible.* almost, close to, nearly, pretty well, virtually, well nigh.

nibble *verb He nibbled his food.* bite, gnaw, munch, peck at, pick at; see also EAT. — *noun a nibble of cake.* bite, morsel, mouthful, taste, titbit.

nice *adjective* **1** *We had a nice day.* agreeable, delightful, enjoyable, fabulous (*informal*), fantastic (*informal*), fine, good, great (*informal*), lovely, marvellous, pleasant, satisfactory, splendid, wonderful; see also EXCELLENT, GOOD. OPPOSITE awful, dreadful. **2** *a nice person.* agreeable, amiable, amicable, attractive, benevolent, benign, caring, charming, compassionate, congenial, considerate, delightful, friendly, good, good-natured, gracious, kind, kindly, likeable, pleasant, polite, sweet, sympathetic, thoughtful, understanding, winsome. OPPOSITE disagreeable, unpleasant. **3** *a nice distinction.* careful, delicate, fine, minute, precise, subtle. OPPOSITE approximate, rough.

nicety *noun the niceties of behaviour.* detail, finer point, refinement, subtlety.

niche *noun* **1** *a niche in the wall.* alcove, bay, nook, recess. **2** *She found her niche in life.* calling, place, slot, vocation.

nick *noun He made nicks in the timber with a knife.* cut, gouge, notch, score, scratch, snick. — *verb* **1** *He nicked himself while shaving.* cut, gash, scratch, snick. **2** (*slang*) *He was caught nicking books.* knock off (*slang*), lift, pilfer, pinch (*informal*), snatch, snitch (*informal*), steal, swipe (*informal*), take. **3** (*slang*) *The police have nicked him.* arrest, catch, nab (*informal*), pick up. □ **in good nick** (*informal*) in good condition, in good health, in good trim.

nickname *noun* alias, pet name, sobriquet. — *verb He was nicknamed 'Professor'.* call, christen, dub, rename.

niggardly *adjective* **1** *He was too niggardly to give a donation.* mean, miserly, parsimonious, penny-pinching, stingy, tight-fisted. OPPOSITE generous. **2** *a niggardly amount.* beggarly, meagre, mean, measly (*informal*), mingy (*informal*), paltry, scanty, stingy. OPPOSITE lavish.

niggle *verb He kept niggling over trifles.* carp, fuss, nag, nit-pick (*informal*), quibble.

niggling *adjective a niggling doubt.* annoying, lurking, nagging, persistent, worrying.

night *noun* dark, darkness, dusk, evening, nightfall, night-time.

nightly *adjective the cat's nightly wanderings.* after-dark, evening, night-time, nocturnal.

nightmarish *adjective a nightmarish experience.* dreadful, frightening, horrible, horrifying, scary, terrible, terrifying.

nil *noun The score was two games to nil.* love, none, nothing, nought, zero.

nimble *adjective a nimble ninety-year old.* active, agile, lithe, lively, nippy (*informal*), quick, sprightly, spry, swift. OPPOSITE clumsy, slow.

nip *verb* **1** *He nipped himself with the tweezers.* pinch, squeeze, tweak. **2** *The cat nipped her ankle.* bite, nibble. **3** *She nipped off the sideshoots.* break, clip, cut, snip.

nippy *adjective* (*informal*) *nippy weather.* biting, bitter, chilly, cold, freezing, icy.

nit-picking *noun* (*informal*) *His constant nit-picking was getting her down.* carping, cavilling, fault-finding, niggling, quibbling.

nobility *noun a member of the nobility.* aristocracy, peerage, upper class, upper crust (*informal*). OPPOSITE commoners.

noble *adjective* **1** *of noble birth.* aristocratic, blue-blooded, lordly, titled. OPPOSITE lowly. **2** *a noble character. noble sentiments.* exalted, generous, high-minded, honourable, lofty, selfless, virtuous, worthy. OPPOSITE base, ignoble. **3** *a noble building.* fine, grand, imposing, impressive, magnificent, majestic, splendid, stately. OPPOSITE modest.

nobleman *noun* aristocrat, grandee, lord, noble, peer; [*kinds of nobleman*] baron, count, duke, earl, marquess, marquis, viscount.

noblewoman *noun* aristocrat, lady, noble, peeress; [*kinds of noblewoman*] baroness, countess, duchess, marchioness, marquise, viscountess.

nobody *pronoun* none, no one. — *noun They treated him as a nobody.* lightweight, nonentity, nothing, pipsqueak (*informal*), small fry, unknown. OPPOSITE somebody.

nocturnal *adjective His nocturnal activities were suspicious.* after-dark, evening, nightly, night-time. OPPOSITE diurnal.

nod *verb* **1** *He nodded to the next customer.* gesture, indicate, motion, signal. **2** *She nodded her head.* bob, bow, incline. — *noun They were given a nod to begin.* gesture, sign, signal. □ **nod off** *Elsie nodded off in front of the TV.* doze off, drop off, drowse, fall asleep.

node *noun a node on a tree trunk.* bump, knob, knot, lump, nodule, protuberance, swelling.

noise *noun She could not sleep because of the constant noise.* bedlam, clamour, clatter, commotion, din, hubbub, hullabaloo, outcry, pandemonium, racket, row, rumpus, sound, tumult, uproar.

noisy *adjective* **1** *a noisy crowd.* boisterous, lively, rowdy, tumultuous, turbulent, uproarious, vociferous. OPPOSITE quiet. **2** *noisy music.* blaring, booming, deafening, discordant, grating, jarring, loud, piercing, raucous, shrill, strident, thundering. OPPOSITE soft.

nomad *noun He sold his house and became a nomad.* gypsy, itinerant, rover, traveller, vagabond, wanderer.

nomadic *adjective The people lead a nomadic life.* itinerant, migratory, peripatetic, roving, travelling, vagabond, vagrant, wandering.

nominal *adjective* **1** *a nominal Christian.* in name only, ostensible, professed, so-called, theoretical. OPPOSITE real, true. **2** *They paid only a nominal rent.* minimal, small, token.

nominate *verb* **1** *Five films were nominated for the award.* name, propose, put forward, recommend, submit, suggest. **2** *He was nominated as their spokesman.* appoint, choose, designate, elect, name, pick, select.

non-believer *noun* agnostic, atheist, freethinker, heathen, infidel, pagan, sceptic, unbeliever.

nonchalant *adjective She tried to appear nonchalant.* apathetic, blasé, calm, carefree, careless, casual, composed, cool, imperturbable, indifferent, laid-back (*informal*), unconcerned, unemotional, unexcited, unflappable (*informal*). OPPOSITE concerned.

non-committal *adjective a non-committal response.* cagey (*informal*), cautious, circumspect, evasive, guarded, indefinite, reserved, temporising, tentative, wary. OPPOSITE decisive.

nonconformist *noun Nonconformists were victimised.* dissenter, eccentric, heretic, iconoclast, individualist, maverick, misfit, radical, rebel.

nondescript *adjective a nondescript house in a dreary street.* bland, characterless, ordinary, plain, unexceptional, uninteresting, unremarkable. OPPOSITE distinctive.

nonentity *noun Some nonentity presented the prizes.* lightweight, nobody, small fry, unknown. OPPOSITE identity (*Australian informal*).

non-event *noun The fair turned out to be a non-event.* anticlimax, damp squib, disappointment, fizzer (*Australian informal*).

non-existent *adjective The monster turned out to be non-existent.* fictitious, hypothetical, imaginary, make-believe, mythical, pretend (*informal*), pretended, unreal. OPPOSITE real.

non-flammable *adjective Pyjamas should be made of non-flammable material.* fireproof, flameproof, incombustible, non-inflammable. OPPOSITE flammable, inflammable.

nonplussed *adjective The strange events left us nonplussed.* amazed, baffled, bamboozled (*informal*), bewildered, confounded, confused, dumbfounded, flabbergasted, flummoxed (*informal*), perplexed, puzzled, speechless, stunned, surprised.

nonsense *noun He talked a lot of nonsense.* balderdash, boloney (*informal*), borak (*Australian*), bunkum, claptrap, codswallop (*slang*), drivel, foolishness, garbage, gibberish, gobbledegook (*informal*), guff (*slang*), hogwash (*informal*), hooey (*informal*), humbug, inanity, kidstakes (*Australian informal*), mumbo-jumbo, piffle (*informal*), poppycock (*slang*), rot (*slang*), rubbish, silliness, stupidity, tommyrot (*slang*), trash, tripe (*informal*), twaddle. OPPOSITE reason, sense.

nonsensical *adjective a nonsensical idea.* absurd, crazy, fatuous, foolish, idiotic, inane, laughable, ludicrous, meaningless, preposterous, ridiculous, senseless, silly, stupid. OPPOSITE sensible.

non-stop *adjective* **1** *a non-stop train.* direct, express, through. **2** *non-stop laughter.* ceaseless, constant, continuous, endless, incessant, persistent, steady.

nook *noun She sat in her nook and sewed.* alcove, corner, cubby hole, niche, recess.

noon *noun* midday, noonday, twelve o'clock.

norm *noun compared to the norm.* average, benchmark, criterion, mean, pattern, rule, standard, usual, yardstick.

normal *adjective* **1** *under normal conditions.* average, conventional, customary, habitual, ordinary, regular, routine, standard, typical, usual. OPPOSITE abnormal. **2** *He wasn't normal after the accident.* balanced, rational, reasonable, sane. OPPOSITE odd, unbalanced.

nose *noun a bump on the nose.* beak (*informal*), conk (*slang*), muzzle, proboscis, snout. — *verb* **1** *The dog nosed her leg.* nudge, nuzzle, smell, sniff. **2** *Someone's been nosing around.* poke, prowl, pry, search, snoop (*informal*), stickybeak (*Australian informal*). **3** *The car nosed past them.* ease, edge, inch.

nosedive *noun The plane took a sudden nosedive.* descent, dive, drop, fall, plunge, swoop. — *verb Prices nosedived after Christmas.* crash, drop, fall, plummet, plunge. OPPOSITE soar.

nostalgia *noun nostalgia for the early days.* longing, pining, yearning.

nostalgic *adjective The photos of home made him nostalgic.* homesick, maudlin, sentimental, wistful.

nosy *adjective* (*informal*) *a nosy visitor.* curious, inquisitive, meddlesome, prying, snoopy (*informal*).

notable *adjective* **1** *a notable success.* conspicuous, important, noticeable, outstanding, remarkable, significant, striking. OPPOSITE insignificant. **2** *a notable historian.* celebrated, distinguished, eminent, famous, noted, prominent, renowned, well-known. OPPOSITE obscure, unknown.

notation *noun musical notation.* code, signs, symbols, system.

notch *noun The walker made notches in the trunks of the trees.* blaze, cut, nick, score, snick. — *verb He notched every tree which he passed.* cut, gouge, nick, score, snick. □ **notch up** *They notched up another victory.* achieve, gain, score.

note *noun* **1** *He made notes of their conversation.* minute, record. **2** *She wrote a note to the principal.* communication, epistle, letter, memo (*informal*), memorandum, message, missive. **3** *Buy an edition of the play with notes.* annotation, comment, endnote, explanation, footnote. **4** *a $100 note.* banknote, bill. OPPOSITE coin. **5** *He detected a note of optimism.* air, element, feeling, sound, tone. **6** *Take note of what she says.* attention, heed, notice. — *verb* **1** *We noted that he was smiling.* notice, observe, perceive, register, see. **2** *Note what he is telling you.* heed, mind, pay attention to. OPPOSITE ignore. **3** *He noted*

it in his diary. enter, jot down, mark, record, write down.

notebook *noun* exercise book, jotter, journal, logbook, memo book, pocketbook.

noted *adjective* see NOTABLE.

nothing *noun We were left with nothing.* nil, nought, zero, zilch (*informal*).

nothingness *noun a state of nothingness.* emptiness, non-existence, nothing, oblivion, vacuum, void.

notice *noun* **1** *He read the notice about coming events.* advertisement, announcement, circular, flyer, leaflet, letter, memo (*informal*), message, note, pamphlet, placard, poster, sign. **2** *She brought the matter to his notice.* attention, consideration. **3** *He gave two days' notice of the test.* advice, notification, warning. — *verb He noticed nothing unusual.* be aware of, catch sight of, detect, discern, note, observe, perceive, see, spot. OPPOSITE disregard, overlook.

noticeable *adjective a noticeable change.* clear, conspicuous, definite, discernible, distinct, manifest, marked, obvious, perceptible, pronounced, striking, visible. OPPOSITE imperceptible.

notification *noun You will receive official notification.* advice, announcement, communication, information, notice.

notify *verb* **1** *They haven't notified the relatives yet.* advise, alert, inform, tell, warn. **2** *He notified his intentions.* announce, declare, disclose, make known, proclaim, publish, report, reveal.

notion *noun a weird notion.* belief, concept, fancy, idea, opinion, thought.

notoriety *noun He achieved notoriety as a drug smuggler.* dishonour, disrepute, ignominy, infamy, scandal.

notorious *adjective a notorious criminal.* disreputable, infamous, scandalous, well-known.

nought *noun* cipher, nil, nothing, zero, zilch (*informal*).

nourish *verb* **1** *She nourishes her children well.* feed, nurture, provide for. **2** *He nourished the hope of becoming a writer.* cherish, foster, nurse, nurture.

nourishing *adjective Eat nourishing food.* healthy, nutritious, nutritive, wholesome.

novel *noun He reads historical novels.* fiction, saga, story, tale. — *adjective a novel idea.* different, innovative, new, original, strange, unfamiliar, unusual. OPPOSITE familiar, old.

novelty *noun* **1** *The novelty has worn off.* freshness, newness, originality, unfamiliarity. **2** *The show bags contain a few novelties.* bagatelle, knick-knack, trifle, trinket.

novice *noun a novice in the trade.* apprentice, beginner, learner, new chum (*Australian informal*), rookie (*informal*), tiro, trainee. OPPOSITE master, old hand.

now *adverb These things are happening now.* at present, at the moment, at this moment, at this point, at this stage, at this time, currently, nowadays.

noxious *adjective a noxious chemical.* damaging, deleterious, destructive, harmful, pernicious, poisonous, toxic. OPPOSITE harmless.

nuance *noun too fine a nuance to be appreciated.* difference, distinction, nicety, refinement, shade, subtlety.

nub *noun the nub of the problem.* core, crux, essence, gist, heart, kernel, nitty-gritty (*informal*), substance.

nuclear *adjective nuclear energy.* atomic.

nucleus *noun the nucleus of a new congregation.* basis, centre, core, heart, kernel.

nude *adjective nude bodies on the beach.* bare, exposed, naked, stripped, unclothed, undressed. OPPOSITE clothed. □ **in the nude** in the altogether (*informal*), in the raw, in your birthday suit (*informal*), starkers (*slang*).

nudge *verb He nudged the boy sitting next to him.* bump, dig in the ribs, elbow, jog, poke, prod, push, shove, touch.

nuggety *adjective* (*Australian*) *a nuggety footballer.* beefy, burly, hefty, husky, stocky, sturdy, thickset. OPPOSITE skinny.

nuisance *noun Her broken leg was a nuisance.* annoyance, bother, drag, hassle (*informal*), inconvenience, irritation, menace, pain (*informal*), pest, problem, trouble.

null *adjective The agreement was declared null and void.* annulled, invalid, nullified, worthless. OPPOSITE valid.

nullify *verb* **1** *The law has been nullified.* abolish, annul, cancel, invalidate, repeal, rescind, revoke, void. OPPOSITE ratify. **2** *One mistake nullified all their efforts.* cancel out, negate, neutralise, undo.

numb *adjective Her fingers were numb with cold.* asleep, deadened, insensible, paralysed. — *verb His foot was numbed by the cold.* anaesthetise, deaden, paralyse.

number *noun* **1** *the numbers from 1 to 5.* digit, figure, integer, numeral. **2** *The December number of the magazine is the biggest.* copy, edition, issue, publication. **3** *She sang two numbers at the concert.* item, piece, song. **4** *the number of those present.* amount, quantity, sum, total. — *verb The crowd numbered five thousand.* add up to, amount to, come to, total. □ **a number of** *a number of friends.* a few, several, some. **numbers of** *numbers of fans.* see MANY.

numeral *noun The children can write all their numerals legibly now.* digit, figure, integer, number.

numerous *adjective numerous examples.* abundant, copious, countless, innumerable, many, myriad, numberless, numbers of, untold. OPPOSITE few.

nun *noun* abbess, prioress, religious, sister.

nunnery *noun* abbey, cloister, convent, priory, religious house.

nurse *verb* **1** *Amy nursed her mother at home.* care for, look after, minister to, take care of, tend. **2** *She nursed the baby for nine months.* breastfeed, feed, suckle. □ **nursing home** convalescent home, hospice, hospital, hostel, institution, rest home, sanatorium.

nurture *verb* **1** *They nurtured their children lovingly.* bring up, care for, feed, look after, nourish, provide for, raise, rear. **2** *The school nurtures the pupils.* develop, discipline, educate, instruct, school, train. — *noun responsible for the children's nurture.* care, development, discipline, education, instruction, rearing, training, upbringing.

nut *noun* **1** *pine nuts.* kernel, seed. **2** (*informal*) *The person who did this was a nut.* crackpot (*informal*), crank, eccentric, fruitcake (*informal*), loony (*informal*), lunatic, madman, madwoman, maniac, nutcase (*informal*), nutter (*informal*), psychopath, weirdo (*informal*).

nutritious *adjective He only eats nutritious food.* healthy, nourishing, nutritive, wholesome. OPPOSITE unhealthy.

nutty *adjective* see CRAZY.

Oo

oath *noun* **1** *They swore an oath of allegiance.* pledge, promise, vow. CONTRASTS WITH affirmation. **2** *In his rage he uttered several unrepeatable oaths.* blasphemy, curse, expletive, obscenity, profanity, swear word.

obedient *adjective an obedient child.* biddable, compliant, disciplined, docile, dutiful, meek, submissive, tractable. OPPOSITE defiant, disobedient.

obese *adjective* see FAT.

obey *verb She obeys all the rules.* abide by, adhere to, comply with, follow, heed, keep to, observe, respect, stick to, submit to. OPPOSITE break, disobey.

object *noun* **1** *an unidentified flying object.* article, body, contraption (*informal*), device, entity, item, thing. **2** *The object of the exercise is to win support.* aim, goal, intention, objective, point, purpose. — *verb* **object to** *He objects to all their ideas.* complain about, criticise, disapprove of, dislike, find fault with, grumble at, knock (*informal*), mind, oppose, protest at, take exception to. OPPOSITE accept, approve.

objection *noun* **1** *Joe voiced his objection to the plan.* disagreement, disapproval, opposition, protest. OPPOSITE approval. **2** *Please state your objections in writing.* complaint, criticism, demur, grievance, quibble, reservation.

objectionable *adjective objectionable behaviour. an objectionable smell.* abhorrent, disagreeable, disgusting, foul, insufferable, intolerable, nasty, nauseating, obnoxious, offensive, on the nose (*Australian informal*), repugnant, repulsive, revolting, unacceptable, unbearable, unpleasant, vile. OPPOSITE acceptable, pleasant.

objective *adjective* **1** *objective evidence.* actual, concrete, factual, observable, real. **2** *an objective assessment.* detached, dispassionate, fair, impartial, just, unbiased, unprejudiced. OPPOSITE subjective. — *noun The group formulated its objectives.* aim, design, goal, intention, mission, object, purpose, target.

obligation *noun He has an obligation to attend practices.* commitment, duty, onus, requirement, responsibility.

obligatory *adjective an obligatory fine.* compulsory, mandatory, necessary, required. OPPOSITE optional, voluntary.

oblige *verb He was obliged to go.* bind, compel, constrain, force, require.

obliging *adjective An obliging man helped change the tyre.* accommodating, considerate, cooperative, courteous, helpful, kind, neighbourly. OPPOSITE unhelpful.

oblique *adjective an oblique line.* angled, diagonal, slanting, sloping.

obliterate *verb* **1** *Time has obliterated the unhappy memories.* blot out, cancel, efface, erase, expunge, rub out, wipe out. **2** *The bomb obliterated the entire camp.* annihilate, demolish, destroy, raze, wipe out.

oblivious *adjective oblivious of her surroundings.* forgetful, heedless, insensible, unaware, unconscious, unmindful. OPPOSITE aware.

oblong *noun* rectangle.

obnoxious *adjective an obnoxious character.* abhorrent, despicable, detestable, disagreeable, disgusting, hateful, horrible, insufferable, loathsome, nasty, objectionable, odious, offensive, repugnant, repulsive, unpleasant, vile. OPPOSITE delightful, likeable.

obscene *adjective obscene language.* blue, crude, dirty, filthy, foul, improper, indecent, lewd, offensive, pornographic, rude, smutty, unprintable, vulgar. OPPOSITE decent.

obscenity *noun* **1** *The book was banned on the grounds of obscenity.* immorality, indecency, lewdness, pornography, smuttiness, vulgarity. OPPOSITE decency. **2** *He uttered obscenities.* curse, expletive, profanity, swear word.

obscure *adjective* **1** *an obscure shape at the window.* dark, dim, faint, fuzzy, hazy, indistinct, misty, murky, shadowy. OPPOSITE distinct. **2** *an obscure writer.* forgotten, little-known, unheard-of, unimportant, unknown. OPPOSITE famous. **3** *The meaning is obscure.* abstruse, arcane, cryptic, enigmatic, esoteric, hidden, inscrutable, mysterious, uncertain, unclear, vague. OPPOSITE plain. — *verb* **1** *The main issue has been obscured.* blur, cloud, confuse, eclipse, muddy. OPPOSITE reveal. **2** *The peak was obscured by mist.* block out, blot out, cloud, conceal, cover, envelop, hide, mask, shroud.

obsequious *adjective The obsequious assistant irritated her.* crawling (*informal*), deferential, fawning, grovelling, kowtowing, servile, slimy, smarmy (*informal*), subservient, sycophantic, toadying, truckling.

observant *adjective The postman is observant.* alert, attentive, aware, perceptive, sharp-eyed, shrewd, vigilant, watchful, wide awake (*informal*). OPPOSITE unobservant.

observation *noun* **1** *The tower is for the observation of wild animals.* surveillance, viewing, watching. **2** *She made an observation about the lateness of the hour.* comment, remark, statement.

observe *verb* **1** *He observed the children playing. He observed changes.* contemplate, detect, discover, look at, monitor, note, notice, perceive, see, spot, study, survey, view, watch, witness. **2** *Observe the law.* abide by, adhere to, comply with, follow, heed, keep, obey. OPPOSITE disobey. **3** *Do they observe Remembrance Day?* celebrate, commemorate, honour, keep, mark. **4** *He quietly observed that they were all wrong.* comment, remark, say, state.

observer *noun He attended as an observer.* bystander, eyewitness, onlooker, spectator, viewer, witness. OPPOSITE participant.

obsess *verb The idea obsessed him.* consume, dominate, grip, haunt, possess, preoccupy.

obsession *noun Cleanliness became an obsession.* fetish, fixation, hobby horse, infatuation, mania, passion, preoccupation.

obsolescent *adjective Videos appear to be obsolescent.* declining, disappearing, dying out, moribund, on the way out (*informal*), waning.

obsolete *adjective The word 'apothecary' is now obsolete.* antiquated, archaic, dead, defunct, disused, old-fashioned, outdated, out of date. OPPOSITE current.

obstacle *noun an obstacle to progress.* bar, barrier, blockage, difficulty, hindrance, hurdle, impediment, obstruction, snag, stumbling block.

obstinate *adjective The obstinate man continued to refuse help.* defiant, dogged, headstrong, inflexible, intractable, intransigent, mulish, perverse, pigheaded, recalcitrant, refractory, resolute, self-willed, stiff-necked, strong-willed, stubborn, uncompromising, unyielding, wilful. OPPOSITE compliant.

obstreperous *adjective The teacher could not control the obstreperous children.* boisterous, disorderly, irrepressible, noisy, rowdy, stroppy (*informal*), uncontrollable, unmanageable, unruly, wild. OPPOSITE docile, well-behaved.

obstruct *verb* **1** *Leaves obstructed the drain.* block, bung up, choke, clog, jam, plug up, stop up. OPPOSITE clear. **2** *The workmen tried to obstruct progress.* block, delay, deter, frustrate, halt, hamper, hinder, hold up, impede, inhibit, prevent, retard, slow down, stall, stop, thwart. OPPOSITE help.

obstruction *noun The obstruction has been removed.* barricade, barrier, blockage, obstacle.

obtain *verb* **1** *She obtained the book from a new shop.* acquire, buy, come by, get, get hold of, pick up, procure, purchase. **2** *He obtained the information.* elicit, extract, gain, gather, get, glean, receive, secure. **3** *He obtained 65% in the test.* achieve, attain, earn.

obtrusive *adjective* **1** *The shop assistant was too obtrusive for my liking.* forward, importunate, interfering, intrusive, meddlesome, nosy (*informal*), pushy. OPPOSITE reserved. **2** *The view was marred by obtrusive signs.* blatant, conspicuous, glaring, noticeable, obvious, prominent. OPPOSITE inconspicuous, unobtrusive.

obtuse *adjective It was impossible to explain it to the obtuse clerk.* dense, dim-witted, dopey (*informal*), dumb (*informal*), slow, stupid, thick. OPPOSITE bright.

obvious *adjective an obvious error.* apparent, blatant, clear, conspicuous, distinct, evident, glaring, manifest, noticeable, palpable, patent, plain, prominent, pronounced, self-evident, unconcealed, unmistakable, visible. OPPOSITE hidden, obscure.

occasion *noun* **1** *The wedding was a joyous occasion.* ceremony, episode, event, function, happening, incident, occurrence. **2** *It was an occasion to use her new camera.* chance, moment, opportunity, time.

occasional *adjective The bureau forecast occasional showers.* fitful, infrequent, intermittent, irregular, odd, random, rare, scattered, spasmodic, sporadic. OPPOSITE constant, frequent.

occasionally *adverb The car breaks down occasionally.* at times, every so often, from time to time, now and then, once in a while, on occasion, sometimes. OPPOSITE constantly, often.

occult *adjective occult powers.* arcane, esoteric, hidden, magic, mysterious, mystic, mystical, secret, supernatural.

occupant *noun the occupant of a house.* dweller, householder, inhabitant, lessee, occupier, resident, tenant.

occupation *noun* **1** *the occupation of gardener.* business, calling, career, employment, job, profession, trade, vocation, work. **2** *enemy occupation of the country.* capture, conquest, invasion, possession, seizure, takeover.

occupied *adjective The sign on the toilet door read 'occupied'.* engaged, in use. OPPOSITE vacant.

occupy *verb* **1** *The family occupied the house for forty years.* dwell in, inhabit, live in, reside in. **2** *The enemy occupied the country.* capture, conquer, invade, seize, take over, take possession of. **3** *The fat man occupied two seats.* fill, take up, use. **4** *He occupies the position of treasurer.* fill, hold, hold down. **5** *She is fully occupied with study.* absorb, employ, engage, engross, involve, keep busy, preoccupy.

occur *verb* **1** *They expected an accident to occur.* befall, come about, come off, come to pass, eventuate, happen, take place. **2** *The problem occurs wherever water is scarce.* appear, arise, be found, crop up, emerge, exist, manifest itself, show up, surface. □ **occur to** *It did not occur to him to tell anybody.* dawn on, enter your head, suggest itself to.

occurrence *noun Blackouts are a common occurrence.* episode, event, happening, incident, instance, occasion, phenomenon.

ocean *noun* the blue, the briny (*humorous*), the deep, sea.

odd *adjective* **1** *odd behaviour.* aberrant, abnormal, anomalous, bizarre, curious, deviant, eccentric, extraordinary, freakish, funny, incongruous, irregular, offbeat, peculiar, queer, quirky, singular, strange, uncommon, unconventional, unnatural, unusual, weird. OPPOSITE normal. **2** *He does odd jobs.* casual, miscellaneous, occasional, random, sporadic, sundry, various. OPPOSITE regular. **3** *an odd number.* uneven. OPPOSITE even. **4** *an odd knitting needle.* leftover, lone, remaining, single, spare, surplus, unpaired. OPPOSITE paired.

oddity *noun* **1** *the oddity of her appearance.* eccentricity, incongruity, peculiarity, singularity, strangeness. **2** *He was considered rather an oddity.* character, curiosity, eccentric, freak, misfit, nut (*informal*), oddball (*informal*), weirdo (*informal*).

oddments *plural noun a sale of oddments.* leftovers, odds and ends, odds and sods (*informal*), remainders, remnants, sundries.

odious *adjective an odious crime.* abhorrent, abominable, contemptible, despicable, detestable, hateful, heinous, horrible, loathsome, monstrous, obnoxious, repugnant, repulsive, vile.

odour *noun* **1** *a pleasant odour.* aroma, bouquet, fragrance, perfume, scent, smell. **2** *an unpleasant odour.* pong (*informal*), reek, smell, stench, stink.

offbeat *adjective an offbeat sense of humour.* bizarre, eccentric, odd, strange, unconventional, unusual, way-out, weird.

offcuts *plural noun The timber offcuts are sold cheaply.* leftovers, remnants, scraps.

offence *noun* **1** *a punishable offence.* crime, felony (*old use*), misdeed, misdemeanour, sin, transgression, trespass (*old use*), wickedness, wrongdoing. **2** *She meant no offence.* disrespect, harm, hurt, insult, wrong. □ **take offence** *He took offence at the remark.* be affronted, be offended, take umbrage.

offend *verb* **1** *Try not to offend anyone.* affront, anger, disgust, displease, hurt someone's feelings, insult, outrage, upset. OPPOSITE please. **2** *He offended against the law.* do wrong, sin, transgress, trespass (*old use*).

offender *noun The offender was punished.* criminal, culprit, felon, lawbreaker, malefactor, miscreant, sinner, transgressor, trespasser (*old use*), wrongdoer.

offensive *adjective* **1** *offensive remarks.* abusive, disrespectful, improper, indecent, insolent, insulting, nasty, objectionable, obscene, odious, rude. OPPOSITE polite. **2** *an offensive smell.* bad, disgusting, foul, nasty, nauseating, obnoxious, off-putting, on the nose (*Australian informal*), repulsive, revolting, sickening, unsavoury, yucky (*informal*). OPPOSITE pleasant. **3** *offensive weapons.* aggressive, attacking. OPPOSITE defensive. — *noun a military offensive.* assault, attack, blitz, drive, invasion, onslaught, raid.

offer *verb* **1** *She offered her guest a biscuit.* give, hand, present, proffer. OPPOSITE deny, withhold. **2** *He offered a suggestion.* propose, put forward, submit, suggest, tender, volunteer. OPPOSITE refuse. — *noun He made an offer too good to refuse.* bid, proposal, proposition, suggestion, tender.

offering *noun a generous offering.* contribution, donation, gift, offertory, present, sacrifice.

offhand *adjective They were hurt by his offhand manner.* brusque, casual, curt, perfunctory, rude, terse, unceremonious, unconcerned. OPPOSITE concerned. — *adverb I can't tell you offhand.* impromptu, off the cuff, spontaneously, without preparation.

office *noun* **1** *One room of the house is an office.* den, study, workroom. **2** *He works in a government office.* agency, bureau, department, secretariat. **3** *She took up the office of treasurer.* appointment, duty, function, job, position, post, role.

officer *noun* **1** *a customs officer.* functionary, official. **2** *a police officer.* see POLICE.

official *adjective our official representative. an official announcement.* accredited, approved, authorised, certified, endorsed, formal, legitimate, proper. OPPOSITE unauthorised, unofficial. — *noun The decision rests with the official.* bureaucrat, functionary, office-bearer, officer.

officious *adjective The clerk was too officious.* bossy, bumptious, cocky, interfering, intrusive, meddlesome, overbearing, self-important.

off-putting *adjective* (*informal*) *He had an off-putting manner.* disconcerting, disgusting, offensive, repellent, repugnant, repulsive, unpleasant. OPPOSITE attractive.

offset *verb The salary increase was offset by a rise in prices.* balance, cancel out, compensate for, counteract, counterbalance, neutralise, nullify.

offshoot *noun* **1** *The plant developed offshoots.* branch, side shoot. **2** *an offshoot of the main research.* by-product, derivative, development, spin-off.

offsider *noun* (*Australian informal*) *He works as an electrician's offsider.* assistant, associate, helper, partner, sidekick (*informal*).

offspring *noun* **1** *The couple have no offspring.* child(ren), descendant(s), family, heir(s), kid(s) (*informal*), progeny. **2** *an animal's offspring.* brood, litter, young.

often *adverb They see each other often.* constantly, continually, frequently, regularly, repeatedly. OPPOSITE never, seldom.

ogle *verb The man ogled the girl at the bus stop.* eye, gawp at (*informal*), gaze at, leer at, stare at.

ogre, ogress *noun* **1** *a fairy-tale ogre.* bogyman, giant, monster. **2** *He wasn't really such an ogre.* beast, brute, bully, fiend, monster, tyrant.

oil *verb She oiled the machine.* grease, lubricate.

oily *adjective The food was oily.* fatty, greasy.

ointment *noun He applied ointment to the sores.* balm, cream, embrocation, liniment, lotion, oil, salve.

OK or okay adjective (*informal*) *The meal was OK.* adequate, all right, fine, passable, reasonable, satisfactory, so-so (*informal*), tolerable. — verb *Will you OK it?* agree to, allow, approve, authorise, clear, consent to, pass, sanction. OPPOSITE veto.

old adjective **1** *an old person.* aged, elderly, geriatric, mature, retired, senior. OPPOSITE young. **2** *The museum houses old cars.* antiquated, antique, archaic, obsolescent, obsolete, outdated, primitive, veteran, vintage. OPPOSITE modern. **3** *They keep the old customs.* age-old, ancient, early, long-standing, time-honoured, traditional. OPPOSITE modern, recent. **4** *Wear old clothes.* decrepit, dilapidated, ragged, tatty (*informal*), worn, worn-out. OPPOSITE new. **5** *He always tells old jokes.* familiar, hackneyed, stale, unoriginal. OPPOSITE fresh, original. **6** *the old days.* bygone, early, former, olden (*old use*), prehistoric. OPPOSITE present. **7** *He went back to his old job.* earlier, former, previous, prior. OPPOSITE new.

old-fashioned adjective *old-fashioned clothes. old-fashioned ideas.* antediluvian (*informal*), antiquated, archaic, behind the times, conservative, conventional, fuddy-duddy (*informal*), obsolete, old hat (*informal*), outdated, outmoded, out-of-date, traditional, unfashionable. OPPOSITE fashionable, up-to-date.

omen noun *The grey clouds were a bad omen.* indication, portent, sign, warning.

ominous adjective *ominous clouds.* inauspicious, menacing, portentous, sinister, threatening. OPPOSITE auspicious.

omission noun **1** *her omission from the party list.* exclusion, non-inclusion. OPPOSITE inclusion. **2** *errors of omission.* neglect, negligence, oversight. OPPOSITE commission.

omit verb **1** *The author omitted an important name.* drop, exclude, ignore, leave out, miss, overlook, pass over, skip. OPPOSITE include. **2** *He omitted to sign the cheque.* fail, forget, neglect. OPPOSITE remember.

omnipotent adjective *omnipotent God.* all-powerful, almighty, sovereign, supreme. OPPOSITE powerless.

omniscient adjective *omniscient God.* all-knowing, all-wise. OPPOSITE ignorant.

once adverb *People once lived there.* formerly, hitherto, in days gone by, in the past, previously.

oncoming adjective *oncoming traffic.* advancing, approaching. OPPOSITE receding.

onerous adjective *an onerous task.* arduous, burdensome, difficult, exacting, hard, heavy, herculean, oppressive, taxing, tiring. OPPOSITE easy.

one-sided adjective **1** *They gave a one-sided version of events.* biased, unfair, prejudiced. OPPOSITE unbiased. **2** *a one-sided contest.* unbalanced, unequal, uneven, unfair. OPPOSITE balanced.

ongoing adjective *an ongoing debate.* continuing, current, running.

onlooker noun *a crowd of onlookers at the scene of the accident.* bystander, eyewitness, looker-on, observer, spectator, viewer, witness. OPPOSITE participant.

only adjective *our only hope.* lone, one, single, sole, solitary. — adverb *He only says it to annoy people.* just, merely, purely, simply.

onset noun *the onset of war.* beginning, commencement, inception, outbreak, outset, start.

onslaught noun *They could not survive the fierce onslaught.* aggression, assault, attack, blitz, bombardment, charge, incursion, offensive, raid.

onus noun *The onus of proof rests with you.* burden, duty, obligation, responsibility.

ooze verb *Blood oozed from the wound.* discharge, dribble, drip, exude, leak, seep, trickle.

opaque adjective *an opaque liquid.* cloudy, milky, muddy, murky, turbid, unclear. CONTRASTS WITH translucent, transparent.

open adjective **1** *The door is open.* ajar, gaping, unbolted, undone, unfastened, unlatched, unlocked. OPPOSITE shut. **2** *She likes the wide open spaces.* broad, clear, empty, extensive, unbounded, uncluttered, uncrowded, unfenced, unobstructed. OPPOSITE confined. **3** *an open meeting.* general, public, unrestricted. OPPOSITE closed, exclusive. **4** *The newspaper was open on the table.* spread out, unfolded, unfurled. **5** *welcomed with open arms.* outspread, outstretched. **6** *He was open about his motives.* candid, communicative, direct, forthright, frank, honest, outspoken, straightforward. OPPOSITE secretive. **7** *open contempt.* blatant, flagrant, obvious, overt, patent, unconcealed, undisguised. OPPOSITE covert, secret. **8** *keeping their options open.* undecided, unresolved, unsettled. — verb **1** *Fran opened the door.* unbolt, unfasten, unlatch, unlock. OPPOSITE close. **2** *Colin opened the package.* undo, unfasten, unseal, untie, unwrap. OPPOSITE close, fasten. **3** *The chairman opened the proceedings.* begin, commence, initiate, kick off (*informal*), launch, start. OPPOSITE close.

open-air adjective *an open-air cinema.* alfresco, outdoor, outside. OPPOSITE indoor.

opening noun **1** *They blocked up the opening.* aperture, breach, break, chink, cleft, crack, cut, fissure, gap, hatch, hole, leak, manhole, mouth, orifice, outlet, passage, rift, slit, slot, space, vent. **2** *the opening of his business.* beginning, commencement, inception, launch, outset, start. OPPOSITE close. **3** *the opening of a book. the opening of the opera.* introduction, overture, preface, prelude. OPPOSITE conclusion, finale. **4** *He sought an opening in the housing industry.* break (*informal*), chance, opportunity, position, vacancy.

open-minded adjective *He remained open-minded as he listened to both sides.* fair, impartial, just, objective, tolerant, unbiased, unprejudiced. OPPOSITE narrow-minded.

operate verb **1** *The torch operates with a battery.* function, go, perform, run, work. **2** *He knows how to operate the machine.* control, drive, handle, manage, manipulate, use, wield, work.

operation noun **1** *a delicate operation. a military operation.* action, business, campaign, exercise, job, manoeuvre, procedure, process, task, undertaking. **2** *The doctor performed a knee operation.* op (*informal*), surgery.

opinion noun *She keeps her opinions to herself.* belief, comment, conclusion, conviction, creed, feeling, idea, impression, judgement, notion, point of view, sentiment, standpoint, thought, view, viewpoint.

opinionated adjective *She disliked this opinionated upstart.* bigoted, cocksure, dogmatic, headstrong,

obstinate, self-assertive, stubborn. OPPOSITE open-minded.

opponent noun *She thought she could beat all her opponents.* adversary, challenger, competitor, contender, enemy, foe, opposition, rival.

opportune adjective *an opportune time.* advantageous, appropriate, apt, auspicious, convenient, expedient, favourable, fitting, fortunate, good, lucky, propitious, timely. OPPOSITE inopportune.

opportunity noun *He never got an opportunity to speak.* break (*informal*), chance, moment, occasion, opening, time.

oppose verb *She opposed the changes.* argue against, buck (*informal*), contest, counter, defy, fight, object to, resist, withstand. OPPOSITE support. □ **opposed to** *She is strongly opposed to capital punishment.* against, anti, averse to. OPPOSITE in favour of, pro.

opposite adjective **1** *the opposite wall.* facing. OPPOSITE same. **2** *opposite points of view.* conflicting, contradictory, contrary, contrasting, incompatible, opposing. OPPOSITE like, same. — noun **1** *He did the opposite of what he was told.* antithesis, contrary, converse, reverse. **2** *The two words are opposites.* antonym. OPPOSITE synonym.

opposition noun **1** *They voiced their opposition to the proposal.* antagonism, disagreement, disapproval, hostility, objection, resistance. OPPOSITE backing. **2** *He left the company and joined the opposition.* competitor, enemy, opponent, rival.

oppress verb **1** *The new government oppressed the people.* abuse, bully, crush, exploit, maltreat, persecute, subjugate, tyrannise. **2** *Her worries oppressed her.* afflict, burden, depress, overwhelm, torment, trouble, weigh down, worry. OPPOSITE cheer up.

oppressive adjective **1** *an oppressive master.* cruel, despotic, hard, harsh, repressive, severe, tyrannical, unjust. OPPOSITE humane, lenient. **2** *The weather was oppressive.* close, humid, muggy, stifling, stuffy, sultry, uncomfortable.

opt verb **opt for** *We each opted for a different chocolate.* choose, decide on, go for, pick, select, settle on, vote for.

optical adjective see VISUAL.

optimistic adjective *She was optimistic about the outcome.* cheerful, confident, expectant, hopeful, positive, sanguine, upbeat (*informal*). OPPOSITE pessimistic.

optimum adjective *Under optimum conditions fuel consumption is 10 litres/100 km.* best, ideal, optimal, peak, perfect. OPPOSITE worst.

option noun *He disliked both the options.* alternative, choice, possibility.

optional adjective *optional subjects.* elective, non-essential, voluntary. OPPOSITE compulsory.

opulent adjective **1** *an opulent family.* affluent, moneyed, prosperous, rich, wealthy, well off. OPPOSITE impoverished. **2** *an opulent hotel suite.* luxurious, plush (*informal*), splendid, sumptuous. OPPOSITE squalid.

oral adjective *an oral examination.* spoken. OPPOSITE written.

orange adjective *an orange colour.* amber, apricot, carroty, coral, ginger, saffron, salmon, tangerine.

oration noun *a funeral oration.* address, discourse, eulogy, homily, lecture, speech.

orbit noun *the orbit of the planet.* circuit, course, path, revolution, track, trajectory. — verb *The spaceship*

orbited the earth. circle, circumnavigate, revolve around.

orchestra noun band, ensemble.

orchestrate verb **1** *She orchestrated the music.* arrange, score. **2** *He orchestrated the protest campaign.* coordinate, mastermind, organise, stage-manage.

ordain verb **1** *He was ordained as a minister.* appoint, consecrate, induct, install, invest. **2** *The king ordained that all prisoners would be pardoned.* command, decree, dictate, order, prescribe, rule.

ordeal noun *She survived the ordeal.* affliction, distress, hardship, nightmare, suffering, test, trial, tribulation, trouble.

order noun **1** *The books are in alphabetical order.* arrangement, classification, grouping, layout, organisation, sequence, series, system. **2** *She had the room back in order quickly.* neatness, orderliness, shape, tidiness. OPPOSITE disarray, disorder. **3** *The car is in good running order.* condition, nick (*informal*), repair, state. **4** *Police restored law and order.* calm, control, discipline, harmony, peace. OPPOSITE anarchy, chaos. **5** *He follows the boss's orders.* command, decree, dictate, direction, directive, edict, injunction, instruction. OPPOSITE request. **6** *He showed courage of the highest order.* degree, kind, level, quality, sort, type. **7** *They belong to a religious order.* association, brotherhood, community, fraternity, group, sisterhood, society. — verb **1** *The medical records are ordered alphabetically.* arrange, classify, dispose, group, lay out, organise, sort. **2** *He ordered them to leave.* bid, charge, command, decree, direct, enjoin, instruct, prescribe, tell. OPPOSITE entreat. **3** *He ordered tickets for the play.* apply for, book, request, reserve. □ **order about** *The supervisor was fond of ordering people about.* boss around, bully, control, push around, tell someone what to do. **out of order** *The machine is out of order.* broken, bung (*Australian informal*), damaged, inoperative, kaput (*informal*), on the blink (*informal*). OPPOSITE working.

orderly adjective **1** *He keeps his things in an orderly fashion.* methodical, neat, ordered, organised, shipshape, spick and span, straight, systematic, tidy. OPPOSITE chaotic. **2** *orderly behaviour.* controlled, disciplined, law-abiding, quiet, well-behaved. OPPOSITE disorderly, unruly.

ordinary adjective *an ordinary man. an ordinary day.* average, common, commonplace, conventional, customary, everyday, familiar, humble, humdrum, mediocre, middling, mundane, nondescript, normal, orthodox, plain, regular, routine, run-of-the-mill, simple, so-so (*informal*), standard, typical, undistinguished, unexceptional, unexciting, unimpressive, uninspired, uninteresting, unremarkable, usual. OPPOSITE exceptional, extraordinary.

organisation noun **1** *They belong to a peacemaking organisation.* alliance, association, body, club, company, corps, federation, fellowship, fraternity, group, league, movement, order, party, society, union. **2** *He works for a large banking organisation.* business, company, corporation, enterprise, establishment, firm, institution. **3** *The organisation of the essay was clear.* arrangement, design, form, format, layout, presentation, structure. **4** *The organisation of the event was a nightmare.* administration, coordination, management, orchestration, planning, running.

organise verb **1** *She organised her collection.* arrange, catalogue, classify, group, order, put in order, sort, structure, systematise, tidy. **2** *The event was organised with military precision.* arrange, control, coordinate, manage, orchestrate, plan, run, stage-manage. **3** *The police organised a search party.* assemble, establish, form, mobilise, put together, set up.

organised adjective *an organised approach.* businesslike, careful, efficient, methodical, neat, orderly, planned, structured, systematic. OPPOSITE disorganised.

organism noun *microscopic organisms.* being, creature, living thing.

orgy noun **1** *a drunken orgy.* binge (slang), party, revelry, spree (informal). **2** *an orgy of spending.* frenzy, splurge (informal), spree (informal).

orientate verb *The course is orientated towards teachers.* aim, direct, gear, orient. □ **orientate yourself 1** *He used the tower to orientate himself.* find your position, get your bearings, orient yourself. **2** *It can take a few weeks for you to orientate yourself.* acclimatise, adapt, adjust, familiarise yourself, orient yourself.

origin noun **1** *the origin of life.* basis, beginning, birth, cause, commencement, creation, derivation, emergence, foundation, genesis, inception, root, source, start, starting point. OPPOSITE end. **2** *a man of humble origin.* ancestry, birth, descent, extraction, lineage, parentage, pedigree.

original adjective **1** *the original vegetation.* aboriginal, earliest, first, initial, native, primeval. OPPOSITE imported. **2** *an original story.* creative, firsthand, fresh, imaginative, innovative, inventive, new, novel, unconventional, unique. OPPOSITE hackneyed, unoriginal. — noun *The original is housed in the museum: this is a copy.* archetype, master, prototype. OPPOSITE copy, replica.

originate verb *The tradition originated centuries ago.* arise, begin, commence, date from, emerge, spring up, start.

ornament noun **1** *She displays her ornaments in a cabinet.* bauble, knick-knack, trinket. **2** *The dress needs some ornament to make it less plain.* adornment, decoration, embellishment, jewellery, trimming.

ornate adjective *ornate furnishings.* baroque, decorated, elaborate, fancy, flamboyant, ornamented, rococo, showy. OPPOSITE plain.

orthodox adjective *orthodox beliefs.* accepted, conformist, conventional, established, mainstream, official, ordinary, standard, traditional. OPPOSITE heretical.

oscillate verb **1** *The pendulum oscillates.* sway, swing. **2** *Her mood oscillates between depression and ecstasy.* fluctuate, see-saw, swing, vacillate, vary, waver.

ostensible adjective *Their ostensible motive for going in was to rescue the children.* alleged, apparent, declared, outward, pretended, professed, seeming. OPPOSITE actual.

ostentatious adjective *an ostentatious house.* conspicuous, extravagant, flamboyant, flash (informal), flashy, grandiose, imposing, pretentious, showy, swanky (informal). OPPOSITE modest.

ostracise verb *He was ostracised by his peers.* avoid, banish, blackball, blacklist, boycott, cold-shoulder, disown, exclude, reject, send to

Coventry, shun, snub. OPPOSITE accept, welcome.

other adjective **1** *He has no other income.* additional, extra, further, more, supplementary. **2** *There can be no other explanation.* alternative, different. OPPOSITE same. □ **other than** *She has no friends other than her family.* apart from, aside from, besides, except.

oust verb *He was ousted from his job.* banish, dismiss, drive out, eject, expel, fire, give the boot (slang), give the sack (informal), kick out (informal), sack (informal), throw out.

out-and-out adjective *an out-and-out scoundrel.* absolute, arrant, complete, downright, thorough, total, utter.

outback noun (Australian) *He grew up in the city but now lives in the outback.* backblocks, back of beyond, bush, inland, interior, never-never, sticks (informal).

outbreak noun *an outbreak of fighting. a new outbreak of cholera.* epidemic, eruption, outburst.

outburst noun *an outburst of anger. an outburst of laughter.* blaze, burst, eruption, explosion, fit, flood, outbreak, spasm.

outcast noun *He was treated as an outcast.* deportee, exile, outlaw, pariah, refugee.

outcome noun *The outcome of the talks was a peaceful settlement.* consequence, effect, end, fruit, result, sequel, upshot.

outcrop noun *a fresh outcrop of spots.* burst, crop, eruption, outbreak.

outcry noun *The umpire's decision brought an angry outcry.* clamour, hue and cry, hullabaloo, objection, outburst, protest, uproar.

outdated adjective *outdated customs.* antiquated, archaic, obsolete, old, old-fashioned, outmoded, out-of-date, unfashionable. OPPOSITE current, modern.

outdo verb *She can outdo all her competitors.* beat, defeat, eclipse, exceed, excel, get the better of, outclass, outshine, outstrip, overshadow, surpass, top.

outdoors adverb *They eat outdoors in summer.* al fresco, in the open air, out of doors, outside. OPPOSITE indoors.

outer adjective **1** *an outer layer.* exterior, external, outside, superficial, surface. OPPOSITE inner, internal. **2** *an outer suburb.* outlying, peripheral, remote. OPPOSITE inner.

outfit noun **1** *She wore her new outfit to the party.* clothes, clothing, costume, gear (informal), get-up (informal). **2** *a bicycle repair outfit.* apparatus, equipment, gear, kit.

outgoing adjective **1** *an outgoing personality.* extroverted, friendly, gregarious, sociable, warm. OPPOSITE retiring, shy. **2** *the outgoing president.* departing, ex-, former, past, retiring. OPPOSITE incoming.

outgoings plural noun *Outgoings must not exceed income.* costs, expenditure, expenses. OPPOSITE income.

outgrowth noun **1** *an outgrowth on the trunk of the tree.* knob, lump, node, nodule, offshoot, shoot, sprout. **2** *outgrowths of the original research project.* by-product, consequence, development, offshoot, outcome, product, result, spin-off, upshot.

outhouse noun barn, outbuilding, shed.

outing noun *an outing to the zoo.* drive, excursion, expedition, hike, jaunt, tour, trip.

outlandish adjective *a contest for the most outlandish outfit.* bizarre, exotic, freakish, odd, outrageous,

peculiar, preposterous, strange, unusual, way-out, weird. OPPOSITE ordinary.

outlaw noun *The carriage was attacked by a band of outlaws.* bandit, brigand, criminal, desperado, fugitive, marauder, outcast. — verb *Smoking is outlawed on public transport.* ban, forbid, prohibit, proscribe. OPPOSITE allow.

outlay noun *a small outlay of ten dollars.* charge, cost, expenditure, expense. OPPOSITE return.

outlet noun **1** *a safety outlet.* duct, escape, exit, hole, opening, overflow, vent, way out. **2** *an outlet for her imagination.* channel, release. **3** *a fast-food outlet.* shop, store.

outline noun **1** *the outline of a person.* contour, profile, shadow, shape, silhouette, tracing. **2** *an outline of the story.* abstract, draft, framework, plan, précis, résumé, run-down, sketch, summary, synopsis.

outlive verb *She outlived her husband by five years.* outlast, survive. OPPOSITE predecease.

outlook noun **1** *a pleasant outlook over the lake.* aspect, panorama, prospect, scene, sight, view, vista. **2** *He has an optimistic outlook.* attitude, frame of mind, perspective, view, viewpoint. **3** *a grim economic outlook.* forecast, prediction, prognosis, prospect.

outlying adjective *outlying areas.* distant, far-flung, outer, remote. OPPOSITE inner.

outnumber verb *Boys outnumbered girls.* exceed.

output noun *Their output was diminished because of the power failure.* production, yield. OPPOSITE input.

outrage noun **1** *an outrage against society.* affront, atrocity, crime, evil, insult, offence, scandal. **2** *He felt outrage at the incident.* anger, disgust, fury, indignation, ire, rage, shock. — verb *He was outraged at the suggestion.* affront, anger, enrage, incense, infuriate, insult, offend, scandalise, shock.

outrageous adjective **1** *outrageous prices.* absurd, excessive, exorbitant, immoderate, preposterous, shocking, unreasonable. OPPOSITE reasonable. **2** *an outrageous crime.* atrocious, barbarous, despicable, disgraceful, heinous, infamous, monstrous, notorious, offensive, scandalous, shocking, unspeakable, vile, wicked.

outright adverb **1** *She was killed outright.* at once, immediately, instantly. **2** *Smoking is banned outright.* absolutely, altogether, categorically, completely, entirely, utterly. **3** *He told him outright.* directly, frankly, openly, straight. — adjective *outright stupidity.* absolute, complete, downright, out-and-out, sheer, thorough, utter.

outset noun *The scheme was doomed from the outset.* beginning, commencement, inception, start. OPPOSITE finish.

outside noun **1** *The food looked perfect on the outside.* case, covering, crust, exterior, shell, skin, surface. OPPOSITE inside. **2** *the outside of the building.* exterior, façade, face. — adjective **1** *an outside wall.* exterior, external, outer. OPPOSITE interior, internal. **2** *an outside chance.* distant, faint, remote, slender, slight, slim. — adverb *They like eating outside.* al fresco, in the open air, outdoors, out of doors. OPPOSITE inside. — preposition *Robert has no interests outside his work.* apart from, aside from, beyond, except, other than.

outsider noun *He felt like an outsider.* alien, foreigner, immigrant, intruder, newcomer, odd man out,

ring-in (Australian informal), stranger, visitor. OPPOSITE member.

outskirts plural noun *on the outskirts of town.* edge, fringe, limits, periphery. OPPOSITE centre.

outspoken adjective *an outspoken critic of the government.* blunt, candid, forthright, frank, open, straightforward, unreserved. OPPOSITE reticent.

outstanding adjective **1** *outstanding work. an outstanding student.* distinguished, eminent, excellent, exceptional, exemplary, extraordinary, great, impressive, memorable, notable, pre-eminent, remarkable, sensational, singular, special, splendid, superior. OPPOSITE mediocre. **2** *The amount outstanding is ten dollars.* due, overdue, owing, unpaid. OPPOSITE paid.

outstrip verb *He outstripped the other runners.* beat, outdistance, outpace, outrun; see also OUTDO.

outward adjective *an outward sign of an inward change.* exterior, external, observable, outer, outside, superficial, visible. OPPOSITE inward.

outweigh verb *The advantages outweigh the disadvantages.* exceed, override, predominate over, surpass.

outwit verb *She outwitted her opponent.* dupe, hoodwink, outfox (informal), outsmart, trick.

oval noun **1** *the shape of an oval.* ellipse. **2** (Australian) *Games are played on the oval.* playing field, sports field, sportsground. — adjective *an oval garden.* egg-shaped, elliptical, ovoid.

ovation noun *The audience gave the pianist a big ovation.* applause, clap, hand (informal).

oven noun *cooked in the oven.* cooker, furnace, kiln, microwave, range, stove.

overact verb *He was criticised for overacting the part.* exaggerate, ham up (informal), overdo, overplay.

overall adjective *the overall effect.* all-inclusive, broad, complete, general, total.

overalls plural noun *Overalls keep his clothes clean.* boiler suit, dungarees.

overbearing adjective *an overbearing official.* arrogant, autocratic, bossy, domineering, high-handed, imperious, officious, peremptory. OPPOSITE unassuming.

overcast adjective *overcast skies.* cloudy, dull, foggy, gloomy, grey, heavy, leaden, louring, misty. OPPOSITE clear, sunny.

overcoat noun greatcoat, topcoat; see also COAT.

overcome verb **1** *They overcame the enemy.* beat, conquer, crush, defeat, master, overpower, overthrow, quell, subdue, thrash, triumph over, trounce, vanquish. OPPOSITE surrender to. **2** *She overcame the problem.* conquer, lick (informal), rise above, surmount, triumph over. OPPOSITE give in to.

overdo verb *He overdid the praise.* exaggerate, lay (it) on a bit thick (informal), overstate, pile (it) on (informal). OPPOSITE understate.

overdue adjective *The payment was overdue.* in arrears, late, outstanding, owing. OPPOSITE early, premature.

overeat verb *If you overeat, you might feel sick.* binge (informal), gorge yourself, overindulge, pig out (informal), stuff yourself. OPPOSITE starve yourself.

overestimate verb *He overestimated the size of the problem.* exaggerate, overrate, overstate. OPPOSITE underestimate.

overflow verb *The water overflowed.* brim over, flood, flow over, pour over, run over, slop over, spill over. — *noun We needed a bucket to catch the overflow.* excess, spillage, surplus.

overgrown *adjective* **1** *an overgrown zucchini.* enormous, gigantic, large, outsize, oversized. OPPOSITE undersized. **2** *The cats liked the overgrown garden.* tangled, uncut, unkempt, untidy, wild.

overhang *verb The tree overhangs the fence.* jut out over, project over, protrude over, stick out over.

overhaul *verb The mechanic overhauled the engine.* recondition, repair, restore, service.

overhear *verb He overheard a private conversation.* eavesdrop on, hear, listen in on.

overjoyed *adjective He was overjoyed at the news.* delighted, ecstatic, elated, euphoric, exuberant, exultant, happy, joyful, joyous, jubilant, over the moon (*informal*), rapt, rapturous, thrilled. OPPOSITE downcast.

overload *verb He is overloaded with work.* overburden, overtax, weigh down.

overlook *verb* **1** *The castle overlooks the lake.* face, front on to, look out on, look over. **2** *He overlooked an important point.* forget, ignore, leave out, miss, neglect, omit, skip. **3** *She overlooks his faults.* condone, disregard, excuse, forgive, ignore, pardon, pass over, turn a blind eye to. OPPOSITE notice.

overpower *verb He overpowered the madman.* beat, conquer, defeat, get the better of, overcome, overwhelm, subdue.

overpowering *adjective an overpowering feeling of tiredness.* irresistible, overwhelming, powerful, uncontrollable.

overrate *verb He overrated his abilities.* exaggerate, overestimate. OPPOSITE underrate.

override *verb* **1** *The manager can override the decision.* see OVERRULE. **2** *Considerations of safety override all others.* have precedence over, outweigh, prevail over.

overriding *adjective the overriding consideration.* chief, foremost, main, major, paramount, primary, principal, supreme.

overrule *verb The court overruled his decision.* disallow, invalidate, override, overturn, reject, reverse, revoke, set aside, veto. OPPOSITE uphold.

overrun *verb The rabbits soon overran the country.* cover, infest, invade, occupy, spread over, swarm over, take over.

overseas *adverb He travels overseas.* abroad. — *adjective an overseas investment.* foreign, offshore.

oversee *verb He oversees the work.* be in charge of, direct, manage, run, superintend, supervise.

overseer *noun He was appointed overseer of the men.* boss, foreman, forewoman, manager, superintendent, supervisor.

overshadow *verb This one achievement overshadowed all the others.* dwarf, eclipse, outshine, put in the shade, surpass, tower over.

oversight *noun The letter wasn't sent because of an oversight.* blunder, carelessness, error, lapse, mistake, omission, slip-up (*informal*).

overstate *verb He has overstated the problem.* blow up, exaggerate, inflate, magnify. OPPOSITE understate.

overstatement *noun* exaggeration, hyperbole. OPPOSITE understatement.

overt *adjective overt hostility.* blatant, evident, manifest, obvious, open, patent, plain, unconcealed, visible. OPPOSITE covert, secret.

overtake *verb The leader could see the others gradually overtaking her.* catch up with, go past, outpace, outstrip, overhaul, pass.

overtax *verb He had overtaxed himself, and was exhausted.* overburden, overload, overwork, strain, stretch.

overthrow *verb The rebels overthrew the government, the president, etc.* bring down, defeat, depose, oust, overturn, topple, unseat. — *noun the overthrow of the government.* collapse, defeat, downfall, fall.

overtone *noun The sermon had political overtones.* connotation, hint, implication, innuendo, insinuation, suggestion, undercurrent.

overture *noun the overture of an opera.* beginning, introduction, opening, prelude.

overturn *verb* **1** *The boat overturned.* capsize, keel over, topple over, turn over, turn turtle. **2** *He overturned the flowerpot.* invert, knock over, spill, tip over, up-end, upset, upturn. **3** *The judge overturned the decision.* see OVERRULE. **4** *They overturned the government.* see OVERTHROW.

overused *adjective an overused phrase.* clichéd, common, hackneyed, overworked, stale, trite. OPPOSITE original.

overview *noun an overview of the subject.* outline, sketch, survey.

overweight *adjective Being overweight is a health risk.* chubby, corpulent, dumpy, fat, gross, heavy, obese, plump, podgy, portly, rotund, stout, tubby. OPPOSITE thin.

overwhelm *verb* **1** *The floodwaters overwhelmed the town.* bury, cover, deluge, drown, engulf, flood, inundate, submerge, swamp. **2** *Their army was overwhelmed by the enemy.* beat, conquer, crush, defeat, overcome, overpower, rout, vanquish.

overwhelming *adjective an overwhelming urge to speak.* irresistible, overpowering, uncontrollable.

overwrought *adjective The parents of the missing child were overwrought.* agitated, beside yourself, distressed, frantic, hysterical, nervous, nervy, on edge, overexcited, uptight (*informal*), worked up. OPPOSITE calm.

owe *verb He doesn't owe you anything.* be beholden to, be indebted to, be in debt to, be under an obligation to.

owing *adjective the amount owing.* due, outstanding, overdue, unpaid. □ **owing to** *She was late, owing to a derailment.* because of, caused by, on account of, thanks to.

own[1] *adjective Bring your own chair.* individual, personal, private. □ **on your own** *She did it on her own.* alone, by yourself, independently, single-handed, solo, unaccompanied, unaided, unassisted, unescorted.

own[2] *verb He owns shares.* be the owner of, have, hold, keep, possess. □ **own up** (*informal*) *The culprit would not own up.* admit, come clean (*informal*), confess.

owner *noun the owner of the property.* holder, landlady, landlord, master, mistress, possessor, proprietor, proprietress.

ox *noun* bull, bullock, steer.

Pp

pace *noun* **1** *Take five paces backwards.* step, stride. **2** *He works at a*

fast pace. rate, speed, velocity. — *verb He paced up and down.* march, stride, walk.

pacifist *noun* conscientious objector, dove, peace lover.

pacify *verb She pacified the baby by feeding him.* appease, calm, placate, quieten, settle, soothe. OPPOSITE agitate, provoke.

pack *noun* **1** *There are six candles in a pack.* bag, box, bundle, carton, package, packet, parcel. **2** *He carried the food in his pack.* backpack, haversack, kitbag, knapsack, rucksack, satchel; see also SWAG. **3** *a pack of thieves.* band, gang, group, mob, push (*Australian*). **4** *a pack of lies.* heap, load, lot, set. — *verb* **1** *She packed the glasses in padded boxes.* load, package, parcel, place, put, store, stow, wrap up. **2** *He packed his bags.* fill, load. OPPOSITE unpack. **3** *We were packed into the room like sardines.* cram, crowd, jam, squash, squeeze, stuff. **4** *She packed the soil down tightly.* compact, compress, press, ram, tamp. □ **pack off** *They packed him off to the country.* bundle off, dispatch, send away, send off.

package *noun a heavy package.* bag, bale, box, bundle, carton, container, pack, packet, parcel. — *verb She packaged the present neatly.* pack (up), parcel (up), wrap (up).

packet *noun Yeast comes in little packets.* bag, envelope, pack, package, parcel, sachet.

pact *noun The two sides signed a pact.* accord, agreement, bargain, compact, contract, covenant, deal, treaty, understanding.

pad *noun* **1** *a protective pad.* buffer, cushion, padding, pillow, wad. **2** *a writing pad.* jotter, notepad. — *verb* **1** *They padded the seat with foam.* cushion, fill, line, protect, stuff, upholster. **2** *He padded out his speech with jokes.* bulk out, expand, fill out, lengthen, protract, spin out, stretch out.

padding *noun The boxes were lined with kapok for padding.* cushioning, filling, stuffing, wadding.

paddle[1] *verb The toddlers paddled in the little pool.* dabble, splash about, wade.

paddle[2] *noun a paddle for a boat.* oar, scull. — *verb She paddled the canoe.* row, scull.

paddock *noun* (*Australian*) *The sheep are in the paddock.* field, lea (*poetical*), meadow, pasture.

pagan *noun a festival celebrated by pagans.* heathen, infidel, nonbeliever, unbeliever.

page *noun a page of a book.* folio, leaf, sheet.

pageant *noun We went to see the Christmas pageant.* display, parade, procession, show, spectacle, tableau.

pain *noun* **1** *She has no physical pain.* ache, discomfort, hurt, pang, soreness, sting, throb, twinge. **2** *The news caused him pain.* affliction, agony, anguish, distress, grief, heartache, hurt, sadness, sorrow, suffering, torment, torture, woe. OPPOSITE joy. — *verb It pained her to have to tell the family the sad news.* distress, grieve, hurt, sadden, trouble. □ **pains** *plural noun He takes pains with his work.* care, effort, trouble.

painful *adjective* **1** *His fingers are swollen and painful.* aching, hurting, raw, sensitive, smarting, sore, stinging, tender, throbbing. **2** *a painful headache.* agonising, excruciating, shooting, splitting, stabbing. **3** *a painful subject.* *a painful situation.* awkward, delicate, distressing, embarrassing, traumatic, uncomfortable, unpleasant, upsetting. OPPOSITE pleasant.

painkiller *noun* anaesthetic, analgesic, palliative.

painless *adjective* **1** *a painless operation.* comfortable, pain-free. OPPOSITE painful. **2** *a painless way to lose weight.* easy, effortless, simple. OPPOSITE difficult.

painstaking *adjective a painstaking craftsman.* assiduous, careful, conscientious, diligent, hard-working, meticulous, precise, punctilious, scrupulous, thorough. OPPOSITE careless.

paint *noun paint for the woodwork.* colour, colouring, dye, pigment, stain, tint. — *verb* **1** *She painted the room blue.* coat, colour, daub, decorate. **2** *She painted the scene.* depict, portray, represent.

painter *noun* artist, decorator.

painting *noun His paintings are in the art gallery.* picture, work of art; [*kinds of painting*] abstract, fresco, landscape, mural, oil painting, portrait, seascape, still life, water colour.

pair *noun* **1** *They make a good pair.* couple, duo, partnership, twosome. **2** *a pair of birds.* brace, couple. — *verb He pairs the socks before putting them away.* match, pair up, put together.

pal *noun* (*informal*) *A good pal won't let you down.* buddy (*informal*), chum (*informal*), cobber (*Australian informal*), comrade, crony, friend, mate. OPPOSITE enemy.

palace *noun The duke lives in a palace.* castle, château, mansion. OPPOSITE hovel.

pale *adjective* **1** *The patient looks pale.* anaemic, ashen, colourless, deathly, ghostly, pallid, pasty, peaky, wan, washed out, white. OPPOSITE ruddy. **2** *a pale colour.* bleached, dim, faint, light, misty, muted, pastel, soft, subdued. OPPOSITE deep, vivid.

paleness *noun The invalid's paleness was disturbing.* pallor, pastiness, whiteness.

palpable *adjective a palpable lie.* palpable hostility.* apparent, blatant, clear, distinct, evident, manifest, obvious, patent, plain, tangible, unmistakable. OPPOSITE intangible.

paltry *adjective a paltry amount.* beggarly, meagre, mean, measly (*informal*), minor, negligible, niggardly, pathetic, petty, puny, trifling, trivial, worthless. OPPOSITE substantial.

pamper *verb They pamper their children.* cosset, humour, indulge, mollycoddle, spoil.

pamphlet *noun He read the pamphlet about immunisation.* booklet, brochure, flyer, handout, leaflet, notice, tract.

pan *noun cooking pans.* billy (*Australian*), casserole, cauldron, Dutch oven, frying pan, frypan, griddle, pot, pressure cooker, saucepan, skillet, wok. — *verb* (*informal*) *The film was panned by the critics.* see CRITICISE. □ **pan out** *Wait and see how things pan out.* come out, end up, turn out, work out.

pancake *noun* crêpe, flapjack, pikelet.

pandemonium *noun There was pandemonium after the earthquake.* bedlam, chaos, commotion, confusion, disorder, hubbub, hullabaloo, racket, rumpus, tumult, turmoil, uproar. OPPOSITE order, peace.

pander *verb* **pander to** *The newspaper panders to the public interest in scandal.* cater for, gratify, indulge.

panel *noun* **1** *a wall panel. a tapestry panel.* insert, piece, section, strip. **2** *a panel of adjudicators.* body, committee, group, jury, team.

pang *noun* **1** *hunger pangs.* ache, pain, spasm, stab, sting, twinge. **2** *pangs of remorse.* misgiving, qualm, scruple, twinge.

panic *noun Panic seized him.* alarm, anxiety, consternation, dismay, dread, fear, fright, horror, hysteria, terror, trepidation. OPPOSITE calmness. — *verb She panics when it is better to stay calm.* drop your bundle (*Australian informal*), freak out (*informal*), get into a flap (*informal*), get into a state, get into a tizzy (*informal*), get the jitters (*informal*), go to pieces, lose your cool (*informal*).

panicky *adjective She was panicky before the exam.* agitated, flustered, frantic, frightened, jittery (*informal*), nervous, nervy, panic-stricken, petrified, scared, terrified, terror-stricken. OPPOSITE calm.

panorama *noun They admired the panorama from the lookout.* landscape, prospect, scene, view, vista.

pant *verb The dog was panting in the sun.* gasp, huff, puff, wheeze.

pantry *noun Flour is kept in the pantry.* cupboard, larder, storeroom.

pants *plural noun* **1** *She prefers skirts to pants.* slacks, trousers. **2** *Pants are sold with other underwear.* boxer shorts, briefs, drawers, jocks (*slang*), knickers, panties, trunks, underpants, undies (*informal*).

paper *noun* **1** *written on paper.* card, letterhead, notepaper, papyrus, parchment, stationery, writing paper. **2** *He reads the paper every day.* see NEWSPAPER. **3** *Keep important papers in a safe place.* certificate, deed, document, form, record.

par *noun Her mark was below par.* average, mean, norm, normal, standard.

parable *noun Jesus told parables.* allegory, fable, story, tale.

parade *noun* **1** *We watched a parade of floats and bands through the city.* cavalcade, march, march-past, motorcade, pageant, procession. **2** *The street is called 'Anzac Parade'.* avenue, boulevard, road, street. — *verb The children paraded in the main street.* file past, march.

paradise *noun* **1** *The dying woman looked forward to being in paradise.* heaven. OPPOSITE hell. **2** *Adam and Eve lived in an earthly paradise.* Eden, Garden of Eden. **3** *a shopper's paradise.* delight, heaven, joy, wonderland.

paradoxical *adjective a paradoxical statement.* absurd, anomalous, illogical, incongruous, inconsistent, self-contradictory.

paragon *noun a paragon of virtue.* example, exemplar, ideal, model, pattern, quintessence.

parallel *adjective parallel situations.* analogous, comparable, corresponding, like, similar. — *noun He drew a parallel between the two situations.* analogy, comparison, correspondence, likeness, similarity. — *verb an achievement which cannot be paralleled.* equal, match, rival.

paralysed *adjective* **1** *The accident left him paralysed.* crippled, disabled, immobile, incapacitated, lame, numb, paraplegic, quadriplegic. **2** *Facing the lion he was paralysed with fear.* frozen, petrified, rigid.

paramount *adjective a matter of paramount importance.* chief, foremost, greatest, highest, main, major, primary, prime, supreme, utmost. OPPOSITE secondary.

parapet *noun The soldiers were protected by the parapet.* battlements, rampart.

paraphernalia *noun He brought lots of paraphernalia for just a weekend.* accessories, belongings, effects, equipment, gear, materials, odds and ends, possessions, stuff, tackle, things.

paraphrase *verb She paraphrased the hymn.* rephrase, reword, rewrite.

parasol *noun* sunshade, umbrella.

parcel *noun a parcel of clothes.* bale, bundle, pack, package, packet.

parched *adjective* **1** *parched ground.* arid, baked, bone-dry, burnt, dry, scorched, waterless. OPPOSITE wet. **2** *The walkers were parched.* dehydrated, dry, thirsty.

pardon *noun The repentant sinner received God's pardon. The prisoner was granted a royal pardon.* absolution, amnesty, exoneration, forbearance, forgiveness, mercy, remission, reprieve. OPPOSITE punishment. — *verb* **1** *She pardoned the offence.* condone, excuse, forgive, overlook. **2** *The judge pardoned the prisoner.* absolve, acquit, exonerate, forgive, let off, release, reprieve. OPPOSITE punish.

parent *noun the child's parents.* father, mother.

parentage *noun proud of his noble parentage.* ancestry, birth, descent, extraction, lineage, origin. OPPOSITE progeny.

park *noun a picnic in the park.* gardens, parklands, playground, recreation ground, reserve.

parka *noun* anorak; see also JACKET.

parlour *noun (old use) The front room is the parlour.* drawing room, living room, lounge, salon, sitting room.

parochial *adjective The newspaper editor has a parochial outlook.* hidebound, insular, narrow, narrow-minded, petty, provincial, small-minded. OPPOSITE cosmopolitan.

parody *noun a parody of the play.* burlesque, imitation, satire, send-up (*informal*), spoof (*informal*), take-off.

parry *verb* **1** *She parried his blows with her handbag.* avert, beat off, block, deflect, fend off, repel, repulse, ward off. **2** *He parried their questions skilfully.* avoid, circumvent, dodge, duck, elude, evade, sidestep.

parson *noun The parson married them.* chaplain, clergyman, clergywoman, minister, padre, pastor, preacher, priest, rector, vicar.

part *noun* **1** *part of the profits. part of a pie.* bit, chunk, division, fraction, fragment, percentage, piece, portion, proportion, section, sector, segment, share, slice, subdivision. OPPOSITE total. **2** *The story is issued in five parts.* chapter, episode, instalment, issue, section, volume. **3** *He comes from another part of the state.* area, district, neighbourhood, region. **4** *He assembled the parts.* component, constituent, element, ingredient, module, unit. **5** *the early part of your life.* period, point, stage. **6** *The actor enjoyed his part.* character, role. — *verb They parted amicably.* break up, divorce, separate, split up. OPPOSITE marry. □ **part with** *She won't part with her teddy.* give away, give up, hand over, relinquish, spare, surrender. OPPOSITE keep. **take part** see PARTICIPATE.

partial *adjective* **1** *a partial eclipse.* imperfect, incomplete, limited. OPPOSITE total. **2** *The judge must not be partial.* biased, partisan, prejudiced, unfair. OPPOSITE impartial. □ **be partial to** *She is partial to chocolate.* be fond of, be keen on, enjoy, like, love. OPPOSITE dislike.

partiality *noun* **1** *The judge showed no partiality.* bias, favouritism, partisanship, preference, prejudice. OPPOSITE impartiality. **2** *a partiality for sweets.* fondness, inclination, liking, penchant, predilection, proclivity, weakness. OPPOSITE dislike.

participant *noun a participant in the discussions.* contributor, party, player.

participate *verb She participated in the game.* be active, be involved, join, partake, play a part, share, take part.

particle *noun* **1** *food particles.* bit, crumb, fragment, grain, morsel. **2** *He hasn't a particle of sense.* atom, iota, jot, scrap, shred, skerrick (*Australian informal*), speck, trace.

particular *adjective* **1** *made for a particular purpose.* distinct, exact, individual, precise, special, specific. OPPOSITE general. **2** *He took particular care.* especial, exceptional, special. OPPOSITE ordinary. **3** *He is particular about what he eats.* choosy (*informal*), fastidious, finicky, fussy, pernickety (*informal*), selective. OPPOSITE indifferent.

particulars *plural noun She was familiar with the particulars of the case.* circumstances, details, facts, information.

partisan *noun* **1** *a partisan of the former leader.* adherent, backer, champion, fan, follower, supporter, zealot. OPPOSITE opponent. **2** *He fought with the partisans.* freedom fighter, guerrilla.

partition *noun Liam hid behind the partition.* barrier, divider, panel, room divider, screen, wall. — *verb The space was partitioned into poky offices.* break up, divide, separate, split up, subdivide.

partly *adverb That's partly true.* half, in part, partially, semi-. OPPOSITE completely.

partner *noun* **1** *a business partner.* a partner in crime. accessory, accomplice, ally, associate, collaborator, colleague, helper, offsider (*Australian informal*), sidekick (*informal*). **2** *None of the guests had partners.* companion, consort, husband, mate, spouse, wife.

partnership *noun Both businesses benefit from the partnership.* alliance, association, collaboration, relationship, union.

party *noun* **1** *The guests enjoyed the party.* at-home, ball, banquet, bash (*informal*), celebration, do (*informal*), feast, festivity, formal, function, gathering, get-together (*informal*), orgy, rave (*informal*), reception, shindig (*informal*), shivoo (*Australian informal*), social, soirée. **2** *a search party.* band, body, crew, force, group, squad, team. **3** *a political party.* camp, faction, league, side.

pass *verb* **1** *We watched the procession pass.* file past, go by, go past, move on, proceed, progress. **2** *The car passed theirs on the bridge.* get ahead of, outstrip, overhaul, overtake. **3** *He passed the ball from one hand to the other.* juggle, shuffle, slide, slip, toss, transfer. **4** *Reading helps to pass the time.* fill, kill, occupy, take up, use up, while away. **5** *Time passed quickly.* elapse, fly, go by, roll by, slip away. **6** *The storm passed.* blow over, die away, disappear, evaporate, fade, peter out, vanish. **7** *The parliament passed the new law.* adopt, approve, authorise, decree, enact, ratify. **8** *Not all the candidates pass.* get through, qualify, succeed. OPPOSITE fail. — *noun* **1** *The students have a travel pass.* permit, ticket. **2** *a mountain pass.* canyon, defile, gap, gorge, ravine. □ **pass away** *Father passed away after a long illness.* see DIE. **pass out** (*informal*) *He passes out at the sight of blood.* black out, collapse, faint, keel over, swoon. OPPOSITE come round. **pass over** **1** *They passed over the next item on the agenda.* disregard, ignore, miss, omit, skip. **2** *He was passed over for the job.* ignore, overlook, reject. **pass round** *She passed the biscuits round.* deal out, distribute, dole out, hand round, offer, share. **pass up** (*informal*) *She passed up an opportunity.* decline, forgo, let go, let slip, neglect, turn down.

passable *adjective* **1** *The road was not passable in snow.* clear, open, traversable. OPPOSITE impassable. **2** *His work was passable.* acceptable, adequate, all right, fair, mediocre, middling, OK (*informal*), reasonable, satisfactory, so-so (*informal*), tolerable. OPPOSITE unsatisfactory.

passage *noun* **1** *We wished the travellers a safe passage.* crossing, journey, trip, voyage. **2** *We walked along the narrow passage.* aisle, alley, arcade, corridor, gangway, hall, opening, passageway, shaft, tunnel. **3** *She copied the passage from a book.* episode, excerpt, extract, paragraph, piece, portion, quotation, section.

passenger *noun a bus passenger.* commuter, traveller.

passing *adjective a passing glance.* brief, casual, cursory, fleeting, hasty, momentary, quick, short, superficial, transient.

passion *noun* **1** *He expressed his hatred with passion.* ardour, earnestness, emotion, feeling, fervour, fire, intensity, vehemence, zeal. OPPOSITE apathy. **2** *sexual passion.* amorousness, ardour, desire, love, lust. OPPOSITE frigidity. **3** *She has a passion for cricket.* craze, enthusiasm, infatuation, mania, obsession.

passionate *adjective a passionate plea.* ardent, burning, eager, earnest, emotional, enthusiastic, fervent, heartfelt, heated, impassioned, intense, vehement, zealous. OPPOSITE apathetic.

passive *adjective His wife is a passive creature.* apathetic, compliant, docile, inactive, inert, resigned, submissive, unassertive, unresisting, unresponsive. OPPOSITE active.

password *noun She gave the password to enter.* countersign, sign, signal, watchword.

past *adjective* **1** *in past times.* bygone, earlier, former, previous, prior. CONTRASTS WITH future, present. **2** *the past president.* ex-, former, previous. — *noun She talked about the past.* antiquity, history, old days, olden days, yesterday, yesteryear. — *preposition He drove past our house.* beyond, by, in front of.

paste *noun* **1** *wallpaper paste.* adhesive, glue, gum. **2** *tuna paste.* pâté, purée, spread. — *verb She pasted the pieces together.* glue, gum, stick.

pastel *adjective painted in pastel shades.* delicate, faint, light, muted, pale, soft, subdued. OPPOSITE bright, dark.

pastime *noun Reading and cricket are his pastimes.* activity, amusement, diversion, entertainment, game, hobby, interest, leisure pursuit, recreation, sport.

pastor *noun The congregation has two pastors.* chaplain, clergyman, clergywoman, minister, padre, parson, preacher, priest, rector, vicar.

pastoral *adjective* **1** *a pastoral scene.* bucolic, country, rural, rustic. **2** *pastoral lands.* agricultural, farming, grazing, stock-raising.

pastoralist *noun (Australian)* cattle farmer, grazier (*Australian*), sheep farmer, squatter (*Australian*).

pasture *noun The sheep are in the pasture.* field, meadow, paddock, run (*Australian*).

pasty¹ *noun Cornish pasties.* pastry, turnover.

pasty² *adjective a pasty-faced child.* anaemic, colourless, pale, pallid, sallow, unhealthy, wan.

pat verb 1 *She patted his back gently.* caress, massage, rub, stroke. 2 *He patted down the pastry.* dab, slap, tap. — noun *He gave him a little pat on the wrist.* hit, rap, slap, smack, tap.

patch noun 1 *She sewed a patch on her jeans.* mend, reinforcement, repair. 2 *He had a patch over the wound.* bandage, cover, dressing, pad, plaster. 3 *black patches on a white background.* area, blob, blotch, mark, speck, speckle, splash, splotch, spot. 4 *a vegetable patch.* area, garden, lot, plot. — verb *He patched his trousers.* mend, reinforce, repair. □ **patch up** *After their quarrel they tried to patch things up.* make up, resolve, set right, settle.

patchy adjective 1 *The colour is rather patchy.* blotchy, dappled, inconsistent, mottled, speckled, uneven, variable. OPPOSITE uniform. 2 *We only have patchy information.* incomplete, rough, sketchy. OPPOSITE complete.

patent adjective *a patent dislike.* apparent, blatant, clear, conspicuous, evident, manifest, obvious, plain, unconcealed.

paternal adjective *a paternal interest.* fatherlike, fatherly, kindly, protective.

paternity noun *He had a DNA test to establish paternity.* fatherhood, fathership.

path noun 1 *They walked up the path.* aisle, alley, footpath, footway, lane, passage, pathway, pavement, sidewalk (*American*), track, trail, walkway, way. 2 *This can trace the path of a moving vehicle.* course, line, orbit, route, trajectory, way.

pathetic adjective 1 *pathetic sights of starving children.* distressing, heartbreaking, heart-rending, moving, piteous, pitiable, pitiful, poignant, sad, touching, tragic, wretched. OPPOSITE heart-warming. 2 *a pathetic amount.* meagre, measly (*informal*), miserable, paltry, stingy, woeful.

patience noun 1 *He showed patience as he waited in the line.* calmness, endurance, forbearance, restraint, self-control, tolerance. OPPOSITE impatience. 2 *With patience he can learn to walk again.* determination, diligence, doggedness, perseverance, persistence, staying power, tenacity. OPPOSITE impatience.

patient adjective 1 *a patient sufferer.* calm, forbearing, long-suffering, resigned, stoical, tolerant. 2 *a patient worker.* determined, diligent, dogged, indefatigable, persistent, tenacious, tireless, unflagging. OPPOSITE impatient. — noun *The doctor has many patients.* case, client, invalid, sufferer.

patio noun *The patio is used for outdoor parties.* courtyard, terrace.

patriotic adjective *patriotic soldiers.* chauvinistic, jingoistic, loyal, nationalistic.

patrol verb *The police patrol the area.* guard, police, watch. — noun *The patrol must stay awake all night.* guard, lookout, sentinel, sentry, watch, watchman.

patron noun 1 *a patron of the arts.* backer, benefactor, champion, promoter, sponsor, supporter. 2 *a restaurant patron.* client, customer, regular.

patronage noun 1 *government patronage of the arts.* aid, backing, help, promotion, sponsorship, support. 2 *The store appreciated our patronage.* business, custom.

patronising adjective *He spoke to us in a patronising way.* condescending, contemptuous, disdainful, haughty, lofty, supercilious, superior.

patter[1] verb *The rain pattered on the windows.* beat, rap, tap. — noun *the patter of the rain.* beating, pit-a-pat, pitter-patter, tapping.

patter[2] noun *the salesman's patter.* line, pitch, spiel (*slang*).

pattern noun 1 *The curtains have a floral pattern.* decoration, design, figure, marking, motif, ornamentation. 2 *a sewing pattern.* design, guide, model, template. 3 *a pattern for living.* example, exemplar, guide, ideal, model, standard. 4 *There was a pattern to the crimes.* consistency, formula, order, regularity, system. — verb *The play was patterned on an older one.* model, mould, shape, style.

patterned adjective *patterned material.* decorated, figured, ornamented. OPPOSITE plain.

patty noun *a fish patty.* cake, croquette, rissole.

paunch noun *With dieting he reduced his paunch.* abdomen, belly, gut, pot-belly, stomach, tummy (*informal*).

pause noun *a pause in the conversation.* break, breather, gap, halt, hesitation, hiatus, interlude, interruption, let-up, lull, rest, spell, stop. OPPOSITE continuity. — verb *She paused for the others to catch up.* break off, delay, halt, hesitate, rest, stop, wait. OPPOSITE continue.

pavement noun *Walk on the pavement.* footpath, path, pathway, sidewalk (*American*).

paw noun *a dog's paw.* foot, pad.

pawn[1] noun *Management treated him as a pawn.* instrument, puppet, stooge (*informal*), tool.

pawn[2] verb *She pawned her watch to get the money.* hock (*slang*), pledge.

pay verb 1 *He paid $200.* advance, contribute, cough up (*informal*), expend, fork out (*slang*), give, hand over, outlay, part with, refund, remit, shell out (*informal*), spend. 2 *He paid his debts.* clear, discharge, honour, meet, pay off, pay up, settle, square. 3 *He had to pay the owner for the damage.* compensate, indemnify, recompense, reimburse, remunerate, repay. 4 *Crime doesn't pay.* be advantageous, be profitable, be worthwhile, pay off. 5 *He paid her a compliment.* bestow, extend, give, grant, present. OPPOSITE withhold. — noun *He saves some of his pay each fortnight.* earnings, emolument, fee, income, remuneration, salary, stipend, wages. □ **pay back** see REPAY, RETALIATE. **pay for** *You'll pay for your foolishness.* be punished for, pay a penalty for, pay the price for, suffer for.

payment noun *She received a handsome payment. They make regular payments.* advance, allowance, award, benefit, bonus, commission, compensation, contribution, donation, fee, instalment, outlay, pay, pay-off (*informal*), payout, premium, recompense, refund, reimbursement, remittance, remuneration, repayment, reward, royalty, salary, settlement, subscription, surcharge, tip, toll, wage(s).

peace noun 1 *a time of peace between the wars.* accord, concord, harmony, order. OPPOSITE war. 2 *the peace of the bush.* calm, calmness, quiet, quietness, repose, serenity, silence, stillness, tranquillity. OPPOSITE noise.

peaceful adjective 1 *a peaceful holiday.* balmy, calm, quiet, relaxing, restful, serene, still, tranquil, undisturbed, untroubled. OPPOSITE hectic. 2 *a peaceful discussion.* amicable, calm, friendly, harmonious, non-violent, peaceable. OPPOSITE hostile, violent.

peacemaker noun *She acted as a peacemaker between the two parties.* conciliator, intercessor, mediator, negotiator.

peak noun 1 *mountain peaks.* apex, crest, pinnacle, summit, tip, top, zenith. OPPOSITE base, foot. 2 *the peak of his career.* acme, apex, climax, culmination, height, heyday, pinnacle, summit, top, zenith. OPPOSITE nadir.

peal noun 1 *the peal of bells.* carillon, chime, knell, ringing, toll. 2 *a peal of thunder.* blast, burst, clap, crash, roar, rumble. — verb *The bells pealed each Sunday.* chime, resound, ring, sound, toll.

pebbles plural noun *a path made of pebbles.* cobbles, gravel, shingle, stones.

peck verb 1 *The bird pecked me.* bite, nip. 2 *She pecks at her food.* nibble, pick.

peculiar adjective 1 *a peculiar person.* abnormal, bizarre, crazy, curious, eccentric, extraordinary, freakish, funny, odd, offbeat, outlandish, quaint, queer, strange, unconventional, unusual, weird. OPPOSITE normal, ordinary. 2 *his own peculiar style.* characteristic, distinctive, exclusive, idiosyncratic, individual, particular, personal, special, specific, unique. OPPOSITE common.

peculiarity noun *She knows all his peculiarities.* characteristic, eccentricity, foible, idiosyncrasy, mannerism, quirk, trait.

pedant noun *She was a pedant in matters of grammar.* dogmatist, pedagogue, purist, stickler.

pedantic adjective *The teacher was pedantic about his use of words.* exact, fussy, hair-splitting, meticulous, nit-picking, particular, pernickety (*informal*), precise.

pedestrian noun *The track was only for pedestrians.* hiker, rambler, walker.

pedigree noun *They studied the dog's pedigree.* ancestry, background, family, genealogy, line, lineage, stock. — adjective *a pedigree poodle.* pure-bred, thoroughbred.

pedlar noun *He never buys from pedlars.* door-to-door salesman, hawker, huckster.

peel noun *grated lemon peel.* rind, skin, zest. — verb 1 *She peeled off the dead skin.* flake, remove, scale, strip. 2 *He peeled the vegetables.* pare, skin.

peep[1] verb 1 *She peeped from behind the curtain.* glance, look, peek, peer. 2 *The sun peeped out from behind the cloud.* appear, come into view, emerge, show. — noun *He took a peep at the presents.* glance, glimpse, look, peek.

peep[2] noun 1 *the peep of sparrows.* cheep, chirp, squeak, tweet, twitter. 2 *not a peep from the children.* cry, murmur, sound, squeak, whimper, whisper. — verb *The sparrows peeped.* cheep, chirp, squeak, tweet, twitter.

peer[1] verb *He peered at them over his glasses.* gaze, look, peek, peep, stare.

peer[2] noun 1 *peers of the realm.* aristocrat, lord, noble, nobleman; [*kinds of peer*] baron, duke, earl, marquess, viscount. 2 *She gets on well with her peers.* contemporary, equal, fellow.

peeress noun aristocrat, lady, noblewoman; [*kinds of peeress*] baroness, countess, duchess, marchioness, viscountess.

peerless adjective *a peerless performance.* incomparable, inimitable, matchless, superlative, supreme, unequalled, unparalleled, unrivalled, unsurpassed.

peeve verb (*informal*) *His remark really peeved her.* annoy, bug (*informal*), irritate, miff (*informal*), needle, pique, provoke, rile, upset, vex.

peevish adjective *She's peevish when she does not get what she wants.* bad-tempered, crabby, cranky, cross, fractious, grouchy, grumpy, irritable, petulant, querulous, snaky (*Australian informal*), sulky, surly, testy. OPPOSITE good-tempered.

peg noun *He hung his coat on the peg.* hook, nail, pin, spike. — verb 1 *She pegged the washing on the line.* attach, fasten, pin, secure. 2 *Prices have been pegged.* control, fix, freeze, limit, set.

pejorative adjective *a pejorative word.* derogatory, disparaging, uncomplimentary.

pellet noun *pellets of pet food.* ball, bead, pill.

pelt[1] verb 1 *She pelted the thieves with stones.* assail, batter, bombard, pepper, shower. 2 *The rain was pelting down.* bucket, pour, teem.

pelt[2] noun *The animals are killed for their pelts.* coat, fleece, hide, skin.

pen[1] noun *He writes with a pen.* ball-point, Biro (*trade mark*), felt-tipped pen, fountain pen, marker, quill, Texta (*trade mark*).

pen[2] noun *The animals are in the pen.* cage, compound, coop, corral, enclosure, fold, hutch, pound, run, stall, sty. — verb *The animals were penned.* close in, confine, coop up, enclose, fence in, impound, restrict, shut in.

penalise verb *He was penalised for using bad language.* fine, handicap, punish.

penalty noun 1 *He paid the penalty for his misdeeds.* fine, forfeit, price, punishment. OPPOSITE reward. 2 *The team is playing with a penalty.* disadvantage, handicap.

penetrate verb 1 *The prongs penetrated the rubber boot.* break through, drill through, enter, perforate, pierce, prick, probe, puncture, spike. 2 *The rain penetrated their clothes.* permeate, saturate, seep through, soak through.

penetrating adjective 1 *a penetrating mind.* astute, discerning, incisive, intelligent, keen, perceptive, sharp, shrewd. OPPOSITE dull. 2 *a penetrating cry.* harsh, loud, piercing, sharp, shrill. OPPOSITE soft.

penitent adjective *The driver was penitent after the accident.* apologetic, contrite, regretful, remorseful, repentant, sorry. OPPOSITE impenitent.

pen-name noun *She writes under a pen-name.* alias, assumed name, nom de plume, pseudonym.

pennant noun *The team carried the school pennant.* banner, ensign, flag, standard.

penniless adjective *He cannot pay his bills: he is penniless.* broke, destitute, hard up (*informal*), impecunious, impoverished, needy, poor, poverty-stricken, skint (*informal*). OPPOSITE affluent, rich.

penny-pinching adjective *a penny-pinching old miser.* mean, mingy, miserly, niggardly, parsimonious, stingy, tight-fisted. OPPOSITE generous.

pension noun *She received a pension after 60.* annuity, benefit, super (*informal*), superannuation.

pensive adjective *photographed in pensive mood.* day-dreaming, dreamy, introspective, meditative, reflective, serious, thoughtful. OPPOSITE carefree.

pent-up adjective *pent-up emotions.* bottled-up, held in, repressed, restrained, stifled, suppressed.

people plural noun 1 *He prefers animals to people.* human beings, humanity, humans, mankind, men and women, persons. **2** *the Australian people.* citizens, community, electorate, inhabitants, nation, populace, population, public, residents, society. — verb *The place was densely peopled.* colonise, inhabit, occupy, populate, settle.

pep noun *They were full of pep after their holiday.* dash, energy, go, life, liveliness, spirit, verve, vigour, vim (*informal*), vitality, vivacity. OPPOSITE lassitude. — verb *The change in the weather pepped him up.* energise, enliven, invigorate, liven up, perk up, vitalise.

pepper noun *green or red peppers.* capsicum. — verb *The body was peppered with bullets.* bombard, pelt, riddle, shower, spray.

perceive verb **1** *He perceived a change in their attitude.* become aware of, detect, discern, notice, observe, recognise, see. **2** *She perceived that there was something wrong.* apprehend, deduce, feel, gather, grasp, realise, sense, understand.

perceptible adjective *a perceptible change.* appreciable, discernible, evident, noticeable, observable, obvious, palpable, tangible, visible. OPPOSITE imperceptible.

perceptive adjective *a perceptive judge of character.* astute, clever, discerning, keen, observant, percipient, perspicacious, quick, sensitive, sharp, shrewd, understanding. OPPOSITE obtuse.

perch noun *a bird's perch.* roost. — verb *The bird perched on the branch.* alight, land, rest, roost, settle, sit.

percolate verb *The water percolated through the soil.* filter, leach, ooze, permeate, seep, trickle.

perennial adjective *Weeds are a perennial problem.* chronic, constant, continuous, eternal, everlasting, lasting, never-ending, permanent, perpetual, persistent, recurring. OPPOSITE occasional, temporary.

perfect adjective **1** *a perfect answer.* accurate, complete, correct, exact, precise, right. OPPOSITE wrong. **2** *a perfect specimen.* excellent, faultless, flawless, immaculate, impeccable, in mint condition, spotless, unblemished, undamaged. OPPOSITE faulty, imperfect. **3** *perfect conditions for sailing.* ideal, model, optimum. OPPOSITE poor. **4** *perfect nonsense.* absolute, complete, out-and-out, pure, sheer, thorough, total, utter. — verb *She has perfected the technique.* polish, refine.

perforate verb *The spikes perforated the skin.* penetrate, pierce, prick, puncture.

perform verb **1** *He performs his job well.* accomplish, achieve, carry out, complete, discharge, do, execute, fulfil. **2** *The car performs well.* behave, function, go, operate, run, work. **3** *He is performing in a new play.* act, appear, play, star. **4** *They performed a play.* enact, present, put on, stage.

performance noun *a performance of the play.* enactment, presentation, production, showing, staging; see also SHOW.

performer noun actor, actress, artist, artiste, busker, dancer, entertainer, instrumentalist, musician, player, singer, star, vocalist.

perfume noun *the sweet perfume of the flowers.* aroma, bouquet, fragrance, odour, scent, smell. OPPOSITE stink.

perfunctory adjective *a perfunctory inspection.* brief, careless, casual, cursory, half-hearted, hasty, mechanical, offhand, routine, slapdash, superficial. OPPOSITE thorough.

perhaps adverb *Perhaps you're right.* maybe, perchance (*old use*), possibly.

peril noun *The walkers were in grave peril.* danger, hazard, jeopardy, risk, threat. OPPOSITE safety.

perilous adjective *a perilous journey across the ice.* chancy, dangerous, dicey (*slang*), hairy (*slang*), hazardous, precarious, risky, unsafe. OPPOSITE safe.

perimeter noun *the perimeter of the school.* border, boundary, circumference, edge, fringe, limits, margin. OPPOSITE centre.

period noun **1** *a period of ill health. He went away for a long period.* bout, duration, interval, patch, phase, season, space, span, spell, stage, stint, stretch, term, time, while. **2** *relics of an earlier period.* aeon, age, epoch, era, time. **3** *They have two art periods a week.* class, lesson, session.

periodic adjective *a periodic change.* cyclical, periodical, recurrent, regular, seasonal.

periodical noun *The library does not lend periodicals.* journal, magazine, newspaper, paper, serial.

peripatetic adjective *a peripatetic music teacher.* itinerant, mobile, travelling.

peripheral adjective *a peripheral issue.* incidental, marginal, minor, secondary, subsidiary, tangential. OPPOSITE central, important.

periphery noun *She lives on the periphery of the city.* boundary, edge, fringe, limits, outskirts, perimeter. OPPOSITE centre.

perish verb **1** *He perished in the desert.* die, expire, lose your life, pass away. **2** *The elastic has perished.* disintegrate, give way, go, rot.

perjure verb **perjure yourself** bear false witness, give false testimony, lie.

perk[1] verb **perk up** *He perked up after the shower.* brighten up, buck up, liven up, pep up, revive.

perk[2] noun (*informal*) *A company car is one of the perks of the job.* bonus, extra, fringe benefit, perquisite.

perky adjective *He felt perky again after his illness.* animated, bright, cheerful, energetic, frisky, lively, sprightly, spry, vivacious. OPPOSITE lethargic.

permanent adjective **1** *a permanent problem.* chronic, constant, continual, continuous, enduring, everlasting, lasting, lifelong, long-lasting, never-ending, ongoing, perennial, perpetual, persistent. OPPOSITE temporary. **2** *a permanent structure.* durable, fixed, indestructible, stable. OPPOSITE impermanent, temporary. **3** *a permanent stain.* indelible, ingrained, persistent. OPPOSITE removable.

permanently adverb *The house is his permanently.* always, constantly, continuously, eternally, forever, for good, for keeps (*informal*), perpetually, persistently.

permeate verb *The brine permeated the olives.* flow through, penetrate, pervade, saturate, soak through, spread through.

permissible adjective *a permissible amount.* acceptable, admissible, allowable, authorised, lawful, legal, legitimate, permitted, proper, right, sanctioned, valid. OPPOSITE forbidden, illegal.

permission noun *He granted them permission to publish his story.* approval, authorisation, authority, clearance, consent, go-ahead, leave, licence. OPPOSITE prohibition.

permissive adjective *a permissive society.* broad-minded, easygoing, indulgent, lenient, liberal, tolerant. OPPOSITE strict.

permit verb *He does not permit smoking.* agree to, allow, approve of, authorise, consent to, legalise, license, put up with, sanction, tolerate. OPPOSITE ban, prohibit. — noun *a parking permit.* authorisation, licence, pass, warrant.

pernickety adjective (*informal*) *a pernickety clerk.* fastidious, finicky, fussy, over-scrupulous, punctilious. OPPOSITE careless.

perpendicular adjective *The walls should be perpendicular.* upright, vertical. OPPOSITE horizontal.

perpetual adjective **1** *a state of perpetual bliss.* abiding, endless, enduring, eternal, everlasting, lasting, never-ending, permanent, unending. OPPOSITE temporary. **2** (*informal*) *Her perpetual whinging was tiring.* ceaseless, constant, continual, endless, incessant, interminable, non-stop, persistent, recurrent, repeated, unceasing. OPPOSITE occasional.

perplex verb *Her behaviour perplexed people.* baffle, bamboozle (*informal*), bewilder, confuse, mystify, nonplus, puzzle, stump (*informal*), throw (*informal*).

persecute verb *He was persecuted for his religious beliefs.* bully, harass, hassle, intimidate, maltreat, mistreat, oppress, terrorise, torment, torture, tyrannise, victimise.

perseverance noun *In the end he was rewarded for his perseverance.* determination, diligence, doggedness, endurance, patience, persistence, pertinacity, stamina, staying power, sticking power, tenacity.

persevere verb *She persevered at the task until it was mastered.* battle on, carry on, continue, endure, keep on, persist, plug away, stick at (*informal*). OPPOSITE give up.

persist verb **1** *He persisted in cheating.* carry on, continue, go on, keep on, persevere, stick at (*informal*). OPPOSITE give up, stop. **2** *The custom persists in some places.* continue, hold, last, live on, remain, survive.

persistent adjective **1** *He was persistent in his fight for truth.* assiduous, determined, diligent, dogged, firm, indefatigable, obstinate, patient, pertinacious, relentless, resolute, steadfast, stubborn, tenacious, tireless, unwavering. OPPOSITE irresolute. **2** *The pain is persistent.* chronic, constant, continuous, endless, eternal, everlasting, incessant, interminable, nagging, permanent, perpetual, recurrent, unceasing, unrelenting, unremitting. OPPOSITE intermittent.

person noun *a lucky person. a funny person.* chap (*informal*), character, creature, fellow (*informal*), human, human being, individual, mortal, sort (*informal*), soul, type (*informal*); see also CHILD, MAN, WOMAN.

personal adjective **1** *He gave the painting his personal touch.* characteristic, distinctive, idiosyncratic, individual, special, unique. **2** *a personal opinion.* individual, private, subjective. **3** *her personal diary.* confidential, intimate, own, private, secret. OPPOSITE public. **4** *personal hygiene.* bodily, physical.

personality noun **1** *He has a charming personality.* character, disposition, make-up, nature, temperament. **2** *a television personality.* celebrity, identity (*Australian informal*), luminary, star.

personify verb *He personifies evil.* embody, epitomise, exemplify, represent, symbolise, typify.

personnel noun *The firm looks after its personnel.* employees, human resources, staff, workers, workforce.

perspective noun *She could see things from his perspective.* angle, outlook, point of view, standpoint, viewpoint.

perspiration noun sweat, wetness.

perspire verb sweat.

persuade verb *She finally persuaded them to go.* cajole, coax, convert, convince, entice, induce, influence, lead, move, prevail on, sway, talk into, tempt, win over. OPPOSITE dissuade.

persuasion noun **1** *It did not take much persuasion to make them come.* argument, cajolery, coaxing, convincing, influence. **2** *They are of a different political persuasion.* belief, conviction, school of thought.

persuasive adjective *a persuasive argument.* cogent, compelling, convincing, eloquent, forceful, plausible, powerful, strong, telling, weighty. OPPOSITE weak.

pertinent adjective *The comment was not pertinent to the subject in hand.* applicable, apposite, appropriate, apt, germane, material, relevant, suitable. OPPOSITE irrelevant.

perturb verb *He was not perturbed by their absence.* agitate, alarm, bother, disconcert, distress, disturb, frighten, scare, trouble, upset, worry. OPPOSITE reassure.

perusal noun *a perusal of the documents.* examination, inspection, reading, scrutiny, study.

peruse verb *They perused the papers before signing them.* examine, inspect, look over, read, scan, scrutinise, study.

pervade verb *A smell of garlic pervaded the house.* diffuse through, fill, permeate, spread through.

perverse adjective *a perverse child, delighting in disobedience.* contrary, disobedient, headstrong, intractable, obstinate, pigheaded (*informal*), rebellious, recalcitrant, refractory, stroppy (*informal*), stubborn, unreasonable, wayward, wilful. OPPOSITE cooperative, reasonable.

pervert verb *He tried to pervert the witness.* bribe, corrupt, lead astray. — noun *a sexual pervert.* deviant, weirdo (*informal*).

perverted adjective *a perverted mind.* corrupt, depraved, deviant, kinky (*informal*), sick, twisted, warped. OPPOSITE normal.

pessimistic adjective *He was pessimistic about his results.* cynical, defeatist, despairing, despondent, fatalistic, gloomy, hopeless, morbid, negative, resigned, unhappy. OPPOSITE optimistic.

pest noun *The telephone is sometimes a pest.* annoyance, bother, curse, inconvenience, menace, nuisance, pain (*informal*).

pester verb *He pestered his mother for his pocket money.* annoy, badger, bother, harass, hassle (*informal*), hound, irritate, keep on at, nag, plague, torment, trouble, worry.

pet noun *the teacher's pet.* apple of someone's eye, darling, favourite. — adjective **1** *a pet wallaby.* domestic, domesticated, tame. **2** *a pet subject.* favourite, special. — verb *She petted the cat.* caress, cuddle, fondle, pat, stroke.

peter verb **peter out** *The supply petered out.* diminish, end, fail, give out, run out, stop, taper off. OPPOSITE continue.

petition noun *The residents signed a petition to keep the bank open.* appeal, entreaty, plea, request, supplication. — verb *He petitioned his local Member of Parliament.* appeal to, ask, beseech, call upon, entreat, plead, pray, request.

petrify *verb The noises petrified her.* appal, frighten, numb, paralyse, scare stiff (*informal*), terrify.

petrol *noun The car needs petrol.* fuel, gas (*American informal*), gasoline (*American*). □ **petrol station** filling station, garage, roadhouse, service station, servo (*Australian informal*).

petty *adjective Don't worry about petty details.* insignificant, minor, paltry, piffling (*informal*), small, trifling, trivial, unimportant. OPPOSITE important.

petulant *adjective They ignored him when he became petulant.* bad-tempered, crabby, cross, grouchy, grumpy, huffy, irritable, peevish, snappy, sulky, sullen, testy, tetchy.

phantom *noun She thought she saw a phantom.* apparition, ghost, hallucination, phantasm, poltergeist, spectre, spirit, spook (*informal*), vision, wraith.

pharmacist *noun The pharmacist made up the prescription.* apothecary (*old use*), chemist, dispenser, druggist, pharmaceutical chemist.

pharmacy *noun Medicines are sold at the pharmacy.* dispensary, drugstore (*American*).

phase *noun the introductory phase.* period, point, stage, step, time.

phenomenal *adjective a phenomenal achievement.* amazing, exceptional, extraordinary, fabulous (*informal*), fantastic (*informal*), great, incredible (*informal*), marvellous, miraculous, noteworthy, outstanding, prodigious, rare, remarkable, sensational, singular, stupendous, uncommon, wonderful. OPPOSITE ordinary.

phenomenon *noun Snow is a rare phenomenon in most parts of Australia.* event, experience, happening, occurrence.

philanthropic *adjective The donation was seen as a philanthropic gesture.* benevolent, charitable, generous, humane, humanitarian, kind-hearted, magnanimous, munificent. OPPOSITE mean, misanthropic.

philistine *adjective an unappreciative and philistine audience.* boorish, ignorant, lowbrow, uncultivated, uncultured, unrefined.

philosophical *adjective He was philosophical about the loss.* calm, fatalistic, logical, rational, reasonable, resigned, serene, stoical, unemotional. OPPOSITE upset.

philosophy *noun a philosophy of life.* belief system, convictions, doctrine, ideology, principles, values, view.

phlegmatic *adjective a phlegmatic temperament.* apathetic, calm, cool, impassive, indifferent, lethargic, nonchalant, placid, serene, sluggish, stolid, unemotional, unexcitable, unflappable (*informal*). OPPOSITE lively.

phobia *noun He was cured of his phobia about cats.* aversion, dislike, dread, fear, hang-up (*informal*), horror. OPPOSITE liking.

phone *noun She doesn't like talking on the phone.* blower (*informal*), telephone. — *verb He phoned his parents.* call, dial, ring (up), telephone.

phoney *adjective* (*informal*) *a phoney diamond.* artificial, bogus, counterfeit, fake, false, forged, imitation, pretend (*informal*), pseudo, sham, synthetic. OPPOSITE genuine. — *noun* (*informal*) **1** *We realised the man was a phoney.* charlatan, con man (*informal*), fake, fraud, impostor, pretender, quack. **2** *The diamond was a phoney.* counterfeit, fake, forgery, imitation, sham.

photocopy *noun a photocopy of the document.* copy, duplicate. — *verb He photocopied the letter for his own records.* copy, duplicate, reproduce.

photograph *noun She likes to look at her baby photographs.* photo, picture, print, shot, snap, snapshot. — *verb He photographed the house before it was demolished.* shoot, snap.

phrase *noun* **1** *a French phrase.* expression, idiom, locution, term. **2** *It became a famous phrase.* catchphrase, cliché, dictum, maxim, motto, proverb, saying, slogan. — *verb He phrased the statement carefully.* couch, express, formulate, frame, put, word.

phraseology *noun legal phraseology.* idiom, language, parlance, terminology, vocabulary, wording.

physical *adjective* **1** *physical punishment.* bodily, corporal. CONTRASTS WITH mental, spiritual. **2** *the physical world.* actual, concrete, material, real, solid, tangible. OPPOSITE intangible.

physician *noun* doctor, medical practitioner.

physique *noun a healthy physique.* body, build, figure, shape.

pick *verb* **1** *He only picks at his food.* nibble, peck. **2** *She picked some grapes.* collect, cut, gather, harvest, pluck, pull off. **3** *She was picked to be captain.* choose, decide on, elect, name, nominate, opt for, select, settle on, single out, vote for. OPPOSITE reject. — *noun* **1** *He had first pick.* choice, option, preference, selection. **2** *the pick of the crop.* best, choice, cream, elite. OPPOSITE worst. □ **pick on** *Stop picking on her.* bully, criticise, find fault with, get at (*informal*), harass, nag. **pick out** *He picked her out easily in the crowd.* distinguish, make out, notice, recognise, spot. **pick up** **1** *Friends picked him up at the airport.* call for, collect, fetch, get. **2** *The police picked him up for shoplifting.* apprehend, arrest, catch, detain, nab (*informal*), nick (*slang*), take into custody. **3** *She picked up a bargain.* acquire, come by, find, get, obtain, snaffle (*informal*). **4** *He picked up a bad cold.* catch, come down with, contract. **5** *Business is picking up.* get better, improve, rally, recover.

picket *noun* **1** *The picket warned of the enemy's approach.* guard, lookout, patrol, sentinel, sentry, watch. **2** *a fence of pickets.* pale, paling, post, stake.

pickle *noun He got himself into a pickle.* fix (*informal*), jam (*informal*), mess, plight, predicament, spot (*informal*). — *verb He pickled the olives in brine.* preserve, souse.

picture *noun* **1** *a picture in a book. pictures on the walls.* cartoon, collage, design, diagram, drawing, engraving, etching, illustration, image, landscape, likeness, mosaic, mural, painting, photo, photograph, plate, portrait, print, representation, reproduction, sketch, snapshot; [*pictures*] graphics. **2** *They watched a picture in black and white.* film, flick (*informal*), motion picture, movie (*informal*), moving picture, video. — *verb* **1** *The artist pictured the judge at his desk.* depict, draw, illustrate, paint, portray, represent, reproduce, sketch. **2** *Picture yourself by a mountain stream.* conceive, dream up, envisage, fancy, imagine, see, visualise.

picturesque *adjective* **1** *a picturesque landscape.* attractive, beautiful, charming, pretty, quaint, scenic. OPPOSITE ugly. **2** *picturesque language.* colourful, descriptive, expressive, graphic, imaginative, striking, vivid. OPPOSITE dull.

pie *noun a baked pie.* flan, quiche, tart.

piebald *adjective a piebald horse.* dappled, mottled, pied, skewbald.

piece *noun* **1** *a piece of chocolate. a piece of timber.* amount, bar, bit, bite, block, chip, chunk, division, fraction, fragment, hunk, length, lump, morsel, part, portion, quantity, remnant, scrap, section, segment, share, shred, slab, slice, sliver, snippet, stick, titbit, wedge. **2** *There are fifty pieces in the set.* component, element, module, part, unit. **3** *a piece of embroidery. a museum piece.* article, example, instance, item, object, sample, specimen, thing. **4** *She played her new piece on the piano.* composition, creation, item, number, opus, work. — *verb* **piece together** *He pieced the saucer together again.* assemble, join together, mend, patch up, put together, reassemble.

pied *adjective a clown in pied costume.* dappled, harlequin, motley, mottled, multicoloured, particoloured, piebald, skewbald, variegated.

pier *noun fishing from the pier.* breakwater, jetty, landing stage, quay, wharf.

pierce *verb The nail pierced his foot.* bore through, enter, gore, impale, jab, lance, penetrate, perforate, prick, puncture, skewer, spear, spike, stab, wound.

piercing *adjective* **1** *a piercing wind.* biting, bitter, cutting, keen. OPPOSITE gentle. **2** *a piercing voice.* deafening, loud, noisy, penetrating, screeching, sharp, shrill, strident. OPPOSITE soft.

piety *noun He was not just a church-goer, but a man of true piety.* devotion, devoutness, faith, godliness, holiness, piousness, reverence, saintliness, sanctity. OPPOSITE impiety.

pig *noun* **1** *a herd of pigs.* boar, hog, piglet, porker, sow (*female*), swine. **2** (*informal*) *Some pig has eaten all of the pie.* see GLUTTON.

pigeon-hole *noun The letter is in your pigeon-hole.* compartment, cubby hole, niche.

pigheaded *adjective She is too pig-headed to listen to your advice.* headstrong, intractable, mulish, obstinate, refractory, self-willed, stiff-necked, stubborn, wilful. OPPOSITE tractable.

pigment *noun painted in natural pigments.* colour, colouring, dye, tint.

pikelet *noun* drop scone, flapjack, pancake.

pile[1] *noun* **1** *a pile of clothes.* batch, collection, heap, hoard, mass, mound, mountain, pyramid, stack, stockpile. **2** (*informal*) *She has a pile of work. piles of work to do.* heap (*informal*), load (*informal*), lot (*informal*), mountain, oodles (*informal*), plenty, stack (*informal*), ton (*informal*). — *verb* **1** *She piled the toys in the corner.* accumulate, assemble, collect, gather, heap (up), load, mass, stack (up), stockpile. OPPOSITE scatter. **2** *They piled into the car.* crowd, huddle, pack, squeeze.

pile[2] *noun The house is built on piles.* column, pillar, post, stilt, support, upright.

pile[3] *noun The carpet has a thick pile.* nap, surface.

pilfer *verb She was caught pilfering lollies from the shop.* filch, help yourself to, lift (*informal*), nick (*slang*), pinch (*informal*), snitch (*slang*), souvenir (*slang*), steal, take.

pill *noun The pills are available on prescription.* capsule, lozenge, pellet, tablet.

pillage *verb & noun* see PLUNDER.

pillar *noun a tall supporting pillar.* column, obelisk, pile, post, prop, shaft, stanchion, standard, support, upright.

pillow *noun She put her head on the pillow.* bolster, cushion.

pilot *noun* **1** *an aeroplane pilot.* airman, airwoman, aviator, captain. **2** *The pilot steered the boat.* coxswain, guide, helmsman, navigator, steersman. — *verb His job is to pilot the boats through the harbour.* conduct, escort, guide, lead, navigate, steer. — *adjective a pilot programme.* experimental, preliminary, test, trial.

pimple *noun a medication to help clear pimples.* blackhead, pustule, spot, whitehead, zit (*slang*); [*pimples*] acne.

pin *noun fastened with a pin.* brooch, drawing pin, hairpin, hatpin, nappy pin, safety pin, skewer, spike, split pin, staple, tack, tiepin. — *verb* **1** *The picture was pinned on the board.* affix, attach, fasten, fix, nail, secure, spike, staple, stick, tack. **2** *He was pinned under the car.* hold down, hold fast, immobilise, pinion. □ **pin down** *He pinned him down to a time.* bind, commit, nail down.

pinch *verb* **1** *She pinched my arm.* nip, squeeze, tweak. **2** (*informal*) *She pinched a watch from behind the counter.* lift (*informal*), nick (*slang*), pilfer, purloin, snatch, snavel (*Australian informal*), snitch (*slang*), steal, swipe (*informal*), take. — *noun* **1** *The baby gave her a pinch.* nip, squeeze, tweak. **2** *a pinch of salt.* bit, smidgen, speck, touch, trace.

pine *verb* **1** *He pined when his wife died.* grieve, languish, mope, mourn, waste away. **2** *The dog is pining for its master.* hanker after, hunger for, long for, miss, yearn for.

pink *adjective a pink colour.* coral, flesh-coloured, peach, rose, rosy, salmon-pink, shell-pink, skin-coloured.

pinnacle *noun* **1** *The pinnacle was covered with snow.* apex, cap, crest, peak, summit, tip, top. **2** *the pinnacle of her career.* acme, apex, climax, culmination, height, heyday, peak, summit, top, zenith. OPPOSITE nadir.

pinpoint *verb He pinpointed their position.* discover, find, identify, locate, spot.

pioneer *noun* **1** *Her ancestors were Australian pioneers.* colonist, discoverer, explorer, settler. **2** *pioneers in the fast-food industry.* founder, innovator, trailblazer. — *verb He pioneered the procedure.* create, develop, discover, establish, found, introduce, initiate, originate, start.

pious *adjective a pious man, inspired by his love for God.* devout, faithful, God-fearing, godly, holy, religious, reverent, saintly. OPPOSITE impious.

pipe *noun The pipe is blocked.* channel, conduit, drainpipe, duct, hose, main, pipeline, tube.

piquant *adjective a piquant flavour.* appetising, flavoursome, pungent, sharp, spicy, tangy, tart. OPPOSITE bland.

pique *verb Losing to his former student piqued him.* affront, annoy, gall, humiliate, hurt, irk, irritate, mortify, needle, nettle, offend, peeve (*informal*), vex, wound. OPPOSITE delight. — *noun a fit of pique.* annoyance, displeasure, humiliation, irritation, mortification, resentment, umbrage.

pirate *noun Pirates took over the ship.* buccaneer, corsair, marauder, privateer.

pit noun **1** *The ball fell into a pit.* abyss, bunker, cavity, crater, depression, ditch, gully, hole, hollow, trench. **2** *The miners went into the pit.* coalmine, colliery, mine, quarry, shaft, working. — *verb* **1** *The surface was pitted.* dent, gouge, nick, pock-mark, scar. **2** *He was pitted against a strong opponent.* match, oppose, set against.

pitch verb **1** *He pitched the ball.* bowl, cast, chuck (*informal*), fling, heave, hurl, lob, sling, throw, toss. **2** *He pitched the tent.* erect, put up, raise, set up. **3** *The ship pitched in heavy seas.* lurch, plunge, rock, roll, toss about. — *noun* **1** *The roof has a gentle pitch.* angle, cant, grade, gradient, incline, slope. **2** *Their excitement had reached fever pitch.* degree, height, intensity, level, point. **3** *He has no ear for recognising differences in pitch.* highness, lowness, tone. **4** *sales pitch.* line (*informal*), patter, spiel (*slang*), talk.

pitcher noun *a pitcher of water.* ewer, jug.

pitfall noun *Would-be writers were warned of the pitfalls.* danger, difficulty, hazard, peril, snag, snare, trap.

pithy adjective *pithy comments.* brief, concise, meaningful, succinct, terse.

pitiful adjective **1** *the pitiful sight of an injured animal.* distressing, forlorn, heartbreaking, heartrending, moving, pathetic, poignant, sad, touching, wretched. **2** *a pitiful attempt.* contemptible, hopeless, miserable, pathetic, poor, sorry, useless, woeful.

pitiless adjective *a pitiless tyrant.* brutal, callous, cruel, hard-hearted, heartless, inhuman, merciless, relentless, remorseless, ruthless. OPPOSITE compassionate, merciful.

pittance noun *He was paid a pittance for his labours.* chicken-feed (*informal*), peanuts (*informal*), trifle. OPPOSITE fortune.

pity noun **1** *He felt pity for the victims.* commiseration, compassion, condolence, fellow-feeling, regret, sorrow, sympathy, tenderness, understanding. OPPOSITE indifference. **2** *The judge showed no pity.* charity, clemency, compassion, forbearance, lenience, mercy. OPPOSITE severity. **3** *What a pity!* shame. — *verb He pitied those who missed out.* commiserate with, feel for, feel sorry for, sympathise with.

pivot noun *The needle turns on a pivot.* axis, fulcrum, shaft, spindle. — *verb The spinning top pivots on this point.* revolve, rotate, spin, swivel, turn, twirl.

placard noun *The wall was covered with placards.* advertisement, bill, notice, poster, sign.

placate verb *She was easily placated.* appease, calm, conciliate, mollify, pacify, propitiate, soothe. OPPOSITE provoke.

place noun **1** *This is the place where it happened.* address, area, locality, location, scene, setting, site, situation, spot, venue. **2** *We visited many interesting places.* area, city, country, district, locality, neighbourhood, region, town, township, village. **3** *The meeting is at his place.* dwelling, home, house, premises, residence. **4** *Someone is sitting in that place.* chair, position, seat, space, spot. — *verb* **1** *She placed the parcels on the table.* arrange, deposit, dump, lay, leave, locate, plant, plonk, position, put, rest, set, situate, stand, station, stick (*informal*). OPPOSITE remove. **2** *I can't place him.* identify, recognise, remember. □ **in place of** *She used raisins in place of sultanas in the rec-*

ipe. as a substitute for, in lieu of, instead of.

placid adjective *a placid nature.* calm, easygoing, equable, even-tempered, level-headed, mild, peaceable, quiet, sedate, serene, tranquil, unexcitable, unruffled. OPPOSITE excitable.

plagiarise verb *The student plagiarised another's essay.* appropriate, copy, crib, lift (*informal*), pirate.

plague noun **1** *bubonic plague.* epidemic, pandemic, pestilence. **2** *a plague of mice.* infestation, invasion, scourge. — *verb We were plagued by mosquitoes.* annoy, bother, bug (*informal*), disturb, harass, hassle (*informal*), irritate, pester, torment, trouble, vex, worry.

plain adjective **1** *The meaning was plain.* apparent, certain, clear, comprehensible, evident, explicit, intelligible, manifest, obvious, patent, transparent, unambiguous, understandable, unmistakable. OPPOSITE obscure. **2** *a plain dress.* austere, basic, homely, simple, unadorned. OPPOSITE elaborate, fancy. **3** *The food tastes plain.* bland, insipid, tasteless, uninteresting, wishy-washy. OPPOSITE tasty. **4** *plain paper.* blank, unlined, unmarked, unpatterned. OPPOSITE patterned. **5** *some plain speaking.* blunt, candid, direct, forthright, frank, honest, open, outspoken, straightforward, unambiguous. OPPOSITE evasive. **6** *She thought she looked plain.* homely (*American*), ordinary, unattractive, unprepossessing. OPPOSITE attractive. — *noun The hills overlook sweeping plains.* flat, grassland, pampas, prairie, savannah, steppe, tundra, veld.

plaintive adjective *a plaintive song.* doleful, melancholy, mournful, pitiful, sad, sorrowful.

plait verb *She plaited the three strands.* braid, interlace, intertwine, interweave.

plan noun **1** *They looked at the plan of the building.* blueprint, chart, design, diagram, drawing, layout, map, sketch. **2** *They worked according to a plan.* formula, method, outline, plot, policy, procedure, programme, project, proposal, schedule, scheme, strategy. — *verb* **1** *The city developed as it had been planned.* design, draw, lay out, map out. **2** *They planned their action.* arrange, contrive, design, devise, draft, formulate, organise, plot, premeditate, prepare, scheme, think up. **3** *Do you plan to come?* aim, intend, mean, propose.

plane noun *They travelled to England by plane.* aeroplane, aircraft, jet, jumbo. — *adjective a plane surface.* even, flat, flush, level, smooth.

plank noun *The floor is made of planks.* board, slab, timber.

planned adjective *a planned attack.* calculated, deliberate, intentional, organised, premeditated. OPPOSITE unplanned.

plant noun **1** *A botanist studies plants.* flora, greenery, vegetation. **2** *an engineering plant.* factory, foundry, mill, works, workshop. **3** *The firm is insured for damage to plant.* apparatus, equipment, gear, machinery. — *verb* **1** *He planted seeds and seedlings.* set out, sow, transplant. **2** *She planted the idea in his head.* fix, implant, put. **3** *He planted the tapes in her house.* conceal, hide, secrete.

plaster noun *She had a plaster on her cut finger.* bandage, dressing. — *verb He plastered the table with finger paint.* coat, cover, daub, smear, spread.

plate noun **1** *a plate for food.* dish, platter. **2** *a plate of glass.* layer, pane, panel, sheet. **3** *His name was*

on a brass plate on the wall. plaque, shingle, sign, tablet.

plateau noun *After an uphill climb we reached a plateau.* highland, tableland.

platform noun **1** *She addressed us from the platform.* dais, podium, pulpit, rostrum, stage, stand. **2** *a political party's platform.* manifesto, policy, programme.

platitude noun *The card expressed many platitudes.* banality, cliché, commonplace, truism.

platter noun *platters of food.* dish, plate, salver, tray.

platypus noun duckbill, water mole (*old use*).

plausible adjective *a plausible explanation.* believable, conceivable, credible, likely, reasonable. OPPOSITE implausible, unlikely.

play verb **1** *She is playing with her sister.* amuse yourself, cavort, enjoy yourself, entertain yourself, fool about, frisk, frolic, gambol, have fun, mess about, romp, skylark. **2** *He plays cricket.* join in, participate in, take part in. **3** *Our team plays your school next week.* challenge, compete against, meet, take on, vie with. **4** *She played the fairy in the play.* act as, impersonate, perform as, portray, pretend to be, represent, star as. **5** *She plays the flute.* perform on. — *noun* **1** *a mixture of work and play.* amusement, diversion, entertainment, fun, leisure, pleasure, recreation, sport. **2** *a stage play.* drama, entertainment, production, show. □ **play down** *He played down the incident.* downplay, gloss over, make light of, minimise. **play for time** delay, hedge, procrastinate, stall, stonewall, temporise. **play up** (*informal*) *The children played up for the babysitter.* be disobedient, be mischievous, be naughty, misbehave, muck up (*informal*).

player noun **1** *a tennis player.* competitor, contestant, participant, sportsperson. **2** *the piano player.* artist, artiste, entertainer, musician, performer. **3** *The players bowed before the curtain fell.* actor, actress, performer.

playful adjective **1** *playful kittens.* active, frisky, high-spirited, lively, mischievous, skittish, spirited, sprightly, vivacious. OPPOSITE sedate. **2** *a playful remark.* arch, facetious, humorous, jesting, jocular, light-hearted, teasing, tongue-in-cheek. OPPOSITE serious.

playground noun park, recreation ground.

playwright noun dramatist.

plea noun **1** *a plea for mercy.* appeal, entreaty, petition, request, supplication. **2** *He declined the invitation on the plea of ill health.* excuse, grounds, pretext.

plead verb *He pleaded ignorance.* allege, assert, claim. □ **plead with** *He pleaded with them to let him go.* appeal to, ask, beg, beseech, entreat, implore, petition, request, urge.

pleasant noun **1** *a pleasant day. a pleasant setting.* agreeable, attractive, beautiful, delightful, enjoyable, fine, good, inviting, lovely, mild, nice, pleasing, pleasurable, relaxing, satisfying. OPPOSITE nasty, unpleasant. **2** *pleasant sounds.* dulcet, euphonious, gentle, harmonious, mellow, melodious, musical, pretty, soothing, sweet, tuneful. OPPOSITE harsh. **3** *a pleasant companion.* affable, amiable, amicable, charming, cheerful, congenial, cordial, friendly, genial, good-humoured, hospitable, jolly, jovial, kindly, likeable, nice, sweet, sympathetic, winsome. OPPOSITE obnoxious.

please verb **1** *The shopkeeper likes to please his customers.* content, delight, gratify, satisfy, suit. OPPOSITE annoy, displease. **2** *You may do as you please.* choose, desire, like, prefer, think fit, want, wish.

pleased adjective *She was pleased when it was all over.* content, contented, delighted, elated, glad, grateful, gratified, happy, joyful, satisfied, thankful. OPPOSITE displeased, unhappy.

pleasure noun *He gets pleasure out of helping people. He walks for pleasure.* amusement, bliss, contentment, delight, diversion, enjoyment, entertainment, fulfilment, fun, gratification, happiness, joy, kick(s) (*informal*), recreation, satisfaction, thrill. OPPOSITE displeasure, pain.

pleat noun *a skirt with pleats.* crease, fold, tuck.

pledge noun *a pledge of loyalty.* assurance, commitment, guarantee, oath, promise, vow, word. — *verb He pledged his support.* guarantee, plight (*old use*), promise, swear, vow.

plentiful adjective *a plentiful supply of tomatoes.* abundant, ample, bountiful, copious, generous, large, lavish, liberal, profuse, prolific. OPPOSITE meagre.

plenty noun *plenty of cream.* abundance, heaps (*informal*), lashings (*informal*), loads (*informal*), lots (*informal*), masses, much, oodles (*informal*), piles (*informal*), stacks (*informal*), tons (*informal*). OPPOSITE shortage.

pliable adjective **1** *a pliable material.* bendable, flexible, malleable, plastic, pliant, springy, supple. OPPOSITE rigid. **2** *a pliable person.* adaptable, amenable, compliant, flexible, malleable, suggestible, tractable, yielding. OPPOSITE intractable.

plight noun *a sad and sorry plight.* difficulty, dire straits, jam (*informal*), mess, pickle (*informal*), predicament, situation, state.

plod verb **1** *She plodded slowly through the mud.* lumber, plough, slog, traipse (*informal*), tramp, trudge. **2** *She plodded on with the work.* beaver on, grind away, peg away, persevere, plug away, soldier on.

plot noun **1** *a vegetable plot.* allotment, block (*Australian*), field, garden, lot, patch. **2** *the film's plot.* outline, scenario, storyline, synopsis. **3** *a plot to bring down the government.* conspiracy, intrigue, plan, scheme. — *verb* **1** *He plotted the course for the rally.* chart, draw, map out, outline, sketch. **2** *They plotted to overthrow the government.* conspire, plan, scheme.

ploy noun (*informal*) *a clever ploy to divert their attention.* dodge, manoeuvre, ruse, scheme, stratagem, tactic, trick.

pluck verb **1** *She plucked some flowers.* gather, harvest, pick, pull off, yank (*informal*). **2** *He plucks his eyebrows.* pull out, remove. **3** *He plucked the letter from her hand.* grab, seize, snatch, tug. — *noun The rescuer showed great pluck.* bravery, courage, daring, grit, guts (*informal*), mettle, nerve, spunk (*informal*), valour.

plucky adjective *the plucky hero.* bold, brave, courageous, daring, fearless, game, hardy, heroic, intrepid, mettlesome, spirited, valiant. OPPOSITE faint-hearted.

plug noun **1** *The plug came out of the hole.* bung, cork, stopper. **2** (*informal*) *The broadcaster gave their product a free plug.* advertisement, boost, commercial, promotion, publicity. — *verb He plugged the* *gaps.* block up, close up, fill, seal, stop up.

plummet *verb The bird plummeted to the ground. Prices plummeted.* crash, drop, fall, nosedive, plunge, take a dive, tumble. OPPOSITE soar.

plump *adjective She needs to lose weight before she becomes too plump.* chubby, corpulent, dumpy, fat, obese, overweight, podgy, portly, roly-poly, rotund, squat, stout, tubby. OPPOSITE skinny.

plunder *verb The soldiers plundered the town.* loot, maraud, pillage, raid, ransack, ravage, rob, sack. — *noun He loaded the plunder in his truck.* booty, loot, pillage, spoils, swag (*informal*), takings.

plunge *verb* **1** *He plunged the sword into his side.* force, jab, push, stick, thrust. **2** *The lift plunged when the cable broke.* descend, drop, fall, nosedive, plummet. OPPOSITE soar. **3** *The boy plunged into the icy water.* dive, duck, fall, jump, leap, sink, throw yourself, tumble. **4** *She plunged the clothes in the water.* dip, douse, immerse, lower, submerge. — *noun a plunge from the ten-metre tower.* dive, drop, fall, header, jump, leap, nosedive, tumble.

plus *noun The scheme has several pluses.* advantage, asset, benefit, bonus. OPPOSITE drawback, minus.

plush *adjective plush furnishings.* costly, lavish, luxurious, opulent, sumptuous. OPPOSITE cheap.

ply *noun* **1** *three-ply wood.* layer, thickness. **2** *eight-ply wool.* strand, thickness.

poach[1] *verb He poached the fish in wine.* simmer.

poach[2] *verb He poached the owner's pheasants.* hunt, steal.

pocket *noun The credit card fits in a plastic pocket.* bag, compartment, envelope, pouch. — *verb He pocketed the money.* appropriate, misappropriate, pilfer, steal, take. □ **pocket knife** clasp-knife, jack-knife, penknife. **pocket money** allowance.

pod *noun She removed the peas from the pod.* case, hull, husk, shell.

podgy *adjective He was teased at school because he was podgy.* chubby, dumpy, fat, overweight, plump, portly, roly-poly, pudgy, rotund, squat, stout, tubby. OPPOSITE skinny.

podiatry *noun* chiropody.

poem *noun* rhyme, verse; [*kinds of poem*] ballad, clerihew, doggerel, elegy, epic, haiku, idyll, jingle, lay, limerick, lyric, ode, sonnet.

poet *noun* bard.

poetic *adjective poetic writing.* lyrical, metrical, poetical, rhythmic.

poetry *noun* poems, verse. CONTRASTS WITH prose.

poignant *adjective The film presented a poignant look at poverty.* distressing, heartbreaking, heartrending, moving, pathetic, pitiful, stirring, touching.

point *noun* **1** *It narrows to a sharp point.* apex, extremity, prong, spike, tine, tip, vertex. **2** *The house is on the point.* cape, headland, promontory. **3** *a decimal point.* dot, spot. **4** *They agreed to meet at a certain point.* location, place, position, site, situation, spot. **5** *At that point she wanted to give up.* instant, juncture, moment, stage, time. **6** *The judges award points.* mark, score. **7** *The house has its good points.* aspect, attribute, characteristic, feature, property, quality, trait. **8** *They differed on several points.* detail, issue, item, matter, particular. **9** *the point of the story.* argument, drift, essence, gist, meaning, message, pith, substance, thrust. **10** *The exercise has no point.* aim, goal, intention, object, purpose, reason, sense,

use, value. — *verb* **1** *He pointed the gun at the fox.* aim, direct, level, train. **2** *He pointed the car towards home.* aim, direct, guide, lead, steer. **3** *These results point to a need for revision.* indicate, show, signal, suggest. □ **on the point of** *She was on the point of leaving.* about to, close to, near to, on the brink of, on the verge of. **point of view** *They have different points of view.* opinion, outlook, perspective, stance, standpoint, viewpoint. **point out** *She pointed out the sights.* draw attention to, indicate, show. **to the point** *The comments were to the point.* apposite, apropos, apt, germane, pertinent, relevant. OPPOSITE beside the point, irrelevant.

pointed *adjective* **1** *a pointed object.* pointy, sharp, tapered, tapering. **2** *a pointed comment.* barbed, cutting, incisive, penetrating, sharp, trenchant.

pointer *noun* **1** *The book has helpful pointers on removing stains.* hint, recommendation, suggestion, tip, wrinkle (*informal*). **2** *pointers to underlying problems.* clue, indication, indicator, lead, sign.

pointless *adjective a pointless discussion. a pointless task.* aimless, fatuous, futile, irrelevant, meaningless, needless, senseless, unnecessary, unproductive, useless, worthless. OPPOSITE useful.

poise *noun* **1** *The gymnasts were awarded marks for poise.* balance, equilibrium, steadiness. **2** *She handled the situation with poise.* aplomb, calmness, composure, confidence, coolness, equanimity, self-assurance, self-confidence, self-control.

poison *noun killed by the poison.* toxin, venom. — *verb* **1** *We poisoned the grass.* kill. **2** *The chemicals poisoned the water supply.* contaminate, infect, pollute, taint. **3** *She was accused of poisoning their minds.* corrupt, defile, pervert, pollute, warp.

poisonous *adjective* **1** *Poisonous substances are locked away.* deadly, harmful, lethal, noxious, toxic. OPPOSITE non-toxic. **2** *a poisonous spider-bite.* deadly, fatal, lethal, venomous. OPPOSITE non-venomous.

poke *verb* **1** *Ted poked him in the back.* butt, dig, elbow, jab, nudge, prod, push. **2** *Poke your fork in your meat.* jab, stab, stick, thrust. **3** *She is poking about in the drawer.* forage, fossick (*Australian informal*), rummage, search, snoop (*informal*). □ **poke fun at** *The other boys poked fun at him.* chiack (*Australian informal*), deride, jeer at, laugh at, make fun of, mock, poke borak at (*Australian informal*), rib (*informal*), ridicule, satirise, sling off at (*Australian informal*), take the mickey out of (*informal*), tease. **poke out** *The label is poking out.* jut out, project, protrude, stick out. **poke your nose in** *He always pokes his nose in other people's affairs.* interfere in, intrude in, meddle in, pry in.

pole *noun a wooden pole.* bar, boom, column, mast, post, rod, shaft, spar, staff, stanchion, standard, stick, stilt, upright.

police *noun The police were called to the accident scene.* constabulary, cops (*slang*), fuzz (*slang*), law (*informal*). — *verb The streets are policed.* control, patrol, supervise. □ **police officer** constable, cop (*slang*), copper (*slang*), detective, inspector, officer, policeman, policewoman, sergeant, superintendent.

policy[1] *noun defence policy. a policy on discipline.* code, guidelines, line,

manifesto, plan, platform, principles, procedure, rules, strategy, system, tactics.

policy[2] *noun an insurance policy.* contract.

polish *verb* **1** *He polished the lamp.* buff, burnish, rub, shine, smooth. **2** *She polished her technique.* brush up, improve, perfect, refine, smarten up, touch up. — *noun The furniture has a fine polish.* brilliance, gloss, lustre, sheen, shine, smoothness, sparkle. OPPOSITE dullness.

polite *adjective a polite person.* attentive, chivalrous, civil, civilised, considerate, courteous, diplomatic, gallant, genteel, gentlemanly, ladylike, refined, respectful, suave, tactful, thoughtful, urbane, well-behaved, well-bred, well-mannered. OPPOSITE impolite, rude.

politic *adjective It seemed politic to remain silent.* advisable, expedient, judicious, prudent, sensible, wise. OPPOSITE impolitic.

politician *noun* Member of Parliament, MP, parliamentarian, polly (*slang*), senator, statesman.

poll *noun* **1** *The people go to the polls this Saturday.* ballot, election, vote. **2** *a public opinion poll.* Gallup poll, straw poll, survey. — *verb She polled sixty per cent of the votes.* gain, get, receive, win.

pollute *verb We must stop polluting our rivers with chemical waste.* contaminate, defile, dirty, foul, infect, poison, soil, taint.

pomp *noun great pomp and ceremony.* ceremony, display, glory, grandeur, magnificence, ostentation, pageantry, show, solemnity, spectacle, splendour, style.

pompous *adjective His pompous manner upsets some people.* arrogant, bombastic, grandiose, haughty, high and mighty, high-falutin (*informal*), hoity-toity, imperious, overbearing, pretentious, self-important, snobbish, stuck-up (*informal*), supercilious, superior. OPPOSITE modest.

pond *noun ducks on the pond.* dam (*Australian*), lake, pool, waterhole.

ponder *verb She likes to sit and ponder.* brood, cogitate, contemplate, meditate, muse, reflect, ruminate, think. □ **ponder over** *He pondered over the problem.* consider, deliberate over, dwell on, mull over, muse over, puzzle over, reflect on, study, think about.

ponderous *adjective* **1** *ponderous furniture.* bulky, cumbersome, heavy, massive, unwieldy, weighty. OPPOSITE light. **2** *The book was written in a ponderous style.* dull, laborious, laboured, long-winded, stilted, stodgy, tedious, turgid, verbose, wordy. OPPOSITE lively.

pong *noun* (*informal*) *The pong from the rotten meat was unbearable.* reek, stench, stink. — *verb* (*informal*) *Bad fish pongs.* reek, smell, stink.

pool[1] *noun* **1** *a swim in a mountain pool.* bogey hole (*Australian*), lagoon, lake, mere (*poetical*), pond, swimming hole, waterhole. **2** *The rain left pools of water.* puddle. **3** *a swim at the municipal pool.* aquatic centre, baths, swimming pool.

pool[2] *noun They each put $2 a week into a pool for joint spending.* bank, fund, jackpot, kitty, pot, reserve. — *verb They pooled their resources.* amalgamate, combine, consolidate, merge, share.

poor *adjective* **1** *too poor to afford new shoes.* bankrupt, broke (*informal*), destitute, hard up (*informal*), impecunious, impoverished, indigent, needy, penniless, penurious, poverty-stricken, skint (*informal*), stony-broke (*informal*). OPPOSITE

affluent, rich. **2** *The food is poor in vitamins.* deficient, insufficient, lacking, low, wanting. OPPOSITE rich. **3** *poor soil.* barren, infertile, sterile, unproductive, useless. OPPOSITE fertile, productive. **4** *poor workmanship. poor quality.* bad, crummy (*informal*), defective, faulty, imperfect, inadequate, inferior, mediocre, rotten, rubbishy, second-rate, shoddy, slipshod, substandard, unsatisfactory. OPPOSITE good. **5** *The poor kitten lost her mother.* hapless, miserable, pathetic, pitiful, sorry, unfortunate, unlucky, wretched. OPPOSITE lucky.

poorly *adjective Billy was feeling poorly.* ill, indisposed, off colour, seedy (*informal*), sick, under the weather (*informal*), unwell. OPPOSITE well.

pop *noun the pop of a balloon bursting.* bang, burst, crack, explosion, snap. — *verb The popcorn started to pop.* bang, burst, crackle, explode. □ **pop in** *The doctor popped in each day.* call in, drop in, nip in (*informal*), stop by, visit. **pop up** *The problem will pop up again.* appear, come up, crop up, emerge, surface.

pope *noun* Bishop of Rome, Holy Father, pontiff.

populace *noun The Prime Minister spoke to the general populace.* masses, mob, multitude, people, population, public.

popular *adjective* **1** *a popular writer.* admired, celebrated, famous, favourite, renowned, sought-after, well-known, well-liked. OPPOSITE unpopular. **2** *popular opinion.* common, conventional, general, mainstream, prevalent, universal, widely-held, widespread.

populate *verb The area was populated by post-war immigrants.* colonise, inhabit, occupy, people, settle.

population *noun The city's population is three million.* citizens, inhabitants, occupants, people, populace, public, residents.

porch *noun The visitors waited in the porch.* entrance hall, lobby, portico, vestibule.

pore[1] *noun skin pores.* hole, opening, orifice.

pore[2] *verb* **pore over** *The student pored over his notes.* examine, go over, peruse, read, scrutinise, study.

pornographic *adjective pornographic films.* blue, dirty, erotic, indecent, lewd, obscene, smutty.

porous *adjective a porous material.* absorbent, permeable, pervious, spongy.

port *noun The ship was in the port.* anchorage, dock, dockyard, harbour, marina, seaport.

portable *adjective a portable cot.* compact, light, movable, transportable.

portent *noun portents of war.* harbinger, omen, presage, sign, warning.

portentous *adjective portentous events.* menacing, ominous, threatening, warning.

porter[1] *noun A railway porter carried our bags.* attendant, carrier.

porter[2] *noun a hotel porter.* commissionaire, concierge, doorkeeper, doorman, gatekeeper, janitor.

portion *noun They each received a portion of the profits, cake, etc.* allocation, allotment, bit, cut (*informal*), division, fraction, helping, part, percentage, piece, quantity, quota, ration, section, segment, serving, share, slice. — *verb* **portion out** *He portioned out the presents.* allocate, allot, apportion, distribute, divide out, dole out, mete out, parcel out, share.

portly *noun a portly bear.* bulky, corpulent, fat, obese, overweight, rotund, stocky, stout, tubby. OPPOSITE thin.

portrait *noun a portrait of her parents.* drawing, image, likeness, painting, photograph, picture, representation, sketch.

portray *verb* **1** *The writer portrays the evil side of the characters.* characterise, depict, describe, picture, represent, show. **2** *She portrayed the duchess in the play.* act as, impersonate, perform as, play, represent.

pose *verb* **1** *They posed for the photo.* model, sit. **2** *She loves to pose when people are looking.* posture, put on airs, show off. **3** *She posed a difficult question.* ask, present, put forward, raise. — *noun photographed in a reclining pose.* attitude, position, posture, stance. □ **pose as** *He posed as an expert.* act as, impersonate, masquerade as, pass yourself off as, pretend to be.

posh *adjective* (*informal*) *a posh hotel.* elegant, grand, luxurious, opulent, plush, smart, stylish, sumptuous, swanky (*informal*), swish (*informal*), upmarket. OPPOSITE downmarket.

position *noun* **1** *We found their position on the map.* locality, location, place, point, site, situation, spot, whereabouts. **2** *out of its correct position.* niche, place, possie (*Australian informal*), setting, slot, spot. **3** *a difficult yoga position.* pose, posture, stance. **4** *a person's financial position.* circumstances, condition, situation, state. **5** *What is his position on asylum seekers?* attitude, line, opinion, stance, stand, standpoint, view, viewpoint. **6** *She has taken up a position in a legal firm.* appointment, job, occupation, office, post, situation. — *verb She took care in positioning the paintings.* arrange, array, dispose, lay out, line up, place, put, set.

positive *adjective* **1** *He was positive that he was right.* assured, certain, cocksure, confident, convinced, definite, sure. OPPOSITE unsure. **2** *They had positive proof.* absolute, categorical, conclusive, definite, firm, incontrovertible, indisputable, irrefutable, sure, undeniable, unequivocal. OPPOSITE inconclusive. **3** (*informal*) *He's a positive scoundrel.* absolute, complete, downright, out-and-out, real, thorough, true, utter, veritable. **4** *She made some positive suggestions.* beneficial, constructive, helpful, practical, useful. OPPOSITE negative, useless. **5** *a positive answer.* affirmative. OPPOSITE negative. **6** *Maintain a positive attitude.* confident, hopeful, optimistic. OPPOSITE negative, pessimistic.

possess *verb* **1** *Zoe possesses a large fortune.* have, hold, own. **2** *Chloe possesses musical talent.* be blessed with, be endowed with, be gifted with, have. **3** *The man was possessed by a demon.* control, dominate, govern, influence, rule.

possessions *plural noun Dan looks after his possessions.* assets, belongings, chattels, effects, gear, goods, property, stuff, things.

possessive *adjective He was possessive about his friends.* clinging, domineering, jealous, proprietorial.

possibility *noun* **1** *There is a slight possibility of rain.* chance, contingency, likelihood, probability, prospect, risk. **2** *The plan has possibilities.* potential, potentiality, promise, prospects.

possible *adjective* **1** *It is not possible to do that.* achievable, attainable, feasible, manageable, practicable, viable, workable. OPPOSITE impossible, impracticable. **2** *a possible solution.* admissible, conceivable, credible, reasonable. OPPOSITE impossible, unthinkable. **3** *a possible winner.* likely, potential, probable, promising. OPPOSITE unlikely.

possibly *adverb Possibly he might come.* maybe, perchance, perhaps.

post[1] *noun The post is leaning over.* bollard, column, newel, pale, paling, picket, pier, pile, pillar, pole, prop, shaft, stake, stanchion, standard, stilt, support, upright. — *verb He posted the notice on the board.* display, paste up, pin up, put up, stick up.

post[2] *noun We received some interesting post today.* correspondence, letters, mail, packets. — *verb He posted two letters.* dispatch, mail, send. □ **keep posted** *Keep me posted on what's happening.* advise, brief, inform, notify.

post[3] *noun* **1** *The sentries are at their posts.* place, point, position, station. **2** *She resigned her post in the company.* appointment, employment, job, occupation, office, position, situation, work. — *verb* **1** *They posted lookouts at the entrances.* install, place, position, put, set, station. **2** *The journalist was posted to New York.* appoint, assign, send.

postbox *noun* letterbox, mailbox, pillar box (*old use*).

poster *noun Posters were stuck up on the walls.* advertisement, announcement, bill, notice, placard, sign.

posterity *noun* **1** *Posterity will judge the merits of his plan.* future generations. **2** *The benefits will go to his posterity.* children, descendants, heirs, offspring, progeny.

post-mortem *noun A post-mortem was carried out on the victim.* autopsy, necropsy.

postpone *verb They postponed the race.* adjourn, defer, delay, hold over, put off, put on ice, shelve. OPPOSITE bring forward.

postscript *noun a postscript to the report.* addendum, addition, afterthought, epilogue, PS, supplement.

postulate *verb He postulated the existence of a new particle.* assume, hypothesise, posit, propose, suppose, theorise.

posture *noun Fitness classes improved his posture.* bearing, carriage, deportment, stance.

posy *noun a posy of carnations.* bouquet, bunch, corsage, nosegay, spray.

pot *noun* **1** *a cooking pot.* billy, casserole, cauldron, crockpot, dixie, pan, quartpot, saucepan, urn, vessel. **2** *He put the plant in a pot.* flowerpot, planter.

potency *noun He underestimated the potency of the drug.* effectiveness, efficacy, might, force, power, strength.

potent *adjective a potent drug.* effective, efficacious, heady, intoxicating, overpowering, powerful, strong. OPPOSITE weak.

potential *adjective a potential genius.* budding, likely, possible, promising, prospective. — *noun This candidate shows a lot of potential.* ability, aptitude, capability, possibility, promise.

potion *noun He drank the magic potion.* brew, concoction, drink, liquid, mixture, philtre.

pottery *noun* ceramics, china, crockery, earthenware, porcelain, stoneware, terracotta.

pouch *noun a money pouch.* bag, dillybag (*Australian*), holder, pocket, purse, sack, wallet.

poultry *noun* chooks (*Australian informal*), domestic fowls.

pounce *verb* **pounce on** *The cat pounced on the sparrow.* ambush, attack, fall upon, jump on, leap on, seize, spring on, swoop down on.

pound[1] *noun Stray dogs are taken to the pound.* compound, enclosure, pen, yard.

pound[2] *verb* **1** *He pounded the seeds into a powder.* crush, grind, pulverise. **2** *She pounded the vegetables into a purée.* mash, pulp, squash. **3** *She pounded on the door. He pounded the man's back.* bang, batter, beat, clobber (*slang*), hammer, hit, knock, pummel, thump. **4** *Her heart was pounding.* beat, palpitate, pulsate, throb, thump.

pour *verb* **1** *Water was pouring out of the burst pipe.* cascade, discharge, flow, gush, issue, run, spew, spill, spout, spurt, stream. **2** *We stayed indoors because it was pouring.* bucket, deluge, pelt, rain cats and dogs (*informal*), teem. **3** *The shoppers poured into the store.* flood, rush, stream, swarm, throng.

poverty *noun Many people live in poverty.* beggary, deprivation, destitution, hardship, impoverishment, indigence, need, penury, want. OPPOSITE wealth.

power *noun* **1** *The problem taxed his mental powers.* ability, capability, capacity, competence, faculty, skill, talent. **2** *a man of great physical power.* energy, force, might, muscle, potency, strength, vigour. OPPOSITE weakness. **3** *political power.* authority, clout (*informal*), control, dominance, dominion, influence, leverage, muscle, sway. OPPOSITE impotence. **4** *They have no legal power to do that.* authority, jurisdiction, licence, mandate, right, warrant.

powerful *adjective* **1** *a powerful athlete.* dynamic, energetic, hefty, invincible, mighty, robust, strong, sturdy. OPPOSITE weak, weedy. **2** *a powerful argument.* authoritative, cogent, compelling, convincing, effective, forceful, influential, persuasive, potent, sound, strong, weighty. OPPOSITE weak. **3** *a powerful voice.* loud, penetrating, resonant, sonorous, stentorian, strong. OPPOSITE gentle, soft.

powerless *adjective* **1** *He takes advantage of powerless people.* defenceless, feeble, helpless, impotent, weak. OPPOSITE powerful. **2** *We were powerless to help.* incapable (of), unable. OPPOSITE able.

practicable *adjective The proposal to interview everyone is not practicable.* achievable, feasible, manageable, possible, practical, realistic, viable, workable. OPPOSITE impracticable.

practical *adjective* **1** *no practical experience.* applied, hands-on. OPPOSITE theoretical. **2** *a practical gadget.* functional, handy, usable, useful, utilitarian. OPPOSITE impractical, useless. **3** *a practical handyman.* capable, competent, handy, proficient, skilled. **4** *It's nice to dream, but let's be practical.* businesslike, down-to-earth, hard-headed, pragmatic, realistic, sensible. OPPOSITE impractical, unrealistic. □ **practical joke** gag, hoax, prank, trick.

practically *adverb There was practically no hope.* almost, close to, essentially, nearly, virtually.

practice *noun* **1** *Your idea works well in practice.* action, effect, operation, use. OPPOSITE theory. **2** *It is his practice to shake each person's hand.* convention, custom, habit, procedure, ritual, routine, tradition, wont. **3** *Practice makes perfect.* drill, exercise, preparation, rehearsal, training.

practise *verb* **1** *Vicki is practising for the exam.* brush up, drill, exercise, rehearse, train. **2** *You must practise what you preach.* apply, carry out, do, perform. **3** *She no longer practises medicine.* engage in, pursue, work at.

praise *verb* **1** *The paper praised the rescuer for his actions.* acclaim, applaud, commend, compliment, congratulate, honour, pay homage to, pay tribute to. OPPOSITE criticise. **2** *The people praised God.* adore, exalt, glorify, hallow, honour, laud (*formal*), magnify (*old use*), revere, venerate, worship. — *noun The praise was deserved.* acclaim, accolade, applause, bouquet, commendation, compliment, congratulations, eulogy, homage, honour, ovation, tribute. OPPOSITE criticism.

praiseworthy *adjective a praiseworthy result.* admirable, commendable, creditable, deserving, exemplary, honourable, laudable, meritorious, worthy. OPPOSITE dishonourable.

pram *noun Mara's baby loves her pram.* baby buggy, baby carriage, perambulator, pushchair, pusher (*Australian*), stroller.

prance *verb They pranced happily around the stage.* caper, cavort, dance, frisk, frolic, gambol, jump, leap, romp, skip.

prank *noun The first day of April is a day of pranks.* antic, caper, escapade, hoax, lark, practical joke, trick.

prattle *verb The child prattled incessantly.* babble, chatter, gabble, natter (*informal*), rabbit on (*informal*), yabber (*Australian informal*).

pray *verb We prayed to God for peace.* appeal, ask, beg, beseech, entreat, implore, plead with, supplicate, urge.

prayer *noun The service included prayers and hymns.* benediction, blessing, collect, devotion, entreaty, intercession, litany, petition, request, supplication, thanksgiving.

preach *verb* **1** *The minister preached a provocative sermon.* deliver. **2** *He preached the gospel.* expound, proclaim, teach. **3** *She's always preaching at them.* lecture, moralise, pontificate, sermonise.

preacher *noun The preacher had an attentive audience.* chaplain, clergyman, clergywoman, curate, evangelist, minister, missionary, padre, parson, pastor, priest, rector, vicar.

prearrange *verb They prearranged the meeting place.* fix, plan, predetermine.

precarious *adjective* **1** *a precarious position on the edge of the cliff.* dangerous, hazardous, insecure, perilous, rocky, shaky, unsafe, unstable, unsteady, vulnerable. OPPOSITE secure. **2** *a precarious operation.* chancy, delicate, dicey (*slang*), dodgy (*informal*), risky, ticklish, touch-and-go, uncertain. OPPOSITE safe.

precaution *noun a precaution against sunburn.* defence, preventive measure, protection, safeguard, safety measure.

precede *verb Summer precedes autumn.* come before, go before, herald, lead into, pave the way for, usher in. OPPOSITE follow, succeed.

precedent *noun The ruling in the case set a precedent.* example, model, pattern, standard, yardstick.

precious *adjective* **1** *precious jewels.* costly, dear, expensive, invaluable, priceless, valuable. OPPOSITE worthless. **2** *precious memories.* beloved, cherished, dear, prized, treasured, valuable.

precipice *noun He injured his back when he fell down the precipice.* bluff, cliff, crag, escarpment, rock-face, scarp.

precipitate *verb* **1** *The horse precipitated its rider.* fling down, hurl down, throw down. **2** *This action precipitated his decline.* accelerate, bring on, expedite, hasten, speed up. — *adjective a precipitate departure.* abrupt, hasty, headlong, hurried, impetuous, impulsive, rapid, rash, reckless, speedy, sudden, swift.

precipitation *noun Annual precipitation is 100 centimetres.* dew, hail, rain, rainfall, sleet, snow, snowfall.

precipitous *adjective a precipitous track.* perpendicular, sheer, steep, vertical.

précis *noun He read a précis of the document.* abstract, outline, résumé, summary, synopsis.

precise *adjective* **1** *at that precise moment.* exact, particular, specific, very. **2** *precise details.* clear, definite, exact, explicit, express, minute, specific. OPPOSITE hazy, imprecise. **3** *He is very precise in his work.* accurate, careful, correct, fastidious, finicky, meticulous, painstaking, particular, pernickety (*informal*), punctilious, scrupulous. OPPOSITE careless, hit-or-miss.

precisely *adverb* **1** *precisely in the middle.* bang (*informal*), exactly, right, smack (*informal*). **2** *at six o'clock precisely.* on the dot, on the knocker (*Australian informal*), punctually, sharp.

preclude *verb Her job precluded her from entering the competition.* bar, block, debar, exclude, prevent, prohibit, rule out.

precocious *adjective a precocious child.* advanced, bright, forward, gifted, mature, quick. OPPOSITE backward.

preconception *noun She came with an open mind, and no preconceptions.* assumption, expectation, prejudgement, prejudice, presumption, presupposition.

precursor *noun the precursor of the modern car.* ancestor, antecedent, forerunner, predecessor.

predator *noun the animal is a predator.* hunter, marauder. OPPOSITE prey.

predecessor *noun a history of the man's predecessors.* ancestor, antecedent, forebear, forefather, progenitor. OPPOSITE descendant.

predestine *verb She believed that she was predestined to work there.* destine, fate, foreordain, intend, mean, preordain.

predicament *noun He found himself in a terrible predicament.* difficulty, dilemma, emergency, fix (*informal*), jam (*informal*), mess, pickle (*informal*), plight, quandary, spot (*informal*), trouble.

predict *verb He predicted that it would be fine.* forecast, foretell, prophesy.

predictable *adjective The result was predictable.* expected, foreseeable, on the cards, unsurprising. OPPOSITE unpredictable.

prediction *noun His prediction turned out to be spot on.* forecast, prognosis, prophecy.

predispose *verb The committee was predisposed in her favour.* bias, dispose, incline, prejudice.

predisposition *noun a predisposition to depression.* inclination, proneness, propensity, susceptibility, tendency, vulnerability.

predominant *adjective The predominant feeling was anger.* chief, dominant, main, major, paramount, prevailing, primary. OPPOSITE subordinate.

predominate *verb Weeds predominated over flowers in their garden.* dominate, preponderate, prevail.

pre-eminent *adjective a pre-eminent flautist.* distinguished, excellent, foremost, leading, outstanding, peerless, superior, supreme, unrivalled, unsurpassed. OPPOSITE unknown.

preen *verb The bird was preening itself.* clean, groom, neaten, plume, primp, smarten, spruce, tidy.

preface *noun He read the preface to the book.* foreword, introduction, preamble, prologue. OPPOSITE epilogue.

prefer *verb She prefers those chocolates.* choose, fancy, favour, like better, opt for, pick out, select.

preference *noun* **1** *Brian has a preference for classical music.* fondness, inclination, leaning, liking, partiality, predilection. OPPOSITE dislike. **2** *They were given their first preference.* choice, option, pick, selection.

pregnant *adjective The woman is pregnant.* expectant, expecting, with child (*literary*).

prehistoric *adjective prehistoric times.* ancient, antediluvian, earliest, olden (*old use*), primeval, primitive, primordial. OPPOSITE future.

prejudice *noun a victim of racial prejudice.* bias, bigotry, discrimination, intolerance, partiality, unfairness.

prejudiced *adjective The adjudicator was prejudiced.* biased, bigoted, discriminatory, intolerant, narrow-minded, one-sided, partisan, unfair. OPPOSITE unbiased.

preliminary *adjective preliminary lessons. preliminary remarks.* early, first, initial, introductory, opening, prefatory, preparatory. OPPOSITE concluding. — *noun He played better in the preliminaries.* elimination round, heat, qualifying round. OPPOSITE final.

prelude *noun The parade was a colourful prelude to the festival.* beginning, curtain-raiser, introduction, opening, overture, preamble, precursor, preface, prologue, start. OPPOSITE conclusion.

premature *adjective a premature decision.* hasty, precipitate, too early, too soon, untimely.

premeditated *adjective The crime was premeditated.* calculated, deliberate, intended, intentional, planned, wilful. OPPOSITE spontaneous.

premise *noun The argument was based on a false premise.* assumption, basis, grounds, hypothesis, postulate, presupposition, proposition, supposition.

premises *plural noun They moved to new premises.* accommodation, building, campus, house, property, site.

premonition *noun He had a premonition that an accident would happen.* feeling, foreboding, hunch, intuition, presentiment, suspicion.

preoccupied *adjective* **1** *Gemma was preoccupied with work.* absorbed, engrossed, immersed, wrapped up. **2** *Her father wasn't listening properly because he was preoccupied.* absent-minded, abstracted, faraway, lost in thought, pensive.

preparation *noun* **1** *All the preparations for the event were completed.* arrangement, groundwork, organisation, plan, planning, setting up, spadework. **2** *She did her preparation for her music lesson.* homework, practice, prep. **3** *The doctor prescribed a skin preparation.* concoction, mixture, product, substance.

preparatory *adjective a preparatory lecture.* introductory, initial, preliminary.

prepare *verb* **1** *Tom prepared the table for dinner.* arrange, get ready, lay, organise, set. **2** *Neil was well prepared for the job.* brief, coach, equip, groom, prime, train. **3** *She prepared her item for the concert.* practise, rehearse, work on. **4** *The teacher prepared an interesting programme.* arrange, design, develop, devise, map out, organise, plan.

5 *Mum prepared a delicious dessert.* assemble, concoct, cook, make, mix, produce, put together, whip up. □ **be prepared to** *He was not prepared to resign.* be minded to, be ready to, be willing to.

preposterous *adjective What a preposterous idea!* absurd, crazy, farcical, laughable, ludicrous, monstrous, nonsensical, outrageous, ridiculous, unthinkable, weird.

prerequisite *noun Ability to drive a car is a prerequisite for the job.* condition, essential, must (*informal*), necessity, pre-condition, requirement, requisite.

prerogative *noun The governor has the prerogative to decide who goes.* authority, power, privilege, right.

preschool *noun* kindergarten, nursery school.

prescribe *verb* **1** *The doctor prescribed an antibiotic.* advise, order, recommend, suggest. **2** *He likes to prescribe what others should do.* dictate, impose, lay down, ordain, order, specify, stipulate.

presence *noun Your presence is required at the meeting.* attendance, company, society. OPPOSITE absence.

present[1] *adjective* **1** *Is there a doctor present?* about, at hand, here, in attendance, on the scene, on the spot. OPPOSITE absent. **2** *the present situation.* contemporary, current, existing, immediate. **3** *the present champion.* current, existing, reigning. — *noun He lives for the present.* here and now, now, today. CONTRASTS WITH future, past.

present[2] *noun They gave a costly present.* contribution, donation, gift, handout, offering, tip. — *verb* **1** *She presented the prizes.* award, bestow, confer, distribute, donate, give, hand out, hand over. **2** *He presented his views clearly.* announce, communicate, declare, expound, impart, make known, put forward, recount, relate, state. **3** *He presented his fiancée to his parents.* introduce, make known. **4** *They presented their latest products at the show.* demonstrate, display, exhibit, reveal, show. **5** *The students presented a French comedy.* act, mount, perform, put on, stage. □ **present itself** *No suitable occasion presented itself.* arise, eventuate, happen, occur. **present yourself** *They presented themselves in court.* appear, arrive, attend, front up (*informal*), turn up.

presentable *adjective He looked presentable in a borrowed suit.* acceptable, all right, decent, neat, OK (*informal*), passable, respectable, satisfactory, suitable, tidy.

presentation *noun* **1** *The project was marked on both content and presentation.* appearance, arrangement, form, layout, structure. **2** *We enjoyed the children's end-of-year presentation.* demonstration, display, exhibition, performance, production, show.

presently *adverb* **1** *We shall see you again presently.* anon, before long, by and by, directly, in a moment, shortly, soon. **2** *He is in a meeting presently.* at present, currently, now.

preserve *verb* **1** *We want to preserve our heritage.* conserve, defend, guard, keep, keep safe, look after, maintain, perpetuate, protect, retain, safeguard, save, secure. OPPOSITE destroy. **2** *She learned ways to preserve fruit, meat, fish, etc.* bottle, can, corn, cure, dry, freeze, pickle, salt, smoke, tin. — *noun She eats quince preserve on her toast.* conserve, jam, jelly.

preside *verb* **preside over** *She is presiding over the meeting.* be in charge

of, chair, conduct, control, direct, officiate at, run.

president *noun the society's president.* chairman, chairperson, chairwoman, chief, director, head, leader.

press *verb* **1** *Press the button.* depress, push. **2** *The recipe says to press the grapes.* compress, crush, mash, squash, squeeze. **3** *She presses her own clothes.* flatten, iron, smooth. **4** *They pressed him to make a speech.* beg, coerce, compel, constrain, entreat, force, implore, order, persuade, pressure, request, urge. — *noun The story received good coverage in the press.* journals, magazines, newspapers, papers, periodicals, print media.

pressing *adjective a pressing need for food aid.* critical, crucial, essential, important, insistent, urgent, vital. OPPOSITE unimportant.

pressure *noun* **1** *He applied pressure to the wound to stop the bleeding.* compression, force. **2** *financial pressures.* burden, constraint, demand, difficulty, hardship, hassle (*informal*), load, oppression, strain, stress, tension. **3** *The board put pressure on him to resign.* coercion, compulsion, duress, force. — *verb They pressured him into signing.* browbeat, bulldoze (*informal*), bully, coerce, compel, constrain, drive, force, lean on (*informal*), persuade, press, pressurise, put pressure on, put the acid on (*Australian slang*), put the screws on (*informal*), railroad.

prestige *noun Her job gave her prestige.* celebrity, distinction, fame, glamour, glory, honour, kudos, renown, reputation, respect, status.

presume *verb* **1** *He presumed that she was telling the truth.* assume, believe, guess, imagine, presuppose, suppose, surmise, take for granted, take it. **2** *He presumed to advise a stranger.* be so bold as, dare, have the audacity, take the liberty, venture.

presumption *noun* **1** *Their action was based on a wrong presumption.* assumption, belief, premise, presupposition, supposition, surmise. **2** *He had the presumption to put himself at the head of the table.* arrogance, audacity, boldness, cheek, effrontery, impertinence, impudence, nerve (*informal*), presumptuousness, temerity.

presumptuous *adjective It was presumptuous to come without an invitation.* arrogant, audacious, bold, cheeky, cocky, forward, impertinent, impudent, overconfident, pushy (*informal*).

presuppose *verb His plans presupposed that the money was available.* assume, presume, suppose, take for granted.

pretence *noun* **1** *Say what you really think: no more pretence.* acting, affectation, deception, fabrication, faking, hypocrisy, invention, lying, make-believe. **2** *Her sympathy was all a pretence.* act, charade, cover, front, hoax, masquerade, pretext, put-on (*informal*), ruse, sham, show, trick.

pretend *verb* **1** *She isn't really sick: she's just pretending.* act, bluff, deceive, fake, feign, kid (*informal*), make believe, put it on (*informal*), put on an act, sham. **2** *He pretended to be a policeman.* act as, impersonate, masquerade as, pass yourself off as, pose as. **3** *He pretended that he knew.* claim, make believe, make out, profess.

pretentious *adjective Ed felt uncomfortable with such pretentious people.* affected, arty (*informal*), la-di-da (*informal*), ostentatious, pompous, self-important, showy, snob-

bish, stuck-up (*informal*), toffee-nosed (*informal*). OPPOSITE unpretentious.
pretext *noun He found a pretext to call on Jane.* excuse, pretence, ruse.
pretty *adjective* **1** *a pretty girl.* appealing, attractive, beautiful, bonny (*Scottish*), captivating, charming, dainty, fair (*old use*), fetching, good-looking, handsome, lovely, nice, pleasing, sweet (*informal*), winsome. OPPOSITE plain, ugly. **2** *pretty scenery.* attractive, beautiful, breathtaking, picturesque, scenic, spectacular. OPPOSITE drab. — *adverb pretty good.* fairly, moderately, quite, rather, reasonably, somewhat.
prevail *verb Common sense prevailed.* be victorious, rule, triumph, win the day. □ **prevail on** *They prevailed on her to present the speech.* convince, induce, persuade, talk into.
prevailing *adjective The prevailing wind is from the north.* chief, common, dominant, main, predominant, usual.
prevalent *adjective the prevalent view.* common, current, dominant, general, popular, predominant, prevailing, usual, widespread. OPPOSITE rare.
prevent *verb The vaccine will prevent the spread of the disease.* avert, avoid, bar, block, curb, deter, fend off, foil, forestall, halt, hamper, hinder, impede, inhibit, obstruct, preclude, prohibit, stave off, stop, thwart, ward off. OPPOSITE cause, enable.
previous *adjective* **1** *his previous boss.* ex-, former, one-time, past. **2** *The article was in a previous issue.* back, earlier, past, preceding, prior. OPPOSITE subsequent.
previously *adverb Jenny had worked there previously.* before, earlier, formerly, in the past. OPPOSITE subsequently.
prey *noun The cat killed its prey.* quarry, victim. OPPOSITE predator. — *verb* **prey on 1** *The cat preys on mice.* devour, eat, feed on, hunt, kill, live off. **2** *It preyed on his conscience.* haunt, oppress, trouble, weigh on, worry.
price *noun* **1** *the price of a new car. Prices have increased.* amount, charge, cost, expense, fare, fee, figure, outlay, payment, rate, sum, terms, toll, value, worth. **2** *That's the price you pay for foolishness.* consequence, cost, penalty, punishment, sacrifice.
priceless *adjective* **1** *priceless antiques.* costly, dear, expensive, invaluable, irreplaceable, precious, pricey (*informal*), valuable. OPPOSITE cheap, worthless. **2** (*informal*) *The story she told us was priceless.* absurd, amusing, funny, hilarious.
prick *verb The needle pricked his skin.* jab, lance, perforate, pierce, puncture, stab. — *noun He felt a sharp prick.* jab, pinprick, prickle, stab, sting.
prickle *noun The plant had sharp prickles.* barb, needle, spike, spine, thorn. — *verb His skin prickled after he touched the plant.* itch, smart, sting, tingle.
pride *noun* **1** *Lucy takes pride in her work.* delight, enjoyment, gratification, happiness, joy, pleasure, satisfaction. **2** *His new baby is his pride and joy.* delight, joy, pleasure. **3** *He wouldn't do that. He has his pride.* dignity, honour, self-esteem, self-respect. **4** *Pride goeth before a fall.* arrogance, conceit, egotism, hubris, self-importance, self-love, self-satisfaction, smugness, vanity. OPPOSITE humility. — *verb* **pride yourself on** *He prided himself on his cooking.* be proud of, boast about, congratulate yourself on, flatter yourself on.
priest *noun a priest in the Christian church.* archdeacon, chaplain, chief priest, clergyman, clergywoman, cleric, father, high priest, minister, padre, parson, pastor, rector, vicar.
priestly *adjective a priestly duty.* clerical, ecclesiastical, ministerial, pastoral.
prim *adjective The children's behaviour offended the prim old lady.* demure, formal, old-fashioned, precise, prissy, proper, prudish, starchy, strait-laced, stuffy. OPPOSITE broad-minded.
primarily *adverb His tasks are primarily administrative.* basically, chiefly, essentially, firstly, fundamentally, generally, largely, mainly, mostly, predominantly, principally. OPPOSITE secondarily.
primary *adjective* **1** *primary education.* basic, elementary, first. OPPOSITE secondary. **2** *Our primary purpose is to save lives.* chief, essential, fundamental, key, main, major, paramount, prime, principal. OPPOSITE secondary.
prime[1] *adjective* **1** *the prime motive.* chief, key, leading, main, major, primary, principal. OPPOSITE secondary. **2** *prime beef.* best, excellent, first-class, superior, top-quality. OPPOSITE inferior. — *noun past their prime.* best, heyday, peak, zenith.
prime[2] *verb* **1** *He primed the woodwork.* make ready, prepare. **2** *They primed him for the interview.* brief, coach, equip, fill in (*informal*), forearm, inform, instruct, prepare, train.
primeval *adjective a primeval forest.* ancient, early, prehistoric, primal, primitive, primordial.
primitive *adjective* **1** *a primitive tribe.* ancient, barbarian, prehistoric, primeval, primordial, savage, uncivilised. OPPOSITE civilised. **2** *primitive methods.* archaic, basic, crude, elementary, obsolete, old-fashioned, rough, rudimentary, simple, unsophisticated. OPPOSITE advanced.
principal *adjective* **1** *the principal features.* basic, cardinal, chief, dominant, essential, foremost, fundamental, leading, main, major, outstanding, predominant, primary, prime, supreme. OPPOSITE minor, secondary. **2** *the principal city.* capital, chief, main, major. — *noun* **1** *the school principal.* head, headmaster, headmistress, head teacher. **2** *She was paid interest on the principal.* capital.
principle *noun* **1** *a scientific principle.* assumption, axiom, law, rule, truth. **2** *She follows certain principles of behaviour.* belief, code, guideline, precept, rule, standard, tenet. **3** *a man of principle.* conscience, ethics, honesty, honour, integrity, morality, morals, probity, scruples, standards, virtue.
principled *adjective a principled businessman.* ethical, high-minded, honest, honourable, moral, scrupulous, upright. OPPOSITE unprincipled.
print *verb* **1** *She printed the design on the fabric.* impress, imprint, stamp. **2** *They print 100 copies of the newsletter.* produce, reproduce, run off; see also PUBLISH. — *noun* **1** *His feet left prints in the cement.* impression, imprint, indentation, mark, stamp. **2** *The book has large print.* font, letters, type, typeface. **3** *a print of the original drawing.* copy, duplicate, facsimile, replica, reproduction.
printout *noun He read the computer printout.* hard copy, output.
prior *adjective a prior engagement. a prior claim.* anterior, earlier, pre-existing, previous. OPPOSITE subsequent. — *adverb* **prior to** see BEFORE.
priority *noun His request was given priority.* precedence, preference.
priory *noun* abbey, cloister, convent, friary, monastery, nunnery, religious house.
prise *verb She prised the lid off.* force, lever, wrench.
prison *noun The prison was built last century.* detention centre, dungeon, jail, lock-up, nick (*slang*), penitentiary (*American*), remand centre.
prisoner *noun The prisoners were kept in individual cells.* captive, convict, detainee, hostage, inmate, internee, jailbird, lag (*slang*).
private *adjective* **1** *a private club.* closed, exclusive, restricted, special. OPPOSITE public. **2** *private property.* individual, own, personal. OPPOSITE public. **3** *private thoughts.* innermost, intimate, personal, secret. **4** *The information was to be kept private.* classified, confidential, hush-hush (*informal*), quiet, secret. OPPOSITE open, public. **5** *a private retreat.* hidden, isolated, off-limits, quiet, remote, secluded. **6** *a private school.* independent, non-government. OPPOSITE state.
privilege *noun a staff privilege.* advantage, benefit, concession, entitlement, exemption, perk (*informal*), prerogative, right.
prize *noun Alan won the prize.* award, crown, cup, jackpot, laurels, medal, reward, trophy. — *adjective a prize pumpkin.* award-winning, champion, excellent, first-rate, prize-winning, top, winning. — *verb Miriam prized the necklace.* appreciate, cherish, esteem, treasure, value.
probability *noun There is little probability of rain.* chance, likelihood, possibility, prospect.
probable *adjective It's probable the match will end in a draw.* expected, likely, on the cards, predictable. OPPOSITE improbable.
probationary *adjective After a probationary period she became permanent.* test, testing, trial.
probe *noun They conducted a probe into his business dealings.* examination, exploration, inquiry, inspection, investigation, study. — *verb* **1** *The doctor probed the wound for bits of glass.* examine, explore, feel around, poke, prod. **2** *She probed his motives.* examine, inquire into, investigate, look into, question, scrutinise, sound out.
problem *noun* **1** *mathematical problems.* conundrum, enigma, mystery, poser, puzzle, question, riddle, sum, teaser. **2** *technical problems. financial problems.* bug (*informal*), burden, complication, concern, difficulty, dilemma, hassle (*informal*), headache, hitch, predicament, setback, snag, strife (*Australian informal*), trouble, worry.
problematic or **problematical** *adjective* **1** *a problematic situation.* complicated, difficult, messy, ticklish, tricky, troublesome. OPPOSITE straightforward. **2** *a problematic assertion.* debatable, disputable, doubtful, questionable, uncertain. OPPOSITE certain.
procedure *noun He followed the procedure for handling enquiries.* approach, method, operation, practice, process, routine, system, technique, way.
proceed *verb* **1** *They proceeded to the hotel.* advance, go on, head, make your way, move on, press on, progress, push on. OPPOSITE retreat. **2** *Business proceeded uninterrupted.* carry on, continue, go on, keep going. OPPOSITE halt.
proceedings *plural noun* **1** *She instituted divorce proceedings.* action, lawsuit, legal action, litigation. **2** *He was present during the entire proceedings.* actions, activities, business, events, goings-on, happenings.
proceeds *plural noun He gave away the proceeds from the sale.* earnings, gain, income, profit(s), revenue, takings.
process *noun* **1** *a process for making paper.* means, method, operation, procedure, system, technique, way. **2** *The house was in the process of being built.* course, progress. — *verb* **1** *They process the raw materials.* change, convert, refine, transform, treat. **2** *They processed her application.* deal with, handle, take care of.
procession *noun Shoppers stopped to watch the procession along the street.* cavalcade, column, cortège, line, march, motorcade, pageant, parade.
proclaim *verb The officer proclaimed the good news.* advertise, announce, broadcast, circulate, declare, make known, pronounce, publicise, publish, tell, trumpet.
procrastinate *verb He procrastinated too long over the decision.* dally, delay, dilly-dally (*informal*), dither, drag your feet, hesitate, hold off, play for time, shilly-shally, stall.
procure *verb The book is difficult to procure.* acquire, buy, come by, find, get, get hold of, lay your hands on, obtain, pick up, secure.
prod *verb* **1** *She prodded him to wake him up.* butt, elbow, jab, nudge, poke. **2** *They need to be prodded into action.* goad, prompt, push, rouse, spur, stimulate, stir, urge. — *noun* **1** *She gave the bundle a prod.* butt, elbow, jab, nudge, poke, push. **2** *He needs a prod to get started on the cleaning.* prompt, reminder, spur, stimulus.
prodigal *adjective the prodigal son.* extravagant, improvident, profligate, spendthrift, wasteful. OPPOSITE thrifty.
prodigious *adjective* **1** *a prodigious achievement.* amazing, astonishing, astounding, exceptional, extraordinary, great, marvellous, miraculous, phenomenal, rare, remarkable, stupendous, terrific (*informal*), wonderful. OPPOSITE ordinary. **2** *a prodigious sum.* colossal, enormous, gigantic, great, immense, massive, monumental, tremendous, vast. OPPOSITE tiny.
prodigy *noun a musical prodigy.* genius, marvel, sensation, virtuoso, whiz-kid (*informal*), wizard.
produce *verb* **1** *She produced new evidence.* bring forward, come up with, disclose, display, exhibit, furnish, offer, present, provide, reveal, show, supply. OPPOSITE withhold. **2** *The tree will produce a lot of fruit.* bear, bring forth, supply, yield. **3** *They produced offspring.* bear, beget, breed, bring forth, give birth to, raise, rear, reproduce. **4** *Their discovery produced a sensation.* bring about, cause, create, generate, give rise to, provoke, raise. **5** *The firm produces electrical appliances.* assemble, build, construct, create, fabricate, form, invent, make, manufacture. **6** *He produced many hit songs.* compose, create, devise, think up, write. — *noun They cook with fresh garden produce.* crops, foodstuffs, harvest, products, yield.
product *noun manufactured products.* artefact, article, commodity, creation, item, object, production, thing; [*products*] goods, merchandise, output, produce, wares.

productive *adjective* **1** *The soil is productive.* fertile, fruitful, prolific, rich. OPPOSITE barren, sterile. **2** *productive workers.* active, busy, dynamic, effective, efficient, energetic, prolific. OPPOSITE unproductive. **3** *a productive meeting.* beneficial, constructive, profitable, rewarding, useful, valuable, worthwhile. OPPOSITE unproductive, useless.

profane *adjective* **1** *He composed both sacred and profane music.* lay, secular, temporal, worldly. OPPOSITE sacred. **2** *His profane language offended many people.* blasphemous, disrespectful, impious, irreligious, irreverent, sacrilegious. OPPOSITE reverent. — *verb They profaned God's name. He profaned the holy shrine.* abuse, debase, defile, desecrate, misuse, violate.

profess *verb* **1** *She professed a liking for opera.* assert, avow, claim, confess, declare, proclaim, pronounce, state. **2** *He professed to be an expert.* allege, claim, make out, pretend, purport.

profession *noun a profession in journalism.* calling, career, employment, job, occupation, vocation.

professional *adjective* **1** *a professional opinion.* expert, knowledgeable, qualified, skilled, trained. OPPOSITE amateur. **2** *The painter did a professional job.* adept, competent, expert, proficient, skilful. OPPOSITE amateurish, unprofessional. **3** *a professional tennis player.* paid. OPPOSITE amateur. — *noun The job was done by a professional.* authority, expert, master, pro (*informal*), specialist. OPPOSITE amateur.

proficiency *noun She showed proficiency in swimming.* ability, aptitude, capability, competence, expertise, mastery, skill.

proficient *adjective a proficient carpenter.* able, accomplished, adept, adroit, capable, competent, deft, dexterous, expert, skilful, skilled, trained. OPPOSITE inept.

profile *noun* **1** *They traced each other's profile.* contour, outline, shape, silhouette. **2** *The book contains profiles of our prime ministers.* account, biography, character sketch, description.

profit *noun* **1** *She could see no profit in further study.* advantage, avail, benefit, gain, good, use, value. OPPOSITE disadvantage. **2** *The company made a big profit.* gain, proceeds, return, surplus. OPPOSITE loss. — *verb* **profit from** *He profited from the time spent in the library.* be helped by, benefit from, capitalise on, exploit, gain from, make the most of.

profitable *adjective* **1** *a profitable meeting.* advantageous, beneficial, helpful, productive, rewarding, useful, valuable, worthwhile. **2** *a profitable enterprise.* commercial, fruitful, lucrative, moneymaking, paying, remunerative. OPPOSITE unprofitable.

profound *adjective* **1** *He expressed profound sympathy.* deep, great, heartfelt, intense, sincere. OPPOSITE insincere. **2** *a profound discussion.* deep, erudite, intellectual, learned, penetrating, serious, thoughtful, wise. OPPOSITE shallow, superficial.

profuse *adjective profuse apologies.* abundant, ample, copious, excessive, extravagant, lavish, plentiful. OPPOSITE sparing.

progeny *noun The man's fortune passed to his progeny.* children, descendants, family, offspring. OPPOSITE ancestry.

prognosis *noun The patient's prognosis was good.* forecast, prediction.

programme *noun* **1** *the programme of events.* agenda, calendar, plan, schedule, timetable. **2** *a TV or radio programme.* broadcast, performance, presentation, production, show, telecast. — *verb She programmed her appointments for Monday.* arrange, line up, organise, plan, schedule.

progress *noun* **1** *The hikers were making good progress each day.* advance, headway, strides. **2** *He surveyed the progress of scientific knowledge.* advance, advancement, development, evolution, expansion, growth, improvement, march, progression. OPPOSITE regression. — *verb The work progressed quickly.* advance, come along, come on, continue, develop, go ahead, improve, make headway, move ahead, move forward, move on, proceed. OPPOSITE regress. □ **in progress** *The demolition is in progress.* going on, happening, proceeding, taking place, under way.

progression *noun The children had a progression of nannies.* sequence, series, string, succession.

progressive *adjective* **1** *a progressive improvement.* continuous, gradual, ongoing, steady. OPPOSITE sudden, uneven. **2** *a progressive company.* avant-garde, enlightened, enterprising, forward-thinking, go-ahead, innovative, modern, up-and-coming (*informal*). OPPOSITE conservative.

prohibit *verb* **1** *Smoking is prohibited in offices.* ban, bar, forbid, outlaw, proscribe, veto. OPPOSITE permit. **2** *His blindness prohibits his becoming a pilot.* preclude, prevent, rule out, stop.

project *verb* **1** *The shelf projects over the fireplace.* extend, jut out, overhang, protrude, stand out, stick out. **2** *He projected the missile at the target.* cast, fling, hurl, launch, propel, shoot, throw. — *noun* **1** *a redevelopment project.* enterprise, plan, proposal, scheme, undertaking, venture. **2** *Students did projects on various subjects.* assignment, exercise, task.

projectile *noun The projectile reached the target.* bullet, grenade, missile, rocket, shell, shot.

projection *noun* **1** *They stood on a narrow projection.* ledge, overhang, ridge, shelf. **2** *projections of unemployment figures.* estimate, estimation, extrapolation, forecast, prediction.

proletariat *noun He did not seek to rise from the proletariat.* commoners, masses, plebs (*informal*), rank and file, wage earners, workers, working class. CONTRASTS WITH aristocracy, bourgeoisie.

proliferate *verb Cafés proliferated.* burgeon, increase, multiply, mushroom, spread.

prolific *adjective a prolific peach tree.* fertile, fruitful, productive. OPPOSITE unproductive.

prologue *noun The play begins with a prologue.* foreword, introduction, preamble, preface, prelude. OPPOSITE epilogue.

prolong *verb He tried not to prolong the pain.* drag out, draw out, extend, lengthen, protract, spin out, stretch out, string out. OPPOSITE shorten.

prominent *adjective* **1** *She had her prominent nose reshaped.* jutting out, projecting, protruding, sticking out. **2** *the prominent features.* conspicuous, noticeable, obtrusive, obvious, pronounced, salient, striking. OPPOSITE inconspicuous. **3** *a prominent academic.* celebrated, distinguished, eminent, famous, illustrious, important, notable, outstanding, pre-eminent, renowned, well-known. OPPOSITE unknown.

promiscuous *adjective a promiscuous woman.* fast, immoral, licentious, loose, wanton. OPPOSITE chaste.

promise *noun* **1** *He broke his promise.* assurance, commitment, contract, covenant, guarantee, oath, pledge, vow, word, word of honour. **2** *His work shows promise.* aptitude, capability, potential, talent. — *verb He promised us that he would be there. He promised to come.* agree, assure, commit yourself, give your word, guarantee, pledge, swear, undertake, vow.

promising *adjective* **1** *a promising start to the day.* auspicious, encouraging, favourable, propitious, reassuring. OPPOSITE discouraging. **2** *a promising actor.* able, gifted, talented, up-and-coming (*informal*).

promontory *noun The view from the promontory out to sea was superb.* cape, head, headland, point.

promote *verb* **1** *He was promoted to a supervisory position.* advance, elevate, move up, raise, upgrade. OPPOSITE demote. **2** *The organisation promotes understanding.* advance, boost, encourage, facilitate, foster, further, help, sponsor, support. OPPOSITE obstruct. **3** *They need to promote their product.* advertise, hype up (*slang*), make known, market, plug (*informal*), publicise, push.

prompt *adjective* **1** *He received a prompt answer.* early, expeditious, immediate, instant, instantaneous, quick, speedy, swift. OPPOSITE belated. **2** *Please be prompt.* on time, punctual. OPPOSITE late. — *verb* **1** *His comments prompted her to apologise.* egg on, encourage, incite, induce, influence, inspire, motivate, move, spur, stimulate. **2** *She prompted the actors when they forgot their lines.* cue, jog the memory of, remind.

promptly *adverb* **1** *He dealt promptly with the problem.* at once, expeditiously, immediately, instantly, quickly, readily, right away, speedily, straight away, swiftly, without delay. **2** *The guests left promptly at eight o'clock.* on the dot, on the knocker (*Australian informal*), on time, punctually. OPPOSITE late.

prone *adjective* **1** *He was lying prone on the bed.* face down, flat, horizontal, prostrate. CONTRASTS WITH supine, upright. **2** *Anne is prone to headaches.* inclined, liable, predisposed, subject, susceptible. OPPOSITE immune.

prong *noun The fork has four prongs.* point, spike, tine.

pronounce *verb* **1** *The b is not pronounced in 'lamb'.* articulate, enunciate, say, sound, speak, utter, voice. **2** *The play was pronounced a success.* announce, declare, proclaim.

pronounced *adjective The differences were becoming more pronounced.* apparent, clear, clear-cut, conspicuous, definite, distinct, evident, marked, noticeable, obvious, prominent, striking, strong, unmistakable. OPPOSITE faint.

proof *noun He has no proof of their guilt.* confirmation, corroboration, demonstration, documentation, evidence, facts, grounds, substantiation, testimony, verification.

prop¹ *noun The fence was held up with props.* brace, buttress, post, reinforcement, stake, stay, strut, support. — *verb He propped his bicycle against the tree.* lean, rest, stand. □ **prop up** *Two posts propped up the wall.* brace, buttress, hold up, reinforce, shore up, stake, strengthen, support.

prop² *verb* (*Australian*) *The horse propped at a fallen tree.* baulk, jib, pull up, stop.

propel *verb She was propelled from her chair when the spring snapped.* catapult, drive, eject, fling, impel, push, send, shoot, throw, thrust.

propensity *noun a propensity to talk too much.* inclination, leaning, penchant, predisposition, proclivity, proneness, tendency.

proper *adjective* **1** *This isn't the proper time to tell her.* appropriate, apt, fitting, right, suitable. OPPOSITE inappropriate. **2** *She learnt to do it the proper way.* accepted, conventional, correct, established, orthodox, right, standard. OPPOSITE wrong. **3** *Her behaviour was generally very proper.* conventional, courteous, decent, decorous, dignified, formal, polite, prim, respectable, seemly. OPPOSITE improper. **4** (*informal*) *We were in a proper mess.* absolute, complete, real, thorough, utter.

property *noun* **1** *Look after your personal property.* belongings, chattels, effects, gear, goods, possessions, things. **2** *His property passes to his children on his death.* assets, fortune, riches, wealth. **3** *He invested in property.* buildings, land, real estate. **4** *a herb with medicinal properties.* characteristic, feature, quality, trait.

prophecy *noun We saw the fulfilment of his prophecy.* forecast, prediction.

prophesy *verb He prophesied a period of war.* forecast, foresee, foretell, predict.

prophet *noun The words of the prophet came true.* augur, forecaster, fortune-teller, oracle, prophetess (*female*), seer, sibyl (*female*), soothsayer.

propitious *adjective a propitious time to make the announcement.* advantageous, auspicious, favourable, fortunate, lucky, opportune, timely. OPPOSITE unfavourable.

proportion *noun* **1** *He is paid a proportion of the profits.* cut (*informal*), division, fraction, part, percentage, piece, portion, quota, section, share. **2** *The proportion of red to blue varies in each of these purple paints.* balance, ratio, relationship. □ **proportions** *plural noun a house of large proportions.* dimensions, extent, magnitude, measurements, size.

proposal *noun The proposal to build the hall needs council approval.* bid, offer, plan, project, proposition, recommendation, scheme, submission, suggestion.

propose *verb* **1** *She proposed a simple solution.* advance, offer, present, proffer, propound, put forward, recommend, submit, suggest, tender. **2** *He proposed to ring them back.* aim, intend, mean, plan.

proprietor *noun a hotel proprietor.* landlady, landlord, manager, owner, proprietress.

propriety *noun He did not act with propriety.* correctness, courtesy, decency, decorum, politeness, respectability, seemliness. OPPOSITE impropriety.

prosaic *adjective His prosaic life contrasted with her exciting one.* banal, boring, commonplace, dull, humdrum, monotonous, mundane, ordinary, pedestrian, routine, uninspiring, uninteresting, workaday. OPPOSITE interesting.

proscribe *verb* see PROHIBIT.

prosecute *verb They were prosecuted for trespassing.* accuse, bring to trial, charge, indict, sue, take to court, try.

prospect *noun* **1** *The prospects of winning were slim.* chance, hope, likelihood, odds, outlook, possibility, probability. **2** *a splendid prospect from the lookout.* outlook, panorama, scene, sight, view, vista. — *verb They prospected for gold.* explore, fossick (*Australian informal*), look, search.

prospective *adjective prospective clients.* future, likely, possible, potential, would-be.

prosper *verb The business prospered.* boom, do well, flourish, grow, make money, succeed, thrive. OPPOSITE fail.

prosperity *noun a life of prosperity.* affluence, fortune, plenty, riches, success, wealth.

prosperous *adjective a prosperous businessman.* affluent, flourishing, moneyed, rich, successful, thriving, wealthy, well-heeled (*informal*), well off, well-to-do. OPPOSITE poor, unsuccessful.

prostitute *noun* call-girl, courtesan (*old use*), harlot (*old use*), hooker (*slang*), sex worker, whore.

prostrate *adjective They rose from their prostrate position.* face down, flat, horizontal, procumbent, prone. OPPOSITE upright. — *verb* **prostrate yourself** *He prostrated himself before the king and asked for mercy.* bow, kneel, kowtow, throw yourself down.

protect *verb* **1** *The shepherd protects his flock.* care for, cherish, defend, guard, keep safe, look after, mind, take care of, tend, watch over. **2** *The house is protected from the wind by a row of trees.* screen, shelter, shield. OPPOSITE expose. **3** *Take insurance to protect yourself against loss.* cover, indemnify, insure, safeguard, secure. **4** *The wax protects the surface.* insulate, preserve, seal, shield. OPPOSITE expose.

protection *noun protection against disease. protection against attack.* armour, barrier, buffer, cover, defence, immunity, insurance, refuge, safeguard, screen, security, shelter, shield.

protective *adjective* **1** *protective towards their children.* possessive, solicitous, vigilant, watchful. **2** *a protective jacket.* covering, fireproof, insulating, protecting, waterproof.

protest *noun* **1** *The changes were accepted without any protest.* beef (*slang*), complaint, demur, grumble, hue and cry, objection, outcry. **2** *The workers staged a protest.* boycott, demo (*informal*), demonstration, rally, sit-in. — *verb* **1** *They protested at the decision.* beef (*slang*), be up in arms, complain, demonstrate, demur, grumble, moan, object, remonstrate, squeal (*informal*). OPPOSITE approve, support. **2** *He protested his innocence.* affirm, assert, avow, declare, insist on, maintain, profess.

protester *noun The protesters became rowdy.* agitator, complainer, demonstrator, dissident, objector. OPPOSITE supporter.

prototype *noun the prototype of the car.* archetype, original, sample, trial model.

protract *verb He tried to protract the conversation.* drag out, draw out, extend, lengthen, prolong, spin out, stretch out. OPPOSITE shorten.

protrude *verb His stomach protrudes.* bulge, jut out, poke out, project, stand out, stick out.

proud *adjective* **1** *proud parents of a new baby.* delighted, gratified, happy, pleased, satisfied. OPPOSITE ashamed, displeased. **2** *They were too proud to ask for help.* dignified, independent, self-respecting. OPPOSITE humble. **3** *She was so proud that we found her insufferable.* arrogant, boastful, cocky, conceited, disdainful, egotistic(al), haughty, high and mighty, hoity-toity, self-satisfied, smug, snobbish, snooty (*informal*), stuck-up (*informal*), supercilious, superior, vain. OPPOSITE humble, modest.

prove *verb* **1** *This evidence proves his guilt.* bear out, confirm, corroborate, demonstrate, document, establish, show, substantiate, verify. OPPOSITE disprove. **2** *It proved to be a mistake.* be found, turn out.

proverb *noun His favourite proverb is 'Too many cooks spoil the broth'.* adage, axiom, catchphrase, dictum, maxim, motto, saying, slogan.

provide *verb* **1** *He provided them with everything they needed.* arm, equip, furnish, supply. OPPOSITE deprive of. **2** *He provided the money.* allot, contribute, donate, endow, give, grant, offer, present, supply. □ **provide for** **1** *He can no longer provide for his family.* keep, maintain, support, take care of. **2** *They tried to provide for every possibility.* allow for, anticipate, cater for, make provision for, plan for, prepare for.

providential *adjective Providential rains saved the harvest.* fortunate, heaven-sent, lucky, opportune, timely.

province *noun* **1** *The country is divided into provinces.* area, district, region, state, territory. **2** *Fixing computers is not her province.* area, domain, field, responsibility, sphere.

provincial *adjective a provincial newspaper.* country, district, local, regional, rural. OPPOSITE national.

provision *noun* **1** *He made provision for their future.* arrangement, plan, preparation. **2** *under the provisions of the will.* clause, condition, proviso, requirement, specification, stipulation, term. □ **provisions** *plural noun They bought provisions for the hike.* food, groceries, rations, stores, supplies.

provisional *adjective a provisional appointment.* interim, stopgap, temporary. OPPOSITE permanent.

proviso *noun She gave her approval with one proviso.* condition, provision, qualification, requirement, rider, stipulation.

provocative *adjective* **1** *a provocative dress.* alluring, inviting, seductive, sexy, tantalising, tempting. **2** *The interviewer was deliberately provocative.* annoying, exasperating, infuriating, irritating, maddening.

provoke *verb* **1** *He provoked people with his snide remarks.* anger, annoy, enrage, exasperate, incense, infuriate, irritate, madden, needle (*informal*), outrage, rile (*informal*), upset, vex, wind up (*informal*). OPPOSITE pacify. **2** *The sharp comment provoked an angry response.* arouse, cause, draw, elicit, evoke, generate, inspire, produce, prompt, spark, stimulate, trigger.

prow *noun the prow of a ship.* bow, front, nose. OPPOSITE stern.

prowess *noun* **1** *mathematical prowess.* ability, aptitude, competence, expertise, genius, proficiency, skill, talent. OPPOSITE incompetence. **2** *a warrior's prowess.* boldness, bravery, courage, daring, grit, guts (*informal*), heroism, mettle, valour. OPPOSITE cowardice.

prowl *verb Wild animals prowled around the tents.* lurk, roam, skulk, slink, sneak, steal.

prudent *adjective It seemed prudent to make further enquiries.* careful, cautious, far-sighted, judicious, politic, sage, sensible, shrewd, smart, wise. OPPOSITE imprudent, unwise.

prudish *adjective The film upset some prudish viewers.* demure, narrow-minded, old-fashioned, prim, prissy, puritanical, strait-laced. OPPOSITE open-minded.

prune *verb He pruned the dead branches of the fruit trees.* chop, cut back, lop, remove, snip off, trim.

pry *verb He's always prying into other people's affairs.* delve, inquire, interfere, intrude, meddle, poke about, probe, snoop (*informal*), stickybeak (*Australian informal*).

pseudo *adjective a pseudo friend.* bogus, fake, false, insincere, phoney (*informal*), pretended, sham. OPPOSITE genuine, real.

pseudonym *noun Lewis Carroll was the pseudonym of Charles Dodgson.* alias, assumed name, false name, nom de plume, pen-name.

psych *verb* **psych up** *He psyched himself up for the interview.* gear up, gird, prepare, steel.

psychic *adjective She claimed to have psychic powers and could read people's minds.* clairvoyant, extrasensory, occult, paranormal, supernatural, telepathic.

psychological *adjective a psychological problem.* emotional, mental. OPPOSITE physical.

pub *noun* (*informal*) *They had a drink at the pub.* bar, hotel (*Australian*), inn, local (*informal*), public house, saloon (*American*), tavern.

puberty *noun The child had reached puberty.* adolescence, pubescence, teens.

public *adjective* **1** *a public library.* civic, community, council, government, municipal, national, state. OPPOSITE private. **2** *the public interest.* common, community, general, national, popular. OPPOSITE private. **3** *The information was now public.* disclosed, familiar, known, official, open, published, unconcealed. OPPOSITE secret. — *noun members of the Australian public.* citizens, community, country, electorate, nation, people, populace, population, society, voters. □ **in public** *She said these things in public.* openly, publicly. OPPOSITE in private.

publican *noun a hotel publican.* hotelier, hotel-keeper, innkeeper, landlady, landlord, licensee, proprietor, proprietress.

publicise *verb The event was publicised in newspapers and on TV and radio.* advertise, announce, hype up (*slang*), make known, plug (*informal*), promote, publish, push.

publicity *noun* **1** *The rescuer tried to avoid publicity.* attention, fame, limelight, notice. **2** *After all the publicity, the show was disappointing.* advertising, build-up, hype (*slang*), marketing, plug (*informal*), promotion, propaganda.

publish *verb* **1** *The book was published in 1839.* bring out, issue, release; see also PRINT. **2** *The results were published in the newspaper.* advertise, announce, broadcast, disclose, disseminate, make known, make public, proclaim, promulgate, publicise, report, reveal. OPPOSITE suppress.

pucker *verb She puckered her brow. The material puckered.* contract, crinkle, furrow, gather, screw up, wrinkle. — *noun She sewed the seam without any puckers.* crease, crinkle, fold, gather, pleat, tuck, wrinkle.

puddle *noun He stepped in a puddle.* pool.

puerile *adjective puerile behaviour.* childish, foolish, immature, infantile, juvenile, silly. OPPOSITE mature.

puff *noun a puff of wind.* blast, breath, draught, gust. — *verb The wolf huffed and puffed.* blow, exhale, gasp, heave, huff, pant, wheeze. □ **puff up** *Her stomach puffed up.* bloat, blow up, distend, expand, inflate, swell.

puffy *adjective His eyes were puffy from crying.* puffed up, swollen.

pugnacious *adjective He was loud and pugnacious after a few drinks.* aggressive, argumentative, bellicose, belligerent, combative, hostile, hot-tempered, militant, quarrelsome. OPPOSITE peaceable.

pull *verb* **1** *The engine could not pull the heavy load.* drag, draw, haul, heave, lug, tow, trail, tug. OPPOSITE push. **2** *He pulled my hair.* jerk, pluck, tug, wrench, yank (*informal*). **3** *He pulled a muscle.* sprain, strain, stretch, tear, wrench. □ **pull down** *They pulled down the building.* demolish, destroy, dismantle, knock down, level, raze, take down, tear down. OPPOSITE erect. **pull in** *The train pulled in to the station.* arrive (at), draw in, enter, stop (at). **pull off** *He pulled off the stunt without much trouble.* accomplish, achieve, carry off, do, manage, succeed in. **pull out** **1** *The train pulled out of the station.* draw out, leave, move out. OPPOSITE enter. **2** *She pulled out her tooth.* draw, extract, remove, take out. OPPOSITE insert. **pull someone's leg** *Don't believe him: he's just pulling your leg.* have on (*informal*), kid (*informal*), tease, trick. **pull through** *The doctor didn't expect him to pull through.* get better, rally, recover, survive. **pull up** *The car pulled up at the lights.* draw up, halt, stop.

pullover *noun He wore a pullover for warmth.* jersey, jumper, sweater.

pulp *noun fruit pulp.* flesh, mash, mush, purée. — *verb She pulped the fruit in the blender.* crush, liquidise, mash, pound, purée, smash, squash.

pulsate *verb He could feel his heart pulsating.* beat, palpitate, pound, pulse, quiver, throb, thump, vibrate.

pulse *noun She could not feel any pulse.* beat, pulsation, rhythm, throb, vibration.

pulverise *verb* **1** *He pulverised the seeds.* crush, grind, mill, pound. **2** *They pulverised the opposition.* beat, clobber (*slang*), defeat, thrash, trounce.

pummel *verb She pummelled his back.* hit, pound, punch.

pump *verb* **1** *The doctor pumped her stomach to remove the poison.* drain, empty. **2** *He pumped the man for information.* grill, interrogate, probe, question, quiz. □ **pump up** *He pumped up the tyres.* blow up, fill, inflate. OPPOSITE let down.

pun *noun* double meaning, play on words.

punch *verb He punched the other man.* bash, box, clout (*informal*), cuff, dong (*Australian informal*), hit, pummel, quilt (*Australian slang*), slog, slug, sock (*slang*), stoush (*Australian slang*), strike, thump. — *noun* **1** *He gave the man a punch in the stomach.* blow, box, clout (*informal*), hit, slog, slug, sock (*slang*), thump. **2** (*informal*) *His sermon lacked punch.* force, forcefulness, power, vigour.

punctual *adjective The doctor was punctual.* on schedule, on the dot, on the knocker (*Australian informal*), on time, prompt. CONTRASTS WITH early, late.

punctuate *verb His speech was punctuated with coughs.* break, dot, interrupt, intersperse, pepper.

puncture *noun The tyre has a puncture.* hole, leak, perforation, rupture, slit, tear. — *verb A thorn punctured the tyre.* penetrate, perforate, pierce, prick.

pundit *noun Political pundits predicted a close result.* authority, expert, sage.

pungent adjective *a pungent smell. a pungent taste.* acid, acrid, aromatic, hot, piquant, sharp, spicy, strong, tangy, tart. OPPOSITE bland, delicate.

punish verb *He was punished for his misdeeds.* castigate, chastise, discipline, make to suffer, penalise, scold, sentence. OPPOSITE pardon, reward.

punishment noun *Make the punishment fit the crime.* castigation, chastisement, discipline, fine, imposition, penalty, sentence. OPPOSITE reward.

punt verb (*informal*) *How much are you prepared to punt?* bet, gamble, risk, speculate, stake, wager. — noun *He had a punt on the outcome.* bet, gamble, wager.

puny adjective **1** *He is too puny to do such heavy work.* feeble, frail, sickly, skinny, small, undersized, weak, weedy. OPPOSITE strapping. **2** *a puny amount.* feeble, paltry, pathetic, petty, small, tiny, trifling, trivial. OPPOSITE large.

pup noun *The dog had a litter of three pups.* puppy, whelp.

pupil noun **1** *Each teacher has twenty pupils.* learner, scholar, schoolboy, schoolchild, schoolgirl, student. **2** *a pupil of the great painter.* apprentice, disciple.

puppet noun *The story was told using puppets.* doll, finger puppet, glove puppet, marionette, string puppet.

purchase verb *They purchased a television.* acquire, buy, get, obtain, pay for. OPPOSITE sell. — noun *She was pleased with her purchase.* acquisition, buy.

purchaser noun buyer, customer. OPPOSITE vendor.

pure adjective **1** *pure gold.* solid, unadulterated, unalloyed, unmixed. OPPOSITE adulterated. **2** *pure water.* clean, clear, fresh, straight, uncontaminated, undiluted, unpolluted, untainted. OPPOSITE impure, polluted. **3** *a pure person.* blameless, chaste, decent, good, guiltless, innocent, modest, moral, sinless, upright, virtuous. OPPOSITE immoral. **4** *pure nonsense.* absolute, complete, downright, perfect, sheer, thorough, total, utter.

purée noun *The baby eats apple purée.* mash, mush, pulp. — verb *Purée the pumpkin.* liquidise, mash, pulp.

purgative noun *The doctor prescribed a purgative.* enema, laxative, purge.

purge verb **1** *They purged the party of traitors.* clear, empty, rid. **2** *They purged the traitors from the party.* clear out, dismiss, eliminate, eradicate, expel, get rid of, remove, weed out.

purify verb *The water has to be purified.* clean, disinfect, distil, filter, refine, sterilise. OPPOSITE contaminate.

purist noun *a purist in matters of language.* dogmatist, pedant, stickler.

puritanical adjective *a serious and puritanical old man.* ascetic, austere, moralistic, prim, prudish, strait-laced, strict, wowserish (*Australian*). OPPOSITE permissive.

purple adjective *a purple colour.* amethyst, hyacinth, jacaranda, lavender, lilac, mauve, mulberry, plum, violet.

purport noun *He explained the purport of the article.* drift, gist, meaning, substance, thrust. — verb *The information is purported to be from official sources.* allege, claim, pretend, profess.

purpose noun **1** *The task has an educational purpose.* aim, function, goal, intent, intention, justification, motivation, motive, object, objective, point, use, value. **2** *He did the work with purpose.* determination, resolution, resolve, single-mindedness. □ **on purpose** *He tripped her up on purpose.* consciously, deliberately, intentionally, knowingly, purposely, wittingly. OPPOSITE accidentally.

purposeless adjective *a purposeless activity.* aimless, meaningless, pointless, senseless, useless. OPPOSITE purposeful.

purse noun **1** *She keeps her money in a purse.* pouch, wallet. **2** (*American*) *She carries her glasses in her purse.* bag, handbag. — verb *He pursed his lips.* press together, pucker, squeeze.

pursue verb **1** *The police pursued the villains.* chase, follow, go after, hound, hunt, run after, shadow, stalk, tail (*informal*), track down, trail. **2** *She pursued a career in social work.* carry on, conduct, continue, engage in, follow, work at.

pursuit noun **1** *The cat gave up her pursuit of the mouse.* chase, hunt, stalking, tracking. **2** *intellectual and recreational pursuits.* activity, hobby, interest, occupation, pastime, recreation.

push verb **1** *He pushed the trolley out of the way.* drive, move, propel, shove, thrust. **2** *She pushed her way through the crowd.* advance, butt, elbow, force, forge, jostle, nudge, press, ram, shoulder, shove, thrust. **3** *She pushed the filling into the hole.* compress, cram, force, pack, press, ram, squash, squeeze, stick (*informal*), stuff. **4** *His friends pushed him into entering the contest.* bully, coerce, compel, dragoon, drive, egg on, encourage, force, goad, hound, press, pressure, spur, urge. OPPOSITE discourage. **5** *The presenter likes to push new products.* advertise, plug (*informal*), promote, publicise.

pusher noun **1** *a drug pusher.* dealer, peddler, seller. **2** (*Australian*) *a baby's pusher.* pushchair, stroller.

pushover noun (*informal*) **1** *She found the test a pushover.* bludge (*Australian informal*), breeze (*informal*), child's play, cinch (*informal*), doddle (*informal*), piece of cake (*informal*), snack (*Australian informal*), snap (*informal*), walkover. OPPOSITE struggle. **2** *He'll be a pushover for that trickster.* dupe, easy prey, mug (*informal*), sitter (*informal*), sitting duck (*informal*), soft touch, sucker (*informal*).

pushy adjective *a pushy salesman.* aggressive, assertive, bumptious, forceful, forward, self-assertive. OPPOSITE retiring.

put verb **1** *He put the ornaments on the shelf.* arrange, bung (*informal*), deposit, dump, lay, leave, locate, place, plant, plonk, pop, position, rest, set down, settle, situate, slap, stand, station, stick. **2** *He put the pictures on the wall.* arrange, hang, mount, place, position. **3** *She put the battery in the camera.* fit, insert, install, load, place. OPPOSITE remove. **4** *Who put that idea in his head?* implant, insert, instil, plant. **5** *They put the damage at $3000.* assess, calculate, estimate, reckon. **6** *He put his theory very simply.* express, formulate, phrase, say, state, word. **7** *He put the idea to us for comment.* advance, offer, present, propose, put forward, submit, suggest. **8** *The government put a tax on wine.* apply, impose, levy, place. **9** *She put the blame on others.* assign, attribute, cast, impute, lay, pin. □ **put away** (*informal*) *The murderer was put away for thirty years.* confine, imprison, jail, lock up. **put by** *They put some money by each week for their holiday.* put aside, reserve, save, set aside, stash (*informal*). OPPOSITE spend. **put down 1** *The army put down the rebellion.* crush, quash, quell, stop, subdue, suppress. **2** *She felt he was putting her down.* belittle, denigrate, disparage, humiliate, slight, snub. **3** *The dog had to be put down.* destroy, kill, put to sleep. **4** *She put it down to tiredness.* ascribe, attribute, blame on. **put forward 1** *They put forward their ideas.* advance, offer, present, propose, propound, put up, submit, suggest. **2** *John's name was put forward.* nominate, propose, recommend, submit, suggest. **put in 1** *He put in many extra hours.* devote, give, spend. **2** *She put in for the job.* apply, go, try. **put off 1** *She had to put off the party.* defer, delay, hold off, postpone, reschedule, shelve. **2** *The fish looked good to eat, but the smell put him off.* disgust, repel, revolt, sicken. OPPOSITE attract. **3** *His father tried to put him off becoming an actor.* deter from, discourage from, dissuade from, talk out of. OPPOSITE encourage. **put on 1** *She put on her new outfit.* change into, don, dress in, slip into, wear. OPPOSITE take off. **2** *They put on a play.* mount, perform, present, produce, stage. **3** *She put on a funny voice.* adopt, affect, assume. **4** *They put cream on their skin.* apply, slap, spread. OPPOSITE remove. **5** *She has put on weight.* gain, increase. OPPOSITE lose. **6** *He put on the heater.* switch on, turn on. OPPOSITE turn off. **put out 1** *He put out his hand to save them.* extend, hold out, reach out, stick out, stretch out. OPPOSITE withdraw. **2** *They tried not to put Granny out by their visit.* annoy, bother, inconvenience, irritate, trouble. **3** *They put out the fire.* douse, extinguish, quench, snuff out. OPPOSITE light. **put together** *He needed glue to put the model together.* assemble, build, construct, join, make. OPPOSITE dismantle. **put up 1** *They put up the house in six weeks.* build, construct, erect. OPPOSITE demolish. **2** *He put up the tent.* erect, pitch, set up. **3** *They are putting up their prices.* boost, bump up (*informal*), increase, jack up (*informal*), raise. OPPOSITE lower. **4** *The company put up the money for the venture.* contribute, donate, pay, provide, supply. **5** *They put us up for the night.* accommodate, billet, house, lodge, take in. **put up with** *She won't put up with any rudeness.* abide, accept, bear, brook, endure, stand for, suffer, take, tolerate.

putrid adjective *The meat had to be thrown out because it was putrid.* bad, decayed, decomposed, foul, rank, rotten, smelly, stinking. OPPOSITE fresh.

puzzle noun *They all tried to solve the puzzle.* brainteaser, conundrum, dilemma, enigma, mystery, paradox, problem, question, riddle. — verb **1** *She was puzzled by the message.* baffle, bamboozle (*informal*), bewilder, confound, confuse, flummox (*informal*), mystify, nonplus, perplex, stump (*informal*), throw (*informal*). **2** *She puzzled over the strange events.* brood, muse, ponder, rack your brains, wonder.

puzzling adjective *puzzling behaviour. a puzzling problem.* abstruse, baffling, difficult, enigmatic, inexplicable, inscrutable, insoluble, mysterious, perplexing, strange, unfathomable. OPPOSITE straightforward.

pygmy noun *a fairy tale of pygmies and giants.* dwarf, lilliputian, midget. OPPOSITE giant. — adjective *a pygmy kangaroo.* dwarf, miniature, small, tiny, undersized. OPPOSITE giant.

Qq

quack noun **1** *He isn't qualified. He's a quack.* charlatan, fake, impostor, phoney (*informal*). **2** (*slang*) *He went to the quack for a check-up.* see DOCTOR.

quadrangle noun *The offices are arranged around a quadrangle.* courtyard, quad.

quaff verb *He quaffed his wine greedily.* drink, gulp, guzzle, swallow, swig (*informal*).

quagmire noun *The tractor was stuck in a quagmire.* bog, fen, marsh, mire, morass, slough, swamp.

quail verb *He quailed at the sight of the cane.* cower, cringe, flinch, recoil, shrink, wince.

quaint adjective *a quaint old cottage.* attractive, charming, curious, odd, old-fashioned, picturesque, twee, unusual.

quake verb *She quaked with fear at the thunder.* quaver, quiver, shake, shiver, shudder, tremble. — noun (*informal*) *The quake caused buildings to collapse.* earthquake, tremor.

qualification noun **1** *Do you have the right qualifications for the job?* ability, aptitude, attribute, competence, competency, credentials, eligibility, experience, knowledge, prerequisite, quality, skill, training. **2** *After four years of study he gained his teaching qualification.* certificate, degree, diploma. **3** *This statement needs some qualification.* condition, limitation, modification, proviso, reservation, restriction, stipulation.

qualified adjective *The work was done by a qualified mechanic.* certificated, certified, competent, licensed, skilled, trained.

qualify verb **1** *His studies qualified him to practise as a therapist.* allow, authorise, entitle, equip, fit, licence, make eligible, permit, prepare, train. **2** *She qualified the phrase 'all students' to 'nearly all students'.* limit, modify, restrict.

quality noun **1** *His work is of the highest quality.* calibre, class, grade, level, standard. **2** *It's quality that matters, not quantity.* excellence, merit, value, worth. **3** *He has many good qualities.* attribute, characteristic, feature, trait.

qualm noun *He has no qualms about stealing.* compunction, misgiving, pang of conscience, scruple.

quandary noun **in a quandary** *She was in a quandary about what to do.* confused, in a dilemma, perplexed, uncertain, unsure.

quantity noun *a small quantity.* amount, dose, extent, load, lot, mass, measure, number, portion, quantum, sum, volume, weight.

quarantine noun *The animals were kept in quarantine after the journey.* isolation, segregation.

quarrel noun *They had a quarrel over money.* altercation, argument, barney (*informal*), clash, conflict, controversy, difference, disagreement, dispute, feud, fight, row, spat (*informal*), squabble, tiff, wrangle. — verb *The children quarrel constantly.* argue, be at loggerheads, bicker, brawl, differ, fall out, fight, row (*informal*), scrap, squabble, wrangle.

quarrelsome adjective argumentative, belligerent, cantankerous, contentious, contrary, cross, disputatious, irritable, petulant, pugnacious, truculent. OPPOSITE peaceable.

quarry¹ noun *They filled in the old stone quarry.* excavation, mine, pit, working.

quarry² noun *a wild animal's quarry.* prey, victim.

quarter noun *the city's student quarter.* area, district, locality, neighbourhood, region. — verb *The officers were quartered in several homes in the town.* accommodate, billet, house, lodge, put up, station. □ **quarters** plural noun *the soldiers' quarters.* accommodation, barracks, billet, digs (*informal*), housing, lodgings.

quash verb *The conviction was quashed.* annul, invalidate, nullify, overrule, overturn, rescind, reverse, revoke.

quaver verb *Her voice quavered.* quiver, shake, tremble, vibrate, waver. — noun *a quaver in her voice.* quiver, shaking, trembling, tremor, vibration, wavering.

quay noun *The ferry drew close to the quay.* berth, dock, jetty, landing stage, pier, wharf.

queasy adjective *He felt queasy after the rich food.* bilious, ill, nauseous, off colour, sick, unwell.

queen noun monarch, ruler, sovereign.

queer adjective **1** *Her behaviour was a bit queer.* abnormal, bizarre, curious, eccentric, funny, odd, offbeat, peculiar, singular, strange, unconventional, unusual, weird. OPPOSITE normal. **2** *She felt a bit queer.* dizzy, faint, giddy, ill, off colour, out of sorts, poorly, queasy, unwell.

quell verb **1** *The rebellion was quelled.* crush, defeat, overcome, put down, quash, subdue, suppress. **2** *He quelled my fears.* allay, alleviate, assuage, calm, quieten, soothe, subdue.

quench verb **1** *The rain quenched the fire.* douse, extinguish, put out, smother. **2** *The drink quenched his thirst.* satisfy, slake.

query noun *The officer answered our query.* enquiry, inquiry, question. — verb *He queried our motives.* challenge, dispute, doubt, question.

quest noun *a quest for knowledge.* hunt, pursuit, search.

question noun **1** *Did you answer her question?* conundrum, enquiry, inquiry, poser, puzzle, query, riddle. OPPOSITE answer, statement. **2** *unresolved questions.* issue, matter, point, problem. **3** *There is no question that he is guilty.* argument, controversy, debate, dispute, doubt, uncertainty. — verb **1** *The police questioned him about the incident.* ask, cross-examine, enquire of, examine, grill, inquire of, interrogate, interview, probe, pump, quiz, sound out. **2** *She questioned the spokesperson's authority.* call into question, cast doubt on, challenge, dispute, doubt, query. □ **out of the question** *An overseas trip is out the question.* impossible, inconceivable, unthinkable. OPPOSITE possible.

questionable adjective *His motives are rather questionable.* doubtful, dubious, suspect, suss (*informal*), uncertain.

questionnaire noun set of questions, survey.

queue noun *a queue of people.* chain, column, file, line, line-up, row, string. — verb *They queued for the bus.* line up.

quibble noun *a quibble about the price.* complaint, objection, protest. — verb *It's not worth quibbling about.* argue, carp, cavil, find fault, niggle, nit-pick (*informal*), object, protest, quarrel, split hairs.

quiche noun *a leek quiche.* flan, pie, tart.

quick adjective **1** *a quick pace.* breakneck, brisk, express, fast, fleet, precipitate, rapid, speedy, swift, zippy. OPPOSITE slow. **2** *The old man was quick on his feet.* agile, lively, nimble, nippy (*informal*), sprightly, spry. OPPOSITE slow. **3** *a quick visit. a quick look.* brief, cursory, fleeting, hasty, hurried, perfunctory, short. OPPOSITE long. **4** *a quick response.* expeditious, immediate, instant, instantaneous, prompt, speedy, swift. OPPOSITE slow. **5** *She is quick at mathematics.* able, alert, astute, bright, clever, intelligent, perceptive, sharp, shrewd, smart. OPPOSITE slow. **6** *He has a quick temper.* fiery, hot, sharp, short.

quicken verb **1** *They quickened their pace.* accelerate, hasten, hurry, speed up. OPPOSITE slacken, slow down. **2** *Our interest was quickened.* arouse, enliven, inspire, kindle, stimulate.

quickly adverb *Wendy ran quickly. She got the job done quickly.* apace, at full pelt, at speed, at the double, briskly, expeditiously, fast, hastily, hell for leather (*informal*), hurriedly, immediately, in a flash, in a jiffy (*informal*), in no time, instantly, like greased lightning (*informal*), post-haste, promptly, rapidly, speedily, swiftly. OPPOSITE slowly.

quiet adjective **1** *The examination room was quiet.* noiseless, silent, soundless, still. OPPOSITE noisy. **2** *The wombat was so quiet that we thought he was dead.* inactive, inert, motionless, quiescent, still. OPPOSITE active. **3** *The streets were quiet after the riot.* calm, peaceful, tranquil, undisturbed. OPPOSITE busy, rowdy. **4** *a quiet voice.* gentle, hushed, inaudible, low, soft. OPPOSITE loud. **5** *She is a quiet person.* gentle, introverted, mild, placid, reserved, reticent, retiring, sedate, serene, shy, silent, taciturn, uncommunicative. OPPOSITE noisy, talkative. **6** *quiet colours.* muted, restful, soft, subdued, subtle, unobtrusive. OPPOSITE loud, showy.

quieten verb *He quietened the children.* calm, hush, pacify, quiet, restrain, shush (*informal*), silence, soothe, subdue.

quietness noun calm, hush, peace, quiet, serenity, silence, stillness, tranquillity. OPPOSITE noise.

quilt noun *a warm quilt for the bed.* continental quilt, coverlet, Doona (*trade mark*), duvet, eiderdown.

quip noun *The speaker's quips kept the audience amused.* jest, joke, sally, wisecrack, witticism.

quirk noun **1** *Most people have a few quirks.* eccentricity, foible, idiosyncrasy, oddity, peculiarity. **2** *one of those quirks of fate.* aberration, fluke, trick, twist, vagary.

quit verb **1** *They quit the campsite at dawn.* depart from, desert, go away from, leave, vacate. OPPOSITE arrive at. **2** *He quit his job.* abandon, abdicate, chuck in (*informal*), forsake, give up, jack in (*slang*), leave, pack in (*informal*), relinquish, resign from, retire from, toss in (*informal*). OPPOSITE continue, start. **3** (*informal*) *Quit moaning.* cease, desist from, discontinue, leave off, stop. OPPOSITE keep on.

quite adverb **1** *Are you quite certain?* absolutely, altogether, completely, entirely, fully, perfectly, positively, totally, utterly. **2** *He is quite fat.* comparatively, fairly, moderately, pretty, rather, reasonably, relatively, somewhat.

quiver verb *The boy quivered with fear.* pulsate, quake, quaver, shake, shiver, shudder, tremble, vibrate.

quiz noun *The teacher gave her students a quiz to see how much they remembered.* competition, exam, examination, questionnaire, test. — verb *She quizzed the witnesses about what they had seen.* ask, examine, grill, interrogate, question, test.

quota noun *They received their quota of the money.* allocation, allowance, cut (*informal*), lot, part, portion, proportion, ration, share.

quotation noun **1** *The essay contained quotations from the Bible.* citation, excerpt, extract, passage, quote (*informal*), reference. **2** *The painter gave us a quotation for the job.* estimate, quote (*informal*), tender.

quote verb **1** *He is fond of quoting Shakespeare.* recite, repeat. **2** *Can you quote a recent example?* call up, cite, instance, mention, name, refer to. **3** *The painter quoted $1000 for the job.* estimate, tender.

Rr

rabbit noun buck (*male*), bunny (*informal*), doe (*female*), kitten (*young*).

rabble noun *He tried to quieten the noisy rabble.* crowd, horde, mob, swarm, throng.

race¹ noun *She won the race.* chase, competition, contest, heat, marathon, rally, relay. — verb **1** *She raced against her brother.* compete. **2** *He raced past me.* career, dart, dash, fly, hurry, hurtle, run, rush, shoot, speed, sprint, sweep, tear, whiz, zip, zoom.

race² noun *the different races of the world.* ethnic group, nation, people, tribe.

racetrack noun circuit, course, racecourse, speedway, track.

racial adjective *racial background.* ethnic, national, tribal.

racism noun racial discrimination, racial intolerance, racialism, racial prejudice.

rack noun *a rack for mugs.* framework, holder, shelf, stand, support.

racket noun **1** *The racket made it impossible to concentrate.* clamour, commotion, din, disturbance, hubbub, hullabaloo, noise, pandemonium, row, ruckus, rumpus, tumult, uproar. OPPOSITE quietness. **2** *He was involved in a tax racket.* dodge (*informal*), lurk (*Australian informal*), rort (*Australian slang*), scam (*slang*), scheme, swindle.

racy adjective *Bill has written a racy description of his adventures.* animated, exciting, juicy (*informal*), lively, spicy, spirited, stimulating. OPPOSITE dull.

radiant adjective **1** *a radiant light.* bright, brilliant, dazzling, gleaming, glowing, incandescent, luminous, shining. OPPOSITE dark, dull. **2** *the radiant mother-to-be.* beaming, beautiful, blissful, ecstatic, glowing, happy, joyful, overjoyed. OPPOSITE unhappy.

radiate verb **1** *Five roads radiate from this point.* branch out, diverge, issue, spread out. OPPOSITE converge. **2** *The heater radiates warmth.* diffuse, emit, give off, give out, send out, shed, transmit.

radical adjective **1** *radical changes.* complete, drastic, far-reaching, fundamental, profound, sweeping, thorough. OPPOSITE minimal, superficial. **2** *radical policies.* extreme, extremist, immoderate, revolutionary. OPPOSITE conservative, moderate.

radio noun *He listened to the programme on the radio.* receiver, set, transistor, tuner, wireless.

raffle noun *We bought a ticket in the raffle.* art union (*Australian*), draw, lottery, sweep, sweepstake, tombola.

rag noun *He wiped his hands on a rag.* cloth, fragment, remnant, scrap.

ragamuffin noun guttersnipe, urchin, waif.

rage noun **1** *a fit of rage.* anger, exasperation, frenzy, fury, ire, paddy (*informal*), tantrum, temper, wrath. **2** *Big hats were all the rage.* craze, fashion, mode, trend, vogue. — verb *He raged at the unfairness of the system.* be angry, be beside yourself, be furious, blow your stack (*informal*), blow your top (*informal*), do your block (*Australian informal*), flare up, fly off the handle (*informal*), fume, go off the deep end (*informal*), let off steam, lose your cool (*informal*), lose your temper, rail, rant, rave, seethe.

ragged adjective **1** *ragged clothes.* dilapidated, frayed, holey, scruffy, shabby, tattered, tatty (*informal*), threadbare, torn, worn-out. **2** *a ragged edge.* irregular, jagged, rough, uneven. OPPOSITE even, smooth.

raging adjective **1** *raging seas.* heavy, roaring, stormy, turbulent, violent, wild. OPPOSITE calm. **2** *a raging headache.* excruciating, intense, severe. OPPOSITE mild.

raid noun **1** *a midnight raid on the town.* assault, attack, blitz, foray, incursion, invasion, offensive, onslaught, sortie, swoop. **2** *a police raid.* bust (*informal*), search. — verb **1** *The soldiers raided the town.* attack, descend on, invade, storm, swoop on. **2** *The thieves raided the store.* loot, pillage, plunder, ransack, rifle, rob.

rail¹ noun *He held on to the rail to steady himself.* banisters, bar, handrail, railing.

rail² verb *He railed against everybody in authority.* complain, declaim, inveigh, lash out, protest, rage, vociferate.

railing noun *He stood on the other side of the railing.* balustrade, barrier, fence, rails.

rain noun *After the rain we can go outside.* cloudburst, deluge, downpour, drizzle, precipitation, rainfall, shower, storm, thunderstorm. — verb *It is raining.* bucket down, drizzle, pelt, pour, rain cats and dogs (*informal*), spit, sprinkle, teem.

raincoat noun anorak, mac (*informal*), mackintosh, oilskin, trench coat, waterproof.

rainy adjective *rainy weather.* damp, drizzly, showery, wet. OPPOSITE dry.

raise verb **1** *He raised the weight off the ground.* elevate, heave, hoist, jack, lift, pick up. OPPOSITE lower. **2** *He raised a monument on the site.* build, construct, erect, put up. OPPOSITE pull down. **3** *The shop raised their prices.* boost, bump up (*informal*), increase, inflate, jack up (*informal*), mark up, put up. OPPOSITE reduce. **4** *She raised our hopes.* arouse, awaken, boost, build up, encourage, heighten, increase, kindle, stimulate. OPPOSITE dash. **5** *He raises roses.* breed, cultivate, grow, produce, propagate. **6** *The couple raised four children.* bring up, nurture, rear. **7** *They raised the amount needed.* accumulate, amass, collect, gather, get, obtain. **8** *She raised the question.* bring up, broach, initiate, introduce, pose, put forward. — noun *He asked for a raise.*

increase, rise. □ **raise from the dead** restore to life, resurrect, resuscitate, revive.

rake *verb* **1** *She raked the leaves.* collect, gather, sweep up. **2** *They raked through the old papers.* comb, forage, fossick (*Australian informal*), rummage, scour, search.

rally *verb* **1** *The people rallied in support.* assemble, come together, convene, gather, unite. **2** *The leader rallied his troops.* assemble, marshal, mobilise, muster, round up, summon. **3** *The old man rallied after weeks of being ill.* get better, improve, pull through, recover, revive. OPPOSITE deteriorate. — *noun* **1** *The students held a rally.* assembly, convention, demo (*informal*), demonstration, jamboree, gathering, meeting. **2** *Fifty cars competed in the rally.* competition, race.

ram *verb* **1** *He rammed the filling into the cushion.* compress, cram, force, jam, pack, push, squeeze, stuff, tamp. **2** *He rammed the nail into the wood.* drive, force, hammer, push. **3** *Her car rammed the one in front.* bump into, collide with, crash into, hit, run into, slam into, smash into.

ramble *verb* **1** *They rambled through the bush.* amble, hike, roam, rove, saunter, stroll, traipse, tramp, trek, walk, wander. **2** *The audience lost interest as the speaker rambled.* digress, go off at a tangent, waffle (*informal*), wander, witter on (*informal*). — *noun a ramble in the bush.* hike, roam, stroll, trek, walk.

rambling *adjective* **1** *a rambling speech.* discursive, disjointed, meandering, wandering, wordy. OPPOSITE succinct. **2** *a rambling plant.* climbing, straggling, trailing.

ramification *noun They did not foresee all the ramifications of their new policy.* complication, consequence, implication, offshoot.

ramp *noun a steep ramp.* incline, slope.

rampage *verb The gang rampaged through the city streets.* go berserk, go wild, run amok, run riot.

rampant *adjective Disease was rampant in the poorer districts.* epidemic, flourishing, out of control, prevalent, rife, unchecked, uncurbed, unrestrained, widespread.

rampart *noun The city was surrounded by ramparts for protection.* bulwark, earthwork, embankment, fortification, parapet, wall.

ramshackle *adjective a ramshackle old cottage.* decrepit, derelict, dilapidated, rickety, run-down, tumbledown.

ranch *noun a cattle ranch.* farm, stud.

rancid *adjective The butter smelt rancid.* bad, high, off, on the nose (*Australian informal*), rank, rotten, sour, stale. OPPOSITE fresh.

rancour *noun He bore no rancour despite what had been done to him.* acrimony, animosity, bitterness, grudge, hatred, hostility, ill will, malice, resentment, spite, venom. OPPOSITE goodwill.

random *adjective a random choice.* accidental, arbitrary, chance, fortuitous, haphazard, hit-or-miss, indiscriminate, unplanned. OPPOSITE deliberate, systematic.

range *noun* **1** *a range of mountains.* chain, line, row, series. **2** *a specific age range.* bracket, group, span. **3** *a wide range of interests.* assortment, gamut, selection, set, spectrum, spread, variety. **4** *outside the range of her duties.* area, bounds, compass, domain, extent, field, limits, orbit, scope, sphere. **5** *She warmed herself by the range.* cooker, fireplace, oven, stove. — *verb* **1** *The prices ranged from $100 to $500.* differ, extend, fluctuate, go, vary. **2** *The sheep ranged over the hills.* ramble, roam, rove, stray, travel, wander. □ **ranges** *plural noun The ranges were covered with stringybarks.* highlands, hills, mountains, tiers (*Tasmania & early South Australia*).

ranger *noun a park ranger.* curator, keeper, warden.

rank[1] *noun* **1** *They stood in two ranks.* column, file, line, queue, row. **2** *a person of lower rank.* class, degree, grade, level, position, standing, station, status. — *verb He ranked them in order of merit.* arrange, class, grade, order, place, rate.

rank[2] *adjective* **1** *rank vegetation.* dense, lush, luxuriant, overgrown, profuse, thick. **2** *a rank smell in the fridge.* bad, foul, noxious, off, offensive, on the nose (*Australian informal*), putrid, rancid, smelly, stinking, strong. **3** *rank injustice.* absolute, complete, downright, flagrant, glaring, gross, obvious, out-and-out, sheer, total, utter.

ransack *verb* **1** *She ransacked her drawer for a safety pin.* comb, fossick in (*Australian informal*), rake through, rummage in, scour, search. **2** *Thieves ransacked the house.* loot, pillage, plunder, raid, rob, sack.

rant *verb He ranted about the decline in manners.* bluster, declaim, hold forth, rave, sound off (*informal*), spout, vociferate.

rap *noun* **1** *He gave him a rap on the back of the hand.* blow, hit, knock, tap, whack. **2** (*informal*) *He took the rap for what happened.* blame, censure, punishment. — *verb He rapped on the window.* hit, knock, strike, tap.

rape *verb The man raped the girl.* assault sexually, ravish, violate.

rapid *adjective a rapid decision. rapid progress.* brisk, expeditious, fast, hasty, high-speed, meteoric, precipitate, prompt, quick, speedy, sudden, swift, whirlwind. OPPOSITE slow.

rapidity *noun They answered with amazing rapidity.* alacrity, dispatch, haste, promptness, quickness, speed, swiftness. OPPOSITE slowness.

rapidly *adverb* see QUICKLY.

rapt *adjective The audience was rapt.* absorbed, captivated, engrossed, enraptured, enthralled, entranced, intent, spellbound. OPPOSITE uninterested.

rapture *noun The music filled her with rapture.* bliss, delight, ecstasy, elation, euphoria, happiness, joy. OPPOSITE sorrow.

rare[1] *adjective* **1** *These animals have become rare.* scarce, uncommon. OPPOSITE common, plentiful. **2** *a rare sight.* abnormal, infrequent, occasional, odd, strange, uncommon, unfamiliar, unusual. OPPOSITE common.

rare[2] *adjective rare steak.* undercooked, underdone.

rarefied *adjective rarefied air.* rare, thin.

rarely *adverb She rarely goes out.* infrequently, once in a blue moon, seldom. OPPOSITE often.

rascal *noun* **1** *The police caught the rascal.* blackguard, knave (*old use*), miscreant, rogue, scoundrel, villain, wretch. **2** *She was a rascal to scare her mother like that.* devil, imp, monkey, scallywag, scamp.

rash[1] *adjective He regretted his rash decision.* foolhardy, hare-brained, hasty, headlong, heedless, hotheaded, impetuous, imprudent, impulsive, madcap, precipitate, reckless. OPPOSITE cautious.

rash[2] *noun an itchy rash on the body.* dermatitis, eczema, eruption, hives, spots.

rasping *adjective a rasping voice.* croaky, grating, harsh, hoarse, husky, raucous, rough, strident. OPPOSITE mellifluous.

rate *noun* **1** *a rate of six kilometres per hour.* pace, speed, velocity. **2** *Cheaper rates apply at weekends.* charge, cost, fare, fee, price, tariff. **3** *council rates.* levy, tax, taxation. — *verb She rated her chances as good.* assess, class, consider, count, deem, estimate, evaluate, gauge, judge, measure, rank, reckon, regard, value.

rather *adverb It is rather dark.* comparatively, fairly, moderately, pretty, quite, relatively, slightly, somewhat.

ratify *verb The parties ratified the agreement.* agree to, approve, assent to, confirm, consent to, countersign, endorse, sign, validate. OPPOSITE veto.

ratio *noun The ratio of blue to red is 2:1.* proportion, relationship.

ration *noun She gave away her ration of butter.* allocation, allowance, helping, portion, quota, share. □ **ration out** *The food was rationed out among the starving people.* allocate, apportion, distribute, dole out, mete out, share out.

rational *adjective* **1** *a rational person.* intelligent, lucid, normal, sane, sensible, well-balanced. OPPOSITE irrational, mad. **2** *a rational explanation.* logical, reasonable, sensible, sound. OPPOSITE illogical, irrational.

rationalise *verb* **1** *She tried to rationalise her fears.* account for, excuse, explain away, justify. **2** *The industry has been rationalised.* make more efficient, reorganise, restructure, streamline.

rattle *verb* **1** *The glasses rattled in the box.* clank, clatter, clink, jangle, shake. **2** (*informal*) *Nothing seems to rattle him.* agitate, alarm, disconcert, disturb, faze (*informal*), fluster, frighten, perturb, shake, throw, unnerve, upset, worry. □ **rattle off** *He rattled off his story.* recite, recount, reel off, relate.

raucous *adjective raucous laughter. a raucous voice.* grating, harsh, hoarse, jarring, loud, noisy, piercing, rasping, shrill, strident. OPPOSITE soft, sweet.

ravage *verb The town had been ravaged by war.* damage, destroy, devastate, lay waste, loot, pillage, plunder, raid, ransack, raze, ruin, sack, wreck. □ **ravages** *plural noun the ravages of time.* damage, depredation, destruction, devastation.

rave *verb* **1** *He ranted and raved like a madman.* carry on (*informal*), go on (*informal*), rant, sound off (*informal*); see also BE ANGRY (at ANGRY). **2** *She raved about my new dress.* be effusive, be enthusiastic, go overboard (*informal*), go wild, gush, wax lyrical (*informal*).

ravenous *adjective They were ravenous after their long hike.* famished, hungry, starving.

ravine *noun The river flows through a ravine.* canyon, defile, gorge, gully, valley.

raw *adjective* **1** *raw meat.* uncooked. OPPOSITE cooked. **2** *raw sugar.* crude, natural, unprocessed, unrefined, untreated. OPPOSITE processed. **3** *The firm took on a raw graduate and trained him.* callow, fresh, green, inexperienced, new, untrained. OPPOSITE experienced. **4** *His knee was raw after the fall.* grazed, red, scratched, skinned, sore, tender.

ray *noun* **1** *a ray of sunlight.* beam, shaft, streak, stream. **2** *a ray of hope.* flicker, glimmer, hint, spark, trace.

raze *verb Workmen razed the building.* bulldoze, demolish, destroy, flatten, knock down, level, tear down, wreck. OPPOSITE erect.

reach *verb* **1** *He reached out his hand to save the man.* extend, hold out, put out, stick out, stretch out. **2** *They reached Sydney in daylight.* arrive at, come to, get to, hit, make. **3** *They reached him by telephone.* catch up with, communicate with, contact, get hold of, get in touch with. **4** *They reached their goal.* accomplish, achieve, attain. **5** *The temperature reached 40°.* climb to, get to, go to, hit, rise to. **6** *Prices reached rock-bottom.* descend to, fall to, hit, strike. — *noun* **1** *The prize was beyond his reach.* capability, capacity, compass, grasp, range, scope. **2** *the river's upper reaches.* part, section, stretch.

react *verb She reacted strangely.* act, behave, respond.

reaction *noun a reaction to a request.* answer, feedback, reply, response.

read *verb* **1** *She could not read his handwriting.* decipher, interpret, make out, understand. **2** *He read the book.* browse through, dip into, glance at, peruse, pore through, scan, skim, study, wade through. **3** *She read the poem to the class.* present, quote, recite, reel off. **4** *He read about it in the newspaper.* discover, find out, hear, learn. **5** *The thermometer reads 20°.* indicate, register, show.

readable *adjective* **1** *readable writing.* clear, decipherable, legible, neat, plain, understandable. OPPOSITE illegible. **2** *a readable book.* absorbing, enjoyable, entertaining, interesting. OPPOSITE boring, unreadable.

ready *adjective* **1** *ready for action.* equipped, fit, geared up, organised, prepared, primed, psyched up (*informal*), set. OPPOSITE unprepared. **2** *She is always ready to help a friend.* disposed, eager, game, glad, happy, inclined, keen, willing. OPPOSITE reluctant. **3** *He always has a ready answer.* immediate, instant, pat, prompt, quick, rapid, speedy. **4** *She has a ready supply of gifts.* accessible, available, convenient, handy, on hand.

real *adjective* **1** *The film is based on real events and real people.* actual, existent, factual, historical, true. OPPOSITE imaginary. **2** *real butter.* authentic, bona fide, dinkum (*Australian informal*), dinky-di (*Australian informal*), genuine, honest-to-goodness (*informal*), natural, proper. OPPOSITE artificial, imitation. **3** *Her faith was real.* genuine, heartfelt, honest, sincere, solid, true, unaffected. OPPOSITE nominal.

realisation *noun a growing realisation of her responsibility.* appreciation, awareness, consciousness, knowledge, perception, recognition, understanding.

realise *verb* **1** *She didn't realise what was going on.* appreciate, apprehend, become aware of, catch on to (*informal*), comprehend, cotton on to (*informal*), grasp, jerry to (*Australian informal*), know, latch on to (*informal*), perceive, sense, suss out (*informal*), twig (*informal*), understand, wake up to. **2** *She finally realised her goal.* accomplish, achieve, attain, fulfil.

realism *noun realism in art.* authenticity, fidelity, naturalism, verisimilitude.

realistic *adjective* **1** *a realistic painting.* accurate, authentic, faithful, lifelike, natural, true-to-life. OPPOSITE unrealistic. **2** *a realistic proposal.* feasible, practicable, practical, pragmatic, viable, workable. OPPOSITE impractical.

really *adverb He really meant it.* actually, certainly, definitely, genuinely, honestly, indeed, in fact, positively, sincerely, surely, truly.

realm *noun* **1** *the queen's realm.* country, domain, dominion, empire, kingdom, monarchy, territory. **2** *the realm of science.* area, domain, field, province, sphere, world.

reap *verb* **1** *The wheat is ready to be reaped.* cut, gather in, harvest. **2** *She reaped the benefits of their experience.* gain, obtain, realise, receive.

rear[1] *noun She stood towards the rear.* back, end, stern, tail. OPPOSITE front. — *adjective the dog's rear legs.* back, hind. OPPOSITE fore, front.

rear[2] *verb* **1** *She reared the family on her own.* bring up, care for, look after, nurture, raise. **2** *The farmer rears pigs.* breed, keep, produce, raise.

rearrange *verb She rearranged the items.* change, interchange, juggle, reorder, reorganise, reschedule, reshuffle, shift, shuffle, swap, switch, transpose.

reason *noun* **1** *the reason for her odd behaviour.* cause, excuse, explanation, grounds, justification, motive, pretext, rationale. **2** *He has lost his reason.* faculties, intellect, intelligence, judgement, mind, rationality, sanity, wits. OPPOSITE insanity. **3** *He won't listen to reason.* common sense, good sense, logic, reasoning, sense, wisdom. — *verb* **1** *She reasoned that they must have been there.* conclude, deduce, figure out, infer, work out. **2** *He tried to reason with her.* argue, debate, discuss, plead, remonstrate.

reasonable *adjective* **1** *any reasonable person.* intelligent, logical, rational, sane, sensible, thinking. OPPOSITE unreasonable. **2** *a reasonable explanation.* logical, plausible, rational, sensible, sound, tenable. OPPOSITE absurd. **3** *The fee was reasonable.* acceptable, equitable, fair, just, justifiable, moderate. OPPOSITE excessive.

reassure *verb She reassured the others that all would be well.* assure, comfort, encourage, set someone's mind at rest. OPPOSITE perturb.

reassuring *adjective a reassuring sign.* comforting, encouraging, favourable, hopeful, promising. OPPOSITE discouraging.

rebel *noun The army fought against the rebels.* dissenter, insurgent, malcontent, mutineer, nonconformist, revolutionary. — *verb They rebelled against the authorities.* buck (*informal*), disobey, mutiny, resist, revolt, rise up. OPPOSITE obey.

rebellion *noun a rebellion against the government.* insurgence, insurrection, mutiny, resistance, revolt, revolution, rising, uprising.

rebellious *adjective The rebellious youth became an ardent reformer.* defiant, disobedient, insubordinate, insurgent, intractable, mutinous, recalcitrant, refractory, unmanageable, unruly, wild. OPPOSITE obedient.

rebound *verb* **1** *The ball rebounded off the wall.* bounce back, ricochet, spring back. **2** *The nasty trick rebounded on them.* backfire, boomerang, recoil.

rebuff *noun His offer of help met with a rebuff.* brush-off, knockback (*informal*), refusal, rejection, snub. OPPOSITE acceptance. — *verb When he tried to help, he was quickly rebuffed.* brush off, decline, knock back, refuse, reject, snub, spurn, turn down. OPPOSITE accept.

rebuild *verb They rebuilt the bridge after it collapsed.* reconstruct, remake, renew, restore.

rebuke *verb Her parents rebuked her for her insolence.* admonish, berate, castigate, censure, chide (*old use*), reprimand, reproach, reprove, scold, tell off (*informal*), tick off (*informal*), upbraid. OPPOSITE praise. — *noun He was given a stern rebuke.* admonition, censure, dressing down (*informal*), lecture, rap over the knuckles, reprimand, reproach, reproof, scolding, serve (*Australian informal*). OPPOSITE commendation.

rebut *verb The speaker rebutted his opponent's arguments.* counter, disprove, invalidate, negate, refute.

recalcitrant *adjective They used to cane recalcitrant children.* defiant, disobedient, headstrong, intractable, obstinate, perverse, refractory, stubborn, wayward, wilful. OPPOSITE compliant.

recall *verb She recalled the incident.* call to mind, recollect, remember.

recap *verb* (*informal*) *The chairman recapped what the other speakers had said.* go over, recapitulate, reiterate, repeat, restate, summarise, sum up. — *noun* (*informal*) *a recap of the previous lesson.* recapitulation, résumé, summary, summing up.

recede *verb The floodwaters receded.* ebb, go back, move back, retreat, subside. OPPOSITE advance.

receipt *noun She returned the goods with the receipt.* docket, proof of purchase.

receive *verb* **1** *She received the award.* accept, acquire, collect, earn, gain, get, land, obtain, take, win. OPPOSITE give. **2** *He received unfair treatment.* be subjected to, experience, meet with, suffer, sustain, undergo. OPPOSITE inflict. **3** *She received her guests at the door.* greet, meet, welcome.

recent *adjective recent news.* contemporary, current, fresh, latest, new, up-to-date. OPPOSITE old.

receptacle *noun a receptacle for rubbish.* carrier, container, holder, repository, vessel.

reception *noun* **1** *We got a cool reception.* greeting, welcome. **2** *a wedding reception.* do (*informal*), function, gathering, party.

receptive *adjective He is receptive to new ideas.* amenable, open, open-minded, responsive.

recess *noun* **1** *The cave had many recesses.* alcove, bay, niche, nook. **2** *She eats an apple at recess.* break, little lunch, morning tea, playlunch, playtime.

recession *noun The country is facing a recession.* decline, depression, downturn, slump.

recipe *noun He made the cake without a recipe.* directions, formula, instructions.

reciprocal *adjective She loved him, but the feeling was not reciprocal.* mutual, reciprocated, requited, returned. OPPOSITE one-sided.

recital *noun an organ recital.* concert, performance.

recite *verb She recited the poem.* deliver, narrate, perform, rattle off, reel off, repeat, say, tell.

reckless *adjective a reckless driver.* careless, daredevil, foolhardy, harebrained, heedless, hotheaded, impetuous, imprudent, impulsive, incautious, irresponsible, mad, madcap, negligent, rash, unthinking, wild. OPPOSITE careful, cautious.

reckon *verb* **1** *He reckoned the cost to be $50,000.* add up, assess, calculate, compute, count, figure out, tally, total, tot up (*informal*), work out. **2** *She reckoned they would win.* believe, consider, fancy, judge, think.

recline *verb He reclined on the sofa.* lean back, lie, loll, lounge, repose, rest, sprawl, stretch out.

reclining *adjective The artist painted her in a reclining position.* horizontal, leaning, lying, recumbent.

recluse *noun The old woman became a recluse.* hermit, loner, solitary.

recognise *verb* **1** *She didn't recognise their faces.* identify, know, pick out, place, recall, recollect, remember. **2** *He recognised the hopelessness of the situation.* accept, acknowledge, admit, appreciate, be aware of, concede, grant, perceive, realise, see, understand.

recognition *noun She eventually received public recognition for her work.* acknowledgement, appreciation, notice.

recoil *verb* **1** *He was injured when his gun recoiled.* kick, kick back, spring back. **2** *She recoiled at the sight of the dead body.* cower, cringe, draw back, flinch, jump back, quail, shrink, shy away, start, wince.

recollect *verb I do not recollect the incident.* call to mind, recall, remember.

recommend *verb* **1** *He recommended a different treatment.* advise, advocate, counsel, prescribe, propose, suggest, urge. **2** *The librarian recommended the book.* approve of, commend, endorse, laud (*formal*), praise, speak well of. OPPOSITE condemn.

reconcile *verb* **1** *The counsellor reconciled the man and woman.* bring together, conciliate, placate, reunite. **2** *They reconciled their differences.* fix up, mend, patch up, resolve, settle.

recondition *verb The mechanic reconditioned the engine.* overhaul, rebuild, renovate, repair, restore.

reconnaissance *noun The aeroplanes were involved in reconnaissance.* exploration, inspection, investigation, observation, recce (*informal*), spying, survey.

reconsider *verb He begged her to reconsider her decision.* consider again, reassess, rethink, review, think again.

reconstruct *verb* **1** *They reconstructed the model.* reassemble, rebuild, remake, repair, restore. **2** *Police reconstructed the crime.* recreate, re-enact.

record *noun* **1** *He kept a record of events. The secretary keeps the club's records.* account, annals, archives, chronicle, diary, document, dossier, history, journal, log, memorandum, minutes, narrative, note, register, report, transcription. **2** *He likes listening to records.* see RECORDING. **3** *She has a good employment record.* background, curriculum vitae, CV, experience, history. — *verb* **1** *She records what is said at meetings.* chronicle, document, enter, jot down, list, log, minute, note, register, take down, transcribe, write down. **2** *They recorded the show.* film, tape, tape-record, video.

recording *noun* album, CD, compact disc, disc, DVD, record, release, tape, video.

recount *verb She recounted the whole sad tale.* describe, detail, narrate, recite, relate, report, tell.

recoup *verb He recouped his losses.* get back, recover, redeem, regain, retrieve, win back.

recover *verb* **1** *Peter recovered his car which had been stolen.* find, get back, reclaim, recoup, redeem, regain, retrieve, salvage, track down. **2** *Grace is recovering from her illness.* convalesce, get better, heal, improve, mend, pick up, pull through, rally, recuperate. OPPOSITE deteriorate.

recreation *noun He fixes cars for recreation.* amusement, diversion, enjoyment, entertainment, fun, hobby, leisure, pastime, play, pleasure, relaxation, sport.

recruit *verb He recruited extra staff.* engage, enlist, hire, sign on, take on. — *noun The new recruits attended a training course.* apprentice, beginner, newcomer, novice, rookie (*informal*), tiro, trainee.

rectangle *noun* oblong, square.

rectify *verb He rectified the problem.* correct, cure, fix, mend, put right, redress, remedy, repair.

recuperate *verb The patient recuperated at home.* convalesce, get better, improve, mend, recover, regain health.

recur *verb The problem recurs each summer.* be repeated, happen again, reappear, repeat itself, resurface, return.

recurrent *adjective a recurrent problem.* chronic, continual, cyclical, frequent, perennial, periodic, perpetual, recurring, regular, repeated. OPPOSITE isolated.

recycle *verb Cans may be recycled.* reprocess, reuse, salvage, use again.

red *adjective* **1** *a red colour.* blood-red, brick-red, burgundy, cardinal, carmine, cerise, cherry, claret, cochineal, crimson, flame, garnet, maroon, ruby, russet, scarlet, vermilion. **2** *red hair.* auburn, carroty, ginger, sandy. **3** *a red face.* florid, flushed, rubicund, ruddy. OPPOSITE pale. **4** *red eyes.* bloodshot.

redden *verb His cheeks reddened.* blush, colour, flush, glow. OPPOSITE whiten.

redeem *verb* **1** *He redeemed his watch at the pawnshop.* buy back, reclaim, recover, repurchase. **2** *Christians believe that Jesus died to redeem sinners.* atone for, ransom, rescue, save, set free.

redress *verb He tried to redress the injustice.* compensate for, make amends for, make up for, put right, rectify, remedy, repair. — *noun She sought redress.* compensation, recompense, reparation, restitution.

reduce *verb* **1** *They reduced their spending.* curtail, cut, cut back, cut down, decrease, diminish, lessen, pare down, slash, trim, whittle down. OPPOSITE increase. **2** *He reduced the price.* cut, decrease, discount, drop, lower, mark down, slash. OPPOSITE increase. **3** *He reduced the message to a few lines.* abbreviate, abridge, condense, prune, shorten. OPPOSITE lengthen. **4** *The treatment reduced the pain.* alleviate, ease, lessen, lighten, minimise, mitigate, moderate. OPPOSITE increase, intensify. **5** *He reduced the page to A4.* scale down, shrink. OPPOSITE enlarge.

reduction *noun* **1** *reductions in staff.* cut, cutback, decrease, downsizing, retrenchment. OPPOSITE increase. **2** *Pensioners are entitled to a 5% reduction on rates.* concession, deduction, discount, rebate. OPPOSITE surcharge.

redundant *adjective The essay included redundant information.* excess, superfluous, surplus, unnecessary, unwanted.

reek *noun the reek of tobacco.* odour, pong (*informal*), smell, stench, stink. — *verb The house reeked after the dinner party.* pong (*informal*), smell, stink.

reel *noun a reel of yarn.* bobbin, spindle, spool. — *verb* **1** *The wounded man reeled, and finally collapsed.* lurch, rock, stagger, stumble, sway, teeter, totter, wobble. **2** *Her head reeled when she tried to get up.* spin, swim, whirl. □ **reel off** *He reeled off the dates.* rattle off, recite.

refer *verb* **refer to** **1** *He didn't refer to the incident again.* allude to, bring up, cite, comment on, mention, speak of, touch on. **2** *He referred the*

matter to his solicitor. direct, pass, send. **3** *She referred to her handbook.* consult, look up in, turn to.
referee *noun The players respected the referee's decision.* adjudicator, ref (*informal*), umpire.
reference *noun* **1** *He made no reference to recent events.* allusion, hint, mention. **2** *a biblical reference.* citation, example, quotation. **3** *The principal wrote a reference for each student.* testimonial.
referendum *noun A referendum was held to decide whether Australia should become a republic.* ballot, plebiscite, poll, vote.
refill *verb Steve has a job refilling shelves at a supermarket.* replenish, restock, top up.
refine *verb The liquid has been refined.* clarify, distil, filter, process, purify.
refined *adjective a refined person.* civilised, cultivated, cultured, dignified, elegant, genteel, gentlemanly, ladylike, polished, polite, sophisticated, urbane, well-bred, well-mannered. OPPOSITE uncouth.
reflect *verb* **1** *The trees were reflected in the lake.* mirror. **2** *His exam mark did not reflect his real ability.* demonstrate, display, exhibit, indicate, reveal, show. □ **reflect on** *He reflected on what had been said.* brood on, cogitate about, consider, contemplate, deliberate on, meditate on, mull over, muse about, ponder, ruminate on, think about.
reflection *noun Sheila studied her reflection in the mirror.* image, likeness.
reform *verb* **1** *The government reformed the tax system.* ameliorate, amend, change, correct, improve, mend, rectify, revise, revolutionise, transform. **2** *She used to be an alcoholic, but she has reformed.* mend your ways, turn over a new leaf.
refractory *adjective a refractory child.* disobedient, headstrong, intractable, obstinate, perverse, pigheaded, rebellious, recalcitrant, stubborn, uncontrollable, unmanageable, wayward, wilful. OPPOSITE manageable.
refrain[1] *verb* **refrain from** *Please refrain from coughing.* abstain from, avoid, desist from, forbear from, stop. OPPOSITE persist in.
refrain[2] *noun They all sang the refrain.* chorus.
refresh *verb* **1** *The holiday refreshed him.* freshen, invigorate, perk up (*informal*), rejuvenate, restore, revive. **2** *Let me refresh your memory.* jog, prod, prompt, stimulate.
refreshments *plural noun* drinks, eats (*informal*), food, nibbles (*informal*), snacks.
refrigerate *verb The milk should be refrigerated.* chill, cool, freeze.
refuge *noun* **1** *The cave was a refuge from the bushfire.* haven, hideout (*informal*), hidey-hole (*informal*), hiding place, retreat, sanctuary, shelter. **2** *He took refuge in the hut.* asylum, cover, protection, safety, sanctuary, shelter.
refugee *noun She came to Australia as a refugee.* asylum seeker, displaced person, exile, fugitive, runaway.
refund *verb He refunded them the money.* give back, pay back, reimburse, repay, return. — *noun She received a tax refund.* reimbursement, repayment.
refurbish *verb He refurbished the house before selling it.* clean up, do up (*informal*), redecorate, remodel, renovate, restore, revamp, spruce up.
refusal *noun Their request met with refusal.* knockback (*informal*), rebuff, rejection, veto. OPPOSITE acceptance.
refuse[1] *verb* **1** *He refused their offers of help.* decline, knock back (*informal*), pass up (*informal*), rebuff, reject, scorn, spurn, turn down. OPPOSITE accept. **2** *They were refused entry.* deny, forbid, prohibit, withhold. OPPOSITE grant.
refuse[2] *noun He put the refuse in the bin.* debris, garbage, junk, litter, rubbish, scrap, trash, waste.
refute *verb He refuted the other man's statement.* disprove, negate, rebut. OPPOSITE prove.
regain *verb He regained the trophy.* get back, recoup, recover, retrieve, win back.
regal *adjective regal splendour.* kingly, lordly, majestic, princely, queenly, royal, stately.
regard *verb* **1** *She regarded him studiously.* behold (*old use*), contemplate, eye, gaze at, look at, observe, scrutinise, stare at, view, watch. OPPOSITE ignore. **2** *We regard the matter as serious.* consider, deem, judge, look upon, reckon, view. **3** *His work is highly regarded.* esteem, respect, value. — *noun* **1** *He pays no regard to the rules.* attention, care, concern, consideration, heed, notice, thought. OPPOSITE disregard. **2** *He is held in high regard.* admiration, approval, esteem, favour, honour, respect. OPPOSITE contempt.
regarding *preposition He spoke to them regarding the matter.* about, apropos, concerning, in regard to, with reference to, with regard to, with respect to.
regardless *adverb Carry on regardless.* anyhow, anyway, heedlessly, nevertheless, nonetheless. □ **regardless of** *Regardless of what you say, I still want to go.* despite, disregarding, in spite of, irrespective of, notwithstanding.
region *noun They live in an arid region.* area, district, land, locality, neighbourhood, part, place, province, spot, territory, tract, vicinity, zone.
regional *adjective regional cookery.* district, local, provincial.
register *noun His name is in the register.* catalogue, directory, index, list, record, roll. — *verb* **1** *He registered for swimming lessons.* enlist, enrol, join up, sign up. **2** *She registered a complaint.* enter, file, log, place on record, record, submit, write down. **3** *The thermometer registered 100°.* indicate, read, record, show. **4** *His face registered his true feelings.* betray, display, express, indicate, reflect, reveal, show.
regress *verb He regressed into babyhood.* backslide, degenerate, go back, lapse, relapse, retrogress, revert, slip back. OPPOSITE progress.
regret *noun He had no regrets about the incident.* compunction, disappointment, penitence, remorse, repentance, sorrow. — *verb She regretted what had happened.* bemoan, be sad about, be sorry about, deplore, lament, repent, rue.
regretful *adjective She was regretful about the accident.* apologetic, contrite, penitent, remorseful, repentant, rueful, sorry. OPPOSITE unrepentant.
regrettable *adjective a regrettable affair.* deplorable, lamentable, reprehensible, sad, shameful, unfortunate.
regular *adjective* **1** *She makes regular visits to her aunt.* frequent, periodic, repeated, routine. OPPOSITE occasional. **2** *a regular bedtime.* consistent, fixed, normal, predictable, set, standard, systematic, unchanging. OPPOSITE variable. **3** *This is not the regular way of doing it.* conventional, correct, customary, established, habitual, normal, official, ordinary, orthodox, proper, routine, standard, traditional, typical, usual. OPPOSITE unorthodox. **4** *regular footsteps.* even, measured, rhythmic, steady, uniform. OPPOSITE uneven. **5** *a regular shape.* even, symmetrical. OPPOSITE irregular.
regulate *verb* **1** *The traffic is regulated by police.* control, direct, govern, manage, oversee, supervise. **2** *The sound is regulated with this knob.* adjust, alter, change, moderate, modulate, vary.
regulation *noun local government regulations.* by-law, decree, directive, law, ordinance, rule, statute.
rehearse *verb They rehearsed the play many times.* go over, practise, prepare, run through.
reign *noun under the reign of Henry VII.* kingship, rule, sovereignty. — *verb The Queen reigned for three years.* be on the throne, govern, rule.
reimburse *verb The company will reimburse you for your expenses.* indemnify, pay back, recompense, refund, repay.
rein *verb* **rein in** *He reined in their spending.* check, control, curb, keep a tight rein on, limit, restrain.
reinforce *verb* **1** *He reinforced the wall.* bolster, brace, buttress, fortify, prop up, shore up, strengthen, support, toughen. OPPOSITE weaken. **2** *This reinforced their argument.* add weight to, assist, bolster, enhance, strengthen, support. OPPOSITE weaken.
reject *verb* **1** *She rejected the offer.* decline, dismiss, knock back (*informal*), pass up (*informal*), refuse, spurn, turn down, turn your nose up at. OPPOSITE accept. **2** *He rejected all their gifts.* discard, get rid of, jettison, scrap, send back, throw out. OPPOSITE accept. **3** *His friends rejected him.* brush off, disown, ditch (*informal*), drop, dump, forsake, jilt, rebuff, renounce, repudiate, snub. — *noun The shop sells rejects.* cast-off, discard, second.
rejection *noun Her application met with another rejection.* brush-off, knockback (*informal*), rebuff, refusal, snub, thumbs down, veto. OPPOSITE acceptance.
rejoice *verb They rejoiced at the good news.* be happy, be joyful, be overjoyed, celebrate, crow, delight, exult, revel. OPPOSITE be sad.
rejuvenate *verb The trip rejuvenated him.* refresh, reinvigorate, renew, restore, revitalise, revive. OPPOSITE age.
relapse *verb It was easy to relapse into bad habits.* backslide, degenerate, fall back, lapse, regress, retrogress, revert, slip back. — *noun The patient suffered a relapse.* deterioration, recurrence, regression, setback.
relate *verb She related their exciting tale.* describe, narrate, recite, recount, report, spin, tell. □ **relate to** **1** *These facts relate to the case.* apply to, bear on, belong to, be relevant to, concern, have to do with, pertain to, refer to. **2** *She does not relate well to children.* emphathise with, get on with, have a rapport with, identify with, interact with, understand.
related *adjective They are related problems.* allied, associated, connected, interconnected, interrelated. OPPOSITE separate.
relation *noun* **1** *the relation between fact and fiction.* association, connection, correlation, correspondence, link, relationship, tie-in. **2** *friends and relations.* see RELATIVE.
relationship *noun The relationship between the two is very close.* affinity, association, attachment, bond, connection, correlation, link, rapport, tie.
relative *adjective She did it with relative ease.* comparative. — *noun She visited her relative.* kinsman, kinswoman, relation; [*relatives*] clan, family, flesh and blood, folk, kin, kindred, kith and kin.
relax *verb* **1** *He relaxed in front of television.* calm down, laze, lounge, rest, take it easy, unwind, veg out (*slang*). OPPOSITE tense. **2** *She relaxed her grip.* ease off, let go, loosen, slacken, weaken. OPPOSITE tighten. **3** *They relaxed the rules.* bend, ease, liberalise, moderate, soften, stretch. OPPOSITE tighten.
relaxation *noun He plays cards for relaxation.* diversion, enjoyment, fun, hobby, leisure, pastime, pleasure, recreation, rest. OPPOSITE work.
relaxed *adjective a relaxed attitude.* calm, carefree, casual, easygoing, informal, laid-back (*informal*), nonchalant, serene, slack. OPPOSITE tense.
relay *verb He relayed the information.* communicate, pass on, send on, transmit.
release *verb* **1** *They released the captives.* deliver, discharge, emancipate, free, let go, let loose, let out, liberate, set free. OPPOSITE detain. **2** *The passengers released their seat belts.* unbuckle, undo, unfasten, untie. OPPOSITE fasten. **3** *The publisher released a new edition.* circulate, distribute, issue, launch, publish. **4** *The names of the victims have not been released.* disclose, divulge, make known, publicise, publish, reveal. OPPOSITE suppress.
relent *verb He finally relented and allowed them to go.* be merciful, capitulate, give in, have pity, soften, yield.
relentless *adjective* **1** *a relentless tyrant.* cruel, harsh, implacable, inexorable, merciless, pitiless, remorseless, ruthless, severe, unyielding. OPPOSITE lenient. **2** *The crying was relentless.* constant, continuous, endless, incessant, persistent, unceasing, unrelenting, unremitting.
relevant *adjective Keep your points relevant to the topic.* applicable, apposite, appropriate, apropos, apt, connected, germane, pertinent, related, to the point. OPPOSITE irrelevant.
reliable *adjective a reliable friend.* constant, dependable, faithful, loyal, staunch, steadfast, steady, sure, true, trusted, trustworthy, trusty (*old use*). OPPOSITE unreliable.
relic *noun relics of the past.* antique, heirloom, keepsake, memento, reminder, remnant, souvenir, survival, vestige.
relief *noun* **1** *He sought relief from the pain.* alleviation, comfort, ease, let-up, palliation, remission, respite, rest, solace. **2** *An emergency fund offered relief to flood victims.* aid, assistance, help, succour, support.
relieve *verb* **1** *Nothing will relieve the pain.* alleviate, assuage, ease, help, lessen, lighten, mitigate, palliate, reduce, soothe, subdue. OPPOSITE aggravate. **2** *The money raised will be used to relieve the bushfire victims.* aid, assist, help, succour, support. **3** *She relieves the teacher when he is ill.* cover for, fill in for, stand in for, substitute for, take the place of.
religion *noun a comparative study of the world's religions.* belief, creed, cult, denomination, faith, sect.
religious *adjective* **1** *a religious service.* devotional, divine, holy, sacred, spiritual. OPPOSITE secular. **2** *reli-*

gious instruction. doctrinal, scriptural, spiritual, theological. OPPOSITE secular. **3** *a religious person.* devout, God-fearing, godly, pious, spiritual. OPPOSITE impious, irreligious.

relinquish *verb She relinquished her rights.* abandon, abdicate, cede, forgo, forsake, give up, renounce, resign, surrender, waive. OPPOSITE keep.

relish *noun She attacked the job with relish.* delight, enthusiasm, gusto, keenness, pleasure, zest. OPPOSITE displeasure. — *verb She relished the thought of sleeping in.* delight in, enjoy, fancy, like, love, revel in, savour. OPPOSITE dislike.

reluctant *adjective They were reluctant to commit themselves.* averse, disinclined, hesitant, loath, unwilling. OPPOSITE eager.

rely *verb* **rely on** *Can you rely on him?* bank on, count on, depend on, reckon on, trust.

remain *verb* **1** *Two pieces of cake remain.* be left. **2** *The old customs remain.* continue, endure, go on, live on, persist, prevail, survive. OPPOSITE die. **3** *She remained in Albury.* hang around, keep on, linger, stay, stick around (*informal*), tarry, wait. OPPOSITE leave.

remainder *noun He kept two coats and threw out the remainder.* balance, excess, leftovers, remnant, residue, rest, surplus.

remains *plural noun* **1** *the remains of the meal.* dregs, leftovers, remnants, scraps. **2** *Roman remains.* relics, ruins. **3** *They buried his remains.* body, carcass, corpse.

remark *noun He addressed his remarks to me.* comment, observation, opinion, reflection, statement, word. — *verb 'You've had your hair cut,' he remarked.* comment, mention, note, observe, reflect, say.

remarkable *adjective a remarkable achievement.* amazing, astounding, conspicuous, exceptional, extraordinary, impressive, marvellous, memorable, notable, noteworthy, outstanding, phenomenal, sensational, signal, significant, singular, special, startling, striking, surprising, uncommon, unusual, wonderful. OPPOSITE ordinary.

remedial *adjective remedial exercise.* corrective, curative, therapeutic.

remedy *noun* **1** *a remedy for many illnesses.* antidote, cure, medication, medicine, panacea, therapy, treatment. **2** *The problem has an easy remedy.* answer, cure, solution. — *verb The technician remedied the problem.* correct, cure, fix, mend, put right, rectify, redress, repair, solve.

remember *verb* **1** *He remembered what we told him.* call to mind, keep in mind, memorise, recall, recollect, retain. OPPOSITE forget. **2** *They were remembering old times.* look back on, recall, recollect, reflect on, reminisce about, think back on.

remembrance *noun They were silent in remembrance of the dead.* commemoration, memory, recollection.

remind *verb Remind her to pay the bill.* jog someone's memory, prompt, refresh someone's memory.

reminder *noun The photo was a reminder of happier times.* keepsake, memento, remembrance, souvenir.

reminiscences *plural noun He wrote his reminiscences.* memoirs, memories, recollections.

remiss *adjective He had been remiss in his duties.* careless, forgetful, lax, neglectful, negligent, slack, slipshod, sloppy. OPPOSITE careful.

remnant *noun She made a quilt out of the remnants.* fragment, leftover, offcut, piece, remainder, remains, residue, scrap.

remorse *noun He felt no remorse for his crime.* compunction, contrition, guilt, penitence, regret, repentance, shame, sorrow.

remote *adjective* **1** *a remote place.* distant, far-away, far-flung, inaccessible, isolated, lonely, outlying, out of the way, secluded, solitary. OPPOSITE near. **2** *a remote chance.* faint, outside, slender, slight, slim, unlikely. OPPOSITE likely.

remove *verb* **1** *The protesters were removed from the building.* banish, drive out, eject, evacuate, evict, expel, kick out (*informal*), throw out, turn out. **2** *He removed a branch of the tree.* chop off, cut off, detach, lop off, prune. **3** *He was removed to a different hospital.* cart off, convey, move, relocate, shift, take away, transfer, transport. **4** *Michelle removed her savings from the bank.* take out, withdraw. OPPOSITE deposit. **5** *He removed the splinter.* extract, pull out, take out. **6** *He removed his clothes.* doff (*a hat*), peel off, pull off, shed, strip off, take off. OPPOSITE don, put on. **7** *He was removed from the job.* depose, dismiss, expel, fire, get rid of, kick out (*informal*), oust, sack (*informal*), transfer. OPPOSITE install. **8** *He removed the offending words.* delete, efface, eliminate, eradicate, erase, expunge, get rid of, obliterate, rub out, wash off, wipe out.

remuneration *noun a job with good remuneration.* pay, payment, recompense, reward, salary, wages.

render *verb* **1** *a reward for services rendered.* do, give, perform, provide, supply. **2** *The accident rendered him helpless.* leave, make.

rendezvous *noun They arranged a rendezvous at four o'clock.* appointment, assignation, date (*informal*), engagement, meeting.

renegade *noun* apostate, defector, deserter, traitor, turncoat.

renew *verb* **1** *Her energy was renewed by the holiday.* refresh, rejuvenate, restore, revive. **2** *The tyres need renewing.* change, replace. **3** *They renewed their friendship.* pick up again, re-establish, resume, resurrect, revive. **4** *They renewed their requests.* begin anew, reiterate, repeat, restate. **5** *He renewed his subscription.* continue, extend, prolong. OPPOSITE cancel.

renounce *verb* **1** *He renounced his rights.* abdicate, abnegate, forgo, forswear, give up, relinquish, surrender, waive. OPPOSITE claim. **2** *They renounced their parents' religion.* abandon, discard, disown, forsake, reject, repudiate. OPPOSITE accept.

renovate *verb The new owners renovated the house.* do up (*informal*), make over, modernise, redecorate, refurbish, rejuvenate, remodel, renew, restore, revamp, update.

renown *noun She won renown as a ballerina.* distinction, fame, importance, note, prestige, reputation, repute. OPPOSITE obscurity.

renowned *adjective the renowned pianist.* celebrated, distinguished, eminent, famed, famous, illustrious, notable, noted, prominent, well-known. OPPOSITE obscure.

rent *verb He bought a houseboat and rents it out.* charter, hire, lease, let.

reorganisation *noun His job was abolished in the reorganisation.* change, rationalisation, rearrangement, reshuffle, restructuring, shake-up, transformation.

reorganise *verb He reorganised the business.* change, rationalise, rearrange, restructure, transform.

repair *verb* **1** *They repaired the car.* fix, overhaul, recondition, restore, service. **2** *She repaired the hole in her stockings.* darn, mend, patch, sew up. — *noun in good repair.* condition, nick (*informal*), order, shape, state.

reparation *noun He demanded reparation for the loss.* atonement, compensation, damages, indemnity, redress, restitution.

repay *verb* **1** *He repaid me the money he had borrowed.* pay back, recompense, refund, reimburse, remunerate. **2** *She could never repay their kindness.* pay back, reciprocate, requite, return, reward.

repeal *verb The law was repealed.* abrogate, annul, cancel, nullify, rescind, revoke, withdraw. OPPOSITE enact.

repeat *verb* **1** *He repeated what he had been told to say.* echo, quote, recite, reiterate, retell, say again, tell again. **2** *They repeated their mistake.* do again, duplicate, redo, reproduce. — *noun The programme was a repeat.* rebroadcast, replay, rerun. OPPOSITE première.

repeated *adjective repeated interruptions.* continual, frequent, recurrent. OPPOSITE one-off.

repeatedly *adverb The phone rang repeatedly throughout dinner.* again and again, continually, frequently, often, over and over, time and time again.

repel *verb* **1** *They repelled the attacker.* drive away, fend off, force back, keep at bay, parry, repulse, stave off, ward off. **2** *The foul smell repelled her.* disgust, nauseate, offend, put off, revolt, sicken. OPPOSITE attract.

repellent *adjective* **1** *a repellent task.* disgusting, distasteful, horrible, loathsome, nauseating, offensive, off-putting, repugnant, repulsive, revolting, sickening. OPPOSITE attractive. **2** *water-repellent fabric.* impermeable, impervious, proof, resistant.

repent *verb He repented of his sins.* be sorry for, bewail, feel remorse for, lament, regret, rue.

repentant *adjective a repentant sinner.* apologetic, contrite, penitent, regretful, remorseful, rueful, sorry. OPPOSITE unrepentant.

repercussion *noun The decision had serious repercussions.* after-effect, backlash, consequence, effect, knock-on effect, result, side effect.

repetitive *adjective a repetitive job.* boring, humdrum, monotonous, repetitious, tedious, unchanging, unvaried.

replace *verb* **1** *He replaced the vase on the shelf.* put back, restore, return. **2** *She replaced the unpopular secretary.* come after, follow, oust, substitute for, succeed, supersede, supplant, take the place of. **3** *She replaces the water daily.* change, renew, replenish.

replacement *noun When Toby left we had to find a replacement.* deputy, locum, proxy, ring-in (*Australian informal*), stand-in, substitute, successor, surrogate.

replica *noun a replica of a painting.* copy, duplicate, facsimile, imitation, likeness, model, reproduction. OPPOSITE original.

reply *verb 'That's not what I've heard,' he replied.* answer, counter, rejoin, respond, retort. OPPOSITE ask. — *noun a reply to a letter or question.* acknowledgement, answer, comeback (*informal*), rejoinder, response, retort, riposte.

report *verb* **1** *They reported their results.* announce, communicate, declare, disclose, divulge, document, notify, publish, record, say, state, tell, write up. OPPOSITE withhold. **2** *He reported them to the Tax Office.* denounce, dob in (*Australian informal*), grass (on) (*slang*), inform on, shop (*slang*), tell on. **3** *Report to the office.* front up (*informal*), introduce yourself, present yourself. — *noun* **1** *He read the report.* account, announcement, article, bulletin, communiqué, description, narrative, news, paper, proceedings, record, statement, story, write-up. **2** *The gun went off with a loud report.* bang, blast, boom, detonation, explosion, noise.

reporter *noun a newspaper reporter.* correspondent, journalist, writer.

repose *noun refreshed by a night's repose.* rest, sleep, slumber. — *verb He reposed on the sofa.* lie, recline, relax, rest, stretch out; see also SLEEP.

reprehensible *adjective His behaviour was reprehensible.* blameworthy, culpable, deplorable, despicable, inexcusable, shameful, unworthy, wicked, wrong. OPPOSITE praiseworthy.

represent *verb* **1** *She represented the Queen in the play.* act as, appear as, perform as, play, portray. **2** *The hotel was not as it had been represented in the brochure.* depict, describe, illustrate, picture, portray, present, show. **3** *An 'X' represents a kiss.* correspond to, denote, express, indicate, mean, signify, stand for, symbolise. **4** *He represents the tourism industry.* act for, act on behalf of, speak for.

representative *adjective a representative sample.* archetypal, characteristic, illustrative, typical. OPPOSITE atypical. — *noun* **1** *an official representative.* ambassador, delegate, deputy, emissary, envoy, mouthpiece, proxy, spokesperson, stand-in, substitute. **2** *the company's sales representatives.* agent, rep (*informal*), salesman, salesperson, saleswoman.

repress *verb* **1** *The government repressed the people severely.* control, crush, keep down, oppress, subjugate. **2** *They repressed the revolt.* put down, quash, quell, subdue, suppress. **3** *She repressed her emotions.* bottle up, check, control, curb, hold back, inhibit, restrain, stifle, suppress. OPPOSITE express, release.

reprieve *noun The judge granted him a reprieve.* pardon, postponement, remission, stay of execution. — *verb The prisoner was reprieved.* let off, pardon, spare.

reprimand *noun He was given a stern reprimand.* admonition, castigation, dressing down (*informal*), lecture, rebuke, reproach, reproof, rocket (*slang*), scolding, serve (*Australian informal*), talking-to (*informal*), wigging (*informal*). OPPOSITE commendation. — *verb She reprimanded them for speaking rudely.* admonish, berate, castigate, censure, chastise, chide (*old use*), go crook at (*Australian informal*), haul over the coals, lecture, rap over the knuckles, rebuke, reproach, reprove, rouse on (*Australian informal*), scold, take to task, tell off (*informal*), tick off (*informal*), upbraid. OPPOSITE praise.

reprisal *noun The neighbours said nothing for fear of reprisal.* retaliation, retribution, revenge, vengeance.

reproach *verb She reproached herself for not doing enough.* admonish, blame, castigate, censure, chide (*old use*), criticise, rebuke, reprimand, reprove, scold, upbraid. OPPOSITE commend. — *noun Her behaviour has always been beyond reproach.* censure, condemnation,

criticism, rebuke, reproof. OPPOSITE approval.
reproduce *verb* **1** *They reproduced the document.* copy, duplicate, fax, photocopy, print. **2** *The situation cannot be reproduced.* mimic, recreate, repeat, replicate. **3** *The rabbits are constantly reproducing.* breed, multiply, procreate, proliferate, propagate.
reproduction *noun* **1** *animal reproduction.* breeding, procreation, proliferation, propagation. **2** *a reproduction of a painting.* copy, duplicate, facsimile, imitation, print, replica. OPPOSITE original.
repudiate *verb She repudiated the accusation.* deny, disclaim, disown, reject. OPPOSITE accept.
repugnant *adjective a repugnant job.* abhorrent, abominable, detestable, disgusting, distasteful, hateful, hideous, horrible, loathsome, nasty, nauseating, objectionable, obnoxious, odious, offensive, off-putting, repulsive, revolting, vile. OPPOSITE attractive.
repulse *verb They repulsed the attackers.* drive back, fend off, force back, repel, ward off.
repulsive *adjective a repulsive sight.* abominable, disgusting, distasteful, foul, gross (*informal*), hideous, horrible, loathsome, nasty, nauseating, objectionable, obnoxious, odious, offensive, off-putting, repellent, repugnant, revolting, sickening, ugly, vile, yucky (*informal*). OPPOSITE attractive.
reputable *adjective a reputable dealer.* above board, honest, honourable, reliable, respectable, respected, trustworthy. OPPOSITE disreputable.
reputation *noun The carpenter had a good reputation.* fame, name, prestige, renown, repute, standing.
reputed *adjective his reputed father.* alleged, putative, supposed.
request *noun He granted her request for funds.* appeal, application, entreaty, petition, plea, supplication. — *verb* **1** *She requested a job.* apply for, ask for, beg for, petition for, plead for, seek, solicit. **2** *He requested them not to smoke.* appeal to, ask, beseech, entreat, implore.
require *verb* **1** *The patient requires help to get dressed.* depend on, need, rely on. **2** *She bought the things she required.* be missing, be short of, lack, need, want. **3** *The job requires keyboard skills.* call for, demand, necessitate, need. **4** *You are required to be there.* command, compel, direct, oblige, order.
required *adjective This book is required reading for the course.* compulsory, essential, mandatory, necessary, obligatory, prescribed, requisite, set.
requirement *noun A degree is a requirement for the job.* essential, must, necessity, prerequisite, requisite, specification, stipulation.
rescue *verb* **1** *The police rescued the hostages.* deliver, free, liberate, release, save. **2** *They rescued a few things from the burning house.* recover, retrieve, salvage. — *noun The officers carried out a daring rescue.* deliverance, liberation, recovery, release, retrieval, salvage.
research *noun He conducts cancer research.* experimentation, exploration, inquiry, investigation, study. — *verb He researched his family's history.* delve into, explore, inquire into, investigate, study.
resemblance *noun There is a resemblance between father and son.* affinity, correspondence, likeness, similarity. OPPOSITE difference.
resemble *verb She resembles her sister.* be like, be similar to, look like, take after.
resent *verb He resents having to pay.* begrudge, dislike, mind, object to, take exception to, take umbrage at. OPPOSITE like.
resentful *adjective a resentful attitude.* aggrieved, angry, bitter, discontented, disgruntled, envious, grudging, huffy, indignant, jealous, piqued, rancorous, sullen.
resentment *noun She felt resentment at their good fortune.* anger, animosity, bitterness, discontent, envy, grudge, hatred, hostility, ill will, indignation, jealousy, pique, rancour.
reservation *noun* **1** *a hotel reservation.* booking. **2** *They had no reservations about the proposal.* doubt, hesitation, misgiving, objection, qualm, scruple.
reserve *verb* **1** *He reserved some chocolates for later.* hoard, hold back, keep, keep back, preserve, put aside, retain, save, spare, withhold. **2** *She reserved a room for the night.* book, order, prearrange, secure. **3** *They reserved judgement.* defer, delay, postpone, suspend, withhold. — *noun* **1** *a reserve of lollies.* cache, fund, hoard, kitty, pool, reservoir, stock, stockpile, store, supply. **2** *The team has two reserves.* backup, deputy, stand-by, stand-in, substitute, understudy. **3** *a nature reserve.* conservation park, game park, preserve, safari park, sanctuary, wildlife park.
reserved *adjective a reserved person.* aloof, bashful, distant, remote, restrained, reticent, shy, standoffish, taciturn, uncommunicative, undemonstrative, unemotional, withdrawn. OPPOSITE open, outgoing.
reservoir *noun The water is low in the reservoir.* dam, lake, pond.
reshuffle *noun a Cabinet reshuffle.* rearrangement, reorganisation, shake-up, spill (*Australian informal*).
reside *verb* **reside in** *She resides in a converted barn.* dwell in, hang out in (*informal*), inhabit, live in, lodge in, occupy, stay in.
residence *noun the governor's official residence.* abode (*old use*), domicile, dwelling, habitation, home, house, place.
resident *noun* **1** *a resident of Hobart.* citizen, denizen, householder, inhabitant, local, native. **2** *a hotel resident.* guest, inmate, lodger, occupant, visitor.
residue *noun He disposed of the residue.* balance, dregs, lees, leftovers, remainder, remains, remnant, rest.
resign *verb She resigned her position.* abdicate, give up, leave, quit, relinquish, stand down from, step down from, vacate. □ **resign yourself to** *She resigned herself to defeat.* accept, reconcile yourself to.
resist *verb* **1** *They resisted their attackers.* battle against, confront, defy, fight, oppose, stand up to, withstand. OPPOSITE surrender to. **2** *He resisted the proposed changes.* buck (*informal*), fight against, jack up at (*Australian slang*), oppose, rebel against. OPPOSITE accept.
resistant *adjective resistant to disease. water-resistant.* immune, impervious, proof, unaffected. OPPOSITE susceptible.
resolute *adjective He was resolute in his opposition to the proposed law.* adamant, determined, dogged, firm, persistent, purposeful, resolved, staunch, steadfast, tenacious, unwavering. OPPOSITE irresolute, vacillating.
resolution *noun* **1** *She has the resolution to complete the job.* determination, doggedness, persistence, purpose, resolve, tenacity, willpower. **2** *a New Year's resolution.* commitment, decision, intention, pledge, promise, resolve. **3** *The meeting passed the resolution.* decision, motion, proposition. **4** *the resolution of a problem.* resolving, settlement, solution, solving, sorting out, working out.
resolve *verb* **1** *She resolved to tell him.* decide, determine. OPPOSITE hesitate. **2** *The problem has been resolved.* clear up, fix, overcome, remedy, settle, solve, sort out, work out. — *noun Her friend's death strengthened her resolve to change the system.* determination, doggedness, resolution, steadfastness.
resonant *adjective a resonant voice.* booming, echoing, full, resounding, reverberating, rich, sonorous, stentorian, vibrant. OPPOSITE thin.
resort *verb* **resort to** *He resorted to violence.* adopt, fall back on, have recourse to, turn to, use, utilise. — *noun* **1** *a tourist resort.* centre, haunt, holiday centre, retreat, spot. **2** *She will only do it as a last resort.* choice, expedient, option, recourse.
resound *verb The organ resounded in the church.* echo, resonate, reverberate, ring.
resounding *adjective The craft fair was a resounding success.* enormous, great, marked, notable, outstanding, remarkable, striking, tremendous (*informal*).
resource *noun The library is full of study resources.* aid, help, material. □ **resources** *plural noun They pooled their resources.* assets, capital, funds, means, money, reserves, riches, wealth.
resourceful *adjective a resourceful student.* clever, creative, enterprising, ingenious, innovative, inventive, shrewd. OPPOSITE unimaginative.
respect *noun* **1** *She treated her parents with respect.* admiration, awe, consideration, courtesy, deference, esteem, honour, politeness, regard, reverence, veneration. OPPOSITE disrespect. **2** *with respect to climate change.* reference, regard, relation. **3** *They differ in several respects.* aspect, detail, facet, feature, particular, point, regard, way. — *verb* **1** *They respected their grandparents.* admire, esteem, honour, look up to, revere, value, venerate. OPPOSITE scorn. **2** *He respected her wishes.* comply with, consider, follow, heed, honour, obey, observe. OPPOSITE ignore.
respectable *adjective* **1** *a respectable family.* decent, honest, honourable, law-abiding, reputable, upright, worthy. **2** *He did not look respectable in his gardening clothes.* decent, presentable, proper, tidy. OPPOSITE disreputable. **3** *a respectable score.* acceptable, adequate, fair, passable, reasonable, satisfactory. OPPOSITE disgraceful.
respected *adjective a respected academic.* acclaimed, celebrated, distinguished, esteemed, highly-regarded.
respectful *adjective The children are respectful towards their elders.* civil, considerate, courteous, deferential, polite, well-mannered. OPPOSITE disrespectful.
respite *noun a respite from the work.* break, breather, intermission, let-up, lull, pause, relief, reprieve, rest, spell (*Australian*).
respond *verb She responded rudely to the question.* answer, counter, react, rejoin, reply, retort. OPPOSITE ask.
response *noun* **1** *an immediate response to the question.* answer, comeback, rejoinder, reply, retort, riposte. OPPOSITE question. **2** *The report met with little response.* acknowledgement, feedback, reaction.
responsibility *noun* **1** *They accepted responsibility for the accident.* blame, culpability, fault, guilt, liability. **2** *He had the responsibility of telling the family.* burden, duty, job, obligation, onus, task.
responsible *adjective* **1** *He was responsible for their safety.* accountable, answerable, in charge (of), liable. **2** *She was responsible for the accident.* at fault, culpable, guilty, to blame. **3** *a responsible person.* conscientious, dependable, dutiful, honest, law-abiding, level-headed, mature, reliable, sensible, trustworthy. OPPOSITE irresponsible. **4** *a responsible job.* executive, important, managerial, senior, supervisory.
responsive *adjective a responsive audience.* alert, alive, awake, impressionable, interested, quick, receptive, sensitive, sympathetic. OPPOSITE impassive.
rest[1] *verb* **1** *He worked hard and then rested.* doze, idle, laze, lie down, pause, relax, sleep, slumber, snooze, take it easy. **2** *He rested the rake against the tree.* lean, perch, place, prop, stand, support. **3** *The case rests on scanty evidence.* be based, be founded, depend, hang, hinge, rely. — *noun* **1** *He had a rest on the sofa.* doze, forty winks, kip (*slang*), lie-down, nap, siesta, sleep, snooze. **2** *The body needs periods of rest.* ease, idleness, inactivity, leisure, relaxation, repose. OPPOSITE activity. **3** *She stopped work for a short rest.* break, breather, holiday, interlude, intermission, interval, pause, recess, respite, smoko (*Australian informal*), spell (*Australian*), time off, vacation. **4** *a rest for a telescope.* base, holder, prop, stand, support, tripod. □ **at rest** inactive, inert, motionless, still. OPPOSITE moving.
rest[2] *noun They sold some of the paintings and gave away the rest.* balance, excess, leftovers, others, remainder, remnant, residue, surplus.
restaurant *noun They dined at a restaurant.* bistro, brasserie, buffet, café, cafeteria, canteen, diner (*American*), eatery (*informal*).
restitution *noun He was ordered to make restitution.* compensation, indemnification, recompense, redress, reparation.
restless *adjective* **1** *a restless horse.* agitated, edgy, excitable, fidgety, frisky, impatient, lively, nervous, restive, skittish, toey (*Australian informal*). OPPOSITE calm. **2** *a restless night.* disturbed, interrupted, sleepless, unsettled, wakeful.
restore *verb* **1** *They restored the old car.* do up (*informal*), fix, mend, rebuild, recondition, reconstruct, refurbish, remodel, renovate, repair. **2** *He was restored to good health.* bring back, rehabilitate, return. **3** *The stolen painting was restored to its owners.* give back, hand back, return. **4** *They restored an old custom.* bring back, re-establish, re-instate, reintroduce, resurrect, revive.
restrain *verb* **1** *He restrained the prisoner.* bind, chain, fetter, hold back, pinion, shackle, straitjacket, tie up. **2** *He restrained his temper.* bottle up, bridle, contain, control, keep in check, repress, suppress. **3** *They restrained their spending.* check, curb, curtail, keep a tight rein on, limit, moderate, rein in, restrict.
restraint *noun* **1** *The car is fitted with child restraints.* harness, seat belt. **2** *She showed great restraint in not saying anything.* control, modera-

tion, self-control, self-discipline, self-restraint.

restrict *verb* **1** *Her movements were restricted.* check, circumscribe, cramp, curb, hamper, handicap, hinder, impede, limit. **2** *The animals were restricted in small cages.* box in, confine, coop up, enclose, hem in, pen, shut in.

restriction *noun* *No restrictions are imposed on how the money is to be spent.* condition, constraint, control, limitation, proviso, qualification, stipulation.

result *noun* **1** *the result of his research.* consequence, effect, fruit, outcome, output, repercussion, upshot. **2** *exam results.* grade, mark, score. **3** *She came up with the correct result.* answer, finding, solution. — *verb* *The headache resulted from too much reading.* arise, come about, ensue, follow, happen, occur, originate, spring, stem. □ **result in** *Disobedience resulted in tragedy.* bring about, cause, culminate in, end in, finish in, give rise to, lead to.

resume *verb* **1** *They resumed their seats.* reoccupy, return to, take again. **2** *They resumed lessons after lunch.* begin again, carry on, continue, recommence, restart.

résumé *noun* **1** *He read a résumé of the article.* abstract, outline, précis, summary, synopsis. **2** *a résumé for a job application.* curriculum vitae, CV.

resurrect *verb* *They resurrected an old law.* bring back, reactivate, reintroduce, restore, resuscitate, revive.

retain *verb* **1** *She retained the lid.* hang on to, hold on to, keep, reserve, save. OPPOSITE discard. **2** *He retains information easily.* learn, memorise, recall, recollect, remember. OPPOSITE forget.

retaliate *verb* *It was hard not to retaliate after having been punched.* counter-attack, get even, get your own back (*informal*), hit back, pay back, reciprocate, seek retribution, take reprisals, take revenge.

retaliation *noun* *This attack will only invite more in retaliation.* counter-attack, reprisal, retribution, revenge, vengeance.

retard *verb* *Poor diet can retard growth.* delay, hamper, handicap, hinder, impede, inhibit, obstruct, slow down, stunt. OPPOSITE speed up.

retarded *adjective* *a retarded child.* backward, slow. OPPOSITE precocious.

reticent *adjective* **1** *a reticent student.* diffident, quiet, reserved, shy, taciturn, uncommunicative. OPPOSITE outgoing. **2** *She was reticent about the matter.* discreet, secretive, silent, tight-lipped, unforthcoming. OPPOSITE outspoken.

retire *verb* **1** *He retired at 55.* give up work, leave work, quit work, stop working. **2** *They retired to the sitting room.* repair, retreat, withdraw. **3** *She retires at 9 o'clock.* go to bed, hit the hay (*informal*), hit the sack (*informal*), turn in (*informal*). OPPOSITE get up.

retiring *adjective* *a retiring disposition.* bashful, diffident, meek, modest, reserved, shy, timid, uncommunicative, withdrawn. OPPOSITE outgoing.

retort *verb* *He retorted angrily.* answer, counter, react, rejoin, reply, respond. — *noun* *His sharp retort took her by surprise.* answer, comeback, rejoinder, reply, response, riposte.

retrace *verb* **retrace your steps** backtrack, go back, return.

retract *verb* **1** *The snail retracted its horns.* draw in, pull in. **2** *She retracted her statement.* cancel, dis-

claim, recant, rescind, revoke, take back, withdraw.

retreat *verb* *They retreated in terror from the scene.* back away, bolt, depart, escape, flee, go away, leave, retire, run away, shrink back, take flight, withdraw. OPPOSITE advance. — *noun* **1** *He made a hasty retreat.* departure, escape, exit, flight, getaway, withdrawal. **2** *They ran to their cosy retreat in the hills.* asylum, haven, hideout (*informal*), hiding-place, refuge, resort, sanctuary, shelter.

retrench *verb* **1** *In hard times the company was forced to retrench.* cut back, downsize, economise, rationalise, tighten your belt. **2** (*Australian*) *They retrenched fifty workers.* dismiss, get rid of, lay off, make redundant, sack (*informal*), shed.

retribution *noun* *He saw the flood as divine retribution.* just deserts, justice, nemesis, punishment, recompense, revenge, vengeance.

retrieve *verb* **1** *The dog retrieved the ball.* bring back, fetch, find, get back, recapture, recover, regain, rescue, salvage. **2** *He retrieved the information.* access, find, recover, track down.

return *verb* **1** *He returns on Monday.* come back, go back, reappear. OPPOSITE leave. **2** *She returned the books.* bring back, give back, hand back, put back, replace, restore, send back, take back. OPPOSITE keep. **3** *She returned the favour.* pay back, reciprocate, repay, requite. **4** *The rash returned.* come back, reappear, recur, resurface. **5** *He kept returning to his pet subject.* backtrack, go back, hark back, revert. — *noun* **1** *She was welcomed on her return.* arrival, homecoming, reappearance. OPPOSITE departure. **2** *a poor return on an investment.* earnings, gain, income, interest, profit, revenue, yield. OPPOSITE outlay.

reunion *noun* *a school reunion.* gathering, get-together.

reuse *verb* *The jars can be reused.* recycle, use again.

revamp *verb* *The whole system needs to be revamped.* overhaul, redo, renovate, revise, transform.

reveal *verb* **1** *The paper revealed the true story.* bring to light, disclose, divulge, expose, leak, let out, let slip, make known, proclaim, publish, tell. OPPOSITE cover up. **2** *He revealed his real feelings.* admit, air, betray, confess, declare, show, voice. OPPOSITE hide. **3** *She lifted her veil to reveal her face.* bare, display, expose, show, uncover, unmask, unveil. OPPOSITE cover.

revel *verb* **revel in** *She revels in all the attention.* bask in, delight in, enjoy, glory in, luxuriate in, rejoice in, relish, savour, wallow in.

revelation *noun* *astonishing revelations about their past.* admission, confession, disclosure, discovery, eye-opener, leak.

revelry *noun* *Neighbours were disturbed by their revelry.* carousing, celebration, festivities, high jinks, jollification, merrymaking, orgy, party, revels, roistering, spree, wassailing (*old use*).

revenge *noun* *He sought revenge for the murder.* reprisal, retaliation, retribution, vengeance. □ **take revenge** *He vowed to take revenge for his wife's murder.* avenge yourself, get even, get your own back, pay back, retaliate, take reprisals.

revenue *noun* Income, proceeds, receipts, return, takings. OPPOSITE expenditure.

reverberate *verb* *The music reverberated through the house.* boom, echo, resonate, resound, ring, thunder.

revere *verb* *She reveres God. They revered their mother.* admire, adore, esteem, glorify, hold in awe, honour, idolise, look up to, respect, reverence, venerate, worship. OPPOSITE despise.

reverence *noun* *They treated his name with reverence.* admiration, adoration, awe, devotion, esteem, homage, honour, respect, veneration. OPPOSITE irreverence.

reversal *noun* *a complete reversal of policy.* about-face, about-turn, backflip, change, turnabout, turnaround, U-turn.

reverse *noun* **1** *Sign on the reverse.* back, flip side (*informal*), other side, underside, verso. **2** *It was the reverse of what she expected.* antithesis, contrary, converse, opposite. — *verb* **1** *They reversed the order.* invert, transpose, turn round, turn upside down. **2** *He reversed his decision.* countermand, do a backflip on (*informal*), override, overrule, overturn, revoke, undo. OPPOSITE uphold. **3** *She reversed the car.* back, drive backwards. OPPOSITE advance.

revert *verb* **1** *He reverted to childish behaviour.* backslide, go back, lapse, regress, retrogress, return. **2** *She reverted to the subject of holidays.* go back, hark back, return.

review *noun* **1** *a review of the firm's performance.* analysis, examination, reappraisal, reassessment, reconsideration, re-examination, stocktaking, study, survey. **2** *The play received good reviews.* criticism, critique, notice, write-up. — *verb* **1** *He reviewed the situation.* analyse, assess, examine, go over, investigate, reappraise, reassess, reconsider, re-examine, scrutinise, study, survey, take stock of, think over. **2** *She enjoyed reviewing the book.* appraise, assess, comment on, criticise, evaluate, judge.

revise *verb* **1** *He revised the article for publication.* alter, amend, change, edit, modify, revamp, rework, rewrite, update. **2** *They revised their physics for the test.* brush up on, cram, go over, learn, study, swot (*informal*).

revival *noun* *a revival of interest in Jane Austen.* reawakening, rebirth, renaissance, renewal, restoration, resurgence, resurrection.

revive *verb* **1** *The doctor revived the patient.* bring round, resuscitate. **2** *The patient did not revive.* come round, rally, recover, regain consciousness. **3** *He revived the custom.* bring back, re-establish, reintroduce, restore, resurrect.

revoke *verb* *The law was revoked.* abrogate, annul, cancel, nullify, quash, repeal, rescind, retract, take back, withdraw. OPPOSITE enact.

revolt *verb* **1** *The people revolted against the government.* disobey, mutiny, rebel, rise up. **2** *They were revolted by what they saw.* appal, disgust, horrify, nauseate, offend, repel, shock, sicken. — *noun* *The people's revolt was quashed.* insurrection, mutiny, rebellion, revolution, rising, uprising.

revolting *adjective* *a revolting smell.* abhorrent, abominable, detestable, disgusting, distasteful, foul, gross (*informal*), hateful, hideous, horrible, loathsome, nasty, nauseating, objectionable, obnoxious, obscene, odious, offensive, off-putting, repellent, repugnant, repulsive, sickening, vile, yucky (*informal*). OPPOSITE attractive, pleasant.

revolution *noun* **1** *the French Revolution.* coup, coup d'état, insurrection, mutiny, rebellion, revolt, rising, uprising. **2** *a medical revolution.* change, reformation, shift, transformation, upheaval. **3** *a revo-*

lution of the wheel. rotation, spin, turn. **4** *the revolution of a satellite around the earth.* circuit, orbit.

revolve *verb* *The planet revolves around the sun.* circle, go round, orbit.

reward *noun* *a reward for a job well done.* award, bounty, compensation, payment, prize, recompense, remuneration. OPPOSITE punishment. — *verb* *He was rewarded for his efforts.* compensate, pay, recompense, remunerate, repay. OPPOSITE penalise.

rewarding *adjective* *a rewarding job.* fulfilling, gratifying, profitable, satisfying, worthwhile.

rewrite *verb* *He rewrote the book.* adapt, edit, paraphrase, revamp, revise, rework.

rhetoric *noun* *He wasn't impressed by the speaker's rhetoric.* bombast, elocution, eloquence, grandiloquence, oratory, pomposity.

rhyme *noun* *a nursery rhyme.* jingle, poem, verse.

rhythm *noun* *the rhythm of music, poetry, etc.* beat, cadence, lilt, metre, pattern, pulse.

rhythmic *adjective* *rhythmic music.* metrical, regular, rhythmical, steady.

ribbon *noun* *The parcel was tied with gold ribbon.* band, braid, strip, tape.

rich *adjective* **1** *a rich businessman.* affluent, flush (*informal*), loaded (*informal*), moneyed, prosperous, wealthy, well-heeled (*informal*), well off, well-to-do. OPPOSITE poor. **2** *rich in natural resources.* abounding, abundant, well endowed, well supplied. OPPOSITE deficient. **3** *rich furnishings.* costly, expensive, grand, lavish, luxurious, magnificent, opulent, plush, precious, splendid, sumptuous, valuable. OPPOSITE cheap. **4** *a rich soil.* fertile, fruitful, lush, productive. OPPOSITE unproductive. **5** *a rich purple.* deep, intense, strong, vibrant, vivid. OPPOSITE pastel. □ **riches** *plural noun* affluence, assets, fortune, means, money, opulence, property, prosperity, resources, wealth.

rickety *adjective* *a rickety table.* decrepit, dilapidated, flimsy, ramshackle, shaky, tumbledown, unstable, unsteady, weak, wobbly. OPPOSITE steady.

ricochet *verb* *The ball ricocheted off the wall.* bounce, rebound.

rid *verb* *He rid the dog of fleas.* cleanse, clear, free, purge, relieve. □ **get rid of** *They got rid of the things they didn't want.* chuck out (*informal*), discard, dispense with, dispose of, ditch (*informal*), drive out, dump, eject, eliminate, eradicate, evict, expel, exterminate, remove, scrap, throw away, throw out, weed out. OPPOSITE acquire.

riddle *noun* *He enjoys solving riddles.* brainteaser, conundrum, enigma, mystery, poser, problem, puzzle, teaser.

ride *verb* **1** *She cannot ride a horse.* control, handle, manage. **2** *He likes riding on buses.* go, journey, travel. **3** *He bought a bike, and now he rides to work.* bicycle, cycle, pedal. — *noun* *She had a ride in his car.* drive, journey, lift, outing, spin (*informal*), trip.

rider *noun* **1** *horses and riders.* equestrian, hoop (*Australian slang*), horseman, horse-rider, horsewoman, jockey. **2** *bicycle riders.* bicyclist, biker, bikie (*Australian informal*), cyclist, motorcyclist.

ridge *noun* *The views from the ridge were spectacular.* brow, crest, hilltop, saddle.

ridicule *noun* *The politician was an object of ridicule.* banter, derision, mockery, sarcasm, satire, scorn. — *verb* *They love to ridicule impor-*

tant people. caricature, chiack (*Australian informal*), deride, gibe at, jeer at, lampoon, laugh at, make fun of, mock, parody, pillory, poke borak at (*Australian informal*), poke fun at, satirise, scoff at, send up (*informal*), sling off at (*Australian informal*), sneer at, take off, take the mickey out of (*informal*), taunt, tease.

ridiculous *adjective a ridiculous idea.* absurd, comical, crazy, derisory, droll, farcical, foolish, funny, harebrained, hilarious, idiotic, laughable, ludicrous, mad, nonsensical, outrageous, preposterous, silly, stupid, zany. OPPOSITE sensible.

rife *adjective Disease was rife in the city.* common, prevalent, rampant, widespread.

rift *noun* **1** *a rift in the rock.* break, chink, cleft, crack, crevasse, crevice, fissure, fracture, opening, slit, split. **2** *a rift between friends.* breach, disagreement, division, estrangement, schism, split.

rig *verb* **rig out** *He was rigged out as a soldier.* dress, equip, fit out, kit out, outfit. — *noun* **1** *an oil rig.* installation, platform. **2** (*informal*) *The cricket team was photographed in full rig.* clothes, gear (*informal*), get-up (*informal*), kit, outfit, rig-out (*informal*).

right *adjective* **1** *right conduct.* decent, ethical, fair, good, honest, honourable, just, lawful, legal, moral, proper, upright, virtuous. OPPOSITE wrong. **2** *the right word for the occasion.* appropriate, apt, fitting, proper, suitable. OPPOSITE inappropriate. **3** *the right answer.* accurate, correct, exact, perfect, precise, proper, true, valid. OPPOSITE incorrect. — *noun* **1** *You don't have the right to do that.* authority, entitlement, licence, permission, power, prerogative, privilege. **2** *a ship's right.* starboard. OPPOSITE port. — *verb* **1** *They managed to right the boat.* set upright, stand upright, straighten up. **2** *She tried to right the wrong.* correct, put right, rectify, redress, repair, set right.

righteous *adjective a righteous person.* blameless, ethical, good, holy, honest, honourable, just, law-abiding, moral, upright, virtuous. OPPOSITE wicked.

rightful *adjective the rightful owner of the vehicle.* lawful, legal, legitimate, proper, true. OPPOSITE unlawful.

rigid *adjective* **1** *rigid materials.* firm, hard, inflexible, stiff, unbending. OPPOSITE flexible. **2** *The rules are rigid.* cut and dried, firm, hard and fast, inflexible, rigorous, strict, stringent. OPPOSITE flexible. **3** *a rigid person.* harsh, intransigent, stern, strict, stubborn, uncompromising, unyielding. OPPOSITE flexible.

rigorous *adjective* **1** *rigorous discipline.* austere, harsh, rigid, severe, stern, strict, stringent, tough, uncompromising. OPPOSITE lax. **2** *rigorous research.* accurate, careful, conscientious, meticulous, painstaking, scrupulous, thorough. OPPOSITE slapdash.

rile *verb* (*informal*) *His lateness riled the others.* anger, annoy, exasperate, infuriate, irk, irritate, madden, nark (*informal*), provoke, vex.

rim *noun the rim of a cup. the rim of a lake.* border, brim, brink, circumference, edge, lip, perimeter, verge.

rind *noun He peeled off the rind.* crust, husk, peel, skin.

ring¹ *noun* **1** *a gold ring. a ring of light.* band, circle, disc, halo, hoop, loop. **2** *a wrestling ring.* arena, enclosure. — *verb Police ringed the house.* circle, encircle, enclose, encompass, hem in, surround.

ring² *verb* **1** *The bell rang.* chime, clang, ding, dong, jingle, peal, tinkle, toll. **2** *The hall rang with cheers.* echo, resonate, resound, reverberate. **3** *He rang the police.* call, phone, ring up, telephone. — *noun* **1** *They heard a ring of bells.* chime, clang, jingle, knell, peal, tinkle, toll. **2** (*informal*) *Give me a ring next week.* bell (*informal*), buzz (*informal*), call, phone call.

ring-in *noun* (*Australian informal*) *They didn't detect that one of the entrants was a ring-in.* impostor, phoney (*informal*), replacement, substitute, swap.

rinse *verb Rinse the plates in clean water.* clean, swill, wash.

riot *noun People were hurt in the riot which broke out.* brawl, commotion, disorder, disturbance, fracas, mêlée, mutiny, pandemonium, revolt, rising, tumult, turmoil, uprising, uproar. — *verb The people rioted in the city.* mutiny, rampage, rebel, revolt, run amok, run riot.

riotous *adjective a riotous crowd.* anarchic, boisterous, disorderly, lawless, mutinous, rebellious, rowdy, unruly, wild. OPPOSITE orderly.

rip *verb The barbed wire ripped his skin.* gash, lacerate, rupture, sever, slash, slit, split, tear. — *noun There was a large rip in his trousers.* gash, laceration, rupture, slash, slit, split, tear. □ **rip off** (*informal*) *The company makes money by ripping people off.* cheat, con (*informal*), defraud, diddle (*informal*), fleece, rob, rook, swindle, take for a ride (*informal*).

ripe *adjective* **1** *The fruit is ripe.* in season, mature, mellow, ready. OPPOSITE green, unripe. **2** *He lived to a ripe age.* advanced, mature, old. OPPOSITE tender.

ripen *verb The cheese needs to ripen.* age, develop, mature, mellow.

rip-off *noun* (*informal*) *Don't buy it. It's a rip-off.* con (*informal*), swindle, swizz (*informal*).

ripple *noun The breeze made ripples on the lake.* wave, wavelet. — *verb The breeze rippled the surface.* agitate, disturb, ruffle, stir.

rise *verb* **1** *The plane is rising.* ascend, climb, go up, mount, soar. OPPOSITE descend. **2** *The building rose above them.* loom, tower. **3** *She rose to greet us.* arise (*old use*), get up, stand up. OPPOSITE lie down, sit down. **4** *The people rose against the government.* mutiny, rebel, revolt, take up arms. **5** *The waves rose.* billow, heave, surge, swell. OPPOSITE subside. **6** *The shares rose in value.* appreciate, escalate, gain, go up, grow, increase, jump, rocket, shoot up, skyrocket. OPPOSITE decrease. **7** *Her spirits rose.* improve, lift, soar. OPPOSITE fall. **8** *The dough rises.* expand, prove, puff up, swell. **9** *The river rises in these mountains.* begin, commence, flow (from), originate, spring (from), start. — *noun* **1** *The car overheated after the steep rise.* ascent, climb. OPPOSITE descent. **2** *The house is visible from the rise.* elevation, hill, hillock, incline, slope. **3** *Employees receive an annual rise.* increase, increment, raise. **4** *her rise to fame.* advance, advancement, climb, march, progress.

risk *noun There was a risk of being caught.* chance, danger, possibility. — *verb* **1** *He risked his life.* endanger, imperil, jeopardise. **2** *He risked his wages on a horse.* bet, chance, gamble, hazard, stake, venture, wager. □ **at risk** *Their lives were put at risk.* in danger, in jeopardy, in peril.

risky *adjective a risky investment. a risky operation.* chancy, dangerous,

dicey (*slang*), dodgy (*informal*), hairy (*slang*), hazardous, perilous, precarious, tricky, uncertain, unsafe. OPPOSITE safe.

ritual *noun* **1** *a marriage ritual.* ceremony, rite, service. **2** *a bedtime ritual.* practice, procedure, routine, tradition.

rival *noun He beat his rival.* adversary, antagonist, challenger, competitor, contender, enemy, foe, opponent. OPPOSITE ally. — *verb* **1** *They rivalled one another for first place.* compete with, contend with, contest, oppose, vie with. **2** *His cooking rivals that of the best chefs.* compare with, equal, match, measure up to.

river *noun The river is muddy since the rain.* brook, creek, rill, rivulet, stream, tributary, watercourse, waterway.

road *noun* **1** [*kinds of road*] alley, avenue, boulevard, bypass, byway, causeway, clearway, close, crescent, cul-de-sac, dead end, drive, expressway, freeway, highway, lane, motorway, orbital, parade, ring road, route, street, thoroughfare, tollway, track, turnpike (*historical & American*), way. **2** *the road to success.* path, route, way. □ **road train** (*Australian*) *The road trains travel faster than the cars.* juggernaut (*informal*), lorry, semi (*Australian informal*), semitrailer, truck.

roadhouse *noun We ate at a roadhouse near Hay.* café, diner (*American*), eatery (*informal*), restaurant.

roadside *noun They parked by the roadside.* edge, kerb, verge, wayside.

roadway *noun* carriageway, road.

roam *verb He roamed through the town.* meander, ramble, range, rove, saunter, stroll, tootle around (*informal*), travel, wander.

roar *noun* **1** *the lion's roar.* bellow, howl, shout, yell. **2** *the roar of the engines.* blare, clamour, din, racket, rumble, thunder. **3** *roars of laughter.* guffaw, hoot (*informal*), howl, scream, shout, shriek. — *verb* **1** *He roared with pain.* bawl, bellow, howl, scream, shout, yell. **2** *They roared at his jokes.* guffaw, laugh.

roast *verb He roasted the turkey.* bake.

rob *verb* **1** *He robbed the man. They robbed a bank.* burgle, hold up, loot, mug, pilfer from, plunder, ransack, steal from, stick up (*informal*). **2** *He robs his customers.* cheat, diddle (*informal*), fleece, overcharge, rip off (*informal*), rook, shortchange, swindle.

robber *noun The robbers were caught with the money still on them.* bandit, brigand, buccaneer, burglar, bushranger, crook (*informal*), highwayman, housebreaker, looter, marauder, mugger, pickpocket, pilferer, pirate, plunderer, shoplifter, thief.

robbery *noun* **1** *The robbery was committed at 9 o'clock.* burglary, heist (*informal*), hold-up, mugging, raid, stick-up (*informal*). **2** *He was in jail for robbery.* larceny, stealing, theft.

robe *noun* [*kinds of robe*] bathrobe, cassock, dress, dressing gown, gown, habit, kimono, vestment.

robot *noun Some tasks can be done by robots.* android, automaton, machine.

robust *adjective a robust youth.* brawny, hardy, healthy, muscular, powerful, strapping, strong, sturdy, tough, vigorous. OPPOSITE weak.

rock¹ *noun The ground was covered with rocks.* boulder, crag, outcrop, pebble, stone.

rock² *verb* **1** *The boat rocked when he stood up.* lurch, pitch, reel, roll, shake, sway, swing, toss, totter,

wobble. **2** *The country was rocked by the news of his death.* disturb, shake, shock, stagger, stun, upset.

rocky¹ *adjective a rocky path.* craggy, gravelly, pebbly, rugged, stony.

rocky² *adjective a rocky start.* precarious, shaky, uncertain, unstable, unsteady.

rod *noun a wooden rod. a steel rod.* bar, baton, cane, cue, dowel, mace, poker, pole, sceptre, staff, stick, wand.

rogue *noun* **1** *The police caught the rogues.* blackguard, con man (*informal*), crook (*informal*), good-for-nothing, knave (*old use*), miscreant, rascal, rotter, scoundrel, villain, wretch. **2** *The little rogue hid their shoes.* devil, imp, monkey, rascal, scallywag, scamp, wag.

role *noun* **1** *She played the title role.* character, part. **2** *the role of computers in schools.* function, job, part, place.

roll *verb* **1** *He rolled the wheelchair down the path.* trundle, wheel. **2** *The child rolled over.* flip, somersault, tumble, turn. **3** *The wheels rolled.* go round, revolve, rotate, spin, turn, twirl, whirl. **4** *She rolled up the flag.* furl, wind. OPPOSITE unfurl. **5** *The cat rolled herself up in a ball.* coil, curl, twist, wind, wrap. **6** *He rolled out the pastry.* flatten, level, smooth. **7** *The ship rolled on heavy seas.* lurch, pitch, reel, rock, sway, toss, totter. — *noun* **1** *a roll of paper.* cylinder, reel, spool. **2** *bread rolls.* bagel, bap, bun. **3** *The teacher read the roll.* list, register. **4** *a drum roll.* boom, reverberation, rumble, thunder.

roller coaster *noun* big dipper, switchback.

romance *noun* **1** *the romance of travel.* adventure, excitement, fascination, glamour. **2** *She reads romances.* love story. **3** *Theirs was a short-lived romance.* affair, courtship, liaison, love affair, relationship.

romantic *adjective* **1** *a romantic film.* emotional, mushy, nostalgic, sentimental, sloppy, soppy (*informal*). **2** *a romantic card for Valentine's Day.* amorous, loving, passionate, sentimental, tender. OPPOSITE unromantic. **3** *a romantic view of the world.* idealistic, impractical, quixotic, starry-eyed, unrealistic, Utopian, visionary. OPPOSITE realistic.

romp *verb The children romped around.* caper, dance, frisk, frolic, gambol, jump, play, prance, run, skip.

rook *verb He knew he'd been rooked.* cheat, defraud, diddle (*informal*), have (*slang*), overcharge, rip off (*informal*), swindle.

room *noun* **1** *There was no room to move.* area, elbow room, space. **2** *Each person has his own room.* cell, chamber (*old use*), office. **3** *There was no room for negotiation.* chance, latitude, leeway, margin, opportunity, scope.

roomy *adjective a roomy bag. a roomy house.* ample, big, capacious, commodious, huge, large, spacious, vast. OPPOSITE small.

roost *verb The birds roosted under the eaves.* nest, perch, settle, sleep.

rooster *noun* cock, cockerel.

root *noun* **1** *plant roots.* radicle, rhizome, rootlet, tuber. **2** *the root of all evil.* basis, bottom, cause, foundation, origin, source. — *verb He was rooted to the spot.* anchor, fix, stick. □ **root out** *They rooted out crime.* eliminate, eradicate, get rid of, remove, weed out. **take root** *The idea took root.* become established, catch on, take hold.

rope *noun tied with a rope.* cable, cord, guy, hawser, lanyard, lariat, lasso, line, noose, painter, stay,

tether. — *verb The car was roped to the one in front for towing.* attach, bind, fasten, hitch, secure, tie.

ropeable *adjective see* ANGRY.

rort *noun (Australian slang) a tax rort.* dodge (*informal*), lurk (*Australian informal*), racket, scam (*slang*), scheme, swindle. — *verb (Australian slang) The man was found to be rorting the system.* cheat, defraud, rip off (*informal*), rob, swindle.

roster *noun the canteen roster.* list, rota.

rostrum *noun She spoke from the rostrum.* dais, platform, podium, stage, stand.

rosy *adjective* **1** *rosy cheeks.* blushing, florid, flushed, glowing, pink, red, rose, rubicund, ruddy. OPPOSITE pale. **2** *a rosy future.* auspicious, bright, encouraging, hopeful, optimistic, promising. OPPOSITE bleak.

rot *verb The food rotted.* decay, decompose, disintegrate, fester, go bad, go off, moulder, perish, putrefy, spoil. — *noun (slang) He talks a lot of rot.* see NONSENSE.

rotate *verb* **1** *The table-top rotates.* go round, gyrate, revolve, spin, swivel, turn, twirl, whirl. **2** *They rotate jobs in the office.* alternate, swap, take turns at.

rotten *adjective* **1** *rotten food.* bad, decayed, decomposed, mouldy, off, perished, putrid, rancid, rank, stinking. OPPOSITE fresh. **2** *Replace the rotten elastic.* crumbling, disintegrating, perished, worn-out. **3** *That was a rotten thing to do.* beastly, contemptible, despicable, lousy (*informal*), low-down, mean, nasty, unkind. **4** (*informal*) *She felt rotten with her cold.* ill, miserable, poorly, seedy (*informal*), sick, unwell, wretched. **5** (*informal*) *rotten weather.* abysmal (*informal*), appalling (*informal*), atrocious (*informal*), bad, dreadful (*informal*), foul, shocking (*informal*), terrible (*informal*). OPPOSITE fine.

rotund *adjective The man grew rotund.* chubby, corpulent, fat, obese, overweight, plump, podgy, portly, stout, tubby. OPPOSITE skinny.

rough *adjective* **1** *a rough surface, edge, etc.* broken, bumpy, coarse, craggy, irregular, jagged, knobbly, pitted, ragged, rocky, rugged, stony, uneven. OPPOSITE smooth. **2** *rough skin.* bristly, calloused, chapped, hard, leathery, scaly, unshaven. OPPOSITE smooth. **3** *a rough person. rough manners.* boorish, coarse, crude, ill-bred, impolite, loutish, rude, uncivil, uncouth, unrefined, vulgar. OPPOSITE refined. **4** *a rough voice.* grating, gruff, harsh, hoarse, husky, rasping, raucous, strident. OPPOSITE gentle. **5** *hurt in rough play.* boisterous, lively, rowdy, unrestrained, wild. OPPOSITE gentle. **6** *rough weather.* blustery, inclement, squally, stormy, tempestuous, turbulent, violent, wild. OPPOSITE calm. **7** *They had a rough time.* difficult, hard, rugged, tough, unpleasant. OPPOSITE easy. **8** *The painter did a rough job.* careless, clumsy, hasty, imperfect, patchy, unfinished. OPPOSITE perfect. **9** *Their dwellings were rough and temporary.* crude, makeshift, primitive, rough-and-ready, rudimentary. OPPOSITE elaborate. **10** *She only had a rough idea.* approximate, ballpark (*informal*), general, hazy, imprecise, inexact, sketchy, vague. OPPOSITE exact.

roughly *adverb There were roughly fifty guests.* about, approximately, around, close to, in the vicinity of, nearly, round about.

round *adjective* **1** *a round object.* bulbous, circular, curved, globular, rotund, spherical. **2** *a round dozen.* complete, entire, full, whole. — *noun* **1** *another round of talks.* course, cycle, series, succession. **2** *She won the first round in the contest.* bout, division, game, heat, section, stage. — *verb The car rounded the corner.* go round, turn. □ **round off** *She rounded off the conversation.* bring to a close, close, complete, conclude, end, finish, terminate. **round up** *They rounded up the cattle.* assemble, collect, gather, herd, muster.

roundabout *noun Let's have a ride on the roundabout.* carousel, merry-go-round, whirligig. — *adjective* **1** *a roundabout way to the shops.* circuitous, devious, indirect, meandering, tortuous. OPPOSITE straight. **2** *He asked in a roundabout way.* circumlocutory, devious, indirect, oblique. OPPOSITE direct.

rouse *verb* **1** *She could not rouse him from his sleep.* arouse, awaken, stir, waken, wake up. **2** *He was easily roused to anger.* excite, incite, move, provoke, stimulate, stir.

rouseabout *noun (Australian) He works as a rouseabout on the property.* blue tongue (*Australian informal*), handyman, knockabout (*Australian*), loppy (*Australian*), odd-job man.

rousing *adjective a rousing speech.* inspiring, moving, powerful, provoking, stimulating, stirring.

rout *verb They routed their opponents.* beat, conquer, crush, defeat, overpower, overthrow, put to flight, scatter, thrash, trounce, vanquish.

route *noun They drove the scenic route.* course, itinerary, path, road, way.

routine *noun a daily routine.* custom, habit, method, pattern, practice, procedure, ritual, system, way. — *adjective* **1** *a routine check of bags.* customary, habitual, normal, regular, scheduled, standard, usual. OPPOSITE one-off. **2** *The work had become routine.* boring, dull, familiar, humdrum, mechanical, monotonous, ordinary, predictable, tedious. OPPOSITE exciting.

rove *verb The cat likes to rove.* prowl, ramble, roam, stray, wander.

rover *noun He doesn't like to stay in one place: he's a rover.* gypsy, itinerant, nomad, traveller, vagabond, wanderer, wayfarer.

row[1] *noun They were arranged in rows.* chain, column, file, line, queue, rank, sequence, series, string, tier.

row[2] *verb She rowed the boat.* paddle, propel, scull.

row[3] *noun* (*informal*) **1** *What's all the row about?* clamour, commotion, din, disturbance, fuss, hubbub, hullabaloo, noise, racket, ruckus, rumpus, shindy (*informal*), tumult, uproar. **2** *They had a row over money.* altercation, argument, barney (*informal*), blue (*Australian informal*), bust-up (*informal*), disagreement, dispute, fight, fracas, quarrel, run-in, scrap (*informal*), squabble, tiff, wrangle.

rowdy *adjective a rowdy crowd.* boisterous, disorderly, lawless, noisy, obstreperous, riotous, rough, unruly, wild. OPPOSITE quiet.

royal *adjective the royal seal.* kingly, monarchic, queenly, regal, sovereign.

rub *verb* **1** *He rubbed her back.* caress, massage, pat, stroke. **2** *She has a blister where the shoe rubs.* abrade, chafe, gall. **3** *He rubbed cream on the sunburn.* apply, smear, spread, wipe, work in. **4** *She rubbed the silver.* buff, burnish, polish,

shine, wipe. □ **rub out** *She rubbed out the mistake.* blot out, cancel, delete, efface, erase, expunge, obliterate, remove, wipe out.

rubbish *noun* **1** *They removed the rubbish.* debris, detritus, dross, garbage, junk, litter, muck (*informal*), mullock (*Australian*), refuse, rubble, scrap, trash, waste. **2** *He talks a lot of rubbish.* balderdash, boloney (*informal*), bunkum, claptrap, cobblers (*slang*), codswallop (*slang*), drivel, garbage, gibberish, gobbledegook (*informal*), guff (*slang*), hogwash (*informal*), humbug, nonsense, piffle (*informal*), poppycock (*slang*), rot (*slang*), stuff and nonsense (*informal*), tommyrot (*slang*), tripe (*informal*), twaddle. OPPOSITE sense. — *verb* (*Australian informal*) *He rubbished their proposal.* bag (*Australian informal*), belittle, criticise, disparage, knock (*informal*), pan (*informal*), pick holes in, pooh-pooh, run down, scoff at, slate (*informal*), tear to pieces.

rubble *noun building rubble.* debris.

rucksack *noun The hikers carried their food in rucksacks.* backpack, haversack, knapsack, pack.

ruddy *adjective a ruddy face.* florid, flushed, red, rosy, rubicund. OPPOSITE pale.

rude *adjective* **1** *a rude person.* abrupt, abusive, bad-mannered, boorish, brazen, brusque, cheeky, churlish, curt, discourteous, disrespectful, foul-mouthed, ill-mannered, impertinent, impolite, impudent, inconsiderate, insolent, insulting, loutish, offensive, offhand, rough, saucy, surly, uncivil, uncouth, vulgar. OPPOSITE polite. **2** *rude jokes.* blue, coarse, crude, dirty, filthy, foul, improper, indecent, lewd, obscene, offensive, pornographic, smutty, tasteless, unprintable, vulgar. OPPOSITE clean. **3** *rude stone implements.* crude, makeshift, primitive, rough, simple. OPPOSITE sophisticated.

rudimentary *adjective* **1** *a rudimentary education.* basic, elementary, fundamental, primary. OPPOSITE advanced. **2** *a rudimentary tail.* immature, incomplete, undeveloped, vestigial.

rudiments *plural noun She only knew the rudiments of the subject.* ABC, basics, elements, essentials, fundamentals.

rue *verb He rued the day he said the fateful words.* lament, mourn, regret, repent.

rueful *adjective She was rueful about the pain she had caused.* apologetic, contrite, penitent, regretful, remorseful, repentant, sorrowful, sorry.

ruffian *noun The old man was attacked by ruffians.* bully, gangster, hood (*informal*), hoodlum, hooligan, hoon (*Australian informal*), larrikin (*Australian*), lout, mugger, rogue, rough, scoundrel, thug, tough, villain, yobbo (*informal*).

ruffle *verb* **1** *The pebble ruffled the surface of the lake.* disturb, ripple, stir. **2** *He was not ruffled by the news.* agitate, disconcert, disturb, faze (*informal*), fluster, perturb, rattle (*informal*), unsettle, upset. OPPOSITE calm. — *noun The dress had ruffles.* flounce, frill, ruff.

ruffled *adjective Her hair was ruffled.* dishevelled, messed up, rumpled, tangled, tousled, untidy.

rug *noun* **1** *a floor rug.* mat. **2** *a rug for the bed.* blanket, coverlet.

rugged *adjective* **1** *rugged country.* bumpy, craggy, irregular, jagged, rocky, rough, stony, uneven, wild. **2** *a rugged face.* craggy, furrowed, leathery, lined, weather-beaten, wrinkled. OPPOSITE smooth.

ruin *noun* **1** *The house was in a state of ruin.* decay, destruction, devastation, dilapidation, disrepair, rack and ruin. **2** *He suffered financial ruin.* collapse, defeat, downfall, failure, fall, loss, ruination, undoing. — *verb She ruined their plans. The crop was ruined.* damage, demolish, destroy, devastate, mess up, muck up, sabotage, scupper (*informal*), shatter, spoil, undermine, vandalise, wreck. □ **ruins** *plural noun They sifted through the ruins of their house.* debris, remains, rubble, shell, wreck, wreckage.

rule *noun* **1** *They followed the rules.* by-law, code, commandment, convention, decree, formula, guideline, instruction, law, order, ordinance, policy, precept, principle, protocol, regulation, ruling, statute. **2** *Getting up at 6 o'clock is the rule.* convention, custom, norm, practice, routine, standard. OPPOSITE exception. **3** *under the rule of Elizabeth I.* authority, command, control, dominion, government, jurisdiction, leadership, regime, reign, sovereignty. — *verb* **1** *He ruled the country for six months.* administer, command, control, direct, govern, lead, manage, reign over, run. **2** *The judge ruled that they were innocent.* adjudicate, decide, decree, determine, find, judge, pronounce. □ **as a rule** *He visits his mother every Sunday as a rule.* for the most part, generally, normally, ordinarily, usually. **rule out** *The possibility has been ruled out.* dismiss, eliminate, exclude, preclude.

ruler *noun* **1** *the ruler of the people.* chief, commander, emir, emperor, empress, governor, head, head of state, king, leader, lord, monarch, overlord, potentate, president, prince, princess, queen, sovereign, sultan. **2** *He measured the distance with a ruler.* measure, rule, yardstick.

rumble *noun the rumble of aeroplanes.* boom, roar, thunder.

rummage *verb Joe rummaged through the drawer to find the key.* comb, ferret, forage, fossick (*Australian informal*), hunt, ransack, rifle, scour, search.

rumour *noun He didn't believe the rumours he heard.* bush telegraph, furphy (*Australian informal*), gossip, hearsay, mulga wire (*Australian informal*), tale, whisper. — *verb It was rumoured that he had been poisoned.* bandy about, gossip, put about, report, say, spread about, whisper.

rumpus *noun They kicked up a rumpus.* commotion, din, disturbance, fuss, hullabaloo, pandemonium, protest, racket, row, ruckus, shindy (*informal*), storm, to-do, uproar.

run *verb* **1** *The boys ran past quickly.* bound, dart, dash, fly, gallop, hasten, hurry, hurtle, jog, race, rush, scamper, scoot, scurry, scuttle, shoot, speed, sprint, spurt, stampede, streak, sweep, tear, trot, whiz, zip. **2** *The car ran down the hill.* plunge, roll, slide. **3** *The colour ran in the wash.* bleed, come out, spread. **4** *The water ran from the tap.* cascade, drip, flow, gush, issue, leak, pour, spurt, stream, trickle. **5** *The car runs well.* behave, function, go, perform, work. **6** *The bus runs every hour.* go, operate, travel. **7** *A friend ran her home.* convey, drive, take, transport. **8** *The lease runs for six months.* be current, be valid, continue, last. OPPOSITE expire. **9** *He runs the business.* administer, carry on, conduct, control, direct, govern, look after, maintain, manage, organise, oversee, supervise. — *noun* **1** *They went for a run in the car.* drive, excursion, jaunt, outing, ride, spin (*informal*), trip. **2** *a run of disasters.* sequence, series, spate, string, succession. **3** *a chicken run.* compound, coop, enclosure, pen. **4** (*Australian*) *He owns a cattle run.* farm, property, station (*Australian*). □ **run after** *The security officer ran after the shoplifter.* chase, follow, pursue. **run away** *Tom was afraid of the consequences and decided to run away instead.* abscond, beat it (*slang*), bolt, clear off (*informal*), decamp, depart, disappear, do a runner (*slang*), escape, flee, go away, hightail it (*informal*), leave, make off, nick off (*Australian slang*), retreat, run off, scarper (*informal*), scoot, scram (*informal*), shoot through (*Australian informal*), skedaddle (*informal*), take flight, take off, take to your heels, withdraw. OPPOSITE arrive. **run down** *The writer is always running politicians down.* bag (*Australian informal*), belittle, criticise, disparage, knock (*informal*), malign, pan (*informal*), revile, rubbish, slate (*informal*). OPPOSITE praise. **run into 1** *They ran into another car.* bump into, career into, collide with, crash into, hit, knock into, ram, smash into, strike. **2** *She ran into an old school friend in town.* bump into, come across, meet, run across. **run over 1** *The water ran over.* brim over, overflow, spill over. **2** *The driver ran over a cat.* hit, knock down, run down. **3** *He ran over his lines.* go over, practise, rehearse, run through.

runaway *noun The runaway eventually returned home.* absconder, bolter, deserter, escapee, fugitive.

run-down *noun a run-down of the day's events.* outline, recap (*informal*), report, review, round-up, summary, survey.

runny *adjective a runny mixture.* fluid, liquid, sloppy, thin, watery. OPPOSITE solid.

runway *noun* airstrip, landing strip.

rupture *verb A blood vessel ruptured.* break, burst, split, tear.

rural *adjective rural scenery.* bucolic, country, pastoral, rustic. OPPOSITE urban.

ruse *noun He thought of a ruse to get them out of the house.* artifice, deception, dodge (*informal*), hoax, manoeuvre, ploy (*informal*), stratagem, subterfuge, trick, wile.

rush *verb* **1** *They rushed to the hospital.* charge, dash, fly, gallop, hasten, hurry, hustle, race, run, scoot, scramble, scurry, shoot off, speed, sprint, storm, tear, whiz, zip, zoom. OPPOSITE dawdle. **2** *The officer rushed her claim through.* accelerate, expedite, fast-track, hurry, push. OPPOSITE delay. **3** *They rushed the building.* attack, capture, charge, seize, storm. — *noun* **1** *They are always in a rush to be on time.* haste, hurry, hustle, race. **2** *a rush for the best seats.* charge, dash, run, scramble, stampede.

rust *verb The iron roof rusted.* corrode, oxidise, rot.

rustic *adjective a rustic atmosphere.* bucolic, country, pastoral, rural. OPPOSITE urban.

rustle *noun a rustle of leaves.* swish, whisper.

rut *noun* **1** *The wheels were caught in the rut.* channel, furrow, groove, track. **2** *He was in a rut.* grind, habit, routine.

ruthless *adjective a ruthless killer.* brutal, callous, cruel, ferocious, harsh, heartless, merciless, pitiless, relentless, remorseless, savage, vicious. OPPOSITE compassionate.

Ss

sabotage *noun The plane crash was the result of sabotage.* damage, destruction, disruption, vandalism. — *verb He sabotaged my plans.* destroy, disrupt, ruin, spoil, undermine, wreck.

sack¹ *noun a sack of potatoes.* bag, pack, package. — *verb* (*informal*) *The boss sacked half his workers.* discharge, dismiss, fire, give notice to, give someone the boot (*slang*), lay off, make redundant. OPPOSITE hire.

sack² *verb The town was sacked by the invaders.* destroy, lay waste, loot, pillage, plunder, raid, ransack, ravage.

sacred *adjective a sacred object. sacred music.* blessed, consecrated, divine, hallowed, holy, religious, revered, sacrosanct, sanctified, spiritual, venerated. OPPOSITE profane, secular.

sacrifice *noun The priest offered a lamb as a sacrifice to their god.* oblation, offering. — *verb Jane sacrificed her day off to take her mother to the doctor.* forfeit, forgo, give up, offer, renounce, surrender.

sacrilege *noun Vandalism of church property is sacrilege.* desecration, disrespect, irreverence, profanation, profanity, violation.

sacrilegious *adjective Whistling in church is considered sacrilegious.* disrespectful, impious, irreverent, profane; see also BLASPHEMOUS.

sacrosanct *adjective His leisure time is sacrosanct.* inviolable, protected, respected, sacred.

sad *adjective* **1** *We were sad when our friends moved away.* blue, broken-hearted, dejected, depressed, desolate, despondent, disconsolate, discontented, dismal, distressed, doleful, downcast, gloomy, glum, heartbroken, heavy-hearted, lugubrious, melancholy, miserable, mournful, sorrowful, unhappy, woebegone, wretched. OPPOSITE happy. **2** *They went to see a sad film.* dismal, distressing, gloomy, heart-breaking, heart-rending, pessimistic, touching, tragic, upsetting. OPPOSITE comic.

sadden *verb He was saddened by their selfishness.* depress, dishearten, dismay, distress, grieve, upset. OPPOSITE cheer.

sadistic *adjective a sadistic killer.* brutal, cruel, inhuman, monstrous, vicious.

sadness *noun Mary was overcome with sadness.* dejection, depression, desolation, despondency, discontent, distress, gloom, glumness, melancholy, misery, sorrow, unhappiness, woe, wretchedness. OPPOSITE happiness.

safari *noun an African safari.* expedition, tour, trip.

safe *adjective* **1** *safe medicines.* harmless, innocuous, non-toxic. OPPOSITE dangerous, harmful. **2** *a safe car.* dependable, reliable, roadworthy, sound. OPPOSITE dangerous. **3** *They remained safe because they stayed inside.* all right, OK (*informal*), safe and sound, unharmed, uninjured, unscathed. OPPOSITE endangered. **4** *The building is safe.* defended, impregnable, protected, secure. OPPOSITE unprotected. — *noun She keeps her jewels in a safe.* strongbox, vault.

safeguard *noun environmental safeguards.* defence, precaution, protection, security. — *verb The lawyer will safeguard their interests.*

defend, guard, look after, preserve, protect. OPPOSITE jeopardise.

safely *adverb Drive safely.* carefully, cautiously, prudently. OPPOSITE dangerously.

safety *noun The helmet is for your safety.* protection, security. OPPOSITE danger.

sag *verb The bed sagged in the middle.* bow, droop, flop, sink, slump, subside.

saga *noun Icelandic sagas.* chronicle, epic, history, legend, romance, story, tale.

sage *adjective sage advice.* judicious, prudent, sagacious, sensible, shrewd, wise. — *noun He sought advice from the sage.* authority, expert, guru, philosopher, pundit, scholar, wise man.

sail *noun Devonport is an overnight sail from Melbourne.* cruise, journey, trip, voyage. — *verb* **1** *We sail next week.* put to sea, set out, set sail, weigh anchor. **2** *Who was sailing the boat?* navigate, pilot, skipper, steer. **3** *They sailed around Australia.* cruise, voyage, yacht. **4** *The clouds sailed across the sky.* drift, float, glide, scud, sweep, waft.

sailor *noun* mariner, navigator, seafarer, seaman, yachtsman, yachts-woman.

saintly *adjective a saintly person.* blameless, blessed, God-fearing, godly, holy, innocent, pious, righteous, upright, virtuous. OPPOSITE ungodly.

salary *noun The manager gets an annual salary of $90,000.* earnings, emolument, income, pay, remuneration, stipend. CONTRASTS WITH wage.

sale *noun* **1** *the sale of goods.* selling, vending. OPPOSITE buying, purchase. **2** *The salesman gets a commission on every sale.* deal, transaction. **3** *He bought the cupboard at a sale.* auction, clearance, sell-out.

salesperson *noun You pay the salesperson at the counter.* sales assistant, salesman, saleswoman, shop assistant.

salient *adjective the salient features.* conspicuous, noticeable, outstanding, prominent, striking. OPPOSITE inconspicuous.

saliva *noun* dribble, spit, spittle, sputum.

sallow *adjective The invalid had a sallow complexion.* pale, pallid, sickly, wan, yellowish.

salon *noun a beauty salon.* establishment, parlour, shop.

salty *adjective salty water.* brackish, briny, saline, salt.

salute *noun He raised his hand in salute.* greeting, salutation, welcome. — *verb* **1** *He saluted each person as they entered.* acknowledge, greet, nod to. **2** *We salute this achievement.* applaud, commend, congratulate, honour, pay tribute to.

salvage *noun They are taking part in a salvage operation.* recovery, rescue, retrieval. — *verb He salvages old bicycles.* recover, recycle, rescue, retrieve, save.

salvation *noun the salvation of souls.* deliverance, redemption, saving. OPPOSITE damnation.

salve *noun lip salve.* balm, lotion, ointment. — *verb He salves his conscience by giving to charity.* appease, ease, relieve, soothe.

salvo *noun a salvo of twenty-one guns.* firing, report, salute, volley.

same *adjective* **1** *We see the same man every day.* identical, selfsame. OPPOSITE different. **2** *The two girls have the same features.* alike, identical, indistinguishable. OPPOSITE dissimilar. **3** *He continued at the same speed.* constant, unchanged, un-

changing, uniform, unvarying. OPPOSITE variable.

sameness *noun There's a sameness about his writing.* evenness, monotony, similarity, uniformity. OPPOSITE variety.

sample *noun He sent them a sample of his work.* example, foretaste, instance, model, specimen, taste. — *verb He sampled the soup.* taste, test, try.

sanatorium *noun The sick man recuperated in a sanatorium.* clinic, convalescent home, hospital, nursing home.

sanctify *verb The priest sanctified the house.* bless, consecrate, hallow.

sanctimonious *adjective a sanctimonious hypocrite.* holier-than-thou, hypocritical, pharisaical, pious, self-righteous.

sanction *noun* **1** *The practice will never be given official sanction.* approval, authorisation, blessing, consent, go-ahead, OK (*informal*), permission, support. **2** *Other countries imposed sanctions against the offending country.* ban, boycott, embargo, penalty. — *verb The government will not sanction euthanasia.* allow, approve, authorise, consent to, legalise, permit, support. OPPOSITE prohibit.

sanctity *noun the sanctity of marriage.* holiness, inviolability, sacredness.

sanctuary *noun* **1** *The priest is in the sanctuary.* chapel, church, sanctum, shrine, temple. **2** *a koala sanctuary.* conservation park, preserve, reservation, reserve, wildlife park. **3** *The refugees were seeking sanctuary.* asylum, haven, protection, refuge, retreat, safety, shelter.

sand *verb He sanded the timber.* polish, sandpaper, smooth.

sandbank *noun* reef, sandbar, shoal.

sandwich *verb The car was sandwiched between two trucks.* jam, squash, squeeze, wedge.

sane *adjective* **1** *The doctors declared the man to be sane.* all there (*informal*), lucid, normal, of sound mind, rational. OPPOSITE insane, mad. **2** *a sane approach to the problem.* logical, rational, reasonable, sensible, sound. OPPOSITE foolish.

sanguine *adjective a sanguine view of the future.* confident, hopeful, optimistic, positive. OPPOSITE pessimistic.

sanitary *adjective a sanitary cooking environment.* antiseptic, aseptic, clean, disinfected, germ-free, healthy, hygienic, sanitised, sterile, sterilised. OPPOSITE unhygienic.

sanity *noun She regained her sanity after a long holiday.* normality, rationality, reason, saneness. OPPOSITE insanity, madness.

sap *noun tree sap.* juice, lifeblood. — *verb The disease had sapped his strength.* deplete, drain, exhaust, rob, weaken.

sarcastic *adjective a sarcastic comment.* derisive, ironic, mocking, sardonic, satirical, scornful, sneering, taunting.

sardonic *adjective sardonic humour.* cynical, derisive, mocking, sarcastic, scornful, sneering, wry.

sash *noun The dress has a sash at the waist.* cummerbund, girdle, obi, tie.

satanic *adjective satanic rituals.* demonic, devilish, diabolic, diabolical, evil, fiendish, hellish, infernal, wicked.

satchel *noun a school satchel.* backpack, bag, pack, schoolbag.

satellite *noun a satellite orbiting the planet.* moon, space station, sputnik.

satin *adjective a satin finish.* glossy, shiny, smooth. OPPOSITE matt.

satire *noun* **1** *He uses satire in his essays.* irony, mockery, ridicule, sarcasm. **2** *The play was a satire on the workings of government.* burlesque, caricature, lampoon, parody, send-up (*informal*), skit, spoof (*informal*), take-off.

satirical *adjective a satirical play.* derisive, ironic, mocking, sarcastic.

satirise *verb The show satirised both politicians and bureaucrats.* caricature, deride, lampoon, make fun of, parody, ridicule, send up (*informal*), take off.

satisfaction *noun Her success was a source of great satisfaction to her parents.* contentment, delight, fulfilment, gratification, happiness, pleasure, pride. OPPOSITE dissatisfaction.

satisfactory *adjective His marks are satisfactory.* acceptable, adequate, all right, enough, fair, fine, OK (*informal*), passable, sufficient, tolerable, up to scratch. OPPOSITE unsatisfactory.

satisfy *verb* **1** *Nothing seems to satisfy him.* content, fulfil, gratify, please. **2** *This should satisfy their needs.* answer, comply with, fill, fulfil, meet, supply. **3** *Water will satisfy his thirst.* appease, assuage, quench, sate, satiate, slake. **4** *She satisfied the examiners that she knew her subject.* convince, persuade, prove to.

satisfying *adjective a satisfying job.* enjoyable, fulfilling, gratifying, pleasing, rewarding.

saturate *verb His clothes were saturated in the rain.* drench, soak, souse, wet through.

sauce *noun The meat was covered with sauce.* condiment, dressing, gravy, relish.

saucepan *noun* cauldron, pan, pot.

saucy *adjective saucy remarks.* bold, brazen, cheeky, forward, fresh, impertinent, impudent, insolent, pert, presumptuous.

saunter *verb The tourists sauntered through the grounds.* amble, mosey (*slang*), ramble, roam, stroll, wander.

sausage *noun barbecued sausages.* banger (*slang*), snag (*Australian slang*).

savage *adjective* **1** *savage animals.* feral, ferocious, fierce, untamed, wild. OPPOSITE domesticated, tame. **2** *a savage attack.* brutal, callous, cruel, ferocious, harsh, inhuman, merciless, ruthless, stinging, vicious, violent. OPPOSITE mild. — *verb The sheep were savaged by a pack of dogs.* attack, maul.

save *verb* **1** *He saved the boy from drowning.* guard, keep safe, preserve, protect, rescue, spare. **2** *They have been saved from their sins.* deliver, liberate, ransom, redeem, set free. **3** *Save water by not washing the car.* conserve, economise on, use sparingly. OPPOSITE waste. **4** *She saves plastic bags.* collect, hoard, hold on to, keep, preserve, reserve, retain, salvage, stockpile, store. **5** *They are saving money for a holiday.* accumulate, bank, deposit, invest, lay by, put aside, put by, set aside. **6** *He saved us the trouble.* obviate, prevent, spare.

savings *plural noun They spent their savings on a new car.* capital, funds, investments, nest egg, reserves.

saviour *noun* **1** *Mandela was seen as his country's saviour.* deliverer, liberator, protector, redeemer, rescuer. **2** *the Saviour.* Christ, Jesus, Messiah.

savour *noun He was enticed by the savour of wild mushrooms.* aroma, flavour, smell, taste. — *verb* **1** *He savoured every mouthful.* appreciate, delight in, enjoy, relish. **2** *His manner savours of conceit.* smack (of), suggest.

savoury *adjective* **1** *savoury biscuits with cheese.* piquant, salty. OPPOSITE sweet. **2** *She enjoyed the savoury smells from the kitchen.* appetising, delectable, delicious, mouth-watering, scrumptious (*informal*), tasty.

saw *noun [kinds of saw]* chainsaw, circular saw, fretsaw, hacksaw, jigsaw. — *verb* see CUT.

say *verb* **1** *'Good,' she said.* announce, answer, bellow, blurt out, call out, comment, cry, declare, exclaim, moan, mumble, murmur, mutter, recite, remark, repeat, reply, scream, shout, shriek, snap, snarl, speak, splutter, squawk, squeal, stammer, state, stutter, tell, utter, whisper, yell. **2** *Does she say much in her letter?* communicate, convey, disclose, divulge, express, impart, mention, refer to, report, reveal, speak of, tell. **3** *What does the sign say.* designate, indicate, specify. — *noun They all had their say.* input, opinion, voice, vote.

saying *noun a famous saying.* adage, aphorism, axiom, byword, catchphrase, cliché, dictum, epigram, maxim, motto, proverb, quotation, slogan.

scab *noun a scab on a sore.* crust.

scabbard *noun He returned his sword to its scabbard.* sheath.

scaffold *noun The prisoner was sent to the scaffold.* gallows, gibbet.

scaffolding *noun The painters erected scaffolding around the building.* frame, framework, gantry, platform.

scald *verb* see BURN.

scale[1] *noun* **1** *a scale of fees.* hierarchy, ladder, progression, range, sequence, series, spectrum. **2** *a map with a scale of 1 cm to 1 km.* proportion, ratio. **3** *the scale of the problem.* dimensions, extent, level, scope, size. — *verb He scaled the cliff.* ascend, clamber up, climb, mount.

scale[2] *noun* **1** *The fish has scales.* flake, lamina, plate. **2** *She removed the scale from the inside of the kettle.* coating, crust, deposit, encrustation.

scales *plural noun* balance, weighing machine.

scallywag *noun* devil, imp, knave, miscreant, rascal, rogue, scamp, wretch.

scaly *adjective scaly skin.* flaky, peeling, rough, scurfy.

scam *noun* see RACKET.

scamper *verb She scampered off before I could talk to her.* dash, hurry, race, run, rush, scoot, scurry, scuttle, skip.

scan *verb* **1** *He scanned their faces for clues.* examine, look at, scrutinise, study, survey. **2** *He quickly scanned the book.* flick through, flip through, glance at, leaf through, skim.

scandal *noun* **1** *His abuse of his position is a scandal!* crime, disgrace, outrage, shame, sin. **2** *Have you heard the latest scandal?* gossip, rumour, tattle, tittle-tattle.

scandalise *verb The ladies were scandalised by his behaviour.* affront, appal, offend, outrage, shock.

scandalmonger *noun* gossip, muckraker (*informal*), mud-slinger (*informal*), rumour-monger, tittle-tat.

scandalous *adjective scandalous behaviour.* disgraceful, improper, outrageous, shameful, shocking, unseemly, wicked.

scant *adjective scant consideration for others.* inadequate, insufficient, limited, little, minimal.

scanty *adjective Their information was scanty.* inadequate, insufficient, limited, meagre, scant, skimpy, sparse. OPPOSITE ample.

scapegoat *noun* bunny (*Australian informal*), fall guy (*slang*), victim, whipping boy.

scar *noun The cut left a scar.* mark, scratch, wound. — *verb His arm was scarred by the cat.* damage, disfigure, mark, scratch, wound.

scarce *adjective Copies of the book were scarce.* in short supply, insufficient, rare, scanty. OPPOSITE plentiful.

scarcely *adverb I scarcely know her.* barely, hardly, only just.

scarcity *noun a scarcity of trained nurses.* dearth, lack, paucity, shortage. OPPOSITE plethora.

scare *verb The man scares people with his wild behaviour.* alarm, dismay, frighten, intimidate, panic, shock, startle, terrify, terrorise, unnerve. OPPOSITE reassure. — *noun The results of the doctor's tests gave her a scare.* alarm, fright, shock, start.

scared *adjective There's no need to be scared.* afraid, alarmed, fearful, frightened, intimidated, nervous, panic-stricken, petrified, terrified.

scarf *noun* bandanna, headscarf, kerchief, muffler, neckerchief.

scary *adjective a scary story.* alarming, creepy, eerie, frightening, hair-raising, spine-chilling, spooky (*informal*), terrifying.

scathing *adjective scathing criticism.* biting, caustic, harsh, savage, severe, withering.

scatter *verb* **1** *The gardener scattered the seeds.* broadcast, disseminate, sow, spread, sprinkle, strew, throw about. **2** *The crowd scattered.* disband, disperse, dissipate.

scatterbrained *adjective* absent-minded, disorganised, dreamy, forgetful, hare-brained, muddle-headed, scatty (*informal*), silly, vague.

scavenge *verb She scavenges in rubbish bins for useful objects.* forage, fossick (*Australian informal*), look, rummage, scrounge, search.

scenario *noun the scenario of the film.* outline, plot, script, storyline, summary, synopsis.

scene *noun* **1** *the scene of the crime.* locale, locality, location, place, setting, site, spot. **2** *Please don't create a scene.* exhibition, fuss, incident, outburst, spectacle. **3** *We admired the scene from the lookout.* landscape, outlook, panorama, prospect, scenery, sight, view, vista.

scenery *noun* **1** *mountain scenery.* landscape, panorama, view, vista. **2** *stage scenery.* backdrop, set.

scenic *adjective a scenic drive.* beautiful, panoramic, picturesque, pretty.

scent *noun* **1** *the scent of roses.* aroma, bouquet, fragrance, odour, perfume, redolence, smell, whiff. **2** *The dogs lost the scent.* spoor, track, trail.

sceptical *adjective He was sceptical about the man's claims.* disbelieving, distrustful, doubting, dubious, incredulous, mistrustful, questioning, suspicious. OPPOSITE convinced.

scepticism *noun She views everything new with scepticism.* disbelief, distrust, doubt, mistrust, suspicion.

schedule *noun The surgeon has a busy schedule.* agenda, diary, itinerary, plan, programme, timetable. — *verb The interview is scheduled for Friday.* appoint, arrange, book, list, plan, programme, timetable.

scheme *noun* **1** *a job creation scheme.* plan, programme, project, strategy. **2** *a tax-avoidance scheme.* conspiracy, dodge (*informal*), lurk (*Australian informal*), plot, ploy, racket, rort (*Australian slang*), ruse, scam (*slang*), stratagem. **3** *a colour scheme.* arrangement, design, system. — *verb They were scheming to oust the President.* collude, conspire, intrigue, plan, plot.

scholar *noun* **1** *a classics scholar.* academic, highbrow, intellectual, pundit. **2** *Many schools have an association of old scholars.* collegian, pupil, student.

scholarly *adjective a scholarly person.* academic, bookish, erudite, intellectual, learned, studious. OPPOSITE ignorant.

scholarship *noun* **1** *The scholarship pays the university fees.* award, bursary, fellowship, grant. **2** *a work of sound scholarship.* erudition, learning, research.

scholastic *adjective scholastic achievements.* academic, educational.

school[1] *noun* **1** *He teaches in a school.* academy, college, educational institution, seminary. **2** *the Heidelberg school of painters.* circle, group, movement, set. — *verb They schooled her in social as well as academic skills.* discipline, educate, instruct, teach, train.

school[2] *noun a school of fish.* shoal.

schoolchild *noun* collegian, pupil, scholar, schoolboy, schoolgirl, student.

schooling *noun He had limited formal schooling.* education, instruction, learning, training, tuition.

schoolteacher *noun* chalkie (*Australian slang*), master, mistress, pedagogue (*old use*), schoolie (*Australian informal*), schoolmaster, schoolmistress, teacher.

scientific *adjective a scientific approach.* analytical, methodical, precise, rigorous, systematic.

scintillating *adjective a scintillating discussion.* animated, brilliant, lively, sparkling, stimulating, witty. OPPOSITE dull.

scissors *plural noun* clippers, cutters, secateurs, shears, snips.

scoff[1] *verb* **scoff at** *He scoffed at her efforts.* belittle, chiack (*Australian informal*), deride, disparage, gibe at, jeer at, knock (*informal*), make fun of, mock, ridicule, rubbish (*Australian informal*), scorn, sling off at (*Australian informal*), sneer at.

scoff[2] *verb (informal) Who scoffed all the food?* devour, eat up, finish off, gobble, guzzle.

scold *verb He scolded them for being late.* admonish, berate, castigate, censure, chastise, chide (*old use*), go crook at (*Australian informal*), haul over the coals, rap over the knuckles, rebuke, reprimand, reproach, reprove, rouse on (*Australian informal*), tell off (*informal*), tick off (*informal*), upbraid. OPPOSITE praise.

scolding *noun He was going to get a scolding from his mother.* dressing down (*informal*), lecture, rap over the knuckles, rebuke, reprimand, reproof, talking-to (*informal*), wigging (*informal*).

scoop *noun a scoop of flour.* ladle, shovel, spoon. — *verb He scooped out a hole in the soil.* dig, excavate, gouge, hollow.

scoot *verb He scooted off suddenly.* dart, dash, go, hurry, run, rush.

scope *noun* **1** *It does not fall within the scope of this inquiry.* area, bounds, compass, extent, limits, orbit, range. **2** *In this job there is scope for initiative.* capacity, latitude, opportunity, outlet, room.

scorch *verb The iron was too hot and scorched the shirt.* brown, burn, discolour, sear, singe.

scorching *adjective* see HOT.

score *noun He improved his score in maths.* grade, mark, points, result, tally. — *verb* **1** *She scored ten points.* achieve, gain, get, make, notch up, win. **2** *The timber had been heavily scored.* cut, gash, gouge, groove, incise, notch,

scorn scratch. **3** *The music was scored for string ensemble.* arrange, orchestrate, write.

scorn *noun* *He treated the suggestion with scorn.* contempt, derision, disdain, ridicule. — *verb* *He scorned their attempts to include him.* despise, disdain, rebuff, refuse, reject, shun, snub, spurn, turn your nose up at.

scornful *adjective* *Her scornful look said it all.* contemptuous, derisive, disdainful, jeering, mocking, sarcastic, scathing, scoffing, sneering, snide (*informal*).

scoundrel *noun* *The scoundrel made off with all their money.* blackguard, cad, crook (*informal*), knave (*old use*), miscreant, rascal, rogue, villain.

scour[1] *verb* *She scoured the pans until they shone.* clean, cleanse, polish, rub, scrub.

scour[2] *verb* *They scoured the area for clues.* comb, rake through, ransack, search.

scourge *noun* **1** *The prisoners were punished with scourges.* lash, whip. **2** *the scourge of war.* affliction, bane, curse, plague, suffering. — *verb* *The prisoners were scourged regularly.* beat, flog, lash, thrash, whip.

scout *noun* *The army sent him ahead as a scout.* lookout, spy, vanguard. — *verb* *He scouted around for evidence.* ferret, fossick (*Australian informal*), hunt, look, search, snoop (*informal*).

scowl *verb* *She scowled angrily.* frown, glare, glower, lour.

scraggy *adjective* *a few scraggy sheep.* bony, emaciated, gaunt, lean, scrawny, skinny, thin. OPPOSITE fat.

scramble *verb* **1** *We scrambled over the rocks.* clamber, climb, crawl, struggle. **2** *They scrambled to the exits.* dash, hurry, race, run, rush, scurry. — *noun* *There was a mad scramble for the ball.* race, run, rush, scrimmage, struggle, tussle.

scrap[1] *noun* **1** *scraps of material.* fragment, piece, rag, remnant, shred, tatter. **2** *not a scrap of evidence.* bit, fragment, grain, iota, jot, shred, skerrick (*Australian informal*), trace. **3** *He makes money out of scrap.* junk, refuse, rubbish, salvage, trash. — *verb* *They scrapped that idea and started again.* abandon, discard, ditch (*informal*), do away with, drop, get rid of, give up, jettison. OPPOSITE retain. □ **scraps** *plural noun* *table scraps.* crumbs, leftovers, scrapings, waste.

scrap[2] *noun* (*informal*) *The boys had a scrap over the toy.* altercation, argument, barney (*informal*), dispute, fight, quarrel, row, squabble, tiff.

scrape *verb* **1** *He scraped the mud off his shoes.* clean, remove, rub, scrub. **2** *The teacher scraped the blackboard with her fingernail.* grate, rasp, scratch. **3** *He scraped his knee.* bark, graze, scratch, skin. — *noun* **1** *It's hard to avoid scrapes especially on knees.* abrasion, cut, graze, injury, laceration, scratch. **2** *He's always getting into scrapes.* difficulty, plight, predicament, trouble.

scrappy *adjective* *a scrappy piece of work.* bitty, disjointed, fragmentary.

scratch *verb* **1** *The timber had been badly scratched.* gouge, mark, score, scuff. **2** *She scratched her leg on the fence.* abrade, cut, graze, lacerate, scrape, skin. **3** *The horse was scratched.* withdraw. — *noun* *scratches on his legs.* abrasion, graze, laceration, scrape, wound.

scrawl *verb* *He scrawls illegibly.* scribble; see also WRITE.

scrawny *adjective* *He lost so much weight that he looked scrawny.* bony, emaciated, gaunt, lanky, lean, puny, scraggy, skinny, thin. OPPOSITE brawny.

scream *verb* *She screamed in pain.* bawl, cry out, howl, screech, shriek, squawk, squeal, wail, yell, yowl. — *noun* **1** *The screams could be heard for some distance.* cry, howl, screech, shriek, squawk, squeal, yell, yowl. **2** (*informal*) *We thought the play was a scream.* hoot (*informal*), laugh, riot (*informal*).

screech *noun & verb* see SCREAM.

screen *noun* **1** *They were separated by a screen.* divider, partition. **2** *a window screen.* blind, curtain, flyscreen. **3** *He planted trees as a screen from the wind.* barrier, protection, shelter, shield. **4** *a computer screen.* monitor, VDU, visual display unit. — *verb* **1** *The house was screened from public view.* camouflage, conceal, hide, protect, shelter, shield. **2** *The television channel screened a series of French films.* broadcast, present, show. **3** *The coal is screened.* filter, riddle, sieve, sift, strain. **4** *Volunteers are screened before being appointed.* check, examine, investigate, test, vet.

screw *verb* **1** *He screwed the cap on tightly.* rotate, turn, twist. **2** *She screwed up the letter.* crumple, scrunch, twist, wrinkle.

scribble *verb* *She scribbled on a sheet of paper.* doodle, jot, scrawl.

scrimp *verb* *They have to scrimp in order to afford new shoes.* economise, save, skimp, stint, tighten your belt.

script *noun* **1** *The letter was written in a neat script.* handwriting, writing. **2** *a film script.* lines, screenplay, text, words.

scripture *noun* *Each religion has its scripture.* sacred writings. □ **Scripture** the Bible, the Word of God.

scrounge *verb* *He's always without money and scrounging off friends.* beg, bludge (*Australian informal*), borrow, cadge, scab (*Australian slang*), sponge.

scrub[1] *verb* **1** *They helped to scrub the pans.* clean, scour, wash. **2** (*informal*) *We had to scrub our plans when it rained.* abandon, call off, cancel, drop, forget, scrap.

scrub[2] *noun* *The land was covered with scrub.* bush, mallee, mulga.

scrubby *adjective* *scrubby trees.* low, small, stunted.

scruffy *adjective* *a scruffy appearance.* bedraggled, dishevelled, messy, shabby, slovenly, tatty (*informal*), unkempt, untidy. OPPOSITE neat.

scrumptious *adjective* (*informal*) *a scrumptious dessert.* appetising, delectable, delicious, luscious, mouth-watering, tasty, yummy (*informal*).

scrunch *verb* see CRUNCH.

scruple *noun* *He hadn't the slightest scruple about taking the money.* compunction, doubt, hesitation, misgiving, qualm, twinge of conscience.

scrupulous *adjective* **1** *He paid scrupulous attention to detail.* careful, conscientious, fastidious, meticulous, painstaking, particular, punctilious, rigorous, thorough. OPPOSITE careless. **2** *A treasurer must be scrupulous.* ethical, honest, honourable, moral, principled, upright. OPPOSITE unscrupulous.

scrutinise *verb* *He scrutinised the document before signing it.* examine, inspect, look over, peruse, study, survey.

scrutiny *noun* *The work was subjected to close scrutiny.* examination, inspection, investigation, perusal, study.

scud *verb* *The clouds scudded across the sky.* fly, race, speed, sweep.

scuff *verb* *A toddler scuffs his shoes very easily.* mark, rub, scrape, wear away.

scuffle *noun* *The policeman was injured in the scuffle.* brawl, fight, fisticuffs, scrap (*informal*), scrimmage, skirmish, stoush (*Australian slang*), struggle, tussle.

sculpture *noun* *a sculpture of a young woman.* bust, carving, cast, figure, figurine, statue, statuette. — *verb* *The man sculptured a dolphin out of wood.* carve, chisel, form, hew, make, model, sculpt, shape.

scum *noun* *the scum on the top of the liquid.* film, foam, froth.

scupper *verb* **1** *They scuppered the ship.* scuttle, sink. **2** (*informal*) *The plan was scuppered.* foil, ruin, spoil, stonker (*Australian slang*), thwart, wreck.

scurrilous *adjective* *a scurrilous attack on his character.* abusive, defamatory, insulting, low, offensive, vilifying.

scurry *verb* *The mice scurried away at the sound of the cat.* flit, hurry, run, rush, scamper, scoot, scramble, scutter, scuttle.

scuttle[1] *verb* *They scuttled the ship.* scupper, sink.

scuttle[2] *verb* see SCURRY.

sea *noun* **1** *a ship on the open sea.* the blue, the deep, the main (*old use*), ocean. OPPOSITE land. **2** *a sea of faces.* expanse, mass. □ **at sea** *Henry was all at sea with the new computers.* baffled, bewildered, confused, perplexed, puzzled, uncertain.

seafarer *noun* mariner, sailor, seaman. OPPOSITE landsman.

seafaring *adjective* *a seafaring nation.* maritime, nautical, naval, sailing, seagoing.

seal *noun* *This seal guarantees its authenticity.* crest, emblem, imprint, insignia, stamp, sticker, symbol. — *verb* **1** *The envelope was sealed.* close, fasten, secure, stick down. **2** *The timber has been sealed.* coat, protect, surface. **3** *His fate was sealed.* decide, determine, secure, settle. **4** (*Australian*) *Most of the roads are sealed.* bituminise, macadamise, tar, tarmac, tar-seal (*Australian*). □ **seal off** *The police sealed off the area.* block off, close off, cordon off. OPPOSITE open up.

seam *noun* **1** *a dress seam.* join, stitching. **2** *the seam of coal.* layer, lode, stratum, vein.

seaman *noun* mariner, sailor, seafarer.

seamy *adjective* *the seamy side of life.* sordid, squalid, unattractive, unpleasant, unsavoury. OPPOSITE pleasant.

sear *verb* *He seared the meat.* brown, burn, scorch, singe.

search *verb* **1** *They searched the area for clues.* comb, examine, explore, hunt, look over, ransack, scour, survey. **2** *She searched through her handbag to find a pen.* check, ferret, forage, fossick (*Australian informal*), look, rummage. **3** *The authorities searched all the new arrivals.* check, examine, frisk, inspect. — *noun* *They abandoned the search for survivors.* examination, exploration, hunt, inspection, investigation, look, quest.

searching *adjective* *a searching examination.* careful, in-depth, probing, testing, thorough.

seasick *adjective* nauseous, queasy, sick.

seaside *noun* *a holiday at the seaside.* beach, coast.

season *noun* *Christmas is a festive season.* period, time. — *verb* **1** *The food has already been seasoned.* flavour, pepper, salt, spice. **2** *The wood has been seasoned.* age, condition, dry, harden, mature. □ **in season** *Plums are in season.* available, ready, ripe.

seasoned *adjective* *a seasoned traveller.* accustomed, experienced, practised, veteran.

seasoning *noun* *What seasoning did you put in the sauce?* condiment, flavour, herb, relish, spice.

seat *noun* **1** *a seat to sit on.* armchair, bench, chair, couch, form, lounge, pew, settee, settle, sofa, stall, stool, throne. **2** *We reserved seats.* place. **3** *a safe Labor seat.* constituency, electorate. **4** *He fell and bruised his seat.* backside (*informal*), behind (*informal*), bottom, bum (*slang*), buttocks, rump. — *verb* **1** *The usher seated them in the front row.* place, position, put, situate. **2** *The hall seats two hundred.* accommodate, hold, take.

secateurs *plural noun* *She uses the secateurs to prune the roses.* clippers, cutters, pruning shears.

secede *verb* *The larger states wanted to secede from the union.* break away, leave, pull out, quit, separate, split, withdraw. OPPOSITE join.

secluded *adjective* *a secluded place.* hidden, isolated, lonely, private, remote, sheltered, solitary.

second *adjective* **1** *There won't be a second time.* following, next, subsequent. **2** *The team has a second driver.* additional, alternative, backup, extra, other, substitute, supplementary. — *noun* (*informal*) *I'll be with you in a second.* flash, instant, jiffy (*informal*), minute, moment, tick (*informal*). — *verb* *He seconded the motion.* back, endorse, support.

secondary *adjective* **1** *a secondary consideration.* lesser, minor, subordinate, subsidiary. OPPOSITE primary. **2** *secondary colours.* derivative, derived. OPPOSITE primary.

second-hand *adjective* *second-hand clothes.* hand-me-down, pre-loved, pre-owned, recycled, used, worn. OPPOSITE new.

secrecy *noun* confidentiality, furtiveness, mystery, privacy, stealth. OPPOSITE openness.

secret *adjective* **1** *The details of the project were kept secret.* classified, concealed, confidential, hidden, hushed up, hush-hush (*informal*), private, under wraps, undisclosed. OPPOSITE public. **2** *a secret meeting.* clandestine, covert, private, stealthy, surreptitious, undercover. OPPOSITE public. **3** *a secret code.* arcane, cryptic, mysterious, occult. — *noun* **1** *She can be trusted with a secret.* confidence. **2** *the secrets of nature.* enigma, mystery, puzzle, riddle. **3** *The secret of her success was hard work.* explanation, formula, key, recipe. □ **secret agent** see SPY.

secrete *verb* **1** *He secreted the key in a flowerpot.* conceal, hide, stash. OPPOSITE display. **2** *Resin is secreted by pine trees.* discharge, emit, excrete, exude, give off, ooze, produce. OPPOSITE absorb.

secretive *adjective* *There is no need to be so secretive.* cagey (*informal*), enigmatic, evasive, furtive, mysterious, reticent, tight-lipped, uncommunicative. OPPOSITE candid, open.

sect *noun* *a religious sect.* cult, denomination, faction, party.

section *noun* **1** *The whole is divided into sections.* bit, compartment, division, fraction, part, piece, portion, sector, segment, slice, subdivision. **2** *The novel was published in six sections.* chapter, instalment, part. **3** *sections of an organisation.* branch, department, division. **4** *a section of a journey.* leg, stage.

sector noun *The city was divided into sectors.* area, district, division, part, quarter, region, section, zone.

secular adjective *secular life. secular music.* earthly, lay, temporal, worldly. OPPOSITE religious.

secure adjective **1** *The people thought their walled town was secure.* defended, impregnable, protected, safe, unassailable. OPPOSITE vulnerable. **2** *He felt his position was secure.* assured, certain, guaranteed, reliable, safe, solid, sound, steady, strong, sure. OPPOSITE shaky. **3** *She felt secure in her mother's arms.* confident, protected, safe, sheltered, snug. OPPOSITE insecure. — verb **1** *They secured the city from attack.* defend, fortify, guard, make safe, protect, safeguard. **2** *Secure the doors and windows before the winds start.* batten down, bolt, fasten, lock. **3** *He secured the necessary items.* acquire, come by, get, obtain, procure.

security noun **1** *lulled into a false sense of security.* assurance, confidence, protection, safety. OPPOSITE anxiety. **2** *The house is the security for the loan.* guarantee, pledge, surety.

sedate adjective *a sedate person. sedate music.* calm, collected, composed, decorous, dignified, peaceful, placid, serious, sober, staid, tranquil. OPPOSITE lively. — verb *The medicine sedated him.* calm, pacify, quieten, relax, soothe, subdue, tranquillise. OPPOSITE agitate, stimulate.

sedative adjective *The medicine had a sedative effect.* calming, relaxing, soothing, soporific, tranquillising. — noun *The doctor prescribed a sedative.* narcotic, opiate, sleeping pill, tranquilliser. OPPOSITE stimulant.

sedentary adjective *a sedentary worker.* inactive, seated, sitting, stationary.

sediment noun *the sediment in a bottle of wine.* deposit, dregs, grounds, lees, precipitate, residue.

seditious adjective *a seditious speech.* insurrectionist, mutinous, rabble-rousing, subversive, treasonous.

seduce verb *He was seduced into betraying his country.* beguile, corrupt, entice, lead astray, lure, persuade, tempt.

seductive adjective *a seductive outfit.* alluring, attractive, enticing, inviting, provocative, sexy, tempting.

see verb **1** *She could see the fine detail with her new glasses.* behold (*old use*), discern, distinguish, espy, glimpse, identify, make out, notice, observe, perceive, recognise, spot. **2** *I don't see what you mean.* appreciate, comprehend, get (*informal*), grasp, perceive, realise, understand. **3** *I just can't see it happening.* conceive, envisage, foresee, imagine, picture, visualise. **4** *I see things differently now.* consider, look at, regard, view. **5** *He saw the programme.* look at, view, watch. **6** *I saw a friend at the shops.* bump into, chance upon, encounter, meet, run into. **7** *He went to see what happened.* ascertain, determine, discover, find out, investigate, learn. **8** *She went to see the principal.* call on, confer with, consult, meet with, speak to, talk to, visit. **9** *Please see her out.* accompany, conduct, escort, lead, show, take, usher. **10** *See that he gets this.* ensure, make sure, mind, take care. □ **see to** *Please see to this matter.* attend to, deal with, look after, sort out, take care of.

seed noun *The plant grew from a seed.* germ, grain, ovule, pip, spore, stone.

seedy adjective **1** *A seedy-looking man was lying on the park bench.* disreputable, scruffy, shabby, untidy. **2** (*informal*) *He felt seedy the day after the party.* ill, off colour, poorly, queasy, sick, under the weather, unwell.

seek verb **1** *She sought help.* ask for, go for, look for, request, solicit. **2** *Whom are you seeking?* look for, search for. **3** *What are you seeking to achieve?* aim, aspire, attempt, endeavour, try.

seem verb *It seems likely that he will leave.* appear, feel, look, sound.

seemly adjective *seemly behaviour.* appropriate, becoming, befitting, decorous, fitting, proper, right, suitable. OPPOSITE unseemly.

seep verb *Oil seeped through the hole.* dribble, exude, filter, flow, leak, ooze, percolate, trickle.

seer noun *The seer's predictions were surprisingly accurate.* augur, clairvoyant, diviner, prophet, sibyl (*female*), soothsayer, visionary.

seethe verb **1** *The waters are seething.* boil, bubble, churn, foam, surge. **2** *She seethed with rage.* be furious, be livid, boil, fume.

see-through adjective *She wore a see-through blouse.* diaphanous, gauzy, sheer, transparent. OPPOSITE opaque.

segment noun *a segment of the pie.* division, part, piece, portion, section, slice, wedge.

segregate verb *Schools used to segregate the girls from the boys.* isolate, keep apart, separate.

segregation noun *racial segregation.* apartheid, isolation, separation.

seize verb **1** *She seized her bag and ran outside.* clutch, grab, grasp, pluck, snatch, take hold of. **2** *He was seized by the police.* apprehend, arrest, capture, catch, collar (*informal*), nab (*informal*), nick (*slang*). **3** *Customs officers seized the goods.* commandeer, confiscate, impound, take away, take possession of. **4** *He seized the opportunity.* grab, jump at, make use of, take advantage of, use, utilise. □ **seize up** *The engine seized up.* become stuck, jam, lock up.

seizure noun *He is in hospital after suffering a seizure.* apoplexy, attack, convulsion, fit, stroke.

seldom adverb *John seldom eats out.* hardly ever, infrequently, once in a blue moon, rarely. OPPOSITE often.

select verb *She was selected as captain.* appoint, choose, elect, nominate, pick. — adjective *one of a select group.* choice, chosen, elite, exclusive, hand-picked.

selection noun **1** *She took time to make her selection.* choice, decision, option, pick. **2** *a selection of chocolates.* assortment, collection, mixture, range, variety.

selective adjective *Ben is selective in what he reads.* careful, choosy (*informal*), discriminating, fussy, particular, picky (*informal*).

self-centred adjective *People avoid him because he is so self-centred.* egocentric, egotistic, self-absorbed, selfish, self-seeking, wrapped up in yourself. OPPOSITE selfless.

self-confident adjective *Jake got the job because he was self-confident.* assured, bold, confident, poised, self-assured. OPPOSITE insecure.

self-conscious adjective *The girl felt self-conscious as she walked across the stage.* awkward, bashful, diffident, embarrassed, insecure, shy, uncomfortable.

self-control noun *She lacked the self-control to resist chocolates.* restraint, self-discipline, self-restraint, will-power.

self-denial noun *Their religion demands complete self-denial.* abstemiousness, asceticism, selflessness, self-sacrifice. OPPOSITE self-indulgence.

self-esteem noun *Her self-esteem is growing.* pride, self-respect, self-worth.

self-governing adjective *a self-governing country.* autonomous, free, independent, self-regulating, sovereign.

self-important adjective arrogant, bumptious, conceited, egocentric, egotistic, high and mighty, pompous, self-centred, self-satisfied, snobbish, snooty (*informal*), stuck-up (*informal*), vain. OPPOSITE self-effacing.

selfish adjective egocentric, greedy, inconsiderate, mean, miserly, self-centred, self-seeking, stingy, thoughtless, wrapped up in yourself. OPPOSITE generous, unselfish.

selfless adjective *a selfless volunteer.* altruistic, generous, kind, self-denying, self-sacrificing, unselfish. OPPOSITE selfish.

self-possessed adjective calm, collected, composed, confident, cool, dignified, sedate, self-assured, self-confident, self-controlled, unflappable (*informal*). OPPOSITE panicky.

self-respect noun dignity, pride, self-esteem.

self-righteous adjective *He rejected the criticism with self-righteous indignation.* holier-than-thou, pompous, priggish, sanctimonious, self-satisfied, smug.

self-satisfied adjective *He showed off his work with a self-satisfied smile.* cocky, complacent, conceited, proud, self-important, smug.

self-sufficient adjective *With his farm he was able to be self-sufficient.* independent, self-contained, self-reliant, self-supporting.

self-willed adjective *a difficult and self-willed child.* determined, headstrong, intractable, obstinate, pig-headed, refractory, stubborn, wilful. OPPOSITE biddable.

sell verb **1** *He sells stamps.* auction, barter, deal in, flog (*slang*), handle, hawk, market, peddle, retail, stock, trade in, traffic in, vend. OPPOSITE buy. **2** *The book sells for $20.* be priced at, cost, retail at.

seller noun dealer, hawker, merchant, peddler, pedlar, pusher, retailer, salesman, salesperson, saleswoman, shopkeeper, stockist, supplier, trader, trafficker, vendor, wholesaler. OPPOSITE buyer.

sell-out noun *The concert was a sell-out.* hit, success, winner.

semblance noun *There was not even a semblance of gratitude.* air, appearance, façade, pretence, show.

seminar noun *a university seminar.* class, discussion group, tutorial.

semitrailer noun articulated vehicle, lorry, road train (*Australian*), semi (*Australian informal*), transport, truck.

send verb **1** *He sent them a message. She sent the parcel.* consign, convey, dispatch, email, fax, forward, pass on, post, relay, remit, ship, transmit, write. **2** *He sent the arrow into the air.* direct, fire, launch, propel, release, shoot. □ **send away** DISMISS. **send for** *We sent for the doctor.* ask for, call, order, summon. **send up** (*informal*) *The show sends up politicians.* caricature, lampoon, make fun of, mimic, parody, satirise, take off.

send-up noun (*informal*) *a send up of parliament.* burlesque, caricature, lampoon, parody, satire, spoof (*informal*), take-off.

senile adjective *She dreaded becoming senile.* decrepit, doddery, feeble-minded, infirm.

senior adjective **1** *Tom Brown senior.* elder, older. OPPOSITE junior. **2** *a senior officer.* higher-ranking, superior. OPPOSITE junior. — noun *concessions for seniors.* pensioner, retiree, senior citizen.

sensation noun **1** *the sensation of pain.* awareness, consciousness, feeling, perception, sense. **2** *The news caused a sensation.* commotion, excitement, stir.

sensational adjective **1** *It was a sensational finish to the tennis match.* dramatic, electrifying, exciting, spectacular, striking, stunning, terrific (*informal*), thrilling. **2** *That newspaper goes for the sensational news.* lurid, scandalous, shocking, startling.

sense noun **1** *a sense of smell.* faculty, perception, power, sensation. **2** *a sense of decency.* awareness, consciousness, perception, recognition. **3** *She has no sense.* brains (*informal*), common sense, gumption, intelligence, judgement, nous (*informal*), reason, sagacity, wisdom, wit. **4** *This word has several senses.* denotation, import, meaning, signification. **5** *What is the sense of doing that?* point, purpose, use, value. — verb *She sensed that something was wrong.* be aware, detect, discern, feel, perceive, realise, suspect, twig (*informal*).

senseless adjective **1** *a senseless act.* absurd, foolish, inane, mad, meaningless, nonsensical, pointless, silly, stupid. OPPOSITE sensible. **2** *He was knocked senseless.* cold (*informal*), insensible, out, unconscious. OPPOSITE conscious.

sensibility noun *Sensibility contrasts with sense.* sensitiveness, sensitivity. □ **sensibilities** plural noun *He had offended her sensibilities.* emotions, feelings, susceptibilities.

sensible adjective **1** *a sensible person.* intelligent, judicious, level-headed, logical, prudent, rational, realistic, reasonable, sagacious, sage, shrewd, thoughtful, wise. OPPOSITE foolish. **2** *sensible clothes.* functional, practical, serviceable.

sensitive adjective **1** *Plants are sensitive to light.* affected by, responsive to, susceptible to. **2** *a sensitive listener.* considerate, empathetic, perceptive, sympathetic, understanding. OPPOSITE insensitive. **3** *Be careful what you say as she's very sensitive.* hypersensitive, reactive, thin-skinned, touchy. OPPOSITE thick-skinned. **4** *The skin was sensitive at the site of the scar.* delicate, painful, sore, tender. **5** *a sensitive subject.* controversial, delicate, ticklish, touchy, tricky.

sensual adjective *sensual pleasures.* bodily, carnal, fleshly, physical, sexual.

sensuous adjective *sensuous music.* appealing, attractive, beautiful, exquisite.

sentence noun *The judge passed the sentence.* decision, judgement, penalty, punishment. — verb *The judge sentenced him to two years' jail.* condemn, penalise, punish.

sentiment noun **1** *I do not share his political sentiments.* attitude, belief, feeling, opinion, thought, view. **2** *She acted out of sentiment rather than reason.* emotion, feeling, sentimentality.

sentimental adjective *a sentimental film.* corny (*informal*), emotional, maudlin, mawkish, mushy, nostalgic, romantic, schmaltzy, soppy (*informal*), weepy (*informal*).

sentry noun *A sentry guarded the entrance to the palace.* guard, lookout, sentinel, watchman.

separable adjective *The two issues are not separable.* discrete, distinct. OPPOSITE inseparable.

separate adjective **1** a separate matter. different, discrete, unconnected, unrelated. OPPOSITE connected, same. **2** They live in separate houses. detached, distinct, free-standing, individual, single. **3** That is a separate organisation. autonomous, independent. — verb **1** The glued parts could not be separated. break apart, detach, disconnect, divide, sever, split, sunder, take apart. **2** The teacher separated the class into three groups. break, divide, segregate, sort, split. OPPOSITE merge. **3** The couple separated. break up, divorce, part, split up.

separation noun **1** separation of the parts. break, detachment, disconnection, dissociation, division, partition, segregation, split. OPPOSITE union. **2** They announced their separation after 20 years of marriage. break-up, divorce, parting, split-up.

sequel noun Have you read the sequel? continuation, development, follow-up.

sequence noun the logical sequence of events. chain, course, order, progression, series, succession, train.

serene adjective She remained serene throughout her ordeal. calm, composed, peaceful, placid, quiet, tranquil, unperturbed, unruffled. OPPOSITE agitated.

series noun a series of disasters. chain, cycle, group, line, order, progression, row, sequence, set, string, succession, train.

serious adjective **1** a serious person. earnest, grave, long-faced, pensive, sedate, sober, solemn, staid, steady, thoughtful. OPPOSITE frivolous. **2** He is serious about doing it. committed, determined, earnest, genuine, keen, resolute, sincere. OPPOSITE joking. **3** a serious decision. crucial, important, momentous, vital, weighty. OPPOSITE unimportant. **4** a serious illness. bad, critical, dangerous, grave, life-threatening, major, severe. OPPOSITE minor.

sermon noun a sermon in church. address, homily, talk.

serpentine adjective a serpentine road. corkscrew, curving, sinuous, tortuous, twisting, winding. OPPOSITE straight.

servant noun The master treats his servants well. attendant, butler, domestic, factotum, footman, help, housekeeper, lackey, maid, maidservant, manservant, menial, minion (derogatory), page, retainer, slave, valet, vassal.

serve verb **1** He served his country. aid, assist, help, work for. **2** That box will serve as a table. act, be suitable, do, function. **3** He has served his sentence. complete, undergo. **4** One person served the food to everybody. dish up, distribute, dole out, give, hand, present. **5** She serves the customers. assist, attend to, look after, wait on. — noun a small serve of potatoes. helping, portion, serving.

service noun **1** He left the firm after 30 years of service. employment, labour, work. **2** The hospital has a good welfare service. facility, provision, set-up, system. **3** Can I be of service? aid, assistance, benefit, help, use. **4** a church service. ceremony, rite, ritual, sacrament. **5** a warranty on service and parts. maintenance, overhaul, repair. — verb The mechanic services our car. check, fix, maintain, overhaul, repair, tune. □ **services** plural noun see ARMED SERVICES (at ARM²).
   service station filling station, garage, petrol station, roadhouse, servo (Australian informal).

serviceable adjective **1** The old steam engine was still serviceable.

functioning, operative, usable. **2** These shoes will be serviceable. durable, functional, hard-wearing, practical, strong, tough.

serviette noun napkin, table napkin.

servile adjective **1** servile tasks. humble, lowly, menial. **2** servile flattery. a servile assistant. abject, fawning, grovelling, obsequious, slavish, submissive, subservient, sycophantic.

serving noun a serving of pudding. helping, portion, serve.

servitude noun bondage, enslavement, slavery, subjection. OPPOSITE freedom.

session noun **1** a parliamentary session. meeting, sitting. **2** a long session on the telephone. period, spell, time.

set verb **1** She set the vase on the shelf. bung (informal), deposit, dump, install, lay, leave, park (informal), place, plonk, position, put, rest, stand. **2** He set the clock. adjust, regulate. **3** She set the table. arrange, lay, prepare. **4** The jelly has set. congeal, firm, gel, jell, solidify, stiffen. **5** They set a date for their next meeting. appoint, choose, decide on, determine, establish, fix, name, settle on, specify. **6** The post is set in concrete. embed, fix, lodge, mount, stick. **7** He set a new record for the 100 metres. create, establish. **8** The teacher set them homework. allot, assign, give, prescribe. — noun **1** a set of stamps. a set of books. assortment, batch, bunch, collection, group, series. **2** a TV set. apparatus, receiver. **3** a stage set. backdrop, scene, scenery, setting. □ **set about** He set about building a bookcase. begin, commence, start. **set back** The work was set back by rain. delay, hamper, hinder, hold back, impede, slow. OPPOSITE advance. **set off 1** They set off for Melbourne. depart, leave, set forth, set out, start. **2** This set off a chain reaction. cause, spark, start, stimulate, touch off, trigger. **3** They set off their fireworks. detonate, explode, ignite, let off. **set out 1** The report sets out the terms of reference. declare, detail, make known, present, state. **2** They set out on a long journey. begin, depart, embark, leave, set forth, set off, start. **set sail** We set sail on Friday. depart, leave, put to sea, sail. **set up 1** He set up the hall before the party. arrange, organise, prepare. **2** They set up a business. begin, create, develop, establish, found, institute, start.

setback noun He succeeded despite many setbacks. blow, complication, hiccup, hitch, obstacle, problem, reverse, snag.

settee noun They sat together on the settee. couch, lounge, sofa.

setting noun a house's setting. a historical setting. background, context, environment, locale, locality, place, scene, site, surroundings.

settle verb **1** They settled in Perth. establish yourself, immigrate, move, put down roots. OPPOSITE emigrate, uproot. **2** Englishmen settled the east coast. colonise, occupy, people, populate. **3** The dove settled on an olive branch. alight, come to rest, descend, land, perch. **4** They left the dust to settle. fall, sink, subside. **5** They settled on a meeting point. agree, choose, decide, determine, fix. **6** The dispute has been settled. clear up, deal with, resolve, straighten out, work out. **7** She couldn't settle the baby. calm, pacify, quieten, soothe. OPPOSITE agitate. **8** The debt has been settled. clear, discharge, liquidate, pay. OPPOSITE incur.

settlement noun **1** The two parties have reached a settlement. agree-

ment, arrangement, reconciliation, resolution. **2** Life was hard in the new settlement. colony, community, outpost, township.

settler noun colonist, immigrant, pioneer.

set-up noun arrangement, format, framework, organisation, structure, system.

sever verb see CUT.

several adjective She sent out several invitations. a few, a good many, a number of, some.

severe adjective **1** a severe person. a severe look. cold, cruel, dour, forbidding, grim, hard, harsh, merciless, pitiless, ruthless, stern, strict, unsmiling, unsympathetic. OPPOSITE gentle. **2** They took severe measures. Draconian, drastic, extreme, harsh, stringent, strong, tough. OPPOSITE lenient. **3** severe storms. fierce, intense, strong, violent. OPPOSITE mild. **4** a severe illness. acute, bad, critical, dangerous, grave, serious. OPPOSITE mild. **5** a severe style of dress. austere, plain, simple, unadorned. OPPOSITE ornate.

sew verb baste, darn, embroider, mend, smock, stitch, tack.

sewage noun effluent, waste.

sex noun **1** the sex of the baby. gender. **2** sex in the life of a couple. coitus, copulation, intercourse, love-making, sexual intercourse.

sexism noun male chauvinism, sexual discrimination; see also PREJUDICE.

sexual adjective **1** sexual organs. genital, reproductive, sex. **2** sexual attraction. erotic, physical, sensual.

sexy adjective a sexy smile. alluring, attractive, erotic, flirtatious, seductive, sensual.

shabby adjective **1** shabby clothes. frayed, ragged, scruffy, tattered, tatty (informal), threadbare, worn. **2** shabby old buildings. dilapidated, dingy, drab, neglected, ramshackle, run-down, seedy, squalid, tumbledown. OPPOSITE neat. **3** a shabby trick. contemptible, despicable, dirty, dishonourable, low-down, mean, unfair.

shack noun a holiday shack in the country. cabin, hovel, hut, shanty, weekender (Australian).

shackle verb He shackled the prisoner. bind, chain, fetter, handcuff, manacle, restrain. □ **shackles** plural noun The prisoners were placed in shackles. bonds, chains, fetters, handcuffs, irons, manacles.

shade noun **1** At midday there is little shade. semi-darkness, shadow. **2** different shades of pink. colour, degree, hue, intensity, tinge, tint, tone. **3** a shade better. bit, degree, fraction, tad (informal), touch, trace. **4** shades of meaning. degree, difference, gradation, nuance, variation. **5** a lamp shade. cover, screen, shield. — verb **1** The tree shades the house. cast shadow on, screen, shelter. **2** He had shaded the area on the map. darken, hatch.

shadow noun **1** The photo was taken in shadow. darkness, dimness, gloom, semi-darkness, shade. **2** The man cast a longer shadow. outline, shape, silhouette. — verb The detective shadowed the suspect. follow, pursue, stalk, tail (informal), track, trail.

shady adjective **1** a shady corner. cool, dark, dim, shaded, shadowy. OPPOSITE sunny. **2** shady dealings. crooked, dishonest, dubious, fishy (informal), questionable, shonky (Australian informal), suspect, suspicious. OPPOSITE above board.

shaft noun **1** He sent a shaft through the air. arrow, lance, spear. **2** a shaft of light. beam, ray, streak. **3** a shaft of lightning. bolt, streak. **4** the shaft

of a tool. handle, pole, shank, stem, stick. **5** a mine shaft. entrance, opening, passage, tunnel. **6** a lift shaft. well.

shaggy adjective shaggy hair. bushy, messy, rough, thick, tousled, unkempt, untidy, woolly; see also HAIRY.

shake verb **1** He shook his stick. brandish, jiggle, swing, wag, waggle, wave, wiggle. **2** The earthquake made the house shake. rock, sway, vibrate, wobble. **3** She shook with fear. quake, quaver, quiver, shiver, shudder, totter, tremble. **4** The news had shaken them. agitate, disconcert, distress, disturb, jolt, perturb, rattle (informal), ruffle, shock, stun, unnerve, unsettle, upset. **5** Her voice shook. falter, quaver, tremble, wobble.

shaky adjective **1** He is a bit shaky on his legs. doddery, trembling, unsteady, weak, wobbly. OPPOSITE steady. **2** a shaky start. doubtful, hesitant, rocky (informal), uncertain.

shallow adjective **1** a shallow wound. skin-deep, superficial, surface. OPPOSITE deep. **2** shallow talk. empty, frivolous, glib, superficial, trivial. OPPOSITE profound.

sham noun **1** His penitence was a sham. act, charade, pretence, put-on (informal). **2** They soon realised the financial adviser was a sham. charlatan, cheat, con man (informal), fake, fraud, impostor, phoney (informal). — adjective sham pearls. artificial, counterfeit, fake, false, imitation, phoney (informal), pseudo, synthetic. OPPOSITE genuine. — verb He shammed death. counterfeit, fake, feign, pretend, simulate.

shambles noun Their bedroom was a shambles. disaster area (informal), mess, muddle, pigsty, shemozzle (informal).

shame noun **1** He felt shame over the incident. embarrassment, guilt, humiliation, mortification, regret, remorse. OPPOSITE pride. **2** He brought shame on himself. discredit, disgrace, dishonour, humiliation, ignominy, scandal, stigma. OPPOSITE honour. **3** It's a shame that you won't be there. disappointment, pity. — verb His father would not shame him in front of his friends. disgrace, embarrass, humble, humiliate, mortify.

shamefaced adjective abashed, ashamed, embarrassed, hangdog, humiliated, mortified, sheepish.

shameful adjective shameful behaviour. contemptible, deplorable, disgraceful, dishonourable, ignominious, reprehensible, scandalous, shocking, unbecoming. OPPOSITE honourable.

shameless adjective shameless conduct. bold, brazen, cheeky, immodest, impudent, unashamed, unseemly.

shanghai noun (Australian) a shanghai for shooting stones. catapult, ging (Australian informal), sling, slingshot.

shanty noun a shanty on the outskirts of town. hovel, hut, shack.

shape noun **1** He recognised the object by its shape. build, contour, figure, form, outline, profile, silhouette. **2** He wasn't in good shape. condition, fettle, form, health, state, trim. — verb **1** The sculptor shaped the head. construct, fashion, form, frame, make, model, mould, sculpt, sculpture. **2** The book is shaping up well. develop, evolve, progress, take shape. **3** He shaped the dress to fit her. adapt, adjust, fit, modify, tailor.

shapeless adjective a shapeless blob. amorphous, formless, nebulous, unstructured, vague.

share *noun They each got their fair share.* allocation, allotment, allowance, bit, cut (*informal*), division, fraction, helping, part, portion, quota, ration, whack (*slang*). — *verb She shared the pencils among the children.* allocate, allot, apportion, deal out, distribute, divide, divvy (*informal*).

sharp *adjective* **1** *a sharp knife.* keen, pointed. OPPOSITE blunt. **2** *a sharp slope.* abrupt, precipitous, sheer, steep, vertical. OPPOSITE gentle, gradual. **3** *a sharp bend.* acute, hairpin, sudden. OPPOSITE gradual. **4** *in sharp focus.* clear, distinct, well-defined. OPPOSITE indistinct. **5** *sharp pain.* acute, excruciating, intense, severe, shooting, stabbing. OPPOSITE mild. **6** *a sharp voice.* high-pitched, penetrating, piercing, shrill, strident. OPPOSITE soft. **7** *sharp words.* acrimonious, angry, bitter, caustic, cutting, harsh, stinging, unkind. OPPOSITE gentle. **8** *a sharp taste or smell.* acid, acrid, bitter, piquant, pungent, sour, strong, tangy, tart, vinegary. OPPOSITE bland, mild. **9** *He is very sharp: you won't fool him.* alert, astute, bright, clever, intelligent, knowing, perceptive, quick, shrewd, smart. OPPOSITE dull, slow. — *adverb* **1** *He arrived at six o'clock sharp.* exactly, on the dot, on the knocker (*Australian informal*), precisely, promptly, punctually. OPPOSITE approximately. **2** *She pulled up sharp.* abruptly, suddenly. OPPOSITE gradually.

sharpen *verb sharpen a knife.* grind, hone, strop, whet. OPPOSITE blunt.

shatter *verb* **1** *The glass shattered.* break, burst, crack, explode, smash, splinter. **2** *All our hopes were shattered.* dash, destroy. **3** *We were shattered by the news.* crush, devastate, disturb, upset.

shave *verb* **1** *He shaved his whiskers.* cut off, snip off, trim. **2** *He shaved a millimetre off the door.* pare, plane, slice, trim. — *noun* **close shave** (*informal*) close call (*informal*), narrow escape.

shawl *noun a woollen shawl.* scarf, stole.

sheaf *noun a sheaf of wheat.* bunch, bundle.

shear *verb He shears sheep.* clip, crop, strip.

shears *plural noun* clippers, cutters, scissors.

sheath *noun He replaced the knife in its sheath.* case, cover, scabbard, sleeve.

shed[1] *noun The garden tools are in the shed.* barn, garage, hut, lean-to, outbuilding, outhouse, shelter, workshop.

shed[2] *verb* **1** *Deciduous trees shed their leaves.* drop, lose. **2** *The snake shed its skin.* cast, lose, slough. **3** *The birds shed their feathers.* lose, moult. **4** *He shed his clothes before stepping into his bath.* cast off, discard, remove, take off, throw off. OPPOSITE don, put on.

sheen *noun The woodwork has a sheen after polishing.* brightness, gleam, gloss, lustre, polish, shine.

sheep *noun* ewe (*female*), jumbuck (*Australian*), lamb, ram (*male*), wether (*male*).

sheepish *adjective a sheepish look.* abashed, ashamed, bashful, coy, embarrassed, hangdog, self-conscious, shamefaced, shy, timid. OPPOSITE brazen.

sheer[1] *adjective* **1** *sheer happiness.* absolute, complete, pure, total, utter. **2** *sheer cliffs.* abrupt, perpendicular, precipitous, sharp, steep, vertical. **3** *sheer fabric.* diaphanous, fine, flimsy, gauzy, see-through, thin, transparent. OPPOSITE opaque, thick.

sheer[2] *verb The car sheered away just in time.* slew, swerve, turn, veer.

sheet *noun* **1** *a sheet of paper.* folio, leaf, page. **2** *a sheet of glass.* pane, panel, plate. **3** *She put a sheet of plastic over the food.* cover, film, layer, overlay.

shelf *noun* ledge, mantelpiece, sill.

shell *noun* **1** *The hard shell protects the soft contents.* case, cover, covering, exterior, outside. **2** *a turtle's shell.* carapace, exoskeleton. **3** *the shell of seeds or nuts.* case, hull, husk, pod. **4** *the shell of a ship.* body, chassis, frame, framework, hull. — *verb The town was shelled.* bomb, bombard, fire on.

shellfish *noun* crustacean, mollusc.

shelter *noun* **1** *The people sought shelter from the bombs.* asylum, cover, haven, protection, refuge, safety, sanctuary. **2** *The walkers crowded into the tiny shelter.* bunker, hut, shed. — *verb* **1** *The wall shelters the garden.* protect, screen, shield. **2** *They sheltered the escapee.* conceal, give refuge to, harbour, hide. **3** *They sheltered under the eaves until the rain had eased.* take cover, take refuge.

shelve *verb The plans have been shelved.* defer, postpone, put aside, put on the back burner (*informal*), put on hold, suspend.

shield *noun* **1** *a warrior's shield.* buckler, escutcheon, hielaman (*Australian*). **2** *a shield against attack.* barrier, defence, guard, protection, refuge, safeguard, screen, shelter. — *verb We were shielded from danger.* defend, guard, preserve, protect, safeguard, screen, shelter. OPPOSITE expose.

shift *verb They are always shifting things around.* change, move, rearrange, relocate, switch, transfer. — *noun a shift in position.* alteration, change, move, relocation, switch, transfer, transposition, variation.

shifty *adjective a shifty character.* deceitful, dishonest, dodgy (*informal*), evasive, shonky (*Australian informal*), slippery, sly, sneaky, underhand, untrustworthy, wily. OPPOSITE trustworthy.

shilly-shally *verb* hesitate, hum and haw, vacillate, waver.

shimmer *verb The lights shimmered in the water.* flicker, gleam, glimmer, glisten, sparkle, twinkle. — *noun the shimmer of the lights reflecting in the water.* flicker, gleam, glimmer, glitter, sparkle, twinkle.

shindig *noun* (*informal*) **1** *invited to a shindig.* see PARTY. **2** *kick up a shindig.* brawl, din, disturbance, fight, fracas, row, rumpus, shindy (*informal*), uproar.

shine *verb* **1** *The lights are shining.* beam, blaze, dazzle, flash, flicker, gleam, glimmer, glint, glisten, glitter, glow, radiate, reflect, scintillate, shimmer, sparkle, twinkle. **2** *The sun shone today.* be visible, come out. **3** *What does she shine at?* do well, excel, stand out. **4** *I had to shine all the brass.* buff, burnish, clean, polish. — *noun The silver cup has lost its shine.* brightness, gleam, glint, gloss, glow, lustre, polish, radiance, sheen, shimmer, sparkle.

shiny *adjective a shiny surface.* bright, burnished, gleaming, glistening, glossy, lustrous, polished, satin, shimmering. OPPOSITE dull.

ship *noun* vessel; [*various ships*] aircraft carrier, battleship, brig, clipper, container ship, corvette, cruiser, destroyer, flagship, freighter, frigate, galleon, galley, gunboat, ice-breaker, liner, man-of-war, merchant ship, minesweeper, sailing ship, steamship, submarine,

tanker, warship, windjammer; see also BOAT. — *verb They had their furniture shipped beforehand.* consign, convey, dispatch, export, freight, send, transport.

shipment *noun a shipment of cars.* cargo, consignment, load.

shirk *verb He shirks the horrible jobs.* avoid, dodge, duck, evade, get out of, shun, shy away from.

shirker *noun The management won't put up with any shirkers.* bludger (*Australian informal*), idler, layabout, loafer, malingerer, skiver (*informal*), slacker.

shirty *adjective* (*informal*) *He got shirty with me when I corrected him.* angry, annoyed, mad, rude, stroppy (*informal*).

shiver *verb The thought made her shiver.* quake, quaver, quiver, shake, shudder, tremble.

shoal *noun a shoal of fish.* school.

shock *noun* **1** *Several minor shocks were detected after the initial earthquake.* impact, jolt, quake, shake, tremor. **2** *The news came as a terrible shock.* blow, bolt from the blue, bombshell, surprise. **3** *The victim was treated for shock.* trauma. — *verb* **1** *News of the murder shocked everyone.* appal, disgust, dismay, horrify, offend, outrage, scandalise, traumatise, upset. **2** *He was shocked by the findings.* amaze, astonish, astound, dumbfound, stagger, stun, surprise, take aback.

shocking *adjective* **1** *a shocking crime.* appalling, atrocious, disgusting, disturbing, horrific, horrifying, monstrous, outrageous, scandalous, terrible. **2** (*informal*) *shocking weather.* abominable (*informal*), appalling (*informal*), atrocious (*informal*), bad, dreadful (*informal*), foul, terrible (*informal*), unpleasant.

shoddy *adjective shoddy work.* bad, careless, gimcrack, inferior, poor, second-rate, slipshod, sloppy, substandard. OPPOSITE careful.

shoe *noun* [*kinds of shoe*] boot, brogue, clog, court shoe, Loafer (*trade mark*), moccasin, pump, sandal, sandshoe, slipper, sneaker, thong, trainer.

shoemaker *noun* bootmaker, cobbler, shoe repairer.

shonky *adjective* (*Australian informal*) *a shonky salesman.* crooked, dishonest, dodgy (*informal*), shady (*informal*), underhand, unreliable, untrustworthy. OPPOSITE honest.

shoot *verb* **1** *He shot the last round of ammunition.* discharge, fire. **2** *He shot a paper plane across the room.* launch, project, propel, send. **3** *He shot the man.* gun down, hit, kill, snipe at, wound. **4** *The others shot past me.* bolt, charge, dash, fly, race, rush, speed, streak, tear. **5** *The film was shot on location.* film, photograph. — *noun The plant has new shoots.* branch, bud, offshoot, sprig, sprout, sucker, tendril. □ **shoot through** see LEAVE. **shoot up** *The child has shot up.* grow, sprout.

shop *noun* boutique, department store, emporium, mart, megastore, outlet, retailer, salon, store, supermarket.

shore[1] *noun* **1** *They walked along the shore, picking up shells.* beach, coast, foreshore, seashore, seaside, strand (*poetical*). **2** *They had their picnic on the shore of the lake.* bank, edge, side.

shore[2] *verb The wall was shored up.* brace, buttress, prop, support.

short *adjective* **1** *a short person a short tree.* diminutive, dwarf, little, miniature, petite, pygmy, small, squat, stubby, stumpy, stunted, tiny, undersized, wee. OPPOSITE tall. **2** *a short visit.* brief, fleeting, momentary, passing, quick, short-lived.

OPPOSITE long. **3** *Money was short.* deficient, insufficient, lacking, light on (*Australian informal*), limited, low, scanty, scarce, wanting. OPPOSITE abundant. **4** *a short speech.* brief, concise, pithy, succinct, terse, to the point. OPPOSITE long-winded. **5** *He was very short with people.* abrupt, blunt, brusque, curt, gruff, impatient, laconic, sharp, snappy, terse. OPPOSITE patient. — *adverb She stopped short.* abruptly, suddenly, unexpectedly.

shortage *noun a shortage of information. food shortages.* dearth, deficiency, deficit, famine, insufficiency, lack, paucity, scarcity, shortfall, want. OPPOSITE abundance.

shortcoming *noun She knows her shortcomings.* defect, deficiency, failing, fault, flaw, foible, imperfection, limitation, vice, weakness. OPPOSITE strength.

shorten *verb He shortened the book for publication.* abbreviate, abridge, compress, condense, curtail, cut down, diminish, prune, reduce, truncate. OPPOSITE lengthen.

short-lived *adjective His joy was short-lived.* ephemeral, fleeting, passing, temporary, transient. OPPOSITE lasting.

shortly *adverb* **1** *I'll be leaving shortly.* before long, directly, presently, soon. **2** *He answered her shortly.* abruptly, brusquely, curtly, gruffly, impatiently, sharply, tersely. OPPOSITE patiently.

short-sighted *adjective She wears glasses because she is short-sighted.* myopic, near-sighted. OPPOSITE hypermetropic, long-sighted.

short-tempered *adjective* cross, grumpy, hot-tempered, impatient, irascible, irritable, quick-tempered, snappy, testy, tetchy.

shot *noun* **1** *He heard five shots.* bang, blast, discharge, explosion, report. **2** *The gunman fired his last shot.* bullet, pellet, slug. **3** *He's a good shot.* archer, marksman, sharpshooter, shooter, sniper. **4** *You get three shots at the bull's-eye.* attempt, chance, go, try. **5** *They don't need any shots before this trip.* immunisation, injection, jab (*informal*), vaccination. **6** *holiday shots of scenery.* photo, photograph, picture, snapshot.

shoulder *verb* **1** *He shouldered his way through to the front.* elbow, jostle, push, shove. **2** *She shouldered the responsibility.* assume, bear, carry, take on, take upon yourself. OPPOSITE shirk.

shout *noun* **1** *We heard a shout.* bellow, cry, outcry, roar, scream, screech, shriek, yell. **2** (*informal*) *He said that it was his shout.* round, treat, turn. — *verb* **1** *He shouted to the people behind him.* bawl, bellow, call, cry out, roar, scream, screech, shriek, thunder, yell. **2** (*Australian informal*) *He shouted everyone a drink.* pay for, stand, treat.

shove *noun He gave the boy a shove.* push, thrust. — *verb* **1** *He shoved his way through the crowd.* elbow, jostle, push, shoulder, thrust. **2** (*informal*) *Shove it in the drawer.* place, put, stash (*informal*), stick (*informal*), stuff.

shovel *verb He shovelled soil.* dig, excavate, scoop, shift.

show *verb* **1** *The gallery is showing all her work.* display, exhibit, present. **2** *He doesn't usually show his feelings.* disclose, express, indicate, manifest, reveal. OPPOSITE conceal. **3** *He showed us how it works.* demonstrate, describe, explain, illustrate, instruct, point out, teach. **4** *This shows that it can be done.* attest, confirm, demonstrate, prove, verify. **5** *Show the man out.* conduct, direct, escort, guide, lead, usher. **6** *The label is showing.* be visible, stick out. — **noun 1** *a craft show.* display, exhibition, expo (*informal*), exposition, fair, pageant, presentation. **2** (*informal*) *In the evening they went to a show.* entertainment, gig (*informal*), performance, play, production. **3** (*informal*) *He runs the whole show.* business, enterprise, operation, undertaking. □ **show off 1** *He showed off his new car.* display, flaunt, parade. **2** *He loves to show off.* boast, brag, skite (*Australian informal*), swagger, swank (*informal*). **show up 1** *This latest incident has shown up his nasty streak.* expose, highlight, reveal. **2** (*informal*) *He always shows up in the end.* appear, be present, come, front up (*informal*), materialise, turn up.

showdown *noun Management can't avoid a showdown with the workers.* clash, confrontation, crisis, moment of truth.

shower *noun A light shower is forecast.* drizzle, rain, sprinkle. — *verb* **1** *He showered them with the hose.* spatter, spray, sprinkle. **2** *He was showered with presents.* deluge, flood, inundate, overwhelm.

show-off *noun* boaster, braggart, exhibitionist, hoon (*Australian informal*), lair (*Australian informal*), skite (*Australian informal*).

showy *adjective a showy outfit.* bright, brilliant, conspicuous, flamboyant, flashy, garish, gaudy, lairy (*Australian informal*), ostentatious, striking.

shred *noun* **1** a *shred of material.* bit, fragment, piece, scrap, strip; [*shreds*] rags, tatters. **2** *not a shred of evidence.* bit, iota, jot, particle, scrap, skerrick (*Australian informal*), trace. — *verb The documents had to be shredded.* cut up, destroy, rip up, tear up.

shrew *noun The woman had become a bitter old shrew.* battleaxe (*informal*), nag, scold (*old use*), termagant, virago.

shrewd *adjective a shrewd businesswoman.* astute, canny, clever, crafty, cunning, far-sighted, ingenious, intelligent, knowing, perceptive, sagacious, savvy (*informal*), sharp, sly, smart, wily, wise. OPPOSITE stupid.

shriek *noun & verb* cry, howl, scream, screech, squeal, yell.

shrill *adjective She spoke in a shrill voice.* high-pitched, penetrating, piercing, screeching, sharp. OPPOSITE low.

shrine *noun* **1** *They worshipped at the shrine.* altar, chapel, church, mosque, sanctuary, temple. **2** *a shrine of remembrance.* cenotaph, memorial, monument.

shrink *verb* **1** *The membership was shrinking as people drifted away.* contract, decline, diminish, dwindle, reduce. OPPOSITE expand. **2** *He shrank from the accident scene in horror.* back away, draw back, flinch, recoil, retire, retreat, shy away, withdraw.

shrivel *verb The plant has shrivelled.* dehydrate, dry up, shrink, wilt, wither, wrinkle.

shroud *noun The corpse was wrapped in a shroud.* winding-sheet. — *verb* **1** *The body was shrouded.* cover, swathe, wrap. **2** *His past life is shrouded in mystery.* cloak, clothe, conceal, cover, envelop, hide, veil.

shrub *noun* bush, plant.

shrug *verb* **shrug off** *He shrugs off criticism.* dismiss, disregard, ignore, laugh off, make light of, play down.

shudder *verb* **1** *He shuddered at the thought.* quake, quaver, quiver, shake, shiver, tremble. **2** *The washing machine shuddered violently.* judder, rock, shake, vibrate. — *noun a shudder of fear.* convulsion, quake, quiver, shake, shiver, spasm, tremble, tremor, vibration.

shuffle *verb* **1** *He is able to shuffle about now.* hobble, shamble. **2** *Please don't shuffle your feet.* drag, scrape, scuff. **3** *He has shuffled the cards.* jumble, mix, rearrange, reorganise, scramble.

shun *verb He shuns publicity.* avoid, dodge, evade, keep away from, recoil from, shy away from, steer clear of. OPPOSITE seek.

shunt *verb The train was shunted on to a siding.* divert, sidetrack.

shut *verb I shut the door.* bolt, close, fasten, latch, lock, secure. OPPOSITE open. □ **shut out** *They were shut out of the meeting.* bar, exclude, keep out, leave out, lock out. **shut up 1** *He will soon be shut up for five years.* confine, imprison, incarcerate, intern, jail, lock up, put away (*informal*). OPPOSITE release. **2** (*informal*) *He told them to shut up.* be quiet, be silent, stop talking.

shy[1] *adjective She was shy with strangers.* bashful, coy, diffident, hesitant, nervous, reserved, reticent, retiring, self-conscious, timid, timorous. OPPOSITE confident. — *verb The horse shied at the noise.* buck, jump, recoil, start. □ **shy away from** *He shied away from confrontation.* avoid, back away from, flinch from, recoil from, shrink from, shun.

shy[2] *verb He shied a stone at the bushes.* cast, fling, hurl, pitch, throw, toss.

sick *adjective* **1** *He is too sick to go to work.* ailing, bedridden, crook (*Australian informal*), diseased, ill, indisposed, infirm, poorly, sickly, unwell. OPPOSITE well. **2** *She had eaten too much and felt a bit sick.* bilious, nauseous, queasy. **3** *What he has done makes me sick.* angry, annoyed, disgusted, distressed, mad, sickened, upset. □ **be sick** *The cat was sick on the carpet.* barf (*slang*), chuck (*informal*), chunder (*Australian slang*), heave, puke (*informal*), retch, sick up (*informal*), spew, throw up, vomit. **sick of** *He is sick of watching TV.* bored with, fed up with (*informal*), jack of (*Australian slang*), tired of, weary of.

sicken *verb She was sickened by what she saw.* appal, disgust, distress, horrify, nauseate, offend, repel, revolt, shock, upset.

sickly *adjective* **1** *a sickly child.* ailing, delicate, frail, ill, sick, unhealthy, unwell, weak. OPPOSITE healthy. **2** *She looks sickly.* ashen, green, grey, pale, pallid, peaky, wan, yellow. **3** *a sickly taste.* cloying, nauseating, over-sweet, saccharine, sugary, syrupy.

sickness *noun* **1** *They promised to love one another in sickness and in health.* ill health, illness, infirmity. OPPOSITE health. **2** *What are the symptoms of this sickness?* affliction, ailment, bug (*informal*), complaint, disease, disorder, illness, malady. **3** *Many people suffer from motion sickness.* biliousness, nausea, queasiness, vomiting.

side *noun* **1** *Write on the ruled side of the paper.* face, surface. **2** *He stood at the side of the pool.* boundary, brink, edge, fringe, limit, margin, perimeter, periphery, rim, verge. OPPOSITE centre. **3** *the side of a hill.* face, flank, slope. **4** *They studied the problem from every side.* aspect, facet, perspective, position, slant, standpoint, view, viewpoint. **5** *the opposing side.* camp, faction, party, squad, team. — *adjective* **1** *a side shoot.* lateral. **2** *a side issue.* incidental, marginal, secondary, subsidiary. OPPOSITE main. — *verb* **side with** *She sided with them.* ally with, back, defend, go along with, stand up for, stick up for (*informal*), support.

sideboard *noun The china goes in the sideboard.* buffet, cabinet, cupboard, dresser.

sideline *noun* see HOBBY.

sidestep *verb He neatly sidestepped the issue.* avoid, bypass, circumvent, dodge, duck, evade, skirt round.

sidetrack *verb He was sidetracked and forgot what he was meant to be doing.* deflect, distract, divert.

sidewalk *noun* (*American*) footpath, pavement.

sideways *adjective a sideways glance.* indirect, oblique, sidelong. OPPOSITE direct.

sidle *verb He sidled quietly out of the room.* creep, cringe, edge, slink.

siege *noun The city was under siege.* blockade. □ **lay siege to** *The enemy laid siege to the city.* beleaguer, besiege, blockade, encircle, surround.

siesta *noun They took a siesta after lunch.* catnap, forty winks, kip, nap, rest, sleep, snooze.

sieve *noun Pass the mixture through a sieve.* colander, filter, riddle, screen, sifter, strainer. — *verb Sieve the flour.* filter, riddle, sift, strain.

sift *verb* **1** *Sift the flour.* see SIEVE. **2** *She sifted the evidence.* analyse, examine, investigate, review, sort through, study.

sight *noun* **1** *His sight is poor.* eyesight, vision. **2** *It was love at first sight.* appearance, glance, glimpse, look, view. **3** *He disappeared from my sight.* range of vision, view. **4** *The tourists were told of the sights to visit.* display, scene, spectacle. — *verb We sighted land.* behold (*old use*), catch sight of, espy, glimpse, make out, observe, see, spot, spy. □ **in sight 1** *Land was in sight.* in view, visible. **2** *The end was in sight.* approaching, at hand, close, imminent, near.

sightless *adjective* blind, visually impaired.

sightseer *noun* holidaymaker, tourist, traveller, visitor.

sign *noun* **1** *a sign of love. no sign of trouble.* clue, evidence, forewarning, hint, indication, manifestation, omen, pointer, portent, proof, symptom, token, trace, warning. **2** *We saw the sign of the red cross and felt safe.* badge, emblem, insignia, logo, mark, symbol. **3** *He read the sign.* notice, placard, plaque, poster, signboard. **4** *The policeman will give you the sign to go.* cue, gesture, motion, nod, signal, wave. — *verb* **1** *He signed to me to come.* see SIGNAL. **2** *She signed the document.* autograph, countersign, endorse, undersign. □ **sign up** *He signed up at the beginning of the war.* enlist, join up, register, sign on, volunteer.

signal *noun* **1** *We waited for the signal to proceed.* gesture, indication, nod, semaphore, sign, wave. **2** *This was her signal to leave.* cue, sign, tip-off, warning. — *verb He signalled to them to come through.* beckon, direct, gesture, indicate, motion, nod, sign, wave.

significance *noun* **1** *What is the significance of this symbol?* implication, import, meaning, point, purport, sense, signification. **2** *an event of historical significance.* consequence, importance, moment.

significant *adjective* **1** *She gave him a significant look.* eloquent, expressive, knowing, meaningful, pregnant, telling. **2** *a significant achievement.* considerable, great, important, momentous, noteworthy, outstanding, remarkable. OPPOSITE insignificant.

signify *verb* **1** *Red signifies danger. What does this word signify?* be a sign of, betoken, denote, imply, indicate, mean, represent, stand for, symbolise. **2** *They signified their appreciation by applauding.* communicate, convey, demonstrate, express, indicate, intimate, make known, show.

silence *noun the silence of the night.* calm, hush, peace, quietness, stillness, tranquillity. OPPOSITE noise. — *verb They managed to silence the protesters.* gag, hush, muzzle, quieten.

silent *adjective* **1** *a silent person, unable to speak.* dumb, mute, speechless, tongue-tied. **2** *a silent night.* calm, peaceful, quiet, soundless, still, tranquil. OPPOSITE noisy. **3** *She was silent about the incident.* laconic, mum (*informal*), quiet, reserved, reticent, secretive, taciturn, tight-lipped, uncommunicative, unforthcoming. OPPOSITE talkative. **4** *a silent telephone number.* ex-directory, unlisted. OPPOSITE listed.

silhouette *noun I could see his silhouette through the curtain.* contour, form, outline, profile, shadow, shape.

silky *adjective silky material.* fine, satiny, sleek, smooth, soft.

sill *noun a window sill.* ledge.

silly *adjective* **1** *a silly thing to do.* absurd, asinine, childish, crazy, fatuous, foolhardy, foolish, hare-brained, idiotic, illogical, inane, ludicrous, mad, mindless, pointless, reckless, ridiculous, senseless, stupid, unwise. OPPOSITE sensible. **2** *a silly person.* barmy (*slang*), batty (*slang*), crazy, daft (*informal*), dopey (*informal*), dotty (*informal*), feeble-minded, foolish, goofy (*slang*), half-witted, immature, insane, mad, naive, potty (*informal*), scatty (*informal*), stupid. OPPOSITE sensible.

silt *verb* **silt up** *The harbour has silted up.* become obstructed, block up, clog up.

similar *adjective The two cases are similar.* akin, alike, analogous, comparable, equivalent, kindred, like, parallel. OPPOSITE dissimilar.

similarity *noun The similarity of the paintings is striking.* affinity, closeness, correspondence, likeness, resemblance, similitude. OPPOSITE difference, dissimilarity.

simmer *verb The casserole simmered for an hour.* boil, bubble, stew.

simple *adjective* **1** *simple arithmetic.* basic, easy, elementary, rudimentary, straightforward, uncomplicated. OPPOSITE complex, difficult. **2** *simple clothes.* austere, modest, plain, unadorned, unsophisticated. OPPOSITE fancy. **3** *a simple person who doesn't put on airs.* artless, genuine, guileless, honest, ingenuous, natural, sincere, straightforward, unaffected, unpretentious, unsophisticated. OPPOSITE sophisticated. **4** *He was a bit simple and people took advantage of him.* backward, childish, dumb (*informal*), feeble-minded, naive, obtuse, simple-minded, slow, stupid.

simpleton *noun* ass (*informal*), blockhead, bonehead, clot (*informal*), cretin, dill (*Australian informal*), dimwit (*informal*), dodo (*informal*), dolt, dope (*informal*), drip (*informal*), drongo (*Australian informal*), dunce, fool, half-wit, idiot, imbecile, moron (*informal*), mug (*informal*), muggins (*informal*), nincompoop, ninny, nitwit (*informal*), nong (*Australian informal*), sap (*informal*), twit (*slang*).

simplistic *adjective a simplistic view.* facile, oversimplified, shallow, superficial.

simulate *verb He simulated a heart attack.* act, fake, feign, imitate, pretend, sham.

simultaneous *adjective simultaneous events.* coexistent, coincident, concurrent, contemporaneous, parallel.

sin *noun* **1** *a world of sin.* corruption, crime, evil, immorality, iniquity, sinfulness, ungodliness, unrighteousness, vice, wickedness, wrongdoing. OPPOSITE righteousness. **2** *Forgive us our sins.* crime, error, fault, iniquity, misdeed, misdemeanour, offence, peccadillo, transgression, trespass (*old use*), vice, wrong, wrongdoing. OPPOSITE virtue. — *verb He confessed that he had sinned and asked forgiveness.* do wrong, err, go astray, offend, transgress, trespass (*old use*).

sincere *adjective a sincere apology. a sincere person.* artless, authentic, dinkum (*Australian informal*), dinky-di (*Australian informal*), earnest, frank, genuine, guileless, heartfelt, honest, natural, open, real, true. OPPOSITE false, insincere.

sinful *adjective They were punished for their sinful conduct.* bad, blasphemous, corrupt, depraved, evil, immoral, impious, iniquitous, sacrilegious, ungodly, unrighteous, wicked, wrong. OPPOSITE righteous, sinless.

sing *verb* **1** *The man was singing.* carol, chant, croon, hum, serenade, trill, yodel. **2** *The birds were singing.* chirp, chirrup, tweet, twitter, warble. □ **sing out** *Sing out if you need me.* bellow, call, call out, cry out, shout, yell.

singe *verb She singed the sheet she was ironing.* burn, scorch, sear.

singer *noun* chorister, crooner, diva, minstrel, prima donna, songster, troubadour, vocalist.

single *adjective* **1** *There was only a single copy of the book left.* isolated, lone, odd, one, sole, solitary, unique. **2** *single beds.* individual, separate. **3** *a club for single people.* unattached, unmarried. OPPOSITE married. — *verb* **single out** *He was singled out for promotion.* choose, earmark, pick out, select.

single-handed *adverb He moved the bed single-handed.* alone, by yourself, independently, solo, unaided, unassisted.

single-minded *adjective* determined, dogged, obsessive, purposeful, resolute, unswerving, unwavering.

singular *adjective* **1** *singular behaviour.* abnormal, bizarre, curious, eccentric, extraordinary, odd, outlandish, peculiar, queer, strange, uncommon, unconventional, unusual. OPPOSITE common. **2** *a singular talent for music.* exceptional, extraordinary, outstanding, rare, remarkable, unique. OPPOSITE ordinary.

sinister *adjective* **1** *a sinister look.* alarming, disturbing, forbidding, frightening, menacing, ominous, threatening. OPPOSITE benign. **2** *sinister intentions.* bad, criminal, diabolical, evil, malevolent, malignant, vile, villainous, wicked. OPPOSITE good.

sink *verb* **1** *She sank to the ground.* descend, dip, droop, drop, fall, slump, subside. **2** *The sun sank below the horizon.* go down, set. OPPOSITE rise. **3** *The ship sank.* founder, go down, submerge. **4** *They sank the ship.* scupper, scuttle. **5** *He was sinking in strength.* decline, deteriorate, diminish, fade, fail, go downhill, languish, slip, weaken. OPPOSITE rally. **6** *sink a*

shaft or well. bore, dig, drill, excavate. — *noun Wash your hands in the sink.* basin, washbasin. □ **sink in** *The news hasn't sunk in yet.* be absorbed, go in, penetrate, register.

sinner *noun a repentant sinner.* evildoer, malefactor, miscreant, offender, transgressor, trespasser (*old use*), wrongdoer.

sip *noun He had one sip and left the rest.* drink, drop, mouthful, sup, swallow, swig (*informal*), taste.

siren *noun* **1** *an ambulance siren.* alarm, signal, tocsin, warning. **2** *The sirens lured sailors to their death.* enchantress, seductress, temptress.

sissy *noun They teased him and called him a sissy.* coward, cry-baby, sook (*Australian informal*), wimp (*informal*), wuss (*slang*).

sit *verb* **1** *He sat on my chair.* be seated, perch yourself, rest, settle, squat. **2** *The car sits in the garage unused.* lie, remain, stand, stay. **3** *The committee will sit again in a month's time.* assemble, be in session, convene, meet.

site *noun the site for the event.* location, place, position, setting, spot, venue. — *verb The house is conveniently sited.* locate, place, position, situate.

sitting room *noun* drawing room, living room, lounge, parlour (*old use*).

situate *verb The post office is situated next to the bank.* locate, place, position, site.

situation *noun* **1** *Their house is in a beautiful situation.* locality, location, place, position, setting, site, spot. **2** *He was in a difficult situation.* circumstances, plight, position, predicament, state of affairs. **3** *He looked every day in the 'Situations Vacant' column.* employment, job, position, post.

size *noun* **1** *the size of a room.* area, bulk, capacity, dimensions, magnitude, measurements, proportions, scale. **2** *the size of a problem.* extent, magnitude, scale, scope. — *verb* **size up** (*informal*) *He sized up the situation very quickly.* appraise, assess, gauge, judge, weigh up (*informal*).

sizeable *adjective a sizeable sum.* ample, big, considerable, generous, handsome, hefty, large, substantial. OPPOSITE small.

sizzle *verb The sausages sizzled in the pan.* crackle, hiss, sputter.

skate *verb She skated across the ice.* glide, skid, skim, slide.

skeleton *noun* **1** *an animal's skeleton.* bones, frame. **2** *the skeleton of a building.* framework, shell, structure.

skerrick *noun* (*Australian informal*) *She didn't leave a skerrick.* bit, crumb, fragment, jot, particle, scrap, shred, trace.

sketch *noun* **1** *a sketch of the finished house.* design, diagram, drawing, picture. **2** *a sketch of the finished book.* abstract, draft, outline, plan, précis, summary, synopsis. **3** *The drama students performed a sketch.* play, skit.

sketchy *adjective He only has a sketchy idea of what he has to do.* cursory, incomplete, patchy, rough, superficial, vague. OPPOSITE detailed.

skew *adjective a table with skew legs.* oblique, slanting.

skid *verb The car skidded on the wet road.* aquaplane, glide, slide, slip.

skilful *adjective a skilful performer. skilful work.* able, accomplished, adept, adroit, brilliant, capable, clever, competent, consummate, deft, dexterous, expert, gifted, ingenious, masterly, professional, proficient, skilled, talented. OPPOSITE incompetent.

skill *noun a job requiring skill.* ability, adroitness, aptitude, art, capability, cleverness, competence, dexterity, expertise, ingenuity, knack, know-how, mastery, proficiency, prowess, talent. OPPOSITE incompetence.

skim *verb* **1** *He skimmed the fat off the stock.* remove, scrape. **2** *He skimmed over the water in his boat.* fly, glide, sail, sweep. **3** *She skimmed through several books.* flick, flip, glance, leaf, scan, thumb. OPPOSITE pore over.

skimp *verb He didn't skimp on materials.* economise, save, scrimp, stint. OPPOSITE squander.

skimpy *adjective* **1** *a skimpy bikini.* brief, scanty, small. **2** *Some restaurants offer very skimpy serves.* inadequate, insufficient, meagre, small, tiny. OPPOSITE generous, large.

skin *noun* **1** *His skin was damaged by chemicals.* dermis, epidermis. **2** *animal skins.* coat, fur, hide, pelt. **3** *a plastic skin.* casing, coating, covering, exterior, film, membrane. **4** *the skin of fruit and vegetables.* husk, jacket (*of a potato*), peel, rind, shell. — *verb He fell and skinned his knee.* abrade, bark, graze, scrape, scratch.

skin-deep *adjective Beauty is only skin-deep.* external, superficial.

skinflint *noun You won't get money from that skinflint.* cheapskate (*informal*), miser, niggard, scrooge.

skinny *adjective Since dieting he has become too skinny.* bony, emaciated, gaunt, lanky, lean, scraggy, scrawny, slender, thin. OPPOSITE fat.

skip *verb* **1** *They skipped off happily.* bob, bound, caper, cavort, dance, frisk, gambol, hop, leap, prance, romp, run, trip. **2** *They skipped from one subject to another.* flit, jump, pass. **3** *He skipped that page.* leave out, miss, neglect, omit, overlook, pass over. **4** *She skipped the lecture that day.* absent yourself from, cut (*informal*), miss, play truant from, wag (*informal*). OPPOSITE attend.

skirmish *noun skirmishes between rival groups.* altercation, argument, brush, clash, conflict, confrontation, fight, scrap (*informal*), scrimmage, scuffle, struggle, tussle.

skirt *verb* **1** *Skirting the property is a low hedge.* border, bound, circle, edge, encircle, fringe, surround. **2** *He skirted the issue.* avoid, bypass, circumvent, dodge, evade, sidestep.

skit *noun The revue consisted of several very funny skits.* burlesque, parody, satire, send-up (*informal*), sketch, spoof (*informal*), take-off.

skite *verb* (*Australian informal*) *He loves to skite about his achievements.* blow your own trumpet, boast, brag, congratulate yourself, crow, show off, vaunt. — *noun* (*Australian informal*) boaster, braggart, show-off.

skittish *adjective a skittish animal.* excitable, fidgety, frisky, jumpy, lively, nervous, playful, restive, restless. OPPOSITE calm.

skulk *verb He skulked in the shadows.* creep, hide, loiter, lurk, prowl.

sky *noun* air, atmosphere, ether, firmament, heavens, stratosphere.

skyrocket *verb Prices have skyrocketed.* escalate, increase, jump, rise, soar. OPPOSITE plummet.

slab *noun a slab of cake.* block, chunk, hunk, piece, slice, wedge.

slack *adjective* **1** *a slack rope.* floppy, limp, loose, relaxed. OPPOSITE taut, tight. **2** *She's been slack in her work.* careless, casual, lackadaisical, lax, lazy, negligent, offhand, remiss, slapdash, slipshod, sloppy. OPPOSITE diligent. **3** *Business is slack.* inactive, quiet, slow, sluggish. OPPOSITE booming, busy. — *verb Don't*

let him catch you slacking. be lazy, ease off, idle, let up, take it easy.

slacken *verb* **1** *You can slacken the rope now.* let go, loosen, relax, release, slack. OPPOSITE tighten. **2** *They slackened their pace too early.* decrease, ease, reduce, relax, slow down. OPPOSITE increase.

slam *verb* **1** *He slammed the door.* bang, close, shut. **2** *The red car slammed into the white one.* bump, crash, knock, ram, run, smash.

slander *noun If he continues to make up stories about me I shall sue him for slander.* calumny, defamation, denigration, libel, misrepresentation, vilification. — *verb The speaker slandered his opponent.* defame, denigrate, libel, malign, misrepresent, slur, smear, vilify.

slanderous *adjective a slanderous comment.* defamatory, denigratory, libellous, malicious, scurrilous, untrue.

slang *noun thieves' slang.* argot, cant, jargon, lingo (*informal*).

slant *verb* **1** *The floor slants downwards near the drain hole.* incline, lean, list, slope, tilt. **2** *The story has been slanted in his favour.* angle, bias, distort. — *noun* **1** *The floor is on a slant.* angle, incline, list, slope, tilt. **2** *The station presents a different slant on the news.* angle, attitude, bias, perspective, prejudice, view.

slap *verb She slapped his face.* cuff, hit, smack, spank, strike, whack. — *noun She received a slap on the bottom.* blow, cuff, hit, smack, whack. — *adverb He ran slap into the teacher.* bang, directly, headlong, smack (*informal*), straight.

slapdash *adjective His work was slapdash.* careless, haphazard, hasty, perfunctory, slipshod, sloppy. OPPOSITE careful.

slash *verb* **1** *The box has been slashed open.* cut, gash, hack, rip, slice, slit, tear. **2** *Prices were slashed.* cut, drop, lower, reduce. — *noun* **1** *a slash made by a knife.* cut, gash, incision, laceration, rip, slit. **2** *Put a slash through the mistake.* line, oblique, stroke.

slaughter *noun the slaughter of innocent people.* bloodbath, bloodshed, butchery, carnage, killing, massacre, murder, pogrom, slaying. — *verb* **1** *The animals were slaughtered.* butcher, destroy, kill. **2** *The soldiers slaughtered civilians.* annihilate, butcher, execute, exterminate, kill, massacre, murder, slay. **3** (*informal*) *We were slaughtered by the other team.* beat, defeat, rout, thrash, trounce.

slave *noun The boy was sold as a slave.* serf, servant, vassal. — *verb She slaves all day in the kitchen.* drudge, grind away, labour, slog, sweat, toil, work hard.

slave-driver *noun He works for a slave-driver.* despot, oppressor, taskmaster, tyrant.

slavery *noun He was sold into slavery.* bondage, captivity, enslavement, serfdom, servitude, thraldom. OPPOSITE freedom.

slavish *adjective* **1** *slavish devotion to his master.* obsequious, servile, submissive, subservient. **2** *a slavish copy.* unimaginative, unoriginal.

slay *verb* assassinate, execute, kill, massacre, murder, put to death, slaughter.

sleazy *adjective* (*informal*) *a sleazy hotel.* dirty, disreputable, seedy, shabby, sordid, squalid, unsavoury. OPPOSITE respectable.

sledge *noun* bob sled, bob-sleigh, luge, sled, sleigh, toboggan.

sleek *adjective She has beautiful sleek hair.* glossy, lustrous, shiny, silky, smooth. OPPOSITE dull.

sleep *noun* **1** *an afternoon sleep.* catnap, doze, forty winks, kip (*slang*), nap, repose, rest, shut-eye (*informal*), siesta, slumber, snooze. **2** *the animal's winter sleep.* dormancy, hibernation. — *verb He can sleep anywhere.* catnap, doze, drop off, kip (*slang*), nap, nod off, rest, slumber, snooze.

sleepless *adjective a sleepless night.* disturbed, restless, wakeful.

sleeplessness *noun* insomnia, wakefulness.

sleepwalker *noun* noctambulist, somnambulist.

sleepy *adjective* **1** *The hot weather makes him feel sleepy.* dopey (*informal*), drowsy, lethargic, somnolent, tired, torpid, weary. OPPOSITE wide awake. **2** *a sleepy little outback town.* dormant, inactive, peaceful, quiet. OPPOSITE busy.

sleeve *noun a protective sleeve.* case, casing, cover, sheath.

sleight *noun* **sleight of hand** *a magician's sleight of hand.* conjuring, dexterity, legerdemain, trickery.

slender *adjective* **1** *a slender figure.* lean, slight, slim, svelte, thin. OPPOSITE stout. **2** *a slender hope.* faint, feeble, remote, slight, slim, small, weak. OPPOSITE strong.

sleuth *noun an amateur sleuth.* detective, investigator, private eye (*informal*).

slice *noun* **1** *a slice of cake.* chunk, piece, portion, segment, sliver, wedge. **2** *a slice of the profits.* cut, part, portion, proportion, share. — *verb* **1** *He sliced the chicken.* carve, cut, divide. **2** *He sliced off the top layer.* pare, peel, shave, trim, whittle.

slick *adjective a slick salesman.* clever, cunning, glib, sly, smarmy (*informal*), smooth.

slide *verb He slid down the hill.* coast, glide, glissade, skate, skid, slip, slither.

slight *adjective* **1** *a slight difference.* imperceptible, infinitesimal, insignificant, little, minor, minute, negligible, small, subtle, superficial, tiny, trivial. OPPOSITE considerable, great. **2** *a girl of slight build.* delicate, frail, lean, slender, slim, thin. OPPOSITE heavy, large. — *verb She felt slighted because she wasn't invited.* affront, ignore, insult, rebuff, scorn, snub.

slim *adjective* **1** *a slim person.* lean, slender, slight, svelte, thin. OPPOSITE fat. **2** *a slim chance.* faint, feeble, remote, slender, slight, small. OPPOSITE strong. — *verb* diet, lose weight, reduce weight.

slime *noun The pipes were full of slime.* goo (*informal*), gunge (*informal*), gunk (*informal*), muck, mud, ooze, sludge.

slimy *adjective* **1** *a slimy substance.* gooey (*informal*), gungy (*informal*), mucky, muddy, oozy, slippery, sludgy, viscous. **2** *a slimy character.* crawling, obsequious, oily, slick, smarmy (*informal*), smooth, unctuous.

sling *noun* **1** *His injured arm was in a sling.* bandage, belt, strap, support. **2** *He shot stones from his sling.* catapult, shanghai (*Australian*), slingshot. — *verb* **1** *He slung the hammock between two trees.* dangle, hang, suspend, swing. **2** (*informal*) *He slung his bag on the floor.* cast, chuck (*informal*), fling, hurl, throw, toss. □ **sling off at** see MOCK.

slink *verb He slunk out of the room.* creep, edge, skulk, slip, sneak, steal.

slinky *adjective a slinky dress.* clinging, close-fitting, sinuous, tight-fitting.

slip *verb* **1** *She slipped on the wet floor.* fall, glide, skid, slide, slither. **2** *She slipped out of the room.* creep, skulk, slink, sneak, steal. **3** *Slip these stitches off the needle.* detach, release. — *noun* **1** *Avoid slips by moving slowly.* fall, glide, skid, slide. **2** *He can be forgiven for a minor slip.* blue (*Australian informal*), blunder, booboo (*slang*), error, lapse, mistake, slip-up (*informal*). **3** *The dress needs a slip underneath.* petticoat. **4** *The pillows need clean slips.* case, cover, pillowcase, pillowslip. **5** *He handed me a slip of paper.* piece, scrap, sheet, strip. □ **give the slip** *He gave me the slip.* avoid, dodge, elude, escape, evade, lose. **slip up** (*informal*) *We rely on you not to slip up.* blunder, err, goof (*slang*), make a mistake.

slippery *adjective a slippery surface.* greasy, oily, slick, slithery, smooth, wet.

slipshod *adjective His work was slipshod.* careless, lax, messy, shoddy, slapdash, sloppy, slovenly, unmethodical. OPPOSITE careful.

slit *noun a slit in the wall. a slit in her skirt.* crack, cut, fissure, gash, hole, incision, opening, rip, slash, slot, split, tear. — *verb She slit the seam.* cut, gash, rip, slash, split, tear.

slither *verb The snake slithered across the path.* slide, slink, slip.

sliver *noun almond slivers.* flake, fragment, piece, shaving, slice, strip.

slobber *verb The dog slobbered on her skirt.* dribble, drool, salivate, slaver.

slog *verb* **1** *He slogged the ball.* hit, strike, thump, whack. **2** *He slogged away at his work for hours.* grind, labour, plod, plough, toil, work. **3** *They slogged on through the scrub for another ten kilometres.* plod, plough, tramp, trek, trudge.

slogan *noun an advertising slogan.* catchphrase, catchword, jingle, motto.

slop *verb She slopped her tea over her books.* slosh (*informal*), spill, splash, splatter. □ **slops** *plural noun The pigs are fed the kitchen slops.* dregs, refuse, swill, waste.

slope *verb The road slopes steeply.* ascend, bank, descend, drop, incline, rise, slant, tilt, tip. — *noun a steep slope.* angle, ascent, bank, descent, escarpment, grade, gradient, hill, hillside, inclination, incline, pitch, rake, ramp, rise, scarp, slant, tilt.

sloppy *adjective* **1** *sloppy food.* gooey (*informal*), liquid, runny, watery. OPPOSITE solid. **2** *sloppy work.* careless, lax, messy, shoddy, slapdash, slipshod, slovenly, unmethodical, untidy. OPPOSITE careful. **3** *sloppy love letters.* mushy, romantic, sentimental, soppy (*informal*).

slot *noun* **1** *He put the coin in the slot.* groove, hole, opening, slit. **2** *Each patient has a ten-minute slot.* place, position, space, spot, time. — *verb The doctor slotted two extra patients in.* fit, schedule.

slothful *adjective The slothful worker was dismissed.* idle, inactive, indolent, lazy, slack, sluggish. OPPOSITE industrious.

slouch *verb When he's tired he tends to slouch.* droop, hunch, loll, sag, slump, stoop.

slovenly *adjective* **1** *a slovenly appearance.* careless, dirty, disreputable, messy, scruffy, slatternly, unkempt, untidy. OPPOSITE neat. **2** *slovenly work.* see SLOPPY.

slow *adjective* **1** *a slow pace.* dawdling, deliberate, leisurely, measured, plodding, sluggish, steady, unhurried. OPPOSITE fast. **2** *a slow process.* drawn-out, endless, gradual, interminable, long, painstaking, prolonged, protracted, time-consuming. OPPOSITE quick. **3** *a slow response.* delayed, dilatory, late, tardy. OPPOSITE hasty, quick. **4** *You may need to explain it again, as he is a bit slow.* dense, dim, dull, dumb (*informal*), obtuse, stupid, thick (*informal*). OPPOSITE clever, quick. **5** *Business is slow today.* dead, dull, quiet, slack, sluggish. OPPOSITE brisk, lively. — *verb* **1** *Cars must slow down for this corner.* brake, decelerate, reduce speed. OPPOSITE accelerate. **2** *Illness has slowed her progress on the work.* delay, hinder, hold back, impede, retard. OPPOSITE speed up.

slowcoach *noun* dawdler, laggard, sluggard, straggler.

slowly *adverb* at a snail's pace, gradually, sluggishly, steadily, unhurriedly. OPPOSITE quickly.

sludge *noun The drain was blocked with sludge.* goo (*informal*), mire, muck, mud, silt, slime, slush.

slug *verb* **1** *He slugged his opponent.* see HIT. **2** (*Australian informal*) *He was slugged with a huge fine.* charge, hit, tax.

sluggish *adjective* **1** *a sluggish person.* inactive, indolent, inert, lazy, lethargic, listless, phlegmatic, slothful, torpid. OPPOSITE lively. **2** *Business was sluggish.* quiet, slack, slow. OPPOSITE brisk, busy.

slumber *noun The princess fell into a deep slumber.* repose, rest, sleep. — *verb He found the princess slumbering.* doze, nap, rest, sleep, snooze.

slump *noun* **1** *The country was facing a slump.* decline, depression, downturn, recession, setback. OPPOSITE upturn. **2** *a slump in prices.* collapse, crash, decline, drop, fall, tumble. OPPOSITE improvement, increase. — *verb* **1** *The value of his shares slumped.* collapse, crash, decline, drop, fall, nosedive, plummet, plunge, tumble. OPPOSITE improve. **2** *She slumped into the chair.* collapse, drop, fall, flop, sink, tumble.

slur *verb When he is tired he slurs his words.* mumble, mutter. — *noun His enemies cast a slur on his reputation.* aspersion, blot, insult, libel, slander, slight, smear, stain, stigma.

sly *adjective* **1** *He is a sly character.* artful, crafty, cunning, devious, foxy, furtive, secretive, shifty, shrewd, sneaky, underhand, wily. OPPOSITE straightforward. **2** *She did it with a sly smile.* arch, knowing, mischievous, playful, roguish.

smack[1] *noun a smack on the bottom.* blow, hit, rap, slap, spanking, whack. — *verb He smacked the child.* belt (*slang*), hit, rap, slap, spank, strike, wallop (*informal*), whack. — *adverb* (*informal*) *He ran smack into the car in front.* bang, directly, slap, straight.

smack[2] *verb His manner smacks of conceit.* savour, suggest.

small *adjective* **1** *a small object.* baby, compact, diminutive, dwarf, little, microscopic, miniature, mini, minuscule, minute, pocket-sized, poky, puny, stunted, teeny (*informal*), tiny, undersized, wee, weeny (*informal*). OPPOSITE big, large. **2** *a small person.* little, petite, short, slender, slight. **3** *a small amount.* imperceptible, infinitesimal, insignificant, little, meagre, measly (*informal*), minimal, negligible, paltry, petty, scant, scanty, trifling, trivial. OPPOSITE big. **4** *He said it in a small voice.* faint, feeble, little, quiet, soft, subdued, weak. OPPOSITE loud, strong.

small-minded *adjective* bigoted, hidebound, intolerant, narrow-minded, petty, prejudiced, selfish, ungenerous. OPPOSITE broad-minded.

smart *adjective* **1** *a smart pace.* brisk, cracking (*slang*), energetic, fast, jaunty, quick, swift, vigorous. OPPOSITE slow. **2** *a smart student.* able, astute, brainy, bright, capable, clever, ingenious, intelligent, keen, sharp. OPPOSITE dull. **3** *That wasn't a very smart thing to do.* clever, prudent, sensible, shrewd, wise. OPPOSITE silly, stupid. **4** *a smart appearance.* chic, dapper, dolled up (*informal*), elegant, fashionable, natty (*informal*), neat, posh (*informal*), snappy (*informal*), snazzy (*informal*), spruce, stylish, swanky (*informal*), swish (*informal*), trim. OPPOSITE dowdy, untidy. — *verb Onions make her eyes smart.* hurt, sting, throb.

smash *verb* **1** *The glass smashed.* break, crash, shatter, shiver, splinter. **2** *He smashed the door down.* bash, batter, break, hammer, hit, knock, pound, strike. **3** *The car smashed into the bus.* bang, bump, collide (with), crash, hit, knock, ram, run, slam. — *noun a smash on the freeway.* accident, bingle (*Australian informal*), collision, crash, pile-up (*informal*), prang (*slang*). □ **smash hit** (*informal*) *The song was a smash hit.* hit, success, triumph, winner. OPPOSITE flop (*informal*).

smear *verb* **1** *The baby smeared her high chair with jam.* coat, cover, daub, plaster, rub, spread. **2** *The newspaper smeared the doctor's reputation.* blacken, defame, denigrate, malign, slander, slur, smirch, sully, vilify. — *noun paint smears on his face.* blotch, mark, smudge, splotch, stain, streak.

smell *noun* **1** *What sort of smell was it?* aroma, bouquet, fragrance, odour, perfume, redolence, scent, whiff. **2** *The smell of rotten meat filled the shop.* pong (*informal*), reek, stench, stink. — *verb* **1** *She smelt the wine before sipping it.* nose, scent, sniff. **2** *The refrigerator smells.* pong (*informal*), reek, stink.

smelly *adjective a smelly rubbish dump.* foul-smelling, high, malodorous, noisome (*literary*), on the nose (*Australian informal*), pongy (*informal*), putrid, rancid, rank, reeking, stinking. OPPOSITE fragrant, odourless.

smile *noun & verb* beam, grin, simper, smirk. OPPOSITE frown.

smirk *noun & verb* grin, simper, smile, sneer.

smitten *adjective He was smitten with her.* besotted, bowled over, captivated, enchanted, enthralled, infatuated.

smoke *noun* **1** *The smoke was choking them.* exhaust, fumes, smog. **2** (*informal*) *a packet of smokes.* cigar, cigarette, fag (*slang*). — *verb The fire is only smoking now.* fume, smoulder.

smoko *noun* (*Australian informal*) coffee break, rest, spell (*Australian*), tea break.

smooth *adjective* **1** *a smooth surface.* even, flat, flush, level, unbroken. OPPOSITE rough. **2** *smooth hair.* glossy, shiny, silky, sleek, soft, velvety. **3** *a smooth batter.* creamy, flowing, runny. OPPOSITE lumpy. **4** *a smooth voice.* dulcet, mellow, pleasant, soothing, sweet. OPPOSITE harsh. **5** *smooth seas.* calm, even, flat, peaceful, still, unruffled. OPPOSITE rough. **6** *the smooth running of the school.* calm, orderly, steady, well-regulated. OPPOSITE disorderly. **7** *a smooth talker.* facile, glib, persuasive, plausible, slick, smarmy (*informal*), suave, unctuous. — *verb* **1** *smooth the sheets.* even, flatten, iron, level, press. **2** *smooth the timber.* file, plane, sand, sandpaper. **3** *He went ahead to smooth the way.* clear, ease, open, pave, prepare.

smoothly *adverb All went smoothly.* easily, straightforwardly, well, without a hitch.

smother *verb* **1** *He smothered his victim with a pillow.* asphyxiate, choke, stifle, suffocate. **2** *They smothered the fire with a blanket.* extinguish, put out, quench, snuff. **3** *The pie was smothered with cream.* cover. **4** *She smothered her resentment.* conceal, hide, hold back, repress, restrain, stifle, suppress.

smoulder *verb* *The fire was still smouldering.* burn, smoke.

smudge *noun* *There were smudges of ink on her book.* blot, blotch, mark, smear, splash, splotch, spot, stain, streak. — *verb He smudged his work.* blot, smear, stain, streak.

smug *adjective* *a smug smile.* complacent, conceited, self-righteous, self-satisfied, supercilious, superior. OPPOSITE humble.

smuggling *noun* bootlegging, contraband, drug running, gunrunning.

snack *noun* **1** *We have a snack at about 11 o'clock.* bite, playlunch, recess, refreshments. **2** (*Australian informal*) *The exam was a snack.* bludge (*Australian informal*), breeze (*informal*), cinch (*informal*), doddle (*informal*), piece of cake (*informal*), pushover (*informal*). □ **snack bar** canteen, deli (*informal*), kiosk (*Australian*), milk bar, sandwich shop, takeaway.

snag *noun* *There's just one snag.* catch, difficulty, hitch, impediment, obstacle, obstruction, problem, stumbling block. — *verb She snagged her stockings.* catch, rip, tear.

snake *noun* serpent.

snaky *adjective* (*Australian informal*) *He got quite snaky when asked for money.* angry, annoyed, bad-tempered, crabby, irritable, shirty (*informal*).

snap *verb* **1** *The teacher snapped his fingers.* click, crack. **2** *The branch snapped.* break, crack, fracture, give way, split. **3** *The dog snapped at his heels.* bite, gnash, nip. **4** *He lost his temper and snapped at them.* bark, growl, snarl. **5** *He snapped the scene with his camera.* photograph, shoot. — *noun* **1** *They heard a snap.* click, crack, crackle, fracture, pop. **2** *a cold snap.* period, spell, stretch. **3** *holiday snaps.* photo, photograph, picture, snapshot. — *adjective a snap decision.* hasty, precipitate, quick, sudden. □ **snap up** *If an opportunity comes, snap it up.* accept, grab, seize, snatch, take.

snappy *adjective* (*informal*) **1** *a snappy performance.* brisk, energetic, fast, lively, vigorous, zippy. OPPOSITE slow. **2** *a snappy dresser.* chic, dapper, elegant, fashionable, neat, smart, trendy (*informal*). OPPOSITE dowdy. **3** *a snappy mood.* crabby, cross, crotchety, grumpy, irascible, irritable, short-tempered, testy, tetchy.

snare *noun* **1** *The wombat was caught in a snare.* gin, net, noose, trap. **2** *I warned him of the many snares.* danger, peril, pitfall, trap. — *verb He snared a fox.* capture, catch, ensnare, entrap, trap.

snarl¹ *verb* *The dog snarled at the postman.* bare your teeth, growl.

snarl² *verb* *The thread has snarled.* entangle, entwine, knot, tangle, twist. — *noun a traffic snarl.* blockage, hold-up, jam, obstruction, tangle.

snatch *verb* *The thief snatched her handbag.* grab, nab (*informal*), pluck, seize, snitch (*slang*), steal, swipe (*informal*), take.

sneak *verb* **1** *He is sneaking out.* creep, slink, slip, steal, tiptoe. **2** (*informal*) *He sneaked a book from the library.* smuggle, snitch (*informal*), steal. **3** (*informal*) *We couldn't trust him not to sneak on us.* betray, dob (*Australian informal*),

grass (*slang*), inform, rat (*informal*), report, shop (*slang*), split (*slang*), tell, tell tales.

sneaky *adjective* *a sneaky person.* crafty, cunning, deceitful, devious, furtive, secretive, shifty, slippery, sly, stealthy, treacherous, underhand, wily. OPPOSITE open.

sneer *verb* **sneer at** *He sneered at their efforts.* deride, disdain, gibe at, jeer at, laugh at, mock, ridicule, scoff at, scorn, snigger at.

sniff *verb* **1** *Blow your nose instead of sniffing.* sniffle, snivel, snuffle. **2** *She sniffed the wine.* nose, smell.

sniffle *verb* *He has a cold and is sniffling.* sniff, snivel, snuffle.

snigger *noun & verb* chuckle, giggle, snicker, titter; see also SNEER.

snip *verb* *She snipped her hair.* clip, crop, cut, lop, prune, trim.

snipe *verb* *The gunman sniped at the president from a tall building.* fire, shoot.

snippet *noun* *He only caught snippets of the news.* bit, extract, fragment, part, snatch.

snivel *verb* *What was she snivelling about?* blubber, cry, sob, weep, whimper, whine; see also SNIFFLE.

snobbish *adjective* *A snobbish person has few friends.* condescending, disdainful, haughty, patronising, pompous, pretentious, snooty (*informal*), stuck-up (*informal*), supercilious, superior, toffee-nosed (*informal*). OPPOSITE humble.

snoop *verb* (*informal*) *The neighbour caught him snooping.* nose around, poke around, pry, spy, stickybeak (*Australian informal*).

snooze *noun* *She had a snooze in the armchair.* catnap, doze, forty winks, kip (*slang*), nap, rest, siesta, sleep. — *verb She snoozed in the chair in the evening.* catnap, doze, kip (*slang*), nap, rest, sleep.

snub *verb* *She snubbed him publicly.* cold-shoulder, give someone the brush-off, humiliate, ignore, insult, rebuff, reject, scorn.

snuffle *verb* *The baby snuffled in her bassinet.* sniff, sniffle, snivel.

snug *adjective* **1** *snug in bed.* comfortable, comfy (*informal*), cosy, secure, warm. **2** *a snug fit.* close, tight.

snuggle *verb* *The cat snuggled up on her lap.* cuddle, curl up, huddle, nestle.

soak *verb* **1** *Soak the stained clothes in bleach.* immerse, souse, steep, submerge, wet. **2** *The dye soaked through.* penetrate, permeate, seep. **3** *The rain soaked the washing.* drench, saturate, wet. □ **soak up** *They soaked up the spill with an old nappy.* absorb, sop up, take up.

soar *verb* **1** *The bird soared higher and higher.* ascend, fly, rise. OPPOSITE descend. **2** *The price of new cars has soared.* climb, escalate, increase, mount, rise, rocket. OPPOSITE drop.

sob *verb* *He sobbed uncontrollably.* bawl, blubber, cry, snivel, wail, weep.

sober *adjective* **1** *Her friends got drunk but she stayed sober.* abstemious, abstinent, clear-headed, lucid, on the wagon (*informal*), teetotal, temperate. OPPOSITE drunk. **2** *She is a sober person, not given to frivolity.* calm, earnest, grave, level-headed, restrained, sedate, self-controlled, sensible, serious, solemn, staid. OPPOSITE frivolous. **3** *sober colours.* drab, dreary, dull, inconspicuous, sombre, subdued. OPPOSITE bright, gaudy.

sociable *adjective* *She has become more sociable as she has grown older.* affable, communicative, companionable, convivial, extroverted, friendly, gregarious, outgoing, social. OPPOSITE unsociable.

social *adjective* **1** *Ants are social creatures.* cooperative, gregarious, interdependent. OPPOSITE independent, solitary. **2** *social problems.* community, public. **3** *She is not a social person.* see SOCIABLE. — *noun They went to the social on Saturday night.* dance, disco (*informal*), do (*informal*), function, gathering, get-together (*informal*), party.

society *noun* **1** *an outrage against society.* community, humanity, mankind, the public. **2** *members of different societies.* civilisation, community, culture, nation, people. **3** *They are happy in each other's society.* companionship, company, fellowship, presence. **4** *They joined a historical society.* association, body, club, group, guild, organisation, union.

sodden *adjective* *Everything was sodden from the rain.* drenched, saturated, soaked, soggy, sopping, waterlogged, wet. OPPOSITE dry.

sofa *noun* couch, settee.

soft *adjective* **1** *soft plastics.* flexible, malleable, pliable, supple. OPPOSITE hard. **2** *a soft pillow.* floppy, limp, spongy, springy, squashy. OPPOSITE firm. **3** *soft fabrics.* fleecy, satiny, silky, sleek, smooth, velvety. OPPOSITE rough. **4** *soft voices.* faint, gentle, hushed, inaudible, low, mellow, muted, quiet, subdued. OPPOSITE loud. **5** *soft colours.* delicate, light, pale, pastel, restful, subdued. OPPOSITE bright. **6** *His muscles have gone soft through lack of exercise.* feeble, flabby, flaccid, weak. OPPOSITE firm. **7** *He's too soft with the children: they need a firmer hand.* easygoing, indulgent, lax, lenient, permissive; see also SOFT-HEARTED. OPPOSITE firm, tough. **8** (*informal*) *a soft job.* comfortable, cosy, cushy (*informal*), easy, undemanding. OPPOSITE demanding, difficult. **9** *soft drink.* non-alcoholic. OPPOSITE alcoholic.

soften *verb* **1** *He softened his voice to speak to the child.* lower, moderate, quieten, subdue, tone down. OPPOSITE raise. **2** *This will soften the impact.* buffer, cushion, dampen, deaden, lessen, reduce. OPPOSITE intensify.

soft-hearted *adjective* caring, compassionate, generous, gentle, kind, merciful, mild, soft, sympathetic, tender-hearted, understanding, warm-hearted.

soggy *adjective* **1** *The washing was still soggy.* drenched, saturated, soaked, sodden, sopping, waterlogged, wet. OPPOSITE dry. **2** *soggy damper.* doughy, heavy, moist, stodgy. OPPOSITE light.

soil¹ *noun* **1** *He tills the soil.* dirt, earth, ground, loam. **2** *on her home soil.* country, ground, land, territory.

soil² *verb* *He soiled his new jumper.* blacken, dirty, stain. OPPOSITE clean.

solace *noun* *She found solace in poetry.* comfort, consolation, relief.

soldier *noun* commando, conscript, fighter, GI (*American*), marine, mercenary, NCO, private, regular, serviceman, servicewoman, trooper, warrior.

sole *adjective* **1** *the sole survivor.* lone, only, single, solitary. **2** *The channel has the sole right to show the tennis.* exclusive. OPPOSITE joint.

solemn *adjective* **1** *We don't want any solemn faces in this room.* earnest, glum, grave, sad, sedate, serious, sober, sombre, staid, unsmiling. OPPOSITE cheerful. **2** *a solemn occasion.* awesome, ceremonial, ceremonious, dignified, formal, grand, important, impressive, stately. OPPOSITE frivolous.

solicit *verb* *He solicited help.* appeal for, ask for, beg for, request, seek.

solicitor *noun* see LAWYER.

solicitous *adjective* *He was very solicitous about my welfare.* anxious, concerned, considerate, thoughtful, troubled, worried. OPPOSITE unconcerned.

solid *adjective* **1** *a solid substance.* compact, dense, firm, hard, rigid, stable. OPPOSITE fluid, hollow. **2** *solid silver.* pure, unadulterated, unalloyed. **3** *They talked for two solid hours.* continuous, unbroken, uninterrupted. **4** *a solid table.* durable, robust, sound, stout, strong, sturdy, substantial. OPPOSITE flimsy. **5** *solid evidence.* concrete, reliable, sound, strong, tangible, weighty. OPPOSITE flimsy. **6** *The members of the union are solid on conservation.* unanimous, undivided, united. OPPOSITE divided.

solidarity *noun* *the solidarity of union members.* agreement, harmony, like-mindedness, unanimity, unity. OPPOSITE disunity.

solidify *verb* *The mixture solidified.* congeal, gel, harden, jell, set. OPPOSITE liquefy.

soliloquy *noun* monologue; see also SPEECH.

solitary *adjective* **1** *a solitary walker.* alone, lone, single, sole, solo, unaccompanied. **2** *a solitary example.* isolated, one and only, single, sole. **3** *He found a solitary spot to meditate and pray.* deserted, desolate, empty, isolated, lonely, remote, secluded, unfrequented. OPPOSITE busy.

solo *adverb* *He flew solo.* alone, by yourself, independently, on your own, single-handed, unaccompanied.

solution *noun* **1** *a solution of salt and water.* blend, mixture. **2** *a solution to the problem.* answer, explanation, key, remedy, resolution, result.

solve *verb* *He has solved the puzzle.* answer, crack, decipher, figure out, resolve, work out.

sombre *adjective* **1** *sombre colours.* dark, drab, dreary, dull, gloomy, sober. OPPOSITE bright. **2** *a sombre mood.* dismal, funereal, gloomy, grave, melancholy, sad, serious, sober, solemn. OPPOSITE cheerful.

sometime *adjective* *her sometime friend.* erstwhile, former, one-time.

sometimes *adverb* *They drop in sometimes.* every so often, from time to time, now and then, occasionally, on and off. OPPOSITE never.

song *noun* *Sing me a song.* air, anthem, aria, ballad, canticle, carol, chant, chorus, ditty, hymn, jingle, lay (*old use*), lied, lullaby, madrigal, number, psalm, serenade, shanty.

sonorous *adjective* *a sonorous voice.* deep, loud, powerful, resonant, resounding, reverberant, rich.

sook *noun* (*Australian informal*) *Don't be such a sook.* baby, coward, cry-baby, sissy, softie (*informal*), wimp (*informal*), wuss (*slang*).

sool *verb* (*Australian informal*) *He sooled the dogs on the intruder.* egg on, goad, incite, urge.

soon *adverb* **1** *They'll be here soon.* anon (*old use*), before long, by and by, presently, shortly. **2** *The rain came too soon.* early, quickly. OPPOSITE late.

soothe *verb* **1** *It was hard to soothe the dissatisfied customer.* appease, calm, mollify, pacify, placate. OPPOSITE upset. **2** *The ointment soothed the pain.* alleviate, assuage, ease, mitigate, palliate, reduce, relieve. OPPOSITE aggravate.

sooty *adjective* **1** *a sooty chimney.* dirty, grimy. **2** *The cat was a sooty colour.* black, blackish, charcoal.

sophisticated *adjective* **1** *a sophisticated audience.* cosmopolitan, cultivated, cultured, experienced, refined, urbane, worldly, worldly-wise. OPPOSITE naive, unsophisticated. **2** *a sophisticated gadget.* advanced, complex, complicated, elaborate, intricate. OPPOSITE crude.

sopping *adjective She came home sopping.* drenched, dripping, saturated, soaked, sodden, wet. OPPOSITE dry.

sorcerer *noun* enchanter, magician, warlock, wizard.

sorceress *noun* enchantress, magician, witch.

sorcery *noun* black magic, enchantment, magic, witchcraft, wizardry.

sordid *adjective* **1** *sordid living conditions.* dirty, filthy, foul, putrid, seamy, seedy, sleazy, squalid. OPPOSITE clean. **2** *a sordid business.* base, dishonourable, mean, mercenary, shabby, vile. OPPOSITE honourable.

sore *adjective* **1** *a sore ankle.* aching, bruised, chafed, grazed, hurting, inflamed, injured, painful, sensitive, smarting, stinging, tender, uncomfortable. **2** *He was feeling sore about losing.* aggrieved, angry, annoyed, distressed, irritated, peeved (*informal*), touchy, upset, vexed. — *noun The sores took a long time to heal.* abrasion, abscess, blister, boil, burn, graze, inflammation, laceration, scratch, ulcer, wound.

sorrow *noun* **1** *His death caused her great sorrow.* anguish, distress, grief, heartache, misery, regret, sadness, suffering, unhappiness, woe. OPPOSITE joy. **2** *She faced many sorrows in her life.* affliction, hardship, misfortune, trial, tribulation, trouble.

sorrowful *adjective* see SAD.

sorry *adjective* **1** *She was sorry about what she had done.* apologetic, contrite, penitent, regretful, remorseful, repentant, rueful, sad, sorrowful. OPPOSITE unrepentant. **2** *She felt sorry for the victims.* compassionate, pitying, sympathetic, understanding. OPPOSITE unsympathetic. **3** *Things were in a sorry state.* bad, deplorable, dreadful, lamentable, miserable, pitiful, terrible, woeful, wretched.

sort *noun different sorts of things.* brand, breed, category, class, form, genus, group, kind, make, species, style, type, variety. — *verb* **1** *The specimens have been sorted into groups.* arrange, categorise, class, classify, divide, grade, group, organise. **2** *Sort the grain from the chaff.* pick out, segregate, select, separate, sift. OPPOSITE mix. □ **sort out 1** *They sorted out the pile of ribbons.* disentangle, organise, straighten out, tidy. **2** *He will sort out the problem.* attend to, clear up, deal with, handle, resolve, solve.

soul *noun* **1** *a person's soul.* psyche, spirit. **2** *not a soul in sight.* creature, individual, person.

soulful *adjective soulful music.* emotional, expressive, inspiring, moving, passionate, profound, stirring.

sound[1] *noun He didn't hear a sound.* noise. — *verb* **1** *The g in 'gnat' is not sounded.* enunciate, pronounce, speak, utter, voice. **2** *It sounds all right.* appear, seem. **3** *The bells sounded the start of business.* announce, signal.

sound[2] *verb He sounded the depth of the river.* fathom, measure, plumb, probe, test. □ **sound out** see QUESTION.

sound[3] *adjective* **1** *sound in mind and body.* fit, healthy, robust, well. OPPOSITE unhealthy. **2** *The house was structurally sound.* intact, solid, strong, sturdy, well-built. OPPOSITE damaged. **3** *a sound argument.* cogent, coherent, logical, rational, reasonable, solid, well-founded. OPPOSITE illogical. **4** *a sound investment.* reliable, safe, secure, solid. OPPOSITE risky. **5** *a sound sleep.* continuous, deep, unbroken, uninterrupted. OPPOSITE disturbed, light.

soup *noun* bisque, broth, chowder, consommé.

sour *adjective* **1** *a sour taste.* acid, acidic, astringent, mouth-puckering, sharp, tangy, tart, vinegary. OPPOSITE sweet. **2** *The milk has gone sour.* bad, curdled, fermented, off, rancid, stale. OPPOSITE fresh. **3** *Nobody liked the new teacher who always looked so sour.* bad-tempered, bitter, crabby, disagreeable, embittered, grouchy (*informal*), irritable, nasty, peevish, sullen, surly, testy, tetchy, unpleasant. OPPOSITE amiable.

source *noun* **1** *Smoking was the source of her ill health.* cause, origin, root. OPPOSITE consequence. **2** *Some dictionaries give the source of words.* derivation, origin. **3** *the source of the river.* beginning, head, spring, start. OPPOSITE mouth. **4** *The evidence comes from a reliable source.* informant.

souvenir *noun He was given a tie as a souvenir of his visit.* keepsake, memento, reminder.

sovereign *noun The sovereign has supreme power.* emperor, empress, king, monarch, potentate, queen, ruler, sultan. — *adjective* **1** *sovereign power.* absolute, paramount, supreme, unlimited. **2** *sovereign states.* autonomous, independent, self-governing, self-ruling.

sow *verb* **1** *The farmer sowed the seeds in the field.* broadcast, disseminate, plant, scatter, strew. **2** *He sowed discontent in the group.* implant, introduce, spread.

space *noun* **1** *There's plenty of space in the hall.* area, capacity, room, volume. **2** *a parking space.* bay, place, position, spot. **3** *Fill in the spaces.* blank. **4** *There was a big space between them.* break, distance, gap, hiatus, hole, interval, opening. **5** *She wanted to be an astronaut and explore space.* the heavens, outer space, the universe. **6** *in a short space of time.* duration, interval, period, span, stretch. — *verb The teacher spaced the children an arm's length apart.* arrange, place, position, separate, spread. □ **space traveller** astronaut, cosmonaut.

spacecraft *noun* space probe, spaceship, space shuttle.

spacious *adjective a spacious house.* big, capacious, commodious, enormous, extensive, large, roomy, sizeable, vast. OPPOSITE compact, small.

span *noun* **1** *the wing span.* breadth, distance, extent, length, measure, reach, spread, stretch. **2** *over a span of five years.* duration, interval, length, period, space, spell, stretch, term. — *verb The viaduct spans the valley.* bridge, cross, extend across, straddle, stretch across, traverse.

spank *verb He would not spank a child.* hit, slap, smack.

spar *verb* **1** *He chose to spar with a professional boxer.* box, fight. **2** *They were always sparring before they separated.* argue, be at loggerheads, bicker, fight, quarrel, squabble, wrangle.

spare *verb* **1** *He wanted to spare me the pain.* protect from, relieve of, save, shield from. OPPOSITE expose to. **2** *He could not spare me his time.* afford, give, grant, part with. — *adjective* **1** *spare space.* additional, available, extra, free, in reserve, leftover, surplus, unoccupied. **2** *a person of spare build.* lanky, lean, skinny, slim, thin, weedy, wiry. OPPOSITE heavy.

sparing *adjective He was sparing with the club's money.* careful, economical, frugal, miserly, niggardly, parsimonious, penny-pinching, stingy, thrifty. OPPOSITE extravagant.

spark *noun a spark of light.* flash, flicker, glimmer, glint, sparkle. — *verb* **spark off** *The article sparked off a heated debate.* provoke, set off, start, stimulate, touch off, trigger off.

sparkle *verb The jewels sparkled in the light.* flash, gleam, glint, glitter, scintillate, shimmer, shine, twinkle.

sparkling *adjective* **1** *a sparkling light.* bright, brilliant, dazzling, gleaming, glittering, glowing, scintillating, shining, twinkling. OPPOSITE dull. **2** *a sparkling personality.* animated, bright, exuberant, lively, vibrant, vivacious, witty. OPPOSITE dull. **3** *sparkling wine.* aerated, bubbly, carbonated, effervescent, fizzy. OPPOSITE still.

sparse *adjective The population of these animals is sparse.* meagre, scanty, scarce, scattered. OPPOSITE dense.

spartan *adjective They have a very spartan life.* ascetic, austere, frugal, hard, harsh, severe, simple, strict. OPPOSITE luxurious.

spasm *noun* **1** *The tablets control the spasm.* contraction, convulsion, cramp, fit, jerk, seizure, shudder, tic, twitch. **2** *a spasm of coughing.* attack, bout, burst, fit, outburst, spell, spurt.

spasmodic *adjective The teacher was displeased by his spasmodic attendance.* erratic, fitful, intermittent, irregular, occasional, sporadic. OPPOSITE regular.

spate *noun He received a spate of enquiries.* deluge, flood, inundation, run, rush, torrent. OPPOSITE trickle.

spatter *verb Her clothes were spattered with fat.* shower, splash, splatter, spot, spray, sprinkle, stain.

spawn *verb The book spawned many smaller publications.* beget, bring about, engender, generate, give rise to, produce, yield.

spay *verb The cat was spayed after one litter.* desex, doctor, neuter, sterilise.

speak *verb* **1** *He does not speak clearly.* articulate, enunciate, pronounce, talk, vocalise. **2** *The two leaders spoke about many matters.* chat, confer, converse, talk; see also DISCUSS. **3** *The minister spoke to the congregation.* address, lecture, preach, talk. **4** *She spoke the thoughts of everyone present.* communicate, convey, declare, express, relate, say, state, utter, voice. □ **speak of** *He never spoke of it again.* allude to, discuss, mention, refer to, talk about. **speak out** *She always speaks out on issues which concern her.* be outspoken, sound off (*informal*), speak up, speak your mind.

speaker *noun* lecturer, orator, preacher, spokesman, spokesperson, spokeswoman, talker. OPPOSITE listener.

spear *noun* harpoon, javelin, lance, pike, trident. — *verb The hunter speared the fish.* harpoon, impale, lance, pierce, stab.

special *adjective* **1** *She has a special way of doing her hair.* certain, characteristic, distinctive, individual, particular, specific, unique. OPPOSITE general. **2** *She has a special gift for music.* exceptional, extraordinary, outstanding, rare, remarkable, singular, uncommon, unusual. OPPOSITE ordinary.

specialist *noun a specialist on frogs.* authority, connoisseur, consultant, expert, master, professional.

speciality *noun Wedding cakes are her speciality.* forte, line, specialty, strength, strong point, talent, thing (*informal*).

species *noun a species of animal.* breed, class, classification, strain; see also SORT.

specific *adjective* **1** *The client described his specific problem.* individual, particular, special, unique. OPPOSITE general. **2** *He gave specific instructions.* definite, exact, explicit, express, precise, unambiguous. OPPOSITE vague.

specify *verb The ingredients are specified on the label.* detail, identify, itemise, list, mention, name, spell out, state, stipulate.

specimen *noun They collected plant specimens from the garden.* example, instance, model, representative, sample.

specious *adjective* see DECEPTIVE.

speck *noun There was not a speck of dust to be seen.* bit, fleck, grain, particle, skerrick (*Australian informal*), speckle, spot, trace.

speckled *adjective a speckled egg.* brindled, dotted, flecked, freckled, mottled, spotted.

spectacle *noun* **1** *the spectacle of snow-capped mountains.* scene, sight. **2** *A large crowd attended the spectacle.* display, exhibition, exposition, extravaganza, pageant, show, spectacular. □ **spectacles** *plural noun* see GLASSES (at GLASS).

spectacular *adjective spectacular feats.* amazing, breathtaking, dramatic, electrifying, exciting, impressive, magnificent, marvellous, sensational, splendid, stunning, thrilling. OPPOSITE ordinary.

spectator *noun The spectators cheered loudly.* bystander, eyewitness, looker-on, observer, onlooker, viewer, witness; [*spectators*] audience, crowd.

spectre *noun* apparition, ghost, phantom, poltergeist, spirit, spook (*informal*), vision, wraith.

spectrum *noun a broad spectrum of abilities.* compass, gamut, range, span, spread.

speculate *verb We were left to speculate about what actually happened.* conjecture, guess, hypothesise, surmise, theorise, wonder.

speculative *adjective* **1** *speculative reasoning.* conjectural, hypothetical, suppositional, theoretical. **2** *speculative investments.* dicey (*slang*), dodgy (*informal*), hazardous, risky, uncertain, unreliable.

speech *noun* **1** *She has lost the power of speech.* communication, speaking, talking, utterance. **2** *He won an award for clear speech.* articulation, diction, elocution, enunciation, pronunciation. **3** *They sat quietly throughout his speech.* address, discourse, harangue, homily, lecture, monologue, sermon, soliloquy, spiel (*slang*), talk, tirade. **4** *in colloquial speech.* dialect, idiom, language, lingo (*informal*), parlance, tongue.

speechless *adjective He was speechless with surprise.* dumb, dumbfounded, inarticulate, mute, silent, thunderstruck, tongue-tied.

speed *noun* **1** *a speed of 60 kilometres per hour.* pace, rate, velocity. **2** *We were bewildered by the speed with which he completed the job.* alacrity, briskness, dispatch, haste, promptness, quickness, rapidity, swiftness. OPPOSITE slowness. — *verb She sped home to tell the news.* bolt, dash, fly, gallop, hasten, hurry, race, run, rush, scoot, scurry, shoot, tear, zip, zoom. □ **speed up 1** *He sped up to get home on time.*

accelerate, get a move on (*informal*), hurry up, quicken, step on it (*informal*). OPPOSITE slow down. **2** *They tried to speed up her application.* accelerate, expedite, fast-track (*informal*), hasten, hurry along. OPPOSITE delay.

speedy *adjective a speedy reply.* expeditious, express, fast, immediate, prompt, quick, rapid, swift. OPPOSITE slow, tardy.

spell[1] *noun a magic spell.* charm, curse, hex, incantation.

spell[2] *noun* **1** *They had not seen each other for a long spell.* interval, period, time, while. **2** *a spell of gardening.* bout, period, session, shift, stint, stretch, term, turn. **3** (*Australian*) *After working for two hours they needed a spell.* break, breather, pause, rest, smoko (*Australian informal*).

spell[3] *verb This decision spelt disaster.* mean, portend, result in, signal, signify. □ **spell out** *All the conditions of employment were clearly spelt out.* detail, explain, set out, specify.

spellbound *adjective The dancer held the audience spellbound.* bewitched, captivated, charmed, enchanted, enraptured, enthralled, entranced, fascinated, hypnotised, mesmerised, rapt, riveted.

spend *verb* **1** *She spent all her money on the holiday.* blow (*slang*), cough up (*slang*), fork out (*slang*), lash out, outlay, pay out, shell out (*informal*), splash out, splurge, squander, use up. OPPOSITE save. **2** *She spends an hour a day reading.* devote, fill, occupy, pass, while away.

spendthrift *noun* prodigal, profligate, squanderer, wastrel. OPPOSITE miser.

spew *verb* **1** *The smell made him spew.* see VOMIT. **2** *The volcano spewed lava for several days.* discharge, disgorge, eject, expel, spit out, spurt.

sphere *noun* **1** *a sphere the size of an orange.* ball, globe, orb. **2** *His sphere of influence is small.* area, circle, domain, field, range, scope.

spherical *adjective* globular, round.

spice *noun He uses spices in his cooking.* condiment, flavouring, herb, seasoning.

spick *adjective* **spick and span** *They left the kitchen spick and span.* clean, neat, orderly, shipshape, smart, tidy. OPPOSITE dirty, untidy.

spicy *adjective a spicy curry.* aromatic, fragrant, hot, piquant, pungent, sharp, strong. OPPOSITE bland.

spike *noun He caught his clothes on the spike.* barb, point, prong, spine, stake, thorn. — *verb The pitchfork spiked his foot.* impale, pierce, skewer, spear, stab.

spill *verb* **1** *She spilt her cup of milk.* knock over, overturn, tip over, upset. **2** *The tea spilt on the saucer.* brim over, overflow, pour, run over, slop.

spin *verb* **1** *He spun round to face us.* gyrate, pirouette, revolve, rotate, swirl, turn, twirl, twist, wheel, whirl. **2** *He can spin a good yarn.* concoct, invent, make up, narrate, relate, tell. — *noun He took us for a spin in his new car.* drive, ride, run, trip. □ **spin out** *He spun the story out over two episodes.* drag out, draw out, extend, prolong, protract.

spindle *noun The disc revolves on a spindle.* axle, pin, rod, shaft.

spindly *adjective spindly legs.* lanky, long, skinny, thin.

spine *noun* **1** *an injured spine.* backbone, spinal column, vertebral column. **2** *a plant with spines.* barb, needle, prickle, spike, thorn. **3** *The porcupine has sharp spines.* bristle, prickle, quill, spike.

spine-chilling *adjective a spine-chilling murder story.* blood-curdling, chilling, frightening, hair-raising, horrifying, scary, terrifying.

spineless *adjective He's too spineless to tell her himself.* chicken (*informal*), cowardly, fearful, gutless (*informal*), irresolute, lily-livered, pusillanimous, timid, timorous, weak. OPPOSITE brave.

spin-off *noun an important spin-off from his research.* by-product, consequence, offshoot, side benefit.

spiral *noun* coil, corkscrew, helix, twist, whorl.

spirit *noun* **1** *I shall be with you in spirit.* mind, psyche, soul. OPPOSITE body. **2** *The castle was said to be haunted by spirits.* apparition, bogy, genie, ghost, gremlin (*informal*), phantom, poltergeist, spectre, spook (*informal*), sprite. **3** *He has a generous spirit.* character, disposition, heart, make-up, nature, temperament. **4** *the spirit of the times.* atmosphere, attitude, feeling, mood. **5** *His captors will never break his spirit.* courage, determination, drive, endurance, fearlessness, grit, guts (*informal*), mettle, pluck, spunk (*informal*), will, zeal. **6** *She played the piece with spirit.* animation, dash, energy, enthusiasm, gusto, liveliness, passion, verve, vigour, vivacity, zest. □ **spirits** *plural noun The patient is in good spirits.* feelings, frame of mind, humour, mood, morale, temper.

spirited *adjective* **1** *a spirited discussion.* animated, ardent, energetic, fervent, lively, passionate, vigorous. OPPOSITE lifeless, spiritless. **2** *the spirited hero of the story.* bold, brave, courageous, daring, determined, fearless, feisty (*informal*), intrepid, mettlesome, plucky, valiant. OPPOSITE timid.

spiritual *adjective* **1** *Spiritual well-being is more important than physical health.* emotional, inner, mental, psychic, psychological. OPPOSITE material, physical. **2** *spiritual music.* divine, ecclesiastical, religious, sacred. OPPOSITE secular.

spit[1] *verb* **1** *He spat out the pips.* eject, spew. **2** *The fat was spitting in the pan.* hiss, pop, splutter, sputter. — *noun a ball of spit.* saliva, slag (*Australian slang*), spittle, sputum. □ **dead spit** *She is the dead spit of her sister.* double, image, likeness, lookalike, ringer (*informal*), spitting image.

spit[2] *noun They keep their boat at the spit.* peninsula, point, promontory.

spite *noun She dobbed him in out of spite.* animosity, bitterness, hatred, hostility, ill will, malevolence, malice, rancour, resentment, revenge, spleen, vengeance, vindictiveness. OPPOSITE benevolence. — *verb She did it to spite me.* annoy, get at (*informal*), hurt, irritate, provoke, put out, thwart, upset, wound. OPPOSITE please. □ **in spite of** *She loved him in spite of his faults.* despite, notwithstanding, regardless of.

spiteful *adjective a spiteful person.* bitchy (*informal*), bitter, catty, malevolent, malicious, nasty, rancorous, resentful, revengeful, unkind, vengeful, venomous, vindictive. OPPOSITE benevolent.

splash *verb* **1** *The passing car splashed mud on the pedestrians.* fling, shower, spatter, splatter, spray, throw up. **2** *She splashed about in the pool.* paddle, slosh, wade. **3** *His picture was splashed across the front page.* blazon, display, plaster, spread. — *noun* **1** *He loves to hear the splash of the waves on the rocks.* battering, breaking, crash, smashing, splatter. **2** *splashes of ink on the page.* blob, blotch, mark, smear, smudge, splotch, stain, streak. **3** *tea with a splash of milk.* dash, drop, touch. □ **splash out** *He likes to splash out occasionally.* lash out, spend, splurge.

spleen *noun He vented his spleen.* anger, animosity, bitterness, gall, hostility, irritability, malice, rancour, spite, wrath.

splendid *adjective* **1** *a splendid display.* beautiful, brilliant, dazzling, fine, glittering, glorious, gorgeous, grand, imposing, impressive, lavish, magnificent, resplendent, rich, showy, spectacular, sumptuous, superb. OPPOSITE poor. **2** *splendid results.* brilliant, excellent, exceptional, fabulous (*informal*), fantastic (*informal*), first-rate, great, marvellous, outstanding, remarkable, stupendous, super (*informal*), superb, terrific (*informal*), wonderful. OPPOSITE poor.

splendour *noun the splendour of Versailles.* beauty, brilliance, glory, grandeur, greatness, magnificence, majesty, resplendence, richness, show, sumptuousness.

splice *verb He spliced the ends of the rope together.* braid, intertwine, interweave, join, plait.

splinter *noun She had a splinter of glass in her foot.* fragment, shard, shiver, sliver. — *verb The timber splinters easily.* fracture, shatter, split.

split *verb* **1** *The axeman split the log.* break, chop, cleave, crack, fracture, hew, splinter. **2** *They split the profits between them.* allocate, apportion, carve up, distribute, divide, dole out, share. **3** *His trousers have split.* burst, come apart, rip, tear. **4** *The students were split into two groups.* break, divide, segregate, separate. OPPOSITE unite. — *noun* **1** *a split in the rock.* breach, break, cleft, crack, fissure, fracture, slit. **2** *There was a split in the party over the issue.* breach, division, rift, rupture, schism. OPPOSITE unity. □ **split up** *His parents have split up.* break up, divorce, part, separate.

splutter *verb* **1** *The sausages spluttered in the pan.* hiss, sizzle, spit, sputter. **2** *She spluttered unintelligibly.* mumble, stammer, stutter.

spoil *verb* **1** *The work was spoilt by carelessness.* blight, botch, bungle, damage, destroy, harm, mar, mess up, ruin, undo, upset, wreck. OPPOSITE improve. **2** *Food spoils if it is left out of the refrigerator.* decay, decompose, deteriorate, go bad, go off, perish, putrefy, rot. OPPOSITE keep. **3** *The parents are spoiling their child with too many toys.* cosset, indulge, lavish, mollycoddle, overindulge, pamper. OPPOSITE deprive.

spoils *plural noun the spoils of war.* booty, loot, pillage, plunder, prizes, swag (*informal*).

spoilsport *noun We don't want that spoilsport at our party.* damper, killjoy, nark (*Australian informal*), party-pooper (*informal*), wet blanket (*informal*), wowser (*Australian informal*).

spoken *adjective a spoken message.* oral, unwritten, verbal.

spokesperson *noun* delegate, mouthpiece, representative, speaker, spokesman, spokeswoman.

sponge *verb She sponged the floors.* clean, mop, wash, wipe. □ **sponge off, sponge on** *He doesn't work and likes to sponge on people.* bludge on (*Australian informal*), cadge from, impose on, live off, scrounge from.

sponger *noun He has a reputation as a sponger.* bludger (*Australian informal*), cadger, freeloader (*informal*), hanger-on, parasite, scrounger.

spongy *adjective spongy ground.* absorbent, boggy, marshy, porous, soft, springy, swampy. OPPOSITE firm.

sponsor *noun The football club has a new sponsor.* backer, benefactor, financier, patron, promoter, supporter. — *verb The match was sponsored by their company.* back, finance, fund, promote, subsidise, support.

spontaneous *adjective* **1** *a spontaneous response.* automatic, impetuous, impulsive, instinctive, involuntary, natural, reflex, unconscious, unforced. OPPOSITE considered. **2** *A spontaneous speech is often better than a prepared one.* ad lib, extempore, impromptu, off-the-cuff, unplanned, unprepared, unrehearsed. OPPOSITE prepared.

spoof *noun The movie was a spoof of 'Macbeth'.* burlesque, parody, satire, send-up (*informal*), take-off.

spook *noun* see GHOST.

spooky *adjective* (*informal*) *It was spooky in the old house.* creepy, eerie, frightening, ghostly, scary, uncanny, weird.

spool *noun The cotton is wound on a spool.* bobbin, reel.

sporadic *adjective sporadic fighting.* fitful, infrequent, intermittent, irregular, isolated, occasional, random, scattered, spasmodic. OPPOSITE regular.

sport *noun His favourite sport is badminton.* diversion, game, pastime, physical activity, recreation.

sporting *adjective It was very sporting of him to let you go first.* considerate, decent, fair, generous, sportsmanlike.

sportsground *noun* arena, field, ground, oval, pitch, playing field, stadium.

sportsman, sportswoman *noun* contestant, participant, player, sportsperson.

sportsmanlike *adjective* see SPORTING.

spot *noun* **1** *a white dog with black spots.* blot, blotch, dot, fleck, mark, patch, smudge, speck, speckle, splash, splotch, stain. **2** *skin without a spot.* birthmark, blackhead, blemish, freckle, mole, pimple, whitehead, zit (*informal*); [*spots*] rash. **3** *a beautiful spot for a house.* area, district, locality, location, neighbourhood, place, position, region, setting, site, situation. **4** *a few spots of rain.* bead, blob, drop. — *verb* **1** *The material is spotted with grease.* dot, mark, smudge, soil, spatter, speckle, splash, splotch, spray, stain. **2** (*informal*) *I could not spot her in the crowd.* catch sight of, detect, discover, distinguish, espy, find, identify, locate, notice, pick out, recognise, see. □ **in a spot** (*informal*) *He was in a bit of a spot and needed help.* in a bind (*informal*), in a fix (*informal*), in a jam (*informal*), in a mess, in a pickle (*informal*), in a plight, in a predicament, in a quandary, in difficulties. **on the spot** *The policeman fined him on the spot.* at the scene, immediately, right away, straight away, then and there.

spotless *adjective* **1** *The floor is spotless.* clean, immaculate, unstained. OPPOSITE dirty. **2** *She has a spotless record.* clean, faultless, flawless, immaculate, impeccable, perfect, unblemished, untarnished. OPPOSITE blemished.

spotty *adjective* **1** *a spotty dog.* dappled, mottled, spotted. **2** *spotty fabric.* dotted, flecked, speckled, spotted. **3** *a spotty face.* blotchy, freckled, pimply, splotchy.

spouse *noun* consort, husband, mate (*informal*), partner, wife.

spout *noun Water comes out the spout.* jet, nozzle, outlet. — *verb* **1** *The water spouted from the hose.* flow, gush, jet, spray, spurt, squirt, stream. **2** (*informal*) *He's always spouting about what's wrong with the world.* carry on (*informal*), declaim, go on (*informal*), hold forth, pontificate, rant, rave, sermonise.

sprain *verb She has sprained her ankle.* twist, wrench.

sprawl *verb He sprawled on the bed.* flop, lie spread-eagled, loll, lounge, recline, slouch, slump, spread yourself out, stretch out. — *noun the urban sprawl.* expansion, spread.

spray[1] *noun* **1** *The liquid comes out in a fine spray.* drizzle, droplets, mist, shower, vapour. **2** *a perfume spray.* aerosol, atomiser, vaporiser. — *verb He sprayed the stove with sauce.* shower, spatter, splash, sprinkle, wet.

spray[2] *noun a spray of flowers.* bouquet, bunch, corsage, nosegay, posy, sprig.

spread *verb* **1** *He spread the newspaper on the floor.* lay out, open out, unfold, unfurl, unroll. **2** *The stain spread as she treated it.* diffuse, disperse, enlarge, extend, grow, permeate, pervade, widen. **3** *She spread the glue thickly.* apply, coat, lay on, paste, plaster, smear. **4** *The gardener spread the seeds.* broadcast, distribute, scatter, sprinkle, strew. **5** *He helped to spread the news.* broadcast, circulate, disseminate, promulgate, publicise, transmit. **6** *The rabbit population is spreading.* expand, grow, increase, multiply, proliferate. OPPOSITE diminish. **7** *The store spread the payments over six months.* distribute, space. — *noun* **1** *They measured the spread of the wings.* breadth, compass, coverage, expanse, extent, range, reach, scope, span, stretch, sweep, width. **2** *the spread of the disease.* advance, expansion, increase, proliferation. **3** (*informal*) *The caterers put on a fine spread for the visitors.* banquet, feast, meal.

spree *noun* (*informal*) **1** *a drinking spree.* bender (*slang*), binge (*slang*), bout, orgy, revel. **2** *a shopping spree.* field day, fling, outing, splurge.

sprig *noun a sprig of parsley.* branch, shoot, spray.

sprightly *adjective a sprightly old gentleman.* active, agile, dynamic, energetic, hale, lively, nimble, perky, spry, vivacious. OPPOSITE doddery.

spring *verb* **1** *He sprang from behind the chair and startled her.* bounce, bound, dart, hop, jump, leap, pounce, shoot out, vault. **2** *Weeds sprang up.* appear, burst forth, come up, emerge, grow, shoot up, sprout. **3** *The enmity sprang from a misunderstanding.* arise, derive, emanate, grow, originate, proceed, stem. — *noun* **1** *With one spring he was by her side.* bound, hop, jump, leap, vault. **2** *There's plenty of spring left in the mattress.* bounce, elasticity, resilience, springiness. **3** *The water comes from a spring.* fountain, geyser, spa, well-spring. — *adjective the spring equinox.* vernal. □ **spring back** *The door sprang back in his face.* bounce back, fly back, rebound, recoil.

springy *adjective a springy cushion.* bouncy, elastic, resilient, spongy.

sprinkle *verb* **1** *He sprinkled the plants with the hose.* shower, spatter, splash, spray. **2** *She sprinkled cocoa on her cappuccino.* dust, scatter, strew.

sprinkling *noun There was only a sprinkling of women in senior positions.* few, handful.

sprint *verb He sprinted to the corner when he heard the crash.* dash, race, run, rush, speed, tear.

sprite *noun* elf, fairy, goblin, hobgoblin, imp, leprechaun, pixie, spirit.

sprout *verb The plants are sprouting.* bud, develop, germinate, grow, shoot.

spruce *adjective He looked spruce in his new suit.* chic, dapper, neat, smart, tidy, trim, well-groomed. OPPOSITE shabby. — *verb* **spruce up** *He spruced himself up before dinner.* clean up, groom, smarten up, tidy up, titivate (*informal*).

spruiker *noun* (*Australian informal*) *Each of the stall owners employs a spruiker to try to attract business.* barker, tout.

spry *adjective a spry old gentleman.* active, agile, dynamic, energetic, hale, lively, nimble, sprightly. OPPOSITE doddery.

spunk *noun* (*informal*) *The job requires someone with spunk.* bravery, courage, determination, grit, guts (*informal*), mettle, pluck.

spur *verb The good reviews spurred him on to greater success.* egg on, encourage, goad, motivate, prompt, stimulate, urge. OPPOSITE discourage.

spurious *adjective a spurious excuse.* bogus, counterfeit, fake, false, phoney (*informal*). OPPOSITE genuine.

spurn *verb Do not spurn her kind offer.* disdain, rebuff, refuse, reject, repudiate, scorn, turn your nose up at. OPPOSITE accept.

spurt *verb* **1** *The water spurted out of the hose.* burst, flow, gush, jet, shoot, spout, spray, squirt, stream, surge. OPPOSITE trickle. **2** *He spurted ahead after the final turn.* dash, race, shoot, speed, sprint, tear. — *noun The water came out in a spurt.* burst, gush, jet, rush, spray, squirt, stream, surge. OPPOSITE trickle.

sputter *verb The bacon sputtered in the pan.* hiss, sizzle, spit, splutter.

spy *noun He worked as a spy during the war.* double agent, informer, intelligence agent, mole, secret agent, undercover agent. — *verb He spied a new star with the telescope.* catch sight of, discern, discover, espy, make out, notice, observe, perceive, see, spot. □ **spy on** *He knew that someone was spying on him.* keep under surveillance, keep watch on, observe, peep on, shadow, snoop on (*informal*), tail (*informal*), watch.

spying *noun* espionage, intelligence, surveillance.

squabble *verb The twins often squabbled over their toys.* argue, bicker, fight, quarrel, scrap (*informal*), wrangle. — *noun They finished their squabble and were friends again.* altercation, argument, barney (*informal*), dispute, fight, quarrel, row, scrap (*informal*), tiff, wrangle.

squad *noun a squad of workers.* band, force, gang, group, team, unit.

squalid *adjective squalid living conditions.* dilapidated, dirty, filthy, run-down, seedy, shabby, sordid, wretched. OPPOSITE clean.

squall *noun The weather bureau has forecast squalls.* gust, storm, wind.

squander *verb He squanders all his money on cigarettes.* blow (*slang*), dissipate, fritter away, throw away, waste. OPPOSITE save.

square *noun* **1** *Put a tick in the square.* box, space. **2** (*informal*) *The students considered her a square.* conservative, fuddy-duddy (*informal*), old fogy, stick-in-the-mud (*informal*). — *adjective* **1** *The corners are square.* right-angled. **2** *We need to get your room square.* in order, neat, orderly, tidy. **3** *The teams are all square at this stage of the competition.* equal, even, level, tied. **4** *three square meals a day.* decent, satisfying, substantial. OPPOSITE inadequate. **5** *a square deal.* above board, equitable, fair, honest, just, straight. OPPOSITE crooked. **6** (*informal*) *She thinks all old people are square.* conservative, conventional, old-fashioned, out of date, out of touch. OPPOSITE trendy (*informal*). — *verb His story squares with hers.* agree, be consistent, correspond, fit, match, tally.

squash *verb* **1** *Don't squash the tomatoes.* compress, crush, flatten, mangle, mash, press, pulp, smash, squeeze. **2** *The children were squashed into a small classroom.* cram, crowd, crush, jam, pack, squeeze. **3** *The army squashed the rebellion.* crush, put down, quash, quell, suppress.

squat *verb She squatted under the table.* crouch. — *adjective a squat figure.* dumpy, nuggety (*Australian*), short, stocky, stubby, thickset. OPPOSITE lanky.

squatter *noun* (*Australian*) *a wealthy squatter.* grazier, pastoralist, sheep farmer.

squawk *verb The ducks are squawking.* cry, scream, screech.

squeak *verb The bird squeaked.* cheep, chirp, cry, peep, screech.

squeal *noun* **1** *the squeal of brakes.* scream, screech. **2** *a squeal of pain.* cry, scream, screech, shriek, wail, yell. — *verb She squealed when she was pinched.* cry, scream, screech, shriek, wail, yell.

squeamish *adjective He is too squeamish to work in an abattoir.* easily nauseated, queasy.

squeeze *verb* **1** *He squeezed the rubbish so that it took up less space.* compact, compress, crush, press, squash, wring. **2** *Squeeze the shampoo out of the bottle.* extract, force, press, push. **3** *We all squeezed into the little car.* cram, crowd, jam, pack, pile, squash. — *noun He gave her an affectionate squeeze.* clasp, cuddle, embrace, hug.

squelch *verb We squelched through the mud.* slosh, splash, wade.

squirm *verb* **1** *Worms squirm.* twist, wiggle, wriggle, writhe. **2** *He squirmed with embarrassment.* fidget, wince, writhe.

squirt *verb* **1** *The doctor squirted water in her ear.* shoot, spray, syringe. **2** *He squirted me with lemon juice.* shower, spatter, splash, splatter, spray, sprinkle, spurt, wet.

stab *verb The man was stabbed to death.* jab, knife, lance, pierce, spear, spike, wound. — *noun* **1** *She felt a stab of pain.* jab, pang, prick, tweak, twinge. **2** (*informal*) *Have a stab at it.* attempt, bash (*informal*), crack (*informal*), go (*Australian informal*), shot (*informal*), try.

stable[1] *adjective* **1** *The base of the structure must be stable.* anchored, firm, fixed, secure, solid, sound, steady, sturdy. OPPOSITE shaky. **2** *A stable partnership had built up over many years.* enduring, established, lasting, permanent, reliable, solid, steady, strong. OPPOSITE insecure. **3** *The patient remains in a stable condition.* constant, steady, unchanged. OPPOSITE fluctuating. **4** *a stable person.* balanced, sane, sensible, steady, together (*informal*). OPPOSITE unstable.

stable[2] *noun The horse is in his stable.* stall.

stack *noun* **1** *a stack of books.* bundle, heap, load, mound, mountain, pile. **2** *stacks of hay.* cock, haycock, hayrick, haystack, rick. **3** (*informal*) *a stack of work. stacks of time.* heap, load, lot (*informal*), mass, mountain, pile (*informal*), plenty, ton (*informal*). — *verb Her job was to stack the plates.* collect, heap, pile.

stadium *noun an athletic stadium.* amphitheatre, arena, ground, sportsground.

staff *noun* **1** *He supported himself on his staff.* cane, crook, crosier, crutch, stick. **2** *a ceremonial staff.* baton, mace, pole, rod, sceptre. **3** *The company has a staff of forty.* crew, employees, manpower, personnel, team, workers, workforce. — *verb The new office is staffed by three officers.* man, run, service, tend.

stage *noun* **1** *The speakers addressed us from the stage.* dais, platform, podium, rostrum. **2** *Negotiations had reached a critical stage.* juncture, period, phase, point. **3** *The first stage of their journey was the longest.* hop, leg, part, section. — *verb* **1** *The school staged a play for the parents.* mount, perform, present, produce, put on. **2** *The workers staged a demonstration.* arrange, carry out, hold, organise, plan.

stagger *verb* **1** *He staggered from his bed to the telephone.* falter, lurch, reel, stumble, teeter, totter. **2** *He was staggered by the news.* astonish, astound, confound, dumbfound, flabbergast, nonplus, overwhelm, shock, startle, stun, surprise, take aback.

stagnant *adjective* **1** *The water in the creek was stagnant.* motionless, stale, standing, still. OPPOSITE flowing. **2** *Business was stagnant.* dead, dormant, slow, sluggish, static. OPPOSITE booming.

stagnate *verb She stagnated in the same job for twenty years.* become stale, idle, languish, mark time, vegetate. OPPOSITE progress.

staid *adjective a staid young man.* dignified, earnest, grave, restrained, sedate, serious, settled, sober, steady. OPPOSITE flighty.

stain *verb Her dress is stained with paint.* discolour, mark, smear, smudge, soil, spot. — *noun* **1** *stains on her dress.* blotch, discoloration, mark, smudge, speck, splotch, spot. **2** *a stain on his reputation.* blemish, blot, flaw, stigma, taint, tarnish. **3** *They used a walnut stain on the timber.* dye, tint.

stairs *plural noun I climbed up the stairs.* staircase, stairway, steps.

stake *noun* **1** *The tomato bushes are supported by stakes.* picket, pole, post, spike, stick. **2** *He could afford the stake of $5 on the game.* bet, wager. **3** *He has a stake in the business.* concern, interest, investment, share. — *verb* **1** *He has staked the plants.* brace, prop, support. **2** *I'll stake my life on it.* bet, chance, gamble, hazard, risk, wager.

stale *adjective* **1** *The bread has gone stale.* dry, hard, mouldy. OPPOSITE fresh. **2** *The room smelt stale because it had been closed up.* close, fusty, musty, stuffy. OPPOSITE fresh. **3** *His jokes are stale.* banal, clichéd, familiar, hackneyed, old, out of date, trite, unoriginal. OPPOSITE new. **4** *After ten years in the same job he is feeling stale.* bored, jaded, stagnant.

stalemate *noun The talks have reached a stalemate.* deadlock, impasse, stand-off, standstill. OPPOSITE resolution.

stalk[1] *noun The flowers have long stalks.* shoot, stem.

stalk[2] *verb* **1** *She stalked out with her nose in the air.* flounce, march, stride, strut. **2** *The murderer stalked his victim.* follow, hound, hunt, prowl after, pursue, shadow, tail (*informal*), track, trail.

stall *noun* **1** *The animals are all in their stalls.* pen, shed, stable. **2** *The room was divided into stalls for privacy.* booth, cell, compartment, cubicle, enclosure. **3** *He helped on the lolly stall at the fair.* booth, counter, kiosk, stand, table. — *verb* **1** *Quit stalling!* delay, hedge, play for time, procrastinate, temporise. **2** *He stalled the visitors until everything was ready.* block, delay, obstruct, put off, stave off.

stalwart *adjective* *stalwart Labor supporters.* dependable, faithful, firm, loyal, reliable, staunch, steadfast, strong.

stamina *noun* *He doesn't have the stamina to run five kilometres.* endurance, energy, fortitude, perseverance, staying power, strength, vigour.

stammer *verb* *He stammers only when he is nervous.* falter, splutter, stumble, stutter.

stamp *verb* **1** *He stamped on the snails.* crush, flatten, squash, step, stomp, tramp, trample, tread. OPPOSITE tiptoe. **2** *He had his initials stamped on his wallet.* brand, emboss, engrave, imprint, inscribe, print. — *noun* **1** *the maker's official stamp.* brand, hallmark, imprint, logo, mark, seal, trade mark. **2** *This job bears the stamp of professionals.* characteristic, hallmark, mark. □ **stamp out** *They tried to stamp out sexism.* abolish, eliminate, eradicate, put an end to, stop.

stamp-collecting *noun* philately.

stampede *noun* *There was a stampede for the exits.* charge, dash, race, run, rush. — *verb* *The crowd stampeded into the arena.* bolt, charge, dash, race, rush.

stance *noun* **1** *a golfer's stance.* bearing, carriage, deportment, position, posture. **2** *What is the government's stance on climate change?* attitude, line, opinion, position, stand, standpoint, viewpoint.

stand *verb* **1** *The court stands when the judge enters.* get up, rise. OPPOSITE sit. **2** *Their house stands on the edge of a park.* be, be located, be situated, lie. **3** *She stood the vase on the table.* deposit, place, position, put, set. **4** *Their marriage has stood the test of time.* bear, endure, survive, weather, withstand. **5** *The traffic stood still.* remain, stay, stop. **6** *She is standing for parliament.* run. **7** *She stood trial for the murder of the child.* face, undergo. **8** *He couldn't stand the noise.* abide, bear, cope with, endure, handle, put up with, stomach, suffer, take, tolerate. **9** *John stood everyone a drink.* pay for, provide, shout (*Australian informal*), treat to. — *noun* **1** *He took his stand near the door.* place, position. **2** *What is his stand on this issue?* see STANDPOINT. **3** *a stand for a camera, vase, etc.* base, pedestal, rack, shelf, support, tripod. **4** *He works on a newspaper stand.* booth, counter, kiosk, stall. **5** *a taxi stand.* rank. **6** *The witness took the stand.* witness box. □ **stand by 1** *She stood by helplessly.* look on, stay on the sidelines, watch. **2** *She will always stand by her children.* back, defend, side with, stick by, support. **3** *Stand by for lift-off.* be ready, wait. **4** *He always stands by his promises.* abide by, adhere to, honour, keep, observe, stick to. **stand down 1** *The chairman was asked to stand down.* resign, step down, withdraw. **2** *The firm has begun standing down workers.* lay off, stand off, suspend. **stand for 1** *What do the letters 'TLC' stand for?* be short for, denote, indicate, mean, represent, signify, symbolise. **2** (*informal*) *He won't stand for any nonsense.* brook, endure, put up with, suffer, take, tolerate. **stand in for** *He'll stand in for me if I can't be there.* cover for, deputise for, fill in for, relieve, replace, substitute for, take the place of. **stand out** *He stood out in his purple shirt.* be conspicuous, be noticeable, be prominent, stick out. **stand up for** *He can be relied upon to stand up for you.* defend, speak up for, stand by, stick up for, support. **stand up to 1** *He was too weak to stand up to the boss.* challenge, confront, defy, face up to, oppose, resist. **2** *This carpet should stand up to heavy use.* endure, last through, resist, survive, withstand.

standard *noun* **1** *Does this meet the company's standards?* benchmark, criterion, guideline, requirement, specification, touchstone, yardstick. **2** *Her work is of a high standard.* grade, level, quality. **3** *the royal standard.* banner, ensign, flag, pennant. — *adjective* *the standard treatment for burns.* accepted, approved, common, conventional, customary, normal, ordinary, orthodox, prescribed, recognised, regular, routine, set, stock, usual. OPPOSITE abnormal, unorthodox.

stand-by *noun* *The team has a second car as a stand-by.* backup, replacement, reserve, substitute.

stand-in *noun* *He acts as a stand-in when someone's sick.* deputy, locum, relief, replacement, reserve, stand-by, substitute, surrogate.

standoffish *adjective* *The new principal was standoffish at first.* aloof, cold, cool, detached, distant, remote, reserved, unapproachable, unsociable. OPPOSITE friendly.

standover *adjective* (*Australian*) *standover tactics.* bullying, intimidating, threatening.

standpoint *noun* *He looked at the situation from a different standpoint.* angle, attitude, opinion, point of view, position, stance, stand, viewpoint.

standstill *noun* *The accident brought work to a standstill.* halt, impasse, stop.

stanza *noun* *The poem has four stanzas.* verse.

staple *adjective* *Bread is their staple food.* basic, chief, essential, main, primary, principal, standard.

star *noun* **1** *the stars in the sky.* celestial body, heavenly body; [*group of stars*] constellation, galaxy. **2** *a printed star.* asterisk, pentagram. **3** *a film star.* celebrity, idol, megastar (*informal*), superstar. — *verb* *Nicole Kidman stars in the film.* act, appear, feature, perform, play.

starchy *adjective* *She comes across as stiff and starchy.* formal, prim, stiff, strait-laced, stuffy.

stare *verb* *He stood and stared in amazement.* gape, gawk (*informal*), gawp (*informal*), gaze, glare, goggle, look, peer, watch. — *noun* *He gave a hard stare.* gape, gaze, glare, look.

stark *adjective* **1** *stark madness.* absolute, complete, downright, pure, sheer, total, utter. **2** *a stark house in need of some decoration.* austere, bare, bleak, desolate, grim, harsh, plain, severe, simple, spartan. — *adverb* *She walked out stark naked.* absolutely, altogether, completely, quite, totally, utterly, wholly.

start *verb* **1** *He started his musical career at seven.* begin, commence, embark on, enter upon, take up. OPPOSITE finish. **2** *He started the machine.* activate, switch on, turn on. OPPOSITE stop. **3** *He started a fund for research into leukaemia.* create, establish, found, inaugurate, initiate, institute, launch, originate, pioneer, set up. **4** *They started for Sydney first thing in the morning.* depart, get going, leave, set off, set out. OPPOSITE arrive. **5** *The sudden noise made him start.* blench, flinch, jump, recoil, twitch, wince. **6** *She started from her seat.* bound, jump, leap, shoot, spring. — *noun* **1** *the start of an era, enterprise, etc.* beginning, birth, commencement, dawn, genesis, inauguration, inception, kick-off (*informal*), launch, onset, opening, origin, outset. OPPOSITE finish. **2** *She was given a fresh start.* break (*informal*), chance, opening, opportunity. **3** *He had a head start.* advantage, edge, lead. **4** *The knock at the door gave her a start.* jolt, jump, shock, surprise.

starting point *noun* *the starting point of a discussion.* base, basis, beginning, foundation, premise.

startle *verb* *The sound of footsteps startled him.* alarm, disturb, frighten, scare, shake, surprise, unsettle, upset.

startling *adjective* *startling news.* alarming, astonishing, disturbing, dramatic, remarkable, shocking, staggering, surprising, unexpected.

starvation *noun* *They will die of starvation.* famine, hunger, malnutrition, undernourishment.

starve *verb* **starve yourself** fast, go hungry, go without food. OPPOSITE overeat.

starving *adjective* (*informal*) *After their long walk they were starving.* famished, hungry, ravenous.

state *noun* **1** *the state of the economy.* circumstances, condition, health, shape, situation. **2** *She remained in a depressed state.* attitude, condition, frame of mind, mood. **3** *She got into a state.* dither, flap (*informal*), fluster, panic, stew (*informal*), tizzy (*informal*). **4** *The funeral was attended by many heads of state.* country, kingdom, land, nation, principality, republic. **5** *Those services are run by the state.* government. — *adjective* **1** *state schools.* government, public. OPPOSITE independent, private. **2** *on state occasions.* ceremonial, formal, official. — *verb* *He stated his opinion.* affirm, announce, assert, declare, express, proclaim, report, say, voice.

stately *adjective* *a stately mansion.* dignified, grand, imposing, impressive, magnificent, majestic. OPPOSITE modest.

statement *noun* **1** *Each person made a brief statement.* account, affidavit, affirmation, announcement, assertion, comment, communication, communiqué, confession, declaration, proclamation, remark, report, utterance. **2** *The company sends me a monthly statement.* account, bill, invoice.

static *adjective* *Prices remained static.* constant, fixed, frozen, pegged, stable, stationary, steady, unchanging, unvarying. OPPOSITE variable.

station *noun* **1** *When the alarm rings report to your station.* location, place, position, post, site. **2** *a radio station.* broadcaster, channel. **3** *a bus station.* depot, stop, terminal, terminus. **4** (*Australian*) *a cattle station.* estate, property, ranch (*American*), run (*Australian*). — *verb* *He is stationed at Richmond.* assign, base, locate, place, position, post.

stationary *adjective* *a stationary vehicle.* immobile, motionless, parked, standing, static, still, unmoving. OPPOSITE moving.

stationery *noun* office supplies, paper, writing materials.

statue *noun* *a statue of Captain Cook.* bust, carving, cast, figurine, sculpture, statuette.

stature *noun* **1** *The child grew in stature.* height, size, tallness. **2** *The school is privileged to have a teacher of her stature.* calibre, eminence, greatness, importance, prominence, standing.

status *noun* **1** *two employees of equal status.* level, position, rank, standing, station. **2** *He thought the new job would give him status.* distinction, importance, prestige, recognition.

statute *noun* act, law, regulation, rule.

staunch *adjective* *a staunch supporter.* dependable, faithful, firm, loyal, reliable, steadfast, strong, trustworthy. OPPOSITE fickle.

stave *verb* **stave off** *He managed to stave off disaster.* avert, defer, fend off, prevent, ward off.

stay[1] *verb* **1** *Her friend stayed until the taxi arrived.* linger, remain, tarry, wait. OPPOSITE leave. **2** *The child stayed awake until everyone had gone.* continue, keep, remain. **3** *She is staying at a friend's house.* dwell, live, lodge, reside, sleep, sleep over, sojourn, visit. — *noun* **1** *They had a brief stay in Hobart.* holiday, sojourn, stop, stopover, time, visit. **2** *He was granted a stay of execution.* deferment, postponement, reprieve.

stay[2] *noun* *The stays supporting the post are loose.* brace, line, prop, rope, support.

staying power *noun* *To run a marathon you need staying power.* endurance, fortitude, grit, perseverance, persistence, stamina, sticking power.

steadfast *adjective* *Her faith remained steadfast throughout her illness.* constant, determined, firm, persistent, resolute, staunch, steady, sure, unchanging, unshakeable. OPPOSITE wavering.

steady *adjective* **1** *The ladder is not steady on that surface.* balanced, firm, immovable, secure, stable. OPPOSITE unsteady, wobbly. **2** *Maintain steady pressure.* consistent, constant, continuous, even, invariable, regular, unchanging, uniform. OPPOSITE variable. **3** *He is a steady worker.* careful, conscientious, dependable, diligent, level-headed, reliable, serious. OPPOSITE unreliable. — *verb* **1** *Nobody helped to steady the ladder.* balance, secure, stabilise, support. **2** *She steadied herself before walking into the examination room.* calm, compose, control.

steal *verb* **1** *He stole the money. He was caught stealing jewellery.* appropriate, duff (*Australian*), embezzle, filch, help yourself to, knock off (*slang*), lift (*informal*), make off with, misappropriate, nick (*slang*), pilfer, pinch (*informal*), poach, pocket, purloin, seize, snaffle (*informal*), snatch, snavel (*Australian informal*), snitch (*slang*), souvenir (*slang*), swipe (*informal*), take, thieve. **2** *He stole out of the room when nobody was looking.* creep, flit, skulk, slink, slip, sneak, tiptoe.

stealing *noun* see THEFT.

stealth *noun* *The new rules were introduced by stealth.* furtiveness, secrecy, secretiveness, slyness, sneakiness, surreptitiousness. OPPOSITE openness.

stealthy *adjective* *stealthy steps towards his prey.* covert, furtive, secret, secretive, sly, sneaky, surreptitious, undercover, unobtrusive. OPPOSITE open.

steam *noun* **1** *The bathroom was full of steam after his shower.* mist, vapour. **2** *He's run out of steam.* energy, momentum, power, puff (*informal*), stamina.

steel *verb* **steel yourself** *Steel yourself for the onslaught.* brace yourself, gird yourself, nerve yourself, prepare yourself, steady yourself.

steep[1] *adjective* **1** *a steep slope.* abrupt, precipitous, sharp, sheer, vertical. OPPOSITE gentle. **2** (*informal*) *Their prices are a bit steep.* dear, excessive, exorbitant, expensive, extortionate, high. OPPOSITE reasonable.

steep[2] *verb* **1** *The olives are steeped in brine.* immerse, impregnate, marinade, soak, souse, submerge. **2** *The old church was steeped in history.* fill, imbue, permeate, pervade.

steer *verb He steered the boat into port.* conduct, direct, guide, lead, navigate, pilot. □ **steer clear of** *They steered clear of one another.* avoid, bypass, dodge, give a wide berth to, keep away from.

stem[1] *noun The plant has a strong stem.* cane, stalk, stock, trunk. — *verb* **stem from** *Her dissatisfaction stems from a misunderstanding.* arise from, derive from, issue from, originate in, result from, spring from.

stem[2] *verb They stemmed the flow of blood from the wound.* check, curb, halt, hold back, stanch, stop.

stench *noun The stench from the dump was intolerable.* pong (*informal*), reek, stink. OPPOSITE fragrance.

step *verb She tries not to step on ants.* trample, tread, walk. — *noun* **1** *Some people take longer steps than others.* pace, stride. **2** *She recognised his step.* footstep, gait, tread, walk. **3** *There are three steps in the solution of the problem.* part, phase, stage. **4** *What steps have you taken to find a job?* action, measure, move. **5** *She finds it difficult to climb steps.* rung, stair. □ **step in** see INTERVENE. **steps** *plural noun* ladder, staircase, stairs, stepladder. **step up** *He stepped up the dose.* boost, build up, increase, raise. OPPOSITE decrease.

stereotyped *adjective a stereotyped phrase.* clichéd, conventional, hackneyed, standardised.

sterile *adjective* **1** *a sterile couple.* barren, childless, infertile. OPPOSITE fertile. **2** *sterile country.* arid, bare, barren, desert, unfruitful, unproductive, waste. OPPOSITE fertile. **3** *a sterile sickroom.* antiseptic, aseptic, clean, disinfected, germ-free, hygienic, sanitary, sterilised. OPPOSITE septic.

sterilise *verb* **1** *The equipment must be sterilised.* clean, disinfect, fumigate, sanitise. **2** *The food was sterilised.* pasteurise, purify. **3** *The animals were sterilised.* castrate, desex, doctor, geld, neuter, spay.

stern[1] *adjective a stern headmaster.* austere, authoritarian, dour, forbidding, grim, hard, harsh, inflexible, rigid, severe, strict, tyrannical. OPPOSITE lenient.

stern[2] *noun the ship's stern.* back, poop, rear. OPPOSITE bow.

stevedore *noun* docker, watersider (*Australian*), waterside worker, wharfie (*Australian informal*), wharf labourer.

stew *verb She stewed the pork for our dinner.* braise, casserole. — *noun* **1** *beef stew.* casserole, fricassee, goulash, hotpot, ragout. **2** (*informal*) *He got in a stew about the exam.* dither, flap (*informal*), fluster, panic, state, tizzy (*informal*).

steward *noun* **1** *an airline steward.* flight attendant, hostess (*female*), hostie (*Australian informal*), stewardess (*female*). **2** *The landowner employs a steward to manage the estate.* agent, bailiff, manager.

stick[1] *noun* **1** *We collected sticks for the fire.* branch, twig. **2** *The gardener uses sticks to support his plants.* cane, pole, stake. **3** *He hit the animal with a stick.* baton, bludgeon, cane, club, cudgel, rod, truncheon, waddy (*Australian*). **4** *The old man walks with a stick.* cane, crook, staff, walking stick. **5** *Some sports use a stick.* bat, club, cue. **6** *a magician's stick.* baton, rod, wand. □ **the sticks** (*informal*) *They left the city and went to live in the sticks.* the backblocks (*Australian*), the back of beyond, the backwoods, the bush, the country, the outback (*Australian*), Woop Woop (*Australian informal*).

stick[2] *verb* **1** *She stuck the needle in her finger.* insert, jab, poke, push, thrust. **2** *They stick their pictures on the pinboard.* attach, fasten, fix, nail, pin, tack. OPPOSITE remove. **3** (*informal*) *He stuck a copy in each letterbox.* place, put, shove (*informal*), thrust. **4** *He stuck the label on the box.* affix, attach, glue, gum, paste, tape. OPPOSITE remove. **5** *The two surfaces have stuck together.* adhere, bind, bond, cement, fuse, glue, join, seal, weld. OPPOSITE separate. **6** *The bone stuck in her throat.* catch, jam, lodge, wedge. OPPOSITE dislodge. **7** *They were stuck for hours in the traffic.* catch, detain, hold up, immobilise, trap. **8** (*informal*) *She likes to stick at home.* remain, stay, stop. □ **stick at** (*informal*) *He stuck at the job.* continue, keep at, last at, persevere with, persist at. **stick by** *She stuck by her friend.* stand by, support. OPPOSITE desert. **stick out** **1** *The branch stuck out through the fence.* extend, jut out, poke out, project, protrude. **2** *The purple house sticks out.* be conspicuous, be noticeable, stand out. **stick to** *He stuck to the rules.* abide by, adhere to, follow, keep to. **stick up for** (*informal*) *She always sticks up for her friends.* back, back up, defend, side with, stand by, stand up for, support. OPPOSITE abandon.

sticker *noun Her suitcase was covered in stickers.* label, notice, seal, sign.

stick-up *noun* (*informal*) *a bank stick-up.* hold-up, robbery.

sticky *adjective* **1** *a sticky mixture.* gluey, glutinous, gooey (*informal*), tacky, viscous. OPPOSITE runny. **2** *sticky tape.* adhesive, gummed. **3** *sticky weather.* clammy, close, humid, muggy, steamy, sultry. OPPOSITE dry. **4** (*informal*) *a sticky situation.* awkward, delicate, difficult, ticklish, tricky.

stickybeak *noun* (*Australian informal*) *She's such a stickybeak.* busybody, Nosy Parker (*informal*), snooper (*informal*).

stiff *adjective* **1** *stiff cardboard.* firm, hard, inflexible, rigid. OPPOSITE flexible. **2** *stiff muscles.* rigid, taut, tense, tight. OPPOSITE relaxed, supple. **3** *a stiff mixture.* dense, firm, heavy, solid, thick. OPPOSITE fluid. **4** *a stiff test.* arduous, challenging, difficult, exacting, formidable, hard, rigorous, tough. OPPOSITE easy. **5** *She always is so stiff and difficult to talk to.* aloof, austere, cold, cool, formal, prim, reserved, starchy, stilted, strait-laced, unfriendly, wooden. OPPOSITE relaxed. **6** *a stiff sentence.* Draconian, drastic, hard, harsh, merciless, severe, tough. OPPOSITE lenient. **7** *a stiff breeze.* brisk, keen, strong. OPPOSITE gentle. **8** *a stiff drink.* potent, powerful, strong. OPPOSITE weak.

stiffen *verb The mixture stiffened.* coagulate, congeal, firm up, harden, jell (*informal*), set, solidify, thicken.

stifle *verb* **1** *He was stifled with a pillow.* asphyxiate, smother, suffocate. **2** *He stifled a giggle.* hold back, restrain, smother, suppress.

stigmatise *verb He was stigmatised as a coward.* brand, condemn, denounce, label.

still *adjective* **1** *Try to keep still.* immobile, inert, motionless, static, stationary, stock-still. OPPOSITE moving. **2** *a still night.* calm, noiseless, peaceful, quiet, silent, soundless, tranquil. OPPOSITE noisy. **3** *a pool of still water.* calm, stagnant, undisturbed. OPPOSITE flowing. — *noun in the still of the night.* calm, peace, quietness, silence, stillness, tranquillity. — *verb He stilled her fears.* allay, appease, calm, lull, pacify, quieten, settle, soothe, subdue. OPPOSITE arouse.

stilt *noun The houses are built on stilts.* block, pile, pillar, post.

stilted *adjective The writer's language is stilted.* artificial, awkward, forced, formal, laboured, pompous, stiff, unnatural. OPPOSITE natural.

stimulate *verb The excursion stimulated an interest in zoology.* activate, arouse, awaken, encourage, excite, inspire, prompt, provoke, rouse, spur, stir up, whet. OPPOSITE discourage.

stimulus *noun The reward acted as a stimulus.* encouragement, goad, incentive, inducement, shot in the arm, spur. OPPOSITE deterrent.

sting *noun The ointment soothes stings.* bite, prick, tingle, wound. — *verb* **1** *The bee stung her on the foot.* bite, nip, prick, wound. **2** *The onion made his eyes sting.* burn, hurt, smart, tingle. **3** *Her cutting remarks stung him into action.* goad, incite, provoke, spur, stimulate, stir.

stinging *adjective stinging remarks.* acid, biting, bitter, caustic, cutting, scathing.

stingy *adjective* **1** *a stingy person.* close-fisted, mean, mingy (*informal*), miserly, niggardly, parsimonious, penny-pinching, tight, tight-fisted. OPPOSITE generous. **2** *a stingy amount.* beggarly, inadequate, insufficient, meagre, measly (*informal*), paltry, scanty, skimpy, small. OPPOSITE lavish.

stink *noun the stink of the rubbish dump.* pong (*informal*), reek, stench. OPPOSITE fragrance. — *verb The place stinks.* pong (*informal*), reek, smell.

stinking *adjective* see SMELLY.

stint *verb She never stints on food.* be niggardly, be stingy, economise, pinch, skimp. — *noun He did his stint of serving on the counter.* period, quota, shift, spell, stretch, term, turn.

stipend *noun The minister is paid a stipend.* allowance, emolument, income, pay, salary.

stipulate *verb The contract stipulates the materials to be used.* demand, designate, insist on, lay down, specify, state.

stipulation *noun a stipulation in a contract.* condition, demand, proviso, requirement, specification.

stir *verb* **1** *Not even the leaves were stirring.* flutter, move, quiver, rustle, twitch. **2** *She stirred the pudding mixture.* agitate, beat, blend, mix, whip, whisk. **3** *The story stirred their interest.* arouse, awaken, excite, inspire, kindle, provoke, quicken, stimulate. **4** (*informal*) *He's only stirring you.* get someone going (*informal*), provoke, tease, wind up (*informal*). — *noun The news caused a stir.* commotion, disturbance, excitement, fuss, kerfuffle (*informal*), sensation, to-do.

stirrer *noun The police knew who the stirrers were.* activist, agitator, rabble-rouser, troublemaker.

stirring *adjective a stirring speech.* exciting, inspiring, moving, provocative, rousing, stimulating.

stitch *noun The wound needed five stitches.* suture. — *verb She stitched the dress.* baste, darn, embroider, mend, sew, tack.

stock *noun* **1** *She keeps a stock of soap.* accumulation, cache, hoard, quantity, reserve, stockpile, store, supply. **2** *The farmer sold half his stock.* animals, beasts, livestock. **3** *He comes of German stock.* ancestry, background, blood, descent, extraction, lineage. **4** *chicken stock.* bouillon, broth. — *adjective That is his stock reply.* customary, regular, routine, set, standard, traditional, usual. — *verb They stock her favourite chocolates.* carry, handle, have, keep, sell. □ **stock up on** *She stocked up on cat food.* accumulate, amass, buy up, hoard, lay in, stockpile.

stockings *plural noun* hose, hosiery, pantihose, tights.

stockman *noun* (*Australian*) drover (*Australian*), herdsman, stockrider (*Australian*).

stocky *adjective a stocky man.* burly, dumpy, nuggety (*Australian*), solid, stout, sturdy, thickset. OPPOSITE lanky.

stodgy *adjective* **1** *stodgy porridge.* heavy, indigestible, starchy. OPPOSITE light. **2** *a stodgy book.* boring, dreary, dull, tedious, uninteresting. OPPOSITE interesting.

stoical *adjective Her stoical acceptance of her illness was impressive.* calm, fatalistic, impassive, patient, philosophical, resigned, self-controlled, uncomplaining. OPPOSITE emotional.

stole *noun She wrapped her stole around her shoulders.* scarf, shawl, wrap.

stolid *adjective a stolid person.* apathetic, dull, impassive, indifferent, phlegmatic, unemotional, unexcitable, uninterested. OPPOSITE animated, emotional.

stomach *noun a protruding stomach.* abdomen, belly, gut, insides (*informal*), paunch, tummy (*informal*). — *verb He couldn't stomach the film.* abide, bear, endure, put up with, stand, take, tolerate.

stomp *verb He stomped up the hall and woke the baby.* clump, stamp, tramp. OPPOSITE tiptoe.

stone *noun* **1** *The surface was covered with stones.* boulder, cobble, gibber (*Australian*), pebble, rock; [*stones*] gravel, scree, shingle. **2** *a ring with a precious stone.* gem, jewel. **3** *cherry stones.* pip, pit, seed.

stoned *adjective* see INTOXICATED.

stonker *verb* (*Australian slang*) *They stonkered their opponents.* beat, defeat, euchre, get the better of, outwit, thwart.

stony *adjective* **1** *stony paths.* cobbled, gravelly, pebbly, rocky, rough, rugged, shingly. OPPOSITE smooth. **2** *a stony look.* blank, chilly, cold, fixed, frosty, hard, icy, indifferent, unfeeling, unresponsive, unsympathetic. OPPOSITE friendly, warm.

stooge *noun He always plays the stooge.* butt, fall guy (*slang*), foil, straight man.

stoop *verb* **1** *He stooped to go through the low doorway.* bend down, crouch, duck, kneel, lean over. OPPOSITE straighten up. **2** *He hasn't stooped to lying, has he?* demean yourself, descend, fall, lower yourself, resort, sink. — *noun She walks with a stoop.* droop, hunch, slouch.

stop *verb* **1** *He stopped the car.* brake, halt, pull up, stall, switch off, turn off. OPPOSITE start. **2** *She danced until the music stopped.* cease, come to an end, end, finish, terminate.

OPPOSITE start. **3** *He tried to stop them from going.* bar, hinder, keep, preclude, prevent. OPPOSITE allow. **4** *The accident stopped traffic.* block, halt, hamper, immobilise, impede, obstruct. **5** *They have stopped these illegal practices.* abolish, discontinue, do away with, put an end to. OPPOSITE introduce. **6** *She stopped reading and looked up.* abandon, break off, cease, conclude, desist, discontinue, finish, give up, halt, interrupt, knock off (*informal*), leave off, pause, quit, refrain from. OPPOSITE begin, continue. **7** *The supply has stopped.* expire, peter out, run out. OPPOSITE continue. **8** (*informal*) *They stopped at a friend's place for the weekend.* put up, rest, sojourn, stay, stop off, stop over. **9** *They cannot stop the bleeding.* arrest, check, curb, stanch, stem. **10** *All the gaps have been stopped.* block, bung, close, fill, plug, seal. — *noun* **1** *Everything has come to a stop.* cessation, close, conclusion, end, finish, halt, rest, standstill, termination. OPPOSITE start. **2** *a stop in proceedings.* break, interlude, intermission, pause, recess, suspension. OPPOSITE resumption.

stopgap *noun He was only employed as a stopgap.* fill-in, relief, stand-in (*informal*), substitute, temporary.

stopover *noun London to Sydney with a stopover in Singapore.* break, stay, stop, stop-off.

stoppage *noun an industrial stoppage.* shutdown, strike, walkout.

stopper *noun a stopper for a cask.* bung, cork, plug.

store *noun* **1** *She has a store of toothpaste in her cupboard.* accumulation, cache, collection, hoard, pile, reserve, stock, stockpile, supply. **2** *The stores stay open until 9 p.m.* department store, emporium, general store, megastore, retailer, shop, supermarket. **3** *The truck collected the furniture from the store.* depot, storehouse, warehouse. — *verb She is storing empty jars for future use.* accumulate, collect, hoard, keep, lay up, preserve, put aside, put away, reserve, save, stash (*informal*), stockpile, stow. OPPOSITE discard.

storey *noun a building of twenty storeys.* floor, level.

storm *noun* **1** *Houses were damaged in the storm.* blizzard, cloudburst, cyclone, deluge, downpour, dust storm, gale, hailstorm, hurricane, rainstorm, sandstorm, snowstorm, squall, tempest, thunderstorm, tornado, typhoon, willy willy (*Australian*). **2** *a storm of protest. a political storm.* commotion, furore, fuss, outcry, row, rumpus, stir, to-do, uproar. — *verb* **1** *She stormed out of the room.* charge, rush, stamp, stomp, tear. **2** *The soldiers stormed the building.* attack, charge, invade, raid, rush, take by storm, take over.

stormy *adjective Stormy weather has been forecast.* blustery, foul, gusty, inclement, squally, tempestuous, turbulent, violent, wild, windy. OPPOSITE mild.

story *noun* **1** *She is reading a story.* allegory, anecdote, fable, legend, myth, narrative, novel, parable, tale, yarn. **2** *He's sticking to his story of what happened.* account, chronicle, record, report, statement, version. **3** (*informal*) *Stop telling stories and tell the truth.* falsehood, fib, fiction, furphy (*Australian informal*), lie, untruth.

storyline *noun The book has a complicated storyline.* plot, scenario, story.

stout *adjective* **1** *a stout stick.* fat, solid, strong, sturdy, thick. OPPOSITE thin. **2** *a stout person.* burly,

corpulent, fat, obese, overweight, plump, portly, rotund, stocky, tubby. OPPOSITE skinny. **3** *stout support.* bold, brave, courageous, determined, fearless, resolute, valiant. OPPOSITE timid.

stow *verb The luggage was stowed in the boot.* load, pack, put, stash (*informal*), store, stuff.

straggle *verb The young ones straggled behind the older children.* dawdle, lag, loiter, spread out, stray, trail.

straggler *noun They had to wait for the stragglers.* dawdler, laggard, loiterer, slowcoach, stray.

straggly *adjective long straggly hair.* lank, loose, unkempt, untidy. OPPOSITE neat.

straight *adjective* **1** *in a straight line.* direct, unbending, unswerving. OPPOSITE curved. **2** *The paintings are straight.* aligned, level, square. OPPOSITE crooked. **3** *The room is now straight.* neat, orderly, shipshape, tidy. OPPOSITE untidy. **4** *He won in straight sets.* consecutive, successive, unbroken. **5** *I want you to be straight with me.* candid, direct, frank, honest, straightforward, truthful, upfront (*informal*). OPPOSITE evasive. — *adverb* **1** *Go straight to bed.* directly, immediately, instantly. **2** *I told him straight.* candidly, directly, frankly, honestly, without beating about the bush. □ **straight away** *He left straight away.* at once, directly, immediately, instantly, on the spot, right away, without delay.

straightforward *adjective* **1** *a straightforward person.* candid, direct, frank, honest, open, straight, truthful. OPPOSITE devious. **2** *a straightforward procedure.* easy, simple, uncomplicated. OPPOSITE complex.

strain[1] *verb* **1** *Our patience was strained to the limit.* push, stretch, tax, test. **2** *He has strained a muscle.* injure, pull, rick, sprain, wrench. **3** *He strained to lift the heavy box.* exert yourself, heave, strive, struggle, try. **4** *He strained the mixture to remove lumps.* filter, percolate, riddle, screen, sieve, sift. — *noun* **1** *She felt under too much strain in her job.* pressure, stress, tension. **2** *muscle strain.* injury, pull, rick, sprain, wrench. **3** *Even the simplest things are a strain for her.* burden, drag, effort, exertion, struggle. **4** *They all joined in the well-known strain.* air, melody, song, tune.

strain[2] *noun a new strain of roses.* breed, kind, type, variety.

strainer *noun a food strainer.* colander, filter, sieve, sifter.

strait *noun The ship crossed the strait.* channel, narrows, passage, sound. □ **in dire straits** in a mess, in a predicament, in a spot (*informal*), in difficulties, in distress, in need, in strife (*Australian informal*), in trouble.

strait-laced *adjective The strait-laced lady did not understand the joke.* old-fashioned, prim, proper, prudish, puritanical, stuffy. OPPOSITE broad-minded.

strand *noun She separated the cotton into six strands.* fibre, filament, thread.

stranded *adjective* **1** *a stranded ship.* beached, grounded, shipwrecked, stuck. **2** *They left us stranded without our luggage.* abandoned, deserted, high and dry, in the lurch, marooned.

strange *adjective* **1** *She likes to visit strange places.* alien, exotic, foreign, unfamiliar, unknown. OPPOSITE familiar. **2** *a strange idea. a strange person.* abnormal, bizarre, curious, eccentric, extraordinary, funny, new, novel, odd, outlandish, pecu-

liar, queer, singular, surprising, uncanny, unconventional, unusual, way-out (*informal*), weird, zany. OPPOSITE ordinary.

stranger *noun They welcome strangers into their home.* alien, foreigner, newcomer, outsider, visitor. OPPOSITE friend.

strangle *verb He strangled his victim.* asphyxiate, choke, garrotte, suffocate, throttle.

strap *noun tied with straps.* band, belt, bowyang (*Australian*), cord, thong, tie; [*straps*] braces. — *verb The baggage is strapped to the roof.* attach, bind, fasten, lash, secure, tie, truss.

strapping *adjective a strapping young man.* healthy, husky, robust, strong, sturdy, tall, vigorous. OPPOSITE puny.

stratagem *noun He devised a clever stratagem to obtain what he wanted.* artifice, dodge, manoeuvre, plan, ploy (*informal*), ruse, scheme, subterfuge, tactic, trick.

strategic *adjective a strategic move.* calculated, planned, politic, tactical.

strategy *noun the strategy for winning the game.* approach, method, plan, policy, scheme, tactics.

stratum *noun* **1** *Several strata were visible in the cliff face.* layer, lode, seam, vein. **2** *They belong to the same stratum of society.* class, echelon, level, rank, station.

stray *verb* **1** *He searched for the sheep that had strayed.* go astray, roam, rove, straggle, wander. **2** *Do not stray from the subject.* deviate, digress, drift, get away, wander. — *adjective a stray animal.* abandoned, homeless, lost, roaming, wandering.

streak *noun* **1** *She has streaks of pink in her hair.* band, line, strip, stripe. **2** *He has a nasty streak.* element, side, strain, vein. **3** *She's on a winning streak.* run, series, spell, stretch, trot (*Australian informal*). — *verb* **1** *Her clothes were streaked with paint.* mark, smear, stain, stripe. **2** *He streaked ahead.* dart, dash, run, rush, speed, tear, whiz, zoom.

stream *noun* **1** *The streams are marked in blue on the map.* brook, creek, rill, river, rivulet, tributary, watercourse. **2** *a steady stream of traffic.* flow, line. **3** *a stream of water.* flood, flow, gush, jet, rush, surge, torrent. **4** *She moves against the stream.* current, flow, tide. — *verb Water streamed from the hose.* flood, gush, issue, pour, run, rush, shoot, spill, spout, spurt, surge.

streamer *noun The streets were decorated with streamers.* bunting, flag, pennant, ribbon.

streamlined *adjective* **1** *a streamlined car.* aerodynamic, sleek, smooth. **2** *a streamlined process.* efficient, rationalised, simplified, smooth.

street *noun They live in the same street.* alley, avenue, boulevard, close, crescent, cul-de-sac, drive, highway, lane, place, road, terrace, thoroughfare.

strength *noun* **1** *a man of great strength.* brawn, endurance, might, muscle, power, robustness, stamina, toughness. OPPOSITE weakness. **2** *the strength of the earthquake.* force, intensity, power. **3** *the strength of the mixture.* concentration, efficacy, intensity, potency. **4** *Diplomacy is one of her strengths.* asset, forte, strong point. OPPOSITE weakness.

strengthen *verb* **1** *The fence needs to be strengthened.* brace, buttress, prop up, reinforce, shore up, support. **2** *The wind strengthened.* heighten, increase, intensify. OPPO-

SITE lessen. **3** *This has strengthened their relationship.* bolster, boost, build up, develop, enhance, fortify, improve. OPPOSITE weaken.

strenuous *adjective* **1** *He made strenuous efforts for their release.* determined, energetic, indefatigable, persistent, sedulous, tenacious, untiring, vigorous. **2** *a strenuous task.* arduous, demanding, difficult, exhausting, hard, herculean, laborious, taxing, tough, uphill. OPPOSITE effortless.

stress *noun* **1** *Her headaches are caused by stress.* anxiety, pressure, strain, tension, worry. **2** *He puts a lot of stress on correct spelling.* emphasis, importance, priority, value, weight. **3** *The stress is on the last syllable.* accent, beat, emphasis, force. — *verb He stressed the point.* accentuate, dwell on, emphasise, highlight, impress, insist on, labour, underline. OPPOSITE play down.

stressful *adjective a stressful job.* demanding, difficult, draining, exhausting, onerous, pressured, taxing, tense, trying, worrying. OPPOSITE easy.

stretch *verb* **1** *He stretched the material.* draw out, elongate, expand, extend, lengthen, pull out. OPPOSITE shrink. **2** *Knitted fabrics stretch.* be elastic, expand. **3** *The land stretches from here to the river.* cover, extend, reach, spread. **4** *My patience was stretched to the limit.* challenge, strain, tax, test. — *noun* **1** *The material has lost its stretch.* elasticity, give, stretchiness. **2** *a stretch of land.* area, distance, expanse, length, section, tract. **3** *a ten-minute stretch of skipping.* period, spell, stint, term.

stretcher *noun* (*Australian*) camp bed, camp stretcher, folding bed.

stricken *adjective stricken with polio.* affected, afflicted, smitten, struck down.

strict *adjective* **1** *a strict translation.* close, exact, faithful, literal, precise. OPPOSITE loose. **2** *strict rules.* absolute, binding, firm, hard and fast, inflexible, rigid, stringent. OPPOSITE flexible. **3** *a strict teacher.* authoritarian, firm, inflexible, rigid, severe, stern, tough, uncompromising. OPPOSITE indulgent, lenient.

stride *verb He strides around the yard.* march, pace, stalk, walk. — *noun He takes long strides.* pace, step.

strident *adjective a strident voice.* discordant, grating, harsh, loud, rasping, raucous. OPPOSITE soft.

strife *noun There is strife between the unions and the government.* conflict, disagreement, discord, dissension, friction, trouble, unrest. OPPOSITE harmony. □ **in strife** (*Australian informal*) *She's always in strife and needing help.* in a mess, in difficulties, in hot water (*informal*), in the soup (*slang*), in trouble.

strike *verb* **1** *He struck the other man.* bash, batter, beat, belt (*slang*), box, clobber (*informal*), clout (*informal*), cuff, dong (*Australian informal*), flog, hit, job (*informal*), knock, lash, punch, quilt (*Australian slang*), rap, slap, smack, smite, sock (*slang*), spank, stoush (*Australian slang*), swipe (*informal*), tap, thrash, thump, thwack, trounce, wallop (*informal*), whack, whip. **2** *The car struck an oncoming car.* bump into, collide with, crash into, hit, knock into, ram into, run into, smash into. **3** *The virus strikes the nervous system.* affect, afflict, attack. **4** *The clock struck one.* chime, peal, sound, toll. **5** *The diggers struck gold.* come upon, discover, find, reach, stumble on. **6** *The idea struck me.* come to, dawn upon, hit, occur to. **7** *How does he* *strike you?* appear to, come across (*informal*), impress, seem to. **8** *The workers are striking for improved rosters.* down tools (*informal*), go on strike, stop work, take industrial action, walk out. — **noun** *The strike was over working conditions.* industrial action, stoppage, walkout.

striking *adjective* *a striking likeness.* amazing, astounding, conspicuous, extraordinary, impressive, noticeable, obvious, remarkable.

string *noun* **1** *He wrapped the parcel with string.* cord, rope, twine. **2** *a string of beads.* chain, necklace, strand. **3** *A string of people were already waiting.* column, file, line, queue, row. **4** *a string of events.* chain, sequence, series, succession. — *verb* **1** *He strung the wire between the tree and the house.* hang, sling, stretch, suspend, tie. **2** *She likes stringing beads.* lace, thread.

stringent *adjective* *Stringent rules apply.* firm, inflexible, rigid, rigorous, strict, tough, uncompromising.

strip^{1} *verb* **1** *He stripped the wallpaper.* peel off, remove, shave off, take off. **2** *The doctor asked him to strip to the waist.* disrobe, expose yourself, undress.

strip^{2} *noun* *a strip of land. a strip of material.* band, bar, belt, ribbon, stripe.

stripe *noun* *The uniform has blue and white stripes.* band, bar, chevron, line, strip.

striped *adjective* *a red and blue striped cloth.* banded, lined, striated, stripy.

strive *verb* **1** *His report praised him for striving to do his best.* aim, attempt, endeavour, make an effort, try. **2** *They strove against impossible odds.* battle, contend, fight, struggle.

stroke^{1} *noun* **1** *As punishment he received six strokes of the cane.* blow, hit, lash, whack. **2** *She suffered a stroke.* apoplexy, cerebral haemorrhage, seizure.

stroke^{2} *verb* *The cat likes having her back stroked.* caress, massage, pat, rub, touch.

stroll *verb* *They strolled beside the river.* amble, promenade, ramble, saunter, walk, wander.

stroller *noun* *a baby's stroller.* pushchair, pusher (*Australian*).

strong *adjective* **1** *strong furniture.* durable, hard-wearing, heavy-duty, indestructible, sound, stout, sturdy, tough, unbreakable. OPPOSITE flimsy. **2** *a man as strong as Hercules.* brawny, burly, hardy, hefty, mighty, muscular, robust, sinewy, stalwart, sturdy, tough. OPPOSITE weak. **3** *a strong argument.* cogent, compelling, convincing, forceful, irrefutable, persuasive, powerful, solid, sound, weighty. OPPOSITE unconvincing. **4** *a strong wind.* mighty, powerful, violent. OPPOSITE mild. **5** *a strong team.* formidable, invincible, powerful, unbeatable, unconquerable. OPPOSITE weak. **6** *strong measures.* drastic, extreme, firm, harsh, severe, stiff, stringent. OPPOSITE weak. **7** *a strong curry.* aromatic, hot, piquant, pungent, sharp, spicy. OPPOSITE mild. **8** *strong colours.* bold, bright, dark, deep, intense, loud, solid, vivid. OPPOSITE pale. **9** *a strong accent.* clear, definite, distinct, marked, noticeable, obvious, pronounced, unmistakable. OPPOSITE faint. **10** *a strong drink.* alcoholic, concentrated, fortified, heady, intoxicating, potent, stiff. OPPOSITE low-alcohol, soft. **11** *a strong faith.* ardent, earnest, fervent, firm, intense, keen, passionate, powerful, steadfast, unshakeable. OPPOSITE half-hearted, weak. □ **strong point** *The applicant listed his strong points.* asset, attribute, forte, quality, speciality, strength. OPPOSITE weakness.

stronghold *noun* *They bombed all the enemy's strongholds.* bastion, castle, citadel, fort, fortification, fortress.

stroppy *adjective* (*informal*) *He gets stroppy when he can't have his own way.* bad-tempered, difficult, irritable, obstreperous, perverse, snaky (*Australian informal*), uncooperative. OPPOSITE tractable.

structure *noun* **1** *the structure of a book, company, etc.* arrangement, composition, configuration, constitution, design, form, framework, layout, make-up, organisation, shape. **2** *The architect has designed a magnificent structure.* building, construction, edifice. — *verb* *The course is structured to meet the different needs of students.* arrange, design, construct, organise, put together.

struggle *verb* **1** *They struggled to make ends meet.* battle, endeavour, labour, strain, strive, toil, try, work hard. **2** *The man struggled with his opponent.* battle, contend, fight, grapple, scuffle, spar, tussle, vie, wrestle. — *noun* **1** *After a brief struggle he surrendered.* battle, conflict, confrontation, contest, fight, scuffle, skirmish, tussle. **2** *She finds writing a struggle.* effort, grind, hassle (*informal*), strain, trial. OPPOSITE cinch (*informal*).

strut *verb* *He strutted into the room wanting to be noticed.* flounce, parade, prance, stride, swagger. OPPOSITE sneak.

stub *noun* **1** *Cigarette stubs leave a stale smell in a room.* butt, end, remains, remnant, stump. **2** *He wrote the details of the cheque on the stub.* butt, counterfoil. — *verb* **1** *He stubbed his toe.* bump, hit, knock, strike. **2** *He stubbed his cigarette out.* extinguish, put out, snuff.

stubbly *adjective* *a stubbly face.* bristly, prickly, whiskery.

stubborn *adjective* **1** *a stubborn person.* adamant, defiant, dogged, headstrong, inflexible, intractable, intransigent, obstinate, pigheaded, recalcitrant, refractory, strong-minded, uncompromising, unyielding. OPPOSITE docile. **2** *stubborn stains.* ground-in, ingrained, persistent.

stuck *adjective* **1** *He was stuck in the traffic.* caught, held up, stranded, trapped. **2** *She was stuck on the hard questions.* at a loss, baffled, beaten, bushed (*Australian informal*), stumped (*informal*).

stuck-up *adjective* (*informal*) *a stuck-up prig.* arrogant, conceited, condescending, haughty, high and mighty, hoity-toity, patronising, pretentious, proud, snobbish, snooty (*informal*), toffee-nosed (*informal*), uppity (*informal*). OPPOSITE modest.

student *noun* apprentice, learner, postgraduate, pupil, scholar, schoolboy, schoolchild, schoolgirl, trainee, undergraduate.

studio *noun* *a craftsman's studio.* workroom, workshop.

studious *adjective* *a studious child.* academic, bookish, diligent, intellectual, scholarly.

study *noun* **1** *She went to university to pursue her studies.* education, instruction, learning, research, scholarship, training. **2** *The government commissioned a study of poverty.* analysis, examination, inquiry, investigation, review, survey. **3** *He works in the study.* den, office, studio, workroom. — *verb* **1** *He is studying law at university.* learn, read, take. **2** *She needs to study for the test.* cram, learn, memorise, revise, swot (*informal*). **3** *The medical team studied the drug's side effects.* analyse, examine, inquire into, investigate, look at, research, survey.

stuff *noun* **1** *sticky stuff.* material, matter, substance. **2** *They leave their stuff everywhere.* belongings, bits and pieces, effects, gear, goods, junk (*informal*), odds and ends, paraphernalia, possessions, things. — *verb* **1** *She stuffed her clothes in the drawer.* cram, jam, pack, push, put, ram, shove (*informal*), squash, squeeze, stash (*informal*), stow. **2** *He stuffed the cushion with feathers.* fill, pack, pad, wad. **3** *She stuffed herself with delicious cakes.* fill, gorge, sate, satiate.

stuffing *noun* *The cushions need new stuffing.* filling, padding, wadding.

stuffy *adjective* **1** *a stuffy atmosphere.* airless, close, fusty, humid, muggy, musty, oppressive, stale, stifling, suffocating, sultry, unventilated. OPPOSITE airy. **2** *Her nose is stuffy.* blocked up, clogged up, congested, stuffed up. OPPOSITE clear. **3** *a stuffy lecturer.* conventional, dreary, dull, narrow-minded, old-fashioned, priggish, prim, staid, strait-laced.

stumble *verb* **1** *She stumbled on the rocky path.* fall, falter, flounder, lurch, reel, sprawl, stagger, topple, totter, trip. **2** *She stumbled through the sonata.* blunder, falter, flounder. □ **stumble on** *I stumbled on the solution by accident.* chance on, come across, discover, find, happen on, hit on.

stumbling block *noun* *The biggest stumbling block to a peaceful end is unfinished business.* barrier, difficulty, hindrance, hitch, hurdle, impediment, obstacle, snag.

stump *noun* *a tree stump. the stump of a tooth.* base, butt, end, remnant, stub. — *verb* (*informal*) *The question stumped him.* baffle, bewilder, confound, mystify, perplex, puzzle, throw (*informal*).

stun *verb* **1** *She was stunned by a blow on the head.* daze, knock out, numb. **2** *The news stunned me.* amaze, astonish, astound, bewilder, bowl over, dumbfound, flabbergast, floor, overwhelm, shock, stagger, stupefy, surprise.

stunning *adjective* (*informal*) *What a stunning dress!* attractive, beautiful, exquisite, fantastic (*informal*), gorgeous (*informal*), sensational (*informal*), spectacular, splendid, striking, stupendous, wonderful. OPPOSITE plain.

stunt^{1} *verb* *His growth was stunted by poor diet.* check, curb, hamper, hinder, impede, inhibit, restrict, retard. OPPOSITE promote.

stunt^{2} *noun* *The crowd was impressed with his brave stunts.* act, exploit, feat, performance, trick.

stupefy *verb* **1** *The drugs had stupefied him.* daze, dull, fuddle, numb. **2** *She was stupefied by the strange events.* amaze, astonish, astound, bewilder, confound, flabbergast, mystify, overwhelm, shock, stagger, stun, surprise.

stupendous *adjective* *a stupendous achievement.* amazing, astonishing, astounding, colossal, enormous, exciting, extraordinary, great, huge, immense, incredible, marvellous, phenomenal, prodigious, sensational (*informal*), spectacular, stunning (*informal*), terrific (*informal*), tremendous (*informal*), unbelievable, unreal (*slang*), wonderful. OPPOSITE ordinary.

stupid *adjective* **1** *a stupid person.* asinine, bovine, brainless, clueless (*informal*), dense, dim (*informal*), dim-witted, dopey (*informal*), dull, dumb (*informal*), feeble-minded, foolish, half-witted, idiotic, obtuse, simple-minded, slow, thick, unintelligent. OPPOSITE intelligent. **2** *It was a stupid thing to do.* absurd, crazy, foolhardy, foolish, idiotic, imprudent, inane, irrational, ludicrous, mad, mindless, nonsensical, reckless, senseless, silly, unwise. OPPOSITE sensible.

sturdy *adjective* **1** *a sturdy person.* brawny, burly, hardy, hefty, husky, mighty, muscular, nuggety (*Australian*), robust, stalwart, stout, strapping, strong, tough, vigorous. OPPOSITE weak. **2** *a sturdy chair.* durable, indestructible, solid, sound, strong, tough, unbreakable. OPPOSITE flimsy.

stutter *verb* *He stutters when he speaks.* falter, stammer, stumble.

style *noun* **1** *The essay was marked for style and content.* expression, language, phraseology, wording. **2** *a modern style of painting.* approach, genre, manner, method, mode, technique, way. **3** *various styles of jacket.* design, fashion, kind, pattern, shape, sort, type, version. **4** *a woman with style.* chic, class, elegance, flair, panache, polish, sophistication. — *verb* *He styled the woman's hair.* arrange, cut, design, shape.

stylish *adjective* *a stylish outfit.* chic, classy (*informal*), elegant, fashionable, smart, snazzy (*informal*), trendy (*informal*), up-to-date, with it (*informal*). OPPOSITE dowdy.

suave *adjective* *suave manners.* bland, charming, debonair, diplomatic, gracious, polite, smooth, sophisticated, urbane.

subconscious *adjective* *a subconscious desire.* instinctive, intuitive, unconscious.

subdue *verb* **1** *The police subdued the demonstrators.* control, defeat, overcome, overpower, quell, repress, restrain, suppress. **2** *They subdued their voices.* hush, lower, moderate, mute, quieten, soften, tone down. OPPOSITE raise.

subject *noun* **1** *Her favourite subject is mathematics.* course, discipline, field. **2** *The subject of her lecture is safety in the home.* issue, matter, substance, theme, topic. — *verb* *The doctor subjected him to a battery of tests.* expose, put through, submit, treat. — *adjective* **subject to 1** *He is subject to colds.* liable to, prone to, susceptible to, vulnerable to. **2** *She accepted the invitation, subject to her parents' approval.* conditional upon, contingent on, dependent upon.

subjective *adjective* *a subjective criticism.* biased, personal, prejudiced. OPPOSITE objective.

subjugate *verb* *The invading forces subjugated the villagers.* conquer, overpower, quell, subdue, subject, vanquish.

sublime *adjective* **1** *sublime music.* awe-inspiring, elevated, exalted, glorious, grand, lofty, magnificent, majestic, noble, wonderful. OPPOSITE ordinary. **2** *sublime indifference.* complete, extreme, supreme, total, utter.

submerge *verb* **1** *The olives must be submerged in brine.* dunk, immerse, plunge, soak, souse, steep. **2** *All the low-lying land was submerged.* cover, drown, engulf, flood, inundate, swamp. **3** *The submarine submerged.* dive, go under. OPPOSITE surface.

submission *noun* **1** *The committee received numerous submissions.* entry, presentation, proposal, suggestion, tender. **2** *a leader who demands submission.* capitulation, compliance, deference, humility, meekness, obedience, passivity, surrender.

submissive *adjective She became bolder and less submissive.* accommodating, acquiescent, compliant, deferential, docile, humble, meek, obedient, passive, servile, tractable, unassertive, yielding. OPPOSITE defiant.

submit *verb* **1** *They had to submit to the enemy in the end.* bow, capitulate, give in, surrender, throw in the towel, yield. OPPOSITE resist. **2** *She submitted her research proposal.* give in, hand in, offer, present, proffer, put forward, tender. OPPOSITE withdraw.

subordinate *adjective* **1** *a subordinate consideration.* lesser, secondary, subsidiary. OPPOSITE primary. **2** *subordinate officers.* inferior, junior, lower. OPPOSITE senior.

subpoena *noun She received a subpoena to appear in court.* order, summons, writ.

subscribe *verb* **subscribe to 1** *She subscribes generously to various charities.* contribute to, donate to, give to, help, support. **2** *She does not subscribe to euthanasia.* accept, agree with, approve of, believe in, endorse, go along with, hold with (*informal*), support.

subscription *noun She has paid her subscription to the club.* contribution, dues, fee, membership fee, sub (*informal*).

subsequent *adjective subsequent discoveries.* ensuing, following, later, succeeding. OPPOSITE previous.

subservient *adjective His subservient manner did not win him promotion.* deferential, fawning, obsequious, servile, slavish, submissive, sycophantic, toadying, truckling. OPPOSITE superior.

subside *verb* **1** *The land has subsided.* cave in, collapse, drop, settle, sink. OPPOSITE rise. **2** *The storm subsided.* abate, decrease, die down, diminish, ebb, lessen, let up, moderate, recede, wane, weaken. OPPOSITE intensify.

subsidiary *adjective She is a full-time teacher with a subsidiary income from writing.* additional, extra, lesser, minor, secondary, subordinate, supplementary. OPPOSITE principal.

subsidise *verb The government subsidised the scheme.* back, contribute to, finance, fund, sponsor, support, underwrite.

subsidy *noun The centre is paid a government subsidy for each user.* assistance, contribution, grant.

subsist *verb They barely manage to subsist on his income.* exist, live, survive.

substance *noun* **1** *They have identified the substance.* material, matter, stuff. **2** *the substance of an argument.* essence, gist, heart, nub, pith, thrust.

substandard *adjective a substandard hotel.* inferior, mediocre, poor, second-class, second-rate, shoddy, unsatisfactory.

substantial *adjective* **1** *a substantial amount.* big, considerable, large, significant, sizeable, tidy (*informal*). OPPOSITE insignificant. **2** *a substantial house.* solid, strong, well-built. OPPOSITE flimsy. **3** *We were in substantial agreement.* basic, essential, fundamental.

substantiate *verb You have to be able to substantiate your statement.* authenticate, back up, confirm, corroborate, prove, support, validate, verify. OPPOSITE disprove.

substitute *noun a substitute for a teacher, doctor, actor, etc.* deputy, fill-in, locum, proxy, relief, replacement, reserve, ring-in (*Australian*

informal), stand-in, stopgap, sub (*informal*), surrogate, understudy. — *verb* **1** *The copy was substituted for the original painting.* exchange, interchange, replace, swap, switch. **2** *He will substitute for you while you are away.* cover, deputise, fill in, relieve, stand in.

subterfuge *noun The con men used a clever subterfuge to get inside the house.* artifice, deception, dodge (*informal*), lurk (*Australian informal*), plan, ploy, pretext, ruse, scheme, stratagem, trick, wile.

subtle *adjective* **1** *a subtle difference.* fine, imperceptible, minor, slight, tiny. OPPOSITE obvious. **2** *a subtle fragrance.* delicate, faint, gentle, mild, understated. OPPOSITE strong. **3** *subtle methods.* clever, cunning, devious, ingenious, sly, sneaky, wily. OPPOSITE crude.

subtract *verb If you subtract 3 from 5 you are left with 2.* deduct, remove, take away, take off. OPPOSITE add.

suburb *noun They live in a quiet suburb.* area, community, district, neighbourhood.

subvert *verb The new government was subverted.* destroy, overthrow, overturn, sabotage, topple, undermine.

subway *noun* tunnel, underpass.

succeed *verb* **1** *His plan succeeded.* bear fruit, be effective, be successful, work. OPPOSITE fail. **2** *She finally succeeded as an actress.* achieve success, do well, make good, make it, prosper. **3** *He succeeded his brother as captain.* come after, follow, replace, supplant, take over from. OPPOSITE precede.

success *noun* **1** *We wished him success.* achievement, attainment, prosperity, triumph, victory. OPPOSITE failure. **2** *The play was a success.* hit, sell-out (*informal*), sensation, smash hit (*informal*), triumph, winner. OPPOSITE failure, flop (*informal*).

successful *adjective* **1** *a successful enterprise.* booming, effective, flourishing, fruitful, productive, profitable, prosperous, thriving. OPPOSITE unsuccessful. **2** *the successful team.* triumphant, victorious, winning. OPPOSITE losing.

succession *noun a succession of mishaps.* chain, cycle, line, round, run, sequence, series, string, train. □ **in succession** *three wins in succession.* consecutively, in a row, one after the other, running, successively.

successive *adjective three successive wins.* consecutive, straight, uninterrupted.

succinct *adjective a succinct report.* brief, concise, condensed, laconic, pithy, terse. OPPOSITE long-winded.

succour *noun She gave succour to the injured.* aid, assistance, help, relief. — *verb He succoured the needy.* aid, assist, help, minister to, relieve.

succulent *adjective succulent strawberries.* juicy, luscious, moist.

succumb *verb He succumbed to the temptation.* bow, capitulate, give in, give way, submit, surrender, yield. OPPOSITE resist.

suck *verb* **suck up** *The vacuum cleaner sucks up the dirt.* draw up, pick up, pull up. **suck up to** (*informal*) *He was despised because he sucked up to the teacher.* crawl to (*informal*), fawn on, flatter, grovel to, kowtow to, play up to, toady to.

sucker *noun* (*informal*) *He was a sucker to fall for that.* dupe, mug (*informal*), muggins (*informal*), pushover (*informal*), sap (*informal*).

suckle *verb The animal suckles its young.* breastfeed, feed, nurse.

sudden *adjective a sudden decision.* abrupt, hasty, impetuous, instant, precipitate, quick, rapid, rash, snap,

surprise, swift, unexpected, whirlwind. OPPOSITE gradual. □ **all of a sudden** abruptly, all at once, in an instant, in the twinkling of an eye, out of the blue, quickly, suddenly, unexpectedly, without warning. OPPOSITE gradually, slowly.

suds *plural noun a sink full of suds.* bubbles, foam, froth, lather.

suffer *verb* **1** *She suffered a lot of pain.* bear, cope with, endure, experience, feel, go through, put up with, undergo. **2** *He wouldn't let the dog suffer.* be in pain, feel pain, hurt. **3** *He will not suffer any insolence.* allow, permit, put up with, stand, take, tolerate.

suffering *noun Nothing could ease the suffering.* affliction, agony, anguish, discomfort, distress, grief, hardship, heartache, hurt, misery, pain, sorrow, torment, torture, tribulation, woe.

suffice *verb That will suffice for the purpose.* answer, be adequate, be ample, be enough, be sufficient, do, satisfy, serve.

sufficient *adjective sufficient food to feed a family.* adequate, ample, enough. OPPOSITE insufficient.

suffocate *verb* asphyxiate, choke, smother, stifle, strangle, throttle.

sugary *adjective a sugary taste.* cloying, saccharine, sickly, sweet. OPPOSITE sour.

suggest *verb* **1** *The rash suggests rubella.* be a sign of, indicate, signal. **2** *Was he suggesting that she was lying?* hint, imply, insinuate, intimate. **3** *He suggested that we take a rest.* advise, advocate, propose, put forward, recommend.

suggestion *noun He would not follow her suggestion.* advice, proposal, recommendation, tip.

suggestive *adjective She was upset by his suggestive remarks.* bawdy, improper, indecent, lewd, obscene, risqué, rude.

suicidal *adjective suicidal behaviour.* self-destructive.

suit *noun* **1** *She wore a green suit.* costume, ensemble, outfit. **2** *a criminal suit.* action, case, lawsuit, proceedings. — *verb* **1** *That time suits me.* be acceptable to, be convenient for, be right for, be suitable for, fit in with, please. OPPOSITE be inconvenient to. **2** *That dress suits her.* become, look good on.

suitable *adjective a suitable remark.* acceptable, apposite, appropriate, apt, becoming, befitting, convenient, fitting, meet (*old use*), pertinent, proper, relevant, right, satisfactory, seemly, timely. OPPOSITE inappropriate, unsuitable.

suitcase *noun* bag, case, grip, port (*Australian*), portmanteau, trunk, valise.

suitor *noun The lady has several suitors.* admirer, beau, boyfriend, lover, swain (*old use*), sweetheart.

sulky *adjective a sulky child.* bad-tempered, brooding, disgruntled, moody, peevish, petulant, pouting, resentful, scowling, sullen.

sullen *adjective a sullen man.* bad-tempered, brooding, dismal, gloomy, grouchy (*informal*), grumpy, melancholy, moody, morose, resentful, sour, sulky, surly, unsociable. OPPOSITE cheerful.

sully *verb His reputation has been sullied.* blemish, disgrace, smirch, soil, spoil, stain, taint, tarnish.

sultry *adjective sultry weather.* close, hot, humid, muggy, oppressive, sticky, stifling, stuffy, suffocating.

sum *noun* **1** *the sum of the first five numbers.* addition, aggregate, subtotal, total. **2** *a tidy sum of money.* amount, quantity. **3** *The teacher set ten sums for homework.* calculation, problem. — *verb* **sum up** **1** *He summed up all that had been said.*

précis, recap (*informal*), recapitulate, review, summarise. **2** *She summed him up quickly.* assess, judge, size up.

summarise *verb* see SUM UP (at SUM).

summary *noun a summary of the report.* abstract, digest, outline, précis, recap (*informal*), recapitulation, résumé, synopsis. — *adjective* **1** *a summary account.* brief, concise, condensed, short, succinct. OPPOSITE lengthy. **2** *summary dismissal.* hasty, instant, instantaneous, prompt.

summit *noun They reached the summit of the mountain.* apex, crest, crown, peak, pinnacle, top, zenith. OPPOSITE base.

summon *verb* **1** *She summoned the fire brigade.* call out, send for. **2** *He was summoned to appear in court.* call, command, order, subpoena, summons. □ **summon up** *He summoned up all his strength.* call on, draw on, gather, invoke, muster.

summons *noun I received a summons to appear in court.* command, demand, order, subpoena, writ.

sumptuous *adjective a sumptuous feast.* costly, expensive, extravagant, grand, lavish, luxurious, magnificent, opulent, posh (*informal*), splendid.

sunbathe *verb She spent too long sunbathing and got burnt.* bask, sunbake, sun yourself.

sundry *adjective Sundry items for sale.* assorted, diverse, miscellaneous, several, various.

sunny *adjective* **1** *a sunny day.* bright, clear, cloudless, fair, fine, sunlit. OPPOSITE dull. **2** *a sunny disposition.* blithe, bright, buoyant, cheerful, gay, genial, happy, jovial, joyful, light-hearted, smiling. OPPOSITE gloomy.

sunrise *noun He wakes at sunrise.* cock-crow, dawn, daybreak, first light, sun-up.

sunset *noun He goes for a walk at sunset.* dusk, evening, gloaming, nightfall, sundown, twilight.

sunshade *noun protected by a sunshade.* awning, canopy, parasol.

superb *adjective a superb meal. a superb performance.* brilliant (*informal*), cool (*informal*), excellent, exceptional, fabulous (*informal*), fantastic (*informal*), fine, first-class, first-rate, grand, great, impressive, magnificent, marvellous, outstanding, remarkable, splendid, stupendous, super (*informal*), superlative, terrific (*informal*), top-notch (*informal*), wonderful. OPPOSITE inferior, poor.

supercilious *adjective His supercilious manner puts people off.* arrogant, condescending, disdainful, haughty, hoity-toity, lofty, lordly, patronising, proud, scornful, self-important, snobbish, stuck-up (*informal*), superior.

superficial *adjective* **1** *a superficial wound.* exterior, external, shallow, skin-deep, slight, surface. OPPOSITE deep. **2** *superficial knowledge of first aid.* cursory, limited, partial, sketchy, slight. OPPOSITE thorough.

superfluous *adjective He gave away the superfluous copies.* excess, extra, redundant, spare, surplus, unnecessary, unneeded.

superhuman *adjective superhuman power.* divine, miraculous, prodigious, supernatural.

superintendent *noun The superintendent has 20 people working under him.* administrator, boss, chief, foreman, head, manager, overseer, supervisor, warden.

superior *adjective* **1** *a superior officer.* higher, senior. OPPOSITE inferior. **2** *superior quality.* better, excellent, first-class, greater, outstanding, super (*informal*), top, unequalled. OPPOSITE inferior, poor. **3** *a superior tone of voice.* arrogant, condescending, disdainful, haughty, high and mighty, hoity-toity, lofty, patronising, self-important, smug, snobbish, stuck-up (*informal*), supercilious.

superlative *adjective a superlative performance.* consummate, excellent, first-class, incomparable, magnificent, matchless, outstanding, superb, supreme, unparalleled, unsurpassed. OPPOSITE mediocre.

supernatural *adjective supernatural power.* extraordinary, metaphysical, miraculous, mysterious, mystic, occult, paranormal, psychic, unearthly.

supersede *verb This model supersedes the original one.* displace, oust, replace, supplant, take the place of.

supervise *verb He supervised the work.* administer, control, direct, head, manage, orchestrate, organise, oversee, preside over, run, stage-manage, superintend.

supervision *noun* **1** *He was praised for his supervision of the project.* administration, direction, management, organisation, oversight. **2** *The prisoners are under close supervision.* control, observation, scrutiny, surveillance, watch.

supervisor *noun She referred the matter to her supervisor.* administrator, boss, chief, director, foreman, head, manager, overseer, superintendent, superior.

supine *adjective a supine position.* face upwards, flat on your back; see also HORIZONTAL. CONTRASTS WITH prone, upright.

supplant *verb He was supplanted in her affections by a newcomer.* displace, oust, replace, supersede, take the place of.

supple *adjective Exercise keeps his body supple.* flexible, limber, lithe, pliable. OPPOSITE stiff.

supplement *noun* **1** *a single-person supplement.* add-on, extra, surcharge. **2** *a supplement to the document.* addendum, addition, appendix, codicil, insert, postscript, rider. — *verb The second job is to supplement his income.* add to, augment, boost, increase, top up.

supplementary *adjective a supplementary income.* additional, extra.

supplication *noun She made her supplications to God.* appeal, entreaty, petition, plea, prayer, request.

supplier *noun a uniform supplier.* dealer, distributor, merchant, retailer, seller, shopkeeper, stockist, vendor, wholesaler.

supply *verb They will supply you with a car.* equip, furnish, give, provide. — *noun* **1** *the supply of gas to homes.* delivery, provision. **2** *He has laid in a supply of matches.* hoard, reserve, stock, stockpile, store.

support *verb* **1** *He used a plank to support the fence.* bolster, brace, buttress, hold up, prop up, reinforce, shore up. **2** *That chair won't support two of you.* bear, carry, hold, take. **3** *He supports a family of five.* keep, maintain, provide for. **4** *She supports the club.* back, barrack for (*Australian*), contribute to, finance, patronise, subsidise. **5** *She supported him in his campaign.* assist, back, champion, defend, endorse, help, side with, stand by, stand up for, stick by, stick up for. **6** *She was supported in her time of sorrow.* comfort, encourage, help, succour, sustain. **7** *Witnesses supported her story.* back up, confirm, corroborate, endorse, substantiate, uphold, verify. — *noun* **1** *He promised his support to the club.* aid, assistance, backing, help, patron-

age, sponsorship. **2** *One of the supports has collapsed.* bolster, brace, bracket, buttress, calliper, column, crutch, foundation, joist, pillar, post, prop, stanchion, stay, stilt, strut.

supporter *noun They thanked their supporters.* ally, backer, benefactor, champion, fan, follower, helper, patron, well-wisher. OPPOSITE opponent.

supportive *adjective a supportive wife.* caring, concerned, encouraging, helpful, sympathetic, understanding.

suppose *verb I suppose that he will show up.* assume, believe, expect, fancy, guess, imagine, presume, surmise, think. □ **be supposed to** *You are supposed to attend.* be expected to, be meant to, be obliged to.

supposition *noun We require facts, not suppositions.* assumption, conjecture, guess, hypothesis, opinion, presumption, speculation, surmise, theory. OPPOSITE fact.

suppress *verb* **1** *The army suppressed the riot.* crush, overcome, overpower, put an end to, quash, quell, squash, stop. **2** *They can't suppress the truth.* censor, conceal, cover up, hide, keep secret, silence, withhold. OPPOSITE expose. **3** *He suppressed his anger.* bottle up, contain, control, keep in check, repress, restrain, stifle. OPPOSITE express.

supreme *adjective* **1** *The king has supreme authority.* chief, highest, leading, paramount, principal, sovereign. **2** *He was awarded a medal for supreme bravery.* consummate, extreme, greatest, highest, utmost, uttermost.

sure *adjective* **1** *I am sure you are right.* assured, certain, confident, convinced, persuaded, positive. OPPOSITE unsure. **2** *The play is sure to be a hit.* bound, certain, guaranteed. **3** *One thing is sure.* certain, clear, definite, indisputable, true, undeniable. OPPOSITE uncertain. **4** *a sure cure.* certain, dependable, failsafe, infallible, reliable, sure-fire (*informal*), trustworthy, unfailing. OPPOSITE unreliable. □ **make sure** *She made sure that there was a train.* ascertain, check, confirm, double-check, make certain, verify.

surf *noun* foam, spume; see also WAVE.

surface *noun a smooth surface.* coating, covering, exterior, façade, finish, outside, shell, skin, top, veneer. OPPOSITE inside. — *adjective surface damage.* exterior, external, superficial. — *verb The diver surfaced.* come up, emerge, rise. OPPOSITE submerge.

surge *verb* **1** *The sea surged.* billow, heave, roll, swell. **2** *The crowd surged forward.* push, rush, stream. — *noun* **1** *a surge of water.* flow, gush, rush, stream, wave. **2** *a surge of interest.* growth, increase, rise, upsurge.

surly *adjective As he got older he became more surly.* bad-tempered, churlish, crabby, crotchety, crusty, grouchy (*informal*), gruff, grumpy, rude, snaky (*Australian informal*), sullen, testy, unfriendly. OPPOSITE friendly.

surmise *verb He could only surmise that she was sick.* assume, conjecture, guess, infer, presume, speculate, suppose, suspect.

surmount *verb* **1** *She has surmounted all the difficulties.* conquer, get over, overcome, prevail over, triumph over. **2** *The roof is surmounted by a cross.* cap, crown, top.

surname *noun* family name, last name.

surpass *verb* **1** *She surpasses the others at mathematics.* beat, do better

than, eclipse, excel, outclass, outdo, outshine, outstrip, overshadow, top. **2** *This result surpasses all expectation.* exceed, go beyond, transcend.

surplus *noun We ate what we could and gave away the surplus.* excess, glut, remainder, residue, surfeit. OPPOSITE deficit.

surprise *noun* **1** *They were filled with surprise.* amazement, astonishment, incredulity, shock, wonder. **2** *The news came as a complete surprise.* bolt from the blue, bombshell, shock. — *verb* **1** *The news surprised them.* amaze, astonish, astound, confound, dumbfound, flabbergast, nonplus, shock, stagger, startle, stun, take aback. **2** *He surprised them eating in the library.* catch, catch red-handed, discover, spring (*Australian informal*), take unawares.

surprised *adjective* amazed, astonished, astounded, dumbfounded, flabbergasted, nonplussed, shocked, speechless, staggered, startled, stunned, taken aback, thunderstruck.

surprising *adjective a surprising result.* amazing, astonishing, astounding, incredible, mind-boggling (*informal*), staggering, startling, unexpected, unforeseen. OPPOSITE predictable.

surrender *verb* **1** *He surrendered his licence to the policeman.* give, hand over, part with, relinquish. **2** *Finally the gunman surrendered.* capitulate, give in, give yourself up, submit, throw in the towel, yield. OPPOSITE resist.

surreptitious *adjective surreptitious copying.* clandestine, covert, furtive, secret, secretive, sly, stealthy, sneaky, underhand. OPPOSITE open.

surrogate *noun* see SUBSTITUTE.

surround *verb* **1** *A fence surrounds the garden.* encircle, enclose, ring, skirt. **2** *She was surrounded by fans.* beset, besiege, encircle, hem in.

surroundings *plural noun He works in pleasant surroundings.* environment, environs, milieu, setting.

surveillance *noun The man was under police surveillance.* observation, scrutiny, supervision, watch.

survey *verb* **1** *He surveyed the scene from the lookout.* contemplate, look at, observe, view. **2** *This chapter surveys other theories.* consider, examine, explore, inspect, investigate, look at, look over, review, scrutinise, study. **3** *His job is to survey the land.* map out, measure, plot. — *noun a survey of voting trends in Australia.* examination, inquiry, inspection, investigation, overview, poll, review, study.

survival *noun the fight for survival.* existence, life, subsistence. OPPOSITE extinction.

survive *verb* **1** *They cannot survive on one income.* exist, live, make ends meet, subsist. **2** *Some traditions have survived.* continue, endure, keep on, last, live on, persist. OPPOSITE die. **3** *He won't survive the winter.* come through, endure, last, live through. **4** *She survived her husband by ten years.* outlast, outlive. OPPOSITE predecease.

susceptible *adjective* **1** *susceptible to colds.* inclined, liable, predisposed, prone. OPPOSITE immune. **2** *susceptible to her charms.* open, receptive, responsive, sensitive, vulnerable. OPPOSITE insensitive, resistant.

suspect *verb* **1** *I suspect that you're right.* believe, fancy, guess, have a feeling, have a hunch, imagine, suppose, surmise, think. OPPOSITE know. **2** *They suspected his reliability.* distrust, doubt, have misgivings

about, mistrust, question. OPPOSITE trust.

suspend *verb* **1** *Decorations were suspended from the ceiling.* dangle, hang, sling. **2** *He suspended the inquiry.* adjourn, defer, delay, postpone, put off, shelve. **3** *They suspended payments while she was sick.* cease, discontinue, halt, interrupt, stop. OPPOSITE continue, resume. **4** *He was suspended from his job.* lay off, stand down.

suspense *noun The suspense was intolerable.* anticipation, expectation, tension, uncertainty, waiting. OPPOSITE certainty.

suspicion *noun* **1** *The jealous husband was filled with suspicion.* distrust, doubt, misgiving, mistrust, scepticism. **2** *She had a suspicion that they would win.* feeling, hunch, idea, notion. **3** *a suspicion of garlic in the soup.* dash, hint, soupçon, suggestion, tinge, touch, trace.

suspicious *adjective* **1** *a suspicious mind.* disbelieving, distrustful, doubting, incredulous, mistrustful, sceptical, wary. OPPOSITE trusting. **2** *suspicious activities.* dubious, fishy (*informal*), questionable, shady, suspect, untrustworthy. OPPOSITE above board.

suss *verb* (*informal*) **suss out** **1** *She sussed out the local shops.* check out, explore, inspect, investigate. **2** *He hasn't sussed out what's going on.* grasp, realise, tumble to (*informal*), twig (*informal*), work out.

sustain *verb* **1** *The walls were built to sustain the weight of the roof.* bear, carry, hold, support, take. **2** *Eat food which sustains you.* keep alive, keep going, nourish. **3** *The book sustained his interest.* hold, keep, maintain. **4** *They sustained heavy losses.* experience, suffer, undergo.

swag *noun* **1** (*informal*) *The thief dropped the swag.* booty, loot, plunder, spoils, takings. **2** (*Australian*) *The tramp carries his belongings in his swag.* bluey (*Australian*), drum (*Australian*), matilda (*Australian*), shiralee (*Australian*). **3** (*Australian informal*) *He had a swag of bills to pay.* heap (*informal*), lot, masses, mountain, pile (*informal*).

swagger *verb All eyes turned as he swaggered down the mall.* parade, prance, strut.

swagman *noun* (*Australian*) bagman (*Australian*), sundowner (*Australian*), swaggie (*Australian*), tramp.

swallow *verb* **1** *She swallowed her food.* consume, devour, eat, gobble, gulp, guzzle, ingest, scoff (*informal*). **2** *He swallowed his drink.* down (*informal*), gulp, guzzle, imbibe, quaff, swig (*informal*), swill. **3** *He swallowed the story.* accept, believe, buy (*slang*), fall for (*informal*). □ **swallow up** *He was swallowed up in the crowd.* absorb, assimilate, engulf, swamp.

swamp *noun The coastal land was a swamp.* bog, fen, marsh, morass, quagmire, slough. — *verb* **1** *The waves swamped the boat.* engulf, fill, flood, inundate, submerge. **2** *They were swamped with orders.* deluge, flood, inundate, overwhelm, snow under.

swan *noun* cob (*male*), cygnet (*young*), pen (*female*).

swap *verb* **1** *They swapped stamps.* barter, exchange, trade. **2** *They swapped the paintings and no one noticed.* exchange, interchange, substitute, switch. — *noun They did a swap while nobody was looking.* exchange, substitution.

swarm *noun a swarm of insects. a swarm of people.* army, cluster, crowd, drove, flock, herd, host, mass, mob, multitude, myriad, throng. — *verb* **1** *The children* *swarmed into the hall.* crowd, flock, pour, rush, stream, surge. **2** *The people swarmed outside the building.* cluster, congregate, crowd, flock, herd, mass, mob, throng. □ **swarm with** *The place swarmed with journalists.* be alive with, be crowded with, be overflowing with, be overrun by, crawl with, teem with.

swarthy *adjective a swarthy complexion.* dark, tanned. OPPOSITE fair.

swathe *verb The wounded leg was swathed in bandages.* bandage, bind up, cover, envelop, swaddle, wrap.

sway *verb* **1** *He swayed unsteadily and then fell.* lurch, reel, rock, stagger, swing, totter, wobble. **2** *We were swayed by his stirring speech.* influence, move, persuade, win over. **3** *She has never swayed in her opinion.* change, fluctuate, swerve, vacillate, waver.

swear *verb* **1** *He swore to tell the truth.* pledge, promise, vow. **2** *He swears when he's angry.* blaspheme, curse. □ **swear word** blasphemy, expletive, four-letter word (*informal*), obscenity, profanity.

sweat *noun in a sweat after exercise.* lather, perspiration. — *verb He sweats heavily.* perspire.

sweater *noun* jersey, jumper, pullover, skivvy (*Australian*), sweatshirt, top, windcheater.

sweep *verb* **1** *He swept the floor.* brush, clean, clear. **2** *They all swept past him.* belt (*slang*), charge, dash, fly, race, rush, sail, speed, tear, zoom. — *noun* **1** *a long sweep of coastline.* arc, curve, expanse, extent, stretch. **2** *She gave the rugs a sweep.* brush, clean.

sweeping *adjective* **1** *He has made sweeping changes.* broad, comprehensive, extensive, far-reaching, huge, massive, radical, wholesale, wide-ranging. OPPOSITE minor. **2** *a sweeping statement.* broad, general, unqualified. OPPOSITE specific.

sweet *adjective* **1** *a sweet taste.* cloying, luscious, saccharine, sickly, sugary, syrupy. OPPOSITE bitter, savoury, sour. **2** *a sweet smell.* balmy, fragrant, perfumed, scented. OPPOSITE foul. **3** *sweet sounds.* dulcet, euphonious, harmonious, mellifluous, mellow, melodious, pleasant, tuneful. OPPOSITE harsh. **4** (*informal*) *She has such a sweet face.* appealing, attractive, cute, lovely, pretty. **5** (*informal*) *What a sweet person she is!* amiable, charming, considerate, dear, delightful, endearing, generous, gentle, good-natured, kind, likeable, lovable, nice, pleasant, thoughtful. OPPOSITE disagreeable. — *noun* **1** *a bag of sweets for two dollars.* candy (*American*), confection, lolly (*Australian*), toffee. **2** *No room for sweet after the roast.* afters (*informal*), dessert, pudding (*British*).

sweetheart *noun a childhood sweetheart.* beloved, boyfriend, girlfriend, love, lover.

swell *verb* **1** *Her stomach swelled after overeating.* bloat, blow up, bulge, distend, expand, inflate, puff up. OPPOSITE shrink. **2** *The visitors swelled the numbers.* augment, boost, increase, inflate. OPPOSITE diminish. **3** *The crowd swelled.* build up, grow, increase, multiply. OPPOSITE decrease. **4** *The music swelled.* grow louder, heighten, intensify. OPPOSITE die away. **5** *The sea swelled.* billow, heave, mount, rise, surge. OPPOSITE fall. — *noun* **1** *The boat was caught in a heavy swell.* billows, surge, waves. **2** *a swell in numbers.* increase, rise, surge.

swelling *noun The swelling went down after a day.* blister, boil, bulge, bump, inflammation, lump, protuberance.

sweltering *adjective a sweltering day.* boiling, hot, scorching, stifling, sultry, torrid. OPPOSITE freezing.

swerve *verb We swerved to avoid hitting the other car.* deviate, sheer, turn, veer.

swift *adjective* **1** *He is swift on his feet.* brisk, fast, fleet, nimble, nippy (*informal*), quick, speedy. OPPOSITE slow. **2** *a swift response.* expeditious, hasty, immediate, prompt, quick, rapid. OPPOSITE slow.

swiftly *adverb* see QUICKLY.

swig *verb* (*informal*) *He swigged his beer.* gulp, quaff, swill; see also DRINK. — *noun* (*informal*) *He took a big swig of wine.* draught, gulp, mouthful.

swill *verb He swilled the glasses under the tap.* clean, rinse, wash. — *noun kitchen swill.* pigswill, slop.

swim *verb She likes to swim after school.* bathe, bogey (*Australian*), have a dip. □ **swimming costume** bathers (*Australian*), bathing suit, bikini, cossie (*Australian informal*), swimmers (*Australian*), swimsuit, togs (*Australian informal*), trunks. **swimming pool** aquatic centre, baths, pool.

swindle *verb They swindled her out of her savings.* cheat, con (*informal*), deceive, defraud, diddle (*informal*), dupe, fleece, hoax, hoodwink, rip off (*informal*), rook, trick. — *noun victims of a swindle.* con (*informal*), confidence trick, deception, fraud, hoax, racket, rip-off (*informal*), rort (*Australian slang*), scam (*slang*), swizz (*informal*), trick.

swindler *noun The swindler had cheated them of their money.* charlatan, cheat, con man (*informal*), crook (*informal*), fraud, racketeer, rogue, shark, sharper, shicer (*Australian slang*), shyster (*informal*), trickster.

swing *verb* **1** *The plank swings up and down.* flap, oscillate, rock, seesaw, sway. **2** *She swung a rope between the trees.* dangle, hang, sling, suspend. **3** *She swung round to face the other way.* rotate, spin, swivel, turn. **4** *Her mood swings from hope to despair.* alter, change, fluctuate, oscillate, shift, switch, vary, waver. — *noun* **1** *He took a swing with the bat.* stroke, sweep, swipe (*informal*). **2** *the swing in the vote.* change, fluctuation, movement, shift, turnaround, variation.

swipe *verb* (*informal*) **1** *He swiped the ball.* belt (*slang*), hit, strike, swing at, whack. **2** *The thief swiped my bag.* grab, nab (*informal*), nick (*slang*), pinch (*informal*), seize, snatch, snitch (*slang*), steal. — *noun* (*informal*) *He took a swipe at the ball.* hit, stroke, swing.

swirl *verb It was windy and the dust was swirling.* eddy, revolve, spin, spiral, twirl, twist, whirl.

swish *adjective* (*informal*) *a swish hotel.* elegant, fashionable, posh (*informal*), smart, snazzy (*informal*), swanky (*informal*).

switch *noun* **1** *He hit the animal with a switch.* lash, rod, stick, whip. **2** *a switch in methods.* about-face, change, changeover, shift, U-turn, variation. — *verb* **1** *Switch on the light.* flick, turn. **2** *He switched their glasses.* change, exchange, interchange, substitute, swap.

swivel *verb She likes to swivel on her chair.* pivot, revolve, rotate, spin, turn, twirl, whirl.

swollen *adjective a swollen abdomen.* bloated, bulging, distended, inflated, puffed-up, puffy. OPPOSITE shrunken.

swoon *verb & noun* see FAINT.

swoop *verb The bird swooped on the mouse.* descend, dive, plunge, pounce, spring. □ **swoop on** *The soldiers swooped on the town.* attack, descend on, raid, rush, storm.

sword *noun The two knights fought with swords.* blade, broadsword, claymore, cutlass, foil, rapier, sabre, scimitar, steel (*literary*).

swot *verb* see STUDY.

sycophant *noun The boss was surrounded by sycophants.* crawler (*informal*), fawner, flatterer, lackey, toady, truckler, yes-man.

symbol *noun* **1** *the company's symbol.* badge, emblem, insignia, logo, sign, token, trade mark. **2** *The table explains the meaning of the symbols.* character, figure, ideogram, letter, mark, pictogram, sign.

symbolic *adjective a symbolic play.* allegorical, figurative, metaphorical.

symbolise *verb White symbolises purity.* betoken, denote, express, indicate, mean, represent, signify, stand for.

symmetrical *adjective a symmetrical shape.* balanced, even, regular. OPPOSITE asymmetrical, lopsided.

symmetry *noun the symmetry of the human body.* balance, evenness, harmony, regularity. OPPOSITE asymmetry.

sympathetic *adjective a sympathetic judge.* caring, compassionate, concerned, humane, kind, kindly, merciful, supportive, tender-hearted, understanding, warm-hearted. OPPOSITE cold-hearted, unsympathetic.

sympathise *verb* **sympathise with** **1** *We sympathised with the unhappy family.* commiserate with, feel compassion for, feel for, feel sorry for, offer condolences to, pity. **2** *I can sympathise with those feelings.* empathise with, identify with, relate to, understand. **3** *He sympathised with their cause.* agree with, approve of, back, side with, support. OPPOSITE disapprove of.

sympathiser *noun a party sympathiser.* comrade, fellow-traveller, supporter. OPPOSITE opponent.

sympathy *noun He felt deep sympathy for the victims.* commiseration, compassion, concern, condolences, empathy, feeling, pity, tenderness, understanding. OPPOSITE indifference.

symptom *noun the symptoms of the disease.* feature, indication, mark, pointer (*informal*), sign, signal.

syndicate *noun The companies formed a syndicate.* alliance, association, cartel, consortium, federation, group, league.

synopsis *noun a synopsis of the play.* abstract, outline, précis, résumé, summary.

synthesis *noun The discussion led to a synthesis of ideas.* amalgamation, blend, combination, fusion, mixture, union.

synthetic *adjective synthetic grass.* artificial, fake, imitation, man-made, manufactured. OPPOSITE natural.

syringe *noun* hypodermic, needle.

system *noun* **1** *a system of highways.* arrangement, network, organisation, set-up, structure. **2** *a system for doing the job.* approach, method, methodology, order, plan, procedure, routine, scheme, structure, technique, way.

systematic *adjective a systematic approach.* businesslike, efficient, logical, methodical, ordered, orderly, organised, planned, scientific. OPPOSITE haphazard.

Tt

table *noun* **1** *He put the things down on the table.* altar, bar, bench, buffet, counter, desk, lectern, stand. **2** *The information was presented in a table.* chart, list, tabulation.

tableland *noun the Atherton Tableland.* highland, plateau.

tablet *noun* **1** *The chemist sells cold tablets.* caplet, capsule, lozenge, pill. **2** *The words were written on a stone tablet.* panel, plaque, plate, slab.

taboo *adjective taboo words.* banned, forbidden, prohibited, proscribed, unacceptable, unmentionable. OPPOSITE acceptable.

tacit *adjective tacit approval.* implicit, implied, silent, unspoken, unstated. OPPOSITE explicit.

taciturn *adjective She was shy and taciturn.* quiet, reserved, reticent, silent, uncommunicative, unforthcoming. OPPOSITE loquacious.

tack *noun* **1** *The poster was fastened with tacks.* drawing pin, nail, pin, staple. **2** *He changed tack.* approach, course, direction, method, policy, strategy, tactic. — *verb* **1** *She tacked the picture to the board.* fasten, fix, nail, pin, staple. **2** *The dressmaker tacks the seam first.* baste, sew, stitch. **3** *She tacked an extra paragraph on the letter.* add, annex, append, attach, tag. OPPOSITE delete.

tackle *noun The sports shop sells fishing tackle.* apparatus, equipment, gear, kit, rig. — *verb* **1** *He tackled the problem systematically.* address, approach, attack, deal with, grapple with, handle, manage, set about. **2** *He successfully tackled the other player.* attack, challenge, intercept, take on.

tacky *adjective* **1** *The paint is still tacky.* sticky, wet. OPPOSITE dry. **2** (*informal*) *tacky ornaments.* cheap, garish, gaudy, kitsch, shabby, tasteless, tawdry.

tact *noun She handled the situation with tact.* courtesy, delicacy, diplomacy, discretion, sensitivity. OPPOSITE tactlessness.

tactful *adjective a tactful comment.* considerate, courteous, diplomatic, discreet, polite, politic, sensitive, thoughtful. OPPOSITE tactless.

tactic *noun He tried a different tactic to win them over.* approach, manoeuvre, plan, ploy (*informal*), policy, scheme, strategy, tack.

tactless *adjective He apologised for his tactless remark.* impolite, impolitic, inconsiderate, indiscreet, insensitive, thoughtless, undiplomatic. OPPOSITE tactful.

tag *noun a name tag.* label, sticker, tab, ticket. — *verb* **1** *The clothes have been tagged.* identify, label, mark, ticket. **2** *He tagged on an extra paragraph.* add, append, attach, tack. □ **tag along** *Do you mind if he tags along with us?* accompany, come, follow, go, trail.

tail *noun* **1** *an animal's tail.* brush, dock, scut. **2** *She was at the tail of the queue.* back, end, rear. OPPOSITE head. — *verb* (*informal*) *The police tailed the suspect.* dog, follow, pursue, shadow, stalk, track, trail.

tailor *noun The tailor makes all their clothes.* clothier, couturier, dressmaker, outfitter.

taint *verb* **1** *The chemicals tainted the water.* contaminate, infect, poison, pollute, spoil. OPPOSITE purity. **2** *His impropriety had tainted his reputation.* blacken, blemish, blot, stain, sully, tarnish. OPPOSITE enhance.

take *verb* **1** *He took her hand.* clasp, clutch, grab, grasp, hold, pluck, seize, snatch. OPPOSITE let go. **2** *They took many prisoners.* abduct, capture, carry off, catch, detain, seize. OPPOSITE release. **3** *She took all the prizes.* acquire, gain, get, obtain, receive, scoop up, secure, win. **4** *Someone has taken my watch.* appropriate, help yourself to, lift (*informal*), make off with, nick (*slang*), pilfer, pinch (*informal*), pocket, purloin, remove, snaffle (*informal*), snatch, snavel (*Australian informal*), snitch (*slang*), souvenir (*slang*), steal, swipe (*informal*). OPPOSITE give back. **5** *He takes the eight o'clock train.* catch, travel by, use. **6** *It takes courage to speak out.* call for, demand, need, require. **7** *He offered to take us home.* accompany, bring, carry, conduct, convey, deliver, escort, guide, lead, run, transport. **8** *She takes delight in teasing the cat.* derive, experience, gain, get, obtain. **9** *He took it that they were satisfied.* assume, conclude, construe, gather, infer, interpret, suppose, understand. **10** *He took the blame.* accept, assume, bear, shoulder. **11** *She took her mother's advice.* accept, adopt, follow, heed. OPPOSITE ignore. **12** *He couldn't take the strain.* bear, endure, put up with, stand, stomach, suffer, tolerate, undergo, withstand. **13** *She took English at university.* learn, read, study. **14** *Which teacher takes Latin?* instruct in, lecture in, teach, tutor in. □ **take after** *She takes after her mother.* be the (spitting) image of, look like, resemble. **take away 1** *The teacher took away the comics.* appropriate, commandeer, confiscate, deprive someone of, impound, remove, seize. OPPOSITE return. **2** *Take 5 away from 7.* deduct, subtract. OPPOSITE add to. **take back** *He took back his statement.* recant, retract, revoke, withdraw. **take in 1** *He did not take in all the information.* absorb, assimilate, comprehend, digest, grasp, realise, understand. **2** *The scoundrel took them in with his smooth talk.* cheat, con (*informal*), deceive, dupe, fool, have on (*informal*), hoodwink, mislead, trick. **take off 1** *He took off his wet clothes.* doff, peel off, remove, shed, strip off. OPPOSITE don. **2** *The actor is clever at taking people off.* caricature, imitate, lampoon, mimic, parody, send up (*informal*). **3** *He took off in a waiting car.* see LEAVE. **take on 1** *She took on the extra responsibility willingly.* accept, assume, shoulder, undertake. **2** *The firm took on two new people.* appoint, employ, engage, hire, recruit. OPPOSITE dismiss. **take out** *He took the splinter out.* draw out, extract, pull out, remove. OPPOSITE insert. **take part** *Ten children took part in the contest.* be involved, compete, enter, join, participate. **take place** *The accident took place at noon.* befall, come about, come to pass, happen, occur. **take up 1** *He took up a new career at 60.* begin, commence, embark on, start. **2** *Sewing takes up her time.* consume, eat up, fill, make inroads into, occupy, use up. **3** *He took up from where he left off.* carry on, continue, pick up, recommence, resume.

take-off *noun* **1** *a brilliant take-off of the politician.* caricature, imitation, lampoon, parody, send-up (*informal*), spoof (*informal*). **2** *the spacecraft's take-off.* blast-off, launch, lift-off. OPPOSITE landing.

takings *plural noun* *The thief stole the day's takings.* earnings, income, proceeds, receipts, revenue.

tale *noun* *a tale of adventure.* account, anecdote, fable, fairy tale, legend, myth, narrative, saga, story, yarn (*informal*).

talent *noun* *artistic talent. a talent for mathematics.* ability, accomplishment, aptitude, bent, capacity, flair, genius, gift, knack, prowess, skill.

talk *verb* **1** *They talked for hours.* chat, chatter, converse, gabble, gossip, jabber, mag (*Australian informal*), natter (*informal*), prattle, rabbit on (*informal*), speak, yabber (*Australian informal*), yak (*informal*). **2** *The baby has just learnt to talk.* babble, communicate, speak, vocalise. **3** *The minister talked to the children.* address, lecture, preach, speak. OPPOSITE listen. **4** *He needs to talk to a counsellor.* confer (with), consult, speak, unburden yourself. — *noun* **1** *The friends had a long talk.* chat, chinwag (*informal*), confabulation, conference, consultation, conversation, dialogue, discussion, gossip, natter (*informal*), tête-à-tête, yabber (*Australian informal*), yak (*informal*). **2** *baby talk.* language, speech. **3** *We went to a talk on global warming.* address, discourse, lecture, oration, presentation, sermon, speech. **4** *There's been talk of a strike.* gossip, hearsay, report, rumour. □ **talk down to** *He talks down to his pupils.* condescend to, patronise. **talk into** *They talked him into staying.* cajole into, coax into, convince to, persuade to. **talk out of** *They talked him out of resigning.* deter from, discourage from, dissuade from, stop.

talkative *adjective* *a talkative child.* chatty, communicative, garrulous, loquacious, voluble. OPPOSITE taciturn.

talker *noun* chatterbox, conversationalist, gasbag (*informal*), orator, speaker, windbag (*informal*). OPPOSITE listener.

tall *adjective* **1** *a tall person.* gangling, gigantic, lanky, leggy. OPPOSITE short. **2** *a tall building.* high, lofty, multi-storey, towering. OPPOSITE low.

tally *noun* *They kept a tally of their spending.* account, count, reckoning, record, score, total. — *verb* *Her story does not tally with theirs.* accord, agree, coincide, concur, conform, correspond, match, square.

talon *noun* *a bird's talon.* claw.

tame *adjective* **1** *a tame animal.* docile, domestic, domesticated, gentle. OPPOSITE wild. **2** *The film turned out to be quite tame.* bland, boring, dull, flat, unexciting, uninteresting. OPPOSITE exciting. — *verb* *He succeeded in taming the horse.* break in, domesticate, subdue, train.

tamper *verb* **tamper with** *Someone had tampered with the controls.* fiddle with, interfere with, meddle with, muck around with, play with, tinker with.

tan *verb* *His skin has tanned.* bronze, brown, suntan. — *adjective* *a tan colour.* bronze, brownish-yellow, khaki, tawny, yellowish-brown.

tang *noun* *Hospital food often lacks tang.* bite, flavour, piquancy, pungency, savour, sharpness, spiciness.

tangible *adjective* *tangible proof.* concrete, definite, objective, palpable, real, solid, substantial. OPPOSITE intangible.

tangle *verb* *He tangled the wires.* confuse, entangle, entwine, knot, ravel, snarl, twist. OPPOSITE untangle. — *noun* *She sorted out the tangle of threads.* confusion, jumble, jungle, knot, maze, muddle, snarl, web.

tangled *adjective* *tangled hair.* dishevelled, knotted, knotty, matted, ruffled, tousled, unkempt. OPPOSITE neat.

tangy *adjective* *a tangy lemon jelly.* acid, piquant, pungent, sharp, sour, tart.

tank *noun* **1** *a water tank.* cistern, reservoir, vat. **2** *a fish tank.* aquarium.

tantalise *verb* *He tantalised the dog with a piece of meat.* entice, lead on, tease, tempt, torment. OPPOSITE gratify.

tantamount *adjective* *Her action was tantamount to stealing.* as good as, equal, equivalent, the same as.

tantrum *noun* fit of temper, hysterics, outburst, paddy (*informal*), rage.

tap¹ *noun* *a water tap.* faucet, stopcock, valve. — *verb* **1** *They tapped the wine from the cask.* drain, draw off, extract, siphon off. **2** *He tapped a new source of information.* draw on, exploit, make use of, milk, use.

tap² *verb* *She tapped on the glass.* beat, drum, hit, knock, patter, rap, strike. — *noun* *a tap at the door.* knock, patter, pit-a-pat, rap.

tape *noun* **1** *The labels are made from cotton tape.* binding, ribbon, strip. **2** *She fastened the package with tape.* adhesive tape, insulating tape, masking tape, packing tape, Sellotape (*trade mark*), sticky tape. **3** *You can buy a tape of the programme.* audiotape, cassette, tape recording, video, videotape. — *verb* **1** *She taped the ends down.* bind, fasten, fix, seal, sellotape, stick. **2** *He taped the concert.* record, tape-record, video, videotape.

taper *verb* *The stick tapers to a point.* narrow, thin. □ **taper off** *Business tapers off in winter.* decline, decrease, die down, diminish, peter out, reduce, slacken off, tail off, wane. OPPOSITE expand.

target *noun* **1** *We reached our target of $100,000.* aim, goal, object, objective. **2** *She was always the target of their jokes.* butt, object, scapegoat, victim.

tariff *noun* **1** *the hotel tariff.* charges, fees, prices, rates. **2** *import tariffs.* customs, duty, excise, impost, levy, tax.

tarnish *verb* **1** *The metal tarnishes in damp conditions.* blacken, discolour, dull, stain. OPPOSITE shine. **2** *His reputation was tarnished by the affair.* besmirch, blacken, mar, smirch, stain, sully, taint. OPPOSITE enhance.

tart¹ *noun* *a baked tart.* flan, pastry, pie, quiche, tartlet.

tart² *adjective* **1** *The apples have a tart flavour.* acid, acidic, astringent, piquant, pungent, sharp, sour, tangy. OPPOSITE sweet. **2** *I was taken aback by her tart reply.* acid, biting, caustic, cutting, sharp, trenchant. OPPOSITE gentle.

task *noun* *They all have tasks to perform.* assignment, charge, chore, commission, duty, errand, function, job, mission, work. □ **take to task** admonish, castigate, censure, chastise, chide (*old use*), criticise, rebuke, reprimand, reproach, reprove, scold, tell off (*informal*), tick off (*informal*), upbraid. OPPOSITE commend.

taskmaster *noun* *The boss was a hard taskmaster.* disciplinarian, martinet, slave-driver, tyrant.

taste *noun* **1** *a pleasant taste.* flavour, savour, tang. **2** *He had a small taste of the cheese.* bit, bite, morsel, mouthful, nibble, piece, sample, titbit. **3** *She had a taste of the juice.* mouthful, sample, sip, swallow. **4** *He developed a taste for travel.* appetite, fondness, inclination, liking, love, partiality, penchant, predilection. OPPOSITE distaste. **5** *He has good taste in clothes.* discernment, discrimination, judgement, refinement, style. — *verb* *He tasted the soup.* sample, savour, sip, test, try.

tasteful *adjective* *The hotel has tasteful furnishings.* aesthetic, artistic, attractive, elegant, graceful, handsome, refined, stylish. OPPOSITE tasteless.

tasteless *adjective* **1** *a tasteless drink.* bland, flavourless, insipid, weak, wishy-washy. OPPOSITE tasty. **2** *a tasteless joke.* coarse, crude, improper, indelicate, offensive, ribald, rude, unseemly, vulgar. **3** *tasteless decorations.* cheap, garish, gaudy, inelegant, kitsch, showy, tacky (*informal*), tawdry, unattractive. OPPOSITE tasteful.

tasty *adjective* *a tasty meal.* appetising, delectable, delicious, flavoursome, luscious, mouth-watering, palatable, piquant, savoury, scrumptious (*informal*), yummy (*informal*). OPPOSITE bland.

tattered *adjective* *tattered clothes.* frayed, holey, ragged, ripped, tatty (*informal*), threadbare, torn, worn-out.

tatters *plural noun* *The old sheets were in tatters.* rags, shreds.

tatty *adjective* *She wears tatty clothes for painting.* frayed, holey, motheaten, old, patched, ragged, scruffy, shabby, tattered, untidy, worn.

taunt *verb* *They taunted him about his accent.* chiack (*Australian informal*), deride, gibe, jeer at, make fun of, mock, poke borak at (*Australian informal*), poke fun at, ridicule, scoff at, sling off at (*Australian informal*), sneer at, take the mickey out of (*informal*), tease, torment. — *noun* *a cruel taunt.* barb, dig, gibe, insult, jeer, sneer.

taut *adjective* *a taut muscle.* taut elastic. stretched, tense, tight. OPPOSITE slack.

tawdry *adjective* *tawdry clothes.* cheap, flashy, garish, gaudy, kitsch, showy, tacky (*informal*), tasteless, tatty (*informal*). OPPOSITE elegant.

tax *noun* *a tax on goods and services.* charge, customs, duty, excise, impost, levy, rates, slug (*Australian informal*), tariff, taxation, tithe (*historical*), toll, tribute (*historical*). — *verb* *The work taxed his brain.* burden, challenge, exhaust, overload, overwork, strain, stretch, tire.

taxing *adjective* *A police officer's work can be taxing.* challenging, demanding, difficult, draining, exacting, exhausting, hard, onerous, strenuous, stressful, tiring, tough. OPPOSITE easy.

teach *verb* **1** *He has taught many students.* coach, drill, edify, educate, enlighten, indoctrinate, inform, instruct, lecture, school, train, tutor. **2** *She taught the children good manners.* drum into, hammer into, implant in, inculcate in, instil in.

teacher *noun* chalkie (*Australian slang*), coach, educator, governess, guide, guru, headmaster, headmistress, instructor, lecturer, master, mentor, mistress, pedagogue (*old use*), preacher, principal, professor, rabbi, schoolie (*Australian informal*), schoolmaster, schoolmistress, schoolteacher, trainer, tutor.

teaching *noun* **1** *foreign language teaching.* education, instruction, training, tuition. **2** *the teachings of the Church.* doctrine, dogma, precept, principle, tenet.

team *noun* **1** *a netball team.* club, line-up, side, squad. **2** *a team of workers.* band, corps, crew, force, gang, group, staff, unit. — *verb* **team up** *They teamed up to do the research.* band together, collaborate, combine, cooperate, join forces, unite.

teamwork *noun* collaboration, cooperation.

tear *verb* 1 *She tore her stockings.* ladder, rend, rip, shred, slash, slit, snag, split. 2 *He tore his leg on the barbed wire.* cut, gash, lacerate, mangle, mutilate, rupture. 3 *He tore the photo away from them.* grab, pluck, pull, rip, seize, snatch. 4 *They tore past us.* bolt, dart, dash, fly, gallop, hurry, hurtle, race, rip, run, rush, shoot, speed, sprint, spurt, streak, sweep, whiz, zip. OPPOSITE crawl. — *noun a tear in his shirt.* hole, rent, rip, slit, split. □ **tear apart** *The issue is tearing the people apart.* break up, divide, split. OPPOSITE unite. **tear down** *The men tore down the old shed.* demolish, level, pull down, raze, rip down. OPPOSITE erect.

tearful *adjective tearful mourners at a funeral.* crying, emotional, lachrymose, maudlin, sobbing, teary (*informal*), upset, weepy (*informal*).

tease *verb* 1 *They teased him because he wore glasses.* chaff, chiack (*Australian informal*), gibe, make fun of, pay out, poke borak at (*Australian informal*), poke fun at, rag, rib (*informal*), ridicule, sling off at (*Australian informal*), stir (*informal*), take the mickey out of (*informal*). 2 *The cat will bite you if you tease her.* annoy, bait, bother, molest, needle, pester, provoke, tantalise, taunt, torment.

technical *adjective* 1 *technical studies.* applied, mechanical, practical. 2 *technical language.* scientific, specialised, specialist.

technique *noun* 1 *a technique for resolving conflict.* approach, knack, manner, method, procedure, system, trick, way. 2 *The artist developed her technique.* art, craft, skill.

tedious *adjective The work was tedious and unrewarding.* boring, dreary, dull, humdrum, laborious, monotonous, tiresome, tiring, unexciting, uninteresting, wearisome. OPPOSITE interesting.

teem¹ *verb The river teemed with fish.* abound, be full (of), be overrun, brim, overflow, seethe, swarm.

teem² *verb It teemed all day.* bucket down, pelt, pour, rain, rain cats and dogs (*informal*).

teenager *noun* adolescent, juvenile, minor, youth.

teeter *verb The old man teetered on the gangway.* lurch, reel, stagger, sway, totter, wobble.

teetotal *adjective* abstinent, non-drinking, temperate.

teetotaller *noun* abstainer, non-drinker, wowser (*Australian*). OPPOSITE drinker.

telepathic *adjective telepathic communication.* psychic.

telephone *verb Telephone me when you arrive.* call, dial, give someone a bell (*informal*), give someone a buzz (*informal*), give someone a call, phone, ring (up).

televise *verb The tennis match will be televised.* broadcast, screen, telecast, transmit.

television *noun* television receiver, television set, telly (*informal*), the box (*informal*), TV.

tell *verb* 1 *He told the story.* announce, broadcast, chronicle, communicate, confess, describe, disclose, divulge, explain, impart, make known, mention, narrate, proclaim, recite, recount, relate, report, reveal, state. 2 *He told them of the dangers.* acquaint (with), advise, apprise (*formal*), inform, notify, warn. OPPOSITE conceal. 3 *She told a lie.* say, speak, utter. 4 *He promised he wouldn't tell.* blab, give the show away, let the cat out of the bag, spill the beans

(*slang*), squeal (*slang*), talk, tittle-tattle. 5 *People can't tell which is which.* determine, discern, discover, distinguish, identify, make out, recognise. 6 *She told them to leave.* bid, command, direct, instruct, order. □ **tell off** (*informal*) *He told them off for being late.* admonish, blast (*informal*), castigate, censure, chastise, go crook at (*Australian informal*), lecture, rebuke, reprimand, reproach, rouse on (*Australian informal*), scold, tick off (*informal*). OPPOSITE commend. **tell on** *He'll tell on you.* betray, blow the whistle on (*informal*), dob in (*Australian informal*), grass (on) (*slang*), inform on, rat on (*slang*), report, shop (*slang*), sneak on (*slang*), split on (*slang*).

telling *adjective a telling argument.* effective, forceful, powerful, significant, strong, weighty. OPPOSITE insignificant.

tell-tale *noun He was accused of being a tell-tale.* blabbermouth, dobber (*Australian informal*), grass (*slang*), informer, sneak (*informal*), tale-bearer. — *adjective a tell-tale blush.* give-away (*informal*), indicative, meaningful, revealing, significant.

temerity *noun She had the temerity to ask for a rise.* audacity, boldness, cheek, effrontery, gall, hide, impertinence, impudence, nerve, presumption, rashness.

temper *noun* 1 *He is in a good temper.* disposition, frame of mind, humour, mood. 2 *She breaks things when she's in a temper.* fury, paddy (*informal*), rage, tantrum. 3 *a fit of temper.* anger, fury, irascibility, ire, irritation, peevishness, petulance, pique, rage, wrath. 4 *He kept his temper.* calmness, composure, cool, equanimity, self-control. — *verb He tempered justice with mercy.* mitigate, moderate, palliate, soften, tone down.

temperament *noun The child has a lively temperament.* character, disposition, make-up, nature, personality, spirit, temper.

temperamental *adjective a temperamental person.* capricious, changeable, emotional, erratic, excitable, fickle, highly-strung, hotheaded, mercurial, moody, touchy, unpredictable, volatile. OPPOSITE steady.

temperate *adjective a temperate climate.* gentle, mild, moderate. OPPOSITE harsh.

tempest *noun The tempest raged.* cyclone, gale, hurricane, storm, tornado, typhoon.

tempestuous *adjective tempestuous weather.* blustery, rough, squally, stormy, turbulent, violent, wild, windy. OPPOSITE calm.

temple *noun* church, gurdwara, mosque, pagoda, sanctuary, shrine, stupa, synagogue, tabernacle.

tempo *noun a fast tempo.* pace, rate, speed.

temporary *adjective* 1 *The feeling of nausea was only temporary.* brief, ephemeral, fleeting, impermanent, momentary, passing, short-lived, transient, transitory. OPPOSITE lasting. 2 *Petrol rationing is a temporary measure.* interim, makeshift, provisional, short-term, stopgap. OPPOSITE permanent.

tempt *verb He tempted the dog with a bone.* allure, attract, bait, coax, entice, inveigle, lure, seduce, tantalise.

temptation *noun The chocolates were a big temptation.* attraction, bait, draw, enticement, incentive, inducement, lure.

tempting *adjective The other firm made him a tempting offer.* alluring, appealing, attractive, enticing, inviting, irresistible, seductive.

tenable *adjective His theory is not tenable in the light of these discoveries.* arguable, defensible, plausible, reasonable, supportable. OPPOSITE untenable.

tenacious *adjective* 1 *a tenacious grip.* firm, iron, powerful, strong, tight. OPPOSITE loose. 2 *John was a tenacious campaigner for human rights.* determined, dogged, obstinate, persistent, resolute, staunch, stubborn, unyielding.

tenant *noun The owner has found a new tenant.* inhabitant, lessee, occupant, resident.

tend¹ *verb The baby tends to cry a lot.* be apt, be disposed, be inclined, be liable, be prone.

tend² *verb The shepherd tends the sheep. The nurse tended the patient.* attend to, care for, cherish, keep an eye on, keep watch over, look after, mind, nurse, take care of, watch. OPPOSITE neglect.

tendency *noun He has a tendency to mope.* disposition, inclination, penchant, predilection, predisposition, proclivity, propensity, readiness.

tender¹ *adjective* 1 *tender meat.* edible, soft, succulent. OPPOSITE tough. 2 *tender plants.* delicate, fragile, frail. OPPOSITE hardy. 3 *of tender age.* callow, immature, inexperienced, vulnerable, young, youthful. OPPOSITE old. 4 *His knee was tender after the accident.* aching, inflamed, painful, raw, sensitive, sore. 5 *Children need tender care.* affectionate, compassionate, fond, gentle, kind, loving.

tender² *verb He tendered his resignation.* give, hand in, offer, present, proffer, submit. — *noun Each company submitted a tender for the work.* bid, offer, proposal, quotation, quote (*informal*).

tender-hearted *adjective* caring, compassionate, humane, kind, kind-hearted, kindly, merciful, soft-hearted, sympathetic, warm-hearted. OPPOSITE hard-hearted.

tenet *noun the basic tenets of a religion.* belief, creed, doctrine, dogma, precept, principle, teaching.

tense *adjective* 1 *a tense muscle.* stiff, strained, stretched, taut, tight. OPPOSITE relaxed. 2 *He was tense before the interview.* anxious, apprehensive, edgy, highly-strung, jumpy, keyed up, nervous, nervy, uneasy, uptight (*informal*). OPPOSITE calm, relaxed. 3 *The negotiator defused the tense situation.* explosive, fraught, nerve-racking, strained, stressful, uneasy, volatile. OPPOSITE calm.

tension *noun* 1 *the tension of a rope.* stiffness, tautness, tightness. OPPOSITE slackness. 2 *Her headaches are caused by tension.* anxiety, apprehension, strain, stress, suspense, unease, uneasiness. OPPOSITE calmness.

tent *noun* big top, marquee, tepee, wigwam.

tentative *adjective a tentative suggestion.* cautious, experimental, hesitant, provisional, trial, unconfirmed. OPPOSITE firm.

tepid *adjective tepid tea.* lukewarm, warm.

term *noun* 1 *a term of office.* course, duration, period, session, spell, stint, stretch, time. 2 *a university term.* semester, trimester. 3 *a scientific term.* expression, name, phrase, word. — *verb What is this condition termed?* call, designate, label, name. □ **come to terms with** *He came to terms with his disability.* accept, face up to, learn to live with, reconcile yourself to. **terms** *plural noun* 1 *The two countries are on friendly terms.* footing, relations, standing. 2 *This was written in the terms of the settlement.* conditions, provisions,

specifications, stipulations. 3 *The company offered interest-free terms.* charges, fees, prices, rates.

terminal *adjective a terminal illness.* deadly, fatal, incurable, mortal. — *noun the bus terminal.* depot, station, terminus.

terminate *verb* 1 *She terminated the conversation.* close, conclude, cut off, end, finish, round off, stop, wind up. 2 *The music terminated abruptly.* cease, come to an end, conclude, end, finish, stop. OPPOSITE start.

terminology *noun He was not familiar with medical terminology.* jargon, language, lingo (*informal*), nomenclature, phraseology, terms, vocabulary, words.

terminus *noun the bus terminus.* depot, last stop, station, terminal.

terrain *noun rocky terrain.* country, ground, land, landscape, region, territory.

terrestrial *adjective* 1 *terrestrial life.* earthly. OPPOSITE extraterrestrial. 2 *Cats are terrestrial animals.* land. OPPOSITE aquatic.

terrible *adjective* 1 *a terrible plane crash.* appalling, catastrophic, disastrous, dreadful, ghastly, gruesome, hideous, horrendous, horrible, horrific, shocking, terrifying. 2 *She suffered terrible pain.* awful, distressing, excruciating, extreme, fierce, frightful, intense, intolerable, severe, unbearable. OPPOSITE mild. 3 (*informal*) *The weather has been terrible.* abominable (*informal*), abysmal (*informal*), appalling (*informal*), atrocious (*informal*), awful (*informal*), bad, dreadful (*informal*), foul, lousy (*informal*), miserable, rotten (*informal*), shocking (*informal*), unpleasant. OPPOSITE pleasant. 4 (*informal*) *He's terrible at tennis.* bad, hopeless, incompetent, pathetic, poor, useless (*informal*), woeful (*informal*). OPPOSITE brilliant.

terrific *adjective* (*informal*) 1 *The boat cost a terrific amount.* astronomical, colossal, enormous, excessive, exorbitant, extravagant, huge, large, monumental, staggering, stupendous, tremendous. OPPOSITE tiny. 2 *We had a terrific storm last night.* colossal, fierce, intense, mighty, severe, terrible, violent. 3 *She does a terrific job.* admirable, brilliant, excellent, extraordinary, fabulous (*informal*), fantastic (*informal*), fine, first-class, great, incredible, magnificent, marvellous, outstanding, phenomenal, remarkable, sensational, spectacular, splendid, super (*informal*), superb, unbelievable, wonderful. OPPOSITE terrible.

terrify *verb The sounds of battle terrified him.* alarm, appal, dismay, freak out (*informal*), frighten, horrify, petrify, scare, terrorise. OPPOSITE reassure.

terrifying *adjective a terrifying experience.* alarming, frightening, hair-raising, horrifying, nightmarish, scary, spine-chilling.

territory *noun foreign territory.* area, country, district, domain, land, province, region, state, terrain, tract, zone.

terror *noun They were seized with terror.* alarm, consternation, dismay, dread, fear, fright, horror, panic, trepidation.

terrorise *verb The child terrorised smaller children.* bully, frighten, intimidate, menace, persecute, terrify, torment.

terse *adjective a terse reply.* abrupt, brief, brusque, compact, concise, crisp, curt, laconic, pithy, short, snappy (*informal*), succinct. OPPOSITE verbose.

test noun **1** *a test of the car's performance.* analysis, appraisal, assessment, check, evaluation, experiment, trial. **2** *a screen test.* audition, check, try-out. **3** *school tests.* exam (*informal*), examination, quiz. — verb **1** *The examiners tested the candidates.* appraise, assess, audition, evaluate, examine, question, quiz, screen. **2** *They tested the drug on volunteers.* check, experiment with, sample, trial, try out.

testify verb *The man testified that the accused had been with him.* affirm, attest, bear witness, declare, give evidence, state under oath, swear.

testimony noun **1** *The witness presented his testimony.* affidavit, declaration, deposition, evidence, statement. **2** *The sacrifice was testimony of his love.* demonstration, evidence, indication, manifestation, proof.

testy adjective *The pressure of work has made him testy.* bad-tempered, cranky, cross, crotchety, grouchy (*informal*), grumpy, irritable, peevish, petulant, prickly, querulous, shirty (*informal*), short-tempered, snaky (*Australian informal*), stroppy (*informal*), surly, tetchy, touchy.

tether noun *The animal is on a tether.* chain, halter, lead, leash, rope. □ **tether** verb *He tethered the horses.* chain up, secure, tie up. OPPOSITE untether.

text noun **1** *the text of the speech.* content, matter, script, transcript, wording, words. **2** *The sermon was based on a biblical text.* passage, quotation, sentence, verse.

textbook noun *a grammar textbook.* manual, primer, schoolbook, text.

textile noun *woven and knitted textiles.* cloth, fabric, material, stuff.

texture noun *a fabric's texture.* appearance, composition, consistency, feel, grain, structure, weave.

thank verb *She thanked them for the gift.* acknowledge, express appreciation to, express gratitude to. □ **thanks** plural noun *He expressed his thanks.* acknowledgement, appreciation, gratefulness, gratitude, thankfulness. OPPOSITE ingratitude.

thankful adjective *They were thankful for our help.* appreciative, grateful, indebted, obliged, pleased. OPPOSITE unappreciative.

thankless adjective *Washing up is a thankless task.* unappreciated, unrewarding, useless, vain. OPPOSITE appreciated.

thaw verb *The ice thawed.* defrost, liquefy, melt, soften, unfreeze. OPPOSITE freeze.

theatre noun *We went to the theatre to see the play.* auditorium, hall, playhouse.

theatrical adjective *He joined a theatrical company.* drama, show business, stage.

theft noun *the theft of a large sum of money.* burglary, embezzlement, larceny, misappropriation, pilfering, poaching, robbery, shoplifting, stealing, thieving.

theme noun **1** *The theme of her speech was authenticity.* argument, keynote, matter, subject, topic. **2** *The theme was played by the violins.* air, melody, motif, tune.

theology noun *a course in theology.* divinity, religion.

theoretical adjective **1** *a theoretical solution.* abstract, academic, conjectural, hypothetical, notional, unproven, untested. OPPOSITE actual, proven. **2** *theoretical physics.* abstract, pure. OPPOSITE applied, practical.

theory noun **1** *He based his theory on observations of many cases.* argument, assumption, conjecture, explanation, hypothesis, idea, notion, supposition, surmise, thesis, view. OPPOSITE fact. **2** *the theory of music.* laws, principles, rules, science, system. OPPOSITE practice.

therapeutic adjective *a therapeutic drug.* curative, healing, medicinal, remedial, restorative.

therapy noun *occupational therapy. speech therapy.* cure, healing, remedy, treatment.

therefore adverb *Petrol prices have gone up; therefore freight charges have increased.* accordingly, consequently, hence, so, thus.

thick adjective **1** *a thick stick.* broad, chunky, fat, squat, stout, stubby, stumpy, wide. OPPOSITE thin. **2** *a thick layer.* deep, dense, heavy, solid. OPPOSITE thin. **3** *a thick jumper.* bulky, heavy, woolly. OPPOSITE light. **4** *thick grass.* abundant, bushy, dense, impenetrable, lush, luxuriant, profuse, rank. OPPOSITE sparse. **5** *a thick paste.* concentrated, condensed, heavy, solid, stiff, viscous. OPPOSITE thin, watery. **6** *He's a bit thick.* dense, dim (*informal*), dull, dumb (*informal*), half-witted, obtuse, slow, stupid, unintelligent. OPPOSITE quick-witted.

thicken verb **1** *The custard thickened.* clot, coagulate, congeal, set, solidify, stiffen. OPPOSITE thin. **2** *He thickened the sauce by boiling it down.* concentrate, condense, reduce. OPPOSITE dilute.

thickness noun **1** *a metre in thickness.* breadth, depth, diameter, width. **2** *several thicknesses of wood.* layer, ply.

thickset adjective *a thickset man.* beefy, brawny, burly, heavy, husky, nuggety (*Australian*), solid, stocky, sturdy. OPPOSITE gangling.

thick-skinned adjective *After years of criticism she became thick-skinned.* hardened, impervious, insensitive, tough. OPPOSITE thin-skinned.

thief noun *The police caught the thief red-handed.* bandit, brigand, burglar, bushranger, crook (*informal*), highwayman, housebreaker, kleptomaniac, looter, mugger, pickpocket, pilferer, robber, shoplifter.

thin adjective **1** *a thin pipe.* fine, narrow. OPPOSITE thick. **2** *Her face was visible through the thin veil.* delicate, diaphanous, fine, flimsy, fragile, light, see-through, sheer, transparent. OPPOSITE thick. **3** *He was thin after his long illness.* bony, emaciated, gangling, gaunt, lanky, lean, puny, scraggy, scrawny, skinny, slender, slight, slim, spare, spindly, weedy, wiry. OPPOSITE fat. **4** *a thin covering of hair.* light, meagre, scant, scanty, sparse, wispy. OPPOSITE profuse. **5** *The sauce is too thin.* dilute, runny, watery. OPPOSITE thick. **6** *a thin excuse.* feeble, flimsy, inadequate, lame. OPPOSITE convincing. — verb *She thinned the soup.* dilute, water down, weaken. OPPOSITE thicken.

thing noun **1** *The shop sells all sorts of things.* article, commodity, device, item, object, product. **2** *They witnessed strange things.* act, deed, doing, event, feat, happening, incident, occurrence, phenomenon. **3** *We have things to discuss.* affair, business, concern, matter. **4** *There are one or two odd things about the case.* aspect, detail, feature, particular, point. □ **things** plural noun **1** *Take all your things when you leave.* belongings, bits and pieces, chattels, clothes, effects, equipment, gear, goods, paraphernalia, possessions, property, stuff. **2** *Things began to improve.* circumstances, conditions, matters, the situation.

think verb **1** *He spent hours thinking.* brood, cogitate, contemplate, deliberate, meditate, muse, ponder, rack your brains, reason, reflect, ruminate. **2** *He is thinking of resigning.* consider, contemplate, entertain the thought, give thought to, mull over. **3** *She can't think where she put it.* bring to mind, call to mind, recall, recollect, remember. OPPOSITE forget. **4** *What do you think will happen?* believe, conjecture, expect, imagine, reckon, suppose, surmise. **5** *It is thought to be a fake.* assume, believe, consider, deem, hold, judge, regard (as). □ **think up** (*informal*) *He thought up a clever scheme.* conceive, concoct, create, devise, dream up, invent, make up.

thin-skinned adjective *A complaints officer cannot afford to be thin-skinned.* hypersensitive, over-sensitive, sensitive, touchy. OPPOSITE thick-skinned.

thirst noun *The young explorer had a thirst for adventure.* appetite, craving, desire, fancy, hankering, hunger, longing, lust, passion, yearning. — verb **thirst for** *He thirsts for knowledge.* crave, desire, hanker after, hunger for, long for, yearn for.

thirsty adjective *She was thirsty after her walk.* dehydrated, dry, parched.

thong noun *He beat the boys with a leather thong.* belt, lash, strap, strip.

thorn noun *The rose thorns pricked her.* barb, needle, prickle, spike, spine.

thorny adjective **1** *a thorny plant.* barbed, prickly, spiky, spiny. **2** *a thorny problem.* complicated, difficult, hard, intricate, knotty, problematic, ticklish, troublesome. OPPOSITE easy.

thorough adjective **1** *He wrote a thorough account.* blow-by-blow, close, complete, comprehensive, detailed, exhaustive, extensive, full, in-depth, minute. OPPOSITE incomplete, superficial. **2** *Mary is a thorough worker.* careful, conscientious, diligent, methodical, meticulous, painstaking, punctilious, rigorous, scrupulous, systematic. OPPOSITE careless, perfunctory. **3** *The meeting was a thorough waste of time.* absolute, complete, downright, out-and-out, outright, total, utter.

thoroughbred adjective *a thoroughbred animal.* pedigree, pure-bred.

thought noun **1** *I was deep in thought when the phone rang.* contemplation, daydreaming, deliberation, introspection, meditation, reasoning, reflection, reverie, rumination, thinking. **2** *What are your thoughts on the matter?* belief, concept, idea, notion, opinion, sentiment, view. **3** *He paid little thought to their feelings.* attention, care, concern, consideration, regard, solicitude.

thoughtful adjective **1** *a thoughtful expression.* absorbed, broody, contemplative, introspective, pensive, reflective, serious, wistful. **2** *It was thoughtful of him to ring.* attentive, caring, considerate, helpful, kind, obliging, solicitous. OPPOSITE thoughtless.

thoughtless adjective **1** *It was thoughtless not to take an umbrella.* absent-minded, careless, forgetful, heedless, negligent, scatterbrained, unthinking. **2** *He regretted his thoughtless remark.* inconsiderate, indiscreet, insensitive, rude, selfish, tactless, unfeeling. OPPOSITE considerate, thoughtful.

thrash verb **1** *He thrashed the pupil for lying.* beat, belt (*slang*), cane, flog, hit, lash, lay into (*informal*), quilt (*Australian slang*), scourge, tan (*slang*), wallop (*informal*), whack, whip. **2** *Our team thrashed their team.* beat, clobber (*slang*), defeat, drub, lick (*informal*), overwhelm, paste (*slang*), pulverise, rout, slaughter, trounce. □ **thrash out** *They thrashed out the problem.* discuss, resolve, settle, talk over, talk through.

thread noun **1** *a silken thread.* fibre, filament, strand, yarn. **2** *He lost the thread of the argument.* drift, plot, storyline, train of thought.

threadbare adjective *Her clothes were threadbare.* frayed, holey, ragged, shabby, tattered, tatty (*informal*), thin, worn.

threat noun **1** *There's a threat of rain.* danger, risk, warning. **2** *Machinery was seen as a threat to people's jobs.* danger, hazard, menace, risk.

threaten verb **1** *The robber threatened them with a gun.* bully, intimidate, menace, terrorise. **2** *The bushfire threatened homes.* endanger, imperil, jeopardise, put at risk.

threatening adjective *threatening clouds.* looming, louring, menacing, ominous, sinister.

threshold noun **1** *He carried his wife over the threshold.* doorstep, doorway, entrance. **2** *the threshold of a new era.* beginning, brink, dawn, outset, start, verge. OPPOSITE end.

thrifty adjective *a thrifty housewife.* economical, frugal, provident, sparing. OPPOSITE extravagant.

thrill noun **1** *He felt a thrill of excitement.* flutter, quiver, shiver, throb, tingle, tremor. **2** *She gets a thrill from diving.* buzz (*informal*), enjoyment, excitement, kick (*informal*), pleasure. — verb *He thrilled the crowd with his stunts.* delight, electrify, excite, rouse, stir, wow (*slang*).

thrilling adjective *Parachuting is a thrilling experience.* electrifying, exciting, exhilarating, heady, rousing, sensational, stirring. OPPOSITE boring.

thrive verb *The plants thrive in wet conditions.* burgeon, do well, flourish, grow well. OPPOSITE wither.

thriving adjective *a thriving building industry.* booming, burgeoning, flourishing, healthy, prosperous, successful. OPPOSITE languishing.

throaty adjective *a throaty voice.* deep, gruff, guttural, hoarse, husky, rasping.

throb verb *His heart was throbbing.* beat, palpitate, pound, pulsate, pulse, thump. — noun *the throb of the drums.* beat, beating, pulse, vibration.

throng noun *She was lost in the throng of shoppers.* crowd, gathering, herd, horde, host, mass, mob, multitude, swarm. — verb *The people thronged round the singer.* congregate, crowd, flock, gather, herd, mill, press, swarm.

throttle verb *The victim had been throttled.* choke, garrotte, strangle, suffocate.

throw verb **1** *He threw the ball.* bowl, cast, chuck (*informal*), fling, heave, hurl, launch, lob, pelt, pitch, project, propel, shy, sling, toss. OPPOSITE catch. **2** *She threw the book down on the table.* bung (*informal*), chuck (*informal*), dump, plonk, slam, toss. **3** *The question threw me.* bewilder, confuse, disconcert, faze (*informal*), fluster, perplex, rattle (*informal*), stump (*informal*). — noun *an accurate throw.* delivery, fling, hurl, launch, lob, pitch, shot, shy, toss. □ **throw away 1** *He threw away his old textbooks.* cast off, chuck out (*informal*), discard, dispose of, ditch (*slang*), dump, get rid of, jettison, reject, scrap, throw out. OPPOSITE keep. **2** *He threw away a golden opportunity.* blow (*informal*), squander, waste. OPPOSITE exploit.

throw out **1** *He was thrown out of the building.* chuck out (*informal*), eject, evict, expel, kick out (*informal*), remove, turf out (*informal*). **2** *He threw out his old coat.* see THROW AWAY. **throw up** *The boy threw up after the party.* barf (*slang*), be ill, be sick, chuck (*informal*), chunder (*Australian slang*), puke (*informal*), sick up (*informal*), spew, vomit.

thrust *verb* **1** *He thrust his way forward.* elbow, force, jostle, propel, push, ram, shoulder, shove. **2** *He thrust the sword into the man's side.* drive, jab, lunge, plunge, poke, stab, stick.

thud *noun They heard a thud when he fell.* bang, bump, clunk, crash, thump.

thug *noun He was assaulted by thugs.* bully, delinquent, gangster, hoodlum, hooligan, mugger, rough, ruffian, tough.

thumb *verb She thumbed through the book.* browse, flick, flip, leaf, skim.

thump *verb* **1** *He thumped the other boy.* bash, batter, beat, clobber (*slang*), clout (*informal*), hammer, hit, knock, pound, punch, quilt (*Australian slang*), slog, slug, sock (*slang*), stoush (*Australian slang*), strike, thwack, wallop (*informal*), whack. **2** *Her heart was thumping.* pound, pulsate, pulse, throb. — *noun She came down with a thump.* bang, bump, clunk, crash, thud.

thunder *noun the thunder of drums.* boom, roar, roll, rumble.

thus *adverb We were early and thus able to get a seat.* accordingly, consequently, hence, so, therefore.

thwart *verb They thwarted his attempts to escape.* baulk, block, foil, frustrate, hamper, hinder, obstruct, prevent, stonker (*Australian slang*), stymie (*informal*). OPPOSITE assist.

tic *noun a facial tic.* spasm, twitch.

tick *noun* (*informal*) *He'll be with you in a tick.* flash, instant, jiffy, minute, moment, second, trice. — *verb Tick the correct answers.* check off, indicate, mark. □ **tick off** (*informal*) *The teacher ticked Paul off for being late.* admonish, castigate, censure, chastise, chide (*old use*), lecture, rap over the knuckles, rebuke, reprimand, reproach, scold, tell off (*informal*), upbraid. OPPOSITE praise.

ticket *noun* **1** *You need a ticket to enter.* coupon, pass, permit, token, voucher. **2** *a price ticket.* label, tab, tag. **3** *a parking ticket.* fine, notice, notification.

tickle *verb* **1** *She tickled the baby under the arm.* stroke, touch. **2** *She was tickled by the thought.* amuse, delight, divert, entertain, please, titillate. — *noun He felt a tickle in his throat.* itch, tingle.

ticklish *adjective a ticklish problem.* awkward, delicate, difficult, knotty, problematic, thorny, tricky. OPPOSITE simple.

tide *noun The fisherman watches the tide.* current, ebb and flow.

tidy *adjective* **1** *The office is tidy.* methodical, neat, orderly, shipshape, spick and span, straight, systematic, uncluttered. OPPOSITE messy, untidy. **2** *She has a tidy appearance.* neat, presentable, smart, spruce, trim, well-groomed. OPPOSITE scruffy. **3** (*informal*) *He left a tidy fortune.* considerable, goodly, handsome, sizeable, substantial. OPPOSITE tiny. — *verb* **1** *He tidied his room.* arrange, clean up, neaten, organise, sort out, straighten. OPPOSITE mess up. **2** *She tidied herself up before going out.* clean up, groom, smarten up, spruce up, titivate (*informal*).

tie *verb* **1** *He tied the two pieces together.* attach, bind, connect, couple, fasten, hitch, join, knot, lace, lash, link, strap, truss, unite, yoke. OPPOSITE separate, untie. **2** *They tied for second place.* be equal, be even, be level, be neck and neck, draw. — *noun* **1** *He wears a tie.* bow tie, cravat, necktie. **2** *The result was a tie.* dead heat, draw, stalemate. □ **tie in** *His statement tied in with the others.* agree, be consistent, correspond, fit, tally. **tie up** *They tied up the boat.* moor, secure. OPPOSITE untie.

tier *noun* **1** *tiers of seats.* line, rank, row. **2** *a wedding cake with three tiers.* layer, level.

tie-up *noun a tie-up between the two ideas.* association, connection, link, relationship.

tiff *noun The friends had a tiff.* altercation, argument, barney (*informal*), blue (*Australian informal*), disagreement, quarrel, row, squabble.

tight *adjective* **1** *a tight screw.* fast, firm, fixed, secure. OPPOSITE loose. **2** *tight jeans.* close-fitting, skintight, snug. OPPOSITE loose. **3** *a tight seal.* airtight, hermetic, impervious, watertight. **4** *tight elastic.* stiff, stretched, taut, tense. OPPOSITE loose. **5** *He's tight with money.* mean, miserly, niggardly, parsimonious, penny-pinching, stingy, tight-fisted. OPPOSITE generous.

tighten *verb* **1** *They tightened the rope.* stiffen, stretch, tauten, tense. OPPOSITE slacken. **2** *The blood vessel tightened.* constrict, contract, narrow. OPPOSITE dilate.

till[1] *noun The money is in the till.* cash drawer, cash register, peter (*Australian slang*).

till[2] *verb He tilled the soil.* cultivate, farm, plough, work.

tilt *verb The boat tilted.* bank, cant, heel over, incline, keel over, lean, list, slope, sway, tip. — *noun The cupboard was on a tilt.* angle, incline, slant, slope.

timber *noun The house is built of timber.* beams, boards, logs, lumber, planks, wood.

time *noun* **1** *in Roman times.* age, days, epoch, era, period. **2** *Do not come at this time.* date, day, hour, instant, juncture, moment, occasion, opportunity, point, stage. **3** *It lasted a long time.* duration, interval, period, phase, season, session, span, spell, stretch, term, while. □ **on time** *The bus arrived on time.* on schedule, on the dot, on the knocker (*Australian informal*), punctually.

timeless *adjective timeless beauty.* abiding, ageless, enduring, eternal, everlasting, immutable, indestructible, permanent, unchanging. OPPOSITE passing.

timely *adjective The autumn rains were a timely warning to repair the roof.* opportune, seasonable, well-timed. OPPOSITE ill-timed.

timetable *noun a bus timetable.* programme, schedule.

timid *adjective The child was as timid as a mouse.* bashful, chicken (*informal*), cowardly, coy, diffident, faint-hearted, fearful, frightened, nervous, pusillanimous, sheepish, shy, sooky (*Australian informal*), timorous, underconfident, unheroic, wussy (*slang*). OPPOSITE bold.

tin *noun* **1** *The sugar is stored in a tin.* can, canister. **2** *a square cake tin.* pan.

tinge *verb The sky was tinged with pink.* colour, dye, stain, tint. — *noun* **1** *a tinge of pink.* colour, shade, tincture, tint. **2** *There was a tinge of sadness in his letter.* hint, suggestion, touch, trace.

tingle *verb The hot water made her toes tingle.* prickle, sting, tickle.

tinker *verb He likes to tinker with cars.* fiddle, mess about, play, potter, toy.

tinkle *noun the tinkle of a bell.* chime, ding, jingle, peal, ring.

tint *noun a bluish tint.* colour, dye, hue, pigment, shade, stain, tincture, tinge, tone.

tiny *adjective* baby, compact, diminutive, dwarf, imperceptible, infinitesimal, insignificant, little, microscopic, midget, mini, miniature, minuscule, minute, negligible, pocket-sized, small, teeny (*informal*), titchy (*informal*), trifling, undersized, wee (*informal*), weeny (*informal*). OPPOSITE enormous.

tip[1] *noun* **1** *a pencil with a sharp tip.* end, extremity, point. **2** *The tip of the mountain was covered in snow.* apex, cap, crest, crown, peak, pinnacle, summit, top. OPPOSITE base.

tip[2] *verb The boat tipped.* cant, heel over, incline, lean, list, tilt. □ **tip over** **1** *The boat tipped over.* capsize, keel over, overturn, topple over. **2** *She tipped over the rubbish basket.* knock over, overturn, spill, up-end, upset, upturn.

tip[3] *noun* **1** *The waitress receives tips.* gift, gratuity, present. **2** *a tip on how to peel onions.* advice, clue, hint, pointer, suggestion, warning, wrinkle (*informal*). **3** *a rubbish tip.* dump.

tipsy *adjective She was tipsy after one drink.* inebriated, intoxicated, jolly, merry (*informal*), slightly drunk, tiddly (*informal*). OPPOSITE sober.

tirade *noun They don't listen to his tirades.* denunciation, diatribe, harangue, lecture.

tire *verb The walk tired her.* drain, exhaust, fatigue, wear out, weary. OPPOSITE invigorate.

tired *adjective He was tired after his hard work.* all in (*informal*), beat (*slang*), bushed (*informal*), dog-tired, done in (*informal*), drained, drowsy, exhausted, fagged (*informal*), fatigued, jaded, languid, listless, pooped (*informal*), sapped, sleepy, weary, whacked (*informal*), worn out, zapped (*slang*), zonked (*slang*). OPPOSITE energetic. □ **tired of** *She was tired of cleaning.* bored of, browned off with (*slang*), fed up with, jack of (*Australian slang*), sick of.

tiredness *noun* drowsiness, exhaustion, fatigue, languor, lassitude, lethargy, listlessness, sleepiness, weariness. OPPOSITE vitality.

tireless *adjective a tireless worker.* energetic, hard-working, indefatigable, industrious, unflagging, untiring. OPPOSITE lazy.

tiresome *adjective* **1** *a tiresome person.* annoying, bothersome, exasperating, irksome, irritating, troublesome. **2** *a tiresome book.* boring, dreary, dull, tedious, uninteresting, wearisome. OPPOSITE interesting.

tiring *adjective Cleaning offices is a tiring job.* arduous, exacting, exhausting, hard, laborious, onerous, strenuous, taxing, tiresome, wearisome, wearying. OPPOSITE easy.

titbit *noun His lunch box contained delicious titbits.* bit, delicacy, morsel, nibble, snack.

titillate *verb The pictures titillated some readers.* arouse, excite, stimulate, tantalise, tickle, turn on (*informal*).

title *noun* **1** *the title of a picture.* caption, heading, inscription, name. **2** *a person's title.* appellation, designation, position, rank, status. — *verb She titled the book 'Dogs'.* call, designate, entitle, label, name.

titter *noun The joke caused a few titters.* chuckle, giggle, snicker, snigger.

tittle-tattle *verb They tittle-tattled about their classmates.* blab, chatter, gossip, tattle, tell tales. — *noun Don't believe all that tittle-tattle you hear.* chatter, chit-chat, gossip, hearsay, tattle.

titular *adjective the titular head of state.* nominal, so-called, theoretical, token.

toady *noun one of the boss's toadies.* crawler (*informal*), flatterer, flunkey, hanger-on, lackey, parasite, sycophant, truckler, yes-man. — *verb He wasn't going to toady to the boss.* crawl (*informal*), curry favour (with), fawn (on), grovel, kowtow, play up, suck up (*informal*), truckle.

toast *verb* **1** *He toasted the muffins.* brown, cook, grill. **2** *The guests toasted the bride and groom.* drink to, raise your glass to, salute.

toddler *noun* baby, child, infant, preschooler.

to-do *noun The new book caused a great to-do.* bother, commotion, disturbance, excitement, furore, fuss, hue and cry, hullabaloo, kerfuffle (*informal*), outcry, palaver (*informal*), rumpus, stir, storm, turmoil, uproar.

toey *adjective* (*Australian informal*) *Let him go: he's getting a bit toey.* agitated, anxious, impatient, nervous, restive, restless, uneasy.

together *adverb* **1** *They work together.* closely, cooperatively, in collaboration, jointly, side by side. OPPOSITE independently. **2** *They answered together.* as one, in chorus, in unison, simultaneously. OPPOSITE separately.

toil *verb She toiled for hours in the kitchen.* beaver away, drudge, labour, slave, slog, strive, sweat, work. — *noun the reward after years of toil.* drudgery, effort, exertion, grind, industry, labour, slog, sweat (*informal*), travail (*old use*), work, yakka (*Australian informal*).

toilet *noun* bathroom, convenience, dunny (*Australian slang*), Gents (*informal*), Ladies, latrine, lavatory, loo (*informal*), men's, powder room, privy, rest room, toot (*Australian informal*), urinal, washroom, water closet, WC, women's.

token *noun* **1** *Accept this gift as a token of our gratitude.* evidence, expression, indication, keepsake, mark, memento, sign, symbol. **2** *The prize was a book token.* coupon, voucher. **3** *The machine takes tokens.* counter, disc.

tolerable *adjective* **1** *The pain was only just tolerable.* bearable, endurable. OPPOSITE intolerable. **2** *He cooked a tolerable meal.* acceptable, adequate, fair, OK (*informal*), passable, reasonable, satisfactory, so-so (*informal*).

tolerant *adjective She is tolerant of other people.* broad-minded, charitable, easygoing, forbearing, forgiving, indulgent, lenient, liberal, long-suffering, open-minded, patient, permissive, understanding. OPPOSITE intolerant, narrow-minded.

tolerate *verb* **1** *They will not tolerate rudeness.* accept, admit, allow, brook, condone, permit, sanction. **2** *He cannot tolerate the pain.* abide, bear, cope with, endure, put up with, stand, stomach, suffer, take.

toll[1] *noun* **1** *They pay a toll to use the expressway.* charge, fee, levy, payment, tax. **2** *the death toll from the hurricane.* cost, damage, loss.

toll[2] *verb The bell tolled.* chime, peal, ring, sound, strike.

tomb *noun The princess was buried in the family tomb.* crypt, grave, mausoleum, sepulchre, vault.

tone noun **1** *the tone of a voice.* inflection, intonation, modulation, note, pitch, sound, timbre. **2** *The letter was written in an apologetic tone.* expression, manner, style, vein. **3** *The room was painted in autumn tones.* colour, hue, shade, tinge, tint. **4** *the tone of the place.* atmosphere, character, feeling, mood, spirit. — *verb The cushions tone with the sofa.* blend, harmonise, match. OPPOSITE clash. □ **tone down** *He toned down his criticism.* moderate, modulate, play down, soften, subdue, temper.

tongue noun *the mother tongue.* language.

tongue-tied adjective *She was tongue-tied in front of an audience.* dumb, inarticulate, mute, silent, speechless. OPPOSITE loquacious.

too adverb **1** *She is too protective.* excessively, extremely, overly, unduly. **2** *intelligent, and good-looking too.* also, as well, besides, furthermore, in addition.

tool noun *a kitchen tool.* apparatus, appliance, contraption, device, gadget, implement, instrument, machine, utensil; [*tools*] equipment, gear, hardware.

toot verb *He tooted the horn.* beep, blast, honk, hoot, sound.

top noun **1** *the top of the hill.* apex, brow, crest, crown, peak, pinnacle, summit, tip, vertex, zenith. OPPOSITE bottom. **2** *the top of the queue.* front, head. OPPOSITE end. **3** *a bottle top.* cap, cover, covering, lid, stopper. — adjective **1** *the top position.* highest, maximum, supreme, topmost, uppermost. OPPOSITE lowest. **2** *the country's top designers.* best, foremost, greatest, leading, outstanding, pre-eminent. — verb **1** *He topped the list.* head, lead. **2** *Nobody could top that score.* beat, better, exceed, improve on, outdo, surpass. **3** *The trifle was topped with strawberries.* cap, cover, crown, finish, garnish.

topic noun *a conversation topic.* issue, matter, point, subject, theme.

topical adjective *a topical issue.* contemporary, current, live, up-to-date, up-to-the-minute.

topple verb **1** *He toppled down the stairs.* collapse, fall, stumble, totter, tumble. **2** *The ornament toppled off the shelf.* crash, fall, tip over, tumble. **3** *The crisis toppled the government.* bring down, oust, overthrow, overturn, unseat.

topsy-turvy adjective *a topsy-turvy house.* chaotic, confused, disorderly, higgledy-piggledy, messy, mixed-up, muddled, upside-down. OPPOSITE orderly.

torment noun *He suffered mental and physical torment.* agony, anguish, distress, hell, misery, pain, suffering, torture. — verb **1** *She was tormented by doubts.* afflict, bedevil, distress, haunt, plague, rack, torture, trouble, worry. **2** *The dog tormented the cat.* annoy, bait, harass, intimidate, molest, oppress, persecute, pester, plague, provoke, tease, victimise.

torn adjective *Mum mended my torn jeans.* holey, ragged, rent, ripped, slit, split, tattered, tatty (*informal*). OPPOSITE intact.

tornado noun *The tornado caused a lot of damage.* twister (*American*), whirlwind; see also STORM.

torpor noun see LETHARGY.

torrent noun *They were swept away in the torrent of water.* cascade, deluge, downpour, flood, rush, spate, stream.

tortuous adjective *a tortuous path.* circuitous, convoluted, crooked, serpentine, sinuous, twisting, winding, zigzag. OPPOSITE straight.

torture noun *He suffered the torture of losing a child.* agony, anguish, pain, suffering, torment. — verb **1** *The prisoner was tortured to try to make him confess.* abuse, maltreat, mistreat, persecute, punish, torment. **2** *She was tortured by self-doubts.* afflict, distress, plague, rack, torment, trouble, worry.

toss verb **1** *He tossed the ball.* bowl, cast, chuck (*informal*), fling, heave, hurl, launch, lob, pitch, propel, shy, sling, throw. OPPOSITE catch. **2** *The boat tossed in heavy seas.* bob, heave, lurch, pitch, reel, rock, roll, welter. **3** *He tossed and turned all night.* squirm, thrash, wriggle, writhe. — noun *a toss of the ball.* delivery, fling, hurl, launch, lob, pitch, throw.

total adjective **1** *The total number is 500.* aggregate, combined, complete, cumulative, entire, full, overall, whole. **2** *The bombing caused total chaos.* absolute, complete, outright, perfect, pure, sheer, thorough, utter. — noun *The total is 500.* aggregate, amount, sum, sum total, whole. — verb **1** *She totalled the bill.* add up, calculate, compute, sum, tot up (*informal*), work out. **2** *The donations totalled $400.* add up to, amount to, come to, make, tot up to (*informal*).

totally adverb *He was totally ruined.* absolutely, completely, entirely, fully, to the hilt, utterly, wholly. OPPOSITE partially.

totter verb *The old man tottered.* dodder, falter, reel, rock, shake, stagger, stumble, sway, teeter, wobble.

touch verb **1** *He flinched when anyone touched him.* brush, caress, dab, feel, finger, fondle, graze, handle, manipulate, massage, maul, nudge, pat, paw, poke, press, prod, rub, strike, stroke, tap, tickle. **2** *Do not touch the switches.* fiddle with, interfere with, meddle with, play with, tamper with, tinker with. **3** *She was touched by their kindness.* affect, impress, move, stir. — noun **1** *He hasn't lost his touch.* ability, dexterity, finesse, flair, knack, skill, technique. **2** *The soup has just a touch of coriander.* dash, hint, pinch, soupçon, suggestion, suspicion, tinge, trace, whiff. □ **in touch with 1** *She kept in touch with her friend.* in contact with, in communication with, in correspondence with. **2** *He keeps in touch with the latest developments.* abreast of, familiar with, informed on, up to date with. **touch down** *The aircraft touched down.* arrive, land. OPPOSITE take off. **touch on** *The article touches on many subjects.* allude to, cover, deal with, mention, refer to, speak of, talk about. **touch up** *He touched up the painting.* enhance, fix up, improve, repair.

touch-and-go adjective *It's touch-and-go whether he'll live.* chancy, dicey (*slang*), doubtful, iffy (*informal*), precarious, uncertain. OPPOSITE certain.

touching adjective *a touching story.* emotional, moving, poignant, rousing, stirring.

touchy adjective **1** *He's very touchy on the subject.* over-sensitive, prickly, sensitive, thin-skinned. OPPOSITE thick-skinned. **2** *It's a touchy subject and best avoided.* delicate, sensitive, sore, thorny, ticklish, tricky.

tough adjective **1** *tough steak.* chewy, gristly, leathery. OPPOSITE tender. **2** *The uniform is made of tough material.* durable, hard-wearing, hardy, heavy-duty, indestructible, resistant, serviceable, strong, sturdy, unbreakable. OPPOSITE weak. **3** *a physically tough person.*

beefy, brawny, burly, fit, hardy, robust, rugged, strapping, strong, sturdy. OPPOSITE weak. **4** *Father was a tough disciplinarian.* firm, inflexible, merciless, rigid, strict, uncompromising. OPPOSITE soft. **5** *a tough job.* arduous, challenging, demanding, difficult, exacting, formidable, gruelling, hard, laborious, onerous, stiff, strenuous, taxing, uphill. OPPOSITE easy.

toughen verb *The glass has been toughened.* fortify, harden, reinforce, strengthen. OPPOSITE weaken.

tour noun *a tour of the city.* excursion, expedition, jaunt, journey, outing, trip. — verb *They are touring Europe.* explore, go round, holiday in, travel round, visit.

tourist noun *Our city welcomes tourists.* globe-trotter, holidaymaker, sightseer, traveller, tripper, visitor.

tournament noun *This match is the last in the tournament.* championship, competition, contest, event, series.

tout verb **1** *The traders touted for custom.* appeal for, ask for, beg for, seek, solicit. **2** *It was touted as the best film of the year.* hype (*slang*), plug (*informal*), promote, push (*informal*), talk up (*informal*).

tow verb *The truck towed the car.* drag, draw, haul, pull, tug. OPPOSITE push.

tower noun belfry, keep, minaret, pagoda, skyscraper, steeple, turret. — verb *The new building towers above the rest.* loom, rise, soar, stand out, stick up.

towering adjective *a towering office block.* high, lofty, multi-storey, tall.

town noun **1** *a small country town.* community, hamlet, settlement, township, village. **2** *They moved from the town to the country.* big smoke (*informal*), city, metropolis. OPPOSITE bush, country.

toxic adjective *a toxic chemical.* deadly, lethal, noxious, poisonous. OPPOSITE non-toxic.

toy noun *a child's toy.* game, plaything. — verb **toy with 1** *She toyed with the cord.* fiddle with, play with, twiddle with. **2** *He toyed with the idea.* consider, flirt with, think about.

trace noun **1** *There was no trace of the hikers.* evidence, indication, mark, sign, track, trail. **2** *a trace of bitterness in her voice.* element, hint, overtone, shade, shadow, tinge. **3** *The sauce had just a trace of vinegar.* bit, dash, drop, hint, pinch, suggestion, suspicion, tinge, touch. — verb **1** *They traced their missing cat.* discover, find, hunt down, locate, recover, retrieve, track down. **2** *The book traces the development of the language.* chart, delineate, map, outline, record. **3** *They traced the map using grease-proof paper.* copy, draw over.

track noun **1** *animal tracks.* footprint, mark, print, scent, spoor, trace, trail. **2** *The researchers seem to be on the right track.* course, line, path, tack. **3** *We walked along a narrow bush track.* lane, path, road, trail, way. **4** *The horses raced round the track.* circuit, course, racecourse, racetrack. **5** *a train track.* line, rails, railway line. — verb *The police tracked the thief.* follow, hunt, pursue, shadow, stalk, tail (*informal*), trail. □ **track down** *They tracked down the missing purse.* discover, find, locate, recover, retrieve, trace.

tract noun *large tracts of land.* area, expanse, region, stretch, zone.

trade noun **1** *overseas trade.* business, buying and selling, commerce, dealing, traffic, transactions. **2** *She works in the clothing trade.* business, field, industry. **3** *He's a*

plumber by trade. calling, career, craft, employment, job, occupation, vocation, work. — verb **1** *The two countries trade with one another.* buy and sell, deal, do business, market, traffic. **2** *She traded her stamps.* barter, exchange, swap. □ **trade mark** brand, crest, emblem, hallmark, logo, name, proprietary name, symbol.

trader noun *suburban traders.* dealer, merchant, retailer, seller, shopkeeper, supplier, vendor.

tradesman, tradeswoman noun *a skilled tradesman.* artisan, craftsman, craftwoman, workman.

tradition noun *Celebrating birthdays is a tradition.* convention, custom, habit, institution, practice, ritual.

traditional adjective *the traditional methods.* classical, conventional, customary, established, habitual, orthodox, set, standard, time-honoured. OPPOSITE new.

traffic verb *They were jailed for trafficking in heroin.* deal, peddle, push (*informal*), sell, trade.

tragedy noun *the bushfire tragedy.* calamity, catastrophe, disaster, misfortune.

tragic adjective **1** *a tragic sight.* distressing, heartbreaking, pathetic, pitiful, sad, wretched. OPPOSITE happy. **2** *a tragic accident.* appalling, calamitous, catastrophic, dire, disastrous, ghastly, terrible, unfortunate. OPPOSITE fortunate.

trail verb **1** *She trailed the blanket behind her.* drag, draw, haul, pull, tow. **2** *Her dress trailed in the mud.* dangle, drag, hang, sweep. **3** *He was tired and trailed behind the others.* dally, dawdle, drop behind, fall behind, lag, straggle. OPPOSITE lead. **4** *They trailed the suspect.* follow, hound, pursue, shadow, stalk, tail (*informal*), track. — noun **1** *The ship left a trail.* mark, trace, wake, wash. **2** *an animal's trail.* footmarks, footprints, scent, spoor, traces, track. **3** *a walking trail.* lane, path, track. □ **trail away** *Her voice trailed away.* die away, fade, grow fainter, peter out.

trailer noun *We watched the trailers for films.* advertisement, clip, extract, preview.

train noun **1** *The pageant consisted of an endless train of floats and bands.* caravan, cavalcade, column, convoy, cortège, file, line, motorcade, procession. **2** *a train of events.* chain, sequence, series, set, string, succession. — verb **1** *He trained the dog to stop at the corner.* coach, condition, discipline, drill, educate, instruct, teach. **2** *He's training for the big race.* exercise, practise, prepare, work out. **3** *She trained the gun on the tree.* aim, direct, focus, level, point.

trainee noun *a trainee chef.* apprentice, beginner, cadet, learner, novice, student.

trainer noun *a fitness trainer.* coach, instructor, teacher, tutor.

traipse verb (*informal*) *They traipsed around the shops.* plod, tramp, trek, trudge, walk.

trait noun *an endearing trait.* attribute, characteristic, feature, idiosyncrasy, peculiarity, quality.

traitor noun *a traitor to your country.* betrayer, collaborator, deserter, informer, Judas, quisling, renegade, snake in the grass, turncoat.

tramp verb **1** *We heard him tramping along the corridor.* clomp, clump, stamp, stomp, stride. **2** *They tramped for miles through the forest.* hike, march, plod, ramble, slog, traipse (*informal*), trek, trudge, walk. — noun *The tramp slept under the bridge.* beggar, down-and-out, hobo, sundowner (*Aus-*

tralian), swagman (*Australian*), vagabond, vagrant.

trample *verb He trampled the flowers.* crush, flatten, squash, stamp on, step on, tramp on, tread on, walk on.

tranquil *adjective* **1** *She felt tranquil at last.* calm, collected, composed, peaceful, placid, sedate, serene, unflappable (*informal*), untroubled. OPPOSITE agitated. **2** *tranquil surroundings.* peaceful, quiet, restful, still, undisturbed. OPPOSITE busy.

tranquillise *verb The medicine tranquillised her.* calm, pacify, quieten, relax, sedate, soothe. OPPOSITE agitate.

transact *verb He transacted the business on their behalf.* carry out, conduct, execute, handle, manage, negotiate, perform.

transaction *noun a business transaction.* deal, dealing, negotiation, undertaking.

transcend *verb* **1** *It transcends human experience.* go beyond, lie outside of. **2** *His wisdom transcends that of any other man.* eclipse, exceed, outshine, outstrip, overshadow, surpass.

transfer *verb They transferred the goods from the warehouse to the shop.* carry, convey, deliver, move, relocate, remove, shift, shunt, switch, take, transplant, transport.

transfix *verb* **1** *The snake was transfixed with a sharp stick.* impale, pierce, skewer, spike, stab. **2** *He stood transfixed with fear.* freeze, paralyse, petrify, rivet, root to the spot.

transform *verb The house was transformed into a hotel.* alter, change, convert, metamorphose, modify, remodel, turn.

transformation *noun The old house has undergone a transformation.* alteration, change, conversion, facelift, makeover, metamorphosis, revolution.

transgress *verb* **1** *He transgressed the law.* breach, break, contravene, infringe, offend against, violate. OPPOSITE keep. **2** *She was forgiven for having transgressed.* do wrong, err, go astray, sin, trespass (*old use*).

transient *adjective a transient feeling.* brief, ephemeral, fleeting, impermanent, momentary, passing, short-lived, temporary, transitory. OPPOSITE permanent.

transit *noun The goods were delayed in transit.* conveyance, movement, passage, shipment, transfer, transport, transportation.

transition *noun* **1** *the transition from kindergarten to school.* change, changeover, move, progression, shift, switch. **2** *the transition from caterpillar to butterfly.* change, conversion, development, evolution, metamorphosis, transformation.

translate *verb Translate this sentence into German.* change, convert, decipher, decode, interpret, paraphrase, render, rephrase, reword.

transmit *verb* **1** *The operator transmitted the message.* broadcast, communicate, convey, dispatch, forward, pass on, relay, send. OPPOSITE receive. **2** *The disease is transmitted by touch.* carry, communicate, pass on, spread, transfer.

transparent *adjective* **1** *transparent material.* diaphanous, filmy, gauzy, see-through, sheer. **2** *a transparent liquid.* clear, colourless, crystal-clear, limpid. OPPOSITE cloudy, opaque. **3** *a transparent lie.* clear, manifest, obvious, patent, plain, unconcealed, undisguised, unmistakable. OPPOSITE obscure.

transpire *verb It transpired that the politician had acted improperly.* become known, be disclosed, be

revealed, come to light, emerge, leak out.

transplant *verb The gardener transplanted the seedlings.* move, relocate, shift, transfer.

transport *verb* **1** *The company transports heavy machinery.* bear, bring, carry, cart, convey, deliver, ferry, fetch, forward, freight, haul, move, shift, ship, take, transfer. **2** (*historical*) *They used to transport convicts.* banish, deport, exile, expatriate. — *noun* **1** *the transport of goods.* carriage, conveyance, freight, haulage, shipping, transportation. **2** *He has no transport to get to work.* conveyance, transportation, vehicle, wheels (*slang*).

transportable *adjective a transportable building.* demountable, mobile, portable. OPPOSITE fixed.

transpose *verb She transposed the two letters.* interchange, reverse, switch.

trap *noun The animal was caught in the trap.* ambush, booby trap, gin, net, pitfall, snare. — *verb* **1** *The farmer trapped the fox.* capture, catch, corner, ensnare, snare. OPPOSITE release. **2** *He felt he'd been trapped into saying it.* deceive, dupe, set up (*informal*), trick. **3** *His leg was trapped under the car.* catch, hold, lock, pin down, stick. OPPOSITE free.

trash *noun* **1** *He reads a lot of trash.* drivel, garbage, junk, nonsense, rubbish. **2** *Throw the trash in the bin.* garbage, junk, litter, refuse, rubbish, scraps, waste.

traumatic *adjective a traumatic experience.* distressing, disturbing, painful, shocking, upsetting.

travel *verb* **1** *He travels to work by bus.* commute, go, journey. **2** *They travelled through South America.* cross, journey, roam, rove, tour, trek, voyage, wander. **3** *Good news travels fast.* be carried, be transmitted, move, spread. **4** *The walkers travelled thirty kilometres a day.* cover, go, progress. □ **travels** *plural noun She was back from her travels.* excursion, expedition, exploration, globe-trotting, journey, peregrination, pilgrimage, tour, trip, voyage, wandering.

traveller *noun interstate and overseas travellers.* backpacker, commuter, explorer, globe-trotter, gypsy, holidaymaker, nomad, passenger, sightseer, tourist, tripper, vagabond, visitor, voyager, wanderer, wayfarer.

travelling *adjective a travelling musician.* itinerant, peripatetic, roving, touring, vagabond, wandering.

traverse *verb The bridge traverses the river.* bridge, cross, extend across, go across, pass over, span.

travesty *noun The trial was a travesty of justice.* burlesque, misrepresentation, mockery, parody, perversion.

treacherous *adjective* **1** *a treacherous person.* deceitful, disloyal, duplicitous, false, perfidious, sneaky, traitorous, two-faced, untrustworthy. OPPOSITE loyal. **2** *The roads were icy and treacherous.* dangerous, hazardous, perilous, precarious, unsafe. OPPOSITE safe.

treachery *noun* betrayal, disloyalty, duplicity, perfidy, treason. OPPOSITE loyalty.

tread *verb She disliked treading on ants.* stamp, step, tramp, trample, walk.

treason *noun The official was executed for treason.* betrayal, disloyalty, high treason, traitorousness, treachery.

treasure *noun The robbers buried the treasure.* cache, fortune, hoard, riches, valuables, wealth. — *verb*

She treasures the photo. appreciate, cherish, esteem, love, prize, value. OPPOSITE despise.

treat *verb* **1** *He treated his staff badly.* behave towards, deal with, handle, manage. **2** *He treated the ceremony as a joke.* consider, look upon, regard, view. **3** *The subject is treated sensitively.* deal with, discuss, handle, present, tackle. **4** *The doctor treated the patient.* attend to, care for, look after, minister to, nurse, tend. **5** *The fabric has been treated with chemicals.* coat, dress, impregnate, process. **6** *She treated her children to an ice cream.* buy for, pay for, shout (*Australian informal*), stand. — *noun* **1** *Going to a concert was a treat.* delight, joy, luxury, pleasure, thrill. **2** *The meal was his treat.* gift, present, shout (*Australian informal*).

treatise *noun He wrote a treatise on virtue and vice.* article, discourse, dissertation, essay, monograph, paper, study, thesis.

treatment *noun cancer treatment.* care, medication, therapy.

treaty *noun The treaty was signed by both countries.* agreement, alliance, armistice, compact, convention, covenant, deal, pact.

trek *noun a three-day bush trek.* excursion, expedition, hike, journey, tramp, walk. — *verb They trekked through mud and long grass.* hike, journey, slog, traipse (*informal*), tramp, trudge, walk.

trellis *noun The plant grows on a trellis.* frame, grid, grille, lattice.

tremble *verb She trembled with fear.* quake, quaver, quiver, shake, shiver, shudder, vibrate, wobble.

tremendous *adjective* **1** *The fountain was a tremendous waste of money.* big, colossal, enormous, gigantic, huge, immense, large, mammoth, massive, terrific (*informal*), vast. OPPOSITE slight. **2** (*informal*) *The singers gave a tremendous performance.* excellent, exceptional, fabulous (*informal*), fantastic (*informal*), fine, great, impressive, magnificent, marvellous, remarkable, stupendous, superb, terrific (*informal*), wonderful. OPPOSITE poor.

tremor *noun* **1** *a tremor in her voice.* quaver, quiver, shake, shiver, shudder, tremble, vibration, wobble. **2** *an earth tremor.* earthquake, quake (*informal*), shock.

tremulous *adjective Her tremulous voice disclosed her fear.* nervous, quavering, quivering, shaky, shivering, timid, trembling. OPPOSITE steady.

trench *noun The soldiers dug a trench.* ditch, furrow, sap.

trend *noun* **1** *an upward trend in prices.* direction, drift, inclination, movement, shift, tendency. **2** *She follows the trend in clothes.* craze, fad, fashion, mode, style, vogue.

trendy *adjective* (*informal*) *trendy clothes.* contemporary, cool (*informal*), fashionable, in, modern, stylish, up-to-date, with it (*informal*). OPPOSITE old-fashioned.

trepidation *noun He faced the interview with some trepidation.* alarm, anxiety, apprehension, consternation, dismay, dread, fear, nervousness, panic, uneasiness. OPPOSITE calm.

trespass *verb* **1** *They trespassed on the farmer's land.* encroach, intrude, invade. **2** (*old use*) *Forgive those who trespass against you.* err, offend, sin, transgress. — *noun* (*old use*) *Forgive us our trespasses.* iniquity, misdeed, offence, sin, transgression, wrong, wrongdoing.

trial *noun* **1** *a legal trial.* case, examination, hearing, inquiry. **2** *The new machine underwent a trial.* check,

evaluation, experiment, test, tryout. **3** *one of life's trials.* adversity, affliction, hardship, ordeal, suffering, tribulation, trouble, woe. — *adjective a trial period.* experimental, pilot, probationary, testing.

tribe *noun Each tribe has its own language.* clan, community, family, people, race.

tribulation *noun trials and tribulations.* adversity, affliction, anxiety, distress, hardship, misery, misfortune, ordeal, suffering, trial, trouble, woe, worry. OPPOSITE joy.

tribunal *noun The matter was reviewed by an independent tribunal.* board, committee, court, forum.

tributary *noun a tributary of the Murray.* branch, creek, rivulet.

tribute *noun a tribute to a great statesman.* accolade, commendation, compliment, eulogy, panegyric, testimonial. □ **pay tribute to** *They paid tribute to his leadership.* commend, compliment, honour, laud (*formal*), pay homage to, praise, salute.

trick *noun* **1** *He fell for that old trick.* bluff, con (*informal*), confidence trick, deception, dodge (*informal*), fraud, hoax, lurk (*Australian informal*), manoeuvre, ploy, ruse, stratagem, subterfuge, wile. **2** *a trick of the light.* illusion, mirage. **3** *There's a trick to making beds neatly.* art, knack, method, secret, skill, technique, way. **4** *conjuring tricks.* illusion, legerdemain, magic, sleight of hand. **5** *She played a trick on the others.* gag, hoax, joke, practical joke, prank. — *verb She tricked them into thinking they'd won.* bluff, cheat, con (*informal*), deceive, defraud, dupe, fool, have on (*informal*), hoax, hoodwink, kid (*informal*), mislead, outwit, pull someone's leg, swindle, take in.

trickery *noun They were taken in by his trickery.* artifice, cheating, chicanery, craftiness, cunning, deceit, deceitfulness, deception, fraud, hocus-pocus, pretence, skulduggery, sleight of hand, wiliness. OPPOSITE honesty.

trickle *verb The water trickled from the hose.* dribble, drip, leak, ooze, percolate, seep. OPPOSITE spurt.

trickster *noun That trickster deceived us.* charlatan, cheat, con man (*informal*), crook (*informal*), fraud, racketeer, rogue, shark, sharp (*informal*), shicer (*Australian slang*), swindler.

tricky *adjective* **1** *a tricky person.* artful, crafty, cunning, deceitful, foxy, shifty, slippery, sly, underhand, wily. OPPOSITE honest. **2** *a tricky task.* awkward, complicated, dangerous, delicate, difficult, hard, knotty, problematical, risky, ticklish. OPPOSITE simple.

trifle *noun She worries over trifles.* inessential, little thing, nothing, triviality. — *verb He trifled with her affections.* dally, flirt, play, toy.

trifling *adjective see* TRIVIAL.

trigger *verb The assault triggered a series of revenge attacks.* initiate, provoke, set off, spark off, start, touch off.

trim *adjective* **1** *He keeps trim by diet and exercise.* fit, lean, slender, slim. OPPOSITE fat. **2** *a trim garden.* neat, orderly, shipshape, spick and span, spruce, tidy. OPPOSITE untidy. — *verb* **1** *She trimmed their hair.* bob, clip, crop, cut, shear, snip. **2** *They trimmed the Christmas tree.* adorn, deck, decorate, ornament. — *noun an athlete in good trim.* condition, fettle, form, health, shape.

trimming *noun the dress trimming.* decoration, ornamentation, trim. □ **trimmings** *plural noun* **1** *wood* *trimmings. garden trimmings.* clippings, cuttings, scraps, shavings. **2** *roast pork with all the trimmings.* accompaniments, extras, frills, garnish, trappings.

trinket *noun a casket of useless trinkets.* bric-à-brac, jewellery, knickknack, novelty, ornament, trifle.

trio *noun* threesome, triad, trilogy, trinity, triplets, triumvirate.

trip *verb* **1** *They tripped lightly to the music.* caper, dance, frolic, gambol, prance, skip. **2** *She tripped on the footpath.* fall over, slip, sprawl, stumble. — *noun an overseas trip. a trip in the car.* cruise, drive, excursion, expedition, flight, holiday, jaunt, journey, outing, run, tour, trek, visit, voyage. □ **trip up** *He tripped up on unfamiliar words.* blunder, bungle, err, slip up (*informal*), stumble.

tripe *noun* (*informal*) *He talks a load of tripe.* see NONSENSE.

triple *adjective* threefold, treble, tripartite.

trite *adjective It sounded trite but she meant it sincerely.* banal, clichéd, commonplace, corny, hackneyed, platitudinous, stereotyped, stock, unoriginal. OPPOSITE original.

triumph *noun* **1** *the triumph of right over wrong.* conquest, success, victory. OPPOSITE defeat. **2** *The play was a triumph.* hit (*informal*), sensation, smash hit (*informal*), success, winner. OPPOSITE failure. **3** *Climbing the mountain was a personal triumph.* accomplishment, achievement, conquest, feat. — *verb He triumphed in battle.* be successful, be victorious, conquer, prevail, succeed, win. OPPOSITE lose. □ **triumph over** *She triumphed over her enemies.* beat, conquer, defeat, overcome, overpower, vanquish.

triumphant *adjective the triumphant team.* successful, victorious, winning; see also EXULTANT. OPPOSITE defeated, losing.

trivial *adjective Speeding is not a trivial matter.* inconsequential, insignificant, little, minor, negligible, paltry, petty, small, superficial, trifling, unimportant. OPPOSITE important.

troop *noun a troop of people.* band, company, crew, flock, gang, group, horde, mob, pack. — *verb The children trooped in to their classroom.* file, march, parade. □ **troops** *plural noun* armed forces, army, military, servicemen, servicewomen, soldiers.

trophy *noun a diving trophy.* award, cup, medal, prize, shield.

trot *noun* **1** *A trot is faster than a walk.* jog, jogtrot, run. **2** (*Australian informal*) *She had a good trot.* innings, period, run, spell, spin (*Australian informal*).

trouble *noun* **1** *He offers help in times of trouble.* adversity, difficulty, distress, hardship, misfortune, sorrow, trial, tribulation. OPPOSITE joy. **2** *She was weighed down by her troubles.* anxiety, burden, care, concern, problem, woe, worry. **3** *It's no trouble to do that.* bother, difficulty, hassle (*informal*), inconvenience, nuisance, problem. **4** *The finished product was worth the trouble it took.* care, effort, exertion, labour, pains, struggle, work. **5** *Don't stir up trouble.* commotion, conflict, discord, disorder, disturbance, fuss, mischief, row, strife, turmoil, unrest. OPPOSITE calm. **6** *The plane had engine trouble.* breakdown, defect, fault, malfunction, problem. **7** *The patient complained of stomach trouble.* affliction, ailment, disease, disorder, illness, pain, problem. — *verb* **1** *What's troubling him?* afflict, agitate, ail, annoy, bother, bug (*infor-*

mal), concern, distress, disturb, hassle (*informal*), hurt, inconvenience, irritate, oppress, perturb, pester, plague, prey on, put out, upset, vex, weigh down, worry. OPPOSITE please. **2** *He didn't even trouble to find out.* bother, make the effort, take the time, take the trouble. □ **in trouble** *A friend can help when you're in trouble.* in a fix, in a jam (*informal*), in a mess, in a pickle (*informal*), in a plight, in a predicament, in a scrape, in a spot (*informal*), in difficulties, in dire straits, in hot water (*informal*), in strife (*Australian informal*), in the soup (*informal*), up the creek (*informal*).

troublemaker *noun He was branded a troublemaker.* agitator, culprit, delinquent, firebrand, hooligan, mischief-maker, rabble-rouser, ratbag (*Australian informal*), ringleader, ruffian, stirrer (*Australian*).

troublesome *adjective* **1** *The mosquitoes are troublesome.* annoying, bothersome, distressing, irritating, pesky (*informal*), pestilential, tiresome, vexing, worrying. **2** *He is good at dealing with troublesome children.* disobedient, naughty, recalcitrant, refractory, trying, uncooperative, unmanageable, unruly. OPPOSITE helpful.

trough *noun Water collected in the trough.* channel, conduit, culvert, depression, ditch, furrow, gully, gutter, trench.

trounce *verb She trounced her opponent.* beat, clobber (*slang*), defeat, drub, lick (*informal*), overpower, paste (*slang*), rout, slaughter, thrash, vanquish.

troupe *noun He joined a troupe of actors.* band, company, group.

trousers *plural noun* pants, strides (*informal*); [*kinds of trousers*] bellbottoms, breeches, chinos, cords, flares, hipsters, jeans, jodhpurs, knickerbockers, moleskins, pantaloons, plus fours, slacks.

truant *noun The school chases up truants.* absentee, malingerer, skiver (*informal*), wag (*informal*). □ **play truant** *Peter often played truant on exam days.* absent yourself, bludge (*Australian informal*), play hookey (*informal*), skive (*informal*), stay away, wag (*informal*).

truce *noun The parties called for a truce.* armistice, ceasefire, moratorium, peace.

truck *noun He drives a truck.* juggernaut, lorry, pick-up, road train (*Australian*), semi (*Australian informal*), semitrailer, van.

trudge *verb He trudged up the hill.* lumber, plod, slog, traipse (*informal*), tramp, trek.

true *adjective* **1** *What I have told you is a true account.* accurate, actual, authentic, correct, exact, factual, faithful, genuine, honest, precise, reliable, right, strict, truthful, veracious. OPPOSITE fictitious, untrue. **2** *He was the true heir.* authorised, genuine, legal, legitimate, proper, rightful. OPPOSITE phoney (*informal*). **3** *Michelle was a true friend.* constant, dependable, dinkum (*Australian informal*), dinky-di (*Australian informal*), faithful, loyal, real, reliable, sincere, staunch, true-blue, trustworthy. OPPOSITE false.

trunk *noun* **1** *the trunk of a tree.* bole, stem, stock. **2** *The rash was only on her trunk.* body, torso. **3** *She stores clothes in the trunk.* box, case, chest, coffer. **4** *an elephant's trunk.* proboscis, snout. □ **trunks** *plural noun* swimming trunks. bathers (*Australian*), costume, shorts, swimmers (*Australian*), togs (*Australian informal*).

truss *verb She trussed the chicken before cooking it.* bind, secure, tie up.

trust *noun* **1** *They have trust in God.* belief, confidence, conviction, credence, faith, reliance. **2** *He was placed in a position of trust.* responsibility. — *verb* **1** *He trusts in God.* believe in, depend on, have confidence in, have faith in, rely on. OPPOSITE mistrust. **2** *She trusted the children to his care.* assign, commend, commit, consign, delegate, entrust, hand over. **3** *We trust you will come to the party.* assume, expect, hope, presume, take it.

trusting *adjective He is too trusting when it comes to strangers.* credulous, gullible, naive, trustful, unsuspecting, unsuspicious. OPPOSITE suspicious.

trustworthy *adjective She confided in a trustworthy friend.* dependable, faithful, honest, loyal, reliable, responsible, staunch, steadfast, steady, sure, true, trusty (*old use*). OPPOSITE unreliable, untrustworthy.

truth *noun* **1** *His story has the ring of truth.* accuracy, authenticity, genuineness, reliability, truthfulness, veracity. OPPOSITE falsity. **2** *Tell me the truth.* facts, reality. OPPOSITE lies. **3** *a generally accepted truth.* axiom, fact, maxim, principle, truism. OPPOSITE fallacy.

truthful *adjective* **1** *Mary was brought up to be truthful.* frank, honest, open, sincere, straight, trustworthy, veracious. OPPOSITE dishonest. **2** *The witness gave a truthful account.* accurate, correct, factual, faithful, honest, reliable, true. OPPOSITE inaccurate.

try *verb* **1** *He tried to answer the questions.* aim, attempt, endeavour, strive, struggle. **2** *He tried the ice cream.* sample, taste, test. **3** *The children tried her patience.* strain, tax, test. **4** *A new judge tried the case.* adjudicate, examine, hear, judge. — *noun I am willing to have a try.* attempt, bash (*informal*), crack (*informal*), go, shot (*informal*), stab (*informal*), whack (*informal*). □ **try out** **1** *They tried out the treatment on volunteers.* check out, experiment with, test. **2** *He tried out for the school play.* audition, test.

trying *adjective With the computers not working we have had a very trying time.* annoying, demanding, difficult, exasperating, frustrating, irritating, stressful, taxing, tiresome, troublesome, vexing.

tub *noun He grew the plants in an old tub.* barrel, bath, butt, cask, drum, pot.

tubby *adjective She grew tubby through overeating.* chubby, dumpy, fat, obese, plump, podgy, portly, rotund, stout. OPPOSITE slim.

tube *noun The water passes through a tube.* conduit, duct, hose, pipe.

tuck *noun The dress has ornamental tucks.* fold, pin-tuck, pleat. — *verb She tucked her singlet into her pants.* insert, push, shove, stick, stuff.

tuft *noun tufts of grass.* bunch, clump, tussock.

tug *verb* **1** *He tugged the button off the mattress.* jerk, pluck, pull, wrench, yank. **2** *The ship was tugged into port.* drag, draw, haul, pull, tow. OPPOSITE push.

tuition *noun Sue's French improved with private tuition.* coaching, education, instruction, lessons, teaching, training.

tumble *verb* **1** *She tumbled down the stairs.* collapse, fall, plunge, roll, stumble, topple. **2** *Prices tumbled.* collapse, crash, drop, fall, nosedive, plummet, plunge, slump. OPPOSITE increase.

tumbledown *adjective an old town of tumbledown houses.* decrepit, derelict, dilapidated, ramshackle, rickety.

tumour *noun The surgeon removed the tumour.* cancer, carcinoma, growth, lump.

tumult *noun The speaker could not be heard above the tumult.* bedlam, chaos, commotion, confusion, din, disturbance, fracas, hubbub, hullabaloo, kerfuffle (*informal*), mayhem, noise, pandemonium, racket, riot, row, ruckus, rumpus, shindy (*informal*), turmoil, uproar. OPPOSITE peace.

tumultuous *adjective The players received a tumultuous welcome.* boisterous, excited, noisy, rowdy, uproarious, wild.

tune *noun They sang a pleasant tune.* air, melody, strain, theme. — *verb The engine needs to be tuned.* adjust, regulate, set. □ **in tune** *in tune with your peers.* in accord, in agreement, in harmony, in step, in sympathy.

tuneful *adjective a tuneful song.* catchy, harmonious, melodious, musical, pleasant. OPPOSITE tuneless.

tunnel *noun He made his way through the tunnel.* adit, burrow, hole, mine, passage, shaft, subway, underpass. — *verb The wombat tunnelled under the fence.* burrow, dig, excavate.

turbulent *adjective* **1** *a turbulent mob.* boisterous, disorderly, obstreperous, restless, riotous, rough, rowdy, unruly, violent, wild. OPPOSITE peaceful. **2** *turbulent weather.* blustery, gusty, rough, stormy, tempestuous, violent, wild, windy. OPPOSITE calm.

turf *noun* grass, lawn, sod, sward.

turmoil *noun The place was in turmoil after the earthquake.* agitation, bedlam, chaos, commotion, confusion, disorder, disturbance, mess, pandemonium, tumult, upheaval, uproar. OPPOSITE order.

turn *verb* **1** *The merry-go-round started to turn.* gyrate, pivot, revolve, rotate, spin, swivel, twirl, whirl. **2** *She turned to face me.* circle, spin round, swing round, twist round, wheel round. **3** *He turned the pages.* flick, flip, leaf, riffle. **4** *She turned the clothes to help them dry.* flip over, invert, reverse, roll over. **5** *The truck turned the corner.* go round, round. **6** *Turn right.* bear, deviate, diverge, veer. **7** *He turned his thoughts to serious matters.* apply, direct, divert, shift, switch. **8** *The grub turned into a moth.* become, be transformed, change, metamorphose. **9** *She turned the essay into a book.* adapt, change, convert, make, modify, transform. — *noun* **1** *a turn of the handle.* revolution, rotation, twist, wind. **2** *The patient took a turn for the worse.* alteration, change, shift. **3** *a road with many turns.* angle, bend, corner, curve, hairpin bend, loop, turning, twist, wind. **4** *She did me a good turn.* act, action, deed, service. **5** *Everyone had a turn.* chance, go, innings, move, opportunity, shot, spell, stint. **6** (*informal*) *He gave me quite a turn.* fright, scare, shock, start, surprise. □ **turn down** *He turned down their offer.* decline, knock back (*informal*), pass up (*informal*), rebuff, refuse, reject, spurn. OPPOSITE accept. **turn off** **1** *He turned off the power.* cut off, disconnect, switch off. **2** (*informal*) *His bad manners turned people off.* alienate, disgust, offend, put off, repel, repulse. **turn on** **1** *She turned on the washing machine.* plug in, put on, start, switch on. **2** (*informal*) *The idea didn't turn them on.* animate, excite, interest, please, thrill.

turn out 1 *He was turned out of his own home.* chuck out (*informal*), eject, evict, expel, kick out (*informal*), remove, throw out, turf out (*informal*). 2 *Things turned out all right.* end up, happen, pan out, work out. **turn up** 1 *The gloves eventually turned up.* be found, be located, materialise. 2 *She finally turned up.* appear, arrive, come, front (up) (*informal*), lob in (*Australian informal*), roll up (*informal*), show up.

turncoat *noun She was seen as a turncoat and lost her seat at the next election.* apostate, defector, deserter, renegade, traitor.

turning point *noun a turning point in the research.* breakthrough, crisis, crossroads, watershed.

tussle *noun Both men were injured in the tussle.* battle, brawl, clash, conflict, fight, fracas, scrap (*informal*), scuffle, set-to, skirmish, squabble, struggle, wrestle.

tussock *noun a tussock of grass.* clump, tuffet, tuft.

tutor *noun The student has a private tutor.* coach, educator, instructor, mentor, teacher. — *verb He tutors students before exams.* coach, instruct, school, teach.

tutorial *noun a university tutorial.* class, discussion group, seminar.

tweak *verb He tweaked the boy's ear.* jerk, pinch, pull, tug, twist, yank.

tweet *verb The birds tweeted.* cheep, chirp, chirrup, peep, twitter.

tweezers *plural noun* pincers.

twiddle *verb He twiddled his pen.* fiddle with, fidget with, play with, twirl.

twig[1] *noun He collected twigs for the fire.* offshoot, shoot, stalk, stem, stick.

twig[2] *verb She didn't twig that they'd cheated.* see REALISE.

twilight *noun Headlights are needed at twilight.* dusk, evening, gloaming, gloom, nightfall, sundown, sunset. — *adjective the twilight hour.* crepuscular.

twin *noun Did you know you have a twin?* clone, double, lookalike, ringer (*informal*), spitting image. — *verb Adelaide is twinned with Austin, Texas.* couple, link, match, pair.

twine *noun The parcel is tied with twine.* cord, string, thread. — *verb The ivy had twined round the pillar.* coil, entwine, twist, weave, wind.

twinge *noun He felt a twinge in his stomach.* ache, cramp, pain, pang, spasm, stitch, throb.

twinkle *verb The lights twinkled.* blink, flash, flicker, glimmer, glitter, shimmer, shine, sparkle.

twirl *verb* 1 *The dancer twirled around the room.* gyrate, loop, pirouette, revolve, rotate, spin, twist, whirl. 2 *He twirled his spaghetti round his fork.* coil, curl, twine, twist, wind.

twist *verb* 1 *He twisted the threads together.* braid, entwine, intertwine, interweave, plait, weave. OPPOSITE unravel. 2 *He twisted the wire round a reel.* coil, curl, twine, twirl, wind, wrap. 3 *The road twists.* bend, curve, kink, loop, meander, turn, wind, zigzag. OPPOSITE straighten out. 4 *She twisted her way through the tunnel.* squirm, worm, wriggle, writhe. 5 *He twisted his ankle.* pull, rick, sprain, wrench. 6 *The collision twisted the car's bodywork.* buckle, contort, crumple, distort, screw up, warp. — *noun* 1 *a road with many twists.* bend, corkscrew, curve, loop, turn, wind, zigzag. 2 *a twist in the hose.* coil, convolution, kink, knot, snarl, tangle. 3 *an unexpected twist in the story.* change, development, turn.

twisted *adjective* 1 *The car was a twisted wreck.* bent, contorted, crooked, deformed, misshapen, screwed up. 2 *a twisted sense of humour.* kinky (*informal*), perverted, sick, warped.

twisty *adjective Mountain roads can be twisty.* crooked, curved, serpentine, sinuous, tortuous, winding, zigzag. OPPOSITE straight.

twit *noun* see FOOL.

twitch *verb He twitched when the needle pricked him.* fidget, flinch, jerk, jump, quiver, start, wince, wriggle. — *noun a facial twitch.* blink, jerk, spasm, tic.

twitter *verb The birds twittered.* cheep, chirp, chirrup, peep, tweet.

two-faced *adjective* deceitful, dishonest, double-dealing, duplicitous, false, hypocritical, insincere. OPPOSITE sincere.

tycoon *noun an advertising tycoon.* baron, magnate, mogul (*informal*).

type *noun* 1 *It isn't the type of thing I like.* breed, category, class, form, genre, genus, group, kind, make, model, order, sort, species, strain, style, variety, version. 2 *The heading is printed in bold type.* characters, font, print, typeface.

typhoon *noun The town was severely damaged by the typhoon.* hurricane, tropical cyclone; see also STORM.

typical *adjective* 1 *a typical winter's day.* average, normal, ordinary, regular, representative, standard. OPPOSITE atypical. 2 *He answered with his typical rudeness.* characteristic, customary, distinctive, usual. OPPOSITE uncharacteristic.

typify *verb He typifies politicians.* epitomise, exemplify, represent.

tyrannical *adjective a tyrannical leader.* autocratic, cruel, despotic, dictatorial, domineering, harsh, imperious, oppressive, severe, tyrannous, unjust. OPPOSITE democratic.

tyrant *noun The new king was a tyrant.* autocrat, bully, despot, dictator, martinet, slave-driver.

Uu

ugly *adjective* 1 *An ugly tower spoilt the view.* frightful, ghastly, grotesque, hideous, horrible, monstrous, repulsive, shocking, unattractive, unsightly. OPPOSITE beautiful, handsome. 2 *The crowd in an ugly mood.* belligerent, hostile, menacing, nasty, threatening, unpleasant. OPPOSITE pleasant.

ulterior *adjective ulterior motives.* covert, hidden, secret, undisclosed. OPPOSITE obvious.

ultimate *adjective* 1 *The stress is on the ultimate syllable.* end, final, last. OPPOSITE first. 2 *The ultimate cause of the accident was a loose nut.* basic, fundamental, primary, root, underlying.

ultimately *adverb Ultimately Jim was proved right.* eventually, finally, in the end, in the long run.

umbrella *noun* brolly (*informal*), parasol, sunshade.

umpire *noun Respect the umpire's decision.* adjudicator, arbiter, arbitrator, judge, moderator, ref (*informal*), referee. — *verb He umpired the contest.* adjudicate, arbitrate, judge, moderate, referee.

unabridged *adjective an unabridged version of the book.* complete, entire, full, uncut, unexpurgated, whole. OPPOSITE abridged.

unacceptable *adjective His behaviour was unacceptable.* improper, inadmissible, intolerable, objectionable, offensive, taboo, unsatisfactory, unseemly, unsuitable. OPPOSITE acceptable.

unaccompanied *adjective The steward looks after unaccompanied minors.* alone, lone, single, sole, solitary, solo, unescorted. OPPOSITE accompanied.

unaccustomed *adjective* 1 *He is unaccustomed to speaking in public.* inexperienced (at), unused. OPPOSITE used. 2 *She spoke with unaccustomed frankness.* atypical, rare, uncommon, unusual, unwonted. OPPOSITE usual.

unafraid *adjective She was strong and unafraid.* bold, brave, courageous, dauntless, fearless, game, intrepid, plucky, undaunted, valiant. OPPOSITE afraid.

unanimity *noun There was unanimity on the issue.* accord, agreement, consensus, solidarity, unity. OPPOSITE disagreement.

unapproachable *adjective He found his boss unapproachable.* aloof, cool, detached, distant, forbidding, remote, reserved, standoffish, unfriendly, unsociable, withdrawn. OPPOSITE accessible, friendly.

unassuming *adjective Alex was quiet and unassuming.* diffident, modest, quiet, retiring, self-effacing, unassertive, unpretentious. OPPOSITE bold.

unattractive *adjective She wore an unattractive dress.* drab, hideous, inelegant, plain, repulsive, tasteless, ugly, unappealing, unbecoming, unsightly. OPPOSITE attractive.

unauthorised *adjective He was sold an unauthorised copy.* illegal, illicit, pirated, unofficial, unsanctioned. OPPOSITE authorised.

unavoidable *adjective* 1 *an unavoidable outcome.* certain, destined, fated, inescapable, inevitable, predestined. OPPOSITE avoidable. 2 *an unavoidable duty.* compulsory, mandatory, necessary, obligatory.

unaware *adjective The swimmer was unaware of the dangers.* ignorant, oblivious, unconscious, uninformed. OPPOSITE aware.

unawares *adverb He was caught unawares.* by surprise, off guard, unexpectedly.

unbalanced *adjective* 1 *The truck's load was unbalanced.* asymmetrical, lopsided, uneven. 2 *unbalanced reporting of news events.* biased, one-sided, partisan, prejudiced, unfair. OPPOSITE fair. 3 *The offender was mentally unbalanced.* crazy, demented, deranged, insane, mad, unhinged, unsound, unstable. OPPOSITE stable.

unbearable *adjective The pain became unbearable.* excruciating, insufferable, intolerable, unendurable. OPPOSITE bearable.

unbeatable *adjective We have an unbeatable team.* invincible, unconquerable, undefeatable, unstoppable.

unbecoming *adjective* 1 *an unbecoming dress.* unattractive, unflattering, unsuitable. 2 *unbecoming behaviour.* improper, inappropriate, indecorous, ungentlemanly, unladylike, unseemly. OPPOSITE becoming.

unbelievable *adjective an unbelievable story.* amazing, astounding, extraordinary, far-fetched, implausible, improbable, incredible, unconvincing. OPPOSITE credible.

unbeliever *noun* see NON-BELIEVER.

unbiased *adjective We need an unbiased adjudicator.* disinterested, even-handed, fair, impartial, just, neutral, non-partisan, objective, open-minded, unprejudiced. OPPOSITE biased.

unblock *verb The plumber unblocked the drain.* clear, free, unclog, unstop.

unbreakable *adjective unbreakable crockery.* indestructible, solid, strong, sturdy, tough. OPPOSITE fragile.

unbroken *adjective an unbroken series.* complete, continuous, entire, intact, uninterrupted, whole. OPPOSITE broken.

uncalled-for *adjective Her comments were uncalled-for.* gratuitous, needless, unjustified, unnecessary, unsolicited, unwarranted, unwelcome. OPPOSITE warranted.

uncanny *adjective* 1 *uncanny noises.* creepy, eerie, frightening, mysterious, scary, spooky (*informal*), strange, supernatural, unearthly, weird. 2 *She has an uncanny knack of turning up when needed.* astonishing, extraordinary, incredible, remarkable, unbelievable.

uncaring *adjective I've never met such an uncaring person.* callous, cold, hard-hearted, heartless, indifferent, insensitive, unfeeling, unsympathetic. OPPOSITE compassionate.

uncertain *adjective* 1 *She is uncertain about whether to go.* ambivalent, doubtful, dubious, hesitant, indecisive, in two minds, irresolute, undecided, unsure. OPPOSITE decided. 2 *The weather is uncertain.* changeable, erratic, unpredictable, unreliable, variable. OPPOSITE predictable.

unchangeable *adjective unchangeable quality.* changeless, consistent, constant, dependable, immutable, invariable, reliable, unvarying. OPPOSITE variable.

uncharitable *adjective an uncharitable remark.* mean, unchristian, unfair, ungenerous, unkind. OPPOSITE charitable.

uncivilised *adjective We were shocked by such uncivilised behaviour.* antisocial, barbarian, barbaric, barbarous, boorish, philistine, primitive, rude, savage, uncouth, uncultured, vulgar, wild. OPPOSITE civilised.

uncomfortable *adjective* 1 *an uncomfortable situation.* awkward, difficult, distressing, embarrassing, painful. 2 *an uncomfortable feeling.* anxious, apprehensive, awkward, embarrassed, nervous, troubled, uneasy, worried. OPPOSITE comfortable.

uncommon *adjective an uncommon sight.* abnormal, curious, exceptional, extraordinary, infrequent, odd, peculiar, rare, remarkable, singular, special, strange, striking, unfamiliar, unusual. OPPOSITE common.

uncommunicative *adjective He is shy and uncommunicative.* quiet, reserved, reticent, retiring, secretive, silent, taciturn, tight-lipped, unforthcoming, unsociable. OPPOSITE communicative.

uncomplimentary *adjective an uncomplimentary remark.* critical, derogatory, disparaging, insulting, pejorative, rude, unkind. OPPOSITE complimentary.

uncompromising *adjective an uncompromising attitude.* hard-line, inflexible, intransigent, rigid, strict, stubborn, unbending, unyielding. OPPOSITE flexible.

unconcerned *adjective They seemed unconcerned about the danger.* apathetic, carefree, indifferent, lackadaisical, nonchalant, oblivious, unperturbed, untroubled. OPPOSITE worried.

unconditional *adjective unconditional love.* absolute, complete, unlimited, unqualified, unreserved. OPPOSITE conditional.

unconnected *adjective The two matters are unconnected.* independent, separate, unrelated. OPPOSITE connected.

unconscious *adjective* **1** *The victim was unconscious.* blacked out, comatose, insensible, knocked out, senseless. OPPOSITE conscious. **2** *unconscious of what was happening.* oblivious, unaware. OPPOSITE aware. **3** *an unconscious act.* automatic, instinctive, involuntary, mechanical, reflex, unintentional, unthinking, unwitting. OPPOSITE conscious.

uncontrollable *adjective* **1** *uncontrollable children.* headstrong, intractable, irrepressible, obstreperous, rebellious, refractory, undisciplined, unmanageable, unruly, wayward, wilful. OPPOSITE manageable. **2** *an uncontrollable urge.* compulsive, irresistible, overwhelming. OPPOSITE resistible.

unconventional *adjective* *unconventional behaviour.* abnormal, eccentric, odd, offbeat, original, peculiar, singular, strange, unorthodox, unusual, way-out, weird. OPPOSITE conventional.

unconvincing *adjective* *an unconvincing excuse.* feeble, flimsy, implausible, lame, unbelievable, unsatisfactory, weak. OPPOSITE convincing.

uncooperative *adjective* *The workers were being deliberately uncooperative.* difficult, obstructive, perverse, rebellious, recalcitrant, stroppy (*informal*), unhelpful. OPPOSITE cooperative.

uncoordinated *adjective* see CLUMSY.

uncouth *adjective* *an uncouth fellow.* bad-mannered, boorish, coarse, loutish, rough, rude, unrefined, vulgar. OPPOSITE polite.

uncover *verb* *The police uncovered the truth.* bare, dig up, disclose, discover, expose, reveal, unearth. OPPOSITE cover up.

uncultivated *adjective* *uncultivated land.* fallow, unused, virgin, waste, wild. OPPOSITE cultivated.

undecided *adjective* *She is undecided about whether to go.* ambivalent, in two minds, irresolute, open-minded, uncertain, unsure, vacillating. OPPOSITE decided.

undeniable *adjective* *The link between smoking and lung cancer is undeniable.* certain, incontrovertible, indisputable, indubitable, irrefutable, positive, sure, unquestionable. OPPOSITE refutable.

under *preposition* **1** *a cellar under the house.* below, beneath, underneath. OPPOSITE above. **2** *selling for under $20.* below, less than, lower than. OPPOSITE over. **3** *He has several staff under him.* below, junior to, subordinate to. OPPOSITE above.

undercurrent *noun* *an undercurrent of discontent.* atmosphere, feeling, hint, undertone, vibes (*informal*).

underdone *adjective* *The meat was underdone.* rare, undercooked. OPPOSITE overcooked.

underestimate *verb* *She underestimated their ability.* misjudge, underrate, undervalue. OPPOSITE exaggerate.

undergo *verb* *She had to undergo more chemotherapy.* bear, be subjected to, brave, endure, experience, go through, put up with, submit to, weather.

underground *adjective* **1** *an underground cave.* subterranean. **2** *We joined an underground resistance group.* clandestine, covert, secret, undercover.

undergrowth *noun* *The rabbit hid in the undergrowth.* brush, bushes, ground cover, shrubs.

underhand *adjective* *He used underhand methods to get what he wanted.* crafty, crooked (*informal*), cunning,

deceitful, devious, dishonest, fraudulent, shonky (*Australian informal*), sly, sneaky, unscrupulous. OPPOSITE above board.

underline *verb* *This accident underlines the need for traffic lights.* emphasise, highlight, point up, stress.

underling *noun* *He disliked being treated as an underling.* flunkey, menial, minion, servant, subordinate. OPPOSITE boss.

undermine *verb* *His enemies sought to undermine his influence.* destroy, erode, ruin, sabotage, sap, subvert, weaken. OPPOSITE strengthen.

underneath *preposition* *The money was hidden underneath the floorboards.* below, beneath, under. OPPOSITE above.

underpants *plural noun* boxer shorts, briefs, drawers, jocks (*slang*), knickers, panties, pants, undies (*informal*).

underpass *noun* subway, tunnel. OPPOSITE overpass.

underprivileged *adjective* *Support is offered to underprivileged families.* deprived, disadvantaged, needy, poor.

underrate *verb* *The restaurant has been underrated.* sell short, underestimate, undervalue. OPPOSITE overrate.

underside *noun* *You don't look at the underside.* back, bottom, reverse, underneath, wrong side.

undersized *adjective* *an undersized tree.* diminutive, dwarf, little, midget, puny, pygmy, short, small, stunted, tiny, underdeveloped. OPPOSITE oversized.

understaffed *adjective* *The office was understaffed.* short-handed, short-staffed, undermanned. OPPOSITE overstaffed.

understand *verb* **1** *He didn't understand what was going on.* apprehend, comprehend, cotton on to (*informal*), fathom, follow, get (*informal*), grasp, interpret, jerry to (*Australian informal*), know, perceive, realise, recognise, see, take in, tumble to (*informal*), twig (*informal*). OPPOSITE misunderstand. **2** *Can you understand what he has written?* decipher, decode, make head or tail of, make out. **3** *He understands how you feel.* appreciate, empathise with, sympathise with. **4** *I understand she is retiring.* believe, gather, hear, learn.

understanding *adjective* *an understanding friend.* compassionate, considerate, forbearing, perceptive, sensitive, sympathetic, tolerant. OPPOSITE unsympathetic. — *noun* **1** *beyond human understanding.* intellect, intelligence, knowledge, mentality, perception, wisdom. **2** *She has no understanding of the problems.* appreciation, awareness, comprehension, conception, insight, perception, realisation. **3** *His friends were lacking in understanding.* compassion, consideration, empathy, feeling, sensitivity, sympathy, tolerance. **4** *The parties reached an understanding.* accord, agreement, arrangement, bargain, compromise, deal, entente, pact, settlement.

undertake *verb* **1** *She undertook to be treasurer.* agree, consent, promise, volunteer. **2** *He undertook the job.* accept, assume, embark on, start, tackle, take on.

undertaker *noun* *After he died she called the undertaker.* funeral director, mortician (*American*).

undertaking *noun* **1** *He has the energy for this undertaking.* endeavour, enterprise, job, project, task, venture, work. **2** *He gave a solemn undertaking.* assurance, commit-

ment, guarantee, pledge, promise, vow.

undertone *noun* **1** *The nurses spoke in undertones.* murmur, whisper. **2** *an undertone of resentment.* atmosphere, hint, suggestion, trace, undercurrent.

underwater *adjective* subaquatic, submarine, submerged, undersea.

underwear *noun* lingerie, underclothes, undergarments, undies (*informal*).

undeserved *adjective* *undeserved praise.* unearned, unjustified, unmerited, unwarranted. OPPOSITE deserved.

undesirable *adjective* *an undesirable state of affairs.* objectionable, offensive, repugnant, unacceptable, unsatisfactory, unwanted. OPPOSITE desirable.

undeveloped *adjective* *existing in an undeveloped state.* embryonic, immature, primitive, rudimentary. OPPOSITE advanced.

undisciplined *adjective* see UNRULY.

undistinguished *adjective* *The soldier had an undistinguished career.* mediocre, ordinary, unexceptional, unimpressive, unremarkable. OPPOSITE distinguished.

undivided *adjective* *She received his undivided attention.* complete, exclusive, full, total, wholehearted. OPPOSITE divided.

undo *verb* **1** *He can't undo the straps.* detach, disconnect, loosen, open, release, unbuckle, unbutton, unclasp, unfasten, unhook, untie, unwrap, unzip. OPPOSITE do up, fasten. **2** *Her carelessness undid all their good work.* cancel, counteract, destroy, nullify, reverse, ruin, spoil, wreck.

undoing *noun* *Drink was his undoing.* destruction, downfall, ruin, ruination.

undoubted *adjective* *Sam was the undoubted winner.* certain, clear, clear-cut, indisputable, sure, undisputed.

undress *verb* *She undressed in the bedroom.* disrobe, peel off, strip, uncover yourself. OPPOSITE dress.

undressed *adjective* bare, naked, nude, unclothed. OPPOSITE dressed.

undue *adjective* *The ambulance arrived without undue delay.* disproportionate, excessive, inordinate, unjustified, unnecessary, unreasonable. OPPOSITE due.

undying *adjective* *undying love.* abiding, constant, endless, eternal, everlasting, immortal, infinite, never-ending, permanent, perpetual, unending. OPPOSITE transient.

unearth *verb* *The archaeologist unearthed several bones.* dig up, discover, disinter, excavate, exhume, uncover. OPPOSITE bury.

unearthly *adjective* *She was woken by an unearthly sound.* creepy, eerie, ghostly, spooky (*informal*), supernatural, uncanny, weird.

uneasy *adjective* *She feels uneasy about talking to strangers.* anxious, apprehensive, edgy, ill at ease, jittery (*informal*), nervous, nervy, tense, uncomfortable, worried. OPPOSITE comfortable.

uneconomic *adjective* *The business had become uneconomic.* non-paying, unprofitable, unviable. OPPOSITE economic.

uneducated *adjective* ignorant, illiterate, unschooled, untaught. OPPOSITE educated.

unemployed *adjective* *He is unemployed but looking for work.* jobless, laid off, on the dole (*informal*), out of work, redundant. OPPOSITE employed

unequal *adjective* **1** *unequal amounts.* different, disparate, dissimilar, uneven. OPPOSITE identical. **2** *The two teams received unequal*

treatment. biased, discriminatory, unbalanced, uneven, unfair, unjust. OPPOSITE even-handed.

unethical *adjective* *unethical business practices.* dishonest, dishonourable, immoral, shady, shonky (*Australian informal*), underhand, unprincipled, unscrupulous, wrong. OPPOSITE ethical.

uneven *adjective* **1** *an uneven surface.* bumpy, irregular, lumpy, rough, rugged, undulating. OPPOSITE level, smooth. **2** *an uneven edge.* crooked, jagged, ragged, wavy. OPPOSITE straight. **3** *an uneven contest.* inequitable, one-sided, unbalanced, unequal, unfair. **4** *uneven work.* erratic, inconsistent, patchy, variable. OPPOSITE uniform.

unexcitable *adjective* *an unexcitable person.* calm, cool, impassive, listless, nonchalant, phlegmatic, serene, stolid, unemotional, unflappable (*informal*). OPPOSITE excitable.

unexciting *adjective* *He has an unexciting job.* boring, dreary, dull, humdrum, monotonous, mundane, ordinary, run-of-the-mill, tame, tedious, uneventful, uninteresting. OPPOSITE exciting.

unexpected *adjective* *an unexpected result.* accidental, chance, fortuitous, startling, surprising, undreamed-of, unforeseen, unlooked-for. OPPOSITE expected.

unfailing *adjective* *his unfailing good humour.* constant, dependable, infallible, reliable.

unfair *adjective* *unfair treatment.* biased, inequitable, one-sided, partial, partisan, prejudiced, unjust, unreasonable. OPPOSITE fair.

unfaithful *adjective* **1** *unfaithful to the party.* disloyal, false, perfidious, traitorous, treacherous. **2** *an unfaithful husband.* adulterous, false, fickle, inconstant, two-timing (*informal*), untrue. OPPOSITE faithful.

unfaithfulness *noun* adultery, disloyalty, inconstancy, infidelity, perfidy, treachery, treason. OPPOSITE faithfulness.

unfamiliar *adjective* *an unfamiliar concept.* alien, exotic, foreign, new, novel, strange, unheard-of, unknown. OPPOSITE familiar.

unfashionable *adjective* *Not all op shop clothes are unfashionable.* dated, obsolete, old-fashioned, outdated, outmoded, out of date. OPPOSITE fashionable.

unfasten *verb* see UNDO, UNLOCK.

unfavourable *adjective* **1** *unfavourable conditions.* adverse, contrary, disadvantageous, inauspicious, unhelpful, unpropitious. **2** *an unfavourable response.* critical, discouraging, hostile, negative. OPPOSITE favourable.

unfeeling *adjective* *an unfeeling person.* callous, clinical, cold, cold-hearted, cruel, hard, hard-hearted, harsh, heartless, inhuman, insensitive, merciless, pitiless, ruthless, uncaring, unsympathetic. OPPOSITE sensitive, sympathetic.

unfinished *adjective* see INCOMPLETE.

unfit *adjective* **1** *The house is unfit for people to live in.* inappropriate, unsuitable, unusable, useless. OPPOSITE suitable. **2** *He is unfit to be their leader.* inadequate, incapable, incompetent, unqualified, unsuited. OPPOSITE qualified. **3** *The exercise showed how unfit she was.* out of condition, out of form, out of training, unhealthy. OPPOSITE fit.

unflappable *adjective* (*informal*) *He remains unflappable even under extreme pressure.* calm, collected, composed, cool, easygoing, imperturbable, nonchalant, phlegmatic, placid, unexcitable. OPPOSITE panicky.

unfold *verb* **1** *She unfolded the cloth.* open out, spread out, unfurl. OPPOSITE fold up. **2** *The story gradually unfolded.* develop, emerge, evolve.

unforeseen *adjective* see UNEXPECTED.

unforgettable *adjective an unforgettable evening.* impressive, memorable, noteworthy, remarkable, striking. OPPOSITE forgettable.

unforgivable *adjective A mortal sin is one that is unforgivable.* indefensible, inexcusable, unjustifiable, unpardonable. OPPOSITE forgivable.

unforgiving *adjective Despite her apology he remained unforgiving.* hard-hearted, implacable, merciless, pitiless, remorseless, vengeful, vindictive. OPPOSITE merciful.

unfortunate *adjective* **1** *an unfortunate error.* calamitous, disastrous, lamentable, regrettable, terrible, tragic. **2** *an unfortunate person.* hapless, ill-fated, jinxed (*informal*), luckless, unlucky, wretched. OPPOSITE fortunate, lucky.

unfounded *adjective an unfounded fear.* baseless, groundless, unjustified, unwarranted. OPPOSITE justified.

unfriendly *adjective an unfriendly person.* aloof, antagonistic, antisocial, clinical, cool, distant, hostile, icy, inhospitable, standoffish, surly, uncaring, unfeeling, unkind, unneighbourly, unsociable. OPPOSITE friendly.

ungainly *adjective He looked very ungainly on the dance floor.* awkward, clumsy, gawky, inelegant, ungraceful. OPPOSITE graceful.

ungodly *adjective He repented of his ungodly life.* evil, godless, immoral, impious, iniquitous, irreligious, sinful, unholy, wicked. OPPOSITE godly.

ungrateful *adjective an ungrateful person.* unappreciative, unthankful. OPPOSITE grateful.

unhappiness *noun* see SADNESS.

unhappy *adjective* **1** *He was alone and unhappy.* blue, dejected, depressed, despondent, disconsolate, discontented, dismal, dispirited, distressed, doleful, downcast, down-hearted, fed up (*informal*), gloomy, glum, heartbroken, heavy-hearted, melancholy, miserable, mournful, pessimistic, sad, sorrowful, woebegone, wretched. OPPOSITE happy. **2** *It turned out to be an unhappy choice.* bad, inappropriate, poor, regrettable, unfortunate, unlucky, unsatisfactory, unsuitable. OPPOSITE satisfactory.

unharmed *adjective They escaped unharmed.* safe, safe and sound, undamaged, unhurt, uninjured, unscathed. OPPOSITE harmed.

unhealthy *adjective* **1** *He looks rather unhealthy.* ailing, diseased, poorly, sick, sickly, unsound, unwell. OPPOSITE healthy. **2** *They live in unhealthy conditions.* deleterious, detrimental, harmful, insalubrious, insanitary, unhygienic, unwholesome. OPPOSITE healthy.

unhelpful *adjective The sales assistant was unhelpful.* obstructive, stroppy (*informal*), uncooperative. OPPOSITE helpful.

unidentified *adjective an unidentified victim.* anonymous, incognito, nameless, unknown, unnamed. OPPOSITE identified.

uniform *noun The employees wear uniform.* habit, livery, regalia. — *adjective food of uniform quality.* consistent, constant, even, identical, invariable, regular, same, stable, steady, unchanging. OPPOSITE varying.

unify *verb* see UNITE.

unimaginative *adjective an unimaginative story.* colourless, dull, hackneyed, ordinary, pedestrian, prosaic, unexciting, uninspired, unoriginal. OPPOSITE imaginative.

unimportant *adjective Let's not worry about unimportant details.* inconsequential, insignificant, irrelevant, minor, obscure, peripheral, petty, trivial. OPPOSITE important.

uninhabited *adjective The house was uninhabited.* deserted, empty, unoccupied, vacant. OPPOSITE inhabited.

uninhibited *adjective uninhibited behaviour.* free, reckless, spontaneous, unrepressed, unrestrained, unselfconscious. OPPOSITE inhibited.

unintelligible *adjective Their conversation was unintelligible to others.* confused, incoherent, incomprehensible, indecipherable, meaningless. OPPOSITE intelligible.

unintentional *adjective an unintentional meeting.* accidental, chance, fortuitous, inadvertent, unforeseen, unintended, unplanned, unpremeditated; see also INVOLUNTARY. OPPOSITE planned.

uninterested *adjective He was uninterested in what was going on.* apathetic, blasé, bored, detached, indifferent, unconcerned. OPPOSITE curious, interested.

uninteresting *adjective an uninteresting book.* banal, boring, commonplace, dreary, dull, humdrum, monotonous, mundane, ordinary, pedestrian, prosaic, stodgy, tedious, tiresome, uneventful, unexciting, unimaginative, uninspiring, vapid. OPPOSITE interesting.

uninterrupted *adjective uninterrupted sleep.* continuous, non-stop, solid, sound, unbroken, undisturbed. OPPOSITE interrupted.

uninviting *adjective an uninviting place.* inhospitable, unappealing, unattractive, unenticing, unwelcoming. OPPOSITE inviting.

union *noun* **1** *a union of several smaller firms.* alliance, amalgamation, association, coalition, combination, consortium, federation, league, merger, syndicate. **2** *the students' union.* club, group, society. **3** *a workers' union.* guild, trade union.

unique *adjective Each singer has a unique voice.* distinctive, inimitable, matchless, one-off, peculiar, singular. OPPOSITE common.

unit *noun* **1** *The cupboard is made up of several smaller units.* component, constituent, element, item, module, part, piece, section. OPPOSITE whole. **2** *a unit of weight.* measure, measurement, quantity. **3** *The company has a research unit.* group, squad, team. **4** *She lives in a unit in the city.* apartment, condominium (*American*), flat, home unit.

unite *verb* **1** *A common goal united them.* bind, bring together, join, link, tie, unify. OPPOSITE divide. **2** *They united the two councils.* amalgamate, combine, consolidate, federate, incorporate, integrate, join, merge. OPPOSITE split. **3** *The people united to block the development.* band together, collaborate, cooperate, join forces, team up. OPPOSITE split.

unity *noun They strove for party unity.* accord, agreement, cohesion, concord, consensus, harmony, oneness, solidarity, unanimity. OPPOSITE disunity, division.

universal *adjective AIDS is a universal problem.* general, global, international, ubiquitous, widespread, worldwide. OPPOSITE localised.

universe *noun our place in the universe.* cosmos, Creation, world.

unjust *adjective an unjust decision.* biased, inequitable, one-sided, partial, prejudiced, unfair, unjustified,

unreasonable, wrong. OPPOSITE just, reasonable.

unkempt *adjective He looked unkempt when he first got up.* bedraggled, dishevelled, messy, scruffy, tousled, untidy. OPPOSITE tidy.

unkind *adjective an unkind person. an unkind act.* beastly (*informal*), callous, cold-hearted, cruel, hard-hearted, harsh, heartless, hurtful, inconsiderate, inhuman, inhumane, malicious, mean, merciless, nasty, pitiless, ruthless, sadistic, spiteful, stern, thoughtless, uncaring, uncharitable, unfeeling, unfriendly, unneighbourly, unsympathetic, vicious. OPPOSITE kind.

unknown *adjective* **1** *The soloist was an unknown pianist.* obscure, undistinguished, unheard-of. OPPOSITE well-known. **2** *The benefactor wanted to remain unknown.* anonymous, nameless, unidentified, unnamed. OPPOSITE identified.

unlikely *adjective an unlikely tale.* far-fetched, implausible, improbable, incredible, unbelievable. OPPOSITE likely.

unlimited *adjective* **1** *a leader with unlimited power.* absolute, unqualified, unrestricted. OPPOSITE restricted. **2** *Her mother has unlimited patience.* boundless, endless, everlasting, inexhaustible, infinite, limitless, never-ending, vast. OPPOSITE limited.

unload *verb* **1** *He unloaded the cargo.* discharge, drop off, dump, offload, remove. **2** *He unloaded the car.* empty, unpack. OPPOSITE load.

unlock *verb She unlocked the door and went inside.* open, unbolt, undo, unfasten, unlatch. OPPOSITE lock.

unlucky *adjective How can somebody be so unlucky?* accident-prone, hapless, ill-fated, jinxed (*informal*), luckless, unfortunate, wretched. OPPOSITE lucky.

unmarried *adjective an unmarried aunt.* maiden, single, unattached, unwed.

unmentionable *adjective an unmentionable word.* forbidden, obscene, rude, shocking, taboo, unprintable.

unmistakable *adjective an unmistakable family likeness.* apparent, blatant, clear, conspicuous, distinct, evident, glaring, manifest, noticeable, obvious, patent, plain, pronounced.

unnatural *adjective* **1** *He was worried by a series of unnatural events.* abnormal, bizarre, freakish, odd, peculiar, strange, supernatural, unusual, weird. **2** *Her behaviour is very unnatural.* affected, artificial, contrived, forced, mannered, phoney (*informal*), stilted, studied, theatrical. OPPOSITE natural.

unnecessary *adjective Try to omit unnecessary details.* dispensable, excessive, expendable, inessential, needless, non-essential, redundant, superfluous, uncalled-for, unwanted. OPPOSITE necessary.

unnerve *verb The eerie noises unnerved the campers.* agitate, disconcert, fluster, frighten, perturb, rattle (*informal*), unsettle, upset. OPPOSITE encourage.

unoccupied *adjective The house was vandalised while unoccupied.* deserted, empty, uninhabited, unlived-in, vacant. OPPOSITE occupied.

unorthodox *adjective an unorthodox view.* heretical, irregular, non-standard, unconventional. OPPOSITE orthodox.

unpaid *adjective* **1** *an unpaid account.* outstanding, overdue, owing. **2** *an unpaid worker.* honorary, unsalaried, unwaged, voluntary. OPPOSITE paid.

unparalleled *adjective unparalleled joy.* incomparable, inimitable, matchless, peerless, supreme, unequalled, unrivalled, unsurpassed.

unplanned *adjective an unplanned meeting.* accidental, chance, fortuitous, unintended, unintentional, unpremeditated, unscheduled. OPPOSITE planned.

unpleasant *adjective an unpleasant person. an unpleasant thing.* abominable, annoying, appalling, atrocious, awful, bad-tempered, beastly (*informal*), diabolical, disagreeable, disgusting, distasteful, dreadful, foul, frightful, ghastly, harsh, hateful, hideous, horrible, horrid, irksome, loathsome, nasty, nauseating, objectionable, obnoxious, offensive, off-putting, repugnant, repulsive, revolting, sickening, sordid, squalid, terrible, troublesome, unattractive, unfriendly, unlikeable, unpalatable, unsightly, upsetting, vile. OPPOSITE pleasant.

unpopular *adjective He was unpopular at school.* disliked, friendless, on the outer (*Australian informal*), shunned, unloved. OPPOSITE popular.

unprecedented *adjective an unprecedented turnout for council elections.* exceptional, extraordinary, unheard-of, unparalleled, unusual. OPPOSITE usual.

unpredictable *adjective We were warned that she was unpredictable.* capricious, changeable, erratic, fickle, inconstant, mercurial, moody, temperamental, unreliable, volatile. OPPOSITE predictable.

unprejudiced *adjective an unprejudiced jury.* disinterested, fair, impartial, objective, open-minded, unbiased. OPPOSITE prejudiced.

unprepared *adjective It was very good for an unprepared speech.* ad lib, extempore, impromptu, off the cuff, spontaneous, unrehearsed. OPPOSITE prepared.

unpretentious *adjective Although he is rich, his house is unpretentious.* homely, humble, lowly, modest, plain, simple, unimposing, unostentatious. OPPOSITE pretentious.

unprincipled *adjective* see UNETHICAL.

unproductive *adjective* **1** *unproductive land.* barren, infertile, sterile, waste. OPPOSITE fertile. **2** *an unproductive discussion.* fruitless, futile, unprofitable, unrewarding, useless, vain. OPPOSITE productive.

unprofessional *adjective* **1** *an unprofessional job.* amateurish, incompetent, inexpert, shoddy. OPPOSITE professional. **2** *unprofessional conduct.* improper, irresponsible, negligent, unethical, unprincipled. OPPOSITE ethical.

unprofitable *adjective* **1** *an unprofitable business.* uncommercial, uneconomic. OPPOSITE profitable. **2** *unprofitable research.* fruitless, unproductive, useless, worthless. OPPOSITE fruitful.

unquestionable *adjective Its authenticity is unquestionable.* certain, definite, incontrovertible, indisputable, indubitable, irrefutable, sure, undeniable, undisputed. OPPOSITE questionable.

unravel *verb She unravelled the wool.* disentangle, untangle, untwist. OPPOSITE entangle.

unreadable *adjective unreadable writing.* illegible, indecipherable. OPPOSITE legible.

unreal *adjective an unreal world.* artificial, fabulous, false, fantastic, fictitious, hypothetical, illusory, imaginary, make-believe, mythical, non-existent. OPPOSITE real.

unrealistic *adjective unrealistic goals.* idealistic, impracticable, impractical, unreasonable, unworkable. OPPOSITE realistic.

unreasonable *adjective* **1** *an unreasonable person.* headstrong, illogical, irrational, mulish, obstinate, opinionated, perverse, pigheaded, stiff-necked, stroppy (*informal*), stubborn, wilful. OPPOSITE reasonable. **2** *an unreasonable price.* excessive, exorbitant, extortionate, steep (*informal*). OPPOSITE moderate. **3** *an unreasonable request.* absurd, ludicrous, outrageous, preposterous. OPPOSITE reasonable.

unreliable *adjective* **1** *The method is unreliable.* chancy, dicey (*slang*), dodgy (*informal*), iffy (*informal*), risky, shonky (*Australian informal*), uncertain, unsound, unsure. **2** *an unreliable worker.* erratic, fickle, irresponsible, undependable, untrustworthy. OPPOSITE reliable.

unrepentant *adjective* *an unrepentant sinner.* hardened, impenitent, remorseless, unashamed. OPPOSITE contrite.

unreservedly *adverb* *He forgave her unreservedly.* absolutely, completely, totally, unconditionally, utterly, wholeheartedly, without reservation.

unresolved *adjective* *an unresolved issue.* debatable, doubtful, moot, pending, undecided, undetermined, unsettled. OPPOSITE resolved.

unrest *noun* *student unrest.* agitation, disquiet, dissatisfaction, rebellion, rioting, strife, trouble, turbulence, turmoil, unease, uprising.

unrestrained *adjective* *unrestrained emotion.* unbridled, unchecked, uncontrolled, uninhibited, unrepressed, wild. OPPOSITE restrained.

unrivalled *adjective* see UNPARALLELED.

unruly *adjective* *an unruly class.* boisterous, disobedient, disorderly, lawless, obstreperous, riotous, rowdy, uncontrollable, undisciplined, unmanageable, wayward, wild. OPPOSITE well-behaved.

unsafe *adjective* *The road is unsafe.* dangerous, hazardous, perilous, precarious, risky, treacherous. OPPOSITE safe.

unsatisfactory *adjective* *an unsatisfactory performance.* defective, deficient, disappointing, faulty, inadequate, insufficient, substandard, unacceptable. OPPOSITE satisfactory.

unscathed *adjective* see UNHARMED.

unscrupulous *adjective* *an unscrupulous businessman.* corrupt, crooked, deceitful, dishonest, dishonourable, immoral, shady, shonky (*Australian informal*), unethical, unprincipled. OPPOSITE ethical, honest.

unseemly *adjective* *unseemly behaviour.* improper, inappropriate, indecent, indecorous, offensive, tasteless, unbecoming, unfitting. OPPOSITE seemly.

unseen *adjective* *She was photographed by an unseen camera.* concealed, hidden, invisible, out of sight, unnoticed. OPPOSITE seen.

unselfish *adjective* *Many people benefited from his unselfish action.* altruistic, considerate, generous, kind, magnanimous, open-handed, philanthropic, selfless, thoughtful, unstinting. OPPOSITE selfish.

unsettle *verb* *The change unsettled him.* agitate, disconcert, distress, disturb, faze (*informal*), perturb, rattle (*informal*), ruffle, trouble, upset.

unsettled *adjective* *unsettled weather.* changeable, erratic, patchy, unpredictable, unstable, variable. OPPOSITE settled.

unshakeable *adjective* *In the face of adversity her faith was unshakeable.*

firm, resolute, staunch, steadfast, unwavering. OPPOSITE wavering.

unsociable *adjective* *He lived alone and was unsociable.* aloof, antisocial, reclusive, retiring, standoffish, unfriendly, withdrawn. OPPOSITE sociable.

unsophisticated *adjective* **1** *She was sweet and unsophisticated.* artless, ingenuous, naive, natural, unaffected, unpretentious, unworldly. **2** *Their methods were unsophisticated.* basic, crude, primitive, simple, unrefined. OPPOSITE sophisticated.

unstable *adjective* *an unstable situation.* changeable, explosive, fluctuating, fluid, unpredictable, volatile. OPPOSITE stable.

unsteady *adjective* *The ladder was unsteady.* precarious, rickety, rocky, shaky, unstable, wobbly, wonky (*informal*). OPPOSITE steady.

unsuccessful *adjective* *an unsuccessful try.* abortive, failed, fruitless, futile, ineffective, ineffectual, unavailing, vain. OPPOSITE successful.

unsuitable *adjective* *an unsuitable outfit for the occasion.* inappropriate, out of place, unbecoming, unfitting, unseemly, wrong. OPPOSITE suitable.

unsure *adjective* see UNCERTAIN.

unsuspecting *adjective* *an innocent and unsuspecting man.* credulous, gullible, ingenuous, naive, trusting, unsuspicious, unwary. OPPOSITE suspicious.

unsympathetic *adjective* *an unsympathetic official.* callous, cold, hard-hearted, heartless, indifferent, insensitive, uncaring, uncompassionate, unfeeling. OPPOSITE sympathetic.

untamed *adjective* *an untamed animal.* feral, savage, unbroken, undomesticated, warrigal (*Australian*), wild. OPPOSITE tame.

untangle *verb* *untangle a ball of wool.* disentangle, unravel, unsnarl, untwist. OPPOSITE tangle.

unthinkable *adjective* *an unthinkable outcome.* inconceivable, incredible, unbelievable, unimaginable. OPPOSITE conceivable.

unthinking *adjective* *His unthinking act caused much pain.* careless, heedless, inconsiderate, mindless, negligent, short-sighted, tactless, thoughtless.

untidy *adjective* **1** *an untidy room.* chaotic, cluttered, disorderly, disorganised, higgledy-piggledy, jumbled, littered, messy, muddled, topsy-turvy. OPPOSITE tidy. **2** *He has an untidy appearance.* bedraggled, dishevelled, ruffled, rumpled, scruffy, shabby, shaggy, slatternly, sloppy, slovenly, straggly, tatty (*informal*), tousled, unkempt. OPPOSITE neat.

untie *verb* see UNDO.

untiring *adjective* *He was thanked for his untiring efforts.* constant, indefatigable, persistent, tireless, unceasing, unflagging.

untold *adjective* **1** *There were untold problems.* countless, innumerable, myriad, numberless, numerous. **2** *untold misery.* great, immeasurable, incalculable, indescribable.

untrue *adjective* **1** *His story was found to be untrue.* apocryphal, erroneous, false, fictitious, invented, made-up, untruthful, wrong. OPPOSITE true. **2** *She was untrue to him.* disloyal, fickle, perfidious, treacherous, unfaithful. OPPOSITE loyal, true.

untruth *noun* *He told an untruth.* fabrication, fairy story, falsehood, fib, fiction, lie, story. OPPOSITE truth.

untruthful *adjective* *an untruthful witness.* deceitful, dishonest, false, lying, mendacious. OPPOSITE honest.

unused *adjective* **1** *She gave back the unused sheets of paper.* blank, clean, empty, fresh, new, untouched. OPPOSITE used. **2** *He was unused to country driving.* inexperienced (at), unaccustomed, unfamiliar (with). OPPOSITE used.

unusual *adjective* *an unusual occurrence. an unusual person.* abnormal, atypical, bizarre, curious, different, eccentric, exceptional, exotic, extraordinary, freakish, irregular, odd, offbeat, outlandish, peculiar, phenomenal, queer, rare, remarkable, singular, special, strange, surprising, uncommon, unfamiliar, unorthodox, way-out (*informal*), weird. OPPOSITE ordinary, usual.

unwanted *adjective* **1** *He gave away the unwanted items.* see UNNECESSARY. **2** *They didn't ask her and she felt unwanted.* excluded, on the outer (*Australian*), rejected, shunned, uninvited, unpopular, unwelcome. OPPOSITE wanted.

unwarranted *adjective* *unwarranted fears. unwarranted rudeness.* groundless, indefensible, inexcusable, uncalled-for, unjustified, unnecessary, unreasonable. OPPOSITE justified.

unwary *adjective* *a trap for unwary investors.* imprudent, incautious, unguarded, unsuspecting, unsuspicious. OPPOSITE wary.

unwell *adjective* *He felt unwell.* ailing, bilious, crook (*Australian informal*), funny (*informal*), ill, indisposed, infirm, nauseous, off colour, out of sorts, poorly, queasy, rotten, seedy (*informal*), sick, sickly, under the weather. OPPOSITE well.

unwieldy *adjective* *an unwieldy tool.* awkward, bulky, clumsy, cumbersome, heavy, hefty. OPPOSITE handy.

unwilling *adjective* *She was unwilling to help.* averse, disinclined, hesitant, loath, reluctant. OPPOSITE keen.

unwind *verb* see RELAX.

unwise *adjective* *It is unwise to go there.* crazy, foolish, impolitic, imprudent, inadvisable, injudicious, silly, stupid, unintelligent. OPPOSITE wise.

unworldly *adjective* *He is young and unworldly.* callow, green, inexperienced, innocent, naive, unsophisticated. OPPOSITE worldly.

unworthy *adjective* **1** *He is unworthy of this honour.* undeserving. **2** *Such conduct is unworthy of a king.* beneath, inappropriate, unbecoming, unbefitting, unfitting, unsuitable. OPPOSITE worthy.

unwritten *adjective* *an unwritten law.* implicit, oral, spoken, tacit, unstated. OPPOSITE written.

unyielding *adjective* *an unyielding master.* adamant, firm, inflexible, intransigent, obstinate, relentless, steadfast, stubborn, tenacious, tough, unbending, uncompromising. OPPOSITE flexible.

upbraid *verb* *He upbraided them for speaking rudely to their mother.* admonish, berate, castigate, censure, chastise, chide (*old use*), rebuke, reprimand, reproach, reprove, scold, tell off (*informal*), tick off (*informal*). OPPOSITE praise.

upbringing *noun* *the children's upbringing.* education, nurture, raising, rearing, training.

update *verb* *They updated their bathroom.* modernise, refurbish, remodel, renovate.

up-end *verb* *The child up-ended his toy box.* overturn, tip up, upturn.

upfront *adjective* *She is always upfront about her motives.* direct, forthright, frank, honest, open.

upgrade *verb* *He upgraded the computer.* enhance, improve.

upheaval *noun* *Their lives were full of upheaval.* change, chaos, disruption, disturbance, havoc, turbulence, turmoil.

uphill *adjective* *Getting changes accepted is an uphill battle.* arduous, demanding, difficult, exacting, gruelling, hard, laborious, strenuous, tough. OPPOSITE easy.

uphold *verb* *The court upheld the earlier decision.* confirm, endorse, maintain, stand by, support, sustain. OPPOSITE overrule.

upkeep *noun* *He paid for the car's upkeep.* maintenance, repairs, running.

uplift *verb* *Our spirits were uplifted by their singing.* buoy up, encourage, inspire, lift, raise. OPPOSITE depress.

upmarket *adjective* *He cannot afford an upmarket hotel.* classy (*informal*), de luxe, expensive, luxurious, superior. OPPOSITE downmarket.

upper *adjective* *They climbed to the upper level.* higher, raised, superior. OPPOSITE lower.

uppermost *adjective* *He rose to the uppermost level.* highest, supreme, top, topmost. OPPOSITE lowest.

upright *adjective* **1** *an upright position.* erect, perpendicular, standing, vertical. OPPOSITE horizontal. **2** *an upright person.* ethical, good, honest, honourable, just, moral, principled, righteous, trustworthy, upstanding, virtuous. OPPOSITE dishonourable.

uprising *noun* *a students' uprising.* insurrection, mutiny, rebellion, revolt, revolution, rising.

uproar *noun* **1** *The party ended in uproar.* bedlam, chaos, commotion, confusion, disorder, mayhem, pandemonium, tumult, turmoil. **2** *The decision caused an uproar.* clamour, fracas, furore, hullabaloo, kerfuffle (*informal*), outcry, protest, riot, row, ruckus, rumpus, stir, storm, to-do.

uproot *verb* *He uprooted the weeds.* dig up, eradicate, get rid of, pull up, remove, root out.

upset *verb* **1** *He upset the trolley and broke a bottle.* knock over, overturn, spill, tip up, topple, up-end, upturn. OPPOSITE right. **2** *Fog upset the timetable.* affect, disrupt, interfere with, mess up. **3** *She upset her mother by not keeping in touch.* agitate, alarm, anger, annoy, bother, distress, disturb, fluster, frighten, grieve, hurt, offend, perturb, provoke, rattle (*informal*), trouble, vex, worry. OPPOSITE pacify. — *noun a stomach upset.* ailment, bug (*informal*), complaint, disorder, malady.

upsetting *adjective* *an upsetting experience.* distressing, disturbing, frightening, painful, traumatic, unnerving, worrying.

upshot *noun* *The upshot of the talks was that an inquiry was set up.* consequence, effect, outcome, result.

upside-down *adjective* *an upside-down cake.* inverted, topsy-turvy, upturned.

upstage *verb* *She upstaged the other guests.* eclipse, outdo, outshine, overshadow, put in the shade, steal the show from, surpass.

uptight *adjective* (*informal*) *He was uptight before the speech.* anxious, apprehensive, edgy, jittery (*informal*), keyed up, nervous, tense, uneasy, worried. OPPOSITE calm.

up-to-date *adjective* *an up-to-date kitchen.* contemporary, current, fashionable, latest, modern, modernised, new, trendy (*informal*), up-to-the-minute, with it (*informal*). OPPOSITE antiquated.

upturn *noun* *an economic upturn.* improvement, recovery, upswing. OPPOSITE downturn.

urban *adjective an urban dweller.* city, metropolitan, town. OPPOSITE rural.
urge *verb* **1** *He urged them on.* drive, egg on, force, goad, impel, prod, spur. **2** *She urged her to enter the contest.* beseech, coax, encourage, entreat, exhort, implore, plead with, press, prompt, push, recommend. OPPOSITE discourage. — *noun Heidi had an irresistible urge to get up and dance.* compulsion, desire, drive, fancy, impulse, itch, longing, wish, yearning, yen.
urgent *adjective The people are in urgent need of medicines.* compelling, desperate, dire, immediate, imperative, important, necessary, pressing, vital. OPPOSITE unimportant.
usable *adjective The car is not usable.* available, functional, operational, working. OPPOSITE unusable.
usage *noun The bag was damaged by rough usage.* handling, treatment, use.
use *verb* **1** *She learned how to use the gadget.* employ, handle, manage, manipulate, operate, ply, utilise, wield, work. **2** *She used her brain.* apply, exercise, exert. **3** *The car uses a lot of petrol.* burn, consume, go through. **4** *He uses people for his own ends.* exploit, make use of, manipulate, take advantage of. — *noun* **1** *The car has received a lot of use.* handling, usage. OPPOSITE disuse. **2** *The product has various uses.* application, function. **3** *What is the use of discussing it?* advantage, benefit, good, point, purpose, usefulness, utility, value. □ **use up** *They used up all their holiday savings.* blow (*slang*), consume, deplete, exhaust, expend, fritter away, spend.
used[1] *adjective The charity shop sells used clothes.* cast-off, hand-me-down, old, recycled, second-hand, worn. OPPOSITE new.
used[2] *adjective* **used to** *He is used to the climate.* acclimatised to, accustomed to, familiar with.
useful *adjective* **1** *A blender is a useful device.* convenient, effective, efficient, functional, handy, practical, productive, serviceable, usable, utilitarian. OPPOSITE useless. **2** *The adjudicator made some useful comments.* advantageous, beneficial, constructive, helpful, invaluable, positive, practical, profitable, valuable, worthwhile. OPPOSITE useless.
useless *adjective* **1** *The gadget is useless.* bung (*Australian informal*), dud (*informal*), impractical, ineffective, unusable, worthless. OPPOSITE useful. **2** *It was useless trying to talk to him.* fruitless, futile, hopeless, ineffectual, pointless, unavailing, unproductive, vain. OPPOSITE productive.
user *noun* consumer, operator.
usher *noun The usher showed us to our seats.* attendant, escort, guide, sidesman. — *verb He ushered them to their seats.* conduct, escort, guide, lead, show.
usual *adjective the usual method.* accustomed, common, conventional, customary, established, everyday, familiar, general, habitual, normal, ordinary, orthodox, regular, routine, set, standard, stock, traditional, typical.
utensil *noun kitchen utensils.* appliance, device, gadget, implement, instrument, machine, tool.
uterus *noun* womb.
utilise *verb* see USE.
utilitarian *adjective The furniture is utilitarian, not decorative.* functional, practical, serviceable, useful.
utility *noun The utility of computers is unquestionable.* benefit, convenience, practicality, service, serviceability, use, usefulness, value.
utmost *adjective First aid training is of the utmost importance.* extreme, greatest, highest, maximum, paramount, supreme.
utter[1] *verb He did not utter a sound.* come out with, emit, express, let out, pronounce, say, speak, voice.
utter[2] *adjective He was speaking utter nonsense.* absolute, arrant, complete, downright, out-and-out, perfect, positive, pure, sheer, thorough, total, unmitigated.
U-turn *noun The politician did a complete U-turn.* about-face, about-turn, backflip, reversal.

Vv

vacancy *noun The firm has a vacancy for a clerk.* job, opening, position, post, situation.
vacant *adjective* **1** *The house is vacant.* deserted, empty, uninhabited, unoccupied, untenanted. OPPOSITE occupied. **2** *I parked in one of the vacant spaces.* available, clear, empty, free, spare, unfilled, unoccupied, unused, void. OPPOSITE filled. **3** *The old lady sat with a vacant stare.* absent-minded, blank, deadpan, empty, expressionless, vacuous. OPPOSITE expressive.
vacate *verb He had to vacate the house by the end of the week.* abandon, depart from, evacuate, leave, quit. OPPOSITE occupy.
vacation *noun He spent his vacation in Tasmania.* break, furlough, holiday, leave, time off.
vaccination *noun a smallpox vaccination.* booster, immunisation, injection, inoculation, jab (*informal*), shot.
vacillate *verb He vacillated between the two courses of action.* dither, fluctuate, hesitate, hum and haw, shilly-shally, swing, waver.
vacuum *noun There was a vacuum inside the container.* emptiness, nothingness, void.
vagabond *noun He left his home and became a vagabond.* beachcomber, gypsy, hobo, itinerant, nomad, rover, swagman (*Australian*), tramp, traveller, vagrant, wanderer, wayfarer.
vagrant *noun He was arrested as a vagrant.* beggar, hobo, homeless person, itinerant, rover, tramp, vagabond.
vague *adjective* **1** *His ideas are pretty vague at this stage.* ambiguous, equivocal, fuzzy, general, hazy, imprecise, indefinite, inexplicit, loose, nebulous, sketchy, uncertain, unclear, woolly. OPPOSITE precise. **2** *She saw a vague shape at the window.* amorphous, blurred, dim, faint, fuzzy, indistinct. OPPOSITE clear, distinct.
vain *adjective* **1** *She was so vain about her good looks.* arrogant, boastful, cocky, conceited, egotistical, narcissistic, proud, stuck-up (*informal*). OPPOSITE modest. **2** *They made a vain attempt to save the man.* abortive, fruitless, futile, hopeless, unavailing, unsuccessful, useless. OPPOSITE successful.
valedictory *adjective a valedictory speech.* farewell, leave-taking, parting.
valiant *adjective a valiant warrior.* bold, brave, courageous, daring, dauntless, doughty, fearless, gallant, heroic, intrepid, lion-hearted, plucky, spirited, stout-hearted, undaunted, valorous. OPPOSITE cowardly.
valid *adjective* **1** *To drive you must have a valid driver's licence.* lawful, legal, legitimate, official. OPPOSITE invalid. **2** *a valid argument.* acceptable, allowable, cogent, logical, permissible, proper, reasonable, sound. OPPOSITE unacceptable.
validate *verb They both signed the contract to validate it.* authorise, confirm, endorse, legalise, ratify, sanction. OPPOSITE invalidate.
valley *noun* basin, canyon, dale, dell, glen, gorge, gully (*Australian*), hollow, pass, ravine, vale.
valour *noun The police officer received an award for valour.* bravery, courage, daring, gallantry, heroism, intrepidity, pluck. OPPOSITE cowardice.
valuable *adjective* **1** *Molly learnt a valuable lesson.* beneficial, constructive, helpful, important, invaluable, profitable, useful, worthwhile. OPPOSITE useless. **2** *Sarah keeps her valuable jewellery in a safe.* costly, expensive, precious, priceless, prized, treasured. OPPOSITE cheap.
value *noun* **1** *The stamps increased in value.* price, worth. **2** *She can see the value of piano practice.* advantage, benefit, importance, merit, profit, use, usefulness, worth. OPPOSITE uselessness. — *verb* **1** *The dealer valued her coin collection.* appraise, assess, estimate, evaluate, price. **2** *She valued their friendship.* appreciate, cherish, esteem, prize, respect, set store by, treasure. □ **values** *plural noun She does not share her parents' values.* ethics, morals, principles, standards.
van *noun All the luggage fitted in the van.* campervan, lorry, panel van (*Australian*), truck, wagon.
vandal *noun Vandals had damaged the fence.* delinquent, hoodlum, hooligan, ruffian, thug.
vanguard *noun* **1** *the vanguard of an army.* advance guard, front line, spearhead, van. OPPOSITE rearguard. **2** *the vanguard of fashion.* avant-garde, cutting edge, forefront, leaders, pioneers, trailblazers, trendsetters.
vanish *verb The stain has vanished.* become invisible, disappear, evaporate, fade away, go away. OPPOSITE appear.
vanity *noun Her vanity prevents her from seeing others' beauty.* conceit, egotism, narcissism, pride, self-admiration, self-love. OPPOSITE modesty.
vanquish *verb He vanquished his enemies.* beat, conquer, defeat, overcome, overpower, overthrow, rout, subdue, subjugate, thrash, triumph over, trounce. OPPOSITE surrender to.
vapour *noun The air was filled with the poisonous vapour.* fog, fumes, gas, haze, mist, smoke, steam.
variable *adjective variable quality. variable winds.* changeable, erratic, fickle, fitful, fluctuating, inconsistent, mutable, patchy, shifting, temperamental, unpredictable, unreliable. OPPOSITE consistent.
variant *adjective 'Jail' is a variant spelling of 'gaol'.* alternative, different.
variation *noun a variation in the order.* alteration, change, deviation, difference, divergence, fluctuation, modification, permutation, shift.
variegated *adjective a variegated fabric.* harlequin, marbled, motley, mottled, multicoloured, particoloured. OPPOSITE plain.
variety *noun* **1** *The job has a lot of variety.* change, contrast, difference, diversity, variation. OPPOSITE monotony. **2** *a wide variety of talents.* array, assortment, collection, combination, miscellany, mixture, range. **3** *a new variety of tomato.* breed, class, form, kind, sort, strain, type.
various *adjective In his work he meets people from various backgrounds.* assorted, different, disparate, diverse, heterogeneous, many, miscellaneous, several, sundry, varied.
varnish *noun The shelves are finished with a varnish.* coating, glaze, gloss, lacquer.
vary *verb* **1** *He varied the tone of his voice.* adjust, alter, change, modify, modulate. **2** *Her mood varies from hour to hour.* change, fluctuate, swing. **3** *Opinions vary on this point.* be at odds, conflict, differ, diverge. OPPOSITE agree.
vast *adjective* **1** *The cattle station covers a vast area.* big, boundless, broad, enormous, expansive, extensive, great, huge, immense, large, spacious, wide. **2** *The property is worth a vast amount of money.* astronomical, colossal, exorbitant, gigantic, massive, sizeable, stupendous, substantial, tremendous. OPPOSITE tiny.
vat *noun a vat of beer.* barrel, tank.
vault[1] *verb She vaulted the rail.* bound over, clear, hurdle, jump over, leap over, spring over. — *noun a vault over the fence.* bound, jump, leap, spring.
vault[2] *noun* **1** *The valuables are stored in a vault.* strongroom. **2** *a cathedral vault.* basement, cellar, crypt.
veer *verb The car suddenly veered to the right.* bear, diverge, sheer, swerve, swing, turn, wheel.
vegetate *verb He stopped work and vegetated for a year.* do nothing, idle, stagnate, veg (*informal*).
vegetation *noun They cleared the natural vegetation.* flora, greenery, growth, plants.
vehement *adjective a vehement denial.* ardent, fervent, fierce, fiery, heated, impassioned, intense, passionate, vigorous, violent. OPPOSITE apathetic.
vehicle *noun All road vehicles must be registered.* conveyance; [*various vehicles*] bus, car, caravan, carriage, coach, cycle, tractor, trailer, tram, truck, van, wagon.
veil *noun* **1** *She wore a veil.* mantilla, yashmak. **2** *The plans were covered in a veil of secrecy.* cloak, cloud, cover, mantle, mask, screen, shroud. — *verb Her face was veiled.* conceal, cover, disguise, hide, mask, obscure, screen, shroud. OPPOSITE expose.
velocity *noun The car was travelling at a high velocity.* pace, rate, speed.
vendetta *noun a vendetta between the families.* conflict, dispute, feud, quarrel.
veneer *noun* **1** *The furniture is finished in teak veneer.* coating, covering, exterior, finish, overlay, surface. **2** *a veneer of politeness.* façade, front, mask, pretence, show.
venerable *adjective our venerable founder. a venerable institution.* aged, ancient, august, esteemed, honoured, old, respected, revered, venerated.
venerate *verb She venerated her parents.* adore, esteem, hallow, honour, look up to, respect, revere, worship. OPPOSITE scorn.
vengeance *noun He sought vengeance for his brother's murder.* reprisal, retaliation, retribution, revenge.
venial *adjective a venial sin.* excusable, forgivable, minor, pardonable, slight. OPPOSITE mortal, unforgivable.

venom *noun snake venom.* poison, toxin.

venomous *adjective* **1** *That snake's bite is venomous.* deadly, fatal, lethal, poisonous, toxic. OPPOSITE harmless. **2** *a venomous attack on the author.* bitter, hostile, malevolent, malicious, malignant, rancorous, spiteful, vicious, virulent.

vent *noun The steam escapes through a vent in the lid.* aperture, duct, hole, opening, outlet, slit. — *verb He vented his anger on his family rather than his colleagues.* air, express, give vent to, release. OPPOSITE bottle up.

ventilate *verb The bathroom needs to be ventilated.* air, freshen.

venture *noun a new business venture.* endeavour, enterprise, project, undertaking. — *verb* **1** *She did not venture to stop them.* be so bold as, dare, presume, take the liberty. **2** *She ventured a suggestion.* advance, offer, put forward, volunteer. **3** *He ventured $20 on the horse.* chance, gamble, hazard, risk, stake, wager.

venue *noun The club meets at a new venue.* location, meeting place, place, site.

verbal *adjective* **1** *verbal skill.* lexical, linguistic. OPPOSITE non-verbal. **2** *verbal evidence.* oral, said, spoken, unwritten. OPPOSITE written.

verbose *adjective a verbose explanation.* circumlocutory, lengthy, long-winded, ponderous, tautological, wordy. OPPOSITE succinct.

verbosity *noun The audience was bored by the speaker's verbosity.* long-windedness, loquacity, verbiage, wordiness. OPPOSITE succinctness.

verdict *noun The jury reached a unanimous verdict.* adjudication, conclusion, decision, finding, judgement, opinion.

verge *noun the verge of the lake.* border, brink, edge, margin, perimeter, rim, side, threshold. — *verb* **verge on** *Her reaction verged on hysteria.* approach, border on, come close to. □ **on the verge of** *on the verge of collapse.* close to, near to, on the brink of, on the point of.

verify *verb His statement can easily be verified.* authenticate, check, confirm, corroborate, prove, substantiate, support, uphold, validate.

vermin *noun* parasites, pests.

vernacular *noun The farm workers had their own vernacular.* dialect, idiom, jargon, language, lingo (*informal*), parlance, patois, phraseology, speech, tongue.

versatile *adjective Ella is a versatile player.* adaptable, all-round, flexible, handy, multi-skilled. OPPOSITE specialised.

verse *noun* **1** *He writes verse.* poems, poetry; see also POEM. **2** *The poem has four verses.* stanza.

version *noun* **1** *She believed his version of the incident.* account, description, narrative, report, side, story. **2** *a modern version of the Bible.* edition, interpretation, paraphrase, reading, translation. **3** *a new version of an old song.* rendering, rendition, variation. **4** *the cheaper version of the sofa.* design, form, model, style, type, variant.

vertex *noun* see TOP.

vertical *adjective* **1** *The dog's tail was in a vertical position.* erect, perpendicular, standing, upright. OPPOSITE horizontal. **2** *a vertical rock face.* bluff, precipitous, sheer.

vertigo *noun As he looked down he experienced vertigo.* dizziness, giddiness, light-headedness, unsteadiness.

verve *noun She played the piano with verve.* animation, dash, energy, enthusiasm, gusto, liveliness, spirit,

vigour, vim (*informal*), vitality, vivacity, zeal, zing (*informal*), zip.

very *adverb The incident was very embarrassing.* awfully, dreadfully (*informal*), especially, exceedingly, exceptionally, extraordinarily, extremely, frightfully, highly, immensely, jolly (*informal*), mightily, most, particularly, really, terribly, thoroughly, tremendously (*informal*), truly. OPPOSITE slightly. — *adjective This pen is the very one I was looking for.* actual, exact, precise, selfsame.

vessel *noun* **1** *The vessel was not seaworthy.* boat, craft, ship; see BOAT, SHIP. **2** *He filled the vessel with clean water.* container, holder, receptacle, utensil; [*various vessels*] crock, ewer, flask, jar, jug, pitcher, pot, urn, vase.

vestibule *noun We were met by our host in the vestibule.* antechamber, ante-room, entrance hall, foyer, hall, porch, lobby.

vestige *noun the last vestige of the fortune she had inherited.* relic, remains, remnant, residue, trace.

vet *noun* veterinarian, veterinary surgeon. — *verb He vetted the applicants.* check out, examine, investigate, screen.

veteran *noun Vietnam veterans.* ex-serviceman, ex-servicewoman, returned serviceman, returned servicewoman, vet (*informal*). — *adjective a veteran politician.* experienced, long-serving, old, seasoned. OPPOSITE inexperienced.

veto *noun the right of veto.* prohibition, refusal, rejection. OPPOSITE approval. — *verb She vetoed the plan.* ban, bar, block, disallow, forbid, give the thumbs down to, prohibit, reject, rule out. OPPOSITE approve.

vex *verb She was vexed by his behaviour.* anger, annoy, bother, bug (*informal*), displease, disturb, exasperate, harass, hassle (*informal*), infuriate, irk, irritate, nark (*informal*), needle, peeve (*informal*), perturb, pique, plague, provoke, put out, rile (*informal*), trouble, try, upset, worry. OPPOSITE please.

viable *adjective a viable project.* feasible, possible, practicable, practical, realistic, workable. OPPOSITE unviable.

vibes *plural noun* (*informal*) *The house has good vibes.* feelings, sensations, vibrations; see also ATMOSPHERE.

vibrant *adjective* **1** *vibrant colours.* bold, bright, brilliant, intense, radiant, striking, strong, vivid. OPPOSITE dull. **2** *a vibrant personality.* animated, dynamic, energetic, enthusiastic, lively, sparkling, spirited, vivacious. OPPOSITE lifeless.

vibrate *verb The glasses vibrated as the plane flew over the house.* oscillate, pulsate, quake, quiver, rattle, shake, shudder, throb, tremble, wobble.

vibration *noun a noisy vibration in the pipes.* oscillation, quaver, quiver, rattle, shaking, shudder, tremor.

vice *noun* **1** *She was tempted into a life of vice.* corruption, depravity, evil, immorality, iniquity, sin, wickedness, wrongdoing. **2** *Smoking was not one of her vices.* defect, failing, fault, flaw, imperfection, shortcoming, weakness. OPPOSITE virtue.

vicinity *noun They live in the vicinity of the school.* area, district, environs, locality, neighbourhood, precincts, proximity, region, zone.

vicious *adjective* **1** *a vicious crime.* atrocious, barbaric, beastly, brutal, callous, cruel, fiendish, heinous, inhuman, monstrous, ruthless, sadistic, savage, vile, violent. **2** *a vicious criminal.* depraved, evil,

immoral, malevolent, malicious, nefarious, spiteful, villainous, vindictive, wicked. OPPOSITE kind. **3** *The dog looked vicious.* bad-tempered, dangerous, ferocious, fierce, hostile, mean, nasty, savage, wild. OPPOSITE tame.

victim *noun* **1** *The train crash claimed dozens of victims.* casualty, fatality. **2** *the victim of a confidence trick.* bunny (*Australian informal*), dupe, fall guy (*slang*), mug (*informal*), pushover (*informal*), scapegoat, sucker (*informal*). OPPOSITE perpetrator. **3** *The snake devours its victim.* prey, quarry, target.

victimise *verb She felt victimised by everyone.* bully, cheat, exploit, oppress, persecute, pick on, torment, use.

victor *noun The trophy was presented to the victor.* champion, conqueror, vanquisher, winner. OPPOSITE loser.

victorious *adjective victorious in battle.* conquering, successful, triumphant, winning. OPPOSITE defeated.

victory *noun The team celebrated another victory.* conquest, success, triumph, walk-over, win. OPPOSITE defeat.

vie *verb The two vied for first place.* compete, contend, contest, rival, strive.

view *noun* **1** *Charles admired the view from the summit.* landscape, outlook, panorama, prospect, scene, scenery, spectacle, vista. **2** *The procession came into view.* sight, vision. **3** *He had strong views on the subject.* attitude, belief, conviction, idea, notion, opinion, sentiment, thought; see also VIEWPOINT. — *verb* **1** *The inspector viewed the murder scene closely.* behold (*old use*), contemplate, examine, eye, gaze at, inspect, look at, observe, scrutinise, stare at, survey, take in, watch. **2** *He viewed the crime as serious.* consider, deem, judge, look upon, regard, see.

viewer *noun a TV viewer.* observer, onlooker, spectator, watcher; [*viewers*] audience.

viewpoint *noun two conflicting viewpoints.* angle, attitude, opinion, outlook, perspective, point of view, position, side, slant, stance, stand, standpoint, view.

vigilant *adjective The supervisor must be vigilant.* alert, attentive, awake, careful, observant, on the lookout, on your guard, wary, watchful. OPPOSITE inattentive.

vigorous *adjective* **1** *a vigorous young man.* active, dynamic, energetic, fit, hardy, lively, robust, spirited, strapping, strenuous, strong. OPPOSITE weak. **2** *He made vigorous efforts to help the man.* determined, forceful, hearty, intense, keen, strenuous, zealous. OPPOSITE feeble.

vigour *noun He attacked the task with great vigour.* animation, dash, drive, dynamism, energy, enthusiasm, gusto, liveliness, pep, power, spirit, stamina, strength, verve, vim (*informal*), vitality, vivacity, zeal, zest, zip. OPPOSITE languor.

vile *adjective* **1** *a vile smell.* disgusting, foul, ghastly, horrible, nasty, nauseating, objectionable, obnoxious, offensive, repugnant, repulsive, revolting, unpleasant. OPPOSITE pleasant. **2** *a vile deed.* abominable, base, contemptible, depraved, despicable, evil, foul, hateful, heinous, hideous, horrible, ignoble, immoral, loathsome, low, nasty, odious, outrageous, shameful, shocking, sinful, sordid, wicked. OPPOSITE honourable

vilify *verb The newspapers had vilified him.* blacken, defame, denigrate, libel, malign, revile, slander, smear.

village *noun They live in a sleepy village.* community, hamlet, settlement, township.

villain *noun The police captured the villain.* baddy (*informal*), blackguard, criminal, crook (*informal*), knave (*old use*), malefactor, miscreant, rascal, rogue, scoundrel, wrongdoer.

vindicate *verb* **1** *The report vindicated the officers.* absolve, acquit, clear, exculpate, exonerate. OPPOSITE blame. **2** *Our policy has been vindicated by this success.* defend, justify, support, uphold.

vindictive *adjective She had been hurt and was feeling vindictive.* revengeful, spiteful, unforgiving, vengeful. OPPOSITE forgiving.

vintage *noun The cars are of the same vintage.* date, era, period, year.

violate *verb* **1** *The manufacturer has violated safety standards.* break, contravene, defy, disobey, disregard, ignore, infringe, transgress. OPPOSITE keep. **2** *The tourists had violated the sacred place.* defile, desecrate, dishonour, profane. OPPOSITE revere.

violation *noun the violation of human rights.* abuse, breach, contravention, disregard, infringement, transgression. OPPOSITE upholding.

violent *adjective* **1** *a violent argument.* fierce, furious, heated, impassioned, intense, passionate, stormy, tempestuous, vehement. OPPOSITE calm. **2** *a violent person.* berserk, desperate, destructive, frenzied, hotheaded, maniacal, uncontrollable, wild. OPPOSITE gentle. **3** *a violent assault.* bloodthirsty, bloody, brutal, cruel, ferocious, fierce, murderous, savage, vicious, wild. **4** *a violent storm.* destructive, fierce, intense, mighty, powerful, raging, severe, tempestuous, turbulent, wild. OPPOSITE mild.

violin *noun* fiddle (*informal*).

VIP *abbreviation The VIPs sit at the top table.* big shot (*informal*), bigwig (*informal*), celebrity, dignitary. OPPOSITE nobody.

virgin *noun* see GIRL. — *adjective* **1** *virgin snow.* clean, fresh, immaculate, new, pristine, pure, spotless, unblemished. **2** *virgin forest.* uncultivated, unspoilt, untouched, unused.

virile *adjective a virile youth.* macho, manly, masculine, red-blooded, robust, strong. OPPOSITE unmanly.

virtually *adverb It is virtually impossible to tell them apart.* almost, effectively, essentially, more or less, nearly, practically.

virtue *noun* **1** *Uphold virtue and hate vice.* decency, goodness, honesty, honour, integrity, morality, principle, probity, rectitude, righteousness. OPPOSITE vice. **2** *The house has few virtues to recommend it.* advantage, asset, good point, merit, plus, strength, strong point. OPPOSITE disadvantage.

virtuoso *noun a violin virtuoso.* expert, genius, maestro, master.

virtuous *adjective virtuous behaviour.* blameless, chaste, decent, ethical, good, honest, honourable, moral, pure, righteous, saintly, upright. OPPOSITE immoral.

viscous *adjective The mixture was too viscous to pour.* gluey, glutinous, sticky, thick, viscid. OPPOSITE runny.

visible *adjective* **1** *The patient showed visible signs of distress.* apparent, clear, conspicuous, discernible, evident, manifest, noticeable, observable, obvious, outward, palpable, patent, plain, unmistakable. OPPOSITE hidden, invisible. **2** *The ship was visible on the horizon.* in sight, in view.

vision *noun* **1** *Spectacles improved her vision.* eyesight, sight. **2** *He saw a vision of his late wife.* apparition, ghost, hallucination, illusion, phantom, spectre, spirit, wraith. **3** *The premier has a vision for the future.* conception, dream, idea, plan. **4** *They elected a man of vision.* far-sightedness, foresight, imagination, insight. OPPOSITE short-sightedness.
visit *verb They visited their relatives in Sydney.* call in on, drop in on, go to see, look in on, look up, pop in on, stay with, stop by. — *noun He paid them a visit.* call, sojourn, stay, stop, visitation.
visitor *noun* **1** *Visitors are always welcome.* blow-in (*Australian informal*), caller, company, guest. **2** *The city attracts many overseas visitors.* holidaymaker, non-resident, sightseer, tourist, traveller. OPPOSITE local.
vista *noun The avenue of trees provided a beautiful vista.* landscape, outlook, panorama, prospect, scene, scenery, view.
visual *adjective visual problems.* ocular, ophthalmic, optic, optical, sight.
visualise *verb It's hard to visualise what it will be like.* conceive, envisage, imagine, picture, see.
vital *adjective a vital component.* basic, critical, crucial, essential, fundamental, important, indispensable, key, necessary, significant. OPPOSITE optional, unnecessary.
vitality *noun His holiday gave him renewed vitality.* animation, dynamism, energy, exuberance, go, gusto, liveliness, pep, strength, verve, vigour, vim (*informal*), vivacity, zeal, zest, zing (*informal*), zip. OPPOSITE lethargy.
vitriolic *adjective vitriolic remarks.* abusive, acrimonious, bitter, caustic, cutting, hostile, savage, scathing, spiteful, stinging, venomous, virulent.
vivacious *adjective a vivacious young woman.* animated, bubbly, exuberant, high-spirited, lively, perky, sparkling, spirited, vital. OPPOSITE listless.
vivacity *noun* see VITALITY.
vivid *adjective* **1** *vivid colours.* bold, bright, brilliant, colourful, deep, garish, gaudy, gay, intense, loud, rich, striking, strong, vibrant. OPPOSITE dull. **2** *a vivid description.* clear, detailed, graphic, lifelike, lively, realistic. OPPOSITE dull, lifeless.
vocabulary *noun The technical words are in the vocabulary at the back of the book.* dictionary, glossary, lexicon, word list.
vocal *adjective* **1** *a vocal communication.* oral, spoken, sung. OPPOSITE written. **2** *She was very vocal about her rights.* forthright, outspoken, vociferous, voluble. OPPOSITE reticent.
vocalist *noun* see SINGER.
vocation *noun* **1** *He had a vocation for the priesthood.* call, calling, mission. **2** *The employment counsellor discussed various vocations.* career, job, line of work, occupation, profession, trade.
vociferous *adjective vociferous protesters.* clamorous, insistent, loud, noisy, outspoken, vocal. OPPOSITE quiet.
vogue *noun Short skirts are the vogue.* craze, fashion, mode, rage, style, trend. □ **in vogue** *Hats are in vogue again.* fashionable, in, in fashion, popular, trendy (*informal*). OPPOSITE unfashionable.
voice *noun* **1** *We heard voices outside.* shouting, singing, speaking, speech. **2** *They have no voice in the matter.* representation, say, vote. — *verb He voiced his opinion.* air, articulate, communicate, declare, enunciate, express, speak, state, utter, ventilate.
void *adjective* **1** *There were no void spaces.* bare, empty, unoccupied, vacant. OPPOSITE full. **2** *The contract was declared void.* invalid, null and void. OPPOSITE valid. — *noun His death left a void which could not be filled.* blank, emptiness, gap, hole, space, vacuum.
volatile *adjective* **1** *a volatile situation.* charged, explosive, tense, unstable. **2** *a volatile person.* capricious, changeable, erratic, fickle, inconstant, mercurial, unpredictable, unstable. OPPOSITE stable.
volley *noun a volley of bullets.* barrage, bombardment, fusillade, hail, salvo, shower.
voluble *adjective a voluble speaker.* chatty, fluent, garrulous, glib, loquacious, talkative. OPPOSITE taciturn.
volume *noun* **1** *The dictionary is in two volumes.* book, part, tome. **2** *the volume of a container.* capacity, dimensions, measure, size. **3** *the volume of mail.* amount, bulk, mass, quantity. **4** *He turned up the volume of the music.* loudness, sound.
voluminous *adjective Her slim figure was hidden under a voluminous skirt.* ample, big, billowing, bulky, full, large, roomy, vast. OPPOSITE skimpy.
voluntarily *adverb You can leave voluntarily or else be forcibly evicted.* by choice, freely, of your own accord, of your own free will, of your own volition, willingly.
voluntary *adjective* **1** *voluntary unionism.* non-compulsory, optional, unforced. OPPOSITE compulsory. **2** *He does voluntary work.* honorary, unpaid, volunteer. OPPOSITE paid.
volunteer *verb* **1** *She volunteered to do the job.* nominate yourself, offer, step forward. **2** *He volunteered for the army.* enlist, join up, register, sign on.
voluptuous *adjective* **1** *voluptuous living.* hedonistic, pleasure-seeking, sensual, sybaritic. OPPOSITE ascetic. **2** *a voluptuous woman.* attractive, buxom, curvy, seductive, sexy, shapely.
vomit *verb After several drinks he vomited.* barf (*slang*), be sick, chuck (*informal*), chunder (*Australian slang*), puke (*informal*), ralph (*slang*), sick up (*informal*), spew, throw up.
voracious *adjective* **1** *The young man had a voracious appetite.* greedy, insatiable, ravenous. **2** *The library satisfies many a voracious reader.* avid, compulsive, eager, insatiable, keen.
vortex *noun* eddy, maelstrom, spiral, whirlpool, whirlwind.
vote *noun* **1** *They held a vote for class captain.* ballot, election, plebiscite, poll, referendum. **2** *Eighteen-year-olds have the vote.* franchise, right to vote, suffrage. — *verb* **vote for** *They each voted for a different candidate.* choose, elect, opt for, pick, select.
voter *noun* elector.
vouch *verb* **vouch for** *He vouched for the boy's reliability.* answer for, attest to, confirm, guarantee, swear to.
voucher *noun a gift voucher.* coupon, token.
vow *noun They made their vows in front of the congregation.* oath, pledge, promise. — *verb She vowed that she would never smoke again.* declare, give your word, pledge, promise, swear, take an oath.
voyage *noun The voyage took three weeks.* crossing, cruise, journey, passage, sail, trip.
vulgar *adjective* **1** *Burping in public is considered vulgar.* bad-mannered, boorish, coarse, common, ill-mannered, impolite, rough, rude, uncouth. OPPOSITE polite. **2** *a vulgar joke.* coarse, crude, dirty, filthy, impolite, indecent, lewd, obscene, offensive, risqué, rude, smutty, tasteless. OPPOSITE tasteful.
vulnerable *adjective* **1** *The country is in a vulnerable position.* defenceless, exposed, insecure, precarious, unguarded, unprotected, weak. OPPOSITE invulnerable. **2** *The town is vulnerable to flooding.* open, subject, susceptible. OPPOSITE immune.

Ww

wad *noun a wad of cotton wool.* bundle, hunk, lump, mass, pad, plug, roll.
wadding *noun The box is lined with wadding.* filling, lining, padding, stuffing.
waddle *verb The toddler waddled out of the room.* shuffle, toddle, wobble.
waddy *noun The man was armed with a waddy.* bludgeon, club, war club.
wade *verb* **1** *She waded through the mud.* paddle, plod, splash, trek, trudge. **2** *He waded through the book.* plod, plough, work your way.
waffle *noun* (*informal*) *His essay was all waffle.* hot air (*slang*), padding, verbiage. — *verb* (*informal*) *The speaker waffled on for over an hour.* prattle, rabbit (*informal*), ramble, witter (*informal*).
waft *verb A delicious aroma wafted through the house.* drift, float, stream.
wag[1] *verb* **1** *The dog wagged his tail.* shake, waggle, wave, wiggle. **2** *His parents discovered he had been wagging school.* absent yourself from, bludge (*Australian informal*), play hookey from (*informal*), play truant from, skive off (*informal*), stay away from.
wag[2] *noun* clown, comedian, jester, joker, wit.
wage[1] *noun He is paid an hourly wage.* earnings, income, pay, payment, remuneration, wages. CONTRASTS WITH salary.
wage[2] *verb The two sides waged a war which lasted six years.* carry on, conduct, engage in, fight, pursue.
wager *noun He had a small wager on the outcome.* bet, flutter (*informal*), gamble, punt, speculation, stake. — *verb She wagered two dollars on the race.* bet, gamble, hazard, punt (*informal*), risk, stake.
wagon *noun a horse-drawn wagon.* cart, dray, wain (*old use*).
waif *noun a home for waifs and strays.* foundling, homeless person, orphan, stray.
wail *verb The child was wailing with pain.* bawl, caterwaul, cry, groan, howl, moan, shriek, sob, weep, whine, yowl.
waist *noun The apron ties around the waist.* middle, midriff, waistline.
waistcoat *noun The suit includes a waistcoat.* jerkin, vest.
wait *verb* **1** *They waited patiently for their turn.* bide your time, hang on, hold on, mark time, pause, sit tight (*informal*), stand by. **2** *They waited behind to help clean up.* dally, hang around, linger, loiter, lurk, remain, rest, stay, stop (*informal*), tarry. **3** *The decision will have to wait until next meeting.* be deferred, be delayed, be postponed, be put off, be shelved. — *noun There was a long wait for the bus.* delay, hold-up, interval, pause, stay. □ **wait for** *She was waiting for a phone call.* await, expect, look out for. **wait on** *She waited on the guests.* attend to, serve.
waive *verb* **1** *He waived his rights to an appeal.* forgo, forsake, give up, relinquish, renounce, surrender, yield. OPPOSITE claim. **2** *They waived the normal rules.* dispense with, set aside. OPPOSITE enforce.
wake[1] *verb* **1** *He did not wake until midday.* awake, get up, stir, surface (*informal*), wake up. **2** *She woke the baby.* awaken, disturb, rouse, waken, wake up. OPPOSITE put to sleep.
wake[2] *noun a wake for the dead man.* vigil, watch.
wake[3] *noun the ship's wake.* backwash, track, trail, wash. □ **in the wake of** after, behind, following, subsequent to.
wakeful *adjective Many people are wakeful on hot summer nights.* awake, insomniac, restless, sleepless. OPPOSITE asleep.
walk *verb She can't run but she walks a lot.* amble, bushwalk (*Australian*), creep, foot it, go on foot, hike, hobble, limp, march, pace, parade, perambulate, plod, promenade, prowl, ramble, saunter, shamble, shuffle, slink, slog, stagger, stalk, stamp, step, stride, stroll, strut, swagger, tiptoe, toddle, totter, traipse (*informal*), tramp, tread, trek, troop, trudge, waddle, wade. — *noun* **1** *They went for a walk.* amble, bushwalk (*Australian*), constitutional, hike, promenade, ramble, saunter, stroll, tramp, trek, walkabout, wander. **2** *He has a brisk walk.* gait, pace, step, stride. **3** *The map shows various walks through the forest.* path, pathway, route, track, trail. □ **walk out 1** *He became angry and walked out.* depart, flounce out, leave, storm out. **2** *The workers walked out.* down tools, go on strike, stop work, strike, take industrial action, walk off the job. **walk out on** *He walked out on the people who needed him.* abandon, desert, forsake, leave, leave in the lurch.
walker *noun paths for walkers and cyclists.* bushwalker, hiker, pedestrian, rambler.
walkover *noun The contest was a walkover for them.* breeze (*informal*), child's play, cinch (*informal*), doddle (*informal*), piece of cake (*informal*), pushover (*informal*), snack (*Australian informal*), snap (*informal*). OPPOSITE struggle.
wall *noun The building was hidden behind a wall.* barricade, barrier, battlements, bulkhead, bulwark, dyke, embankment, fence, parapet, partition, rampart, stockade.
wallet *noun She keeps her money in a wallet.* notecase, pocketbook, purse.
wallop *verb & noun* see HIT.
wallow *verb* **1** *The hippopotamus was wallowing in the mud.* roll about, splash about. **2** *He wallowed in self-pity.* bask, delight, indulge, luxuriate, revel.
wall-painting *noun* fresco, mural.
wan *adjective He felt better but still looked wan.* pale, pallid, pasty, peaky, sickly, washed out, waxen. OPPOSITE ruddy.
wand *noun She waved her magic wand.* baton, cane, rod, staff, stick.
wander *verb* **1** *They wandered around the town.* meander, mooch (*informal*), mosey (*slang*), prowl, ramble, range, roam, rove, saunter, stroll, tootle (*informal*), traipse (*informal*), travel, walk. **2** *She wandered from the subject.* deviate, digress, drift, stray.

wanderer noun *He's a wanderer: he'll never settle down.* drifter, gypsy, hobo, itinerant, nomad, rambler, rover, swagman (*Australian*), traveller, vagabond, vagrant, wayfarer.

wane verb *Her strength is waning.* decline, decrease, diminish, dwindle, ebb, fade, lessen, subside, taper off, weaken. OPPOSITE increase.

wangle verb (*slang*) *You might be able to wangle an invitation.* contrive, engineer, fix (*informal*), get, pull off, swing (*informal*).

want verb **1** *He wants a new car.* covet, crave, desire, fancy, hanker after, hunger for, long for, pine for, wish for, yearn for. **2** *They don't want for anything.* be short of, lack, need, require. — noun **1** *Janet is a person of few wants.* desire, need, requirement, wish. **2** *a want of common sense.* absence, dearth, deficiency, insufficiency, lack, paucity, scarcity, shortage. OPPOSITE abundance.

wanting adjective *His driving skills were found wanting.* deficient, inadequate, insufficient, lacking, unsatisfactory. OPPOSITE sufficient.

wanton adjective *wanton vandalism.* arbitrary, groundless, irresponsible, malicious, motiveless, reckless, senseless, unprovoked, wilful.

war noun **1** *The two countries were engaged in war.* battle, combat, conflict, fighting, hostilities, strife, warfare. OPPOSITE peace. **2** *a war against poverty.* attack, battle, blitz, campaign, crusade, fight, struggle. □ **war cry** *The teams chanted their war cries.* battle-cry, motto, slogan, watchword.

ward noun **1** *The child became a ward of the state.* charge, dependant, protégé(e). **2** *a council ward.* area, district, division, section. — verb **ward off** *He warded off his attackers.* avert, beat off, deflect, fend off, keep at bay, parry, repel, repulse, stave off, thwart.

warden noun **1** *a traffic warden.* superintendent, supervisor. **2** *a church warden.* attendant, sexton, sidesman, steward, verger.

warder noun *a prison warder.* guard, jailer, keeper, prison officer.

wardrobe noun *He hung his shirts in the wardrobe.* closet, cupboard.

warehouse noun *The goods are stored in a warehouse.* depot, repository, store, storehouse.

wares plural noun *Traders displayed their wares.* commodities, goods, merchandise, products, stock.

warfare noun see WAR.

warlike adjective **1** *a warlike people.* aggressive, bellicose, belligerent, combative, hostile, militant, militaristic, pugnacious. OPPOSITE peaceable. **2** *warlike music.* martial, military.

warm adjective **1** *warm food.* lukewarm, tepid. OPPOSITE cool. **2** *warm weather.* balmy, mild, sunny. **3** *warm clothes.* cosy, thermal, thick, woolly. **4** *a warm welcome.* cordial, enthusiastic, friendly, hearty, hospitable, rousing, sincere. OPPOSITE cool, hostile. — verb *She warmed the milk.* heat, heat up, hot up (*informal*), reheat, scald, warm up. OPPOSITE chill. □ **warm up** *The runner warmed up with gentle exercises.* limber up, loosen up, prepare.

warm-hearted adjective *a warm-hearted person.* affectionate, amiable, caring, compassionate, friendly, genial, kind, kind-hearted, kindly, loving, sympathetic, tender-hearted, warm. OPPOSITE cold-hearted.

warn verb *He was warned of the dangers.* advise, alert, apprise (*formal*), caution, counsel, forewarn, inform,

make aware, notify, remind, tell, tip off.

warning noun **1** *They did not heed his warning.* admonition, advice, caution, caveat. **2** *There was no warning of any trouble.* forewarning, hint, indication, notice, notification, omen, sign, signal, threat, tip-off.

warp verb **1** *The timber warped because it had been left in the sun.* bend, bow, buckle, contort, curve, distort, twist. OPPOSITE straighten out. **2** *His mind has been warped.* corrupt, pervert, twist.

warrant noun *The police have a warrant to search his house.* authorisation, authority, entitlement, licence, permit. — verb *Nothing can warrant such insolence.* authorise, call for, excuse, justify, permit, sanction.

warranty noun *The clock has a one-year warranty.* guarantee.

warren noun *a rabbits' warren.* burrow, maze.

warrigal adjective (*Australian*) *They were busy rounding up warrigal cattle.* feral, unbroken, untamed, wild.

warrior noun *Their warriors were victorious.* brave, combatant, fighter, gladiator, soldier.

warship noun aircraft carrier, battleship, corvette, cruiser, destroyer, frigate, gunboat, man-of-war, submarine, torpedo boat, trireme (*historical*).

wary adjective **1** *She was wary of anything new.* careful, cautious, chary, circumspect, distrustful, guarded, suspicious. OPPOSITE unwary. **2** *A security guard needs to be wary.* alert, observant, on the lookout, on your guard, vigilant, watchful. OPPOSITE careless.

wash verb **1** *She washed the clothes. The floors must be washed.* clean, cleanse, douse, drench, flush, launder, mop, rinse, scour, scrub, shampoo, sluice, soak, soap, sponge, swab, swill, wipe. **2** *He washed before dinner.* bath, bathe, clean yourself, perform your ablutions, shower, wash yourself. **3** *The waves washed over the rocks.* break, flow, splash, sweep. **4** *The bottle was washed out to sea.* carry, sweep, transport. **5** (*informal*) *That argument won't wash.* be accepted, hold water, stand up. — noun **1** *He had a wash before dinner.* bath, scrub, shower. **2** *the wash of the boats.* backwash, wake. □ **washed out 1** *His clothes had a washed-out look.* bleached, dull, faded. OPPOSITE new. **2** *He was washed out after his long day.* all in (*informal*), done in (*informal*), drained, exhausted, jaded, tired, weary, worn out. OPPOSITE invigorated.

washing noun *She pegged out the washing.* clothes, laundry, wash.

washout noun (*informal*) *The concert was a complete washout.* damp squib, debacle, disaster, failure, fiasco, fizzer (*Australian informal*), flop (*informal*).

waste verb **1** *He wasted his money on the pokies.* blow (*slang*), dissipate, fritter away, misspend, misuse, squander. OPPOSITE save. **2** *She wasted her opportunity.* let slip, miss, throw away. OPPOSITE use. — adjective **1** *The council recycles waste paper.* discarded, leftover, superfluous, unwanted, useless. **2** *waste land.* arid, barren, desert, uncultivated, unusable, wild. — noun **1** *a waste of resources.* misuse, squandering. **2** *The waste is dumped in a pit.* debris, dregs, dross, effluent, garbage, junk, litter, refuse, rubbish, scraps, sewage, trash. □ **waste away** *If she doesn't eat soon, she'll waste away.* become emaciated, fade away, grow thin, pine, shrivel, wither.

wasteful adjective *a wasteful use of paper.* extravagant, improvident, prodigal, profligate, uneconomical. OPPOSITE frugal, thrifty.

watch verb **1** *He watched what was happening.* attend to, behold (*old use*), concentrate on, contemplate, eye, gaze at, keep your eyes on, look at, mark, monitor, note, notice, observe, pay attention to, peep at, peer at, regard, scrutinise, stare at, survey, take notice of, view. OPPOSITE ignore. **2** *He knew he was being watched.* keep an eye on, keep under observation, keep under surveillance, spy on. **3** *Watch what you say.* be careful, beware, be wary, mind. **4** *He watched the baby while she went out.* guard, keep an eye on, look after, mind, protect, supervise, take care of, tend. OPPOSITE neglect. — noun *She read the time on her watch.* chronometer, pocket watch, stopwatch, timepiece, wristwatch. □ **keep watch** *He stayed outside to keep watch.* be on the lookout, keep guard, keep vigil.

watchdog noun *a consumer watchdog.* guardian, monitor, protector.

watchful adjective *They were under their teacher's watchful eye.* alert, attentive, careful, eagle-eyed, observant, vigilant, wary. OPPOSITE careless.

watchman noun *The watchman checks each floor of the building.* guard, nightwatchman, patrol, security guard.

watchword noun *The company's watchword is 'service'.* byword, catchphrase, catchword, maxim, motto, slogan.

water noun *She fell in the water and nearly drowned.* creek, dam, lake, ocean, pond, pool, reservoir, river, sea, stream. — verb **1** *He watered his vegetable plot.* dampen, flood, hose, irrigate, moisten, soak, spray, sprinkle, wet. OPPOSITE parch. **2** *Onions make her eyes water.* run, stream, weep. OPPOSITE dry up. □ **water down** *She waters down the juice for the baby.* adulterate, dilute, thin, weaken. OPPOSITE concentrate.

watercourse noun *Watercourses are marked in blue on the map.* brook, channel, creek, river, rivulet, stream, waterway.

waterfall noun *The waterfall only flows after heavy rain.* cascade, cataract, falls.

waterhole noun *All the waterholes were full after the rain.* claypan (*Australian*), gilgai (*Australian*), gnamma hole (*Australian*), mickery (*Australian*), rockhole, soak, watering hole.

waterlogged adjective *The ground is waterlogged.* boggy, marshy, saturated, soaked, sodden, swampy.

waterproof adjective *Raincoats are made of waterproof material.* impermeable, impervious, showerproof, water-repellent, water-resistant, watertight, weatherproof.

watershed noun *The decision was considered a watershed in the nation's history.* crossroads, turning point.

watertight adjective **1** *Store nails in a watertight container.* sealed, waterproof. OPPOSITE leaky. **2** *He presented a watertight argument.* irrefutable, sound, unassailable.

waterway noun *The barges travel along a system of waterways.* canal, channel, river, stream, watercourse.

watery adjective **1** *a watery substance.* aqueous, fluid, liquid. OPPOSITE solid. **2** *watery soup.* diluted, runny, thin, watered down, weak, wishy-washy. OPPOSITE thick. **3** *watery eyes.* bleary, damp, lachrymose, moist, streaming, tearful, teary, weepy, wet. OPPOSITE dry.

wave noun **1** *He goes to the beach to watch the waves.* billow, boomer, breaker, comber, dumper (*Australian*), ripple, roller, surf, swell, wavelet. **2** *The town has suffered a wave of bombings.* outbreak, rush, spate, surge, upsurge. **3** *He gave a farewell wave.* gesticulation, gesture, salutation, signal. — verb **1** *She waved her handkerchief.* flap, flutter, shake, wag, wiggle. **2** *He waved his knife about as he spoke.* brandish, flourish, swing. **3** *They waved goodbye.* gesticulate, gesture, signal. **4** *She waves her hair.* coil, curl, kink, twirl. □ **wave aside** *The committee waved his objection aside.* brush aside, dismiss, disregard, ignore, reject.

waver verb **1** *His courage never wavered.* change, falter, vary. **2** *The light from the lantern is wavering.* flicker, quiver, shake, tremble, wobble. **3** *He wavered between accepting and declining their offer.* dither, hesitate, hover, oscillate, shilly-shally, swing, vacillate.

wavy adjective **1** *wavy hair.* crimped, curly, kinky, permed. OPPOSITE straight. **2** *a wavy line.* curving, squiggly, undulating. OPPOSITE straight.

wax verb *The moon waxes and wanes.* enlarge, grow, increase. OPPOSITE wane.

way noun **1** *Which way did he take?* course, direction, path, road, route, track, trail. **2** *It's a long way to the nearest town.* distance, haul, journey. **3** *His way of doing things is different.* approach, fashion, manner, means, method, mode, procedure, process, style, system, technique. **4** *You'll soon get into our ways.* custom, habit, practice, routine, tradition. **5** *It was good in some ways.* aspect, detail, feature, particular, respect, sense. **6** *The patient is in a bad way.* condition, shape, state. □ **way in** see ENTRANCE[1]. **way out** see EXIT.

wayfarer noun gypsy, rover, traveller, vagabond, walker, wanderer.

waylay verb *The gang waylaid him outside the school.* accost, ambush, assail, bail up (*Australian*), buttonhole, corner, detain, hold up, intercept, lie in wait for, pounce on, set upon.

way-out adjective *Jenny has some way-out ideas.* bizarre, eccentric, odd, offbeat, outlandish, outrageous, strange, unconventional, unusual, wacky (*slang*), weird. OPPOSITE conventional.

wayward adjective *a wayward child.* contrary, disobedient, headstrong, incorrigible, intractable, naughty, obstinate, perverse, rebellious, recalcitrant, refractory, self-willed, stroppy (*informal*), stubborn, unmanageable, unruly, wilful. OPPOSITE obedient.

weak adjective **1** *The patient is still weak.* debilitated, delicate, exhausted, feeble, frail, infirm, listless, puny, sickly, weedy. OPPOSITE robust. **2** *a weak fence.* decrepit, flimsy, fragile, rickety, shaky, unsteady. OPPOSITE sturdy. **3** *a weak leader.* cowardly, feckless, impotent, ineffective, ineffectual, namby-pamby, powerless, pusillanimous, soft, spineless, timorous, unassertive. OPPOSITE strong. **4** *a weak excuse.* flimsy, implausible, lame, pathetic, thin, unconvincing, unsatisfactory. OPPOSITE persuasive. **5** *weak coffee.* dilute, insipid, tasteless, thin, watery, wishy-washy. OPPOSITE strong.

weaken verb **1** *The disease weakened him.* debilitate, enervate, enfeeble, exhaust, sap. OPPOSITE strengthen. **2** *The government is trying to weaken the group's influence.*

decrease, diminish, erode, lessen, reduce, undermine.

weakling *noun* coward, drip (*informal*), milksop, runt, sissy, softie (*informal*), sook (*Australian informal*), weed, wimp (*informal*), wuss (*slang*).

weakness *noun* **1** *He suffered increasing weakness in his muscles.* debility, decrepitude, feebleness, fragility, frailty. OPPOSITE strength. **2** *He knows his own weaknesses.* defect, deficiency, failing, fault, flaw, foible, imperfection, shortcoming, weak point. OPPOSITE forte, strength. **3** *She has a weakness for chocolate.* fondness, liking, partiality, passion, penchant, predilection, soft spot. OPPOSITE dislike.

wealth *noun* **1** *He accumulated considerable wealth.* assets, capital, fortune, means, money, property, riches. **2** *They lived in wealth.* affluence, opulence, prosperity. OPPOSITE poverty. **3** *Their website contains a wealth of information.* abundance, fund, mine, profusion, store. OPPOSITE dearth.

wealthy *adjective* *a wealthy merchant.* affluent, flush (*informal*), loaded (*informal*), moneyed, opulent, prosperous, rich, well-heeled (*informal*), well in (*Australian informal*), well off, well-to-do. OPPOSITE poor.

weapons *plural noun* armaments, arms, munitions, weaponry.

wear *verb* **1** *She wore a dress to the party.* be attired in, clothe yourself in, don, dress in, have on, put on, sport. **2** *Constant rubbing has worn the surface.* abrade, corrode, eat away, erode, grind down, rub away, scuff, wear away, wear down. **3** *This fabric wears well.* endure, last, stand up, survive. — *noun* **1** *summer wear.* formal wear. apparel (*formal*), attire (*formal*), clobber (*slang*), clothes, clothing, dress, garb, garments, gear (*informal*), raiment (*old use*). **2** *The carpet is showing signs of wear.* damage, deterioration, disrepair, wear and tear. **3** *This coat has a lot of wear left in it.* service, use. □ **wear off** *The effect of the sedative wore off.* decrease, diminish, dwindle, fade, lessen, subside. OPPOSITE intensify. **wear out 1** *The baby wore her parents out.* drain, exhaust, fatigue, tire out, weary. **2** *His clothes wear out quickly.* become shabby, become threadbare, fray, wear thin.

weariness *noun* *His illness left him with constant weariness.* exhaustion, fatigue, languor, lassitude, lethargy, listlessness, tiredness. OPPOSITE vitality.

weary *adjective* *She felt weary after her long day.* all in (*informal*), beat (*slang*), dog-tired, done in (*informal*), drained, drowsy, exhausted, fagged out (*informal*), fatigued, jaded, knackered (*slang*), pooped (*informal*), sleepy, spent, tired, whacked (*informal*), worn out, zonked (*slang*). OPPOSITE energetic. — *verb* *Her job wearied her.* drain, exhaust, fatigue, sap, tire, wear out. OPPOSITE invigorate.

weather *noun* climate, the elements. — *verb* **1** *They weathered the timber before using it.* dry, season. **2** *They weathered the storm together.* brave, come through, endure, ride out, stand up to, survive, withstand. □ **weather bureau** meteorological bureau.

weather-beaten *adjective* *weather-beaten skin.* brown, dry, leathery, sunburnt, tanned, wrinkled.

weave¹ *verb* **1** *She wove the different strands together.* braid, entwine, interlace, intertwine, interweave, plait. **2** *He weaves an interesting story.* compose, create, put together, spin.

weave² *verb* *The car weaved its way through the traffic.* meander, wind, zigzag.

web *noun* *a spider's web.* cobweb, gossamer, mesh, net, network.

wed *verb* *They will wed in December.* get hitched (*informal*), marry, tie the knot (*informal*).

wedded *adjective* *wedded bliss.* conjugal, marital, married, matrimonial, nuptial.

wedding *noun* marriage, nuptials.

wedge *noun* **1** *A wedge held the door open.* block, chock. **2** *a wedge of cake.* chunk, hunk, piece, slab, slice. — *verb* *It was wedged between two books.* jam, pack, ram, sandwich, squeeze, stick, stuff.

wedlock *noun* *Bob and Jackie are joined in wedlock.* marriage, matrimony.

wee *adjective* see TINY.

weed *verb* weed out *He weeded out the rotten ones.* eliminate, eradicate, get rid of, remove, root out.

weedkiller *noun* herbicide, weedicide.

weedy *adjective* **1** *The garden was neglected and weedy.* overgrown, rank, wild. **2** *a weedy youth.* delicate, frail, puny, scrawny, thin, undersized, weak. OPPOSITE strapping.

weep *verb* **1** *He wept when his dog died.* bawl, blubber, break down, cry, howl, shed tears, snivel, sob, wail. **2** *The wound is weeping.* ooze, seep.

weepy *adjective* (*informal*) *She was weepy throughout the sad film.* crying, lachrymose, maudlin, tearful, teary.

weigh *verb* **1** *He weighs sixty kilograms.* measure, tip the scales at. **2** *This evidence weighed strongly with the jury.* be important, carry weight, count, have an influence, matter. □ **weigh down** *He was weighed down with his problems.* burden, depress, encumber, load, oppress, overload, saddle, trouble. **weigh up** *Weigh up the pros and cons.* assess, balance, compare, consider, evaluate.

weight *noun* **1** *the weight of the package.* heaviness, mass. **2** *a weight off his mind.* burden, load, millstone, onus, pressure, strain. **3** *His opinion carried little weight.* authority, clout (*informal*), force, importance, influence, power.

weighty *adjective* **1** *a weighty object.* burdensome, cumbersome, heavy, hefty, massive, ponderous. OPPOSITE light. **2** *a weighty problem.* grave, important, momentous, pressing, serious. OPPOSITE trifling.

weir *noun* barrage, dam.

weird *adjective* **1** *weird events.* creepy, eerie, extraordinary, mysterious, peculiar, queer, spooky (*informal*), strange, supernatural, uncanny, unnatural. OPPOSITE everyday, normal. **2** *a weird person.* abnormal, bizarre, curious, eccentric, freakish, funny, kinky (*informal*), odd, offbeat, outlandish, peculiar, queer, strange, unconventional, unusual, wacky (*slang*), way-out (*informal*), zany. OPPOSITE conventional, normal.

weirdo *noun* (*informal*) *He associates with some weirdos.* crackpot (*informal*), crank, dingbat (*informal*), eccentric, freak, fruitcake (*informal*), nut (*informal*), nutcase (*informal*), oddball (*informal*).

welcome *adjective* *The charity received a welcome donation.* appreciated, gratifying, pleasing. OPPOSITE unwanted. — *verb* **1** *She welcomed her guests.* greet, meet, receive. OPPOSITE ignore. **2** *The club welcomes new members.* accept, admit, let in, receive, take in. OPPOSITE reject. — *noun* *She received a warm welcome.* greeting, reception, salutation.

welcoming *adjective* *The host was most welcoming.* cordial, friendly, hospitable, kind, warm.

welfare *noun* **1** *The school is concerned for its students' welfare.* good, happiness, health, security, well-being. **2** *The family is on welfare.* assistance, benefit, income support, social security.

well¹ *noun* *They draw water from the well.* bore, shaft.

well² *adverb* **1** *He handled the problem well.* ably, commendably, competently, correctly, effectively, fairly, justly, proficiently, properly, satisfactorily, skilfully. OPPOSITE unsatisfactorily. **2** *Things went well.* famously, like a house on fire, nicely, smoothly, splendidly, successfully. OPPOSITE badly. **3** *She cleaned it well.* carefully, completely, conscientiously, meticulously, thoroughly. OPPOSITE perfunctorily. **4** *He knows the man well.* closely, intimately, personally. OPPOSITE superficially. **5** *He is well over eighty.* considerably, decidedly, much. OPPOSITE slightly. **6** *They think well of him.* admiringly, approvingly, favourably, glowingly, highly. OPPOSITE unfavourably. — *adjective* **1** *She isn't well.* fit, hale and hearty, healthy, robust, sound, strong. OPPOSITE sick. **2** *All's well.* all right, fine, OK (*informal*), satisfactory. OPPOSITE unsatisfactory. □ **well off** *Her parents are not well off.* affluent, comfortable, loaded (*informal*), moneyed, prosperous, rich, wealthy, well-heeled (*informal*), well in (*Australian informal*), well-to-do. OPPOSITE hard up (*informal*), poor.

well-behaved *adjective* disciplined, good, law-abiding, obedient, orderly, polite, well-mannered. OPPOSITE naughty.

well-being *noun* *She looks after their well-being.* good, happiness, health, welfare.

well-groomed *adjective* clean, neat, smart, spruce, tidy, well-dressed. OPPOSITE untidy.

well-known *adjective* **1** *a well-known author.* eminent, famous, illustrious, notable, noted, notorious, prominent, renowned. OPPOSITE obscure, unknown. **2** *a well-known saying.* everyday, familiar, household, popular, proverbial.

well-mannered *adjective* *He is considerate and well-mannered.* civil, correct, courteous, genteel, polite, refined, respectful, suave, thoughtful, urbane, well-behaved, well-bred. OPPOSITE impolite.

welt *noun* *The whipping left a red welt on his back.* ridge, scar, stripe, weal.

wet *adjective* **1** *The ground is wet.* boggy, damp, dewy, moist, muddy, saturated, soaked, sodden, soggy, waterlogged. OPPOSITE parched. **2** *His umbrella broke and he ended up quite wet.* drenched, dripping, saturated, soaked, sopping. OPPOSITE dry. **3** *wet weather.* drizzly, rainy, showery, stormy. OPPOSITE dry, fine. **4** *His skin felt wet.* clammy, damp, dank, humid, moist, sticky, sweaty. OPPOSITE dry. **5** *wet paint.* sticky, tacky. OPPOSITE dry. — *verb* **1** *She wetted the clothes before rubbing them with soap.* dampen, immerse, moisten, soak. OPPOSITE dry. **2** *He wetted them with the hose.* douse, drench, saturate, splash, spray, sprinkle, squirt, water. □ **wet blanket** *Don't invite him. He's such a wet blanket.* damper, killjoy, party-pooper (*informal*), pessimist, spoilsport, wowser (*Australian*).

wetness *noun* clamminess, condensation, damp, dampness, humidity, liquid, moisture, perspiration, sweat.

whack *noun & verb* see HIT.

wharf *noun* *The ship is in at the wharf.* dock, jetty, landing stage, pier, quay.

wharfie *noun* (*Australian informal*) docker, longshoreman, stevedore, watersider (*Australian*), waterside worker (*Australian*), wharf labourer.

wheel *noun* **1** *The bed is on wheels.* castor, roller. **2** *a wheel of fire.* circle, disc, ring. — *verb* **1** *He wheeled the trolley up the ramp.* push, trundle. **2** *He wheeled round in astonishment.* pivot, spin, swing, swivel, turn, veer, whirl. **3** *The birds wheeled above us.* circle, gyrate.

wheeze *verb* *She stopped wheezing once she took her medicine.* gasp, pant, puff.

whereabouts *noun* *They don't know his whereabouts.* location, position, situation.

whet *verb* **1** *He whetted the blade.* grind, hone, sharpen, strop. OPPOSITE blunt. **2** *The newspaper article whetted their curiosity.* arouse, awaken, excite, kindle, stimulate, stir. OPPOSITE dampen.

whiff *noun* **1** *He went outside for a whiff of fresh air.* breath, puff. **2** *She caught a whiff of the curry.* aroma, fragrance, odour, smell, stink.

while *noun* *He stayed for a while.* period, spell, time. — *verb* **while away** *She whiled away the time reading.* fill, occupy, pass, spend.

whim *noun* *She bought the dress on a whim.* caprice, desire, fancy, impulse, urge.

whimper *verb* *The child whimpered after stubbing his toe.* cry, grizzle (*informal*), moan, snivel, wail, whine. — *noun* *There wasn't a whimper from the baby.* cry, moan, peep, whine.

whine *verb* *The dog whines when its owners go out.* cry, moan, whimper. — *noun* *The child's whines were irritating.* cry, moan, wail, whimper, whinge (*informal*).

whinge *verb* (*informal*) *He's never happy, always whinging about something.* complain, gripe (*informal*), grizzle (*informal*), grumble, moan, whine. — *noun* (*informal*) *She rang her friend to have a whinge.* complaint, gripe (*informal*), grizzle (*informal*), grumble, moan, whine.

whip *noun* *The culprit was flogged with a whip.* birch, crop, lash, rawhide, scourge, strap, switch. — *verb* **1** *He whipped the horse.* beat, birch, flog, lash, scourge, tan (*slang*), thrash. **2** *She whipped the eggs and sugar.* beat, mix, whisk. **3** *He whipped the letter out of her hand.* pull, seize, snatch, swipe, whisk.

whirl *verb* **1** *The carousel whirled round and round.* gyrate, revolve, rotate, spin, swirl, swivel, turn, twirl. **2** *His head was whirling.* reel, spin. — *noun* *Her mind was in a whirl.* confusion, daze, muddle, spin, turmoil.

whirlpool *noun* eddy, maelstrom, vortex.

whirlwind *noun* tornado, twister (*American*), vortex, willy willy (*Australian*). — *adjective* *a whirlwind courtship.* lightning, quick, rapid, speedy, swift.

whirr *verb* *The machine whirred.* buzz, drone, hum.

whisk *verb* **1** *He was whisked away to hospital.* snatch, sweep, whip. **2** *She whisked the egg whites.* beat, mix, whip.

whiskers *plural noun The man shaved his whiskers.* beard, bristles, facial hair, moustache, sideburns, stubble.

whiskery *adjective a whiskery face.* bristly, hairy, hirsute, stubbly, unshaven, whiskered. OPPOSITE clean-shaven.

whisper *verb He whispered the words so softly that nobody else heard.* breathe, murmur, mutter, say under your breath. OPPOSITE shout. — *noun* **1** *He spoke in a whisper.* hushed tone, murmur, undertone. **2** *Don't believe those idle whispers.* furphy (*Australian informal*), gossip, hearsay, hint, rumour, suggestion.

whistle *noun* **1** *We heard a loud whistle.* catcall, hoot. **2** *He blew the whistle.* hooter, siren.

white *adjective* **1** *a white colour.* chalky, cream, hoary, ivory, lily-white, milky, off-white, platinum, silvery, snow-white, snowy. OPPOSITE black. **2** *a white race of people.* Caucasian, fair-skinned, light-skinned. **3** *His illness had made him turn very white.* anaemic, ashen, bloodless, colourless, pale, pallid, pasty, wan, waxen. OPPOSITE ruddy. — *noun Separate the white and yolk of the egg.* albumen.

whiten *verb The bleach whitened the nappies.* blanch, bleach, fade, lighten.

whitewash *verb He tried to whitewash all their mistakes.* camouflage, conceal, cover up, gloss over, play down.

whiz *verb The cars whizzed past her.* dash, fly, hurry, hurtle, race, shoot, speed, tear, zip, zoom.

whiz-kid *noun* (*informal*) *a computer whiz-kid.* expert, genius, prodigy, wizard.

whole *adjective* **1** *Tell me the whole story.* complete, entire, full, total, unabridged, uncut. OPPOSITE partial. **2** *There's not a plate left whole.* intact, unbroken, undamaged. OPPOSITE broken. □ **on the whole** *On the whole she likes her new school.* all in all, altogether, by and large, for the most part, generally, in general, in the main.

wholehearted *adjective wholehearted support.* complete, dedicated, devoted, earnest, enthusiastic, full, hearty, sincere, total, unconditional, unreserved. OPPOSITE half-hearted.

wholesale *adjective wholesale destruction.* comprehensive, extensive, general, large-scale, mass, sweeping, universal, widespread. OPPOSITE partial.

wholesome *adjective wholesome food.* healthy, nourishing, nutritious. OPPOSITE unhealthy.

wicked *adjective* **1** *a wicked person. a wicked action.* atrocious, bad, base, beastly, contemptible, corrupt, degenerate, depraved, despicable, devilish, diabolical, evil, fiendish, foul, heinous, immoral, incorrigible, infamous, iniquitous, lawless, malicious, monstrous, nefarious, satanic, shameful, sinful, sinister, spiteful, ungodly, unholy, vicious, vile, villainous. OPPOSITE good, righteous. **2** *a wicked grin.* arch, devilish, impish, mischievous, naughty, roguish. OPPOSITE angelic.

wickedness *noun He repented of his wickedness.* depravity, evil, immorality, iniquity, sin, sinfulness, turpitude, ungodliness, unrighteousness, vice, villainy, wrongdoing. OPPOSITE righteousness.

wide *adjective* **1** *a wide chasm.* big, broad, expansive, extensive, immense, large, open, spacious, vast, yawning. OPPOSITE narrow. **2** *He recommended wide changes.* big, broad, comprehensive, extensive, far-reaching, global, sweeping, vast, wide-ranging. OPPOSITE limited.

widen *verb The river widens here.* broaden, dilate, enlarge, expand, open out, spread. OPPOSITE narrow.

widespread *adjective* **1** *These machines are in widespread use.* common, extensive, general, universal, wholesale. OPPOSITE limited. **2** *The disease is widespread.* epidemic, pervasive, prevalent, rife, ubiquitous. OPPOSITE rare.

width *noun* breadth, diameter, girth, span, thickness. OPPOSITE length.

wield *verb* **1** *He wielded the axe clumsily.* handle, hold, manage, manipulate, ply, swing, use. **2** *She wields considerable power in the firm.* command, exercise, exert, have.

wife *noun* bride, consort, partner, spouse.

wig *noun* hairpiece, switch, toupee.

wiggle *verb She wiggled her hips.* shake, sway, twitch, wag, waggle, wobble, wriggle.

wild *adjective* **1** *a wild animal.* feral, ferocious, free, myall (*Australian*), savage, unbroken, undomesticated, untamed, warrigal (*Australian*). OPPOSITE tame. **2** *wild plants.* indigenous, myall (*Australian*), native, natural, uncultivated, warrigal (*Australian*). OPPOSITE cultivated. **3** *The island was inhabited by a wild tribe.* barbarian, barbaric, barbarous, primitive, uncivilised. OPPOSITE civilised. **4** *He was hiking in wild country.* bleak, desolate, rough, rugged, uninhabited, waste. **5** *wild behaviour.* berserk, boisterous, crazy, disorderly, excited, frenzied, hysterical, lawless, obstreperous, rebellious, reckless, riotous, rowdy, uncontrolled, undisciplined, unrestrained, unruly, violent. OPPOSITE calm, orderly. **6** *wild weather.* blustery, rough, squally, stormy, tempestuous, turbulent, violent, windy. OPPOSITE calm. **7** *a wild idea.* absurd, crazy, foolish, hare-brained, impracticable, mad, madcap, rash, ridiculous, silly, unreasonable. OPPOSITE sensible.

wilderness *noun He is trying to conserve the wilderness.* bush, desert, wasteland, wilds.

wilful *adjective* **1** *a wilful child.* determined, dogged, headstrong, intractable, mulish, obstinate, perverse, pigheaded, recalcitrant, refractory, self-willed, strong-willed, stubborn, wayward. OPPOSITE submissive. **2** *wilful murder.* calculated, deliberate, intentional, premeditated. OPPOSITE accidental.

will *noun* **1** *He has the will to live.* desire, determination, inclination, intention, resolution, resolve, wish. **2** *He went along against his will.* choice, desire, inclination, volition, wishes. **3** *She wrote her will.* testament. — *verb He willed the house to his son.* bequeath, hand down, leave, pass on.

willing *adjective* **1** *She was willing to participate.* disposed, eager, game, happy, inclined, keen, prepared, ready. OPPOSITE reluctant. **2** *a willing helper.* amenable, consenting, cooperative, enthusiastic, keen, obliging. OPPOSITE unwilling.

willingly *adverb He signed up willingly.* eagerly, happily, like a shot, of your own accord, of your own free will, of your own volition, readily, voluntarily. OPPOSITE reluctantly.

will-power *noun It takes will-power to quit smoking.* commitment, determination, resolution, resolve, self-control, self-discipline, will.

wilt *verb* **1** *The flowers wilted in the heat.* become limp, deteriorate, droop, shrivel, wither. OPPOSITE thrive. **2** *The runners wilted after ten kilometres.* droop, flag, languish, tire.

wily *adjective He was as wily as a fox.* artful, astute, clever, crafty, cunning, devious, foxy, knowing, scheming, shrewd, sly, tricky, underhand. OPPOSITE straightforward.

wimp *noun* (*informal*) *He's such a wimp when it comes to injections.* baby, coward, milksop, sissy, sook (*Australian informal*), wuss (*slang*).

win *verb* **1** *May the best team win.* be victorious, come first, come top, prevail, succeed, triumph. **2** *He won first prize.* attain, earn, gain, get, land, obtain, pick up, receive, secure, walk away with (*informal*). OPPOSITE lose. — *noun They scored another win.* conquest, success, triumph, victory. OPPOSITE loss. □ **win over** *He won his audience over.* convert, convince, persuade, sway, talk round.

wince *verb She winced as the splinter was removed.* blench, cringe, flinch, grimace, recoil, start.

winch *verb The tow-truck winched the car from the gully.* hoist, lift, pull.

wind[1] *noun* **1** *The wind blew.* air current, blast, breeze, draught, gale, gust, squall, zephyr; [*various winds*] cyclone, doctor (*Australian*), hurricane, mistral, monsoon, sirocco, southerly buster (*Australian*), tornado, typhoon, whirlwind, willy willy (*Australian*). **2** *After eating cabbage he has a lot of wind.* flatulence, gas. **3** *The piper has run out of wind to keep playing.* air, breath, puff.

wind[2] *verb* **1** *The river winds through pretty country.* bend, curve, meander, snake, twist, wander, zigzag. **2** *She wound the wool over her hand.* coil, curl, loop, roll, turn, twine, twirl, twist, wrap. OPPOSITE unwind. □ **wind up 1** *He wound up the business.* close down, dissolve, liquidate. **2** (*informal*) *He wound up in jail.* end up, finish up, land.

windbreak *noun The trees act as a windbreak.* barrier, breakwind, screen.

windcheater *noun Their windcheaters keep out wind and spray.* anorak, cagoule, jacket, parka; see also SWEATER.

windfall *noun He has spent his little windfall.* bonanza, godsend.

winding *adjective a winding road.* corkscrew, crooked, serpentine, sinuous, tortuous, twisting, zigzag. OPPOSITE straight.

window *noun* **1** *He looked out of the window.* aperture, opening; [*kinds of window*] bay window, bow window, casement, dormer window, fanlight, French window, oriel window, porthole, quarterlight, skylight, transom, windscreen. **2** *The ball smashed the window.* glass, pane.

windswept *adjective The survivors found themselves on a windswept beach.* bleak, desolate, exposed, unprotected, windy. OPPOSITE sheltered.

windy *adjective a windy night.* blowy, blustery, breezy, gusty, squally, stormy, tempestuous. OPPOSITE calm.

wine *noun* booze (*informal*), grog (*Australian informal*), plonk (*informal*), vino (*informal*).

wing *noun* **1** *a bird's wing.* pinion. **2** *the south wing of the hospital.* addition, annexe, extension. **3** *He belongs to the right wing of the party.* branch, faction, section.

wink *verb* **1** *He winked at her.* bat an eyelid, blink. **2** *The stars were winking.* blink, flash, flicker, sparkle, twinkle.

winner *noun* **1** *the winner of the competition.* champion, conqueror, victor. **2** *The soufflé was a real winner.* hit, knockout (*informal*), smash hit (*informal*), success.

wipe *verb* **1** *She wiped the floor with a cloth.* clean, dry, dust, mop, polish, rub, sponge, towel. **2** *He wiped grease on the moving parts.* apply, rub, smear, spread. **3** *The tape was wiped.* erase, scrub (*informal*); see also DELETE. □ **wipe out 1** *He wiped out my debts.* cancel, erase, expunge, get rid of, remove. **2** *The whole army was wiped out.* annihilate, destroy, eliminate, exterminate, kill, obliterate. **wipe up** *She wiped up the spill.* blot, clean up, mop up, soak up, sponge.

wire *noun electrical wire.* cable, flex, lead.

wiry *adjective a wiry youth.* lean, muscular, sinewy, strong, thin, tough. OPPOSITE flabby.

wisdom *noun He had knowledge but lacked wisdom.* astuteness, discernment, insight, intellect, intelligence, judgement, nous (*informal*), prudence, reason, sagacity, sense, shrewdness, understanding. OPPOSITE folly.

wise *adjective* **1** *He made a wise decision.* advisable, appropriate, judicious, politic, prudent, sensible, shrewd, smart, sound. OPPOSITE stupid, unwise. **2** *He sought advice from a wise old friend.* astute, discerning, intelligent, knowing, perceptive, prudent, sagacious, sage, savvy (*informal*), sensible, shrewd, understanding. OPPOSITE foolish. **3** (*informal*) *He was wise to what was going on.* awake, aware, informed, in the know (*informal*), knowledgeable. OPPOSITE ignorant.

wisecrack *noun* (*informal*) *His wisecracks ceased to amuse them.* gag, jest, joke, quip, sally, witticism.

wish *noun They tried to satisfy his wishes.* ambition, aspiration, craving, desire, hope, longing, objective, request, want, whim, yearning, yen. — *verb* **1** *They wished for peace.* aspire, crave, desire, hanker, hope, long, want, yearn. **2** *She wished them good evening.* bid. **3** *Do as you wish.* desire, fancy, like, please, want.

wishy-washy *adjective wishy-washy soup.* bland, flavourless, insipid, tasteless, watery, weak. OPPOSITE flavoursome.

wisp *noun a wisp of hair.* piece, strand.

wistful *adjective a sad and wistful look.* doleful, forlorn, longing, melancholy, nostalgic, pensive, pining, sad, yearning.

wit *noun* **1** *We enjoyed the speaker's sparkling wit.* banter, humour, jokes, puns, repartee. **2** *She had a reputation as a wit.* comedian, comic, humorist, jester, joker, punster, wag. **3** *Use your wits.* brains, common sense, intellect, intelligence, judgement, nous (*informal*), sense, understanding, wisdom. OPPOSITE stupidity.

witch *noun* **1** *The witch cast a spell on the princess.* enchantress, magician, sorceress. **2** *She was frightened by the ugly old witch.* bag (*slang*), battleaxe (*informal*), hag, shrew, termagant, virago.

witchcraft *noun* black magic, magic, the occult, sorcery, voodoo, witchery, wizardry.

witchdoctor *noun* medicine man, shaman.

withdraw *verb* **1** *He withdrew his troops.* pull out, recall, remove, take away. **2** *She withdrew her money from the bank.* remove, take out. OPPOSITE deposit. **3** *He withdrew his statement.* cancel, recant, rescind, retract, revoke, take back. OPPOSITE stand by. **4** *The troops withdrew.* back off, depart, go, leave, pull out, retire, retreat. OPPOSITE advance.

withdrawn *adjective After her husband's death she became withdrawn.* antisocial, detached, introverted, reclusive, reserved, retiring, shy, unsociable. OPPOSITE outgoing, sociable.

wither *verb The flowers withered in the heat.* dehydrate, droop, dry out, dry up, shrivel, wilt. OPPOSITE thrive.

withhold *verb* **1** *He withheld his permission.* deny, refuse. OPPOSITE give. **2** *You must not withhold information.* conceal, hide, hold back, keep back, suppress.

withstand *verb The town can withstand any attack.* bear, cope with, endure, oppose, resist, stand up to, survive, tolerate, weather. OPPOSITE yield.

witness *noun There were no witnesses to the accident.* bystander, eyewitness, looker-on, observer, onlooker, spectator, viewer. — *verb* **1** *She witnessed the crime.* behold (*old use*), be present at, observe, see, view, watch. **2** *A JP witnessed his signature.* countersign, endorse, validate. □ **bear witness to** *His friend bore witness to his bravery.* attest to, confirm, testify to, vouch for, witness to.

witty *adjective a witty writer.* amusing, clever, droll, funny, humorous, quick-witted, scintillating, sharp-witted. OPPOSITE dull.

wizard *noun* **1** *The wizard made a magic potion.* magician, medicine man, sorcerer, warlock (*old use*), witchdoctor. **2** *He's a wizard at chess.* expert, genius, maestro, master, virtuoso, whiz (*informal*).

wobble *verb She wobbled as she tried to stand up.* quake, quiver, reel, rock, shake, stagger, sway, teeter, totter, tremble, waver. — *noun There was a slight wobble in her voice.* quaver, quiver, shaking, tremble, tremor.

wobbly *adjective* **1** *The child has a wobbly tooth.* loose, wiggly. OPPOSITE secure. **2** *The patient was a bit wobbly when she first got up.* groggy, shaky, unsteady, wonky (*informal*).

woe *noun* **1** *Her life was full of woe.* anguish, distress, grief, hardship, heartache, misery, misfortune, pain, sorrow, suffering, unhappiness. OPPOSITE joy. **2** *She told them all her woes.* adversity, affliction, burden, misfortune, problem, trial, tribulation, trouble.

woman *noun* bird (*informal*), chick (*slang*), dame (*old use* or *American slang*), damsel (*old use*), female, girl, lady, lass, maid (*old use*), maiden (*old use*), matron, sheila (*Australian slang*).

womanish *adjective He is rather womanish.* effeminate, sissy, unmanly, unmasculine. OPPOSITE mannish.

womanly *adjective She now has a womanly figure.* feminine, ladylike. OPPOSITE masculine.

womb *noun* uterus.

wonder *noun* **1** *He stared at the stars in wonder.* admiration, amazement, astonishment, awe, bewilderment, fascination, surprise, wonderment. **2** *the wonders of nature.* curiosity, marvel, miracle, phenomenon, rarity. — *verb* **1** *He wondered at their ingenuity.* be amazed, be stunned, be surprised, marvel. **2** *He wondered why they came.* ask yourself, be curious, conjecture, muse, ponder, puzzle, question, speculate, think.

wonderful *adjective a wonderful achievement. wonderful scenery.* admirable, amazing, astonishing, astounding, awe-inspiring, awesome, breathtaking, brilliant (*informal*), excellent, extraordinary, fabulous (*informal*), fantastic (*informal*), fine, first-class, impressive, incredible, magnificent, marvellous, miraculous, outstanding, phenomenal, prodigious, remarkable, sensational, spectacular, splendid, staggering, stunning, stupendous, superb, terrific (*informal*), tremendous (*informal*), unbelievable, unreal (*slang*), wondrous (*old use*). OPPOSITE ordinary, terrible.

woo *verb* **1** (*old use*) *He wooed the woman for five years.* court, pursue, seek the hand of. **2** *He did it to woo supporters.* attract, seek, seek to win. OPPOSITE deter.

wood *noun* **1** *The house is made of wood.* boards, logs, lumber (*American*), planks, slabs, timber, weatherboards. **2** *He put the wood on the fire.* firewood, kindling, logs. **3** *The heroine got lost in the wood.* bush, copse, forest, grove, jungle, scrub, spinney, thicket, woodland, woods.

woodcutter *noun* logger, lumberjack (*American*), sawyer, splitter, tree-feller.

wooded *adjective The plane came down in wooded country.* forested, silvan, timbered, tree-covered. OPPOSITE treeless.

wooden *adjective* **1** *a wooden house.* timber, weatherboard. **2** *The dancer's movements were rather wooden.* clumsy, leaden, rigid, stiff. OPPOSITE supple. **3** *The old lady sat with a wooden stare.* blank, deadpan (*informal*), empty, expressionless, glassy, impassive, poker-faced, vacant, vacuous. OPPOSITE animated, expressive.

woodwork *noun* cabinetmaking, carpentry, joinery.

wool *noun* **1** *The sheep is kept for its wool.* fleece, hair. **2** *knitting wool.* yarn.

woolly *adjective* **1** *a woolly animal.* fleecy, fluffy, furry, fuzzy, hairy, shaggy. **2** *a woolly jumper.* wool, woollen. **3** *woolly ideas.* fuzzy, hazy, imprecise, indefinite, muddled, unclear, vague. OPPOSITE clear.

Woop Woop *noun* see BACKBLOCKS.

word *noun* **1** *What is the word for a corkscrew in French?* appellation, expression, locution, name, term. **2** *Bring me word of where they are.* advice, information, intelligence, message, news, report, tidings. **3** *He gave us his word that he would do it.* assurance, guarantee, pledge, promise, undertaking, vow, word of honour. **4** *Don't fire till I give you the word.* command, direction, instruction, order. — *verb She worded the request carefully.* couch, express, formulate, phrase, put. □ **word for word** *He recorded the speech word for word.* accurately, exactly, faithfully, literally, precisely, verbatim. **words** *plural noun* **1** *scientific words.* jargon, language, terminology, vocabulary. **2** *the words of the opera.* libretto, lyrics, script, text.

wording *noun The wording of the contract is important.* expression, language, phraseology, phrasing.

wordy *adjective* **1** *a wordy speaker.* diffuse, garrulous, long-winded, loquacious, rambling, talkative, verbose, voluble. OPPOSITE brief, succinct. **2** *a wordy definition.* circumlocutory, roundabout, tautological. OPPOSITE concise.

work *noun* **1** *Getting the house ready for sale requires hard work.* drudgery, effort, elbow grease, exertion, graft (*slang*), grind, industry, labour, slog, sweat (*informal*), toil, travail (*old use*), yakka (*Australian informal*). OPPOSITE play. **2** *Each person was given his work to do.* assignment, chore, duty, homework, job, project, task, undertaking. **3** *literary and musical works.* book, composition, creation, opus, piece, writing. **4** *She enjoys her work and does not want to retire.* business, career, employment, job, occupation, profession, trade, vocation. OPPOSITE hobby. — *verb* **1** *He worked for two years on the project.* apply yourself, beaver away, be busy, drudge, exert yourself, graft (*slang*), grind away, labour, peg away, plug away, slave, slog, strive, sweat, toil. **2** *He worked until he was 65.* be employed, have a job. OPPOSITE be unemployed. **3** *The dishwasher is not working properly.* act, function, go, operate, perform, run. **4** *She showed me how to work the juicer.* control, handle, manage, manipulate, operate, use, wield. **5** *The trick worked.* be effective, succeed. OPPOSITE fail. **6** *He works miracles.* accomplish, achieve, bring about, effect, execute, perform. □ **worked up** *He became worked up over the issue.* agitated, excited, het up (*informal*), hot under the collar, stirred up, upset. OPPOSITE calm. **work out** **1** *He worked out what was going on.* analyse, deduce, discover, fathom, figure out, gather, infer, reason. **2** *She worked out the answer.* calculate, compute, figure out, solve. **3** *They worked out a plan.* concoct, contrive, develop, devise, draw up, formulate, produce. **4** *Things worked out well.* develop, evolve, go, pan out, turn out. **works** *plural noun* **1** *He opened up the clock to look at the works.* insides (*informal*), machinery, mechanism, movement, workings. **2** *One hundred people are employed at the cement works.* factory, foundry, mill, plant, workshop.

workable *adjective a workable scheme.* feasible, practicable, practical, viable. OPPOSITE unworkable.

worker *noun* artisan, craftsman, craftswoman, employee, hand, labourer, operative, operator, tradesman, tradeswoman, wage-earner, workman. OPPOSITE employer.

workforce *noun The company looks after its workforce.* employees, human resources, labour force, manpower, personnel, staff, workers.

working *adjective* **1** *a working person.* employed. OPPOSITE unemployed. **2** *a working computer.* functioning, going, operational, running, usable. OPPOSITE broken.

workman *noun The council employs workmen to do repairs.* handyman, labourer, navvy, tradesman, worker.

workmanship *noun He deplored shoddy workmanship.* craftsmanship, handiwork, skill, technique.

workout *noun a workout at the gym.* drill, exercise, practice, training session.

workshop *noun Repairs are done at the workshop.* factory, laboratory, mill, plant, workroom, works.

world *noun* **1** *the whole created world.* cosmos, Creation, universe. **2** *He has travelled the world.* earth, globe, planet. **3** *the world of politics.* area, circle, domain, field, realm, sphere.

worldly *adjective The convert began to despise worldly things.* earthly, material, materialistic, mundane, secular, temporal. OPPOSITE spiritual.

worldly-wise *adjective She became worldly-wise at a young age.* cosmopolitan, experienced, knowing, sophisticated, worldly. OPPOSITE naive.

worldwide *adjective a worldwide shortage of oil.* global, international, universal.

worm *verb He wormed his way through the tunnel.* crawl, slither, squirm, twist, wriggle, writhe.

worn *adjective* **1** *The clothes were too worn to pass on.* dilapidated, frayed, holey, ragged, shabby, tattered, tatty (*informal*), thin, threadbare. OPPOSITE new. **2** *The car has worn tyres.* bald, smooth. OPPOSITE new. **3** *She looked worn.* careworn, drawn, exhausted, haggard, tired, weary, worn out. □ **worn out** *She was worn out after a hard day's work.* bushed (*informal*), dog-tired, done in (*informal*), drained, exhausted, fagged out (*informal*), fatigued, jaded, knackered (*slang*), spent, tired out, whacked (*informal*). OPPOSITE energetic.

worried *adjective They comforted the worried parents.* afraid, agitated, anxious, apprehensive, concerned, distraught, distressed, fearful, fretful, frightened, nervous, perturbed, troubled, uneasy. OPPOSITE serene.

worry *verb* **1** *Don't worry him now: I'll ring back later. The loud music does not worry her.* annoy, bother, disturb, harass, hassle, irritate, perturb, pester, plague, trouble, upset, vex. **2** *She worries about their safety.* be agitated, be anxious, brood, fret. — *noun* **1** *They were caused a lot of worry by the absence of news.* anguish, anxiety, apprehension, bother, concern, disquiet, distress, stress, trouble, uneasiness. OPPOSITE reassurance. **2** *Finances are his major worry.* bugbear, burden, concern, hassle (*informal*), headache, menace, nightmare (*informal*), problem, trial, trouble, vexation.

worrying *adjective a worrying situation.* alarming, distressing, disturbing, nerve-racking, stressful, upsetting, worrisome.

worsen *verb* **1** *Her condition worsened.* decline, degenerate, deteriorate, go backwards, go downhill (*informal*), go to the pack (*Australian informal*), retrogress. **2** *Exercise worsened the painful condition.* aggravate, exacerbate, intensify. OPPOSITE improve.

worship *noun* **1** *the worship of God.* adoration, exaltation, glorification, homage, honour, praise, respect, reverence, veneration. **2** *He attends worship once a week.* church, service. **3** *an object of worship.* admiration, adoration, deification, devotion, hero-worship, idolisation. — *verb They worship many gods.* admire, adore, dote on, exalt, extol, glorify, hallow, honour, idolise, laud (*informal*), look up to, love, magnify, praise, respect, revere, venerate. OPPOSITE despise.

worth *noun the worth of education.* benefit, good, importance, merit, use, usefulness, value. OPPOSITE worthlessness. — *adjective* **be worth** **1** *The book is worth $20.* be priced at, be valued at, cost, sell at. **2** *The book is worth reading.* be worthy of, deserve, justify, merit.

worthless *adjective a worthless exercise.* futile, insignificant, meaningless, pointless, unimportant, unproductive, unprofitable, useless, vain, valueless. OPPOSITE valuable.

worthwhile *adjective a worthwhile experience.* advantageous, beneficial, important, productive, profitable, rewarding, useful, valuable. OPPOSITE pointless.

worthy *adjective* **1** *a worthy cause.* commendable, deserving, good, meritorious, worthwhile. OPPOSITE undeserving. **2** *our worthy leader.* admirable, creditable, estimable, honourable, praiseworthy, respectable. OPPOSITE unworthy.

wound *noun* **1** *The nurse bandaged his wounds.* cut, gash, graze, incision, injury, laceration, lesion, scratch, sore. **2** *psychological wounds.* blow, damage, distress, hurt, injury, pain, trauma. — *verb* **1** *The madman wounded ten people.* cut, damage, gash, graze, harm, hurt, injure, knife, lacerate, maim, mutilate, shoot, stab. **2** *The criticism wounded her.* hurt, mortify, offend, pain, sting.

wowser *noun* (*Australian*) *You won't have any fun with those wowsers present.* killjoy, party pooper (*slang*), puritan, spoilsport, teetotaller, wet blanket.

wrangle *verb They wrangled endlessly about minor details.* argue, bicker, debate, disagree, dispute, fight, haggle, quarrel, quibble, squabble. — *noun a protracted legal wrangle.* altercation, argument, barney (*informal*), brawl, clash, controversy, disagreement, dispute, quarrel, row, squabble, tiff.

wrap *verb She wrapped the bottle in paper. He wrapped himself in the blanket.* bind, cocoon, cover, encase, enclose, enfold, envelop, insulate, lag, muffle, pack, package, parcel up, shroud, surround, swaddle, swathe. — *noun Put on a wrap to go out.* cape, cloak, coat, mantle, poncho, shawl, stole.

wrapper *noun The magazine comes in a plastic wrapper.* case, casing, cover, envelope, jacket, packet, sleeve.

wrath *noun Do not incur his wrath by deliberate disobedience.* anger, displeasure, exasperation, fury, indignation, ire, rage, temper.

wreath *noun The flowers were woven into a wreath.* chaplet, festoon, garland, lei.

wreck *verb* **1** *The ship was wrecked on the coral reef.* break up, destroy, ruin, scupper, scuttle, shatter, shipwreck, smash. **2** *The building was wrecked by the rioters.* demolish, destroy, devastate, raze, ruin, trash (*informal*), vandalise. **3** *He wrecked their plans.* botch, bungle, dash, destroy, muck up, ruin, sabotage, shatter, spoil, undermine, undo, upset.

wreckage *noun He scavenged amongst the wreckage.* debris, flotsam, remains, remnants, rubble, ruins, wreck.

wrench *verb He wrenched the knob off the door.* force, jerk, lever, prise, pull, tear, tug, twist, wrest, yank (*informal*).

wrestle *verb* **1** *He wrestled with his attacker.* battle, contend, fight, grapple, scuffle, struggle, tussle. **2** *He wrestled with the problem.* contend, grapple, struggle.

wretch *noun* **1** *He gave his last dollar to the starving wretch.* beggar, down-and-out, unfortunate. **2** *This is the wretch who stole my car.* blackguard, miscreant, rascal, ratbag (*informal*), rogue, rotter (*slang*), scoundrel, swine (*informal*), villain.

wretched *adjective* **1** *She was all alone and feeling wretched.* dejected, depressed, despondent, disconsolate, dismal, forlorn, hopeless, miserable, sad, sorrowful, unhappy, woebegone. OPPOSITE happy. **2** *She felt sorry for the wretched creature.* hapless, pathetic, pitiful, poor, sorry, unfortunate. OPPOSITE fortunate.

wriggle *verb He wriggled through the narrow opening.* crawl, slither, squirm, twist, wiggle, worm your way, writhe. □ **wriggle out of** *She is able to wriggle out of anything.* avoid, back out of, escape, evade, extricate yourself from, get out of.

wring *verb* **1** *He wrung the clothes to remove the excess water.* mangle, press, squeeze, twist. **2** *She wrung a promise from them.* extort, extract, force, obtain, screw, wrest.

wrinkle *noun* **1** *He ironed out the wrinkles in the trousers.* crease, crinkle, crumple, fold, pleat, pucker. **2** *facial wrinkles.* crow's-foot, furrow, line. — *verb* **1** *He wrinkled his sleeves.* crease, crinkle, crumple, rumple. **2** *She wrinkled her face.* pucker, screw up.

wrinkled *adjective a wrinkled face.* craggy, lined, rugged, shrivelled, wizened, wrinkly. OPPOSITE smooth.

write *verb* **1** *He wrote his name on the form.* inscribe, pen, pencil, print, scrawl, scribble, sign. **2** *He writes books.* compose, create, produce. **3** *He wrote a letter.* compose, dash off, draft, pen, send. **4** *They agreed to write to each other.* correspond, drop a line, send a letter. □ **write down** *She wrote down what the man said.* document, jot down, list, make a note of, note, record, register, take down, transcribe. **write off** **1** *The company wrote off the debt.* cancel, erase, forget about, wipe out. **2** *He wrote off his car.* destroy, ruin, wreck.

writer *noun* **1** *a neat writer.* calligrapher, scribe. **2** *She earns her living as a writer.* author, columnist, correspondent, dramatist, essayist, journalist, novelist, playwright, poet, screenwriter, scriptwriter.

write-up *noun The play received a good write-up.* critique, notice, report, review.

writhe *verb The snakes writhed.* squirm, twist, wriggle.

writing *noun* **1** *legible writing.* calligraphy, copperplate, graffiti, hand, handwriting, hieroglyphics, inscription, longhand, printing, scrawl, scribble, script, shorthand. **2** *an author's writings.* article, book, composition, diary, document, essay, journal, letter, literature, novel, poem, prose, publication, story, text, work.

wrong *adjective* **1** *He knows it is wrong to lie.* bad, corrupt, criminal, crooked, dishonest, evil, illegal, illicit, immoral, improper, iniquitous, naughty, reprehensible, sinful, unethical, unfair, unjust, unlawful, wicked. OPPOSITE right. **2** *a wrong answer. a wrong impression.* erroneous, fallacious, false, imprecise, inaccurate, incorrect, inexact, mistaken, untrue. OPPOSITE correct, true. **3** *She chose the wrong colour.* inappropriate, incongruous, undesirable, unsuitable. OPPOSITE perfect. **4** *There is something wrong with the car.* amiss, awry, defective, faulty, kaput (*informal*), out of order, wonky (*informal*). OPPOSITE right. **5** *the wrong side of the material.* reverse, under. OPPOSITE right. — *noun Two wrongs don't make a right. He knows the difference between right and wrong.* abuse, crime, evil, immorality, iniquity, injustice, misdeed, misdemeanour, offence, sin, sinfulness, transgression, trespass (*old use*), vice, wickedness, wrongdoing. OPPOSITE right. — *verb She felt that she had been wronged.* abuse, harm, ill-treat, maltreat, misrepresent, mistreat.

wrongdoer *noun The wrongdoer was punished.* baddy (*informal*), criminal, crook (*informal*), culprit, delinquent, evildoer, felon, lawbreaker, malefactor, miscreant, offender, sinner, transgressor, villain.

wry *adjective He pulled a wry face.* askew, contorted, crooked, distorted, twisted. OPPOSITE straight.

Yy

yabber *verb* (*Australian informal*) *I can't understand what he's yabbering about.* babble, blather, chatter, gabble, jabber, prattle, talk, yap (*informal*).

yakka *noun* (*Australian informal*) *Clearing the yard was hard yakka.* effort, exertion, graft (*slang*), grind, labour, slog, sweat, toil, work.

yank *verb* (*informal*) *She yanked out her loose tooth.* jerk, pull, tug, wrench. — *noun* (*informal*) *The button came off with one sharp yank.* jerk, pull, tug, wrench.

yap *verb The dog wouldn't stop yapping.* bark, yelp.

yard *noun The children play in the yard.* backyard, courtyard, garden, quad (*informal*), quadrangle.

yardstick *noun a yardstick for assessing your home's energy efficiency.* benchmark, criterion, gauge, guide, measure, standard, touchstone.

yarn *noun* **1** *woollen yarn.* fibre, strand, thread. **2** (*informal*) *He tells a good yarn.* anecdote, narrative, story, tale.

year *noun They are in Year 12.* class, form, grade, level.

yearly *adjective a yearly festival.* annual.

yearn *verb He yearns for recognition.* crave, hanker, have a yen, hunger, long, pine, thirst; see also DESIRE.

yell *verb I yelled for help.* bawl, bellow, call, cry, holler (*American*), howl, roar, scream, screech, shout, shriek. — *noun yells of pain.* bellow, cry, howl, roar, scream, screech, shout, shriek.

yellow *adjective a yellow colour.* amber, buttercup, canary, daffodil, gold, golden, jaundiced, lemon, mustard, primrose, saffron.

yelp *verb The dog yelped after being hit by the bicycle.* bark, cry, howl, squeal.

yen *noun She had a yen to travel.* craving, desire, fancy, hankering, hunger, longing, thirst, yearning.

yet *adverb* **1** *They haven't seen the play yet.* so far, thus far, up till now, up to now. **2** *She hates plays, yet she went to see this one.* however, nevertheless, nonetheless, still.

yield *verb* **1** *The land yields good crops.* bear, bring forth (*old use*), give, produce. **2** *The investment yields 5%.* bring in, earn, generate, net, pay, return. **3** *He yielded to pressure.* bow, capitulate, cave in, give in, give way, submit, succumb, surrender. OPPOSITE resist. — *noun a farmer's yield.* crop, harvest, output, return.

yobbo *noun* (*informal*) *He was attacked by a bunch of yobbos.* hooligan, hoon (*Australian informal*), larrikin (*Australian*), lout, ruffian, thug, yob (*informal*).

yokel *noun* bushie (*Australian informal*), country bumpkin, countryman, countrywoman, hick (*informal*), hill-billy (*American informal*), rustic. OPPOSITE city slicker (*informal*).

young *adjective* **1** *a young industry.* developing, fledgeling, growing, new, undeveloped. OPPOSITE established, old. **2** *her young brother.* adolescent, baby, junior, little, newborn, youthful. **3** *too young to understand.* babyish, childish, immature, inexperienced, infantile, juvenile, puerile. OPPOSITE adult, mature. — *noun The animals look after their young.* babies, brood, family, litter, offspring, progeny.

youngster *noun a club for youngsters.* adolescent, boy, child, girl, juvenile, kid (*informal*), lad, lass, teenager, youth.

youth *noun* **1** *He lived in Sydney in his youth.* adolescence, teenage years, teens, young days. OPPOSITE old age. **2** *a youth of 16.* adolescent, boy, fellow, juvenile, kid (*informal*), lad, teenager, young man, youngster. **3** *the youth of the country.* kids (*informal*), the young, young people.

youthful *adjective a youthful grandmother.* active, energetic, sprightly, spry, young, young-looking. OPPOSITE old.

yucky *adjective* (*informal*) *The food tastes yucky.* disgusting, gross (*informal*), repulsive, revolting, sickening.

yummy *adjective* (*informal*) *a yummy dinner.* appetising, delectable, delicious, mouth-watering, scrumptious (*informal*), tasty.

Zz

zany *adjective David has a zany sense of humour.* absurd, bizarre, comical, crazy, eccentric, funny, mad, odd, offbeat, peculiar, unconventional, unusual, wacky (*slang*), weird. OPPOSITE conventional.

zap *verb* see DESTROY, KILL.

zeal *noun He attacked the work with zeal.* ardour, dedication, devotion, diligence, eagerness, earnestness, energy, enthusiasm, fanaticism, fervour, gusto, keenness, passion, verve, vigour, zest. OPPOSITE apathy.

zealot *noun She was considered a religious zealot.* bigot, crank, enthusiast, extremist, fanatic.

zealous *adjective The parking inspector was overly zealous in fining people.* ardent, conscientious, devoted, diligent, eager, earnest, energetic, enthusiastic, fanatical, fervent, keen, passionate. OPPOSITE apathetic.

zenith *noun The prime minister was at the zenith of his popularity.* acme, apex, climax, height, peak, pinnacle, prime, summit, top. OPPOSITE nadir.

zero *noun The score was zero.* cipher, duck (*Cricket*), love (*Tennis*), nil, nothing, nought, zilch (*slang*). □ **zero in on** *The government has zeroed in on youth unemployment.* concentrate on, focus on, home in on.

zest *noun* **1** *The eighty-year-old pianist has a great zest for life.* eagerness, energy, enjoyment, enthusiasm, gusto, interest, keenness, pleasure, relish, zeal. OPPOSITE apathy. **2** *The performance lacked zest.* excitement, liveliness, oomph (*informal*), sparkle, spirit, vigour, zing (*informal*).

zigzag *adjective We followed a zigzag path up the slope.* crooked, serpentine, sinuous, tortuous, twisting, winding. OPPOSITE straight. — *verb The road zigzags up the mountain.* curve, meander, snake, twist, wind.

zip *noun At eighty-five she still has plenty of zip in her.* energy, go, gusto, life, liveliness, oomph (*informal*), pep, vigour, vim (*informal*), vitality, zest, zing (*informal*). OPPOSITE languor. — *verb* **1** *He zipped his jacket.* close, do up, fasten. OPPO-

SITE open, unzip. **2** *She zipped through her work in no time.* race, rush, speed, tear, whiz.

zit *noun* see PIMPLE.

zone *noun an arid zone. a commercial zone.* area, belt, district, locality, place, region, sector, territory.

zoo *noun We went to the zoo to see the lions.* conservation park, menagerie, safari park, sanctuary, wildlife park, zoological gardens.

zoom *verb She zoomed off before I could tell her the news.* dash, fly, hurry, race, rush, speed, tear, whiz, zip.